Praise for this Book

"*The Internet Kids & Family Yellow Pages* is an excellent reference for a household with a computer and kids."

John Frazer Dobson
Computer Shopper

"Jean Armour Polly makes the Internet a lot more kid-friendly."

Ira Flatow, host of public radio's Science Friday

"It's a jungle out there on the Internet, and for families needing guidance to steer them to suitable Web sites for children, *The Internet Kids & Family Yellow Pages* is a great resource."

San Francisco Chronicle

"*The Internet Kids & Family Yellow Pages* gives you summaries of the sites so your kids will really know where they're going, and it's also a place for you and your kids to begin a dialogue about what's out there. Besides, they list some REALLY cool sites."

Krissy Harris
Los Angeles Times

"...a totally cool—and useful—guide."

Disney Adventures

"A great book for kids and parents....More than just a collection of sites, it's full of ideas."

Independent Web Review

"Whether your child needs a copyright-free map of Afghanistan, help with quadratic equations, or just wants to spend time with the Power Rangers, this book will save hours of connect time and arguments."

New York Newsday

"Jean Armour Polly is the perfect Internet guide for kids and families."

Cheryl Kravetz
Lake Worth Herald

"One of the most thorough collections of Web sites that are safe for kids."

Melinda Miller
Buffalo New York News

"*The Internet Kids & Family Yellow Pages* will help almost any teacher quickly locate quality Web pages on student interests and will help any teacher find the Web resources they need to support lessons."

Joyce Kasman Valenza
Philadelphia Inquirer

"*The Internet Kids & Family Yellow Pages* is an educational environment in a fun setting, where kids can learn about their world and not even realize they're learning."

Lane Beauchamp
KidsCom co.

"When you need information, there's no better guide than a librarian, even in cyberspace. In her new book...cyber-librarian Jean Armour Polly offers some wise advice about which way to click on line....Polly's book makes good computer sense, as she sends your family down that superhighway primed for new fangled ways to learn *and* have fun."

Syracuse New Times

"...perfect for classroom research, homework assignments, and rainy day exploring."

Philadelphia Inquirer

"*The Internet Kids Yellow Pages* offers nothing less than the world at your fingertips."

DOS World

"*The Internet Kids Yellow Pages* is a great resource as well as a fun read....The descriptions contain lively detail that will have you itching to explore."

MacHome Journal

"This book is a great resource for those who have kids or spend time with them."

Computer Currents

"*The Internet Kids Yellow Pages*...a book that offers a plethora of child-safe online destinations for preschoolers to teens...this book is jam-packed...easy to use."

Computer User

"*The Internet Kids Yellow Pages* is a great resource for parents who want to plan their children's Web excursions and point them toward worthwhile pursuits in cyberspace."

c | net

"This is a very good book to have on reserve if you have a children's computer lab. With Polly's well-chosen tips, they will spend hours clicking, pointing, and scrolling all over the web without the need for SurfWatch or NetNanny."

Library Journal

THE INTERNET KIDS & FAMILY YELLOW PAGES

SPECIAL EDITION

ABOUT THE AUTHOR

Jean Armour Polly is the author of *The Internet Kids & Family Yellow Pages, Third Edition* (Osborne/McGraw-Hill), a family-friendly directory to over 3,500 of the best children's resources the Internet has to offer. Author, librarian, and mom, Jean is an internationally recognized expert on the Internet from a family's point of view. She wrote the *original* "Surfing the Internet" back in 1992, which coined the phrase, according to Lexis-Nexis. She was one of the first two women elected to the Internet Society Board of Trustees and is now a Trustee Emerita.

Under her Net-mom® brand, she is a private consultant, researcher, and speaker. Her client list includes America Online, The Bertelsmann Foundation (Germany), Disney Online, Leadership Texas, The Morino Institute, and TCI.Net. She also writes Best of the Web reviews for Children's Television Workshop's family area on Webcrawler. Other current clients include GuardiaNet and Landmark Community Interests, as well as MCI Foundation.

Jean was recently elected to the board of the Recreational Software Advisory Council on the Internet (RSACi), a group promoting rating of Internet resources by their authors. She has also served as cochair of the children's category of the international Global Information Infrastructure Awards competition as well as a finals judge in the ThinkQuest competition, sponsored by Advanced Network and Services, Inc.

Publisher of Net-mom News, Jean authors a regular 2,000-word electronic newsletter. It is aimed at Internet families trying to make sense of new Net resources, issues, and ideas.(Subscriptions are free at Jean's Web site.) Additionally, Jean cohosted a weekly call-in radio show (now discontinued) called "The On-Ramp" with John Levine, author of *The Internet For Dummies.* WSYR–570 AM, a Cox affiliate, produced the show.

Formerly the Director of Public Services and Internet Ambassador at NYSERNet, Inc. Jean was coprincipal investigator on the landmark *Project GAIN: Connecting Rural Public Libraries to the Internet* study (1994) and producer of the accompanying video.

Prior to that, Jean was a public librarian for 16 years. During Jean's watch, the Liverpool Public Library began many innovative programs, including an electronic BBS (1983–85), a public computer lab (1981–present), and a circulating software collection (1984–present), which was later named in her honor.

She is cofounder and moderator emerita of PUBLIB, the oldest and largest Internet discussion list for public librarians.

Jean received her B.A. in medieval studies at Syracuse University in 1974, and her master's degree in library science from the same university in 1975.

She is a member of the American Library Association and is a former director of the Library and Information Technology Association's board.

A popular and entertaining regular on the demo and speaking circuit, Jean has jacked into the Net in places as diverse as: Alaska, the Czech Republic, Italy, Hawaii, Kuala Lumpur, and historic booth number one at Rogers Frontier Bar in Old Colorado City, Colorado.

She lives on a hill in central New York, above a woods full of raccoons, fox, and deer. Mom to a 12-year-old son, Stephen, Jean also enjoys her cats, ducks, and a garden pond full of goldfish and lilies. Her husband, Larry, works as a Web programmer and computer systems integrator at the State University of New York Health Science Center at Syracuse, New York, and is system administrator of the netmom.com and pollywood.com server network at home.

More about Jean is available at her current home page at <*http://www.netmom.com*>.

To send communications about this book, kindly use the form at <*http://www.netmom.com/feedback.htm*>.

THE INTERNET KIDS & FAMILY YELLOW PAGES

SPECIAL EDITION

Jean Armour Polly

Osborne/McGraw-Hill

Berkeley New York St. Louis San Francisco Auckland Bogotá Hamburg
London Madrid Mexico City Milan Montreal New Delhi Panama City Paris
São Paulo Singapore Sydney Tokyo Toronto

THE INTERNET KIDS & FAMILY YELLOW PAGES

SPECIAL EDITION

OSBORNE/MCGRAW-HILL
2600 TENTH STREET
BERKELEY, CALIFORNIA 94710
U.S.A.

For information on translations or book distributors outside the U.S.A., or to arrange bulk purchase discounts for sales promotions, premiums, or fund-raisers, please contact Osborne/**McGraw-Hill** at the above address.

1234567890 QPD QPD 90198765432109

ISBN 0-07-212206-4

Publisher
Brandon A. Nordin
Editor-in-Chief
Scott Rogers
Project Editor
Janet Walden
Copy Editor
Kathryn Hashimoto
Proofreaders
Morton Flask, Pat Mannion
Indexer
David Heiret
Computer Designers
Roberta Steele, Mickey Galicia, Jani Beckwith, Peter F. Hancik
Illustrators
Leslee Bassin, Brian Wells
Series Design
Peter F. Hancik
Cover Illustration
Cristina Deh-Lee

For our son, Stephen,

and my mother,

who both have a lot to teach about love

and respect for children.

And for Larry: husband, mentor, friend.

Put it before them briefly so they will read it, clearly so they will appreciate it, picturesquely so they will remember it, and, above all, accurately so they will be guided by its light.

Joseph Pulitzer

Table of Contents

Acknowledgments

There are a number of people I want to thank, and this is the page where I get to do that.

You wouldn't be holding this book in your hands if it weren't for my husband, Larry Polly. He developed the custom database for this project, he runs the servers, and he manages the Web site. I write the prose and organize the book, but Larry manipulates the data back out of the database and makes it into a real chapter to be sent to the publisher. It is always a mammoth task, and he never loses his sense of perspective and humor.

And to my 12-year-old son, Stephen, a big hug and thanks for giving Dad and me the time to do something for kids all over the world.

At Osborne/McGraw-Hill, I would like to thank Brandon Nordin, publisher, for believing in ruby slippers and happy endings. Many thank you's to Scott Rogers, editor-in-chief, for pulling the CD-ROM together under impossible deadlines and for his continued support—even though he hasn't managed to send me on a book signing tour of South Pacific Island bookstores. Yet. Also bugging him to do that are Anne Ellingsen and Caroline Keller, who do all the public relations for the book. If you've read a review, heard me on the radio, or seen me on TV, Anne and Caroline were probably responsible. So, they will have to come along on the Pacific signing trip, too! Senior project editor Janet Walden, project editor Jennifer Wenzel, copy editor Kathryn Hashimoto, proofreaders Morton Flask and Pat Mannion, indexer David Heiret, illustrators Leslee Bassin and Brian Wells, and page layout artists Roberta Steele, Jani Beckwith, Michelle Galicia, and Peter F. Hancik should be praised for the time they took with the book and the care and commitment they displayed towards making it right for families.

Thanks go to my friend Harley Hahn, author of about a zillion computer and Internet books. Harley is always a ready source of counsel and encouragement. And he has his own sportswear line.

Now that I think of it, so does John Levine, author of *The Internet For Dummies* and many other computer books. Maybe it's a trend. John's deep understanding of the computer book publishing industry, and how to work with it anyway, was a great source of comfort.

I would be remiss if I did not thank my friend Steve Cisler for continually pushing my thought and action toward finding my own Right Path.

On the same journey, I met the interfaith teachings of His Holiness Baba Virsa Singh Ji, whose work and words helped inspire me to complete this book. I was introduced to Babaji through the friendship of Ralph Singh Rakieten, his wife, Joginder, and sons Chetan and Tegbir. Interested? Check out <http://www.GobindSadan.org/>.

To Vicki, Diane, Peg, Melinda, and all the girlfriends, thanks for the support.

To Dr. Charles and Myrna Hall, thanks for the gardening tips and trading publisher stories.

To Ursula and Christian Braun, my walking partners, I hope we can hit the road again soon, now that this is over!

To my sister-in-law, Mary Kay Polly, the teacher, thanks for giving me all the great leads on trends in education.

To Dewayne, thanks for coaching me on How to Be an Entrepreneur 101. I think I am ready for the graduate course now.

When you're writing a book, you don't get out much, so whatever informs and entertains you while you're working becomes extremely important. Specifically, I'd like to credit all the fine people at National Public Radio for educating me on what was happening around the world while I was stuck at my computer for five months!

Also, did you know you can listen to radio via the Internet? NetRadio's audio broadcasts became a favorite, specifically "Celtic Mix" created by Gordy (Dj Free) Schaeffer from the Ambient World Music band Soulfood on Rykodisc: <http://www.netradio.net/soulfood>.

Additionally, we'd like to thank both Ben and Jerry for creating what we endorse as the Official Ice Cream of Net-mom®: DILBERT'S WORLD™ Totally Nuts™ Ice Cream. We recommend it: <http://web.benjerry.com/product/totally-nuts.html>.

Thanks also to the Syracuse office of DHL, the courier company used by Osborne/McGraw-Hill. Specifically, Betsy Kosecki, Paul Auber, Claretha Cargo, and Bob Humeniuk. Also, Bob Piazza, Christopher Robinson, Robert Atkins, Bob Lindsay, and Steve Schumle. They really helped in shipping out edited material, review copies, press kits, and so much more. Usually I called them at the end of the day, and they'd have to drive here in a blinding snowstorm, uphill both ways. These folks are *good*.

I want to acknowledge the work of members of research teams of past editions, whose work also appears in this book: Kitty Bennett, Peg Elliott, Ron Evry, Jan K. France, Charles and Frankie Grace, Brian M. Harris, John Iliff, Gayle Keresey, Vicki Kwasniewski, Steve Marks, Neal Meier, Keith Parish, Laurel Sharp, Bernie Sloan, Mark A. Spadafore, and Diane Towlson.

Additional advisors for this edition include: Maureen, Colin, and Dylan; Brian; Jennifer, Christian, and Justin; Jill and Todd; and Chris and Sarah.

Also, Kyle, Nikki, and Noah helped with homeschooling questions.

Stephen wants to acknowledge the support of Mr. Hugh Jones, Head of the Manlius Pebble Hill Middle School, as well as the entire seventh grade class. In addition, he credits his favorite research associates, T.J. and Tyler.

I also want to thank Mom for providing outstanding moral support services, including cooking a few random dinners and washing the occasional dish.

Finally, thank you to the parents, families, teachers, and librarians who bought the first two editions of the book and made it a best-seller. Kids do belong on the Net.

Respectfully,

Jean Armour Polly
Jamesville, New York
August 1998

About the Research Team

Sharon R. Fulmer's career as an editor of a weekly newspaper in central New York brought her numerous writing and design awards over a 20-year period. She also served on the board of directors and executive committee of the New York Press Association, an organization of 350 community newspapers across the state. She was its president in 1993–94. More recently, she founded Myredith Press, a small company that provides writing, design, and production services for small businesses. Sharon and her husband, David, have three grown children, Melissa, Andrew, and Scott. Scott and his wife, Michele, have one daughter, one-year-old Morgen—a perfect and beautiful child, according to Grandma and Great-Grandma, Emma Ridgeway.

Larry M. Polly works as a Web programmer and computer systems integrator at the State University of New York Health Science Center at Syracuse, New York. He created the original campus gopher and is now heavily involved in Web development, and he manages a variety of academic servers at the university. He is also webmaster of the www.netmom.com Web site. When he is not dodging Jean's cats, he enjoys soldering old electronic parts together with his son, Stephen. He also enjoys traveling to exotic locales.

Stephen Jade Polly, 12, served as the Official Kid Advisor and arbiter of humor in the book. He is occasionally introduced at bookstore book signings as Net-mom's Vice President of Marketing, since he likes to hand out bookmarks and T-shirts and encourage people to buy the book. He likes to use the Net to learn things about science, and his favorite season is Hawaii. In the future he is interested in developing a bionic plant that senses when to water itself. He has memorized the entire script of *Monty Python and the Holy Grail.* His cat, Pooshka, is incredibly large. And last night, awakened from a visionary half-dream, Son of Net-mom wrote down the Meaning of Life: "The Meaning of Life is to hdgsdbv and krhsdni for all eternity." Perhaps he needs more sleep.

Introduction

Welcome! This book is a labor of love for us, and we are happy it seems to have fulfilled a need for so many readers worldwide.

Here's what you'll find in this third edition:

- Thousands of fully annotated educational and entertaining Internet sites, all handpicked and family-friendly. Sites are arranged in broad subject headings, organized alphabetically. The main A–Z section is written for kids in grades K–8, although many general reference works for all ages are included.

- In "W" there is a new section called WHY? In that area you'll find Internet sites where kids (and parents) can go to find out such things as

  Why is the sky blue?
  Why is the sunset red?
  Why do the leaves change color in the fall?
  What makes a cat's eyes glow in the dark?
  Why is the ocean salty?
  Where does the water go during low tide?
  How many stars are in the sky?
  What color is snow?

- More than 250 "Net Files" trivia questions to encourage interest in Net exploration. Don't worry, the answers are there, too!

- Free online updates at <http://www.netmom.com/>. We track changes to the addresses in this book and post them online to help our readers stay up to date. We also offer a free e-mail newsletter; see the Web site for details.

- A CD-ROM containing a clickable version of all the site addresses, plus a Family Internet Safety Toolkit, which includes tutorials, children's Net safety comics, and special filtering software demos and offers for families. There are also special offers in the back of the book.

- A newly updated hotlist section featuring 100 "Best of the Net" sites in categories like homework help, sports, and science, plus sites for preschoolers, parents, teachers, and more! This year, Son of Net-mom makes his debut with an additional ten surefire sites kids love (including some their parents might consider yucky, such as the ever-popular Belch Page). Also new in this edition is a "Best of the Rest" list, with additional don't-miss sites.

- Don't forget our Countries of the World section, where you can explore the globe through official government sites, embassies, departments of tourism, and more. This section is very helpful for school reports!

- At the end of the book is a special collection of materials for parents and teachers. Resources for preschoolers and sites for family fun are also included in this section, as well as answers to commonly asked questions about the Internet. You'll also find an excerpt from a new book on how to keep kids safe online—written by Donna Riçe Hughes, a nationally recognized advocate for children's safety on the Internet.

WHAT'S DIFFERENT ABOUT THIS BOOK?

Other books are collections. This book features *selections*. You're holding the first and only directory of Internet resources for kids and families selected by a librarian. You'll find a thoughtful and intuitive organization of Internet knowledge here, which is driven by the types of questions I used to answer at the public library reference desk.

I selected these sites with care, respect, and yes, love. I was thinking hard about kids and parents worldwide. I was thinking about inclusion, and tolerance, and disturbing events on the news. I believe that the Net can help humans learn to get along, and there is hope for a better world ahead.

WELCOME KIDS!

It's great to meet you! I can't wait to show you some of my favorite places on the Net!

First, though, you need to know that the Net changes all the time. Some places I thought were cool when I wrote this book might not be the same by the time you follow in my footsteps. So if, on the Net, you find yourself someplace that just doesn't "feel right" to you, or you are "talking" to someone and start to feel uncomfortable with what is going on, go get a parent, teacher, or caregiver. If there is no one around, just turn off the computer.

The good news is, while you're reading this, I'm still finding outstanding new places for the next edition of this book! Please think of me as your friend—come on, let's explore!

WELCOME PARENTS, TEACHERS, AND CAREGIVERS!

Because of my unique background as a public librarian, Internet pioneer, and mom, I wrote this book because I believe kids belong on the Net. There has been some movement to ban kids entirely, and I believe that is entirely wrong. Still, I know that there are places on the Net that I would not want my son to go without me. There are places in the city where I live that I wouldn't let him go to alone, either.

So, I set out to find places on the Net that were built expressly for children or where people of any age could find value. You're holding in your hands thousands of such locations. Almost all of them are Web sites, the handful remaining are Gopher, FTP, or other archives. They are located all over the world, from Washington, D.C., to Moscow. You'll visit servers on tiny Pacific islands, one inside the Vatican, and an Internet video camera aimed at a research station on Antarctica. You'll visit the Library of Congress, NASA, the British Museum, and even some school and family home pages.

SELECTION POLICY: WHAT YOU WILL FIND IN THIS BOOK

Every good library needs a selection policy, so naturally, we have one. Here it is. In general, I select sites based on the following criteria:

- The resources include compelling, engaging material for children from preschool through eighth grade, or approximately ages 3 to 14. There are also many sites for general audiences of all ages. I also collect for adults in the PARENTING AND FAMILIES section.
- They display outstanding organization and navigation/search capabilities.
- They use a judicious mix of graphics and text, so that they will be useful to a user with text-only Web access. Many times, these resources will offer a text-only option.
- They are authoritative and list their sources.
- They are timely and have a date on them.
- They exist on a stable Internet site with good connectivity.

SELECTION POLICY: WHAT YOU WON'T FIND IN THIS BOOK

I have explored all these sites myself, in great detail. This book does not knowingly include resources that contain violent, racist, sexist, erotic, or other adult content.

You will find health information, such as resources on puberty. However, I have not included other resources involving sexuality and gender issues. My research informs me that most parents want to decide how, and when, to introduce their children to these topics, so I have respected that. If you feel otherwise, please see the section of the book called INTERNET—SEARCH ENGINES AND DIRECTORIES for guidance on finding things on the Net.

You'll see that I have marked some annotations with a "Parental Advisory." Some sites contained too many links for me to follow to their ends. Please be sure to preview these sites yourself.

The Internet is always in motion, and resources may change. Something I found appropriate for inclusion in the book today may be inappropriate tomorrow. So, I cannot guarantee that your Internet experience, based on my recommendations, will always meet your needs.

I strongly recommend that parents, caregivers, and teachers always use the Internet alongside their children and preview sites if at all possible.

Still, all that said, let me say that when in doubt, I left the site out. I was guided by the following, which I found on a server in Honolulu:

You cannot make people see stuffs they no can see. So, jus worry about yourself...no make hassles, treat everyone like how you like be treated, and everything should be okay dokey.

—Bu La'ia

WHAT YOU NEED TO KNOW TO USE THIS BOOK

This book won't teach you how to use your Net browser. There are too many of them. I use Netscape, but you may use Internet Explorer, America Online's browser, Lynx, or some other application. If you just know how to use your browser, you can find out how to use the Internet. Go to the INTERNET—BEGINNER'S GUIDES section of this book and start learning.

You do need to know what a "smiley" is. Here's one coming at you :-) now, put your left ear on your left shoulder and look at those characters again. See the little smiley face? This is a "winkie" ;-) and it means we're joking about something. We use these throughout the book. You can read more about smilies in the INTERNET—NETIQUETTE, FOLKLORE, AND CUSTOMS section of this book.

TROUBLESHOOTING: WHEN URLS DON'T WORK

Unfortunately, I can't help you with connectivity problems. Contact your Internet service provider and ask them to help you with setting up your browser or configuring other Internet software applications. They may also be able to help you with modem settings or other hardware-related concerns.

However, I can help you with the following problem:

I typed in the address, but it doesn't work. I got "404 Not Found," "Not found on this server," "No DNS entry exists for this server," or some other cranky-sounding message. What should I do?

If you come across this problem, just follow these steps:

1. Try it again. The Internet isn't perfect. Along the way, from where the information lives to your computer, something may have blinked. At the beginning of the PARENTING AND FAMILIES section is a special feature called "Ask Net-mom: What Parents Ask Me About Kids and the Internet." In it, and among other things, I explain how Web pages get from host computers to your desktop, and what can go wrong in-between.

2. Check your spelling. Many of these addresses are long and complex, so it's easy to make a mistake. You might try having another person read you the address while you type it. Or you could use the CD-ROM version!

3. Make sure you are careful to use capital letters or lowercase when they are printed in this book. They are not interchangeable, and the computer won't recognize its file called "foo.html" if you have typed "FOO.HTML."

4. Check to see if I have found where the page has gone. The free updates to this book are all at <http://www.netmom.com/>.

5. The location or file name may have changed since I visited the page. That means its address will be different. Computer files (making up the pages you see on the World Wide Web) are stored in directories on remote servers all over the world. Sometimes people move these files to different places, so you need to find where they have been moved.

6. And if you're pretty smart (and you are, because you've got this book), you'll know four tricks to help you find pages that have moved.

Trick #1: Solve File Name Change Problems

The first trick is to shorten the address and look there. Say that you've been looking for Dorothy and Toto's home page. It used to be at:

http://land.of.oz.gov/munchkinland/mainstreet/ dorothy.html

Perhaps Dorothy changed the name of her home page, so let's go "back" a level and look around. Let's try:

http://land.of.oz.gov/munchkinland/mainstreet/

That takes you "higher" in the directory path, and you may be able to find where Dorothy has moved from there. On the "mainstreet" Web page, we might see several new choices:

/the.scarecrow.html
/the.tin.man.html
/the.cowardly.lion.html
/dorothy.and.toto.html

Great! Dorothy's just changed the name of her home page to include her little dog, too. Choose that one, and make a note of it for future visits. Write the changes directly into this book; I won't mind. Another mystery solved!

If you still can't find what you're looking for, try going "back" yet another level. You may have to try several levels back until you locate what you want.

Trick #2: Solve Server Name Change Problems

It's also possible that the Wizard of Oz has ordered that the new name of the World Wide Web server containing all home pages will now be called "www.land.of.oz.gov" instead of "land.of.oz.gov." That creates a problem for people looking for home pages under the *old* server name, which isn't there anymore. How are you supposed to find it?

Fortunately, the crafty old Wizard chose a common name change. If a computer server's name is going to be changed, it's often given a prefix to reflect the type of services it runs. Common prefix names are gopher (for those operating Gopher servers), ftp (for those offering File Transfer Protocol), and www (for sites running Web servers.)

If you don't know what the new server name might be, try *guessing*, using one of these prefixes. For a Web server, try putting "www." in front of whatever name it originally had (unless it already had that prefix). For example, here's the old name:

http://land.of.oz.gov

Here's your guess at the new name:

http://www.land.of.oz.gov

Bingo—that was it! Be sure to make a note of the change in this book, so you won't have that problem again.

Trick #3: Use Search Engines to Find Pages That Have Moved

If none of the above works, it's possible that Dorothy has taken her home page Someplace Else. In that case, the previous two tricks won't work, since you will no longer find an entry for her anywhere in the Land of Oz domain.

Your next trick involves trying one of the Net search or Net directory indexes, such as Infoseek, Yahoo, and AltaVista. Many of them are listed under those Net buttons on Netscape's browser. If you are using another browser, it probably has similar choices to help you search the entire World Wide Web. Look in the section of this book called INTERNET—SEARCH ENGINES AND DIRECTORIES for more information on searching techniques.

Choose one of the search engines, and search on the word "dorothy." Chances are, she's put up her home page on a computer server in her new domain. Wow, the search returns hundreds of pages containing the word "dorothy." How do you know which one you want, without having to look through all of them?

Look at the original entry for Dorothy's home page in this book. We have been very careful to print whatever Dorothy used as her home page's title. It is very possible that she is still using that home page title, even though it is located on a different computer server.

We don't really have a home page for Dorothy in this book, this is just an example: Dorothy and Toto's Wicked Good Adventure.

Go to one of the search indexes again. Instead of just searching on "Dorothy," try the page's *title* as it is printed in this book. You want to make the search engine look for the entire phrase "Dorothy and Toto's Wicked Good Adventure." You don't want to search on "Dorothy," "Toto's," "Wicked," "Good," and "Adventure" separately. If you did that, you would get hundreds of items again, and

we are trying to narrow it down. Searching on the entire phrase will help do that. Check the directions for the particular index you are using (typically, a Help button will take you there); many indexes allow you to keep the entire phrase together by putting it between quotation marks. So, for example, you would try this:

Search on: "Dorothy and Toto's Wicked Good Adventure"

Alternative guess: "Dorothy and Toto"

Another alternative guess: "Wicked Good Adventure"

If that doesn't work, a final trick is to guess what Dorothy might have said in the *content* of her home page. She probably talks about Toto, the Scarecrow, the Tin Man, and the Lion in there somewhere. Therefore, these words will be indexed, and you should be able to use that knowledge when you search using one of the indexes.

Go back to your search engine (we like Infoseek or the advanced mode of the AltaVista search engine for this). Try the following (be sure to check the Help files to learn the correct way to phrase your search):

Search on: Dorothy AND Toto AND Scarecrow

Alternative: Dorothy AND Lion

Another alternative: Dorothy AND Scarecrow AND Lion

Trick #4: Check with Us

When all else fails, don't forget to look on my home page at <http://www.netmom.com/>. While you were trying all these tricks, we may have already found where the page has been moved. If you can't get to my home page at www.netmom.com, try its mirror site at <http://www.well.com/user/polly/>.

These are just some tips to help you find where Dorothy's gone. I know they will help!

For Kids Who Love Art and Music

Play it, sing it, paint it, or color it—virtual crayons never break, and cyber-instruments never go out of tune!

Aunt Annie's Craft Page ™
http://www.auntannie.com/

She won't pinch your cheeks and talk about how much you've grown! Aunt Annie *will* give you ideas, patterns, and great directions for making interesting crafts. She has a new project for you each week, and lots of creative links, too.

Eyeneer Music Archives
http://www.eyeneer.com/

Find links here to world music, contemporary classic, new jazz, and American music. Each link will keep you busy exploring. In the International Music Archive, you'll find an abundance of photos, sound samples, and descriptions of instruments.

The Incredible Art Department
http://www.artswire.org/kenroar/

Explore this intriguing toolbox of art lessons, projects, cartoons about art, and art news. You'll find projects for everyone, from little preschoolers all the way up to college kids. There's also a wonderful section on how persons with disabilities are able to create artwork using new and old technologies.

Joseph Wu's Origami Page
http://www.origami.vancouver.bc.ca/

You don't care if you ever see another folded paper crane in your life! OK, relax, you don't have to fold any more cranes. Now you're ready for some intermediate and advanced origami projects. From this page you can download incredible diagrams and instructions for a windmill, butterfly, or basket, among other things!

Kids' Space
http://www.kids-space.org/

What fun—this is everybody's home page! Here your family can submit music or drawings and hear and see what other children around the world have done, too. The Story Book is where kids write their own stories, using the pictures and themes provided. There is even a beanstalk that keeps growing each month in the Craft Room.

Mark Kistler's Imagination Station
http://www.draw3d.com/

The real world is in three dimensions: objects have width, length, and depth. In a drawing, you have to use special techniques to simulate the third dimension of depth. No problem—Mark's here to give you 3-D drawing lessons.

Mozart's Magical Musical Life
http://www.stringsinthemountains.org/m2m/1once.htm

What if your parents named you Johannes Chrysostomus Wolfgangus Theophillus Amadeus Mozart. Can you imagine writing that on the top of your paper in school? This great story, complete with audio clips, tells about "Wolfie," or Mozart as we know him today.

RCA: Idiot's Guide to Classical Music
http://www.rcavictor.com/rca/hits/idiots/cover.html

You probably recognize more classical music than you'd think! Take a listen to some of the sound bites at this site, and see which ones you know from TV commercials, shows, and movies.

Songs for Scouts
http://www.macscouter.com/Songs/

Gather 'round the campfire and share some singing—here are silly songs, lots of gross songs, and songs that are just plain fun. If you want the definitive version of "Greasy Grimy Gopher Guts," look no further.

Welcome to Piano on the Net '97
http://www.artdsm.com/music.html

Would you like to learn how to play the piano or how to read music? You can! This easy, reassuring series of modules includes QuickTime movies, audio files, even online metronomes.

For Kids Who Love Comics, Cartoons, and Animation

If the first thing you read in the Sunday paper is the funnies, these sites are for you!

Cartoon Corner
http://www.cartooncorner.com/
This site will tell you the secrets of cartooning, but you have to promise *not* to tell anyone else! Learn some drawing tips, and try to guess some tricky riddles here.

Draw and Color a Cartoony Party with Uncle Fred
http://www.unclefred.com/
"Uncle Fred" Lasswell has been drawing the "Barney Google and Snuffy Smith" comic strip since 1934, and he still stays on the cutting edge of today's technology. His Web page includes numerous fun cartoon drawing lessons.

Garfield's Official Web Site
http://www.garfield.com/
This purr-fect home page is hosted by a big fat hairy deal: Garfield! Check out the recipes for Garfield's favorite food (lasagne) and read some great jokes.

Nickelodeon Online-The Web Site for Kids
http://www.nick.com/
Ooze into this Web site, but please avoid the mess Ren and Stimpy made! Find your way into the TV Shows area to read up on the latest with all your favorites: *Kablam, Alex Mack, AAAHH!! Real Monsters, Doug,* and those wacky guys *Keenan and Kel.* Download some cool games for Mac or Win, and make sure the rest of your family notices the links to Nick Jr. and Nick-at-Nite!

Non-Stick MGM Cartoon Page
http://www.nonstick.com/mgm/
Here is everything you always wanted to know about Tom and Jerry, Droopy, and all the other classic MGM cartoons and how they were made. The site features downloadable sounds, graphics, and includes links to other terrific animation pages as well.

The Official Snoopy Home Page
http://www.snoopy.com/
All your favorites are here! Charlie Brown, Lucy, Linus, Woodstock, Peppermint Patty, and Snoopy, of course! The history section is especially fascinating. You'll find some fun Shockwave games here and electronic postcards to send to your friends.

The Official Thomas The Tank Engine & Friends Web Site
http://www.thomasthetankengine.com/
Do you know *Thomas the Tank Engine & Friends*? If you're a fan of *Shining Time Station,* then you'll love the coloring book pictures and information on Thomas and the whole gang, plus some new Really Useful Engines.

RON KURER'S TOON TRACKER HOME PAGE
http://ftp.wi.net/~rkurer/
With so many long-forgotten animated cartoons of the past showing up on cable TV these days, this site is a gold mine of information on many of them. Find pages devoted to Mighty Mouse, Beany and Cecil, Clyde Crashcup, Clutch Cargo, Bullwinkle, Woody Woodpecker, and dozens more!

Warner Bros. Kids Page
http://www.kids.warnerbros.com/
Anyone with the slightest interest in animated cartoons needs to drop in here. The step-by-step tour of how a cartoon gets made is the World Wide Web at its best! The site also includes Loony Tunes Online Karaoke and Looney Tunes Web Postcards!

Welcome to the Comic Zone
http://www.unitedmedia.com/comics/
Catch up on your favorite comic strip characters and see what they are doing on the Internet. Find out about the artists and how they thought up the characters, and play games based on the comic strip. Then take a detour from the main page to the National Cartoonists Society, where the *real* cartoonists behind the strips hang out!

For Kids Who Love Games and Interactive Stuff

Why surf the Internet when you can PLAY with it instead?

The Amazing Fish-Cam!
http://www1.netscape.com/fishcam/
Yes, from wherever you are on the Web, you can watch live fish swim around a tank in someone's office. These fish can be viewed by two different cameras (you get to pick), or you can choose the Continuously Refreshing Fish-Cam if you have a browser that is capable of automatic updates.

Apple Corps
http://apple-corps.westnet.com/apple_corps.html
Similar to Mr. Potato Head, this site lets you choose to disguise other vegetables and fruit. Try a moustache on an artichoke or maybe some spectacles on a pumpkin. Not a veggie fan? Try the head of a famous politician instead.

Build Your Own Snowman Contest
http://tn.areaguide.com/games/snowman/
Do you live in a place where there is lots of snow in the winter? Or do you live where there's never any snow? It doesn't matter, because here on the Web, you can build a snowman any day of the year. Plus, you can save your creation online so he never melts!

Cyber Jacques' Cyber Seas Treasure Hunt
http://www.cyberjacques.com/
Avast ye, me hearties, from whatever else you're doing, and come try the games at Cyber Jacques' seagoing arcade. They all require Shockwave, so you'd best have a current version or you'll be walking the plank real soon!

Interactive Model Railroad
http://rr-vs.informatik.uni-ulm.de/rr/
This one is pretty cool. You get to give commands to an actual model train at the University of Ulm in Germany! You pick the train, tell it which station to go to, and if you're quick (and lucky) enough, you're in charge.

Kid's Domain – KIDS
http://www.kidsdomain.com/kids.html
Lots of games and pictures to color, software downloads, clip art, and a list of links to similar sites. Click on Surf Safe and talk to your youngsters about what rules they should follow when using the computer. This is a must-see site for all families!

Ringling Bros. and Barnum & Bailey Circus
http://www.ringling.com/home.asp
It's billed as the Greatest Show on Earth, and now you can visit it whenever you choose! Do you have what it takes to perform in the circus? It takes ability, grace, skill, and did we mention nerves of steel? Take the online aptitude test and see how well you do. There's also a loads-of-laughs "make a clown" game for little kids, as well as other games.

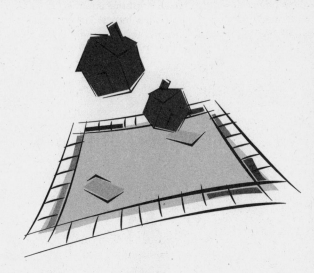

Seuss Lorax Introduction
http://www.randomhouse.com/seussville/games/lorax/
Even very little children will have fun trying to catch seeds in this Shockwave game inspired by Dr. Seuss. Use your mouse to position your basket just right. If you catch ten seeds, you'll be able to replant the Truffula Forest, and the Truffula Forest is what everyone needs.

Welcome to Lemonade Stand
http://www.littlejason.com/lemonade/
In this easy-to-learn simulation game of high finance, you start with a fistful of dollars, a dream, and a weather forecast. Balance the cost of rent, lemons, and your advertising budget into your sales price per cup. Watch that weatherperson! Can you squeeze out a lemonade empire or will you lose all your lemons?

Welcome to Theatrix/Sanctuary Woods
http://www.theatrix.com/fun/fun.html
Got Shockwave? You'll love this site. It has ten of the most engaging, fun, and nutty games we've ever seen on the Web.

For Emergency Homework Help

Just the facts, just in time!

Ask An Expert Page
http://njnie.dl.stevens-tech.edu/curriculum/aska.html
Got a question no one seems to know how to answer? Maybe you need to call in an expert. Many scientists and others have offered to answer questions about science, math, medicine, history, and other topics. You won't usually get an answer overnight, though, so think ahead.

Ask Jeeves for Kids
http://www.ajkids.com/
Why doesn't someone invent a kid-safe search engine that lets you type in a real question rather than all those plusses and minuses and quotes and other weird terms? And if you weren't the World's Greatest Speller, the search engine would check the spelling of your question, too. Why doesn't someone invent a search tool like that? Guess what, someone did. Why not go and Ask Jeeves?

B.J. Pinchbeck's Homework Helper
http://tristate.pgh.net/~pinch13/
"Beege" is 11 years old and has collected over 440 resources that he uses with his school homework. Maybe they will work for you, too! You'll find everything from biographical dictionaries to flags of the world.

IPL Reference Center
http://www.ipl.org/ref/
With a Reference Desk and book shelves arranged by subject, the only thing missing here is the smiling librarian! This site links to sites all over the Net, so be prepared to take some time to check all the different sources at the Internet Public Library.

LibrarySpot
http://www.libraryspot.com/
Just in time for term paper season, a new one-stop reference desk has opened on the Web. Acronym dictionaries, biographical dictionaries, inventions, useful calculators (how much grass seed to buy? how to convert cooking measurements?)—all are here for your use. There are also links to hundreds of library card catalogs all over the world.

Martindale's 'The Reference Desk'
http://www-sci.lib.uci.edu/HSG/Ref.html
Hotlist this one now. First off, find out what time it is, not only where you live but all over the world. You'll learn what the weather is, where the earthquakes are, and where the surf's up. Then move on to the calculators. There are over 6,400 of them. In fact, there is so much compelling information here we bet you can't take just one link!

Research-It! - Your one-stop reference desk
http://www.itools.com/research-it/
This site's cool! Spell a word, conjugate a verb, find a quote, or locate facts about a famous person. Almost 30 quick reference tools are all rolled into one easy-to-use site.

Study WEB
http://www.studyweb.com/
Whatever your homework assignment is, this site is sure to have something you can use, with "more than 69,000" research-quality links, listed by subject category. The Reference Shelf is a good place to start, but the brief reviews of each site will also help you select just the right place to look.

Welcome to TheBig6.com
http://big6.syr.edu/
Would you like to be able to answer any question? Try this six-step methodical approach, which lets you break down your research into manageable steps. At the official site, you'll find lots more detail, examples, and sample lesson plans. Forget study tricks: go Big Six!

You Don't Have to Play Football to Score a Touchdown
http://www.mtsu.edu/~studskl/hsindex.html
This page will help you take notes, manage your time, and learn to do your best to make and meet your goals. Be sure to take the link to "Study Skills Help Page" for more.

For Parents

These are Net-mom's favorite sites for parents-to-be, new parents, old parents, grandparents, caregivers, and kids who want to look ahead to their own futures!

Family.com Home Page
http://family.disney.com/

Presented by Disney Online, Family.com offers lots of intriguing feature articles on family activities, travel, recipes, education, and more.

Homeschooling Information and Homeschool Resource Pages
http://www.home-ed-press.com/

This is a fine ecumenical resource with information about everything you want to know about homeschooling and unschooling, sponsored by *Home Education* magazine and its online version.

KidSource OnLine Welcome Page
http://www.kidsource.com/

Wasn't that toy recalled? Find out here! Families, be sure to check out this outstanding parenting site. The reviews of kid-tested software are written from a family perspective, with both negative and positive comments. The Education section includes articles and book lists and, best of all, annotated links and more links! The Health section has everything from vaccination schedules to growth charts, and the ComputingEDGE is a way to match needy schools with computer equipment. We highly recommend this site for annotated pointers to sites about dealing with angry kids, raising only children, and figuring out such things as alternative assessment in education.

Parent Soup
http://www.parentsoup.com/

The content here is based on what other users can add to the mix of real-time chat and discussion groups. Want to ask for help with your shy preschooler? Want someone to talk to while your partner watches football? Want some health, crafts, or entertainment suggestions? Try the Parent Soup community!

Parents Place.com: Pregnancy, Parenting, Parents, Baby, Pregnancy, Kids, Family
http://www.parentsplace.com/

Parents, whether you are on your first child, your tenth, or somewhere in between, join the hundreds of other parents who come to ParentsPlace to chat, get support, and share information on the adventures and challenges of child rearing. Whether you are looking for directions to make invisible ink or the latest in toy safety labeling requirements, you'll find it here.

Pregnancy & Childbirth Information - Childbirth.org
http://www.childbirth.org/

This is an excellent site, offering good, factual information about fertility, episiotomies, doulas, breast-feeding, and more. But it's not all serious stuff. Wondering if your baby will be a boy or a girl? A handy "calculator" here may give you the answer, based on a combination of old wives' tales and folk wisdom.

SCREEN IT! ENTERTAINMENT REVIEWS FOR PARENTS
http://www.screenit.com/

These movie, video, and music reviews are astonishingly complete, scoring each title in a variety of sensitive areas that might be of concern to parents. How much violence? How much bad language? How many instances of disrespectful behavior or nudity? This site helps parents "know before you go" so there will be no surprises later.

Technology Inventory
http://www.research.att.com/projects/tech4kids/

There's been a lot of talk in the news about the Internet having stuff on it that is inappropriate for kids, and parents may feel they want to use filtering software and other tools in the digital toolbox. This page, from research by Dr. Lorrie Cranor at AT&T, will tell you what's available. Tools are arranged into categories and are explained in great detail in the report.

The Teel Family Web Site
http://www.teelfamily.com/

Brrrr! Snow is falling all around, and you're harnessing the dogs to the sled. Get ready for a trip to Alaska to visit the Teel family and find out what interests them on their homeschool Web page. See what curriculum they are working on this week, and explore some of their favorite links. Watch out for the polar bears, though!

Tips & Tools for Parents: Keeping Kids Safe Online
http://www.childrenspartnership.org/safety.html

The Children's Partnership, in cooperation with The National PTA and The National Urban League, presents a very nice overview of some of the dangers kids face on the Net and what parents can do about each one. One of the main things parents should know is that when kids meet the Internet, it always merits parental attention.

For Preschoolers

These engaging sites will amuse, excite, amaze, educate, and entertain your little ones.

Billy Bear's Playground — Billy Bear 4Kids.com
http://www.billybear4kids.com/
The graphics here are superb! You can play these games online, or offline on paper. The "Make Your Own Cartoon Bear" and the "Mix & Match Em Up" games are sure to be winners. Billy Bear has storybooks you will enjoy reading. Also, there's a lot of clip art you can use on your Web pages! Just be certain to read the rules for its use.

funschool.com - Free Interactive, educational software for Kids
http://www.funschool.com/
This site has more fun, engaging, and educational Java games than any other site we've seen for this edition. There are separate sections for preschoolers, kindergartners, first graders, and second graders. If your kids fall into third through sixth grade, there is one section for them. The Java games may take quite a while to load, but you can play with this site's online kaleidoscope while you wait.

GusTown: Fun, Games, Cartoons, and the CyberBuds!
http://www.gustown.com/home/gustownsummer.html
Meet Gus, Rant, Rave, and the rest of the Cyberbuds in this colorful town full of animations, articles, recipes, crafts, and links for kids and parents! Be sure to head over to the toy store for some fun games. Hint: Click on the Index link to look at a quick map to all the fun on this site.

Hop Pop Town
http://www.kids-space.org/HPT/
Precious musical games let preschoolers record a song or experiment with notes and instruments. Here's a writing activity that makes a cute, illustrated story. It's easy to use, with a little adult or older brother or sister help—the little ones learn about music and the mouse, and the "helpers" learn how to think more creatively!

Idea Box - Early Childhood Education and Activity Resources
http://www.theideabox.com/
Crafts for little hands, finger plays, recipes, games, and online stories are just a few of the ideas we found here. Parents will love these on a rainy day!

Kindergarten Kafe
http://members.aol.com/CharleneWP/kkafe.htm
Each issue of the newsletter offers a finger play, a story, suggested books, crafts, activities, and more. Look through back issues for holiday crafts and other activities.

LITTLE EXPLORERS by Enchanted Learning Software
http://www.EnchantedLearning.com/Dictionary.html
Try this on very little kids. They can click on any letter in the alphabet and link to lots of Web sites and activities that begin with that letter. This is an interactive picture dictionary with hours of fun just waiting behind the letters. This page also has English-French, English-German, English-Portuguese, and English-Spanish versions. Much of the site is also available in Japanese.

Meddybumps
http://www.meddybemps.com/
On the island of Meddybumps, jelly beans grow on vines, like grapes. You can learn all about the ritual and lore of gourmet bean tasting (yes, they sell them here, too). But that's not the best part. You can check out some wonderful and imaginative stories, or visit the Learning Activities section and the Young Writer's Workshop, where you can read a "story starter" to your child and ask him to finish the story. In the Learning area, click on Online Activities. Then have some fun playing games with frogs, fire engines, clowns, and rutabagas.

Nikolai's Web Site
http://www.nikolai.com/default.htm
Lots of creative stuff to do here! Make finger puppets, print out and build a town or a circus, cook easy recipes, dress paper dolls, read stories. Watch out for pirates!

The Theodore Tugboat Online Activity Centre
http://www.cochran.com/theodore/
Here's a tugboat with a smile and appealing eyes, straight from the Canadian TV series. Toddlers will love the interactive story, in which they get to choose what happens next. Downloadable coloring book pages sail via the Net to your printer or graphics program. Little ones can even get their own postcard in the mail from Theodore Tugboat himself!

For Kids Who Love Reading, Writing, Chat, or Pen Pals

Have you read these URLs? They are on Net-mom's "best-seller" list.

CLWG: Children's Literature Web Guide
http://www.acs.ucalgary.ca/~dkbrown/

This is the FIRST place to look for Internet resources related to books for children and young adults! Here you will find online children's stories, information about authors and illustrators, children's book awards, and lots of lists. Also available at this site are lists of book discussion groups, sources for book reviews, online resources, publishers, booksellers, and children's literature associations.

For Young Writers
http://www.inkspot.com/young/

If you dream about writing, this is your site! Get advice from professional writers and editors. Participate in chat sessions and discussions with other young writers. Find links to other useful writing sites. Submit your work to the Young Writer's Collection for Web publication. You may even get your first paid writing job by visiting the Market Info page.

FreeZone for kids: chat, e-pals, homepages, and much more!
http://www.freezone.com/

This place is so cool. In BrainStorm, you can do a puzzle, write a poem, and learn weird facts. And in Homework Helpers, you can find someone to assist you in the most difficult problem a teacher assigns! You can create your own home page, meet an e-pal, find out about your favorite band, TV show, or movie and even write a review! Son of Net-mom highly recommends this site's chat room.

HEADBONE ZONE - Be Weird, Be Wired, Be Inspired!
http://www.headbone.com/

If you're looking for someone to talk to, this is the place. There are four chat rooms, including two for teens and one for younger kids. Before you sign on, remember to read their rules: don't give out personal information in chat because if you do, you'll be booted. Bummer.

Mighty Media Keypals Club
http://www.mightymedia.com/keypals/

A part of the safe, fun Keypals Club, this is a good place to learn about others and the world around you as you practice the art of writing. This site acts as a remailer and does not divulge your e-mail address.

The Neverending Tale
http://www.coder.com/creations/tale/

Start reading one of the stories and when you get to the bottom of the page you'll find a number of choices about what to do next. You can follow a path someone else has written, or you can easily add your own series of choices.

Poetry Pals Internet Poetry Publishing Project for K-12 Students
http://www.geocities.com/EnchantedForest/5165/

Do you like to write poetry? If so, then by all means visit this site and share your poems with other kids. If you've never written a poem in your life, and you'd like to give it a try, click on Magnetic and take a peek at an online version of "magnetic poetry." Click on the words you like and drag them around to make a poem on your computer screen.

The Prince and I
http://www.nfb.ca/Kids/

The teenage prince has a problem. How can he be king someday if he can't read? Become a "Friend of the Prince", and you can help him learn by submitting stories to be posted at this site.

Treasure Island – Home
http://www.ukoln.ac.uk/services/treasure/

It's a tale of adventure, pirates, tropical islands, and murder! Robert Louis Stevenson's book, *Treasure Island*, is available online at this site. Besides a biography of the author, you'll find links to sites about pirates, islands, and buried treasure! This finely designed site also has some suggestions for things to do—besides reading, of course.

WORLD Magazine @ nationalgeographic.com
http://www.nationalgeographic.com/media/world/

National Geographic has been a family favorite for decades. Here is an online version of their magazine just for kids, called *WORLD*. The contents of the issues vary, but recently we found articles on the space station, pirates, and movies of an avalanche in action! There are links to challenging games, plus a way for you to get an international pen pal, too (click on "Kids" at the top of the screen).

For Kids Who Love Science and Math

Are you building a rocket out of old pieces of junk? Are you growing mold in your sock drawer? Do you celebrate Pi Day on 3/14 at 1:59? Then try these sites at home.

Bill Nye the Science Guy's Nye Labs Online
http://nyelabs.kcts.org/
It's Bill Nye the Science Guy, and is he loaded with science goodies to show you! Check out Today's Demo or visit the U-Nye-Verse to see what's happening in Bill's world of science. Lots of experiments and lessons on things scientific can be found here, plenty of fodder for your next science fair project.

Cool Math - Welcome to COOLMATH.COM by Karen!!
http://www.coolmath.com/
This is the greatest math site ever. Really, it has no equals. Want to multiply your fun on the Net? You can learn about tessellations, or meet the Icosidodeca family and others in the divisions of the Polyhedra Gallery. There are no limits to what you can do at Cool Math—or are there?

Exploratorium: ExploraNet
http://www.exploratorium.edu/
Do you know what makes a fruit fly grow legs out of its head? How would you like to take a "light walk" and explore the world of shadows? The Exploratorium, in San Francisco, California, is a huge hands-on science laboratory for kids of all ages. Discover the many interesting wonders that they have ported to the Web!

The NEW What's It Like Where You Live?
http://www.mobot.org/MBGnet/
Explore six different biomes here: grassland, rain forest, taiga, deciduous forest, desert, and tundra. You'll learn about the features of each area and its plants and animals. You don't have a clue what living in the taiga is like? Ask a kid at a school in Finland or Russia—links to schools in each biome area are included here!

Questacon
http://sunsite.anu.edu.au/Questacon/
Australia's National Science and Technology Centre has a fabulous online museum! You can explore lots of interactive exhibits, puzzles, games and more. Dinosaurs, meteors, optical illusions, and clever science activities abound here. This is one of the best sites on the Net for kids interested in science.

StarChild: A learning center for young astronomers
http://heasarc.gsfc.nasa.gov/docs/
    StarChild/StarChild.html
This is a wonderful beginner's guide to astronomy. It's written for smaller children and presents itself in an easy-to-read text. This site also includes sections on Earth, planets, stars, galaxies, the Sun, and more.

Volcano World Starting Points
http://volcano.und.nodak.edu/vw.html
How do you become a volcanologist? Look at this site to find out what becoming a volcanologist is all about and what courses you'll need to take. Oh yeah, there's also the BEST information here about volcanoes, including lessons and activities for teachers and students.

Welcome to Chem4Kids! Your Chemistry Website!
http://www.chem4kids.com/
You've got your solids, your liquids, and your gases, but did you know there's also something called *plasma*? It has nothing to do with blood, though. This kind of plasma includes ball lightning and the aurora borealis, or northern lights. You can also view plasma in the electrically charged matter contained in a fluorescent light or a neon sign. Find out lots about matter, elements, atoms, ions, and reactions at this fascinating site! Also included are brief biographies of famous scientists.

Welcome to Thinking Fountain!
http://www.sci.mus.mn.us/sln/tf/
From A to Z, you're going to find a lot of wonderful ideas and information here. Allow us to demonstrate! A—Read about Anansi the Spider and then find out how to make your own sliding spider toy. N—Noodle-ing around where you can build a structure out of spaghetti, (the secret is in the mini-marshmallows!). Finally, Z—Zoo Machines. Invent a machine to take care of all those animals. Keep going, you're sure to find lots more activities and ideas, galleries to show your work, books you can use, and surprises inspired by the Thinking Fountain!

Whelmers Science Activities
http://www.mcrel.org/whelmers/
Is there iron in your cereal? Can a penny dance on the top of a soda bottle? Want to find out? At this really cool site, you can open up 20 different "whelmers" and have a lot of fun while actually learning some useful information! It will require gathering some simple materials and then reading instructions on how to complete the task.

For Kids Who Love Sports and Outdoor Fun

Somebody had to make the call. Net-mom says these sites are "safe at home," and they are all winners!

ESPN SportsZone
http://espnet.sportszone.com/
Get the latest in up-to-the-minute sports reporting, including scores at this site, from the folks who bring you ESPN, the all-sports cable TV network.

The Exploratorium's Science of Hockey: Home
http://www.exploratorium.edu/hockey/
There you are—center ice at the San Jose Arena. Join the San Jose Sharks as they explore the science of one of the most exciting sports. Follow the Sharks as you learn about the ice, the skills, the equipment, and more. And when your mom tells you to be careful with your teeth, listen—she knows what she's talking about!

The Fishing Network
http://sbinnie.rogerswave.ca/tfn/
Something smells *fishy* here! That's because this page is full of fish-type information. Interested in learning about fly-fishing, or just want to talk with others interested in this art? Speaking of art, how about some color clip art of fish? You can find that at this site, too. There are also lots of links to other fishing pages on the Web, for people who like to fish for everything from panfish to deep sea monsters!

kcarroll's Horse Country
http://www.horse-country.com/
This is the ultimate horse site for juniors! Horse history, care, stories, sounds, images, and associations are all here. Several fantasy games let you create your own dream stable, "buy and sell" virtual horses, "compete" in virtual horse shows, and share the results with your fellow dream stable owners. Other musts here are the Junior Riders Mailing Digest and an International Pen Pal List.

The Locker Room....Sports For Kids!
http://members.aol.com/msdaizy/sports/locker.html
Do you need basic information on how to hold a bat, kick a football, serve a volleyball, or shoot a hockey puck? Get in here. Besides "skills and drills," you'll find the rules of these sports and many others, their histories, fun facts about them, and a glossary of terms. There is also advice on how to do warm-up exercises and how to deal with team problems.

NBA.com: The Official Site of the National Basketball Association
http://www.nba.com/
The official NBA Web site really lets you interact with the players and teams. You can't go one-on-one (yet), but they do have live chat sessions with all your favorite players, which are saved, so if you miss one you can go back and read the transcript! This site also gives you the latest news, schedules, results, and links to the home pages of the NBA teams. You can also read reports in Spanish and French, as well as follow international hoop tournaments.

NFL.COM
http://www.nfl.com/
The official NFL site provides the latest headlines and league statistics and even offers an opportunity to chat with the players. In the Fan area, you'll also find a complete digest of NFL rules (in English, Thai, Chinese, and Malay), the Pro Football Hall of Fame, and a library of historical facts and timelines.

The Official Site of Major League Baseball
http://www.majorleaguebaseball.com/
All the information you'd ever need to settle any World Series argument is here: all the stats, all the teams, everything but the hot dogs. Here, you'll find official information on all the major league teams, expanded box scores for all the games, and a great photo gallery! A baseball team shop is here, too, as well as contests for kids and others.

the olympic movement . le mouvement olympique
http://www.olympic.org/
This is the official site for the Olympics, where you can explore the past, present, and future of the Games. When new Olympic cities are announced, you can read news and updates here first. You can keep track of progress through the Olympic.org page or go directly to the official link they provide at <http://www.athens2004.gr/>.

Sports Illustrated for Kids
http://www.sikids.com/
This online magazine is all about athletic challenges. If you've been wanting to try your hand at a new sport, this is where you can find out all about the moves, the lingo, and the equipment. Don't miss the interviews with sports heroes, hilarious comics, games, and a whole lot more.

For Teachers

Here are some tried-and true shortcuts, sites, lesson plans, and more for busy teachers, administrators, and parents who care about education and technology.

Access Excellence
http://www.gene.com/ae/
This site is renowned for its design, content, and collaborative activities. Focusing on the biological sciences, the activities collection is truly excellent. Online "seminars" put you in touch with scientists and science teachers. Offerings include "Local Habitats," "Science of Amber," and "Emerging Diseases." Collaborative classroom projects like "Fossils Across America" help in sharing resources.

Blue Web'n Learning Library
http://www.kn.pacbell.com/wired/bluewebn/
This site collects the cream of the crop of learning-oriented Web sites. All sites are rated and categorized by area, audience, and type. Each subject category has links to related tutorials, activities, projects, lesson plans, and more. You can also use their keyword search to explore their collection.

Classroom Connect
http://www.classroom.net/
Classroom Connect is one of our favorite magazines. Their Web site doesn't disappoint, either. Check it out for info on upcoming conferences, a jumpstation to great Web links, newsgroups, ftp sites, a Web toolkit, and more. This is a commercial publisher, but they know their market, so stop in and browse!

From Now On—Educational Technology for Schools
http://fromnowon.org/
Internet use policies. Assessment. Libraries of the future. Grants. Parenting. *From Now On* tackles all those topics and more. It is a vast collection of feature articles, Web sites, and other resources, which you can use in your family, your classroom, and your community. Learn how to cut out the "mind kandy" and the "new plagiarism" of indiscriminate cut and paste.

Global SchoolNet Foundation Home Page
http://www.gsn.org/
"Where in the World Is Roger?" "Roots and Shoots with Jane Goodall," "International CyberFair," "Global Schoolhouse Videoconferencing"—the folks in charge of GSN just keep collecting and coming up with more terrific ideas all the time! Always fresh and exciting, this is where K–12 innovation lives on the Net. Kids can find new contest announcements at this site, including ThinkQuest and other opportunities.

Kathy Schrock's Guide for Educators - Home Page
http://www.capecod.net/schrockguide/
The links in this guide are organized according to subject area. In World History, for instance, you'll get a breakdown of Web pages, from "Ancient World Web" to "World War II: The World Remembers." Each month, a list of new resources will point you to the latest and greatest. Kathy Shrock's list is a lifesaver for teachers!

TEACHERS HELPING TEACHERS
http://www.pacificnet.net/~mandel/
Don't you just hate to read "advice" from someone who has never set foot in the classroom? Instead, here are your teaching peers, who know *exactly* what you are going through and how to help.

Web Sites And Resources For Teachers
http://www.csun.edu/~vceed009/
Many subject areas are covered here, but let's take math as an example. You'll not only get lesson plans but also online math applications, like a calorie calculator and even a magic square checker. Online board games such as Mancala (the great strategy game that teaches critical thinking) and dozens of puzzles will challenge you to go beyond worksheet math.

Web66 Home Page
http://web66.coled.umn.edu/
This is the largest collection of all the schools with Web sites in the world! If your school doesn't have a Web site yet, a cookbook here will give you the recipe to create one: where to get the software, how to write the HTML, and more. Teachers: Can't tell a LAN from a WAN? You'll find technical info anyone can understand, plus acceptable use policies as well as other technology planning musts.

The Well-connected Educator
http://www.gsh.org/wce/
This site features real teachers doing real things with technology in real classrooms. Read articles and find out how to get a multimedia, multidisciplinary project going—with classrooms on the other side of the planet. Talk to your peers about what works and what doesn't.

You've seen the sites that my mom thinks you'll like, but now you'll see the ones I *know* you will like! These sites are Son of Net-mom approved!

Ambrosia Software, Inc.
http://www.ambrosiasw.com/Ambrosia.html
This page has all kinds of shareware games that you can download and play. Personally, my favorite game is "Escape Velocity," but there are many others. Ambrosia also has mailing lists to tell you about upcoming games and such. Some of the games they have can be enhanced by downloading plug-ins. And like any good game maker, they have hidden cheats and Easter eggs. A word of advice: Make sure your computer has enough free storage space before downloading.

The Belch Page
http://www.rahul.net/renoir/
Do you like the pleasant sound of a burp? Do you wish you did not have to hurt yourself trying to get just the right tone? And do you want the reassurance that when your mother comes to yell at you, you can truthfully say it was not your fault? Well, this site is for you! It contains five high-quality burps that you can listen to and one "Grade A" snore! Caution: Do *not* have your volume up too loud for some of these, in the interest of good taste and possible regurgitation.

Bug Cuisine
http://www.orkin.com/html/cuisine.html
I bet you'd never purposely eat a bug, even a "chocolate-covered ant." You might change your mind when you see this site. It's filled with recipes containing common insects like grasshoppers and mealworms. If you try to make the "Dry Roasted Bugs" and your parents are wondering if that's such a good idea, just tell them that bugs give you protein!

The Codebook
http://www.codebook.pp.se/
CAUTION—SPOILER ALERT! This site has more cheats than you can shake a computer game at! Extra lives, unlimited funds, hints, walk-throughs, Easter eggs—it's all here! The Codebook is constantly updated, so if you've just gotten a new game and Codebook doesn't have the cheats for it yet, don't worry, it will! A word from Son-Of-Net-mom: This is the only program I use to get cheats.

Deb and Jen's Land O' Useless Facts
http://www-leland.stanford.edu/~jenkg/useless.html
If you are the kind of know-it-all who likes to impress people with obscure facts, then this site is for you. It has more useless facts than one person could ever need! Here are some examples: In English, "four" is the only digit that has the same number of letters as its value. Or how's this: ZIP code 12345 is assigned to General Electric in Schenectady, New York. Try this one on Aunt Mabel: "The Panama Canal was excavated from the coasts inland; the final short segment was cleared by explosives detonated by President Woodrow Wilson, who sent the signal by wire from New York City." Now we're not sure any of this stuff is true. Don't use this page to do your homework. But if you just want to have some fun with facts that not many people know, you should definitely check out this Web site.

The Internet Pizza Server
http://www.ecst.csuchico.edu/~pizza/
It's a little hard to explain this site. You can order a pizza with tons of weird toppings and have it delivered to your screen. You buy the pizzas with "Beej-Bux," a type of currency of which you have an unlimited supply. This is not just any kind of pizza, mind you. You can get a pizza with EYEBALLS on it. Or GOBLINS. Heck, you can even order kitchen sinks on your pizza! When making your selections, don't put too many toppings on at a time (some kinds of toppings have a tendency to get buried). Is it silly? Yes, but remember, you get what you pay for.

Name That Candybar
http://www.sci.mus.mn.us/sln/tf/c/
    crosssection/namethatbar.html

Do you like candy bars? Do you like them so much that you could recognize them anywhere? At this site you can test your skills! There are 24 pictures of candy bars that have been cut in cross-section so you can see what is inside them. Twelve of these are harder to guess and in a different section of the site. See if you can beat Son of Net-mom! I was able to get 18 of them right. Most of the ones I got wrong were some sort of local generic-brand candy. If you beat me, well, give yourself a pat on the back!

THE SIMPSONS
http://www.foxworld.com/simpsons/simpcity.htm

The Simpsons page. Need I say more? This page is for anyone who has ever used the phrase "Homer Simpson" when someone else is acting dumb. It also has some cool facts about the characters and the shows. Keep looking, maybe there is an answer to the question "Why doesn't baby Maggie ever grow?" But then again, maybe not. If you take the quiz, here's a clue. On his famous ride, Paul Revere did not say to the British, "Hey Redcoats, eat my shorts, man!"

Super Soaker
http://www.supersoaker.com/

My mom thinks I don't know about this site. Ha! She thinks I don't know about the CSP 3000! HA! At this page you can find out about any kind of Super Soaker. From the Original S.S. 15 to the CSP 3000, it's all here. You can also enter a contest to WIN Super Soakers (ask your parents first). And don't forget about the mini soaker series! If you like getting wet, this is the page for you. If you like getting OTHER people wet this is REALLY the page for you. And by the way, Mom, I've been saving up—better get your poncho!

U.S.S. Jaguar
http://worldkids.net/jaguar/

Have you always wanted to be a crew member on a Starfleet mission? At this free online club for kids, you can—but first you have to pass a *Star Trek* trivia test. I really enjoy the mailing list, which includes discussions on real-life transporters, the uselessness of Borg assimilation techniques, and general rants about the Ferengi. If you see Junior Lieutenant Oten'nan, that's Son of Net-mom.

THE BEST
OF THE REST OF THE BOOK

The other 11 hotlists represent major topics, like Science and Sports. Sites appearing on Net-mom's hotlists should be considered the "Best of the Book" in those categories. On each hotlist we include only ten sites. Sometimes we had too many great sites, though, and we wanted to showcase them in another special way. The following don't-miss sites are scattered throughout the book, and some might be tucked away in subject headings you might think wouldn't interest you. Trust Net-mom, if you visit any of these resources, you'll be impressed. They are too good to miss.

Amazing Space Web-Based Activities
http://oposite.stsci.edu/pubinfo/education/amazing-space/

The Hubble Space Telescope folks have a whole spectrum of fun Web-based activities here. In Star Light, Star Bright you can explore the nature of light waves and prisms. Don't miss the brain teasers in this section. Learn fast facts about planets to collect virtual Solar System Trading Cards. If neither of those are challenging enough, fasten your seat belts and enter the Hubble Deep Field Academy for some advanced training. Still think you're pretty good? Help plan a Hubble Space Telescope mission. Soon: No escape—the truth about black holes!

ArtLex - dictionary of visual art
http://www.artlex.com/

From Baroque to Pop Art, from Realism to Renaissance—all those confusing art terms are defined here, along with notes on how to pronounce them. Included are over 2,600 techniques, styles, and art history words. Here's the best part: the dictionary is illustrated, and not only that, there are links to other Web pages with more information.

Ballparks by Munsey & Suppes
http://www.ballparks.com/

Interested in baseball, football, hockey, or basketball? You should be interested in where the games are played, too, and this site will tell you about those fields, rinks, and courts. This site offers stadium facts, statistics, aerial views, and more! For example, explore baseball's American and National League parks of the past, present, and future.

Band-Aides and Blackboards
http://funrsc.fairfield.edu/~jfleitas/contents.html

Subtitled "When Chronic Illness...Or Some Other Medical Problem...Goes To School," this site is about growing up with a medical problem. Just because kids and teens have an illness, it doesn't mean they aren't interested in pets, TV, music, video games, and other stuff. Meet kids with cancer, kids with cerebral palsy, kids with ADD, and many more. You'll also find poems written by kids with chronic illness, take virtual hospital tours, and find out once and for all what to do about teasing.

Baseball Links: Main Menu
http://www.baseball-links.com/main.shtml

This is a neat, annotated collection of Web sites, newsgroups, and graphics from all over the Net. You'll find links to baseball history, stats, Little League, coaching, and lots more here. How about softball, whiffleball, and the Irish and Swedish baseball teams? Yes, they are here, too, as well as a link to the U.S. Olympic baseball team's home page. Bring some peanuts and hot dogs—you'll be here all day!

Bluedog can count!!
http://www.forbesfield.com/bdf.html

Blue Dog is a classic Web celebrity, and she's been around for quite a while. She's had a lot of time to practice basic arithmetic, and she's willing to help anyone learn how to do simple math problems. Just type in your numbers, and Blue Dog will bark the answer. She's always right, patient, and so...colorful.

Bottom Dollar
http://www.bottomdollar.com/

Find the best price for a book, CD, toy, movie, hardware, software, or other merchandise. For example, just type in the name of the book you want, and the search engine queries several online bookstores to discover the lowest price.

CMCC - Mysteries of Egypt - Title page
http://www.civilization.ca/membrs/civiliz/
    egypt/egypt_e.html

Tutankhamun's tomb, discovered in 1922 by Howard Carter, contained over 3,000 wonderful things, including a golden mask of the boy king himself. Although he became king at age nine, he was dead by about age 17. What really happened to Tutankhamun? What was his life like? Was he murdered? Find out possible answers here. Gaze in awe at the treasures found, displayed for you in the virtual galleries. There are also many additional links collected at this excellent site.

CNN Interactive
http://www.cnn.com/

CNN, the 24-hour news channel, has made it easy and fast to get the news of the moment over the Internet. And it's in a multimedia format that brings you lots more than words. You'll find that QuickTime movies and sound turn up in the most amazing places! Look for them in stories about belly-flop contests as well as space shuttle dockings. And if you want to know more about the news CNN is covering, you can link to thousands of newspapers, magazines, and broadcasts from all over the world. Don't forget that CNN covers entertainment, sports, style, and other fun stuff. Check out Billboard's weekly Top Ten list, featuring sound clips of each popular song.

Destination: Himalayas - Where Earth Meets Sky
http://library.advanced.org/10131/

This ThinkQuest contest grand prize winner was created by a team of geographically and culturally diverse kids! It gives an overview of the Himalayan region, its flora and fauna, and its environmental problems. "Himalaya" is a Sanskrit word, which literally means "Abode of Snow." You'll find multimedia if you choose the high-bandwidth version, otherwise the text will inform and enlighten. This excellent site proves what value kids bring to the Net.

Discovery Online
http://www.discovery.com/

You'd expect to find background articles on many of the Discovery Channel's programs here, and you'd be right. There are stories and pictures from shows on history, nature, science, and people. Here are some examples: You can visit a baseball factory in Costa Rica or take a close-up look at elephants. And there's more: links to The Learning Channel and Animal Planet programming and a way to search the archives of past fascinating stories!

Down Syndrome
http://tqjunior.advanced.org/3880/

This site was created by kids to explain Down Syndrome to other kids. One of the kids on the Web team has Down Syndrome. You can read all about him at this page and also see a video of him in a wrestling competition. This resource explains that kids with Down Syndrome are not so different after all. You'll also find out about the history of the syndrome as well as other facts. This resource does its job so well, it was a winner in the 1998 ThinkQuest Junior awards competition!

Earth and Moon Viewer
http://www.fourmilab.ch/earthview/vplanet.html

When it's 10 A.M. and bright and sunny in Florida, what's it like in Japan? Stop by this site and ask their server, which will show where it's light and dark any place in the world. You can choose the satellite location to view from, or you can tell it to look at Earth from the Sun's or Moon's perspective. You can even create a custom request and specify the desired longitude and latitude you want to see; the computer then picks the best viewpoint.

ENERGY QUEST — Energy Education from the California Energy Commission
http://www.energy.ca.gov/education/

What was Ben Franklin's energy-saving invention? Join Ben in a word game to find out the answer. He also has other games, crafts, and even a Declaration of (Energy) Independence. This site has activities and games about different kinds of energy, from wind to solar and nuclear to hydroelectric! This site is a must for the energy-efficient, but it loads very slowly. There is a text only and low-bandwidth version you might try.

Foam Bath Fish Time
http://www.savetz.com/fishtime/

Bathtub foam fish toys can have more than one use, after all. This site will tell you the time in several time zones—using FISH. Just get in here and see one of Net-mom's all-time favorite Internet toys.

Fynbos - Kingdom Threatened
http://www.lizard.org/jfd/cf/narrate.html

Fynbos refers to "the characteristic shrubland of the southwestern and southern Cape of South Africa." To continue to amaze you, we offer this tidbit: "The 470 square kilometers of the Cape Peninsula, including Table Mountain, is home to 2,256 different plant species - more than the whole of Great Britain (which only supports 1,500 species), an area 5,000 times bigger!" This outstanding site will introduce you to Fynbos and its plant life. You'll also learn about the threats to this shrubland, which include everything from Man to alien plants. The best part is that the entire site was done by KIDS—it was a winner in this year's CyberFair, and for good reason.

Harcourt Brace School Publishers Math
http://www.hbschool.com/justforkids/math/math.html

Choose your grade and get ready for fun. It is amazing that you can learn a lot of math stuff while you are having such a good time. Take fourth grade, for example. With one click of the mouse, you can be working with Dr. Gee in the 3-D lab, helping her figure out what flat maps could be folded into which solids. Each grade has several areas you'll enjoy, along with a great glossary of mathematic terms.

How To Love Your Dog
http://www.geocities.com/~kidsanddogs/

Getting a dog is a big responsibility. You will care for your pet for many years to come. Are you ready for that? If so, print out the I Love My Dog contract here, and sign it. Show the contract to your dog. He will be very, very impressed. If you're still wondering if dog ownership is for you, study this site. It goes through everything: what dogs cost, what various types of dogs are like, how to train dogs, and how you feel when you lose your dog. This impressive site doesn't just teach how to love your dog. There are lessons here about kindness and humane treatment that carry over into dealings with people too.

Inventions! @ nationalgeographic.com
http://www.nationalgeographic.com/features/
    96/inventions/

You'll need Shockwave to play these inventing games, but if you don't have it, you can use the neat selection of links to other pages on inventions around the Web. There are five games; one is guessing the purpose of a wacky patent drawing. Hmmm, is it an automatic baby-patting machine or a mitten stretcher? If you guess right enough times, you'll get a token. Get five tokens, and you can operate the wackiest machine of them all back at the Lab: the Action Contraption!

Investing for Kids
http://tqd.advanced.org/3096/

How can you use money to make more money? What's the deal with stocks, anyway? And what the heck are mutual funds? This page, developed by kids for other kids, will let you check your knowledge of the stock market, play some money games, and learn about the world of financial investments. Study this ThinkQuest entry, then give your parents some advice!

J.J.'s Adventure: A Baby Gray Whale's Rescue and Release
http://tqjunior.advanced.org/4397/

J.J. the gray whale has made lots of news this year. First she was found on the beach at the tender age of seven days old. Although very sick, she was rescued, cared for, and eventually released back to her home in the Pacific Ocean. Three schoolgirls loved the story so much they decided to make a Web page and enter the ThinkQuest Junior contest. Guess what? They won Best of Contest! View lots of great photos and learn how J.J. got her name at this terrific site.

Kids Farm Where do you want to go?
http://www.kidsfarm.com/wheredo.htm

Any idea what the difference is between alfalfa and regular grass? Familiar with the sounds a turkey makes? Did you know you should stay away from the back of a horse and the front of a bull? You'll know the answers to these perennial questions if you visit this site. You'll also become an expert on farm equipment and learn all about hay baling and other fun on a working Colorado farm.

KidsHealth - Children's Health & Parenting Information
http://kidshealth.org/

This is the best kids' health resource out on the Net. Now, you might be thinking, "Diseases, ick! Why would I want to visit a Web page about health?" Well, haven't you always wanted to know what causes hiccups? The answer's here! And what if we said the Shockwave games here are awesome? Play Plak Attack: shoot toothpaste or crack your floss whip to fight back at the plaque monsters and keep your teeth healthy. Or try the animations about how your body works. Hit the kitchen for some healthy recipes (try Ants on a Log or Pretzels), or read some reviews of hot toys and see how they rate on the Fun-o-meter. There is a LOT more here; we recommend the whole site for learning about nutrition, feelings, and lots of ways to stay healthy.

Learn2.com - The ability utility
http://www.learn2.com/

Do you know how to use chopsticks or how to clean a freshly caught fish? Could you use a lesson in putting a golf ball or breaking in a new baseball mitt? How about tips on folding a shirt or cleaning up a stain? This truly great site will teach you all of the above and more!

LEGO Worlds
http://www.lego.com/

Your dog chewed all the little pieces, and now you need some new ideas for other Lego projects to make with what's left! On the LEGO Information page, you can see pictures of other people's creations and discover how to make and play Lego games. You'll also find fun online games, screen savers, and other things to download for Lego-maniacs everywhere.

Main Menu @ nationalgeographic.com
http://www.nationalgeographic.com/main.html

Take a road trip with *National Geographic* as they take you on a series of adventures around the world. Tour the fantastic forest, discover dinosaur eggs, and even stop at the White House. These people are exploring professionals!

Mark Newbold's Animated Necker Cube
http://www.sover.net/~manx/necker.html

Do not try this illusion at home. Remember we warned you. OK, well maybe you can try it at home, but make sure you have your seatbelts fastened first and that your tray and seat backs are fully upright. Prepare for your brain cells to get messed up as your perception of this seemingly innocent cube switches around. According to this site, "The Necker Cube is named after the Swiss crystallographer Louis Albert Necker, who in the mid-1800s saw cubic shapes spontaneously reverse in perspective." But don't try the Counter-Rotating Spirals Illusion. Unless you want to have fun!

Mission to Mars Homepage
http://library.advanced.org/11147/

This exemplary site was the winner of the 1998 ThinkQuest competition's Math and Science category, entirely built by kids. You can learn all sorts of information about Mars, the Red Planet, here at Mars Academy. But the real fun starts when you can outfit and fly your own mission! You have to know a lot to design your mission, so you'd better go back to the Academy and make sure you did all the assigned homework! This site takes a long time to explore, and your mission may take many visits to complete. That's why they ask you to set up an "account" so they can keep track of your spacecraft, but don't worry, it's free.

NativeTech: Native American Technology and Art
http://www.lib.uconn.edu/NativeTech/

This site is really neat! It talks about a lot of Native American art and technologies like beadwork, clay and pottery, leather and clothes, toys and games, and more. We started at beadwork because it seems so interesting. There is information about the kinds of beads and their meanings. Wampum beads were made from shells and often decorated clothing. Long woven wampum belts were often exchanged at treaty signings or other formal occasions. You can find out how the beads were made—it was a very difficult process! Let's mosey on over to porcupine quillwork, perhaps the oldest form of Native American embroidery. Native American artists sometimes decorate their clothing and birchbark containers with quills. At this site, not only do you learn the history of these fascinating art forms, you can also learn these crafts. Maybe you should start with the cornhusk doll instructions, though, since corn's easier to find than porcupine quills.

Neuroscience for Kids - Explore the NS
http://weber.u.washington.edu/~chudler/introb.html

When you bite into a chocolate bar, how do you know it's delicious? How do you know to say "Ouch!" when you get stung by a mosquito? Little sensors, called *neurons*, are all over your body, and they carry messages to your brain through a system of nerves. Your brain then sorts everything out. This resource is crammed with great info about brains, your senses, spinal cords, and careers in neuroscience. Be aware, though, that many of these folks go to school for 20 *years* before they become neuroscientists!

New Jersey Online: Wendell's Yucky Bug World
http://www.nj.com/yucky/roaches/

Visit the yuckiest site on the Internet. You can find out about cockroaches and other bug stuff. Take the Cockroach World quiz, or tell your cockroach story to the rest of the forum. Stop by Cockroach World's multimedia library for yucky sights and sounds. Hear the hiss of the Madagascar hissing cockroach or watch the "Smelly Roach" QuickTime movie. You'll also learn that cockroaches spend 75 percent of their time resting up for those late-night snack runs!

OneLook Dictionaries (Dictionary), The Faster Finder
http://www.onelook.com/

Did you know that a lot of specialized online dictionaries are scattered all over the Net? There are dictionaries for medicine, sports, religion, art, music, and more. This site has cobbled together 287 of them to create a huge dictionary you can search with just one look (can you guess what it is called?). Be sure to check out the survey, too. It will ask you how you pronounce certain Net-related words. Past surveys have sampled world opinion on the correct way to say "GIF," "URL," and "FAQ." Vote for your favorite audio file and let your voice be counted!

The Otto Club
http://www.ottoclub.org/

The California State Automobile Association has a terrific site to help very young kids learn about traffic safety. Visit Otto the car and his interactive town; talk about "street smarts"—Otto is a real know-it-all! There is a full-featured animation and sound version or a lighter version for those who believe less is more. Sing along with the Seat Belt Song by pressing the radio buttons on Otto's dashboard. Play the traffic light game and see if you can compare the two pictures and decide who's stopped for red based on the signals you can see. There are little games on helmet safety and playground safety, too. Be sure to click on the question mark in each area, though, to find out what you can do in each section.

PBS Online
http://www.pbs.org/

If it's on PBS, it's educational, entertaining, excellent, or all three. Viewers support their local public stations, and these stations provide quality local programs as well as programs from PBS (Public Broadcasting Service). From Muppets to money, PBS brings us important issues and delightful special events. The Web site invites you to investigate what's on the schedule, what's going on inside the network, and what to try on in the network store. The online news reports keep you up to date, and links to your local station keep you in touch. Look for all the PBS kids shows in the Kids' area of this site. Did you know that you're the public? So it's your network!

Quotations Home Page
http://www.geocities.com/~spanoudi/quote.html

"A child of five could understand this. Fetch me a child of five." The comedian Groucho Marx said that. To find all kinds of quotes, from long ago and just yesterday, be sure to try this page. You'll find quotes from Miss Piggy to David Letterman here. There's a collection of the world's most annoying proverbs ("Haste makes waste") as well as Miscellaneous Malapropisms and student bloopers ("The Egyptians built the Pyramids in the shape of a huge triangular cube"). Don't miss "The Best of Anonymous" either ("Remember, a day without sunshine is like night"). This site is highly recommended!

A Science Odyssey
http://www.pbs.org/wgbh/aso/

We don't care what you're doing right now. Just get on the Net and visit this site. You will not be disappointed. Check out the Shockwave simulations in the You Try It section. In the Technology at Home area, you can scroll through the twentieth century and see what changes happen in the virtual home. Appliances appear and disappear, telephone equipment changes—what else will you notice? You can mouse over each item, and it will give you some facts about it: what it is, who invented it, and when it came into vogue or went out of style. Now try the other explorations: human evolution, radio transmission, probe the brain, atomic structure, and several more. When you get done with those, read the On the Edge comic books about various scientists and their discoveries. Did radio astronomer Jocelyn Bell really think she'd gotten a message from little green men in outer space? Find out here! Don't miss the hit game show That's My Theory! Question the three contestants to see which one is the real Einstein, the real Freud, and the real ENIAC.

Space Day
http://www.spaceday.com/

Every year, Space Day is celebrated on the Thursday prior to the anniversary of U.S. President John F. Kennedy's 1961 challenge to "land a man on the moon and return him to the Earth." There are loads of related online events that day, but the official Web page is fun anytime. Try the Night Watchman and see if you can click and drag the constellations to the correct place in the sky (if you've got sound, you'll even hear the crickets!). In The Phaser, you'll learn all about the phases of the Moon (hope you know your waxing from your waning gibbous; if not, this site will teach you). And don't forget to send your friends some space postcards to show that you really get around.

ThinkQuest
http://www.thinkquest.org/

Would you like to win thousands of dollars in scholarship money? Do you have a great idea for a new Web resource? You might be a fabulous C++ programmer, but you can't write interesting English prose very well. Or maybe you're terrific at graphics but can't code. Maybe you're not a computer nut at all but you really know how to research a topic. There is a place for all of you at ThinkQuest. First, you have to create a team to work on your project. Advertise your skills and your ideas at the Team Maker part of the site. Typically, teams are formed with four or five kids from all over the world; they have usually never met, and they usually come from schools or homeschools with widely varying levels of technology. You also need a coach or two, usually a teacher or a parent, but it could be someone else. You decide how to tackle the project, and then spend many months building your Web resource on the server space provided by ThinkQuest. You and your team members use chat rooms to discuss the project as well as e-mail and other forms of communication. Eventually the contest deadline rolls around and your project is frozen in time so that the judges can take a look. If your site if chosen as a finalist, you and your team (and your coaches) are flown (all expenses paid) to Washington, D.C. Your site is inspected by the finals judges. You and your team are interviewed, and at long last, winners are chosen and placements are made. The winning team members each get $25,000 scholarships, and many of the finalist teams who place lower receive scholarships as well. ThinkQuest has given away over one million dollars in scholarship money. There are two contests, one for elementary grades, called ThinkQuest Junior, and the original one for older kids. At this site you can explore past winners' sites and get information about the latest ThinkQuest competition schedule.

Trendy Magic - Interactive Style
http://pw2.netcom.com/~sleight/interactivemagic.html

Check this one out! Here are some interactive tricks that are guaranteed to catch you off guard. We thought, hey, how mysterious can it be, it's only a rabbit. Wrong! It fooled us! Then we tried Color Theory. How'd they do that? Maybe we're just too susceptible. But after the Psycho Test, we just turned off the computer, backed away, and kept a safe distance for a while.

USA Today WEATHER
http://www.usatoday.com/weather/wfront.htm

This site is the best-kept secret on the Net for weather information! You'll find a ton of special articles, fun facts, and lots of other goodies at this site, from information on tornadoes and hurricanes to tips on weather forecasting. Check the index. If you have a weather-related report due or if you're just interested in things meteorological, do not miss this excellent site.

The Weather Channel - Home Page
http://www.weather.com/homepage.html

How's the weather where you are, or anywhere else, for that matter? Actually, anyone can find out just by visiting this page. Sure, you'll find up-to-date weather information from around the world, but that's only the beginning. This site has more weather stuff than anyone could imagine. It includes shareware to download, colorful maps, video clips, tips on getting started as a meteorologist, and special forecasts for sports fans. This site is really cool (in the north) and hot (down south)!

Welcome to FOTW (Flags of the World)
http://fotw.digibel.be/flags/

If you were going to design a flag for the Internet, what would it look like? Fans of this site have chosen one—see what you think. We liked one of the losers (the one with the two crossed computer mice), but there is no accounting for taste. You'll also find pages and pages of flags of the world here. An extra bonus: you'll see national symbols, anthems, and other patriotic links for many countries.

Welcome to Geo-Globe: Interactive Geography!
http://library.advanced.org/10157/

This ThinkQuest contest finalist site, built by kids, will rock your world! How much do you know about geography? In Geo-Find, you can play at the beginner, intermediate, or advanced levels. Is Santiago the capital of Chile? What countries contain part of the Sahara Desert? Is Egypt south or north of the equator? Right or wrong, you'll get more links for you to explore on that topic. Geo-Quest involves ten questions: try to guess the right animal or bird, based on the answers to the questions you pose. Don't stop there—there are several more games that will test your knowledge of the seas, lands, and skies of Planet Earth.

White House for Kids
http://www.whitehouse.gov/WH/kids/
  html/kidshome.html

Let Socks, the First Cat, take you on a fascinating kid's-eye tour of the White House in Washington, D.C. You'll learn how the White House was built (bricks were made on the front lawn), tour the rooms, and find out the First Family pets that have lived there (don't miss President Harrison's goat or Caroline Kennedy's pony). We learned something we didn't know before: the president's desk was once part of a ship, abandoned north of the Arctic circle in 1854!

Winnie the Pooh - An Expotition
http://www.worldkids.net/pooh/

Explore this interactive map of the "100 Aker Wood" and try to find and visit all 20 wonderful places. Check out the Bee Tree, Rabbit's house, and the ever-popular Heffalump Trap! You'll find interactive games and more at each site.

The Wonderful World of Trees
http://www.domtar.com/arbre/english/start.htm

This resource has several sections. You can follow a Canadian tree through its four seasons. Click on the buds, the branches, the roots, and the leaves and see what's going on at each time. In the Formidable Forms section, you can learn how to classify trees by the properties they have in common. Other areas of this site discuss protecting trees, paper recycling, and an update on the devastating ice storms of the winter of 1997–1998. Hint: Click on the camera icon to open an encyclopedia of trees, with photos and information on each. If you click on the tic-tac-toe icon, you'll discover several tree-related games and word find puzzles.

Yak's Corner
http://www.yakscorner.com/

Imagine a magazine for kids run by a yak. There would be hard-hitting investigative journalism (Is Lake Champlain Really a Great Lake?), survey reports (How High is Your Allowance?), and even behind-the scenes-sports stories (How to Talk Hockey). You'd also find some Yaktivities, such as the Neverending Yak Story, where you can add to the adventures kids have already written, some yak jokes, and lots of fun and games. You don't have to imagine it—you can visit it!

Zoom Dinosaurs - Enchanted Learning Software
http://www.EnchantedLearning.com/subjects/dinosaurs/

This is a great site—it can be enjoyed by all age groups. Everyone, including your little brother and your parents, will love it. There are lots of pictures, animations, and tons of great scientific information. There's a geologic time scale, a dino dictionary, and lots of activities and links. You'll also find some fun, and some really bad jokes such as this: Question: "Why did the dinosaur cross the road?" Answer: "Because the chicken hadn't evolved yet!"

AFRICAN AMERICANS

CULTURE

Africa Online: Kids Only

At this site, you can find a key pal at a school in Africa! Did you know that over 1,000 different languages are spoken in Africa? For some quick lessons in Kiswahili, some fun word search and other games, and biographies of Nelson Mandela and other famous Africans, check this site.

http://www.africaonline.com/AfricaOnline/
coverkids.html

The Encyclopedia of African Music

Spanning musical styles from the entire Black diaspora, you'll hear everything from the Kenyan national anthem to Caribbean reggae and Brazilian samba at this most comprehensive site! But wait, there's more: lots of country-specific information, including languages, history, and geography. There are way too many links here for Net-mom to check them all, so explore with caution and with a parent.

http://matisse.net/~jplanet/afmx/ahome.htm

It appeared on the cover of *Mad* magazine back in 1965. It has been called the Poiuyt, the Devil's Fork, the Three Stick Clevis, the Widgit, the Blivit, even the Triple Encabulator Tuned Manifold. No, it is not Alfred E. Neuman. What is it?

Answer: It is an impossible drawing that looks like a pitchfork with three tines, but if you look closely, it has only two. Find out more at
*http://www.illusionworks.com/html/
impossible_trident.html*

HISTORICAL FIGURES

The African American History Challenge

Learn about 12 famous African American men and women from the nineteenth century, then see if you can score high on the quiz!

http://www.brightmoments.com/blackhistory/

Did you know that Mary Church Terrell was the first president of the National Association of Colored Women or that Mary Ann Shadd was the first Black woman editor of a North American newspaper?

Read about other African American pioneers at The African American History Challenge!

African American inventors, inventions, and patent dates

This is a list of some African American inventors and their patented inventions. These inventions include a pencil sharpener, refrigeration equipment, elevator machinery, and railroad telegraphy discoveries.

http://www.ai.mit.edu/~isbell/HFh/black/
events_and_people/009.aa_inventions

African American Online Exhibit Homepage

Profiles of significant African Americans in science, medicine, and technology were developed by students at the University of California at Irvine. This site also has a great timeline of events, inventions, and people, and you'll find educational opportunities and organizations in support of African Americans pursuing a career in the sciences.

http://sun3.lib.uci.edu/~afrexh/AAhomepage.html

A B C D E F G H I J K L M N O P Q R S T U V W X Y Z

A
B
C
D
E
F
G
H
I
J
K
L
M
N
O
P
Q
R
S
T
U
V
W
X
Y
Z

A Deeper Shade of History: Events & Folks in Black History

What happened this week in Black history? Search on any date at this Web site. You can also search on a name, and if you're lucky, there will be a short biography. For example, there's Benjamin Banneker, born in Maryland in 1731. His father was a slave although his mother was free. He was a real tinkerer and was always taking things apart and putting them back together. He built the first wooden clock in America! He was also interested in astronomy, geology, physics—and surveying. Thomas Jefferson appointed Banneker to the team that planned the layout of Washington, D.C. He is probably best known for his almanac series, called Benjamin Banneker's Almanac and Ephemeris.

http://www.ai.mit.edu/~isbell/HFh/black/bhist.html

Everyone knows diamonds are made out of carbon, right? So is graphite, the "lead" in your pencil. How can one be so hard and the other so soft, if they are both made out of the same thing?

Answer: *It all depends on the chemical structure of the carbon. Scientists are experimenting with a new carbon structure, called buckminsterfullerene (or fullerene for short, also known as "buckyballs"). This structure looks something like a geodesic dome, which was invented by Buckminster Fuller. One cool thing you can do with buckyballs is put other atoms inside the buckyball "cage." This can create all sorts of new materials, with interesting properties! Read more about buckyballs and other structures at* http://www.lbl.gov/MicroWorlds/MaterialWorld/MatWorld.html *in the Material World section.*

Education World™ - Lesson Planning: A Black History Treasure Hunt!

This is a fun and educational Black History Month activity—a treasure hunt that will take you all over the Web to find the answers! Don't worry, there are suggested Web sites for you to try first. Be sure to choose the right hunt for your grade level. There are four different treasure hunts: one for fourth grade and below, one for fifth and sixth graders, one for seventh and eighth graders, and one for ninth graders and above. Sample question for fourth graders: "This person refused to give up a seat on the bus. That led to a 382-day bus boycott by black people in Montgomery, Alabama." Do you know the answer? Find out here!

http://www.education-world.com/a_lesson/ lesson052.shtml

The Faces of Science: African Americans in the Sciences

This site gives you biographical information for about 100 African Americans who have made important contributions to science. The articles are well documented, and their sources are cited. You can also see a selection of patents issued to some of these scientists.

http://www.lib.lsu.edu/lib/chem/display/faces.html

Ronald E. McNair

Dr. McNair was a mission specialist aboard the 1984 flight of the space shuttle *Challenger*. Read about his life at this site.

http://www.aad.berkeley.edu/uga/osl/mcnair/ Ronald_E._McNair.html

Have a whale of a time in MAMMALS.

HISTORY
The African-American Mosaic Exhibition (Library of Congress)

The Library of Congress is in Washington, D.C., and it has a huge collection of materials, some of which cover about 500 years of African history in the Western Hemisphere. The materials include books, periodicals, prints, photographs, music, film, and recorded sound. This exhibit samples these materials in four areas: Colonization, Abolition, Migrations, and the Work Projects Administration period. You'll be able to look at pages from original materials, such as an abolitionist children's book. Sometimes it's useful to look at these original materials, also called "primary sources," for yourself, rather than use books other people have written about these same sources—this way, you're closer to what really happened. This site has lots to use for school reports!

http://lcweb.loc.gov/exhibits/african/intro.html

Anacostia Museum Homepage

Did you know that February is Black History Month? This site will give you many examples of the contributions of African Americans to U.S. history and culture. You will discover online exhibits of inventions, art, music, and more. The museum is located in Washington, D.C. Hint: Click on the Exhibitions and Programs menu choice and not the navigation bar at the bottom.

http://www.si.edu/anacostia/anachome.htm

NET FILES

In a recipe, what does the symbol XXX mean?

Answer: No, it's not when you throw in a mystery ingredient of your choice! It's the symbol for light, fluffy confectioners' sugar. Check http://www.foodstuff.com/cgibin/glos-x.cfm?alpha=X for a great food glossary.

Black History: The African American Journey

This excellent site from the editors of *World Book Encyclopedia* traces the history of African Americans from slavery to freedom. It offers information on the civil rights movement as well as a brief history of Black History Month itself. The idea began all the way back in 1926, with the observance of Negro History Week. It was originally proposed by Carter G. Woodson, among others. Woodson was a black historian and is now known as the "Father of Black History." Black History Week began during the early 1970s and Black History Month was first celebrated in 1976. It is sponsored each year by the Association for the Study of Afro-American Life and History in Washington, D.C., which Woodson founded in 1915.

http://www.worldbook.com/features/blackhistory/

CNN Million Man March - Oct. 16, 1995

On October 16, 1995, Nation of Islam leader Louis Farrakhan called thousands of African American men to go to Washington, D.C., to make their voices heard. This historic event is chronicled here. CNN's site includes pointers to the "official" MMM site but adds audio and video to the print record. Read many related stories, quotes, and support material, including biographies of some of the main participants.

http://www3.cnn.com/US/9510/megamarch/march.html

Education First: Black History Activities

This comprehensive and thoughtful collection of links in support of Black History Month will take you all over the Web on a treasure hunt to find the answers to some very big questions. You'll also find information on many prominent Africans and people of African descent, from Bob Marley to Nelson Mandela. This site has study questions and activities for classes as well.

http://www.kn.pacbell.com/wired/BHM/AfroAm.html

A
B
C
D
E
F
G
H
I
J
K
L
M
N
O
P
Q
R
S
T
U
V
W
X
Y
Z

A
B
C
D
E
F
G
H
I
J
K
L
M
N
O
P
Q
R
S
T
U
V
W
X
Y
Z

Exploring Amistad: Race and the Boundaries of Freedom in Antebellum Maritime America

What has come to be known as the Amistad Revolt began in 1839 as a shipboard slave uprising off the coast of Cuba. It intensified into a debate on slavery, race, Africa, and the foundations of American democracy itself. Popularized by a recent movie, you can read the original accounts of the story at this informative site. The schooner the slaves took over was named *Amistad*, which means "friendship."

http://amistad.mysticseaport.org/main/welcome.html

Harriet Tubman and the Underground Railroad for Children

An escaped slave could work his way north to Canada and gain his freedom, but the journey was often hundreds of miles long. He had to remain hidden, his route secret. Along the way, he would be helped by a loose organization of sympathetic people who provided a hot meal, shelter, and, often, help traveling to the next "station" on the Underground Railroad. You'll also find links to other Web resources on the Underground Railroad and the brave "conductors" who made it run, without regard to their own personal risk. One of the most famous was Harriet Tubman. A second-grade class created this page so you could learn all about her.

http://www2.lhric.org/pocantico/tubman/tubman.html

National Civil Rights Museum

Take the virtual tour to discover what it was like when African Americans had to sit at the back of the bus and avoid "Whites Only" restaurants, swimming pools, and drinking fountains. As bizarre as this seems to us now, before the civil rights movement of the 1960s, this was standard, everyday life in many places in the U.S. The Freedom Summer of 1964 included student sit-ins, boycotts, and marches. This museum in Memphis, Tennessee, re-creates some of the sights, sounds, and scenes of that era. Remember, the struggle for civil rights continues around the world today, and it involves people of many races.

http://www.mecca.org/~crights/

Roots

During the winter of 1977, a very powerful miniseries appeared on television. It was a dramatization of Alex Haley's Pulitzer Prize-winning book, *Roots*. The series of programs traced Haley's ancestors back to the days of slavery. The compelling story made it the most-watched miniseries of all time, with 130 million viewers during its initial telecast. Although Americans had learned about slavery in school, this was the first time it was portrayed in such close and personal detail, and adults and kids all over the country couldn't wait until the next show to see what happened to Kunta Kinte and the other characters. This online exhibit gives a chronological background and introduction to slavery in America as well as a listing of inventions by African Americans.

http://www.historychannel.com/community/roots/

AMPHIBIANS

See also PETS AND PET CARE

Frogs and Other Amphibians

Aah—the sweet singing of frogs in the springtime...but did you know that frogs are disappearing all over the world? This phenomenon has been linked to depletion of the ozone layer in the atmosphere, which lets too much ultraviolet light through, which harms the frogs. Recently, scientists have also discovered a connection between the health of frogs and a buildup of ozone in the lower atmosphere due to pollution. Watch your frogs carefully, everybody—they are important! Did you know that Australian tree frogs give off a chemical that helps heal sores when it's put on a person's skin? Doctors expect to find lots of other ways the chemical can be used. You'll find additional links that lead to information about rain forest amphibians and Australian frogs. You can even make your way to the Interactive Frog Dissection Kit, where you can test your knowledge of frog anatomy by playing the Virtual Frog Builder Game.

http://fovea.retina.net/~gecko/herps/frogs/

Herp Link- Care Sheets and FAQ's

What's the best way to care for that nifty newt you have just bought? This site tells you all about how to care for various kinds of frogs, salamanders, and other amphibians. Further down in the list you'll find reptile care sheets—even how to take care of your very own alligator, if you have one (but we don't recommend it!). This site has numerous unchecked links.

http://home.ptd.net/~herplink/care.html

FROGS AND TOADS

Netfrog—The Interactive Frog Dissection— Title Page

Did you ever wonder what's inside a frog? Now you can look for yourself. There's a special way to take animals apart to learn about them, and it's called *dissection*. Learn to identify the locations of a frog's major organs. Click on one button and watch movies of dissections. Click on another button and practice what you've learned. Only one frog had to lose its life for this Web page, and many simulated dissections can be performed over and over, by kids all over the world.

http://curry.edschool.Virginia.EDU/go/frog/

A Thousand Friends of Frogs

Are you a friend of frogs? If so, you can join 999 others and send in your frog art and writings to this page, which celebrates all that is green or brown and croaks or sings. From the Center for Global Environmental Education in Minnesota you can learn fantastic frog facts, see and hear various types of frogs, and read field (or pond) reports regarding frog research from scientists all over the world. You can help them by answering questions about frogs in your area.

http://cgee.hamline.edu/frogs/

SALAMANDERS AND NEWTS
Autodax: Salamander Feeding

Visit a scientific research lab, where the spotlight is on salamanders and how they feed. High-speed movies of various types of salamanders feasting on termites, waxworms, and crickets makes for an interesting if not appetizing educational experience!

http://socrates.berkeley.edu/~deban/salfeed.html

Newts & Salamanders Homepage

Salamanders sometimes live in the water, but eventually they turn into land dwellers. Newts are generally aquatic. Don't confuse them with lizards! Lizards have scaly skin and claws, while these fragile animals have smooth skin and delicate feet. Did you know some newts have lived for over 50 years in captivity? This page gives hints on the care and feeding of these interesting creatures, which many people keep as pets.

http://www.users.interport.net/~spiff/main.html

Which state has an official prairie grass, and what is it?

Answer: Illinois, also known as the Prairie State, honors the big bluestem grass. It was an important member of the tall-grass prairie that formerly covered much of the state. Big bluestem grows to a height of between one and three meters (three to ten feet), and you can find out more at http://www.museum.state.il.us/exhibits/symbols/grass.html

A
B
C
D
E
F
G
H
I
J
K
L
M
N
O
P
Q
R
S
T
U
V
W
X
Y
Z

A
B
C
D
E
F
G
H
I
J
K
L
M
N
O
P
Q
R
S
T
U
V
W
X
Y
Z

AMUSEMENT PARKS

See also DISNEY

Anheuser Busch Theme Parks

Anheuser-Busch Company operates many theme parks you may want to visit: SeaWorld, Busch Gardens, Sesame Place, and various water parks. This site will give you details on attractions, rides (and minimum height requirements), hours, parking, maps, ticket prices, and sources of more information. For example, let's look at the info on Sesame Place in Langhorne, Pennsylvania. You can find out about water attractions such as Slimey's Chutes, Little Bird's Birdbath, and the Count's Fount. Learn how to get involved in one of the Girl Scout weekends and maybe earn a special Sesame Place patch for your sash! You'll also discover what Anheuser-Busch is doing to help the environment and wildlife.

http://www.4adventure.com/

HUIS TEN BOSCH, Dutch City in NAGASAKI, JAPAN

This is the largest theme park in Japan. It's based on the theme of Holland, with its canals and historic buildings. It's also an ecological showplace. Wander around and click on things—you may end up at a ride, a restaurant, or a palace!

http://www.huistenbosch.co.jp/english/index_e.html

National Amusement Park Historical Association

Here's a group dedicated to saving old amusement parks, on the theory that a once-amusing ride can never, ever cease to be amusing. Read about the history of amusement parks and some of your favorite rides.

http://www.napha.org/

It never rains in cyberspace.

Paramount's Great America - The Official Web Site

This park in northern California has a lot going for it. It has the largest IMAX theater in the world, the largest and most expensive carousel in the world, and the only stand-up coaster west of the Mississippi. It also has award-winning roller coasters, such as the Top Gun—an inverted looping coaster—and our personal favorite, the Green Slime Mine Car Coaster!

http://www.pgathrills.com/

Santa Cruz Beach Boardwalk

The Santa Cruz Beach Boardwalk in Santa Cruz, California, lets you take a walk into America's past. Check the live videocam to see what the weather's like in Santa Cruz today. Maybe you'll see the classic 1911 Looff Carousel or the 1924 Giant Dipper roller coaster. If you are interested in going to Santa Cruz, you can plan your whole vacation (including hotel information) right from this page!

http://www.beachboardwalk.com/

NET FILES

What are zoonoses?

Answer: No, they're not elephant trunks, alligator snouts, or even parrot beaks. Zoonoses are viruses, infections, or diseases that can be passed from an animal to a human. For example, there are lots of things you can get from your cat! The good news is that zoonoses are very hard to "catch." Read more about them at http://www.fanciers.com/off/zoonoses.html

Six Flags Theme Parks

They say that 85 percent of Americans live within a day's drive of a Six Flags theme park; there are now eight of them, all over the United States. They are part of the Time-Warner family, so you'll see Batman, Superman, and all your favorite Looney Tunes characters when you visit. From this jumping-off point, you can take a virtual vacation at all of the parks and explore the similarities and differences of each. You'll find a park calendar, a list of the latest and greatest rides, a suggested "perfect day" itinerary, directions to each park, and job opportunities!

http://www.sixflags.com/

Universal Studios

Did you ever want to explore a real movie studio's backlot? You'd find old props and scenery, closets full of costumes, and maybe some new things they are working on, like—DINOSAURS! Visit the virtual Jurassic Park ride at this site, as well as the world-famous Universal Studios tram ride. It will take you into the fist of King Kong, through the gaping maw of Jaws, and spit you out just in time to escape an earthquake and a very believable flood. Try the Florida version of the theme park for an interactive tour of Back to the Future: The Ride. Doc Brown's wild trip through time will take you down into live volcanoes and bring you way too close to long-extinct dinosaurs. Hint: Don't eat lunch before looking at this site!

http://www.mca.com/unitemp/

CAROUSELS

1911 Looff Carousel Page

Along the Boardwalk in Santa Cruz, California, is a National Historic Landmark. It's a hand-carved carousel, and you can read about its history here. See a few close-ups of some of the horses, and download a QuickTime movie of the carousel in action.

http://www.beachboardwalk.com/looff.html

Carousel! Your Carousel Information Center

Everyone has seen carousel horses, but did you know that some carousels have frogs, roosters, and fantastic creatures like sea monsters on them? Find out about the history of carousels, see some detailed wooden horses, and listen to carousel music—guaranteed to make you smile! This site tells you where antique carousels can still be found and ridden. They are something of a rare species, since many old carousels have been taken apart and the horses and other figures have been sold. Maybe you can help save an old carousel in your town.

http://www.carousel.org/

ROLLER COASTERS
Coasters.Net

It all starts innocently enough. You get into a little car, you slowly click-clatter click-clatter up the track to the top of a huge and dangerous mountain, when all of a sudden, you're at the top and the whole world is below you. It might be nice to enjoy the view, but with a rush of wind, you're catapulted over the hill, screaming out your last breath, speeding towards uncertain doom at the bottom. You twist, you turn, you wish you had not eaten lunch. At last, the car slows and it's all over. You hear yourself yell, "AGAIN!" Roller coaster fans will love this page, complete with reviews of coasters all over the world. You'll also find frequently asked questions, photos, statistics, and an overview of roller coaster history right here. This is a "no hands" Web site, and remember, in cyberspace, no one can hear you scream! One note: This site is often slow to load.

http://www.coasters.net/

Roller Coaster Physics Book by Tony Wayne

As you swoosh around a roller coaster, you're probably not thinking very much about physics. But it's lucky for you that the designer of the roller coaster thought about physics a lot when he planned the engineering for the ride! A good coaster strikes a balance between thrills, speed, and safety—find out how the laws of physics can make sure you have fun at the amusement park.

http://pen.k12.va.us/Anthology/Pav/Science/
   Physics/book/

A B C D E F G H I J K L M N O P Q R S T U V W X Y Z

A
B
C
D
E
F
G
H
I
J
K
L
M
N
O
P
Q
R
S
T
U
V
W
X
Y
Z

ANCIENT CIVILIZATIONS AND ARCHAEOLOGY

See also HISTORY—ANCIENT HISTORY and COUNTRIES OF THE WORLD under the specific present-day country name.

Abzu: Guide to Resources for the Study of the Ancient Near East Available on the Internet

ABZU is based at the Oriental Institute in Chicago. Resources are indexed by author, directory, region, and subject. The resources also include online journals, online library catalogs, and online museum collections. There's a lot to look through here, but some things may interest you right away, such as information on Tutankhamun, mummies, and other mysteries of ancient Egypt.

http://www-oi.uchicago.edu/OI/DEPT/RA/ABZU/ABZU.HTML

NET FILES

Who bought the first car from the Ford Motor company?

Answer: Dr. Pfennig, from Chicago, bought the first car, which was sold by the Ford Motor Company in 1903. Back then, auto makers didn't name cars after fast animals and reptiles; they just named models of cars after the letters of the alphabet! Henry Ford started what is today one of the largest corporations, and his Model N was a big success, but the Model K, well!....Find out all about the fascinating history of Ford at http://www.ford.com/archive/ FordHistory.Html#Beginning

The Ancient World Web: Main Index

This site is chock-full of links to information about the ancient world. Topics include ancient documents, architecture, and cooking. In addition, links are provided to information about geography, history, the history of science, military, money, music, sciences, theater, towns, and cities.

http://www.julen.net/aw/

AncientSites: The Ancient History Community Welcomes You!

Did you ever feel like you were born in the wrong century? Want to return to the past? Try on another lifetime by exploring one of the realms of Ancient Sites. You can take guided 3-D tours of Rome, Athens, and Egypt. Learn about history, play simulation games, and participate in trivia contests. To do some of these things, you have to become a member, but it's free. They ask for your name and address, although many people just make up something rather than give personal information. After you register, you can select a city, for example, Rome. Now select a character name, and choose a family. But read the descriptions of the families, because some of them might be nicer to join than others. You can even pick an "avatar," which is a physical screen representation of your character. Once you're a registered member, you can also choose a 3-D "house" in Rome and make it your home page. You can participate in chats and discussions on Latin, among other things. The folks here debate grammatical points with the same enthusiasm that others might discuss baseball! As in all online chat and discussion areas, parents should monitor use.

http://www.ancientsites.com/

Archaeological Pieces of the Past - Introduction - ROM

What's it like to be a real archaeologist? Get your equipment together, because you're about to find out! Canada's Royal Ontario Museum invites you to visit a simulated "dig" on the site of an old farmstead. Examine various artifacts, puzzle over their meaning, and emerge with a clearer understanding of the past.

http://www.rom.on.ca/digs/munsell/

Archaeology

How do archaeologists take a few items from a pile of rubble and re-create an entire picture of how people lived long ago? This explanation from the TV show *Newton's Apple* includes many resource ideas as well as a glossary. There are also some hands-on activities to help you learn how historic sites are surveyed and, sometimes, excavated.

http://ericir.syr.edu/Projects/Newton/11/
   archeogy.html

ArchNet: WWW Virtual Library - Archaeology

ArchNet, housed at the University of Connecticut, is a virtual library for all things archaeological. Look up resources by geographic region or by subject. This is a don't-miss site for budding archaeologists. Indiana Jones probably stops here all the time!

http://spirit.lib.uconn.edu/ArchNet/

Exploring Ancient World Cultures

Move the mouse, click the buttons, and be prepared to enter a different world. Eight cultures from the past can help you to understand the cultural diversity of today. Go on a journey through time to visit the following ancient cultures: the Near East, India, Egypt, China, Greece, the Roman Empire, the Islamic World, and Medieval Europe. Although the text is very dense, you'll get a lot of information from the photos and thoughtful links to other places on the Net.

http://eawc.evansville.edu/

Mr. Donn's Ancient History Page

Look no further for information on ancient Mesopotamia, Egypt, Greece, Rome, China, India, Africa, Inca, Maya, Canada, Holidays, Map Skills, and more. Online resources, games, lesson plans, quizzes—it's all here!

http://members.aol.com/donnandlee/

Odyssey Online

Explore the ancient cultures of the Near East, Greece, Rome, and Egypt via cool puzzles and games. For example, click on Greece and find out all about famous Greek heroes, rulers, and athletes. Examine artifacts and see if you can guess which ones relate to athletic events or prizes. In other games, you try to put fragments of statues back together—don't forget to bring your super glue on this adventure!

http://www.emory.edu/CARLOS/ODYSSEY/

UCSB Anthropology Web Links

What makes this collection of links about anthropology so cool is that you can search on just the "New" ones or just the "Hot!" ones. Another way to search through this huge resource is to browse via a geographic region or organization, such as museums or college departments. You will find everything from Bristlecone Pines to Human Languages here, but we have not checked every link, and new things are added all the time.

http://www.anth.ucsb.edu/netinfo.html

ANCIENT AMERICA
CMCC - Mystery of the Maya

Did you know that there are about six million Maya today? Most live in Mexico, Guatemala, and Belize. Besides loss of culture, they face many political and environmental problems. This sensitive site will tell you about the Maya culture as it exists today, as well as teach you all about the ancient Maya, whose civilization flourished about A.D. 250.

http://www.civilization.ca/membrs/civiliz/maya/
   mminteng.html#menu

Be swampwise in EARTH SCIENCE.

A
B
C
D
E
F
G
H
I
J
K
L
M
N
O
P
Q
R
S
T
U
V
W
X
Y
Z

CMCC - Retracing An Archaeological Expedition

Canada's arctic Northwest Territories are very remote. They are at the very northwest corner of the continent of North America. People have lived in this region for thousands of years, but archaeologists have been studying it for only a short time. This site follows a group of archaeologists and the progress of their research over almost a decade. See how an expedition is planned, what happens, and how conclusions are reached based on the artifacts found. Sometimes scientists change their minds as more discoveries are made! This site is in both French and English, and you can ask for brief or detailed information on most of the resources.

http://www.civilization.ca/membrs/archaeo/ nogap/pilhome.htm

MayaQuest '98

Who were the Maya, and what happened to their civilization? This site tells you all about the history and cultures of this lost nation. The ancient Maya had an apparently healthy culture from around A.D. 250. They were masters of mathematics, building huge pyramids in the jungles of what is now Mexico and Central America. They had complex astronomical calendars and engineering for improving agriculture. During the ninth century, their civilization collapsed. No one knows exactly where they went or what happened to them. From this site, you can follow an expedition team called MayaQuest, searching the jungle for archaeological answers in 1998, or check the archives available for earlier expeditions.

http://www.classroom.com/mayaquest/

Shawnee Minisink Site

How did people live 10,000 years ago? What did they eat? What were their houses like? This Web page features an archaeological dig in the Delaware Water Gap area near what is now the border of Pennsylvania and New Jersey. The dig, conducted by the American University Department of Anthropology, reveals the history of the region, exactly what was dug up at the site, and how the artifacts were pieced together to give a picture of that time period's culture.

http://www.american.edu/academic.depts/cas/ anthro/sms/sms.html

You be the Historian

This site isn't really about ancient times; it's about an American family's life in the 1700s. By examining artifacts and documents at this site you may be able to get a fairly good picture of what life was like for Thomas and Elizabeth Springer's family in New Castle, Delaware, 200 years ago. Compare your guesses to what historians have concluded. What could future archaeologists and historians learn about your family from what's on the floor of your closet, under your bed, or in your trash?

http://www.si.edu/organiza/museums/nmah/ notkid/ubh/00intro.htm

ANCIENT EGYPT

Ancient Egypt

Ms. Kerdoncuff and her sixth-grade class have studied up on fast times in ancient Egypt, and they are here to share their research with you. Find out about housing, foods, clothing, hieroglyphs, transportation, mummification, and more. Did you know that King Tutankhamun was the ruler of all Egypt at the age of nine?

http://northport.k12.ny.us/~nms/egypt.html

CMCC - Mysteries of Egypt - Title page

Tutankhamun's tomb, discovered in 1922 by Howard Carter, contained over 3,000 wonderful things, including a golden mask of the boy king himself. Although he became king at age nine, he was dead by about age 17. What really happened to Tutankhamun? What was his life like? Was he murdered? Find out possible answers here. Gaze in awe at the treasures found, displayed for you in the virtual galleries. There are also many additional links collected at this excellent site.

http://www.civilization.ca/membrs/civiliz/ egypt/egypt_e.html

See Your Name in Hieroglyphic language (Egypt's Tourism Net)

If you want to know how you'd have to sign your homework if you were in ancient Egypt, go here. "Net-mom" looks like a squiggle, an arm, a half circle, a couple of falcons, and a baby chick. What does your name look like?

http://www.idsc.gov.eg/tourism/tor_trn.htm

ANCIENT EUROPE

Flints and Stones

Do you have the "right stuff" to survive in Stone Age times? Meet the shaman, who will show you what life is like in his village of Ice Age hunters and gatherers. You'll also meet the archaeologist, who will show you how he interprets the lives of the village folk from the objects, art, and other signs they have left behind. Everyone thinks cavemen were big, hairy guys who carried clubs and dragged women around by the hair. This site explodes that myth and others. You'll also be able to take a Stone Age food quiz—hmmm, should you eat that mushroom or not?

http://www.ncl.ac.uk/~nantiq/menu.html

The Viking Network Web

Experience the Viking way of life: raiding, trading, and exploration. This site is aimed at kids and teachers all over the world who are interested in Viking heritage and culture. Did they wear horns on their helmets, or not? Find out here! For extra fun, check out the Viking math quiz.

http://www.viking.no/

Virtual Excavation Medieval Archaeology

What do archaeologists do? They find ancient artifacts such as tools, pottery, bones, or other debris and try to find out about the people who left these things. At this site, you'll learn how archaeologists do their jobs and you'll have a chance to go on a virtual excavation of a medieval monastery. Can you find the room that served as the hospital?

http://web.lemoyne.edu/~begieral/start.html

ANCIENT GREECE

Perseus Project Home Page

The Perseus Project is "an evolving digital library on Ancient Greece" that is headquartered at the Department of Classics at Tufts University. Information is offered about art and archaeology as well as primary texts and Greek dictionaries. Included are pictures and descriptions of 523 coins, 1,420 vases, 179 sites, and 381 buildings. There's lots of new information about Julius Caesar. This is a don't-miss site for anyone studying ancient Greece!

http://medusa.perseus.tufts.edu/

ANCIENT ROME

ROMARCH: Roman Art and Archaeology

Romarch, housed at the University of Michigan, is the home to Web resources about Roman art and archaeology from 1000 B.C. to A.D. 700. General-interest resources include central sources of information and images, museums, society, as well as culture, religion, law, and war. Resources that are especially good for students are marked. A geographic approach to the sources is available, but beware: You may accidentally stumble into a site in another language!

http://www-personal.umich.edu/~pfoss/
ROMARCH.html

ANTHROPOLOGY

People and Climatic Change Index

Anthropologists study people, their cultures, and the setting in which they live. A community, whether a small band of hunters or a large sprawl of city dwellers, always affects the land. This gem of a site explores the Great Plains area of the U.S. and traces the hand of man upon it. You'll learn about these vast grasslands and the human habitation of them. Beginning with the first peoples thousands of years ago, through the Dust Bowl of the 1930s, to today—see what you can predict for the future based on what has happened in the past. Look for the parental advisory regarding the photo of a mass grave site, dating from an A.D. 1325 massacre.

http://www.usd.edu/anth/epa/

UCSB Anthropology Web Links

The study of families, cultures, and communities is called cultural anthropology. There's also physical anthropology and archaeology. This colorful, well-designed page has unearthed many of the most interesting and important anthropological sites, annotating and organizing them for easy accessibility. Here you'll find links described and cataloged in alphabetical order, by topical and geographical focus, and by departmental and museum sites. Looking for a listing of all the stone circles in Scotland? Confused by the Maya's calendar? Interested in tribal masks? All this and more are available at this don't-miss resource!

http://www.anth.ucsb.edu/netinfo.html

AQUARIUMS

See also FISH

Aquaria

Can you raise native fish and minnows in your fish tank? Is your aquarium getting smothered by too many snails? Interested in finding out about African Clawed Frogs? Wondering about the lighting in your tank, but don't know how to spell "fluorescent"? (This site explains how: *U* comes before *O*. Just remember there is no flour in fluorescent lights.) Some of these answers are otherwise hard to find, but here they are collected all in one place!

http://www.geocities.com/CapeCanaveral/4742/aquaria.html

Cathy's Homepage of Tropical Fishkeeping Main Menu

A tank of colorful fish can be an educational and fun hobby, but keeping the aquarium looking nice can be a lot of work. How much work? Check out the beginner information and the answers to frequently asked questions, and then send some fishy electronic postcards to your friends. The annotated link of links alone is well worth your visit!

http://www.geocities.com/Heartland/Plains/3515/main.htm

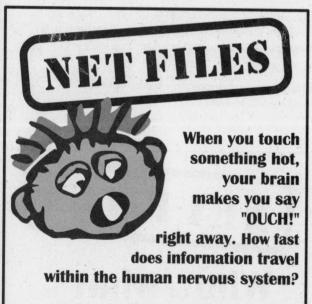

NET FILES

When you touch something hot, your brain makes you say "OUCH!" right away. How fast does information travel within the human nervous system?

Answer: It depends on which type of neuron is sending the message. According to the Neuroscience for Kids - Explore the NS page, "Transmission can be as slow as 0.5 meters per second or as fast as 120 meters per second. That's the same as going 250 miles per hour!!! Check the math out yourself." Speed over to http://weber.u.washington.edu/~chudler/what.html for more fun facts from the world of neuroscience.

Fish Information Service (FINS) Index

That little goldfish you bought has outgrown its bowl, so you're going to get it a new tank. Visit this archive of information about aquariums! It covers both freshwater and marine, tropical and temperate fish tank culture. You'll find beginning to advanced information, especially on marine and reef tanks. Click on a picture to identify a fish and get more information, or use the glossary full of aquarium terms. Be sure to see the live video from a camera overlooking a garden pond, and check out the live Fish Cam activity at a saltwater tank in someone's office.

http://www.actwin.com/fish/index.cgi

The Florida Aquarium

Watch out! Whew, didn't you see that stingray? You almost stepped on it! Because stingrays live in shallow offshore water, beachgoers often step on them by accident and get stung. Stingrays will lie partly buried in the sand, with only their eyes, spiracle, and tail exposed. Stingray stings are easy to avoid, though—just shuffle your feet as you wade. Learn more about stingrays and other creatures that inhabit Florida's waterways. Ask the Aquarium experts a question or check out one of many experiments and games available for kids of all ages.

http://www2.sptimes.com/aquarium/

The Monterey Bay Aquarium

Did you ever wonder what it would be like to swim with fish—even sharks? Would you dare feed them? Watch your hand, that shark looks hungry! Look at the sea otter pup—isn't it cute? Visit the Monterey Bay Aquarium page and get a diver's-eye view of hand-feeding the fish in the Kelp Forest Tank. Watch the QuickTime movies as divers hand-feed various sharks, rockfish, and eels that inhabit the underwater seaweed forests.

http://www.mbayaq.org/

Curl up with a good URL in BOOKS AND LITERATURE!

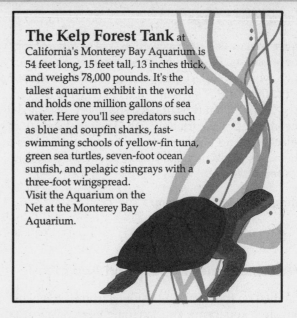

The Kelp Forest Tank at California's Monterey Bay Aquarium is 54 feet long, 15 feet tall, 13 inches thick, and weighs 78,000 pounds. It's the tallest aquarium exhibit in the world and holds one million gallons of sea water. Here you'll see predators such as blue and soupfin sharks, fast-swimming schools of yellow-fin tuna, green sea turtles, seven-foot ocean sunfish, and pelagic stingrays with a three-foot wingspread. Visit the Aquarium on the Net at the Monterey Bay Aquarium.

Oregon Coast Aquarium - Official Keiko Home Page

Did you ever see the *Free Willy* movies about the whale that was rescued from a small display aquarium? Did you know that "Willy" is really named Keiko? For the last few years he's been living in a two-million-gallon aquarium in Oregon. People have been watching him in person and over the Web every day. In September, 1998, Keiko will be moved to a sea tank in Iceland, where he was originally captured. You may be able to see him in a webcam there.

http://www.aquarium.org/keikohome.htm

Sea World/Busch Gardens Animal Information Database

Do you ever wish you could visit Sea World in either Florida, Ohio, Texas, or California? You can find out about all kinds of fish here and also learn about parrots, polar bears, gorillas, lions, and more. Interested in setting up a tropical saltwater aquarium? This page tells you how to keep an aquarium as a hobby. Write, e-mail, or phone Shamu the Killer Whale to ask questions about the ocean and marine animals. Try your hand at the animal information quiz and receive a free animal information booklet. Check out the wide variety of educational programs and curriculum materials on endangered rain forests, ecosystems, and habitat. Surprise your grandmother with her very own pet coral reef—find out how to grow one at this site!

http://www.seaworld.org/

A B C D E F G H I J K L M N O P Q R S T U V W X Y Z

Tetra Home Page

Tetra makes fish food as well as lots of other things for aquarists. Even if you don't have a tank of your own, you can experience playing with the Virtual Aquarium at this site. You don't even have to get wet! Just choose what type of tank you want. The site will recommend some friendly fish. Then make your selections, and watch the fun! There are also links to the home pages of major public aquaria around the United States.

http://www.tetra-fish.com/

Welcome to the New England Aquarium

Perched on the wharf in Boston Harbor is the New England Aquarium. You can join Stefan on a virtual whale watch—maybe you'll see some humpbacks on your day trip out on the water. When you come back, you can see the Giant Ocean Tank inside. It's over four stories high and contains more than 200,000 gallons of water! The 46-year-old sea turtle, Myrtle, can usually be found snoozing on the bottom, so be sure to look for her.

http://www.neaq.org/

ARCHITECTURE

See also HISTORY—HISTORIC SITES

The World-Wide Web Virtual Library: Architecture

The resources here will guide you from the covered bridges of New Hampshire to the architecture of Islam. You'll find yourself looking at churches in Australia, contemporary buildings in Hong Kong, and Soleri's desert Arcosanti experiments. What a great way to experience many different architectural building styles all at once!

http://www.clr.toronto.edu:1080/VIRTUALLIB/ARCH/proj.html

BRIDGES AND TUNNELS
The Building of the San Francisco Bay Bridge

The San Francisco–Oakland Bay Bridge opened to traffic in November 1936. It was called "the greatest bridge in the world for the versatility of its engineering." This bridge is one of seven toll bridges in the Bay Area that connect the city to its surrounding suburbs and are key to making San Francisco the city it is today. Here you'll see photos of the building of this historic bridge.

http://www.wco.com/~jray/baybridg/baystart.htm

CONFEDERATION BRIDGE/Le Pont de la Confédération

Eight miles long, it's the longest continuous multispan marine bridge in the world. It links the Canadian mainland of New Brunswick Province to Prince Edward Island. Ferries have been the only other way to get vehicles to and from the island. This site will tell you all about the construction of the bridge, which opened on May 31, 1997. There was even a lottery to be one of the first to cross it!

http://www.confederationbridge.com/

Covered Bridges

Why are some bridges covered? To avoid rot, according to Dr. McCain, who also says that the structures were once called "kissing bridges." Take the Northeastern Chester County Driving Tour and read about the renovation of Bartram's Bridge. Stop by the Covered Bridges page today and enjoy your virtual tour of the bridges of various counties in Pennsylvania, Oregon, and New Hampshire.

http://william-king.www.drexel.edu/top/ bridge/cb1.html

Eurotunnel Official Web Site

The Eurotunnel (also known as the "Chunnel") goes under the English Channel, between England and France. Actually, there are three tunnels, not just one. Two are for rail travel while the third is a smaller, service and emergency tunnel. Each is 50 kilometers long (about 30 miles). Cars, trucks, and passengers are loaded onto high-speed trains to make the journey, which takes 35 minutes. This site describes the history of the Eurotunnel as well as its construction, one of the major engineering feats of this century!

http://www.eurotunnel.com/

Golden Gate Bridge, Highway and Transportation District

San Francisco's most beautiful bridge is the Golden Gate. It's not painted gold; it's painted a color called international orange. The name of the bridge comes from the location it spans: the Golden Gate Strait, which is the entrance to the San Francisco Bay from the Pacific Ocean. This site offers history, photos, and answers to trivia questions such as "Has the bridge ever been closed?" The answer is yes; it was closed several times due to 70 mph winds and again a few times for visiting dignitaries.

http://www.goldengate.org/

Be swampwise in EARTH SCIENCE.

Newton's Apple- Bridges

How do bridges stay up? London Bridge didn't. It was always falling down, falling down. What are the different kinds of bridge designs, anyway, and why would you pick one over another? If you're ready to build your very own bridge, better stop here first. Create a blueprint and model of your bridge before you begin construction. This *Newton's Apple* TV show will help!

http://ericir.syr.edu/Projects/Newton/12/Lessons/ bridges.html

CASTLES AND PALACES

Castles of the United States

There are lots of castles and castle-like buildings in the United States. King James the Castlefinder and his lady, Princess Patricia, enjoy going to Renaissance festivals, and along the way they like to collect castles. They have quite a list here; is there a castle located near you? Look in the listings for your state. If the castle has a home page, you will find a link to it as well.

http://www.dclink.com/castles/INDEX.HTM

Castles on the Web

King Arthur, eat your heart out! If you want to know anything (and we mean *anything*) about castles, this is the page for you. You'll find Castle Tours, Castle of the Week, Castle Questions and Answers, Castle Image Archive, and Castles for Sale. Maybe you can look up your family's ancestral castle. There's also a Glossary of Castle Terms so that even the novice castle lover can feel at home. Hey! Watch out for the (splash) moat.

http://fox.nstn.ca/~tmonk/castle/castle.html

CHURCHES, MOSQUES, AND SYNAGOGUES

Città del Vaticano

Take a virtual tour of St. Peter's Basilica in Rome, Italy, designed by Michelangelo. See photos of the domes and vaults, piazzas, and gardens at this multilingual site.

http://www.christusrex.org/www1/citta/0-Citta.html

A B C D E F G H I J K L M N O P Q R S T U V W X Y Z

A
B
C
D
E
F
G
H
I
J
K
L
M
N
O
P
Q
R
S
T
U
V
W
X
Y
Z

Dome of the Rock

Built in A.D. 692, the Dome of the Rock is one of the great Muslim monuments. The building looks like an enameled, multicolored jewel, capped by a shining, golden dome. The Dome protects and houses the Sacred Rock of Jerusalem sandstone at the summit of Mount Moriah. Muslims believe that the prophet Muhammad, guided by the archangel Gabriel, traveled to Jerusalem and rose to the presence of God from this Rock. The area is also sacred to other faiths, as it was formerly the location of the Temple of Solomon. This site also details costumes, foods, and other important places in early Muslim history.

http://jeru.huji.ac.il/ee21.htm

Washington National Cathedral

On the highest point in Washington, D.C., is a beautiful interfaith cathedral. It is decorated with 107 carved stone gargoyles and untold numbers of grotesques. A grotesque is like a gargoyle, except it has no pipe inside and the water runs over the outside of the carving. The cathedral also has wonderful stained glass windows inside. The western rose window contains over 10,500 pieces of glass! Along the inside aisle is another window commemorating the flight of *Apollo 11*. It holds a real piece of moon rock! In addition to many U.S. presidents, Dr. Martin Luther King, Jr. and Indira Gandhi have spoken from the pulpit. Helen Keller is among the famous Americans buried beneath the cathedral.

http://www.cathedral.org/cathedral/

Westminster Abbey

This London landmark has been the site of every British coronation since 1066. Many kings and queens are entombed at the Abbey, notably Elizabeth I. You'll also find Chaucer's grave in the Poets' Corner, along with those of other famous English authors, including Lewis Carroll. The Abbey has been the scene of numerous royal ceremonies, including royal weddings and other occasions. The funeral of Diana, Princess of Wales, was held at Westminster Abbey on September 6, 1997. Admire the inspiring Gothic architecture as you wander around with the other tourists at this site.

http://www.westminster-abbey.org/

GOVERNMENT AND PUBLIC BUILDINGS

Empire State Building

It's big, it's historic, it's got a big gorilla climbing up it! OK, we were just kidding about that last part—that only happened in the movies! Besides the monkeyshines you remember in *King Kong*, about 90 other movies have featured the Empire State Building. In case you were wondering, the building is about 1,454 feet (OK, exactly 1,453 feet, 8 9/16 inches) or 443.2 meters tall, to the top of the lightning rod. There are 1,860 stairs from street level to the 102nd floor. Every year a race is held to see who can climb them the fastest. In 1998, the winning time was 10 minutes, 49 seconds.

http://www.esbnyc.com/html/
    empire_state_building.html

Moscow Kremlin 3W Guide

The Kremlin is an architectural marvel located in Moscow, Russia. Its walled city is the site of Red Square, cathedrals, and many government buildings. Take a virtual tour and learn some fascinating facts about this complex. Don't miss the world's largest bell!

http://www.online.ru/sp/cominf/kremlin/kremlin.html

THE OFFICIAL SITE OF THE EIFFEL TOWER

Symbol of Paris, the Eiffel Tower was finished on March 31, 1889. How tall is it? Well, in 1889 it was 312.27 meters high, including the flagpole. But in 1994 it grew an antenna and got taller: now it's 318.7 meters high. Visit this site to learn all about the history of the tower and activities and things you can see at each level. Don't like the color of this famous landmark? Choose the Play with the Tower section and try various fashion statements of your own. We like the giraffe look or perhaps the cloud camouflage.

http://www.tour-eiffel.fr/

> "Use the source, Luke!"
> and look it up in
> REFERENCE WORKS.

Tower of London Virtual Tour

The Traitor's Gate. The Bloody Tower. The Ceremony of the Keys. The Crown Jewels. What an incredible history this building has. The Tower of London has been a treasury, a prison, and a government building for a thousand years. It is said that if the ravens that inhabit the Tower green ever leave, the Commonwealth of Great Britain will fall. You can take a tour of the Tower and its grounds right here. But don't scare the ravens!

http://www.camelot-group.com/tower/

A Virtual Tour of the US Capitol

This page lets you tour the U.S. Capitol in Washington, D.C. You can take a Guided Tour or explore using a Tour Map, which allows you to have control over what you visit. You'll learn the history of the building, too. On September 18, 1793, George Washington laid the first cornerstone for the Capitol. The dome is made of cast iron and was erected during the Civil War. The pictures of the construction of the building are fascinating.

http://www.senate.gov/capitol/virtour.html

LIGHTHOUSES

Bill's Lighthouse Getaway

It's a foggy night, and a ship is lost amid the black waves, with shoals and rocks somewhere out ahead. Suddenly, the darkness is pierced by a friendly light in the distance. It's the lighthouse! Checking the navigational map, the ship's captain notes the location of the lighthouse on shore and is able to steer clear of danger. Part of American lore and legend, lighthouses all over America (and now, Ireland) can be visited via this home page. You'll find pictures and descriptions of lights from New England, through the Great Lakes, around the South Atlantic, and to the West Coast. There are also links to Lighthouse Societies and something about the history of the Fresnel lens, which produces the powerful light needed.

http://zuma.lib.utk.edu/lights/

The WWW Virtual Library: The World's Lighthouses, Lightships & Lifesaving Stations

Are lighthouses all over the world? You bet—and this site will let you visit a lot of them. Learn all about the history of lighthouses and lightships from a real lighthouse keeper! Lightships are just that: very well-lighted ships stationed at sea, guarding shoals and other navigational hazards.

http://www.maine.com/lights/www_vl.htm

UNUSUAL

Gargoyle Home Page

Have you ever seen a gargoyle? Gargoyles have been added into the roof lines of large buildings since the eleventh century. Originally, they were placed for functional purposes—they helped drain water off the roof. They also had symbolic religious significance. Today, gargoyles are still used as decorations on buildings. Tour this site and find out more about the history and design of these little monsters. Be sure to keep an eye up as you walk along the street—you never know what may be looking back down at you!

http://ils.unc.edu/garg/garghp4.html

lucy_the_elephant

Lucy is a famous elephant-shaped building in Margate City, New Jersey. She dates back to 1888, built by a realtor to advertise his business development plans. It took one million pieces of lumber for the structure and 12,000 feet of tin for the elephant's skin. You can climb up spiral staircases inside the legs to get to the rooms inside. She is 65 feet high—as tall as a six-story building. From the top, you get a great view of the beach. Remember to keep your cool souvenir ticket to prove you walked through an elephant!

http://www.citycom.com/dm3/lucy_the_elephant.html

A
B
C
D
E
F
G
H
I
J
K
L
M
N
O
P
Q
R
S
T
U
V
W
X
Y
Z

ART

ArtLex - dictionary of visual art

From Baroque to Pop Art, from Realism to Renaissance—all those confusing art terms are defined here, along with notes on how to pronounce them. Included are over 2,600 techniques, styles, and art history words. Here's the best part: the dictionary is illustrated, and not only that, there are links to other Web pages with more information.

http://www.artlex.com/

The Incredible Art Department

Get beyond the shifty-eyed *Mona Lisa* and explore this intriguing toolbox of art lessons, projects, cartoons about art, and art news. You'll find projects for everyone, from little preschoolers all the way up to college kids. There's also a wonderful section on how persons with disabilities are able to create artwork using new and old technologies.

http://www.artswire.org/kenroar/

Inside Art: An Art History Game

You're being dragged around the art museum with your parents. It's hot, your feet hurt, and you're simply bored, bored, bored. Wait—the colors in that painting: they look like they are moving. The swirling vortex leaps off the wall and inches towards you. Suddenly, you're sucked in and now you're caught up in a painting! Which one? You'll have to ask the help of a fish named Trish and learn some things about art technique and art history before you can escape. If you manage to get out of this painting, there's another adventure to try, called A. Pintura, Art Detective.

http://www.eduweb.com/insideart/

KinderArt - Art Education - free art lessons for k-8

Tired of coloring books and crayon drawing? Get ready for a whole new artist's palette of ideas, techniques, and tools at this site. Lots of hands-on projects, holiday activities, and even how to make your own chalk, clay, and painted sand! There's a glossary of art terms and even a virtual fridge to display your work and others from around the globe.

http://www.bconnex.net/~jarea/lessons.htm

CLAY AND CERAMICS
KUTANI

Kutani is a very attractive form of Japanese pottery. The enameled vases look like jewels when they emerge from the kiln. The KUTANI pages show the elaborate process that leads to a finished piece of ceramic art. You can view a map of Japan showing Terai-Machi (the cradle of Kutani) and see a picture of the tools used in Kutaniware. Explore the history of the process and see examples of this beautiful art form.

http://www.njk.co.jp/kutani/

**Nothing to do?
Check CRAFTS AND HOBBIES
for some ideas.**

NET FILES

How much blood is in the average human body?

Answer: The average human has about five liters of blood. About 55 percent of your blood is plasma. Check out the inside story on blood at http://sln.fi.edu/biosci/blood/blood.html

Nathan Youngblood, From Earth to Object

Everyone likes to play with clay, but most people buy their clay at the store. Not Nathan Youngblood. He digs his own special clay and sand, which are mixed to form a slurry. When the clay mixture reaches the right consistency, it is allowed to set until the perfect texture is achieved. Later, he begins to form his pots. You can follow the whole process from earth to object here and see the beautiful results!

http://nmaa-ryder.si.edu/whc/artistshtml/
   youngbloodearthtoobject.html

DRAWING AND PAINTING

See also COLOR AND COLORING BOOKS

Art Studio Chalkboard

Wondering about "one point perspective"? What type of paintbrush offers which effect? Confused by color theory? This excellent tutorial focuses on the technical fundamentals of perspective, shading, and color in drawing and painting.

http://www.saumag.edu/art/studio/chalkboard.html

The Chauvet Cave

Admit it, you would love to draw all over the walls in your home. The only problem is that you would get in trouble. A long time ago, kids your age didn't have crayons or finger paint. In fact, ancient civilizations apparently encouraged drawing on the walls. At least 30,000 years ago, cave people drew all over this cave, and their artwork can still be seen today. These paintings were discovered by archeologists in the Ardèche gorges of southern France. The photographs are gorgeous, too.

http://www.culture.fr/culture/arcnat/chauvet/
   en/gvpda-d.htm

Draw a Trochoid

Do you love to draw patterns? A mechanical toy that traces the path of one circle as it moves around another circle will draw complicated patterns for you. When your parents were kids, they had to draw these patterns using clumsy toys that were actually geared tools. Their pens and gears were always slipping, and it took forever to draw the final image. Now you can "draw" them by typing in numbers and hitting the Generate Image button. Isn't technology wonderful?

http://www.vanderbilt.edu/VUCC/Misc/Art1/
   trochoid.html

If you were to place every Oreo cookie ever made in a tall stack, one on top of the other, how high would the pile reach?

Answer: Since the Beginning of Time (1912), more than 362 billion Oreos have been made. The pile would reach all the way to the moon and back more than five times. Placed side by side, they would encircle Earth 381 times at the equator! Find out more fun facts about the Oreo, America's favorite sandwich cookie, at http://www.oreo.com/allabout/aa_index.html

Fresco Workshop

Do you know what a fresco is? It isn't a can of diet soda or a city in California. It's a form of artwork, and—get this—it's painted right on the walls. Traditionally, plaster is poured in layers and is tinted as it dries. The end result is a lasting piece of art. The world's earliest known frescoes are the cave paintings of Lasceaux, France. They were made some 30,000 years ago—that's old! Historically, the technique was developed in ancient Greece, and it was incorporated into Minoan and Roman artwork. This series of pages takes you through the process step by step, as a group of people create a fresco of a playground scene.

http://www.artswire.org/Community/afmadams/
   afm/fresco.html

Everyone's flocking to BIRDS!

A B C D E F G H I J K L M N O P Q R S T U V W X Y Z

Global Children's Art Gallery - The Natural Child Project

Would you like to see pictures drawn by kids from all over the world? You can even send in your own artwork, if you're between the ages of 1 and 12. Check the vibrant energy in "Jamaican Dancing" or the cool fish and creatures in "El Mar (The Sea)." If you can't send in an electronic picture, you can mail a photograph.

http://www.naturalchild.com/gallery/

The Greatest Painters on the Web

Your art teacher has assigned a report on a famous artist! Relax. At this well-designed site, you will find about 30 well-known artists represented. For each entry, you'll discover a brief biography, a picture or photo of the artist (if available), and lots of links to online works and commentary. Don't miss the section on Escher, known for his strange graphic illusions, impossible buildings, and repeating geometric patterns (tessellations). Was he an artist? A mathematician? Or both?

http://kultur-online.com/greatest/

Kali

Math is fun! Kali is a geometry program written at the Geometry Center. It makes cool symmetrical patterns (suitable for framing or just coloring) based on your instructions, which are easily entered by clicking on pictures and buttons.

http://www.geom.umn.edu/apps/kali/about.html

Landscape Painting

In three easy lessons, the Smithsonian Institution provides an interesting look at landscape painting. Do the paintings of the American West faithfully represent the country? Can you paint a realistic view of a rocky shoreline using a photograph as your model? You'll learn about this and more!

http://educate.si.edu/lessons/art-to-zoo/landscape/
   cover.html

Mark Kistler's Imagination Station

The real world is in three dimensions: objects have width, length, and depth. In a drawing, you have only two dimensions to work with: length and width. You have to use special techniques to simulate the third dimension of depth. No problem—Mark's here to give you 3-D drawing lessons. You say you can't even draw a straight line? Mark claims it doesn't matter. Soon you'll be talking about the 12 Renaissance secrets of 3-D drawing right along with him!

http://www.draw3d.com/

The Refrigerator Art Contest

If you came to visit Net-mom, one thing you would not be able to see is the refrigerator. That's because the entire appliance is covered with artwork, school papers, dentist appointment slips, and other stuff that's too important to lose! If you want the world to see your artistic masterpiece, send it here. Every week, several kids' drawings appear on this Internet site, and people vote for their favorites. Yours could make it to the Hall of Fame!

http://www.artcontest.com/

Sistine Chapel Extended Tour

The ceiling of the Sistine Chapel in Rome, Italy, is considered to be one of the most incredible works of art in human history. It was painted by Michelangelo in the 1500s. It took him many years to paint it. Take the tour and download the lovely images.

http://www.christusrex.org/www1/sistine/0-Tour.html

Web-a-Sketch!

You know that fun drawing screen with the two knobs? If you thought that was hard, wait until you try Web-a-Sketch! Look through the gallery and see what other people have created. Some of them have way too much time on their hands. Other people didn't quite get it. See how well you can do.

http://www.digitalstuff.com/web-a-sketch/

GLASS

The Chagall Windows

The Synagogue of the Hadassah-Hebrew University Medical Center, in Jerusalem, is lit by sunlight streaming through the world-famous Chagall Windows. Marc Chagall, the artist, worked on the project for two years. The Bible provided his main inspiration. The Chagall Windows represent the 12 sons of the patriarch Jacob, from whom came the Twelve Tribes of Israel. Chagall's brilliantly colored windows also have floating figures of symbolic animals, fish, and flowers. See this beautiful example of stained glass art without having to wait for a sunny day!

http://www.md.huji.ac.il/chagall/chagall.html

A Resource for Glass

No one knows who first made glass. Pliny, the Roman historian, said the first glass was made by mistake. According to his account, Phoenician sailors landed on a beach to make a cooking fire. They propped up their pot using a block of *natron*, a naturally occurring alkali used in the mummification process, which they were carrying as cargo. As the fire got hotter, the sand beneath it melted. When it later cooled, the material hardened into glass. This site, from the Corning Museum of Glass, will tell you about the history of glassmaking and the properties of glass. Learn how making fudge can teach you about the making of glass!

http://www.pennynet.org/glmuseum/edglass.htm

NET FILES

The comic strip "Peanuts" was first printed on October 2, 1950. In what year did Snoopy the beagle first appear standing on two legs instead of four?

peanuts/d_history/html/date/1958.html
http://www.snoopy.com/comics/
You'll find more Snoopy facts at
Answer: Snoopy first stood on two legs in 1958.

Welcome to Kokomo Opalescent Glass

Visit a stained glass factory, where they create beautiful glass shimmering with opalescent colors. Take the virtual tour to see this process. A mixture of glass is shoveled, by hand, into the "twelve-pot furnace," which is heated to a temperature exceeding 2400 degrees Fahrenheit. Over a 17-hour period, all the glass melts into a liquid. The "table man" rings a bell every minute and a half, which means it's time to pour another sheet of glass. The men use large ladles to scoop up the fiery hot glass. Then, "ladles full and cooling fast, the ladlers run to the mixing table. They keep the glass in constant motion to keep it from cooling unevenly on the way. Trailing molten threads behind them, as many as five people (one for each color in the sheet) converge on the mixing table. Tread carefully, assume everything is hot, and if you smell rubber burning you better check your own shoes first!" Visit the site to learn the rest of the process, see many samples of colors and patterns, and be inspired by the windows displayed in the online gallery.

http://www.kog.com/

MASKS

masks.org

Doctors wear masks so they won't spread germs. Kids celebrating Halloween wear masks for a different reason: they want you to believe they are someone or something else! Sometimes masks have religious or sacred meaning, while others are worn just for fun. Explore the world of masks at this colorful site. A caution to parents: Some of these masks may be frightening (but then, that's the idea).

http://www.masks.org/

METAL AND JEWELRY CRAFT

Fabergé Easter Eggs 3W Guide

At the turn of the century, Peter Fabergé was named "The Jeweler of his Emperor's Majesty and the Jeweler of the Emperor's Hermitage" to Emperor Nicholas II of Russia. His skill in designing and crafting intricate, jeweled Easter eggs was unsurpassed. Would you like to see examples of these magical eggs, encrusted with gemstones such as diamonds and rubies? Step right up!

http://www.online.ru/sp/cominf/faberge/faberge.html

A B C D E F G H I J K L M N O P Q R S T U V W X Y Z

Fremlin's Forgery: the Art of Blacksmithing, Horseshoeing & Metal Art

Not only can this journeyman blacksmith shoe a horse, but he can also craft a beautiful rose out of metal! How does he do it? Online tutorials reveal some of his secrets, and while you're oohing and aahing over his work, you can hear audio of his hammer ringing on the anvil.

http://www.siriusweb.com/Fremlin/

MUSEUMS

Asian Arts

See the rich art of many cultures in this electronic journal devoted to Asian arts. You'll be linked to online museum exhibits, articles about new discoveries, and many graphics of traditional Asian art. Explore the different media that the artists used. Weavings, sculpture, metal engravings, masks, paintings, clay tablets, carvings, and more await you.

http://www.asianart.com/

FAMSF - Education - Publications - Ghost of the de Young

If you think visiting an art museum sounds more boring than, say, sorting out the letters in your bowl of alphabet soup, then you should read this online comic book. Seems Irene and Farley are trying to take Irene's daughter, Olive, to the De Young art museum in San Francisco's Golden Gate Park. Olive wants to go to Disneyland instead. Mom and Farley leave Olive on a lobby bench (with a guard nearby) while they visit a special exhibit. Suddenly, the ghost of Mr. De Young himself appears to take Olive on a very special tour of some of the museum's masterpieces! Follow along on this humorous 72-page story. Hint: Load all the pictures first, then read them with the family.

http://www.thinker.org/fam/education/publications/
   ghost/

Leonardo Home Page

If you think this site is about the hero of *Titanic*, sorry. This Leonardo is famous for painting the *Mona Lisa*. But did you know Leonardo da Vinci also designed a helicopter, a hang glider, a parachute, and several other contraptions that didn't actually get built until hundreds of years later. Which ones can you recognize from their original drawings? This special exhibit comes from Boston's Museum of Science.

http://www.mos.org/sln/Leonardo/

Metropolitan Museum of Art Education Page

That's a nice painting, but can you explain why you like it? This site defines what elements go into works of art: composition, texture, pattern, and light are some you'll learn about as you explore the pages of the Metropolitan Museum of Art in New York City.

http://www.metmuseum.org/htmlfile/education/
   edu.html

Museums Index at World Wide Arts Resources

From this jumping-off point, you can explore over 950 museums all over the world! You'll find art museums galore, but you'll also experience science, folk, maritime, and other specialized exhibits if you explore the lists. Many countries from Africa to Asia are represented.

http://wwar.com/museums.html

National Museum of American Art

Look at all those paintings of yours that Mom has hung proudly on the refrigerator! One day you may become a famous American artist. Then your work would become part of a tradition of American art, and it might find a home in this museum. The museum boasts a grand collection of the best artwork produced by American artists. Which page will your artwork be on? Maybe the White House Collection of American Crafts, or part of the permanent collection? Browse these pages and take a walk through history.

http://www.nmaa.si.edu/

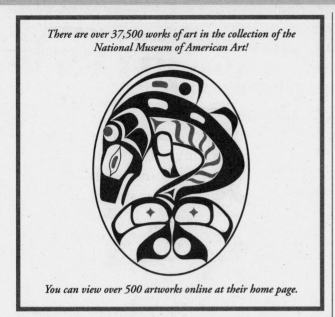

There are over 37,500 works of art in the collection of the National Museum of American Art!

You can view over 500 artworks online at their home page.

The Robert C. Williams American Museum of Papermaking

Young Roman students did their homework on wax tablets. Thanks to innovative thinking in China over 1,700 years ago, today you turn your homework in on paper. By the time you are out of school, students will probably hand in their assignments on computer disks. The American Museum of Papermaking highlights the development of papermaking. From clay tablets to the modern paper mill, follow the winding history of paper. After all, without paper how would you make paper airplanes?

http://www.ipst.edu/amp/

Splendors of Christendom

The Vatican, an independent city-state, is located in Rome, Italy. It has its own postage and souvenir coinage, but it is best known as being the worldwide center of Roman Catholicism. The Head of the Catholic Church, the Pope, lives here. The world-famous Vatican Museums are here; the Popes have been collecting art since 1503, so there is a lot to see! If you go to the Vatican, you'll have to wait in line to get in, but here in the virtual museum, you can walk right in. View over 500 images of paintings, tapestries, and sculptures.

http://www.christusrex.org/www1/splendors/
    splendors.html

WebMuseum: Bienvenue! (Welcome from the curator)

Browse through an incredible collection of famous paintings and other artwork. See the *Mona Lisa*, the most recognized piece of art in the world, or listen to some classical music in the auditorium. You can even take a mini-tour of Paris! The opening page of the WebMuseum includes a list of its mirror sites. Choose one close to you to provide a faster connection.

http://sunsite.unc.edu/wm/

Welcome to The Metropolitan Museum of Art

Let's read the tour brochure: "The Metropolitan Museum of Art's collections include nearly three million works of art spanning 5,000 years of world culture, from prehistory to the present." Hmmm, maybe we should think about spending the whole day exploring this one site! This world-class art museum is located in New York City. If you visit the virtual version, you'll see suits of armor, Egyptian antiquities, Asian art, twentieth century art, sculpture, and lots of famous art masterpieces. This site is also available in Japanese.

http://www.metmuseum.org/

SCULPTURE

Christo & Jeanne-Claude Home Page

Most sculptors make artwork from stone, metals, or other substances. Christo and Jeanne-Claude make artwork out of landscapes. For example, there was the *Running Fence*. Made of shimmering white fabric, it was 5.5 meters (18 feet) high and ran 40 kilometers (24.5 miles). It began north of San Francisco and followed rolling hills until at last it dropped down to the Pacific Ocean at Bodega Bay. It was completed on September 10, 1976, and remained in place for two weeks. What do you think this artistic statement meant? Visit the Web site to be astounded by more of Christo and Jeanne-Claude's impressive and thought-provoking large-scale sculptures.

http://www.beakman.com/christo/

A B C D E F G H I J K L M N O P Q R S T U V W X Y Z

A
B
C
D
E
F
G
H
I
J
K
L
M
N
O
P
Q
R
S
T
U
V
W
X
Y
Z

The Rolling Ball Web - Main Page

If we said, "Kinetic sculpture," you might say, "Huh?" How about marble runs—do you know what they are? No? OK, then how about those cool machines you see in museums, airports, and malls with the balls that travel around mazes of tracks, doing strange things like ringing bells, inflating balloons, traveling in elevators, only to get to the bottom and travel up to the beginning again? *Now* you know what we mean! This no-frills page is a collection of kinetic art resources that reside on the Web.

http://www.msen.com/~lemur/rb-rolling-ball.html

Walter S. Arnold / Sculptor - Virtual Sculpture Gallery

Have you ever tried to hold as still as a statue? Statues are a form of art called sculpture. A sculpture starts as a block (usually wood or stone) and ends up as a piece of art. Walter S. Arnold is a sculptor who makes all sorts of art. He sculpts a lot of really neat things, such as gargoyles and park fountains. Learn about the tools sculptors use under the Resources link at "carving tools." Stop by the Virtual Sculpture Gallery and treat yourself to a very creative collection of art and ideas. Send gargoyle postcards to your friends. There is also a visual dictionary of types of marble.

http://www.stonecarver.com/

TEXTILE ARTS

Textiles Through Time

What if we didn't have any malls? Where would people go to buy their clothes? Throughout most of history, people have had to make their own clothes, fabric, and fibers. This site links museum textile collections around the world. See handmade fabrics, including clothing, quilts, ceremonial artifacts, and a whole lot more. You'll also find links to the Bayeux Tapestry, Hmong needlework, and exquisite Japanese kimonos.

http://www.interlog.com/~gwhite/ttt/tttintro.html

NET FILES

You're making a new recipe for dinner, but the cookbook has some words you've never heard of. What, for example, is a roux?

Answer: According to *Webster's Dictionary*, it's "a cooked mixture of flour and fat," and it's pronounced "roo." Get out the butter, and learn more new words at http://work.ucsd.edu:5141/cgi-bin/http_webster?roux

Welcome to the World Wide Quilting Page

Of course you know what a quilt is, but do you know what goes into making one? Did you know that quilts can be computer designed, watercolor painted, or tie-dyed, and they can even have pictures transferred onto them? The page has a detailed how-to section with every step of the quilting process, from basic quilt design to advanced stitch technique. Peek in and see the shameful losing quilt in the Third and Final Worst Quilt In The World Contest!

http://quilt.com/MainQuiltingPage.html

Find your roots in GENEALOGY.

ASIAN AMERICANS

See also HOLIDAYS—ASIAN HOLIDAYS and COUNTRIES OF THE WORLD under specific entries.

CERN/ANU - Asian Studies WWW Virtual Library

Interested in the Pacific island of Tonga, or maybe the country of Malaysia, or perhaps Japan? Check this site for resources for school reports.

http://coombs.anu.edu.au/WWWVL-AsianStudies.html

Kid's Window

This little window on things Japanese will bring a smile to your face. Learn several origami folded figures, select items from a Japanese restaurant menu, and hear some Japanese letters and words.

http://jw.nttam.com/KIDS/kids_home.html

CULTURE
Asian Astrology

Find out about Chinese, Vietnamese, and Tibetan calendar and astrological systems here. You'll also find calendar conversion utilities and information on Asian divination. The site also has an informative FAQ on *Feng Shui*, the art of locating buildings according to the most favorable geographic influences. Recently, this practice has migrated to interior decoration. To find out whether you should relocate your bed or not, check here.

http://users.deltanet.com/~wcassidy/astro/
  astroindex.html

**Nothing to do?
Check CRAFTS AND HOBBIES
for some ideas.**

Body Language and Gestures in Asia and the Pacific

How well can you speak "body language"? If your mom were to cross her arms, frown, and start tapping her foot, you'd be able to read her body language well enough to tell she was mad! In other cultures, various body motions or gestures may mean something completely different than they do to you. This site focuses on proper body languages of the Asia-Pacific region. Find out how to cross your legs in Singapore, how to accept a gift in Korea, and when to applaud in China.

http://www.worldculture.com/gesturea.htm

Chinese Calligraphy

This beautiful site explains the tools and techniques used in traditional Chinese writing, or calligraphy. You'll also learn a lot about Chinese lettering and what the various characters mean. This site was built by kids and is a Thinkquest Junior contest finalist.

http://tqjunior.advanced.org/3614/

Chinese Historical and Cultural Project

The Golden Dragon is reawakening! Discover how this 200-foot long, historic creature appeared at Chinese festivals around the turn of the century.
And now it's coming back! Have a look at the colorful modern photos as well as the historic photos and get a glimpse into Chinese history and culture. Teachers note: There are also complete lesson plans and materials for use in the award-winning Golden Legacy program.

http://www.chcp.org/

Hmong Textiles

The Hmong people of Vietnam and Laos have a language, but it is a spoken language, not a written one. So, their culture passes down its stories by telling them orally or by telling them in cloths. Here are some cloths made by Hmong Americans and native Hmong. What stories might they be telling?

http://www.lib.uci.edu/sea/hmong.html

A
B
C
D
E
F
G
H
I
J
K
L
M
N
O
P
Q
R
S
T
U
V
W
X
Y
Z

NET FILES

Where was cheese first made?

Answer: It was probably first made in the Middle East. Cheese was known to the ancient Sumerians in 4000 B.C. The ancient Greeks credited Aristaeus, a son of Apollo and Cyrene, with its discovery; it is also mentioned in the Old Testament of the Bible (don't eat cheese *that* old, though). You can read all about the aromatic world of cheese at CheeseNet

http://www.wgx.com/cheesenet/info/

Living in Tokyo is....

This excellent winner from last year's Cyberfair was created by over 40 kids from a school in Japan. They will tell you from experience that living in Tokyo is fun, delicious, interesting, challenging, and inspiring! You'll discover the fascinating material they present on Japanese customs, theater and music, sumo wrestling, foods, and more.

http://cyberfair.gsn.org/smis/contents.html

Teaching (and Learning) About Japan

Festival puppets, flower arranging, the tea ceremony: these are all traditional parts of Japanese culture. But what do you know about popular things kids in Japan like to do? This site gives an overview of the traditional and the popular! A caution to parents: Characters in Japanese children's stories (anime, Manga) often die and do not live happily ever after. Also, not every link has been reviewed from this site.

http://www.csuohio.edu/history/japan.html

Fetch some fascinating info in DOGS AND DOG SPORTS.

HISTORY

Asian Pacific American Heritage Month Site

How many famous Asian Americans can you name? Kristi Yamaguchi (Olympic skater), Vera Wang (fashion designer), and Ann Curry (news anchor) are a few. At this site, you can read about these people and others, including Robert Nakasone, CEO of Toys 'R' Us!

http://www.abcflash.com/apa/

ASTRONOMY, SPACE, AND SPACE EXPLORATION

Abrams Planetarium

Are you interested in astronomy but don't know where to look? Would you like to know what interesting events are happening in the night sky? Visit this site for a day-by-day list of what to look for and where to look for it. The list is updated each month and includes an archive of past diaries. Check out the archive near the end of the month to take a peek at next month's diary.

http://www.pa.msu.edu/abrams/diary.html

Amazing Space Web-Based Activities

The Hubble Space Telescope folks have a whole spectrum of fun Web-based activities here. In Star Light, Star Bright you can explore the nature of light waves and prisms. Don't miss the brain teasers in this section. Learn fast facts about planets to collect virtual Solar System Trading Cards. If neither of those are challenging enough, fasten your seat belts and enter the Hubble Deep Field Academy for some advanced training. Still think you're pretty good? Help plan a Hubble Space Telescope mission. Soon: No escape—the truth about black holes!

http://oposite.stsci.edu/pubinfo/education/
   amazing-space/

Ambit NASA Live Cams and Mission Display

How would you like to see pictures live from space? NASA has a slew of video cameras taking pictures of Earth, of weather in the vicinity of the Kennedy Space Center, and more. If there is a mission going on, you can view the shots as they come in. Otherwise, old footage is shown. It's out of this world!

http://www.ambitweb.com/nasacams/nasacams.html

The Astronomical Society of the Pacific

So, you think you might be interested in astronomy? Well, things are looking up! The Astronomical Society of the Pacific is here to help. This organization has been serving astronomers for over 100 years. They publish *The Mercury*, a monthly magazine, and *The Universe in the Classroom*, a free quarterly newsletter for teachers. Of course, there's also loads of information for astronomers here on their Web site.

http://www.aspsky.org/

The Astronomy Cafe

Do you have what it takes to be an astronomer? Do you have the same interests and curiosities that astronomers have? Ask the Astronomer, and you might just find the answers right here. Dr. Sten Odenwald starts by telling you about his childhood and how a TV show sparked his own interest in astronomy. He tells you how his knowledge of mathematics and astronomy developed through college and then describes his career as a research scientist and astronomer. You can also read about the experiences of other astronomers and how they became interested in astronomy. Lots of links, articles, and other astronomy resources for you here!

http://www2.ari.net/home/odenwald/cafe.html

Earth and Sky Homepage

Earth and Sky is a daily radio feature about science, heard on 950 stations around the world. Their topics range from deep-ocean vents to the farthest-flung star nurseries in deep space. They also answer intriguing listener questions, some of which have been collected on this Web site. Why is the sky blue? Are soap bubbles round in weightless conditions? Why do leaves change color in the fall? *Earth and Sky* knows!

http://www.earthsky.com/

Frequently Asked Questions About NASA

Want to know how to become an astronaut? Maybe you just want to get those cool space mission patches to sew onto your backpack. Or you've just got to know if the space shuttle has a bathroom. You might say that NASA (National Aeronautics and Space Administration) has the mother ship of all space pages. The answers are here!

http://www.nasa.gov/qanda/index.html

Naked Eye Astronomy

If you're serious about learning about astronomy, you should read this introductory essay. It will give you older kids a good perspective on what astronomy is all about. It starts with the concept of time and distance, which is important if you want to learn the whys and hows of astronomy. If there's something you don't understand, try reading it with your parents and then explain it to them. We're sure they will appreciate it. ;-)

http://www.bc.cc.ca.us/programs/sea/astronomy/
    nakedeye/nakedeya.htm

NASA Spacelink - An Aeronautics & Space Resource for Educators

You could visit the NASA Home Page at <http://www.nasa.gov>, but for kids and teachers, we like this jumping-off place better. Did you read a space-related story in yesterday's newspaper? Chances are there is something about it here, in the Hot Topics area. For more general topics, you can browse some of the most popular sites on the Web in the Cool Links area. If it's about space and it's the latest and greatest, then this site is a convenient shortcut!

http://spacelink.nasa.gov/index.html

The Planetary Society

This nonprofit group was founded by astronomer Carl Sagan and others. Its mission is to encourage planetary exploration and the search for extraterrestrial life. Naturally, the Web site has links to the SETI (Search for Extra Terrestrial Intelligence) pages, but there is more. How about building your own Mars rover, which distant kids can control (don't worry, you can also drive their rovers).

http://www.planetary.org/

A
B
C
D
E
F
G
H
I
J
K
L
M
N
O
P
Q
R
S
T
U
V
W
X
Y
Z

A
B
C
D
E
F
G
H
I
J
K
L
M
N
O
P
Q
R
S
T
U
V
W
X
Y
Z

SKY Online - Your Astronomy Source on the World Wide Web

If you really want to know what's up in the sky this week, today, NOW!, then you've got to visit this site. This is the publisher of *Sky & Telescope* magazine and other magazines, books, star atlases, and much more. Included are check tips for backyard astronomers, including how to find and see the Russian space station *Mir* as it orbits overhead. You can also track the latest comet sightings, meteor forecasts, and eclipse data. There is a fabulous collection of links, too. If it's happening in space or astronomy this week, you'll find something about it here.

http://www.skypub.com/

Space Calendar (JPL)

Keep this calendar on hand if you like to keep up with what's happening in space. How close will that asteroid come to Earth? When will the Orionids Meteor Shower peak? It's all here! The calendar also lists anniversaries of past space events, along with upcoming earthly meetings and conventions of space-related activities.

http://NewProducts.jpl.nasa.gov/calendar/

Space Day

Every year, Space Day is celebrated on the Thursday prior to the anniversary of U.S. President John F. Kennedy's 1961 challenge to "land a man on the moon and return him to the Earth." There are loads of related online events that day, but the official Web page is fun any time. Try the Night Watchman and see if you can click and drag the constellations to the correct place in the sky (if you've got sound, you'll even hear the crickets!). In The Phaser you'll learn all about the phases of the Moon (hope you know your waxing from your waning gibbous; if not, this site will teach you). And don't forget to send your friends some space postcards to show that you really get around.

http://www.spaceday.com/

Space Environment Center Home

Check out today's space weather! Here's a partial listing: "The geomagnetic field should remain disturbed for the next three days. Generally active to minor storm conditions are forecast. Periods of major storming are expected for high latitudes. Energetic electron fluxes at geosynchronous orbit should increase to high levels late on 31 Oct." Not exactly what you might hear on TV, but it's how the weather in space is described by the scientists who study it. You'll also find images of the Sun and charts showing how strong X-rays from space are today. Don't forget to wear your shades!

http://www.sel.bldrdoc.gov/

Star Journey: The Heavens - Star Chart @ nationalgeographic.com

Explore a map of visible stars as they appear from the North and South Poles. All 2,844 of these stars (plus nebulae and star clusters also pictured on the map) can be seen with the unaided eye. As you click on the various quadrants you'll come across special blue squares. That means a Hubble Space Telescope photo of that star is available to view as a close-up. Letters from the Greek alphabet are used to describe the apparent brightness of various stars within a constellation. "Alpha" is the brightest, followed by beta, gamma, and so on. It's all explained in the Star Chart Notes section.

http://www.nationalgeographic.com/features/97/stars/chart/

StarChild: A learning center for young astronomers

This is a wonderful beginner's guide to astronomy. It's written for smaller children and presents itself in an easy-to-read text. This site includes sections on general astronomy, Earth, planets, stars, galaxies, the Sun, and more. Use these pages to introduce a child (or brother or sister) to the wonders of space. You may even learn some new stuff yourself.

http://heasarc.gsfc.nasa.gov/docs/StarChild/StarChild.html

AURORA BOREALIS

The Aurora Page

Shimmering curtains of light in the night sky—it's the aurora borealis! Find out about aurora borealis sightings and forecasts. Various aurora maps and images are here, including images taken from the space shuttle. Ever heard the northern lights? They also make sounds! Learn all about the theories on why this happens. There's even a survey for those lucky people who have "heard" one.

http://www.geo.mtu.edu/weather/aurora/

COMETS, METEORS, AND ASTEROIDS

Asteroid Comet Impact Hazards

Fueled by recent blockbuster disaster movies, everyone's gotten worried about the possibility of a huge chunk of space rock crashing into Earth. Will this occur in the future? If it does, what happens to us? This site helps clear up the facts from the hype. Check the very complete Links section for more!

http://impact.arc.nasa.gov/

Asteroids: Deadly Impact @ nationalgeographic.com

Can you solve the mystery in this adventure? Were the craters left by comets, meteors, or *something else*? Log in and see what you can discover! Here's your mission: "TOP SECRET — LEVEL 4 CLEARANCE REQUIRED — CLASSIFIED DATA. Welcome back, Agent Your Name Here. Sorry to clutter your desk in your absence, but I need you on these mysterious cases. All involve extraterrestrial perpetrators. You know the drill: Examine the evidence in the files and on your desk, then finger the most probable culprits. Close every case correctly and you'll get to download a clip from National Geographic Television's classified videotape of 'Asteroids: Deadly Impact.' I know you'll get to the bottom of these cases. Click here to destroy this message. —The Director."

http://www.nationalgeographic.com/features/97/
    asteroids/index.html

Blast from the Past Home Page

Sixty-five million years ago, it was a very bad day for dinosaurs and a lot of other living things on Earth. That day, a huge asteroid crashed into the Gulf of Mexico, near what is now known as the Yucatan Peninsula. The hypothesis is that the asteroid, which was about 10 kilometers (six miles) wide, vaporized on impact, but the collision blasted trillions of tons of debris into the atmosphere. All this stuff, plus ash and soot, managed to create a dark day. In fact, there were so many dark days in a row that plants couldn't get sunlight to grow, the plant-eaters didn't have anything to nibble on, and lots of them couldn't survive. Read why we know what we think we know here.

http://www.nmnh.si.edu/paleo/blast/

NET FILES

Where is the Plimsoll Line, and why shouldn't you cross it?

Answer: These days, it's more of a pictograph than a line. It's painted on the hulls of merchant ships, showing the safe load limit for that ship. In 1870s England, Samuel Plimsoll, a member of Parliament, proposed this "line" to help halt the number of shipwrecks and casualties caused by overloading. If this line was under water, the ship was overloaded and therefore unsafe. Calculating the placement of the line is not easy! It's dependent on the type of ship, cargo, season, and geographic area of operation. So there are really several "Plimsoll Lines" painted on every merchant ship. See a picture of one at http://pacifier.com/~rboggs/PLIMSOLL.HTML

A
B
C
D
E
F
G
H
I
J
K
L
M
N
O
P
Q
R
S
T
U
V
W
X
Y
Z

A
B
C
D
E
F
G
H
I
J
K
L
M
N
O
P
Q
R
S
T
U
V
W
X
Y
Z

Build Your Own Comet

If your parents won't let you stay up late to look for comets and meteors on a school night, maybe you can get your teacher to help you make one during the day, in class! This "comet recipe" includes dry ice and ammonia, so you'll need some help working with these materials, which need careful handling. You'll also find tips for introducing this activity to the classroom and comet facts and other links to educational resources.

http://www.noao.edu/education/igcomet/
    igcomet.html

Comet Hale-Bopp is coming!

Zinging its way through the sky at two million miles per hour is Comet Hale-Bopp, and lots of kids saw it in spring of 1997, when it was "nearby." If you weren't one of them, it's not too late! You can see a GIF of it here and read lots of information on this spectacular visitor to our solar system.

http://www.skypub.com/comets/hb01.html

NET FILES

Two eggs appear to be the same size, yet one comes from a carton marked "Medium" and the other from a box marked "Large." How are eggs sized, anyway?

jumbo (over 69 grams)
extra large (64-69 grams)
large (56-63 grams)
medium (49-55 grams)
small (42-48 grams)
peewee (under 42 grams)

and the weight range for each of the most popular sizes:

Answer: By weight! According to the Canadian Egg Marketing Agency at http://www.canadaegg.ca/english/educat/educat2.html#grade, here are the sizes

Comet Introduction

Comets! They're made up of rock particles and frozen gases (it's cold out there in space!). They move around the Sun in highly elliptical orbits, which take them very close to the Sun, then very, very far away. The show starts when they get close enough to the Sun for their frozen gases to start to "boil" away. These boiling gases are part of what forms the bright tail that blazes across the sky. Find out more about comets, and look at pictures of some of our recent visitors, including Comet West, Comet Shoemaker-Levy 9, Halley's Comet, and others.

http://www.hawastsoc.org/solar/eng/comet.htm

Comet Shoemaker-Levy Home Page (JPL)

For centuries, comets have been well known by the astronomers that scan the night skies searching for its mysteries. Gene and Carolyn Shoemaker and David Levy spotted something on March 24, 1993, which was to become a major event. The comet they identified was found to have an orbit around Jupiter. Only this time, it was on a collision course! The fragmented comet, P/Shoemaker-Levy 9, after intense observation and study, collided with Jupiter between July 16 and July 24, 1994. It took over a week for all the fragments to reach the planet, but it provided a light show for anyone with a strong enough telescope pointed in the right direction. See the results here.

http://www.jpl.nasa.gov/sl9/

Make Asteroid Potatoes

This activity explains where asteroids come from and gives a recipe to make edible asteroids, complete with realistic-looking craters. If you don't want to eat the result of this experiment, you can always keep your new asteroid as a pet. It won't eat much, we guarantee!

http://spaceplace.jpl.nasa.gov/ds1_ast.htm

The Natural History Museum, London — The Cosmic Football

Scientists often explore the ice of Antarctica for micrometeorites. These tiny space travelers are so small, you need a microscope to see them! They have to be collected and studied under very special conditions so that they are not contaminated. This is the story of one very unusual micrometeorite and the British scientist who unraveled its mystery. See if you can follow the clues and make the correct hypothesis about how it got its distinctive shape.

http://www.nhm.ac.uk/sc/cf/cf1.html

Sign Up for a Round Trip on STARDUST

The Jet Propulsion Lab invites you to send your name to a comet. STARDUST will launch in February 1999 to visit Comet Wild-2 to collect particles and return them to Earth for analysis. The names will be placed on a microchip, which will be carried back to Earth after the dance through the comet. It will probably end up in a museum after that.

http://stardust.jpl.nasa.gov/microchip/signup.html

Small Bodies

Did you ever make a wish on a "falling star"? It isn't a star, of course, but a meteor—a bit of rock captured by Earth's gravity, burning as it enters our atmosphere. Sometimes these space rocks don't burn completely, and they can reach Earth. When this happens, they are known as meteorites. You can get a close-up look at some well-traveled rocks at this site, which also features fascinating Hubble Space Telescope photos of Comet Shoemaker-Levy 9 fragments hitting Jupiter in 1994. Compare various portraits of Comet Halley, the world's most famous comet, which swings by Earth about every 75 or 76 years. The spectacular 1910 appearance over Flagstaff, Arizona, makes the more recent 1986 visitation look like a fizzled firecracker!

http://pds.jpl.nasa.gov/planets/welcome/smb.htm

Curl up with a good Internet site.

Spacelink - Comets Asteroids and Meteoroids

Do you want just an overview of facts about comets and meteors? Check here for basic coverage, including such information as how many meteors fall to Earth each day (tons!), how many meteors you can expect to see an hour during the Perseid shower every August (68 at maximum), and what the heck a *tektite* is (a glassy rock that may be the remains of a meteor or a comet fragment—scientists are still arguing about it).

http://spacelink.nasa.gov/Instructional.Materials/
    Curriculum.Support/Space.Science/
    Our.Solar.System/Small.Bodies/
    Comets.Asteroids.and.Meteoroids

ECLIPSES

Educator's Guide to Eclipses

Have you ever seen an eclipse? It's certainly an eerie event. It takes the Moon, the Sun, and Earth to make an eclipse. A solar eclipse happens when the Moon gets between Earth and the Sun and casts a shadow on Earth. A lunar eclipse happens when Earth gets between the Moon and the Sun and casts a shadow on the Moon. All three objects have to be lined up just right in the sky for this to happen. Read about eclipses and discover the special words astronomers use to describe the event.

http://bang.lanl.gov/solarsys/edu/eclipses.htm

Eye Safety

Did you know that it's dangerous to look directly at a solar eclipse? The infrared and ultraviolet light can be very bad for your eyes! Visit this NASA site to learn how you can safely watch a projected image of an eclipse using a straw hat, a big leafy tree, or even your interlaced fingers!

http://planets.gsfc.nasa.gov/eclipse/safety2.html

A B C D E F G H I J K L M N O P Q R S T U V W X Y Z

A
B
C
D
E
F
G
H
I
J
K
L
M
N
O
P
Q
R
S
T
U
V
W
X
Y
Z

May 10th, 1994 Eclipse

It was a dark day in New Mexico on May 10, 1994. No, the weather wasn't bad—it was a total solar eclipse! Scientists and astronomers traveled there from all over the world just to get a good look. To see the rare event that caused all this excitement, check out this site.

http://www.ngdc.noaa.gov/stp/ECLIPSE/eclipse.html

Total Eclipse of the Sun

When's the next solar or lunar eclipse? Where is the best place in the world to see it? Check this site! You'll also find a calendar of space events, a mailing list so you can keep up on eclipses, meteor showers, occultations, sightings, sunspots, rumors, and more. Lots of eclipse Web pages have great photography, and this one is no exception. But how many sites offer audio files? No, you can't hear the Sun say, "Hey Moon! Get out of my way!" but the assembled crowd of astronomers and spectators does have a reaction, and you can hear it here if you use Internet Explorer.

http://eclipse.span.ch/total.htm

PLANETARIUMS

Adler Planetarium & Astronomy Museum Web Site

The Adler Planetarium opened in 1930 in Chicago and was the first planetarium to open to the public in the Western Hemisphere. This well-done page tells you about the available shows and what's on exhibit. Read about upcoming events and programs. If you're ever in the area, be sure to pay a visit.

http://astro.uchicago.edu/adler/

Loch Ness Productions: Planetarium Web Sites

Have you ever been to a planetarium show? You sink back in your seat, then the lights go down and the stars come out across the domed ceiling of the planetarium. It's a special treat each and every time you go. Here is a list of planetariums around the world, sorted by location. Find the planetarium closest to you to see what shows are available. If you're going on a trip, check out the schedule of a planetarium near your destination. Enjoy the show.

http://www.lochness.com//pltweb.html

SOLAR SYSTEM AND PLANETS

How Big is the Solar System?

Let's say you had a bowling ball to represent the Sun and a peppercorn to represent Earth, and you chose other objects to stand in for the other planets. Do you think you could make a scale model of the solar system that would fit on a tabletop? No. Well then, would it fit in your classroom? Still no. OK, how about your school playground? Truth is, you would need 1,000 yards (or slightly less than one kilometer in the metric version) to perform this fascinating and unforgettable "planet walk." This is a great activity for a family picnic, too, since it's fun for both children and adults. Complete instructions are provided here!

http://www.noao.edu/education/peppercorn/
pcmain.html

Mars Atlas home page

Fasten your seat belts. The Mars shuttle will be leaving just as soon as you get the courage to start clicking! You'll soon be served with a map of Mars that you can click to zoom in on. Then move around by selecting directional arrows. Stay as long as you like on Mars. You can either pack a lunch or just go to the fridge if you get hungry. Hint: The actual map link is further down the page, in the To Use This section.

http://ic-www.arc.nasa.gov/ic/projects/bayes-group/
Atlas/Mars/

Mission to Mars Homepage

This exemplary site was the winner of the 1998 ThinkQuest competition's Math and Science category, entirely built by kids. You can learn all sorts of information about Mars, the Red Planet, here at Mars Academy. But the real fun starts when you can outfit and fly your own mission! You have to know a lot to design your mission, so you'd better go back to the Academy and make sure you did all the assigned homework! This site takes a long time to explore, and your mission may take many visits to complete. That's why they ask you to set up an "account" so they can keep track of your spacecraft, but don't worry, it's free.

http://library.advanced.org/11147/

The Nine Planets

Here's a site with pictures of all the planets and their moons and much, much more. How did they get their names? Find out what planets are made of and which are most dense, brightest in the sky, and so on. Many of the words are linked to a glossary; just click on a highlighted word for an explanation. Also find out which planets have the best prospects for supporting life. Earth is listed first!

http://seds.lpl.arizona.edu/
    nineplanets/nineplanets/nineplanets.html

Primer on the Solar Space Environment

How well do you know our nearest star? Have you ever wondered how long the Sun will last before it burns out? How big are sunspots? Are they bigger than your school? Visit this site for a comprehensive description of the Sun as an energy source and its effects on life on Earth. Did you know that geomagnetic storms on the Sun can alter current flow in pipelines and really confuse homing pigeons?

http://www.sec.noaa.gov/primer/primer.html

Sign up for Mars

Send your name to Mars on the Mars Polar Explorer, scheduled to launch January 1999. You get a nice certificate of participation and perhaps some future junk mail from Martians!

http://spacekids.hq.nasa.gov/mars/

Solar System Live

This is Solar System Live, and they mean it! You can tell the computer to draw a picture of the solar system almost any way you'd like it. You can even see what it looked like in the past or what it will look like sometime in the future, by giving it that date. If you're adventurous, you can even get a stereo view, but you'll need to train yourself in how to look at the twin pictures—this may take a bit of practice or help from someone older, but it's worth it. You can even include a comet in the drawing to discover how it travels through the solar system on its long journey.

http://www.fourmilab.ch/solar/solar.html

Sun

It's big, it's hot, and it's the brightest thing around. No, we're not talking about glow-in-the-dark slime. We're talking about our very own star: the Sun. The Sun makes plants grow and keeps us warm. It's over 4.6 billion years old and is big enough to hold 1.3 million Earths. Read all about what it's made of and how it works.

http://www.hawastsoc.org/solar/eng/sun.htm

The Sun

It's pretty hot stuff! With a temperature of 15 million degrees Kelvin at its center, the Sun is the source of energy for all life on Earth. Each second, the Sun burns enough fuel to produce 386 billion-billion megawatts of energy (that's a lot of lightbulbs!). But don't worry, it has enough fuel to burn another five billion years. There are many more interesting facts here to discover about the Sun.

http://seds.lpl.arizona.edu/nineplanets/
    nineplanets/sol.html

Views Of the Solar System

What do you think of when you hear the word "Mars"? Mars, ah yes, one of my favorite candy bars. How about "Pluto"? Hey, that's Mickey's pet dog! "Saturn"? My dad's got one of those in the garage! OK, now what do they all have in common? They're all planets, of course. Did you know that Mars has volcanoes and that the biggest one is 15 miles high (the biggest one on Earth is only six miles high)? Did you know that (at least until 1999) Pluto is closer to the Sun than Neptune? Scientists also think that Pluto's atmosphere freezes and falls to the ground when it gets further away from the Sun—imagine shoveling clouds off your front walk! Did you know that you can drive a Saturn, but you can't make it sink? At least not the planet—it floats! There's lots more here, including many images and animations of planets, comets, and asteroids.

http://bang.lanl.gov/solarsys/

A
B
C
D
E
F
G
H
I
J
K
L
M
N
O
P
Q
R
S
T
U
V
W
X
Y
Z

A
B
C
D
E
F
G
H
I
J
K
L
M
N
O
P
Q
R
S
T
U
V
W
X
Y
Z

NET FILES

In 1899, New York police made their first arrest of a speeding motorist. How fast was the car going?

Answer: The car had been whizzing along at 12 miles per hour! The police officer was able to catch the motorist even while riding a bicycle. More strange-but-true car facts are here at *http://www.autoshop-online.com/auto101/facttext.html*

Weight on Different Planets

Do you know how many kilograms you weigh on Earth? (Hint: To convert pounds to approximate kilograms, take the number of pounds and divide by 2.2.) What would your weight be on other planets? Use this Shockwave simulation to experience the unbearable lightness of being on Pluto, then experiment with the others.

http://sunsite.anu.edu.au/Questacon/comet/weight.htm

Welcome to the Planets

This collection centers on images taken from NASA's planetary exploration program. There are different annotated views of each planet, including close-ups. You'll also find pictures and facts about the spacecraft NASA used to take these photos, including *Mariner, Viking, Voyager, Magellan, Galileo,* and the Hubble Space Telescope.

http://pds.jpl.nasa.gov/planets/

The Sun never sets on the Internet.

Woman in the Moon

You may have heard of the Man in the Moon, but have you ever seen the Woman in the Moon? Some people think she's actually easier to see! She looks a little like Wilma Flintstone to us, but study the pictures here and see what you think.

http://www.tufts.edu/as/wright_center/fellows/georgepage.html

SPACE EXPLORATION AND ASTRONAUTS

Biosphere 2

Did you know there is a rain forest in the middle of the Arizona desert? There's also an ocean. It's true, and the most amazing part: they are both indoors! Biosphere 2 is a 7,200,000-cubic-foot sealed glass and space frame structure, and inside are seven wilderness ecosystems, or biomes, including a rain forest and a 900,000-gallon ocean. The idea was to find out how people could survive inside a sealed environment, in case we wanted to colonize other planets. Could they grow all their own food? Manufacture their own air? Recycle their own waste? The first crew of biospherians (four women and four men) entered Biosphere 2 on September 26, 1991. They remained inside for two years, emerging again on September 26, 1993. Biosphere's original experiments were very controversial, but the results were undisputed: we don't know how to successfully accomplish this mission—yet. Columbia University now operates the facility as a learning center about the greenhouse effect. See what they are up to, take a cybertour, and check out some of the over 750 sensors to see what the temperature happens to be right now.

http://www.bio2.edu/

History of Space Exploration

Humans have been observing the stars for hundreds of years. It wasn't until 1959, with *Luna 1*, that we were able to actually break away from the gravity of Earth to visit another heavenly body—the Moon. In 1968, *Apollo 8* made the first manned space flight around the Moon. Read about all the other spacecraft that we have launched in our quest for knowledge about our universe.

http://www.hawastsoc.org/solar/eng/history.htm

Jim Lovell and the Flight of Apollo 13

This is a brief biography of astronaut Jim Lovell, from his childhood to his retirement. Read about how his interest in rocketry developed into a love for flying and space travel. Jim's most famous mission was the ill-fated *Apollo 13* flight to the Moon. This disastrous flight ended with the crew "escaping" back to Earth by way of the lunar module that was supposed to land on the Moon. Various links are included that explain more about some of the terms used in the story.

http://www.mcn.org/Apollo13/Home.html

KidSAT Mission Operations Center

Did you know kids have taken over the space shuttle? Not the whole shuttle, just a special camera on several of the shuttle missions. This NASA project teams middle school and high school kids with mission specialists. Read about past projects and look out for a new resource on this site, called Launchpad, coming soon.

http://www.kidsat.ucsd.edu/kidsat/

Mission and Spacecraft Library

There have been over 5,000 orbital spacecraft launches and attempted launches since the beginning of the Space Age. It's sometimes hard to imagine what various kinds of spacecraft really look like. For example, what does *Mir* look like? If you're curious, you can search this site by name or by mission. See if you can find the TV satellites from Luxembourg! You'll find out who made the equipment, when it was launched, what its mission is, its orbit, and more. This database is small but growing.

http://leonardo.jpl.nasa.gov/msl/

Space FAQ - How to Become an Astronaut

Being an astronaut must be a cool job. How do you get to be one? Getting a Ph.D. and being a flight pilot are two very important qualifications for becoming an astronaut. Good eyesight and excellent physical condition are also a must. Also, don't be shy—astronauts need to be able to speak to the public. This page tells you all about how to impress NASA in order to get a job as an astronaut.

http://www.gene.com/ae/WN/SU/howto.html

The Space Shuttle Clickable Map

Isn't it amazing how much stuff we recycle these days, when we used to throw it away? NASA is doing the same thing with the space shuttle. NASA recycles its booster rockets after they fall into the ocean and they fly the main cabin and cargo bay back to Earth to use again and again. This page has a clickable picture of a space shuttle, which will take you on a descriptive tour of its different parts. Explore the shuttle and find out what makes it click, er, tick.

http://seds.lpl.arizona.edu/ssa/docs/Space.Shuttle/

Space Shuttle Launches

Here's the official schedule for all upcoming space shuttle launches. This site also describes each of all the past flights. Find out about the crew and cargo for each of the missions. You'll also see descriptions of the scientific experiments the astronauts performed while in space. Some of these experiments include studying the growth of crystals in microgravity and the effects of gravity on the growth of newt eggs (flight STS-65).

http://www.ksc.nasa.gov/shuttle/missions/
    missions.html

The Ultimate Field Trip - Section 1

Here's a field trip that you're unlikely to forget. Astronaut Kathy Sullivan is your host and guide on this incredible journey. She tells you about her decision to switch careers from marine biologist to astronaut. As she talks about her experiences as mission specialist aboard the space shuttle, she guides you on a tour of Earth photos taken from the shuttle. Kathy describes each photo in her own personal way, which gives you a special insight into her own experience.

http://eol.jsc.nasa.gov/uft/uft1.html

Lots of monkey business
in MAMMALS.

A B C D E F G H I J K L M N O P Q R S T U V W X Y Z

A
B
C
D
E
F
G
H
I
J
K
L
M
N
O
P
Q
R
S
T
U
V
W
X
Y
Z

> **Earthquakes are only part of what's shakin' in EARTH SCIENCE.**

SPACE PHOTOS AND IMAGES

ASP List of NGC Images

The Astronomical Society of the Pacific (ASP) offers a list of space images, many of them with descriptions and sky locations. This collection includes images from the Hubble Space Telescope and observatories around the world. Browse and discover the wonders that exist out in the universe!

http://www.aspsky.org/html/resources/ngc.html

Astronomy Picture of the Day

Today we see an image of NGC 4261, a Hubble Space Telescope photo of a neighboring galaxy that has a giant black hole at its center. Tomorrow will be a picture called "24 hours from Jupiter." Guess we'll have to return tomorrow to see that one. The descriptive captions are peppered with links to other materials.

http://antwrp.gsfc.nasa.gov/apod/astropix.html

Chesley Bonestell Gallery

Do you ever watch old Hollywood movies about outer space? You know, the ones where the rockets look like firecrackers. Since people hadn't even started to explore space yet, moviemakers had to rely on imagination when they wanted to show the surface of an alien planet. Most of those outer space scenes were filmed against painted backdrops. To film Martians in their natural habitat, for example, movie directors dressed actors in silly costumes and plopped them in front of the paintings of Chesley Bonestell. His work isn't just a great backdrop for 1930s movies—it helped shape the way scientists design space suits and rocket ships.

http://www.secapl.com/bonestell/Top.html

NASA - JSC Digital Image Collection Home

So many pictures, too little time! This is the Johnson Space Center's collection of space images taken from various space missions. Over 10,000 press release images and 300,000 Earth observation images are available. You'll see pictures here from the first Mercury flight to the latest space shuttle mission. If you know your latitude and longitude, you might be able to find a space photo of where you live. Hint: You can get your latitude and longitude for most places in the U.S. at the How Far Is It? page at <http://www.indo.com/distance/> if you want to check.

http://images.jsc.nasa.gov/

SEDS Messier Database

This would definitely make E.T. feel homesick: 110 images of the brightest and most beautiful objects in the night skies. This is the Messier catalog of star clusters, galaxies, and nebulae. Charles Messier started this catalog in the eighteenth century as a collection of objects that were most often mistaken for comets. It serves as an excellent reference list for both beginner and seasoned astronomers. You'll also find the celestial position for each object, which will help you locate it in the sky. Stars: they are hot stuff!

http://seds.lpl.arizona.edu/messier/Messier.html

STARS AND CONSTELLATIONS

3-D Starmaps

Hey! You in the Alpha sector! Any idea at all how I get to the Gamma Quadrant? Hopelessly lost in space? No problem! Get your space tourist maps right here. As this site says, "Science fiction fans and authors of SF novels have often wondered 'where everything is.' Is Sirius closer to Procyon than Tau Ceti? Is 82 Eridani safely within the Terran Federation, or is it perilously close to the dreaded Blortch Empire? And just where exactly is Babylon 5?" A fascinating site!

http://www.clark.net/pub/nyrath/starmap.html

The Milky Way

Did you know that they named our galaxy after a candy bar—or was it the other way around? Anyway, our Earth is part of the solar system that centers on the Sun, our closest star. Our Sun is only one of a few hundred billion stars that make up the Milky Way galaxy. If you think that's big, the Milky Way (the galaxy, not the candy bar) is only one of millions of galaxies in the universe. This introduction to our home galaxy was written by a fourth grader.

http://pen1.pen.k12.va.us/Anthology/Div/Albemarle/
Schools/MurrayElem/ClassPages/Butler/SPACE/
THEMILKYWAY.HTML

Out of This World Exhibition

You may have heard the names of some of the star constellations: the Big Dipper, Taurus the Bull, and Aquarius, to name a few. You may have even seen their figures drawn along with the stars that form them. Probably not like the figures you'll find here. These pages are filled with etchings and drawings of star charts and maps from hundreds of years ago. They show the constellations drawn with detailed figures and objects. Early astronomers might not have had the fancy instruments we have now, but they sure had imagination!

http://www.lhl.lib.mo.us/pubserv/hos/stars/
welcome.htm

The Universe in the Classroom, Spring 1986

Can you imagine weighing 10,000 tons? That's how much you would weigh if you were able to stand on one of our neighboring stars, Sirius B. Although this star is only about the size of our Earth, it weighs almost as much as our own Sun. That tremendous weight is what gives it such strong gravity. Our Sun is over 300 times brighter than Sirius B. However, Sirius A, its twin, is twice as big as our Sun. Sirius A would look over 20 times brighter if it were in the same spot as our Sun. If these facts sound interesting, there's lots more here about these and other stars that share our corner of the universe.

http://www.aspsky.org/html/tnl/05/05.html

NET FILES

How many peanuts does it take to make a 12-ounce jar of peanut butter?

Answer: 540, says the Peanut Butter Lovers Club site at http://www.peanutbutterlovers.com/ Trivia/index.html

Did you know that the average American kid consumes 1,500 PB&J sandwiches by high school graduation?

TELESCOPES AND OBSERVATORIES

Bradford -Robotic -Telescope

OK, here's the deal. You register (free) with this site, then you get to use their telescope. Unfortunately, the 46-centimeter 'scope is high on the moors in West Yorkshire, England. Fortunately, the Bradford Robotic Telescope is robotic, and an astronomer does not need to be present. Anyone can direct the telescope to look at anything in the northern night sky. The observations are completed as time allows, so be prepared to wait awhile for your results. If you don't want to wait that long, you can browse through some of the completed jobs. Oh wow! Look at that! Wait, who's that waving from the Moon?

http://www.eia.brad.ac.uk/rti/

Wolves are a howl in MAMMALS.

A
B
C
D
E
F
G
H
I
J
K
L
M
N
O
P
Q
R
S
T
U
V
W
X
Y
Z

HST Greatest Hits 1990-1995 Gallery

They say on a clear day, you can see forever. However, astronomers would rather do without the air, no matter how clear. Light waves get distorted as they travel through the air, and it's hard to get a good picture when you're trying to see very far away. That's the idea behind the Hubble Space Telescope (HST). With a powerful telescope in orbit above the atmosphere, scientists can get a much better picture of our universe. The images are sent back to Earth electronically. This way, they are not affected by the atmosphere. Be sure to check out the telescope's greatest hits!

http://oposite.stsci.edu/pubinfo/BestOfHST95.html

Mount Wilson Observatory

Located above Los Angeles, California, this observatory has been at the forefront of astronomy for many years. The lights in nearby L.A. are about as bright as a full moon, so observations are limited to bright objects such as nebulae or star clusters. Still, scientific competition to use the telescopes at this facility is fierce! On the virtual tour, you'll visit all the 'scopes on the mountain. Plus, you'll get a tour of the Monastery, which is the building where scientists sleep when not performing their duties. The building is divided into two parts: the "day" side (for scientists who sleep at night and work during the day) and the "night" side (for scientists who sleep during the day and use the telescopes at night).

http://www.mtwilson.edu/

NASA K-12 Internet: Live From the Hubble Space Telescope

In March and April 1996, three Hubble Space Telescope orbits were dedicated to student observations of Neptune (for two orbits) and Pluto (for one). You can see the results here plus diagrams of the telescope itself.

http://quest.arc.nasa.gov/hst/

Telescopes

Read all about reflection, refraction, parabolic mirrors, and spherical aberration. These are some of the definitions used to describe telescope features and how they are made. Telescopes need to magnify light from weak, distant sources and make the images visible to the observer. There's a lot more available on astronomy if you click on "Return to lecture notes homepage" at the bottom of the page.

http://www.bc.cc.ca.us/programs/sea/astronomy/
telescop/telescop.htm

NET FILES

Every year The Worshipful Companies of the Vintners and Dyers participate in an unusual and ancient ritual on the River Thames in London. What is it?

Answer: This group is charged with the royal duty of rounding up and taking a census of all the swans! For many centuries, mute swans in Britain were raised for food, like other poultry. Individual swans were marked by nicks on their webbed feet or beak, which indicated ownership. Somewhat like cattle brands in the American West, these markings were registered with the Crown. Any unmarked birds become Crown property. The swans are rounded up at a "swan-upping," and although they are no longer used for food, the Royal Swanherd continues the tradition to this day. Check http://www.airtime.co.uk/users/cygnus/muteswan.htm for more information.

Wolves are a howl in MAMMALS.

Sidebar navigation: A B C D E F G H I J K L M N O P Q R S T U V W X Y Z

UNIVERSE

Black Holes

You can check in, but you can't check out! As far back as 1793, astronomer Rev. John Mitchell reasoned that if something were big enough, its gravity would be so strong that even light could not escape. Since then, Einstein's Theory of Relativity has helped explain how this is possible. These objects are now called black holes. Some scientists think that black holes are formed from stars that collapse into themselves when they burn out. That's hard to imagine, but we're finding out more and more about black holes all the time. Maybe you'll be the one who makes a big discovery someday about the mystery of black holes.

http://www.aspsky.org/html/tnl/24/24.html

Cosmology

What do you think of when you hear someone say "big bang"? (You probably picture fireworks on the Fourth of July!) Astronomers use that phrase to talk about one of the most popular theories of how the universe began—with a Big Bang! Read on to get an explanation of how it all started around 20 billion years ago.

http://www.ast.cam.ac.uk/pubinfo/leaflets/
cosmology/cosmology.html

General Astronomy Information

If you feel the need to learn more about astronomy, then you're well on your way to becoming an astrophysicist (someone who studies the universe) and you may want to look at the informative pamphlets listed here.

http://www.ast.cam.ac.uk/pubinfo/leaflets/

Steven Hawking's Universe

What's the deal with the universe, anyway? Where did it come from? Where is it going? Stephen Hawking, a British physicist, has spent most of his life thinking about these questions. The answers he's come up with are here. Two of the answers are "Yes" and "Maybe, if you use exotic matter." (Oh, you want the questions? OK, here they are: Do black holes really exist? Do wormholes really exist?) But there is a lot more here, including a galaxy of links and reading suggestions.

http://www.pbs.org/wnet/hawking/html/

NET FILES

What plants attract butterflies?

Answer: Many flowering plants attract butterflies, and others help feed their caterpillars. Some of these are milkweed, lantana, lilac, cosmos, goldenrod, and zinnia. You can find out more at http://www.butterflies.com/guide.html if you flutter by!

World Builders

If you could create your own planet, starting with a handful of stellar dust, what would you build? Maybe a water planet, or a desert planet? What sorts of animal and plant life would develop? What elements would make up the atmosphere, and—here's the big question—what kind of fast-food restaurants would be there? OK, we were kidding about that last question. But some college kids took a course in world building, and this page documents their results. See what you think about these virtual worlds, then follow the instructions and see if you can create your own planet!

http://curriculum.calstatela.edu/courses/builders/

AVIATION AND AIRPLANES

AeroWeb: The Aviation Enthusiast Corner

Whoa—did you see that precision flying team, the U.S. Air Force Thunderbirds? Those F-16 Fighting Falcons sure do put on a great air show! If you want to learn more about this drill team in the skies and see when they will be coming to your area, check this Web site. You'll also find the schedules of lots of other air show performers, plus specifications on different types of aircraft. There are also links to aircraft manufacturers and aviation museums and lots more. Warning: This site is graphics-intensive and takes a long time to load.

http://aeroweb.brooklyn.cuny.edu/air.html

A B C D E F G H I J K L M N O P Q R S T U V W X Y Z

A
B
C
D
E
F
G
H
I
J
K
L
M
N
O
P
Q
R
S
T
U
V
W
X
Y
Z

AirNav: Airport Information

Type in the three-letter airport code for the airport you want, and you'll get detailed information back. If you don't know the code, you can just type in the name of the nearest city. You can try to look for nearby balloonports, gliderports, heliports, seaplane bases—pretty much everything but a starship dock! You'll get back a map of the airport, its radio frequencies, runway descriptions, yearly traffic statistics, and more, including a list of obstructions in the general area, such as tall radio towers or buildings. You'll also find out if migratory birds or animals are sometimes on the runways.

http://www.airnav.com/airports/

The Earhart Project

Howland Island is famous because of someone who never made it there. In 1937, an airstrip was constructed on Howland as a refueling stop on the round-the-world flight attempt of Amelia Earhart and Fred Noonan. They had left Lae, New Guinea, for Howland Island, but something happened, and they were never seen again. Their disappearance is truly one of the world's great unsolved mysteries. Earhart Light, on the island's west coast, is a day beacon built in memory of the lost aviatrix. The airfield is no longer serviceable. For a possible solution to the mystery and the latest news, see this site.

http://www.tighar.org/Projects/AEdescr.html

History of Flight

Click anywhere on The Runway of Flight to explore various milestones in aviation history. You'll start with the dreams of Leonardo da Vinci, whose ideas were ahead of available technology. Keep going up the runway to learn about test pilot Chuck Yeager, military aircraft, and commercial flight service. Along the way, you can test your knowledge with some fun simulations. This site, built by kids, is a ThinkQuest Junior contest finalist.

http://tqjunior.advanced.org/4027/

ITN's Airlines Of The Web - Information, Reservations, Aviation

Every airline with a Web page is collected here! Cruise links to all the big airlines (Delta, United, TWA, British Airways), and check out the little ones. You'll find Tigerfly, the U.K.-based "world's smallest airline." You'll learn lots of airline statistics here too, like how much airlines spend on food per passenger and current monthly statistics about which airlines generally take off and land on time.

http://www.itn.net/cgi/get?itn/cb/aow/
    index:XX-AIRLINES

The K-8 Aeronautics Internet Textbook

How much do you know about the principles of aeronautics? That's the science of how planes, balloons, and other aircraft fly. Knowing how airfoils work can also help you throw a baseball or improve your tennis game—visit this site to learn how this works!

http://wings.ucdavis.edu/

LANDINGS Welcomes all Pilots & Aviation Enthusiasts to the Busiest Aviation Cyberhub

What in the world is a flight plan? A flight plan helps you prepare for the best route of flight before taking off, just as you would map out your summer vacation road trip. A flight plan will include items such as departure and destination airports, navigation aids, fuel consumption rates, and wind information. This will aid in a safer flight for all. You can download software to assist with flight planning, or you can stay on the ground and use the flight simulator games available here. Make your reservations now; this is a feature-rich site!

http://www.landings.com/aviation.html

Learn to Fly - the Cybercockpit homepage

Wow—you're taking a flight lesson! The weather is nice, but the winds are from 15 to 20 mph, which means plenty of practice with crosswinds. Yikes, too crooked—better go around and try it again. Wondering what *that* switch does? A very informative graphic describes all those confusing-looking gauges in the cockpit.

http://www.grouper.com/francois/

NATIONAL AIR & SPACE MUSEUM HOMEPAGE

See pictures and learn about milestones in aviation. For example, Charles Lindbergh was one of the most famous pilots in history. In his plane, *Spirit of St. Louis*, he was the first to cross the Atlantic alone. He took off from Roosevelt Field, in New York State, early on the morning of May 20, 1927. After 33 hours, Lindbergh landed at Le Bourget Field, near Paris, welcomed by a cheering crowd. This was the first solo crossing of a major ocean by air, and it was a very big deal at the time. Come in for a landing at this online museum, where you'll also see famous spacecraft and even a real moon rock! The National Air and Space Museum is part of the Smithsonian Institution, and it is located in Washington, D.C.

http://www.nasm.edu/

Pratt & Whitney: The Jet Engine

Let's just quote from this page: "You think you've got problems? How would you like to be a molecule of air minding your own business at 30,000 feet when all of a sudden you get mugged by five tons of Pratt & Whitney jet engine?" That sort of sets the tone for this introduction to the inner workings of a jet engine. There is also a sound file so you can hear those screaming decibels!

http://www.pratt-whitney.com/engine/jetengine.html

Thirty Thousand Feet - Aviation Links

If you're interested in military aircraft, helicopters, hang gliding, and ultralights, or you just want to find out where you can get hold of a used blimp, this site should be your first stop. In the Youth section, you can learn about the Young Eagles program, a network of plane enthusiasts who make sure every kid between the ages of 8 and 17 who wants to try an airplane flight can get up in the air with an experienced pilot. Read more about it here!

http://extra.newsguy.com/~ericmax/

NET FILES

What is a group of crows called, and why?

Answer: A "murder" of crows is based on the false folktale that crows judge each other and if it's decided a particular crow has done something bad, the others gang up on him and kill him. According to the American Society of Crows and Ravens at http://www.azstarnet.com/~serres/crow/faq.html occasionally crows will kill a dying crow that doesn't belong in their territory. Much more commonly, they feed on carcasses of dead crows, since they are scavengers.

Time Line

Look, it's a bird! No, it's a plane! In fact, it's a whole bunch of things that fly. From the Montgolfier brothers' hot-air balloon (built in 1783) to the world's largest passenger airplane, the Boeing 747, you'll discover it all here. You'll learn the history of flight and the people and technology behind it. Warning: This page is graphics-intensive, and it comes all the way from the Science Museum of London.

http://www.nmsi.ac.uk/on-line/flight/flight/history.htm

Chase some waterfalls in EARTH SCIENCE.

A B C D E F G H I J K L M N O P Q R S T U V W X Y Z

NET FILES

What did Nero, emperor of ancient Rome, use to improve his viewing of the gladiators?

Answer: The emperor was known to use a large emerald to give him a better view of "the games." Concave gemstones were discovered to be useful as magnifying lenses in ancient times. Beam over to *http://www.utmem.edu/personal/thjones/hist/hist_mic.html* to read more about the history of lenses and optics.

BALLOONING, BLIMPS, AND AIRSHIPS

Airship and Blimp Resources

What's the difference between an airship and a blimp? The airship usually has a rigid internal frame, while a blimp does not. Some of them fly using hot air, while others use lighter than air gases, like helium. Looking for a link to the Goodyear Blimp home page? It's here, along with many other fascinating resources. You'll also find good information on the history of airships and blimps, plus selected links on ballooning.

http://www.hotairship.com/

Hot Air Balloon Cyber-Ride

Up, up, and away! What happens when you take a balloon ride? This little adventure will let you experience it all on a virtual trip. Will you fly over the barn or make for that big mountain in the distance? The choice is up to you. Remember, although champagne is traditional at the end of a balloon journey, you'll have to stick to a nonalcoholic beverage!

http://www.hot-airballoons.com/cybride.html

Metlife Online SM: The Blimp

Have you ever noticed that large sporting events tend to attract blimps, like flies around a picnic? The blimp carries a joystick-controlled camera, which gets a live overhead shot of the playing field. You may have seen the MetLife Blimp—it has everyone's favorite beagle, Snoopy, on it. But is it Snoopy One or Snoopy Two? There are two MetLife blimps, one based on each coast. While they normally are tasked to help televise sporting events, the western Snoopy recently helped track some whales as part of an environmental research project. This site will tell you all about the blimp's construction, its history, and how the heck they park it!

http://www.metlife.com/Blimp/

The official Virgin Global Challenger site

According to this site, in aviation there are records and there are milestones. Records—for the fastest flight, the longest flight, and so on—are made to be broken by someone going faster or farther. But milestones, well, you can only set a milestone event, like the first flight, once. After that, the history of aviation moves on, but the milestone remains. There's one goal that has escaped aviators for years: circling the globe nonstop by balloon. This site focuses on the attempt by Virgin Challenger, but you can read about its competitors and their progress here, too.

http://www.challenger.virgin.net/

BIOLOGY

See also SCIENCE

Beginner's guide to Molecular Biology: Cell Structure

Learn all about the basics of cell structure, complete with colorful drawings and photographs. You'll learn about not only the parts of a cell but also their functions and chemistry.

http://www.res.bbsrc.ac.uk/molbio/guide/cell.html

Cell Basics

Cells are the basic building blocks of life. You need a microscope to see most cells and the tiny structures inside them, which are called *organelles*. This page, part of a biology hypertextbook for the Massachusetts Institute of Technology, gives you an overview of cell biology. See the differences between plant and animal cells, and if you're really into it, go back to the home page for this resource and learn about photosynthesis, genetics, and more!

http://esg-www.mit.edu:8001/bio/cb/cellbasics.html

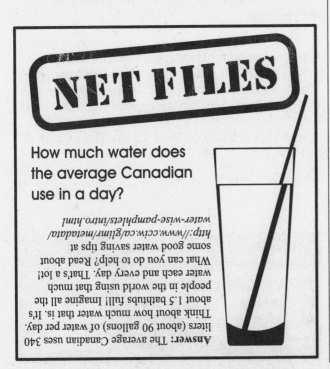

NET FILES

How much water does the average Canadian use in a day?

Answer: The average Canadian uses 340 liters (about 90 gallons) of water per day. Think about how much water that is. It's about 1.5 bathtubs full! Imagine all the people in the world using that much water each and every day. That's a lot! What can you do to help? Read about some good water saving tips at http://www.cciw.ca/glimr/metadata/water-wise-pamphlets/intro.html

---

> CATS are purrfect.

The Heart: An Online Exploration

The heart is more than just a symbol for Valentine's Day. It's the pump that keeps your life's blood flowing throughout your body. Your blood distributes food to your cells and carries away the waste. Since blood can't move on its own, it would be quite useless without the heart to keep it moving! Visit this page to read about the heart and all its functions.

http://sln.fi.edu/biosci/

Neuroscience for Kids - Explore the NS

When you bite into a chocolate bar, how do you know it's delicious? How do you know to say "Ouch!" when you get stung by a mosquito? Little sensors, called *neurons*, are all over your body, and they carry messages to your brain through a system of nerves. Your brain then sorts everything out. This site is crammed with great info about brains, your senses, spinal cords, and careers in neuroscience. Be aware, though, that many of these folks go to school for 20 *years* before they become neuroscientists!

http://weber.u.washington.edu/~chudler/introb.html

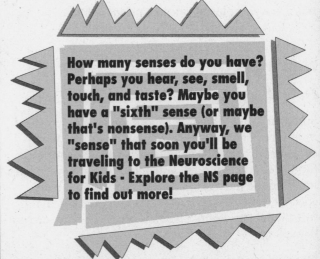

How many senses do you have? Perhaps you hear, see, smell, touch, and taste? Maybe you have a "sixth" sense (or maybe that's nonsense). Anyway, we "sense" that soon you'll be traveling to the Neuroscience for Kids - Explore the NS page to find out more!

A
B
C
D
E
F
G
H
I
J
K
L
M
N
O
P
Q
R
S
T
U
V
W
X
Y
Z

GENETICS

Electronic Desktop Project - Virtual Flylab

Have you heard someone say "he has his father's eyes" or "his mother's smile"? That's because a child is made from genetic instructions contributed by each parent. They combine in different ways, so you'll see people in the same family look similar to each other but not exactly the same. Well, unless they are twins. Confused yet? This science is called genetics, and scientists learned a lot about its rules by studying fruit flies and their offspring (that's their kids). We know it sounds weird. You can try it yourself here. What happens when you mate a purple-eyed fruit fly to one with fluffy wings?

http://vearthquake.calstatela.edu/edesktop/VirtApps/
VflyLab/IntroVflyLab.html

Interactive Genetics

If breeding virtual flies isn't your first choice, you may like learning about genetics using cute little virtual mice! This simulation requires Shockwave. First you'll have to answer some questions about statistics and probability, but don't worry, there's a cool little tutorial that will have you flipping virtual coins in no time. When you think you know a gene from a chromosome, just enter the Simple Mouse House and breed some critters! When you've got that one figured out, move on to the trickier Advanced Mouse House. Can you discover how to make a pink-eyed black mouse?

http://www.explorescience.com/mouse.htm

MICROSCOPES

Early History of the Lens

Sure, we could tell you all about the person who first thought of using a lens to magnify things, or when eyeglasses came into vogue (earlier than you might think!). Or we could tell you about the dude who later invented the microscope. But wouldn't you rather check it out yourself? Lots of pictures and fascinating facts about early optics and scientists are here for you to explore.

http://www.utmem.edu/personal/thjones/hist/c1.htm

NET FILES

What are the most endangered species in the world (not counting your little brother)?

Answer: Find the answer at http://www.wwf.org/species/most_endangered.html

The list includes the Indo-Chinese tiger, the giant panda, the Asiatic black bear, and the black rhino, among others. The only plant on the list is the North American lady slipper orchid (Cypripedium spp.).

Molecular Expressions: Images From the Microscope

Yoo-hoo! I'm right down here. Right under your nose. No, silly, not on the floor! Under the microscope. Take a look at me and a bunch of other images on the Molecular Expressions page. How about a close-up of that microprocessor chip inside your computer? It's here! So is a microscopic tour of beers of the world, as they appear under polarized light. There's more, including how to set up a microscope of your own.

http://micro.magnet.fsu.edu/

SCIMEDIA: Light Microscopy

You'll find a great little diagram here with all the parts of a microscope. This site also has links to info on lenses, electron microscopy, and more.

http://www.scimedia.com/chem-ed/imaging/
  lmicrosc.htm

BIRDS

See also FARMING AND AGRICULTURE—LIVESTOCK; PETS AND PET CARE

Audubon in Your Area

Did you know that the greatest threat to wild birds is the loss of habitat? That's why special places called wildlife sanctuaries have been set aside. There, you can often see the birds and animals really close-up. Imagine walking down a trail and seeing a wood stork in a cypress tree or a sandhill crane family strolling along the river sandbar. Visit this home page and learn about sanctuaries across the United States that protect these wild birds and other wildlife. At this site you can find refuges near you as well as local chapters of birding associations.

http://www.audubon.org/local/

The Aviary - Your Avian Information Resource for Birds!

Join the flock here for a large variety of information about birds. Whether you own a companion bird or enjoy watching wild birds, this home page is a gathering place and resource center for all bird lovers. You'll find information about bird health as well as food and nutrition tips. You'll discover the importance of toys for your pet bird and learn about wild bird rescue. Fly on over and ask an avian vet a question about your pet bird today.

http://theaviary.com/

Try actual reality.

Bird Extremes - Enchanted Learning Software

How fast can a bird fly? The peregrine falcon has been clocked at 90 mph, and the spine-tailed swift is right up there, too, at 90–100 mph. The fastest land bird is the ostrich, which can speed along at 43 mph on a good day. If you're looking for the biggest, smallest, highest, most unusual bird facts ever, this is a good place to start!

http://www.enchantedlearning.com/subjects/birds/
  Birdextremes.shtml

Bird-Pals

For something a little different, why not try illustrating your own field guide to common birds in your area? These kids did! First graders were paired with college students, and together they researched lots of birds. The kids also drew pictures of the birds for the reports. The songs of the birds are also included.

http://www.wce.wwu.edu/smate/birdpals.html

Common Birds of the Australian National Botanic Gardens

It's such a nice day for a walk in the garden. What beautiful birds! And listen—their songs are so pretty. The Australian National Botanic Gardens are so peaceful, it almost feels as if you are actually there. Watch out, though. During the spring breeding season, male magpies protect their territory by "swooping" intruders: a painful experience for those unlucky enough to be hit. Did you know that the tongue of the New Holland honeyeater has a "brush" at the end, which helps it gather the sweet nectar in flowers? Visit the gardens and learn about the other fascinating birds in the sanctuary.

http://osprey.anbg.gov.au/anbg/birds.html

Satellite Tracking of Threatened Species

"Graak, #12345, last seen March 15, 1995 at 19:48:22." This is a sample of monitoring a migratory, threatened species. The bird's activity, latitude, and longitude can be measured via satellite data transmissions. Discover why and how these birds are being tracked by visiting this interesting site!

http://sdcd.gsfc.nasa.gov/ISTO/satellite_tracking/

A B C D E F G H I J K L M N O P Q R S T U V W X Y Z

Virtual Birding - Educational Materials

Have you ever noticed that all birds don't have the same size and shape of bill? That's because they eat different types of things: some peck at seeds while others gobble down insects. This resource offers a series of lessons that will teach you how to discover a bird's diet by inspecting its beak. Besides that, you'll learn how birds are classified, how they build nests, and how they communicate. This is a simple and informative beginner birding guide!

http://www.inhs.uiuc.edu/chf/pub/virtualbird/educational.html

BIRD WATCHING

Backyard Bird Feeding

The bird food store has so many choices: black oil sunflower, safflower seed, niger seed, or maybe peanut hearts. How do you sort it all out? The good news is that you don't have to sort the various seeds—the birds do that for you! You'll find a handy guide to what species of birds like which foods plus some tips about feeders and placing them in the right spots to attract the most birds.

http://www.fws.gov/~r9mbmo/pamphlet/feed.html#0

Bird Song

When you go on a bird watching hike, odds are that you'll hear a lot more birds than you'll see. Wouldn't it be cool to be able to identify a bird by the sounds it makes? For example, you're out for a walk in the woods and you hear a bird that seems to be singing, "Sweet Canada, Canada, Canada"—instantly, you know that's a white-throated sparrow. Or maybe you're walking in the meadow and hear a high-pitched "chortle-deeeeee," drawn out on that last syllable. You recognize at once that's a red-winged blackbird. How did you get so smart? You've memorized a list of birds and little hints to help you remember what their songs sound like. One's available on this home page! The fancy word for memory-joggers like these is *mnemonics*.

http://www.1000plus.com/BirdSong/

Bird Song Central: Birding By Ear — Spring Tune-Up

Have you ever heard a bird's song and wondered who wrote the music? You might find its composer here, where they have many of the latest bird tunes on file for your listening pleasure. If you can't go out in the woods and fields to look for birds, this site also offers virtual birding in many types of habitat. You can also participate in the contests and perhaps win a prize!

http://www.virtualbirder.com/bbestu/

BirdSource

Sponsored by the National Audubon Society and the Cornell Laboratory of Ornithology, BirdSource attempts to chart the large-scale movements of bird populations over time. Where is the first robin of spring? These folks know. Occasionally they ask for your help. Identify what birds are in your area, then add them to the database at this site. You'll also find links to Cornell's classroom bird watch project so you can get your whole class involved.

http://birdsource.cornell.edu/

Feeder Cams - Birding Net Links

Would you like to peek into a bald eagle's nest to see the babies? If you'd prefer not to climb so high, visit a Web page featuring a live camera trained on an eagle nest in Massachusetts! When you're done with that, try other nest and "feedercams" from all over the world. For example, check on storks in Germany, falcons in Montreal, or squirrels in the U.S.-based Wild Birds Unlimited feedercam!

http://birding.miningco.com/msub5-cams.htm

Patuxent - Migratory Bird Research

Learn all about the Audubon Christmas bird count, migratory bird research, the bird identification info center and more! You'll find lots of pictures, song files, and tips for identifying our feathered friends.

http://www.mbr.nbs.gov/

Virtual Birding in Tokyo

Wouldn't it be fun to see what kinds of birds are in other kids' backyards—say, in Tokyo, Japan? This site lets you compare your local birds to their counterparts on the other side of the world! Does the puddle duck mallard you have strutting around your park pond look the same as the ones in Japan? Find out here at this beautiful site.

http://ux01.so-net.or.jp/~koike/

BIRDHOUSES

Bird House Placement and Care

Everyone needs a home, even our fine feathered friends, the birds. You'll find that different types of birds require different types and placements of their homes. A birdhouse is appreciated by its tenants, and boys and girls, young and old, can also enjoy the presence of a birdhouse—and no batteries are required!

http://www.multiscope.com/hotspot/bhcare.htm

HOMES FOR BIRDS

Home, home on a metal pole? Sure, if you're talking about a birdhouse! Did you know that more than two dozen North American birds will nest in birdhouses? Stop by this Web site, and you will discover very complete advice about how to design a birdhouse to attract different types of birds to your neighborhood.

http://www.bcpl.lib.md.us/~tross/by/house.html

NC State University - NCCES - Working With Wildlife - Building Songbird Boxes

Did you know that you can build houses for specific kinds of birds? Just by varying the diameter of the entrance hole, you can make a house for bluebirds, flycatchers, or flickers. You also have to make the hole a certain distance above the floor of the birdhouse. There are other building considerations to keep in mind for various species. Check this site for plans and specifications for birdhouses and predator guards for them. Then place your new homes in the trees and fields in March or April, while the birds are still home-hunting!

http://www.ces.ncsu.edu/nreos/forest/steward/
www16.html

NC State University - NCCES - Working With Wildlife - Woodland Wildlife Nest Boxes

Learn how you can find and build homes for larger birds such as woodpeckers and owls. Instructions for squirrel, raccoon, and other wildlife nest boxes are also included.

http://www.ces.ncsu.edu/nreos/forest/steward/
www17.html

PET BIRDS

(Parrots) The Pet Bird Page (Parrots)

Thinking about buying a bird for a pet? If so, this is the place to stop before making your purchase. They'll help you choose the bird that's best for you. You'll find important information on what to feed your bird and on how to train it as well as guidelines to finding a good vet. You'll have an opportunity to talk to professionals and experienced breeders in the chat room, and you'll learn about the daily and periodic care required for your feathered friend.

http://hookomo.aloha.net/~granty/

Everybody loves budgies, those colorful little birds also known as parakeets. Budgie is short for budgerigar, from an Aboriginal word that translates as "good eating." If you'd rather admire and not eat your budgies, try perching on (Parrots) The Pet Bird Page (Parrots).

A B C D E F G H I J K L M N O P Q R S T U V W X Y Z

SPECIES: ALBATROSSES AND PETRELS

Virtual Antarctica Science: Seabirds

In the early seventeenth century, seagoing mariners believed the souls of drowned sailors were reincarnated as albatrosses, and killing them brought very bad luck. The poet Samuel Taylor Coleridge even wrote a famous poem about it, called "The Rime of the Ancient Mariner." The largest species, the Wandering Albatross, has a wingspan of around 11 to 11.5 feet (2.9–3.45 meters) and weighs around 18 pounds (88.2 kilograms). According to this resource, adult birds have been recorded flying up to 550 miles per day, at speeds of 50 mph! In a single food-foraging flight they can cover an incredible 1,800 to 9,300 miles, a distance greater than the diameter of Earth.

http://www.terraquest.com/va/science/seabirds/
　　seabirds.html

SPECIES: CRANES, RAILS, AND COOTS

Whooping Crane

These endangered birds are BIG! They can be up to 60 inches (150 centimeters) tall, and their wingspan is 7.5 feet (2.3 meters). They live in shallow wetlands and coastal areas, but they migrate from the Gulf of Mexico all the way to Alberta and the Northwest Territories of Canada. They mate for life, and in Japan, it is traditional to have a crane design on wedding clothing to symbolize true love and long life.

http://www.amnh.org/Exhibition/Expedition/
　　Endangered/crane/crane.html

SPECIES: CUCKOOS AND ROADRUNNERS

The Roadrunner

In cartoons, the very intelligent Roadrunner always escapes from the very confused Coyote. Do you think that's true in real life? At this site you can read about the true-life adventures of the real bird, and by the way, he never says "Beep-beep!"

http://www.desertusa.com/road.html

SPECIES: DUCKS, GEESE, AND SWANS

Carter's Rare Birds

Duck, duck, goose! You probably know Daffy Duck, Donald Duck, and even Mother Goose, but let's look at some of the less-famous ducks and geese, such as cackling Canada geese, cinnamon teal, American widgeons, and wood ducks. Stop by this site and meet some of these birds and hear what they sound like. You'll learn about their nests and eggs and also about their status in both the wild and in captivity.

http://www.rarebird.com/carter/

North West Swan Study

Do you know what a *cob* is, besides something corn grows on? What's a *pen*, besides something you write with? A cob is an adult male swan, and a pen is an adult female swan. The three to seven eggs the pen lays is called a *clutch*, and young swans are called *cygnets*. To learn more about swans, visit this page, and listen to the warning call swans give humans who get too close to their nests.

http://www.airtime.co.uk/users/cygnus/swanstud.htm

SPECIES: EAGLES, FALCONS, VULTURES, AND HAWKS

Old Abe the War Eagle

During the Civil War, many military units adopted an animal mascot. Usually it was a dog or a goat, but the Eighth Wisconsin Infantry Regiment had something really unique: a bald eagle, which they named "Old Abe," after President Abraham Lincoln. You can read about Old Abe's war stories and see pictures. Old Abe's legacy lives on in the logos of Wisconsin companies, in replicas at the Wisconsin State Assembly and elsewhere, and in the names of school sports teams. Additionally, the insignia patch of the U.S. Army's 101st Airborne Division, originally formed in Wisconsin during World War I, carries a graphic of Old Abe. According to this page, the "Screaming Eagles" saw extensive action in World War II and the Vietnam and Persian Gulf Wars.

http://badger.state.wi.us/agencies/dva/museum/
　　cybergal/oa-main.html

SERRC'S Home Page

Did you ever wonder how injured wild birds are rehabilitated? What if they don't fully recover? Visit the Southeastern Raptor Rehabilitation Center (SERRC) and discover what it takes to rehabilitate injured birds before they can be released to the wild. Meet the special permanent residents that will never be released due to the severity of their injuries. Learn the importance of raptors and how you can help ensure that these birds get the finest care available. Maybe your class could participate in the Adopt-A-Raptor program!

http://www.vetmed.auburn.edu/raptor/

NET FILES

Each box of Barnum's Animal Crackers

contains 22 cookies, with an assortment of 17 animals. How many animals can you guess?

Answer: *According to the Nabisco page of Animal Cracker History at http://www.nabisco.com/museum/ barnums.html you may find any of the following animals in your box: tiger, cougar, camel, rhinoceros, kangaroo, hippopotamus, bison, lion, hyena, zebra, elephant, sheep, bear, gorilla, monkey, seal, and giraffe. But it wasn't always like that. Learn how the animal lineup has changed since the cookies were first made in 1902.*

Adopt a raptor today!
Find out more about how these birds of prey need your help and what you can do for them at SERRC'S Home Page.

Welcome to the Raptor Center

You find a hawk with an injured wing. What do you do? You need to call a special kind of animal doctor, called a wildlife rehabilitator, who helps the bird get better so it can be released to the wild again. This site tells you what to do in an emergency, but the most important rule is that the less contact you have with the bird, the better its chances of survival will be. You can also call the Raptor Center 24 hours a day to get advice. They treat many sick or injured birds of prey, also known as *raptors*. For example, a bald eagle was found with a severe bacterial infection. The Raptor Center cured it and released it the next month. Years later, the same lucky bird was found caught in a steel-jawed trap, and it had another visit to the Raptor Center. The injury was successfully treated, and the eagle was once again released in February 1995. Visit this Web site to find more materials about the Raptor Center and the birds they treat, including information about endangered/threatened birds and the environmental issues that affect them.

http://www.raptor.cvm.umn.edu/

Crack open CODES AND CIPHERS.

A B C D E F G H I J K L M N O P Q R S T U V W X Y Z

A
B
C
D
E
F
G
H
I
J
K
L
M
N
O
P
Q
R
S
T
U
V
W
X
Y
Z

SPECIES: FLAMINGOS

Virtual Galápagos: Wildlife - Flamingo

Flamingos get their exotic pink coloring from the food they eat, and the ones on the Galápagos Islands are looking just a little pale. But they sound OK (listen to the call of the wild flamingo). You'll also find a brief movie of how a flamingo feeds (by straining water though a net-like bill).

http://www.terraquest.com/galapagos/wildlife/
   coastal/flamingo.html

SPECIES: HERONS, SPOONBILLS, AND STORKS

Everglades National Park Roseate Spoonbill

The beautiful, exotic-looking pink spoonbill soars overhead. It's hard to believe that these birds narrowly escaped extinction. Why? In the 1800s they were killed for their wings and feathers, which were popular on women's hats. Their bills are an unmistakable shape—can you guess what it might look like?

http://www.nps.gov/ever/eco/spoonbil.htm

Hinterland Who's Who—Great Blue Heron

If you've ever watched a great blue heron in the wild, you know it's got two feeding behaviors: standing and walking slowly. With the standing method, this long-legged bird stands motionless in shallow water until a fish, frog, or snake happens by. Then it grabs the creature with its long yellow bill and eats it for lunch! The walking slowly method is similar, except the bird carefully picks up each leg and sets it down slowly as it moves down the shoreline, so as not to disturb any waiting snacks in the water. A flying heron is something to see; its wingspan is about six feet wide, and it can fly between 20 and 29 mph.

http://www.ec.gc.ca/cws-scf/hww-fap/heron/
   heron.html

SPECIES: HUMMINGBIRDS AND SWIFTS

Hummingbirds!

Did you know that in the spring male hummingbirds start heading north as early as three weeks ahead of the females and immature birds? This is so the male can scout ahead for food for the females and young during migration. For more information on attracting hummingbirds to your yard, hummingbird feeders, the natural history of hummingbirds, and more, visit this hobbyist's outstanding page.

http://www.derived.com/~lanny/hummers/

SPECIES: KINGFISHERS

Belted Kingfisher

First grader Rachel and a college student pal researched the belted kingfisher. You'll find lots about kingfishers here, including a drawing Rachel made, and an audio file of the kingfisher's call.

http://www.wce.wwu.edu/smate/BirdPals/
   studentpages/JeffRachelK/RachelK.html

SPECIES: LOONS

North American Loon Fund

Loons are among the oldest of all bird species. They are water birds and go ashore only to mate and to incubate their eggs. They eat fish, which they catch by diving. They scrape up pebbles on the lake bottom to help them digest their food. Sometimes the "pebbles" are really abandoned lead fishing sinkers. Studies show that eating these sinkers poisons loons! If you find some old fishing lines, hooks, or sinkers, be sure to throw them away in a trash can. This organization aims to help save loons through education, research, and preservation of habitat. Visit here to learn all about loons.

http://facstaff.uww.edu/wentzl/nalf/
   aNALFHOMEPAGE.HTML

SPECIES: OWLS

Jamie Stewart's Screech Owl Page

What a wonderful collection of photos, taken of a family of screech owls nesting near Jamie Stewart's house. Be sure to fill out the guest book, and tell Jamie you saw his page referred to in this book. When you do this, you get to see another cute owl picture!

http://www.voicenet.com/~jstewart/scrchowl/scrchowl.html

NC State University - NCCES - Working With Wildlife - Owls

Do you know a barn owl from a screech owl? You will if you visit this site. A barn owl has a heart-shaped face and can be between 15 to 20 inches tall. A screechie, on the other hand, has tufted ears and is much smaller—only about 10 inches long. You can learn to build owl houses here and help increase the owl population where you live. Let's "owl" build some bird houses soon!

http://www.ces.ncsu.edu/nreos/forest/steward/www22.html

SPECIES: PARROTS

Online Book of Parrots (Psittaciformes)

Parrot species can live in all kinds of environments. We usually think of them as tropical, but there are also some mountain-dwelling parrots that live under alpine conditions! Parrots have a long life span—large cockatoos can live 75 years. Whether you're looking for budgies or cockatiels, greys or macaws, this colorful resource will tell and show you about parrots of the world.

http://www.ub.tu-clausthal.de/PAhtml/

SPECIES: PELICANS AND CORMORANTS

The Redberry Pelican Project Research Station

Visit the Redberry Lake research station, near Saskatoon, Saskatchewan, Canada. It's a prime nesting area for the American white pelican, and since they have a live webcam, you may be able to spot one yourself! Worldwide there are eight species of pelican; see photos and get information here. There are also links to other pelican researchers, plus pelican poetry and prose.

http://www.redbay.com/redpel/pelicans.htm

SPECIES: PENGUINS
The Penguin Page

We all know what macaroni and cheese is, but have you ever heard of macaroni penguins? They live in the Antarctic and nearby islands, and they eat crustaceans, fish, and squid. Visit the Aggressive Behavior section and discover the difference between the "sideways stare" and the "alternate stare" given by penguins to other penguins and other animals. You'll also learn about various penguin species and their predators.

http://www.vni.net/~kwelch/penguins/

NET FILES

What national park has more geysers than any other place on Earth?

Answer: Don't get steamed up, but Yellowstone in Wyoming/Montana/Idaho has over 400 geysers. Yellowstone was the first national park in the world, established in 1872! Read all about this famous and amazing place at http://www2.wku.edu/www/geoweb/geyser/about2.html

A B C D E F G H I J K L M N O P Q R S T U V W X Y Z

SPECIES: PERCHING BIRDS

ASCAR Home Page

The American Society of Crows and Ravens (ASCAR) is a group of folks who support the "caws" of crows and ravens. Ravens look like crows, but they are about one-third larger. Did you know that some of these species can be taught to talk? That explains Edgar Allan Poe's raven, who was always saying "Nevermore!" At this site you can find raven T-shirts and coffee mugs as well as lots of links to other information about these smart creatures.

http://www.azstarnet.com/~serres/index.html

Patuxent Bird Identification InfoCenter

Basic information on a variety of perching (and other) birds can be found at this site. Look for photographs, songs, identification tips, maps, and life history information for North American birds.

http://www.mbr.nbs.gov/id/framlst/framlst.html

SPECIES: PHEASANTS, TURKEYS, AND QUAIL

Newton Central on Prairie Chickens

Third and fourth graders wrote these reports. They got interested in the prairie chicken when they found the once-abundant bird was now an endangered species. In the mid-1800s, there were 10 to 14 million prairie chickens in Illinois. In 1990, there were less than 50 left. What happened? Mostly it was loss of habitat. The good news is that prairie chicken sanctuaries have been set aside, and the birds are starting to repopulate them. These fascinating birds have a winter habit called "snow roosting." At night, they let the snow cover them up, and this insulates and keeps them warm. In the morning, they burst out of their "igloo"—which must startle passers-by! You will also read about what types of grasses are found in a prairie and be surprised to learn that Illinois has an official prairie grass: the big bluestem.

http://www.museum.state.il.us/mic_home/newton/
    project/

The Return of the Wild Turkey

Down the road by Potter's farm, Net-mom saw a pair of wild turkeys with nine curious baby turkeys—called *poults*—clustered around them. The babies were about as big as cats! In recent years, the wild turkey population hereabouts has really surged. If you want to see a picture and learn more about wild turkeys, which are found in all of the lower 48 states as well as Hawaii, try this link.

http://www.esf.edu/pubprog/brochure/turkey/
    turkey.htm

SPECIES: PIGEONS AND DOVES

Project Pigeon Watch

Have you ever noticed the variety of color patterns in pigeons? The original wild pigeons from Africa and Europe are of a coloration called "blue bar." Now there are almost 30 different variations of that, and you can see a number of them on this page! Scientists don't understand it, and they want inner-city kids to help them figure it out. There is a nominal cost for your classroom or family to get an official research kit. You'll need to make observations of pigeons in your area and send in reports to Cornell's Laboratory of Ornithology. Even if you don't plan on joining, you can learn about pigeon color variations here.

http://birdsource.cornell.edu/ppw/

SPECIES: SHOREBIRDS AND GULLS

California Gull

The California gull is the state bird of Utah. It commemorates the fact that these gulls saved the harvest of the state back in 1848. The crops were being destroyed by Rocky Mountain crickets, and gulls "terned" up to save the day. Read more about that, and gulls, here.

http://www.state.lib.ut.us/symbols/gull.htm

A
B
C
D
E
F
G
H
I
J
K
L
M
N
O
P
Q
R
S
T
U
V
W
X
Y
Z

BOATING AND SAILING

See also SPORTS—CANOEING AND KAYAKING;
SPORTS—ROWING AND SCULLING;
SPORTS—WIND SURFING

GORP - Paddling - for paddlers, kayakers, rafters, and canoeists around the world!

Tired of surfing the Net? Why not try kayaking the keyboard or canoeing the computer? This resource is a great casting-off point from which to paddle Net resources about canoeing, kayaking, rafting, and similar water vehicles! Parental advisory: Not all links have been checked.

http://www.gorp.com/gorp/activity/paddle.htm

Interactive Marine Observations

This site falls into the category of the truly amazing. A network of sea buoys and CMAN (Coastal Marine Automated Network) stations is maintained by the National Data Buoy Center (NDBC), a division of NOAA (National Oceanic and Atmospheric Administration). The observations are updated continuously, and an eight-hour history is usually available for each station. They report temperature, dew point, wind (sustained and gust) direction and speed, surface pressure, wave heights, and the period between waves. How are the waves off Maui, Hawaii? What's the temperature off Anchorage, Alaska? You can check even closer to home, if you're going boating in the coastal waters of the U.S. or maritime Canada.

http://www.nws.fsu.edu/buoy/

Navigation Information Connection

The U.S. Army Corps of Engineers sponsors this informative site, which offers maps of navigable rivers in the U.S. as well as daily reports on the status of navigation locks along those rivers. Never seen locks in operation before? They allow boats to go around waterfalls or rapids by providing a water "elevator" for the boat to climb or descend the river.

http://www.ncr.usace.army.mil/nic.htm

You are your own network.

Ocean Challenge/Class Afloat

If your teacher told your class to go get your coats because you're going on a field trip, you'd probably be pretty excited, right? What if he or she led you right onto the deck of a tall ship and said to get comfortable because you are all going on a round-the-world cruise? Still interested? You're then told that your class is going to be the crew and that you'll be gone for months! That's exactly what happened to some high school kids, their teachers, and only a handful of actual, old salt crew members. You can follow some of the progress of their journeys on the Net, for free. You can also sign on as a member, for a fee, and get access to more material.

http://www.oceanchallenge.com/

NET FILES

Little Bo Peep has lost her sheep and doesn't know where to find them! They probably went to the country that has the most sheep in the world. Where is that, anyway?

Answer: *Australia has the most sheep: over 138 million! Don't let anyone pull the wool over your eyes—go to "About Wool" at http://www.ansi.okstate.edu/library/youth.html to find out about sheep breeds and wool production.*

A
B
C
D
E
F
G
H
I
J
K
L
M
N
O
P
Q
R
S
T
U
V
W
X
Y
Z

Online Boating Courses and Boating Safety Information

At this site you can learn a lot about personal floatation devices, tying knots, running lights, and all sorts of boating information. There's a special area just for kids where you can ask questions like "How far is the horizon?" and "Why are life jackets orange?" You can even take an online boating safety course that's approved by the National Association of State Boating Law Administrators (NASBLA) and recognized as acceptable to the United States Coast Guard Recreational Boating Program. To get your official Boating Safety ID card and certificate, you must pass the final exam with a score of at least 80 percent. Good luck!

http://boatsafe.com/nauticalknowhow/

The Semaphore Flag Signaling System

You want to say "Hi" to your buddy in a boat across the bay, but it's too far to yell. You could use the semaphore alphabet and two flags to send messages. How? Boaters spell words by holding a flag in each hand and moving them into different positions. An *H* is made by holding the right-hand flag out straight and the left-hand flag down and across the body. You can learn the whole semaphore alphabet from the pictures and descriptions you'll find at this page. Get your flags and practice!

http://osprey.anbg.gov.au/flags/semaphore.html

Terra.org's Glossary of Boating Terms

Where's the *bow*? What if your *scupper* is plugged? How do you know when to *luff*? If you're going to be talking to boaters or sailors (or if you're going to be one), then you'll have to check out this site. And you thought you were a sailor because you knew your *port* (left) from your *starboard* (right)! Sail on over and find the definition of any sailing word.

http://terra.org/journey/glossary/glossary.html

Be swampwise in EARTH SCIENCE.

United States Power Squadrons ®

Can you pass the online navigation quiz offered by the Power Squadron? Try it! You'll be asked which color running light is on the port side, and similar questions. You can compare your scores with others, and no, you don't have to sign your name! If your score could use some improvement, check to see if there is a local Power Squadron group near you. They offer free classes in boating and sailing safety and navigation. You can preview what will be taught in the classes here.

http://www.usps.org/

YOUNG SAILOR

Ah, the slap of the waves against your boat, the wind in your face, the cry of the gulls overhead as the sun shines on and on. Sailing—there's nothing like it! This site provides online chapters from the book by the same name. You'll learn how to choose a boat, how to be fluent with nautical terms, the inside story on ropes and knots, and, oh yes, basic sailing.

http://www.sheridanhouse.com/site/youngstoc.html

BOOKS AND LITERATURE

Carol Hurst's Children's Literature Site

Sometimes it's fun to learn about a topic by reading a story about it rather than slogging through a regular textbook. For example, there is something called "historical fiction." Here's how it works. Instead of reading about, for example, the Revolutionary War in a fact-after-fact, date-after-date history book, you can read a novel written about that time period. By following the story of the characters and how they interact with events and their environment you can really learn a lot about the time period at hand. This Web site lists stories on historical periods, themes, topics, and lots more. An added bonus for teachers: activities and discussion questions are suggested for many titles.

http://www.carolhurst.com/index.html

Children's Bestsellers

What are kids reading today? Now *Publisher's Weekly* puts its Children's Bestsellers List on the Net. For Picture Book, Fiction, Paperback Series, and Nonfiction, you'll get the week's top ten sellers, including the title, author, publisher, price, and ISBN number. There's also the all-time children's best-seller list for paperback and hardcover books—*The Pokey Little Puppy* is at number one with 14,000,000 copies. Wow!

http://www.bookwire.com/pw/bsl/childrens/
   current.childrens.html

Children's Book Awards

Every year, thousands of books are written for kids. Most of the books are good, but trying to decide which books to borrow from the library can be difficult. Fortunately, there are several organizations that pick the finest books for children each year. These books are judged best by a variety of criteria, including which are best for young children, elementary-school-aged kids, etc. Some of the awards for the best children's books are listed on the Internet, and you can find convenient links to many of those lists here. Besides the Caldecott and the Newbery Awards, you'll find the Coretta Scott King Award and the Laura Ingalls Wilder Medal winners. There are also many international awards, plus awards given to books selected by kids. If you're looking for a good book to read, take a glance here!

http://www.acs.ucalgary.ca/~dkbrown/awards.html

CLWG: Children's Literature Web Guide

This is the FIRST place to look for Internet resources related to books for children and young adults! Here you will find online children's stories, information about authors and illustrators, children's book awards, and lots of lists. Also available at this site are lists of book discussion groups, sources for book reviews, online resources, publishers, booksellers, and children's literature associations. David K. Brown updates this site frequently and provides a convenient What's New section.

http://www.acs.ucalgary.ca/~dkbrown/

How a Book is Made

These pages give you an inside look at how a book is published. Illustrations from Aliki's book, *How a Book Is Made*, help to tell the story. Cats pose variously as a book's illustrator, author, and editor as well as workers in production, advertising, and sales. They show the steps involved in the writing and publishing of a book! You can also see how a pop-up book is made in other areas of this site.

http://www.harperchildrens.com/howabook/
   bkstep1.htm

Author, author, lend me your words. If you like writing and want to find out what it's all about, check out How a Book is Made.

IPL Youth Division

Welcome to the Internet Public Library, or IPL! Join the Story Hour and read from a selection of five stories, including "Do Spiders Live on the World Wide Web?", *The Tortoise and the Hare,* and "Molly Whuppie." Got a book report coming up soon? Completed FAQs for Avi, Matt Christopher, Robert Cormier, Lois Lowry, Phyllis Reynolds Naylor, Daniel Pinkwater, and Jane Yolen are available. Biographical information for David Lee Drotar, Timothy Gaffney, Katherine Paterson, Gary Paulsen, and Seymour Simon is also found here.

http://www.ipl.org/youth/

Middle School Book Review Website

Read any good books lately? These kids have! And they have put their reviews up on the Net for you to read. You can add your own reviews, too. If you're having trouble picking something to read, search for a book in a *genre* (special categories like Science Fiction or Mysteries) you like.

http://www.xrds.org/xrds/BookReviews/intro.html

A B C D E F G H I J K L M N O P Q R S T U V W X Y Z

A
B
C
D
E
F
G
H
I
J
K
L
M
N
O
P
Q
R
S
T
U
V
W
X
Y
Z

Stone Soup magazine

Stone Soup is a well-known magazine of stories, poems, and artwork by kids, for kids. Here at their home page you can peek at a sample issue, plus read some online stories and poems. Maybe you'll be able to send them some of your own work! There is nothing like seeing your name in print next to something you wrote, whether it's printed in a magazine, a book, or on the Net!

http://www.stonesoup.com/

ADVENTURE STORIES

Choose Your Own Adventure

Sixth graders wrote this interactive adventure. Cruise along with Buzz Rod in his candy apple red Dodge Viper. He's pretty upset after a fight with his parents. He sees a bright flash of light—look out! To find out what happens after Buzz loses control of his car, surf on over to Hillside Elementary School. Every time you click on the Random SpaceTime Warp button, you will find a different ending to Buzz's story. You find out what happens to Buzz, and you can also read about the author of each ending and hear sound effects recorded by the authors.

http://hillside.coled.umn.edu/class1/Buzz/Story.html

Theodore Tugboat: Interactive Stories

Theodore Tugboat is the star of a Canadian television series. In this set of links, Theodore and part of the story appear on each page. At the end of each page, you get to choose which of two things Theodore will do next! This choice is offered on almost every page, so you'll be actively involved in the story and its ending.

http://www.cochran.com/theodore/noframe/
    stories.html

CLASSICS

The BookWire Electronic Children's Books Index

Many online children's books are collected at this Web resource, including Mark Twain stories and Hans Christian Andersen fairy tales.

http://www.bookwire.com/links/readingroom/
    echildbooks.html

Children's Literature Selections Page

This page features first chapters of some of the books selected as Newbery Award and Honor Book winners by the American Library Association/Association for Library Service to Children. It doesn't include all winners, just those available from Dial-A-Book. Links include background on the Newbery Awards, the terms and criteria used to select winners, and information about the committee that selects the books. There is an option to order some of the books online, but check your local library first!

http://www.dialabook.inter.net/ChapterOne/Children/

Classics for Young People

Many books your parents read as kids are collected at this site; some of the ones they may remember include the *Wizard of Oz* books, *The Wind in the Willows*, and *Treasure Island*. You'll also find the *Anne of Green Gables* stories and *Alice in Wonderland*. Maybe you can read these books to your parents just before you tuck them in for their naps!

http://www.acs.ucalgary.ca/~dkbrown/storclas.html

Fairrosa Cyber Library of Children's Literature

You'll find lots of links to online kids' books, such as *A Little Princess*, *Peter Pan*, and *A Journey to the Center of the Earth*. One of the coolest things, though, is the selection of links to authors' home pages. Need some biographical author info to complete your book report? Try here!

http://www.users.interport.net/~fairrosa/

Incomplete Online Works of Edgar Allan Poe

This home page collects many of Poe's works, including his poetry and short stories. Some of the works are available in HTML; all are available in ASCII. Access to Poe's writings is alphabetical, so you can quickly find what you're looking for. Surf on over to read "The Raven" or another one of Poe's 122 poems and stories!

http://www.comnet.ca/~forrest/works.html

LM Montgomery Institute Entrance

The Kindred Spirits WWW site is dedicated to the works and life of Lucy Maud Montgomery (or LMM, for short), the Canadian author of the *Anne of Green Gables* series. Here you will find information about Cavendish, which is the model for Avonlea. A comprehensive FAQ contains a list of all of Montgomery's works, books about her, and other materials based upon her characters and her works. Other links take you to The Road to Avonlea Home Page, a LMM Art Gallery, as well as information about Ontario, where LMM lived as an adult, and PEI (Prince Edward Island), where she grew up.

http://www.upei.ca/~lmmi/cover.html

My Little House on the Prairie Home Page of Laura Ingalls Wilder

Whether you're a fan of the book or the television series, you need to visit this little house on the cyberprairie to find out everything about Laura Ingalls Wilder and her life. You'll be able to track her travels from the big woods to the prairie, chronicled in her book series about Ma, Pa, Mary, and, of course, herself. You can visit the Heritage Sites, which are now located in the places Wilder describes in her novels.

http://www.vvv.com/~jenslegg/

The Page at Pooh Corner

Somewhere in the Internet's Hundred-Acre Wood is The Page at Pooh Corner. It's the home of information about A. A. Milne's Winnie-the-Pooh books. Find general information about Pooh and facts about author Milne and the illustrator, E. H. Shepard. Learn about the area in England where the Pooh stories are based and the real Christopher Robin. Sing along with your favorite Disney Pooh songs or download pictures of Pooh and his companions. This page also gives you links to more sites that feature Pooh, that "tubby little cubby all stuffed with fluff."

http://chaos.trxinc.com/jmilne/Pooh/

Piglet Press Audio Books

Jump on this page and prepare to be swept away by a Kansas twister and totally immersed in Oziana. Piglet Press has gone way beyond the call of duty in promoting their small collection of Oz audio tapes by putting together a most thorough collection of pictures, descriptions, and notes to L. Frank Baum's beloved series of books. There are pages devoted to each and every Baum book as well as material on those done by Ruth Plumly Thompson and other successors. Look up specific characters, places, and things from the first 14 books via the 878-page Encyclopedia Oziana, reference the movies (several have been made), get details about Baum himself, and find out about two different international Oz Clubs. There are also sample sound files from the Piglet tapes, sections on Baum's songs and short stories, and a bibliography. To exit from the page, just click your heels together and say, "There's no place like home..."

http://www.halcyon.com/piglet/

Right next to Walt Disney's star on the Hollywood Walk of Fame you will find a star honoring another famous cartoonist. Who is he?

Answer: Charles Schulz, creator of Snoopy, Charlie Brown, and other beloved characters from the comic strip "Peanuts." See a picture of the star at *http://www.snoopy.com/comics/peanuts/d_history/html/date/1996.html*

A
B
C
D
E
F
G
H
I
J
K
L
M
N
O
P
Q
R
S
T
U
V
W
X
Y
Z

Project Gutenberg

Among the classic children's books you'll find here are:

Aesop's Fables.

Alcott, Louisa May   *Little Women.*

Barrie, Sir James Matthew   *Peter Pan.*

Baum, Lyman Frank   *The Wonderful Wizard of Oz* series.

Burnett, Frances [Eliza] Hodgson   *The Secret Garden; Sarah Crewe.*

Burroughs, Edgar Rice   *Tarzan* series.

Carroll, Lewis [Dodgson, Charles Lutwidge]   *Alice in Wonderland* series.

Dickens, Charles   *Oliver Twist* and many other titles.

Doyle, Arthur Conan, Sir   Find Sherlock Holmes stories.

Hope, Laura Lee   The Bobbsey Twins series.

Lang, Andrew   Many fairy tales.

London, Jack   *White Fang, The Call of the Wild*

Montgomery, Lucy Maud   *Anne of Green Gables* series.

Potter, Beatrix   Many favorite tales of Peter Rabbit and other animals.

Pyle, Howard   *Robin Hood* and other titles.

Sewell, Anna   *Black Beauty.*

Stratton-Porter, Gene   *A Girl of the Limberlost* and others.

Twain, Mark [Clemens, Samuel Langhorne]   *Adventures of Tom Sawyer* and other favorites.

Verne, Jules   *Around the World in 80 Days* and other titles.

Wiggin, Kate Douglas Smith   *Rebecca of Sunnybrook Farm.*

http://www.promo.net/pg/

Treasure Island - Home

It's a tale of adventure, pirates, tropical islands, and murder! "If this don't fetch the kids, why, they have gone rotten since my day," said Robert Louis Stevenson, when he wrote this book in 1881. The book is available online at this site. Besides a biography of the author, you'll find links to sites about pirates, islands, and buried treasure! This finely designed site also has some rainy-day suggestions for things to do—besides reading, of course.

http://www.ukoln.ac.uk/services/treasure/

Winnie the Pooh - An Expotition

Explore this interactive map of the "100 Aker Wood" and try to find and visit all 20 wonderful places. Check out the Bee Tree, Rabbit's house, and the ever-popular Heffalump Trap! You'll find interactive games and more at each site.

http://www.worldkids.net/pooh/

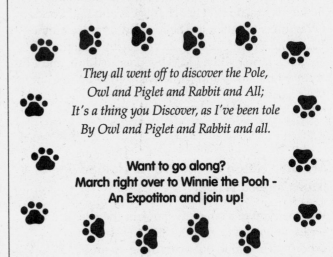

They all went off to discover the Pole,
Owl and Piglet and Rabbit and All;
It's a thing you Discover, as I've been tole
By Owl and Piglet and Rabbit and all.

Want to go along?
March right over to Winnie the Pooh -
An Expotiton and join up!

The Wizard of Oz

Visit this site for the fabulous illustrations by the kindergarten and first-grade kids at Carminati Elementary School in Tempe, Arizona. They retell *The Wonderful Wizard of Oz* in a way that will delight you. Notice that Dorothy sometimes has ruby slippers (as in the movie) and other times has silver slippers (as in the original book)!

http://seamonkey.ed.asu.edu/oz/wizard1.html

CONTEMPORARY FAVORITES

HarperCollins

This Web site gives you the latest news from this publisher of children's books. Read how classics like *If You Give a Mouse a Cookie* were developed. Check out the author interviews and add that info to your next book report. There's a lot at this site—you might even enter and win one of the contests!

http://www.harperchildrens.com/

Series Books

Links from the Booklover's Den give a mystery fan information about a ton of series books and other mysteries. Series for girls featured include Nancy Drew, Trixie Belden, Judy Bolton, and the Dana Girls. Take the link to the Boy's Series page for the Hardy Boys, Encyclopedia Brown, and The Three Investigators.

http://members.aol.com/biblioholc/gseries.html

Welcome to Goosebumps!

Are you a fan of R. L. Stine? His *Goosebumps* series is the subject of this home page. Follow creepy links that lead you to Stine's biography, his photo, and the transcript of an online Halloween chat with Stine. Also read a ghoulish chapter from recent books in his series. Did you know you can get *Goosebumps* from TV? A link includes synopses of the TV episodes, identifying the featured book. Did you hear a noise? We're sure we heard something...

http://place.scholastic.com/goosebumps/

Go to Welcome to Goosebumps! for a thrilling look at R. L. Stine's Goosebumps book and TV series.

Welcome to the Baby-Sitters Club

The Baby-Sitters Club books are very popular! Who is your favorite character? Read profiles of all of them here. You can also enjoy learning some information about the author, Ann M. Martin, as well as find a complete checklist of all the books, their characters, and their plots. Did you miss any?

http://scholastic.com/babysittersclub/

MYSTERIES

Kids mysteries: TheCase.com for Kids

Do you like collecting clues to solve a mystery? If you do, you'll love this site! Mysteries are in abundance here; each one should take you three to five minutes to complete. Every month you'll find contests too, as well as magic tricks and other goodies. Mysteries are a ton of fun, but did you know they also teach you critical thinking skills? Follow the link to Learning With Mysteries <http://www.MysteryNet.com/learn/sites/> for a history of mystery authors and their stories as well as mysterious lesson plans you can share with your teachers.

http://www.TheCase.com/kids/

PICTURE BOOKS

Alex's Scribbles - Koala Trouble

Alexander Balson wanted to write some stories about Max, a koala bear who's always getting into trouble. Alex is only five years old, so he got some help from his parents. Together they have created a fine Web page for your enjoyment. Alex's illustrations really make the interactive story come alive! Hint: When you go to this page, it asks your name. They just want to greet you with your name, but you can make one up if you like.

http://www.scribbles.com.au/max/

BAB Books: On-line Stories for Kids

This site has lots of online stories. One of our favorites is "When I Grow Up." One little boy dreams of the future, when he'll be a firefighter, a cowboy, or an astronaut. What would you like to be when you grow up? There are also links to other charming stories around the Net.

http://www.amtexpo.com/babbooks/

A B C D E F G H I J K L M N O P Q R S T U V W X Y Z

A
B
C
D
E
F
G
H
I
J
K
L
M
N
O
P
Q
R
S
T
U
V
W
X
Y
Z

CANDLELIGHT STORIES - Children's Stories

Storybooks right on the Web! The illustrations are beautifully done by the author of this site. It's amazing how kids can learn to use the mouse when they are reading these stories. Try "Sally Saves Christmas" for a look at what happens when a little girl travels on a moonbeam. As you look at each page, try asking your little brother or sister what will happen next—will Sally decide to follow the Moon Queen? You can also get your own stories published on this site!

http://www.CandlelightStories.com/

Children's Stories

Lucy Van Hook is a really cranky pirate. She wants to steal the King's cookies! Where can they be hidden so her evil plan will fail? Kids of all ages will enjoy the tales here. When you finish the story, you can enjoy making the cookies—the recipe is included!

http://www.itsnet.com/~outward/childstory.html

Concertina - Books on the Internet

Concertina is a Canadian children's publisher. Current titles featured include *Waking in Jerusalem, I Live on a Raft, My Blue Suitcase*, and *The Song of Moses*. Additional links tell the reader about the authors and illustrators as well as the design techniques used to create the online versions of the book. Each book includes the illustrations and all of the pages. *Waking in Jerusalem* is enhanced by the addition of sound clips for each page.

http://www.iatech.com/books/

Cyber-Seuss

Welcome to the world of "the great glorious and gandorious...Dr. Seuss!" You remember him as the author of *The Cat in the Hat, The Grinch Who Stole Christmas, Green Eggs and Ham, Fox in Sox*, and *Yertle the Turtle*. See a photo of the author, read quotes from him, and visit Dartmouth, where Ted (Dr. Seuss) went to college. Check out the scavenger hunt and other contests. Admire the collection of Seuss images, and if you still want to read more, peruse the list of Dr. Seuss books in print!

http://www.afn.org/~afn15301/drseuss.html

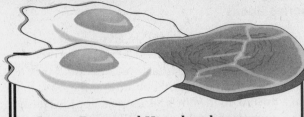

Green Eggs and Ham has been a favorite breakfast of ours since as far back as we can remember. Rumor has it that's a long time, so you know this is a tried-and-true feast. Read all about this and more recipes for treats you can enjoy at any meal at Cyber-Seuss.

Disney Books - Read a Story!

Everyone knows Disney makes terrific movies. Did you know they also publish books? Some of them are online here! Currently, you can read *Aladdin, Toy Story, Oliver & Company, The Lion King, 101 Dalmatians, The Hunchback of Notre Dame, Pocahontas*, and more.

http://www.disney.com/DisneyBooks/Readastory/

Fabler Fox's Reading Room

Fabler Fox has seen many things Under the Big Blue Sky. Best yet, he can really spin a story! Everyone in the meadow wants to hear them, and you can too. Read about Buster the Robin, Eeny-Miney the Mole, Kyoko Peacock, and more. Just bring him a blueberry muffin, stretch out on the comfortable grass, and enjoy!

http://www.bookgarden.com/fox.html

Grandad's Animal Book Contents

Grandad, Thomas Wright, lives on the Hawaiian island of Maui. He's written an interactive animal English alphabet book, in which a picture of an animal is shown with each letter of the alphabet. You know the drill: Z is for Zebra. But you'll also find a vocabulary list, notes on classifying animals, and facts about various classes of animals. You can also choose a letter of the alphabet and then identify which animal begins with that letter of the alphabet. There is also a version of this page in Spanish.

http://www.maui.com/~twright/animals/htmgran.html

How to tell the Birds from the Flowers

Think you know the difference between a bird and a flower? Can you spot a crow among the crocus? Can you tell a tern from a turnip? How about a clover from a plover? These clever pictures are taken from a book originally published in 1907, and although they may not fool you, they are fun to read!

http://www.geocities.com/Vienna/2406/cov.html

IPL Story Hour

Bored? Parents not telling you any good stories these days? Just want to read something new? Point your browser towards the IPL (Internet Public Library) Story Hour. Many traditional stories are available, as well as newer ones. Some are illustrated by kids, too!

http://www.ipl.org/youth/StoryHour/

Mr. Flibby-Cover

Mr. Flibby is a nice man, but he loses job after job because of his clumsiness and his extra-long arms. This story has a happy ending, but you won't be able to guess the very special and exciting job he finally gets! Read all about it in this 28-page story.

http://home.navisoft.com/bcd/flibcov.htm

The Theodore Tugboat Online Activity Centre

Here's a tugboat with a smile and appealing eyes, straight from the Canadian TV series. Toddlers will love the interactive story, in which they get to choose what happens next. Downloadable coloring book pages sail via the Net to your printer or graphics program. Little ones can even get their own postcard in the mail from Theodore Tugboat himself!

http://www.cochran.com/theodore/

Welcome to Ika

"Stop, Don't Read This Page." Who could resist a story that begins like that? It's scary but not too scary. Here you'll find off-the-edge tales about wacky planets, a princess with no hair, and some really baaaad riddles! This site is in English, German, and Spanish.

http://www.ika.com/stories/

PLAYS AND DRAMA
Playbill On-Line

All the world's a stage at this site, which contains links to theater-related pages from all over the world. This site is dedicated to all kinds of theater, from professional companies to scholastic groups to online magazines. You can find schedules of theater companies and information about associations, people involved in theater, educational resources, stagecraft, publications, and film resources. This is a great site if you're interested in drama!

http://www1.playbill.com/playbill/

Reader's Theater Editions

Looking for a play you can perform with the rest of your class? This site has nine complete plays for grades two through eight. A wide range of subjects is covered, from folktales to science fiction. Most are adapted from short stories by Aaron Shepard.

http://www.aaronshep.com/rt/RTE.html

NET FILES

What is the official official dance of South Carolina?

(Hint: It's not the Macarena!)

Answer: It's square dancing! Square dancing is a traditional form of family entertainment and fun in South Carolina. Its many variations include squares, rounds, clogging, contra, line, and other historical or "heritage" dances. Check http://www.lpitr.state.sc.us/square.htm for more of the state's symbols.

A B C D E F G H I J K L M N O P Q R S T U V W X Y Z

Shakespeare

Ah, the Bard himself comes to the Net! Visit this site for the complete works of Shakespeare. You can search the texts, find lists of his plays (chronologically and alphabetically), read Bartlett's familiar Shakespearean quotations, as well as find a picture of William himself. The list of Shakespeare's works is divided into comedy, history, tragedy, and poetry. After you choose a play, you will move to a Web page where you can read one scene per page. The text includes hyperlinks to the glossary, making it easy to understand what Shakespeare was writing. This is a don't-miss destination for all drama students.

http://the-tech.mit.edu/Shakespeare/

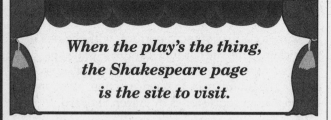

When the play's the thing, the Shakespeare page is the site to visit.

POETRY

Glossary of Poetic Terms from BOB'S BYWAY

Your teacher has assigned a poetry project that's just gone from bad to "verse." There are many unfamiliar words and lots of confusing jargon! Do you know the difference between a *sestina* and a *sonnet*? Can you write a poem in *iambic pentameter*? Visit this site to learn all these terms and more. Many are also illustrated with examples.

http://shoga.wwa.com/~rgs/glossary.html

The Poets' Corner

Some of your favorite poems are collected on the Web, but you'll have to search through these archives to find such works as "Hiawatha," "Jabberwocky," and other classics. Try the one we've listed below first—it has over 3,600 famous poems, and it's easy to use. Didn't find what you wanted? You might also like the archives at <*http://www.hti.umich.edu/ english/amverse/*> and <*http://library.utoronto.ca/www/ utel/rp/intro.html*>.

http://www.geocities.com/~spanoudi/poems/

POETRY—HAIKU
A Haiku Homepage

Haiku is a form of poetry that began in Japan but is popular all over the world. How poets can evoke so many thoughts in only 17 syllables amazes us. Tips for aspiring haiku writers are given here. One of the links leads to The Haiku Attic, where you can post poems to share with others.

http://www.dmu.ac.uk/~pka/haiku.html

The Shiki Internet Haiku Salon

Poet Shiki Masaoka was born in Japan in 1867 and helped popularize the arts as well as haiku, Japan's short poem form. Haiku consists of three lines of five, seven, and five syllables each, and it usually includes a special word to evoke the season. Here is a haiku we made up about the Internet:

*The Net's a garden.
See, my modem light is on.
Netscape slowly blooms.*

http://mikan.cc.matsuyama-u.ac.jp/~shiki/

POETRY—NURSERY RHYMES
Dreamhouse: Nursery: Books: Rhymes

Everyone loves these gentle rhymes of childhood. The rhymes are subdivided by subject, including animals, bedtime, folks and things they do, food, places to go, and weather and things around us. An alphabetical listing is available as well as a list of recommended books. The rhymes chosen are favorites of the collector and her children. This is a useful site for finding those elusive words you can't quite remember from a long-forgotten nursery rhyme!

http://pubweb.acns.nwu.edu/~pfa/dreamhouse/
    nursery/rhymes.html

Find your roots in GENEALOGY.

Nursery Rhymes for Our Times

According to Douglas Crockford, most nursery rhymes are archaic because of their language. He says the rhymes fail to teach kids about the one thing they need in order to live full productive lives: technology. Crockford rewrites 11 nursery rhymes to make them relevant for modern children. A sample rhyme from his page rewrites Old King Cole:

> *Mister Cole has remote control*
> *And remote control has he*
> *He gets CNN*
> *He gets HBO*
> *And he gets his MTV.*

http://www.communities.com/paper/nursery.html

> *Are you beeping?*
> *Are you beeping?*
> *Brother Jack?*
> *Brother Jack?*
> *Get your pocket pager.*
> *Get your pocket pager.*
> *Call them back.*
> *Call them back.*

Poetry always reflects its cultural context, and this is one you can find at Nursery Rhymes for Our Times.

SCIENCE FICTION

The Good Reading Guide - Index

This is a comprehensive index to works by science fiction authors arranged by author. It includes standard authors as well as many children's authors, including Lloyd Alexander, John Christopher, Madeline L'Engle, C. S. Lewis, and Ursula K. LeGuin. While not all of the lists are complete, this is an excellent site for finding other titles by your favorite science fiction authors. You can also read comments other people have about the authors and their works.

http://skogsviol.ce.chalmers.se/SF_archive/SFguide/

Raccoons from Mars

They're atomic-powered robotic raccoons from Mars, and they're aiming for Earth! This wacky science fiction tale comes from the Mount Arlington Public Library. They say, "The following files were found on three sets of stone disks in the supply room of the Mount Arlington Library at the bottom of a box that held issues of National Geographic from the year 1939. The symbols chiseled into their surfaces suggest that they date from the year 4500 B.C. A local artisan managed to manufacture a stone SCSI cable and a rather lovely disk drive made of silver filigree. We were able to read the disks' contents. We remain baffled. Dare we say, at sea." Remember: "If you can read this, you're too close!"

http://www.gti.net/mountarlington/RACMAR/

NET FILES

Which large, plated dinosaur is known for having a brain the size of a walnut?

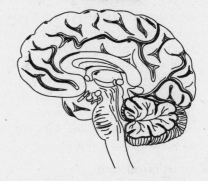

Answer: *The stegosaurus. This plant eater was really a strange combination of parts. Were those bony plates for protection or to help its body stay cool? How about those spikes on the tail — what did they do? Check out all the dinos at http://tyrrell.magtech.ab.ca/tour/stego.html*

CARS

Art Cars in Cyberspace

Hey, look at that car! It's got a giant BUG on top of it! And the one behind it looks more like a temple than a car. And check the van—every inch of it is covered with old cameras! Are these things really cars, or are they some kind of mutant sculptural art form? Yes. Parental advisory: We have not explored all the links. Avoid the poetry.

http://www.artcars.com/cover.html

The Auto Guide

Looking for great car sites on the Web? Check The Auto Guide for new cars, used cars, old cars, and links to just about anything you can think about when it comes to matters automotive.

http://www.theautoguide.com/

AUTOZonLINE Classic Car Museum

There are cars, and then there are *classic* cars. This site has pictures of the coolest classic cars ever. There's even a 1926 Nash and a 1926 Chrysler (yes, they had cars in 1926). And they look just like the Viper…not!

http://www.azl.com/autozonline/carbarn.html

Car and Driver Magazine Online

Cars are fun to look at and interesting to talk about; *Car and Driver* magazine writes about them every month. Driving is fun too, unless you get stuck in traffic. You may not be a driver yet, but you know you will be. You need a place to find out what's happening in the world of cars this year, this month, today! This site has great resource information on every kind of car you can think of, and it also has "Daily Auto Insider" with today's news on cars. Shockwave games, links, car shows—it's all here. Drive on in, there's a parking space!

http://www.caranddriver.com/

Everyone's flocking to BIRDS!

Engine Catalog Page

Start your engines. Are you ready to go?
Press on the pedal and the fuel will flow.
Down goes the piston, in comes the gas.
The mixture is compression and you'll go really fast!

That's part of "The Engine Song." You can hear it at this site while you watch animations of fuel injectors, pistons, crankshafts, and other parts of the internal combustion engine. A lesson plan is available for teachers and parents.

http://www.ca.sandia.gov/outreach/html/
    eng-catpg.html

Ford Worldwide Connection: Historical Library

The history of the world-famous Ford Motor Company would be a great topic for your history, technology, or science report, or…wait a minute—you don't need a report due to go to this site! It's got awesome information, pictures, and stories about cars from 1903 right up to today. For the real sports car fan, the "Jaguar Historical Library" is here, too.

http://www.ford.com/archive/intro.html

License Plate Collector's Home Page

Visit the License Plate Collector's Home Page to find out how to get inexpensive sample plates from state motor vehicle departments. Unfortunately, the addresses are not here, but look in this book under the "United States" heading for the official page of the state you're interested in—the address is probably listed there. This page also lists other sites for license plate collectors.

http://users.aol.com/EdE/plates.htm

License Plates of the World

Sure, you may be familiar with Maine's red lobster, or Georgia's peach, or maybe even Hawaii's rainbow—but what does an Argentine license plate look like, or a Mongolian one, or…well, you get the picture. You *will* get the picture if you visit this Web site!

http://danshiki.oit.gatech.edu/~iadt3mk/index.html

THE PM ZONE HOMEPAGE

You can see next year's models *now* and classic cars too? This must be the PM Zone's Automotive section, where you can get the latest on all the cars out there from *Popular Mechanics* magazine. *Popular Mechanics* surveys users and reports on cars, which means that you get the real story on how the cars perform from the people who drive them and not just from the manufacturer. They report on every kind of car—from Ferrari Spiders to Dodge Caravans—and they spy on the new models, so you can be the first to see them. Put the key in, start 'er up, and head into the PM Zone.

http://popularmechanics.com/

Everyone is talking about the new car being unveiled next fall, but nobody has seen it. Is it just a revamp of this year's model, or is it really as hot as they claim? You might just get that sneak preview at THE PM ZONE HOMEPAGE.

Investigate the "Spy Reports" in the Automotive section for the latest information.

Recreation: Automotive: Makes and Models

The Yahoo directory of car manufacturers lists familiar names, such as General Motors, Toyota, and Volkswagen. You'll also find the Kia, the DeLorean, and the Lada—they are all here. Hey, there are even some links on Hummers! Naturally, this vast array of links has not been checked for family-friendliness, so your mileage may vary.

http://www.yahoo.com/Recreation/Automotive/
   Makes_and_Models/

A Student's Guide to Alternative Fuel Vehicles

What if your family didn't have to drive to the gas station anymore? What if you had an electric car and could just plug it in? Electric cars exist right now! There are lots of other alternative fuels, too, such as ethanol, methanol, propane, natural gas, and of course solar power. No dilithium crystals yet, but somebody somewhere is probably working on it, and when there is news about it, that news will be here! The California Energy Commission also has an excellent series of pages on energy.

http://www.energy.ca.gov/education/EVs/EV-html/
   EVs.html

The web site of Car Talk - cartalk.msn.com

Would you let Click and Clack, the Tappet brothers, work on your family car? They have a very funny radio show, newspaper column, and Web site all about car maintenance and repair. And oh, yes, they used to run a garage in Cambridge, Massachusetts; now, only one brother works there (the other one got tired of breathing exhaust fumes). The Web site has clips from the radio show, advice columns, and other useful stuff, like car reviews, a directory of truly great mechanics, and—what's this?—a guide to raising kids. Maybe they should stick to cars!

http://www.cartalk.com/

WebINK: Auto Tour: So You Want To Make A Car...

Have you ever wondered how cars are made? This site takes you through all the steps, saving you from walking the 16 miles of conveyors that transfer car bodies from start to finish. That's more than 230 football fields in length! At this auto factory, over 260 programmable robots install, weld, and paint in order for those shiny new vehicles to roll off the line. Look over their shoulders (or whatever robots have) and see how cars are built. There are also some great links on car history, solar cars, and race cars.

http://www.ipl.org/autou/

A B C D E F G H I J K L M N O P Q R S T U V W X Y Z

RACING

NASCAR Online: Home Page

If you're into car racing, you already know that NASCAR is the organization that coordinates stock car races. At this site, you can get all the latest news, insider information and history on race tracks, teams, drivers, upcoming schedules, and more.

http://www.nascar.com/

Rockets on Wheels Electronic Field Trip

Why not try to design your own online race car? First pick your wheels. There's a no-tread variety, one with a deep tread, and one that seems to be made out of stone. Which will go faster? Now pick the rest of the car's parts and features, and see how well you do! There is a lot about the science of racing here, too, so start your engine and zoom on over.

http://www.pbs.org/tal/racecars/

CATS

See also MAMMALS—CARNIVORES—CAT FAMILY; PETS AND PET CARE

Cat Fanciers Web Site

Crazy about cats? This is the place for you! It will give answers to questions you didn't even know you had. It contains information about cat breeds, colors, cat shows, the welfare of animals, and lots of other cat-related subjects. You'll find lots of links to everywhere, including cat health information at veterinary schools around the world. Also, find out how to get started showing your cat under Cat Fanciers' Association (CFA) rules. Read up on breeder information and learn about CFA scoring and how titles are earned. If you think you and Fluffy are ready to enter the realm of cat shows, check out CFA's show schedule, and good luck!

http://www.fanciers.com/

Cats @ nationalgeographic.com

Chuck's given you a task: design the best, most effective predator you can. Choose a skeletal base, a muscle structure, and various other goodies such as senses, behavior, and bitey, scratchy parts. What will your predator look like?

http://www.nationalgeographic.com/features/97/cats/

Cats! Wild to Mild

The Natural History Museum of Los Angeles County had an exhibit in 1997 all about cats. Encyclopedia-type entries for 19 feline species from around the world are represented here on their Web site, including jaguars, lions, tigers, leopards, bobcats, and wildcats, as well as house pets. You can see wonderful color pictures of the cats, plus range distribution maps for each. Many of them are endangered species; for example, only 50 Florida panthers are estimated to be left in the wild. Some still exist on the Web, though: you'll find a collection of links for each species. Do you have a cat? Chances are that you do or that you know someone who does. About 65.8 million cats live in the United States, which beats the 54.9 million dogs. Garfield would be so pleased!

http://www.lam.mus.ca.us/cats/

KittyCam

Kitty is a real working cat. Her job involves holding down office conference room chairs and sleeping in sunny spots all day long. You can often view her blistering pace on her live webcam, but if she's out at the cappuccino machine on a break, you can see the "Best of KittyCam." Naturally, she has collected some links you might enjoy, and you can "paws" to drop her a note or join her newsletter if you wish.

http://www.kittycam.com/

rec.pets.cats FAQ Homepage

This is the FAQ from the Usenet cats newsgroup, arranged in HTML so it's easy to read. Find out all about cat breeds, colors, health, training, and more!

http://www.io.com/~tittle/cat-faqs/

CHEMISTRY

ChemDex

This site is a huge collection of links, news, and resources on chemistry. You'll also find pages on the history of chemistry, software to help you learn about chemistry, and more. We want to point out the WebElements 2.0b9 Periodic Table. It is notable because of the graphics and other visualization information for each element. In the Other Periodic Tables links, you will find sources for software that will help you learn the names and properties of the elements discovered so far! There is also a song that teaches you this; find it at <http://paul.merton.ox.ac.uk/science/elements.html>. Not all links have been checked.

http://www.shef.ac.uk/~chem/chemdex/

General Chemistry

Do you love chemistry? Does the idea of equilibrium, states of matter, or quantum mechanics give you goose bumps? If that's the case, then this page is for you! Here you'll find a multimedia course on chemistry that should satisfy even the most intense chemistry nut.

http://www-wilson.ucsd.edu/education/gchem/gchem.html

NET FILES

Where did the word "geyser" originate?

Answer: The Geysir, which means "gusher," is a geyser located in Haukadalur, Iceland. All other geysers in the world were named after it. It erupts only rarely these days, but when it does, the water and steam may reach 200 feet in the air! Go to *http://www2.wku.edu/www/geoweb/geyser/location.html* and read all about geysers around the world. There's also a colorful map of worldwide geyser locations.

Home Page "Understanding Our Planet Through Chemistry"

How do scientists know the age of Earth or when a meteor struck our planet? How can scientists predict and understand volcanoes—when no one can look closely at an eruption and survive? The answers to these and many other questions about our planet can be found in the study of chemistry. To learn more, take a peek at this site.

http://helios.cr.usgs.gov/gips/aii-home.htm

MathMol

Everything around you is made of chemicals—from your computer to your favorite book to you! Scientists sometimes learn how chemicals work by studying the math, algebra, and geometry behind the chemical molecules. The resources here let you visualize and manipulate important ones.

http://www.nyu.edu/pages/mathmol/

Miami Museum of Science-The pH Factor

Is something an acid or a base? Use the online "pH panel" machine to explore the pH of common household solutions, such as lemon juice, borax, vinegar, and Lava soap. Then check out the real experiments you can try with an adult. Some involve toothpicks and gumdrops, while others require more elaborate preparations.

http://www.miamisci.org/ph/

Microworlds- Exploring the Structure of Materials

Scientists are learning more and more about the world by studying its tiniest parts. By looking at atoms and molecules, scientists find out why some objects are hard, some are brittle, and some are strong. You can view this miniature world here. You'll see a new machine that is helping to explore inner space, and you can also view discoveries about materials you use every day.

http://www.lbl.gov/MicroWorlds/

A B C D E F G H I J K L M N O P Q R S T U V W X Y Z

Molecule of the Month

Some parts of chemistry are, well, a mystery! For example, what do molecules really look like? When someone mentions ozone, vitamin B12, or even something as simple as water—are these chemical structures hard for you to visualize? No worries. Just visit the Molecule of the Month archive!

http://www.bris.ac.uk/Depts/Chemistry/MOTM/
    motm.htm

Welcome to Chem4Kids! Your Chemistry Website!

Where, exactly, are the states of matter? Are they anywhere near Cleveland? Does it matter? Of course, you know that anything that takes up space or weight is also called matter. You've got your solids, your liquids, and your gases, but did you know there's also something called *plasma*? It has nothing to do with the type of plasma associated with blood, though. Examples of this kind of plasma include ball lightning and the aurora borealis, or northern lights. You can also view plasma in the electrically charged matter contained in a fluorescent light or a neon sign. Find out lots about matter, elements, atoms, ions, and reactions at this fascinating site. Also included are brief biographies of famous scientists. For some reason they are all pictured with green hair.

http://www.chem4kids.com/

EXPERIMENTS

Bread Chemistry

Everyone likes bread: it's great as toast, makes for good sandwiches, and sometimes is excellent for missiles in a food fight. Bread, though, is a good lesson in chemistry. Every time bread is made, all kinds of interesting chemical reactions result. Don't "loaf" around! Check out this episode from the award-winning *Newton's Apple* TV program for a lesson in bread as science.

http://ericir.syr.edu/Projects/Newton/12/Lessons/
    bread.html

Physical Science and Chemistry Lesson Plans

You have to do a science fair demonstration, and you think a chemistry experiment is the way to go. Problem is, what experiment should you do? Wouldn't it be great if you could get hold of a teacher's lesson plans for chemistry experiments? Well...you can! You'll find a whole slew of great experiments at this gopher page. Be careful, though, and always check with an adult before doing these experiments. You can never be safe enough when it comes to mixing chemicals.

gopher://ec.sdcs.k12.ca.us:70/11/lessons/
    UCSD_InternNet_Lessons/
    Physical_Science_and_Chemistry

Slime Time

Polymers are chemicals that we use all the time. Plastic is a polymer, nylon is a polymer, the keyboard of your computer is probably largely made of polymers. The greatest polymer of all, though, is SLIME! No kidding. You can read all about slime and polymers on this page, produced by Mr. Lemberg's first-period chemistry class in Washington State's Battle Ground Public School.

http://phs.bgsd.wednet.edu/doc/projects/chem/doc/
    slime.html

Solving Dissolving Activity - Science Museum of Minnesota

How can rainwater make an acid and dissolve rock? Actually, that's how many caves are formed. Here is an experiment to try at home that will explain it, complete with pictures and instructions. Be sure to ask for help from a parent or teacher.

http://www.sci.mus.mn.us/sln/ma/sdact.html

Virtual Science Fair

If you're looking for a way to dazzle the rest of the class with your science fair know-how, put your safety goggles on and take a look in here! You'll find out how objects float, how to grow crystals, and how to tell if something is an acid or a base. Most of these kitchen chemistry experiments were designed by kids.

http://www.parkmaitland.org/sciencefair/

The World of Chemistry

The Chemical Institute of Canada and the Halifax West High School have teamed up to present 15 different experiments you can try at home or in school. For example, how do chemists test substances to find out what they are made of? Try the Unknown Powder experiment—you'll need an adult to help you set it up, so you don't already know which powder is which! Hint: The secrets behind all the experiments are in the Teacher's Notes sections, which are in the Investigation areas. This site is available in English and French.

http://www.schoolnet.ca/math_sci/chem/worldofchem/

How do we know what time it is?

Answer: In the U.S., we ask the U.S. Naval Observatory. They have been keeping the nation's time since the 1800s. In 1845, they installed a time ball atop their telescope dome. According to their Web site, "the time ball was dropped every day precisely at Noon, enabling the inhabitants of Washington to set their timepieces. Ships in the Potomac River could also set their clocks before putting to sea." Times have changed since then. Now, hydrogen maser clocks are used, which keep atomic time. There is a good correlation of atomic time to more traditional celestial observations, but every now and again the atomic clock has to be given a whack, known as a "leap second," to bring it into alignment with the heavens. If you have time, read more about it at
http://tycho.usno.navy.mil/history.html

PERIODIC TABLE OF THE ELEMENTS

Chemicool Periodic Table

You can learn a lot about chemistry at the Chemicool Periodic Table. Just click on any element and you'll be transported to all the info you need. There's a list of the "top five requested elements" and links to chemistry calculators around the Net.

http://wild-turkey.mit.edu/Chemicool/

The Periodic Table of the Elements on the Internet

Chemistry is easy to understand—it's "elementary." Actually, chemistry is all about elements, the primary parts of all chemicals. For years, scientists have learned what the elements of chemistry are, and they've grouped the elements in a chart called the periodic table. To see all of the elements and their properties, take a look at this page, written by a ninth grader! It's easy to use, and you'll learn much.

http://domains.twave.net/domain/yinon/default.html

CIRCUSES AND CLOWNS

See also JUGGLING

CIRCUSTUFF Juggling and Circus On-Line

Interested in circus tricks? Start your clowning around here. At this site, you can download digital animations of juggling tricks. You can slow the animation down and even freeze the frames to be sure you "catch" every move. Only one is free; you'll have to pay for the others. But check out the Devil Sticks tricks and other fun. You'll also find juggling props to keep you busy for a long time!

http://www.circustuff.co.uk/

Let balloonists take you to new heights in AVIATION AND AIRPLANES.

A
B
C
D
E
F
G
H
I
J
K
L
M
N
O
P
Q
R
S
T
U
V
W
X
Y
Z

A
B
C
D
E
F
G
H
I
J
K
L
M
N
O
P
Q
R
S
T
U
V
W
X
Y
Z

CircusWeb! Circus Present and Past

As a new circus employee, there is so much to learn! For example, there are a lot of superstitions. If you're walking in a circus parade, it's bad luck to look behind you. And don't even think about whistling in the dressing room! After the show, if you're hungry, don't ask where the kitchen is—you want the "Pie Car." This page gives a glimpse of circus life, including how the heck they get those big tents up! There are also links to circuses and performers all over the world. Parental advisory: Preview them, and caution kids not to try these tricks at home.

http://www.circusweb.com/circuswebFrames.html

Cirque du Soleil

Since its beginning in 1984, over ten million people have seen a Cirque du Soleil show. They have performed all over the world, and often several of their circus companies are touring at any one time. What makes Cirque du Soleil so different? For one thing, there are no animal acts. For another, this is a reinvented circus, one that is part theater, part magic, part imagination, and mostly just plain fun! To see the impossible become reality, visit this site and find out where they will be performing next.

http://www.cirquedusoleil.com/

Clowns of America International Home Page

Send in the clowns. What, you forgot to order the clowns? Help, we need emergency clowns! No time to waste—just log on to this site and check the clown directories for a clown near you. If you need to replace your supply of clown noses, oversized elf shoes, or lapel flowers that shoot water, look no further than the Clown Mall. Don't miss the fascinating history of clowns, where you'll learn the origin of the phrase "jump on the bandwagon."

http://www.clown.org/

Strike up the bandwidth in MUSIC.

The FSU Flying High Circus Home Page

Did you know you can go to college *and* be in a circus at the same time? At Florida State University, you can! Learn about lots of circus tricks performed by students. Some stunts—such as triple somersaults on the flying trapeze and seven-man pyramids—are so hard that lots of professional circus performers won't even try them. What's really surprising is that most of the students haven't had any circus training before joining the Flying High Circus. Don't miss the "cloudswings," especially the kind done without a net. Other circus schools around the world are also listed, as well as links to related sites, like unicycle and juggling home pages.

http://mailer.fsu.edu/~mpeters/fsucircus.html

The Great Circus Parade - Wisconsin's National Treasure

Hey, look at this poster. It reads: "Come to the Great Circus Parade! A two-hour processional over a three-mile route, authentically re-creating turn-of-the-century circus street parades. Features 60 historic wagons, 700 horses, cavorting clowns, wild animals in cage wagons, and the fabulous 40-Horse Hitch." Sounds like FUN! Look over there—isn't that Buffalo Bill Cody in that beaded buckskin jacket? You can learn something about circus history, including circus trains, at this colorful, animated site. If you have Java, you'll also hear vintage calliope music!

http://www.circusparade.com/

On the Internet, nobody knows you're a frog. Craving some "Bee Grubs in Coconut Cream"? Where on Earth can a frog find a cookbook?

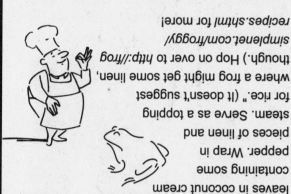

Answer: At the Froggy Page, of course! "Marinate bee grubs, sliced onions, and citrus leaves in coconut cream containing some pepper. Wrap in pieces of linen and steam. Serve as a topping for rice." (It doesn't suggest where a frog might get some linen, though.) Hop on over to http://frog simplenet.com/froggy/ recipes.shtml for more!

Ringling Bros. and Barnum & Bailey Circus

It's billed as The Greatest Show on Earth, and now you can visit it whenever you choose! The first performance of the Ringling Bros. and Barnum & Bailey Circus was held in New York City's Madison Square Garden, on March 29, 1919. Do you have what it takes to perform in the circus? It takes ability, grace, skill, and did we mention nerves of steel? Take the online aptitude test and see how well you do. There's also a loads-of-laughs "make a clown" game for little kids, as well as other online games. Some are also available as downloads, and there are free screen savers and wallpaper, too. Read about the special care given to the animals in the circus and the retirement home for elephants!

http://www.ringling.com/home.asp

Lots of monkey business in MAMMALS.

CLOTHING

Art Deco-Erté

When you think of a special event costume, you probably think of Halloween. In Hollywood, movie stars put on costumes for special events, such as parties or awards ceremonies. The costumes they wear today are usually just tuxedos and gowns. Long ago, famous people used to incorporate a lot more imagination into their costumes! Designers such as Romain de Tirtoff, better known as Erté, went to great efforts to create one-of-a-kind costumes. Erté was an Art Deco fashion creator, and this site is full of great costume ideas.

http://www.webcom.com/ajarts/welcome.html

CMCC - Hold onto Your Hats! History and meaning of headwear in Canada

What kind of hat do you wear? Sometimes hats are worn to keep your head warm, or to keep the sun out of your eyes. Other hats have sports, religious, or other ritual meanings. Still other hats are just plain fun! Can you learn about history and culture just by studying styles and trends in headgear? You bet.

http://www.civilization.ca/membrs/canhist/hats/ hat00eng.html

The Costume Page

Digging through this resource is like exploring an old clothing trunk you found in Grandma's attic. The deeper you go, the more interesting things you discover! Want to know what was fashionable in Roman times, Elizabethan times, or any other time? There is probably a link here. You can also find great ideas for Halloween costumes or other dress-up fancy wear for imaginative play. There's even a link to "How to tie a tie." If you're looking for anything to do with fashion and its history, try here first!

http://members.aol.com/nebula5/costume.html

A B C D E F G H I J K L M N O P Q R S T U V W X Y Z

Column of letters (A–Z index tab) along left margin.

The History of Costume by Braun & Scheider

Your school is having an Ancient Rome day and you don't know how to tie your toga? No problem, just drop in here, where there are 500 costumes pictured, from ancient times through the nineteenth century. The original German text was written in the Victorian period. This page concentrates on the pictures, which are detailed. Whether you intend to dress as a fourteenth-century German knight or a late-nineteenth-century Swiss Heidi, you'll find a model here! Hint: Choose the TEXT version, which loads faster, then focus on the time period you need to explore.

http://www.siue.edu/COSTUMES/history.html

Textiles Through Time

What if we didn't have any malls? Where would people go to buy their clothes? Throughout most of history, people have had to make their own clothes, fabric, and fibers. This site links museum textile collections around the world. See handmade fabrics, including clothing, quilts, ceremonial artifacts, and a whole lot more. You'll find links to the Bayeux Tapestry, Hmong needlework, and exquisite Japanese kimonos.

http://www.interlog.com/~gwhite/ttt/tttintro.html

NET FILES

In the famous painting by Leonardo da Vinci, what color are Mona Lisa's eyes?

Answer: Brown.

This painting is also known as La Gioconda, and you can read all about the woman in the picture at http://sunsite.unc.edu/wm/paint/auth/vinci/joconde/

Welcome to Levi.com

Levi's jeans have been around for over 125 years. Explore the "jean-eology" historic timeline offered at their alternate site at <http://www.levistrauss.com/>. This link, though, is purely fun and fashion—see all the new styles, participate in contests, link to concerts and events sponsored by the company, and more!

http://www.levi.com/

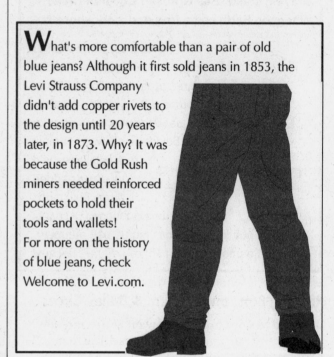

What's more comfortable than a pair of old blue jeans? Although it first sold jeans in 1853, the Levi Strauss Company didn't add copper rivets to the design until 20 years later, in 1873. Why? It was because the Gold Rush miners needed reinforced pockets to hold their tools and wallets! For more on the history of blue jeans, check Welcome to Levi.com.

CODES AND CIPHERS

See also WORDS

A-Z Cryptology!

From the simple cipher of lumpingletterstogetherlikethis to messages concealed within other messages, this site explains it all. You'll find lesson plans, lingo, history, and links on all things cryptological.

http://www.achiever.com/freehmpg/cryptology/crypto.html

KO6YQ's Introduction to Morse Code

How do you begin to learn Morse code in order to pass the higher-level amateur radio license tests? Check here. It's a site where you listen to the code rather than see it written out as a series of visible dots and dashes. You can also type in your name and get it translated into audible Morse code. Don't worry, you can choose to have the code played at 5, 13, or 20 words per minute. That will help you to start slowly and gradually build up speed.

http://www.ati.com/~ikluft/ham/morse-intro.html

Morse Code and the Phonetic Alphabets

Morse code was invented by Samuel Finley Breese Morse as a way to send messages over telegraph lines. Morse is known as the inventor of the "electromagnetic recording telegraph," although he had help from others. The first message transmitted over a telegraph line was in 1844. "What hath God wrought" went 36 miles, from Washington, D.C. to Baltimore, Maryland, in code sent by Morse himself. What happens if you make a mistake in sending code? You can't erase or backspace, so to indicate that a mistake has been made and tell the receiver to delete the last word, send .... (eight dots).

http://dplinux.sund.ac.uk/~manga/refer/alphabet.html

National Cryptological Museum

Years ago, the road signs pointing to the CIA (the spy guys—the Central Intelligence Agency) building in Virginia read "Bureau of Public Roads." Everybody knew what it was, but nobody was willing to admit it publicly. A lot of this has changed. The National Security Agency, a similar government agency that does all kinds of James Bond–type things, opened (in 1993) this public museum devoted to secret codes and code breaking. This page has a nice sampling of museum exhibits, complete with photographs. You'll see once-secret cryptology devices, such as the Cipher Wheel, the Black Chamber, and Enigma. Museum hours and instructions on how to get to the place (including a map) are available here as well. Thank goodness they didn't put the directions in code!

http://www.nsa.gov:8080/museum/

What is the Black Chamber?

Despite its ominous-sounding name, it was a highly secret MI-8 code-breaking project during the 1920s. Herbert O. Yardley worked for the Army and the State Department and broke the diplomatic codes of several nations, including Japan. Before the meetings of the Washington Naval Conference of 1921–22, the U.S. State Department broke the codes detailing the Japanese bargaining position. Everyone was dumbfounded, because the Americans seemed to be reading the minds of the Japanese. They were, of course. The Japanese quickly figured this out and changed their codes. Find out more at the National Cryptological Museum home page.

Secret Language

Psssst! Want to send a secret message to a friend, one that nobody else can possibly decipher? Head on over to this page at San Francisco's Exploratorium, where you can print out a copy of some substitution cipher wheels. Put one inside the other, twirl them around a little bit, and you're in the spy biz!

http://www.exploratorium.edu/ronh/secret/secret.html

Go climb a rock in OUTDOOR RECREATION.

A B C D E F G H I J K L M N O P Q R S T U V W X Y Z

A
B
C
D
E
F
G
H
I
J
K
L
M
N
O
P
Q
R
S
T
U
V
W
X
Y
Z

Some Classic Ciphers and Their Weaknesses

Using a secret code can add intrigue and excitement to the rather ordinary activity of sending a note or letter to a friend (especially via e-mail). While personal computers have made it possible for anybody to have access to encryption programs, sometimes it's just more fun to use a code that you can scribble on a piece of paper. Some of these ciphers go back to the time of Julius Caesar, and a good handful of them can be found on this page. Each code is simply explained, and each is taken apart—deciphered—as well. Even more fun than writing in code is breaking someone else's. Here, you can learn how to use the Caesar, Vigenère, Augustus, and Playfair ciphers, among others, and you'll also find out what it takes to rip them up. Then for people who really want to keep a secret, there is a link to modern encryption systems for e-mail, such as PGP (Pretty Good Privacy).

http://rschp2.anu.edu.au:8080/cipher.html

The Story of the Beale Ciphers

The Beale ciphers hold the key to one of the greatest unsolved puzzles of all time. The story goes that around 1820, a fellow named Beale hid two wagonloads of silver, gold, and jewels someplace near Roanoke, Virginia. He left three coded letters, supposedly detailing the location of the treasure, with a trusted friend. Then he left for the West and was never seen again. One of the letters, describing the treasure, has been deciphered. It is in a code based on the Declaration of Independence. It is believed the other letters are similarly coded to the same document or other public documents. You can read about the status of the Beale ciphers, and you might want to try solving them yourself (if you find this treasure, please let us know!).

http://www.treasure.com/j195.htm

Pony up to HORSES AND EQUESTRIAN SPORTS.

COLLECTORS AND COLLECTING

See also CARS; EARTH SCIENCE—GEOLOGY—GEMS AND MINERALS; TOYS

Antiques

Have you ever been to a flea market? They don't sell fleas there, just lots of old things people have in their basements, garages, and attics. At these types of sales, you can find everything from old clothing to jewelry to toys to fishing gear. Sometimes you will be able to find a treasure inside a pile of junk! How do you know what to look for? You could take along an expert, or you could study this Web page before you go. It will give you the basics on how to talk to antique dealers, plus what to look for in collecting various items, including dolls, marbles, tools, and more.

http://willow.internet-connections.net/web/antiques/

The Ball

Have you ever wadded up some old aluminum foil into a nicely satisfying ball? So has this guy, except he didn't stop with a few old candy wrappers. He kept going, and going, and well, you get the idea. The Ball is now (drum roll please) almost two pounds! Tune in to this site to see The Ball in its many incarnations, and don't miss the links to pages by other people who have the same hobby. If you can spare York Peppermint Patty wrappers or any other foil, this webmaster wants them.

http://sunsite.unc.edu/lou/ball/

Quasi Comprehensive Candy Bar Wrapper Image Archive

Here's a guy who is easily amused. He collects candy bar wrappers, scans them, and puts them on the Web. Apparently, he's not the only one: he has links to people who do the same thing for gum wrappers, European candy, and Mentos! If you can get past the M&M's, Skittles, Snickers, and Kit-Kats, you may need the Pepto-Bismol pink background.

http://www.bradkent.com/wrappers/

Welcome to Collectors Universe: Collectors Universe

This site claims to be "the largest collectible oriented site on the Internet." Whether this assertion is true or not, if you collect coins, stamps, comics, or trading cards, this page is not to be missed. Using professional-quality, vividly colored graphics, each separate "universe" link includes lists of dealers, shows, classified ads, news, and chat sections and clubs. They also have promised to be on the cutting edge with innovations that will "change collectibles on the Internet forever." This may be worth checking out every once in a while just to see what they mean!

http://www.collectors.com/

Welcome to the Burlingame Museum of Pez Memorabilia

Have you ever had PEZ? They are a fruit-flavored candy and are best known for their famous collectible dispensers. The first PEZ dispensers didn't have any heads at all, and now there are over 250 different models. The PEZ Exhibit has detailed pictures of all of the dispensers, with the date of manufacture for each one. You can see which dispensers were made when your parents, and maybe even your grandparents, were born!

http://www.spectrumnet.com/pez/

Welcome to the Scout Patch Auction

Last time you were rummaging in Grandma's attic, you found a lot of old Boy Scout stuff. There were a lot of old merit badges, pins, and even some old manuals. "That's a lot of junk," said Grandma. "Just throw it out." But you want to check the Net first. Hey, this merit badge is worth over $3,000! You may have a real treasure chest there and not even know it. The Scout Patch Auction tracks sales of Boy Scout and Girl Scout memorabilia, so start here.

http://www.tspa.com/

Fetch some fascinating info in DOGS AND DOG SPORTS.

WHEATIES and THE HOBBY OF COLLECTING SPORT CEREAL BOXES

Did you eat your Wheaties today? If they are all gone, you might think about saving the box! Some of the boxes are very collectible and command high prices from people interested in them. This page tells you how to get started in collecting these boxes, many of which are released only in certain regions of the U.S. (that's what makes some Wheaties boxes rare). Find out if your breakfast food box is worth anything at this very interesting site.

http://pages.prodigy.com/funnybusiness/cbox.htm

COIN COLLECTING
Coin Collecting FAQ Part 1

Have you already put together a nice collection of coins, or did you just stumble onto a few old ones in your change? Not really sure what to do with them? Roll on over to this page and get some of the more basic coin collecting questions answered. "How can I determine what a coin is really worth?" and "How can I sell my coins?" are two of the questions that are answered here, clearly and with logic and detail.

http://www.telesphere.com/ts/coins/faq.html

You've got a good start on a coin collection, but some of them are pretty dirty. Should you clean your coins? Probably not. Collectors today value the originality of a coin, and any attempt to clean a coin may alter this originality and lower its value. Read more about this controversy and many other questions about numismatics at the Coin Collecting FAQ Part 1 page.

A
B
C
D
E
F
G
H
I
J
K
L
M
N
O
P
Q
R
S
T
U
V
W
X
Y
Z

A
B
C
D
E
F
G
H
I
J
K
L
M
N
O
P
Q
R
S
T
U
V
W
X
Y
Z

AMPHIBIANS!
Visit them
before you croak.

Coin World Online - Information Vault

Whether you're a beginner or a pro at collecting coins, Coin World will have something of interest. There is a history of the U.S. Mint, including information on coin goofs and mint errors. Sometimes coins are struck in the wrong metal, and other times they are struck twice ("double die") with the second strike slightly offset. These rarities can be worth a lot of money! Check this site to find out what to look for, then ask Mom if you can look through her pocket change! This site also offers some coin-related trivia games and crossword puzzles.

http://www.collect.com/coinworld/infovault.html

One-Minute Coin Expert

Scott Travers has excerpted one entire chapter from his popular book, *One Minute Coin Expert*, on this site. He answers many frequently asked questions from both beginner and experienced coin collectors. Most of these questions are based on ones he has often been asked on radio and television programs. The information posted here is solid and useful, and of course it is designed to entice you to buy the book and get the rest of what you need to become a "one-minute coin expert" yourself. One of the tips he recommends for kids is that they join the Young Numismatist coin collecting club (it's free). Send a postcard with your name, address, age, and telephone number to: Lawrence J. Gentile, Sr., 542 Webster Avenue, New Rochelle, NY 10805. His program for kids includes "free seminars, free coins, free books, and a wealth of information that youngsters find helpful."

http://www.inch.com/~travers/1min.htm

SHELL COLLECTING

Conchologists of America — Conch-Net HomePage

Florida's Sanibel Island's lack of offshore reefs and perpendicular heading, compared to its neighboring islands, make it a natural interceptor of shells from the South Seas. People come from all over the world to comb Sanibel's beaches for washed-up natural treasures, and bending down to pick up shells is called the "Sanibel Stoop"! To learn all about mollusks, bivalves, and univalves, be sure to visit this site. You'll find some fun shell facts in the kids' area, as well as collecting tips and hints to organize your collection.

http://coa.acnatsci.org/conchnet/

Can you do the Sanibel Stoop?
Stand on the shore, bend over, and scoop up a handful of rare and beautiful seashells found on Florida's Sanibel Island. Kick off your flip-flops and head over to Conchologists of America—Conch-Net Home Page to find out more.

Sea Shells

Tony Printezis has graciously put together this page of detailed photographs of his shell collection. The unique thing about his collection is that it doesn't exist! Printezis has devised a computer program from scratch that creates delicate, multicolored images of seashells, which look like they came off a magical beach. Click on the thumbnails and see full-screen pictures of these shells.

http://www.dcs.gla.ac.uk/~tony/ss/

SPORTS AND OTHER TRADING CARDS

Beckett Online - The Sports Card and Collectibles Authority

For over a decade, Dr. James Beckett and his organization have tracked and published the prices of baseball, football, basketball, hockey, and many other sports trading cards. BeckWorld offers a free membership that allows visitors to drop in and dig up information on selected popular cards. A paid subscription plan is also available for unlimited online searches in their extensive guides.

http://www.beckett.com/

STAMP COLLECTING

Stamps and Postal History

Bob Swanson has a collection of stamps, cancellations, first-day covers, and postcards that would make any collector drool, and he has put lots of the best images right here. He has a monthly "Mystery Cover" and links to the American Philatelic Society, the Military Postal Society, and plenty of other fascinating stamp-oriented sites. If you want to try scanning in your own stamps, you'll find advice on that, too.

http://swansongrp.com/posthist.html

Welcome to the National Postal Museum

Check out one of the Smithsonian Institution's newest museums! Its exhibits are organized into several major galleries that tell the story of postal history, and it includes a great collection of rare and wonderful stamp images. In many ways, the study of U.S. postage stamps is the study of American history and tradition. Whether you collect stamps or just use them to mail letters, you'll find a visit to this site well worth the time.

http://www.si.edu/postal/

The Penny Black and the [Two] Penny Blue were the world's first adhesive postage stamps, issued in Great Britain in 1840. They featured a portrait of a very young Queen Victoria. The U.S. issued its first postage stamps in 1847. Benjamin Franklin cost five cents, while George Washington was worth ten cents. The Smithsonian Institution's National Postal Museum offers a glimpse into the intriguing—and sometimes sticky—world of stamps and stamp collecting at Welcome to the National Postal Museum.

COLOR AND COLORING BOOKS

See also ART—DRAWING AND PAINTING

Color Matters

Red means "stop" and green means "go"—everyone knows that without giving it much thought. But did you know that color can affect the way you feel? It can make you feel relaxed or jumpy. It can make you feel interested or bored, even make you feel warmer or colder! And color sometimes means different things in different countries: for example, black is the color of grief and mourning in the U.S., while in some Asian countries the appropriate color is white. Find out more about the fascinating world of color here.

http://www.lava.net/~colorcom/

Have you written to your PEN PALS lately?

A
B
C
D
E
F
G
H
I
J
K
L
M
N
O
P
Q
R
S
T
U
V
W
X
Y
Z

A
B
C
D
E
F
G
H
I
J
K
L
M
N
O
P
Q
R
S
T
U
V
W
X
Y
Z

ARTtoon: Color

What color is your favorite? This page describes where colors come from and what they're made of. Read about what happens when you add colors together. You'll learn about complementary colors, warm and cool colors, and shades and hues.

http://www.wallyweb.com/at_color.htm

Crayola

What's your favorite Crayola color? How do they make crayons anyway? In 1903, the Binney & Smith company manufactured the first box of Crayolas. Explore the history of Crayolas, read the latest "Fun Facts" and learn about Crayola trivia. There is more trivia awaiting you in the "Questions" area, and make sure you visit the Art Education link for lots of craft ideas!

http://www.crayola.com/crayola/

Crayola Art Education * Art Techniques

Inspirations! When you look at this site, you'll be amazed at all the ways you can use crayons, markers, watercolors, and other art products. There are examples of other kids' drawings too.

http://education.crayola.com/techniques/

Crayons

Possibly inspired by Crayola's success, a class at Niskayuna High School (near Albany, NY) decided to try its hand at making crayons. They filled test tubes with chalk and wax and eventually got the proper consistency. See what they found out!

http://www.wizvax.net/nisk_hs/departments/science/
    stures/labs/crayons.html

Crayons and Computers Home Page

Pretend you're a bumblebee, flying into a flower. Past the petals, oops, watch out for that pollen! Wow, you've got a really close-up look. That's also the view you get when you see one of Georgia O'Keeffe's flower paintings. Learn to look very closely as you try some of the colorful crafts at this site.

http://members.aol.com/Sabbeth/
    CrayonsandComputers.html

Introduction to Color in the Graphic Arts

When you mix paints, you already know that if you mix red and blue you get purple, and if you mix blue and yellow you get green, right? That works with paint, but it doesn't work when you mix different colors of light. Light is a different story: for example, red and green light make yellow. How can that be? It's all explained in words and pictures here. This is important stuff to know if you want to print pretty color pictures in magazines, calendars, and even on the cover of this book!

http://www.anitec.com/faithful/intro_to_color/

COLORING BOOKS

Coloring.com

Did you ever use a computer and the Internet to color? At this site, you can color a birthday cake, a snowman, and other fun pictures on the World Wide Web with your computer. The best thing about this coloring book is that you can color over and over, and the pages don't fall out!

http://www.coloring.com/

How big is the audio-animatronic Stegosaurus on the Jurassic Park ride at the Universal Studios Hollywood theme park?

Answer: It's 18 feet tall and over 40 feet long. Its pal, the incredible Ultrasaurus, is over five stories tall, and, gee, it's coming your way! Run over to the Jurassic Park site at http://www.mca.com/unicity/attractions/jp/dinosaurs.html and learn if it's a carnivore or a vegetarian.

Kendra's Coloring Book

Coloring used to be so hard. There's that "stay within the lines" thing. Plus, it can be tough to find the right color crayon or marker. When you do find it, it's always broken or out of ink. If you make a mistake, you might as well start over. Your worries are over at this site. All you have to do is pick a picture, select a color, and click where you want the color to go. No more wondering where you left the "peach."

http://www.geocities.com/EnchantedForest/7155/

More of the Best Coloring Books and Coloring Pages Online - Art for Kids

There are two different ways you can color using the Internet. The first is to try an online coloring book. An outline picture appears on the screen, and you use your mouse to select colors and "paint" them in wherever you want. Some of these programs also let you pick the size of your "crayon" so that you can get a finer level of control. Sometimes you can download your completed picture and save it to print out later. More often, though, this isn't possible. If you always want to be able to save your picture, keep reading. The second type of coloring book is a series of traditional coloring pages. Just select the one you want to color, and download it. This saves it to your home computer. You print it out and color it with actual, not virtual, crayons. This Web resource (and the links from it) is a selection of the best and most fun coloring books on the Net.

http://artforkids.miningco.com/library/weekly/
  aa012898.htm

COMICS AND CARTOONS

See also DISNEY; PUPPETS AND MUPPETS;
TELEVISION

Message to parents and kids: Unfortunately, many of the standard cartoon and comic sites did not meet our book's selection policy this year. They often featured violent and other inappropriate content. If these sites separate kids content from adult content and try to monitor their message boards and chat rooms, we'll reconsider them for next year's edition. Meanwhile, we know you will love the sites we have selected!

Argonne Rube Goldberg Home Page

Reuben Lucius Goldberg, better known as Rube Goldberg, was a cartoonist with a wacky sense of humor. He loved to draw machines that would perform simple tasks, like pouring a glass of milk. First he would draw a way to open the refrigerator, then a way to get the bottle, then a way to open it—before he would ever get the milk into the glass! He accomplished this easy job by using the most complex, roundabout methods possible, often using common household objects in uncommon ways. You can see some examples of this here. A contest is held every year to see which team of students can perform a simple assignment using the weirdest, wackiest, and most complex machine. The assignment for 1998 was to "build the zaniest machines possible to turn off an alarm clock." Come here and find out what they invent. You can also find out how to get your school involved in the fun!

http://www.anl.gov/OPA/rube/

Cartoon Corner

How do people get jobs as cartoonists? Seems like a terrific job, using crayons and markers all day and thinking up funny things. This site will tell you the secrets of cartooning, but you have to promise *not* to tell anyone else! Learn some drawing tips, and try to guess some tricky riddles here.

http://www.cartooncorner.com/

Disney comics

This site does devote a lot of extra space to the Duck Universe of comics (with good reason—they quack us up, too), but there's plenty of information on Mickey, Goofy, and all of Walt Disney's other beloved characters. Did you know they have been in comic books around the world? Sometimes the names are a little strange in translation.

http://www.update.uu.se/~starback/disney-comics/

Be dazzled by the laser shows in PHYSICS.

A
B
C
D
E
F
G
H
I
J
K
L
M
N
O
P
Q
R
S
T
U
V
W
X
Y
Z

A
B
C
D
E
F
G
H
I
J
K
L
M
N
O
P
Q
R
S
T
U
V
W
X
Y
Z

Draw and Color a Cartoony Party with Uncle Fred

"Uncle Fred" Lasswell has been drawing the "Barney Google and Snuffy Smith" comic strip since 1934, and he still stays on the cutting edge of today's technology. His Web page includes numerous fun cartoon drawing lessons and features from his videodisk of the same name. Even the youngest of Web surfers will have no trouble drawing these characters.

http://www.unclefred.com/

The Droodles Home Page

What's a "droodle"? Well, it's a little drawing, called a doodle, crossed with a riddle—droodle, get it? In other words, it's a drawing with a puzzle in it. Picture a vertical (up-and-down) line, wearing what looks like a bow tie. According to this page, it could be "a butterfly climbing up a piece of string, or a vain triangle kissing its reflection in a mirror." What did the originator think the picture represented? Stop by the site and see! You can puzzle over lots of droodles here and submit your guesses as to their meaning.

http://www.webonly.com/droodles/

FOX KIDS TAKEOVER

The Fox Network has some great taste in 'toons. You may also like *Space Goofs*, *The X-Men*, *Ninja Turtles*, and *Casper*, among others. You can find some fun sound files and get news on the shows and contests here.

http://www.foxkids.com/

Garfield's Official Web Site

This purr-fect home page is hosted by a big fat hairy deal: Garfield! Check out the recipes for Garfield's favorite food (lasagne) and read some great jokes. Still can't get enough of this cantankerous kitty? Grab a Garfield screen saver for your computer!

http://www.garfield.com/

Lee's (Useless) Super-Hero Generator

Wouldn't it be great to have superpowers? You could just snap your fingers and your homework would do itself! You need a cool superhero name first, and this site will make one up for you! Net-mom herself is now going to turn into the wondrous Spyder Arrow, taking off on her space stilts!

http://home.hiwaay.net/~lkseitz/comics/herogen/

Looney Tunes Karaoke-Home

Your favorite Looney Tunes characters from Warner Brothers probably include Bugs Bunny, Tweety Bird, and Daffy Duck. Everyone always forgets that after Looney comes TUNES—and now you can sing right along with those characters, karaoke-style! This hilarious site is sure to make you smile.

http://www.kids.warnerbros.com/karaoke/

Mother Goose & Grimm

Does your dog eat out of the garbage can? If so, then your dog has something in common with Grimm! Mother Goose and Grimm are the lovable duo that appear in newspapers around the world as well as on Saturday morning cartoons. At this site, you can read biographical information about Mother Goose, Grimm, Atilla, and Mike Peters (the guy who draws these zany characters). Note to parents: "Toilet Trivia" is really a caption-the-cartoon contest.

http://www.grimmy.com/welcome.html

Non-Stick MGM Cartoon Page

Here is everything you always wanted to know about Tom and Jerry, Droopy, and all the other classic MGM cartoons and how they were made. The site features downloadable sounds and graphics and includes links to other terrific animation pages as well.

http://www.nonstick.com/mgm/

The Official Marmaduke® Site

It's Marmaduke—the greatest of Great Danes. You've seen his cartoons in the comic pages, but did you know he's the official "spokesdog" for a program in which volunteers and their pets visit hospitals to cheer up the patients? Find out more about this big-hearted dog, whose adventures appear in the newspapers of 20 different countries!

http://www.unitedmedia.com/comics/marmaduke/

The Official Snoopy Home Page

All your favorites are here: Charlie Brown, Lucy, Linus, Woodstock, Peppermint Patty, and Snoopy, of course! The history section is especially fascinating. The first "Peanuts" cartoon appeared in newspapers on October 2, 1950. But it wasn't until 1958 that Snoopy stood up on two legs. You'll find some fun Shockwave games here and electronic postcards to send to your friends.

http://www.snoopy.com/

RON KURER'S TOON TRACKER HOME PAGE

With so many long-forgotten animated cartoons of the past showing up on cable TV these days, this site is a gold mine of information on many of them. Find pages devoted to Mighty Mouse, Beany and Cecil, Clyde Crashcup, Clutch Cargo, Bullwinkle, Woody Woodpecker, and dozens more! Warning: This site takes forever to load!

http://ftp.wi.net/~rkurer/

The Simpsons

Bart is just a good kid with a "few bad ideas...that are still being reviewed by the Springfield district attorney." Better get over to the official Fox Network Simpsons Web page before you have a cow! You'll find some fun Simpsons games, news about the show, and contests here in virtual Springfield.

http://www.foxnetwork.com/simpsons/simpson2.htm

TBS Superstation Disaster Area

The TBS (Turner Broadcasting System) Web site is a real Disaster Area—at least, that is what they call their kids' site on the Web! You're probably a fan of a lot of TBS cartoons, including *The Jetsons*, *Scooby Doo*, or *Captain Planet*, so you'll love this site. If you have never heard of any of these, check out the games and contests anyway for some guaranteed fun.

http://TBSsuperstation.com/disaster/

The Wallace & Gromit Homepage

Wallace is an eccentric inventor, while Gromit is his faithful dog. Their adventures are depicted in Claymation, a special animation technique that uses clay figures as actors. You can learn more about this process, plus relive the plots of the W&G movies from the links at this site. There are also cool W&G downloads, cursors, and other fun.

http://rummelplatz.uni-mannheim.de/~mfeld/
wallace&gromit.html

If you could find a big enough pond, what planet would float in it?

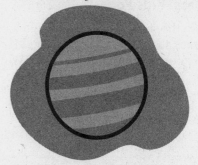

Answer: *Saturn is the lightest of all the planets. Since it's mostly made up of gas, it's actually lighter than water, and would float just like a beach ball. Read more at http://seds.lpl.arizona.edu/nineplanets/nineplanets/saturn.html*

Warner Bros. Animation 101

Do you love to watch cartoons? Do you ever wonder how cartoons are made? Go on a tour and watch the whole process. See how the pictures go from pencil sketches to handpainted art. Follow along as voices, sound effects, and music are added. Just watch out for falling anvils!

http://www.wbanimation.com/cmp/ani_04if.htm

Cartoons sure have a lot of sound effects! Did you know that the ones they use over and over are stored on computers? Then, whenever they are needed in a cartoon, they are "played" with a special computer-connected piano keyboard. Other sound effects are created on the spot. Draw on Warner Bros. Animation 101 for more information.

Warner Bros. Kids Page

Anyone with the slightest interest in animated cartoons needs to drop in here. The step-by-step tour of how a cartoon gets made is the World Wide Web at its best! The site also includes Loony Tunes Online Karaoke and Looney Tunes Web Postcards!

http://www.kids.warnerbros.com/

What is the sound of one router flapping?

Welcome to the Comic Zone

Every week they make families around the world laugh. They have names like Snoopy, Dilbert, and Marmaduke. Who are these wacky characters? They are the drawings that make up the comic strips in your newspaper. Catch up on your favorite comic strip characters, and see what they are doing on the Internet. Find out about the artists and how they thought up the characters, and play games based on the comic strip. Then take a detour from the main page to the National Cartoonists Society, where the *real* cartoonists behind the strips hang out!

http://www.unitedmedia.com/comics/

Welcome to the Home of the International Museum of Cartoon Art

This museum, located in Boca Raton, Florida, features 160,000 original drawings spanning every phase of this art form: animation, comic books, comic strips, editorial cartoons, greeting cards, caricature, computer-generated art, and others. This site offers samples from many different cartoonists and styles.

http://www.cartoon.org/home.htm

NET FILES

Everyone knows frogs can jump pretty far. How far? What's the longest recorded length a frog has leaped?

Answer: According to the Center for Global Environmental Education, a Mascarene frog holds the record for leaping 17.5 feet in a single jump! Hop to it!

http://cgee.hamline.edu/frogs/facts.html

You Can with Beakman and Jax

Put on your thinking cap and log on to this site. This newspaper feature has become so popular, there is now a *Beakman's World* TV series! Check out important historical facts in the You Can Calendar. Discover the answers to important questions, like "What are fingernails made of?" Help Beakman and Jax with their research project. See pictures from the Hubble Space Telescope, and read about what they mean.

http://www.beakman.com/

Your brother always stands too close to the dart board when he plays. What's the rule about how far back you're supposed to stand?

http://www.cyberdarts.com/basics/dartsbasics.html
more of the rules at
bull, is 173 centimeters, or 5 feet, 8 inches." You can read
9-1/4 inches. The height of the center of the
the plane of the face of the dartboard. In feet, this is 7 feet,
countries, is 2.37 meters, as measured along the floor, from
Cyber/Darts page, "The official throwing distance, for most
Answer: According to the Darts Basics area of the

COMPUTERS

alt.folklore.computers FAQ

The word "folklore" generally conjures up images of Davy Crockett or Paul Bunyan. While not as rustic, the world of computers is just as rich in legends and lore. This Usenet newsgroup has amassed a barrage of legends, and this site puts the most popular of them into easy-to-follow HTML format. Learn the truth about the NASA probe that rumors say was destroyed because of a computer typo. Who really wrote MS-DOS? Find out about the origins of Usenet and Unix, various computer firsts, and where in the world Jolt's high-caffeine cola is illegal.

http://www.best.com/~wilson/faq/

Did you hear about the guy who missed the chance to sell his operating system to IBM (which instead used Bill Gates's MS-DOS), because he was flying around in his airplane at the time?

What is the longest discussion thread *ever* in a newsgroup?

Where can you buy slide rules these days? Find out the fascinating answers to these and other questions at alt.folklore.computers FAQ.

BABEL: A Glossary of Computer Related Abbreviations and Acronyms

Sometimes it seems that you can't have a computer anything unless you have an acronym or geeky-sounding term to go with it. If you need to know your GUI (Graphical User Interface) from your ADSL (Asymmetric Digital Subscriber Line), look up this site!

http://www.access.digex.net/~ikind/babel.html

A B C D E F G H I J K L M N O P Q R S T U V W X Y Z

A
B
C
D
E
F
G
H
I
J
K
L
M
N
O
P
Q
R
S
T
U
V
W
X
Y
Z

Dave's Guide

How do you figure out which computer is the right one for you? What size and speed of microprocessor do you need? You don't want to waste your allowance money on a computer that is more than you need, but you do want a system that will be usable for a number of years. Read these guides for tips and suggestions on purchasing and installing a PC. Find out what to ask the store salesperson and what to look for in features. The opinions expressed here are just that—opinions—but you'll find some valuable information here. Hint: Click on the names of the guides in the frame on the left.

http://www.css.msu.edu/pc-guide.html

Guide to Computer Vendors

Want to write to the programmers of your favorite game, to suggest some new features? Here they are: over a thousand computer hardware and software vendors with Web pages ready to be accessed with a click. It's all filled with an easy-to-use alphabetical index, and as a bonus, a telephone directory lists several thousand computer companies. Want more? Link to the computer magazine and newsletter list maintained on this page, and drop in on your favorite periodical's Web site! A caution to parents: Not all links have been viewed. A similar site, Hardware Companies: The Web List is at <http://www.venus.it/homes/spumador/driver.htm>.

http://guide.sbanetweb.com/

Help-Site Computer Manuals - Over 800 free documents and faqs!

Wow! If you're looking for a quick source of online tutorials, manuals, hand-holding help, and more, start here. You'll find everything from Internet beginner's guides to what to do when confronted with a "new" VAX/VMS account. Mac, Win, DOS, and the rest of the expected platforms and hardware are here too. Enjoy!

http://help-site.com/

Introduction to PC Hardware

Are today's computers a *RISC*? How much *cache* do you need to buy a computer? *IDE*'d like a bigger hard drive, but what kind? Is our spelling that bad, or are we trying to make a point? Well, it so happens that those "misspelled" words are computer terms that you can read about on this Web page. You'll learn all about the various types of memory and how they are used in a computer system. Read about what's inside a microprocessor chip and about the different kinds of hard drives. By the time you're through, you'll be able to impress the salespeople in your local computer store—and maybe get a good deal to *boot*.

http://pclt.cis.yale.edu/pclt/pchw/platypus.htm

IPL Youth Division: Do Spiders Live on the World Wide Web?

Take your baby sister to story time at the University of Michigan's Internet Public Library! This picture book dictionary will help her learn the difference between the mouse on your desk and the mouse in your barn. In case you were wondering, the one in the barn eats up all the corn, while the one on your desk eats up all your time.

http://www.ipl.org/youth/StoryHour/spiders/mousepg.html

NET FILES

Sand castles, algae-coated slime, and lava balls are some of the features you've come all this way to see.

Where are you, anyway?

Answer: *You've reached a vacation spot known as Ape Cave, a geologic feature near Mount St. Helens in Washington. It's an ancient lava tube with a hiking trail inside, where you can meet millipedes, banter with bats, and commune with the cave slime. Don't touch the slime, though, because it will die! The slime is really made of algae and bacteria, and it performs a special function in the cave. Read about Ape Cave at* http://volcano.und.nodak.edu/vwdocs/msh/ov/ovb/ovbac.html

Something fishy going on? Visit AQUARIUMS.

THE JARGON FILE

In the beginning, computers were understood by only a small group of insiders. These insiders developed their own language and made up their own words, all of which served to further isolate them from the rest of the world, which was, after all, a distraction from computers and programming. ;-) For years, hacker lore and legend has been collected into this file. Now it has made it to the Web, and you will laugh at the funny computing terms and lingo heard daily in machine rooms all over the Net. Some have even made it into popular conversation! You can search the file for specific terms or just browse for fun. Parental advisory: Some of these terms have mildly adult origins.

http://www.wins.uva.nl/~mes/jargon/

Ever attended a disk drive race?.

In the olden days of computing, disk drives were about the size of washing machines. Bored programmers wrote routines to command the drive heads to seek back and forth on the disks, which built up a momentum that often allowed the drives to totter across the floor. Walking drive races are a legendary part of computing history, and you can read more at THE JARGON FILE.

RING!OnLine | Computer Advisor

Here's some advice on how to buy a computer. This two-part column will help you if you're looking for your first computer or looking to upgrade that old "slowpoke." How much RAM do you need, how big a hard drive should you get, and what is a cache, anyway? Check this site to find out.

http://www.ring.com/vts/advisor/main.htm

AMIGA

Amiga Report Magazine

The Amiga may be the phoenix of computers, rising out of the ashes to new heights. It never achieved the measure of popularity in the U.S. that it did in Europe. But the purchase of the rights to the once-discontinued system by the Amiga Technologies group, and thence to Gateway 2000 has created the possibility of new developments. Whether you already own an Amiga and are looking for sources of support and new software (there are Web browsers for Amiga users!) or you are just interested in keeping track of what's happening, drop in on this site regularly.

http://www.omnipresence.com/Amiga/News/AR/

AmigaZone

For all the very latest Amiga news, rumors, links, contests, and more, you need to see this site! Some of the resources are free while others require a for-fee membership. If you're really into Amiga, you'll want to join.

http://www.amigazone.com/

Aminet at de.aminet.net

"Aminet is the Internet's largest collection of Amiga software." Check out the recent uploads list to keep up to date with your favorite shareware. Visit the "Tree of Aminet directories" for a list of their archives sorted by category. A search tool and help files are also available for those Amigaphiles in need of Amiga files.

http://www.germany.aminet.org/aminet/

A
B
C
D
E
F
G
H
I
J
K
L
M
N
O
P
Q
R
S
T
U
V
W
X
Y
Z

A
B
C
D
E
F
G
H
I
J
K
L
M
N
O
P
Q
R
S
T
U
V
W
X
Y
Z

APPLE II

Nathan Mates's Apple II Resources

While Apple Computer may have discontinued the Apple II line a few years ago, millions of these work-horse machines are still in use in homes and schools everywhere. Plenty of new Apple II hardware and software is still being developed. Nathan Mates (who *really* hates software pirates—he has a few words to say about them) has collected as many Apple II links as he could find, including newsgroups, FTP sites chock-full of programs and information, lists of BBSs, and companies producing Apple II products. The FAQ here is a labor of love. Once the corporate slogan for Apple Computer, "Apple II Forever!" seems to be a fact of life for the dedicated bunch of folks you'll find here.

http://www.visi.com/~nathan/a2/

ARTIFICIAL INTELLIGENCE

BotSpot ® : The Spot for all Bots & Intelligent Agents

Someday soon you may not interact with the Net yourself—you'll have a "bot" or "agent" to go out on the Web for you and bring back what you want. This resource helps you track the latest news in intelligent agents, and we don't mean Fox Mulder.

http://www.botspot.com/main.html

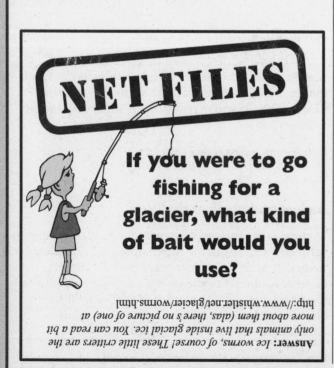

NET FILES

If you were to go fishing for a glacier, what kind of bait would you use?

Answer: *Ice worms, of course! These little critters are the only animals that live inside glacial ice. You can read a bit more about them (alas, there's no picture of one) at* http://www.whistler.net/glacier/worms.html

Cog, the Robot

Back in 1921, playwright Karel Capek coined the word "robot," and since then, books, movies, and television programs have all speculated about the form these mechanical creatures will take. Now a group of researchers at the Massachusetts Institute of Technology's Artificial Intelligence Lab are actually attempting this feat. Artificial intelligence is the process in which a computer takes in information and uses it to create new knowledge—a simulation of human thinking. Cog the Robot is a collection of sensors and motors that attempt to duplicate the sensory and manipulative functions of the human body. Coupled with artificial intelligence programming, Cog may eventually succeed in bringing science fiction's fantasies to reality. Move over Data, here comes Cog!

http://www.ai.mit.edu/projects/cog/Text/
    cog-robot.html

Shallow Red

Shallow Red (SR) is a distant relative of Deep Blue, the famous chess-playing computer program. SR answers questions about its company and their products. He can even play a little samba music (and better yet, turn it OFF!). For a look at some artificial intelligence, have a conversation with Shallow Red.

http://www.neurostudios.com/html/
    ShallowRedFrame.htm

ATARI

What's an Atari 8-bit?

The Atari 8-bit computer was a natural outgrowth of the company's phenomenally popular game cartridge machine. In fact, all of these machines, whether the 400, 800, or any of the XL or XE series, had a port or two for popping in game or program cartridges. Plenty of folks are still getting lots of mileage out of them, and this site is a great starting point if you're wondering what you can do with the one Dad just bought at a garage sale. It includes plenty of links to active Atari 8-bit home pages as well as the important "Atari 8-bit Omnibus."

http://zippy.sonoma.edu/~kendrick/nbs/whatisatari/

COMMODORE

Commodore Ring

Whether you're looking for that old workhorse the Commodore 64 or that young upstart the VIC-20, you'll find information about it here! This is a Web ring of like-minded resources, and not all links have been viewed.

http://www.webring.org/cgi-bin/
    webring?ring=cbmring&id=114&list

HISTORY

Classic Video Games Nexus

There's an old arcade game Dad loved—in fact, he gets all misty-eyed whenever he talks about all those quarters he put into the machines. And what the heck is a Pac-Man? (Download a Java version at <*http://www.csd.uu.se/~alexb/*>. If the letter keys don't work, try your arrow keys.) Lead Dad to this site and you're bound to hear a lot of nostalgic commentary on how great all those games were. In fact, you may be able to play some of them. There are many emulators available, and if you can get your hands on any old ROM game cartridges, you may be able to relive the sights and sounds of yesteryear when Dad played as many video games
as you do now.

http://home.hiwaay.net/~lkseitz/cvg/nexus/

Does the word "vexillology" leave you vexed? What does it mean anyway?

Answer: Vexillology is the study of flags. Find out more about it at
*http://www.math.technion.ac.il/
mirror/flags.cesi.it/flags/vexilla.html*

The Computer Museum: Registration Page

In an old building on Museum Wharf in Boston sits a walk-through computer. The trackball is as big as your sofa. The keyboard is as big as your school bus. And you ought to see the size of that motherboard. Welcome to the Computer Museum! You can visit its Web page and get a taste of the exhibits. Here's a twist: When you enter this site, you can put in a name (any name will do) and you can put in the name of your country or your ZIP code if you are in the U.S. This Web page keeps track of all connected users, and when you select "Who's Out There?" you will get a world map with all current users—if you have a Java-enabled browser. You can click on Paolo from Brazil or Geoff from Australia or Sarah from the U.K. and send a message. Then you can explore the galleries together!

http://www.tcm.org/

Historic Timeline of Computing

This timeline lets you surf through the history of computing from 1945 to 1990. Each year you'll find illustrated entries about significant advances made in hardware, software, and commercial applications. You'll also find biographical info on some of the famous computing pioneers, such as Admiral Grace Hopper, who in 1945 discovered the first "computer bug."

http://www.tcm.org/history/timeline/

Obsolete Computer Museum

You're digging around in the basement one day and come across this big box full of old keyboards, disk drives, and computer hardware of unknown origin. "Hey Mom," you say, "what's this stuff?" She says that is a box of old computer parts she used long ago and doesn't even remember how to put them together anymore. Now there is hope. Not only does this resource show you old computers (outside and inside), but there's a help line to assist you in finding usable boot disks, cables, and replacement parts! Lots of these machines still have a lot of life in them—see how to bring them back.

http://www.ncsc.dni.us/fun/user/tcc/cmuseum/
    cmuseum.htm

A
B
C
D
E
F
G
H
I
J
K
L
M
N
O
P
Q
R
S
T
U
V
W
X
Y
Z

A
B
C
D
E
F
G
H
I
J
K
L
M
N
O
P
Q
R
S
T
U
V
W
X
Y
Z

The Virtual Museum of Computing

The world's largest museum devoted to computers is appropriately located in Downtown Hyperspace. Don't worry about putting coins in the parking meter. Just stroll around and check out the ever-growing collection. You'll find galleries featuring local virtual exhibits, corporate histories, and entire wings with histories of computing organizations and societies, plus general computer history. Special exit doors here will take you to a couple of dozen other online computing museums. While there is no virtual snack bar here yet, you can drop in on an assortment of selected computer-oriented newsgroups to chat about what you've seen. You'll even find a gallery of mousepads old and new at *<http://www.expa.hvu.nl/ ajvdhek/index.html>*! Parental advisory: This is a large site with many links, and they have not all been checked.

http://www.comlab.ox.ac.uk/archive/other/
    museums/computing.html

MACINTOSH

Apple Computer

This is the computer "for the rest of us" that launched the mouse, the Graphical User Interface, and the networked laser printer into the consumer main-stream. Apple's home page has product information to help you choose a system and a technical support area to help answer questions. You'll also find down-loadable upgrades to Apple software and information on the "cool Apple technologies" that Apple is working on to improve their products for the future. The Apple Classrooms of Tomorrow (ACOT) research program was a collaboration among public schools, universities, research agencies, and Apple Computer, Inc. itself. For the past ten years, ACOT studied technology's impact on education. A compilation of the lessons learned is available for a few dollars. It's called "Changing the Conversation about Teaching, Learning, and Technology: A Report on Ten Years of ACOT Research." Other research studies are also available at *<http://www.research.apple.com/ go/acot/ACOTResearch.html#anchor25466881>*.

http://www.apple.com/

Cult of Macintosh

An unofficial evangelistic effort promoting the Macintosh is actively attempting to place page mirrors on every continent. Frequently updated, it has become a friendly all-around resource for Mac users, with hundreds of links to just about anything a Mac user could desire.

http://cult-of-mac.utu.fi/

MacFixIt (Home Page)

Eventually, every Macintosh computer owner will run across a problem and will need some kind of support. We like the info at this site, which is constantly being kept up to date. If you have a bizarre problem you just can't seem to troubleshoot, just search here on keywords describing the situation. You may strike gold!

http://www.macfixit.com/

NET FILES

What is the function of the "hat" in the card game called Hungarian Tarokk?

Answer: Only on the Net would you learn this one! Tarokk is played with a deck of 42 cards. "An important part of the apparatus of this game is the hat, which should look as silly as possible. The traditional version is a sort of Austrian hunting hat with too many large feathers stuck into it at odd angles, but anything ridiculous-looking will do. Any player who has the XXI of trumps captured by an opponent's Skíz must wear the hat until someone else suffers the same misfortune." For a description of the deck and the rules, go to *http://www.netlink.co.uk/users/pagat/ tarot/pasktev.html* from the Card Games home page.

Macintosh Educator's Site

This is billed as an "educators" page, and anyone with a Mac (and even those without one) will have a blast visiting here. Short descriptions are provided for each of the links, which include all the major Macintosh archives, magazine pages, and help sites, as well as Science, General Education, and Fun pages.

http://www.hampton-dumont.k12.ia.us/web/mac/

The ULTIMATE Macintosh

Hundreds of Macintosh-related links are piled on this one page, making it possible to conduct a search using your browser's Find command (on Lynx, use the / command). The best thing about this page is the What's HOT! section, which provides up-to-the-minute news and links to the latest information (including promotions from Apple and major vendors) and software updates. Not all links have been viewed.

http://www.flashpaper.com/umac/

PC COMPATIBLES, MICROSOFT WINDOWS

Dell Computer Corporation - Home Page

According to their Web site, "Dell is the fastest growing among all major computer-systems companies worldwide. The company is the No. 2 computer systems manufacturer in the U.S., where it is a leading supplier of PCs to corporate customers, government agencies and educational institutions." Dell computers are cropping up in more and more K–12 classrooms, and here's the best place to see the latest and greatest.

http://www.dell.com/

IBM Corporation

Here's where the personal computer (PC) all started. IBM introduced the PC in 1983. Today, computers based on the same design account for about 85 percent of the microcomputer market. Talk about popular! Before the PC, and even now, IBM's stronghold has been with big-business computers that run governments, corporations, banks, and other institutions. Explore this Web site to see what this computer giant is up to these days.

http://www.ibm.com/

Microsoft in Education

In February 1975, Bill Gates and Paul Allen completed the first computer language program written for a personal computer: a BASIC interpreter for the Altair. In 1981, Microsoft shipped MS-DOS 1.0 for IBM's new personal computer. In the years to come, MS-DOS became the standard operating system bundled with the millions of PCs shipped to businesses and individuals. In 1985, Windows was introduced to the public. Since then, Microsoft has shipped millions of copies of Windows. Needless to say, Microsoft is the largest software company in the world! Visit these K–12 pages and see what Microsoft is doing in the way of sponsoring programs to promote education, computers, and networking.

http://www.microsoft.com/education/

Welcome to Gateway 2000 USA

Did you know Gateway computers are shipped in boxes that look like they are part dairy cow? What's with those cows, anyway? Ted Waitt's family had been in the cattle business for many generations. When he created a new computer company, Gateway 2000, he brought some of his heritage with him. Apparently, he also brought some luck with him, because his company is now the largest seller of computers through direct marketing.

http://www.gw2k.com/

A
B
C
D
E
F
G
H
I
J
K
L
M
N
O
P
Q
R
S
T
U
V
W
X
Y
Z

A
B
C
D
E
F
G
H
I
J
K
L
M
N
O
P
Q
R
S
T
U
V
W
X
Y
Z

Welcome to WinFiles.com!

WinFiles now offers shareware, drivers, and other information for Windows 95, 98, and NT. You'll find all kinds of information in an easy-to-use format, including the scoop on what happened to "Windows95.com," the site that formerly occupied this space.

http://www.winfiles.com/

The Windows 95 QAID

"How much RAM is required to run Windows 95?" "I lost multiboot option, how do I get it back?" These are two of the many questions that are answered on this Question-Answer Information Database (QAID). The questions are listed by category, such as CD-ROM, booting, printers, and sound. You'll also find news, tips and tricks, and other Windows 95-related areas to browse through. Some of the dialog can get quite technical, but then, computers can get that way sometimes. The QAID is also available for download, allowing you to search for answers while offline.

http://www.kingsoft.com/qaid/win40001.htm

Windows 98 Home Page

So the new code for Windows 98 was all ready to be shipped to retailers and then the U.S. Department of Justice and lots of state attorneys general said, "Hold on there a minute, Bill." By the time you read this, it may all be settled, or you may find there is still a lot of legal maneuvering to be done. Still, you want to know all you can about the operating system—so, for news direct from Microsoft, stop in and get the latest.

http://www.microsoft.com/windows98/default.asp

PROGRAMMING

The Programmer's Vault

If you're really into computers, you might think of writing your own program, maybe even a cool new game! How do you get started? One way is here. Check the tutorials on everything from C and C++ to Java. Lots on game design, how to detect sprite collisions (that's when your spaceship collides with a photon torpedo and you want to show an explosion), and more, and MORE.

http://www.chesworth.com/pv/vault/vault.htm

RECYCLED EQUIPMENT

Computers for Learning

The federal government uses lots of computers in its offices all over the U.S. When they upgrade to new systems, sometimes the old computers become available for schools (yes, even home schools) and other educational or nonprofit purposes. Find out if your organization qualifies, and maybe you can get some free recycled computers!

http://www.computers.fed.gov/

PEP National Directory of Computer Recycling Programs

There is a growing list of clearinghouses for matching donated computer equipment to needy educational and nonprofit causes. This resource highlights groups in Africa, Australia, the United Kingdom, and other countries concerned with helping kids get computers. There are also many U.S. state and national programs. Overloaded with old floppy disks? Donate them to Floppies for Kiddies—the contact info is here.

http://www.microweb.com/pepsite/Recycle/
   recycle_index.html

SOFTWARE ARCHIVES

CNET resources-software central

This is an intro page to the shareware.com software archives. We've selected this page because of its three must-read sections, called "virus check?", "survival kits," and "beginner's guides." Each section has a Mac- and PC-specific selection that contains valuable information on downloading software, especially for first-time users.

http://www.cnet.com/Resources/Software/

INFO-MAC HyperArchive ROOT

Over the years, info-mac has become the master list for Macintosh software archives, with mirror sites around the world. Now you can use your Web client to search or browse this mirror collection at MIT. This is a great way to find shareware, demos, clip art, help, and information about Macintosh. If you own a Mac, this will become one of your favorite links.

http://hyperarchive.lcs.mit.edu/HyperArchive.html

JUMBO! The Download Network

Shareware? What's that? You can try out shareware software before you buy it. Sometimes the shareware version will do everything that the full version will do. Jumbo also has lots of free programs for most computers and operating systems. It's easy to find what you want, since everything is classified by subject. The short descriptions will help you find that arcade game, er, math tutorial you want! They have just added a message board and a chat room (the chat room is monitored).

http://www.jumbo.com/

Kid's Domain

Families who drop in on this site will find it a severe test of the storage capacity of their hard drives. :-) A wealth of kids' software is available on the Internet, and this is the place to look. This extensive, fully annotated collection gives each program its own page, including age recommendations, program sizes, and shareware fees, if any. The page is divided between Mac and PC archives, and a third section is devoted to downloadable commercial demo programs. This last section includes links to many pages of kids' software review sites.

http://www.kidsdomain.com/

What are
Mancos milk-vetch, clay-loving wild buckwheat, Dudley Bluffs bladderpod, and Penland beardtongue?

Answer: Well, they are not the names of new rock groups! They are all plants on the endangered species list for Colorado. Find out more about endangered and threatened species at *http://www.fws.gov/~r9endspp/endspp.html*

Oak Software Repository

Check out this archive site for access to just about all the DOS and Windows software available. Besides listing many of the other software archives, you can browse the legendary SimTel archives here with your Web browser. The SimTel collection goes back to the early DOS years, and it is one of the largest collections of PC programs and information in the world. There is even a CP/M archive here (ask your parents if they remember the CP/M operating system). Of course, a search function is available to help you find the "needle in the haystack" you might be looking for.

http://www.acs.oakland.edu/oak.html

Shareware Zone, Galt Shareware Zone, hottest shareware downloads, reviews, free newsletter

If you're looking for reviews on shareware software for Windows 3.*x* or Windows 95, you might try this extensive collection. You can look for the hottest game downloads and the hottest recommended downloads, and you can wander through over 500 screen savers. You can also get a free newsletter that highlights each month's new additions to the archive. Parents, check it out: some of these games are of the Mortal Kombat variety.

http://www3.galttech.com/

TUCOWS World Wide Affiliate Site Locations

Tucows says it is the world's most popular collection of Internet software for Windows 95, Windows 3.1, and Macintosh software—and we believe it! This collection is mirrored at over 150 sites around the globe, so pick a site close to you. (Another suggestion is to pick a server located somewhere where the local time is in the middle of the night—that server will probably not be overloaded.) This is your source for plug-ins, helper applications, and games.

http://www.tucows.com/

A B C D E F G H I J K L M N O P Q R S T U V W X Y Z

A B **C** D E F G H I J K L M N O P Q R S T U V W X Y Z

SOFTWARE REVIEW

Children's Software Revue

There's so much new software coming out, how do you know which ones are worth your time and money? The *Children's Software Revue* magazine is one terrific way to keep up with this ever-growing marketplace. Many features from the print version are also available here, and you can search the database of over 3,000 reviews! Also valuable is the selection of links to other qualified review resources on the Web.

http://www2.childrenssoftware.com/childrenssoftware/

SuperKids Educational Software Review

This site is aimed at parents and teachers, but you can use it too! Find out if that new software title you've seen advertised on TV is really any good. Each month, a team of reviewers (parents, teachers, kids) check out a selection of the newest programs in a specific subject area, like math, reading, or science. What do they really like? What really made them yawn? Find out here!

http://www.superkids.com/aweb/pages/contents.html

TIMEX SINCLAIR

ZX81 Home Page

At first glance, the ZX81, more commonly known in the U.S. as the Timex Sinclair computer, appears to be a sleek and snappy palmtop. Actually, this tiny, membrane-keyed device is a desktop computer, and at one time it sold like hotcakes. As the first computer in history to break the $100 price barrier, over a million were purchased. They came with a "whopping" one kilobyte of RAM and used cassette tapes to store data—no floppies or hard drives. Writing programs for the machine was an exercise in precision coding. If you've found a ZX81 in the attic or at a garage sale, this is the page to turn to for lots of fascinating information about it and where to go for help in using it. We had two of them. Net-mom's dad often enjoyed showing us cool programs he wrote for it, while we were still figuring out the manual for our Apple IIe. Loading from cassette tape was quite a trick, though. This was back in the olden days, when we had to trudge through the snow to buy RAM...

http://www.gre.ac.uk/~bm10/zx81.html

UNIX

Unix is a Four Letter Word

Unix is cool. Because of its power, Unix is the operating system that is used by engineers and networking professionals most often. Unix systems don't have to "add" TCP/IP to "plug" into the Internet—it's their native networking language. Now try to guess what operating system was used to expand the Internet into what it is today. You're right, it's Unix. Unix was even used to run Jurassic Park in the movie! This nicely designed site gives beginners a good feel for the Unix operating system. There is also a good introduction to the Vi text editor for you real purists out there.

http://www.linuxbox.com/~taylor/4ltrwrd/

UNIXhelp for users

Excuse me, but you "grepped" my file while I was "rm"ing it! Unix geeks like to talk like that a lot. At this site you can learn basic Unix commands and be able to translate what the Unix wizards are saying.

http://www.geek-girl.com/Unixhelp/

NET FILES

Eight miles long, the Confederation Bridge is the longest continuous multispan marine bridge in the world. It links the Canadian mainland of New Brunswick Province to Prince Edward Island. How many streetlights illuminate it at night?

Answer: 310. Read more about the building of this fascinating structure at http://www.confederationbridge. com/english/ fastfact.htm

VIRTUAL REALITY

There are two ways to think of virtual reality, or VR.

The first is a continuous panoramic picture of something real. You can explore it by clicking and dragging your mouse. You are usually "standing" right in the middle of the scene, and can usually "look" at least right and left, sometimes all the way around you, up and down too. You can sometimes click on something you see, and you'll "walk" towards it to get a better view.

The second type of VR lets you "walk" around in a virtual world, one that doesn't exist anywhere but inside the computer. You may be represented in this world by something called an *avatar*. Sometimes programs let you select what your avatar will look like, so you might be a smiley face, a big spotted dog, or even a monster! The VR world you may explore is computer-created, so anything may happen!

The following selected links give you a small sampling of both types of virtual reality. To find more, look in your favorite search engine under VRML (Virtual Reality Modeling Language), virtual reality, QuickTime VR, photo bubble, and similar terms.

CNET features - how to - beyond the browser, part 2 - what are virtual worlds?

This multipage quick-start guide will get you going with what you need to explore the virtual worlds peopled by avatars and wire-framed trees and buildings. It's a lot of fun, but we recommend you explore these worlds with your parents because some of the worlds are nicer than others.

http://www.cnet.com/Content/Features/Howto/
   Beyond2/ss03.html

Galaxies in VRML

If you're a *Star Trek* fan, you'll love this. Fly through hundreds of nearby galaxies and explore strange new worlds. Just don't boldly go too fast, or you'll get not-so-virtually airsick!

http://www.honeylocust.com/Stars/galaxies/

Greatest Places Virtual Reality

All you'll need is QuickTime to explore 360-degree photos from Iguazu Falls in Brazil. Hope you're not afraid of heights. Hold onto the handrail!

http://www.sci.mus.mn.us/greatestplaces/medias/
   media_html/qtvr.html

Interactive Origami in VRML

This little demo allows you to start with a sheet of paper, walk around it, get close to it, and then run farther away. If you click directly on the paper, it will advance to the next stage of paper folding. It's not the greatest exhibition of origami we've ever seen, but it does provide nice practice for your VR driving skills!

http://www.neuro.sfc.keio.ac.jp/~aly/polygon/
   vrml/ika/

IPIX- The World Leader in Immersive Imaging

You will need to download the IPIX plug-in for this one to work. But after you have it, you'll be able to walk around sports stadiums, real estate, famous landmarks, even sharks. Just check the gallery area and start your exploration. One place not mentioned here is the IPIX interactive tour to Westminster Abbey, which was created by CNN for the sad occasion of Princess Diana's funeral. Visit it. One place you'll love is the Poet's Corner at *<http://cnn.com/WORLD/ 9708/diana/london.pix/route.html>*. Be sure to look up over your head and beneath your feet to see memorials to famous authors.

http://www.ipix.com/

Media Storm Home Page

Now here's something cool. You can see current water temperatures all over the planet. Check out El Niño yourself. Then inspect cloud cover over Earth. Spin the globe to see if there's rain in Spain or clouds in China. You can also try the same thing on the VR moon, but it never rains there at all. You'll have to content yourself with locating the Man in the Moon. Wait—is that him over *there*? Move in, move in!

http://www.pacificnet.net/~mediastorm/

A
B
C
D
E
F
G
H
I
J
K
L
M
N
O
P
Q
R
S
T
U
V
W
X
Y
Z

A
B
C
D
E
F
G
H
I
J
K
L
M
N
O
P
Q
R
S
T
U
V
W
X
Y
Z

Trick roping secrets are revealed in KNOTS.

Mediadome - Explore Titanic

This Java-based VR experience lets you explore the wreck of the *Titanic* as you search for the missing safe. We didn't see Leonardo around anywhere, and we didn't find the safe either, but we did feel sort of wet after sloshing around in the sunken staterooms and corroded corridors for a while! There is a similar VR simulation at the official home page for the movie at <*http://www.titanicmovie.com/*>.

http://www.mediadome.com/Webisodes/Titanic/
Explore/

V R M L - iiONLiNE

This little VR simulation is fun. You can trying skiing down some virtual slopes at major ski resorts. What's strange about this one is that you can find yourself skiing *under* the mountain if you're not careful!

http://www.iion.com/Winternet/vrml/

CONSUMER INFORMATION

See also MONEY

Consumer Education for Teens

This site was developed by a class of high school students in Des Moines, Washington. It's right on the money when it comes to answering questions and concerns about investing your hard-earned cash. How much do you know about bank accounts and credit cards? How do you avoid being cheated when you buy merchandise? Learn how to tell the difference between scholarship scams and the real thing. Do you really think you can get rich quick? If it sounds too good to be true, it probably is!

http://www.wa.gov/ago/youth/

Consumer World: Everything Consumer

OK, you've bought that skateboard you've been wanting. Now it won't even roll! Hustle over to this site to find out what you can do about it. It doesn't matter that you're a kid. You have consumer power, and manufacturers listen to consumers, regardless of their age. While you're there, you can also find out how to avoid online scams, determine if the skateboard has been recalled, and link to the Better Business Bureau. You'll also find out how to contact many companies and other sources of consumer information. Be sure to show this site to your parents—they will love it.

http://www.consumerworld.org/

Street Cents Online

Young people make money, save money, and spend money, just like everyone else! But sometimes there just isn't much advice for young people about handling their money. Do you spend money on entertainment, sports, music, and food? What's the deal on using horse shampoo on people? Does Duracell really outlast the Energizer bunny? All of these topics and more are covered by *Street Cents,* a popular Canadian television show. And now it's online in an informative and fun Web page. *Spend* some time here!

http://www.halifax.cbc.ca/streetcents/

Welcome to Consumer Reports® Online

Consumer Reports is a nonprofit organization that tests appliances, audio and TV equipment, cameras, cars, and all sorts of other things. They issue their opinions on which items are the best, based on the results of the tests they run on competing products. They accept no advertising in their magazine, so you can really trust what they have to say. Next time you want to buy something, see if it has been reviewed lately. You'll be glad you did. By the way, be sure to tell your parents this is online.

http://www.consumerreports.org/

Have an order of pi in MATH AND ARITHMETIC.

COOKING, FOOD, AND DRINK

See also COLLECTORS AND COLLECTING

Coca-Cola

This page is The Real Thing. Pause here, and you'll feel refreshed. A class of kids in Tennessee decided to enter the ThinkQuest Junior contest with this resource on the history of the Coca-Cola company. It's been a very popular beverage for over 100 years—did you ever wonder why? This site has links to Coke and its biggest competitors, as well as experiments you can do with soda, games, and a "share your Coca-Cola stories" section.

http://tqjunior.advanced.org/4501/

FOOD FOR SPACE FLIGHT

Have you ever wondered what the astronauts eat while they are zooming around up in space? Cuisine in space has come a long way from the early days of crumbly freeze-dried fodder and squeeze-tube gels. Now astronauts chow down on normal types of foods, including snacks such as candy-coated peanuts and Life Savers. Get a menu list here, and learn about all the ways they prepare meals while in flight.

http://shuttle.nasa.gov/sts-69/factshts/food.html

SpiceGuide

Once, spices were as precious as gems. The demand for spices drove expeditions and opened up new trade routes. You can discover the history of spices at this nicely designed site. A spice encyclopedia tells you where the spice grows, what its uses are, and more. For example, according to its entry, spearmint and peppermint are both native to Asia. Peppermint was used by Egyptians, and spearmint is mentioned in the Bible. Spearmint grew wild in the United States after the 1600s, and peppermint was cultivated commercially before the Civil War. You'll also find recipes and a list of must-have spices for the average kitchen. The Kid's Sugar and Spice section will tell you some interesting facts about a highlighted spice.

http://www.spiceguide.com/

BREAD, CEREAL, RICE, AND PASTA

Frito-Lay

Frito-Lay is more than just corn chips. Their site offers fun, interactive advertising games. You can create your own "dream date" ("Is your dream date punk or preppie?"). Use corn chips to spice up your recipes, and create Chili Pie or a Fiesta Burger. Ever wonder who invented the pretzel? It was invented by a monk in A.D. 610. In other news, Frito-Lay goes through seven and a half *million* pounds of potatoes every day to make potato chips. That's a lot of Ruffles!

http://www.fritolay.com/

In medieval times, knights wore suits of armor as protection in battle. Since all knights looked alike with their armor on, they needed some way to tell each other apart at a distance. A coat of arms was originally a silk T-shirt worn over the armor. This garment had a picture of items important to the knight's family, arranged in specific ways and in various colors, which also had meaning. Everyone in the same family wore the same coat of arms. In the Bible, Adam was the first man and Eve was the first woman. Did either have a coat of arms?

Answer: Heralds in medieval times thought every important person should have a coat of arms. So, although it was thousands of years later, they decided to assign arms to Adam and Eve. Adam's shield is plain red and Eve's is plain silver. See the shields at http://www.fred.net/jefjaivey/jefthera.html

A
B
C
D
E
F
G
H
I
J
K
L
M
N
O
P
Q
R
S
T
U
V
W
X
Y
Z

I Love Pasta - National Pasta Association Home Page

I Love Pasta is the perfect place to head when you're just noodlin' around! Mom and Dad can choose from the more than 250 recipes developed in the National Pasta Association's Test Kitchen, while you might try the kids menu of Turtle Shells or Cheesy Noodle Saucers. You can have your pasta with pork or beef or poultry or seafood! When you've twirled the last spoonful, check the Pasta 101 course where you can learn about every shape and size noodle that's made. "I Love Pasta" and bet you do too!

http://www.ilovepasta.org/

COOKING FOR BEGINNERS

Big Top's Fun Recipes

If you're having a party or other special occasion, why not take a chance and try some Keroppi Frozen Treats or some Hello Kitty Chocolate Truffle Hearts? The Big Top Frozen Krazy Punch sounds delicious, and the Wacky Popcorn would be a great snack for watching TV.

http://www.bigtop.com/kids/recipes1.html

Cooking with Blondee - Kids

Check Blondee's easy pizza recipes, porcupine salad, and butter graham crackers. These nutritious snacks and finger foods are fun to make and delicious, too. You can also send in your own recipe, and Blondee may choose it for her online cookbook!

http://www.familyinternet.com/cooking/kids/

Idea Box Recipes

Visit this site to find over 20 Web sites with easy recipes for kids and interested adults or anyone who is just learning to cook! You'll find recipes for holidays and regular days, breakfasts, lunches, and dinners.

http://www.theideabox.com/ideas.nsf/recipe

It never rains on the PARADES in cyberspace.

KidsHealth Kid's Recipes

KidsHealth is one of the best family sites on the Net, and their recipes page doesn't disappoint. Whether you're looking for a breakfast treat (pancakes, oatmeal) or a dinner delight (chili, macaroni and cheese), you'll find some great ideas here. Don't miss the snacks either, especially Ants on a Log and Train and Trail Mix.

http://kidshealth.org/kid/games/recipe/

FRUITS AND VEGETABLES

Dole 5 a Day - Nutrition Education for Kids

Do you mind your peas and carrots? Learn the nutritional values of the fruits and vegetables that you eat every day. Then fun stuff awaits when you meet Adam Apple, Bobby Banana, and their friends. Try the 5 A Day Game along with them, as they point out how important they are to your well-being. Try some of the delicious recipes provided, and you'll want to bring these friends to your dinner table every day! There's also a virtual tour to the Dole Salad factory—oops, watch out for that radicchio—you'll want to try it!

http://www.dole5aday.com/

It was a breakthrough back in 1913. Henry Ginaca, engineer and inventor, unveiled his masterpiece: a machine that could peel, core, and pack 35 pineapples per minute. Wow, the people at the Dole factory were ecstatic! The Ginaca Machine is still used in pineapple canneries today. Dole is more than pineapples, though; check out the Dole 5 a Day Nutrition Education for Kids home page.

> ## Surf, and you shall become empowered (or wet).

Florida Department of Citrus Web Site

Did you know that citrus fruit must be picked ripe? It will not continue to ripen after it leaves the tree. Here's another interesting fact: although mechanical tree-shakers are sometimes used, 98 percent of Florida oranges are picked by hand. Follow the story of tree-to-juice at this sunny delight of a site.

http://www.floridajuice.com/floridacitrus/
   whereojbar.htm

The Garlic Page

You know that smell from a mile away—it's garlic! Garlic has a wonderful flavor. It makes spaghetti and pizza taste great. It's also good for chasing away garden pests, and it may even be helpful in avoiding cancer. Garlic is also legendary for repelling vampires. Find out more about this fascinating food. The Garlic Page has recipes, health facts, growing tips, and, of course, garlic news. Don't, please don't choose the link from this page labeled "Garlic Surprise." We warned you. Although perhaps there might be one of you out there interested in the effects of garlic on medicinal leeches.

http://www.garlicpage.com/

Mann's Broccoli Table of Contents

From seed to your dinner plate, follow the virtual path of broccoli, the healthy dark green vegetable! In the Kid's Club you can play some neat games (none involving broccoli, crown jewel of nutrition), but you'll have to visit the Mann's Farm section to learn that broccoli has as much calcium per ounce as milk! You can also get some vegetable clip art and recipes at this leafy green site.

http://www.broccoli.com/

MEAT, POULTRY, FISH, DRY BEANS, EGGS, AND NUTS

Butterball

Which do you prefer: light or dark meat? ("Hey!" says the turkey, "It's all the same meat to me!") Not only is turkey a very popular food during the holiday season, it's also a great meal any time of the year. ("Yeah, well so is vegetarian pizza!") Turkey is great, because after the first meal, the leftovers are good for a zillion sandwiches and a delicious soup. ("Ever heard of falafel, pita, and hummus?") At this page, you will find great stuffing recipes, gravy recipes, carving tips, and creative garnishing ideas. ("I'm outta here!")

http://www.butterball.com/

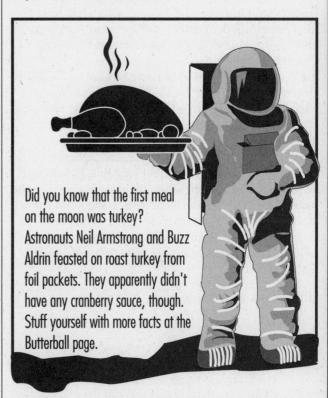

Did you know that the first meal on the moon was turkey? Astronauts Neil Armstrong and Buzz Aldrin feasted on roast turkey from foil packets. They apparently didn't have any cranberry sauce, though. Stuff yourself with more facts at the Butterball page.

Canadian Egg Marketing Agency

We could say this page is *eggciting*. We could say it's *eggzactly* what you're looking for. We don't think that would be an *eggzageration*. Here's an *eggzample* of what you'll find: egg nutrition, egg recipes, information on egg farming, grading eggs, and lots of *eggtivities*. We *eggspect* you'll have fun here!

http://www.canadaegg.ca/

A
B
C
D
E
F
G
H
I
J
K
L
M
N
O
P
Q
R
S
T
U
V
W
X
Y
Z

A
B
C
D
E
F
G
H
I
J
K
L
M
N
O
P
Q
R
S
T
U
V
W
X
Y
Z

Food Fun for Kids

Everything you ever wanted to know about pork, but were afraid to ask Mom, is here. Get some free recipes sent to you by mail (go to "You're Invited" to get these freebies). While you're at this site, look around at all the recipes and pictures. Yum!

http://www.nppc.org/foodfun.html

Oscar Mayer® Virtual Lunchbox: Home

If you wish you were an Oscar Mayer wiener, you'll want to spend a lot of time at this site. There are the usual recipes, contests, and company jabbering, but what caught our eye was the interactive History of the Wienermobile. With or without Real Audio, it's hot! The first hot dog on wheels toured the streets of Chicago in 1936. It was only 13 feet long. By the 1950s, the Wienermobile had grown to 22 feet. It had a sound system and a sunroof. By 1958, though, it finally got what it had been lacking all these years. No, it wasn't mustard—it was a bun! Six "Wienebagos" were touring the world by 1988, with the comforts of onboard microwave ovens and other conveniences. In 1995, the latest model is 27 feet long and 10 feet high. We cannot do any better than to quote from the home page: "The model underwent tests in the wind tunnel at the California Institute of Technology in Pasadena and could really, theoretically speaking, haul buns as it reached speeds in excess of 90 miles per hour." Hot dog!

http://www.oscar-mayer.com/

Peanut Butter Lovers Club

Did you know that about one-third of the U.S. peanut crop goes toward making that famous American staple: peanut butter? Runner peanuts, grown primarily in Georgia, Alabama, and Florida are the preferred type to use. This is because they are uniform in size and it's easier to get them all evenly roasted. At this site you can find out how peanut butter is made, discover how nutritious peanut butter is, and play a fun trivia game.

http://www.peanutbutterlovers.com/index.html

MILK, YOGURT, AND CHEESE
CheeseNet

You can slice it, grate it, melt it, and of course you can eat it. What's your favorite way to eat cheese? How is cheese made? Read about the cheese making process, or tour the cheese picture gallery. Read about the differences among cheeses around the world. If you have questions, you can send them to "cheeseologist Dr. Emory K. Cheese" in the Ask Dr. Cheese section. You might be amused by the cheese poetry, then again, maybe not.

http://www.wgx.com/cheesenet/

Milk - it's on everybody's lips!

Who should be the next celebrity pictured with a milk mustache? How many milk facts do you know? Check in with the Milk Mystic (is he a dumb computer or an annoying human?), then head into the Taste Buds department to find the recipe for Peanut Butter Cup Milk. Yum!

http://www.whymilk.com/

Tours - #1 The Story of Milk

Cows make milk to feed their baby calves. But after the baby is eating other food, the cow continues to make up to eight gallons of milk a day! Cows are milked in a special room called a milking parlor, and their milk is pumped to stainless steel holding tanks and immediately chilled to 38 degrees. It waits until the milk tanker truck comes to pick it up. This happens twice a day. When it gets to the milk processing facility, the milk goes through two other steps, homogenization and pasteurization, but you'll have to read about those at this Web site. The main level has cow-related Shockwave games and other fun.

http://www.moomilk.com/tours/tour1-0.htm

> ## The Web in Pig Latin? Make it so in LANGUAGES.

NUTRITION

10 Tips to Healthy Eating and Physical Activity

Is a big, gooey, pepperoni pizza part of a healthy diet? For pizza lovers, thank goodness, it is! According to the International Food Information Council Foundation, pizza can be used with other foods to keep you healthy. And the ten tips are only the beginning. You'll also learn how to evaluate food advertising, so you won't be fooled into eating the prize and playing with the cereal.

http://ificinfo.health.org/brochure/10TIPKID.HTM

Dairy Council of Wisconsin Nutrition Activities

This is a great site to get "blackline masters" to hand around in class. You'll find material on the Food Pyramid, Lunch in Any Language, Breakfast Around the World, and Nutritious Nibbles. There are also some very tasty links to other nutrition sites on the Net.

http://www.DCWnet.org/nutritionactivities.html

Food and Fitness

This wonderful site is part of Kids Health, one of Net-mom's favorites. Sure, you'll find recipes here, but you'll also discover what vitamins and minerals do, how to eat to play your best at sports, and why water is the beverage of choice when it comes to quenching your thirst.

http://kidshealth.org/kid/food/

The Food Zone

This site is really for eighth through twelfth grade, but we're listing it because we believe you'll be able to enjoy it even if you don't do all the science experiments. Find out how nutrition happens at the cellular level, learn about food chemistry, and delve into the mysterious realm of digestion.

http://kauai.cudenver.edu:3010/

Healthy Choices for Kids Online

Produced by the growers of Washington state apples, this site offers stories, plays, and lesson plans about the food groups. You'll learn about choosing healthy snacks plus find lots of tips for healthy eating.

http://www.healthychoices.org/

Kids Food Cyberclub

You already know your body needs food to keep you healthy, but do you have a good idea about which foods are best for you? Take the nutrition quiz and then see if you can put the Food Pyramid together. Remember: junk food is not a food group!

http://www.kidsfood.org/kf_cyber.html

Nutrition Cafe

Try the Grab a Grape game to see how you'll do playing nutrition Jeopardy. Then try to pick a good breakfast, lunch, or dinner in the Have-A-Bite Cafe. This site is a joint project of the Pacific Science Center and the Washington State Dairy Council.

http://www.exhibits.pacsci.org/nutrition/

Nutrition On the Web

Written by teens for other teens, this site was an award-winner in the ThinkQuest competition. The site is in Spanish, German, and English. It has two parts, the Informative section and the Interactive section. In the first part, you'll read some nutrition horror stories, find out what makes up a good diet, and explore some myths. For example, some kids believe that eating a vegetarian diet is always more healthy. The fact is that "vegetarian diets, which contain absolutely no animal products, are very low in vitamin B12 and, unless carefully planned, may be deficient in vitamin B6, riboflavin, calcium, iron, and zinc. Strict macrobiotic diets, which include everything except grains, are extremely hazardous. More moderate vegetarian diets that include milk and eggs and perhaps fish, and/or poultry, meet the nutritional needs of growing teenagers if carefully planned. This is why many adolescents that are vegetarians are also anemic." The interactive section of this resource asks you to input your weight, height, and age, and it will tell you how many calories you need to eat per day to maintain your weight. There's also a diet planner, a nutrition database, and more! Some things require an account (free!), but you don't have to give your real name.

http://library.advanced.org/10991/

A
B
C
D
E
F
G
H
I
J
K
L
M
N
O
P
Q
R
S
T
U
V
W
X
Y
Z

A
B
C
D
E
F
G
H
I
J
K
L
M
N
O
P
Q
R
S
T
U
V
W
X
Y
Z

RECIPES

Parents: We get so many requests for recipes, we're including a few large sites. However, be advised they may contain links or recipes involving alcohol as an ingredient. You may want to stick to the COOKING FOR BEGINNERS section.

Cookie Recipe .com | Cookie Recipes

What's your favorite kind of cookie? Chocolate chip? Sugar or sugar-free? Peanut butter? Or do you prefer those luscious holiday cookies, or filled cookies, or no-bake cookies, or maybe some international recipes? The cookie of your dreams is here. Take a bite.

http://www.cookierecipe.com/

CopyKat Recipes [Main Page]

If you can't get enough of trademarked foods, such as Cinnabon cinnamon rolls, or Red Lobster Cheese Biscuits, or even Girl Scout Thin Mints cookies—try using these copycat recipes. Fans say a lot of them are pretty close to the originals! A similar site you might try is called Top Secret Recipes on the Web at <http://www.topsecretrecipes.com/>, but it is extensive so please explore with a parent.

http://www.copykat.com/

The Dinner Co-op Home Page: for cooks and food-lovers

What's Dad making for dinner? The next time he has no idea, help him try the links on this page. For one thing, there are recipes—LOTS of recipes! We haven't checked all the links, but this site certainly has some interesting stuff. For example, can the color of food suppress your appetite? Have you ever noticed that besides blueberries, no blue food exists in nature? Our brains are just not keyed into seeing a blue thing as a food source. If you want to eat less, put a blue light in your dining room or eat from a blue plate.

http://dinnercoop.cs.cmu.edu/dinnercoop/
home-page.html

EPICURIOUS FOOD: RECIPE FILE

If you're looking for a recipe from another country, search here for some delicious meal suggestions. Click on "Cuisine" and select from 15 choices, including African, Caribbean, Greek, Indian, and others. You can even choose to find recipes that match what's in your pantry!

http://food.epicurious.com/e_eating/e02_recipes/
recipes.html

EXPO Restaurant Le Cordon Bleu

Are you hankering for some French cooking? Do you want to try some recipes for true gourmet chefs? These recipes are for expert cooks, so don't ask your parents to help you whip up some *Feuilletés de Saumon aux Asperges* after they've just come home from a hard day at the office. These recipes are for special days when everyone is ready for a treat. The site includes recipes for seven special days of cooking. Imagine, a whole week of French food. *Bon appétit*!

http://sunsite.unc.edu/expo/restaurant/restaurant.html

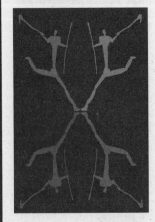

Some early scientists thought they grew from seeds dropped by stars. Others were sure these objects were carved from stone by ancient, forgotten artists. What are they?

Answer: Fossils. *You can even make your own fossils using the handy recipe at this site. First you take a dead insect, follow the simple instructions, and wait about 400 million years. Check http://www.fmnh.org/exhibits/ttr/TTT1b.html for an explanation.*

Hawaii's Favorite Recipes

Come tune into Aunty Leilani's Cooking Show and find recipes for tasty Hawaiian dishes. Check out the Internet Island Fruit Salad or the Pineapple Cream Cheese Pie. Although it is more fun to cook these recipes while wearing a traditional Hawaiian print shirt, a lei, sandals, and a straw hat, the results are just as good if you don't. Be sure to drop in and get your name in Hawaiian here, too!

http://www.hisurf.com/Recipes.html

HomeArts: Eats

Who doesn't like food? When you think about food, do you think about what is on the plate or how it got there? This site puts together information about food, collected from *Redbook, Good Housekeeping, Country Living,* and other great sources of food news. There are tons of hints on cooking and food preparation for you to explore.

http://homearts.com/depts/food/00dpfdc1.htm

Mama's Cookbook

Do you want to be a great cook? Mama's Italian cookbook is a great place to start! It has recipes for all your favorite Italian meals, plus cooking and pasta glossaries for beginners. If you're not sure which one you want, you can let Mama pick "one of her favorites." There is also a searchable database of recipes if you know what you want and don't want to hunt through the list to find it.

http://www.eat.com/cookbook/

Pearl's - Food Glossary

Have you ever read a recipe in a cookbook and come across an ingredient that's unfamiliar? This site is a collection of terms to make reading recipes easier. From "abalone" to "Zuppa Inglese," the glossary provides mouth-watering definitions. The terms cover all types of food from all walks of life. There are recipes for every meal of the day and every course of the meal, plus some delightful extras. Check your knowledge against the glossary, but be warned: Don't do it on an empty stomach.

http://www.foodstuff.com/cgi-bin/gloss.cfm?alpha=A

The Pie Page

When is the best time for pie? If you answered, "Anytime!" you are definitely going to enjoy this site, which has recipes for all of your favorite dessert pies and even one for venison pie...mmmm. Seriously, you'll find tips for better pie making here. There's also a step-by-step tutorial on how to make a perfect pie crust.

http://www.teleport.com/~psyched/pie/pie.html

Yum, everyone likes pie! Did you know that a glass pie plate is the best kind to use when you're baking one? Find out more at The Pie Page.

Recipes for Traditional Food in Slovenia

Can you point to Slovenia on the world map? Can you name any Slovenian foods? Get with the program! Check out the recipes for traditional food in Slovenia. There are pictures of the foods and downloadable sound files of the names for many of the dishes. You'll find recipes for all kinds of foods, including a wonderful spring soup and a delicious fish stew.

http://www.ijs.si/slo/country/food/recipes/

Catch a ride on
a Carousel
in AMUSEMENT PARKS.

A
B
C
D
E
F
G
H
I
J
K
L
M
N
O
P
Q
R
S
T
U
V
W
X
Y
Z

Curl up with a good URL in BOOKS AND LITERATURE!

Rolling Your Own Sushi

Do you know how to eat with chopsticks? If not, don't worry—sushi is a wonderful finger food. Sushi is a Japanese delicacy that is fun and relatively easy to make. A common misunderstanding about sushi is that it is raw seafood. There is a form of sushi called *sashimi*, which does have raw seafood, but this is different than sushi. Sushi is delicious and (don't tell your parents) it's good for you. Warning: Making sushi involves the use of a sharp knife; be sure to let your parents help you prepare your sushi.

http://www.rain.org/~hutch/sushi.html

What are the ingredients for a California Roll?

If you said imitation crab, avocado, cucumber, rice, and nori (toasted seaweed sheets), you'd be a winner! Find out all about Rolling Your Own Sushi.

WELCOME TO Epicurious

You still can't find that extra-special recipe for your doll's dinner party? The publishers of *Bon Appetit* and *Gourmet* magazines give you recipes and a restaurant forum, and they share tips on how to make being in the kitchen a rewarding experience. Check the recipe file and search the forum to locate those hard-to-find holiday cookies. Get basic cookery tips from the original *Fannie Farmer* cookbook!

http://www.epicurious.com/

RECIPES—SPECIAL DIETS

Asian Kashrus Recipes

Cooking Kosher is a very precise and delicate operation. Finding recipes can be a tedious task. With this collection of Asian Kosher recipes, the job is made easy. There are dozens of recipes for cooking food in a variety of cuisine. Thai, Chinese, and Vietnamese are just a few of the delicious styles listed.

http://www.kashrus.org/recipes/recipes.html

Low-Fat Lifestyle Forum Home Page

Do you hate to eat food that is classified as good for you? The truth of the matter is that "good for you" isn't all liver and spinach. There are a lot of arguments about what "healthy eating" means, but most agree that a low-fat lifestyle is best. This site has cooking and eating tips, as well as recommended cookbooks and loads of easy recipes.

http://www.wctravel.com/lowfat/

Nancy's Kitchen

This is a nifty jumping-off spot for loads of special recipes for folks on low-fat, low-carbohydrate, diabetic, or other diets. There are also links to favorite recipes from state governors and U.S. Congress members, among other fascinating diversions.

http://members.amaonline.com/nrogers/Kitchen/
   index.html

What is the *green flash?*

http://mintaka.sdsu.edu/GF/

Answer: No, it's not a new superhero! It's the atmospheric effect seen when the sun's first rays rise above or set below the horizon. The first (or last) sliver of sun is colored bluish-green. The scientific explanation for this is complex. Read about it at

The Vegetarian Society of the United Kingdom - Home Page

Ewwww! Do you dread being told to eat your veggies? Do Brussels sprouts make you hide in the closet? Vegetarian cooking doesn't have to mean tons of icky green food. The Vegetarian Society of the United Kingdom has assembled a list of tasty recipes for every meal, from breakfast to dessert. These pages are also loaded with important facts about nutrition. You'll find some animal rights information here too.

http://www.vegsoc.org/

How many onions should you put in an asparagus and peanut strudel?

One (yum!). Find out about this and other delicious vegetarian recipes at The Vegetarian Society UK.

SWEETS

Ben & Jerry's Ice Cream, Frozen Yogurt and Sorbet HomePage

Admit it. How many times have you run to the grocery store because you needed a Ben & Jerry ice cream cone? Now you can get it here without leaving your seat. If you love their ice cream, you will love their site. It's chock-full of the philosophy and wit that makes them so popular. Find out who these guys are, and play with their fun stuff. If you still grieve over the discontinuation of your favorite flavor, make sure to visit the flavor graveyard and find peace of mind knowing that at least they have gone to the great Web page on the Net. If you get a craving for the real thing, don't even try to lick the screen—just go to the store like everyone else. Funny thing, though. They make over 50 products, but only 34 of them are available in supermarkets. For the rest, you have to go to one of their Scoop Shops. Their hottest ice cream flavor is Chocolate Chip Cookie Dough! Run to the store right now to try their newest flavor: DILBERT'S WORLD™ Totally Nuts™ Ice Cream!

http://www.benjerry.com/

What can you get from one bushel of corn?

http://www.ohiocorn.org/usage/bushel.htm

Answer: A backache, if you try to lift it by yourself! A bushel of corn weighs about 56 pounds and contains approximately 72,800 kernels. Most of the weight is the starch, oil, protein, and fiber, along with some natural moisture. From that one bushel you could make: 32 pounds of cornstarch or 33 pounds of corn sweetener or 2.5 gallons of fuel ethanol, plus 11.4 pounds of 20 percent gluten feed, 3 pounds of 60 percent gluten meal, and 1.6 pounds of corn oil! You'll find this answer at

A
B
C
D
E
F
G
H
I
J
K
L
M
N
O
P
Q
R
S
T
U
V
W
X
Y
Z

A
B
C
D
E
F
G
H
I
J
K
L
M
N
O
P
Q
R
S
T
U
V
W
X
Y
Z

DINOSAURS are prehistoric, but they are under "D."

Candy USA

If you eat all that good, healthy food Mom gives you, maybe she'll let you have a treat for dessert. Until then, visit this site, where you'll learn a lot about candy and chocolate. There are candy statistics, nutritional info, candy in the news, and even candy contests! According to this site, "The best-selling kids' candy these days is anything an adult wouldn't normally choose to eat: super sour suckers, candies that color the mouth, anything blue raspberry-flavored, and anything with 'gross out' appeal." Is that true for you and your friends?

http://www.candyusa.org/

Godiva Chocolatier

See how sweet life can be. Godiva Chocolate welcomes you to their playground for chocolate lovers. They tempt your palate with chocolate recipes, trivia, and an online catalog for instant gratification. If only the Web would implement those aroma attribute protocols! You will never forget another anniversary or birthday if you register with their free gift reminder service. If that still isn't enough, they have plenty of links to other chocolate sites to help satisfy your cravings.

http://www2.godiva.com/

Hershey Foods Homepage

Crunchy, creamy, drippy like hot fudge or steaming like cocoa—what could be more delicious than chocolate? Where do they make chocolate? Lots of places, but one of them is in Hershey, Pennsylvania, at Hershey's Chocolate Town, U.S.A. This site has fun facts about chocolate at <http://www.hersheys.com/~hershey/hcna/facts/> and a tour of the largest chocolate factory in the world at <http://www.hersheys.com/~hershey/tour/plant.index.html>. This site offers a text-only option for those with slower connections.

http://www.hersheys.com/~hershey/

JELL-O: 100 Years and Still the Coolest

Wow—in a year 413,997,403 million packages of Jell-O gelatin dessert are produced. If you laid the boxes end to end, they would stretch three-fifths of the way around the globe with plenty of room to spare! This site traces the cool history of America's favorite dessert and also offers recipes as well as a place to buy special molds online.

http://www.kraftfoods.com/jell-o/history/

M&M's ® Factory

When you eat M&M's, which colors do you eat first? Which colors do you avoid? Take a tour of the M&M factory, and play some funny Shockwave games like "Melt the Candy Bar." If you don't have Shockwave, just download the games (Windows or Mac) for use later. Remember, virtual M&M's don't melt in your hand *or* your mouth, but you'll be hungry for some serious chocolate after you visit this site! You can also get screen savers and wallpaper to make sure there is always chocolate in the house when you want some.

http://www.m-ms.com/factory/

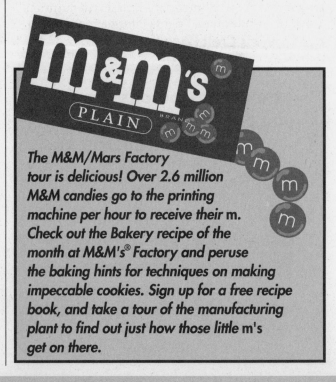

The M&M/Mars Factory tour is delicious! Over 2.6 million M&M candies go to the printing machine per hour to receive their m. Check out the Bakery recipe of the month at M&M's® Factory and peruse the baking hints for techniques on making impeccable cookies. Sign up for a free recipe book, and take a tour of the manufacturing plant to find out just how those little m's get on there.

Nabisco: America's Favorite Food Company!

Are you a twister or a dunker? Any way you eat Oreos, they are America's favorite sandwich cookie treat! Discover the stories behind how your favorite snacks came to be—like Fig Newtons, Barnum's Animal Crackers, and Chips Ahoy cookies. Nabisco also offers a section for healthy living, cooking tips, and recipes, and they challenge you to lots of fun games, including finding the Nabisco antenna-thing in *Where's Waldo?*–type crowd pictures.

http://www.nabisco.com/

Planet Twinkie

How do you feel about Twinkies—you know, those delectable cream-filled sponge cakes? Most people either love them or hate them, but they must be doing something right because millions are sold each year! Here you'll find a whole "planet" dedicated to this snack food, including games about Twinkies, Web sites about Twinkies, and even wacky scientific experimentation with, you guessed it: Twinkies!

http://www.twinkies.com/

CRAFTS AND HOBBIES

Aunt Annie's Craft Page (tm)

She won't pinch your cheeks and talk about how much you've grown! Aunt Annie *will* give you ideas, patterns, and great directions for making interesting crafts. She has a new project for you each week, and it's not the usual "handprint-in-the-plaster" craft. Many are paper crafts, like table decorations, paper hats, or toys. Lots of creative links, too. Who could ask for a cooler aunt? Try her link to the Craft Exchange for lots more project ideas at *<http://www.geocities.com/ EnchantedForest/3053/exchange/>*.

http://www.auntannie.com/

Fetch some fascinating info in DOGS AND DOG SPORTS.

CraftNet Village FREE projects

Whether it's tips on "scrapbooking," making cards with rubber stamps, or just general crafts, there will be something that interests you in the many project libraries here. In the Kid's Crafts library, we especially liked the spider made from an old tuna fish can and the scale model of the solar system made from Styrofoam.

http://www.craftnet.org/projects/

IDEA BOX- Early Childhood Education and Activity Resources

There is a wealth of craft ideas here for kids of all ages. They have everything from holiday crafts to bean bags to finger puppets to...well, you get the idea we like this site!

http://www.the ideabox.com/

Michaels Kids Club Online

Michaels is a huge craft store, and they are always dreaming up new ways for you to use their materials. At their Web site, though, you are just using recycled electrons, and there is never a mess to clean up. Don't miss the make-and-decorate-it-yourself gingerbread architecture game—we played with it for a long time, but then we got hungry and had to stop.

http://www.michaels.com/kids/kid-main.html

Minnetonka Science Center - Ooey Gooey Recipes

If you want to make your own slime, gak, play dough, sparkly paint—or any other messy stuff that's too much fun, you should check the recipes here. If you try the Singing Cake, let us know how it *tunes* out.

http://www.minnetonka.k12.mn.us/support/science/ tools/ooey.html

Nikolai's Web Site

Lots of creative stuff to do here! Make finger puppets, print out and build a town or a circus, cook easy recipes, dress paper dolls, read stories. Watch out for pirates!

http://www.nikolai.com/nnn.htm

A B C D E F G H I J K L M N O P Q R S T U V W X Y Z

A
B
C
D
E
F
G
H
I
J
K
L
M
N
O
P
Q
R
S
T
U
V
W
X
Y
Z

You Can Make Paper

Have you ever seen homemade paper? The rough, uneven edge (called a deckle) gives it that homemade look. You can recycle old newspaper or other printed materials into paper pulp. You can even throw in a bit of yucca, lawn grass, flowers, or other plants. Then make your own homemade, natural paper. Try it here!

http://www.beakman.com/paper/paper.html

NEEDLECRAFT AND SEWING

How to X-Stitch

Type in your name, and this site will generate a free pattern for you in Celtic-style letters. There is also a brief tutorial with animated stitches, which will show you where to put the needle in your cross-stitch canvas. This site is one of the incredible links on 2 Busy Stitching at *<http://www.2busystitching.com/links.htm>*, which we also recommend.

http://www.ils.ie/celtic/learnhow.html

The Needlework Gazette's Wonderful Stitches: Celebrating Decorative Stitch

Are you hooked on cross-stitch or needlepoint? If the answer is yes, then this site is guaranteed to keep you in stitches. Check out what other stitchery enthusiasts have been creating with their busy fingers, then try out some of the decorative stitches featured in the monthly sampler. If you are in need of supplies or want to join a needlework group, put down your needle and look here!

http://www.needlework.com/

Welcome to the World Wide Quilting Page

Who would be crazy enough to take something whole, cut it up into a lot of little pieces, and then sew it all back together again? Quilters! What they end up with usually looks pretty spectacular—unless you are the person who created the winning quilt in the Worst Quilt in the World Contest (see it here!).

http://quilt.com/MainQuiltingPage.html

ORIGAMI

See also PEACE

Arts & Crafts Class

Origami is the Japanese art of paper folding. The word literally means "to fold" (*oru*) "paper" (*kami*). Find a few sheets of square paper, and you can get started with some easy paper-folding projects. Here's an origami crane and a *yakko* (yes, a *yakko* and that's not someone who talks too much!). This site provides graphics and helpful instructions to show you how to fold them.

http://sequoia.nttam.com/KIDS/SCHOOL/ART/

Joseph Wu's Origami Page

You don't care if you ever see another folded paper crane in your life! OK, relax, you don't have to fold any more cranes. Now you're ready for some intermediate and advanced origami projects. From this page you can download incredible diagrams and instructions for a windmill, butterfly, or basket, among other things!

http://www.origami.vancouver.bc.ca/

OrigamiUSA Home Page

Looking for a good pattern for an origami pterodactyl? Search through the database of patterns for all manner of birds, beasts, and flowers! There are also diagrams, videos and puzzling things to fold for young and old alike.

http://www.origami-usa.org/

PAPER AIRPLANES

DSW Games

"Next time someone tells you to go fly a kite, you can fly a paper airplane instead!" This graphically amusing site gives you two airplane templates to print out and fold, "guaranteed to make you the Red Baron of the office!" You may need a paper clip and some tape to help trim your flyer, too.

http://www.dsw.com/airplane.htm

kenblackburn's Home Page

Until recently, Ken had the Guinness World Record for longest flight of a paper airplane. However, some upstarts have just surpassed his record by a few seconds. Ken's going to try and beat them. Why not? He's an expert! He's the author of *The World Record Paper Airplane Book*, the *Kids Paper Airplane Book*, and the *1998 Paper Airplane Calendar*. His Web site offers lots of material to help your airplanes fly faster, higher, and longer, too.

http://www.geocities.com/CapeCanaveral/1817/

Paper Airplane Hangar Page

This site is the ultimate locale for learning about, building, and—best of all—flying paper airplanes! You'll find step-by-step instructions, safety tips, and of course, LINKS!

http://www.tycs.demon.co.uk/planes/

CREATION STUDIES

Creation Science

How did life on Earth begin? Some scientists believe life evolved over millions of years. Others believe there are some real problems with the theory of evolution. For instance, how did life originate from dead chemicals? How could man have come from the apes? To see the arguments against the theory of evolution, go to this site.

http://emporium.turnpike.net/C/cs/

THEORY OF EVOLUTION vs. CREATION SCIENCE

Have you ever thought about how Earth began? Or how all the plants and animals came to be? Creation scientists are those who believe that it all came about as described in the Bible. To help form your own theories, investigate this page from a larger site. Parents, please preview this site.

http://www.religioustolerance.org/evolutio.htm

CULTURAL DIVERSITY

Guide to Museums and Cultural Resources

The Natural History Museum of Los Angeles County invites you to take a virtual tour of all the continents (including Antarctica) and explore museums in each. You may peek inside the Wool Museum in Australia, check out the Information Highway exhibit in Canada, or visit an art museum in Singapore. This will give you a good idea of how many different cultures are in the world and an understanding of what each has to teach.

http://www.lam.mus.ca.us/webmuseums/

NET FILES

There are 29,000 plastic bathtub ducks afloat on the Pacific Ocean.
How did they get there and where are they going?

Answer: The ducks were originally safely packed in shipping containers, on their way from China to Tacoma, Washington. There was a fierce storm on January 10, 1992, and many containers went overboard, including the one with the quackers. When it burst open, the ducks became a science experiment to track sea currents. Computer models believe some may make it to the Washington coast. Others will turn up in Hawaii, while others may make it through the polar ice pack to reach Europe. If you find a plastic duck on the beach, inform the folks at *http://www.yoto98.noaa.gov/books/puffy/page2.html*

OPTICAL ILLUSIONS: now you see them, now you don't!

Multicultural Home Page

This site offers just what it says: a sampling of different cultures from all around the world. Hear Chinese folk music, or learn more about the history of the Canadian fur trade, or read details about historic Canadian women. How about a recipe for *brigadeiro* (a delicious Brazilian dessert) or a visit to the Taj Mahal in India? Not every country is listed here, but you'll find a good selection of diverse cultures from around the world, each listed with a color picture of the country's flag. If you haven't found the information you are looking for somewhere else, check out this site compiled by Purdue University.

http://pasture.ecn.purdue.edu/~agenhtml/agenmc/

The Web of Culture

From this site you can explore world religions, currencies, recipes, holidays, headlines, embassies, and the etiquette of body language, or gestures. There are also contests and chat sessions with people from other countries. The whole idea of this site is to help us to learn about other cultures from the folks who know them best.

http://www.worldculture.com/

CURIOSITIES AND WONDERS

Birthstones

Did you know that if you were born in April, your lucky birthstone is the diamond? To find out more about various gemstones and their properties, check this site!

http://mineral.galleries.com/minerals/birthsto.htm

The Jackalope Page

Have you ever seen something that looks like a rabbit with antlers? Chances are good that you've never seen such a beast! Do they really exist? Some kids in Wyoming have put together some information on jackalopes, so check it out and see what you think! (Here's a hint, though: You can only hunt jackalopes on June 31.)

http://monhome.sw2.k12.wy.us/projects/ jackalope.html

The Notorious Spam Cam

Spam is a registered trademark of a fine product manufactured by the Hormel company. Every month or so, some people with too much time on their hands take out some Spam and put it on a plate with other food items. Then they leave this plate out to decompose. Every afternoon they take another picture of the plate and put it up on the Web. By the 25th day or so things look pretty gruesome. Molds of all colors, fungus, even some things science has not identified yet—this is what you're likely to see as the days lurch on. Don't let your baby sister watch. Please.

http://www.fright.com/cgi-bin/spamcam/

The Seven Wonders of the Ancient World

Everyone's heard about them, but who can name them? Well, there are the Pyramids, of course, and uh…hmmm. Luckily, there is a list of all of them here, along with pictures and links. Since there are not many of the ancient wonders of the world around anymore, you'll also find a list of the Modern Wonders of the World, as well as the Natural Wonders of the World. There are also pictures and links for wonders such as these: the Great Wall of China, Victoria Falls, and the Eiffel Tower.

http://pharos.bu.edu/Egypt/Wonders/

Be an angel and check what we've found in RELIGION.

DANCE

C. K. Ladzekpo - African Music and Dance

"The Africans Are Coming, The Africans Are Coming" is the largest seasonal, professional African cultural arts extravaganza in the U.S. Directed by C. K. Ladzekpo, the African Dance Ensemble has been performing since 1973 and continues to stand for tradition and creativity. Dance, especially ethnic dance, is characterized by music, costume, and tradition, and you'll find all of that here! Lots of video (and audio) clips feature the colorful and vibrant dance and percussion ensemble music of West Africa.

http://cnmat.cnmat.berkeley.EDU/~ladzekpo/

Cajun/Zydeco Music & Dance

Cajun two-step dancing is hotter than pepper sauce! You can explore the links here to find out basic and advanced moves. There are sources of online Cajun music, links to sites about Louisiana culture, and more! Parental advisory: Off-site links have not been viewed.

http://www.bme.jhu.edu/~jrice/cz.html

NET FILES

The Riddle of the Sphinx was this:

"What goes on four feet, on two feet, and three, But the more feet it goes on, the weaker it be?"

What is the answer?

Answer: The riddle's answer is MAN! He crawls (four feet) as a baby, walks (two feet) as an adult, and uses a cane (three feet) when older. You can read more about the riddling Greek Sphinx at http://www.quinion.demon.co.uk/words/gry.htm (This Greek Sphinx was a sea monster, while the more familiar Egyptian Sphinx was half human, half lion.)

Dance UK - Home Page

Try to keep your feet still while you explore this page—we dare you! You'll find links to ballroom dancing, square dancing, round dancing, and contra dancing. Try a Highland fling or maybe a samba. Dance your way through cyberspace, and start by pointing your mouse here.

http://www.dance.co.uk/

Dancescape™ Ballroom Dancing and Dance Sport Index

In 1997, the International Olympic Committee (IOC) announced that it had granted outright recognition to the International Dance Sport Federation (IDSF) as a "recognized federation" and full member of the IOC. This is the first step to making competitive ballroom dancing an Olympic sport, possibly as early as 2008. According to this site, "DanceSport Championships are held in four different disciplines:

STANDARD comprises the Waltz, Tango, Viennese Waltz, Slow Foxtrot, and Quickstep.

LATIN AMERICAN comprises the Samba, Cha Cha, Rumba, Paso Doble, and Jive.

TEN DANCE is all of the above, performed at a one-day event.

FORMATION features eight couples dancing in either the Standard or the Latin American discipline."

At this site you can find out who's dancing where and what's shakin' in the world of competitive ballroom dancing. There are also sections on the history of each dance.

http://www.dancescape.com/info/

Dancing for Busy People Home Page

You may have heard of square dancing, but how good is your round dance? When someone yells, "Hey, how about a Sicilian circle!" do you jump on the dance floor, ready to go? Whether your mescolanza needs a makeover or your line dance needs to be straightened, visit this site to get an encyclopedia of popular community dances, instructions, and links to other featured Web sites!

http://www.henge.com/~calvin/

B
C
D
E
F
G
H
I
J
K
L
M
N
O
P
Q
R
S
T
U
V
W
X
Y
Z

Visit the BRIDGES of Internet County in ARCHITECTURE!

Riverdance - The Official Website

Riverdance has become its own phenomenon, and through it, Irish music and dancing have gained new popularity worldwide. Read the story behind the musical, and experience a virtual "day in the life" of a *Riverdance* troupe as it prepares for another show. No detail is left to chance, even in rehearsal. There are also brief audio and video clips for you to download.

http://www.riverdance.ie/

Stomp

Oh, man! Your parents are dragging you to see some stage show at the theater, and you think you'll be bored. All of a sudden, some guys come out on stage banging on trash cans and pipes, dancing a rhythm with push brooms, and in general making so much noise that no one hears you when you yell, "Hey! Who *are* these guys?" You've just been introduced to STOMP, the hot dance show from the British Isles. This Web page lets you hear some fantastic beats created with everyday materials, and if you go to the study area of this site you'll find some sound and noise experiments that you can try at home.

http://www.usinteractive.com/stomp/

The US Swing Dance Server

Swing dancing has gotten hot! If you're a little confused by the names of the dances—lindy hop, West Coast swing, and the hustle—just triple-step in here. There are instructions, videos, an events calendar, and links.

http://simon.cs.cornell.edu/Info/People/aswin/
SwingDancing/

BALLET

Body and Grace

Here you can learn about the history of the American Ballet Theatre (ABT) through photographer Nancy Ellison's electronic exhibition, "Body and Grace." This is a wonderful collection of photos, which starts with the ABT's beginning in 1940 and includes such historical greats as Agnes de Mille, as well as portraits of the current ABT hierarchy: principals, soloists, and corps de ballet.

http://www.i3tele.com/photo_perspectives_museum/
faces/bodyandgrace/html/abt.html

NET FILES

You're at a picnic, and boy is it hot! You want a can of soda, so you go to the ice chest to get one. All the ice has melted, and the cans are in cold water. You notice all the diet soda is floating, while the stuff with real sugar in it has sunk to the bottom.

Why is that?

Answer: Although both cans are the same size and hold the same amount of soda, they don't weigh the same. The extra sugar in the regular soda makes it weigh more, so it sinks to the bottom. This property is called density, and chemists use it to identify various substances. You know that a glass of chocolate milkshake with ice cream is denser than a glass of chocolate milk. Density is the amount of mass in a certain volume. You can learn more and try some cool experiments at http://www.sci.mus.mn.us/sln/tf/d/density/density.html

CyberDance — Ballet On The Net - Home Page

If ballet is your life, you may want to take a break from your barre exercises long enough to check out this wonderful collection of U.S. and Canadian classical and modern ballet resources. Included is a complete list of professional, regional, and school-affiliated ballet companies. You'll find their addresses and phone numbers, ticketing information, and their touring schedules. The link to the Boston Ballet, among others, even includes a spotlight on their solo and principal dancers. Find out what motivates 20-year-old Pollyana Ribeiro to keep trying new things. It doesn't stop there: you'll find articles, reviews, FAQs, e-zines, and lots of great links, including one to the New York Public Library, which boasts the best dance collection in the world!

http://www.thepoint.net/~raw/dance.htm

Arthur Mitchell

made history as the first African American male to become a permanent member of a major ballet company when he joined the New York City Ballet in 1955. His talents helped him rise quickly to the position of principal dancer. When Dr. Martin Luther King, Jr. was killed in 1968, Mitchell decided to do something to provide children in Harlem (in New York City) with the kinds of opportunities he had been given. That same summer, he began giving dance classes in a remodeled garage. The next year, he founded the Dance Theatre of Harlem. Now, this world-renowned organization has grown into a multicultural facility, serving students and dancers from the United States as well as from around the world. Learn more about this dance company, and others, at CyberDance —Ballet on the Net-Home Page.

WebMuseum: Degas, Edgar

Edgar Degas was a French Impressionist painter in the late 1800s, and he's acknowledged as a master of drawing the human figure in motion. What better subject for his paintings than the ballet dancer? This special Degas exhibit includes works from the Fogg Museum in Cambridge, Massachusetts, the Metropolitan Museum of Art in New York, the National Gallery in Washington, D.C., and the Musée d'Orsay in Paris. Come browse and enjoy these wonderful pastel drawings and oil paintings portraying the grace and form of ballet dancers on stage and off. While you're in the WebMuseum, be sure to check out the works by other famous painters as well.

http://sunsite.unc.edu/wm/paint/auth/degas/

FOLK AND HISTORICAL DANCING

Bassett Street Hounds Morris Dancers

As early as the 1500s, groups of dancers in the Cotswold region of western England were donning their bells and colorful ribbons and welcoming the spring season with a ritual folk dance. Morris dancing on the Net now boasts a worldwide representation from well over 100 teams. Read more about the history of Morris dancing and its various styles (Cotswold, Border, Longsword, and Northwest), all of which are part of the Hounds' repertoire. From this site, you can connect to a searchable archive of the Morris Dance Discussion List and other Morris-related Web pages.

http://web.syr.edu/~htkeays/morris/hounds/

ClogText

If you've ever thought it would be fun to try clogging, read this explanation of what cloggers look like, what they wear, and what's on their feet! You'll learn about the music cloggers move to and the steps they take to complete the dance.

http://members.aol.com/mdevin/clogtext.html

A
B
C
D
E
F
G
H
I
J
K
L
M
N
O
P
Q
R
S
T
U
V
W
X
Y
Z

B
C
D
E
F
G
H
I
J
K
L
M
N
O
P
Q
R
S
T
U
V
W
X
Y
Z

I F D O Home Page

Folk dancing is both fun to watch and fun to do. The International Folk Dancers of Ottawa brings together the traditional social dances and authentic music of many countries and cultures. Here you can find lots of information about folk dancing in Ottawa and then link to many additional resources on the WWW.

http://lucas.dfl.doc.ca/ifdo.html

SCA Dance Cheat Sheets

Your mom's dragging you to the Renaissance Faire again (you *know* it's only because she likes to wear her Princess costume!) and you *know* she'll make you dance all those goofy dances with her. Be prepared. They can be fun if you know the steps! Click through here to find the Society for Creative Anachronism's "Cheat Sheets" for about 50 of the Renaissance's greatest dance crazes.

http://www.pbm.com/~lindahl/dance/Top.html

What is Scottish Country Dancing, Anyway?

Dancing in Scotland isn't always done to the drone of the bagpipes! This site tells you about Scottish country dancing with music played on the fiddle, the flute, and other instruments.

http://www.tm.informatik.uni-frankfurt.de/strathspey/
what-is-scd.html

HULA AND POLYNESIAN DANCING

Hawai'i's H4 - Hula Section

Aloha from Hawaii! The *hula* (Hawaiian for "dance") expresses the culture of the islands in a unique combination of colorful costumes and rhythmic hip and arm movements. This "photo album" contains screen shots from the TV coverage of the 20th Annual Queen Liliuokalani Keiki Hula Festival and Competition. You don't have to cross the *moana* (ocean), *kai* (sea), or *mauna* (mountain) to enjoy the spirit of the hula—just grab your *lei* (wreath of flowers worn around the neck) and point your browser toward this colorful site!

http://www.hotspots.hawaii.com/hula.html

Hula, Hawaii's Art and Soul

The origin of hula is a mystery, but everyone agrees that it began as a sacrament, not an entertainment for tourists. You can read about how goddesses brought hula to the Hawaiians and how it is performed with reverence today in many hula schools around the islands. You can also hear a chant accompanied by traditional instruments, such as the pahu hula drum. It is constructed from a partially hollowed-out tree trunk with a shark skin stretched over the top.

http://www.aloha-hawaii.com/hawaii_magazine/
hula/index.shtml

NATIVE AMERICAN DANCE
PowWow Dancing

The powwow drum brings the heartbeat of the Earth Mother to the gathering of Native American tribes. You can see many traditional dances at these spiritual festivals, from the colorful and exciting Fancy Dress dance to the sacred Kiowan Gourd Dance. This site explains some of the dances and the traditions surrounding the costumes. You'll also learn proper etiquette regarding the drum and the head singer. Check the schedule to see if a powwow is planned near your home!

http://www.scsn.net/users/pgowder/dancing.htm

NET FILES

Congratulations!
You've just won a fabulous Krskopolje!
What is it?

Answer: Hope you've got a barn. Another name for it is the black-belted swine. It's a rare and very old breed of pig, originally from Slovenia. You can read about its attributes and history at http://www.ansi.okstate.edu/breeds/swine/krskop/index.htm

There's a real gem of a site in EARTH SCIENCE—GEOLOGY!

Southern Native American PowWows

This site was created by kids for the ThinkQuest competition. In it, you'll learn where to sit (and where not to sit) to watch the dancing, and you'll know what to do if you are a dancer. Don't forget to honor the Head Man and the Head Lady and give respect to the Drum, which has probably traveled a long way to give you beautiful music. Listen to the audio files of various songs, and check out the various styles of dances for both men and women. There is even advice for the new dancer and someone wishing to get involved with this tradition.

http://tqd.advanced.org/3081/

TAP DANCE

E-TAP

This site not only tells you about tap dance, it also lets you *hear* the various steps and variations. Remember: step right, shuffle, step left—and don't wear sneakers to tap class!

http://www.e-tap.com/

Tap Dance Homepage

Did you know that May 25 is National Tap Dance Day, signed into law by President Bush in 1989? Don't wait until then to find all the neat information about tap dancing at this site. If you're getting your shim sham confused with your paddle and roll, then refer to the Tap Steps glossary (and instructions) to set you straight. The Sites and Sounds of Tap section includes video clips and recordings. There's an events calendar, book list, tap trivia, and lots more. The Who's Who section lists tap companies and has bios of some of tap's greatest from today and yesterday, such as Gregory Hines, Hank Smith, Fred Astaire, and Bill "Bojangles" Robinson, whose birthday was—you guessed it—May 25, 1878!

http://www.allegheny.edu/~corrp/tap/

"My toes are the sticks, and the floor is the drum," says Ira Bernstein, dancer. Not just any dance, though. Ira does tap dancing, Appalachian clogging, English clogging, French-Canadian step dancing, Cape Breton step dancing, Jitterbug swing dancing, and Cajun and Zydeco dancing. Because the sound of each dance is just as important as the look of it, he wears a variety of footwear when he performs: tap shoes, wooden clogs, fiberglass-tipped shoes, and rubber boots. These produce different tones, volumes, and dynamics of sound necessary for the different dances. You can hear a brief audio clip of Ira clog dancing in the Sounds of Tap area on the Tap Dance Homepage.

DINOSAURS AND PREHISTORIC TIMES

bone yard

Funding has run out at the museum! All your reference materials have been moved to a library off-site. All the more-experienced scientists have been reassigned. It's up to you to sort through all the old fossil specimens and bones and try to put them back together again. Just pick the level of difficulty you want in this fun game, pull open a drawer, and get started. Let's see, the hip bone's connected to...?

http://www.abc.net.au/science/holo/dembone.htm

Can't tell a hawk from a handsaw? Look it up in BIRDS.

B
C
D
E
F
G
H
I
J
K
L
M
N
O
P
Q
R
S
T
U
V
W
X
Y
Z

DINO-MITE Dinosaur Site

Kids love dinos, but these kids in Wyoming are downright dinosaur crazy! Wyoming even has a state dinosaur, the triceratops. Check out the DINO-MITE Web page and see comments, facts, pictures, and other dino-related info geared just for kids.

http://www.trib.com/DINO/

Dinosaur Art and Modeling

Now here's something different! If you really love dinosaurs, you won't want to miss these exhibits. Here are the works of the world's most well-known dinosaur artists and model makers, including animatronic model makers, known for creating the moving dinosaurs in movies. Lifelike paintings, action sculptures, and life-size models created for museums are all included here.

http://www.indyrad.iupui.edu/dinoart.html

Dinosaur Eggs @ nationalgeographic.com

According to *National Geographic,* dinosaur eggs and nests have been found at 199 sites around the world, mostly in China, Mongolia, Argentina, India, and the Great Plains of North America. So, unless you live in one of those places, that egg-shaped rock you found in your backyard is probably just a rock! Some of the eggs found in China and elsewhere have had tiny fossilized dino embryos inside them. See what happens when scientists "hatch" dino eggs and try to model what the dino babies would have looked like.

http://www.nationalgeographic.com/features/96/
   dinoeggs/

Dinosaur Extinction Middle School Earth Science Explorer

You may have heard the theory that dinos became extinct after a giant meteor or asteroid hit Earth, creating a chain of disasters that wiped out their food supply. But that's not the only explanation. There might have been an orbital shift of Earth or possibly a supernova of a nearby star. Another theory says volcanoes made life too hot, while another guess is that disease took its toll. What's true? Visit this site and see which you think is correct.

http://www.cotf.edu/ete/modules/msese/
   dinosaur.html

Dinosaur Interplanetary Gazette - All the Dinosaur News that's Fit to Print

The motto at this site is *Scientia, Sapientia, Joci Ridiculi,* which is Latin for "Science, Wisdom, Silly Jokes"! That pretty much sums it up. You can get all the latest dino news at this site, such as the recent discovery of *Giganotosaurus* (which makes *T. rex* look like the runt of the litter). If you like Monty Python, you'll love this site.

http://www.users.interport.net/~dinosaur/
   frontpage.html

The Dinosauria

Can we start making new live dinosaurs from DNA, as in the movie *Jurassic Park*? No way! There are a lot of good scientific reasons why cloning dinosaurs would be impossible—read about it in DinoBuzz. From this site you can get lots of interesting information about dinosaurs.

http://www.ucmp.berkeley.edu/diapsids/dinosaur.html

NET FILES

What is the most easterly point in North America?

Answer: Cape Spear in Newfoundland, Canada. It is the site of one of Newfoundland's more than 200 lighthouses, built in the early 1800s to help transatlantic mariners and local fishermen navigate the treacherous coastline. The keeper's house at Cape Spear was constructed on top of a 300-foot sandstone cliff with a stone light tower built at its center, which anchored the house to the rock. Come visit this and other historic Newfoundland lighthouses at http://www.ucs.mun.ca/~dmolloy/lighthouse.html

Field Museum of Natural History On-Line Exhibits

Where can you see pictures of dinosaurs, hear their names pronounced, and then watch them run? You can do all of this and more by visiting the exhibit pages at the world-famous Field Museum of Natural History. Here you can see birds dodge Jurassic dinosaurs and listen to the Triassic forecast (1-900-CLIMATE) on the dinosaur weather report. Tours include the following: "Life Before Dinosaurs"; "Dinosaurs!"; "Teeth, Tusks, and Tarpits: Life After Dinosaurs." Make tracks to go see it!

http://www.fmnh.org/exhibits/web_exhibits.htm

Giganotosaurus

The Academy of Natural Sciences in Philadelphia exhibits a reconstruction of one of the largest meat-eating dinosaurs ever to walk the earth: *Giganotosaurus*. Although the display is called "T. rex Meets His Match," the creatures never would have met in real life. For one thing, they lived 30 million years apart, and for another, *T. rex* lived in North America and *Giganotosaurus* turf was South America. This fossil was discovered in Argentina. One of the most fascinating parts of the story is that the bones could not leave Argentina, since the law forbids removal of such materials. The bones had to be copied in resin and then reconstructed for the museum. There were many obstacles to be overcome in this process, and you can read them all at <*http://www.giganotosaurus.com/dinosaurs/wherenow.html*>.

http://www.acnatsci.org/gigapage/

Hadrosaurus foulkii

Where in the world was the first, nearly complete skeleton of a dinosaur found? It was found in Haddonfield, New Jersey. In the summer of 1858, vacationing fossil hobbyist William Parker Foulke led a crew of workmen digging "shin deep in gray slime." Eventually he found the bones of an animal, larger than an elephant, that once swam and played about the coastline of what is now Pennsylvania. Read about the discovery that started our fascination with dinosaurs!

http://www.levins.com/dinosaur.html

Nothing to do? Check CRAFTS AND HOBBIES for some ideas.

Honolulu Community College Dinosaur Exhibit

Sometimes it's great to read all about dinosaurs. And sometimes it's more fun to look at pictures. Hey, how about looking at all kinds of fossils and sculptures while someone reads to you? Here you can see the dinosaur bones and sculptures while listening to one of the exhibit's founders talk about them! These fossils are replicas of the originals at the American Museum of Natural History in New York City.

http://www.hcc.hawaii.edu/dinos/dinos.1.html

Introduction - The Mammoth Saga

This virtual exhibition of mammoths, other animals, and plants of the ice ages is based on an exhibition held at the Swedish Museum of Natural History in Stockholm, Sweden. In it, you'll explore the U.S. Midwest of 16,000 years ago and take a look at a woolly rhinoceros, a sabertooth cat, and ancient reindeer. Siberian nomads lived in huts made of mammoth bones, and you can see a re-creation of one here! There are also nice links to other places on the Web that will help you learn more.

http://www.nrm.se/virtexhi/mammsaga/
welcome.html.en

NOVA Online/Curse of T. rex

Dinosaurs roamed the earth between 250 million years ago and 65 million years ago, but they didn't have the place to themselves. There were other animals, insects, and plants! This site gives you an overview of those other species we don't hear too much about. If you were going to look for dino fossils, where would you look? This takes you through that process.

http://www.pbs.org/wgbh/nova/trex/

A
B
C
D
E
F
G
H
I
J
K
L
M
N
O
P
Q
R
S
T
U
V
W
X
Y
Z

B C D E F G H I J K L M N O P Q R S T U V W X Y Z

Welcome to the Dinosaur Society

Usually, people join wildlife societies to help save endangered species; this organization helps save animals *already* extinct. Read all about Sue the dinosaur: seems she died about 65 million years ago, and her fossilized remains were discovered in 1980, near Faith, South Dakota. There was a dispute about who really owned the skeleton, the FBI seized her, and she was held, pending an auction! The Field Museum of Chicago eventually got her, but the Dino Society folks haven't put that info here yet. Read about Sue's current status at *<http://www.fmnh.org./new/ press/press_sue.htm>*. There's a lot of other dino info at the Dino Society though, and you can also visit a dig and join the Society online.

http://www.dinosociety.org/

Welcome to the Royal Tyrrell Museum Homepage

Take a virtual tour of this famous museum in Alberta, Canada. You can stay on the guided tour, or you can use the virtual maps to go from exhibit to exhibit in any order you want! There are fantastic dinosaur exhibits with lots of pictures, and you'll find information on the second floor in Dinosaur Hall. In addition to all of the dinosaurs, you can visit a paleoconservatory, which is a greenhouse full of primitive plants. Try the link to Dinosaur Provincial Park, where most of the museum's exhibits have been excavated.

http://tyrrell.magtech.ab.ca/

Zoom Dinosaurs - Enchanted Learning Software

This is a great site, it can be enjoyed by all age groups. Everyone will love it, including your little brother and even your parents. There are lots of pictures, animations, and tons of great scientific information. There's a geologic time scale, a dino dictionary, and lots of activities and links. You'll also find some fun and really bad jokes, such as this: Why did the dinosaur cross the road? Answer: Because the chicken hadn't evolved yet!

http://www.EnchantedLearning.com/subjects/ dinosaurs/

DISNEY

CyberNetiquette

You want to help your little sister learn about Internet safety rules? If she likes Disney characters, just take her to this site, pull up a chair, and settle back for a story. The stories do take a while to download, but they teach you what you need to know to stay safe. There are two stories currently available: "Who's Afraid of Little Sweet Sheep?" and "The Bad Apple."

http://www.disney.com/cybernetiquette/

Disney.com — The Web Site for Families

Oh yes, the magical world of Disney! The Walt Disney Company produces movies, television shows, and music, and they are nearly all fun. If you want to keep up on the latest from the folks at Disney, take a look at their official home page. You'll find clips from recent Disney movies, which you can play on your computer. You can listen to recordings from the Disney Channel. You can also get all kinds of great graphic images of your favorite Disney characters. Don't forget Disney Online and Radio Disney. There is much, much more. If you like Disney, this is a must-see.

http://www2.disney.com/

NET FILES

If you wanted to walk up the Eiffel Tower in Paris, how many stairs would you have to climb?

Answer: 1,585! Boy, would you be tired! Visit http://www.tour-eiffel.fr/teiffel/tour_uk/histodoc/ page/pg_identite.html for more information.

Get on board, little children, in RAILROADS AND TRAINS.

Lampwick's Disney on the Web

Want to find out about the new Tomorrowland? What about Animal Kingdom—is it a hit or a miss? Keep up on all the news here. And check the surveys— in the Magic Kingdom, everyone's favorite ride is Splash Mountain. And the scariest ride in all of Walt Disney World? A whopping 63 percent said it was Alien Encounter. Wouldn't it be cool to have a relative who works at a Disney theme park? Maybe your older brother could get a job on the new Disney Cruise Line! There are links to careers with Disney here. You can also test your knowledge of Disney lyrics, so "Come on, join in and sing your troubles away." (Hint: It is from a song in *Peter Pan*.)

http://pages.prodigy.com/lampwick/

The Ultimate Disney Link Page

Disney is all over the Internet. This is a good place to begin exploring all those sites. Here you'll find links to Disney theme parks, a hodgepodge of Disney fan pages, and connections to just about anything else that's Disney. Created by cast member Ed Sterrett, this truly is the ultimate Disney site!

http://www.tudlp.org/

Walt Disney Pictures

The folks who brought you *Pocahontas, The Lion King, A Goofy Movie,* and *Toy Story* have their home page here. There's a bunch of video, sound, and color images of movies that have been released and also of movies currently in production. If you're hopelessly "techno-clueless" and can't get your audio or movie files to play, Disney's help files can really help (click on the HELP button). Find out how to see the video and hear the movie themes by linking to whatever software you need.

http://www.disney.com/DisneyPictures/

Welcome to Walt Disney Records

"Be Our Guest" at this treasure chest of sounds from Disney movies. Whether you're in the mood for just "The Bare Necessities" (*The Jungle Book*) or something a little more exotic like "Hakuna Matata" (*The Lion King: Rhythm of the Pride Lands*), you'll find it here. Samples of all the latest music are available, but don't forget about the music from oldies such as *Fantasia* and *Mary Poppins.* Also, you'll find some information about each movie and how it was made.

http://www.disney.com/DisneyRecords/

THEME PARKS

Disneyland® Paris Online

Disneyland Paris gives folks in Europe a more convenient opportunity to visit a Disney park. If you'd like to visit Disneyland Paris, this is the Web page for you. There are also some games for you to play, including a downloadable "Visit to Disneyland Paris" game board. Who will get to Sleeping Beauty's Castle first?

http://www.disneylandparis.com/smain.htm

NET FILES

The Empire State Building, in New York City, often uses special-colored building lights to celebrate holidays, wins by the NY Yankees, and other special occasions. How many different colors can be displayed?

Answer: The different colors are red, green, blue, yellow, and white. Additionally, there is a ring of high-pressure sodium vapor lights above the 103rd floor, which creates a golden "halo" effect around the top of the mast from dusk to dawn. Read http://www.esbnyc.com/html/tower_lights.html for more fascinating tower trivia.

Explore underwater archaeology in SHIPS AND SHIPWRECKS.

Disneyland Park - Anaheim, California

Disneyland is the first of all the Disney parks, and some claim it has a special charm no other can match. At this Web site, dedicated Disneyland fan Doug Krause has pulled together a slew of information and pictures for anyone interested in visiting Disneyland in California. You'll find the usual park info here, plus some really unusual stuff. For example, there's a list of the memorabilia inside the Disneyland 40th Anniversary time capsule, which won't be opened until 2035. There's also Walt Disney's own chili recipe, so get in here and chow down!

http://www.lido.com/disney/parks/disneyland/

Hidden Mickeys of Disney

Look at a picture of Mickey Mouse: notice that his head is made of three circles—a big one for the head and two smaller ones for his ears. Did you know that the people who designed the Disney theme parks have hidden Mickey Mouse all over the place? It's true. At the Magic Kingdom, Epcot Center, Disney–MGM Studios, and even in the Disney hotels, Mickey Mouse's image is hidden in all kinds of unusual places. At Disney World, these three circles are concealed everywhere, from lakes to ceiling fans. Check this site to find out where Mickey is hiding, plus discover loads of other Disney secrets.

http://www.oitc.com/Disney/

Take a Live Look at the Parks!

What if you could check the Magic Kingdom's Main Street U.S.A. right now to see if Mickey Mouse is there? You can, through the real magic of Internet videocams. See what's happening, live, at the Magic Kingdom, Epcot Center, and Disney–MGM Studios in Florida.

http://www.disney.com/DisneyWorld/
ThemeParks/Par49.html

Tokyo Disneyland Official Home Page

Disneyland's Japanese version is called Tokyo Disneyland. With all the appeal of other Disney parks, you can see the sights of Disneyland—the Far East version. It's fun to see what's familiar and what's different at this park. There are also some interactive games you can play. This site is available in English as well as Japanese and Chinese.

http://www.tokyodisneyland.co.jp/

A Visit to Yesterland - The Discontinued Disneyland

Disneyland hasn't always been as it is now. New attractions have been added and old ones have been replaced. Some of those old attractions were really good, and it's too bad they are gone. With the magic of the Internet, though, you can visit many of those attractions here. You can wander into Adventure Through Inner Space, take a ride on the Flying Saucers, or mosey down the People Mover. You'll learn when these and other rides started and ended, and you'll get a good idea of what Disneyland was like for your parents or maybe your older brothers and sisters.

http://www.mcs.net/~werner/yester.html

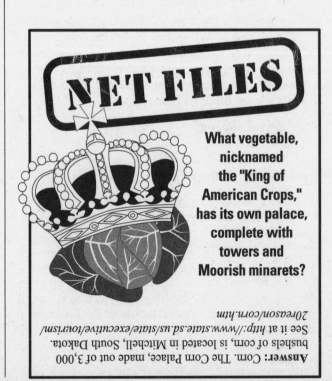

NET FILES

What vegetable, nicknamed the "King of American Crops," has its own palace, complete with towers and Moorish minarets?

Answer: Corn. The Corn Palace, made out of 3,000 bushels of corn, is located in Mitchell, South Dakota. See it at http://www.state.sd.us/state/executive/tourism/20reason/corn.htm

Walt Disney World Home Page

Going to Disney World? At this site, you'll find out everything you need to know about The Magic Kingdom, Epcot, Disney–MGM Studios, plus other attractions in the Orlando, Florida, area.

http://www.travelweb.com/TravelWeb/dw/common/wdw.html

DOGS AND DOG SPORTS

See also MAMMALS—CARNIVORES— DOG FAMILY; PETS AND PET CARE

2000 DOG NAMES: Naming Your Puppy

Dad says you can keep that puppy who followed you home; now all you need is a name. Let's see, how about Sammy? That's the most popular dog name in North America, according to this Web site. Of course, if you want a really unusual name, you could pick one of the thousands of names here, like Angstrom or maybe Tsunami. This site also ranks dog breeds by their intelligence. The Border collie is listed first— after *your* dog, of course!

http://www.petrix.com/dognames/

Belgian Games

Stupid dog tricks—sure, this site has some really silly tricks, but you'll find some useful ones here, too. How about teaching your dog to start pawing you when your alarm clock goes off? You could teach your dog to collect your toys and put them away for you or to look for your mom's lost car keys. Or you could teach your dog to nod on command; then, when you ask your furry friend to respond to a question like "Aren't I the best, smartest, and most good-looking owner you could ever have?" the dog will always nod an enthusiastic "Yes!" The directions for how to teach these tricks are found when you click on the words "dog training page."

http://www.hut.fi/~mtt/belg_tricks.html

Canine Companions National WebSite

Have you ever seen a blind person and guide dog team? Did you ever wonder how dogs for the blind are trained? How about a hearing or signal dog, who teams up with deaf people? These animals go to their owners to "signal" when a noise is heard. They will signal on ringing door bells and phones, smoke alarms, crying babies, and much more. There are also therapy dogs and special canine companions who know how to help disabled people. Find out about this very interesting class of working dogs here.

http://www.caninecompanions.org/

Clifford, the Big Red Page

If you can't decide on a real dog, how about a toy one? The owner of this Web site says, "In 1974, Clifford was discovered in the JC Penney's toy department in Birmingham, AL. Now, Clifford is a successful business dog, award-winning stuffed animal, and an icon of cute-and-fuzziness." Clifford is well-traveled and has had some fabulous adventures, including a trip to the Olympics! Meet him here, and don't forget to try some digital donuts at his bakery.

http://www.scott.net/~kristi/RedPage.html

Dog Fancy On-Line

Does your dog love to watch the Pet Channel on TV? Then your dog will really wag his or her tail at this Web version! If you're looking for a canine companion, you can look through pages on over 200 breeds. There are also links to dog names, health care, dog food companies, and much more. You can also submit your own dog poetry, stories, and tributes to your pet. If you want to make your own home page to honor your dog, you can build one here.

http://www.petchannel.com/dogs/

You can always count on the info in MATH AND ARITHMETIC.

A
B
C
D
E
F
G
H
I
J
K
L
M
N
O
P
Q
R
S
T
U
V
W
X
Y
Z

B
C
D
E
F
G
H
I
J
K
L
M
N
O
P
Q
R
S
T
U
V
W
X
Y
Z

How To Love Your Dog

Getting a dog is a big responsibility. You will care for your pet for many years to come. Are you ready for that? If so, print out the I Love My Dog contract here, and sign it. Show the contract to your dog. He or she will be very, very impressed. If you're still wondering if dog ownership is for you, study this site. It goes through everything: what dogs cost, what various types of dogs are like, how to train dogs, and how you feel when you lose your dog. This impressive site doesn't just teach how to love your dog. There are lessons here about kindness and humane treatment that carry over into dealings with people too.

http://www.geocities.com/~kidsanddogs/

IDITAROD OFFICIAL SITE - MAIN PAGE

The Iditarod is a 1,150-mile dogsled race in Alaska, from Anchorage to Nome. It commemorates an emergency medical mission back in 1925, when diphtheria serum traveled the same route. Usually over 60 teams compete in this annual race. Most teams have an average of 16 dogs each. If you go, you'll traverse some of the roughest, most beautiful country on Earth—behind a team of furry dogs, many of them wearing booties to protect their feet. Whoever drives the team is called a musher. This site has lots of classroom connections, musher bios, activities, and more.

http://www.iditarod.com/

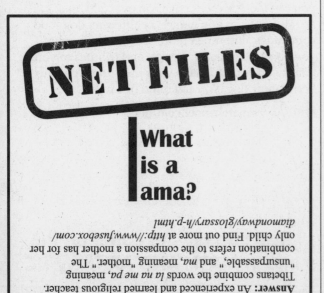

NET FILES

What is a ama?

Answer: An experienced and learned religious teacher. Tibetans combine the words *la na me pa*, meaning "unsurpassable," and *ma*, meaning "mother." The combination refers to the compassion a mother has for her only child. Find out more at http://www.fusebox.com/diamondway/glossary/h-p.html

Pearlie the WonderDog

Not every dog can make it into this book, but Pearlie the Wonder Dog is an exception. What kind of dog is she? Take your pick: Monk Seal Retriever, Brazilian Fruit Bat Terrier, Rare Black Ukrainian Vatzamacalit Spaniel, Toothless Curlyback Highland Poodlehound (Standard size). Huh? Don't miss this dog and her many talents, including her ability to remove every molecule of peanut butter from the inside of the jar in only one hour!

http://www.artsnacks.com/pearlie/

Pro Dog Networks Highlights

Gee, those puppies in the pet store look awfully cute! But wait—before you buy a registered dog, you should know a lot more, and you may not find the answers in the pet store. Some breeds have medical problems that are genetically passed on to the pups. How do you know you won't be getting a puppy with these health problems—many of which can be expensive to treat, if not life-threatening to your best pal? The best way to avoid these problems is to buy from a trustworthy dog breeder. These folks will often let you meet your pup's mom and dad, as well as show you their medical test results and health records. A good breeder will know about and discuss any genetic problems with the breed you're investigating. Maybe you're looking for a quiet dog or an energetic dog. Breeders often "temperament test" their puppies, and they can help match you with a dog that fits your personality.

This site lists breeders for various recognized dog breeds, but you could also find a list in an established dog magazine at the bookstore or public library. You should know that there are "good" pet stores as well as "bad" dog breeders. But the important thing is that you need to know a lot about where the dog's been and the parents' health background. At this page, you'll also find information about the many "breed rescue clubs" around the world. These are people who love, for example, golden retrievers. They "rescue" these dogs from animal shelters and try to place them in adoptive homes. You'll also learn about groups that try to find homes for retired racing greyhounds.

http://www.prodogs.com/frmst5.htm

Pug Park

The admission booth to this amusement park says "Pugs: FREE! Humans FREE when accompanied by a Pug!" Pick up your map to Pug Park and learn all about these little dogs and their big fans! Although focused on pugs, the general information about dog care provided in this site applies to every breed. Don't miss the pug bumper cars or the recipes for pug cakes and cookies.

http://alohi.ucdavis.edu/~len/pugpark/pugpark.html

rec.pets.dogs FAQ Homepage

This comprehensive site will give you information on everything, from picking the best breed for you, to showing your dog in obedience trials, to health care. The Working Dogs area will tell you about sled dogs, search and rescue dogs, and even narcotics-sniffing dogs. Don't bark up the wrong tree—curl up with your puppy and this Web site.

http://www.k9web.com/dog-faqs/

Don't try to get your sled dogs running by yelling

"MUSH!"

*The word the dogs are expecting is "HIKE!" Now you're moving! Mushers know that to turn teams right, they yell "Gee," and for a left turn, "Haw!" You'll have to check the Working Dogs area of the **rec.pets.dogs FAQ Homepage** to find out how to get them to slow down!*

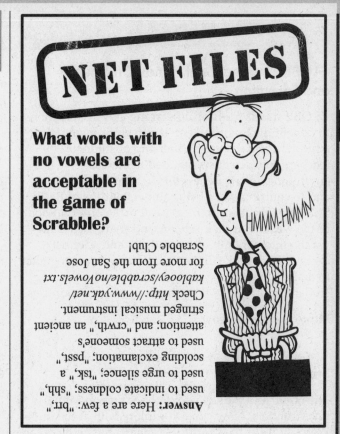

NET FILES

What words with no vowels are acceptable in the game of Scrabble?

HMMM-HMMM

Answer: Here are a few: "brr," used to indicate coldness; "shh," used to urge silence; "tsk," a scolding exclamation; "psst," used to attract someone's attention; and "crwth," an ancient stringed musical instrument. Check http://www.yak.net/kablooey/scrabble/noVowels.txt for more from the San Jose Scrabble Club!

So - you think you want a Dalmatian?

You saw *101 Dalmatians* and now you're seeing spots everywhere? Before you run out to get your own spotted pup, check what the Central Maryland Dalmatian Club says! This breed has a very high energy level—do you and your family? Make sure the breed fits your lifestyle. It's not true that you also have to own your own fire truck, though.

http://www.magpage.com/~kdee/newown.html

Welcome to the AKC

The American Kennel Club (AKC) is the largest registry of purebred dogs in the United States. Here you'll find a list of the breeds they recognize, a roster of recent obedience and show winners, and information on the AKC's many educational activities. You'll also find a list of breed clubs and contacts, as well as a breeder's directory.

http://www.akc.org/

A B C D E F G H I J K L M N O P Q R S T U V W X Y Z

EARTH SCIENCE

GLOBE - International Hands-On Science and Education

GLOBE stands for Global Learning and Observations to Benefit the Environment. It's an environmental education and science partnership of students, teachers, and scientists initiated to increase environmental awareness throughout the world and to contribute to a better understanding of Earth. Students take measurements and make observations of the weather at their schools and share their data via the Internet with other students and scientists around the world. All the details are patched together to make a view of the world as it's seen through the student findings at 3,000 schools in over 40 countries.

http://www.globe.gov/

Sea and Sky

The ocean and the sky—sometimes known as the final frontiers. Now you can explore both at the same Web site. Take the Cousteau submersible to the ocean part of this resource, where you'll find photos and information about all sorts of sea creatures, everything from coral to marine mammals. Then stop in at the games areas to try some word searches, crossword puzzles, and Shockwave fun. There are some carefully chosen links, as well as Java applets with a sea theme, too. If you want, explore the "Sky" side of the house on the Starship Sagan!

http://www.seasky.org/

CLIMATE—ACID RAIN

You Can & Acid Rain

How can rain be an acid? It starts out as regular rain, but then it falls through air pollution. It becomes a weak acid that can dissolve marble, kill trees, and ruin a lake's entire ecosystem. You can help. Here's how to make an acid finder and how to test rainwater. Let Beakman and Jax explain this phenomenon, first identified in England in 1872. Smoke from burning coal was the cause then, as it remains now.

http://www.beakman.com/acid/acid.html

CLIMATE—GREENHOUSE EFFECT

Biosphere 2

Did you know there is a rain forest in the middle of the Arizona desert? There's also an ocean. It's true, and the most amazing part: they are both indoors! Biosphere 2 is a 7,200,000-cubic-foot sealed glass and space frame structure, and inside are seven wilderness ecosystems, or biomes, including a rain forest and a 900,000-gallon ocean. The idea was to find out how people could survive inside a sealed environment, in case we wanted to colonize other planets. Could they grow all their own food? Manufacture their own air? Recycle their own waste? The first crew of biospherians (four women and four men) entered Biosphere 2 on September 26, 1991. They remained inside for two years, emerging again on September 26, 1993. Biosphere's original experiments were very controversial, but the results were undisputed: we don't know how to successfully accomplish this mission—yet. Columbia University now operates the facility as a learning center about the greenhouse effect. See what they are up to, take a cybertour, and check out some of the over 750 sensors to see what the temperature happens to be right now.

http://www.bio2.edu/

Climate Change Home Page - Environment Australia

Someone in a colder climate might think the greenhouse effect is a good thing, especially for those who don't like feeling chilly. However, there are consequences connected with having more planetwide heat than usual, and this doesn't just mean less snow to play in. Find out all about the greenhouse effect from the fact sheets at the Australian Environmental Resources Information Network.

http://kaos.erin.gov.au/air/air.html

DAY AND NIGHT

Earth and Moon Viewer

When it's 10 A.M. and bright and sunny in Florida, what's it like in Japan? Stop by this site and ask their server, which will show where it's light and dark anyplace in the world. You can choose the satellite location to view from, or you can tell it to look at Earth from the Sun's or Moon's perspective. You can even create a custom request and specify the desired longitude and latitude you want to see; the computer then picks the best viewpoint.

http://www.fourmilab.ch/earthview/vplanet.html

ECOLOGY AND ENVIRONMENT

Earthwatch Teacher & Student Homepage

Earthwatch takes ordinary people on extraordinary research expeditions. Of course, you pay for the privilege of counting katydids or helping to save a coral reef. But when you get back, you'll have a great story to tell about how you spent your summer vacation! This page archives some of the field notes and lesson plans developed from past trips, and it's interesting to see which ecological "hot spots" they will attend to next. There are also a few virtual field trips online, where you don't even have to get your boots wet.

http://www.earthwatch.org/ed/

EDF — Environmental Defense Fund WorldWide

You can learn a lot about our environment at this home page of the Environmental Defense Fund. There's a special area for kids called Earth to Kids that has lots of neat things—like an Alpha Bestiary. Don't know what that is? Then check this site. Don't miss the animal Concentration game called Kokoto— it's fun to play, and you'll learn something about the birds and beasts as you make your match.

http://www.edf.org/

Fynbos - Kingdom Threatened

Fynbos refers to "the characteristic shrubland of the southwestern and southern Cape of South Africa." To continue to amaze you, we offer this tidbit: "The 470 square kilometers of the Cape Peninsula, including Table Mountain, is home to 2,256 different plant species—more than the whole of Great Britain (which only supports 1,500 species), an area 5,000 times bigger!" This outstanding site will introduce you to Fynbos and its plant life. You'll also learn about the threats to this shrubland, which include everything from Man to alien plants. The best part is that the entire site was done by kids—it was a winner in 1998's CyberFair, and for good reason.

http://www.lizard.org/jfd/cf/narrate.html

NET FILES

When was the first PEZ candy made?

Answer: In 1927, Austrian candy executive Eduard Haas invented PEZ as a diversion for adults trying to quit smoking! The original little candy bricks were only peppermint and not the many different flavors they are now. The word PEZ is an abbreviation of the German word for peppermint (Pfefferminz). At http://www.best.com/~spectrum/pez/pezinfo.html you can read more about this collectible candy.

A
B
C
D
E
F
G
H
I
J
K
L
M
N
O
P
Q
R
S
T
U
V
W
X
Y
Z

A
B
C
D
E
F
G
H
I
J
K
L
M
N
O
P
Q
R
S
T
U
V
W
X
Y
Z

Harlem Environmental Access Project Home Page

Did you know that a family of four throws away 80 to 150 pounds of garbage a week? If we recycle rather than buy new items, we can generate less garbage. This home has facts on starting your own compost heap and what types of materials are best for composting. Don't miss the instructions for starting a composting program in your school!

http://www.edf.org/heap/

National Wildlife Federation's Homepage

Looking for projects and information on a variety of environmental subjects? Check these out: air, habitat, people and the environment, wildlife and endangered species, and water. Sound good? Each topic includes general background information, class activities, fun facts, and a glossary of terms. How about a random riddle from Ranger Rick? There are also suggestions of things you can do to help!

http://www.nwf.org/

The NEW What's It Like Where You Live?

A biome is the collection of creatures and plants living in a particular region. Explore six different biomes here: grassland, rain forest, taiga, deciduous forest, desert, and tundra. You'll learn about the features of each area and its plants and animals. You don't have a clue what living in the taiga is like? Ask a kid at a school in Finland or Russia—links to schools in each biome area are included here!

http://www.mobot.org/MBGnet/

WWF:North America's Living Legacy

It always seems that some of the most spectacular places in the world are so far away. This site wants to show you ten of the "coolest places you've never seen"—all in the United States. They range from Camp Pendleton, the Marine Corps base in Southern California, to the Eckert James River Bat Cave in Texas. You'll learn about their ecosystems and what you can do to help protect them. When you think you're ready, take the quiz and see how well you do.

http://www.wwf.org/legacy/

GEOLOGY
USGS: Ask-A-Geologist

Have you ever wondered why earthquakes happen in some places but not in others? Why does Hawaii have volcanoes but Florida doesn't? Just ask a geologist. This page tells how to e-mail your questions to a United States Geological Survey scientist for an answer. Before you send your mail, be sure to read about what kinds of questions to ask and how to ask them.

http://walrus.wr.usgs.gov/docs/ask-a-ge.html

GEOLOGY—EARTHQUAKES
Electronic Desktop Project - Virtual Earthquake

How do scientists figure out where the starting point, or epicenter, of an earthquake was? In this cool simulation, you pick the general region for your test earthquake (California, Japan, Mexico). Use the easy-to-follow instructions to examine seismograms and pinpoint the epicenter as well as the relative strength of your quake.

http://vearthquake.calstatela.edu/edesktop/VirtApps/
    VirtualEarthQuake/VQuakeIntro.html

Record of the Day

Where in the world was the biggest earthquake today? The answer is just a click away. This site will show you the most recent large earthquake recorded by the Cal Tech Seismological Laboratory in California. You can look at the actual graph that was recorded by their seismograph. Hmm, where are the Ryukyu Islands? Maps show you where the earthquake's epicenter was. Be sure to check often. Earthquakes are happening around the world all the time.

http://www.gps.caltech.edu/~polet/recofd.html

Seismic Event Bulletins

How many earthquakes do you think occur in the world every day? Probably a lot more than you realize. Seismic activity is monitored day and night, and any recorded activity is posted to this site within 48 hours of each event. Check here and you'll be surprised to find there's a whole lot of shakin' goin' on.

http://www.cdidc.org:65120/web-bin/recentevents

Seismo-Cam

What to know what's shaking in L.A.—literally? Live shots of a seismograph as it's tracking activity in the Southern California area can be monitored here. If nothing's happening while you're watching, you can look at some archived shots from past events, including some BIG temblors. There are also lots of great links to sites with info on earthquakes, including one at the University of Nevada that explains how seismographs work at <*http://www.seismo.unr.edu/Webcam/ explanation.html*>.

http://www.scecdc.scec.org/seismocam/
   SeismoCam.html

This Dynamic Earth—Contents [USGS]

Have you ever seen a bumper sticker that says "Stop Plate Tectonics!"? It's something that's an impossible task. Although continental land masses look pretty stable, they are actually moving all the time. Sometimes they just drift along very very slowly. Other times they shift or move suddenly, and that causes an earthquake. The plates don't just cruise around at random, but scientists aren't completely sure what's "driving" them, either. This nicely illustrated site will explain it all.

http://pubs.usgs.gov/publications/text/dynamic.html

NET FILES

How do two traditional Maoris greet each other?

Answer: They don't shake hands or wave; they rub noses. Check out proper gestures and other cultural behavior at *http://www.worldculture.com/ gesasia.htm* so you'll look and feel right at home when you visit another country!

GEOLOGY—FOSSILS

Charlotte, The Vermont Whale: Directory of Exhibits

Just how did a whale get in the state of Vermont, which has no seacoast? Find how the bones of this 12-foot beluga whale ended up buried in Charlotte, Vermont, about 10,000 years ago. Very nice descriptions with drawings show how the whale probably died and was eventually preserved and fossilized in the sediment.

http://mole.uvm.edu/whale/TableOfContents.html

Discovery Centre, Fossils Cyber-Display - ROM

A fossil is a sort of stone souvenir from the past. When you hold a fossil in your hand, you're really looking at an animal or plant that was buried on a beach, mud puddle, or sandbar of long, long ago. If you need a quick refresher course on fossils and how they formed, better start here. There are also sections on where fossils are found and how they are prepared and preserved by scientists. We liked the fossil game: see if you can match a real fossil with its modern-day equivalent creature. This is harder than you'd think—how well can you do?

http://www.rom.on.ca/quiz/fossil/

Teeth, Tusks, and Tarpits 1

Early scientists thought fossils were carved by ancient artists or were seeds dropped from stars. Chicago's famous Field Museum of Natural History explains fossils and gives a recipe for making your own. Of course, you'll need a dead animal or plant and a million years or so to wait, but go ahead, try it at home!

http://www.fmnh.org./exhibits/ttt/TTT1.htm

A
B
C
D
E
F
G
H
I
J
K
L
M
N
O
P
Q
R
S
T
U
V
W
X
Y
Z

I wonder what
the QUEENS, KINGS,
AND ROYALTY are
doing tonight?

GEOLOGY—GEMS AND MINERALS

A Gem of a Story

Gems and jewels: before they become treasures, they look like, well, rocks. You might be able to spot a diamond in the rough if you study this site. You'll see a collection of pictures and descriptions of rocks and minerals from the Smithsonian Institution's National Museum of Natural History in Washington, D.C. You can also click on each small picture to get a larger picture of that mineral.

http://www.academy.bsu.edu/gems/welcome.html

He Ain't Nothing But a Rock Hound, A Diggin' All The Time

Elvis was spotted digging around on this page recently. If you have rocks in your head and love to collect minerals, fossils, and crystals, you will love this site and its extensive information on collecting and studying rocks. There's also a neat rock hound crossword puzzle.

http://loki.ur.utk.edu/ut2kids/rocks/rocks.html

Rock 'U'

"Rocks are our friends," says this tutorial on various types of minerals. This site explores diamonds, oxides, and silicates, though not in great detail. Still, you'll find interesting stuff, like how to turn amethyst into citrine and how quartz was used to detect submarines during World War I.

http://www.ucs.usl.edu/~amg6262/rocku.html

GEOLOGY—GEYSERS

Fantastic Journeys: Yellowstone @ nationalgeographic.com

Hey, what's all that mist up ahead? Wait—it's steam. Hold on, hear that gurgling and rumbling noise? RUN! Oops. This is the Net, isn't it. That's not a real geyser; that's QuickTime virtual reality. That glopping sound you hear is coming from a virtual mudpot. Still, it's pretty exciting to see and hear the various things that can happen when you mix hot water and minerals together. Don't forget to put on your wet suit and dive down into the depths of the Grand Prismatic Spring to see what's below.

http://www.nationalgeographic.com/features/97/
   yellowstone/

Geysers

A geyser is simply a hot spring that erupts, shooting water into the air. There are only about 700 geysers left in the world! Four hundred of them are located in Yellowstone National Park, but they can also be found in such faraway places as Siberia and Chile. Find out how a geyser builds up steam, and discover why geothermal energy production has destroyed many of the geyser fields and threatens some of the few remaining ones. See what happens when they leave the water running? ;-)

http://www2.wku.edu/www/geoweb/geyser.html

GEOLOGY—VOLCANOES

Excursion to Stromboli summit

Between Sicily and southern Italy lie the Aeolian Islands. Stromboli is the northernmost of this volcanic chain, and it has an active volcano called—Stromboli. If a volcano can have a fan club, this page is theirs. You can find out everything from the current eruption conditions to the current weather on the main page. However, you'll be most interested in the virtual climb to the summit. Remember, if you don't like heights, you can always click the browser's BACK button. If you do get to the summit, sign the guest book.

http://www.ezinfo.ethz.ch/ezinfo/volcano/
   verschiedenes/walk/walk0e.html

Mount St. Helens

Imagine that you're living near Mount St. Helens, a sleeping volcano, and suddenly it blows up! There's dust and debris everywhere, mud slides, and boulders shooting into the air. Read exciting stories from people who were there. Sponsored by Educational Service District 112 in Vancouver, Washington, this graphics-intensive site provides maps, photos, and classroom projects to help bring this devastating eruption to life. The site is also supported by NASA, the National Forest Service, and Volcano World.

http://volcano.und.nodak.edu/vwdocs/msh/msh.html

Volcano World Starting Points

How do you become a volcanologist? Just ask Mr. Spock for lessons, of course! Well, not quite. Look at this site to find out what becoming a volcanologist is all about and what courses you'll need to take. Also, you'll learn about computers (hey, you're halfway there, since you wouldn't be reading this if you didn't know about computers already). Oh yeah, there's also the BEST information here about volcanoes, including lessons and activities for teachers and students.

http://volcano.und.nodak.edu/vw.html

Volcanoes in the Learning Web

From here, it's safe to explore several different volcano labs, including Cascades Volcano Observatory, Alaska Volcano Observatory, and Hawaii Volcano Observatory. At the Hawaiian site, you might feel some heat, but that's probably just your computer monitor! In Alaska, things are hot. Check the archives for the 1995–96 winter: they were monitoring several active volcanoes on both sides of the North Pacific, including Pavlof and 40 others! You'll see satellite maps of activities and plume trails almost as they occur at this amazing site.

http://www.usgs.gov/education/learnweb/volcano/

> It's hard to remember,
> but mnemonic memory tricks
> are in WORDS.

LAND FEATURES—CAVES AND CAVING

Mount St. Helens & Other Volcanoes, Ape Cave

Ape Cave is a special geologic formation called a lava tube. Formed when Mount St. Helens (Amboy, Washington) erupted 1,900 years ago, it is 12,810 feet long—that's almost two and a half miles! It is the longest intact lava tube in the United States and the second longest in the world. You can read all about its amazing features, such as sand castles, "lava-sicles," and lava balls. Don't miss the creatures of Ape Cave, which include cockroaches, millipedes, and cave slime. There have never been any apes in Ape Cave, however. The name came from a local youth group that explored Mount St. Helens, climbing all over it like monkeys!

http://volcano.und.nodak.edu/vwdocs/msh/ov/ ovb/ovbac.html

The Official NPS Mammoth Cave National Park Expanded Page, Mammoth Cave, Mammoth

"Captain, Spock here. According to the informative sign, I am exploring the longest recorded cave system in the world. There seem to be more than 336 miles mapped, but sensors indicate much more to this labyrinth. I chart my location as Kentucky. My Star Fleet tricorder reads ambient temperature at 53 degrees Fahrenheit. Here is a sign; I will read it aloud: 'Violet City Lantern Tour, 3 hours, 3 miles (strenuous). A nostalgic tour into a section of the cave that is not electrically lit. The tour features saltpeter mining, prehistoric exploration, historic tuberculosis hospital huts, and some of the largest rooms and passage ways in the cave. The first half-mile follows the Historic Tour route. Do not bring flashlights. Restrooms not available.' No rest rooms? Illogical. Beam me up. No, wait—it says that other tours are available; some are handicapped-accessible and some are short, fun walks for kids, too. And they have rest rooms!"

http://www.nps.gov/maca/macahome.htm

A B C D E F G H I J K L M N O P Q R S T U V W X Y Z

A
B
C
D
E
F
G
H
I
J
K
L
M
N
O
P
Q
R
S
T
U
V
W
X
Y
Z

Stick to the beekeeping sites in FARMING AND AGRICULTURE, honey

Virtual Cave

Now you can explore the mineral wonders of the perfect cave without leaving your house or school! This site has pictures of many geologic features besides stalactites and stalagmites. For example, you'll see popcorn, bathtubs, and cave pearls. For a bat-free cave experience, try spelunking here. There's also a handy list of public "show caves" arranged by state so that you can find a real cave to visit.

http://www.goodearth.com/virtcave.html

STALACTITES are the ones that hang "tite" from a cave's ceiling. For another way to remember which ones grow up and which hang down, explore the Virtual Cave!

LAND FEATURES—DESERTS

Arizona-Sonora Desert Museum

When you hear the word "desert," does it conjure up visions of sand dunes? Even Africa's Namib, perhaps the sandiest desert in the world, is only about 30 percent dunes! In Arizona's Sonora Desert, sand covers only 1 or 2 percent of the area. It doesn't mean there are no plants, either. Sloping and flat desert lands host so many plants, you can't walk without bumping into bushes! Also, flowers bloom most of the year. Learn more about the interrelationships of the plants, animals, and geology of this arid environment, as presented by the Arizona–Sonora Desert Museum.

http://www.desert.net/museum/index.htmlx

Desert Biome

What is a desert like? It's a land of temperature extremes, usually very rocky and dry. How do deserts form? What kind of plants and animals live there? Because it's so hot during the day, many desert animals live underground most of the time, and others are active only during the cool night. These are the types of questions answered at this page, prepared by the Missouri Botanical Garden. Visit other deserts the easy way.—in the links section!

http://www.mobot.org/MBGnet/vb/desert/

DesertUSA Magazine

What's blooming in the Arizona, California, and Nevada deserts this week? Why is salty Owens Lake red? And has anyone ever found the legendary "black gold" a prospector named Pegleg lost years ago? You can find out at this very interesting site. You'll also meet up with the Animal of the Month (as well as the plant of the month, the rock of the month, and the person of the month) and find out what's hot in the desert these days.

http://www.desertusa.com/

LAND FEATURES—GLACIERS

Blackcomb Glaciers - Main

Glaciers are not just found near the polar caps. They also exist along the equator, although only at high altitudes. Find out how a glacier forms and what happens when glacier meets volcano. You'll find lots of "cool" glacier facts here! The Blackcomb Glacier is in British Columbia, Canada.

http://www.whistler.net/glacier/

Did you know that 75 percent of the world's fresh water is locked up in glaciers? That's equivalent to 60 years of nonstop rain all over the world! Dig into the Blackcomb Glaciers—Main page, and watch out for the ice worms.

LAND FEATURES—MOUNTAINS

Destination: Himalayas - Where Earth Meets Sky

This ThinkQuest contest grand prize winner was created by a team of geographically and culturally diverse kids! It gives an overview of the Himalayan region, its flora and fauna, and its environmental problems. "Himalaya" is a Sanskrit word that literally means "Abode of Snow." You'll find multimedia if you choose the high-bandwidth version; otherwise, the text will inform and enlighten. An excellent site that proves what value kids bring to the Net.

http://library.advanced.org/10131/

Shangri La Home Page

Welcome to a real-life Shangri-La! Around long before people created boundaries, the Himalayas are not just rock and snow but a breathtaking range of mountains teeming with life. The exclusive home of the spiny babbler bird, they also lay claim to some impressive records, including the highest mountain and the deepest canyon. Learn more about the geography and inhabitants of this beautiful region and discover how humankind has left a mark on these majestic peaks.

http://aleph0.clarku.edu/rajs/Shangri_La.html

LAND FEATURES—POLAR REGIONS

Australian Antarctic Division

Discover why these Australian scientists put on their parkas and went way down under to set up shop in Antarctica. Their research includes issues of global change, management of the marine ecosystem, and protection of the Antarctic environment. It's tough to go to the Pole for a research season, and you can read all about life there to see if it's for you by clicking on "Antarctic Separation" under the Expeditions button. Learn more about their expeditions, and find out why they are so interested in what those penguins just had for lunch.

http://www.antdiv.gov.au/

Center for Astrophysical Research in Antarctica

Join April Lloyd, a third-grade teacher from Charlottesville, Virginia, on the adventure of a lifetime. April describes her journey to New Zealand and then to McMurdo Station in Antarctica. Her journey takes her all the way to the South Pole, where she takes part in the first ever, live television broadcast from that site.

http://quest.arc.nasa.gov/antarctica/team/april/

A B C D E F G H I J K L M N O P Q R S T U V W X Y Z

A
B
C
D
E
F
G
H
I
J
K
L
M
N
O
P
Q
R
S
T
U
V
W
X
Y
Z

LFA2*Related Materials

This site lets you take a virtual visit to the South Pole as well as several scientific outposts in Antarctica. This collection of links is outstanding. You'll learn about penguins, plankton, and polar ice, and you can also learn about how you'd prepare to go to the Pole: what you'd need to pack and how you'd go about getting there.

http://quest.arc.nasa.gov/antarctica2/main/related/

Did you know that Antarctica contains 90 percent of Earth's ice and has regions drier than the Gobi Desert?

Find out more about the way cool world of Antarctica at LFA2* Related Materials!

The Polar Regions

Dress up warmly to visit this site, which covers the Arctic and the Antarctic regions. You'll find everything from Santa Claus (who lives at the North Pole) to information on dog mushing. Follow various polar expeditions, and explore scientific research stations and projects involving schoolchildren all over the world. You'll find lots about wildlife and polar land forms here. Truly a labor of love, this site welcomes you to learn more about all things arctic.

http://www.stud.unit.no/~sveinw/arctic/

Do you know the way to San Jose? If not, check a map in GEOGRAPHY.

NET FILES

What is the largest soap bubble ever made?

SOAP

Answer: *David Stein holds the official Guinness record for the longest bubble: 50 feet by 2 feet in diameter. He used his own patented invention, The Bubble Thing. See some pictures at http://bubbles.org-html/biggest.htm*

The South Pole Adventure Web Page

Science is cool, and one of the coolest places to do science is the South Pole. If you're too busy to go today, just visit this page. You'll find out the current weather, but that's not all. The site answers lots of nagging questions. For example, there are the pure science questions: Is the boiling point of water the same everywhere? Which direction does the globe spin? Then there are the questions that are really fun: can you blow a soap bubble when it's that cold? What happens to a Bic pen when it freezes? You can ask your question, and maybe the scientists will answer it. If you have a good idea for an experiment that you think will interest other kids—send it in!

http://www.southpole.com/

Virtual Antarctica

This is a slick resource, with audio and cool Web graphics sure to grab your attention. This site documents an expedition to Antarctica as seen though the eyes, cameras, diaries, and e-mail of the participants. You'll find lots here on geology, weather, and wildlife, as well as history.

http://www.terraquest.com/antarctica/

LAND FEATURES—PRAIRIE
TERRY the PRAIRIE DOG HOME PAGE

Follow Terry the Prairie Dog and discover facts about the plants and animals that live on the tallgrass prairie in the American Midwest. This page was created by fourth graders for the CyberFair '98 contest. You'll love the animated drawings the kids made to help you learn about this ecosystem. They do take a long time to load, but it's worth the effort. Can you guess who might *want* to start a prairie fire?

http://cyberfair.gsn.org/villages/

LAND FEATURES—RAIN FORESTS
MBGnet's Rainforest Biome

When you think about a rain forest, you probably think about a tropical jungle, right? Sure, this site will tell you all about those kinds of rain forests. But did you know that a temperate kind of rain forest exists in cooler parts of the world? These types are located along sea coastlines. In the U.S., you'll find one that stretches for 1,200 miles between Alaska and Oregon. In this type of forest, you will find redwoods, the world's tallest trees! Explore the features and creatures of all kinds of rain forests at this page, prepared by the Missouri Botanical Garden. Don't miss the extensive list of links to info on rain forests both tropical and temperate.

http://www.mobot.org/MBGnet/vb/rforest/

Welcome to the Rainforest Action Network Home Page

You may have already heard that there are more kinds of plants and animals in tropical rain forests than anywhere else on Earth. And you probably already know that about half of all the world's species live in rain forests. But did you also know that in the rain forest you can find an antelope that's as small as a rabbit, a snake that can fly, and a spider that eats birds? The Kids' Corner is packed with just this kind of wild information about the rain forest, and it has lots of pictures of the creatures and native people living there. We all have a big problem, though: rain forests might be gone by the time you grow up. They're already disappearing at the rate of 150 acres per minute! Find out what you can do to help.

http://www.ran.org/ran/

NET FILES
Who (or what) is Deep Blue?

http://library.advanced.org/10746/deepblue.html

Answer: It's a chess-playing computer built by IBM. In 1997, it beat world champion Gary Kasparov in a controversial series of matches. Read more at

Think that just because you're a kid, you can't do anything to help save the rain forest?
Wrong.
Here's one way: protect endangered species in the rain forest by asking your family not to buy anything made of ivory, coral, reptile skins, tortoise shells, or cat pelts.
Go to Welcome to the Rainforest Action Network Home Page to find out more ways.

A B C D E F G H I J K L M N O P Q R S T U V W X Y Z

LAND FEATURES—SWAMPS AND BOGS

Can the Everglades Survive?

It's not really a swamp and not really a bog; it's known as the River of Grass, and there is no other place like it in the world. Birds, alligators, fish, amphibians, and reptiles make it their home. You can find out about the challenges facing this important Florida watershed at this official National Park Service site.

http://www.nps.gov/ever/home.htm

Okefenokee Swamp Natural Education Center

Between northern Florida and southern Georgia lie the 700 acres of the Okefenokee Swamp, home to critters as diverse as coral snakes, alligators, and—yes, TOURISTS! You'll be amazed at the dark, mirrorlike water of the swamp, with its overhanging trees draped in swaying strands of Spanish moss. Explore old Seminole canoe routes and learn about the fragile ecology of this very special area. Just remember, don't turn your back on that gator!

http://www.gravity783.com/joe1.html

WATER

Wise Use of Water - Brochures

The world is three-quarters water, isn't it? That means there is plenty to go around, right? Well, if you're talking about water that's healthy for us to drink, it's really in short supply. Consider the millions of people in the world, all of them thirsty. Now think of all the animals and birds in the world, all of them thirsty. Hmmm—better use that water wisely. Here's a list of tips and ideas to help you conserve this natural resource for future dried-out kids on hot, summer days. This site is also available in French.

http://www.cciw.ca/glimr/metadata/
water-wise-pamphlets/intro.html

You won't believe how the PLANTS, TREES, AND GARDENS section grew!

WATER FEATURES—CORAL REEFS

Contrasts in Blue

On coral reefs of the Bahamas and the rocky shore of Maine, marine ecosystems are very different. Do you know why? This edition of *Art to Zoo*, a publication of the Smithsonian Institution, will help you understand, and it provides lots of interesting projects to make this fun!

http://educate.si.edu/lessons/art-to-zoo/contrast/
cover.html

Coral Reefs

There are many different kinds of coral reefs, but all of them support special types of ecosystems. They may be made up of algae, mollusks, or special animals called coral. An atoll is a ring of coral that encloses a circular lagoon. Most often, atolls are formed on the crater of a volcano that has sunk below the surface of the sea. Read more about the world of the coral at this site.

http://dekalb.dc.peachnet.edu/~pgore/students/f95/
starmoss/coral.htm

WATER FEATURES—OCEANS AND TIDES

Climate Change Fact Sheet 22

What's controlling tomorrow's weather? Winds? Air pressure? Nope. The answer is the oceans, which cover two-thirds of our planet. They affect our weather more than anything else on Earth. What's current on the oceans? Dive in here.

http://www.unep.ch/iucc/fs022.html

Education Center Activities: Let's Make Waves

Water doesn't make its own waves; wind stirs up those waves and swells! If you have ever sailed, you know that the windier the day, the more waves there are. Through some simple experiments designed with kids in mind, you can use a fan and marbles to create waves and model the movement of energy through water. These activities should help you sailors remember that the wind in your sail also causes the waves beneath your boat!

http://www.eduplace.com/rdg/gen_act/ocean/
    wave.html

International Year of the Ocean - Kid's & Teacher's Resources

"1998 is the Year of the Ocean—Get into it!" So begins a site with a sea of information and activities designed to "wet" your imagination. You'll find fun science as well as fun coloring books. Don't miss the "Adopt a Buoy" (or maybe a gull?) section to see photos of marine weather station buoys and learn how you can get real-time wave, temperature, and other readings from around the world. Speaking of reading, enjoy the story "The Whale and the Plover" in English or Hawaiian.

http://www.yoto98.noaa.gov/kids.htm

Ocean Planet Homepage

How many forests grow in the deep sea? Plenty—they're forests made of kelp and other seaweed. These kelp forests are home to many sea creatures, just like the trees on land that shelter and provide homes for many birds and animals. Kelp forests also need good-quality water to survive; pollution and overharvesting is a threat to them. Visit the Smithsonian Institution's National Museum of Natural History in Washington, D.C. This is their Ocean Planet exhibit, where you can read about the kelp forest and much more.

http://seawifs.gsfc.nasa.gov/ocean_planet.html

Surf today, smart tomorrow.

OCEAN98 Victor-Intro

Victor the Vector is searching for his mother. Seems they caught different ocean currents, and he's traveling the seas to find her again. If you hitch a ride with Victor, you'll learn all about the great currents of the world and maybe a little bit about geography, too.

http://www.ocean98.org/vicin.htm

Why is the Ocean Salty

You could describe seawater as being a very diluted soup of pretty much everything on Earth: minerals, organic matter, even synthetic chemicals. Here's the strange thing: the ocean has the same degree of saltiness everywhere. There isn't one place that is saltier than another. Where did the salt come from? If freshwater rivers and streams keep flowing into the sea, why doesn't the sea become less salty? Find out here!

http://www.ci.pacifica.ca.us/NATURAL/SALTY/
    salty.html

NET FILES

How many cubic feet of helium does it take to fly the MetLife Snoopy blimp?

Answer: It takes 68,000 cubic feet. The envelope part of the blimp is 130 feet long and 45 feet tall. The blimp carries three passengers plus the pilot, and its top speed is 57 mph. You can read more at the MetLife Blimp page at http://www.metlife.com/Blimp/

A
B
C
D
E
F
G
H
I
J
K
L
M
N
O
P
Q
R
S
T
U
V
W
X
Y
Z

ENDANGERED AND EXTINCT SPECIES

Alive AS A DODO

Most people know the Dodo bird is extinct. They may also know one was a character in Lewis Carroll's *Alice's Adventures in Wonderland*. What few people know is the island of Mauritius, in the Indian Ocean, was probably the only place on Earth where the Dodo was ever seen. But that was hundreds of years ago, because the Dodo died out sometime in the seventeenth or eighteenth century. This page (and the link from it) explains what happened. It was a combination of lack of people skills on the part of the 50-pound bird (it didn't know how to run away!) and the introduction of dogs and other animals to the islands by the Dutch explorers. However, the Dodo still appears on the coat of arms of the Republic of Mauritius, a reminder of a creature the world will never see again.

http://www.mauritius-canada.com/mtius/dodo.html

AMNH - Expedition : Endangered!

The American Museum of Natural History is in New York City, but you can take a trip around the world of endangered species and habitats at this fascinating site. Check "Invasion of the Lake-Snatchers" about zebra mussels. Then read the "Legend of the Meeps Island Flying Frog" for an amusing and educational look at how a creature becomes endangered. Will the flying frog become extinct? Look here and see.

http://www.amnh.org/Exhibition/Expedition/
   Endangered/intro.html

Endangered Species Home Page, U.S. Fish & Wildlife Service

In the United States, 553 plants and 349 species of animals are on the threatened and endangered lists (as of April 1998). *Extinct* means they are gone from planet Earth forever. *Endangered* species are animals and plants that are in danger of becoming extinct. *Threatened* species are animals and plants that are likely to become endangered in the future. Learn which species are listed as threatened and endangered where you live, in the United States, and internationally.

http://www.fws.gov/r9endspp/endspp.html

The Passenger Pigeon

A hundred years ago, the passenger pigeon was the most abundant bird on the face of the Earth. Their numbers were in the billions, and their flocks often blackened the sky for miles. Unfortunately, their habitat was destroyed in the name of progress. Also, their meat tasted good, and people of the day thought it was fun to kill them. The birds could fly 60 mph. Within 50 years, humans drove this species to extinction. The last bird died in a zoo September 19, 1914. Do you think we have learned anything?

http://www.ris.net/~tony/ppigeon.html

World Wildlife Fund

Want to hear a black rhino sneeze? Want to see what's on and off the endangered species list worldwide? Get in here and see what this organization does to help animals and environments all over the globe. Destruction of tropical forests means the winter habitat of your favorite spring songbirds is at risk. What will happen to the summer tanager and the northern warbler if their winter home disappears completely? Find out how you can help.

http://www.wwf.org/

ENERGY

ENERGY QUEST — Energy Education from the California Energy Commission

What was Ben Franklin's energy-saving invention? Join Ben in a word game to find out the answer. He also has other games, crafts, and even a Declaration of (Energy) Independence. This site has activities and games about different kinds of energy, from wind to solar and nuclear to hydroelectric! This site is a must for the energy-efficient, but it loads very slowly. There is a text only and low-bandwidth version you might try.

http://www.energy.ca.gov/education/

FUSION ENERGY

Did you know that the Sun is a fusion power plant? Solar energy is produced by a reactor in the Sun's core with a temperature of 15 million degree Celsius. It would be great to be able to produce energy this way on Earth. Scientists are working on it, but they have a long way to go. They have already achieved the necessary temperatures—as high as 510 million degrees, more than 20 times the temperature at the center of the Sun. Now, the problem is keeping the deuterium-tritium fuel magnetically suspended inside the reactor. Say that ten times! Who knows, maybe you'll be the one to solve this problem. Will fusion power plants be the energy source of the future? Visit this site to start your quest for the answer.

http://www.pppl.gov/oview/pages/fusion_energy.html

"Every time you look up at the sky, every one of those points of light is a reminder that fusion power is extractable from hydrogen and other light elements, and it is an everyday reality throughout the Milky Way Galaxy." Carl Sagan, the famous astronomer, said that. How are we doing on producing fusion power here on Earth? Get an update at the FUSION ENERGY site!

Maine Solar House

This is Bill Lord's solar house. He built this house in southern Maine, on a property specially chosen for the project. Everything was planned with the goal of constructing a house that would make the most out of solar energy. Descriptions and diagrams show how he uses heat from the sun to warm the house and produce his own electricity. He even sells electricity to the power company when he has a surplus!

http://solstice.crest.org/renewables/wlord/

Watch the building of a solar house on the Maine Solar House page. You will see it take shape, from the dream and planning stages to the building of the house to actually living in the home. The owners of this solar house in Maine actually *make* money from the power company!

Renewable Energy Education Module

For sale to a good home: five types of renewable energy. Choose yours today, before the world runs out of energy! You have a choice of solar, wind, hydroelectric, geothermal, or biomass energy. Shots and history are included, suitable for a beginner.

http://solstice.crest.org/renewables/re-kiosk/

Rocky Run Energy Projects

There are all kinds of things kids can do for energy. Drink more soda? No—that's not the kind of energy we have in mind! These students from Virginia have an energy-efficient house online as part of a village that they're designing. You can click on a room in the house and get energy-saving tips. Virginia has three different kinds of power plants. How many do you have where you live?

http://k12.cnidr.org/gsh/schools/va/rrms/energy.html

Windmills and Whirlygigs

Meet Vollis (and his dogs and ducks) and explore his magical world of spinning whirligigs, or wind toys. You can take a virtual tour to the yard and the shop and try some fun wind power activities, including making whirligigs from plastic soda bottles. If you just want an overview, take the Whirlwind Tour, but watch out for the spitting fungus!

http://www.sci.mus.mn.us/sln/vollis/top.html

A
B
C
D
E
F
G
H
I
J
K
L
M
N
O
P
Q
R
S
T
U
V
W
X
Y
Z

A
B
C
D
E
F
G
H
I
J
K
L
M
N
O
P
Q
R
S
T
U
V
W
X
Y
Z

ETIQUETTE AND CUSTOMS

American Table Manners

You might have seen the movie *Titanic*—in it, the rough-and-ready Jack Dawson is invited to a formal dinner party. He is overwhelmed with all the plates and silverware and doesn't know which to use first. That will never happen to you if you study this page. It even tells you which foods are OK to pick up with your fingers. Now you might think this is silly, but eventually you'll be at a wedding or other special occasion, or you'll even be eating lunch at a fast-food restaurant with someone you want to impress. Luckily, it is OK to eat fries with your fingers!

http://www.cuisinenet.com/glossary/tableman.html

Home and Family: Parenting - Table Manners Through the Ages

When your mom tells you to stop playing with your food, that's about good table manners. In the 1700s, a Colonial mom would have said: "Grease not thy fingers or napkin more than necessity requires..." "Smell not thy meat nor put it to thy nose..." "Spit not in the room but in the corner," and, well, you get the idea. Compare table manners from the eighteenth century and 25 years ago with current standards here!

http://homeandfamily.com/features/parent/
    tablemanners.html

Japanese Customs - Table Manners

If you are invited to a traditional Japanese dinner, you'll want to know how to behave so that you won't offend your hosts. This page will tell you what the hot towel is for, how to use chopsticks, and why you don't want to put soy sauce on your rice. Compare this with the table manners you use in your home.

http://www.shinnova.com/part/99-japa/abj21-e.htm

**Attention everyone.
The Internet is closing. Please
go play outside.**

Learn2 Set a Table - Intro

Which side does the fork go on? Does the knife edge go towards the plate or away from it? You'll find the answers to these and other mysteries of life as you learn to set a table. This is not just a casual breakfast table, mind you, but a full-fledged formal dinner table with lots of silver and glassware! Practice the napkin-folding tricks and really show off a terrific table.

http://learn2.com/06/0608/0608.html

Learn2 Use Chopsticks - Intro

We used to feel ridiculous using chopsticks, but not anymore! While we once had to spear our shrimp tempura, now we deftly handle even the smallest morsels of sticky rice. And it's all because of the terrific techniques taught at this page.

http://learn2.com/06/0607/0607.html

NET FILES

Did you know that sunspots rotate around the sun? How long does a sunspot take to go completely around and get back to where it was?

ANSWER:
A sunspot takes 27 days to rotate around the Sun's surface. Read all about sunspots at
http://www.sel.bldrdoc.gov/
primer/primer.html

Trans-Cultural Study Guide

It's all too easy to assume that people in other countries have the same customs as you do. But once you've found yourself saying or doing something that seems innocent at home but provokes anger somewhere else, you may wish you'd studied a bit more before traveling. This guide was put together by a group called Volunteers in Asia, but it works well for just about anywhere. This is a list of hundreds of questions you could ask in order to systematically study another culture. You will have to supply your own answers.

http://www.moon.com/trans_cultural/

EVOLUTION

See also BIOLOGY—GENETICS

Evolution Entrance

The University of California at Berkeley has set up a separate "exhibition area" for the subject of evolution in its online Museum of Paleontology. Here you are greeted by Charles Darwin speaking of the course of evolution being much like a "great tree of life." From there, you can link to sections on Dinosaur Discoveries and Systematics (the classification system used in charting the families of species) and find out about the most important scientists to develop this field.

http://www.ucmp.berkeley.edu/history/evolution.html

Mutant Fruit Flies

Great, now it's teenage mutant ninja fruit flies! The basis for evolution is the ability of some individuals to adapt and change, which may result in a genetic mutation of the species. To demonstrate the varieties of genetic mutation, San Francisco's Exploratorium has transferred this amazing exhibit to their Web site. Detailed color illustrations of naturally mutated fruit flies graphically demonstrate better than pages of text how this phenomenon works. Just when you thought it was safe to go near the fruit bowl....

http://www.exploratorium.edu/exhibits/mutant_flies/
mutant_flies.html

VIDEO AND SPY CAMS let you look in on interesting parts of the world.

Neandertals: A Cyber Perspective

How much do you think you know about early human evolution? This page gives a fascinating peek into the life of Neandertal, who lived 30,000 years ago in Europe and the Near East. You may know this hominid as "Neanderthal"—but according to this page, that's incorrect. Its fossilized remains were found in 1856, in Feldhofer Cave, in a German valley called Neander Tal. Included are sections on the art, language, culture, and social aspects of the lives of these cave people. It's not big dumb guys dragging clubs around, after all. There are also excellent links on human evolution, as well as a suggested reading list.

http://thunder.indstate.edu/~ramanank/

The Sci.Bio.Evolution Home Page

Two Usenet newsgroups have rousing discussions of evolution: this one and talk.origins (see the following entry). You'll find links to the archives of each group here, ready to download. There are also links to two of Darwin's most important texts, *Voyage of the Beagle* and *The Origin of Species*. But you may like the formatting better at <http://www.literature.org/Works/Charles-Darwin/origin/>.

http://weber.u.washington.edu/~jahayes/evolution/

The Talk.Origins Archive

People love to argue about whether the theory of evolution is "true" or not. This newsgroup is one of the places where this discussion goes on. (Check the entries under CREATION STUDIES in this book for more information.) Though you probably won't want to enter into this newsgroup's conversation, the FAQ section is interesting, and you can check out a nice collection of fossil images and other related links. An interactive browser and a keyword file searcher are included here to make things easy.

http://www.talkorigins.org/

A B C D E F G H I J K L M N O P Q R S T U V W X Y Z

EXPLORERS AND EXPLORING

1492 Exhibit

This Library of Congress display examines Columbus, the man and the myth. Why do we talk about the "discovery" of America when people were living there all along? What was life like in the America that Columbus encountered? What changes, immediate and long term, befell both the Europeans and the people of the Americas?

http://sunsite.unc.edu/expo/1492.exhibit/Intro.html

Crossed the West: The Adventures of Lewis and Clark

In 1804, President Thomas Jefferson looked out the window and said, "Hmm, I wonder if there is a water route, maybe a river or something, that goes all the way across the continent and ends up at the Pacific Ocean? Something we could navigate with boats, so we could get supplies there, and settle, and eventually build theme parks." OK, so he didn't *really* say that. But he did want the West explored, and Lewis and Clark were just the guys to take on the task. Want to join their expedition and see what happens?

http://www.nationalgeographic.com/features/97/west/

Exploration of the Americas Title Page

This shows that kids can create a Web site where no other exists! A fifth-grade class in New York has created an encyclopedia of exploration that has no rivals on the Net. It's divided into sections: northeastern North America, southeastern North America, Mexico and western North America, and South America. Some of the explorers you'll read about include Cabot, Hudson, La Salle, Ponce de León, and Cortés.

http://pen1.pen.k12.va.us/Anthology/Div/Albemarle/
  Schools/MurrayElem/ClassPages/Prudhomme/
  Explorers/exploretitle.html

FAQ on Antarctica

Read astronomer Chris Bero's hilarious FAQ on life in Antarctica. Here's a sample: "How much are you paid for going to the South Pole?" "Not enough! Trust me kids, get it in writing before you start working at the pole. Also, don't make the same mistake I made. There is no such thing as Antarctic dollars!"

http://205.174.118.254/nspt/question/chrisfaq.htm

Forbidden Territory @ nationalgeographic.com

"Dr. Livingstone, I presume?" Who said those famous words, and what were the circumstances? Between 1841 and 1873, a young Scots missionary named David Livingstone made several journeys to Africa, at a time when the continent was largely unexplored. He was the first European to see many of the sites, including Victoria Falls, which he named in honor of his sovereign, Queen Victoria. His writings about his exploits were always eagerly awaited back home. In 1866, Livingstone set off to discover the source of the Nile, the world's longest river. He was 53. No news came for years. Finally, in 1869, a reporter named Henry Morton Stanley was sent to look for Livingstone. According to this site, "On October 27, 1871, Stanley 'discovered' Livingstone at the village of Ujiji on Lake Tanganyika, greeting him with the now-famous words: 'Dr. Livingstone, I presume?'" What happened next? Visit this Web page to find out.

http://www.nationalgeographic.com/features/
  97/lantern/

Global Online Adventure Learning Site

Magellan. de Soto. Columbus. You've already heard of these famous explorers from the past. Right now, all over the world, people are still exploring and having adventures! You can catch up with them and read their travel reports on the Net. For example, there's the Laffitte family, sailing the South Pacific for two years. You can read about their experiences, plus lots of other trips, here!

http://www.goals.com/

The Heroic Age: A Look at the Race to the South Pole

Soon after the North Pole was reached by Robert E. Peary in 1909, the race was on to see who could get to the South Pole first. This page looks at three explorers: Ernest Shackleton, Robert Scott, and Roald Amundsen. All three attempted to reach the South Pole in the early 1900s, but only Amundsen and Scott made it. Investigate their strategies and what went wrong, or right, in each case.

http://magic.geol.ucsb.edu/~geo10/Students/heroic.html

La Salle Shipwreck Project of the THC

The Texas Historical Commission has quite a find on their hands! They are excavating a shipwreck believed to be that of the *Belle*, one of the ships brought by the French explorer René Robert Cavelier, sieur de La Salle. La Salle was the explorer who claimed the Mississippi and all its tributaries for France. His ship was lost in 1686. It lies in about 12 feet of water in a bay about halfway between Galveston and Corpus Christi. Archaeologists built a special double-walled coffer dam around the wreck, then pumped out the water in the middle of this "doughnut." They were then free to explore and carefully record their findings. You can read about La Salle and the recovery of his ship and its artifacts at this very special site!

http://www.thc.state.tx.us/belle/

Lewis & Clark Trail

This is an ambitious project from Washington State, which began in October 1995. It has begun to collect information about the lives and times of Meriwether Lewis and William Clark. During the years 1804–1806, Lewis and Clark led the first transcontinental expedition to the Pacific coast. In commemoration of the 190th anniversary of the explorations, the journey has been re-created online. Their most fascinating travel journals are here, as well as some suggested classroom projects. What was life like on the trail before hiking boots and lightweight backpacks existed?

http://134.121.112.29/wahistcult/trail.html

Main Menu @ nationalgeographic.com

Take a road trip with National Geographic as they take you on a series of adventures around the world. Tour the fantastic forest, discover dinosaur eggs, and even stop at the White House. These people are exploring professionals!

http://www.nationalgeographic.com/main.html

NET FILES

What was Michelangelo's last name? (The artist, not the teenage turtle!)

Answer: Buonarroti. In 1508, he was commissioned by Pope Julius II della Rovere to paint the Sistine Chapel's ceiling; the work was completed between 1508 and 1512. He also painted *The Last Judgment*, over the altar, between 1535 and 1541.

http://www.christusrex.org/www1/sistine/0-Tour.html

**Know your ALPHABET?
Now try someone else's
in LANGUAGES AND
ALPHABETS.**

A
B
C
D
E
F
G
H
I
J
K
L
M
N
O
P
Q
R
S
T
U
V
W
X
Y
Z

The Mariners' Museum - Newport News, Virginia

This is a very handy timeline of exploration, which starts with 3200 B.C., when Pharaoh Snefru brought 40 ships from Byblus to Phoenicia. You can trace events and explorers from there, including Marco Polo, Magellan, and James Cook, among others. Some explorer descriptions have additional links where you can go to find out more. For example, Cook was one of the first to carry a chronometer, a special device that helped captains figure out their positions on the sea, before the days of GPS satellite navigation.

http://www.mariner.org/age/histexp.html

New South Polar Times

This site offers a dramatic account of man's touch on the Antarctic Continent, from the earliest dog sled explorers to modern scientists in airplanes. Fascinating stuff, the story is better than Saturday superhero cartoons, and it's all true! There are a lot of great stories on traveling to the South Pole, so plan on spending some time at this site.

http://205.174.118.254/nspt/home.htm

NET FILES

There's a 900,000 gallon ocean in the middle of the Arizona desert. Why isn't it on the map?

Answer: It's inside the Biosphere 2 structure, which also houses a marsh, a savannah, and a rain forest, among other environments. Read more about this experiment in off-planet colonization at
http://www.bio2.edu/
By the way, it's in Oracle, Arizona, north of Tucson.

THE RACE TO THE SOUTH POLE

Why did Roald Amundsen reach the South Pole before Robert Falcon Scott? This in-depth look at Amundsen explains the differences between the men and the methods they used to make the journey.

http://magic.geol.ucsb.edu/~geo10/Students/race.html

Rune Stone

Columbus was a latecomer to the Americas; the Vikings had been there long before. Want proof? Look at the Heavener Rune Stone, in a state park near Heavener, Oklahoma. A Viking land claim was apparently made there about A.D. 750. It is believed that these Norse explorers crossed the Atlantic, sailed around Florida into the Gulf of Mexico, and entered the Mississippi River. From there, they explored its tributaries, the Arkansas and Poteau Rivers, leaving five or so rune stones along the way. At least, that's the theory. See what you think!

http://admin.hps.osrhe.edu/hps/htmls/runtest.htm

Terraquest

Tired of reading about all those musty old explorers from long ago? This site allows you to go along on some fantastic present-day journeys. You'll find pictures, virtual reality panoramas, audio, and text that documents real expeditions with real people just like you! Try virtual Antarctica and discover the wonders of the South Pole. Or perhaps you'd like a sea voyage to the virtual Galápagos Islands—learn about how this remote island's unique animals helped Charles Darwin formulate his theories of evolution. If that's not enough, tag along with blind mountaineer Erik Weihenmayer as he scales the 3,000-foot sheer wall of El Capitán in Yosemite National Park.

http://www.terraquest.com/

FAMILY HOME PAGES

In earlier editions of this book we listed a handful of home pages from families all over the world. We got lots and lots of letters. *Everyone* wanted to be listed in the next edition of the book! We thank the families who suggested their own home pages. So many of them were outstanding that we couldn't decide which ones to include, so we are retiring this subject heading. If you want to find out how to make your own family home page, check the INTERNET section of this book.

FARMING AND AGRICULTURE

See also HORSES AND EQUESTRIAN SPORTS; PLANTS, TREES, AND GARDENS

Kids Farm Where do you want to go?

Any idea what the difference is between alfalfa and regular grass? Familiar with the sounds a turkey makes? Did you know you should stay away from the back of a horse and the front of a bull? You'll know the answers to these perennial questions if you visit this site. You'll also become an expert on farm equipment and learn all about hay baling and other fun on a working Colorado farm.

http://www.kidsfarm.com/wheredo.htm

Virtual Farmland

At Davis' Farmland in Massachusetts, you can discover what's old in farming: rare and endangered farm animal breeds. Click on the farm fun page to see a variety of common farm animals and hear the sounds they make; click on "more animal sounds" to hear elephants, lions, and other nonbarnyard creatures! You can also download coloring pages of farm life and activities, plus play a farm crossword puzzle.

http://www.davisfarmland.com/index2.htm

BEEKEEPING

Billy Bee Honey Products Limited - Canada's #1 Honey

To *bee* or not to *bee*...but the question is, what do you know about bees? Worker honeybees have many jobs in taking care of their hives. They do the feeding, cleaning, guarding, the long-distance and short-distance flying; they carry pollen, produce honey, and build the honeycomb. To learn more about beekeeping, visit this site, and *bee* careful!

http://www2.billybee.com/billybee/

CROPS, PRODUCE, AND ORCHARDS

The Corn Growers Guidebook (Purdue University)

The corniest people in the United States bring you everything you need to know about the top crop: corn. Maybe you want to raise corn, or you need a corn recipe or a corn song. Perhaps you want to find out what products have corn in them or what ancient civilizations used corn. Well, you've *corn* to the right place. When you have had your fill of corn, you can link to the maize page and read about—more corn.

http://www.agry.purdue.edu/agronomy/ext/corn/
    cornguid.htm

Don't Panic Eat Organic

Farmer, don't harm your environment. Nature's pesticides include ladybugs, which eat aphids, and owls, which catch rodents. Did you know that barn owls are called "flying cats"? You can also use "companion" plants, which help to repel bugs from each other! By understanding and using the natural biological systems on a farm, you can leave the sprays and chemicals on the store shelf and let nature do most of the work. Let these certified organic farmers show you how to cultivate in harmony with your surroundings.

http://www.rain.org/~sals/my.html

A
B
C
D
E
F
G
H
I
J
K
L
M
N
O
P
Q
R
S
T
U
V
W
X
Y
Z

Jim's Farming Page

If you don't live close to a farm, you probably have no idea what a "harrower" is or how corn and beans are grown and harvested. Farmer Jim takes you on a tour of his fields through the growing season. See the big equipment Jim uses. If you explore this resource a little further, you can "Ask a Farmer" a question and see some neat agricultural links.

http://toybox.asap.net/farmsite/

Lundberg Family Partnership with Nature — Welcome

The Lundbergs have been growing rice on their Northern California family farm since 1937. Follow along as they explain how they enrich the soil with cover crops and attract waterfowl and other wildlife to naturally supplement the fertility of the fields. Before they plant, they carefully stake any pheasant or other nests, so they can avoid them with the big machinery. Stored rice is sometimes infused with carbon dioxide to keep bugs out. Rice is nice!

http://www.lundberg.com/partnership/welcome.html

Massachusetts Maple Producers Association

Did you know that depending on the sweetness of the sap, it can take anywhere from 25 to 75 gallons of maple sap to make one gallon of maple syrup? The average, though, is 40 gallons raw to one gallon finished. It doesn't hurt the tree to be tapped, as long as you do it the right way. This page explains how you can make your own maple syrup. If you'd rather visit a commercial "sugar bush" and see how it's done, there's a directory of maple producers as well as lots of sticky links.

http://www.massmaple.org/

The Story of Florida Orange Juice - From the Grove to Your Glass

This page explains how citrus farmers decide when their crop is ripe and ready to be picked. Citrus fruits do not continue to ripen after they are picked, so oranges have to be harvested at their peak. Crews pick most of the crop by hand, then the oranges are transported to the processing plant for grading and juice extraction. The whole journey is pictured and described here.

http://members.aol.com/citrusweb/oj_story.html

LIVESTOCK

Bacon Links, Life & Potbellied Pig FAQ and Resource Page

Does the thought of swine make you swoon? Does having a pig as a pet make your day? Then a pot-bellied pig is the way to go. Read about where the pot-bellied pig came from, see other people's pigs, and join the Pot-Bellied Pig List, where you can talk to others who think hogs are heaven.

http://www.voicenet.com/~johnpac/bacon.html

Big Dave's Cow Page

Cow lovers alert! People's fascination with cows tends to *mooo*ve in the direction of humor, using pictures, sounds, poetry, and songs. This site contains all of that and more, including information for that *udder*ly serious scholar in search of bovine research.

http://www.gl.umbc.edu/~dschmi1/links/cow.html

NET FILES

Where is the world's largest bell?

Answer: The Tsar Bell, weighing 210 tons, is in Moscow, Russia. It stands 20 feet high and has a diameter of 22 feet at the base. A fire swept Moscow in 1737, and it engulfed the Kremlin. When water was poured on the hot bell, it cracked, and a huge piece broke off. The bell now rests on a special granite stand at the foot of the Ivan the Great bell tower. See a picture of it at http://www.online.ru/sp/com/inf/kremlin/31img.html

Did you know...

President Harry Truman once said, "No man should be allowed to be President who does not understand hogs." Even if you don't have political aspirations, you can learn a lot about pigs here. Peruse pig trivia, discover porcine pithy sayings, and meditate on the history of pork. Hogwash? Not here.

http://www.nppc.org/hog-trivia.html

The city of Cincinnati, Ohio, was so strongly associated with pork production that it was nicknamed Porkopolis. Read more intriguing pig facts at the Did you know... page.

FeatherSite - The Poultry Page

If you are more interested in what breed of chicken crossed the road rather than why it crossed the road, then strut on over to the Featherside Farm and inspect their collection of colorful chick pics and descriptions. If you say there is more to poultry than *foul* chickens, you're right! They've also included ducks, geese, turkeys, and peafowl guaranteed to smooth your feathers. Hint: Take the link back to the home page to view a dancing chicken.

http://www.cyborganic.com/People/feathersite/
Poultry/BRKPoultryPage.html

CATS are purrfect.

Goats and more Goats

It has some quirky habits, smells a little, and has been hanging around you all day. Do you call the police? No, all the poor goat wants is a good scratch between the shoulders! The Irvine Masa Charros 4-H Club raises dairy and pygmy goats and knows what a rewarding experience raising goats can be. With the dedication and knowledge demonstrated at this site, how can anyone not approve of these kids raising *kids*? Never heard of 4-H before? Check the ORGANIZATIONS section of this book.

http://www.ics.uci.edu/~pazzani/4H/Goats.html

LlamaWeb, Llamas on the Internet!

Llamas make wonderful pets. They are used as pack animals, golfing caddies, and watch or guard animals. Their coat fiber is used to produce rugs, ropes, and sweaters and other clothing. All camelids (the camel family of mammals) have a bad reputation for spitting. Usually they spit at other llamas, though, and not at people in particular. Be careful not to get in the middle of a spitting contest between two camelids! Stop by to learn all about raising these interesting animals, and vote for the cutest baby llama.

http://www.webcom.com/~degraham/

OSU's Breeds of Livestock

Oklahoma State University's breed archive is extensive. You'll find pictures and info on breeds of the following animals: horses, cattle, swine, sheep, goats, and poultry. Oh, yes, did we mention the "other" category? There you'll find llamas, donkeys, and—buffalo! But let's talk cattle. Everyone's heard of the Jersey cow: "With an average weight of 900 pounds, the Jersey produces more pounds of milk per pound of body weight than any other breed." They have a nice photo here, too. Have you ever heard of the Australian Friesian Sahiwal? It's a breed being developed in Australia for use in tropical areas. How about the Florida Cracker/Pineywoods, the Florida equivalent of the Texas longhorn? Visit this site for a virtual barnyard of breeds.

http://www.ansi.okstate.edu/breeds/

A B C D E F G H I J K L M N O P Q R S T U V W X Y Z

A B C D E F G H I J K L M N O P Q R S T U V W X Y Z

Pigs

Are you interested in raising pigs for fun and/or profit? The 4-Hers in this site learn integrity, good sportsmanship, and communication through raising hogs. Investigate the steps required to start your own pig raising venture, what breeds are available, and how to care for these large but gentle swine. And don't forget the added bonus (forget the health spa): unlimited free mud baths! Never heard of 4-H before? Check the ORGANIZATIONS section of this book.

http://www.ics.uci.edu/~pazzani/4H/Pigs.html

Sheep

If you are looking for a farm animal to raise, take a good look at the multipurpose sheep. Stay warm with wool sweaters made from their fleece. Feast on cheese produced from their milk. Stop mowing the lawn; instead, let sheep keep your grass closely clipped. Get your daily exercise by walking a mile a day with your lamb. Make a profit when you take them to the market. "BAAAAAA!" OK, the sheep request that you skip that last one. Here is where 4-Hers show you how fun and rewarding sheep raising can be. Never heard of 4-H before? Check the ORGANIZATIONS section of this book.

http://www.ics.uci.edu/~pazzani/4H/Sheep.html

Tours - #1 The Story of Milk

Cows make milk to feed their baby calves, but even after the baby is eating other food, the cow continues to make up to eight gallons of milk a day! Cows are milked in a special room called a milking parlor, and their milk is pumped to stainless steel holding tanks and immediately chilled to 38 degrees Fahrenheit. Then the milk tanker truck comes to pick it up. This happens twice a day. When it gets to the milk processing facility, the milk goes through two other steps, homogenization and pasteurization, but you'll have to read about those at this Web site. You'll find cow-related Shockwave games and other fun at the main level.

http://www.moomilk.com/tours/tour1-0.htm

WWW Library - Livestock Section (Youth)

Are you interested in 4-H or maybe even a career in animal science? This is the place for you! You can learn about sheep and wool, check out the National Dairy Database, or get information on your favorite breed of livestock. Maybe you'd like to attend the Judging Camp this summer for hands-on experience. Not sure about the livestock-judging thing? Kids gain a lot from competing on a livestock evaluation team. It builds character, and it may even give you confidence if you are shy or tone you down a bit if you are a little less reserved. Never heard of 4-H before? Check the ORGANIZATIONS section of this book.

http://www.ansi.okstate.edu/library/youth.html

FESTIVALS AND FAIRS

The Gathering of the Clans

Scroll down to the Highland Games part of this page. 'Tis a stirring sight, indeed: the gathering of the clans, marching behind the drums and blaring bagpipes. You can sample Scots recipes, admire clan tartans, listen to folktales, and watch a dancer step nimbly over crossed swords. Try the caber toss if you're very strong, throw the stone, or pitch the sheaf in these traditional games of Scotland. Learn about them, as well as Gaelic culture in general, at this site.

http://www.tartans.com/culture.html

Internet 1996 World Exposition

You may have learned all about the various world's fairs and expositions of the last century. The idea was to show people what new inventions—like railroads, telephones, lights, and cars—could do for them. Well, if you've been wondering what this new invention called the Internet can do for you, then welcome to this site. It's a world's fair for the Information Age. One of the most important parts of this expo is the Global Schoolhouse Pavilion, which links schools around the world, showcases young artists, and features activities to help kids learn (and like) the Internet.

http://park.org/

KTCA Productions: PowWow

Please rise, as the flags and eagle staffs enter the arena for the powwow. It's OK, everyone is welcome at Native American powwows. Learn about the dance, regalia, drum, and song of powwows. If you're thinking about attending a powwow, this page will teach you its customs. Learn more by reading the entries in the NATIVE AMERICANS AND OTHER INDIGENOUS PEOPLES and the DANCE sections in this book.

http://www.ktca.org/powwow/

Shrewsbury Renaissance Faire

Art thou off to the faire? Don't forget your Renaissance-era costume and your muffin hat (you can learn to make one here). Yum, those gingerbread cookies look good! Care for some fried dragon scales? What is your U.S. currency worth in Elizabethan English pounds? See what goes into a reenactment of a sixteenth-century Welsh village—this one is located near Corvallis, Oregon. Remember to learn history by playing *faire*, anon!

http://www.peak.org/shrewsbury/

World's Columbian Exposition

Back in 1893, a wonderful fair took place in Chicago, Illinois, and it was called the Columbian Exposition. It introduced the American public to the wonders of the day: electric lights, the cotton gin, typewriters, and all manner of nineteenth-century technology. It was also the first appearance of food products we know so well today: carbonated soda, hamburgers, Juicy Fruit gum, Cracker Jacks, and Aunt Jemima syrup, among many others. There were strange displays, too, such as a map of the United States "made entirely of pickles" and "not one, but two Liberty Bell models—one in wheat, oats, and rye, and one entirely in oranges." Take a virtual visit to the past here!

http://users.vnet.net/schulman/Columbian/
  columbian.html

World's Columbian Exposition: Idea, Experience, Aftermath

You'll find a thoughtful essay and more pictures about the World's Columbian Exposition. Click on "Legacy" and learn how it has influenced places such as Disney World! Find out which famous composer wrote a piece in honor of the Exposition and more as you explore this site.

http://xroads.virginia.edu/~MA96/WCE/title.html

FISH

See also AQUARIUMS; OUTDOOR RECREATION—FISHING; SHARKS

The Amazing Fish-Cam!

Something fishy is happening on the Net right now! See a live picture of a saltwater fish tank in Lou's office. Who is Lou? No one knows, but his fish tank is famous. Can you spot a moray eel or maybe a *humuhumunukunukuapua'a* (humu-humu-nuku-nuku-apu-a'-a), which is the state fish of Hawaii?

http://www1.netscape.com/fishcam/

DINOSAUR EVOLUTION FISH : THE COELACANTH LIVING FOSSIL OF THE COMOROS AFRICA AND MADAGASCAR

In 1938, fishermen off the coast of South Africa found the first living coelacanth in recent history, and there was another reported find in 1952, off the Comoros Islands (to the northeast, in the Mozambique Channel). This isn't just another fish story, either. The *coelacanth* (pronounced see-la-kanth) is a 400-million-year-old "living fossil" fish, once thought to have become extinct long ago. This account of its amazing discovery reads like a mystery novel.

http://www.dinofish.com/

Trick roping secrets are revealed in KNOTS.

A
B
C
D
E
F
G
H
I
J
K
L
M
N
O
P
Q
R
S
T
U
V
W
X
Y
Z

Sidebar letters: A B C D E F G H I J K L M N O P Q R S T U V W X Y Z

Fish and Fisheries in the Great Lakes Region

Do you know your alewife from your yellow perch? OK, how about your lamprey eel from your brook trout? If not, or if you just want information on over 25 different freshwater fish species, dive in here. There is also a special trout and salmon identification guide, if you want the *angle* on them.

http://www.great-lakes.net/envt/wildlife/fish.html

Fish FAQ

Did you know that salmon generally lay from 2,500 to 7,000 eggs, depending on the species and its size, or that some lobsters hardly move more than one mile? What is the most common fish in the sea? Why do scientists classify fish? How long do fish live? How is the age of a fish determined? Visit the profusely illustrated home page, where you'll find the answers to all these questions and more. You'll discover how porcupine fish inflate themselves, too!

http://www.wh.whoi.edu/faq.html

Foam Bath Fish Time

Bathtub foam fish toys can have more than one use, after all. This site will tell you the time in several time zones—using FISH. Just get in here and see one of Net-mom's all-time favorite Internet toys.

http://www.savetz.com/fishtime/

marine-biology Fishes

What's the *porpoise* of this site? Well, if you can't tell a yellowfin tuna from a cookie-cutter shark or a ratfish from a queenfish, then your troubles are over! This Cal Poly marine biology site has descriptions and photos of many common Pacific fish.

http://www.calpoly.edu:8010/cgi-bin/db/db/
marine-biology/Fishes/templates/index

The Salmon Page

The Riverdale Elementary School in Oregon loves salmon: catching it, cooking it, and saving it and its environment. They have also illustrated the page with colorful fishy paintings. For a collection of unchecked links about this king of fishes, cast your line here.

http://www.riverdale.k12.or.us/salmon.htm

FITNESS AND EXERCISE

10 Tips to Healthy Eating and Physical Activity

There are lots of ways you can get fit without putting in hundreds of miles on your family's treadmill. How about taking a hike once a week with a group of friends? You can climb stairs instead of taking an elevator or an escalator. And you can encourage Mom to park a little farther from the mall so that you both get in some good walking. Check for more tips here.

http://ificinfo.health.org/brochure/10tipkid.htm

Aerobics at www.turnstep.com!

One, two, three—kick! Aerobic exercises get your heart beating and your lungs heaving, and they make your muscles strong. Many aerobic exercises are fun when done to music, as dance steps that tone your body. You can learn some new aerobic steps and a ton about aerobics by checking out this Web page and its associated fitness links.

http://www.turnstep.com/

NET FILES

How many days are there in a year, based on the ancient Maya calendar system?

Answer: Either 260 or 365 — it depends on which type of year you mean! The Maya calendar system is very complex. There were two calendar years: the 260-day Sacred Round, or *tzolkin*, and the 365-day Vague Year, or *haab*. Each year had 20 months. Every 52 years, the calendars would coincide. The 52-year period of time was similar in meaning to our century, and it was called a "bundle."

http://www.civilization.ca/membrs/civiliz/maya/mmc06eng.html#calendar

Benny Goodsport

Meet Benny and the Goodsport gang, who teach tips on nutrition and exercise. Did you know that walking and even hobbies like fishing are good exercise? You'll also like the online games and pointers to other resources around the Net. For example, Benny offers links ranging from resources on Garfield and Hello Kitty to some on Arnold Schwarzenegger! Garfield must get all his exercise by thinking up jokes and hoisting lasagna.

http://www.bennygoodsport.com/

Fitness Fundamentals

The President of the United States wants you to be physically fit. The President's Council on Physical Fitness and Sports is an organization whose single goal is to help Americans become fit—to aid citizens in learning how to be physically healthy. One of the many resources the Council provides is the booklet at this site. It provides all the basics in starting an exercise and fitness program for people of all ages, including figuring out what your target heart rate during exercise should be.

http://www.hoptechno.com/book11.htm

STRETCHING AND FLEXIBILITY

When you exercise—whether you're going for a run or a short jog or you're dancing up a storm—stretching your muscles before you begin is important. At this page on the World Wide Web, you'll learn everything there is to know about stretching and how muscles contract. You'll also learn about fast and slow fibers, connective tissue, and cooperating muscle groups. As a matter of fact, if you read all this, you'll be a foremost expert on this subject! If you just want to see a few easy stretching exercises, try <http://www.fitnesslink.com/ changes/ kidsfit.htm>.

http://www.ntf.CA:8082/papers/rma/
  stretching_toc.html

It never rains on the PARADES in cyberspace.

What Time Is It? Time to Exercise!

What's your excuse? It's too cold out? It's too hot out? There's only you and you'd rather exercise with friends? You're stuck at home? This site gives ideas for all those situations and more. For example, if it's too hot, take your dog outside and give him a bath. Or run through a sprinkler (be careful not to slip, though). Lots of good ideas here.

http://KidsHealth.org/kid/food/what_time.html

FLAGS

Ausflag - Reference Library

Vexillology is the study of flags, and many people find it a topic of deep consequence. This site gives some general flag terms, plus worthwhile links to flag resources all over the Net. You can also see the winners in an unofficial contest to design a new flag for Australia.

http://www.ausflag.com.au/info/info.html

Betsy Ross Home Page

Betsy Ross is credited with having sewn the very first U.S. flag in 1776. But did she? You can learn about the questions surrounding this cherished American figure, as well as take a virtual tour to her house in Philadelphia. Apparently George Washington wanted six-pointed stars on the flag, as they appear on his original pencil sketch. Betsy recommended five-pointed stars instead. Everyone scoffed, saying that the stars were too hard to draw, let alone cut. Then they stood amazed as Ross folded a piece of paper, made one snip with scissors, and unfolded a perfect five-pointed star! You can learn the secret of this trick by clicking on "Cut a 5-point star in one snip" on the flag at the top of the page.

http://www.libertynet.org/iha/betsy/

A
B
C
D
E
F
G
H
I
J
K
L
M
N
O
P
Q
R
S
T
U
V
W
X
Y
Z

A
B
C
D
E
F
G
H
I
J
K
L
M
N
O
P
Q
R
S
T
U
V
W
X
Y
Z

Surf, and you shall become empowered (or wet).

The Flag of the United States of America

For a country that is barely over two hundred years old, the United States has a vast and rich accumulation of lore and tradition regarding its flag. Old Glory gets its due from this page in red, white, and blue embellishment. Images of every single official and unofficial U.S. flag are stored here, as well as a variety of documents, songs, poems, speeches, and letters. Red Skelton's famous version of the Pledge of Allegiance can be found here, as well as the information you'll need if you'd like to acquire a flag that has flown over the Capitol. A series of intriguing questions and answers are posted here, along with the (complete!) words to the National Anthem. The site also carries "opposing views" about flags, national symbols, and patriotism.

http://www.usflag.org/

Did you know that you can buy a flag that has flown over the U.S. Capitol?

It doesn't stay up there very long, just a minute or so, but think of the tradition and history and, heck, the fun of having a flag like that! You can even request a flag that has flown over the Capitol on your birthday or other special occasion.

The flags cost between $7.50 and $18.75 plus shipping, and the ordering information can be found at The Flag of the United States of America page.

Flags

Dyed-in-the-wool flag fans will find some delightful goodies on this Australian page. Besides a fine selection of international flag images, you'll find sections featuring motor racing flags, international maritime signal flags ("I am discharging explosives!"), and the complete semaphore flag code—all graphically displayed.

http://osprey.anbg.gov.au/flags/flags.html

The FlagWire Channel

Just as you're putting the final touches on your school report on the flag of Zaire, you hear on the radio that they have not only just changed the name of the country, but it has a new flag! No worries. This site keeps up on all flag changes, and you can find a picture of the new banner here. There are also special reports on various flag topics and current news involving flags of the world.

http://www.flagmakers.com/flagwire/menu.html

Folding The U.S. Flag

You're finally going to participate in a flag ceremony, maybe for school or for scouts. You've always admired how the big kids fold the flag into that neat triangle shape—but wondered how it's done. This site provides a nice animation to show you the moves.

http://www.crwflags.com/folding.html

The Heraldry and Vexillology Page

Discover why flags are flown at half-mast, which flags get to fly higher than others, and more on this neat page. There are links to pages throughout the world, including one that features heraldic clip art. There's a heraldry dictionary, a collection of flags, and so much more that you'll be waving a flag of your own for this site.

http://www.du.edu/~tomills/flags.html

Kidlink Small Flag Icons

Here you will find more than 116 tiny flag icons representing countries participating in the KIDCAFE and KIDLINK discussion list projects. This page loads rapidly, since the GIFs are so small. You can use these to dress up your school reports or home pages.

http://www.kidlink.org/WWW/miniflags.html

NAVA Homepage

Over 500 Native American nations are recognized by the U.S. government, and some of them have their own flags, which are shown and described here. The Nez Perce have a salmon and a deer on their flag, as well as an eagle, which is sacred to their nation. There is also a drawing of Chief Joseph, one of the greatest Native American leaders. The Iroquois flag has linked squares, symbolizing the nations of the Iroquois confederacy, designed to look like linked wampum shell beads. There are many more flags to admire at this unique site.

http://www.nava.org/

Quinn Flags and Banners

Chances are good that your local mall doesn't have a flag store. This site is where you will probably want to go when the occasion calls for purchasing a flag, whether it's the Stars and Stripes, a state flag, the Jolly Roger, sports flags, or flags from many nations. You can even get the flag for Vatican City here! Flag poles, mounting brackets, and indoor display equipment are all available here as well. There are also some guidelines on flag etiquette.

http://www.qflags.com/

USPS and other Nautical Flags

Have you ever seen a tall ship "dressed"? That means it has all its colorful flags and pennants flying for a special occasion. Those flags also represent a common maritime language. Some flags stand for letters, numbers, or words. Some combinations of flags have special meanings, too. Check this site to see messages like "I am on fire!" or "I need a tow." You'll also learn a lot about nautical flag etiquette, as well as international and U.S. flag customs in general. This excellent site is prepared by the U.S. Power Squadron.

http://www.usps.org/f_stuff/flag.html

Welcome to FOTW (Flags of the World)

If you were going to design a flag for the Internet, what would it look like? Fans of this site have chosen one—see what you think. We liked one of the losers (the one with the two crossed computer mice), but there is no accounting for taste. You'll also find pages and pages of flags of the world here. An extra bonus: you'll see national symbols, anthems, and other patriotic links for many countries.

http://fotw.digibel.be/flags/

FOLKLORE AND MYTHOLOGY

Bulfinch's Mythology, 'The Age of Fable or Stories of Gods and Heroes'

This famous work, published in 1855 by author Thomas Bulfinch, is arguably one of the books most responsible for our current-day notions about Greek and Roman gods and goddesses. You may find the language somewhat quaint, but persevere and you'll discover wonderful stories that are often referred to in current literature, movies, and TV. Keep up—with the past.

http://www.showgate.com/medea/bulfinch/

The CAMELOT PROJECT at the UNIVERSITY OF ROCHESTER

Avalon is the mystical isle where King Arthur was taken after he was mortally wounded in battle. According to legend, Arthur is still sleeping in Avalon until a modern-day hero can awaken him. This home page offers lots of information for Camelot fans, including a list of Arthurian characters, symbols, and places. They have also collected a lot of artwork illustrating the Age of Chivalry. You'll also find links to other sites, but our favorite is Arthurian Resources on the Internet at <http://www.lib.montana.edu/~slainte/arthur/top.html>.

http://www.lib.rochester.edu/camelot/cphome.stm

A
B
C
D
E
F
G
H
I
J
K
L
M
N
O
P
Q
R
S
T
U
V
W
X
Y
Z

A B C D E F G H I J K L M N O P Q R S T U V W X Y Z

Dictionary of Phrase and Fable

Are you forever forgetting the Riddle of the Sphinx? Want to know who Apollo was? Can't wait to find out what the seven wonders of the ancient and medieval worlds were? The current edition of this classic book is one of Net-mom's favorites, but you have to get it at the store. The 1894 edition is online and searchable.

http://www.bibliomania.com/Reference/
PhraseAndFable/

The Encyclopedia Mythica

This encyclopedia on mythology, folklore, and magic contains well over 4,300 definitions of gods and goddesses, supernatural beings, and legendary creatures and monsters from cultures and beliefs all over the world. You'll find Chinese, Etruscan, Greek, Haitian, Japanese, Latvian, Maya, Native American, Norse, Persian, Roman, Welsh, and other mythologies here. Check up on gnomes, unicorns, fairies, and other legendary beings in this award-winning reference source!

http://www.pantheon.org/

NET FILES

What are stovebolts and why would you find them in the ocean?

Answer: They are the knobby tubercles on the upper jaw of a humpback whale. They appear in distinctive patterns and are used to distinguish whales from each other. No one knows their exact function, but they are thought to be touch-sensitive hair follicles. You can see a picture at http://www.nead.org/explore/vww/stovebolts.html

Gryphons, Griffins, Griffons!

This page is dedicated to gryphons: mythological beasts with the head, forelegs, and wings of an eagle and the hindquarters, tail, and ears of a lion. They are symbols of strength and vigilance in mythology. Sections of this home page include gryphons in literature, art, and architecture and other gryphon sightings on the Internet. Fly over to this site to check out these wondrous beasts!

http://www.enteract.com/~tirya/gryphon.html

The Johnny Appleseed Homepage

His name was John Chapman, but you probably know him better as Johnny Appleseed. Sometime in the early nineteenth century, Chapman decided his life's mission was to travel through the wilderness on foot and plant apple seeds wherever he went. He hoarded seeds gleaned from cider mills, and soon the countryside bloomed with his efforts. No one knows very much about him, but recently the U.S. Postal Service honored him with a postage stamp. You can find out more about this legendary American figure here.

http://www.msc.cornell.edu/~weeds/SchoolPages/
Appleseed/welcome.html

Mythology

Type in the URL below. Then click "Enter the Site" and then choose "Myths." After that you'll be ready to explore. For example, just click on The Sun. Immediately you'll have links to almost 20 different myths and legends about this celestial body, from cultural traditions all over the world. Maybe you're interested in myths about the sky and its constellations? There are almost 40 of those listed. If you'd rather read all the stories by geographical region, you can just click on a world map! Plus: in case you can never remember which god is related to which other god, there are convenient family trees for the Greek, Roman, and Norse mythologies.

http://www.windows.umich.edu/

Myths and Legends

This impressive set of links contains pointers to resources from Australian Aboriginal myths to modern science fiction and fantasy. It is the single, best source for a comprehensive listing of world mythological resources. You'll find Celtic, Slavic, Greek, Roman, Norse, and many other kinds of stories here. A caution to parents: This site had too many links for us to explore individually.

http://pubpages.unh.edu/~cbsiren/myth.html

Pegasus' Paradise

A lot of these ancient heroes and mythological beasts have really strange names: Bellerophon, Daedalus, Odysseus—how do you pronounce them? This ThinkQuest Junior site, created by kids, solves that problem. Not only can you look up animals, heroes, villains, and gods and find out all about them, but you can also hear their names pronounced! There's also a neat game that asks you to match the Greek gods with the names of their Roman counterparts.

http://tqjunior.advanced.org/4553/

Reed Interactive's Online Projects

On this page, you'll find creation stories and traditional wisdom as told by schoolchildren from around the world. Included are animal legends, creation stories, tales about the environment, and other stories. Stories have been submitted by children from Australia, Iceland, Canada, Alaska, and Israel.

http://www.ozemail.com.au/~reed/global/
mythstor.html

Stories and Fairy Tales Theme Page

If you're looking for some stories to scare your friends as you sit around the campfire, try here. Other tales include fairy tales, Native American legends, and folklore from other countries. There are also many spiritual teaching stories, including some from the Bible as well as the Sufi tradition, among others.

http://www.cln.org/themes/fairytales.html

FABLES

Aesop's Fables - Online Collection

All the fables you're looking for are here, and some are in Real Audio files so you can listen to them as well as read them. There are also Grimm and Andersen fairy tales, as well as a very cool scrolling timeline from 1000 B.C. to A.D. 1000, showing contemporary thinkers, religious leaders, and scientists.

http://www.pacificnet.net/~johnr/aesop/

S.R.O's Aesop's Fables Page

These very short stories teach lessons you won't soon forget. Although Aesop's fables have been told and retold for thousands of years, people never get tired of hearing them. "The Tortoise and the Hare" and "The Wolf in Sheep's Clothing" are two that you may already know from cartoons or books, but there are many more here for you to discover.

http://attila.stevens-tech.edu/~soh1/aesop.html

NET FILES

SOUTH POLE

Is there really a striped pole stuck in the ice at the South Pole?

Answer: According to astronomer Chris Bero, "There is the ceremonial pole, which is several yards away from the actual South Pole. It is striped red and white like a barber's pole with a metallic mirror ball on top. The real geographic South Pole is marked by a metal rod with a U.S. Geological surveyor marker on top." You'll see a little picture at *http://205.174.118.254/nspt/question/question.htm* but be sure to read his hilarious FAQ on life in Antarctica at *http://205.174.118.254/nspt/question/chrisfaq.htm*

A B C D E F G H I J K L M N O P Q R S T U V W X Y Z

Surf today, smart tomorrow.

FAIRY TALES

Cinderella Project: Home Page

You may have seen Disney's animated story of Cinderella, but do you know that there are lots of other pictures and stories about her? Here is a collection of 12 different versions of the story, some with illustrations. She's really an old lady: the earliest version here is dated 1729! From here you can also explore variations of the following stories: Little Red Riding Hood and Jack and the Beanstalk.

http://www-dept.usm.edu/~engdept/cinderella/
   cinderella.html

Cinderella fans should immediately drive their carriages to the Cinderella Project: Home Page! This site is a text and image archive containing a dozen English versions of the Cinderella tale. The texts may be read horizontally (one version at a time) or vertically (one episode at a time) for comparisons among the versions. You can also choose to look at only the images. This is a good site to visit if you'd like to read variations on a common fairy tale.

Faerie Lore and Literature

Move over, Tinkerbell, this is the fairyland of legend and literature. Check the archive of fairy drawings, Irish and other fairy tales, and the fairy dictionary. You'll also find the texts of Andrew Lang's *Red Fairy Book* and *Yellow Fairy Book*. Read about some funny fairies and some that aren't so nice. Don't believe in fairies anymore? See a photo of one at a Texas Renaissance Fair here (well, sort of). A caution to parents: There are also some links to Wiccan fairy stories included in this very complete collection of stories, poems, and lore.

http://faeryland.tamu-commerce.edu/~earendil/faerie/

Tales of Wonder

This site features folk and fairy tales from around the world. Geographic areas represented include Russia, Siberia, central Asia, China, Japan, and the Middle East. Tales from Scandinavia, Scotland, England, Africa, India, and Native American nations are also included. The source used for the stories is listed. This is an excellent site for exploring the world of folk and fairy tales.

http://darsie.ucdavis.edu/tales/

Every time you baby-sit your little brother, he wants a story, and you've told him all the stories you know! Get some new ones at Tales of Wonder, which contains folk and fairy tales from around the world. You'll find stories from China, Scotland, Japan, and the Middle East, as well as many stories told by Native Americans.

GAMES AND FUN

See also CRAFTS AND HOBBIES; VIDEO GAMES

CARD GAMES

Card Games

This page is an excellent place to get the rules of many different types of card games from all over the world. If you have a question about who goes first in Go Fish, then this is the page for you! A caution to parents: Not all of the world's card games have family-friendly names.

http://www.netlink.co.uk/users/pagat/

The House of Cards

Do you ever just sit alone on a rainy day and realize that there is nothing else to do but play Solitaire? If you only knew *how* to play Solitaire! Think of this site as the place you can go to learn the rules of card games: new, old, and never before heard-of.

http://www.sky.net/~rrasa/hoc.html

Did you know

that jokers were added to American card decks in the 1870s? You can learn about different types of decks and try out lots of fun card games at The House of Cards!

Watch your steps in DANCE.

It never rains in cyberspace.

CHESS

Chess Dominion

Resistance is futile! Chess is a game, a culture, a way of life. To join the Dominion, you must learn to play this classic game of kings, knights, and pawns. But how? You could show your teacher the extensive chess lesson plans at this site and ask to add chess to the school curriculum, or you could just use the interactive tutorials on your own. Developed by ThinkQuest kids who are also chess masters, you'll learn basics, study championship games, and even meet Deep Blue, the chess champion with a power cord!

http://library.advanced.org/10746/

Play Chess against tkChess

If you know your rooks from your pawns, you'll definitely want to make your move here. There are two versions: one is Java-enabled, so can drag your pieces around; the other should work fine on both text and graphical browsers. Be sure to read the FAQ to learn how to use the algebraic notation system, which is easier than it sounds. You'll also find links to other Net chess pages, including one that will let you challenge another online player so you can play together in real time.

http://pine.cs.yale.edu:4201/cgi-bin/chessplayer/

USCF: Scholastic Chess Resources

You know you love chess, and your buddies love to play chess, too. How about starting a chess club at school? The U.S. Chess Federation tells you how to do that at this site. You'll also see who's leading in the national tournament standings. If you need to improve your game, there is a list of recommended books, too.

http://www.uschess.org/scholastic/

A
B
C
D
E
F
G
H
I
J
K
L
M
N
O
P
Q
R
S
T
U
V
W
X
Y
Z

Side alphabet: A B C D E F G H I J K L M N O P Q R S T U V W X Y Z

FRISBEE

The Freestyle Frisbee Page

Ever notice how Frisbees never come with directions? How do you learn those cool tricks? Now you can visit this Web site and learn from the experts. Put a spin on it, and don't forget the silicon spray!

http://www.frisbee.com/

Frisbee Dog Club: National Capital Air Canines Homepage

Don't leave your dog home when you want to play—take your pet along. This page features world-class disc dogs in action photos. Bone up on how to train your dog to catch and fetch a flying disc.

http://www.vais.net/~krobair/ncac.htm

NET FILES

How did the chipmunk get her stripes?

Answer: A Native American tale has the answer. Because the winters were cold and people were starving, Coyote went to the mountains to steal fire from the Fire Beings. As he was returning with it, the easily annoyed Fire Beings ran after him. Coyote threw the fire to Chipmunk, who began to run with it. One of the Fire Beings reached out to grab her, but the rodent was too fast, and she got away. However, the clawed white burn marks can be seen on Chipmunk's fur to this day. Read more about this story at http://www.ozemail.com.au/~oban/coyofire.htm

The History of the Disc

Ever wondered who invented the toy Frisbee? It began life as either a pie plate or a cookie tin lid from the Frisbie Pie Company in New Haven, Connecticut, long ago in the early 1870s. You can read the incredible history of this toy here and even see the original patent. Never heard of a "patent"? This page explains it all!

http://www.upa.org/~upa/upa/frisbee-hist.html

Ultimate Player's Association

"When a ball dreams, it dreams it's a Frisbee!" And you thought it was just a simple game. This stuff is serious fun. Ultimate had a modest beginning back in 1968 in New Jersey at Columbia High School. By 1972, the game had escalated to an intercollegiate sport, and today it's played in over 30 countries around the world. As with any sport, there are rules, but the list is short and the play is simple.

http://www.upa.org/~upa/

FUN ACTIVITIES
See also CRAFTS AND HOBBIES

The Bubblesphere

You don't need a lot of skills to learn to blow soap bubbles, right? So what is with this guy who calls himself "Professor"? Turns out he really is an expert. At his home page, he reveals the ultimate soap solution for making the most colorful, sturdy bubbles. He explains how to make your own bubble-blowing tools from soup cans and coat hangers (ask your parents for help). You don't even need anything special—he teaches you how to blow bubbles using only your HANDS! But wait, there's more. Check the bubble FAQ, bubble games, and the other wonders of the Bubblesphere.

http://bubbles.org/

Have a whale of a time in MAMMALS.

Graffiti Wall

Let's be honest. Graffiti is ugly: it makes buildings and signs look hideous. On the other hand, it is kind of fun to be able to leave a mark somewhere. The problem is that graffiti makes whatever is marked look awful. Now, through the wonder of the Internet, you can leave your mark and never worry about defacing property. It's at this site, and there is one for kids aged 11 and younger and one for kids aged 12 and up. Spray paint, scratch, do what you like. It's designed for fun with no unsightly mess to clean up! The walls are closely monitored for appropriate content to keep the site enjoyable for all.

http://www.kidscom.com/orakc/GraffitiWall/
   wallright.html

John's Word Search Puzzles

John certainly is a creative guy. He's developed word search puzzles about many different themes, including holidays, states, sports, the Bible, and other topics. Hidden words may be frontwards, backwards, on a diagonal, vertical, or horizontal.

http://www.thepotters.com/puzzles.html

North American Stone Skipping Association (NASSA)

"If you can throw a stone at the water and make it touch down and lift off, just once, you have skipped a stone and thereby join one of the most ancient recreational activities of humankind," says Jerdone. He's the current Guinness world record holder for stone skipping! In 1994, he made a small piece of flat black slate jump 38 skips, on the Blanco River in Texas. This site tells you all about the history of stone skipping, also known as "Ducks and Drakes" in England, "ricochet" in France, and "stone skiffing" in Ireland. It even tells you how to challenge the world record holder and asks you to send in your favorite stone skipping locations so they can be mapped worldwide. The huge links list on this page has not been checked.

http://www.yeeha.net/nassa/a1.html

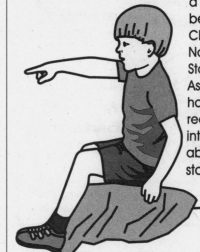

Sitting on a beach, you idly pick up a small flat stone and shoot it across the surface of the water. Wow! It sure skipped a lot of times! Could be a world record! Check the North American Stone Skipping Association (NASSA) home page and read lots of interesting things about skipping stones.

Puzzlemaker

This is a neat site that shows how to make some fun party games or how to make puzzles to add some interest to a school assignment or class newsletter. You can very easily create word search puzzles, hidden message puzzles, crossword puzzles, mazes, math squares, and more. Print them out and send them to your friends and family—everyone will wonder how you did it!

http://www.puzzlemaker.com/

GAMES

DARTS! CYBER/DARTS Dart Info!

Do you see bull's-eyes when you surf the Net? Maybe you'd better turn off the computer and take a walk outside, in actual reality! If you're *looking* for bull's-eyes, though, you've come to the right place. This is the page for those who are obsessed with the game of darts. This page includes press releases from the American Dart Association, a listing of international dart groups (you can find one near you), and wild and crazy dart stories. It's a must for dart enthusiasts. Links are too numerous, and we could not check them all.

http://www.cyberdarts.com/

A B C D E F G H I J K L M N O P Q R S T U V W X Y Z

A
B
C
D
E
F
G
H
I
J
K
L
M
N
O
P
Q
R
S
T
U
V
W
X
Y
Z

NET FILES

What color is a lobster's blood?

Answer: It's colorless, but when it is exposed to air, it turns sort of blue. Read fascinating fish FAQs at http://www.yoto98.noaa.gov/books/fish/fish3a.html#6

Footbag WorldWide Information Service

Some call it a footbag, while others know it by the trademark Hacky Sack. The object of the game is to keep the footbag in the air—with your foot—as you "hack" the "sack" around in the circle with others. Check out this site for the full story. Patterns are here, too, so you can make your own.

http://www.footbag.org/

Games Kids Play

Remember that game you played at camp last summer? It was called Steal the Bacon, wasn't it? Or was it Red Light/Green Light? Maybe you're mixing it up with What Time Is It, Mr. Wolf? If you're a little hazy on the rules of those terrific games you had fun playing once—and then forgot—visit this site. You'll find an archive of the best kids' games EVER!

http://www.corpcomm.net/~gnieboer/gamehome.htm

Introduction to Go

Played by millions of people around the world, Go was originally developed in China, about 3,000 to 4,000 years ago. These days, some players have reached professional status, and tournaments are followed as avidly as baseball's World Series. Get the basics on rocks and bowls, rules and moves, and try the game this Web page says is "the one computers can't beat us at."

http://www.well.com/user/mmcadams/gointro.html

Milkcaps in Hawaiian

Has the game of milkcaps, or POGS, hit your school yet? Don't worry, it will; or maybe this fad has come and gone where you are. This very easy game has kids everywhere clamoring for POGS, POGS, and more POGS! But did you know that the game may have started 600 years ago in Japan? Find out about the mother of POGs, Blossom Galbiso, who reinvented the game for schoolchildren.

http://www.ukulele.com/milkcaps.html

HORSESHOE PITCHING

Horseshoe Pitching Information Site

You can't just borrow shoes from the pony in the paddock; you've got to use regulation horseshoes if you want to play with folks from the National Horseshoe Pitchers Association (NHPA). According to this home page, the horseshoes used by the NHPA are very different from shoes actually used on horses—they are much bigger. Any shoe used in a tournament must not exceed 7 1/4 inches in width and 7 5/8 inches in length. The opening of the horseshoe can't be wider than 3 1/2 inches from just inside both points of the shoe. Most of them weigh about 2.5 pounds. For more of the fine points of horseshoe pitching, trot on over here.

http://members.iquest.net/~tsearsxx/Horseshoe-Pitching.html

Rules of Horseshoes

Here are the court dimensions, rules, and scoring for the game of horseshoes. You'll find everything you'll need to set up the game. Add two steel stakes, a set of horseshoes, some sand for the pits, and a yard. A partner is also a must.

http://www.ece.neu.edu/personal/stricker/horseshoes/horseshoe_rules.html

Curl up with a good URL in BOOKS AND LITERATURE!

WASHERS ~ A Great American Game!

Do you love to pitch horseshoes but are challenged by a lack of space? Try the new all-American game—Washers! You'll learn the history of this wonderful game, the equipment needed, the rules and regulations, and a lot more. In no time at all, you'll be tossing washers and wondering why you waited so long to become a Washers champ.

http://washers.org/

MAZES

3D riDDle - Home Page

Single image stereograms, or SIS—what are they? Ever seen those pictures that look like a bunch of squiggly lines or repeating images but supposedly have hidden pictures in them? Some people can "see" the hidden images, and some, try as they might, just can't. If you're one of the former group, try the puzzles here. Solve one, click in the right place, and you are allowed to go on to the next level. Warning: This maze is HARD and it could drive you crazy! We told you so, so don't complain to us later.

http://cvs.anu.edu.au/andy/rid/riddle.html

Glenn Teitelbaum's Maze

Hang a left—no, a right! Now you're lost (you can always use that BACK key on your browser). Have fun exploring these interactive mazes, but watch out for The Minotaur. Every now and again The Wumpus will turn up and show where you are on the map. Unfortunately, the Wumpus will run away again—with the map!

http://home.pb.net/~tglenn/maze.htm

Mazes - Hands On Children's Museum

Don't let the really easy maze at the beginning fool you. They get harder. If you think you're not challenged enough, try the Face Maze or the Name Maze. We thought we were pretty good too, until we tried this page.

http://www.wln.com/~deltapac/maze/mazepage.html

PeterCat's Maze of Treasures

Gosh, which way should you go? You have a choice of three directions: should you try the Twisting Little Maze of Passages, the Maze of Little Twisting Passages, or the Twisty Maze of Little Passages? Sometimes when you choose a direction, a "treasure" Web site is selected, and you can choose to go "off-maze" to check it out. Choose the right directions, and angels and leprechauns will escort you to the exit! A caution to parents: Not all the "treasure" sites have been checked; kids should use this site with their parents.

http://www.servtech.com/~petercat/maze/

www.MAZES.com - Perplexing Puzzles by John@Mazes.com

Totally amazing! The Maze Man has invented mazes that spell messages, hexagonal mazes, word mazes, movie mazes, and more delights to puzzle over. Don't miss the pizza maze, where you start at the jalapeno pineapple pizza and try to make your way around to the sausage one. Hungry? You will be by the time you finish this game.

http://members.aol.com/themazeman/

You've seen the U.S. flag, with its 50 stars. What other world flags display stars?

Answer: A whole sky-full of flags have stars on them! Flags with constellations on them include those of Australia, Brazil, and New Zealand. Flags with stars in other arrangements include those of China, Panama, and Somalia, among many others. At http://fotw.digibel.be/flags/keyworda.html you can explore more on world flags.

A B C D E F G H I J K L M N O P Q R S T U V W X Y Z

ONLINE GAMES

ACEKids_Java_Games

Is your browser Java-enabled? If you're not sure, this page explains how you can tell. Make sure you don't enable Java without asking your parents first, since there are lots of reasons they may have chosen to disable it. But if you've got it, you can play Master Mind, Connect Four, Stars, Hunt the Wumpus, and Hit Me!

http://www.acekids.com/javagame.html

Activities! Wangaratta Primary School

Say "G'Day" to some friendly kids in Australia, who have created some fun Aussie games for you to try. Listen to the cackle of the kookaburra, then try a dot-to-dot, a word search, and a coloring page—all based on Australian animals. Don't forget to come back up from "down under."

http://www.ozemail.com.au/~wprimary/acts.htm

The Animal Game

Can a computer really think? Try this test. Think of any kind of animal, and the computer will try to guess it by asking you "yes or no" questions. Answer as best you can. The computer will narrow down the choices until it finally makes a guess. If it's wrong, you win, and you get to "teach" the computer that animal with a question it can ask a future player so that it can win next time.

http://www.bushnet.qld.edu.au/animal/

Apple Corps

Similar to Mr. Edible Starchy Tuber Head (see the entry later in this section), this site lets you choose other vegetables. Try a moustache on an artichoke or maybe some spectacles on a pumpkin. Not a veggie fan? You could try a famous politician instead.

http://apple-corps.westnet.com/apple_corps.html

Billy Bear's Playground — Billy Bear 4Kids.com

The graphics here are superb! You can play these games online or offline on paper. The "Make Your Own Cartoon Bear" and the "Mix & Match Em Up" games are sure to be winners. Billy Bear has storybooks you will enjoy reading. Also, there's a lot of clip art you can use on your Web pages! Just be certain to read the rules for its use.

http://www.billybear4kids.com/

Bluedog can count!!

Blue Dog is a classic Web celebrity, and she's been around for quite a while. She's had a lot of time to practice basic arithmetic, and she's willing to help anyone learn how to do simple math problems. Just type in your numbers, and Blue Dog will bark the answer. She's always right, patient, and so...colorful.

http://www.forbesfield.com/bdf.html

Build Your Own Snowman Contest

Do you live in a place where there is lots of snow in the winter? Or do you live where there's never any snow? It doesn't matter, because here on the Web, you can build a snowman any day of the year. Plus, you can save your creation online so he never melts! Just select the hat, mittens, shoes, and other things your snowman will need, give him a name, and you're ready to warm up with some cocoa.

http://tn.areaguide.com/games/snowman/

Build-a-Monster

This is a sweet little game to amuse the little kids in your family. Pick a head for your monster—how about that frog? OK, now choose a body—do you like that chicken? Now, which feet should you select? Yikes, that makes a very strange-looking monster, but it won't scare anyone.

http://www.rahul.net/renoir/monster/monster.html

Build-a-Rocket

If you've been trying to build a rocket out of stuff in the basement, forget about it. Even the youngest children can be rocket scientists at this page. Choose among several pictures and design your own spacecraft. If you have Java capability (ask your folks about this if you're not sure), you can blast your ship into the sky.

http://www.droid.com/renoir/rocket/rocket.html

Checkers

Here's a nice little friendly checkers game, if you have a Java-enabled browser. Can you beat the computer? Click on your red game piece and move diagonally. Jump over a black piece to claim it. Watch out, the computer's good.

http://tn.areaguide.com/games/checkers/checkers.htm

Why has Darth Vader been spotted hanging around the Washington National Cathedral?

Answer: Don't worry, everyone knows he's there. Get out your binoculars. That's him high up on the Northwest Tower; he's a grotesque, which is similar to a gargoyle. The design was one of four winning suggestions by kids. Find out about the others at http://www.cathedral.org/cathedral/kids/gargoyles.shtml

Cyber Jacques' Cyber Seas Treasure Hunt

Avast ye, me hearties, from whatever else you're doing, and come try the games at Cyber Jacques' seagoing arcade. They all require Shockwave, so you'd best have a current version or you'll be walking the plank real soon! What's here? In Fish, you throw pies at a bear but avoid the flying fish jumping up between the two of you. In What's Inside, you take apart a pirate to see what's underneath (a hamster running around an exercise wheel is one thing we found) and retrieve letters to a word puzzle. Figure out the secret word, and you've won! You'll find several more equally wacky games here.

http://www.cyberjacques.com/

Desdemona: Interactive Othello

This site lets you play Othello, or Reversi, against the computer. Play at several different skill levels. If you're a beginner, choose to view your legal moves before you select one. You can also read about the rules and strategy as well as see statistics on the game as played at this server.

http://www.math.hmc.edu/~dmazzoni/cgi-bin/desmain.cgi

The Electric Origami Shop

Actually, this site is not about origami at all, but the stuff here will bend your mind. Check the Fridge Gallery, where you can display your art in cyberspace. None of those tacky magnets are needed—just a bit of cyberglue and your imagination. Or take the temperature of the mood of the Internet today—is it blissfully unaware, grumpy, or happy? Add your mood. Be sure to seed some alien snow, and watch it grow into drifts before your eyes!

http://www.ibm.com/Stretch/EOS/

The Fruit Game

Don't get the idea this is a PEACHy game. It may apPEAR simple, but LEMON tell you, it's impossible to win the way they have it set up. Play against the computer, but don't be the last to take a fruit from the table! ORANGE you glad I told you it's a mathematical trick?

http://www.2020tech.com/fruit/

A
B
C
D
E
F
G
H
I
J
K
L
M
N
O
P
Q
R
S
T
U
V
W
X
Y
Z

Fun Brain

How about playing some math baseball? You pick how difficult the math questions should be and decide if you want addition, subtraction, multiplication, division, or all of the above. Then the computer will ask you an arithmetic question. Can you get it right? Swing—wow, it's a triple! After that see how good you are at making change of a dollar. How many pennies, nickels, dimes, and quarters should you give back after a certain purchase is made? This site has other fun games, too, including a concentration matching game.

http://www.funbrain.com/

Gid's Games

Gid admits he doesn't get out very often. He spends a lot of time playing his own games, we bet. They are fun, colorful, and very, very hard to stop playing. Check out Webtris, The Logic Board, The Cube, Berries, and several other interactive games you'll recognize immediately. But remember to turn off your computer and go play outside occasionally. In case you forgot, that really bright thing up in the sky is called the *Sun*.

http://www.gids-games.com/

Happy Fun Physics Ball

Here's another strange Java game. Click on the Happy Fun Ball and drag your mouse over to the nearest wall of the game square. Now release the button. Happy Fun Ball bounces off the wall. Not impressed yet? OK, now click on Happy Fun Ball and drag it as fast as you can around and around the screen. Now let it go. Keep doing it. Happy Fun Ball has some random tricks that you'll see, sooner or later.

http://links.math.rpi.edu/java/students/sander/
   Friction/

Be swampwise in EARTH SCIENCE.

Headbone Zone Free Games and Prizes!

Headbone Zone offers lots of fun games, and in some of them you may be able to win prizes if you've got the high score of the day. See if you can guess the riddles in Riddleopolis. Pick a category and answer the trivia questions—just watch out for the Randomizer, which can make your score go up or down! Then there is the Rags to Riches game, where you play the part of a big-time rock band promoter and try to rake in cash. Take your band, Groovy Gravy, on a ten-week concert tour. You set the venues and ticket prices, decide when to record new songs, and plan out your advertising campaign. Don't miss the Headbone Derby, either. This popular and long-running series challenges you to travel the Net looking for clues to help you solve mysteries. There is a lot more on this site too, including monitored chat rooms, and we're sure this will be one of your favorite Internet destinations!

http://www.headbone.com/games/

Hunt the Wumpus

What's a Wumpus? We don't know, but there's one sneaking up behind you! In this game, your mission is to shoot the Wumpus before he takes you home for dinner—HIS dinner. Search the caves for clues, and watch out for bats and pits. Be careful, you must also dodge arrows from other online players!

http://scv.bu.edu/htbin/wcl

I Spy

Before we all wondered where Waldo was, we loved a game called I Spy. Now that game's come to the Web, and it's perfect entertainment for young children. Choose a picture, say, a screen full of colorful postage stamps. The first player looks at the picture and says, "I spy a rocket!" Player two points to the stamp with the rocket on it, if he or she can find it. Then it's player two's turn: "I spy a stamp with a dog!" And so on. See if you can find the stamp with Mt. Rushmore!

http://www.geocities.com/~spanoudi/spy/

Kid's Corner * Oasis Telecommunications, Inc.

Here is one wing. Where is the other one? Hmm, the body goes here, and oops, leave room for the antennae to go here. Can you guess what kind of puzzle we're doing and what picture we will have when we are done? Check it out, and while you're here, try a hangman game and a very nice collection of links. Then maybe you can send some of your work to the Kids Art Archive.

http://kids.ot.com/

Kids' Clubhouse

For some wacky word puzzles, math and logic brain teasers, or Net scavenger hunts, visit this site hosted by publisher Houghton Mifflin. There are also author interviews and book reviews for kids, by kids.

http://www.eduplace.com/kids/

Marcel's WebMind

This is a Web version of the popular Master Mind game. You can play this game right over the Internet. The objective is to break the "code" by finding the right combination of colors. The computer will show a black peg, which means that you have the right color in the right position, or a white peg, which means that you have the right color in the wrong position. Confused yet? You can play at several different skill levels, too, and this version gives you hints.

http://einstein.et.tudelft.nl/~mvdlaan/WebMind/
WM_intro.html

Mr. Edible Starchy Tuber Head Home Page

If you are a big fan of Mr. Potato Head, this is the next best thing. Select online options for eyes, ears, hair, and so on to determine what your Mr. ESTH looks like. The author of the page has also created stories about Mr. ESTH, as well as places he's been spotted in the movies and on TV. Inspect the link to a cheap imitation: Mr. Edible Fibrous Stalk Head. Just scroll down and click on "Our cohorts over in the Networking Group don't get out much."

http://winnie.acsu.buffalo.edu/potatoe/

Platypus Garden of Goodies

Do you like puzzles? Here you'll find mazes, word search puzzles, jigsaws, and more. Many of them were designed for kids, by kids! You'll also find family activities, music, pages that *talk* and *sing* (if you have the right plug-ins and hardware), and much more. We particularly enjoyed the "Shareware Carol." This site is available in English and Spanish, and there are some songs in Japanese.

http://www.platypus-share.com/

PonyShow's Kids - Paradox's Puzzles

Paradox has created some really charming puzzles here. If you like to look for hidden animals and objects in drawings, try Pop's Pizza Puzzle or the Secret of the Spiral Notebook. Other puzzles attempt to teach math concepts such as tangents or repeating images, but they are not interactive. For more fun, go back to the main page (click on "Home") and read stories, write to pen pals, or try more links!

http://www.ponyshow.com/kidsnet/puzzle/puzzle.htm

NET FILES

Across the water, you see a distant fellow boater holding a yellow and red flag in each hand, held straight out from his sides. Is he trying to tell you something?

Answer: He might be. If he is signaling you using the semaphore flag system, he is sending the code for the letter R. Want to know what the rest of his message is? Better check *http://osprey.amb.gov.au/flags/ semaphore.html* to find out.

A B C D E F **G** H I J K L M N O P Q R S T U V W X Y Z

Seuss Lorax Introduction

Even very little children will have fun trying to catch seeds in this Shockwave game inspired by Dr. Seuss. Use your mouse to position your basket just right. If you catch ten seeds, you'll be able to replant the Truffula Forest, and the Truffula Forest is what everyone needs.

http://www.randomhouse.com/seussville/games/lorax/

Sony PlayStation Homepage

Bandicoots are the coolest thing to come out of Australia since koalas! Great games on a new and upcoming game system are the rule here. Take a "crash" tour of the Bandicoot's world, get some game tips, play some online games, and check out the latest titles for the Sony PlayStation.

http://www.playstation.com/global.html

NET FILES

The Iditarod is a 1,150-mile dogsled race in Alaska, from Anchorage to Nome. It traverses some of the roughest, most beautiful country on earth, and often the dogs wear booties to protect their feet. According to race rules, how many booties per dog are mushers required to bring?

Answer: Eight per dog, according to the rule book. As this site explains: "In fact most competent mushers keep their dogs bootied from Anchorage to Nome and use about 2,000 booties all together. Booties are usually made of polar fleece and one bootie will last several hours and up to 100 miles."

http://www.iditarod.com/iditarod/question.htm

The Tribe Connect4 Applet Page

Tired of the same old tic-tac-toe? Then maybe you'd like to try Connect Four. Play against the computer and see if you can outsmart it—we couldn't! The best thing about playing over the Net is that you never lose the game pieces.

http://www.thetribe.com/Connect4.htm

Web-a-Sketch!

You know that fun drawing screen with the two knobs? If you thought that was hard, wait until you try Web-a-Sketch! Look through the gallery and see what other people have created. Some of them have way too much time on their hands. Other people didn't quite get it. See how well you can do.

http://www.digitalstuff.com/web-a-sketch/

WebBattleship

Fight naval battles against a computer, and see how good your strategy is! Score a hit on each of the squares occupied by the computer's hidden ships to win. Easy to learn, WebBattleship is similar to the popular board game.

http://gen.ml.org/battle/

Welcome to Lemonade Stand

In this easy-to-learn simulation game of high finance, you start with a fistful of dollars, a dream, and a weather forecast. Balance the cost of rent, lemons, and your advertising budget into your sales price per cup. Watch that weatherperson! Can you squeeze out a lemonade empire or will you lose all your lemons?

http://www.littlejason.com/lemonade/

Welcome to Percy's Puzzles!

OK, these are educational games, but they really will *spark* your curiosity about electricity and solar, wind, and nuclear power. Don't miss playing the hilarious game called Watt's That? If you run out of energy, take a nap and come back later for more fun.

http://www.energy.ca.gov/education/puzzles/
    puzzles-html/puzzle.html

Welcome to Theatrix/Sanctuary Woods

Got Shockwave? You'll love this site. It has ten of the most engaging, fun, and wacky games we've ever seen on the Web. We loved warping the photo of "The Employee of the Week" and we quickly became addicted to Brain Drain (a concentration matching game with a lot of quirks) and Knock-out (a baseball pitch game where you're trying to ring the Liberty Bell—don't ask). Face the Music was all about fractions, and Franklin Dress-up let us try different outfits on a very patient turtle.

http://www.theatrix.com/fun/fun.html

Where's Waldo? on the Web! Contests! Games! Chat! and Prizes!

That Waldo—he's lost again. Can you find him in the center of town? He's hidden in the crowd somewhere. Maybe if you click on some of these objects, they will make noises—try it! After you find Waldo, try one of the games. There are downloadable demos for both Mac and Windows platforms, or you can play the games online.

http://www.findwaldo.com/

Wonka — Enter the Gates to the Wild World of Wonka!

If you loved the movie, *Willy Wonka and the Chocolate Factory*, you'll love this set of Shockwave games. If you don't have that plug-in, you can still download the games and play them offline. There's a coloring book with a twist so even the youngest kids can play. Older kids will enjoy the science games and the various arcade-type challenges. Note that the company is trying to sell you their candy. Remember to ask a parent before you type your name or any other personal information.

http://www.wonka.com/

"Use the source, Luke!" and look it up in REFERENCE WORKS.

SCRABBLE

The Official SCRABBLE® Homepage

At the official Web site, you'll be offered the choice of two sites: one for folks in North America and one for everybody else. Check out both variations, because there is much to learn and see at both sites! Learn the history of the game, see a live Scrabble game as it's played, and get some hot tips to improve your skills. You can even find out how to get replacements for those Scrabble tiles your dog chewed up as well as a complete set of rules for your downloading pleasure.

http://www.scrabble.com/

San Jose Scrabble® Club No. 21

Did you know that a'a is an acceptable Scrabble word? It's a type of rough, cinderlike lava. If you're a fan of the game, this page will go a long way to settle arguments and food fights over which word is legal or not. This page provides links to other Scrabble pages on the Web and even has information on the world championships!

http://www.yak.net/kablooey/scrabble.html

The Scrabble FAQ and other crossword game resources

In addition to the FAQ, this site links you to other Scrabble clubs around the world. You'll also find many Scrabble and crossword puzzle links.

http://www.teleport.com/~stevena/scrabble/faq.html

STRING FIGURES

This + That - String Figures

Have you ever taken a loop of string and woven it around your fingers in a pattern, like Cat's Cradle? Do you sometimes feel like you're "all thumbs"? Check out the animated lessons to learn some fairly easy string figures. It takes practice, but this site will help. Tired of string? This site also offers some very cool animations to show you how to juggle!

http://home.eznet.net/~stevemd/stringar.html

A B C D E F G H I J K L M N O P Q R S T U V W X Y Z

World-Wide Webs

Everybody's taken a loop of string and played Cat's Cradle with a friend. Here's a collection of string figures from around the world to keep you busy all afternoon and into the evening. Try The Banana Tree or Four Boys Walking in a Row, both from Pacific islands.

http://darsie.ucdavis.edu/string/

GENEALOGY AND FAMILY HISTORY

Cyndi's List of Genealogy Sites on the Internet

This is a companion Web site to Cyndi Howell's book *Netting Your Ancestors*. It's a comprehensive and easy-to-use directory to thousands of Internet resources: ship passenger lists, adoption research, handy online starting points, and what to do when you've hit the wall and can't seem to get any further in your quest to find out about your ancestors.

http://www.CyndisList.com/

Deciphering Old Handwriting

Your grandma just gave you a whole trunk full of old family photos and letters. Trouble is, the handwriting is very strange. It just doesn't seem to use the same letters we do these days. The words seem to be abbreviated too. What's going on? This Web site explains it all. There's a mystery at the end, too: what was the name of the woman who inherited the "horse named Clumse"? Based on the clues here, can you figure it out?

http://www.firstct.com/fv/oldhand.html

Everton's Genealogical Helper: Web Site

Here's the Web site of the world's largest genealogical magazine, *Everton's Genealogical Helper*. Sure, it's not the print version, which usually runs around 300 pages, but some great features and lots of help for beginning genealogists are available—for free! There are also for-fee services here for real enthusiasts.

http://www.everton.com/

Family History Centers

Where's the biggest collection of genealogical material in the world? The Family History Library in Salt Lake City, Utah, is the biggest one of its kind. The library is part of the Church of Jesus Christ of Latter-Day Saints. The Church thinks it's very important to find out about family history, so they send researchers around the world to copy public records. You can see these records in person by going to a Family History Center—a branch of the Family History Library—near you. There's at least one in every U.S. state, and there are others in the British Isles, New Zealand, Australia, Canada, and other countries. They're free and open to the public. Take a look at this list to find one close to you.

http://www.genhomepage.com/FHC/fhc.html

The Genealogy Home Page

Ever thought about drawing your family tree? No, not the one in your front yard! We're talking about your relatives. Picture a tree with you at the bottom. On the first two branches are your parents. On the next highest branches are their parents, who are your grandparents. Further up the tree are their parents, or your great-grandparents. Guess what—that tree reaches up higher than you can see! Get started here with help from experienced family researchers, called genealogists. Computers and the Internet are two of the most important tools being used today by genealogists. You can get your own free family tree tracking software here and learn how to be part of a project to share family histories over the Net. The project already includes millions of names! Wouldn't it be amazing if someone's already working on your family history? Find out here.

http://www.genhomepage.com/full.html

Nothing to do?
Check CRAFTS AND HOBBIES
for some ideas.

Genealogy Toolbox

Sure, your dog has a pedigree, but do you? Search for your family name and history here. You may find out your friends should be calling you Duke, Prince, or Princess! Would you like to see what your grandparents' (or maybe even great-grandparents') birth or death certificates looked like? Find out how to send away for your own copies from state Vital Records offices. And if your family has its own coat of arms, the section on heraldry will explain what all those colors and symbols mean.

http://genealogy.tbox.com/

Guide for Interviewing Family Members

"Who was your best friend?" That's just one of the questions you need to include on a family history questionnaire. What are the other 118? Check this site, print out the questions, then go visit your grandma and grandpa for some amazing stories. Don't forget to bring your tape recorder or your videocamera!

gopher://ftp.cac.psu.edu/00/genealogy/roots-l/
    genealog/genealog.intrview

How much does it cost to rent the 100-inch telescope at the Mount Wilson Observatory for a night of observing the stars?

Answer: Only $1,300 a night, and it includes the services of one telescope operator. Such a deal! Not only that, but you get use of two dorm rooms in the refurbished monastery and kitchen access for that late night cookies and milk break. Check it out at http://www.mtwilson.edu/Services/Professional/100in.html

What is a First Cousin, Twice Removed?

You're pretty clear on your parents, your brother and sister, and maybe even your aunts and uncles. But where do your first cousins come in—and what's this "twice removed" stuff? If you've gotten a little fuzzy on relationships and the terms that describe them in our Western culture, check here. Can you really be your own grandpa?

http://www.familytreemaker.com/16_cousn.html

GEOGRAPHY

23 Peaks

Phil Buck had a dream. He wanted to be the first person to climb the tallest mountains in all nations in North America, Central America, and South America. In May 1998, he realized his goal, but along his ten-year journey he encountered land mines, civil war, poisonous snakes and spiders, tropical diseases, avalanches, hidden crevasses, and recently, frostbite. You can follow along in his trip diaries, ask questions, and add to the resources available in this very intriguing site. What goal will Phil tackle next?

http://www.23peaks.com/

3D Atlas Online Geographic Glossary

If you've forgotten what a fjord is, or you're wondering how to define a delta, visit this site's handy dictionary of geographical terms. There are plenty of hyperlinks to help you keep your definitions *strait*.

http://www.3DAtlas.com/letters_gl.html

GeoBee Challenge @ nationalgeographic.com

Each year, thousands of schools participate in the Geography Bee, using materials and questions prepared by the National Geographic Society. Millions of kids compete for a chance at winning a $25,000 scholarship and other prizes. Some of the questions are easy, and some are real stumpers! How many of these questions can you get right? They change them every day, so play often.

http://www.nationalgeographic.com/features/
    97/geobee/

A B C D E F G H I J K L M N O P Q R S T U V W X Y Z

A
B
C
D
E
F
G
H
I
J
K
L
M
N
O
P
Q
R
S
T
U
V
W
X
Y
Z

GeoGame Project

The GeoGame was created to help kids learn geographical terms, read and interpret maps, and to have fun finding out all about cultural diversity. Your class must register to participate in the organized version of the game, but look for a Web version you can play today, called GeoSeek.

http://www.gsn.org/project/gg/

License Plate Game

Try to guess the name of the U.S. state or Canadian province before you click on it on the colorful outline map. See a picture of that area's license plate!

http://www.klutz.com/treefort/travel/plates/intro.html

Operation Webfoot

It's always more interesting to learn about a far-off place from someone who has actually been there. How would you like to learn about geography from a stuffed animal? Tweety Bird, Miss Piggy, Gumby, and Kermit are just a few of the toys now traveling the world and sending back reports. As teacher Paul Meyers says, "Operation Webfoot originated as an idea to help stimulate young minds in the area of geography, history, and science. Stuffed animals traveled around the United States, Australia, Canada, Germany, Guam, and Israel, to various host families. These families took the animals on outings in their local areas, wrote in journals about the animal's experiences, and sent pictures and postcards and/or e-mail from their local area to Cucamonga Middle School in Rancho Cucamonga, California. The host families then mailed the animal to another host family." Follow along on the Web site and see where they will be next. Maybe your school or family can host one of them in the future!

http://www.csd.k12.ca.us/cucamonga/webfoot.html

Get on board, little children, in RAILROADS AND TRAINS.

HAY! Gallop over to HORSES AND EQUESTRIAN SPORTS.

"Pole to Pole" Projects

What would happen if you started at the North Pole, picked any line of longitude, and walked along it until you came to the South Pole? You'd travel through many different countries, need lots of different types of clothing, eat quantities of unusual foods, and carry numerous types of strange bills and coins. A class of fifth graders in the Netherlands pretended to do just that, and they wrote reports about their virtual travels. See how it's done at this interesting page.

http://www.xs4all.nl/~swanson/origins/
    pole_menu.html

The Professor's Postcards

The Professor takes trips to UNESCO World Heritage sites all over the world, and she's great about sending postcards back to her friends. Unfortunately, she always seems to leave out the most important words—like where she is! Can you figure it out from the clues on the postcards?

http://www.un.org/Pubs/CyberSchoolBus/special/
    profesr/

Welcome to Geo-Globe: Interactive Geography!

This ThinkQuest contest finalist site, built by kids, will rock your world! How much do you know about geography? In Geo-Find, you can play at the beginner, intermediate, or advanced levels. Is Santiago the capital of Chile? What countries contain part of the Sahara Desert? Is Egypt south or north of the equator? Right or wrong, you'll get more links for you to explore on that topic. Geo-Quest involves ten questions: try to guess the right animal or bird, based on the answers to the questions you pose. Don't stop there—you'll find several more games that will test your knowledge of the seas, lands, and skies of Planet Earth.

http://library.advanced.org/10157/

Xpeditions @ nationalgeographic.com

Quick—you need an emergency map of Idaho to complete your homework! Relax, this site offers a fast way to get one onto your screen, and then you can save it or print it. (Note: National Geographic's Map Machine, described below, will get you a color map plus information on each state. The Xpeditions atlas is fast, but you'll just get black-and-white maps.) The atlas at this site offers over 600 maps from around the world, all optimized for printing to paper or screen. In the Xpeditions Hall galleries, explore physical, natural, and cultural aspects of geography, using multimedia and QuickTime virtual reality. There is also a forum to ask and answer geography questions.

http://www.nationalgeographic.com/resources/
    ngo/education/xpeditions/

MAPS

Bodleian Library Map Room - The Map Case

This is a project presented by the Bodleian Library Map Room in Great Britain. The Bodleian Library is one of the oldest libraries in the world, and it contains the seventh largest collection of maps. This is a perfect site if you have a report on British history, and they have some unusual maps from the New World, too. For example, there's Boston, Old Montréal, and "Part of Virginia Discovered... by John Smith 1612" (maybe Pocahontas helped him draw it!).

http://www.rsl.ox.ac.uk/nnj/mapcase.htm

Color Landform Atlas of the United States

What state are you interested in? They are all here, but let's use New York as an example. At this site you can see a color physical map of the state, or a black-and-white map, or an 1895 map, or a counties map. There is also a satellite photo of the state, with its outlines marked. Here's the fun part. You'll find links to other specific types of information. See New York watershed maps, find out where the toxic waste dumps are, explore national parks and historic sites in New York, and find out about roadside attractions such as the Cardiff Giant hoax. Parents: Be sure to explore the Roadside America part of the site with your kids.

http://fermi.jhuapl.edu/states/states.html

Make a Map

If you ever wanted to make a detailed map of a country, this is the perfect place for you. You'll use your forms-capable browser to instruct a Graphical Information System (GIS) what you want it to do. Here you can build many different maps of Canada and learn tons about geography in the process. Want to know the Canadian range of the grizzly bear or the location of wetlands? Try this site!

http://atlas.gc.ca/schoolnet/issuemap/

Map Machine @ nationalgeographic.com

Everyone knows how wonderful the National Geographic Society's maps are. Now many of them are online. Need a quick map, facts about a country, state, or province, and a picture of its flag? You'll find it right here at the Map Machine Atlas. Try View From Above (then click on the spinning globe) for colorful maps of the world pieced together from satellite images, digitally enhanced to make it a global cloudless day! You can also get political and physical maps, as well as view some maps of yesteryear in the Flashback area off the main table of contents.

http://www.nationalgeographic.com/resources/
    ngo/maps/

Mapmaker, Mapmaker, Make Me a Map

If you wanted to get to your friend's house but didn't know the way, how would you get there? One way would be to have your friend write the directions on a sheet of paper. That might work if your friend only lived a few blocks away, but it could get very complicated and wordy if he or she lived farther away. The answer: draw a map! This page tells you how maps are made and explains some of the terms used in mapmaking. You'll also find out about the different kinds of maps and how they are used.

http://loki.ur.utk.edu/ut2kids/maps/map.html

DINOSAURS are prehistoric, but they are under "D."

A B C D E F G H I J K L M N O P Q R S T U V W X Y Z

A
B
C
D
E
F
G
H
I
J
K
L
M
N
O
P
Q
R
S
T
U
V
W
X
Y
Z

PCL Map Collection

Available from the University of Texas Library, this collection includes maps from around the world and links to some of the best map collections on the Internet. Check out the historical maps and the current events maps of Bosnia and Iraq. If you need a map, start here!

http://www.lib.utexas.edu/Libs/PCL/Map_collection/
Map_collection.html

Rare Map Collection

Of course, maps have been around for a long time. You can view one of the finest collections of historic maps on the Internet at this University of Georgia Web site. Included are some great maps of U.S. Civil War battlefields, as well as material on Colonial and Revolutionary America.

http://www.libs.uga.edu/darchive/hargrett/maps/
maps.html

NET FILES

What are "utilidors"?

Answer: When Walt Disney World's Magic Kingdom was built in Florida, special "utility corridors," or utilidors, were built. These allow vehicle and pedestrian deliveries to the various "lands" throughout the park; they also allow cast members to travel to various areas of the park without being seen by visitors, who might be disconcerted to see a Frontierland cowboy walking through Tomorrowland. Learn more about this "tunnel system" at http://www.otc.com/Disney/WDW/MagicKingdom/Secrets/General.html

NET FILES

What insect is being used to help design fighter jets?

Answer: Dragonflies are able to change direction very quickly in flight. Engineers at the University of Tennessee are trying to find out how to make jets do the same by studying dragonfly wings. They "fly" large models of these insects in wind tunnels to study how their wing shape keeps them up. Read about the project at http://loki.ur.utk.edu/ut2kids/dragonfly/dragonfly.html

Round Earth, Flat Maps

How do mapmakers manage to portray a round planet on a flat paper surface? It all starts with a *projection*, and there are several types, each having good points and bad ones. Find out why you might choose to use the conic projection over a planar or cylindrical one if you were drawing a map of the United States. On the other hand, a planar projection would be a great idea for a map of Antarctica. Depending on the point of view of the map on your wall, your view of the world may be true or distorted. Clear things up at this site.

http://www.nationalgeographic.com/features/2000/
exploration/projections/

Star Journey: The Heavens - Star Chart @ nationalgeographic.com

Explore a map of visible stars as they appear from the North and South Poles. All 2,844 of these stars (plus nebulae and star clusters pictured on the map) can be seen with the unaided eye. As you click on the various quadrants you'll come across special blue squares. That means there is a Hubble Space Telescope photo of that star available to view as a close-up. Letters from the Greek alphabet are used to describe the apparent brightness of various stars within a constellation. Alpha is the brightest, followed by beta, gamma, and so on. It's all explained in the "Star Chart Notes" section.

http://www.nationalgeographic.com/features/97/
    stars/chart/

TIGER Mapping Service The "Coast to Coast" Digital Map Database.

This site will give you color maps with cities, highways, lakes, and other features clearly marked, based on 1992 data. Try searching by ZIP code, latitude - longitude, as well as city name. You can mark your maps with a variety of symbols. It's also linked to the Census Bureau's *U.S. Gazetteer*, with information on population. You can save your map as a GIF image (select that button, then click on the map itself) and print it. Enclose it with your next letter to Santa or your relatives or anyone else who needs directions to your house!

http://tiger.census.gov/

USGS: What Do Maps Show

This site has comprehensive lesson plans and hands-on student activity sheets for students—all related to understanding maps. You can also download student map packets, which you can print out for use with the lessons. This is a great geography teaching and learning tool.

http://info.er.usgs.gov/education/teacher/
    what-do-maps-show/WDMSTGuide.html

Welcome to MapQuest!

Get customized maps for places all over the world using the interactive atlas. You can get street-level information covering 78 countries and 300 international travel destinations. It's outstanding, it's fun, and it's free! There's also a TripQuest driving planner. How long have you been begging Mom and Dad to drive you to Disneyland? Maybe they say, "Oh, it's so far, and we'd get lost on the way." No problem. Just go to this site, type in the name of your town, and type in the nearest city to Disneyland (Anaheim, California, is close enough). Magically, you'll get back not only a map but also detailed driving directions, complete with the mileage of each segment! It works for U.S. and Canada only (driving to Disneyland from Halifax, Nova Scotia is 3,574.6 miles). Unfortunately, you can't drive from Hawaii, but you get the idea.

http://www.mapquest.com/

Xerox PARC Map Viewer

This site gives you public domain, copyright-free maps on demand, for the United States and world regions, using several different projections. The maps show only coastlines, rivers, and borders; they don't have marked cities or roads. (If you need a more detailed map, see the Xpeditions entry in this category.) For those using a text-only browser, the following hint is suggested by Xerox's Palo Alto Research Center: Select the Map Viewer's "Hide Map Image" option and then the "Retrieve Map Image Only" option. Some browsers will then allow you to save the image to a file on your computer. But note well: the data used to generate these maps is not up-to-the-minute. Read the FAQ to find out which borders may be different. The FAQ also suggests other sources of online maps.

http://mapweb.parc.xerox.com/map/

Fetch some fascinating info in DOGS AND DOG SPORTS.

A
B
C
D
E
F
G
H
I
J
K
L
M
N
O
P
Q
R
S
T
U
V
W
X
Y
Z

HEALTH AND SAFETY

Children's Sleep Problems

Sleep is a good time for dreams, when your body rests for a new day of fun. Sometimes, though, sleep is interrupted by nightmares, sleepwalking, or even really bad dreams called sleep terrors. If you would like to learn more about sleep problems that kids have, take a look here. This page is available in English and French.

http://www.psych.med.umich.edu/web/aacap/
factsFam/sleep.htm

Hospital Tour, Chronic Illness, Children

Nine-year-old Julia has discovered that hospitals can actually be fun! She and some of her friends will take you through the hospital and explain some of the scary parts of being sick. Once you understand what they are, you won't be scared any longer. For example, sometimes patients are fed liquids through a slender, flexible tube and needle stuck into their arms. That is called an IV, and although it might hurt a little at first, once it is in place the doctors and nurses can give medication through this tube. There are a lot of interesting pictures, and each has a great explanation about what is happening. Oh, and don't be scared when you meet up with Chris—he's just wearing a mask, gown, and gloves so he doesn't get any germs from the people around him!

http://funrsc.fairfield.edu/~jfleitas/hospital.html

NET FILES

What is the sound of one cow mooing?

Answer: We're not sure, but you can hear what we mean at http://www.gl.umbc.edu/~dschni1/cows/sounds.html Besides solo cow sounds, you'll hear a cow duet, a cow chorus, and cacophony of cowbells. Mooove over, Garth, here comes Bossie!

KidsHealth - Children's Health & Parenting Information

This is the best kids' health resource out on the Net. Now, you might be thinking, "Diseases, ick! Why would I want to visit a Web page about health?" Well, haven't you always wanted to know what causes hiccups? The answer's here! And what if we said the Shockwave games here are awesome? Play Plak Attack: shoot toothpaste or crack your floss whip to fight back at the plaque monsters and keep your teeth healthy. Or try the animations about how your body works. Hit the kitchen for some healthy recipes (try Ants on a Log, or Pretzels), or read some reviews of hot toys and see how they rate on the Fun-o-meter. There is a LOT more here; we recommend the whole site for learning about nutrition, feelings, and lots of ways to stay healthy.

http://kidshealth.org/

BEDWETTING

Bedwetting

Bedwetting is embarrassing! Did you know that 15 percent of all kids older than three years old wet the bed? It's true, and there are reasons for this. To learn more about bedwetting, check out the page produced by the American Academy of Child and Adolescent Psychiatry. This page is available in English, French, and Spanish.

http://www.psych.med.umich.edu/web/aacap/
factsFam/bedwet.htm

NATIONAL ENURESIS SOCIETY HOME PAGE

It's estimated that between five to seven million kids in the U.S. wet the bed at night. Fortunately, most kids will grow out of it—no kid likes to wake up in a wet bed! This page offers some treatments and further information from the National Enuresis (en-yur-ree-sis) Society. There is a little more at the Kid's Health site at <http://kidshealth.org/parent/healthy/enuresis.html>.

http://www.peds.umn.edu/Centers/NES/

DENTAL CARE

Ask the Dentist Home Page

There is nothing better than a beautiful set of choppers. After all, how can you eat corn on the cob or bite into a big, juicy apple if your teeth aren't in tip-top shape? You can look over other questions to the dentist or ask your own. What's toothpaste made of? Should you pull out your loose tooth? What's the deal with that fluoride goop they put on your teeth? The answers are here!

http://www.smiledoc.com/smiledoc/

The Tooth Fairy

Some children believe that when they lose a tooth, it should be left under their pillows for the Tooth Fairy. She takes the tooth and may leave behind some coins. There is a lot about that gentle story at this Web site. You will also find quick tips on how to keep your teeth healthy and cavity-free. How often should you brush your teeth, and what's that gunky stuff called plaque? Learn how to floss, and remember: the only teeth you have to floss are the ones you want to keep!

http://www.toothfairy.org/

DRUGS, TOBACCO, AND ALCOHOL
CAMPAIGN FOR TOBACCO-FREE KIDS

The CENTERS for Disease Control and Prevention reports that every day, 3,000 kids become regular smokers, and about one-third of them will die because of smoking-related diseases. One of the problems is that tobacco companies target ads at kids. They also sponsor a lot of events kids like, particularly sports events such as auto racing. They give away clothing that kids like—baseball caps, T-shirts—with the ads and tobacco logos all over them. Another problem is that nicotine in cigarettes and smokeless tobacco is addictive, so once someone starts smoking, it may be difficult to quit. The 1996 Food and Drug Administration's rule on tobacco (currently being challenged by the tobacco industry in federal court) and the proposed tobacco settlement agreement would ban tobacco brand sponsorship of sports and entertainment events. Keep up with the latest news, join the tobacco-free kids campaign, learn a lot about what tobacco can do to your body, and find out about the annual "Kick Butts" day.

http://www.tobaccofreekids.org/html/
kid_s_corner.html

NET FILES

"Uncle Sam" is a drawing of a man wearing a flag suit, and in cartoons he is often used to represent the United States, if the U.S. were a person. Early drawings were based on a real person, who happened to be a clown. Who was he, and what famous phrase is also associated with him?

Answer: According to the Clowns of America International, "Dan Rice (1823–1901) was a clown of the Civil War era. Rice had a goatee and wore a patriotic costume he referred to as his flag suit. Political cartoonist Thomas Nast based his drawings of Uncle Sam on Rice and his costume. [Rice] campaigned for Zachary Taylor for President. One of the things he would do was invite Taylor to ride on the circus bandwagon in the circus parades. Local politicians would clamor to ride as well, hoping his popularity would benefit them. People would comment, 'Look who's on Taylor's bandwagon,' inspiring the phrase 'jump on the bandwagon.'" Find out more at http://www.clown.org/history.html

A B C D E F G H I J K L M N O P Q R S T U V W X Y Z

A B C D E F G H I J K L M N O P Q R S T U V W X Y Z

D.A.R.E. Kids

D.A.R.E. stands for Drug Abuse Resistance Education. It's a series of lessons led by a police officer to help give you the skills you need to resist pressure to try drugs or alcohol or to join a gang. This year, over 35 million kids around the world will become involved in a D.A.R.E. program. At this site you can learn about the mission of the organization, read the latest news, and, if you *dare*, join Daren the Lion in his clubhouse where you can talk to other kids.

http://www.Dare-America.com/

Dogs Against Drugs

Yofee is a very special working dog. She's trained for search and rescue as well as disaster and drug work. She takes her "person" around to schools and community events to help teach kids about safety, smoking, and drug addiction. Meet her here, grab some of her coloring book pages, and learn about all kinds of safe practices. There is even a coloring book about safety around strange dogs, called "Does He Bite?" Go fetch it!

http://www.sonic.net/yofee/

National Clearinghouse for Alcohol and Drug Information For Kids Only

Pick a brain, any brain. You'll find out what effects marijuana, alcohol, inhalants, and tobacco have on brains. Does someone you know abuse drugs or alcohol? There's a section called How to Help Someone that will tell you what you can do. Wally Bear and the Know Gang offer word search puzzles, coloring books, and even information on Internet safety. Just say yes and visit this site.

http://www.health.org/kidsarea/

The Smoking Handbook

Written by eighth graders for other middle schoolers, this site examines the allure of smoking as well as the addictive qualities of nicotine. Even if you don't smoke you should be aware of the dangers of secondhand or sidestream smoke. Want to help someone quit smoking? Various methods are outlined on this well-researched page, which also offers a useful set of links.

http://www.westnet.com/~rickd/smoke/smoke1.html

HUMAN BODY

Anatomy

Your body is so amazing. It's a combination of muscles, bones, arteries, and various organs, including your great brain. To get an inside peek at some parts of your incredible body, take a look at this page from Levit Radiologic-Pathologic Institute. Your body looks a whole lot different from the inside! Hint: The term "inferior brain" just means it is looked at from below; "superior brain" means the view is from above.

http://rpisun1.mda.uth.tmc.edu/se/anatomy/

NET FILES

How many transistors are there in the world?

Answer: The folks at Lucent Technologies (who should know) say: "There are some 200 million billion transistors in the world—about 40 million for every man, woman and child." Not for long, though. The same page says that more than half a billion transistors are manufactured every second. Visit *http://www.lucent.com/liveson/html/q10historylinks.html* for more on the history of the transistor.

"We like the INVERTEBRATES best."—The Nields

Anatomy of the skin

What's your body's biggest organ (and we don't mean pipe organ)? It's your skin! You probably don't think too often about your skin, but it's there holding your body like a great big wrapper. To see your skin from the vantage point of an electron microscope, take a look at the "ultrastructure of skin" from this page at the Mie University (Japan) School of Medicine. Get a close-up look at the various skin layers and see what happens if they get infected.

http://www.medic.mie-u.ac.jp/derma/anatomy.html

Come To Your Senses

This site makes a lot of sense. You can *see* what we mean if you *touch* base here. In fact, we *hear* that there are really nine senses: taste, sight, hearing, touch, smell, hunger, thirst, pain, and balance. This page was created by kids as an entry in the ThinkQuest Junior contest. In it, you'll get a *taste* of all the senses; the research here *smells* OK to us.

http://tqjunior.advanced.org/3750/

The Heart: An Online Exploration

Probably the only time you think about your heart is when you run fast and you feel it beating in your chest. Or maybe you think about your heart when you put your hand over it and you feel it go thump, thump. Even if you don't think much about your heart, everybody knows the heart is important. After all, without hearts, what shape would valentines be? To learn all kinds of cool things about the heart, check out the Franklin Institute's info. You'll never take your heart for granted again!

http://sln.fi.edu/biosci/

Human Anatomy On-line - InnerBody.com

This site is fun if only for the animations. See a cutaway view of a mouth and throat as a pizza is eaten and swallowed. See blood pumping through the various chambers of the heart. See sound hitting the eardrum and the adjacent structures. You'll find a human anatomy tutorial here, but it's not written in simple language, so you may be more interested in looking at all the cool diagrams.

http://www.innerbody.com/indexbody.html

Neuroscience for Kids - Explore the NS

When you bite into a chocolate bar, how do you know it's delicious? How do you know to say "Ouch!" when you get stung by a mosquito? Little sensors, called *neurons*, are all over your body, and they carry messages to your brain through a system of nerves. Your brain then sorts everything out. This resource is crammed with great info about brains, your senses, spinal cords, and careers in neuroscience. Be aware, though, that many of these folks go to school for 20 *years* before they become neuroscientists!

http://weber.u.washington.edu/~chudler/introb.html

VA Image Browser

Did you ever wonder what your body would look like with transparent skin? Did you ever wonder what your heart looks like while it's beating inside your chest? You don't have to wonder any longer! At this site, you can see images (including moving pictures) of these and many other parts of the human body.

http://www.vis.colostate.edu/cgi-bin/gva/gvaview/

ILLNESS AND DISEASE
Asthma Tutorial for Children and Parents

Asthma is no fun: wheezing, coughing, struggling to breathe; anyone with asthma knows what problems this illness causes. To learn about asthma, take a look at this site, provided by the Children's Medical Center of the University of Virginia. You'll see cool graphics and hear some great audio files, including what the doctor hears when listening through the stethoscope.

http://hsc.virginia.edu/cmc/tutorials/asthma/
    asthma1.html

What is the sound of one router flapping?

A
B
C
D
E
F
G
H
I
J
K
L
M
N
O
P
Q
R
S
T
U
V
W
X
Y
Z

A
B
C
D
E
F
G
H
I
J
K
L
M
N
O
P
Q
R
S
T
U
V
W
X
Y
Z

Something fishy going on? Visit AQUARIUMS.

Band-Aides and Blackboards

Subtitled "When Chronic Illness...Or Some Other Medical Problem...Goes To School," this site is about growing up with a medical problem. Just because kids and teens have an illness doesn't mean they aren't interested in pets, TV, music, video games, and other stuff. Meet kids with cancer, kids with cerebral palsy, kids with ADD, and many more. You'll also find poems written by kids with chronic illness, go on virtual hospital tours, and find out once and for all what to do about teasing.

http://funrsc.fairfield.edu/~jfleitas/contents.html

NET FILES

Which would you rather be in the middle of:
"Mills Mess"
or
"Burke's Barrage"?

Answer: Actually, if you aren't a juggler (and a good one at that), you'd better not get in the middle of either one! These are two difficult juggling tricks. Hey, don't worry—even if you're just starting out, you'll find juggling help and information at http://www.juggling.org/

Bugs in the News!

What is microbiology? It's the study of really, really little "critters" that can only be seen under a microscope. This includes stuff like bacteria and viruses. Ick, you say? You might be surprised to know that bacteria are our friends. In fact, bacteria are absolutely necessary for all life on this planet—but not too many of them, and not the "wrong" kinds in the "wrong" places. You'll learn what an antibiotic does and what to expect from viruses such as the flu. You'll read the very latest on breaking "bug" news stories, such as the live bacteria they found in an insect trapped in amber for millions of years. Just like *Jurassic Park!* (Look in the General Interest..... area.)

http://falcon.cc.ukans.edu/~jbrown/bugs.html

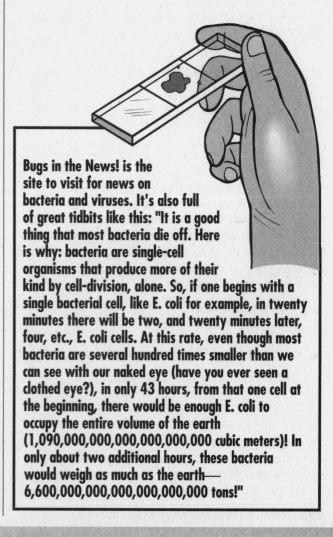

Bugs in the News! is the site to visit for news on bacteria and viruses. It's also full of great tidbits like this: "It is a good thing that most bacteria die off. Here is why: bacteria are single-cell organisms that produce more of their kind by cell-division, alone. So, if one begins with a single bacterial cell, like E. coli for example, in twenty minutes there will be two, and twenty minutes later, four, etc., E. coli cells. At this rate, even though most bacteria are several hundred times smaller than we can see with our naked eye (have you ever seen a clothed eye?), in only 43 hours, from that one cell at the beginning, there would be enough E. coli to occupy the entire volume of the earth (1,090,000,000,000,000,000,000 cubic meters)! In only about two additional hours, these bacteria would weigh as much as the earth— 6,600,000,000,000,000,000,000 tons!"

CELLS Alive!

You get a bad case of the sniffles, and your doctor gives you a shot of penicillin. Ouch! That hurt, but in a few days you feel better. What happened? To see how penicillin works and to learn plenty of information about cells, take a look at this site. If you're really sharp, you'll also find the "anatomy of a splinter" section.

http://www.cellsalive.com/

A Children's Book About HIV/AIDS

What questions do kids have about HIV and AIDS? To find out, kids in grades four through nine were surveyed by other kids. Here are some of the questions: "Does HIV/AIDS have a cure?" "If you're HIV-positive, how long do you have until you die of HIV/AIDS?" "Can you inherit HIV/AIDS from your parents?" "How does HIV/AIDS spread?" "How can you tell if a person has HIV/AIDS?" All of these questions and many more are answered very simply by health care professionals. The kids also interviewed people with HIV and with AIDS and found out they were just regular people with a sad disease. There is a short list of links to other sites on the Net; parents should preview this site and the links.

http://www.sonic.net/yofee/hivaids/

Communicable Disease Fact Sheets

Ahh chooo! Nobody likes getting sick. Chicken pox, mumps, influenza (that's the long way to say the flu) are among the many illnesses you can catch. Sicknesses you catch are called communicable diseases, and you can learn about lots of these from this info provided by the New York State Department of Health. So, remember to always cover your face when you sneeze, wash your hands before you eat, and be health-smart!

http://www.health.state.ny.us/nysdoh/consumer/
   commun.htm

KidsHome

This part of the Internet is just for kids who have cancer, HIV, and other serious illnesses. Meet other kids who hate taking their medicine. Share some stories and poems: welcome to KidsHome.

http://cancernet.nci.nih.gov/occdocs/KidsHome.html

Welcome to the On-line Allergy Center

Itchy skin, red eyes, runny nose, and headache are all symptoms of allergies. You may wonder why Mother Nature would ever let people suffer with allergies, but according to Dr. Russell Roby, allergies happen because your body is working extra hard to keep you healthy! Get the facts about allergies, so the next time you sneeze after the lawn is mowed you can understand why.

http://www.sig.net/~allergy/welcome.html

PERSONS WITH DISABILITIES

Apple Computer's Disability Connection

Now we're talking MICE! Mice of different sizes and speeds, remote-controlled mice, and head-controlled mice. But don't look here for information about cute, little, furry rodents, or toys, or the latest on hypnosis— this site is for you and your family if you're looking for adaptive technology solutions for your computer. The Mac Access Passport is a comprehensive database of access products. You'll find expanded keyboards and other neat gadgets for the physically challenged, innovative software for the visually impaired, and lots of special education software. There is a list with links to popular shareware for you to download and a list of organizations that provide other adaptive technology resources.

http://www2.apple.com/disability/welcome.html

Cerebral Palsy Tutorial

Cerebral palsy, also known as CP, is a medical condition causing uncontrolled muscle movements. It's not a disease, and you can't "catch" it from someone who has it. People with CP have it all of their lives. Many times kids who have CP use wheelchairs around school, and sometimes they can't speak clearly. To learn more about CP, take a look at this site.

http://hsc.virginia.edu/cmc/tutorials/cp/cp.htm

People are the true treasures of the Net.

A
B
C
D
E
F
G
H
I
J
K
L
M
N
O
P
Q
R
S
T
U
V
W
X
Y
Z

A B C D E F G **H** I J K L M N O P Q R S T U V W X Y Z

Visit the CHEMISTRY section periodically.

DEAFKIDS

Most people don't understand what it's like to be deaf. Join other kids who know exactly what it is like to be deaf. Spend a little time on these e-mail discussion lists for some written conversation!

List Address: deafkids@sjuvm.stjohns.edu
Subscription Address: listserv@sjuvm.stjohns.edu

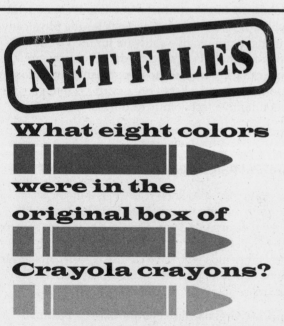

NET FILES

What eight colors were in the original box of Crayola crayons?

Answer: Black, brown, blue, red, purple, orange, yellow, and green.
Binney & Smith, maker of Crayola products, produces more than two billion crayons each year, an average of five million daily. That's enough to encircle the globe four and a half times, or to make one giant crayon 35 feet wide and 400 feet long—100 feet taller than the Statue of Liberty! Find out more at http://www.crayola.com/history/1903.html

Down Syndrome

This site was created by kids to explain Down Syndrome to other kids. One of the kids on the Web team has Down Syndrome. You can read all about him at this page and also see a video of him in a wrestling competition. This resource explains that kids with Down Syndrome are not so different after all. You'll also find out about the history of the syndrome as well as other facts. This resource does its job so well, it won the 1998 ThinkQuest Junior competition!

http://tqjunior.advanced.org/3880/

Future Reflections

The biggest hassle with being blind is not the lack of eyesight; it's the lack of understanding by other people. For anyone interested in what's happening with blind kids, *Future Reflections* is *the* magazine for blind children and their parents. It is available on the Internet, sponsored by the National Federation of the Blind. What color is the sun? How do you do arithmetic in Braille? Know what blind kids know!

http://nfb.org/reflects.htm

National Sports Center for the Disabled

If you love outdoor recreation, adventure, and freedom, then read about all of the fun programs sponsored by the National Sports Center for the Disabled. The NSCD, a nonprofit organization located in Winter Park, Colorado, celebrated its 25th year of "enabling the spirit through sports" in 1995. If you're a winter sports fan, you can join their Ski Pals Program, where disabled and able-bodied kids of ages 8 to 14 hit the slopes. If skiing, snowboarding, or snowshoeing aren't for you, then how about the Family Camp in June? You and your family can enjoy white-water rafting or hiking on nature trails designed to accommodate any special needs. There's even a rock climbing course for the blind and visually impaired.

http://www.nscd.org/nscd/

North American Riding for the Handicapped Association

Many, many kids and adults with disabilities find that with some help, they can ride a horse. Net-mom herself used to volunteer at a therapeutic riding facility, so she's speaking from experience! Everything is done with the greatest safety in mind. Depending on the rider's abilities, the instructor usually has a side walker on each side of the horse, watching and spotting the rider and helping with a leg position if needed. There is also a person leading the horse (that was Net-mom's job) who just pays attention to the horse's gait and also takes care of most of the steering. It's amazing what the warmth of a horse can do to ease a muscle spasm or the horse's rhythmic gait can do for confidence. You can read about specific therapies on this site and perhaps find a facility near you. If you don't need their services yourself, consider volunteering to help as a side walker or groom. You can even help by cleaning tack!

http://www.narha.org/

How fast does a glacier move?

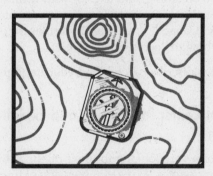

Answer: The fastest moving glacier, the Quarayaq in Greenland, moves about 2.7 to 3.3 feet per hour. Most glaciers move much slower than that. Surprisingly, scientists didn't know glaciers moved at all until 1827. A Swiss scientist built a small hut on a glacier. When he came back three years later, the hut had moved more than 100 yards downhill! Read more fun glacier facts at http://www.whistler.net/glacier/coolfact.html

PUBERTY

In Your Face! What Acne Is and What You Can Do

It seems like you always get a pimple right before a school dance, or party, or some event where you want to look and feel your best. What's to blame? Was it that chocolate you ate? All that dark cola you drank? That greasy cream you put on your face? The truth is, acne in teens is normal, and it's caused by all the hormones you have pumping around in your body during puberty. What can you do about it? Visit this site to clear things up.

http://KidsHealth.org/kid/normal/acne.html

Puberty in Boys

It happens to every boy. All of a sudden, his voice starts croaking, his Adam's apple starts growing, and peach fuzz turns into whiskers. These changes are due to puberty. To learn more about puberty in boys, read the text-only information provided by Planned Parenthood of Ontario. You may want to talk this over with someone you trust, like a parent, teacher, or pastor.

http://www.ncf.carleton.ca/freenet/rootdir/menus /social.services/ppo/info/sex/s103.txt

Puberty in Girls

As a girl grows into a woman, her body changes in many ways. This change is puberty, and sometimes it can be scary and confusing. To learn about puberty, read the text-only information here, provided by Planned Parenthood of Ontario. You may want to talk this over with someone you trust, like a parent, teacher, or pastor.

http://www.ncf.carleton.ca/freenet/rootdir/menus /social.services/ppo/info/sex/s101.txt

Have you written to your PEN PALS lately?

A B C D E F G H I J K L M N O P Q R S T U V W X Y Z

SAFETY

See also INTERNET—SAFETY

Bicycle Helmet Safety Institute Home Page

Bicycle helmets make good sense. Fifteen states and more than 55 localities in the U.S. plus all of Australia and parts of Canada require helmets. Other places are studying such laws and may require helmets as well. This all-volunteer organization tells you what types of helmets meet safety standards, where you can get inexpensive ones, and what's new and trendy at the bike equipment trade shows. If your dad is bald or has a very large head, there is advice for him here, too. According to this site, a round, smooth helmet is better than one with points that can snag on pavement. Visit this site for much, much more about bike and helmet safety.

http://www.helmets.org/

NET FILES

Mastodon, mammoth, bison, and musk ox traveled one way, passing the camels, horses, and cheetahs going in the other direction. What were they doing?

Answer: *They were migrating across the land bridge that connected Asia and North America during the Ice Age, when massive ice packs covered more of Earth's surface than they do today. Falling sea levels exposed enough land to make the connection possible. The first group of animals came to North America from Asia, while the second group originated in North America. Behind both groups were humans, chasing their respective food sources! The chilling truth is out there at* http://tyrrell.magtech.ab.ca/tour/iceages.html

KIDDE Home Safety Foundation Internet Site

Take a look at the Java games at this new resource promoting fire safety. It's presented by a company that makes extinguishers and alarms of various types. Captain Kidde, a colorful superhero, teaches children about fire protection equipment, how to conduct fire safety checks and fire drills, and ways to save themselves and others in the event of a fire. We had fun creating blueprints of imaginary houses and dragging around various appliances, smoke alarms, and fire extinguishers until we figured we'd done a pretty good job. Captain Kidde evaluated our work and luckily he agreed. There are various games for ages 5 to 12 and lots of information for parents, too. Teachers will find lesson plans designed for grades K–8 and safety tips on preventing fires and carbon monoxide poisoning. There are also home safety education tools for firefighters to use during community open houses, in-school visits, and similar outreach activities. You'll find loads of links, too.

http://www.kiddesafety.com/

My 8 Rules for Safety

What are "Checking first," "Using the buddy system," and "Trusting your feelings"? These are three of the eight rules for safety developed by the National Center for Missing and Exploited Children. To stay safe, it's important to stay with friends when you are outside, to always tell your parents or caregiver where you are going, and to trust your feelings if you think something is wrong. This site is presented by Child Find Canada. You'll also find rules for older kids and how to keep safe on the Net.

http://www.discribe.ca/childfind/educate/8tips.hte

National Center for Missing and Exploited Children

Some families are looking for their missing children. Check their photos. Have you seen any of these kids? Maybe you can help! This site lets you search by state, physical description, and other characteristics. If you have a Web page of your own, check the How You Can Help area. It will tell you how to put a link at your page that will show photos of recently missing kids to your Web site visitors, like the pictures on milk cartons.

http://www.missingkids.org/

Operation Lifesaver, Inc.

Trains are fascinating, but dangerous. Did you know that a big 150-car freight train traveling at 50 mph can take up to 1.5 miles to come to a complete stop? In the U.S. there are about 6,000 deaths and injuries per year involving trains and cars or pedestrians walking on the tracks. Most train accidents occur when the train is traveling 30 mph or slower. Even at 30 mph, the approximate stopping distance is 3,500 feet or two-thirds of a mile! Operation Lifesaver educates adults and kids on trains and train safety. Make tracks to visit here soon.

http://www.oli.org/oli/

The Otto Club

The California State Automobile Association has a terrific site to help very young kids learn about traffic safety. Visit Otto the car and his interactive town. Talk about "street smarts"—Otto is a real know-it-all! There is a full-featured animation and sound version or a lighter version for those who believe less is more. Sing along with the Seat Belt Song by pressing the radio buttons on Otto's dashboard. Play the traffic light game and see if you can compare the two pictures and decide who's stopped for red, based on the signals YOU can see. There are little games on helmet safety and playground safety, too. Be sure to click on the question mark in each area, though, to find out what you can do in each section.

http://www.ottoclub.org/

OUDPS Kid Safety Topics Menu

Sometimes it's hard to stay safe and play safe. What do you do if a bully starts picking on you? What do you do if you are in an accident? What do you do if a stranger contacts you on the Internet? Find the answer to these and many other safety questions on this site, provided by the University of Oklahoma Department of Public Safety. If you read all the information here, you'll be a safety expert!

http://www.uoknor.edu/oupd/kidsafe/kidmenu.htm

RCMP / GRC Welcome to CCAPS - Bienvenue à la SPCCA

If you're lost in the woods, what should you do? The Royal Canadian Mounted Police say you should "Hug a Tree!" Not only because the tree is your friend, but also because it will help you to remember to stay put and not wander around. Lost kids are easier to find that way. There's a Hug a Tree coloring and story book at this site, as well as a general safety coloring book. This site is also available in French.

http://www.rcmp-ccaps.com/kidzone.htm

Ryder School Bus Safety Site

It's time to review those school bus safety rules, and there's a nice presentation of them at this address. Do you know where the "Danger Zone" is? You can avoid it by exiting the bus and taking FIVE GIANT STEPS away from the bus. See an animation of this and study other safety tips at the Ryder site.

http://www.ryder.com/schoolbussafety/

Smokey Says

Who can prevent forest fires? Only you, of course! You need to know how to safely handle matches and fire, and Smokey the Bear and his friends can help you learn how. Try the Shockwave games, and you won't get burned, even though this site is *hot!*

http://www.smokeybear.com/

Vince & Larry's Safety City

Larry and Vince are real dummies—crash test dummies, that is. They have been in over 10,000 car crashes over the years, in order to test car safety. What happens at the Car Testing Grounds? What's the correct way to wear a seat belt? Are air bags more trouble than they are worth? What's the best way to be safe around school buses? What's up with bicycle safety? Larry and Vince give you the answers. They also give you the questions in the Safety Challenge Trivia game—can you beat the current high score?

http://www.nhtsa.dot.gov/kids/

A B C D E F G H I J K L M N O P Q R S T U V W X Y Z

HISTORY

1492 Exhibit

"1492: An Ongoing Voyage" is an exhibit at the Library of Congress. Explore the New World before the Europeans got there, what happened when they arrived, and how both the Old and New Worlds were forever transformed by their contact. This is a hypertext exhibit that includes both text and GIF images. It's a good resource for information about Columbus and the early history of America. Read more in the EXPLORERS AND EXPLORING section of this book.

http://sunsite.unc.edu/expo/1492.exhibit/Intro.html

ANYDAY Today-in-History PAGE of SCOPE SYSTEMS

Want to know who shares your birthday or what famous events throughout history happened the day you were born? Just visit this site and type in the month and year you want. For example, famous people born on February 8 include author Jules Verne, actor James Dean, and actress Audrey Meadows, who played Alice in *The Honeymooners*. Find out when and where these folks were born, too; Meadows, for example, was born in China. You can also find out who died on this day (Mary, Queen of Scots) and find out what important historical events took place. On February 8, the Boy Scouts organization was incorporated (1910), radio first came to the White House (1922), and Walt Disney Studios was formed (1926). Know anyone with a brand-new baby? Give the proud parents a printout of their baby's birth date!

http://www.scopesys.com/anyday/

Ari's Today Page

What happened on today's date throughout history? Ari knows. Look here for current and historical events, birthdays, horoscopes, and even sunset times in "seven corners of the World"!

http://www.uta.fi/~blarku/today.html

EDUNet's Timemachine - Home Page

About 1,200 years ago, some people wanted to name a country. They came up with Aotearoa (which means Land of the Long White Cloud). Now we call that country New Zealand! You can find out about it by taking a ride on EduNET's Time Machine. Did Italy ever invade Ethiopia? Yes, indeed—it happened on October 7, 1935, and it was one of the first major wars to use combined arms tactics. You can learn so much at this site that all your friends and family members will think you are a genius! You probably are if you take our advice and give this site a try.

http://www.baxter.net/edunet/cat/timemachine/

The History Channel

Who says history's boring? If you get this cable channel, you know the truth is out there! Even if you don't have cable, you can visit this Web site. There are activities for kids (including contests) and classrooms. Plus, explore listings to places where you can see historic events and time periods re-created and background info on many of the History Channel's special programs. Check the coloring book with pictures of historic sites. Try This Day in History (little menu bar box at the bottom of the page—type the date you want), and get historical facts, plus the top ten in music for past years. Even if you think you have no interest in history, stop in—we think you'll be pleasantly surprised.

http://www.historychannel.com/index2.html

History/Social Studies Web Site for K-12 Teachers

Wow! Finally, an easy way to learn and teach social studies. Subjects available in the menu include archaeology, diversity sources, electronic texts, genealogy, geography, government, and kids and students. Also included are general history, non-Western history, European history, American history, and news and current events. Announcements and relevant TV specials are also listed. Impress your social studies teacher by introducing him or her to this excellent site!

http://www.execpc.com/~dboals/boals.html

Mr. Donn's World History Page

There's enough information at this site for every term paper you will ever have to write! Well, almost every one. We started right at the top in the Age of Exploration and discovered explorers by the dozen as well as interesting bits of information about them and their travels. Then we headed to the Middle Ages section where lots of home pages devote space to castles and cathedrals and—gosh, there are some pictures drawn by children in Net-mom's home school district "Middle Ages Characters (Wetzel Road Elem–6th)"! Time to move along: Renaissance and Reformation, World History, Pirates...we'll never finish reading it all. Maybe we should send a thank you to Mr. Donn for helping make world history so very interesting!

http://members.aol.com/Egyptkids/World.html

World Cultures

Welcome to the Internet portion of a course taught by Richard Hooker at Washington State University. While this site is background for a college course, it also offers much information for the world history student. You can find a glossary of world cultures, including concepts, values, and terms, readings about the world, and Internet resources. A caution to parents: Not all links have been explored.

http://www.wsu.edu:8080/~dee/

NET FILES

How many flowers must honeybees visit to make one pound of honey?

Answer: *Two million flowers! A hive of bees has to fly an average of 55,000 miles to visit that many flowers and bring you that sweet pound of honey. Find out more fun bee facts at http://www.billybee.com/infocenter.html*

World History to 1500

This excellent site contains links to resources on the Internet dealing with world history prior to 1500. This material was collected as a supplement to materials covered in a course at Brigham Young University (Hawaii). The information is mostly arranged geographically. Geographic regions covered include Mesopotamia, India, Rome, Europe, Egypt, China, Greece, Africa, Eurasia, and East Asia. Topics addressed include prehistory, cultural evolution, Islam, Christianity, Judaica, and cultural diffusion. This is a good beginning site for world history reports that cover the early years of civilization.

http://www.byuh.edu/coursework/hist201/

The World-Wide Web Virtual Library: History

This home page contains history indexes, conferences, world news, historical newsgroups and discussion lists, and Carrie: An Electronic Library. Kansas students will particularly like the Kansas sites! You can explore history by era, subject, or world region.

http://history.cc.ukans.edu/history/
WWW_history_main.html

ANCIENT HISTORY

See also ANCIENT CIVILIZATIONS AND ARCHAEOLOGY

Exploring Ancient World Cultures

This site is an excellent introduction to ancient cultures in cyberspace. Eight cultures are represented: the Near East, India, Egypt, China, Greece, the Roman Empire, the Islamic World, and Medieval Europe. Anthony Beavers, an assistant professor at the University of Evansville (Indiana), has tried to provide a variety of resources with balance among the cultures. Some of the Internet sites included in this home page are materials for the study of women in the ancient world, world art treasures, a collection of world scripture, and the International Museum of the Horse. This home page is rich in information for the student of ancient history. Think you're pretty good? Take one of the ten-question online quizzes on Genesis, Greek mythology, or another subject!

http://eawc.evansville.edu/

A
B
C
D
E
F
G
H
I
J
K
L
M
N
O
P
Q
R
S
T
U
V
W
X
Y
Z

Vatican Exhibit Rome Reborn

Rome is one of the most glorious cities in the world. Today, millions of visitors come to admire its architecture, art, and history and to find peace in St. Peter's Basilica. It has not always been that way, though: once it was a miserable village! Explore the past in this exhibit of materials from the Vatican Library's most precious manuscripts, books, and maps. This exhibit was at the Library of Congress in 1993, but it lives on—on the Net.

http://sunsite.unc.edu/expo/vatican.exhibit/
   Vatican.exhibit.html

HISTORIC DOCUMENTS

The Declaration of Independence

If you want a transcription of the Declaration of Independence with the original "Dunlap Broadside" capitalizations preserved, visit this site. It will also take you to other U.S. founding documents such as the Constitution and the Federalist Papers.

http://www.law.emory.edu/FEDERAL/independ/
   declar.html

Declaring Independence:
Drafting the Documents

You know of the Declaration of Independence, written on July 4, 1776. It begins: "When in the course of human Events, it becomes necessary for one People to dissolve the Political Bands which have connected them with another...." The colonists didn't one day just wake up and decide to send this letter to King George III of England. This Library of Congress exhibit presents a chronology of events. You'll find fascinating information about how the documents were drafted, plus photos of important objects. Some of these include fragments of the earliest known draft, the original draft, and various prints relevant to the exhibit, as well as correspondence from Thomas Jefferson. Did you know he was the one who wrote the original?

http://lcweb.loc.gov/exhibits/declara/declara1.html

Watch your steps in DANCE.

EuroDocs: Western European Primary Historical Documents

Venetian sailing directions from 1499? A medieval illuminated manuscript? If you're looking for something newer, how about a World War I archive, or D-Day documents from World War II? The links at this Brigham Young University (Utah) Library home page connect to Western European historical documents that are transcribed, scanned in, or translated. The documents are in the public domain. This home page is an excellent starting place for students who are researching Western European history and want to use primary source material.

http://library.byu.edu/~rdh/eurodocs/homepage.html

NET FILES

How many meteors fall to Earth each day?

Answer: According to Dr. Harry B. Herzer III, of the NASA Aerospace Education Services Project, the number is probably more than you think. It's estimated that 1,000 to more than 10,000 tons of meteoritic material falls to Earth every day! Luckily, most of this material is very tiny, like particles of dust. They are so small, their fall is slowed by air resistance, so they don't burn as they descend. They settle gently to the ground, and you may be walking on them without ever knowing it.

http://spacelink.nasa.gov/Instructional.Materials/
Curriculum.Support/Space.Science/Our.Solar.System/
Small.Bodies/Comets.Asteroids.and.Meteoroids

Can't tell a hawk from a handsaw? Look it up in BIRDS.

The Gettysburg Address

The Library of Congress has devoted this page to President Abraham Lincoln's Gettysburg Address. Lincoln was invited to dedicate the Union cemetery only three weeks before the ceremony, so he did not have much time to write the speech. View the working drafts of the eloquent speech Lincoln eventually delivered. You'll also see the only known photo of Lincoln taken at Gettysburg, Pennsylvania. These precious original documents have been preserved for future generations; find out how!

http://lcweb.loc.gov/exhibits/G.Address/ga.html

Abraham Lincoln, the 16th President of the United States, gave the speech known as the Gettysburg Address on November 19, 1863. The occasion was the dedication of a cemetery for many of the Civil War dead.

It was a very short but important speech, because it began to heal the war-torn states into one nation again. Read more at The Gettysburg Address.

THE HISTORICAL TEXT ARCHIVE

Choose the area of the world you're interested in—click—wow, here is an archive of that country's, or region's, important documents and resources. Try this for elusive information you haven't found anywhere else. The Women's Studies links contain several Godey's Lady's Books from the 1850s. Parents: not all links have been checked.

http://www.msstate.edu/Archives/History/

What were women reading in the 1850s? Many of them loved to look through the Godey's Lady's Books, and now several are online. Here's part of an etiquette column, regarding proper behavior in the theater: "We may as well mention here, for the sake of the other sex, that loud thumping with canes and umbrellas, in demonstration of applause, is voted decidedly rude. Clapping the hands is quite as efficient and neither raises a dust to soil the dresses of the ladies, nor a hubbub enough to deafen them." You can find more at http://www.history.rochester.edu/godeys/, which is a link off THE HISTORICAL TEXT ARCHIVE.

CATS are purrfect.

A B C D E F G H I J K L M N O P Q R S T U V W X Y Z

A
B
C
D
E
F
G
H
I
J
K
L
M
N
O
P
Q
R
S
T
U
V
W
X
Y
Z

The History Channel - Great Speeches

Hear some of the words that changed the world. You'll be able to hear speeches made by Mahatma Gandhi, Barbara Jordan, Douglas MacArthur, as well as historic words like those from Apollo 13: "Houston, we've had a problem."

http://www.historychannel.com/gspeech/

Inaugural Addresses of the Presidents of the United States

George Washington's second-term inaugural speech remains the shortest on record, requiring only 135 words. William Henry Harrison delivered one of the longest, speaking for an hour and 45 minutes in a blinding snowstorm. He then stood in the cold and greeted well-wishers all day; he died a month later, of pneumonia. Read the speech here, but make sure you keep your hat on! Project Bartleby, at Columbia University in New York, houses a home page containing the inaugural addresses of the presidents. Also included is an article about presidents sworn in but not inaugurated and the Oath of Office itself. This is a good site for finding inaugural factoids, such as the revelation that Geronimo, the great Apache, attended the inauguration of Teddy Roosevelt and that attendees at Grover Cleveland's second inaugural ball were all agog at the new invention: electric lights!

http://www.columbia.edu/acis/bartleby/inaugural/

Initiatives for Access: Treasures - Magna Carta

In 1215, the English barons were fed up. They thought that their king had gone too far, on more than one occasion. They wanted a line drawn that would explain the difference between a king and a tyrant. They defined laws and customs that the King himself had to respect when dealing with free subjects. That charter is called the Magna Carta. It's made it all the way from 1215 to the Net, as part of the Treasures Digitisation Project at the British Library. You can view the whole manuscript and read a translation of it. A brief history and further reading are included.

http://www.bl.uk/diglib/magna-carta/magna-carta.html

National Archives Online Exhibit Hall

The National Archives and Records Administration (NARA) is a nationwide system that preserves United States government records of permanent value. The online exhibits help to bring some of the rich and varied holdings of the National Archives to the public. In the Exhibit Hall, you will find some cool special exhibits: for example, "The Charters of Freedom" features the Declaration of Independence, the Constitution of the United States, and the Bill of Rights. You'll also find a special exhibit on the Emancipation Proclamation, issued by President Abraham Lincoln, which ended slavery. Other featured documents include the nineteenth Amendment and Japanese surrender documents. Visit this site for firsthand looks at the historic documents of the United States, several of them written in longhand!

http://www.nara.gov/exhall/exhibits.html

U.S. Founding Documents

We like this archive of U.S. documents, particularly for its searchable version of the Constitution of the United States. Do you know where your nineteenth Amendment is? You'll also find the Federalist Papers and the Declaration of Independence.

http://www.law.emory.edu/FEDERAL/

US Historical Documents

The University of Oklahoma Law Center hosts "A Chronology of United States Historical Documents." The chronology begins in the pre-Colonial era, with the Magna Carta and the Iroquois Constitution, and concludes with the State of the Union Address given by President Bill Clinton in 1997. Along the way, you'll find the Mayflower Compact, the famous "Give Me Liberty or Give Me Death" speech by Patrick Henry, the Monroe Doctrine, the Emancipation Proclamation, and Martin Luther King, Jr.'s "I Have a Dream" speech. Take a peek at the "other" verses of the National Anthem, too:

> *Oh! thus be it ever, when freemen shall stand*
> *Between their loved homes and the war's desolation!*
> *Blest with victory and peace, may the heaven-rescued land*
> *Praise the Power that hath made and preserved us a nation.*
> *Then conquer we must, for our cause it is just,*
> *And this be our motto: "In God is our trust."*
> *And the star-spangled banner forever shall wave*
> *O'er the land of the free and the home of the brave!*

http://www.law.uoknor.edu/ushist.html

NET FILES

Who was Blossom Galbiso?

(Hint: You have her to thank for one of your favorite games!)

Answer: She was the Hawaiian teacher who popularized POGs, or milkcaps, in 1991. You can see a photo of Blossom and read her own essay about the birth of POGS at *http://www.ukulele.com/blossom.html*

Various Historical Documents

Jon Shemitz, who also runs a Home Schooling Web site at <http://www.midnightbeach.com/hs/>, has put the U.S. Declaration of Independence, the Constitution of the United States, and the United Nations Convention on the Rights of the Child, into HTML (HyperText Markup Language) so that the documents can be read more easily with a Web browser. This presentation also makes the documents easy to search!

http://www.midnightbeach.com/jon/histdocs.htm

HISTORIC SITES

The Alexander Palace Time Machine

Once, a second-grade boy visited the library and found a book about the great tsars of Russia. He became fascinated with their stories and their palace lifestyle. As time went on, he read everything he could about the great palace, hoping someday to visit Russia to see it for himself. Incredibly, this boy grew up to do that very thing, and now he's written a comprehensive Web page all about it. This outstanding multimedia tour will give you a look into the past as you explore the life and times of Tsar Nicholas II and his family and friends.

http://www.alexanderpalace.org/palace/

AMERICA'S HOMEPAGE!! PLYMOUTH, MASS

Take a virtual tour of "Plimoth Plantation." In this living history museum, all the employees dress and act as they would in 1627. Visit the re-created village and farm site, then tour other Plymouth and Pilgrim historical resources. Some of the best biographical and other information is in the Historical Reference area. The only thing missing from this page is a good clear picture of Plymouth Rock, but we have pointed out this oversight to the webmaster, so maybe by the time you read this you can gaze on a photo of a gray rock with 1620 carved in it.

http://wwx.media3.net/plymouth/

Watch your steps in DANCE.

A B C D E F G H I J K L M N O P Q R S T U V W X Y Z

A
B
C
D
E
F
G
H
I
J
K
L
M
N
O
P
Q
R
S
T
U
V
W
X
Y
Z

Colonial Williamsburg Foundation

What would it be like to be suddenly transported back in time to the 1700s? For fun, you would play cards and board games, or you'd work at puzzles; outside, you would roll hoops, walk on stilts, and play a rousing game of ninepins bowling. What kinds of foods would you eat? How would people behave—are manners the same now as they were back then? What kind of job would you have? Experience the eighteenth century by visiting this site! Colonial Williamsburg is a living history museum in Virginia, where the people dress and act as if they were living in Colonial times. They have to know a lot about history to do that, and some kids work at the museum, playing the roles of kids back in the 1700s. This is a great site to learn how people lived in early times in America.

http://www.history.org/

NET FILES

What lighthouse is also one of the Seven Wonders of the ancient world?

Answer: The Lighthouse of Alexandria, on the island of Pharos, off Egypt, is one of the Seven Wonders of the ancient world. Built around 300 to 220 b.c., it was as tall as a modern-day 40-story building, making it the tallest structure in the world at that time. It had a miraculous mirror lit by the sun during the day and by fires at night. The light could be seen 35 miles away. By the mid-1400s it was in ruins, and for a long time its exact location was not known. In September 1995, French divers announced they had found large pieces of granite underwater, believed to be pieces of the ancient lighthouse. Find out more at http://pharos.bu.edu/EgyptWonders/pharos.html

Ford's Theater NHS Home Page

The theater where President Lincoln was shot is now a National Historic site. If you scroll down to the bottom of the page, you will learn some fascinating facts about the assassination. Why was there no guard—or was there? Where is the chair Lincoln was sitting in? And where is the bullet that killed him? The surprising answers are all here. This site offers information in 11 languages besides English.

http://www.nps.gov/foth/

The Gift of the Statue of Liberty

Student authors from a fourth-grade classroom in Somers, New York, wrote some articles and drew some great pictures about the Statue of Liberty's history. Did you know it was a gift from the people of France?

http://www.kusd.edu/s_projects/statue_liberty/
     statue_liberty.html

Great American Landmarks Adventure

At this page you can download pages of historic landmarks to color. But it's not the usual type of famous landmark. Here you'll find some really weird stuff, such as a huge elephant-shaped building (Margate City, New Jersey) and Independence Rock (Casper, Wyoming), where folks traveling along the Oregon Trail got out of their covered wagons long enough to scratch their names. You'll find the U.S. Capitol here, but you can also choose to color the Taos pueblo. If you send in your drawing, they may put it on the Web. Check it out!

http://www2.cr.nps.gov/pad/adventure/landmark.htm

Historic Mile

Take a tour of over 50 famous landmarks in Philadelphia, Pennsylvania! You'll visit Independence Hall, where the Declaration of Independence was signed, and see Betsy Ross' House, where some say she sewed the very first American flag. Along the way, stop in at the Pretzel Museum for a quick snack.

http://libertynet.org/iha/virtual.html

Everyone's flocking to BIRDS!

Historic Mount Vernon-The Home of Our First President, George Washington

Seeing where our first president lived makes him more real to us. Walking up his front steps, lounging on his lawn—these things connect us to a real person instead of an historical figure. Maybe you can't visit Mount Vernon, Virginia, in person, but you can stop in via the Net. At Mount Vernon, you can take a tour, read some astounding facts, and even work out a Washington word search puzzle. You can also learn about archaeology at Mount Vernon and explore related links. The Mount Vernon virtual tour includes the East Front, the large dining room, study, master bedroom, gardens, the Washingtons' tomb, and a slave memorial. Washington was the only one of the Founding Fathers to free his slaves.

http://www.mountvernon.org/

Did Washington really chop down a cherry tree?

How about that "throwing the silver dollar across the Potomac River" story—is that bogus?

True or false: he had wooden teeth?

All of these are false. One thing is true, though: many people wanted to crown Washington as King; he declined, accepting the presidency instead. Read more facts you never knew at the pages of Historic Mount Vernon-The Home of Our First President, George Washington.

IC - Ellis Island -

Between 1892 and 1954, Ellis Island was the gateway to America for over 12 million immigrants. Before they could set foot in America, they had to be "processed" on this island in the New York harbor. This meant a three- to five-hour wait, medical and legal questions, and inspections. Some were eventually turned away. Learn about the journey, the processing center, and life in the new land at this excellent example of multimedia education. You will hear audio recollections of some of the immigrants themselves. There is also an "immigrants' cookbook" with recipes such as cabbage rolls and gingersnaps.

http://165.90.42.35/features/ellis/

Moscow Kremlin 3W Guide

Tour the Moscow Kremlin Exhibition! Inside, you'll find wonderful pictures and stories. Some of the sites you will see and read about are the Cathedral of Annunciation, Red Square, the Residence of the President, the Senate Building, and the Tsar-Cannon.

http://www.online.ru/sp/cominf/kremlin/kremlin.html

National Civil Rights Museum

The National Civil Rights Museum is located at the Lorraine Motel (Memphis, Tennessee), where Dr. Martin Luther King, Jr., was assassinated on April 4, 1968. Here you will find continuing exhibits, events, and links of interest. The virtual tour is arranged in chronological order. You'll learn about the Montgomery bus boycott, the freedom rides, Dr. Martin Luther King, Jr., the student sit-ins, the march on Washington, and the Chicago freedom movement. You can take a chronological tour or choose the exhibit you want to see. Each exhibit has a short paragraph about the subject and why it is important in civil rights history.

http://www.mecca.org/~crights/

Did the groundhog see his shadow? Find out if it will be an early spring in HOLIDAYS.

A B C D E F G H I J K L M N O P Q R S T U V W X Y Z

National Trust for Historic Preservation Home Page

Many historic sites are old—so how come they look so nice? Because people like you care enough to save them from deterioration. This is called historic preservation. This resource will help you find out how to save historic sites in your area.

http://www.nthp.org/

OLD STURBRIDGE VILLAGE

Do you think it would be fun to live in the past? Why not visit the nineteenth century and see how you like it? You can experience the sights and sounds of this re-created New England village by taking a virtual visit. Let's visit the blacksmith shop—can you hear the clang of the hammer on the anvil? Listen for the team of horses pulling a sleigh. Why not stroll over to the confectionery shop for some horehound drops or rock candy? Got a question? Ask in the Kids Club, where you'll also find puzzles and a mystery sound contest! If you visit the real Sturbridge Village in Massachusetts, you'll find a fascinating living history museum, where all the kids and other villagers dress, talk, and act like they are living in 1830.

http://www.osv.org/

NET FILES

What's the world's record for the number of balls a juggler's been able to keep in the air at one time?

Answer: *The record is 12 balls. 12 catches! Bruce Sarafian, in 1996, authenticated this to the Juggling Information Service with a personal video. Read about more records for juggling clubs and rings at* http://www.juggling.org/records/records.html

The Statue of Liberty

Give me your tired, your poor,
Your huddled masses yearning to breathe free,
The wretched refuse of your teeming shore.
Send these, the homeless, tempest-tost to me,
I lift my lamp beside the golden door!

This is part of the poem inscribed on the Statue of Liberty. It was written by Emma Lazarus, and you can learn more about the statue's history at the official National Park Service site.

http://www.nps.gov/stli/

Temple of Liberty: Building the Capitol for a New Nation

Visit the Capitol, courtesy of the Library of Congress. The United States Capitol was envisioned as a "Temple of Liberty" by George Washington and Thomas Jefferson. Read the various proposals for how this most important of all U.S. public buildings should look. Then study the approved plans and visit the porticoes and the wings of our Capitol as it was built. The original building took 34 years, six architects, and six presidents to build. When you're finished touring this historic site, you'll be an expert, and your feet won't be tired!

http://lcweb.loc.gov/exhibits/us.capitol/s0.html

Tower of London Virtual Tour

The Traitor's Gate. The Bloody Tower. The Ceremony of the Keys. The Crown Jewels. What an incredible history this building has. The Tower of London has been a treasury, a prison, and a government building for a thousand years. It is said that if the ravens that inhabit the Tower green ever leave, the Commonwealth of Great Britain will fall. You can take a tour of the Tower and its grounds right here. But don't scare the ravens!

http://www.camelot-group.com/tower/

> **"A ship in the harbor is safe, but that is not what ships are built for." —John A. Shedd**

VBoston: Walk Boston

It's only 2.5 miles long, but you'll be walking through years of Boston's history. Check out the Paul Revere House and the Old North Church ("one if by land, two if by sea...."). Don't miss the Boston Massacre site or the Bunker Hill Monument. Bring a cup of tea and take the virtual tour.

http://www.vboston.com/boswalks/

Vietnam Veteran's Memorial

The U.S. National Park Service administers this memorial site, which is in Washington, D.C. Over 58,000 American men and women died in the Vietnam War, a conflict so controversial it divided the generations as well as the country. All their names are engraved on a mirrorlike granite wall. People leave flowers, poems, military gear, and other objects around the wall. It is a very moving place to visit, and we guarantee you will never forget your experience there.

http://www.nps.gov/vive/

Visiting Independence National Historical Park

Welcome to Independence National Historical Park. Is this your first trip to Philadelphia? Yes? Then you'd better begin your tour at the Visitor Center, where you will see the film "Independence." Next you will want to check out the Liberty Bell. No new cracks, please! Do you know when the bell was rung for the last time? You can find out before moving along to Independence Hall. No pushing ahead, there is plenty of time for all of the stops along the way in historic Philadelphia. You'll end at the Deshler Morris House, which served as the official residence for President George Washington during the yellow fever epidemic of 1793. Enjoy your visit!

http://www.nps.gov/inde/visit.html

Looking for the State Bird or the State Motto? It's in the UNITED STATES— STATES section.

White House for Kids

Let Socks, the First Cat, take you on a fascinating kid's-eye tour of the White House in Washington, D.C. You'll learn how the White House was built (bricks were made on the front lawn), tour the rooms, and find out the First Family pets that have lived there (don't miss President Harrison's goat or Caroline Kennedy's pony). We learned something we didn't know before: the president's desk was once part of a ship, abandoned north of the Arctic circle in 1854! The HMS *Resolute* was later found by the crew of an American whaling ship. It was repaired and refitted, then sent to Queen Victoria as a gesture of goodwill. Later, when the ship was taken out of service and dismantled, a desk was made from some of its timbers. Queen Victoria presented the desk to President Hayes in 1880. The desk has been used by most presidents since then. Socks never gets to sit on it, though. Well, maybe he does, late at night, when no one is around.

http://www.whitehouse.gov/WH/kids/html/
   kidshome.html

Did you know that although George Washington, the first President of the United States, directed the construction of the White House, he never got to live in it? It was our second President, John Adams, elected in 1796, who first lived there. His term was almost over by the time he moved in, and only six rooms had been finished. Take the tour, led by Socks, the First Cat, at the White House for Kids page.

A B C D E F G H I J K L M N O P Q R S T U V W X Y Z

NET FILES

A fossil, found by an auto mechanic in Argentina in 1994, turned out to be from a dinosaur bigger than *T. rex.* What was it?

(Hint: it wasn't Barney.)

Answer: It was the *Giganotosaurus* (JYE-gah-NO-tuh-SAW-rus)! Scientists estimate the creature was 40 to 50 feet long and about five tons in weight. *Giganotosaurus* lived about 30 million years before *Tyrannosaurus rex.* According to this site, "Rodolfo Coria, a paleontologist from the Carmen Funes Museum in Neuquen, Argentina, excavated the *Giganotosaurus*, which was originally found by a local auto mechanic whose hobby is hunting dinosaur bones. In honor of the discoverer, Ruben Carolini, the huge dinosaur has been named *Giganotosaurus carolinii.*" Find out more at *http://www.EnchantedLearning.com/subjects/dinosaurs/dinos/Giganotosaurus.html*

MIDDLE AGES
Journey Through the Middle Ages

On your quest to rise from a squire to a knight you'll have to solve puzzles and answer questions relating to medieval history and castle life. The answers are all on this site, and never fear, because you'll have James the Jingling Jester to help you out with some clues. This site, created by kids, was a finalist in the 1998 ThinkQuest Junior contest.

http://tqjunior.advanced.org/4051/

Visit the BRIDGES of Internet County in ARCHITECTURE!

Try actual reality.

Labyrinth Home Page

Welcome to the Labyrinth, a World Wide Web server for medieval studies, located at Georgetown University in Washington, D.C. The Middle Ages are those years after the fall of the Roman Empire and before the Renaissance, so think the years 500–1500 (some authorities say 1300 or 1400). You can navigate the Labyrinth by selecting a main menu item or by using the search engine to search all Labyrinth files. Sources available include bibliographies, text, images, and archives. Also offered are Daedalus' guides to the Net and Web. Find your own Ariadne's thread to hold onto as you surf the Labyrinth!

http://www.georgetown.edu/labyrinth/labyrinth-home.html

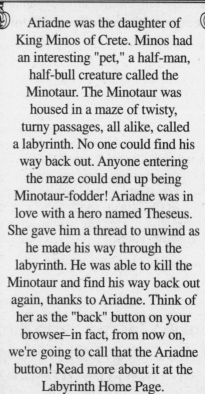

Ariadne was the daughter of King Minos of Crete. Minos had an interesting "pet," a half-man, half-bull creature called the Minotaur. The Minotaur was housed in a maze of twisty, turny passages, all alike, called a labyrinth. No one could find his way back out. Anyone entering the maze could end up being Minotaur-fodder! Ariadne was in love with a hero named Theseus. She gave him a thread to unwind as he made his way through the labyrinth. He was able to kill the Minotaur and find his way back out again, thanks to Ariadne. Think of her as the "back" button on your browser–in fact, from now on, we're going to call that the Ariadne button! Read more about it at the Labyrinth Home Page.

RENAISSANCE

Virtual Renaissance

Built by a class in Buffalo Grove, Illinois, for the ThinkQuest competition, this site allows you to visit such historical locales as the Globe Theater, the Sistine Chapel, and the Tower of London, among others. You'll learn about the sites from people of the Renaissance as they tell of medical knowledge, art techniques, and even games of the times. There are also links to more Renaissance materials around the Web.

http://www.twingroves.district96.k12.il.us/
Renaissance/VirtualRen.html

TIME LINES

Modernism Timeline, 1890-1940

This time line highlights significant events from 1890 to 1940. When you click on a year, you get a list of events that happened in that year, including political and literary events and social customs. For example, in 1917, bobbed hair was popular, the Senate rejected Wilson's suffrage bill, Freud's *Introduction to Psychoanalysis* was published, and there was a famine in Germany. The issue of what is significant is up for grabs here, and you can make suggestions for additions to the list.

http://weber.u.washington.edu/~eckman/timeline.html

NET FILES

At what event were these famous firsts?

❏ George Ferris built the first Ferris wheel.

❏ The U.S. Postal Service produced the first picture postcards.

❏ Cracker Jacks were introduced.

❏ The hamburger became America's favorite fast food.

Answer: The 1893 Columbian Exposition, in Chicago, Illinois. Read more at
http://users.vnet.net/schulman/Columbian/columbian.html

World History

Hey, your mom says you can have some friends over for lunch! She says to invite three people you admire from history—which heroes would you choose? You might get some ideas here. This site will teach you about important people from 1000 B.C. to the present. You'll find scientists, artists, musicians, authors, politicians, explorers, and many others. But that is not all: you can also trace events through history as well as look at important maps of time periods and the spread of civilizations.

http://www.hyperhistory.com/chart/chart.html

U.S. HISTORY

See also UNITED STATES—PRESIDENTS AND FIRST LADIES

The African-American Mosaic Exhibition (Library of Congress)

This exhibit is a sampler of materials found in the Library of Congress illuminating the last 500 years of the African American experience in the Western Hemisphere. This exhibit covers four areas—Colonization, Abolition, Migrations, and the WPA (Work Projects Administration) era. This is an excellent starting point to search for materials about African American history. Be sure to check the AFRICAN AMERICANS section of this book, too.

http://lcweb.loc.gov/exhibits/african/intro.html

The Birth of A Nation

This site won the social science division in the 1998 ThinkQuest Junior contest. You can learn all about the events of April 18-19, 1775. You remember, that's when Paul Revere rode to warn the countryside that "the British are coming!" If you're not up to speed on the minutemen, this site will give you an overview of the important names, places, and deeds. There's also a neat game on daily eighteenth century wear for men, women, and kids. You can mix and match parts of the photos and try to come up with a complete historical costume.

http://tqjunior.advanced.org/3803/

A
B
C
D
E
F
G
H
I
J
K
L
M
N
O
P
Q
R
S
T
U
V
W
X
Y
Z

If you feel funny, think what we went through when we wrote the JOKES AND RIDDLES section!

From Revolution to Reconstruction

The main body of this home page comes from the booklet "An Outline of American History," distributed by the United States Information Agency. The text is illustrated with stamps! It has very dense text, so you may want to look at this site for heavier research only. Additional original sources with hypertext links (which go all over the Net) have been added. This site covers American history from the Colonial period until World War I. Check it out; it's fun just to know there was a stamp with the Carolina charter on it.

http://grid.let.rug.nl/~welling/usa/

Home Page: American Memory from the Library of Congress

You have memories of your own life. Your parents have memories of their lives, and your grandparents have memories of theirs. Wouldn't it be great to find a place to archive all those memories, so they wouldn't be lost when someone died? You could call it the American Memory Project! Look no further. Browse through 25,000 turn-of-the-century postcards; maybe some are from your home town. Look in the Prints and Photographs Division under Detroit Publishing Company (show this to your parents—they will love it). Check old movies of New York City made by Edison himself in 1903. Look into the eyes of the immigrants coming to America—so much hope is expressed there. The historical periods covered are from the Civil War to World War II. Each collection is annotated, and broad topics are listed. This is an excellent source for students looking for non-print sources to accompany an American history report. Don't forget to remember American Memory.

http://rs6.loc.gov/amhome.html

What happened on 23rd Street, during the summer of 1901, in New York City? Move over, Marilyn Monroe! Inventor Thomas A. Edison was experimenting with films that year. The film is now in the Library of Congress' American Memory collection, and it's also on the Internet. From a contemporary Edison film company catalog: "The scene as suggested by the title is made on 23rd Street, New York City. In front of one of the large newspaper offices on that thoroughfare is a hot air shaft through which immense volumes of air are forced by means of a blower. Ladies crossing these shafts often have their clothes slightly disarranged, (it may be said much to their discomfiture). As our picture was being made a young man escorting a young lady, to whom he was talking very earnestly, comes into view and walks slowly along until they stand directly over the air shaft. The young lady's [ankle-length] skirts are suddenly raised to, you might say an almost unreasonable height, greatly to her horror and much to the amusement of the newsboys, bootblacks and passersby. This subject is a winner. Class B. 50 ft. $6.00." It should be noted that the dress blows up "almost" to her knees. It was shocking for those times! To see the film, go to *http://rs6.loc.gov/papr/ paprquery.html* and search on the term "twenty-third" (don't forget the hyphen). For more, remember Home Page: American Memory from the Library of Congress.

"Ships are only hulls, high walls are nothing, When no life moves in the empty passageways." —Sophocles

Library of Congress Home Page

The Library of Congress, founded in 1800, uses the World Wide Web to present materials from its collections so that people all over the world can see them without traveling to Washington, D.C. You can view exhibits, search and view documents in digitized historical collections, search the LC card catalog, and learn about Congress and the government by using the collection known as Thomas. This is an excellent starting point to find information about the United States government and history, both present and past.

http://lcweb.loc.gov/

The Mayflower Web Pages

In 1620, the *Mayflower* set off on a 66-day voyage from England to the New World. At least 30 of the passengers were under age 17. The kids on board got into all sorts of trouble, which was recounted in journals of the time. Read about it at this site: one of the boys shot off a gun and set part of the ship on fire! By the way, boys and girls wore almost the same type of clothes—long dress-like garments! At this well-researched page, you'll also find historical information, books and journals by the Pilgrims, myths about the *Mayflower*, and all sorts of details about the voyage.

http://members.aol.com/calebj/mayflower.html

Presidential Libraries IDEA Network

"PresidentS" is located at the University of North Carolina at Chapel Hill. Its mission is to help to bring presidential library materials to the Internet for improved public access and to link America's past to her future. Presidential libraries from Herbert Hoover through President Clinton and Vice President Gore are included. Some of the more recent libraries have their own home pages. The earlier presidential papers are available via Gopher. Photographs are also housed at the newer libraries. This is an excellent site for accessing info on the twentieth-century presidents and first ladies and links to their homes, libraries, and other resources.

http://sunsite.unc.edu/lia/president/pres.html

The Presidents of the United States

For some kids growing up in the United States, becoming president is the highest ambition. So far, only a few people have achieved that goal, and the job of president is a tough one. At this site, you can read quick facts about each president, find links to other informative Web pages, and get a sense of the times and struggles of each leader of the U.S. Who knows, maybe some day you'll grow up to be president, and your picture will be on these Web pages!

http://www1.whitehouse.gov/WH/glimpse/
presidents/html/presidents.html

Roanoke: A Mystery in History

This 1998 ThinkQuest Junior finalist explores the lost colony of Roanoke Island, in what is now North Carolina. In 1586 it was a tiny garrison of 15 men, but it was later found abandoned in July of 1587. One mysterious human skeleton was found on the beach, but no other trace was found. Ninety-one men, women, and children arrived from England and started fixing up the fort so they could live in it. They had the beginnings of a thriving settlement and had begun to make friends with the Native Americans. In August, some of the colonists went back to England for more supplies. Because England was at war with Spain, no ships could be spared to resupply Roanoke until three years later. When the search party arrived in 1590, no one could be found, although a large fire blazed on the north end of the island. Where did the colonists go? Examine some of the theories at this site and see what seems believable to you.

http://tqjunior.advanced.org/3826/

Wm. Murray's Time Page

Murray categorizes the generations in American history based upon his reading of the book *Generations*. You can then trace his links by eras, generations, and the future. One of the most valuable aspects of this site is the collection of links to resources in American history, although his take on who the visionaries were in each era is also interesting.

http://www.seanet.com/Users/pamur/time.html

A B C D E F G H I J K L M N O P Q R S T U V W X Y Z

A
B
C
D
E
F
G
H
I
J
K
L
M
N
O
P
Q
R
S
T
U
V
W
X
Y
Z

You be the Historian

This site invites you to find out all you can about an American family's life in the 1700s. By examining artifacts and documents at this site you may be able to get a fairly good picture of what life was like for Thomas and Elizabeth Springer's family in New Castle, Delaware, 200 years ago. Compare your guesses to what historians have concluded. What could future archaeologists and historians learn about your family from what's on the floor of your closet, under your bed, or in your trash?

http://www.si.edu/organiza/museums/nmah/
    notkid/ubh/00intro.htm

U.S. HISTORY—1920S
The 1920s

How much do you know about the 1920s? You may know about flappers, gangsters, and the stock market crash at the end of the decade, but how about filling in the blanks a little? Also called the Jazz Age, music is a big part of this site, which also offers time lines, other links, and well-written prose on the art, literature, and culture of the time. Parental advisory: You may want to check the tabloid stories.

http://www.louisville.edu/~kprayb01/1920s.html

NET FILES

What is an atoll ?

Answer: An atoll is a ring of coral that encloses a circular lagoon. Most often atolls are formed on the crater of a volcano that has sunk below the surface of the sea. Read more about atolls and discover other interesting facts about coral reefs by diving into *http://dekalb.dc.peachnet.edu/~pgov6/students/j95/starmoss/coral.htm#Different Types*

Staring off into space? Discover ASTRONOMY!

Flapper Station

This site is the *bee's knees*. Now we're not thinking you're a *pushover* or giving you a *line; everything is Jake*. If you have no idea what we mean, you need to visit the 1920s slang area of this fun historical site. You'll also find info on Prohibition, trends, trains, cars, music, and much more.

http://www.sns.com/~rbotti/

Roaring 1920s Concert Extravaganza

Before television, people gathered around the radio to listen to live concerts from distant places. This popular form of entertainment is re-created here, as you listen to minute-long sound files from such 1920s artists as Al Jolson, Maurice Chevalier, Fanny Brice, and Helen Kane, "the Boop Boop A Doop Girl."

http://bestwebs.com/roaring1920/

U.S. HISTORY—1930S

The American Experience: Riding the Rails

It was a hard time to be a teenager in the 1930s. There was widespread poverty and many troubled families. Over 250,000 teens ran away from home, looking for better lives. Unfortunately, life on the road was often more desperate and lonely than the lives they left. Although it was dangerous and illegal, many crisscrossed the country by hopping the freight trains of the time. These "kids" are now in their 70s and 80s, and they told their stories for a PBS television program. You can read them at this site.

http://www.pbs.org/wgbh/pages/amex/rails/

The American Experience: Surviving the Dust Bowl

The dust storms during the 1930s were horrendous. People thought the world was at an end. Being inside was the safest, but dust sifted in behind closed doors, getting into the dishes, glassware, food, and water. The people of Kansas were being pelted with the landscape of Oklahoma and even Texas. When the dust storm was over, people found their homes and farms buried. A reporter called it "the Dust Bowl." Although some left for better lives elsewhere, others stayed on waiting for the rains to come. They would wait five years. Why was there so much dust? Blame it on the wheat production for World War I. Farmers plowed under the intricate weave of prairie grasses in their zeal to increase food production to help win the war. After the harvest, and without the roots of those grasses, nothing could hold the dry soil in place. Could it happen again?

http://www.pbs.org/wgbh/pages/amex/dustbowl/

NET FILES

Here's a knotty problem: What's the difference between a hitch and a bend?

Answer: Know the ropes! A *hitch* is a knot that ties a line onto something else, and a *bend* ties two lines together. If tying knots leaves you in a snarl, then be sure to drop in on http://www.pcmp.caltech.edu/~tobi/knots/ for a new twist in learning.

Mr. Spock agrees it is highly logical to want to know all about STAR TREK.

The Day of the Black Blizzard

"To talk about April the 14th, 1935...it was a beautiful clear Sunday afternoon, and I was out skipping rocks on the horse pond," recalls Harley "Doc" Holladay. Although the temperature was 90 degrees that Palm Sunday, over a few hours it dropped more than 50 degrees. Suddenly, a "black as coal" cloud of dust rolled into town. People couldn't see to cross the street. You couldn't walk anywhere because the flying sand and dirt would sting your face and legs. Be sure to listen to the audio files of people who lived through this event.

http://www.discovery.com/area/history/dustbowl/dustbowl1.1.html

New Deal Network

As America struggled to get back on its economic feet after the Great Depression, President Franklin Delano Roosevelt announced the New Deal during the presidential race of 1932. It pledged many new government projects to increase financial stability and help along social reform. Remember, one out of four people was unemployed at this time, and many schools had to close because they didn't have the funds to stay open. Poor children wrote to the President's wife, Eleanor Roosevelt, and begged her for cast-off clothing for themselves and their parents. Read some of the children's letters, and Mrs. Roosevelt's responses, at this site. You'll also learn about the CCC (Civilian Conservation Corps) camps and the TVA (Tennessee Valley Authority) water projects, which brought affordable electricity to many Americans for the first time.

http://newdeal.feri.org/

A B C D E F G H I J K L M N O P Q R S T U V W X Y Z

U.S. HISTORY—1940S

See also HISTORY—WORLD WAR II

What did you do in the war, Grandma?

During World War II, food, shoes, sugar, and gasoline were rationed. You could only get so much for your coupon, and if you ran out, too bad until you could use your next coupon, because you couldn't hoard supplies, either. Find out what life was like during the war years by listening to these women who made important contributions as teachers, news reporters, nurses, and in other professions. There is also a time line and glossary so you will be able to understand some of the references. Parents: Not all oral histories at this site have been checked.

http://www.stg.brown.edu/projects/
    WWII_Women/tocCS.html

U.S. HISTORY—1950S

The Fifties

Net-mom has a friend who grew up in the 1950s—even graduated from high school in the last year of the decade! According to this friend, the History Channel has a lot of really good facts about the era they call "vibrant and wholesome." You will learn a lot and might even find an idea for a school term paper right here. After all, in the '50s, a general was the president, and television came in two colors only: black and white!

http://www.historychannel.com/fifties/

Fifties Website Home Page

Take a spin through this Web site and you'll hear lots of music from the '50s, including that of Elvis, Patsy Cline, and even old TV theme music. If you ever find your dad kicking himself trying to remember the lyrics to the songs he and your mom used to dance to—just point him here. This site is a little gem of popular culture, but parents should be forewarned that there are occurrences of PG-13 language and behavior.

http://www.fiftiesweb.com/home.htm

U.S. HISTORY—1960S

What Happened in the Sixties?

Meanwhile, in 1964: a gallon of gasoline costs 30 cents; Hasbro introduces the G.I. Joe doll; the Beatles appear on *The Ed Sullivan Show;* and President Johnson announces a substantial increase in U.S. aid to South Vietnam "to restrain the mounting infiltration of men and equipment by the Hanoi regime in support of the Vietcong." Read about the swinging sixties at this site, but parents should be advised that this is part of a larger site on baby boomers and not all links have been checked.

http://www.bbhq.com/sixties.htm

U.S. HISTORY—1970S

DeeT's 70s Page

Take a ride on the time machine and step back into the 1970s. Some things haven't changed much. Kids watched *Sesame Street* and *The Electric Company* on television, and back then *Gilligan's Island* was being shown for the first time! If you'd like to see these and lots of other '70s stuff, Dee T's is the place to be.

http://www.rt66.com/dthomas/70s/70s.html

U.S. HISTORY—1980S

The 80s Server

In "A Child of the Eighties" you'll find out all about Saturday morning cartoons, sleep-overs at your friend's house, and backseat fights with your brother to pass away the time on those long family car trips. Try your favorite home page in Valley URL and see it magically transform into "Valley-speak." Try some of the trivia games, but be warned, you'll have to be a real '80s expert to win. Parents: A chat room is here and not all links have been checked.

http://www.80s.com/

Pony up to HORSES AND EQUESTRIAN SPORTS.

U.S. HISTORY—CIVIL WAR

The Battle of Gettysburg

It was the turning point of the Civil War: on July 1, 2, and 3, 1863, at Gettysburg, Pennsylvania, more men fought and died than in any other battle on North American soil. A total of 51,000 were killed and wounded. Today, the battlefield is a national military park, with over 1,000 monuments. Follow the maps of the battles and explore other Civil War links from this site.

http://www.gettysbg.com/battle.html

Old Abe the War Eagle

During the Civil War, many military units adopted an animal mascot. Usually it was a dog or a goat, but the Eighth Wisconsin Infantry Regiment had something really unique: a bald eagle, which they named "Old Abe," after President Abraham Lincoln. You can read about Old Abe's war stories and see pictures. Old Abe's legacy lives on in the logos of Wisconsin companies, in replicas at the Wisconsin State Assembly and elsewhere, and in the names of school sports teams. Additionally, the insignia patch of the U.S. Army's 101st Airborne Division, originally formed in Wisconsin during World War I, carries a graphic of Old Abe. According to this page, the "Screaming Eagles" saw extensive action in World War II and the Vietnam and Persian Gulf Wars.

http://badger.state.wi.us/agencies/dva/museum/
  cybergal/oa-main.html

U.S. Civil War Center — Index of Civil War Information available on the Internet

The Civil War is a fascinating event in American history. Many people have spent a great deal of time studying the war and collecting material on it. The "Civil War related Web Links Index" will lead you to hundreds of sites. Diaries, forts, miniatures, maps, music, and much more are all a click away. This is your starting point for any topic on the Civil War. Pictures? Oh yes, there are plenty of those, too!

http://www.cwc.lsu.edu/civlink.htm

U.S. HISTORY—WESTWARD EXPANSION

Adventures of Wells Fargo - Original Information Superhighway

These days, you can hop on a jet plane and travel the width of the U.S. from coast to coast in five or six hours. In the 1800s, however, there were no planes, so people traveled as far as they could by rail, ship, and other transportation, then made the rest of the trip by a bouncy overland stagecoach pulled by a team of horses. They often began their stagecoach journey from places halfway across the country, such as St. Louis, Missouri. The trip from St. Louis to San Francisco, California, generally took about 24 days! Wells Fargo was one of the companies to offer this form of travel, and they present some maps, stories, and tall tales about it all here.

http://wellsfargo.com/about/stories/ch11/

NET FILES

WHAT DO YOU GET WHEN YOU DON'T IRON YOUR MOOSE?

Answer: A Bullwrinkle! Find more jokes like this at http://www.edbydesign.com/jokess1.html

A
B
C
D
E
F
G
H
I
J
K
L
M
N
O
P
Q
R
S
T
U
V
W
X
Y
Z

America's West - Development and History

Return with us now to the days of yesteryear—of gold rush and ghost town, the heyday of cowboy and gunslinger. At this site, you'll discover links to information on America's westward expansion, famous Western trails, pioneers, trappers, and biographies of Kit Carson, Davy Crockett, Daniel Boone, Billy the Kid, Sitting Bull, Roy Rogers, and lots of famous folks in between. There are links to movies about the West as well as to Western theme parks and dude ranches. A caution to parents: Not all the outbound links have been reviewed.

http://www.AmericanWest.com/

Crossed the West:
The Adventures of Lewis and Clark

In 1804, President Thomas Jefferson looked out the window and said, "Hmm, I wonder if there is a water route, maybe a river or something, that goes all the way across the continent and ends up at the Pacific Ocean? Something we could navigate with boats, so we could get supplies there, and settle, and eventually build theme parks." OK, so he didn't *really* say that. But he did want the West explored, and Lewis and Clark were just the guys to take on the task. Want to join their expedition and see what happens?

http://www.nationalgeographic.com/features/97/west/

NET FILES

What's the world's
longest
insect?

Answer: According to The Insect Home Page, the longest insect in the world is the stick insect (*Pharnacia serritypes*), the female of which can be over a foot long! To find out more incredible facts, check http://info.ex.ac.uk/~gjlramel/six.html

Gold Rush

Written by Son of Net-mom for a sixth grade project, this site provides details about the California Gold Rush, which began after gold was discovered at Sutter's Mill in January, 1848. It took over six months for the news to reach the east coast, and by then it was too late in the year to set out via wagon. Some took ships and went around the tip of South America. Others took a dugout canoe shortcut through the jungles and wetlands where the Panama Canal is today, however this route was dangerous and travelers often caught malaria and other diseases. Many waited until the following spring of 1849 and set off in overloaded wagons, heading for the gold fields. This site will teach you about the various routes and what could be expected on the journeys. You'll also find information on sourdough bread, staple food of the miners. There is also a nice set of links to other useful Gold Rush sites.

http://www.net-mom.com/stephen/gold/

GORP - Great Outdoor Recreation Pages -
National Historic Trails

Ever wondered if you could find any of the old pioneer routes, like the Oregon Trail? You can! To this day, some of the old wagon ruts are still visible, and you can walk in the footsteps of early settlers during the westward expansion of the United States. You'll find maps and detailed descriptions of the Oregon Trail, plus the following: Santa Fe Trail; Trail of Tears; Iditarod National Historic Trail; Juan Bautista de Anza National Historic Trail; Lewis and Clark National Historic Trail; Mormon Pioneer National Historic Trail; Nez Perce National Historic Trail; and the Overmountain Victory National Historic Trail.

http://www.gorp.com/gorp/resource/us_trail/
   historic.htm

Surf, and you shall become empowered (or wet).

My Little House on the Prairie Home Page of Laura Ingalls Wilder

Whether you're a fan of the book or the television series, you need to visit this little house on the cyberprairie to find out everything about Laura Ingalls Wilder and her life. You'll be able to track her travels from the big woods to the prairie, chronicled in her book series about Ma, Pa, Mary, and, of course, herself. You can visit the Heritage Sites, which are now located in the places Wilder describes in her novels.

http://www.vvv.com/~jenslegg/

New Perspectives on THE WEST

This is a companion site to the eight-part PBS television series *The West*. It is a history of the expansion of the American West, and we are including it because of the richness of its information about people, places, and events during the westward expansion.

http://www.pbs.org/weta/thewest/

Pioneer Spirit

In the 1800s, many settlers left the east coast and headed west to make better lives for themselves. Trying to carve out places of their own from wilderness prairie wasn't easy. This excellent site shows in pictures and words the struggles of the Dakota pioneers. You'll read a diary written by a physician in the 1870s Dakota territory. And you will be fascinated by a series of "then and now" photographs comparing photos of long ago to the same spot in photos from today. How things have changed!

http://www.gps.com/Pioneer_Spirit/

WORLD WAR II
A-Bomb WWW Museum ~ June, 1995

Hiroshima, Nagasaki, Little Boy, Fat Man, and Enola Gay are all words that bring to mind a picture of the bomb of all bombs, the A-bomb. This site is set up as a place to come and learn about the history and result of the atomic bomb. It contains information about the destruction caused by the bombs, interviews with children and adults who experienced the bombs first hand, health problems faced by the survivors, and much more.

http://www.csi.ad.jp/ABOMB/

Anne Frank Online

She was a kid just like you. Her diary helps us remember that she lived and then died in a German concentration camp. Who is she? Anne Frank. Here is her history, along with photos of Anne and her family. Read some of the things that she wrote in her small red-and-white plaid diary. Maybe you would like to start keeping a journal about your life. Also see the Anne Frank entry in the PEOPLE AND BIOGRAPHIES section of this book.

http://www.annefrank.com/

D-Day

This archive of World War II facts, pictures, movies, and memories was built by students at Patch American High School, located at the United States European Command in Stuttgart, Germany. You'll find battle plans, newsreel footage, and famous speeches connected with D-Day and World War II.

http://www.stut-hs.odedodea.edu/D-Day/
Table_of_contents.html

Enola Gay Perspectives

War is an ugly thing, and it's hard to understand how people could want to harm other people. In 1945, the United States dropped an atomic bomb on the Japanese city of Hiroshima. This Web resource, developed by library school students as part of a project for the University of Maryland, tries to make sense of it all. You'll find out the reasons government leaders decided to drop the bomb. You'll learn about the crew of the plane *Enola Gay* and about the consequences of their mission. There is also a section on the controversy surrounding the *Enola Gay* exhibit at the Smithsonian Institution's National Air and Space Museum. For an objective look at the issue, try this site. Look in the PEACE section of this book for more on this subject.

http://www.glue.umd.edu/~enola/welcome.html

The Web in Pig Latin? Make it so in LANGUAGES.

A
B
C
D
E
F
G
H
I
J
K
L
M
N
O
P
Q
R
S
T
U
V
W
X
Y
Z

A
B
C
D
E
F
G
H
I
J
K
L
M
N
O
P
Q
R
S
T
U
V
W
X
Y
Z

The Holocaust: A Tragic Legacy

This award-winning site was created by high school students as part of the ThinkQuest competition. It traces the roots, events, and legacy of the worst of times, when many European civilians, especially Jews, were killed by the Nazis during World War II. You can visit a VRML concentration camp, and while you're in that area see how you would react when faced with making a terrible decision. Parents: This site is not for young children.

http://library.advanced.org/12663/

United States Holocaust Memorial Museum

The United States Holocaust Memorial Museum in Washington, D.C., offers general information on this painful chapter of world history. The education page offers a guide to teaching about the Holocaust, a brief history, FAQ, a heartbreaking article about children in the Holocaust, and a videography. An online reservation form for groups is available. Parents: Descriptions may be too graphic for youngsters.

http://www.ushmm.org/

World War II, An American Scrapbook

World War II has been in the news a lot lately since it happened just about 50 years ago. One school's assignment was to develop a Web site on World War II and to get the information for it by talking to family members who had been involved in the war. They shared their memories, and here they are! You may also explore links to a number of other World War II Web sites. This site was a finalist in the ThinkQuest Junior competition. The students are from McRoberts School in Katy, Texas.

http://tqjunior.advanced.org/4616/

Never give your name or address to a stranger.

HOLIDAYS

Billy Bear's Holidays

Billy Bear offers special sites for more than ten fun holidays. Each one has games, activities, and facts about the holiday that may be new to you. If we don't have a separate listing for a holiday in this book, check with Billy Bear. Net-mom loves Billy Bear because he gives such great *bear hugs*!

http://www.billybear4kids.com/holidays/fun.htm

Events for ...

Ho hum, today is just another day, right? It seems there are so few special days—like Christmas, your birthday, or the Fourth of July. Actually, every single day has been important in history, or there is some momentous event taking place somewhere, or someone great was born. To see why today is important, take a look here. Maybe you can use the information here as a good excuse for a party!

http://erebus.phys.cwru.edu/~copi/events.html

Festivals Home Page

Somewhere at this site is a European, Chinese, or New Zealand holiday or festival for every occasion. In Austria during February, they prepare for a carnival. All people dress up as "some thing" (ghosts, clowns, witches). There's also a carnival parade. In Sweden, crayfish parties are very popular in August. You can celebrate the Treaty of Waitangi in New Zealand on February 6, and in China, Spring Festival is on the lunar new year. On the eve of the Spring Festival, everyone leaves their lights on all night long in order to drive away ghosts. It is said that ghosts are scared of the light. You can see at least one red lantern is hanging from every family's roof.

http://wfs.vub.ac.be/cis/festivals/

Festivals.com

Can you do the "Beauty Queen Wave"? On floats in big parades, you might wonder how the queens and princesses manage to wave to the crowds all the way down the miles-long parade route—without getting a repetitive motion problem, that is. See an animation of the secret wave at *<http://festivals.com/holiday/ ritual.htm>*. You may want to alternate it with Net-mom's variant: elbow-elbow-wrist-wrist-wrist. While you're practicing, wander through the rest of this site. It is a fascinating look at more than 20,000 seasonal celebrations around the world. Click on any area of the Big Map and get a list of festivals there throughout the next six months. You'll find lots of features and fun, but we haven't looked at everything on the site, so browse with care.

http://www.festivals.com/

Heather's Happy Holidaze Page!! For Kids Only!!

Heather is in elementary school, and she came up with the concept and design of this neat home page all by herself! With a little help from her dad and mom, it's been up and running since September 1995. Pictures go with each of her favorite holidays, so children of all ages can enjoy this site. You'll find scary Halloween links and a search for Tom Turkey for Thanksgiving. For some little-known tree facts, traditions, and folklore, be sure to try her links for Christmas.

http://www.shadeslanding.com/hms/

KIDPROJ'S Multi-Cultural Calendar

Around the world, every day is a holiday somewhere, and kids just like you are celebrating something. Now kids have a place to tell the rest of the world about their holiday foods, decorations, parades, songs, and other ways they make this day special from all the others. You can look at the holidays by month, by country, or by name. Do you have a special holiday you want to talk about? Add it here!

http://www.kidlink.org/KIDPROJ/MCC/

100TH DAY

100th Day of School

Lots of kids are counting the days they go to school—it's because they want to be sure not to miss the 100th day! Teachers and kids are celebrating the 100th day of school in lots of special ways; read about them at this site and its links. For example, each child might bring in 100 pennies to donate to charity. The school nurse might collect 100 healthy handprints, finger painted on a big sheet of paper outside the office. Kids could try to dance for 100 seconds, or (even harder) be quiet for 100 seconds. Some kids like to draw pictures of what they will look like when they are 100 years old! The possibilities are endless—get started at this site.

http://www.siec.k12.in.us/~west/proj/100th/

APRIL FOOL'S DAY

April Fool's Day (April 1)

How did the tradition of April Fool's Day begin? According to this page, it was all because of a calendar change decreed by Pope Gregory in 1562. All of a sudden, New Year's Day was celebrated at a new time of year—it took a while for word to get around (there was no such thing as the Internet then). People still celebrating the New Year on April 1 were fools indeed. Find out more at this site.

http://www.usis.usemb.se/Holidays/celebrate/ april.htm

ASIAN HOLIDAYS

Chinese Holidays & Festivals

June 1 is when China celebrates its Children's Day. Kids are showered with presents, and their schools give them big parties. Sound like fun? Read about this and more Chinese traditions here.

http://www.chinascape.org/china/culture/holidays/ hyuan/holiday.html

A B C D E F G H I J K L M N O P Q R S T U V W X Y Z

A
B
C
D
E
F
G
H
I
J
K
L
M
N
O
P
Q
R
S
T
U
V
W
X
Y
Z

Chinese New Year

This is a really interesting site that describes the Chinese calendar system. The Chinese calendar has 24 solar terms closely related to the changes of Nature—a very useful tool for farmers, providing knowledge on the proper time for planting and harvesting.

http://www.cf.ac.uk/uwcc/suon/chinese/year.html

Happy Chinese New Year

The Chinese calendar is based both on the Gregorian and a lunar-solar system. It divides a year into 12 months, each with 39 1/2 days. Twenty-four poetic solar terms describe seasonal changes, including the Beginning of Spring, the Waking of Insects, Grain in Ear, Frost's Descent, and Great Cold. There is also a system that names the years in a 12-year cycle: Rat, Ox, Tiger, Hare, Dragon, Snake, Horse, Sheep, Monkey, Rooster, Dog, and Boar. Find out how the Chinese New Year is celebrated, and remember, in China, 1998 is year 4696, the Year of the Tiger!

http://www.chinascape.org/ChineseNewYear/

NET FILES

Who were the world's first air passengers? (Hint: They flew in a hot-air balloon.)

Answer: In 1783, the Montgolfier brothers flew the first hot-air balloon in Versailles, France, safely landing a duck, a rooster, and a sheep. Although there was no in-flight movie, the flight must have been very entertaining! Read more at http://www.nmsi.ac.uk/on-line/flight/flight/mont.htm

NET FILES

What languages are spoken in Vatican City?

Answer: The main languages are Italian and Latin. And don't forget Monastic Sign Language, which is used by those in religious orders who have taken a vow of silence. You can learn a lot about languages and where they are spoken at http://www.sil.org/ethnologue/

Festivals & Culture (Keeping Faith With the Past)

Learn the traditions of the Taiwanese Dragon Boat Festival, the Birthday of the Goddess of the Sea, and the Lantern Festival, among many others. You'll also read a bit about Chinese knots, rice-dough figures and candy sculpture, and lion dances.

http://peacock.tnjc.edu.tw/ADD/TOUR/keep.html

Festivals in Japan

A wonderful collection of photos taken during festivals in Japan make you feel a part of the crowd. Hey, watch out for those snow sculpture dinosaurs!

http://www.mainichi.co.jp/photogallery/omatsuri/index-e.html

Festivals of Wakayama

The festivals of Wakayama, Japan, are described at this site—complete with photos. On March 3, unwanted dolls are set adrift in a small boat and pushed out to sea. On February 8, a requiem service is held for unwanted needles. Seeing is believing!

http://fumi.eco.wakayama-u.ac.jp/English/Kishu/festival.html

Hawai'i's Greeting of the Season

Many folks in Hawaii come from a Japanese, Chinese, or other Asian heritage. As in many countries, the coming of the New Year deserves a big celebration. One of the symbolic Japanese decorations you might see is the *kadomatsu* (gates of pine). These graceful arrangements of pine and bamboo, symbolizing good wishes for a long, prosperous life, are displayed for several days before January 1, then burned or tossed into flowing water. The Chinese celebrate New Year's Day according to another calendar system (see the CalendarLand entry in the TIME—CALENDARS section in this book); in 1998, the Year of the Tiger began in February. One of the exciting traditions is the lion dance, many of which are performed by martial arts clubs in Hawaii. The lion is a symbol of life, luck, and health. Colorfully costumed lion dancers parade down the streets accompanied by the sounds of gongs and drums. Merchants and others throw firecrackers at the feet of the "lions," symbolically chasing away bad luck. Read more about these joyous Asian celebrations here.

http://www.aloha-hawaii.com/c_greetings.shtml

Hong Kong Terminal - Chinese Festival

Arranged by moon, or lunar month, you can learn about everything from Chinese New Year to the Day the Kitchen God Visits Heaven. In between you'll find the Dragon Boat Festival, the Hungry Ghosts Festival, and a lot more in this fascinating peek into the culture of both traditional and modern China.

http://zero.com.hk/hkta/culture.html

Japan Travel Updates

Did you know that May 5 is Children's Day in Japan? You'll also learn about the beautiful Star Festival (July 7), in which children tie their wishes to tree branches, and other beautiful Japanese traditions.

http://www.jnto.go.jp/08events/annualevents/
    08frame.html

Catch a ride on a Carousel in AMUSEMENT PARKS.

BIRTHDAYS

ANYDAY Today-in-History PAGE of SCOPE SYSTEMS

Want to know who shares your birthday or what famous events throughout history happened the day you were born? Just visit this site and type in the month and year you want. For example, famous people born on February 8 include author Jules Verne, actor James Dean, and actress Audrey Meadows, who played Alice in *The Honeymooners*. Find out when and where these folks were born, too; Meadows, for example, was born in China. You can also find out who died on this day (Mary, Queen of Scots) and find out what important historical events took place. On February 8, the Boy Scouts organization was incorporated (1910), radio first came to the White House (1922), and Walt Disney Studios was formed (1926). Know anyone with a brand-new baby? Give the proud parents a printout of their baby's birth date!

http://www.scopesys.com/anyday/

Billy Bear's Birthday Party

Happy Birthday to YOU! Happy Birthday to YOU! This site is a present from Net-mom to you! You can play virtual pin the tail on the donkey, bake a virtual cake, pick out some virtual party favors, color some pictures, and more. This site also suggests you make your own Web page with the party icons supplied here.

http://www.billybear4kids.com/holidays/
    birthday/party.htm

World Birthday Web

This site is kind of silly and cool at the same time. Whose birthday is today? Find out here. Enter your own name and birthday. You can also enter your e-mail address and your home page, if you want. The info gets added to the database immediately. When your birthday rolls around, you'll get e-mail greetings from all sorts of well-wishers. This year, we got one from the Klingon Language Institute!

http://www.boutell.com/birthday.cgi/

A B C D E F G H I J K L M N O P Q R S T U V W X Y Z

A
B
C
D
E
F
G
H
I
J
K
L
M
N
O
P
Q
R
S
T
U
V
W
X
Y
Z

CHRISTMAS

Christmas Around The World

Here's a trip you can take without even packing your suitcase! Travel through cyberspace to countries in Europe, South America, the United Kingdom, and elsewhere to learn the different ways children celebrate Christmas. The spirit of the Christmas season, of giving and goodwill toward everyone, is shared by many countries worldwide, each with its own unique traditions and customs.

http://www.the-north-pole.com/around/

Christmas Down Under

Here at Pollywood Farm, we celebrate Christmas with lots of snow, ice, and hot chocolate. But that is because we live in the northeastern U.S., in the Northern Hemisphere, where December is a winter month. In the Southern Hemisphere, the seasons are reversed. In Australia, for example, Christmas comes during the summer. Because we couldn't imagine it, we visited this site. Lots of families go on Christmas picnics, and it is a festive time for all! Some people are afraid Santa and the reindeer may suffer from the Aussie heat, so they are thinking of letting Swag Man deliver the presents in his four-wheel-drive truck. Read all about it by clicking first on "Traditions," then on "Australian Traditions."

http://www.ozkidz.gil.com.au/Christmas/

Christmas Stories

It's the night before Christmas, and you need some new holiday stories. Here's a collection in the St. Nick of time! You'll find the complete text of L. Frank Baum's *The Life and Adventures of Santa Claus,* as well as lesser-known tales from European and other cultural traditions.

http://www.acs.ucalgary.ca/~dkbrown/christmas.html

Grinch Net

Do you remember the Grinch and how he "stole" Christmas from Whoville in *How The Grinch Stole Christmas*? If you are a Who fan, or even a Grinch fan, this site is for you!

http://www.ntr.net/~dave/grinch/

A Holy Christmas

Visit this wonderful site for a family-centered emphasis on the true meaning of Christmas, the Advent season, and the Epiphany. This site also has Christmas clip art, audio files, and recipes.

http://www.rockies.net/~spirit/sermons/
  christmaspage.html

National Christmas Tree Association

Too bad they don't have "smell attribute" plug-ins (yet)! If they did, this site would smell terrific! The National Christmas Tree Growers page provides a dictionary of 16 evergreen types, from the Arizona cypress to the white spruce. You'll also find a directory of tree farms close to you (if you want to cut your own), selection tips, and interesting facts and figures.

http://www.christree.org/

NECCO Wafer Gingerbread House

Several years back, Net-mom and family made a totally cool gingerbread house. Every year we display it during the holidays, and it looks as good as new! Just put the whole thing into a plastic trash bag and keep it in a cool place. If ours ever breaks, though, we're going to use the recipe at this site to make another one.

http://www.necco.com/gingerhouse.htm

NET FILES

In what sport would you find the following terms: bump and run, fried egg, and smothered hook?

Answer: They are all golfing terms. Find out what they mean at http://www.pga.com/FAQ/glossary.html

SANTA CLAUS AT CLAUS.COM

Do you know how to get on Santa's Naughty list? He hates it when you put out cookies and milk for him—and the milk is a WEEK beyond the freshness expiration date! He also doesn't like it when kids shove toys under the bed instead of putting them away. To get on Santa's Nice list—that's easy. Just volunteer to do a chore! What's Santa got written down about you this year? See if you're naughty or nice in the archives. Then visit Mrs. Claus' kitchen for some easy-to-make, elf-tested favorites. Take a walk through the toy shop and see what's new (this is a commercial site and you will see some marketing going on, but it is not very heavy-handed). Sing along with the holiday karaoke band, and send some special Santa e-mail. The best fun, though, is on Christmas Eve. Track Santa's location on the radarscope, keep count of how many cookies he's eaten, and see how close he is to your own house! Then you'd better pop into bed, because as everyone knows, Santa doesn't come to a house until the kids are asleep.

http://www.claus.com/

SANTA'S SECRET VILLAGE (sm) @ NORTHPOLE.COM

Net-mom likes this site and recommends it for preschoolers. It contains no marketing messages. Sure, you can write a letter to Santa in the mail room and click on the toys you want, but you'll be clicking on a generic-looking doll rather than Holiday Magic Barbie. Best yet, come back in a day or two and find a personal response from Santa himself! What enchanted us about this simple site was its innocence. Spruced up with a few animations, it is not overdone like so many other Web sites we see these days. It reminded us of the olden days, back in the early '90s when the Net was still a wilderness area. The read-aloud stories all have lessons, the reindeer all pull on the same team, and the cocoa's never hot enough to burn your tongue. Yes, those were the days. Some parts of the site succeed better than others. We loved the heirloom recipes in Mrs. Claus' Kitchen and the stories in the Reindeer Barn. But we got bored with Santa's video collection and the Festival of Trees.

http://www.northpole.com/

> ## Curl up with a good Internet site.

Santa's Workshop

"'Twas the night before Christmas, when all through the house...." Wait a minute, you don't have to wait until Christmas Eve to visit this site. It's fun anytime of the year, especially if you enjoy reading this poem made famous by Clement Moore in the 1820s. This is a great place to find answers to lots of Santa Claus FAQs (frequently asked questions), as well as learn other holiday traditions and fun historical facts about Christmas. Have you ever wondered about the origins of Santa Claus? Dutch settlers in New Amsterdam (later renamed New York) brought the idea of Santa Claus, or *Sint(e) Klass*, to America. Even though Christmas songs date back to the fourth century, the lighter and more joyous Christmas songs that we know today as carols came from Renaissance times in Italy. The word "carol" comes from the French word *caroler*, meaning "to dance in a ring." And for the Scrooge in your family, you'll find that famous Charles Dickens story, *A Christmas Carol*. This site is available in English, Spanish, and Portuguese.

http://home1.gte.net/santa/

A Search for the Meaning of Christmas

Are you searching for the true meaning of Christmas? Here's a don't-miss noncommercial site with religious traditions, family traditions, customs, songs, thoughtful links, and more. This is part of a larger site with information on Kwanzaa and Hannukah.

http://techdirect.com/christmas/

The Very First Story of Christmas

Do you know that Christmas really celebrates the birth of the baby Jesus? To read the traditional Bible story about Mary and Joseph and the birth of Jesus in Bethlehem, try this beautifully done site. Listen to holiday background music while you read the familiar story, illustrated by Renaissance and contemporary artwork.

http://www.geocities.com/Heartland/8833/xmas.html

A B C D E F G H I J K L M N O P Q R S T U V W X Y Z

Left margin vertical alphabet: A B C D E F G H I J K L M N O P Q R S T U V W X Y Z

A World Wide Christmas Calendar

This worldwide Christmas calendar has a tree with gift-wrapped packages below it. Open a package and discover how a youngster in another country might celebrate this holiday. In Denmark, according to one nine-year-old writer, they make oatmeal balls, decorate their homes with elves, and eat duck and pig for dinner on Christmas Eve.

http://www.algonet.se/~bernadot/christmas/
   calendar.html

CINCO DE MAYO

Cascarones: A Smash at Fiesta

It's almost time to start making *cascarones,* one of the messiest and most charming things about fiesta! These confetti-filled eggs are most often smashed gleefully on other people's heads, creating an instant Kodak moment fit for any travel brochure. For directions on making your very own *cascarones,* or confetti eggs, visit this site.

http://www.silcom.com/fiesta/cascaron.html

Cinco de Mayo

Do you like a really good party? Well, every May 5, many Latino Americans and citizens of Mexico celebrate a grand event, and they have a party in the process. In 1862, on Cinco de Mayo (that's Spanish for May 5), a handful of Mexican troops defeated a much larger and better-armed force of soldiers from France. This victory showed that a small group, strengthened by unity, can overcome overwhelming odds. Ever since, Cinco de Mayo is celebrated with music, tasty food, parades, and a party.

http://latino.sscnet.ucla.edu/cinco.html

Learn More About Cinco de Mayo

While May 5 is a national holiday in Mexico and is celebrated with the usual speeches and parades, it is reportedly a far more important date to Mexicans in America. In the U.S., it is seen as an opportunity to celebrate Hispanic culture in general, with huge fairs that include Mexican singing, dancing, food, and other amusements. Read about Cinco de Mayo and the history of the celebration at this site.

http://soundprint.brandywine.american.edu/
   ~soundprt/more_info/nogales_history.html

DAY OF THE DEAD
Day of the Dead

In November, Mexicans celebrate the annual Day of the Dead. It's not a sad occasion. They make special foods and prepare a feast to honor their ancestors. They have picnics on their relatives' graves so the dead can join in the festivities, too. One of the special foods is called "Bread of the Dead" *(pan de muerto).* The baker hides a plastic skeleton in each rounded loaf, and it's good luck to bite into the piece with the skeleton! People also give each other candy skeletons, skulls, and other treats with a death design. The holiday has complex social, religious, and cultural meanings. Learn more about this celebration here.

http://www.public.iastate.edu/~rjsalvad/
   scmfaq/muertos.html

DAY OF THE DEAD - DIA DE LOS MUERTOS

Learn many of the traditions and rituals surrounding this Mexican holiday, when the dead pay a visit to their old homes and are welcomed with special foods and festivities. There is a rich section with links to explore, but parents should note that we didn't get to look at all of them.

http://www.mexconnect.com/mex_/feature/
   daydeadindex.html

NET FILES

What do Julius Caeser, Annie Oakley, Betsy Ross, and Leonardo da Vinci have in common?

Answer: According to the Chinese zodiac's 12-year cycle, these famous people were all born in the Year of the Monkey. The Chinese belief is that people born in the Year of the Monkey are very intelligent and are always well liked. Find out more at http://pasture.ecn.purdue.edu/~agenhtml/agenmc/china/zmonkey.html

EARTH DAY
Earth Day, 1998

It's the only planet most of us will ever have—why not celebrate it and keep it green? This site suggests individual and classroom activities for both younger and older kids. You'll also be intrigued by a large number of appropriate links to other resources, including a site about the history of Earth Day.

http://www.eduplace.com/ss/earth/

The Earth Day Challenge

Enjoy playing an environmental scavenger hunt that challenges students grades K–6 to learn more about the environment and how to help take care of it. Go to this site for details and to register. This is a free activity—registration is required only if you want to win prizes!

http://www.marshall-es.marshall.k12.tn.us/
jobe/earthday98/main.html

NET FILES

There's lots of stuff below the street: wires, pipes, and tunnels. Access to them is through an opening in the street called a manhole. Why is a manhole round? Why isn't it square?

Answer: According to Dr. Math, it's so the manhole cover won't fall through the hole and hit something underneath! A circle is the only shape that won't fall through its own hole. If it were a square, for example, you could drop it through diagonally, because the diagonal diameter of a square is longer than the diameter straight across. Other polygons will have diameters of different lengths, allowing you to turn the cover so that the shortest diameter of the cover lines up with the longest diameter of the hole, allowing it to fall through. Read more from Dr. Math at http://forum.swarthmore.edu/dr.math/problems/mosh26.html

EASTER
1998 White House Easter Egg Roll Cybercast

Sometime during the presidency of James Madison (1809–1817), the beloved Washington tradition of the Easter Egg Roll was initiated at the suggestion of Madison's wife, Dolley. Its original site was the U.S. Capitol grounds. By 1877, some members of congress got tired of complaining about the leftover hard-boiled eggs (they kept slipping on ones the kids hadn't found), debris, and general disorder of the whole event. Policemen shooed that year's Easter crowds away. Tearful children converged on the White House lawn to petition President Hayes to hold an impromptu egg roll there. He did. The idea caught on. In 1878, President Hayes and his wife, Lucy, officially opened the White House grounds to the children. It's been held there ever since, except for brief breaks during the war years. Visit this site to learn a basketful of facts and trivia about this colorful event, which includes games as well as an egg hunt. The most precious eggs are those with the signatures of famous sports players and other celebrities, who are asked to sign the wooden eggs when they visit the White House. You can buy a souvenir egg from the White House link you will find at this site.

http://www.easter.earthlink.net/

Cathy's Picnic

After you've colored all your Easter eggs, what do you do with them? Do you put them in a bowl on the table? That looks pretty, but try something new—check the Easter Village! Just print out the pictures and color them. In fact, some of them are already in color. Then wrap the pictures around the eggs, set them up, and play with your beautiful creation. Six-year-old Cathy made this page with her family.

http://www.geocities.com/Heartland/7134/

Be dazzled by the laser shows in PHYSICS.

A B C D E F G H I J K L M N O P Q R S T U V W X Y Z

Easter Fun

Easter is a very *egg-citing* occasion! This site gives terrific ideas for making Easter crafts, including lots of ways to dye eggs and make your own candy. We made our own duck mask and some no-bake clay and planted an Easter basket with wheat seeds to make our own Easter grass. We can hardly wait to try the other Easter links here.

http://www.ok.bc.ca/TEN/easter/easter.html

The Great American Egg Hunt

If it's around Easter when you're reading this, Net-mom's friend, Hazel Jobe, is no doubt running another virtual egg hunt. It's aimed at K–3 students, but anyone can play! Students have designed colorful eggs that have been hidden on school sites around the World Wide Web. Hazel says, "Participants will visit the school sites to hunt for the egg and then follow the link to answer the questions. It will give these young students practice navigating the Web for a purpose. Participants will receive a certificate when they have found all the eggs and answered all the questions." You can also win great prizes!

http://www.marshall-es.marshall.k12.tn.us/
  jobe/egghunt/info.html

A Holy Easter

OK, Christmas is always on December 25, Valentine's Day is on February 14, and St. Patrick's Day is always celebrated on March 17, so what about Easter? Why is it on a different date each year? The answer is a long one, but here goes: Easter is observed on the first Sunday following the first full moon after the first day of spring (vernal equinox) in the Northern Hemisphere. This can occur anytime between March 22 and April 25. Although this extensive site collects links about bunnies, eggs, clip art, and audio files, its main emphasis is on the religious observances of Easter and the Passover season.

http://www.rockies.net/~spirit/sermons/
  easterpage.html

How to Make Ukrainian Easter Eggs

This page explains everything you need to know about the art of *Pysanky*, the Ukrainian Easter egg. You need an adult to help, because this process involves a candle and hot wax. First, you must decide on the designs you're going to use. Many geometric patterns have traditional meanings—for example, curlicues mean protection and diamonds signify knowledge. You'll find suggested beginner designs here, so get your equipment and get started (the page lists several sources for materials). Using a special stylus, called a *kistka*, apply wax to the egg wherever you want the shell to remain white. Then dip the egg in colored dyes. When completed, you melt the wax off. It takes a long time to make one of these, but in the end you'll have a true work of art. If handled carefully, you'll be able to give these eggs to your children and maybe even your grandchildren. This may be *eggs-actly* the hobby you've been looking for!

http://www3.ns.sympatico.ca/amorash/ukregg.html

FATHER'S DAY
Billy Bear's Happy Father's Day

What should you give your dad this year? He has enough ties. You know he can never have enough hugs! You can give him a Promise Card, too. Look at the example on this page, then make one yourself. You can promise to rake the leaves, walk the dog, or help Dad clean out the garage. There is also Father's Day clip art, a fun little fishing game, and lots more.

http://www.billybear4kids.com/holidays/father/
  dad.htm

Kid's Domain Father's Day

Mazes, coloring pages, cards, and crafts you can make—all for your dad on Father's Day. Don't miss the paper car craft—Dad would love his own Ferrari!

http://www.kidsdomain.com/holiday/dad/

Something fishy going on? Visit AQUARIUMS.

GERMAN HOLIDAYS

German

This cultural gem originates at the Patch American School, on a U.S. military base in Germany. Because a lot of American kids, who live there with their military families, find some of the local customs unusual, this site attempts to explain them. For example, this site explains the differences between a German Christmas and an American one. You'll also learn all about St. Martin's Day, the witches of May, and the beautiful, candlelit traditions of the Advent season.

http://www.stut-hs.odedodea.edu/Academic/
   German/Ger_Home.htm

GROUNDHOG DAY

CNN - Groundhog quartet agrees on early spring - Feb. 2, 1997

Punxsutawney Phil, the granddad of all weather-predicting groundhogs, was the lead rodent in this CNN report on weather-predicting animals. A cult hero of sorts, Phil has been making news with his February 2 shadows for many years. There are others in the field—and you can "read all about them" right here!

http://www.cnn.com/US/9702/02/
   groundhog.conspiracy/

Groundhog Day - February 2, 1998

Long before we had weather satellites, Doppler radar, and the Weather Channel, we got our winter weather forecasts from a rodent. Yes, it's part of what has made America great, and the tradition continues in Punxsutawney, Pennsylvania. Now you can get up close and personal with Punxsutawney Phil, groundhog extraordinaire. Some may call him a woodchuck, and some may call him a gopher. We call him a great publicity stunt, but we always pay attention to his predictions for an early or late spring. As the legend goes, if Phil comes up out of his hole on February 2 and sees his shadow, he'll be frightened back for six more weeks of winter; if, on the other hand, it's cloudy, we'll get an early spring. Will he see his shadow? Film at 11!

http://www.groundhog.org/

"Groundhog Day— half your hay."

That's an old saying connected with February 2, Groundhog Day. New England farmers knew that despite how sunny or cloudy the day was, there was still a lot of winter to come. If less than half the year's store of hay was left in the hayloft, the cows were in for a stretch of rationing before spring rains brought the new grass. Discover the strange and fanciful traditions of this unusual holiday at the Groundhog Day - February 2, 1998 page, which celebrates the weather forecasting abilities of a rodent.

Wiarton Willie's World Wide Website

Lest you think Canadians don't have a weather rodent (*en Français, météo marmotte*) of their own, meet Wiarton Willie, an albino marmot. "Born on the 45th parallel, exactly midway between the Equator and the North Pole, this white groundhog has the uncanny ability to signal the end of winter. Weather watchers around the world look to Willie's shadow and its 90 percent accuracy rate to see just how long winter is going to continue!" The statue of the critter is not to be missed, and Willie has fun games and mazes to play with, too. You can even send him e-mail (he must have a modem in his burrow). Come join the fun in southwestern Ontario on Lake Huron.

http://www.wiarton-willie.org/welcome.htm

Fetch some fascinating info in DOGS AND DOG SPORTS.

A
B
C
D
E
F
G
H
I
J
K
L
M
N
O
P
Q
R
S
T
U
V
W
X
Y
Z

GUY FAWKES DAY

Guy Fawkes Day

On November 5, people in the United Kingdom gather around roaring bonfires and burn a "guy" in effigy. What's it all about? You can find out at this nicely designed page, but the short form is that Guy Fawkes tried to blow up the Houses of Parliament back in 1601. It was because they were really mad at the King. The plot was discovered in time—or were Fawkes and the others framed?

http://web.idirect.com/~redsonja/guy/

HALLOWEEN

Billy Bear's Halloween

This site has great ideas for holiday parties! Also, you'll find lots of online Halloween-related games, like "Witch's Wart" and "Carve a Virtual Pumpkin." Check the free downloads to make your holiday the creepiest ever! This site was in the process of moving at press time, so visit the main holiday page and just click on Halloween.

http://www.billybear4kids.com/holidays/fun.htm

Family.com: FamilyFun Magazine - Fabulously Slimy Halloween Party

From bloodcurdling beverages (with insects in the ice cubes) to devilish desserts (with chocolate spiders), your Halloween party is sure to be ghoulish if you follow some of the ideas here. There are Halloween decorations and activities that any witch, wizard, or goblin will love. Don't forget to tiptoe through the pumpkin patch for design do's and don'ts about carving and lighting the best jack-o'-lantern ever!

http://family.disney.com/Categories/Activities/
   Features/family_1997_10/famf/famf107party/
   famf107party.html

Lots of monkey business in MAMMALS.

MidLink Magazine's Virtual Haunted House

This was created by middle grade kids for other middle grade kids, so be prepared for a lot of *horror-ible* stuff!

http://www2.ncsu.edu/ncsu/cep/ligon/haunted96/
   haunted96.menu.html

SafeSurf's Halloween Fun Page

Tricks and treats abound at this great Halloween site! (That reminds us of a seasonal joke: Why does a witch ride on a broom? Because vacuum cleaners have to be plugged into the wall!) Stroll through the site (keep your eyes closed if you're scared) and get some tips on easy-to-make costumes, decorations, and party food. You'll find lots of links to other haunted Web sites, none of *witch* we have checked.

http://www.safesurf.com/halloween/

Great tricks and treats for the entire family along with games and other holiday fun will be found on SafeSurf's Halloween Fun Page.

INDEPENDENCE DAY

4th of July - Independence Day

This patriotic site features a message from Vice President Al Gore, an audio file of the U.S. National Anthem, links to lots of government resources around the Net, and last but very important: fireworks safety tips!

http://banzai.neosoft.com/citylink/usa/

The World Wide Holiday and Festival Page

The United States celebrates its birthday on July 4. There are parades, picnics, and at night—fireworks! Most countries celebrate national holidays that are their equivalents of the American Independence Day. You'll find a list of them here.

http://smiley.logos.cy.net/bdecie/

INTERNATIONAL DAY OF PEACE

International Day of Peace at the United Nations

As part of the United Nations International Day of Peace (September 16), kids from all over the world have collaborated on a "Peace Poem." Over 400 schools in 38 countries participated in the project. Each grade in each school could submit only one poem. Parts of the poem are in French and Spanish as well as English. If you could write just two lines describing your feelings about peace, what would they be? Here are some samples:

*Peace on earth is like groovy tie-dyed shirts
Or tranquil baby birds on a bright spring morning.*
(Cleveland Middle School, Cleveland, Oklahoma, U.S.A.)

*As she soars through the hate, all wrong leaves her wing
It's amazing how much peace a small dove can bring.*
(International School of Kuala Lumpur, Kuala Lumpur, Malaysia)

*Peace doesn't need any words
just good hearts.*
(Basic school, Masarykova, Kosice, Slovakia)

Intrigued? Read about the International Day of Peace, check out a discussion area, and find out more at this site.

http://www.un.org/Pubs/CyberSchoolBus/peaceday/

OPTICAL ILLUSIONS: now you see them, now you don't!

JEWISH HOLIDAYS

Ben Uri Art Society

Here is a great site to learn about art, history, and the Jewish holidays, all rolled into one! The Ben Uri Art Gallery is a collection of over 700 paintings, drawings, prints, and sculpture by Jewish artists—selections from which are shown regularly in the gallery in London, England. The first two art selections show the Shabbat, the Hebrew word for Sabbath, which begins at sundown each Friday. Because the Jewish calendar is based on the lunar calendar (cycles of the moon), the new "day" begins at this time. Rosh Hashanah, the Hebrew phrase for the "Head of the Year," is the Jewish New Year celebration, and so our illustrated tour begins with this holiday in September. Continue through the Gallery and the months of the year, to learn more about the other Jewish holy days and festivals and the food, songs, and dances that are part of these traditional celebrations.

http://www.ort.org/benuri/

Billy Bear's Pesach Holiday

Billy Bear's really outdone himself this time. Get ready for lots of print and play mazes: help people cross the Red Sea, help Moses find the Ten Commandments, and more. Then get ready for the Java Chametz Game, in which you try to find and remove all the pieces of bread and cake in the house before Passover begins. Note that it works very slowly on Macs running Netscape; see the instructions. There are also links to other Pesach (Hebrew for Passover) sites for kids.

http://www.billybear4kids.com/holidays/
    pesach/pesach.htm

Calendar of Jewish Holidays

This resource, offered by B'nai B'rith, gives the dates for all important Jewish holidays through the year 2000. Mark your calendars in advance.

http://bnaibrith.org/caln.html

A
B
C
D
E
F
G
H
I
J
K
L
M
N
O
P
Q
R
S
T
U
V
W
X
Y
Z

A
B
C
D
E
F
G
H
I
J
K
L
M
N
O
P
Q
R
S
T
U
V
W
X
Y
Z

Hanukkah-Festival Of Lights

It's the year 165 B.C., and after a three-year struggle, the Jews in Judea have successfully defeated the Syrian tyrant, Antiochus. Now they are ready to hold festivities and celebrate the reclaiming of their Temple, but only a very small bottle of oil is left with which to light all the holy lamps. Miraculously, this small amount of oil lasts for eight days. Hanukkah, the Jewish Festival of Lights, involves the lighting of candles each night for eight days during a special ceremony. Every year, Jewish families celebrate Hanukkah by lighting candles held by a *menorah*, a candleholder with nine branches. And, just like the holiday celebrations of other cultures, there are special foods and music for Hannukah. It's all here: the history, the goodies, and three traditional Hanukkah songs with music and lyrics, in both English and Hebrew. You'll even find a pattern for making a dreidel (a four-sided spinning top), which is part of a traditional children's game of luck.

http://www.ort.org/ort/hanukkah/title.htm

Maven - Jewish/Israel Index Festivals & Holidays

Search the subject index or browse alphabetically to find interesting topics, such as "Hebrew children's songs for the holidays," "Choreographic descriptions of Israeli folk dances," and our personal favorite, "Uncle Eli's Special-for-Kids Most Fun Ever Under-the-Table Passover Haggadah."

http://www.maven.co.il/subjects/idx121.htm

A Search for the Meaning of Chanukah or Hanukkah

Searching for the true meaning of Hanukkah? Here's a don't-miss noncommercial site with religious traditions, family traditions, customs, songs, thoughtful links, and more. This is part of a larger site with searches for the true meaning of Kwanzaa and Christmas.

http://techdirect.com/christmas/chanukah.html

Be an angel and check what we've found in RELIGION.

Temple Israel Celebrates Chanukah

At this site you'll find history, games, how to make latkes (potato pancakes), and more. Also included are the correct procedure for lighting the menorah candles and audio of the traditional Hebrew blessings associated with their kindling.

http://tiwestport.org/chanukah/chanukah.html

Uncle Eli's Special-for-Kids Most Fun Ever Under-the-Table Passover Haggadah

During the Passover meal, there is a special story everyone reads, called a Haggadah. Uncle Eli and Dr. Seuss have a lot in common; Haggadah was never like this! A sample from this site: "We were slaves to King Pharaoh, that terrible king, and he made us do all kinds of difficult things. Like building a pyramid of chocolate ice cream when the sun was so hot that the Nile turned to steam, and digging a ditch with a spade of soft cotton. That Pharaoh was wicked and nasty and rotten!"

http://www.acs.ucalgary.ca/~elsegal/Uncle_Eli/Eli.html

NET FILES

How fast is a "snail's pace"?

Answer: According to the Conchologists of America, "Helix aspersa, a common garden snail, can travel about two feet in three minutes. At that rate, it would travel one mile in five and a half days!" For more on snails, read http://coa.acnatsci.org/conchnet/facts.html

Virtual Seder Plate

The Passover Seder meal is very symbolic. This site features a special Seder plate; click on it to learn about the various foods eaten during this ritual meal. For example, bitter herbs (usually horseradish) symbolize the bitterness of slavery. This plate has room for six foods; others have five—the page explains why this is so.

http://www.shamash.org/reform/uahc/congs/
nj/nj006/seder/plate.html

JOHN MUIR DAY

John Muir Day Study Guide - John Muir Exhibit - (John Muir Education Project, Sierra Club)

Every April 21, students in California celebrate the life of John Muir and his contribution to conservation and appreciation of the environment. He founded the Sierra Club and pushed the U.S. government to establish the national parks system. Yosemite, designated a national park in 1890, is located in California. You can visit it via this site, as well as an online Muir exhibit. There is also a biography of Muir and accounts of his travels around the world.

http://www.sierraclub.org/john_muir_exhibit/
john_muir_day_study_guide/

JUNETEENTH

JUNETEENTH: Freedom Revisited

Celebrate freedom! African Americans recall June 19, 1865, as the date when many slaves in the state of Texas learned that they had been freed, over two years earlier, by President Abraham Lincoln. This celebration is known as Juneteenth, and it is usually marked by historical displays, feasts, songs, and dancing. Learn about the origins of Juneteenth at the Anacostia Museum in Washington, D.C.

http://www.si.edu/anacostia/june.htm

KWANZAA

Kwanzaa Information Center

The symbolic lighting of candles is associated with many holidays. And so it is with Kwanzaa, an African American spiritual holiday emphasizing the unity of the family and encouraging a festive celebration of the oneness and goodness of life. Learn how the seven candles, the Mshumaa, represent the seven principles of Nguzo Saba. Read about the history and meaning of the other symbols used in the celebration of this holiday. A list of children's books about Kwanzaa is also provided here.

http://www.melanet.com/kwanzaa/

The Meaning of Kwanzaa

In 1966, a man named Maulana Ron Karenga and the U.S. Organization invented a new American holiday based on harvest celebrations in Africa. They called this celebration Kwanzaa, a Swahili word meaning "first," signifying the first fruits of the harvest. Many Americans of African heritage celebrate this holiday each December.

http://www.si.edu/anacostia/kwanz.htm

NET FILES

Mom? Dad?

You're looking over some old family history records, and you see you had an ancestor described as an "amanuensis." What does that mean?

Answer: According to a list of old-time job titles, that means your ancestor was the equivalent of a modern-day secretary. An amanuensis was "A person who copied manuscripts or took dictation." Find more fascinating careers of the past described at http://www.onthenet.com.au/~tonylang/occupa.htm

A
B
C
D
E
F
G
H
I
J
K
L
M
N
O
P
Q
R
S
T
U
V
W
X
Y
Z

A Search for the Meaning of Kwanzaa

Searching for the true meaning of Kwanzaa? Here's a don't-miss noncommercial site with spiritual traditions, family traditions, customs, songs, thoughtful links, and more. This is part of a larger site with searches for the true meaning of Hannukah and Christmas.

http://techdirect.com/christmas/kwanzaa.html

MOTHER'S DAY

Billy Bear's Happy Mother's Day

Mom might love a hug, but if you want to give her more, how about a Promise Card? There's one at this site that you can use as a sample. You might promise to walk the dog, do the dishes, or clean your room! You'll also find some fun mazes (Help Mom Find All the Dirty Socks) and other games. As usual, Billy Bear offers other links for further exploration.

http://www.billybear4kids.com/holidays/mother/mom.htm

NET FILES

It seemed like such a normal day. Suddenly, you turn around, only to discover that you're being chased by a grizzled skipper, a red admiral, and a painted lady!

What should you do?

Answer: Enjoy the beautiful sight! These are three types of butterflies found in New York state. You can see their pictures at http://www.npwrc.usgs.gov/resource/distr/lepid/bflyusa/bflyusa/ny/toc.htm and if you live somewhere else in the U.S., pick your state from the list at http://www.npwrc.usgs.gov/resource/distr/lepid/bflyusa/bflyusa.htm

Mom's Day Fun at Kid's Domain

You know you want to make something to give your mom on Mother's Day—but what? This site gives you lots of ideas: you could make her breakfast in bed (if you had a little help from an adult), or you could make her a nice card or a picture frame. There's even an easy recipe for making soap using your microwave, but get more help from that friendly adult, OK?

http://www.kidsdomain.com/holiday/mom/

PI DAY

The Ridiculously Enhanced Pi Page #3

Every March 14, at 1:59 P.M., the Exploratorium museum celebrates Pi Day. Get it? The value of pi to a few decimal places is 3.14159! This irrational celebration happens to coincide with Albert Einstein's birthday. Read about the ceremonial addition of a pi bead to the strand (they are up to 1,600 decimal places) and other events that make San Francisco a unique place to live. There are also plenty of links to places where pi is elevated to new heights of acclaim by its many fans around the world.

http://www.exploratorium.edu/learning_studio/pi/

ST. PATRICK'S DAY

Billy Bear's Happy St. Patrick's Day

They say that on St. Patrick's Day everyone is Irish! Come join the parade as you *March* through this site. Try the Pot o' Gold Money Math game, print out some coloring book pages, or dress up the leprechaun. If you don't get upset playing tricky games, try the Catch the Leprechaun game. Every time you move the mouse to where he is, he moves away! Is it possible to catch him? Yes, but you may go nuts trying! By the way, if you think the shamrock is the official emblem of Ireland, guess again—it's the harp, a favorite musical instrument in Ireland, dating back hundreds of years.

http://www.billybear4kids.com/holidays/stpatty/fun.htm

Get on board, little children, in RAILROADS AND TRAINS.

A Wee Bit O' Fun

Have you ever wondered who St. Patrick really was and why we celebrate St. Patrick's Day? Is there really such a thing as a leprechaun? Americans have been celebrating this holiday for over 200 years. Read all about the history of St. Patrick's Day at this site. Also check out the list of other Web sites dominated by the color green, including one called 40 Tips To Go Green, which has ideas for saving the environment.

http://www.nando.net/toys/stpaddy/stpaddy.html

NET FILES

What happens in London every night at exactly seven minutes before ten o'clock?

Answer: The Chief Warder of the Tower of London begins the Ceremony of the Keys, a ritual locking of the Tower gates that has continued every night, virtually unchanged, for 700 years. Look over his shoulder and know the passwords, which may be found at http://www.camelot-group.com/tower/trad/twyframe9.html where "All's well."

THANKSGIVING

THE FIRST THANKSGIVING

Would you like to fix the perfect Pilgrim-style Thanksgiving dinner? Check out this site to learn about the Pilgrims and the first Thanksgiving in 1621. Great recipe ideas will help you re-create that seventeenth century harvest feast. The interpretive guides, dressed in historic period costumes, will take you on a virtual tour of "Plimoth Plantation," the first permanent European settlement. You'll also see Hobbamock's Homesite, a reconstructed Native American hamlet, complete with a wigwam and a bark-covered longhouse.

http://wwx.media3.net/plymouth/thanksgiving.htm

DON'T want to eat your Brussels sprouts? What would you do if your mom made you finish all your furmenty, a dish from Colonial times? You'd probably be happy! Furmenty is a delicious dish containing cracked wheat, milk, and brown sugar. It's sort of like a sweet oatmeal. Find this recipe and others at THE FIRST THANKSGIVING.

Curl up with a good URL in BOOKS AND LITERATURE!

A
B
C
D
E
F
G
H
I
J
K
L
M
N
O
P
Q
R
S
T
U
V
W
X
Y
Z

Not Just for Kids! An American Thanksgiving for Kids and Families

This site has tasty recipes, directions for carving the turkey, and even Thanksgiving games and fun. Historical information on the first Thanksgiving and additional links to other sites are included.

http://www.night.net/thanksgiving/

VALENTINE'S DAY

Billy Bear's Be My Valentine

Net-mom loves a good holiday, and Valentine's Day really fits the bill! At this site you'll find cute online games, electronic greeting cards, and screen savers and wallpaper.

http://www.billybear4kids.com/holidays/
    valentin/fun.htm

Bonnie's Valentine Page

This site features links to lots of holiday games and activities from all over the Web. Net-mom hasn't looked at every one Bonnie suggests, though, so parents, please preview them for your kids!

http://www2.arkansas.net/~mom/hol2.html

Valentine's Day

At this site designed for kids, you can send a fun or a sappy e-mail valentine to your friend or your true love. You can also find Valentine's Day party ideas, recipes, and crafts and read all about the history of this *love*-ly holiday.

http://www.teelfamily.com/activities/valentine/

Get on board, little children, in RAILROADS AND TRAINS.

HORSES AND EQUESTRIAN SPORTS

See also MAMMALS—PERISSODACTYLA—HORSES AND ZEBRAS

The BLM National Wild Horse and Burro Program

Ever thought of adopting a wild horse? This site tells you all about what you have to do to adopt one from the U.S. Bureau of Land Management. There are requirements though, and remember, these are wild animals that have never been around people before, so folks sometimes have difficulty getting the horses tamed. This site has a schedule of adoption locations and dates and plenty of information for the potential adoptive family.

http://www.blm.gov/whb/

NET FILES

The mail must go through!

These days, letters traveling around the U.S. go by airplane, but it wasn't always like that. When did airmail service start in the U.S., and which cities had it first?

Answer: In 1918, you could have a letter sent via airmail to these cities: New York, Washington, D.C., and Philadelphia. Commercial passenger air service developed as a spin-off from airmail postal service. Find out more at
http://www.si.edu/postal/collect/movemail.htm

Breeds of Livestock - Horse Breeds

Sure, you've heard of Thoroughbreds, and Morgans, and maybe even Dutch Warmbloods and Trakehners, but you haven't heard of all of the breeds mentioned here! Some of them are quite rare and you don't see them very often. Check out the Zhemaichu—a Lithuanian forest breed—or the Ukrainian Saddle Horse, or Guangxi pony. Most breed descriptions include a photo, too.

http://www.ansi.okstate.edu/breeds/horses/

The Hay.net A comprehensive list of almost all the horse sites on the 'net

This site is the Internet equivalent of sweet feed for horse owners: all sorts of delicious grains, dripping with molasses, each crunchier than the last. Start with the Pick of the Week—maybe it's about x-raying large animals or an interactive guide to horse health care. Let's move into the barn and see all the different breeds: Arabians, quarter horses, Thoroughbreds, sure; you'll also find Icelandic ponies, Halflingers, and all kinds of drafts. What's this little one here, not moving at all? Oh, it's a model horse—you'll find lots here on them, too. Check the Olympic events, the Denver Stock Show, and lots of racing and driving information. Pull up a hay bale and make yourself comfortable!

http://www.haynet.net/

NET FILES

Who invented the first solar energy collector?

Answer: *The Swiss scientist Horace de Saussure invented the first solar collector, or "hot box," in 1767. Read more about solar and other types of energy at* http://www.crest.org/ renewables/re-kiosk/solar/solar-thermal/history/index.shtml

---

Origami: the fold to behold!
Check out CRAFTS AND
HOBBIES.

The Horselovers Club

This site (and its sister site, Horsefun.com) is aimed at kids who just can't get enough stories, games, and information about horses! Are you having trouble with your pony? Ask the experts at "Horsefun." Do you want to enter a contest and win some horsy prizes? You can do that here, too. You'll find lots of links (of course) and a horse club you can pay to join (if you want to). They have lots of free samples though, so just close the gate after you go in.

http://www.horselovers.com/

Janet's Horsin' Around on the Web Page

It's raining, and you hate to ride in the rain! It's a pain to clean the mud off your tack afterwards, to say nothing of making your horse look presentable again. Why not give your horse an apple and the day off, and ride the trails of this great Web site instead? Janet's pulled together a nice group of links, including breed home pages, horse health, sports, wild horses, and electronic horse magazines. The back issues of these e-zines alone will keep you busy for hours. Hey, it's stopped raining! Not all links have been reviewed from this site.

http://www.cowgirls.com/dream/jan/horse.htm

kcarroll's Horse Country

This is the ultimate horse site for juniors! Horse history, care, stories, sounds, images, and associations are all here. Several fantasy games let you create your own dream stable, "buy and sell" virtual horses, "compete" in virtual horse shows, and share the results with your fellow dream stable owners. Other musts here are the Junior Riders Mailing Digest and an International Pen Pal List for horse lovers. This site is the best thing to happen to junior riders since *Misty of Chincoteague.*

http://www.horse-country.com/

A
B
C
D
E
F
G
H
I
J
K
L
M
N
O
P
Q
R
S
T
U
V
W
X
Y
Z

Explore underwater archaeology in SHIPS AND SHIPWRECKS.

Kentucky Horse Park & International Museum of the Horse

"Our history was written on his back," says this site, dedicated to the history of horses and horsemanship. Learn about horses in war, in sport, in work, and in recreation. There are also some fascinating online special exhibits: "The Draft Horse In America: Power for an Emerging Nation"; "The Buffalo Soldiers on the Western Frontier"; and the famous Thoroughbreds at "Calumet Farm: Five Decades of Champions." Don't miss the fabulous online equine art gallery, as well as a comprehensive selection of links to horse farms, racetracks, breed clubs, and commercial sites all over the Web.

http://www.imh.org/

Do you love horses?

Are you into rodeo or racing?

Did you know that the horse evolved from an animal no bigger than a modern-day fox? If horses are your thing, then this is your page. Everything from the history of horses to a gallery of breeds to horse sports will be found here. Gallop on over to the **Kentucky Horse Park & International Museum of the Horse.**

The Model Horse Gallery

If you love horses, we mean *really* love horses, then chances are you have a model horse or two. Did you know there are horse shows for model horses, too? At this site you can find out where they are and what classes you and your model horse can enter. You'll also get tips about painting and otherwise reworking your Breyer or other collectible horse models.

http://www.astroarch.com/modelhorse/

North American Riding for the Handicapped Association

Many, many kids and adults with disabilities find that with some help, they can ride a horse. Net-mom herself used to volunteer at a therapeutic riding facility, so she's speaking from experience! Everything is done with the greatest safety in mind. Depending on the rider's abilities, the instructor usually has a side walker on each side of the horse, watching and spotting the rider and helping with a leg position if needed. There is also a person leading the horse (that was Net-mom's job) who just pays attention to the horse's gait and also takes care of most of the steering. It's amazing what the warmth of a horse can do to ease a muscle spasm or the horse's rhythmic gait can do for confidence. You can read about specific therapies on this site and perhaps find a facility near you. If you don't need their services yourself, consider volunteering to help as a side walker or groom. You can even help by cleaning tack!

http://www.narha.org/

The Royal Canadian Mounted Police Musical Ride

The Musical Ride of the Royal Canadian Mounted Police developed from a desire by early members to display their riding ability and entertain the local community. The series of figures that form the basis of the Musical Ride were developed from traditional cavalry drill movements. The Ride is performed by 32 regular member volunteers (male and female) who have had at least two years of police experience. The Ride contingent consists of 36 horses. It travels throughout Canada and sometimes into the U.S. Visit this site to learn more about the Ride and to check their tour schedule.

http://www.rcmp-grc.gc.ca/html/ride.htm

The United States Equestrian Team On Line

Who's on the USET (United States Equestrian Team) this year, and where are they riding next? What were the results of the Devon Horse Show? How old is Anne Kursinski's horse, Eros? At this site you can read interviews with the team, find out little-known facts, and see lots and lots of photos! You've got to be at least 16 to be considered for the team, so you'd better go practice that sitting trot some more.

http://www.uset.com/

FOXHUNTING

Horse Country's Horse and Hound Pages

Nowadays, many hunts don't actually hunt foxes; instead, they follow a scent of fox urine that has been dragged over the ground hours before. Still, the sight of hounds running across a field with a herd of bold horses and riders galloping behind is pretty exciting! Here you'll find some interesting history about foxhunting and learn some of the special jargon you'll need to know in the hunt field. You can also hear some hunting horn fanfare and learn why those bright red hunting jackets are called "pink coats."

http://www.horse-country.com/hunt.html

NET FILES

Everyone's heard of the 4-H Club. What are the four Hs?

Answer: In 1911, they stood for "Head, Heart, Hands, and Hustle...head trained to think, plan and reason; heart trained to be true, kind and sympathetic; hands trained to be useful, helpful and skillful; and the hustle to render ready service, to develop health and vitality." Now, however, they signify Head, Heart, Hands, and Health. The 4-H four-leaf clover emblem was patented in 1924. Read more about the program at http://www.fourhcouncil.edu/nhistory.htm

NET FILES

Can you solve this riddle?

In a marble palace white as milk,
Lined with skin as soft as silk,
In a fountain crystal clear,
A golden apple does appear.
There are no doors to this stronghold,
Yet thieves break in to steal the gold.

Answer: It's an egg! Find more of these riddles at http://www.dujour.com/ riddle/ where you can compete for prizes with others around the world.

HORSE RACING

Racing Memorabilia Pages

Swaps, Man O' War, and Citation are some of racing history's most well-known horses. You can see color postcards of them here, as well as some of the racetracks and breeding farms they made famous. Don't miss the photo of the only three-way tie in stakes race history: at the Carter Handicap race at Aqueduct in 1944, Brownie, Bossuet, and Wait a Bit all finished first!

http://members.xoom.com/horsecards/

POLO

PoloNet UK - Polo Links

Polo is a four-person, four-horse team sport, requiring a mallet and a ball about the size of a baseball. The object is to score points by hitting the ball to a goal. The outdoor variation of polo is played on a grass surface measuring 300 by 160 (or more) yards, about the size of six football fields! Learn about the tactics and strategy of the game, and link to polo clubs and other players around the world.

http://www.polonet.co.uk/links.html

A
B
C
D
E
F
G
H
I
J
K
L
M
N
O
P
Q
R
S
T
U
V
W
X
Y
Z

INSECTS AND SPIDERS

See also INVERTEBRATES

ATOMICWEB.COM

This is a happenin' place. In fact, it's a crawlin' place. Steve's got an ant farm, and he's got a camera pointed at it. Every five minutes, the camera posts a new picture to this Web site. You can watch ants build tunnels, construct bridges, and make molehills out of mountains.

http://www.atomicweb.com/antfarm.html

Entomology for beginners

This very basic page gives an introduction to insect anatomy and metamorphosis. Click on a part of the insect to find out what that part is called and what it's for. If you click on the mouth parts, you'll find that butterflies and moths have coiled tongues, while other insects have mouths that are good for chewing or sucking. In the metamorphosis section, you can see how a caterpillar changes from a crawler to a flier as it morphs into a moth.

http://www.bos.nl/homes/bijlmakers/ento/begin.html

Gordons Entomological Home Page

Did you know that insects were often used as medical treatment? Bedbugs were thought to be a cure for malaria, beetle grubs were used as a cure for toothaches, and acid from ants was often used as a cure for neurotic troubles. Others perceived insects as a delicious addition to their diet. On the other hand, insects make great pets! OK, so you may need to convince your mom and dad. Not only are insects small and less intrusive, but generally they are quieter and cheaper to feed. You can even learn how to care for your pet tarantula or cricket.

http://www.ex.ac.uk/~gjlramel/front.html

Insect Recipes

They say that insects can be tasty! Check this site and you will learn how to make Banana Worm Bread, Chocolate Chirpie Cookies, and more. "As seen on the Jay Leno Show," according to this page.

http://www.ent.iastate.edu/Misc/InsectsAsFood.html

Minibeast Homepage

Question: Why was the inchworm angry? Answer: He had to convert to the metric system! For more insect jokes sure to *bug* you, try this site. You'll also find educational resources here, so you can learn fascinating bug trivia, bug care, and bug facts.

http://members.aol.com/YESedu/welcome.html

New Jersey Online: Wendell's Yucky Bug World

Visit the yuckiest site on the Internet. You can find out about cockroaches and other bug stuff. Take the Cockroach World quiz or tell your cockroach story to the rest of the forum. Stop by Cockroach World's multimedia library for yucky sights and sounds. Hear the hiss of the Madagascar hissing cockroach or watch the "Smelly Roach" QuickTime movie. You'll also learn that cockroaches spend 75 percent of their time resting up for those late-night snack runs!

http://www.nj.com/yucky/roaches/

The O. Orkin Insect Zoo

Ugh, it's a bug! Bugs aren't really so bad. Butterflies are pretty, ladybugs are cute, and praying mantises are helpful in a garden. Insects produce valuable items too, such as honey, silk, wax, and dyes. Some insects are used for human food, and others have proven to be very useful in scientific and medical research. Explore the world of insects here—they are the most successful life form on the planet! This site takes you on a virtual tour of the O. Orkin Insect Zoo at the Smithsonian Institution.

http://www.orkin.com/html/o.orkin.html

University of Kentucky Department of Entomology

Have you ever been to the Olympics? How about the insect Olympics? See a flea go for the gold in the high jump competition. Watch a bolus spider go for a "bolus-eye" in archery. Check out insect world records and discover which insects are the ugliest, have the longest legs, and have the smallest wings. Is your class looking for a mascot? How about an insect? Here you'll find some guidelines to help pick the best choice for your classroom. Interested in an insect treat? How about ants on a log? Come on, it's just a stalk of celery spread with peanut butter and sprinkled with raisins!

http://www.uky.edu/Agriculture/Entomology/ythfacts/
    entyouth.htm

NET FILES

How many miles do the Cotter High School (Winona, Minnesota) marching band members march in a year? How many total bars of music are played by the Cotter band each year?

Answer: *They march 95 miles, give or take a few, er, feet, and they play 21,434,058 musical bars. By the way, there are 165 members in the band. The number of hamburgers consumed by Cotter band members in an average summer is 6,312, and at least 12 T-shirts go unclaimed on the band bus after every road trip. Find more funny facts about this band at http://www.mps.org/~chsband/marching/facts2.html*

BEES

Billy Bee Honey Products Limited - Canada's #1 Honey

To *bee* or not to *bee*...but the question is, what do you know about bees? Worker honeybees have many jobs in taking care of their hives. They do the feeding, cleaning, guarding, the long-distance and short-distance flying; they carry pollen, produce honey, and build the honeycomb. To learn more about beekeeping, visit this site, and *bee* careful!

http://www2.billybee.com/billybee/

gears: internet classroom

You'll have a great time buzzin' through these pages, *honey*! Learn lots about bees and how they make our lives a lot sweeter. Then when you're sure you know everything, click on the "Tri*bee*al Pursuits" site and learn a lot more!

http://gears.tucson.ars.ag.gov/ic/

BUTTERFLIES AND MOTHS
Butterflies of North America

If you can't find your favorite butterfly here, it's possible you really want the Moths of North America page (see separate entry). Pick your state and see a checklist of the butterflies to be found there. Most entries offer at least one color photo, as well as lots of information, like what types of plants you might find that species' caterpillars eating.

http://www.npwrc.usgs.gov/resource/distr/
    lepid/bflyusa/bflyusa.htm

Butterfly Gardening Article

This brief article gives directions for raising a caterpillar to its adult phase as a moth or butterfly. You use a two-liter plastic soda bottle, add daily leaves from the caterpillar's host plant, and use a paintbrush to remove "droppings" from the sides of the plastic dome every day. Once your caterpillar is in the chrysalis stage, it will take about two weeks to hatch into a butterfly. Be sure to let it go in a few hours after its wings are dry and rigid.

http://www2.garden.org/nga/EDU/butterf4.htm

A B C D E F G H I J K L M N O P Q R S T U V W X Y Z

The Butterfly WebSite

Do you know what the first butterflies of spring are? Here's a hint: they have a blue sparkle about them. Give up? The azure butterflies are the first, followed by the sulphurs, then the whites. But you don't have to wait for spring to see butterflies. There are hundreds of butterflies and moths waiting for your discovery year-round. Find out how to locate moths and butterflies any time of the year. Learn about butterfly gardening and which flowers and plants attract butterflies and encourage them to lay eggs.

http://www.mgfx.com/butterflies/

BALLOONS look so pretty against the sky—but those massive balloon launches aren't a good idea. The balloons travel on high-speed winds, high in the sky. Eventually they lose their helium, and they come down, sometimes in the ocean. Seals, dolphins, whales, sea turtles, fish, and marine birds mistake balloons for food. Up to 100,000 whales and seals die each year from eating plastic objects floating in the sea. All seven species of sea turtles are seriously endangered, partly due to swallowing balloons. Check out The Butterfly WebSite to find out about the conservation and ecology of these and other animals.

Try actual reality.

Children's Butterfly Site

This great little page has a coloring book featuring the metamorphosis of a caterpillar to a butterfly. There's also a terrific frequently asked questions file. What's the difference between a butterfly and a moth? How do butterflies go to the bathroom? Where do butterflies go in the rain? Can butterflies communicate with each other? The answers are surprising!

http://www.mesc.nbs.gov/butterfly.html

Journey North

Journey North is a project where the Internet really shines. Each year, monarch butterflies migrate from Canada and the U.S. to their wintering grounds in Mexico and California. In the spring, they start their journey north again. Where are they now? Go outside—see any monarch butterflies? OK, now go back inside, and go to this site to report your findings. Your results will be combined with other reports from all over the U.S., and a map will be created to show where the migratory monarchs have landed. Butterflies aren't the only things monitored here. Besides tracking various animals and birds, this site tracks when the ice goes out of various lakes and rivers, where the tulips are blooming, and where the spring frogs are peeping.

http://www.learner.org/jnorth/spring1998/critters/
  monarch/

Moths of North America

If you can't find your favorite moth here, it's possible you really want the Butterflies of North America page (see separate entry). While you're here, check out the delicate beauty of the luna moth (*Actias luna*).

http://www.npwrc.usgs.gov/resource/distr/
  lepid/moths/mothsusa.htm

SPIDERS AND ARACHNIDS

THE ARACHNOLOGY HOME PAGE

Why do you think they call it the Web, anyway? It's to honor that famous arachnid—the spider! But this site doesn't stop with spiders. It moves right on into scorpions and other creatures with lots of legs and bitey parts. You'll love it. Check the kids' section for links to origami spiders and scorpions and lots of other fun stuff.

http://www.ufsia.ac.be/Arachnology/Arachnology.html

A B C D E F G H I J K L M N O P Q R S T U V W X Y Z

Construction of a Web

If you've ever wondered how spiders make those beautiful wheeled webs, this very simple site will show you the ropes. Do you think you could duplicate this feat with a ball of yarn?

http://www.xs4all.nl/~ednieuw/Spiders/Info/
    Construction_of_a_web.html

You Can - Spider Webs

Why doesn't a spider stick to its web? Try this experiment with Beakman and Jax to find out. Then look at the many different kinds of spider webs, and maybe even collect some using the method described here. But be sure to wait until Charlotte's done with hers before you take it home!

http://www.beakman.com/spider/spider.html

INTERNET

Glossary of Internet Terms

Use this glossary to attach some meaning to the unfamiliar words you will no doubt run across while wandering through the Web. Some descriptions will enlighten and some will confuse, while others may be so technical they make no sense at all. Whether you're interested or just curious, you will definitely increase your "Net" knowledge if you stop by this site.

http://www.delphi.com/navnet/glossary/

Hobbes' Internet World

Everything you need to know about the Internet is probably on this page. We haven't checked every possible link, but we're pretty sure everything is here. If you're looking for an Internet service provider, try the POCIA link. Want to control your own domain name? The forms are here. Curious about Internet organizations, including The Internet Society? Looking for beginner's guides, standards documents, or security alerts? Told you it was all here. Links galore and even more!

http://info.isoc.org/guest/zakon/Internet/

ILC Glossary of Internet Terms

Confused by all those Internet terms? Can't tell an IMHO from a TTFN? Don't SLIP in the MUD, come on over to this terrific glossary, and all will be revealed.

http://www.matisse.net/files/glossary.html

 in the can? No, on the Net! On the Internet, people sometimes send e-mail messages to many, many people on electronic conferences like listservs and Usenet. Usually these messages advertise some product or service having nothing to do with the topic of the discussion. This is called SPAMming. This is just like junk mail, and you can throw it away. Read more new words at the ILC Glossary of Internet Terms.

The Scout Toolkit Homepage

The Internet Scout has put together a page that will help you. If not today, then tomorrow. Trust us when we say that you will need this page. All the tools you need are right here in the toolbox: browsers, search options, specialized applications like Real Audio (radio and other audio over the Net), and CU-SeeMe (video over the Net). There's also a great section on how to keep up with what's current on the Net. Remember, if you don't have the newest stuff in your toolkit, everything looks like a *This Old Net* rerun.

http://wwwscout.cs.wisc.edu/scout/toolkit/

RAILROADS are on track.

A B C D E F G H I J K L M N O P Q R S T U V W X Y Z

A
B
C
D
E
F
G
H
I
J
K
L
M
N
O
P
Q
R
S
T
U
V
W
X
Y
Z

BEGINNER'S GUIDES

Accessing The Internet By E-Mail

A lot of people don't know it, but you can use e-mail to surf the Web and retrieve files. Yes, you read that right. It's possible to read the information on Web pages even if all you have is e-mail access to the Net. Doctor Bob's Guide to Offline Internet Access reveals this secret. OK, so it's not that easy, but it is possible.

http://www.cis.ohio-state.edu/hypertext/faq/
    usenet/internet-services/access-via-email/faq.html

Beginner's Central (Intro)

We consider this an advanced beginner's site. While it covers all the basics on the Internet and Web, you'll find enough in-depth information to keep you reading (and rereading) for a while. Although the site states that it's updated monthly, we found some material to be a bit dated. We still think this is a good page to bookmark for future reference. Want to know how to make your own name and address "signature file" for your e-mail? Need to know just a little about Telnet and FTP? Want to print out the contents of a Web frame? What are e-mail attachments and how do you send one? These are examples of some of the questions answered by this very nice site.

http://www.northernwebs.com/bc/

A Beginner's Guide to URLs

From the inventors of Mosaic comes this brief guide to URLs, or uniform resource locators. If something's out there on the Internet, you can "point" to it using a URL and your favorite Web browser. This page will give you the syntax for pointing at Gopher servers, FTP archives, Usenet news, and of course Web resources!

http://www.ncsa.uiuc.edu/demoweb/url-primer.html

CyberU Internet Elective

This online tutorial aimed at high school kids explains how to use the Web, organize bookmarked resources, and use Net tools like Telnet and FTP. It also goes into Internet history, netiquette, and more.

http://dune.srhs.k12.nj.us/WWW/contents.htm

EFF's (Extended) Guide to the Internet

The EFF (Electronic Frontier Foundation) Guide to the Internet is very dated, but it still contains good information on Internet lore and legend. In addition to English, you'll find versions in Hungarian, Japanese, Russian, Italian, and several other languages. A caution to parents: This site gives addresses, but does not link to various resources that may be inappropriate for your family.

http://www.eff.org/papers/eegtti/eegtti.html

The Internet Companion, 2nd Edition

One of the best books ever written about the Internet is called *The Internet Companion*, by Tracy LaQuey. The entire book is available on the Internet for free! If you want to learn how the Internet came about, what you can do with the Internet, and how to become more familiar with the Internet in general, take a look here.

http://www.obs-us.com/obs/english/books/editinc/

Internet Courses

The author of this site has over a decade of experience creating Internet training courses and materials. Choose the tutorial for your favorite browser's features from the side menu, or select the tutorial on how to create and modify your own Web pages. Then sit back and absorb all the author has to offer of his knowledge of the Internet and World Wide Web.

http://www.uwannawhat.com/NetCourse/
    InternetCourses/

InterNIC 15 Minute Series

These very short tutorials were developed to help people who need to train other people about the Net. The lessons are both on the Web and in a downloadable presentation software file. You'll find lots of useful basic info here in bite-size chunks. Recent additions include: "What is a Web page?" "What is a Domain Name?" "What is an Internet Service Provider?" "What is a network?" and more.

http://rs.internic.net/nic-support/15min/

Mary Houten-Kemp's Everything E-Mail™

What do you want to know about e-mail? How to get a free e-mail account? Where to get the latest and greatest e-mail client software? How to write the most effective message you can? How to stop unsolicited commercial e-mail? How to code your mail so only your buddy can read it? Look no further—all that and more is at this address.

http://www.everythingemail.net/

Walking the Web: Table of Contents

If your parents are hopelessly clueless about what the Web is and how to use it, just take them by the hand and lead them here. Then go away and have a sandwich. When you get back, they will know all about hypertext, inline graphics, and how to fill out an online form. Their eyes won't even be glazed over! This course is short, snappy, and simple.

http://www.edf.org/Earth2Kids/walking/
a_contents.html

Your Internet Consultant - Table of Contents

Kevin Savetz is one of Net-mom's favorite people, especially because he invented telling time with Foam Bath Fish Time (see separate entry). Kevin's book, *Your Internet Consultant: The FAQs of Life Online*, is on his home page. It was originally published in 1994, but every so often Kevin updates it just a little bit more, and it's great for general info, like how the Net works and what you need to know about Net culture.

http://www.savetz.com/yic/

CHAT, MUDS, MOOS, AND IRC

MUDs and MOOs (you'll also hear of similar MUSHs and MUSEs) are programs that let you explore, and sometimes create, computer-generated, text-based worlds. For example, you can build a stream next to a mountain and maybe put a magical fish in it. You can talk live, via your computer keyboard, to kids from all over the world and learn about science, history, and computers. Best of all, these are a ton of fun! You'll also see one recommended IRC (Internet relay chat) in this section. It involves a multichannel real-time chat with kids all over.

Chat Rooms

Net-mom lists only chat rooms that are monitored and safe for kids. You may also want to try some of the free "instant message" or "pager" services that let you chat with your online buddies. Typically these are one conversation and one buddy per chat window. Be sure to ask your parents first, and then you may want to check out ICQ at <*http://www.mirabilis.com/*>, Yahoo! Pager at <*http://pager.yahoo.com/pager/*>, or AOL Instant Messenger (AIM) at <*http:// www.aol.com/aim/*>, among many others. Note that you do not have to be an AOL member to use AIM.

CW95 MUD Workshop

Mind your MOO! Here's a collection of links to MUD guides, resources, MOO FAQs, definitions, and a MOO manners guide. There's a teachers' tip sheet for using MUDs for teaching along with other MUD resources for teaching. Parental advisory: There are links to MUD directories from this site that are general in nature and may contain MUDs unsuitable for younger audiences.

http://www.daedalus.com/net/border.html

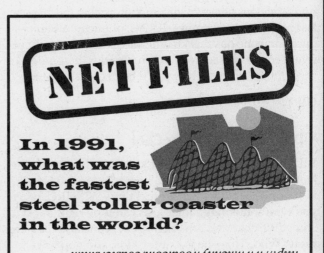

NET FILES

In 1991, what was the fastest steel roller coaster in the world?

Answer: The Steel Phantom at Kennywood in West Mifflin, Pennsylvania, got top honors at 80 mph. This coaster also tied with the Desperado at Buffalo Bill's in Jean, Nevada, for having the longest drop at that time: 225 feet. For more stomach-lurching statistics on the roller coasters at Kennywood, see *http://www.kennywood.com/coasters.htm*

A
B
C
D
E
F
G
H
I
J
K
L
M
N
O
P
Q
R
S
T
U
V
W
X
Y
Z

FreeZone for kids: chat, e-pals, homepages, and much more!

This place is so cool that you'll need to spend an entire afternoon just checking it out! For example, in BrainStorm you can do a puzzle, write a poem, and learn weird facts. In Homework Helpers you can find someone to assist you in the most difficult problem a teacher assigns! You can create your own home page, head to the fully supervised chat box, or find a key pal. You can find out about your favorite band, TV show, or movie and even write a review. Time to check this place out! TTYL. (You've got to go to the Slang Translator to find out what that means.) Son of Net-mom highly recommends this site's chat room.

http://www.freezone.com/

HEADBONE ZONE - Be Weird, Be Wired, Be Inspired!

If you're looking for someone to talk to, this is the place. According to the Headbone chatter, they've got 300,000 kids signed on. There are four chat rooms, including two for teens and one for younger kids. Before you sign on, remember to read their rules: don't give out personal information in chat (addresses, last names, school names, ICQ#s, phone numbers)— once someone has this kind of info, it takes only about five seconds to track you down. Besides, if you do give out this info in chat, you'll be booted. Bummer.

http://www.headbone.com/

KIDLINK Internet Relay Chat

KIDLINK is one of the oldest kid-friendly sites on the Net. Internet relay chat (IRC) is a way for you to talk to kids all over the globe in real time. With IRC, when you type something, other kids can type right back! Some IRC channels are open to everyone and they are pretty wild. This one is just for kids, and you have to register before they will let you use it. It is carefully monitored. Don't pass by, give IRC a try!

http://www.kidlink.org/IRC/

You are your own network.

MOOSE Crossing Information

Would you like to build your own world with other kids from around the planet? Would you like to work on special projects with kids age 13 and under? Would you like to work on a computer at MIT, the foremost center of computer innovation? Do you own or have access to a Macintosh computer? If you answered "Yes" to these questions, then MOOSE Crossing is the place for you!

http://www.cc.gatech.edu/fac/Amy.Bruckman/moose-crossing/

SchoolNet MOO

You've never seen a school like this. Housed in a computer in Canada (it's a multilingual system for French and English speakers), this is the place where you can build all sorts of virtual things while interacting with kids from all over. To connect to this site, you'll need Telnet capability, so ask your parents or teachers if you have that.

http://schoolnet2.carleton.ca/english/moo/

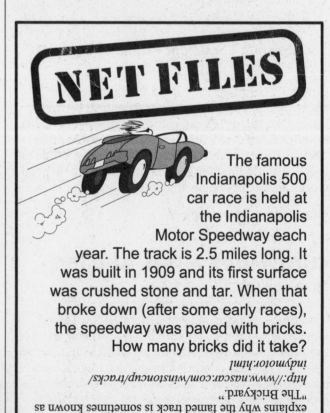

NET FILES

The famous Indianapolis 500 car race is held at the Indianapolis Motor Speedway each year. The track is 2.5 miles long. It was built in 1909 and its first surface was crushed stone and tar. When that broke down (after some early races), the speedway was paved with bricks. How many bricks did it take?

Answer: 3.2 million. Most are still there, sealed under the speedway's current driving surface of asphalt! This explains why the famed track is sometimes known as "The Brickyard."

http://www.nascar.com/winstoncup/tracks/indymotor.html

DISCUSSION LISTS
NEW-LIST

When someone creates a new e-mail discussion list, they often announce it to—what else—a discussion list! As you can imagine, NEW-LIST has a lot of postings, also called *traffic*. If you don't want to subscribe to that, you can just visit this Web resource. It is a collection of all postings to NEW-LIST, so you can browse to your heart's content. This new archive began July 1, 1998. For older postings, see <*http://listserv.nodak.edu/ archives/ new-list.html*>Parental advisory: This list includes material that may be unsuitable for your family.

http://scout.cs.wisc.edu/new-list/

CataList, the official catalog of LISTSERV lists

Whether it's MOMSONLINE, MISSING-KIDS (the Missing Kids Announcement List), or YOUTH-TECH (A Weekly Newsletter For The Kids & Teens Technology Community), you're sure to be able to find an e-mail discussion list to join. This site indexes more than 17,600 lists managed using LISTSERV software. To find still more lists, check the Liszt entry in this section. Parental advisory: This list includes material that may be unsuitable for your family.

http://www.lsoft.com/lists/listref.html

What is the most popular type of evergreen cut for use as a Christmas tree?

Answer: The top-selling Christmas trees are: balsam fir, Douglas fir, Fraser fir, noble fir, Scotch pine, Virginia pine, and white pine. Also, the top Christmas tree–producing states are Oregon, Michigan, Wisconsin, Pennsylvania, California, and North Carolina. Find out more facts about Christmas trees at *http://www.christree.org/factnfig/facts.html*

Discussion Lists: Mailing List Manager Commands

Your pen pal in Michigan says you should subscribe to a favorite discussion group mailing list on snakes. That's great, but how the heck do you subscribe? And does it cost money? You'll be glad to know that usually list discussion groups are free. To subscribe, you send a mail message to a computer running the mailing list software. Because the subscription process is done by that remote computer, you need to send your request in a way the computer can understand. This means you have to use certain common commands to tell the computer what you want to do. That wouldn't be too hard, except that discussion lists use different software packages to distribute mail—some popular ones are called Revised Listserv (also called BITNET Listserv), Unix ListProcessor (or Listproc), Mailbase, Mailserv, and Majordomo. And they all use different commands! James Milles has sorted it all out. Check this site to learn how to talk to all the major discussion group list mailers.

http://lawwww.cwru.edu/cwrulaw/faculty/milles/ mailser.html

KIDLINK: Global Networking for Youth through the age of 15

You know the world's got some big problems: pollution, hunger, poverty. Why not talk to other kids and see if you can help solve some of them? Make new friends, and have some fun with kids from 117 different countries on the KIDCAFE discussions. Take a look at the KIDLINK mailing list page, and start e-mailing new friends. Show this to your teacher and parents, too. They'll find lots of good information about how to share a project with a class in another country. Many of the discussions are held in languages other than English, too!

http://www.kidlink.org/

A B C D E F G H I J K L M N O P Q R S T U V W X Y Z

A
B
C
D
E
F
G
H
I
J
K
L
M
N
O
P
Q
R
S
T
U
V
W
X
Y
Z

Liszt, the mailing list directory

Need a mailing list or a newsgroup? This site has almost 85,000 lists and 30,000 newsgroups, all searchable by word or phrase. Just enter a word, such as "horse," and you'll get a list of items containing that word. For example, your "horse" search will pull up EQUINE-L and 30 others. To get more information on a particular list, follow the instructions on the screen. Your Internet service provider may not give you access to all these newsgroups, but at least you'll know they exist. Maybe you can ask your provider to carry it for you. A caution to parents: Many of these lists and newsgroups are not for children.

http://www.liszt.com/

FINDING PEOPLE

As you use the Internet, you may start wondering if people you know have Internet accounts. Maybe you have a favorite uncle who lives on the other side of the country or a friend from a town where you used to live, and you'd like to communicate with them via the Net. Problem is, how can you determine if they are on the Internet? The surest way is to call or write the person and ask. There are a variety of experimental programs on the Internet, though, that you can use to track people down. Listed here are a few places you can look that provide links to different people-finding tools. Happy hunting, but be sure to read the instructions for these programs. Some are much easier to use than others.

Ahoy! The Homepage Finder v3.0

Oops. It's time for a little extra-credit school project. You suddenly remember a conversation you overheard at your last family reunion. It was Aunt Matilda jabbering to your cousin Oscar. Something about her neighbors, the Joneses, who had a very interesting home page about gene splicing a firefly gene to a pepper plant to get glow-in-the-dark hot peppers. You think it sounds like a neat science topic and realize you have no idea how to look for that home page, and since Aunt Matilda and Oscar live on the other side of the country, you need some help. You could call Aunt Matilda and ask her yourself, but you might try this resource first. Ahoy will hunt for home pages containing the names you specify.

http://ahoy.cs.washington.edu:6060/

Four11 Directory Services

Similar to WhoWhere? (see separate entry), Four11 claims to be the largest directory of its kind, with over ten million e-mail address listings. If you don't find who you're looking for, they have a notification service. You'll get e-mail if your friend's name turns up in the directory. If you're looking for a phone number, they have over 100 million! There are also directories of celebrities and famous folks in sports, entertainment, business, and government. You'll find lots of other useful services, too, such as free Web-based e-mail accounts.

http://www.Four11.com/

Internet E-mail and Finding Internet People on the Internet

Here's a general introduction to the problem and some solutions. Try these ideas if WhoWhere? and Four11 (also listed in this book) don't help.

http://www.sil.org/internet/email.html

Jean's People-Finding Internet Resources

Here's another general one to try as a last resort, with the added strategy of checking college Web phone books and more.

http://www.benoit.com/jean/find.html

Welcome to WhoWhere?!

Finding addresses should always have been this easy. We don't just mean e-mail addresses. We mean street addresses and phone numbers! You can also find people's home pages with the search tools here. Another cool thing is to find other people interested in the same things you are—or people who went to the same school or summer camp. That's called the "Communities" feature, so check it out! You can also find business home pages, toll-free phone numbers, and more (we find something new every time we visit). There are English, French, and Spanish versions of this page. And if you didn't find who you were looking for, WhoWhere? will keep looking and e-mail you if your friend ever turns up in the database.

http://www.whowhere.com/

HISTORY

Internet Society (ISOC) All About the Internet: History - Hobbes' Internet Timeline

How did all this Internet stuff get started, anyway? The unofficial history of the Internet is here. You'll find lots of facts and lots of definitions that you'll probably need help defining from the ILC Glossary of Internet Terms (see separate entry).

http://www.isoc.org/guest/zakon/Internet/
   History/HIT.html

WWW History

A big part of the Internet is the World Wide Web, also known as the WWW or the Web. The World Wide Web makes it easier to use pictures (or graphics) and also helps to link information on the Internet. To better understand the WWW and get a good dose of Internet history in the process, take a peek at this page.

http://edweb.gsn.org/web.history.html

MACHINES ON THE NET

Anthony's list of Internet Accessible Machines

For some time, various folks on the Internet have attached computers to all kinds of machines. With the machines hooked up, the owners are then able to give updates on those machines live on the Net. Soft drink vending machines, refrigerators, toasters, and cameras (with live pictures) are among the types of devices connected. For example, you can learn how many cans of soda are available in a machine and what the temperature in a refrigerator is; you can also see students live in a college dorm room. Why have people done this? It's probably better to ask, "Why ask why?" Take a look at this site to see what it's all about! Parents, not all remote links have been checked.

http://www.geocities.com/~anderberg/ant/machines/

Lots of monkey business in MAMMALS.

What country "spans 11 time zones, 2 continents, and comes within 50 miles of North America"?

Answer: *Russia, of course! The Official Guide to Russia ought to know, and it will show you more at* http://www.interknowledge.com/russia/

MYTHS AND HOAXES

CERT Coordination Center

The most current information on viruses and hoaxes comes from the Computer Emergency Response Team (CERT). When someone forwards e-mail to you about a dire new virus warning, please take a minute and check it out before you pass it on. It's possible the virus alert is bogus. Stopping hoax junk mail is also part of good Internet citizenship. It conserves Internet bandwidth and makes for a faster Internet for us all. :-)

http://www.cert.org/

CIAC Internet Hoaxes

How do you spot a hoax? These folks know. The U.S. Department of Energy's Computer Incident Advisory Capability wants you to know, too. Check their Web page for tips on hoax busting! (Hint: Bill Gates does not want to give you $1,000).

http://ciac.llnl.gov/ciac/CIACHoaxes.html

Computer Virus Myths Home Page

Hi. Thank you for thinking of me when you forwarded that e-mail, but what you sent me is an Internet hoax. There is no such thing as the Good Times Virus, the "Join the Crew" hard drive killer e-mail, or the $250 cookie recipe. Furthermore, Craig Shergold has recovered from cancer and no longer collects business cards. You can read all about these hoaxes at the following site. Have a nice day.

http://www.kumite.com/myths/

NETIQUETTE, FOLKLORE, AND CUSTOMS

The Net: User Guidelines and Netiquette, by Arlene Rinaldi

Everybody knows that politeness and good etiquette make life easier. Waiting your turn in line, keeping your locker in order, or being nice to your friends helps you as much as the people around you. The same is true on the Internet. There are some basic rules of etiquette (on the Internet it's called *netiquette*) that help keep things running smoothly. Check out some of these basic rules of Internet good behavior. To find this document in other languages, just click on the words "TRANSLATED VERSION OF THE GUIDE" at the top of the home page.

http://www.fau.edu/~rinaldi/net/

NetLingo: Smileys & Emoticons

When writing e-mail messages, sometimes it's hard to express what you are really feeling. This has been a problem for folks on the Internet for a long time, and to help better express emotions, smileys were created. For example, turn your head sideways to the left, and look at this :-). Do you see this makes a little smiley face? There are many variations of these smileys—to see more, take a peek at this page. A note to parents: There are lots of smiley lists on the Net that are more comprehensive, but this one is family-oriented.

http://www.netlingo.com/smiley.html

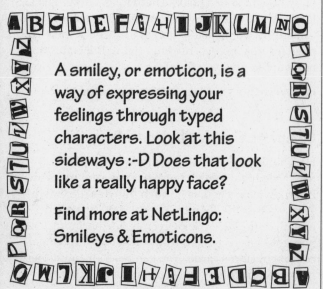

A smiley, or emoticon, is a way of expressing your feelings through typed characters. Look at this sideways :-D Does that look like a really happy face?

Find more at NetLingo: Smileys & Emoticons.

SAFETY

See also PARENTING AND FAMILIES—INTERNET—INTERNET TOOLBOX

CyberNetiquette

You want to help your little sister learn about Internet safety rules? If she likes Disney characters, just take her to this site, pull up a chair, and settle back for a story. The stories do take a while to download, but they teach you what you need to know to stay safe. There are two stories currently available: "Who's Afraid of Little Sweet Sheep?" and "The Bad Apple."

http://www.disney.com/cybernetiquette/

PBS Kids : t e c h k n o w

One of the features found here is a ten-question quiz. "Get Your Web License Here" asks you what information is safe to give out online. You may know those answers by now, but how good are you at answering more technical questions, say, on the fine points of domain names? You can print out a certificate once you have passed the test. Watch for future contests here, too.

http://www.pbs.org/kids/techknow/

Rules for Kids on the Internet/ Information Highway

It's OK to keep a secret, especially when you meet people on the Internet. Never give anyone personal information about yourself, and never send a picture to someone or agree to meet someone without talking to your parents or your teacher about it first. To learn many other safety rules of the road on the Information Superhighway, view this site!

http://www.discribe.ca/childfind/educate/kidrule.hte

Staring off into space? Discover ASTRONOMY!

A
B
C
D
E
F
G
H
I
J
K
L
M
N
O
P
Q
R
S
T
U
V
W
X
Y
Z

Teen Safety on the Information Highway

If you cross a road unsafely you could be hurt. But that doesn't mean you should never cross a road. Once you learn to "look both ways" and stay aware, it becomes a safe, instinctive task. The same rules apply to using the Internet. Learn the turf, follow the rules, and know the dangers, and it, too, can become a safe, instinctive journey. This lively site shows the dangers and explains the rules to keep your Internet travels safe.

http://www.larrysworld.com/safeteens.htm

A Warning for Parents and Kids - The Police Notebook

The Internet is a fun place to be. It is important, though, that you learn to use the Internet safely and wisely. What if someone asks for your phone number? What if someone asks for your password? What if you stumble into something that's "too old" for you? The University of Oklahoma Department of Public Safety gives loads of great tips on using the Internet in a good way.

http://www.ou.edu/oupd/kidsafe/warn_kid.htm

What do Wa'ahila Ridge (Honolulu, Hawaii), The Cathedral of St. Vibiana (Los Angeles, California), and Ellis Island National Cemetery (New York Harbor) have in common?

Answer: *They are on the 1997 America's most endangered historic sites list, published by the National Trust. You should visit these sites soon because they may not be around for long. You can learn more about these sites and others at* http://www.nthp.org/main/endangered/heritage.html

SEARCH ENGINES AND DIRECTORIES

If you're short on time, just read "Net-mom's Seven Secrets of Internet Searching." For more details, continue and read "A Little More Information."

Net-mom's Seven Secrets of Internet Searching

When you look for something on the Internet, do you get the answers you want, or do you get 400,000 possible answers to wade through? A *hit* is an answer the computer sends back in response to your question. Sometimes a question is also called a *query*. Net-mom knows some secrets to cut down on the number of hits and focus on the resources that will help you find what you need. Remember these tips and tricks!

Secret Number 1: Think Before You Search

You'd be surprised how many people forget this step! You need to think about what you want to find and how much information you need. Here are some questions you can ask yourself before beginning your search:

- Do you need a lot of background material, or are you looking for only a few resources?

- What words can you think of to describe the answers you want?

- Are you looking for text, audio, pictures, movies, or all of these?

- Are you looking for something specific or something more general? For example, you may be interested in overall information on endangered species, or you may want to know a specific fact, such as the exact number of cheetahs left on the planet.

Thinking about what kind of answers you want will help you decide how to ask your question and where to look for it.

Secret Number 2: Look in the Right Place

You wouldn't look for your sneaker in the refrigerator, would you? Of course not! So you need to know a little bit about how Internet Web pages and other resources are discovered, sifted, and sorted so that you can figure out the best places to look for that sneaker!

You need to know about directories and search engines and how they are different. The next section ("A Little More Information") will explain more about this difference and why it's important, but here's a brief summary:

Directories are collections of Web sites created and arranged by humans. These people find useful resources and sort them into logical subject categories. For example, the next time you go into a bookstore, notice that all the books on soccer, or pets, or computers are shelved together so you can find them easily. A directory works the same way. Directories are often better to use if you are looking for quick general information.

Search engines create a "collection on demand" for you, based on your search question. It's as if you walked into the bookstore and all the books were on the floor! The important thing to remember here is that the indexes to this "collection" are machine-made, built of actual words used on Web pages and in other resources. Software "robots" comb Web pages throughout the world, indexing all their words and adding them to the master list. This is good, because it means that search engines offer a huge amount of material for you to use. But it is sometimes bad, because having too much information is often worse than having none at all! People using search engines for the first time often get thousands of answers back, way more than they want. The good news is that you can learn how to ask a carefully crafted question so that the search engine is forced to give you just a few targeted answers. To find out how to do this, just go to Secret Number 3.

Secret Number 3: Check the HELP Files to Learn How to Ask Your Question

If you're using a directory, just find the entry box and type in what you're looking for, or browse through the appropriate category. For example, if you're looking for "Beanie Babies" you might browse through the category marked "Toys."

If you're using a search engine, you need a little more information. Each search engine has its own specific tricks, so be sure to read the HELP screens for the ones you want to use. They each have rules about how they want questions structured. This is called *syntax*. For example, say you are looking for the lyrics to "Yellow Submarine" by your favorite group, The Beatles. One engine's syntax may want you to ask it this way:

```
"Yellow Submarine" AND lyrics AND Beatles
```

But another one wants the question asked this way:

```
+"Yellow Submarine" +lyrics +Beatles
```

Be sure to take the time to read those HELP files! And remember:

> *As we live a life of ease*
> *Everyone of us has all we need*
> *Sky of blue and sea of green*
> *In our yellow submarine.*

Secret Number 4: Check Your Spelling

There are a lot of slippery fingers out there. In fact, the most frequently mistyped word is "the"! If your search words aren't spelled correctly, they won't match up with the words in the indexes, and you won't find what you want. Keep a dictionary close by, or use one of the online dictionaries listed in the REFERENCE WORKS section of this book. Now go ahead and send in your search, then meet us at Secret Number 5.

Secret Number 5: Narrow Your Search

Too many hits? Learn how to narrow your search by reading the search engine's HELP files. Often, you can better retrieve the answers you need by searching on a phrase rather than on individual words. To do this, you typically put quotation marks around the phrase in order to keep the words together. For example, a search on the phrase "Hubble Space Telescope" will find only resources containing that entire phrase. It will ignore resources on space and telescopes and people named Hubble. Occasionally, you may have the opposite problem, noted in the next Secret.

Secret Number 6: Broaden Your Search

Not enough hits? Learn how to broaden your search. What words can you use that are more general? The "wider" the terms you can use, the more hits you will get back. Not enough hits when you searched on beagle AND training? Try searching on dog AND training instead.

In most cases, it is best to use lowercase, singular terms. Example: searching on dog will usually find both Dog and Dogs and dog and dogs. If you had searched on Dogs (uppercase, plural) the results would not contain dog (lowercase, singular). Strange, but true.

Secret Number 7: Evaluate Your Results

Is it true? Is it outdated? Does it come from a source you, your parents, your teachers, or others trust? Don't forget to evaluate your results! It may well be the most important step of all.

A Little More Information

There is a lot of treasure out there on the Internet, but the problem is trying to find exactly the gold you want, hidden somewhere in the millions of grains of sand. Now you know a little about how search engines and Internet directories can help.

Here are a few more things I want to tell you about searching on the Internet. Just because a word appears in a document doesn't mean the document will really be about the topic you want! Searching on the word "cat" will pull up thousands of hits. Asking for a search on CAT will return information on CAT and CATS, but also CATalog, CATapult, and CATacombs. There are advanced ways of using search engines to pare down the number of unwanted hits and narrow the focus more towards what you want. The best way to learn how to do this is to read the search help tips each search engine offers. They are all different.

There have also been instances of people stuffing their Web resources with keywords that have nothing to do with their real topics, just so they will turn up as hits in more searches. One guy wanted to sell his new product. He reasoned that if more people saw his product, he'd sell more of it. So, he put his ad on an Internet Web page. Then, he padded the Web page with about a thousand extra indexable words (called *keywords*)! The keywords had nothing to do with the product, but that trick did make his ad turn up in millions of searches about "skiing" and "sports" and "Beanie Babies."

A directory takes Internet information resources and puts them in some kind of logical subject order. In other words, a real person looks at the resources, then decides what they are about and where they should go on the directory's subject "shelves." A directory will return hits that should be generally on target. But, because the Internet is growing so fast and there are so many documents, most subject directories are not fully up to date. Some have Current Events shelves, though, for recent news, so look for them.

Another thing to notice is that some search engines and directories are concerned with only *part* of the Internet. Some deal with Web resources only. Some include Web, Gopher, and maybe FTP or Usenet newsgroup information. Some include press releases. Some include e-mail addresses or telephone books. Some will index sounds, pictures, movies, and maps! Pay attention and know what region of the Internet you're really searching.

There is one more thing you need to know. Not everything on the Net is true. Some of the information is out of date. Some of it is just plain wrong. And some of it is put there as a way to mislead you. How do you tell the good stuff from the bad stuff? One of the ways is to use this book, which you're holding in your hands. We've found some of the good stuff for you. Other authorities in which to place your trust will vary. Ask your parents, a teacher, or a trusted adult. They may help you to decide if the information you find on the Net is right for your purpose.

A good Internet searcher knows how to use lots of searching tools to advantage. Read on to find out about some we use all the time.

AltaVista: Main Page

AltaVista indexes Web pages plus Usenet newsgroups. You can search for sites written in 25 languages, and if you don't speak that language, you can always use the "Translate Page" feature. It works great! We use this search engine because it is easy, it is straightforward, and it doesn't try to distract us with a lot of extra stuff we don't want. It does, however, offer free e-mail accounts.

AltaVista allows special searches on URLs, images, and host names, among other things. Do you have a cool home page? Do you want to know if other pages around the Web have linked theirs to yours? Then type this into the AltaVista Simple Search form: **link:***your page name here*.

> ## Have an order of pi in MATH AND ARITHMETIC.

A
B
C
D
E
F
G
H
I
J
K
L
M
N
O
P
Q
R
S
T
U
V
W
X
Y
Z

A
B
C
D
E
F
G
H
I
J
K
L
M
N
O
P
Q
R
S
T
U
V
W
X
Y
Z

Did you ever search on something and get 400,000 hits? You need to narrow your search. Are you searching on a phrase, something more than one word? (For example, "Major League Baseball" is a phrase.) Then you should tell the computer to search on the phrase, not just single words. How? Say you are looking for something on the Hubble Space Telescope. If you just type **hubble space telescope**, then the search engine will look for all occurrences of hubble, add them to all occurrences of space, and add *them* to all occurrences of telescope. And then you *will* have 400,000 sites to look through!

Instead, type your search terms inside quotation marks, like this: "Hubble Space Telescope." Putting the words inside quotation marks tells AltaVista that the words must be right next to each other—you want to look for the phrase, not just the individual words. This one tip will help you focus in on the best resources to answer your question.

Use lowercase letters, not capitals. If you search on Dogs, AltaVista will be forced to look for Dogs that begin with a capital letter, ignoring dogs. Lowercase search terms will find *both* uppercase and lowercase hits.

Hint: Be sure you type the address just as we have it here. Do not try <*http://www.altavista.com*>. It *looks* like AltaVista, but it is not the real thing, so don't be fooled.

http://www.altavista.digital.com/

Ask Jeeves for Kids

Why doesn't someone invent a kid-safe search engine that lets you type in a real question rather than all those plusses and minuses and quotes and other weird terms? So that you could just type in "I want information on the SuperSoaker 3000" and you'd get back just a few targeted sites, not 23,000 choices! And if you weren't the World's Greatest Speller, the search engine would check the spelling of your question, too. You could type in "I need a map of Arizonia" and it would ask you if you really wanted Arizona. Why doesn't someone invent a search tool like that? Guess what, someone did. Why not go and Ask Jeeves?

http://www.aJKids.com/

HotBot

HotBot is a service from Wired Ventures, Inc., the publisher of *Wired* magazine, a "what's next" journal that focuses on the future of our culture. It's a search engine, a Web directory, and a place where you can search and browse *Wired*'s new and archived collections of articles. If you like to keep tuned in with tomorrow, this is a good site that combines search services with adventurous reading. The HotBot search engine consistently ranks high in "search engine bake-offs," and it's also one of Net-mom's favorites.

http://www.hotbot.com/

Infoseek

Infoseek is a combination search engine and directory, and it is one of Net-mom's favorites. The simple search defaults to searching the Web, but is easily changed to looking at news, companies, or newsgroups. Check the Tips for how to get the most from your search entries. The Advanced Search uses a "smart form" where you select search options from menu pop-ups to help define your search. If browsing is more your style, select a category from one of the various Channels to find sites of particular interest. Other features include map searches, personalized news services, and an online dictionary and thesaurus. Infoseek also offers its services in various languages.

http://www.infoseek.com/

KidsClick! Web Search

Browse almost 1,800 educational and fun Web sites in 15 different categories. All of them have been selected, categorized, and described by a team of librarians who know what kids want. How do they know? Because kids come into their libraries and ask for these types of things! There is a neat and fast search engine to get you where you want to go. You can search for sites by your reading level as well as the amount of graphics you care to load. Compare this site to Yahooligans! (separate entry).

http://sunsite.berkeley.edu/KidsClick!/

Welcome to Excite

Excite combines the features of a search engine and a directory, indexing both Web pages and Usenet newsgroups. But there's more: sites in 16 categories, all of them reviewed; links to Big Yellow's address and telephone directory; and City.Net's mapping and travel information. Create your own personalized page that will display the topics you choose each time you reconnect to Excite. Excite's search results page gives you a "confidence" rating alongside your hits, and it gives you what it thinks are its "best" hits first. Do you agree? If not, look through the hit list until you find a site that you do like. To see similar resources, just click the "more sites like this" button.

http://www.excite.com/

Welcome to Lycos

Lycos has been around a relatively long time. It's easy to use, but we still like Infoseek and AltaVista better as search engines and Yahoo! better as a directory. Still, this is very useful for searching for pictures and sounds ("I need a picture of Mount Rushmore right now!"). Use the Web Guide categories to browse your favorite subjects, or check out the news and weather areas. Lycos offers free e-mail, free home pages with 11MB of storage, and a personalization service where you can create your own customized Lycos page. Lycos is also available in over ten languages.

http://www.lycos.com/

Welcome to Magellan!

This search engine and directory of reviewed sites has a feature called "green light" sites. If, at the time of review, "no objectionable material" was found, the site gets a green light (safe for kids) rating. You can either search "The Entire Web" or limit your searches to "Reviewed Sites Only" or "Green Light Sites Only."

http://www.mckinley.com/

Trick roping secrets are revealed in KNOTS.

It never rains on the PARADES in cyberspace.

Yahoo! and Yahooligans!

Yahoo! is a directory. In other words, Yahoo! does not index the whole Internet but a selected view of it. However, it is allied with AltaVista (see separate entry), which does search the entire Net, so from this site you can have it all!

This directory is fun and easy to use. Browse 14 general categories, like science or education. Under those are smaller subdivisions, which branch into still smaller sub-subtopics, and on and on. Don't worry, it's simpler than it sounds! You can also choose to search the entire database or just a small part of it. Every so often you'll see a pair of sunglasses next to a listing. That means the folks who create Yahoo! thought the resource was way cool.

Yahoo! tries to organize resources into collections with a geographical focus. Try Yahoo! Canada, Germany, Japan, or Yahoo! Metro Boston, Chicago, Los Angeles, New York, or the San Francisco Bay Area. If you don't live in one of those areas, don't despair, "Get Local." Type in your U.S. ZIP code for links to your local TV stations, weather, and other news.

They also have a resource with "kid safe" listings, called Yahooligans!—you can reach it by clicking on the word at the bottom of the page. Try it! We have found a lot of dead links there, so it is not as well maintained as we think it should be. Still, it may be improved by the time you read this.

We particularly like their My Yahoo! service. It creates a home page for you, based on your preferences. Want to follow the scores for just your favorite teams? Want to see the weather for your city and for someone you know in another state? Want to read news about computers but not news about entertainers? Set your news up *your* way by clicking the "My" button (or "Personalize" link) at the top of the page.

http://www.yahoo.com/

A
B
C
D
E
F
G
H
I
J
K
L
M
N
O
P
Q
R
S
T
U
V
W
X
Y
Z

A
B
C
D
E
F
G
H
I
J
K
L
M
N
O
P
Q
R
S
T
U
V
W
X
Y
Z

WEB RINGS
Welcome to WebRing!

Did you know there's now a way to surf the Web "sideways"? Web rings are user-built and maintained directories that are focused on a particular subject or idea. Anyone can start a Web ring and invite other similar sites to join the collection, or ring. You navigate a ring by selecting links to the previous and next sites on the ring. A link to the ring's index and home page are also available at each site.Welcome to WebRing! is the mother ship of rings. Here, you can either search the collection of rings or browse through the various ring categories. Parental advisory: This is a general collection of sites, and some may contain objectionable material.

http://www.webring.com/

NET FILES

Who invented the first pretzel?

Answer: Legend has it that a sixth-century Italian monk used to give out these doughy treats to children who were good during Mass. The pretzel shape is supposed to represent arms crossed in prayer, and the three holes represent the Father, Son, and Holy Spirit. It may be the world's oldest snack food! Read more about the pretzel and its fascinating history at http://libertynet.org/iha/tour/_pretzel.html

WEBWEAVING AND HTML
BUILDER.COM - Web Authoring

If you're trying to advance your Web site building skills, this site is a good place to start. Find reviews for Web authoring software, tips from experts, and advanced tips on subjects such as frames, Dynamic Hypertext Markup Language (DHTML), and cross-platform compatibility. There is also beginner's stuff, but if the material here sounds too complicated, check out some of the other sites in this book first. If you decide to take the plunge into webweaving and need to learn more, remember this site.

http://builder.cnet.com/Authoring/

Free webpages created in minutes - WebSpawner Ltd.

This site offers the basics in free Web pages. Don't look for any bells and whistles, but, as the title states, you can create a page and put yourself on the Web in minutes. The page limit is only 24K, excluding any graphics. Once created, features such as a page counter, search engine interface, and colorized text become available through the page modifier. All operations are performed using a Web form, so you don't have to learn how to upload files via FTP or some other method. Upgrades to enhanced pages are available for a small monthly fee ($4.99 as of this writing), and WebSpawner offers a $29.95 service that will register your page with over 120 search engines.

http://www.webspawner.com/

GeoCities - Free Home Pages

Here's a place where you set up your own free home page on the World Wide Web. When we reviewed the site, GeoCities offered 11MB of disk storage to members along with some basic tools to help build a site. Upgrade paths are available when you outgrow your storage space or page enhancement requirements.

http://www.geocities.com/join/freehp.html

Watch your steps in DANCE.

What are the Seven Wonders of the ancient world?

(Hint: The list does not include Sneezy or Dopey or have anything to do with Snow White.)

?????????

http://pharos.bu.edu/EgyptWonders/Home.html

Answer: The list of the Seven Wonders of the ancient world was originally compiled around 2 B.C. In chronological order, they are: the Great Pyramid of Giza, the Hanging Gardens of Babylon, the Statue of Zeus at Olympia, the Temple of Artemis at Ephesus, the Mausoleum at Halicarnassus, the Colossus of Rhodes, and the Lighthouse of Alexandria. Immerse yourself in the history of these beautiful structures and then see if you can guess the Seven Wonders of the modern world at *http://pharos.bu.edu/EgyptWonders/Home.html*

How to write HTML files

Would you like to be a webweaving expert, a person who knows the ins and outs of HTML? Then this tutorial is for you. Soon, you'll be making the most rad pages ever! The author, Peter Flynn, will be your step-by-step guide.

http://kcgl1.eng.ohio-state.edu/www/doc/
    htmldoc.html

Internet Free Parking-Web Page Resources the Fun Way

If you're a Web page author, do not pass Go, but do connect to this site immediately. This is a refreshingly different approach for a meta-site design, and it's chock-full of free resources for Web authors and webmasters. Categories include "HTML Help and code validators," "Search Engines and their HTML Code," "Advertise your site on other sites," and more.

http://www.freeparking.net/

NCSA—A Beginner's Guide to HTML Home Page

Itching to write your own cool home page? This is a very good place to learn Hypertext Markup Language (HTML), so you can write your own code to amaze the world with your Web creation. At this site, you'll find step-by-step descriptions and instructions.

http://www.ncsa.uiuc.edu/General/Internet/
    WWW/HTMLPrimer.html

ThinkQuest

Would you like to win thousands of dollars in scholarship money? Do you have a great idea for a new Web resource? You might be a fabulous C++ programmer, but you can't write interesting English prose very well. Or maybe you're terrific at graphics but can't code. Maybe you're not a computer nut at all but you really know how to research a topic. There is a place for all of you at ThinkQuest. First, you have to create a team to work on your project. Advertise your skills and your ideas at the Team Maker part of the site. Typically, teams are formed with four or five kids from all over the world; they have usually never met, and they usually come from schools or homeschools with widely varying levels of technology. You also need a coach or two, usually a teacher or a parent, but it could be someone else. You decide how to tackle the project and then spend many months building your Web resource on the server space provider by ThinkQuest. You and your team members use chat rooms to discuss the project as well as e-mail and other forms of communication. Eventually the contest deadline rolls around and your project is frozen in time so that the judges can take a look. If your site if chosen as a finalist, you and your team (and your coaches) are flown (all expenses paid) to Washington, D.C. Your site is inspected by the finals judges. You and your team are interviewed, and at long last, winners are chosen and placements are made. The winning team members each get $25,000 scholarships, and many of the finalist teams who place lower get scholarships as well. ThinkQuest has given away over one million dollars in scholarship money. There are two contests: one for elementary grades, called ThinkQuest Junior, and the original one for older kids. At this site you can explore past winners' sites and get information about the latest ThinkQuest competition schedule.

http://www.thinkquest.org/

A B C D E F G H I J K L M N O P Q R S T U V W X Y Z

Tripod's Homepage Builder

Become a Tripod member for free and receive 11MB of free disk storage for your Web pages. Create your own Web site using only your browser, not those pesky FTP tools. You can use the "quickpage builder" to help guide your way using prompts and forms. Or, use the "custom page builder" to do it your own way. HTML features include a free guest book and online answering machine. More disk storage space is available through their premium membership, at $3 a month. The premium service also includes your own personal chat room, an image library to enhance your pages, and statistics on hits to your Web page.

http://homepager.tripod.com/

NET FILES

In Greece, do people celebrate Christmas by decorating a tree?

Answer: Christmas trees are seldom seen in Greece. More common is a wooden bowl containing a cross wrapped in a sprig of basil (an aromatic herb). The bowl has some water in it to keep the plant fresh. According to the Christmas in Greece home page, "Once a day, a family member, usually the mother, dips the cross and basil into some holy water and uses it to sprinkle water in each room of the house." This ritual is done to keep pesky spirits, called Killantzaroi, away from the house. They do things like put out hearth fires, make milk sour, and generally cause trouble. Luckily, they only come out for the 12 days of Christmas, and since they come down the chimney, keeping the fire burning the entire time is also a good deterrent. Read more at http://www.the-north-pole.com/aroundgreece.html about Christmas traditions.

Web Site Garage - One Stop Shop for Servicing Your Web Site

You've created this wonderful Web page that you're really proud of, but you're getting complaints from some users that the page looks awful. After your first reaction that they must be using some text-based browser on an old DOS system, you realize that you're getting so many complaints that something must be wrong. The Web Site Garage offers some free services that could help you through this mess. Try the free tune-up and run seven different diagnostics on your URL. It will report bad links, questionable HTML tags, cross-platform browser compatibility, spelling, and more. Other services include free Web site registration to 16 search engines, a GIF tune-up, and a META tag generator. They also have "Plus" services that the garage charges for if you need a complete overhaul. Check it out!

http://www.websitegarage.com/

Web66: Classroom Internet Server Cookbook

Wouldn't it be great to have your very own home page on the World Wide Web? You could write funny stories, talk about your pets, or discuss your favorite hobby. Creating a Web page is not too hard—especially if you have one of those newfangled programs that builds Web pages for you. If not, you'll need to learn a simple computer language called Hypertext Markup Language (HTML). There are many free tutorials to help you learn HTML, and the Web 66: Cookbook is a good one. Now that you've got a home page, where are you going to put it? Did you know you can also run your own server? You'll want a direct line to the Internet to do that in the most effective way, and that can be pretty expensive. Maybe you can help your school create its own Web server, instead. The directions are here for Macintosh, Windows 95, and Windows NT.

http://web66.coled.umn.edu/Cookbook/

Nothing to do? Check CRAFTS AND HOBBIES for some ideas.

Welcome to International Schools CyberFair 98!

The International Schools CyberFair invites schools to participate in a collaborative project to create world-class Web sites. Projects should "exploit the unique abilities of the World Wide Web to build relationships and alliances with different people and groups within their local community." One of the goals is to promote an "Internet style of learning" that encourages participants to reach out and use the Web for information gathering. There are prizes and incentives to encourage participation. Check out the list of prizes, rules, and past winners' sites. Be the hero who gets your school started in the CyberFair competition.

http://www.gsn.org/cf/

INVENTIONS AND INVENTORS

3M Collaborative Invention Unit

Could you be an inventor? Before you answer, how do you think a product is invented? Many times, it's not just one person dreaming up a new product. It's a collaboration of several people, or even teams of people, who bring a new item to the market. First, a Scout identifies a problem that needs a solution. Next, a Wizard takes a look at the problem and brainstorms possible solutions. After that, a Critic examines what the Wizard suggests and weighs factors like how much the product will cost to make, how much demand for the product there is, and other factors. Whatever survives this process is given to the Trailblazer, who balances the Five Ps: product, price, promotions, publicity, and place (where the product will be available). This site spells it all out!

http://mustang.coled.umn.edu/inventing/
inventing.html

Pony up to HORSES AND EQUESTRIAN SPORTS.

Argonne Rube Goldberg Home Page

Reuben Lucius Goldberg, better known as Rube Goldberg, was a cartoonist with a wacky sense of humor. He loved to draw machines that would perform simple tasks, like pouring a glass of milk. First he would draw a way to open the refrigerator, then a way to get the bottle, then a way to open it—before he would ever get the milk into the glass! He accomplished this easy job by using the most complex, roundabout methods possible, often using common household objects in uncommon ways. You can see some examples of this here. A contest is held every year to see which team of students can perform a simple assignment using the weirdest, wackiest, and most complex machine. The assignment for 1998 was to "build the zaniest machines possible to turn off an alarm clock." Come here and find out what they invent. You can also find out how to get your school involved in the fun!

http://www.anl.gov/OPA/rube/

NET FILES

On May 18, 1980, Mount St. Helens erupted! Huge mud slides traveled at up to 30 mph, carrying boulders measuring 20 feet across. Wait—volcanoes erupt lava, don't they? So, where did all the water and mud come from?

Answer: Mount St. Helens did erupt hot lava and volcanic gases, as well as rocks, ash, and other debris. These combined to trigger enormous avalanches. Most of the water that poured across the surface of the mountain came from the debris itself. This included water that had been trapped inside the volcano and melting blocks of ice that had been glaciers before the mountain erupted. Find out more at http://volcano.und.nodak.edu/vwdocs/msh/ov/ovd/ovdmf.html

Left margin alphabet: A B C D E F G H I J K L M N O P Q R S T U V W X Y Z

Internet 1996 World Exposition

You may have learned about all the world's fairs and expositions of the last century. The idea was to show people what new inventions—like railroads, telephones, lights, and cars—could do for them. Well, if you've been wondering what this new invention called the Internet could do for you, then welcome to this site. It's a world's fair for the Information Age. One of the most important parts of this expo is the Global Schoolhouse Pavilion, which links schools around the world, showcases young artists, and features activities to help kids learn (and like) the Internet.

http://www.park.org/

The Invention Dimension!

Would you like to win half a million dollars? All you have to do is invent something so cool, so unique, and so compelling that everyone says, "Wow!" That's the idea behind the Lemelson-MIT Prize, which is presented every year to an American inventor-innovator for outstanding creativity. You can find out about the prize and its past winners here, and you'll also find a collection of material about other great inventors and inventions. Check the Inventor of the Week archives, but be prepared for a lengthy wait: the page loads over 60 drawings of famous (and not-so-famous) inventors. Why they don't have a text-only option yet is unknown; perhaps they will by the time you read this. Don't miss the Links area for more inventions and resources.

http://web.mit.edu/afs/athena.mit.edu/org/i/invent/ www/invention_dimension.html

Inventions

The students at Park Maitland School in Maitland, Florida, have completed the entries for their annual science fair, and they're here for you to see! These kids completed their inventions and then built a Web page to share them with the universe. For example, if you click on "Ice Cream Brownie Surprise" by Sam Y., you'll find a recipe for a terrific dessert he created.

http://www.parkmaitland.org/sciencefair/ inventions.html

Inventions! @ nationalgeographic.com

You'll need Shockwave to play these inventing games, but if you don't have it, you can use the neat selection of links to other pages on inventions around the Web. There are five games; one is guessing the purpose of a wacky patent drawing. Hmmm, is it an automatic baby-patting machine or a mitten stretcher? If you guess right enough times, you'll get a token. Get five tokens, and you can operate the wackiest machine of them all back at the Lab: the Action Contraption!

http://www.nationalgeographic.com/features/96/ inventions/

Leonardo Home Page

If you think this site is about the hero of *Titanic*, sorry. This Leonardo is famous for painting the *Mona Lisa*. But did you know Leonardo da Vinci also designed a helicopter, a hang glider, a parachute, and several other contraptions that didn't actually get built until hundreds of years later? Which ones can you recognize from their original drawings? This special exhibit comes from Boston's Museum of Science.

http://www.mos.org/sln/Leonardo/

Lucent Technologies - 50 Years of the Transistor

Any idea how important the invention of the transistor is to modern life? Transistors are in your video games, your television set, your computer—virtually every electronic device. The invention of transistors meant things could be miniaturized, too. According to this site, "The first electronic computer was the size of some suburban homes (about 1,800 sq. ft.) and used 18,000 vacuum tubes to perform the same basic mathematical operations the transistors in a wristwatch do today." They have been around over 50 years, but who invented them? Meet the team at this site. Find out the inside story on silicon, germanium, vacuum tubes, and semiconductors. You can visit many science museums around the world and perhaps win prizes by answering a transistor quiz beginning at this level of the site <*http://www.lucent.com/ liveson/*>. Just keep clicking on the orange ticket at the top of the screen.

http://www.lucent.com/ideas2/heritage/transistor/

Looking for the State Bird or the State Motto? It's in the UNITED STATES—STATES section.

Pencil Inventions

Look at your pencil. How would you improve it? Make it longer, shorter, fatter, or thinner? Maybe put a light on it, or a pretzel on it, or maybe even add a calculator? Getting your brain going on a problem like this is the first step towards being a real inventor. See what this class of kids came up with to improve their pencils.

http://www.noogenesis.com/inventing/pencil/
   pencil_page.html

PM TIME MACHINE MAIN PAGE

Popular Mechanics is *the* magazine for anyone interested in machines. They have built an Internet time machine to help you see how machines have improved over the last 90 or so years. See high-flying French balloons from the early 1900s and crazy car designs from 1960. It's a walk through history, and you won't even have to leave the chair in front of your computer! Your time machine comes with a lot of shiny buttons, and there's even an owner's manual. Let's see, what happens if we press this button right here?

http://popularmechanics.com/popmech/sci/time/
   1HOMETIME.html

The Robert C. Williams American Museum of Papermaking

This book is made of paper, and so is your milk carton, your cereal box, and your report card! How was paper invented? It started in China long ago, but there have been many improvements since then. You'll also discover how modern paper is made, used, and recycled.

http://www.ipst.edu/amp/

The Rolling Ball Web - Main Page

If we said, "Kinetic sculpture," you might say, "Huh?" How about marble runs—do you know what they are? No? OK, then how about those cool machines you see in museums, airports, and malls with the balls that travel around mazes of tracks, doing strange things like ringing bells, inflating balloons, traveling in elevators, only to get to the bottom and travel up to the beginning again? *Now* you know what we mean! This no-frills page is a collection of kinetic art resources that reside on the Web. You can also use it to plan your vacations around visiting these fun sculptures, since there is a checklist by city and state. Don't miss the audio-kinetic "Tower of Bauble" at the Vancouver Science World at <*http://www2.portal.ca/~raymondk/Spider/QuickTime2/scienceWorld.html*> and be sure to listen for the gongs, xylophones, and cymbals. If you can wait long enough, you can see a QuickTime VR movie of the area, but alas, not the sculpture in action!

http://www.msen.com/~lemur/rb-rolling-ball.html

A Science Odyssey

We don't care what you're doing right now. Just get on the Net and visit this site. You will not be disappointed. Check out the Shockwave simulations in the You Try It section. In the Technology at Home area, you can scroll through the twentieth century and see what changes happen in the virtual home. Appliances appear and disappear, telephone equipment changes—what else will you notice? You can mouse over each item and see some facts about it: what it is, who invented it, and when it came into vogue or went out of style. Now try the other explorations: human evolution, radio transmission, probe the brain, atomic structure, and several more. When you get done with those, read the On the Edge comic books about various scientists and their discoveries. Did radio astronomer Jocelyn Bell really think she'd gotten a message from little green men in outer space? Find out here! Don't miss the hit game show That's My Theory! Question the three contestants to see which one is the real Einstein, the real Freud, and the real ENIAC.

http://www.pbs.org/wgbh/aso/

A B C D E F G H I J K L M N O P Q R S T U V W X Y Z

A
B
C
D
E
F
G
H
I
J
K
L
M
N
O
P
Q
R
S
T
U
V
W
X
Y
Z

Welcome to Invention!

Girl Tech will introduce you to some cool inventions by women throughout history. The first U.S. patent granted to a woman went to Mary Dixon Kies. In 1809, Kies got a patent for inventing a new way to process and weave straw with thread. But you may want to read about more recent inventions, such as the one by ten-year-old Becky Schroeder! She thought up a way to write in the dark, using a phosphorescent clipboard! She got a patent on her invention and became famous. Have you got a brilliant idea like that?

http://www.girltech.com/HTMLworksheets/
   IN_menu.html

INVERTEBRATES

See also INSECTS AND SPIDERS

The Cephalopod Page

An octopus is more than just a tentacled cephalopod that squirts ink and runs. It is the smartest of the invertebrates, with both a long- and a short-term memory. It learns through experience and solves problems using trial and error. Check out this site about the octopus and its relatives, and you'll soon realize that these octopi are not just a bunch of *suckers*.

http://is.dal.ca/~ceph/wood.html

Charmaine's KILLER SNAIL HomePage

Run away! It's the Revenge of the Killer Snails! Cone shells are found in reefs throughout the world, but more often in the warm seas of the IndoPacific region. They prey on other organisms, immobilizing them with a powerful venom. There have even been some fatalities from this poison! Want to learn more? Or see photographs? Stop here for plenty of info on these unusual snails.

http://grimwade.biochem.unimelb.edu.au/
   ~bgl/content.htm

Discovery Online, Jellyfish: My Life as a Blob

How do jellyfish eat? No heading to the freezer for something delicious! Some of them troll through the water, others "open their enormous lips and engulf their hapless victims." But eating isn't the only interesting thing about jellyfish. They're cool to look at, and there are some great photos at this site. It also links to other resources about these fascinating underwater creatures.

http://izzy.online.discovery.com/area/nature/
   jellyfish/jellyfish2.html

Kaikoura @ nationalgeographic.com

Let us travel to New Zealand and the Kaikoura Canyon in search of a giant squid. Join researchers, writers, and photographers from *National Geographic* as they begin a search for the elusive squid. Dr. Clyde Roper, teacher-scientist, is known as "Dr. Squid," seemingly knowing all there is to know about the giant squid. Yet neither he nor any other scientist had ever seen an intact giant squid alive in the sea. Dr. Roper often compares giant squids with dinosaurs. But, unlike the dinosaur, the giant squid exists today and is swimming in the depths of Kaikoura Canyon. Somewhere. Join the hunt!

http://www.nationalgeographic.com/features/
   97/kaikoura/

What's "short track"?

Answer: Nope, it's not track and field for little kids! This is a sport kids can participate in, though. It's speed ice skating, usually skated on indoor hockey rinks. Long-track skating is the older sport, skated on huge ovals, usually outdoors. These two sports are fast and they take hard work, but they're lots of fun and terrific exercise. Find out more at http://web.mit.edu/jeffrey/speedskating/intro.html

Sea Urchins Harvesters Association - California

Sea urchins may look spiky and threatening, but when you come right down to it they have no *backbone*. Harvested by divers, these colorful invertebrates are part of a growing industry, as they have become a popular food source. You can find out more about these creatures and how they saved the economy of the north coast of California, although urchins aren't particularly happy about it.

http://www.seaurchin.org/

Welcome to the Lobster Institute

Can lobsters bite? No, they may be able to pinch you with their claws, but their teeth are in their stomachs. Take the lobster quiz and learn more about this large shellfish. Then, if you want, join a lobster chat. But if you feel the only way to appreciate a lobster is to eat it, the Lobster Institute proudly presents their cookbook pages, with recipes and tips for choosing the perfect lobster.

http://inferno.asap.um.maine.edu/lobster/

NET FILES

What are the historical Origins of the Frisbee toy?

Answer: It depends if you go with the "Pie Plate" theory or the "Cookie Tin" theory. But everyone agrees that the Frisbie Pie Company, operating in New Haven, Connecticut, in the early 1870s, had a lot to do with the origin of the game. Yale college students had a lot to do with it, too. You can learn about the history of the disc at *http://www.upa.org/~upa/upa/frisbee/frisbee-hist.html*

WORMS

The Burrow

Just the dirt, please. This is the serious worm place, where worms are elevated to new heights, er, depths. Dig deep here, and you'll find something about worms of all ages, sizes, and squirms.

http://www.gnv.fdt.net/~windle/

The Worm Page

Tractors and earthworms both plow the land, but you don't have to gas up worms. Just give them some garbage or organic material, and watch them go! Learn more about the different types of worms and how slimy, yet beneficial, they are. Then choose your side, as notable worm minds debate the greatest unsolved mystery of all: Why are there so many worms all over the pavement after it rains?

http://users.multiverse.com/~wibble/worm.html

More than one million worms might be found in an acre of land!
Visit The Worm Page to learn about our friend, the worm.

Worms

These first graders made chocolate-covered worms, and then they ate them. As it turned out, they were delicious (made of butter, corn syrup, chocolate, and other yummy stuff). Then they did some gummi worm math experiments, followed up with some worm poetry and songs, and finally they drew some worm pictures. It makes you wonder what's left to do in second grade.

http://www.sci.mus.mn.us/sln/tf/w/worms/worms/worms.html

A
B
C
D
E
F
G
H
I
J
K
L
M
N
O
P
Q
R
S
T
U
V
W
X
Y
Z

JOKES AND RIDDLES

The Droodles Home Page

What's a "droodle"? Well, it's a little drawing, called a doodle, crossed with a riddle—droodle, get it? In other words, it's a drawing with a puzzle in it. Picture a vertical (up-and-down) line, wearing what looks like a bow tie. According to this page, it could be "a butterfly climbing up a piece of string, or a vain triangle kissing its reflection in a mirror." What did the originator think the picture represented? Stop by the site and see! You can puzzle over lots of droodles here and submit your guesses as to their meaning.

http://www.webonly.com/droodles/

Education by Design Publishing Kids Jokes Online

This site has an awful collection of jokes—awfully funny, that is. Real groaners. You'll be faced with such so-called humor as this:

Why did the rabbit go to the barber shop?
To get a hare-do!

And don't forget to iron your moose—if you don't, you may get a Bullwrinkle! (We learned that at this joke page.)

http://www.edbydesign.com/jokesst.html

Fleabusters' Kids Fun Page - Jokes

Submit your own jokes here and see if you can top these:

Where does a general keep his armies?
In his sleevies!

Where do you put a noisy dog?
In a barking lot!

http://www.fleabuster.com/kids/kjokes.htm

Watch your steps in DANCE.

Kaitlyn's Knock Knock Jokes and Riddles

Kaitlyn's only in elementary school, but she has dreams of being a children's doctor or maybe a figure skater! She's got some jokes and riddles here on her home page that may make you chuckle. Here's an example:

Why did it take the monster ten months to finish a book?
Because he wasn't very hungry!

You can also send Kaitlyn your jokes and riddles, and she'll add them, giving you credit!

http://www.bayne.com/kaitlyn/

Riddle du Jour

This site offers a new riddle or brainteaser every day and archives the last week's worth of riddles for your amusement. Other games on this site include a trivia contest, word games, a guess-the-GIF, and more!

http://www.dujour.com/riddle/

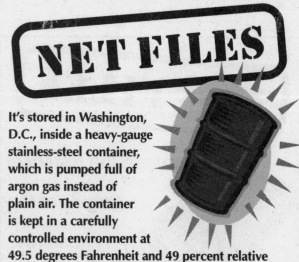

NET FILES

It's stored in Washington, D.C., inside a heavy-gauge stainless-steel container, which is pumped full of argon gas instead of plain air. The container is kept in a carefully controlled environment at 49.5 degrees Fahrenheit and 49 percent relative humidity. Special quarter-inch Plexiglas sheets filter out ultraviolet light.

What on earth is inside?

Answer: Actually, two items are inside, both of them drafts of Lincoln's Gettysburg Address, in the Library of Congress collection. You can see the storage containers and read about the rare documents inside them at http://www.loc.gov/exhibits/gadd/gapres.html

Science From Kids' Perspective

"Most books now say our Sun is a star. But it still knows how to change back into a Sun in the daytime." This is a little collection of things kids have said on class exams, and you may think they are pretty funny. Don't use any of these on your next test, though!

http://w3.mit.edu/afs/athena/user/h/e/hershey/www/
   humor/random/random43.html

Tree and Forest Jokes - Hands On Children's Museum

The jokes here change all the time; you can even submit your own, and maybe the museum will use them! These are some of the jokes we liked when we visited:

How can you tell your dog is slow?
He brings you yesterday's newspaper!

How did the skunk call home?
With a smellular phone!

http://www.wln.com/~deltapac/treejokes.html

JUGGLING

See also CIRCUSES AND CLOWNS

High-tech Juggling Jukebox

The worlds of technology and entertainment really come together here. If you ever run into the Juggling Jukebox, put your money in the machine and then watch and listen. Depending on your selection, you see a variety of juggling routines, and the "wired" juggler makes high-tech music your ears won't believe. It's a fascinating real-life invention you can see and hear on the Net!

http://www.jamesjay.com/juggling/jukebox/hightech/

How to Devil Stick

The first time we tried these juggling sticks, cats were running for cover in all directions. With a little practice, we got so we could do some simple flips, but what we really needed were the pictures and explanations at this Web page. You'll learn how to start the sticks into motion, plus how to do tricks we haven't mastered yet: the helicopter and the propeller spin!

http://www.yoyoguy.com/info/devilstick/

NET FILES

What four languages are spoken in the African country of Cameroon?

Answer: *French, English, Sudanic, and Bantu,* according to the Africa Online: Kids Only site! Learn more about this country and the fascinating continent of Africa, where over 1,000 languages are spoken, at http://www.africaonline.com/AfricaOnline/kidsonly/languages/cam.html

IJA - International Jugglers Association Homepage

One of the things the International Juggler's Association does is work with the Special Olympics to help kids learn to juggle. You can read about that worthy activity on this page, along with other association news. Want some juggling merchandise, such as a Mickey Mouse juggling tie? Buy one here. There's also a great selection of annotated links, including sites about boomerangs, Christian jugglers, Ethiopian jugglers, Swedish jugglers, jugglers in New Zealand, and another organization called Clowns Without Borders. Check out the plans for World Juggling Day—if you guess the number of participants this year, maybe you'll win a prize!

http://www.juggle.org/

Juggling Information Service

Believe it or not, the first thing a new juggler learns is how to juggle only one ball! But it gets much harder after that. This site is for every juggler, from beginner to experienced. There are tips and tricks, links to jugglers' home pages, a photo gallery, and even a movie theater with great performances and demonstrations.

http://www.juggling.org/

A B C D E F G H I J K L M N O P Q R S T U V W X Y Z

A
B
C
D
E
F
G
H
I
J
K
L
M
N
O
P
Q
R
S
T
U
V
W
X
Y
Z

KARTING AND SOAP BOX DERBY

All American Soap Box Derby

No motorized vehicles are allowed on this page! Since 1934, kids have been hauling their gravity-powered racers up a hill in Ohio to see who has the fastest vehicle. World Championship finals are held each August, and kids from all over the United States and several foreign countries turn up to race their homebuilt beauties to victory. You can learn all about soap box derbies here, including how to get your community to sponsor a qualifying race!

http://www.aasbd.org/

The Inside Track - America's Karting Newspaper

This magazine covers the karting scene in the U.S., and some of their articles are online here. You can also explore the links to manufacturers and parts suppliers, as well as participate in the bulletin board forums. Looking for an indoor track in San Antonio? Want to know what to look for when buying a used kart? Ask the experts here!

http://www.theinsidetrack.com/

THE Karting Web Site

Karting is a worldwide sport that hardly resembles the go-cart races of yesteryear. If you watch an old movie or TV show, you might see kids rolling down the hill in go-carts, which were homemade little "cars" put together by kids with their parents' help. Sometimes the wheels came from a baby stroller or an old wagon; other parts came from almost anywhere else. Well, times have changed! Today's karts are complicated, streamlined racing vehicles. Here, you'll find out all about the various forms of this racing hobby practiced all over the world. Latest news, track listings, organizations, and pictures are all here. A caution to parents: Not all links have been checked.

http://www.muller.net/karting/

National Kart News

This site is the online version of "America's favorite karting magazine since 1986." You'll find event news, tune-up tricks, articles from the magazine, and a weekly live chat, often with special guests. Need an engine, chassis, or have some spare parts to sell? Check the online classified ads.

http://www.nkn.com/

KITES

20 Kids * 20 Kites * 20 Minutes

What if the kite-flying conditions are perfect, but you left your kite in the back of your mom's car and she just drove to work? Do you have a piece of typing paper? You'll also need some bamboo shish kebab sticks and some long, plastic nonsticky tape (surveyor's tape or equivalent). Make a kite in 20 minutes! The directions at this site have been time-tested in many Hawaiian classrooms.

http://www.molokai.com/kites/20kidskites.html

Bob's Java Kite

Sometimes there's just not enough wind to fly a kite. Or it's raining. Or it's snowing. Or it's too dark, or...it doesn't matter anymore. Here on a beach beside the Golden Gate Bridge, the conditions are always perfect! You need a Java-enabled browser, and be sure to read the instructions carefully. Otherwise, your virtual kite will spend more time in the sand than in the sky.

http://www.best.com/~bsteele/java/kite.html

clem's homemade kites

You don't need to spend hundreds of dollars on a fancy stunt kite—just try Clem's homemade pattern, made of newspaper and adhesive tape. The directions for making one are all at this site, including some important safety rules for flying your creation.

http://www.ndirect.co.uk/~clem/

Kel's MicroKite Site...(MN_KiteNut)

"Any day is a good day to fly a kite," says Kel, "if you remember to put one in your pocket!" At this site you'll see the world's smallest kite (1/16 square inch) and learn how to make microkites of your own. You can fly these sub-one-inch kites indoors, or fly them outside on windless days. Or tie one to your wheelchair, and take off!

http://www.millcomm.com/~kitenut/

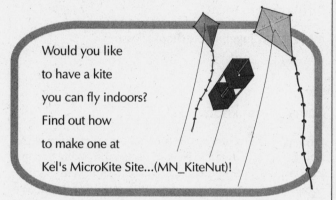

Would you like to have a kite you can fly indoors? Find out how to make one at Kel's MicroKite Site...(MN_KiteNut)!

Kite Aerial Photography

Ever wonder what the view is like from your kite as it soars high above your head? Now there's a way for you to see it. Check the tools and techniques at this site, then go fly a kite!

http://www.ced.berkeley.edu/arch_faculty_cris/kap/

Kites for Kids Only

You'll find links to lots of kite plans for kids, although some are easier to put together than others. At this site, you can go around the world on a kite: learn to make a box kite from Australia, a sled kite from England, or a Bermuda kite from—that's right—Bermuda! There is also a link to software that will help you design your kite.

http://www.sound.net/~kiteguy/kidspage/
kidspage.htm

It never rains in cyberspace.

The Virtual Kite Zoo

Start here for a tour to the various types of kites and their fascinating histories. Did you know that some people use kites for fishing? Or that you can make a tetrahedral kite from drinking straws? Maybe you want to attend a kite festival, or you just want to get some online tips for flying technique. This is the site you'll want to visit! Be sure to click on Kites in the Classroom for many easy-to-make kite plans.

http://www.kfs.org/kites/zoo/

KNOTS

42nd Brighton (Saltdean) Scout Group, UK

Have you ever tried to learn to to tie a knot that's new to you? Sometimes just reading a description and trying to figure it out from a text description doesn't work. The animated knots at this site pay an excellent tribute to the phrase "a picture is worth a thousand words." Watch as each of these 15 knots show you the ropes.

http://www.mistral.co.uk/42brghtn/knots/
42ktmenu.html

NET FILES

WHAT COLOR IS A GIRAFFE'S TONGUE?

Answer: It's black, and it's over 20 inches long! Read up on giraffes at http://www.personal.psu.edu/users/m/r/mrp141/camel.html

A
B
C
D
E
F
G
H
I
J
K
L
M
N
O
P
Q
R
S
T
U
V
W
X
Y
Z

Knots on the Web (Peter Suber)

Have you come to the end of your rope? If so, it's time to *whip* it. That means to tie a special thread around and around the end of the rope to keep it from fraying. "An untidy rope end is a sign of a careless sailor," says this site, which will teach you how to whip a rope as well as tie several useful knots for sailing and other uses. It's *knot* hard—give it a try!

http://www.earlham.edu/~peters/knotlink.htm

The Knotting Dictionary of Kännet

Clear black-and-white drawings and explanations of how each knot should be used (and not used) make this a must-see page for kids wanting to improve their rope skills. Besides common ones like reef knots, fisherman's knot, and the sheet bend, here you'll find the round turn, the prussick, and the jug sling hitch, among others. The page is also available in Swedish, and Jan Andersson (who put the page together) is looking for people to help translate to lots of other languages. Also look for a link to Swedish Scouting's Home Page here.

http://www.netg.se/~jan/knopar/english/

A lot of us learned to tie a bowline by thinking of the end of the rope as a rabbit and making a loop to represent its burrow hole. We memorized this little speech by Elmer Fudd:
"The wabbit goes up, out of his hole, 'wound the back of the twee, and back down into his buwwow."
Visit The Knotting Dictionary of Kännet if you want to learn the ropes!

The Lasso: A Rational Guide to Trick Roping

We're always impressed when we see trick roping in old Western movies. The intricate patterns cowboys make with their twirling ropes take a lot of practice, and we always wished we could learn how to do it. Carey Bunks, holder of a Ph.D. from MIT, has written a book on this subject, and it's all online. Now we know our flat loops from our merry-go-rounds and our wedding rings from our Texas skips. All we need now is a really big cowboy hat and some of those furry chaps to wear!

http://www.juggling.org/books/lasso/

Some useful knots

Are you all thumbs when it comes to tying knots? Do you try to follow diagrams in books, but your fingers get tangled up like pretzels? Here's a site with some remarkably clear live-action MPEG movies that make the bowline, sheet bend, clove hitch, and tautline hitch knots seem as easy as tying a shoelace!

http://www.pcmp.caltech.edu/~tobi/knots/

Untangling the Mathematics of Knots

Boy Scouts, sailors, ladies, and gentlemen. Step right up and join the fun. Here's a site that will have you literally tied up in knots. Mathematical knots, that is! Stop by and read all about the theories behind these special knots, which have no loose ends. The ends are joined to form one single, twisted loop, like an electrical extension cord plugged into itself. Activities and experiments exploring this very knotty problem are included in the discussions.

http://www.c3.lanl.gov/mega-math/workbk/
  knot/knot.html

LANGUAGES AND ALPHABETS

ALPHABET SOUP

When you're eating alphabet soup, have you ever tried to spell your name on the edge of the soup bowl? Ever notice you never have the right assortment of letters? We're including this site as an example of two things: one, it's amazing the type of information you can find on the Net; and two, some people have way too much time on their hands if they can count the letters in a can of soup!

http://www.gigaplex.com/food/soup.htm

AltaVista: Translations

This great Web page is also known as Babelfish. You may not need it right now, but it's a good one to remember, just in case. Say you're exploring the Web and your search engine turns up a resource that looks useful for your school report—at least it looks that way because of the pictures. If you could only understand the language the page is written in! But you don't speak German, or French, or Spanish, or Italian, or even Portuguese. Ask Babelfish. He speaks those languages, and if you give him a Web page address, he will do his best to return a translated page to you. This is fun to try—check it out! Remember, if your original search was using the AltaVista search engine at <http://www.altavista.digital.com>, there is a handy "Translate" button next to the appropriate foreign-language hit. It will automatically take you to Babelfish to perform the translation.

http://babelfish.altavista.digital.com/

Ethnologue, 13th edition, 1996

What languages do they speak in Croatia? Did you know that in Kenya, more than 60 languages are spoken, including Kenyan Sign Language? You can select any of the 228 countries on this page and then discover which languages are spoken there. Also find out how different languages are related, using the language family tree. The Inuit language, Aleut, is related to the Russian Siberian language, Yupik. Do you know why that could be?

http://www.sil.org/ethnologue/

Foreign Languages for Travelers

Just select a language you already speak and then click on a language you'd like to learn. You'll find over 60 of them here, including Hindi, Mandarin, and Zulu. Then you can decide to learn basic words and phrases ("How are you?" "What is your name?" "Where is the bathroom?") or other words or phrases in these categories: numbers, shopping/dining, travel, directions, places, or time/dates. You can read the phrase and hear it (just click on the underlined words). There are also useful links to grammars and translation dictionaries.

http://www.travlang.com/languages/

The Human-Languages Page

Do you like to amaze people by saying things in a different language? Here's the place to get more vocabulary words in your favorite language. There are tons of links to over 1,800 different tongues. You'll also find lots of translating dictionaries, including a project called The Internet Dictionary, which is a multilingual dictionary created by Internet users.

http://www.june29.com/HLP/

NATIVE LANGUAGES PAGE

Would you like to learn a little Navajo or a smattering of Ojibwe? Maybe you'd like to try using a Cherokee font or learn something about Mayan hieroglyphs. This page offers links to all of this and more.

http://www.pitt.edu/~lmitten/natlang.html

A Web of On-line Dictionaries

This exceptional resource collects links to over 500 online dictionaries and word lists in over 140 different languages. You'll also find other reference sources, such as thesauri, rhyming dictionaries, grammars, and more. Parental advisory: Some dictionaries may contain profanity and obscenity.

http://www.bucknell.edu/~rbeard/diction.html

A B C D E F G H I J K L M N O P Q R S T U V W X Y Z

A B C D E F G H I J K L M N O P Q R S T U V W X Y Z

Yamada Language Guides

This is a neatly organized set of guides to over 100 languages. Let's say you wanted to learn some Italian because you're going to Italy on vacation. You could look up phrases that you'd need to know, find information about Italian culture and history, get the daily news in Italian, and even dissect a frog in Italian (that last one is *really* useful!). Besides languages, this gives links to cultural and historical information about the people who speak these languages. Check the Lakota or the Inuit home pages, for example; there are even pages for Klingon and the languages from J. R. R. Tolkien's books!

http://babel.uoregon.edu/yamada/guides.html

ARABIC
Foreign Languages for Travelers: Arabic

Go to the address below and click on Arabic. You'll be taken to a series of lessons that will teach you basic words and phrases. You'll be able to see the special Arabic script (written from right to left) and hear the words. There are also links to learn more about the language and the countries where it is most frequently spoken.

http://www.travlang.com/languages/

BENGALI
Foreign Languages for Travelers: Bengali

Visit the address below and click on Bengali. This site offers words and phrases of particular use to travelers. You'll be able to see the script and hear the pronunciation of the words via audio files. In Bengali, sometimes also called Bangla, there is no such thing as uppercase and lowercase letters. Follow the links to learn where to tune a shortwave radio to hear Bengali speakers.

http://www.travlang.com/languages/

BRAILLE
General Braille Information

Imagine if you could read words by the way they feel to your touch. That's one of the ways blind people read, by feeling the little bumps, which represent letters. This is Braille, and you can learn about it at this page. Included is a cool tutorial that shows how all the Braille letters look.

http://disserv.stu.umn.edu/AltForm/brl-guide.html

The Internet Braille Wizard Access 20/20

Ask the Internet Braille Wizard to translate your phrase into Braille. You can also learn a lot about the inventor of the system, Louis Braille, both at this resource and by exploring the various links provided.

http://www.access2020.com/

CHINESE
Chinese Multimedia Tutorial

This little tutorial is divided into three sections: greetings, expressing thanks, and some phrases about food. For each, you can see the sentence and hear it if you have audio capabilities. Now you know how to order another glass of orange juice in Mandarin!

http://www.inform.umd.edu:8080/EdRes/Topic/
    Humanities/.C-tut/C-tut.html

How tall is the Oscar award, and how much does it weigh?

Answer: The Academy Awards statuette, known as "Oscar," is 13 1/2 inches tall and weighs 8 1/2 pounds. It was born at a Hollywood banquet on May 11, 1927, one week after the Academy of Motion Picture Arts and Sciences was organized. At that meeting, Louis B. Mayer, president of Metro-Goldwyn-Mayer (MGM) Studios, urged that the Academy create a special film award. Cedric Gibbons, an art director for MGM, quickly sketched a figure of a knight holding a crusader's sword standing atop a reel of film, whose five spokes signified the five original branches of the Academy (Actors, Directors, Producers, Technicians, and Writers). Learn more about the award winners at http://www.ampas.org/ampas/awards/history.html

SPEAKING CHINESE

This site offers three short lessons in Chinese and includes audio files. Learn some useful words and phrases to help you meet new Chinese friends. Don't think you'll ever need to know how to say hello in Chinese? Don't be too sure. Once we used CU-SeeMe's Internet video to meet students in China, and they were very impressed we could at least say "*Ni hao*"!

http://redgum.bendigo.latrobe.edu.au/~zhang/
speaking.htm

DAKOTA

The Dakota Language Homepage

As you were growing up, you learned your language. You heard other people speak, and then you imitated the sounds yourself. Here's a way to do just that while you learn the Dakota language, one of many Native American languages. Native speakers help you make the sounds of the Dakota language as you explore a color-coded language "keyboard."

http://www.geocities.com/Paris/9463/

EGYPTIAN

Middle Egyptian

Want to be Indiana Jones someday? Better learn about hieroglyphs so you can read the markings inside the pyramids! Hey, where's the exit sign? This is just the site for that, and you can even type in your name and get it back in hieroglyphs. Be sure to check the ANCIENT CIVILIZATIONS AND ARCHAEOLOGY section of this book for more on ancient Egypt.

http://khety.iut.univ-paris8.fr/~rosmord/
EgyptienE.html

ENGLISH

Aussie English

The kids at the Springwood Central State School in Australia want to explain how Australian English is just a little bit different from what you may be used to hearing. So they have created a *fair dinkum* glossary that's the best thing *this side of the black stump.* Don't *winge,* get in here and translate!

http://www.uq.net.au/~zzlibrar/aussie.html

Dave's ESL Cafe

If your first language isn't English, you'll find a lot of company at Dave's ESL Cafe. ESL is shorthand for English as a Second Language. Check out the hints for both learning and teaching, and have some fun with Hangman and other games. Ever heard of an idiom? That's a word or phrase used in a somewhat unusual way, and there is a dictionary of English idioms at this site. For example, sometimes moms say "there, there" in order to comfort their crying kids. That may make a new learner of English say, "Huh? There—where, where?" Or how about this one: you ask for a cookie and you get a really small one. You say, "That's a pretty small cookie." A new learner of English would wonder if you meant the cookie was beautiful. Even if you're not a new learner, you'll enjoy Dave's site, since he puts so much energy and fun into everything he does.

http://www.pacificnet.net/~sperling/eslcafe.html

ESL Home Page

A new family has moved into your neighborhood. You and your sister decide to visit them and invite them to play. As you knock on the door, three kids race to greet you. They don't speak English, but they want to learn! Here's a page to help you teach them. One of the best ways to learn a language is to hang around other kids. Bet you'll pick up some of their language, too. You'll find links to lots of ESL-related info around the Web.

http://www.lang.uiuc.edu/r-li5/esl/

NET FILES

What are *Goudse Stroopwafels*?

Answer: They are treacle (molasses) pancake cookies found in the Dutch city of Gouda! Although considered a kids' treat, most adults like one with their morning coffee. You can see a picture of one at
http://www.xs4all.nl/~eleede/prod/wiew.htm

A B C D E F G H I J K **L** M N O P Q R S T U V W X Y Z

Left margin vertical alphabet: A B C D E F G H I J K L M N O P Q R S T U V W X Y Z

Grammar and Style Notes

Are you a little shaky on the parts of speech? Can you tell a preposition from a present participle? The names may be strange, but you use these elements in everyday conversation. A preposition usually describes the object of the sentence and its location in time, space, or relationship to the rest of the sentence. For example, in the next sentence, the prepositions are capitalized: BEFORE the alarm rang, the cat was ON the table. A present participle just adds "-ing" to the rest of the verb: singing, sitting, walking. This resource teaches the parts of speech in a fun and easy way. You'll also learn about punctuation, building sentences and paragraphs, and yes—even spelling! Knowing the correct names for these grammatical terms becomes very important when you begin to learn another language. You'll want to know what the teacher means when talking about French subjunctives and superlatives!

http://www.english.upenn.edu/~jlynch/grammar.html

Where on earth can you climb *inside* a huge elephant and live to tell your friends about it?

Answer: *Lucy is a famous elephant-shaped building in Margate City, New Jersey. She dates back to 1888, built by a realtor to advertise his business development plans! It took one million pieces of lumber for the structure and 12,000 feet of tin for the elephant's skin. You can climb up spiral staircases inside the legs to get to the rooms inside. See a picture of Lucy at http://www.cityscom/dm3/lucy_the_elephant.html.*

How Does A Word Get In the Dictionary?

Have you ever wondered how editors of dictionaries choose which words to list and which definitions to use to describe words? This page explains how Merriam-Webster does it, and they should know the best way, because they have been doing it since the 1880s. There are almost 15 million citations for word uses in their database today.

http://www.m-w.com/about/wordin.htm

ESPERANTO

Esperanto: Multilingual Information Center

Esperanto is a fairly new language as these things go: it's been around 100 years or so. It is no one's native language. Rather, it's an attempt to have a common world language many people can easily learn to speak. According to the information at this resource, "About 75 percent of Esperanto's vocabulary comes from Romance languages (especially Latin and French), about 20 percent comes from Germanic languages (German and English), and the rest comes mainly from Slavic languages (Russian and Polish) and Greek (mostly scientific terms)." In Esperanto, every word is pronounced exactly as it is spelled. There are no "silent" letters or exceptions. This makes Esperanto one of the easiest languages to learn quickly, according to experts. Here is how to say "I love you" in Esperanto : *Mi amas vin*. Try it on your mom.

http://www.esperanto.net/

FRENCH

French Language Course Pages

The author of this Web page admits his first five lessons on French grammar are b-o-r-i-n-g! But he promises the rest of the lessons will really help you learn to read French street signs, newspapers, and magazines. There are also audio files so you can hear words and brief phrases. *Papa*? That's French for daddy. See, it's not so hard!

http://www.jump-gate.com/languages/french/

GAELIC

Gaelic and Gaelic Culture

If you're interested in Irish or Scottish variants of Gaelic or other Celtic languages, check this site. You'll find lots on the various Gaelic languages, plus links to music, products, literature, and more. One of the links has a tutorial in Welsh.

http://sunsite.unc.edu/gaelic/gaelic.html

GERMAN

Foreign Languages for Travelers: German

Go to the address below and click on German. You'll find basic words and phrases of interest to the traveler and casual learner. Of course there are audio files so that you can hear the correct way to pronounce everything. There are also links to other places to learn German on the Net and to explore German- speaking countries of the world as an armchair traveler.

http://www.travlang.com/languages/

HAWAIIAN

Ernie's Learn to Speak a Little Hawaiian

Mahalo nui loa (thank you very much), Ernie, for this page, which teaches just a little Hawaiian. You'll find pronunciation notes and a little glossary.

http://www.mhpcc.edu/~erobello/homepage_ernie/
    ernie1.html

Native Tongue - Discover the Hawaiian Language

Learn about petroglyphs: ancient pictographs found on rocks all over the Hawaiian islands. What do they mean? Who left them there for us to discover? Listen to audio clips of Hawaiian vowels and many common words and phrases. Check out this site *wiki-wiki* (fast)!

http://www.aloha-hawaii.com/0common/
    speaking.shtml

HEBREW

Foreign Languages for Travelers: Hebrew

Go to the address below and click on Hebrew. There are brief audio and text lessons on basic words and phrases for the traveler. By the time you read this, the links at the bottom of the Travel Language page may take you to other Hebrew lessons, but at press time a major site has disappeared from the face of the Net. The link is currently broken. We hope it comes back because the site was great!

http://www.travlang.com/languages/

Nurit Reshef: Funland

This is chock-full of fun little Java games to help you practice Hebrew. For example, check out Word Match. There are four pictures of common objects. Click on English and match the words with the pictures. Now click on Hebrew and see if you can do as well! Hint: Play the audio of each word, listen to how it sounds, and match the picture to the word that looks the closest to what you heard. Press Score to see how well you did, then click on New to get four new words to try.

http://www.bus.ualberta.ca/yreshef/funland/
    funland.html

Only men were allowed to compete in the Olympic Games of ancient Greece. But could women watch them?

Answer: *Some young, unmarried girls were allowed to watch the games, and priestesses were welcome, but other women were barred. Read about what happened if one broke the rule at http://devlab.dartmouth.edu/olympic/anecdote/#kall*

A
B
C
D
E
F
G
H
I
J
K
L
M
N
O
P
Q
R
S
T
U
V
W
X
Y
Z

HINDI

Hindi at SU

Hindi is written from left to right in the Devanagari script, which may look very unusual to you at first. This easy-to-use resource puts the basics of the alphabet, numbers, and color names up front in the first lessons. On the alphabet page, sound files let you hear the names of the letters and you can see an animation of the intricate strokes used to write each letter. When you get into lessons with longer phrases and dialog, you can hear the audio files at two different speeds: "normal" is how two native speakers would talk, while "slow" allows you to really hear each word separately.

http://syllabus.syr.edu/hin/jshankar/hin101/hindi.html

ICELANDIC

The Icelandic Alphabet

If you're wondering what those strange runes in Icelandic words are, check this page. There's also a handy pronunciation guide.

http://simon.cs.cornell.edu/home/ulfar/
    IcelandicAlphabet.html

ITALIAN

Foreign Languages for Travelers: Italian

Go to the address below and click on Italian. You'll find a nice little introduction to the Italian language (and it's less goofy than the next entry). Basic words and phrases are listed so you can both see and hear the correct pronunciation. At the bottom of the site are many additional links and other resources to help you learn even more.

http://www.travlang.com/languages/

Mama's Learn to Speak Italian

Ragu, maker of Italian sauces and foods, presents Mama to teach you a little useful Italian. Some are actually phrases your parents might use, such as *Hai già fatto il tuo compito per casa*? (Have you done your homework yet?) It's funny and entertaining, plus there are Real Audio files so you can hear the phrases.

http://www.eat.com/learn-italian/

JAPANESE

The Japanese Tutor

This extensive guide to Japanese culture and language will let you hear everyday words and phrases, spoken by a native speaker. You'll also learn the polite way to count on your fingers and how to use chopsticks!

http://www.missouri.edu/~c563382/

Kid's Window

This little window on things Japanese will bring a smile to your face. Learn how to fold several origami figures, select items from a Japanese restaurant menu, and hear some Japanese letters and words.

http://jw.nttam.com/KIDS/kids_home.html

KOREAN

Korean through English

The Korean alphabet consists of 40 letters. This site has Real Audio files so you can hear the pronunciation of the letters. Then try practicing putting the sounds together to make words: click on the image of the baby or the hippopotamus to hear how these words sound in Korean. Scroll further down the Study page to find dialog practice for greetings and other common situations.

http://ohm.kaist.ac.kr/hangul/

LATIN

Little Venture Latin Pages

Wouldn't it be great to have a chat room in which to talk Latin declensions with people who really understood? A place where you could go to trade mnemonic devices for remembering stuff like which nouns are masculine? A place where you could find tons of resources, including fun stuff like a Latin crossword puzzle and maybe some trivia questions? Guess what? It's all at this site!

http://www.compassnet.com/mrex/

Translated Songs

If you've ever wanted to know how to sing "Happy Birthday to You" or "Row, Row, Row Your Boat" in Latin, this site has that information. But the students at Homestead High School (Mequon, Wisconsin) have taken things a little bit closer to the edge: they have translated other popular lyrics into Latin, for example: *Vale, vale Domina America crusta....* Can you guess what that says? (Hint: it's the chorus from "American Pie"). The top level of this page is worth a look, too. These kids are sure Elvis is alive, and so is Latin!

http://www.mtsd.k12.wi.us/MTSD/homestead/
latin/songs.htm

PIG LATIN

Pig Latin Converter.. or something

Now here's something to confuse your teacher. Go to this site and enter the location of a familiar Web page you've seen a million times. You'll get to the site, all right—but the whole thing will be in Pig Latin! "Oh, teacher, there's something wrong with my browser!" Worse, every link you follow from that site will be in Pig Latin, too. Your only hope is to open a new site. Ave-hay un-fay!

http://voyager.cns.ohiou.edu/~jrantane/menu/pig.html

O-day ou-yay et-gay a ick-kay out of eading-ray Ig-pay Atin-lay?

En-thay oint-pay our-yay rowser-bay o-tay Pig Latin Converter.. or something. Ave-hay un-fay!

PORTUGUESE

Foreign Languages for Travelers: Portuguese

Go to the address below, then click on Portuguese. You'll be all set to learn this language, which is spoken in such countries as Brazil, Mozambique, Angola, and of course, Portugal. Check out text and audio files of various words and phrases, and visit some of the additional links to learn more.

http://www.travlang.com/languages/

RADIO ALPHABET AND MORSE CODE

Morse Code and the Phonetic Alphabets

In addition to Morse code, various United States and other military alphabets are here. Words are sometimes easier to understand than letters when broadcast over radios. For example, it's clearer for a listener to hear "Victor" instead of the letter V. V by itself sounds like E or B or D and may be misunderstood. So, many military and civilian radio broadcasters use an alphabet made of words rather than letters.

http://www.soton.ac.uk/~scp93ch/refer/alphabet.html

RUSSIAN

Foreign Languages for Travelers: Russian

Go to the address below and click on Russian. Then sit back and explore the Russian alphabet (and sounds!) as well as handy travel phrases. There are also numerous links to additional information on the Cyrillic alphabet and its sounds, as well as travel information about—Russia!

http://www.travlang.com/languages/

Friends and Partners - Cyrillic Text

The Russian alphabet is very different from the one we use in English (the Latin alphabet). To get a look at it and learn how to pronounce the letters, try this site. You'll also find links to Cyrillic fonts on the Net and instructions on how to view Web pages in Cyrillic, as well as get them to display the right way on your computer screen.

http://www.friends-partners.org/oldfriends/cyrillic/
cyrillic.html

A
B
C
D
E
F
G
H
I
J
K
L
M
N
O
P
Q
R
S
T
U
V
W
X
Y
Z

A
B
C
D
E
F
G
H
I
J
K
L
M
N
O
P
Q
R
S
T
U
V
W
X
Y
Z

SIGN LANGUAGES

A Basic Guide to ASL

If you have the QuickTime plug-in for your browser, you can see animations of many American Sign Language words. Every word is also described in text, so if the animation doesn't run, you'll still be able to learn that the sign for "home," for example, is made like this: "The closed fingers of the right hand are first placed against the lips (eat), then opened to a flat palm and placed on right cheek (sleep)."

http://www.masterstech-home.com/ASLDict.html

Interactive Finger Spelling & Braille Guide

Finger spelling is one way to communicate with folks who can't hear. Or it's a secret language you and your friend can use when the teacher says, "No talking!" Here's an interactive finger spelling guide and a quiz. See how fast you can "sign" your name! This site also has a Braille guide.

http://www.disserv.stu.umn.edu/AltForm/

What U.S. President once invited all of Washington into the White House to help him eat a 1,400-pound (636-kilogram) wheel of cheese?

Answer: According to National Geographic at *http://www.nationalgeographic.com/features/96/whitehouse/instruct.html* "Toward the end of Andrew Jackson's administration (1829–1837), admirers presented Old Hickory with a large cheese. He placed this mammoth gift in the north hall of the White House and invited all of Washington, D.C., to come taste it. Thousands of people did, tracking cheese all over the mansion. The stench lingered for weeks."

SignWritingSite

Did you know that there is a sign language alphabet? You may be familiar with finger spelling alphabets, but this is one is different. It's an alphabet for the motion of the hands and body as well as the facial expressions used in making the sign for a particular word. The result looks somewhat like hieroglyphics to someone seeing it for the first time! This type of notation has been around since the 1960s; the idea came from DanceWriting—a pictorial shorthand for writing down dance movements. Why not do the same type of thing for sign language movements? The results are here. Be sure to see if you can read "Goldilocks and the Three Bears" and the other children's stories: all the words are in SignWriting!

http://www.SignWriting.org/

SPANISH

Hot Internet Sites ¡en Español!

This is an annotated list of Web sites in Spanish, appropriate for kids as well as their teachers! For those a little rusty on their language skills, the page offers a reminder to use the AltaVista Web page translator, Babelfish.

http://www.kn.pacbell.com/wired/fil/pages/listspanish.html

Spanish Alphabet

Do you know the alphabet? "Sure," you say, "I learned that in nursery school." However, every language has a different alphabet. Sometimes the letters are completely different from English, and other times the letters may be the same but are pronounced differently. With Spanish, the alphabet is the same as English, but the pronunciation is different. You can learn how a good part of the Spanish alphabet is pronounced by taking a glimpse at the Ralph Bunche School *El Alphabeto Español* page. Each letter also has a nice drawing.

http://mac94.ralphbunche.rbs.edu/spanish.html

Web Spanish Lessons, by Tyler Jones

Sometimes it's tough to learn a new language if you don't know how it sounds. Here are some Spanish lessons, complete with pronunciations that you can hear. This page will also test you on translations of written phrases. It's like having your own built-in Spanish teacher!

http://www.june29.com//Spanish/

Webspañol

Did you know that English and Spanish share many similar-sounding and similar-meaning words? For example the English "delicious" sounds very like the Spanish word for "tastes good"—*delicioso*. Over a thousand of these are collected and explained at the Espanglés section of this page. You can hear pronunciation sound files, puzzle over some devilish verbs, try some lessons and links, and even get a Spanish-speaking key pal here.

http://www.cyberramp.net/~mdbutler/

TAGALOG

Foreign Languages for Travelers: Tagalog

Go to the address below and click on Tagalog to get some basic words and phrases. Tagalog is the official language of the Philippines. Do you have audio? You can also hear the words if you have the right plug-ins. At the bottom of the page are additional links that direct you to more information on this language and its country.

http://www.travlang.com/languages/

THAI

Foreign Languages for Travelers: Thai

Go to the address below and click on Thai. Guess where this language is spoken? That's right, in Thailand! You can learn some very basic Thai and look at its script letters. You can hear basic words and phrases pronounced. The links at the bottom of the page will lead you to more information on the language and Thailand in general.

http://www.travlang.com/languages/

TURKISH

Foreign Languages for Travelers: Turkish

Go to the address below and click on Turkish. This page explains that there are two letters in Turkish that cannot be represented by the standard Latin font, so they use substitutes. See and hear Turkish as it is written and pronounced. The links at the bottom of the page will take you to additional resources to learn basic Turkish and view travel information about Turkey.

http://www.travlang.com/languages/

VIETNAMESE

Foreign Languages for Travelers: Vietnamese

Go to the address below and click on Vietnamese. Learn a few basic phrases and listen to the audio files to compare the written word with the spoken word. Then explore some of the additional links to learn more.

http://www.travlang.com/languages/

LATINO

See also HOLIDAYS—CINCO DE MAYO and HOLIDAYS—DAY OF THE DEAD

ELECTRIC MERCADO: Juventud / Latino Youth

This is a hot little page! There are some articles by kids on how to buy great fashions at secondhand stores and how to develop Web sites. Check the poetry and the Mexico bingo game, *Lotería*.

http://www.mercado.com/juventud/

Hot Internet Sites ¡en Español!

This is an annotated list of Web sites in Spanish, appropriate for kids as well as their teachers. For those a little rusty on their language skills, the page offers a reminder to use the AltaVista Web page translator, Babelfish.

http://www.kn.pacbell.com/wired/fil/pages/listspanish.html

A
B
C
D
E
F
G
H
I
J
K
L
M
N
O
P
Q
R
S
T
U
V
W
X
Y
Z

A
B
C
D
E
F
G
H
I
J
K
L
M
N
O
P
Q
R
S
T
U
V
W
X
Y
Z

Latin American Children

What are the good sites for kids, with a Latin American flair? You'll find many listed at this page. With sites from the U.S., Brazil, Argentina, Chile, and Mexico, *Zona Latina* covers a wide territory. Some of the sites listed here may be familiar to you, but we bet you'll find at least a few that are unique and loads of fun! Parents—not all links have been checked.

http://www.zonalatina.com/Zlchild.htm

A Latino Virtual Community - LatinoWeb

Bienvenido! That's Spanish for "Welcome," one of the first things you'll see on LatinoWeb, one part of the Internet set aside for things Latino. If you want to see what's hot on the Internet, this site has much to offer: news, music, cool sites—they are all here. Parents, the extensive set of links from this page has not been checked.

http://www.latinoweb.com/index.html

CULTURE

The Art of Mexican Native Children

Kids everywhere like to paint and draw. True to form, kids in Mexico like to do artwork, and it's fantastic. See samples of drawings from Mayo, Tzeltal, and Maya children at this Web page. The colors will grab you, and the world they paint is filled with animals, musicians, and festivals. Brighten your day and take a look now!

http://www.embamexcan.com/KidsPage/k-artof.html

The Azteca Web Page

Did you know many kids in the United States are of Mexican descent? They are proudly called *Chicanos y Chicanas*. Understanding what it means to be Chicano is about many things: music, history, culture, and language. To learn about this fascinating culture, this page is a good place to start. Parental advisory: Not all links have been checked.

http://www.azteca.net/aztec/

Chicano Mural Tour

Can you picture an art museum that's completely outside? Murals are paintings on buildings, and they turn the outdoors into an art gallery. Some of the best mural artists are Latino. In the past, many Latino artists couldn't get their work placed in art museums. Instead, they painted walls, hallways—all kinds of places—producing some beautiful murals. In Los Angeles, with its large Latino population, there are many, many murals. Take a tour of some of the best of these murals, and see what an outdoor art museum looks like!

http://latino.sscnet.ucla.edu/murals/
    Sparc/sparctour.html

Diego Rivera Web Museum

Diego Rivera was a famous painter originally from Mexico, but his paintings have been enjoyed throughout the world. You can sample some of this great artist's works here. You'll see fantastic murals, learn about Rivera's life, and enjoy Latino art at its best.

http://www.diegorivera.com/diego_home_eng.html

Electric Mercado: Latino Juventud presents Lotería: Mexican Bingo Games

Latinos like to play a fun game called *Lotería*. It's like bingo, but it has colorful pictures with Spanish names instead of numbers and letters. Would you like to play the game? Go to the Lotería page on the World Wide Web. It's fun!

http://www.mercado.com/juventud/loteria/loteria.htm

HISTORY

Chicano! Homepage

Mexican-Americans have had a long struggle to assert their civil rights. The most turbulent period was 1965–1975. A PBS television series traced the events of that period, and you can read about some of them at this site. There are also biographies and photos of prominent figures such as César Chávez, Ruben Salazar, and Elizabeth Martinez.

http://www.pbs.org/chicano/

Galvez

Who is Marshall Bernardo de Gálvez? Well, among other things, the city of Galveston, Texas, is named after him! He was a hero of the American Revolutionary War. This Web page says, "Between 1779 and 1785, Marshall Bernardo de Gálvez... defeated the British in Baton Rouge, Mobile, Pensacola, St. Louis, and Fort St. Joseph, Michigan. These victories relieved British pressure on General George Washington's armies and helped open supply lines for money and military goods from Spain, France, Cuba, and Mexico." There might not have been a United States of America if de Gálvez hadn't helped. Learn more about this American hero at the Hispanics in American History page.

http://207.239.68.174/galvez.html

Hispanos Famosos

What do Roman Emperor Hadrian, Nobel Prize–winning scientist Luis Leloir, and painter Pablo Picasso have in common? They are all famous Hispanics—people with a Spanish heritage. Throughout history, Hispanic people have been great scientists, soldiers, political leaders, artists, and musicians. Read about many famous and accomplished Hispanics here. This page is in both English and Spanish.

http://coloquio.com/famosos.html

Did you know that the longest-held, confirmed POW (prisoner of war) in U.S. history was Lieutenant Everett Alvarez? During the Vietnam War, he flew a jet plane from an aircraft carrier and was shot down, but he somehow landed safely. He was then captured as a POW and held for eight and a half long years. Read about other famous folks by taking a peek at Hispanos Famosos.

The truth is out there in UFOS AND EXTRATERRESTRIALS. Maybe.

LANDMARKS OF HISPANIC L.A.

What do you think of when you hear someone say Los Angeles, California? Maybe movie stars come to mind, or surfers, or rock musicians. Los Angeles, though, is a very old center of American Hispanic and Latino culture. To understand Los Angeles, you have to understand its Latin roots. This page is a good place to begin. Here you'll read about some of Los Angeles' earliest history and you'll see the landmarks where the history took place.

http://www.usc.edu/Library/Ref/LA/
    la_landmarks_hispan.html

NET FILES

How do blind people know if they have a $1 or a $10 bill?

Answer: According to the National Federation of the Blind, many blind people fold the bills in a special way. They ask the bank or store clerk to indicate to them which bills are fives, which are tens, and so on. Then, they don't fold the $1 bills at all and they fold the $5 bills the long way, the $10 bills the short way, and the $20 bills both ways. With this system, they can tell what's in their wallets. For more interesting information about how kids cope with blindness, check out ftp://nfb.org/nfb/fulref/
pasfir/95spiss.txt

A
B
C
D
E
F
G
H
I
J
K
L
M
N
O
P
Q
R
S
T
U
V
W
X
Y
Z

NET FILES

WHY DO BATTERS LOVE TO PLAY BASEBALL AT COORS STADIUM IN DENVER, COLORADO?

(Hint: Denver is known as the "Mile-High City.")

Answer: Batters can hit a ball farther at higher elevations than they can at lower elevations! Why? "The air pressure at Denver and other high elevations is lower than the pressure at lower elevations, which means fewer air molecules occupy a given volume...The collision of air molecules with the baseball creates the 'drag,' or friction that slows the ball down. Since more air molecules are packed into a given volume at New York City, more collisions occur...and as a result, the baseball slows down more quickly [there] than in Denver." Find out more at *http://www.usatoday.com/weather/wbasebal.htm*

LIBRARIES

ALSC HOMEPAGE — AWARDS AND NOTABLES

There's no doubt that librarians know tons about books. Every year, children's librarians in the American Library Association give two awards to authors and illustrators of the best books for kids. The Caldecott Medal <http://www.ala.org/alsc/caldecot.html> goes to the best illustrator of a children's book, and the Newbery Medal <http://www.ala.org/alsc/newbery.html> is given to the author of the finest kids' book. See the winners at these Web sites; you'll find some librarian-tested and approved books!

http://www.ala.org/alsc/awards.html

The Internet Public Library

Wouldn't it be great to have a public library available 24 hours a day? Well, you have one! The Internet Public Library is a project by the library school at the University of Michigan, and you'll find a whole host of material available to you for research projects. There are links to many useful resources on the Internet, guides to help you use the Internet, and librarians available to help you with your studies in a really cool MOO (a MOO is a type of software that lets you interact live with other people in a computer-created world).

http://www.ipl.org/

Library of Congress Home Page

The U.S. Library of Congress is the world's largest single collection of library materials anywhere. It would be great if everything in the library were available to be viewed on the Internet, but that hasn't happened yet. However, the folks at the Library of Congress have made a large amount of information available here. From their home page on the World Wide Web, you can view beautiful graphic images of exhibits, such as original photographs from the U.S. Civil War, or you can see replicas of documents from Columbus' voyages to America. You can also connect easily to the Library of Congress online catalog (if you have Telnet software), and there are convenient links to many U.S. government sites.

http://www.lcweb.loc.gov/

NET FILES

The world's largest waterfall is 16 times the height of Niagara Falls! Where can it be found?

Answer: Angel Falls, in Venezuela, is one of that country's numerous natural wonders. To find out more, visit http://www.lonelyplanet.com/dest/sam/ven.htm

Who is credited with inventing the concept of computer programming?

Answer: Ada Byron Lovelace (1815-1851) is credited with the invention of programming, for her work with Charles Babbage's analytical engine. A military programming language, Ada, is named after her in commemoration. Read more about this mathematician at http://www.scottlan.edu/lriddle/women/love.htm

LibrarySpot

This site says it's "the best of libraries, newspapers, encyclopedias, maps, and more in one Spot." They certainly have made a good start. There are links to public libraries, state libraries, national libraries, medical libraries, school libraries, music libraries, virtual libraries, and more. You can find book reviews, useful reference works, magazines, and lots more to help you with homework assignments. But don't wait until you have an assignment due—this place is amazing any old time.

http://www.libraryspot.com/

SJCPL's Public Libraries with Gopher/ WWW Services

Public libraries all over the world are active on the Internet. Some have their library online catalogs available, others have gopher sites, and yet others have great World Wide Web home pages. To see a list of many public libraries with Internet services, take a look at this site. On most of the public library sites, you'll find links to great resources on the Internet. Maybe you'll see your own neighborhood library on the list!

http://sjcpl.lib.in.us/homepage/PublicLibraries/ PubLibSrvsGpherWWW.html

Smithsonian Institution Libraries' Home Page

The Smithsonian Institution Libraries in Washington, D.C., are among the world's best libraries. As part of the Smithsonian, these libraries are dedicated to spreading knowledge. Take a look at this home page and see outstanding online exhibits, browse through a huge library catalog, and read unique Smithsonian electronic publications.

http://www.sil.si.edu/

The Chinese inventor Pi-Cheng (1016–1076) is credited with inventing...what?

(Hint: It was a moving type of experience!)

Answer: According to HyperHistory Online, "Pi-Cheng is the inventor of printing with moveable types. Pi-Cheng cut characters into cubes of clay and put them into an iron frame. When it was full, the whole frame made one solid block of type ready to print." Find out more at http://www.hyperhistory.com/online_n2/History_n2/a.html (select "People" from the left menu, then "1000-1500" from the right menu).

A B C D E F G H I J K L M N O P Q R S T U V W X Y Z

MAGIC TRICKS

Can the Hall's of Magic Find Your card

Just pick a card, any card. Who will figure it out first? "Mojo: Using gut instinct and street smarts? The Sheik: Using psychic powers? Dr. Megabyte: Using cybernetic calculations?" Now remember whose hand the card is in and click on the appropriate illusionist. Unfortunately, they're none too smart and you'll have to tell them again—and again. But by the third time they've got it right, and sure enough the card they choose is the same one you picked. Try it again—it works!

http://www.hallsofmagic.com/cards/cards.htm

"Hocus Pocus Palace"

Dare to challenge The Great Mysto in a game of mind reading and clairvoyance. Through magical and as yet unexplainable Internet protocols, The Great Mysto will astound you with his long-distance feats. Doubters may scoff and say these are simple "magic square" tricks, but we're not so sure (how did he know we were thinking of Marge Simpson?). You'll laugh out loud at the catalog of old magic trick apparatus, revealed and explained. O Great Mysto, you have a truly fun site!

http://www.teleport.com/~jrolsen/

M&M Magic Product Reviews

If you're really into performing magic tricks, you may be tempted by some of the equipment sold in magic stores and in catalogs. Some of these devices are very expensive—are they worth it? Do they really work? Are the tricks hard to perform or easy? This site reviews commercial magic tricks so that you won't waste your money on a "turkey" when what you want is a magical white rabbit! They also sell magic tricks here, but they don't accept advertising. Users may add their own reviews as well, so you don't have to take just one person's opinion.

http://home.pb.net/~maione/magic.htm

The Magic Secrets Basement - Magic for beginners

Want to try your hand at magic? This is the place to start. The creator of this Web site is a long-time magician who is willing to share a few ideas to get you started. The basic rules are important, but the card and coin tricks described at this site are a lot more fun! Remember that practice is the key to performing a trick that's believable.

http://www.spiderlink.net/users/ralcocer/
    basement/imc.html

Magic Show

Abracadabra! The magic trick amazes the people in the audience, who whisper to each other, "That's impossible! How do they do it?" Everyone loves a magic show. The only thing better than watching a magic show is being the magician. This Web magazine has articles about professional magicians who astound people, show after show. Each issue also contains the secrets of how to perform these magical feats yourself. There are even movie clips so you can watch the professionals. Whether you want to learn magic or you just enjoy it, this site has something for you. Don't forget the hat (and the rabbit)!

http://www.uelectric.com/magicshow/

NET FILES

How many times will your heart pump in your lifetime?

Answer: According to the Franklin Institute's The Heart: An Online Exploration, it will beat two and a half billion times. That's a lot of ba-bump, ba-bump. If you want to learn just about everything there is to know about the heart, take a look at http://sln.fi.edu/biosci/heart.html

> What did grandma do when she was a kid? There is a list of questions to ask in GENEALOGY AND FAMILY HISTORY.

Mathemagic Activities

Put one end of a rope in each of your friend's hands and ask her to tie a knot without dropping the rope. Or amaze your friends with the card tricks and other stunts you'll discover at this site. It's not magic; it's math!

http://www.scri.fsu.edu/~dennisl/CMS/activity/
  math_magic.html

Trendy Magic - Interactive Style

Check this one out! Here are some interactive tricks that are guaranteed to catch you off guard. We thought, hey, how mysterious can it be—it's only a rabbit. Wrong! It fooled us! Then we tried Color Theory. How'd they do that? Maybe we're just too susceptible. But after the Psycho Test we just turned off the computer, backed away, and kept a safe distance for a while.

http://pw2.netcom.com/~sleight/interactivemagic.html

Welcome to The Magic of David Copperfield

A lot of people think David Copperfield is the greatest magician and illusionist alive today. After all, he "vanished" the Statue of Liberty in front of a live audience (even its radar blip went away), and he walked through the Great Wall of China. We attended one of his stage shows, and it sure looked like he was flying around the stage to us. This page will tell you about David's childhood, his current schedule, and his illusions, but it does not give away any of his secrets!

http://www.dcopperfield.com/

MAMMALS

See also CATS; DOGS AND DOG SPORTS; FARMING AND AGRICULTURE; HORSES AND EQUESTRIAN SPORTS; PETS AND PET CARE

Australian A to Z Animal Archive

Not every animal listed at this site is a mammal, so don't get confused. But there are a lot of unusual mammals in Australia. Do you know how the kangaroo got its name? When European explorers first saw a strange animal jumping around, they asked the Aborigines what it was. The Aborigines replied, "Kangaroo," which means "I don't understand," but the Europeans thought that was the strange animal's name. Check out this site and learn about other Australian animals.

http://www.aaa.com.au/A_Z/

NET FILES

Twin sisters of identical height walk into the same room. All of a sudden, one of them looks tiny, while one is a giant! Their parents are upset, but they calm down when one of the twins points out that it's only an Ames Room.

What's that?

Answer: It's a specially constructed room that creates an optical illusion. It's named for American psychologist Adelbert Ames, Jr., who was the first to build one, back in 1946. If you look into the room through a carefully placed peephole, the person standing in the left corner always appears small, while the person in the opposite corner looks much bigger. The room looks like a normal rectangle—but the floor, windows, ceiling, and doors are all trapezoids! Read more about this tricky room and how you can build one at *http://www.illusionworks.com/html/ames_room.html*

A B C D E F G H I J K L M N O P Q R S T U V W X Y Z

A
B
C
D
E
F
G
H
I
J
K
L
M
N
O
P
Q
R
S
T
U
V
W
X
Y
Z

California Department of Fish and Game

Look at that cute little dog—wait, that's not a dog; it's a San Joaquin kit fox! They look just like small dogs with big ears. This endangered animal is about 32 inches long, and 12 inches of that is its luxurious tail. You can see one at this site, along with great photos of lots of other mammals, such as bobcats, porcupines, and raccoons.

http://darkstar.delta.dfg.ca.gov/species/mammal.html

The Electronic Zoo

This page is the best place to start your search for animal info on the Web. For zoo animals and wildlife, check in the Exotics category under the Animals selection. Other mammals (dogs, cats, ferrets, pigs, cows, horses, and more) have their own sections.

http://netvet.wustl.edu/e-zoo.htm

The Hall of Mammals

Take a tour to four major groups of mammals and discover the differences among them and how they are classified. One group, the multituberculata, is extinct. Once widespread and successful, our knowledge of these pre-rodent creatures comes only from observation of their fossils. As you explore this site, try the occasional audio sound bite (it doesn't hurt!).

http://www.ucmp.berkeley.edu/mammal/
    mammal.html

Mammals Home Page

Living mammals are divided into three subclasses. Placentalia is the subclass to which most mammals belong. The other two subclasses include pouched mammals (look, a kangaroo!), known as marsupials, and monotremes, or egg-laying mammals, such as the platypus and the spiny anteater, or echidna. See pictures of these unusual mammals at this page.

http://edx1.educ.monash.edu.au/~juanda/vcm/
    mammals.htm

Nature-Wildlife

Need to know what a warthog looks like? Desperate to discover what a zebra does when he's threatening to bite? Want to see over 60 high-quality photos of elephants? A professional wildlife photographer's page, illustrated with his own photos, also contains lots of information about these and other African mammals.

http://nature-wildlife.com/mammals.htm

Sounds of the World's Animals

Everybody knows that a dog's bark is "woof-woof," right? Well, not everybody knows that! A French dog says "*ouah ouah*," while a Japanese dog says "*wanwan*." In Sweden, the dogs say "*vov vov*," and in the Ukraine, you'll find them saying "*gaf-gaf*." This is a Web page full of what the world thinks various animals sound like. There's an audio sound file for each animal, so you can hear and decide for yourself which language "says it best."

http://www.georgetown.edu/cball/animals/
    animals.html

ARTIODACTYLA

Hinterland Who's Who - Bison

Two hundred years ago, millions of bison, also called buffalo, roamed the Great Plains areas of North America. They were hunted by Native Americans and provided food, clothing, and shelter to the native people. In the 1800s, the animals were killed by the millions and hunted to near extinction. The activities of the commercial buffalo hide hunters, pioneers, and others may have opened up the grasslands for cultivation, but the native peoples were left with a bitter legacy. Now, bison are protected in national parks and other sanctuaries. They are the largest land animal in North America, and you can learn much more at this site.

http://www.ec.gc.ca/cws-scf/hww-fap/bison/
    bison.html

Hinterland Who's Who - Mountain Sheep

Mountain, or bighorn, sheep have a varied lifestyle. Some of them live in the below-sea-level deserts of Death Valley, while others inhabit the steep alpine cliffs of the snowy Rocky Mountains. Their huge curving horns are never shed, and biologists can estimate a sheep's age by examining his horns. Mountain sheep are brown, not white like the domesticated ones you may have seen on farms. They are also very much larger, standing over three feet tall at the shoulder.

http://www.ec.gc.ca/cws-scf/hww-fap/mtnsheep/
  mtnsheep.html

Introduction to the Artiodactyla

Artiodactyla may seem like a strange name, but you're already familiar with many members of this group. It includes the cloven-footed mammals, such as sheep, goats, cows, camels, and giraffes. This site is also where the deer and the antelope play; join them!

http://www.ucmp.berkeley.edu/mammal/artio/
  artiodactyla.html

ARTIODACTYLA—CAMELS

arab.net — A-Z of the Arabian Camel

Source of transport, food, and clothing, the camel is an important part of desert life in many parts of the world, notably Africa and Asia. There are also wild and domesticated camels in Australia. This site teaches many surprising facts about camels. They have two fleshy toes on each foot. When walking, the toes splay out against the sand, providing a snowshoe (sandshoe?) effect that keeps the camel from sinking. All camels shed their coats in the spring and grow new ones by the fall. Their hair is sought after for making fine artist's brushes, garments, and rugs.

http://www.arab.net/camels/welcome.html

> **You know something the Net doesn't—create your own home page! Look in the INTERNET—WEBWEAVING AND HTML section to find out how!**

ARTIODACTYLA—DEER FAMILY

Hinterland Who's Who - Moose

The moose is the largest member of the deer family, often as large as a saddle horse. Old antlers are shed each autumn and new ones are grown in the spring. An adult bull moose can have an antler spread as wide as six feet or more; usually, though, they are about four feet wide. Moose eat twigs, leaves, and water plants. They are often seen wading in shallow ponds, munching water lilies. They swim well and have been known to dive over 18 feet deep to reach a succulent plant!

http://www.ec.gc.ca/cws-scf/hww-fap/moose/
  moose.html

ARTIODACTYLA—GIRAFFES

Giraffe Cam

You've got to see the giraffes at the Cheyenne Mountain Zoo in Colorado Springs, Colorado. Sometimes they are in, sometimes they are out, but keep tuning in and you're bound to see a giraffe or two eventually. We did! They are normally visible from 10 A.M. to 4 P.M. (mountain time). This zoo is famous for successfully breeding giraffes in captivity.

http://c.unclone.com/zoocam.html

Giraffes

Tall and majestic, giraffes cruise the grasslands of Africa with grace and style. But don't even think of messing with them! These 15-foot reticulated wonders are into neck wrestling and head banging, and if threatened, they can kill a predator with a single kick. You definitely want to keep on the good side of this 4,000-pound animal. Even the babies are six feet tall at birth.

http://planetpets.simplenet.com/plntgraf.htm

A B C D E F G H I J K L M N O P Q R S T U V W X Y Z

A
B
C
D
E
F
G
H
I
J
K
L
M
N
O
P
Q
R
S
T
U
V
W
X
Y
Z

CARNIVORES—BEARS

THE BEAR DEN Home Page

This page says: "For bears everywhere, and for those humans who are on their side." We don't know how many bears are actually using the Internet. For one thing, there is the problem of getting a telephone line installed in their dens. For another, there is the difficulty of hitting the right keys when they type with their big, furry paws. However, we are sure that when bears finally get all those problems solved, they will love this Web page. It has two sections, one for everyone and one just for "cubs," so check out both of them! You'll learn about eight species of bears, catch up on current news in the world of bears, and discover some tips on what to do if you ever meet up with a wilderness bear who doesn't act like Yogi and Boo-Boo.

http://www.nature-net.com/bears/

Hinterland Who's Who - Polar Bears

The scientific name for the polar bear is *Ursus maritimus,* which in Latin means "bear of the sea." Although polar bears are good swimmers, they are really large land carnivores. An average adult male weighs 1,200 to 1,300 pounds. Their fur is translucent, which allows sunshine all the way down the hair shaft to the black skin below. The black skin helps absorb heat from the sun. This helps keep the bear warmer.

http://www.ec.gc.ca/cws-scf/hww-fap/plbear/
   pbear.html

North Cascades National Park:Grizzly Bear

Think you can tell the difference between a grizzly and a black bear? Guess what—black bears are not always black, and grizzly bears are not always gray-grizzled, making it very difficult at times to tell which is which. Learn the distinguishing characteristics that set these highly intelligent animals apart. Discover what precautions you can take to avoid a confrontation when you are camping or hiking in the places they call home. Will you know what to do if an encounter becomes unavoidable? You will, if you stop in here.

http://www.halcyon.com/rdpayne/ncnp-grizzly.html

Polar Bears

Do polar bears really like winter? You bet they do! If fact, polar bears would rather live on ice than on land. Discover more about their chilly lifestyle, and learn why you can't sneak up on a polar bear (they can smell you coming up to 20 miles away).

http://www.seaworld.org/polar_bears/pbindex.html

San Diego Zoo - Giant Pandas

So is the giant panda a bear, or a racoon, or what? According to this page, "The giant panda is a bear. It is different enough from other bears to be placed in its own subfamily, but it is still a bear." In the wilds of China, there are only about 1,000 giant pandas left. In captivity, there are another 110, again mostly in China. The San Diego Zoo has a pair of pandas, and this is their home page. Read up on panda habitat, panda characteristics, and panda snacking behavior. There's also a camera in their enclosure. The cam view is at <*http://www.discovery.com/cams/panda/ pandamain.html*> and here's the address to see a QuickTime video of Panda Day: <*http:// www.sandiegozoo.org/special/ pandas/panda_day.html*>.

http://www.sandiegozoo.org/special/pandas/
   panda_home.html

NET FILES

You'd like to do a neat trick, but you need a piece of equipment with a spoke, a honda, and a loop to do it.

What in the world are those?

Surf today, smart tomorrow.

CARNIVORES—CAT FAMILY

Big Cats On-line

Here, kitty kitty! Almost 40 members of the cat family are curled up on this page, waiting for you to discover them. Want to see the big cats up close and *purr*sonal? This is the right place. What's the biggest cat of all? The smallest? How do cats see in the dark? Learn about the evolution of the cat family as well as conservation efforts underway to save those that are endangered. There's also a litter of links that will make big cat lovers purr with pride.

http://dialspace.dial.pipex.com/agarman/

NET FILES

What are the major food groups? (Isn't one of them chocolate?)

Answer: The Food Pyramid lists six food groups:
- Bread, cereal, grains, pasta
- Fruit
- Vegetables
- Meat, poultry, fish, dry beans
- Milk, cheese, yogurt
- Oils, fats, sweets (yes, that's chocolate, but eat only a little!)

Find out more at http://ificinfo.health.org/brochure/pyramid.htm

Cats! Wild to Mild

The Natural History Museum of Los Angeles County has a travelling exhibition all about cats. This companion site to the exhibit has encyclopedia-type entries for 19 feline species from around the world. Represented are jaguars, lions, tigers, leopards, bobcats, and wildcats, as well as house pets. You can see wonderful color pictures of the cats, plus range distribution maps for each. Many of them are endangered species; for example, only 50 Florida panthers are estimated to be left in the wild. Some still exist on the Web, though: you'll find a collection of links for each species. Do you have a cat? Chances are that you do or that you know someone who does. About 65.8 million cats live in the United States, which beats the 54.9 million dogs. Garfield would be so pleased!

http://www.lam.mus.ca.us/cats/

Cyber Tiger

At this site, first you name your tiger, then you write in your name (or a name you make up for yourself). Now it's time to become a zookeeper and save this six-year-old Siberian male tiger. There's a lot of work involved in keeping this fellow alive and happy, and we want him to be happy. Otherwise, he might decide to jump out of his virtual cage (he can leap 10 feet off the ground), and that wouldn't be good for anybody! You're going to have a lot of fun—and learn something, too—as you build a home, feed, and care for your virtual tiger.

http://www.nationalgeographic.com/features/97/tigers/maina.html

Hinterland Who's Who - Canada Lynx

The Canada lynx is a secretive creature. It is most active at night and is rarely seen in the wild. Its main food source is the snowshoe hare, and as hare populations go up, lynx numbers increase as well. The lynx has large, tufted feet, which act as snowshoes in the wintertime. This is good for the lynx, but bad for the hare.

http://www.ec.gc.ca/cws-scf/hww-fap/lynx/lynx.html

A B C D E F G H I J K L M N O P Q R S T U V W X Y Z

Sidebar: A B C D E F G H I J K L **M** N O P Q R S T U V W X Y Z

Hinterland Who's Who - Cougar

Sometimes also known as a mountain lion, puma, or panther, this large cat's favorite prey is the white-tailed deer. It'll also attack bighorn sheep, moose calves, and anything else below its link on the food chain. As solitary hunters, these cats inhabit a wide variety of forested foothills and mountains. Although adults have tawny to chocolate brown coats, kittens are spotted at birth. Their spots disappear by the time they become a year old.

http://www.ec.gc.ca/cws-scf/hww-fap/cougar/
  cougar.html

Tiger Information Center

Why is this server's domain named "5tigers"? Because only five subspecies of tigers remain on Earth today. Three other subspecies have disappeared into extinction in the last 70 years. There are estimated to be only about 5,000 to 7,500 wild tigers left. This organization will teach you something about conservation efforts and how you can help. You can also take a quiz and see how much you already know about the natural history of tigers, play a fun adventure, and listen to tiger sounds, scratches, and growls.

http://www.5tigers.org/

*Tyger! Tyger! burning bright
In the forests of the night...*

So begins the poem by William Blake. Besides those forests of the night, tigers inhabit both the snowy woods of Siberia and the steamy jungles of Sumatra. Visit the Tiger Information Center and see some tigers close-up.

CARNIVORES—DOG FAMILY

Adam's Fox Box

When Fox went out on a chilly night, it was probably heading to this home page. Learn to fox-trot, view some great fox photos, and read stories, songs, and poems about foxes. Links off the "fox fringe" have not been checked, and the fox hunting section is not for the sensitive.

http://www.foxbox.org/

The BoomerWolf Page

BoomerWolf is a real howl! *Paws* at his Web site for terrific wolf information packed with wolf songs, poetry, history, wolf sounds, and more. See if you can help Boomer's detective agency solve mysteries. If you have wolf questions, ask away, and get the answers straight from the wolf's mouth!

http://www.boomerwolf.com/

Desert Wolf's Wolves on the Web Page

Wolves are large, powerful, wild canines that depend on large prey, such as deer, elk, moose, and bison, for survival. Some of their prey weigh more than 1,000 pounds! The wolf has powerful jaws, capable of exerting about 1,500 pounds per square inch, or about twice that of the domestic dog. It is a highly social animal, generally living within the same pack for most, if not all, of its life. To learn more about wolf natural history, lore, and legend, visit this page—and listen for the howling wolves.

http://www.geocities.com/RainForest/Vines/2410/

Hinterland Who's Who—Coyotes

This is one of the few mammals whose range is increasing rather than decreasing, despite efforts to control the coyote population. The clearing of forests and the loss of wolves as a competitor has allowed coyotes to prosper. Here's another fact: the coyote can be a very fast runner, reaching speeds of 24 to 40 mph! This page says that greyhounds can catch up with coyotes, but it takes them quite a long time to do so.

http://www.ec.gc.ca/cws-scf/hww-fap/coyote/
  coyote.html

The International Wolf Center

Imagine this: You are on your way home, and you decide to take a shortcut through the woods. As you enter the forest, the night gets darker. You start hearing things. Suddenly, you hear an animal howling nearby. You're sure it's a wolf, and you're convinced it is getting closer. Should you be afraid of wolves? No! In fact, wolves are very shy around people and try very hard to avoid them. They do not eat people. Also, wolves will howl any time of the day, but they are most often heard at night, when they are most active. Wolves will howl to defend their territory or to reunite pack members. And they will howl whether the moon is full or not! Visit this page and learn more about wolf communication and how wolves live.

http://www.wolf.org/

NOVA Online | Wild Wolves

What's in a howl? What are wolves trying to communicate? At this site, you can listen to a community howl and read a scientific explanation of what's going on. You'll learn a lot from an interview with one of the people responsible for reintroducing wolves to Yellowstone National Park, and then you can try a quiz to test your knowledge of how wolves and dogs are similar and different.

http://www.pbs.org/wgbh/nova/wolves/

CARNIVORES—RACCOONS

Hinterland Who's Who - Raccoons

According to this site, "The name raccoon is derived from the Algonquin Indian word *arakun*, meaning 'he scratches with his hand.' The species name, *lotor*, refers to the raccoon's supposed habit of washing food with its front paws. This activity, however, is probably associated with the location and capture of aquatic prey such as crayfish." Read up on the rakish raccoon at this home page.

http://www.ec.gc.ca/cws-scf/hww-fap/raccoon/
    raccoon.html

The World Wide Raccoon Web

Who's that bandit prying off the lid of your garbage can? It's a family of raccoons! Their nimble paws, black masks, and long, ringed tails make them unmistakable. Visit this home page to meet a true fan of raccoons and their natural—and unnatural—history. You'll find lots of photos, legends, and links, and you can read the incredible story of how one raccoon saved a student's life at Cornell University!

http://www.loomcom.com/raccoons/

CARNIVORES—SEALS, SEA LIONS, WALRUS

The Marine Mammal Center

This San Francisco area wildlife rehabilitation center specializes in pinnipeds: California sea lions, northern elephant seals, and harbor seals. Do you know why elephant seals' eyes are so big? So they can see in low light levels when they dive deep. They get most of their food this way. They prefer to be offshore, up to 35 miles, diving to 4,000 feet and possibly even deeper! On land, because they have nonreversible rear flippers, elephant seals must slide, wriggle, and roll, using movements that resemble those of a caterpillar. To learn more about other marine mammals, visit this home page.

http://www.tmmc.org/

CARNIVORES—SKUNKS

Hinterland Who's Who - Skunks

You know that skunks can spray a foul-smelling musk in order to deter a predator, but what else do you know about them? They are useful because they eat mice, shrews, grasshoppers, crickets, and insect larvae such as white grubs, army worms, and cutworms. According to this page, "They will even eat wasps and bees, which they kill with their front feet. It has been estimated that almost 70 percent of a skunk's diet constitutes a benefit to people and only 5 percent is harmful to human property."

http://www.ec.gc.ca/cws-scf/hww-fap/sskunk/
    skunk.html

A
B
C
D
E
F
G
H
I
J
K
L
M
N
O
P
Q
R
S
T
U
V
W
X
Y
Z

OPTICAL ILLUSIONS: now you see them, now you don't!

The Wonderful Skunk and Opossum Page

What would you do if your dog got sprayed by a skunk? Does a tomato juice bath really work? Sort of, but it may turn your dog pink for a while! You can also try a newer remedy, involving hydrogen peroxide, baking soda, and liquid soap; the recipe is here. There's advice on keeping skunks as pets, plus loads of lore on both skunks and opossums. Opossums are marsupials, meaning they carry their babies in a pouch. Another little-known fact is that a 'possum has 50 teeth—more than any other North American mammal.

http://granicus.if.org/~firmiss/m-d.html

What causes the distinctive odor of skunks?

About a century ago, T.B. Aldritch published his analysis, which said that it was primarily 1-Butanethiol (also known as n-Butyl Mercaptan). Many books still think Aldritch got it right. However, a 1990 analysis of the volatile components of skunk musk reveals it's actually made of seven chemicals. The Wonderful Skunk and Opossum Page reports: "One component had never before been seen in nature and another had never been reported anywhere (natural or man-made), yet none of them were 1-Butanethiol!"

Did times change or did skunks?

CETACEANS

WhaleTimes SeaBed - whales, sharks, penguins, dolphins and more

Did you ever look for a dolphin in a tree? If you're looking for boutos, or Amazon River dolphins, sometimes that's the place to look. They live in South America. During the rainy season, when the rivers flood and the water gets as deep as 40 or 50 feet, the dolphins and other animals in the river actually swim through the trees. Can you tell the difference between a shark and a whale? Many sharks have two dorsal fins; a whale has only one dorsal fin, if at all. Also, a shark's tail is vertical and a whale's tail is horizontal. If you're fishing for fishy facts, you can ask Jake the Sea Dog, who will answer questions online. You can even help write an ocean story! Take a swim to this Web page and see for yourself.

http://www.whaletimes.org/

CETACEANS—WHALES

J.J.'s Adventure: A Baby Gray Whale's Rescue and Release

J.J. the gray whale made lots of news in 1997. In January, she was found on the beach at the tender age of seven days old. Although very sick, she was rescued, cared for, and eventually released back to her home in the Pacific Ocean. Three schoolgirls loved the story so much they decided to make a Web page and enter the ThinkQuest Junior contest. Guess what? They won Best of Contest for 1998! View lots of great photos and learn how J.J. got her name at this terrific site.

http://tqjunior.advanced.org/4397/

Looking for the State Bird or the State Motto? It's in the UNITED STATES—STATES section.

Welcome to WhaleNet at Wheelock College, Boston

Have you ever wanted to go on a whale watch? Big boats of whale seekers leave from port cities all over the world, every day, in search of sighting one or more of the big mammals. Well, you can go on a whale watch right here! There's a slide show where you will begin by climbing aboard the boat and heading out into the Atlantic Ocean, where you are guaranteed to see some whales. That's better than what some of the expensive trips promise! Net-mom knows some people who went out into the ocean in Maine hoping to see a lot of whales. All they saw were big waves. Then it got foggy and they couldn't even see their hands in front of their faces! We know you'll have a lot of fun on this trip and will want to return again with your classmates or your mom and dad. There's lots of great information about whales available at this site, too.

http://whale.wheelock.edu/

NET FILES

Before 1889, Italian pizzas were topped with olive oil, cheese, and basil. Who came up with the idea of putting tomato sauce on pizza, and why?

Answer: According to Seeds of Change at *http://horizon.nmsu.edu/garden/recipes/pizza.html* "Tomato made its debut as a pizza topping in 1889 when Raffaele Esposito, a famous baker, made a special pizza topped with tomato, mozzarella cheese, and basil for Queen Margherita (the pizza still retains her name today). Incidentally, the color of the toppings correspond to the colors of the Italian flag—tomato red, white cheese, and green basil."

Whale Songs

Follow in the footsteps of Saucon Valley School District (Pennsylvania) bioethics teacher Lance Leonhardt as he joins the crew of the sailing yacht *Song of the Whale*. Before his journey, he had his students research the island of Dominica, in the Azores of the Caribbean. They learned about the climate, landscape, wildlife, and especially the marine mammals of the vicinity. Their findings on each whale are here, as well as their teacher's journals, which describe encounters with many kinds of dolphins and whales during the two-week voyage. The detailed entries include rich multimedia resources, such as links to photos, audio files, and a handy glossary.

http://whales.ot.com/

Whales

Have you ever heard of friendly whales? No, not Baby Beluga or Shamu. The term "friendly whale" usually refers to the gray whale. In the lagoons in Mexico, sometimes gray whales will approach small boats. Scientists are not sure why the whales do this, since most wild animals are too wary to approach people or allow people to approach them. Maybe they just want to be friendly! Is a whale a fish? No. Although they share the same environment, there are important differences between a fish and a whale. Visit this page to discover differences in the way fish and whales breathe, swim, and eat. This page is full of references for teachers, activities for students, and whale projects for all.

http://curry.edschool.Virginia.EDU/go/Whales/

CHIROPTERA—BATS
Bat Conservation International Top Page

Did you know that the world's smallest mammal is the bumblebee bat? It weighs less than a penny does. Nearly 1,000 different kinds of bats account for almost 25 percent of all mammal species. Most bats are very good to have around. One little brown bat can catch 600 mosquitoes in just one hour. Visit this site to learn more about bats and bat houses, or stop in at North America's largest urban bat colony by clicking on "Congress Ave. Bridge."

http://www.batcon.org/

A B C D E F G H I J K L M N O P Q R S T U V W X Y Z

A
B
C
D
E
F
G
H
I
J
K
L
M
N
O
P
Q
R
S
T
U
V
W
X
Y
Z

The Buzbee Bat House Temperature Plot

At this batty site, you can check the temperature inside the Buzbee's bat house, and remember, bats like to be warm. After that, discover a whole colony of educational links about bats. You'll find pictures, facts, even tours to bat caves. In addition, groan over bat jokes, bat poetry, and even (ick) bat recipes.

http://www.nyx.net/~jbuzbee/bat_house.html

INSECTIVORES

Hedgehog Hollow

Hedgehogs: the trendy pet of the '90s! Have you been considering getting a hedgehog as a pet, or are you just wondering what all the interest in those hedgehog things is about? Either way, Hedgehog Hollow is the place to visit. Contrary to popular belief, hedgehogs are not related to porcupines. They make great pets, but some kinds make better pets than others; find out here. Some hedgehogs can even be trained to use a litter box! They eat a variety of food, such as cat food, hard-boiled eggs, cottage cheese, oatmeal, fruit, mealworms, crickets, grasshoppers, earthworms...well, you get the picture.

http://www.pci.on.ca/~macnamar/hedgehogs/

Hedgehogs of steel!

These cute critters have an amazing immunity to most things that are toxic. Toxins that would kill a human hundreds or even thousands of times over often have no visible effect on a hedgehog. Scientific research has even confirmed this fact. Visit Hedgehog Hollow to learn more about these adorable little creatures.

LAGOMORPHS—RABBITS AND HARES

Hinterland Who's Who - Snowshoe Hare

Although brown in summer, snowshoe hares turn completely white in the winter. That's good, because it camouflages them in the snow. Their big furry feet help them stay on top of the snow rather than sink in, like a deer would. They have large ears with which to detect nearby predators, but the ears serve another purpose: they help regulate body temperature by dispersing excess heat!

http://www.ec.gc.ca/cws-scf/hww-fap/snowshoe/ snowshoe.html

Official House Rabbit Society Home Page

"Wanted: A patient human with a sense of humor who spends a lot of time at home and doesn't mind hanging out on the floor with me. I am a bunny rabbit in need of a good home. I am inquisitive, sociable, litterbox-trained, and would make a wonderful companion for the right person. I need to be protected from predators, poisons, temperature extremes, electrical cords, and rough handling. I may even purr when I am happy. Stop by to find out what life would be like if you adopted me. Please hurry, my friends and I need your help!" The House Rabbit Society has rabbits for adoption all over the U.S. You'll also find out a lot about rabbit care and handling, so hop on over!

http://www.rabbit.org/

MARSUPIALS (POUCHED MAMMALS)

Pittsburgh Zoo - Gray Kangaroo

Did you know that male kangaroos are called boomers and females are called flyers? Read a little bit about the gray kangaroos at the Pittsburgh Zoo, conservation efforts, and more at this site.

http://zoo.pgh.pa.us/wildlife/grey_kangaroo.html

Ruth's Sugar Glider Page

Sugar glider? Do you eat it or fly it? Neither. It's only the cutest marsupial to come up from "down under." About the size and shape of a flying squirrel, these creatures are soft, striped, and captivatingly cute. Native to Australia, they are considered exotic to the U.S., so you need a license to buy and own one. But owners will tell you they make great pets and are well worth any paperwork hassle. Think twice before checking out this site—once you see one, you're going to want one!

http://www.teleport.com/~jeffruth/sugar_gliders/

MARSUPIALS (POUCHED MAMMALS)—KOALAS

Koala's Page

What seldom drinks, has a big rubbery nose, large fluffy ears, and little or no tail, and looks like a cuddly toy? Why, a koala bear, of course! Koalas live in trees, eat eucalyptus leaves, and are categorized as marsupials because they nourish their young in abdominal pouches. A mother koala only has one baby at a time, and she carries it around in her pouch for seven months; after that, the baby clings to its mother's back until it is about one year old. An old Australian story tells how the first koala was created. Stop by this page and check it out.

http://www.geom.umn.edu/~jpeng/KOALA/koala.html

Koalas at Lone Pine Koala Sanctuary

Visit a wildlife park near Brisbane, Australia! It is home to over 150 koalas and 100 species of unique Australian wildlife. Besides koalas, you'll meet kangaroos, Tasmanian devils, and wombats, among others. You can vote for the cutest koala, download some screen wallpaper, or follow some of the other animal links. This page is available in Chinese, Indonesian, Korean, Japanese, and Thai.

http://www.koala.net/

MARSUPIALS (POUCHED MAMMALS)—OPOSSUMS

National Opossum Society

What animal gives birth only 13 days after mating? What animal has thumbs on its hind feet? What animal plays dead if unable to escape from a predator? Give up? Or are you just "playing possum"? Learn all about the amazing opossum at this home page.

http://www.teleport.com/~opossums/

The Wonderful Skunk and Opossum Page

Opossums are marsupials, meaning they carry their babies in a pouch. Another little-known fact is that a possum has 50 teeth—more than any other North American mammal. Track down facts on opossums and skunks at this critter-friendly page.

http://granicus.if.org/~firmiss/m-d.html

MONOTREMES (EGG-LAYING MAMMALS)

Australian Platypus Conservancy

This page offers a little information on habitat, breeding, and range of the duck-billed platypus. Click in the "Platypus" area to find it. Did you know the "duck bill" is really soft, not hard? It is sensitive to touch and helps the animals find food underwater.

http://www.ozemail.com.au/%7ewildscap/
   conservancy.html

Introduction to the Monotremata

All species of living monotremes come from either Australia or New Guinea. They include the duck-billed platypus and two species of echidna, sometimes called spiny anteaters. These animals produce milk to nurse their young like other mammals, but they lay eggs—setting them apart from all other mammal species. Learn about the fascinating monotremes at this page.

http://www.ucmp.berkeley.edu/mammal/
   monotreme.html

A
B
C
D
E
F
G
H
I
J
K
L
M
N
O
P
Q
R
S
T
U
V
W
X
Y
Z

A
B
C
D
E
F
G
H
I
J
K
L
M
N
O
P
Q
R
S
T
U
V
W
X
Y
Z

MONOTREME EXTREME

The momma echidna lays one egg directly into her pouch. It's about the size of a green grape. It hatches after about ten days, and then it spends about 50 days nestled inside the pouch. By then it has started growing spines of its own (ouch!), so Mom moves it into a special nursery burrow she digs in the earth. Not much is known about the natural history of these strange mammals, but this scientist is trying to change all that. Follow her research and learn about these critters, whose ancestors roamed with the dinosaurs.

http://www.nexus.edu.au/schools/kingscot/pelican/
   monohome.htm

PERISSODACTYLA—HORSES AND ZEBRAS

Animal Bytes: Grevy's zebra

Did you know that each zebra's stripe pattern is as unique as a fingerprint? Zebras help other plant-eaters on the grassland plains, since they eat off the coarse forage at the top of plants, leaving the tender new growth for other animals.

http://www.seaworld.org/animal_bytes/grevysab.html

Bexley's Zebra Page

Some great photographs of zebras are found on Bexley's Zebra Page, but that's about it. If you're looking for zebra pictures, this is the place you want.

http://www.wildfire.com/~ag/zebras.html

Discovery Online, Wild Discovery Wired — Zebra

Are zebras white with black stripes or black with white stripes? What are the stripes for? Why don't people ride zebras like they do horses? What sounds do zebras make? Why are zebras found only in Africa? The answers to these questions, originally posed during a live Internet chat, are archived at this site for you to enjoy.

http://eagle.online.discovery.com/cgi-bin/
   conversations_view/dir/
   Wild%20Discovery%20Wired/Zebra

Go climb a rock in OUTDOOR RECREATION.

Woodland Park Zoo

Meet some Damaraland zebras at Woodland Park Zoo in Seattle, Washington. They have not only black and white stripes but also brownish "shadow" stripes. This camouflage helps them disappear in the sun-on-shifting-grasslands habitat of their native Africa. Unfortunately, fewer than one-half million of these herd animals remain in the wild. You'll learn a lot about the natural history of zebras and also something you probably did not know about legendary rock star Jimi Hendrix and why a plaque in his honor is at the Seattle zoo.

http://www.zoo.org/animals/zebra.stm

NET FILES

Every August, kids from all over the world can't wait to get to Akron, Ohio, and go as fast as they can down a 954-foot hill.

Why?

Answer: They're in the World Championships of the All-American Soap Box Derby! You won't find any motorized vehicles here—these are gravity-powered! Three division winners get to wear the traditional gold championship jackets at the end of Derby Day. Read more about it at *http://www.aasbd.prg/*

PERISSODACTYLA—RHINOCEROS

Animal Bytes: black rhinoceros

Fewer than 2,500 of these animals exist on the planet today. Some people believe that the rhino "horn" has medicinal properties, and the animals are killed by poachers who want to harvest the horn. The rhino "horn" isn't attached to the skull, and it's made out of keratin (the same substance found in fingernails), so it is not a true horn at all. Some zoos, such as the San Diego Wild Animal Park, have had some success breeding these animals, but they will never return to the wild, since their habitat is mostly gone.

http://www.seaworld.org/animal_bytes/
  black_rhinocerosab.html

Save the Rhino Home Page

It may be a little thick-skinned, but its reputation for aggressiveness is totally overblown. Normally timid and with no natural enemies, a white rhino will charge only when confronted. Yet the loss of home and poaching of its horns has nearly destroyed its population. Here you can learn more about this rhino and its relatives and see how one organization is attempting to keep the 97 percent extinction rate from becoming 100 percent.

http://www.cm-net.com/rhino/

In the last 30 years, 97 percent of the world's rhinoceros population has been wiped out, and less than 10,000 are left!

What can kids do to make sure *their* kids get to see live rhinos?

Check the Save the Rhino Home Page.

Be dazzled by the laser shows in PHYSICS.

PRIMATES

African Primates at Home

Uh-oh. There's something moving in the trees overhead. It must be a grey-cheeked mangabey—that "whoop-gobble" call is unmistakable. How did Net-mom get so good at identifying the call of the ape, er, monkey? By listening to the sounds at this Web site, of course. It's really a swingin' place!

http://www.indiana.edu/~primate/primates.html

Global SchoolNet Supports the Jane Goodall Institute

Chimpanzees are biologically close to humans; there is only a two percent genetic difference. This is why they are frequently used in research. The Jane Goodall Institute is committed to improving the lives of chimpanzees both in the wild and in captivity. Goodall's wildlife research in Africa is internationally known and respected. You can get involved with her Roots and Shoots program or the Youth Summit sponsored by the Institute.

http://www.gsn.org/project/jgi/index.html

The Gorilla Foundation

Koko the gorilla was born in San Francisco, California. Koko loves to eat corn on the cob, play with a rubber alligator, and watch *Wild Kingdom* on television. Gorillas sleep about 13 hours each night and rest for several hours at midday. They build new sleeping nests every night by bending nearby plants into a springy platform, usually on the ground or in low trees. When not resting, they spend most of their time looking for food and eating it. Want to know more about these shy mammals? This is a great place to learn!

http://www.gorilla.org/

A
B
C
D
E
F
G
H
I
J
K
L
M
N
O
P
Q
R
S
T
U
V
W
X
Y
Z

Orang Utan

The current number of orangutans left in the wild is estimated at between 20,000 and 27,000. They are an endangered species and are the only big apes found in Asia. Unlike other primate species, they do not live in groups, preferring a solitary life. They feed on fruits, bark, leaves, and insects, such as ants, termites, and bees. Male orangutans feed at ground level; the females never leave the trees. Stop by this page and meet Grungy the Orangutan, and learn more about projects in support of orangutan rehabilitation and preservation around the world.

http://www.tourismindonesia.com/orang.htm

Primate Gallery - Images of Monkeys and Apes

What's all the monkeying around? Why, it's the Primate Gallery Web site! You'll find information on over 200 living primate species, including links to images, animations, and primate audio files. Stop by and see which primate is being featured this week. This comprehensive site will lead you to other monkey business on the Net as well!

http://www.selu.com/~bio/PrimateGallery/

PROBOSCIDEA—ELEPHANTS

Elephant Managers Association

Did you ever wonder what an elephant does all day in the zoo? Elephants demand instruction and guidance to flourish in a man-made environment. The Elephant Managers Association tries to help, and you can read about them at this site. In the Other Links area, you will find lots of additional info about elephants. For example, the Indianapolis Zoo strives hard to provide the psychological, physiological, and social fulfillment needed to keep elephants happy and healthy. Spend a virtual day with the elephants and the trainers as they go about their busy schedules by clicking on the "Other Elephant Links" and then the link for the Indianapolis Zoo's Elephant Program.

http://www.indyzoo.com/ema/

Elephanteria

Do you love elephants? This is probably the site you'll like best—not only can you find information on these precious pachyderms, but also there's an elephant dance and an elephant cake and cookies!

http://www.wildheart.com/

How Can You Go to Bed With an Elephant in Your Head?

This 30-page rhymed story is about a kid who has a dream about getting stuck on a log in a river. The reindeer, monkeys, cow, Tasmanian devil (it looks like a devil with horns, not the animal by that name—don't be fooled) and an angel (whose wings get stuck in the trees) can't help. An elephant happens by, then goes off to get all of its friends. The boy dreams he is rescued, but we won't spoil the surprise. The elephant asks the boy for a favor: to help spread the word about people killing elephants for their ivory. The boy wrote this book to tell everyone that we should share the earth with the elephants.

http://brian.com/Romain/Ele/Ele0.html

Ivory Haven - Laura The Elephant's House on The Web

Meet Laura, an African elephant who now lives in a protected sanctuary in Michigan. She has a lot to say about the fact that elephants are threatened, so take her informative Web tour! You will love Laura and Buster as they teach you all about elephants. Want to help? Join some school classrooms and support the sanctuary by donating a month of elephant feed—it's not peanuts! Laura and Buster's grain bill is about $125 a month. They eat a special chow made just for elephants. The hay bill is $25 per day. Laura's keeper told Net-mom, "We also have a fund going to help finish the breeding barn so any extra money goes towards that building." Check the Wish List for the feed mill address and additional information about how to donate towards this worthy cause.

http://www.geocities.com/RainForest/2248/

"We like the INVERTEBRATES best."—The Nields

RODENTS

The Capybara Page

What would you get if you crossed a guinea pig and a hippopotamus? Probably something that looks like a capybara. These large, friendly rodents are rather vocal, making a series of strange clicks, squeaks, and grunts. Although they adapt easily to captivity, mice and rodent collectors will have to pass this one by as a pet: capybaras are the largest living rodents on earth, weighing in at 100 pounds or more! Great-grandma calls them "outdoor hamsters."

http://www.rebsig.com/capybara/

Gerbil links

One of the places kids learn about gerbils might be in their classrooms. Another place is right here at this page. A lot of sites about gerbils have been collected at this location. You can read about how to take care of gerbils, and you can even read about gerbils owned by kids all over the world. We liked the one about Itchy and Scratchy. Why don't you check it out?

http://ourworld.compuserve.com/homepages/e_ehr/
    gerbils/links.htm

Guinea Pigs on the Net

In English, it's called a guinea pig or cavy. In German: *Meerschweinchen*. Spanish: *conejillos de Indias*. French: *Cobaye*. Italian: *Porcellino d'India*. Japanese: *Tenjiku nezumi, marumotto*. No matter how you say it, these little whistling guys are cute! We love this page, and not just because of the "surfing guinea pig" pictures. There is a pet cavy care FAQ, plus links to other guinea pig pages and loads of "family portraits" of beloved "pigs" everywhere. This pig page is on a server in Italy; the Hawaiian mirror is at <*http://www.hawaii.edu/mirrors/w3.ing.unico.it/carlo/gplinks.html*>.

http://matisse.ing.unico.it/carlo/cavie.html

Hinterland Who's Who - Beavers

This site makes the case that the beaver has greatly influenced the development and settlement of Canada, from the 1600s on. Explorers and trappers pushed farther and farther into the wilderness seeking more beaver for their pelts, which could be sold at a high price. Beavers now appear on Canadian stamps and coins, as well as on North American wilderness lakes. This page shows beaver tracks, illustrates how they engineer their dams and lodges, and explains the many uses of those broad, flat tails.

http://www.ec.gc.ca/cws-scf/hww-fap/beaver/
    beaver.html

Hinterland Who's Who - Chipmunks

Who can resist these friendly little striped creatures? They are fun to watch and can easily be tamed to take peanuts or seeds from your hand. They sit on your hand and push peanuts into cheek pouches, turning the nut over and over, trying it this way, then trying it that way, until they get the perfect fit. Then they run off to store the nuts in their burrows. They have "dominance areas" of territory usually ranging from one to three acres, which includes their burrow. They usually don't go into another chipmunk's territory, but if one trespasses, there is general chasing and chattering and lots of excitement.

http://www.ec.gc.ca/cws-scf/hww-fap/chipmunk/
    chipmunk.html

Hinterland Who's Who - Eastern Grey Squirrel

We have three types of squirrels banging on our windows for food: gray, black, and red. Actually, the first two are just color variations of the same species: *Sciurus carolinensis*, the eastern grey squirrel. The average life span of one of these squirrels is 12.5 years, although there has been at least one instance of a captive squirrel living for 20 years! Apparently, squirrels exist everywhere but Australia, southern South America, and some desert regions. Want to see a squirrel in action? Get over to The Squirrel Cam at <*http://www.rhowick.com/squirrelcam.html-ssi*> where you'll see a new "almost live" photo every few minutes!

http://www.ec.gc.ca/cws-scf/hww-fap/squirrel/
    squirrel.html

A
B
C
D
E
F
G
H
I
J
K
L
M
N
O
P
Q
R
S
T
U
V
W
X
Y
Z

Left margin vertical alphabet: A B C D E F G H I J K L M N O P Q R S T U V W X Y Z

Hinterland Who's Who - Lemmings

Is it true that arctic herds of these mouselike critters throw themselves into the sea if there's a lack of food available? Although there is no firsthand evidence of this, their numbers do fluctuate dramatically from year to year. Sometimes there are lemmings everywhere you look, while other years you'd be hard pressed to find a lemming for miles of treeless tundra. What's going on? The cycle seems to take four year from "lots of lemmings" to "hey, did these guys just go extinct, or what?" This site takes some guesses as to the reasons; what do you think?

http://www.ec.gc.ca/cws-scf/hww-fap/lemming/
lemming.html

Hinterland Who's Who - Muskrat

It's not a beaver, it's not even a rat—it's really an overgrown field mouse that has adapted to life in and around wetlands all over North America. They don't build dams, but they do dig burrows in the soil along riverbanks. Muskrats have thick waterproof fur and can remain totally submerged for more than 15 minutes. This helps them dig underwater, root out tasty plants, and escape predators.

http://www.ec.gc.ca/cws-scf/hww-fap/muskrat/
muskrat.html

Hinterland Who's Who - Porcupine

How do you pet a porcupine? *Very* carefully, of course. His long brown guard hairs conceal barbed quills, which can be five inches in length! Some people believe that porcupines can "throw" their quills, but that's not true. Some of the porcupine's favorite foods include water lilies and other water-loving plants. Sometimes these creatures can be seen swimming (the air trapped in their quills helps keep them afloat). Learn more about this unusual rodent at this site.

http://www.ec.gc.ca/cws-scf/hww-fap/porcupin/
porcupin.html

What is the sound of one router flapping?

Hinterland Who's Who - Woodchuck

The woodchuck is one creature that has actually benefited from forest clearings to plant pastures and crops. If the land is well drained, there is probably a woodchuck or two about somewhere. At this site you can see a cross-section of an underground woodchuck burrow. In the winter, they hibernate, going into a deep sleep. They are able to lower their body temperature, reduce their heart rate, and reduce their oxygen consumption. In the spring, they awaken and come out to munch on the tender new vegetation—like the seedlings coming up in your garden! See also the HOLIDAYS—GROUNDHOG DAY section of this book.

http://www.ec.gc.ca/cws-scf/hww-fap/woodchuc/
woodchuc.html

Prairie Dogs @ nationalgeographic.com

Wow! Did you know that prairie dogs live underground? They are burrowing rodents a foot or so in length, weighing from one to three pounds. They're related to squirrels, but some early settlers thought their barks sounded like those of dogs, thus the name. At this site, you can listen to that sound (and others—do you wonder what a group of prairie dogs sound like when they all bark at once?), see what they like for dinner, and check out their tunnel!

http://www.nationalgeographic.com/features/98/
burrow/

RODENTS—RATS AND MICE

www.rmca.org/

Move over, Mickey—it's the Rat and Mouse Club of America (RMCA)! These pages are absolutely stuffed with more information and resources about mice and rats than you can ever imagine. Show standards, photos, pet info—this site is a pack rat's dream come true.

http://www.rmca.org/

SIRENIA—MANATEES

Manatees

Have you ever heard of the manatee? Found in waters around Florida, throughout the Caribbean, and into South America, manatees are gentle vegetarians that are also called sea cows. They are, believe it or not, related to elephants, and some think the myth of mermaids may have come from sailors who saw these graceful creatures swimming. To learn more about manatees, take a look at this page.

http://www.dep.state.fl.us/psm/webpages/
manatee.htm

MATH AND ARITHMETIC

Cool Math - Welcome to COOLMATH.COM by Karen!!

This is the greatest math site ever. Really, it has no equal. Want to multiply your fun on the Net? You can learn about tessellations and all kinds of other really neat math stuff here. Meet the Icosidodeca family and others in the divisions of the Polyhedra Gallery. There are no limits to what you can do at Cool Math—or are there? See for yourself! We'd add more, but we don't want to take away the surprise.

http://www.coolmath.com/

CTC's Trigonometry Explorer

This site offers a few Java demos from a larger CD-ROM about trigonometry. The easy-to-use applets include a little game of measuring angles with a protractor as well as a brief introduction to angles and their functions and pi. There is a bit on sextants, navigation, and latitude and longitude, too.

http://www.cogtech.com/EXPLORER/

Something fishy going on? Visit AQUARIUMS.

History of Mathematics

All kinds of math historical events and discoveries have been gathered here, including drawings and background information. Want to trace the history of calculus or check up on pi through the ages? Perhaps you need to know all about Egyptian math or find some facts on famous mathematicians. You'll discover a lot of fascinating information by wandering around this site. Who knows, you might one day be listed here for discovering some new mathematical wonder!

http://www-groups.dcs.st-and.ac.uk/~history/

Manipula Math with Java

Did you know everyone learns in different ways? Some kids learn by hearing something explained; other kids have to see something in a drawing or model; still other kids have to manipulate something themselves to really understand it. These wonderful Java applets let you manipulate geometric figures as never before. The Pythagorean theorem was never like this! Don't stop there—try clicking and dragging your way around some trigonometric functions. You'll also find applets in calculus as well as that ever-popular category: miscellaneous!

http://www.ies.co.jp/math/java/iesjava.html-ssi

NET FILES

Your grandpa has sent your dad a ticket for a lottery drawing out of state. How can you find out if your family has won?

Answer: *Check http://www.usatoday.com/leadpage/ lottery/lotto.htm for lottery winners in over 30 states. Good luck!*

A B C D E F G H I J K L **M** N O P Q R S T U V W X Y Z

A
B
C
D
E
F
G
H
I
J
K
L
M
N
O
P
Q
R
S
T
U
V
W
X
Y
Z

Staring off into space? Discover ASTRONOMY!

The Math Forum - Ask Dr. Math

Mom and Dad don't understand your math homework; neither does your best friend. But you can ask Dr. Math! You'll enjoy finding out the answers to some of the questions that kids have already asked Dr. Math, for instance: Can one infinity be larger than another? Why can't you divide a number by zero?

http://forum.swarthmore.edu/dr.math/dr-math.html

The Math Forum: Student Center

Part of a larger forum devoted to geometry, this page focuses on links that could be useful or of interest to students. Lots of games, projects, and downloadable software can be found here. Most interesting is the High School/Elementary Partnership program, which allows high school kids to act as Math Mentors for younger kids. There is also a Problem of the Week and an Internet Hunt, where you can search for answers to math trivia on the Net. In addition, there is a whole archive of math tricks so you can beat a calculator anytime you want!

http://forum.swarthmore.edu/students/

Online Math Applications

Here's a question for you: What does math have in common with investing? How about music, history, science, or travel? Some kids who wanted to enter the 1998 ThinkQuest Junior competition decided to create a Web page about math and its connections with each of these areas. It was so good that it was named one of the finalists! Stop by and learn about Mozart's effect, scientific notation, compound interest, pattern recognition of routes between cities, and lots more. And you thought math was only 2+2!

http://tqjunior.advanced.org/4116/

BRAIN TEASERS

Brain Teasers

If you're looking for some cool puzzles to stretch your brain cells, try this site. Every week you'll find new brain teasers, arranged by grade level. Typical puzzles include map reading, word problems, and puzzles that require a genuinely different outlook. Stumped? If you need a clue, the solutions are provided.

http://www.eduplace.com/math/brain/

Chapters of the MegaMath Book

Kids from 9 to 90 will have hours of fun playing the thinking games here, which involve flat and topological geometry as well as other math and logical concepts. Everything is presented in a colorful, simplified manner, so you may be surprised by the complexity of thought that is needed for some of these games. The Most Colorful Math of All, Games on Graphs (which can be played on a table or playground), Algorithms and Ice Cream for All, and The Hotel Infinity are some of the activities awaiting you here.

http://www.c3.lanl.gov/mega-math/workbk/
    contents.html

Puzzlequest: Main Page

Down under in Australia they've come up with a really neat way to understand math. There are more than 500 puzzles in the Quentacon Maths Centre, which travels around the country. Many of them are shared at this Web site, including a really interesting Williams family photo session. You see, there are all of these kids and the photographer is trying to line them up from tallest to shortest and...well, maybe you'd better head there yourself and help them figure it all out!

http://sunsite.anu.edu.au/Questacon/pq_main.html

Trick roping secrets are revealed in KNOTS.

CALCULATORS

The Abacus

As early as 500 B.C., the Chinese were using calculators! Not battery or solar ones, as we have today. An abacus has a graceful hardwood frame, divided into upper and lower decks. Within these decks are beads, representing numbers, which may be moved up and down thin bamboo rods. You can perform addition, subtraction, multiplication, and division on an abacus. To learn how to use one, try this site. There are also directions on how to make your own abacus out of Lego blocks.

http://www.ee.ryerson.ca:8080/~elf/abacus/

The Home Page for Users of TI Calculators and Educational Solutions

Some schools require kids to use a Texas Instruments (TI) graphing calculator when they start pre-algebra classes. It has a lot of neat functions and a nice little screen, but what everyone *really* wants to know is "Where do I get games and software for it?" You get them here. You'll also be able to join a free discussion list on TI calculators and find out what's new on the calculator scene. There are also some discount and refund offers at this site; tell your parents.

http://www.ti.com/calc/

SOL Web Calculator

Have you ever run all over the house looking for your calculator, then remembered you left it at school? There's probably a simple calculator located somewhere on your PC, but if you always forget where it is, just bookmark this site. It has all the usual basic functions and it never needs batteries!

http://www.sol.com.sg/classroom/simplecalc.html

The world's smallest abacus

Consider this tiny abacus. It is made up of molecules of carbon moved across a copper surface one at a time. If you use a soccer ball to represent the size of one of these molecules, the pointer that moves them would have to be as tall as the Eiffel Tower! View a movie of this abacus in action here, and say you saw it on the Net.

http://www.zurich.ibm.com/News/Abacus/

COUNTING

Bluedog can count!!

Painter George Rodrigue's famous character, Blue Dog, has appeared in paintings, books, and an animated film. Now she will solve simple math problems for you! Simply enter the problem on this page, then listen to Blue Dog bark out the answer. Actually, your browser will download and play a sound file of Blue Dog—the more barks, the longer it will take to load. Make sure your cat isn't around!

http://www.forbesfield.com/bdf.html

LifeLong Universe Monster Math

There's a monster of a party going on for some funny-looking and not-so-scary creatures. The trouble is, these monsters need you to help them count and add. They can speak in both English and Spanish, if you have the right plug-ins for your browser.

http://www.lifelong.com/CarnivalWorld/
MonsterMath/MonMathHP.html

Print A Googolplex

Mathematician Edward Kasner's nine-year-old nephew coined the name for a very large number. That number—ten to the power of 100, otherwise written as a one with a hundred zeroes trailing it—was named a googol. While this was a very large number indeed, perfect for trotting out at parties to impress people, another mathematician was unimpressed and came up with something even more immense: googolplex, a 10 to the power of googol. This page examines exactly what this incredibly huge number is, and it explains why no computer of today could ever print out something that large. You'll find a downloadable program here that will store a much-abbreviated version of a googolplex in about ten hours on a 10-gigabyte hard drive. The program is only 1,235 bytes in size and is triple-zipped so your Web browser won't try to unpack it automatically. Be the first (and probably the last) on your block to have your very own pet googolplex!

http://www.informatik.uni-frankfurt.de/~fp/Tools/
Googool.html

A
B
C
D
E
F
G
H
I
J
K
L
M
N
O
P
Q
R
S
T
U
V
W
X
Y
Z

A
B
C
D
E
F
G
H
I
J
K
L
M
N
O
P
Q
R
S
T
U
V
W
X
Y
Z

DRILL AND PRACTICE
Click on Bricks

Those darn multiplication tables can be so difficult sometimes. It was a real relief to find this ThinkQuest Junior site, where these different-color bricks can help you learn multiplication from one to four. There are also links to other math sites, so if you need more help, click here. Now if we could only find someone who knows about long division!

http://tqjunior.advanced.org/3896/

CSMP Home Page

Are you suffering the strings and arrows of CSMP (Comprehensive School Mathematics Program) at your school? Here is the home page for the publisher of these math materials. Each month there are new sample problems (and solutions in case you're stumped). If your mom and dad just don't get CSMP, have them read the introductory materials at this site. Then you can subscribe (free) to the CSMP listserv discussion group and talk to other families using these math materials.

http://www.mcrel.org/products/csmp/

NET FILES

Why is the Library of Congress' Legislative Information on the Internet named "Thomas"?

Answer: "Thomas" is named in honor of Thomas Jefferson. He was the third President of the United States and drafted the Declaration of Independence. The inscription "In the spirit of Thomas Jefferson, a service of the U.S. Congress through its Library" can be found at the THOMAS home page at http://thomas.loc.gov/.

Dave's Math Tables

Dave must be the smartest guy in the entire universe when it comes to math. He has written down just about everything you could possibly need to know, and he even helps you understand what it's all about. That's more than most mothers and fathers can do. In fact, your parents will probably be thrilled if you let Dave help you understand the solutions to your problems. General math, algebra, trigonometry, calculus—they're all here, and you can even download the information to study at your leisure!

http://www.sisweb.com/math/tables.htm

Flash Cards for Kids!

This set of flash cards for math was originally developed for an elementary school tech fair. They had so much fun with the program that it was put on the Web so everyone could use it. If you are having problems with a particular aspect of simple mathematics, or if you just like practicing your addition or division or other math tables, stop by here and have some fun!

http://www.wwinfo.com/edu/flash.html

Math for Kids A Medieval Adventure in Problem-solving

Two fourth graders developed this page, and it was one of the finalists in the 1998 ThinkQuest Junior competition. Using a medieval knights and castles theme, they offer lots of sample word problems complete with step-by-step instructions on how to come up with the correct answer. They also have an area where you can determine the proper strategy for solving a word problem. "Sir Godfrey has been collecting gemstones for three years. His favorite gems are rubies. Out of his 233 gems, 75 are rubies. How many gems does he have that are not rubies, if there are three other types of gemstones?" Did you get it? No? Read all the help messages and try again. Then try some of the other problems.

http://tqjunior.advanced.org/4471/

Mighty m&m Math Experiment

It is important to purchase proper supplies for this math experiment page. Go to the store at once and buy two big bags of M&M candies. One bag is for the homework. The other is to eat. This lesson was developed by a teacher in California who obviously knows a good way to teach fractions and percentages. Now this is our prediction: 100 percent of the students will enjoy 100 percent of the supplies when 100 percent of the work has been completed!

http://www.iphysique.com/school/main.htm

Welcome to the Math League

If this page had been around many years ago, Net-mom might have conquered long division when she was expected to! As it is, she still has trouble when it comes to fractions and decimals. But now that we have this page to practice with, there is renewed hope. There are lots of answers to lots of questions about mathematics here. There is also a great section explaining Math League contests and how to get involved in them. If you are a math whiz, you will love this place. In fact, even if you have problems with math, you're going to love this place!

http://www.mathleague.com/

FORMULAS AND CONSTANTS

Appendix E: Weights and Measures

You'll find a lot more about this topic in the REFERENCE WORKS section of this book. Still, we thought you'd find some of this Central Intelligence Agency resource interesting. For example, you've heard of megabytes (1,000,000 bytes) of hard drive space, right? The next step is a gigabyte (1,000,000,000 bytes), but did you know the next largest threshold is a terabyte (1,000,000,000,000 bytes)? And after that, well, we can't count that high, but this site says it's a petabyte (1,000,000,000,000,000 bytes). A petabyte of hard disk storage: bliss!

http://www.odci.gov/cia/publications/factbook/
  appe.html

The Joy of Pi

Pi is that endless mathematical number that helps us understand the relationship between the circumference of a circle and its diameter. You may think of it as about 3.14159..., but the number keeps going and going and, well, you get the idea. Lots of people have experienced the Joy of Pi; now you can, too. Parental advisory: Not all links have been checked.

http://www.joyofpi.com/

The Ridiculously Enhanced Pi Page #3

Every March 14, at 1:59 P.M., the Exploratorium museum celebrates Pi Day. Get it? The value of pi to a few decimal places is 3.14159! This irrational celebration happens to coincide with Albert Einstein's birthday. Read about the ceremonial addition of a pi bead to the strand (they are up to 1,600 decimal places) and other events that make San Francisco a unique place to live. There are also plenty of links to places where pi is elevated to new heights of acclaim by its many fans around the world.

http://www.exploratorium.edu/learning_studio/pi/

FRACTALS

Fantastic Fractals

For a fabulously fun-filled fling through the fascinating field of fractals, flip no further! Wait a minute! Just what is a fractal? This ThinkQuest site will fill you in on fractals on three different levels: for kids, for advanced kids who understand fractology, and for advanced fractologists (sorry, we just had to make up those words!). Now use your newly developed skills and create a fractal using Fantastic Fractals 98. Enter it in their (famous?) fractal contest and you just might win Fantastic Fractals 98 software of your own. At the very least, you will have discovered a lot about this interesting mathematical concept.

http://tqd.advanced.org/12740/netscape/

A B C D E F G H I J K L M N O P Q R S T U V W X Y Z

It never rains on the PARADES in cyberspace.

IFSoft Home Page

Fractalina is a program for making fractals and Franimate! is a program for animating fractals, and you will find them both right here. The programs were developed to allow middle school and high school students to illustrate problems dealing with fractals. Even elementary school students can try it if they wish, although it is beneficial to know at least a little about fractals before you begin using this site.

http://www.geom.umn.edu/java/IFSoft/

Sprott's Fractal Gallery

What is a "Julia set," a "strange attractor," or an "iterated function system"? They are all math equations that generate beautiful fractal images. A fractal drawing is the picture a computer makes as it maps out one of these equations. Sprott's Gallery includes sample programs to download and run on your computer so you can see fractals for yourself. There is a FAQ section and also lots of cool fractal pictures to download. Don't miss the animated GIF attractors!

http://sprott.physics.wisc.edu/fractals.htm

Is there order in chaos?
Discover the wonders of the Mandelbrot set.

Check out the fractals created daily using a program from the book Strange Attractors: Creating Patterns in Chaos *at Sprott's Fractal Gallery.*

GEOMETRY
The Fibonacci Numbers and the Golden Section

Leonardo of Pisa, Italy, was known as Fibonacci, the son of Bonacci. He was the greatest European mathematician of his time. In 1202, he wrote a book introducing the Hindu-Arabic number system to Europe. That is the base ten number system we use today, including the decimal point and zero. He also wrote about a sequence of numbers that could be found over and over again in nature. These later became known as *Fibonacci numbers*, and they describe the spirals of pine cones and the leaf growth patterns of plants. You can learn more about Fibonacci and his numbers here as well as investigate where they appear in art, architecture, science, math, and nature. Closely related is the *golden section*, and you will see how it is used in everything from origami to flags of the world.

http://www.mcs.surrey.ac.uk/Personal/R.Knott/ Fibonacci/fib.html

The Geometry Center Welcome Page

If you're looking for interactive geometry, you've come to the right place. Perhaps you'd prefer manipulating some of the Java or other Web-based geometric drawing programs. You can also download many of these to play on your own computer. One of our favorites is KaleidoTile for the Mac, which lets you create geometric figures you've never heard of before and can't pronounce (fortunately, a voice tells you what they are). The interactive "math you can manipulate" programs have big names, but don't let that put you off. Get into them, and have fun with the unique drawing tools. Check out the directions for building the world's largest 20-sided icosahedron. You probably need one for your room.

http://www.geom.umn.edu/

Surf, and you shall become empowered (or wet).

Math Tessellations

You may not know the word "tessellation", but you've seen the results of it before. Ever seen those M. C. Escher drawings with repeating geometrical patterns, where a fish turns into a bird? That's tessellation! But what does it have to do with math? Look at the tessellation art done by students at Highland School; then you can download a Tesselmania Demo and try it out yourself! These students live in Libertyville, Illinois.

http://www.mcs.net/~highland/tess/tess.html

MAGIC SQUARES AND TRICKS

Mathemagic Activities

Put one end of a rope in each hand and tie a knot without dropping the rope. Or amaze your friends with card tricks and other stunts. It's not magic; it's math!

http://www.scri.fsu.edu/~dennisl/CMS/activity/
math_magic.html

Smart Media - The Magic Square

Magic squares are those pesky little grid puzzles that require you to fill in the boxes with numbers so that they add up to the same total in every direction. Visitors to this site not only will find out what a magic square is, and generate odd-numbered squares with a click, but also will find out the amazingly simple solution for creating and solving their own. With a little practice, you can mystify your friends by easily writing out magic squares with any odd number per side! Next, try a magic square word puzzle; the examples here are amazing.

http://www.smartmedia.co.uk/games/games.htm

MATH GAMES

Fun Brain

How about playing some math baseball? You pick how difficult the math questions should be and decide if you want addition, subtraction, multiplication, division, or all of the above. Then the computer will ask you an arithmetic question. Can you get it right? Swing—wow, it's a triple! After that, see how good you are at making change of a dollar. How many pennies, nickels, dimes, and quarters should you give back after a certain purchase is made? This site has other fun games, too, including a concentration matching game.

http://www.funbrain.com/

Harcourt Brace School Publishers Math

Choose your grade and get ready for fun. It is amazing that you can learn a lot of math stuff while you are having such a good time. Take fourth grade, for example. With one click of the mouse, you can be working with Dr. Gee in the 3-D lab, helping her figure out what flat maps could be folded into which solids. Each grade has several areas you'll enjoy, along with a great glossary of mathematical terms.

http://www.hbschool.com/justforkids/math/math.html

NET FILES

How do you play "Chicken Skins"?

Answer: Chicken Skins refers to a version of competition golf where players play for points on each hole. In the popular "skins game," players get a point for each hole they win. If any two players tie, the point is added to the next hole (now worth two). In Chicken Skins, the points do not carry over to the next hole. Do you just love playing golf? Don't be chicken, try http://www.golfweb.com/glbb/glbbfun.htm to learn the rules of any golf game you can imagine!

The Web in Pig Latin? Make it so in LANGUAGES.

A B C D E F G H I J K L M N O P Q R S T U V W X Y Z

A
B
C
D
E
F
G
H
I
J
K
L
M
N
O
P
Q
R
S
T
U
V
W
X
Y
Z

Welcome to Lemonade Stand

In this easy-to-learn simulation game of high finance, you start with a fistful of dollars, a dream, and a weather forecast. Balance the cost of rent, lemons, and your advertising budget into your sales price per cup. Watch that weatherperson! Can you squeeze out a lemonade empire or will you lose all your lemons?

http://www.littlejason.com/lemonade/

STATISTICS AND PROBABILITY

Ken White's Coin Flipping Page

The teacher gives an assignment: write a 20-page paper on statistical analysis in modern-day America, or flip a dime 100 times and see what the odds of heads versus tails ends up to be. The decision is fairly simple to make, since you don't have 20 pieces of paper. Unfortunately, a quick check of the pockets, lunch bag, and locker shows that you also don't have a dime. Thank heavens for the SHAZAM Econometrics Team, which is willing to do the flipping project for you. Just punch in the number of flips you need and click on the flipping button. It'll be done before your mother can say, "Sweetie, do you have any homework to do?"

http://shazam.econ.ubc.ca/flip/

Statistics — Cast Your Vote!

You are about to become a statistic. Before you can learn about how statistical data is developed, you will be asked to complete a survey. Once you've posted your last answer, you will be ushered to an area where you can learn how polls are taken and what factors are used in weighing the results. This is an excellent place to visit if you'd like to understand more about the electoral process and how public opinion affects the end result.

http://www.learner.org/exhibits/statistics/

Never give your name or address to a stranger.

MODELS AND MINIATURES

Revell-Monogram—Model Mania

You're putting your model together and—oops—you've gotten glue all over the windshield. You try to wipe it off, but it just smears. Is there anything you can do? Yes. It will take some work, but if you follow the techniques at this site you'll be able to make your model look exactly like the one on the box. It's also possible to strip old paint off a model and start all over with a new painting scheme. You can also look through the new product catalog and find a history of this model company.

http://www.revell-monogram.com/

Scale Models: Front Page

Did you know that an old dental pick is great for cleaning up filler and carving plastic when you're building a model? It feels great to know you started with pieces, then put it together, painted it, and finished it off yourself. It doesn't matter if you like model ships, vehicles, figures, or fighter planes; it's all assembled here. Find out what new kits are available, and read reviews before you buy them. Learn how to build your model from the excellent online beginner's course. Get building!

http://www.clever.net/dfk/

Welcome to the Testors Web Site!

When you're building a model, chances are you'll want to paint it. You'll need to stock up on forest green, chrome yellow, and metallic flake, or maybe olive drab, flat black, and candy apple red. And you may choose to use Testors paints. This site gives extensive tips and tricks for painting and cementing like a pro. There is also a gallery of superb models—finished using Testors materials, of course!

http://www.testors.com/

AIRPLANES

EAST COAST MODEL CENTER - Introduction to R/C Aircraft

All you hear is a faint buzzing. Then, suddenly, a model airplane flies right over your head! Models fly at anywhere between 20 and 150 mph, although the average speed is about 40 to 60 mph. You need space to fly these sleek planes, and you need expert advice to get started in the hobby. Come in for a landing at this site.

http://www.ecmc.com/document/introrc.html

RAILROADS

See also RAILROADS AND TRAINS

The Lionel Station - Home of Lionel Trains

The Lionel Manufacturing Company was founded in New York on September 5, 1900. In 1901, they sold animated display trains called "The Electric Express" to draw customers to store windows. A year later, they published a 16-page catalog, but it wasn't until 1906 that their product line included steam locomotives, trolleys, passenger cars, freight cars, and a caboose. Since then, Lionel has become a name famous in model railroading. You can check out their history, catalogs, cool accessories (we liked the "Plutonium Purple" toxic tanker, but there is no accounting for taste), and tips for hobbyists. And there's lots of neat new stuff at Kids Station!

http://www.lionel.com/

National Model Railroad Association

Information on everything from garden trains—larger than O scale (1:48) but smaller than the trains that are large enough to ride on—to tiny Z gauge (1:220) trains is collected here. Want a track layout that does more than go around a Christmas tree? It's probably here. All aboard—the track's clear as far as you can see on the Net!

http://www.mcs.net:80/~weyand/nmra/

Welcome to Model Railroader

Some people like to collect precision-made miniature railroad cars, accurate down to the last bolt. Others like to build elaborate layouts, with running water and real plants for their model trains to roll past. Lots of people are in-between. If you're just getting started in model railroading, you'll find an online introduction here.

http://www.kalmbach.com/mr/modelrailroader.html

ROCKETRY

Irving Family Web Pages: Rocketry

Thinking about blasting off into the wide world of model rocketry? At this site, you can learn about it, see some rockets, and explore this exciting hobby. There's basic information on small, large, and high-powered rockets and some great picture samples to give you a look at what you can do. Now that you're this far, you may want more, so plenty of links to other rocketry resources are listed. Just consider this your launchpad to model rocketry!

http://www.irving.org/rocketry/

Everyone's heard of the 4-H Club. What are the four Hs?

Answer: In 1911, they stood for "Head, Heart, Hands, and Hustle…head trained to think, plan and reason; heart trained to be true, kind and sympathetic; hands trained to be useful, helpful and skillful; and the hustle to render ready service, to develop health and vitality." Now, however, they signify Head, Heart, Hands, and Health. The 4-H four-leaf clover emblem was patented in 1924. Read more about the program at http://www.fourhcouncil.edu/nhistory.htm

Catch a ride on a Carousel in AMUSEMENT PARKS.

rec.models.rockets FAQ Table of Contents

Here are the answers to many questions you might have about model rocketry, including basic questions such as: How do you do it? Where do you do it? Is it dangerous? Is it legal? Or, you may be experienced in model rocketry, and your questions are more like these: Where can I find engines that are discontinued? How can I prevent body tube damage from the shock cord? Should I invest in a piston launcher? Come on in, too! This site has categorized questions and answers for every level of rocket enthusiast. Now, should we use a thermalite fuse...?

http://www.ninfinger.org/~sven/rockets/
rmrfaq.toc.html

"Don't linger too long at the pewter wash basin at the station. Don't grease your hair before starting or dust will stick there in sufficient quantities to make a respectable 'tater' patch. Tie a silk handkerchief around your neck to keep out dust and prevent sunburns. Don't imagine for a moment you are going on a pic-nic; expect annoyance, discomfort and some hardships. If you are disappointed, thank heaven."

What is going on here?

Answer: *These are some of the hints given to passengers traveling by stagecoach from St. Louis, Missouri, to San Francisco, California, in 1877. The trip generally took about 24 days! Read more about it at* http://wellsfargo.com/about/stories/ch1/

MONEY

164 Currency Converter by OANDA

When is a dollar not a dollar? Wait a minute! Where did you get that dollar? Is that a U.S. dollar, or an Australian dollar, or a Namibian dollar? If it's a Namibian dollar, then it is likely worth less than half the U.S. dollar. The Australian dollar is worth more than the Namibian dollar but is still not worth as much as the U.S. dollar. Confused yet? What about the German mark, the Japanese yen, or the Slovenian tolar? Whoa! This stuff can get confusing. Luckily, at this site, with just a couple of clicks you can compare 164 currencies all over the world. Try it!

http://www.oanda.com/cgi-bin/ncc

Amateur Paper Currency Collecting

Most people like money. Most people like to spend money. Some people also like to collect it. At this site you'll be able to learn a lot about paper currency and what to look for when you begin a collection. Large denomination (that means how much the bill is worth) bills often have a watermark. That's a mysterious little pattern or portrait seen only when the currency is held up to the light. Lots of bills have a picture of someone famous on them, as well as a long serial number for identification. But in various countries there may be many other interesting components in a bill—bar codes, the name of the printer, or colorful threads. Stop here and learn it all.

http://www.wco.com/~chappell/

"We're flooding people with information. We need to feed it through a processor. A human must turn information into intelligence or knowledge. We've tended to forget that no computer will ever ask a new question."
—Admiral Grace Hopper

Bureau of Engraving and Printing

Did you know that Martha Washington is the only woman whose portrait has appeared on a U.S. currency note? It appeared on the face of the $1 silver certificate of 1886 and 1891 and on the back of the $1 silver certificate of 1896. There are lots more interesting facts to learn when you visit the Bureau of Engraving and Printing (BEP). If you are in Washington, D.C., you can visit in person, or you can do it right here if you are surfing the Internet. The BEP also has a really neat area especially for kids. Did you know that if you had 10 billion $1 notes and spent one every second of every day, it would require 317 years for you to go broke? Bill Gates had better start spending!

http://www.bep.treas.gov/

The Coin Collection/Pièces de collection

In 1996, the Royal Canadian Mint introduced a two-dollar coin. The reasoning was simple: coins last longer than paper money. A metal coin can survive circulation for about 20 years! The two-dollar bill was very popular, but the government had to replace them every year as they wore out. It costs more to make a coin, but over the coin's lifetime, Canadians will save millions. It's a very cool-looking coin, too. There is a smaller circle in the center, made of gold-colored aluminum bronze, while the outer ring is silver-colored nickel. There's a polar bear on the back. Kids call these coins "twonies." Why? Just for fun, and to differentiate them from the one-dollar coins. The one-dollar coin has a loon on it, and those coins are called "loonies." Learn a lot about the Royal Canadian Mint and the history of currency at this site.

http://www.canniff.com/mint/

Currency Comparison Page

Can you believe there's a project on the Internet dedicated to finding out just how much food you can buy for five dollars? And they mean you! The idea is to compare the value of your five dollars to the same amount of money in other countries. It's fun, and the interactive currency conversion chart lets you compare different money from all over the globe. If you're not from Albania, you might still be interested in just how much lunch the lek (Albanian monetary unit) will buy!

http://www.wimmera.net.au/CurrComp/
   CurrComp.html

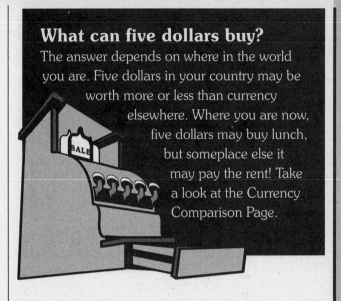

What can five dollars buy?

The answer depends on where in the world you are. Five dollars in your country may be worth more or less than currency elsewhere. Where you are now, five dollars may buy lunch, but someplace else it may pay the rent! Take a look at the Currency Comparison Page.

EURO

Soon there will be one currency for Europe, the euro. No more shillings, marks, or francs. Read about it at this site in the 11 languages of the European Union. This page is designed to help people make the switch from the present currency to the new one. There is even a calendar listing dates when events will happen during the changeover.

http://europa.eu.int/euro/

EduStock

EduStock is designed to explain what the stock market is and how it works. It includes tutorials on how to pick good stocks, information on a select group of companies, and a free 20-minute-delayed stock market simulation. Check it out and learn how to make your fortune. This site was the best entry in the 1996 ThinkQuest Contest for educational Web sites created by teens.

http://tqd.advanced.org/3088/

If you feel funny, think what we went through when we wrote the JOKES AND RIDDLES section!

A B C D E F G H I J K L **M** N O P Q R S T U V W X Y Z

A
B
C
D
E
F
G
H
I
J
K
L
M
N
O
P
Q
R
S
T
U
V
W
X
Y
Z

Foreign Currency - Bank Notes from Around the World

Instead of buying trinkets and doodads in his travels around the world, Randy Johnson returned with paper currency from the countries he visited. He has photo samples of currency from 27 countries, chosen for their beauty and interest. He includes a little bit of information on each and also provides a few links to other Web sites on collecting money.

http://www.ease.com/~randyj/money1.htm

Fun Brain

See how good you are at making change from a dollar. How many pennies, nickels, dimes, and quarters should you give back after a certain purchase is made? This site has other fun games too, including a concentration matching game and math baseball.

http://www.funbrain.com/cashreg/

The Inflation Calculator

Inflation is an interesting concept. Lots of times you will hear an older person talk about "the good old days" and how much—actually, how little—something cost back then. This inflation calculator lets you figure out just how much monetary values have changed over the years. A nickel candy bar in 1959 (yes, they did cost just five cents then!) would be priced at 27 cents today. Actually, they cost more than that, don't they? How do you explain that? Anyway, one of those '59 candy bars would be pretty stale by now! You can also explain to your dad that the $5 weekly allowance he used to get should really be translated into more than $26 today!

http://www.westegg.com/inflation/

Investing for Kids

How can you use money to make more money? What's the deal with stocks, anyway? And what the heck are mutual funds? This page, developed by kids for other kids, will let you check your knowledge of the stock market, play some money games, and learn about the world of financial investments. Study this ThinkQuest entry, then give your parents some advice!

http://tqd.advanced.org/3096/

Klutz Press: The Buck Book

Klutz Press publishes lots of very cool books (which are described in their catalog at this site), and one of the most fun is *The Buck Book*. It teaches you fun things to do with a U.S. dollar bill. For example, would you like to know how to fold a dollar to make a ring you can wear on your finger? The directions are here!

http://www.klutz.com/treefort/buck.html

Money Curriculum Unit

Money: you see it every day. You probably have some in your pocket right now. But how much do you know about its history and how it's made? Recently, the government has made many changes in U.S. money to make it harder to be copied. See what the new tricks are to stop counterfeit cash. And if you don't know what all the symbols on U.S. bills mean and whose portrait is on each one, then you will by the time you finish spending some time at this site!

http://woodrow.mpls.frb.fed.us/econed/curric/
money.html

NOVA Online/Secrets of Making Money

This is a fascinating look at the new security features built into the U.S. $100 bill. You'll discover color-shifting ink made possible by the metallic flakes mixed into it. Check the special engraving techniques used to foil counterfeiters, as well as the special items embedded into the paper the bill is printed on. These include the red and blue fibers, the microprinted security thread, and other items too secret to mention in print. But you can read about them on the Web! Then see if you can spot the bogus bill in the online quiz.

http://www.pbs.org/wgbh/nova/moolah/

Printing money

It takes 65 distinct steps to print a U.S. dollar bill. You can follow the process here at *Newton's Apple* and also learn how to make and print your own "pretend" money!

http://ericir.syr.edu/Projects/Newton/12/Lessons/
money.html

Everyone's flocking to BIRDS!

Sovereign Bank Presents: KidsBank.Com!

How does a checkbook work? What's interest? What does the bank do with the money in your account? Find out how banks work, how money is made, and even how electronic funds transfer takes place.

http://www.kidsbank.com/

Street Cents Online

Young people make money, save money, and spend money, just like everyone else! But sometimes there just isn't much advice for young people about handling their money. Do you spend money on entertainment, sports, music, and food? What's the deal on using horse shampoo on people? Does Duracell really outlast the Energizer bunny? All of these topics and more are covered by *Street Cents,* a popular Canadian television show. And now it's online in an informative and fun Web page.

http://www.halifax.cbc.ca/streetcents/

The part-time job in the newspaper sounds good, since you need a way to make some spending money. The boss says, "Let's try you out for one afternoon and see if you can do the job." That sounds like a fair request, but should you be paid for the tryout? Does it depend on whether you get the job? What are your rights? Young people have money concerns too, and Street Cents Online is worth "spending" some time to visit. It makes "cents"!

U.S. National Debt Clock

Did you know that if you're an American citizen, you owe the government about $20,000? That is currently every citizen's share of the national debt, and that is a lot of weekly allowance money! What's the national debt? The U.S. government spends more money than it takes in. When this happens, it has to borrow money from someplace else. The amount it owes to other sources is called the national debt. This site explains more about how this happened and what the government is trying to do to pay off the debt and keep this from happening again. Canada's also got a national debt clock, which is linked here, too.

http://www.brillig.com/debt_clock/

Welcome to Econopolis!

Let's join up with Mega Money and his pets Bill the horse and Dollar the dog. They're prepared to lead us on a tour through Econopolis, a ThinkQuest Junior Web page designed to help children learn about economics. There's a quiz at the end of each part of the tour, and an incorrect answer will take you back to the beginning.

http://tqjunior.advanced.org/3901/

MONSTERS

Build-a-Monster

This is a sweet little game to amuse the little kids in your family. Pick a head for your monster—how about that frog? OK, now choose a body—do you like that chicken? Now, which feet should you select? Yikes, that makes a very strange-looking monster, but it won't scare anyone.

http://www.rahul.net/renoir/monster/monster.html

Want a snack? Learn to make one in COOKING, FOOD, AND DRINK.

A
B
C
D
E
F
G
H
I
J
K
L
M
N
O
P
Q
R
S
T
U
V
W
X
Y
Z

A B C D E F G H I J K L **M** N O P Q R S T U V W X Y Z

HERE BE DRAGONS!

There are real dragons, you know! The Komodo dragon is the world's largest lizard, and it lives (among other places) on Komodo Island, which is part of Indonesia. Other dragons live in the fantasy worlds of literature, lore, and legend. This home page celebrates all kinds of dragons. You'll find dragon art, history, songs, and more. There's even a place where you can "adopt" your very own dragon! A parental advisory goes on this site because we haven't explored all the links.

http://www.draconian.com/

LifeLong Universe Monster Math

There's a monster of a party going on for some funny-looking and not-so-scary creatures. The trouble is, these monsters need you to help them count and add. They can speak in both English and Spanish, if you have the right plug-ins for your browser.

http://www.lifelong.com/CarnivalWorld/
MonsterMath/MonMathHP.html

Mind's Eye Monster Project: A Free Curriculum Based Language Arts Writing Project

This is a site that everyone is going to love—students, parents, teachers—you name it, stop here! It's simple. Your class draws a monster, but then you have to describe it well enough so that another class can re-create the monster just from the description! Teachers, take a tour of the site and see how your classes can discover new excitement in creative writing.

http://www.win4edu.com/minds-eye/monster/

Monsters in the Dark

You're not afraid of a few little monsters in the dark, are you? If you could just find the right light switch, you would see there's nothing to be afraid of. Uh— which light switch is it? If you ever get the right one, you can download a Windows-only monster-making kit demo.

http://www.imaginengine.com/dark/

Nessie, the Loch Ness Monster

Mark Chorvinsky has put together a remarkable Web site exploring the controversies surrounding Scotland's world-famous Loch Ness Monster. Nessie, as the lake monster is affectionately known, has been the subject of numerous credible sightings over the past 60-plus years, even though extensive scientific efforts to track it down have been a lesson in frustration. This page presents well-researched and clearly written essays on the sightings, the searchers, and the debunkers, as well as investigations into other, lesser-known lake monsters from around the world. For example, ever heard of Canada's Ogopogo? He/she's been spotted regularly since 1926 in Lake Okanagan, British Columbia.

http://www.strangemag.com/nessie.home.html

You've heard of Nessie—the Loch Ness Monster. But have you ever heard of Champ? It was first spotted in July 1883 cavorting in New York's Lake Champlain. This was 50 years before Nessie was first seen! Since then, Champ has been sighted over 240 times. Read more about Champ and other lake monsters at Nessie, the Loch Ness Monster home page.

**"Ships are only hulls, high walls are nothing,
When no life moves in the empty passageways."
—Sophocles**

The North American Science Institute

These folks take their Sasquatches seriously! Back issues of their newsletter, *The Track Record,* which include plenty of up-to-date Bigfoot sightings, are available here, as well as information about the ongoing Digital Bigfoot Conference. Links to other Bigfoot sites are also included. One of the best is The Bigfoot Research Project, which coordinates many of the efforts to gather solid evidence of the existence of this large, hairy, elusive creature. A caution to parents: Other links (in the "Skeptics" area) lead to places you may want to preview.

http://www.teleport.com/~caveman/wbs.html

A Yeti Tale: Introduction

The Abominable Snowman has been spotted high up in the Himalayas by a number of respectable mountaineers. He's known as Yeti, to folks in Nepal and Tibet, where he has been sighted countless times for hundreds of years. If Yeti does exist, chances are the creature is not possessed of magical powers, although legends about it persist. Read some of those legends here.

http://www.dzogchen.org/yeti/ytale1.html

MOVIES

See also DISNEY

The Academy of Motion Picture Arts and Sciences

If you're a movie fanatic, don't miss the Official Interactive Guide to the Academy Awards, designed to help you explore Oscar nominees and winners, past and present. There are pictures and lots of information on all of them. You may be surprised to find out that the Academy of Motion Picture Arts and Sciences does a lot more than just give out awards. They have an amazing movie history library, too. They also sponsor Student Academy Awards, designed to recognize excellence among college students enrolled in film courses throughout the United States.

http://www.ampas.org/ampas/

The truth is out there in UFOS AND EXTRATERRESTRIALS. Maybe.

Introducing the Internet Movie Database

Wow—this international volunteer effort covers over 150,000 movies! You can find info on the following: biographies of actors; plot summaries; character names; movie ratings; trivia; famous quotes from movies; goofs and things that went wrong but didn't get cut out; sound tracks; filming locations; sequel/remake information; advertising tag lines; and Academy Award information. If the movie is based on a book, you'll get that information here too. Butter up some popcorn and enjoy this site!

http://us.imdb.com/introduction

Viewers around the world have voted *Star Wars* as their all-time favorite movie. Did you know that part of it was filmed in Tunisia? The movie has a lot of famous mistakes in it, such as the scene in which a storm trooper hits his or her head on a door. To see famous quotes from the movie other than "Use the force, Luke!" and to learn lots of great trivia, be sure to check Introducing the Internet Movie Database.

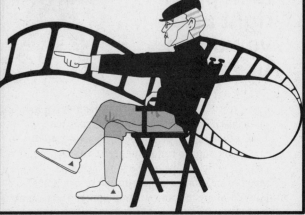

A B C D E F G H I J K L M N O P Q R S T U V W X Y Z

What time is it, anyway? Check with the atomic clock in TIME.

The Motion-Picture Industry: Behind-the-Scenes

Zap some popcorn, lean back, and be prepared to watch a movie produced by students with computer-generated special effects. Once you've scarfed down the snacks and seen the feature presentation, "Fat Man and Little Boys," head backstage and see just how they did it all. One thing you'll realize is that there's a lot of work involved in making a film, and a lot of work went into this ThinkQuest entry, which became a finalist in the 1997 competition.

http://library.advanced.org/10015/

NET FILES

What is likely to happen right after you do an Air Kedidi?

Answer: You'll fall down. Come on, admit it. Anytime you catch that much air and your legs start to pedal without a bicycle, you're probably going to hit the ground. Hey, we're talking inline skating here! Whether you're hard-core or just a flatlander, skate over to http://www.seas.smu.edu/~justin/inline/inline_terms.html where it's radical (and vertical)!

SOUNDS AND THEMES

IMDb Soundtracks Section Search

You loved a song you heard at the movies last night, but you have no idea what it's called or who sang it. Here's what you do: pop a word from the movie title into this searching machine to get all the details in a flash. You can do the same thing with your favorite group. We typed the word "Mozart" into the search box and found out his music has been in lots of movies, even *Operation Dumbo Drop*!

http://us.imdb.com/Search/soundtracks/

Newton's Apple: Movie Sound Effects

Grab your rubber bands, sandpaper, popsicle sticks, and tape recorder and head over to this site to learn how to be a foley artist. Foley artists decide which movie sounds need to be fixed, replaced, or just improved a little. They even invent sounds nobody's ever heard before, like the sound of a dinosaur egg hatching. They're named after Jack Foley, a film sound pioneer from the days when talking pictures were first invented.

http://ericir.syr.edu/Projects/Newton/12/Lessons/movisnd.html

Skywalker Sound

Learn how movie sound tracks are made from the pros at Skywalker Sound, where the famous sounds of the *Star Wars* movies, *Jurassic Park,* and *Toy Story* were made. One of Skywalker's specialties is creature sounds, like the ones made by Imperial Walkers, Chewbacca, and other aliens. To make these characters sound sad, happy, or scary, sound artists use everything from bicycle chains dropping on concrete to the voices of lots of different animals mixed together.

http://www.thx.com/thx/skywalker/skywalker.html

Earthquakes are only part of what's shakin' in EARTH SCIENCE.

www.filmmusic.com

Whether you're looking for movies with bagpipe music, the theme to *Jurassic Park* (watch out—it's 1.5 megabytes!), or music to shoot aliens by, this is the place. Movie music composers, collectors, and fans will find all the reviews, music clips, discussions, and guides they could ever possibly want at this site. External links have not been reviewed.

http://www.filmmusic.com/music/

MUSIC AND MUSICIANS

CDnow : Main : Homepage

This is an online store, where you can get your parents to order cassettes and CDs. It's also the home of the volunteer-built All Music Guide (AMG), which is a huge review archive for—guess what?—all music. You can search for albums by artist, title, or record label. This site also links to Real Audio files, so you can listen to some albums. A caution to parents: There are lots of artist home page and concert links.

http://www.cdnow.com/

The All Music Guide (AMG) will steer you to whatever music pleases you. Hundreds of independent music and film writers evaluate albums and give short reviews. Whether you seek rap or rock, country or classical, you'll find it at CDnow : Main : Homepage.

Eyeneer Music Archives

Find links here to world music, contemporary classic, new jazz, and American music. Each link will keep you busy exploring. In the International Music Archive you'll find an abundance of photos, sound samples, and descriptions of instruments. You can see and hear a Chinese *qin* or a Japanese *shakahachi*. Elsewhere, look for biographical information, photos, QuickTime videos, interviews, and information on new recordings.

http://www.eyeneer.com/

GRAMMY® Awards

Music is a universal language. Everybody likes music, whether it's pop sounds, rock and roll, rap, or R&B. Most music we listen to is recorded, either on tapes, CDs, the radio, or TV. The National Academy of Recording Arts and Sciences is an organization of recording specialists who vote on the best recordings each year. The winning recording artists receive an award called a Grammy. To see (and hear) who has won in the past and who is nominated for the upcoming awards, take a look at this page. It's the place to look if you like music!

http://www.grammy.com/

K-12 Resources For Music Educators

You can show this page to your music teacher, and it will really make his or her day. Resources are collected in categories for band, orchestra, and choral music teachers, and there are links for classroom music teachers. The selection is really interesting for the rest of us, too. You'll find composer biographies, newsgroups, MIDI resources, and hints on how to really *listen* to music. There are also links to free piano lessons by Web, online sheet music, and lots more.

http://www.isd77.k12.mn.us/resources/staffpages/shirk/k12.music.html/

Volcanoes are an explosive subject. Find one in EARTH SCIENCE.

A
B
C
D
E
F
G
H
I
J
K
L
M
N
O
P
Q
R
S
T
U
V
W
X
Y
Z

A
B
C
D
E
F
G
H
I
J
K
L
M
N
O
P
Q
R
S
T
U
V
W
X
Y
Z

Musi-Cal: Free Concert Calendar Search Engine

So you want to go to a concert or a festival. You like acoustic music (or blues, or ska) and your dad is willing to travel up to 20 miles from your home. Musi-Cal's advanced search will pinpoint the very concert you seek. The site strives to provide easy access to current worldwide music information. They promise no weird pictures, no old information, no 200K graphics to download. Search by performer, city, venue, or event, or go to "Options" for a detailed search form. It includes artist(s), event, city, radius around city (up to 200 miles, or 400 kilometers), dates, venue, musical genres, and even keywords. You can also contribute concert information. There are sometimes links to performers' Web pages as well.

http://concerts.calendar.com/

Music Education Online.html

This is a fabulous page with lots of links to everything musical. You can learn about a tuneful place in Los Angeles called the Children's Music Workshop, read about the various instruments in the band and orchestra (click on Music Links), and even find a music teacher who gives lessons in your very own community (in Music Links in the Music Staff category)!

http://www.geocities.com/Athens/2405/

Musical Sands

Here's something unique: did you know walking on some types of sand makes "music"? Here's a Web page about it—don't miss the sound of sand audio files!

http://www.yo.rim.or.jp/~smiwa/

On Air Concert

Sshh! It's time to listen to a musical performance featuring kids from all over the world! You'll hear Anne-Raphaelle (age nine, France) play the piano, Max (age six, U.S.A.) playing his violin, and many others. You can also send in your own audio files if you want to join the "band."

http://www.kids-space.org/air/air.html

VIBEonline: [The Mammoth Music Meta-List]

This site is like one of those nesting Russian dolls. Every link opens up a new world of music. Where else could you find Morris dancing, the San Francisco Symphony, and a sight and sound demo of different Renaissance consorts and instruments? The webmaster hopes to keep a relatively complete set of all music resources available at the site. If you have an interest in Christian music—or Indian, or Russian, or reggae (pick your subject)—it's probably here. The pop/rock section is huge, with bands both well known and obscure. Also there are links to the home pages of specific bands and musicians, as well as reviews and "top 40" and other countdown charts. The links to specific instruments are very complete. For whatever information you need or want on any aspect of music, start here. A caution to parents: Outside links have not been viewed.

http://www.vibe.com/mmm/music.html

WELCOME TO THE SAN FRANCISCO SYMPHONY

This site has specific information about the San Francisco Symphony (tickets, concert hall, and so on), and it also has real Web value. You can meet some of the 106 musicians—you'll see what they look like, why they chose their instruments, who likes baseball, and what other kinds of music they like. The Web Links lead you to searchable archives of listservs, reference guides to composers, music, and recordings, and an array of other symphonic ensembles.

http://www.sfsymphony.org/

CHILDREN'S MUSIC

The Banana Slug String Band

It's a concert! No, it's an education on ecology, wetlands, and oceans! No, wait, it's getting down and dirty with guys who play guitars and talk like insects. Hold on, it's all about how dirt made your lunch. We've got news: it's all of that and more.

http://www.bananaslugstringband.com/

The Bobby McFerrin: Home Page

Maybe he's not really a children's musician, but kids are fascinated by Bobby McFerrin, the "Don't Worry—Be Happy" recording artist. How does he make all those different sounds with his voice? This site provides biographical details as well as a discography and some of those amazing sounds.

http://www.bobbymcferrin.com/

Children's Music List

Here you can find *mucho* info on children's performers, recordings, kids playing music, and where to order tapes and CDs. Run down all those links: Resources, Children's Musicians, Record Labels, Retail Outlets, Songbooks, and Children's Musical Theater. They'll lead you to yet more musical information!

http://www.cowboy.net/~mharper/Chmusiclist.html

Children's Music Web

Want to know when your favorite performer is coming to a town nearby? Looking for a radio station that just plays music for kids? Want to find some online songbooks? Check here for an extensive collection of links about all this and more.

http://www.childrensmusic.org/

The Judy and David Page

This Canadian duo started performing in 1993. Are they the next Raffi(s)? Time will tell. In the meantime, they've put together a sweet home page. If you are in the audience when Judy and David perform, you'll find that every song they sing also has a part for you. Their online presence is similar. The Online Songbook includes the words (and some sound clips) of traditional children's songs and their original songs as well. After you listen to or sing "Alice the Camel," go to the coloring page, print out a picture of her, and color her to your liking.

http://judyanddavid.com/

Sharon, Lois & Bram Club-E

Club E? Of course! That's E for Elephant! Sharon, Lois, and Bram and their pal Elephant have been singing wonderful songs on TV, in concerts, and now on the Web. Well, Elephant doesn't actually sing. But he does dance. Sort of. OK, he moves around a lot! Look around and you'll find games, activities, lyrics, audio clips, and concert dates and locations.

http://www.destinyweb.com/elephant/

Welcome to Red Grammer's Homepage

Red Grammer is a wonderful songwriter and singer who travels all across the country performing at schools and in concert. He and his wife, Kathy, have written a lot of great tunes, including "Teaching Peace." It won a Classic Children's Audio Recording Award from Parents' Choice, an award few albums ever achieve. The All Music Guide declared "Teaching Peace" to be one of the top five children's recordings of all time. You can listen to some of Red's songs and see if he's coming to your school.

http://www.redgrammer.com/

COMPOSERS AND CLASSICAL MUSIC

BMG: Classics World

This is the place to satisfy your raging curiosity about early music, the Romantic period, the Renaissance, or even what's happening today in classical music. You can search by composer, read a short biography, and listen to sound clips from notable works.

http://www.classicalmus.com/

Burkat Notes

If you're going to an orchestra or chamber music concert, take a look at this site. You'll find good biographical information on many famous classical composers and maybe even be able to read the story behind the piece you'll hear.

http://www.culturefinder.com/composers.htm

A B C D E F G H I J K L M N O P Q R S T U V W X Y Z

A
B
C
D
E
F
G
H
I
J
K
L
M
N
O
P
Q
R
S
T
U
V
W
X
Y
Z

Classical MIDI Archives © 1998 Pierre R. Schwob

Take a musical tour of the greatest classical hits from the fourteenth century to the twentieth, sampling the tunes of more than 400 composers along the way. You can listen by time period, search for a composer's name, or explore by type of music: ballet, choral, motets, waltzes, and many others.

http://www.prs.net/midi.html

Classical Music - Classical Net - Classical Music

Parental warning: Off-site links have not been checked. People new to classical music have two questions: Which pieces should I listen to? What are the best recordings of those pieces? This dense site answers both questions. The "List of Basic Repertoire" is a tutorial on styles and forms of music organized by period, from Medieval to Modern. You'll also learn about each composer. Then there are reviews of recommended CDs. There's even a "Composer Data" section, with birth dates, further links to home pages, lists of works, and more classical links. Classical music spans nearly a thousand years. This site will give you a good start at understanding it.

http://www.classical.net/

Classical Music Cube ... The Music Beat

If you are a newcomer to classical music on the Internet, this site is a great place to start. It's a jumpstation to conductor's Web sites, music timelines, the history of classical music, musical terms, women composers, colonial music, and a whole lot more. The Music Beat spotlights various styles of classical music—opera, early music, and orchestral. Novice or expert, you'll like what you discover here. Parental advisory: We have not viewed all external links.

http://www.search-beat.com/classic.htm

> ## You never lose the pieces to the online games in GAMES AND FUN!

The J.S. Bach Home Page

The home page of J. S. Bach really does lead you to his home. Under "Biography," a clickable hypermap shows you the relatively limited geographical space he inhabited from 1685 to 1750. You can travel through time and space from Eisenach, Germany, where he was born, to Leipzig, Germany, where he died. Either click on the map or go from link to link in the right order. You'll see portraits of significant people and photos of buildings. Also, check the entry for his birth in the official birth registry in Eisenach. It's quite a time capsule! You'll also find directory information on his complete works here: by catalog number, category, instrument, and title. There is a similar listing for Bach recordings.

http://www.tile.net/tile/bach/

Mozart's Magical Musical Life

What if your parents named you Johannes Chrysostomus Wolfgangus Theophillus Amadeus Mozart? Can you imagine writing that on the top of your paper in school? This great story, complete with audio clips, tells about "Wolfie," or Mozart as we know him today. Wolfie had a sister named Nannerl and a dog named Bimperl. He also had a tremendous talent for music and a father who realized that his son was a genius. Is there a genius in your family?

http://www.stringsinthemountains.org/m2m/1once.htm

RCA: Idiot's Guide to Classical Music

Did you know that when you listen to the Elmer Fudd theme song ("Kill da wabbit! Kill da wabbit!") you're really tapping your foot to "Ride of the Valkyries" by Wagner? You probably recognize more classical music than you'd think! Take a listen to some of the sound bites at this site, and see which ones you know from TV commercials, shows, and movies. You'll also find a Beginner's Guide at this site which includes an online music mini-encyclopedia. It covers eras (no, not ears) and famous composers, with good graphics and solid information. You can get a little background on the composer of that new piece you're playing in orchestra this week.

http://www.rcavictor.com/rca/hits/idiots/cover.html

COUNTRY

COWPIE Bunkhouse

COWPIE stands for Country and Western Pickers of the Internet Electronic Newsletter. Look here to find country music songs: lyrics, tablature, and chords. They were gleaned from various newsgroups and other Net sources. Take a look at the archives of the newsletter. If you like it and you have an e-mail address, you can subscribe for free, and new issues will be e-mailed to you. The country music archives are worth a look, too. You'll find such gems as Jimmy Buffett's "Love in the Library" ("Surrounded by stories/Surreal and sublime/I fell in love in the library/Once upon a time").

http://www.roughstock.com/cowpie/

Great American Country Home Page

LeeAnn Rimes is a country superstar! She won a Grammy award as the Best New Artist of the year in 1997. You can find out all about LeeAnn's life, including her musical influences, her favorite foods, and things she likes to do when she's got a day off. All your other favorite country stars are here too, many with video and audio clips.

http://www.countrystars.com/

FOLK MUSIC

folkmusic dot org

This is the place to be if you're looking for info on acoustic music and musicians. There are artist biographies, collections, pictures, audio, lyrics, guitar tablature, tour schedules, and more! Want to see Mary-Chapin Carpenter in person? Try the festival and concert listings and information organized by date and by region. You'll also find pointers to other folk-related World Wide Web and Internet information. Parental advisory—we have not chased down all the links, so you should use this site with your kids.

http://www.folkmusic.org/

Richard Robinson's Tunebook

Haul out your fiddle (or flute, sax, or tuba) and try some of these great tunes. This is real sheet music! If you hang out with acoustic or traditional musicians, you'll recognize some of these tunes. Jigs, reels, polkas, schottisches, and more were selected from France, Finland, Turkey, and Cape Breton, as well as lots from the British Isles. There's bound to be some bourrée or other you've never played before. The real fun comes when you share the tunes with other players. Anybody can play them. If you've been taking Suzuki method lessons for a while, try something new. It's the 32-bar pause that refreshes!

http://www.leeds.ac.uk/music/Info/RRTuneBk/
tunebook.html

A
B
C
D
E
F
G
H
I
J
K
L
M
N
O
P
Q
R
S
T
U
V
W
X
Y
Z

Welcome to Arlonet!

Arlo Guthrie calls himself a "folkperson and part-time thinker." He made it big in the '60s with "Alice's Restaurant," a 20-minute song that eventually became a feature film. He's been around ever since, touring, writing songs, producing albums, and hanging out. He's even acquired the church that used to be Alice's Restaurant. Now it's home to the Guthrie Foundation (a charitable organization), the Guthrie Center, and Arlo's record label, Rising Son Records. The site has lots of lyrics, album covers, and some liner notes. You can link up to Pete Seeger, Bob Dylan, Bonnie Raitt, and other folk singers at this Web page.

http://www.arlo.net/

INSTRUMENTS

The In Harmony With EducationSM program

This is so cool. Think about those days when you are really bored and can't think of anything to do. You are so bored that even fighting with your sister doesn't sound interesting. You are thumbing through this book and suddenly—stop right here!—you discover a place where you can learn to make really cool musical instruments. We've been busy constructing a Splashaphone, an instrument involving empty soda bottles and a lot of water. Be sure to practice it only outdoors! OK, time to stop reading and start choosing the instrument you want to make. Hmm, this slide clarinet looks promising.... Have fun! You will need some help with the ones that require a drill, though.

http://www.menc.org/IHWE/ihwes1.html

Instrumental Music Resource Page

Here's help for "students, parents, and teachers of Instrumental Music." It's a good gathering place for much musical information. There are links to home pages for various instruments, a place where you can take a free drum lesson, and a list of great excuses you can use on your teacher when you forget to practice! But watch out—the teacher might be reading them too!

http://fcweb.fcasd.edu/~Dan_Traugh/imrp.html

Lark In The Morning

Where could you buy a hurdy-gurdy, or an Italian bagpipe, or an eighteenth century oboe? This site specializes in hard-to-find musical instruments, music, and instructional materials. They also sell recordings from all over the world and have sound samples to entice you to buy. Their picture dictionary, describing music makers strange only to us, is complete and fascinating. Read the articles on instrument repair, the interviews with musicians, the essays on various unusual instruments, humor, and dance, and other resources. Lark in the Morning is truly more than a music store. If you don't happen to live in Mendocino, California, you can still visit via the Net!

http://www.mhs.mendocino.k12.ca.us/

Renaissance Consort

Have you ever heard a shawm played? No? Well then, how about a crumhorn? A tabor? A bass viole? These were instruments of the hottest bands of the Medieval and Renaissance eras! You can see them and hear some rockin' audio files at this page from Japan.

http://www.hike.te.chiba-u.ac.jp/cons1/

WashingtonPost.com: Sounds of the Symphony

If you want to know a little about each instrument of the orchestra and hear a brief sound file of that instrument, this is the page that will ring your chimes.

http://www.washingtonpost.com/wp-srv/interact/
  longterm/horizon/121196/symphony.htm

Windplayer Online

Woodwind and brass musicians, take note. At this site, you'll find tips and advice from those in the know—professional musicians. The featured instruments are an unlikely quintet: trombone, trumpet, sax, clarinet, and flute. In each category you'll find player profiles (of artists like clarinetist Don Byron). Then you might take a master class from Herbie Mann on Brazilian flute playing. New products from many instrument makers are presented. And if you're in the market to buy or sell an instrument, check out the classified ads.

http://www.windplayer.com/

CATS are purrfect.

INSTRUMENTS—BRASS

The Canadian Brass

A review in the *Columbus Dispatch* called this group "the best thing to happen to brass music since the invention of the spit valve" (Barbara Zuck). They play music from Bach to blues, and some say they put brass music on the map. Their witty arrangements, vast repertoire, and humorous commentary beguile their audiences. Here you'll find biographies of each member, a history of the group, and brass-related articles from the *New York Times* and other sources. You can read mostly glowing reviews, check out the popular, classical, and Christmas discographies, and find out about their line of brass instruments and arrangements.

http://www.canbrass.com/

It's the eighteenth century. Do you know where your augers, gimlets, and bitstocks are? What kind of work do you do, anyway?

Answer: *You're a carpenter or woodworker of some kind. In Colonial times, these were very important tools for drilling holes of various sizes. Holes were needed to build everything from ships to harpsichords! Augers made the biggest holes, while gimlets drilled tiny pilot holes. Bitstocks were made of iron and had interchangeable bits, which could bore holes of several sizes. Find out more about Colonial tools at* http://www.history.org/life/tools/tlaug.htm

The Trombone Page

At this site you can explore the soul of the trombonist. There are also sound clips, a mouthpiece chart, and selected bibliographies. The Trombone-L listserv is a discussion list dedicated to "any aspect of the trombone"—even messy slide treatments. The archives are here, too. If you like what you read, sign on for daily reports from the Land of Trombone. The links include Web sites for other brass instruments, for example, trumpet, French horn, and euphonium.

http://www.missouri.edu/~cceric/

Trumpet Players' International Network Web Page

Trumpet players of the world, unite! At the TPIN site you'll find advice, lists of literature, facts about jazz and orchestral playing, and notes (so to speak) on improvisation. If you want a daily dose of trumpet lore, sign up on the e-mail Trumpet List. There's also an online chat server at this site. The graphics file includes pictures of performers such as Dizzy Gillespie as well as trumpets old and new. Go through the more than two dozen Web pages for individual trumpet players—some famous, some not. There's also a miscellaneous section on valve alignment, humor, performance anxiety, and trumpet myths. How do you get to Carnegie Hall? Practice, practice, practice—then stop, and read essays on practice routines you might try, written by famous performers and teachers. Even nontrumpeters can benefit from these specific ideas.

http://trumpet.dana.edu/~trumpet/

Who (or what) is a "haw-eater"?

Answer: *Haw-eaters are what Canadians born and raised on Manitoulin Island, in Lake Huron, call themselves. They like hawberries, the dark-red fruits of hawthorn species common in northern Ontario. Haws make delicious pies, tarts, and strudels. Find colorful tidbits of Canadian language trivia at* http://www.cangeo.ca/ND96Tongue.htm

A
B
C
D
E
F
G
H
I
J
K
L
M
N
O
P
Q
R
S
T
U
V
W
X
Y
Z

A
B
C
D
E
F
G
H
I
J
K
L
M
N
O
P
Q
R
S
T
U
V
W
X
Y
Z

INSTRUMENTS—KEYBOARD

All About Pianos

The King of Instruments. That's what they call the piano, for its tonal range (the piano covers the full spectrum of any instrument in the orchestra, from below the lowest note of the double bassoon to above the top note of the piccolo), its ability to produce melody and accompaniment at the same time (try that on a flute), and its broad dynamic range. It is also the largest musical instrument (excluding the pipe organ), most versatile, and probably the most interesting. You can learn just about anything you want to know—or need to know—about a piano here. Then you can order a book and begin your lessons!

http://www.tiac.net/users/pianos/

The Piano Education Page

Having fun while practicing the piano—isn't that a contradiction in terms? Maybe not. The "Just for Kids" section of this page features piano-related advice from Taz, tips for practice fun (really!), and an interview each month with a famous (sometimes dead) composer. There's a section on how to choose a piano teacher, studio etiquette, and lots of MIDI piano files.

http://www.unm.edu/~loritaf/pnoedmn.html

Welcome to Piano on the Net '97

Would you like to learn how to play the piano or maybe just how to read music? You can! The first few lessons don't even require a piano, but for later lessons you will want one. Even a small portable keyboard will do. This easy, reassuring series of modules includes QuickTime movies, audio files, even online metronomes to keep you in time with the music.

http://www.artdsm.com/music.html

INSTRUMENTS—PERCUSSION
The Bodhrán Page

Just what is a bodhrán? How do you even pronounce it? Find out here: it's "the heartbeat of Irish music," and it rhymes with "cow brawn." A large wooden round frame is loosely covered with goat skin (or donkey or greyhound skin!). The resulting large shallow drum is played with a double-headed stick. The head can be damped with the player's hand to make different tones. Look here for advice about making, buying, playing, and caring for the bodhrán. The usual assortment of tasteless musician jokes are also included (example: What do you call a bodhrán player with a broken wrist? A huge improvement!). Chieftains fans and Irish music lovers, check it out!

http://celtic.stanford.edu/instruments/bodhran/ bodhran.html

NET FILES

Happy Maewyn Succat's Day! You probably celebrate this holiday under another name what is it?

(Hint: It's in March.)

Answer: It's Saint Patrick's Day! Maewyn Succat is believed to be his original name. He changed his name to Patricus, or Patrick, when he became a priest. Did you know he was not Irish? He was born either in Scotland or Roman Britain. Read more at http://www.nando.net/toys/stpaddy/stpaddy.html

Change Ringing Information

Have you ever heard the sound of bells from a church and thought how much fun it would be to pull the bell ropes and work the levers yourself? If a church has several bells, sometimes a group of people can perform what is called change ringing. The object is to ring the bells in succession, according to specific patterns, which are often complex and lengthy. A change ringer needs to be very aware of timing, to pull the bell through a ring and have it stop at the top of the arc, mouth up. If it stays there for a split second, the next bell in line becomes the "lead" bell and the "round" starts with that bell. Each bell takes a turn at being the lead bell, and the others switch positions in the order of ring. According to this page, "Twenty-four changes [is called] Plain Bob Minimus, and twenty-four changes are all the permutations possible on four bells. It takes less than a minute to ring. If you add a bell, you have Plain Bob Doubles: 120 different permutations are possible on five bells. Each new bell brought into the pattern multiplies the number of changes which can be rung without repetition. Six bells offer 720 changes; seven: 5,040, and a peal. A peal entails five thousand or more changes without break, without irretrievable errors, and (when seven or more bells are being rung), without repetition. It takes six or more people working together coordinating hand and eye, minding permutations and bells for three hours or more." You will learn all about the history of change ringing here and find out where you might be able to hear it, learn it, and participate in it!

http://web.mit.edu/bellringers/www/html/
   change_ringing_info.html

The Drums and Percussion Page

Is there a drumming circle near you? If so, this site will lead you to it. You'll also find specifics about drumming, like choosing and caring for drums, drum etiquette, and percussion folktales. The standard methods of drumming are included. And there are grooves—transcriptions and patterns, like paradiddle, Latin rhythms, and ska. Check out the hand drum grooves, from Abakua (Cuban) to Zebolah (Congolese). You'll find an illustrated encyclopedia of percussion instruments and lots of other drum-related sites linked here, too. Once you find one, you're on to them all.

http://www.cse.ogi.edu/Drum/

Kids, Percussion, and Stomp

Is pure rhythm really music, or is it just a cacophony of noise? If you go to a performance of STOMP, you will see and hear the cast members "play" Zippo lighters, push brooms, trash cans, newspapers, and other common objects. Visit this Web site to see and hear audio from the show and learn more about the science of rhythm.

http://www.usinteractive.com/stomp/instruments/
   instruments.html

INSTRUMENTS—STRINGS

The Classical Guitar Home Page

Suppose you've been playing classical guitar since three weeks ago last Tuesday. Is there anyplace you can find quality guitar music with fingerings? Try the Classical Guitar Beginner's Page on this site. Whether you're a beginning or experienced classical guitarist, you'll have fun browsing here. The Beginner's Page suggests recordings, books, and videos to get you off to a good start. Suggested playing includes pieces by Carulli and Sor in GIF format, with MIDI files to go along with them. More complicated music is available in "Guitar Music," with pieces by Bach and Satie and a flamenco exercise. If you like the flamenco exercise, look at the Flamenco Guitar Home Page. There are links to guitar organizations, with reviews of concerts and recordings and guitar-related articles.

http://www.guitarist.com/cg/cg.htm

Dansm's Home Page, Acoustic Guitar

So you have never picked up a guitar and you're not really sure what the word acoustic really means. This is the place where you belong. Dan Smith, a Cornell University student and guitar player, has developed one of the greatest Web pages—if not the greatest Web page—on the subject. He explains everything you need to know. Take some time first to let Dan help you choose the guitar meant just for you. Then get yourself an instrument and play.

http://www.dreamscape.com/esmith/dansm/

A
B
C
D
E
F
G
H
I
J
K
L
M
N
O
P
Q
R
S
T
U
V
W
X
Y
Z

A
B
C
D
E
F
G
H
I
J
K
L
M
N
O
P
Q
R
S
T
U
V
W
X
Y
Z

The Internet Cello Society

Cellists young and old, amateur and pro, will love this site. Here's an introduction to the instrument, including an interactive multimedia presentation. You'll find out about repertoire, history, and famous artists and teachers. If you're a young cellist, there's a special section just for you on getting started and on picking what to play and what to listen to. In a photo tour, Baby Alec will introduce you to the parts of the cello. Don't miss the sound samples in the "Guide for the Clueless" (the harmonic bugle call would make a great start-up sound). The Tutor includes a few goofy exercises—hey, everyone, time to hug your cello!

http://www.cello.org/

INSTRUMENTS—WOODWINDS

Bagpipes at Best

Where else but on a page devoted to the playing of bagpipe music could you hear a tune named "The Clucking Hen"? Bagpipes are interesting to listen to, and this page has more than two hours of bagpipe music. This can be useful. When you're trying to get everyone up early to go fishing, head to this site, choose "Scotland the Brave," and turn up the volume. Everyone will be very surprised.

http://www.geocities.com/Area51/Corridor/7562/
    MUSIC.htm

David Daye's Bagpipe Page

Chances are that your instrumental music teacher won't ask if you want to learn the bagpipes. For one thing, they're not played in most bands. For another, the pipes are a difficult instrument to master. The first lesson is that you blow into the bag and then move your arm on the bag to pipe the air into the chanter, where your fingers—if placed on the proper keys—make the music. You should also know that there are no flats or sharps in bagpipe music. If you're still interested, check this page out. This guy sounds like he knows everything about playing the bagpipes.

http://www-bprc.mps.ohio-state.edu/~bdaye/
    bagpipes.html

The Recorder: Instrument of Torture or Instrument of Music?

Nicholas Lander, webmaster of this site, ponders the above question. While mulling it over, he imparts information on history, technique, and repertoire of the recorder. His notes on fingerings and vibrato techniques are very complete. He also has links to recorder makers, catalogs, MIDI files, and references to journals and books.

http://www.iinet.net.au/~nickl/torture.html

NET FILES

In the Chinese calendar, when is the Waking of Insects?

Answer: It's from the fifth or sixth of March, as the earth awakes from hibernation, according to the Chinese New Year page at http://www.chinascape.org/china/culture/holidays/hyuan/newyear.html

JAZZ

Jazz Improvisation

How does jazz work? This site can tell you. Not for performers only, these lessons on jazz theory and practice fill you in on history, fundamentals, and playing with others. You'll get new insights into the heart of jazz. Also take a look at the shorter "Jazz Improvisation Primer." The rest of this site is an entire jazz library. Other links are to Pop and Commercial Music, Jazz Education resources, and World Music, where you'll find Chinese, Russian, and Bulgarian sounds, and the Mbira Home Page! Also take a look at European jazz, more photos, and jazz literature. Bring a sandwich and spend the day here.

http://hum.lss.wisc.edu/jazz/

Marsalis on Music Online Home Page

Wynton Marsalis, the great jazz and classical trumpet player, says, "We play at music, we don't work at it." This site is a great place to play with music. It's an overview of the four-part PBS special, *Marsalis on Music*. Marsalis taped this show at Tanglewood, Massachusetts, in front of a live, young audience. Yo Yo Ma and Seiji Ozawa also appeared on the show. You'll get an idea of what each episode is about. "Why Toes Tap" introduces rhythm and meter. You'll get some background on wind bands and early jazz in "From Sousa to Satchmo." Marsalis also has advice on "taming the monster"—how to practice productively and enjoy it. You can take the interactive quizzes for each show. The Blow Your Horn link allows you to express yourself: ask a question, share a musical anecdote, or talk about your favorite performer. Musical Accompaniments has software you can download so you can listen to the audio examples. Ordering information for the video and book of the series is also included. On the Welcome page is the complete transcript of a live chat appearance in November 1995. Marsalis answers questions about the television series and his experiences, and he gives advice to aspiring musicians. As Wynton Marsalis says, "The world of music always accepts new citizens. It's never too early or too late."

http://www.wnet.org/archive/mom/

WNUR-FM JazzWeb

Look in "The Styles of Jazz" at the clickable hypermap. It's a chart that somehow manages to place everything from blues to bebop in the proper perspective, both time- and place-wise. When you click on "ragtime," for example, you are given a fascinating article on the history and particulars of that style of jazz. You'll find artist biographies, discographies, and reviews in "Artists." In "Performance," you'll find out about festivals, venues, and regional jazz information. You can also pick an instrument, such as the guitar, organ, trombone, or violin, and find more information on resources and musicians. There are also links to media: radio stations on the Web, magazines, and a few books (remember books?).

http://www.nwu.edu/WNUR/jazz/

LYRICS

Delmont Scout Reservation and Resica Falls Scout Reservation 1996 SONGBOOK

Summer camp is known as a great place for mosquitoes, strange food, and learning songs to annoy your parents! If you need the words to favorites like "Do Your Ears Hang Low?" this is the place! Simple skits are also included.

http://cac.psu.edu/~jxm181/songs.html

The Digital Traditions Folksong Database Search Page

What makes a song a folk song? Folks sing them, of course! The Mudcat Cafe's Digital Tradition Folk Song Database is a "not-for-profit, not-for-sale, not-for-glory" collection. The 5,000-plus (and growing) songs are searchable by keyword, title, and tune. If you're interested, look at the detailed notes on how to search and how songs get included in the database. A caution to parents: Not all songs are for children.

http://www.deltablues.com/folksearch.html

A B C D E F G H I J K L **M** N O P Q R S T U V W X Y Z

Folksong Index / Volkslieder Verzeichnis

This is a wonderful place to visit if you remember part of a folk song but not all of it. Head for the USA section—you can also find folk songs from a lot of other countries—and choose a letter of the alphabet. Let's say you hear your father singing something about Alexander's Ragtime Band, but he can't remember if it's the "best band that am" or the "best band in the land." The answer is here! You'll also read the lyrics to a lot of songs you've never heard before. Did you know there is a song entitled "The Dutch Came to Missouri"? Surprise your music teacher with that one.

http://acronet.net/%7Erobokopp/folkindx.htm

Songs for Scouts

Gather 'round the campfire and share some singing—here are silly songs, lots of gross songs, and songs that are just plain fun. If you want the definitive version of "Greasy Grimy Gopher Guts," look no further.

http://www.macscouter.com/Songs/

Welcome to the Tower Lyrics Archive!

At Tower Lyrics Archive, you'll discover lyrics to Broadway and Disney shows. Take a look at Andrew Lloyd Webber's *Cats.* Since it's based on T. S. Eliot's *Old Possum's Book of Practical Cats*, you'll find wonderful cat poetry here. The Disney archive has words to songs from *Aladdin, Beauty and the Beast, The Jungle Book,* and *The Little Mermaid.* For Gilbert and Sullivan fans, *The Pirates of Penzance* (with the song "Modern Major General") and three other entire plays, with dialogue as well as lyrics, are available. The rock opera *Tommy* and movies such as *The Nightmare Before Christmas* and *Grease* are also here.

http://www.ccs.neu.edu/home/tower/lyrics.html

MARCHING BANDS
John Philip Sousa (1854-1932)

If you are listening to a band parading down the street, chances are good it is playing a tune written by John Philip Sousa. He wrote more than 130 marches during his lifetime. Although he died in 1932, Sousa is still known as The March King and his pieces are played thousands of times each year by bands throughout the world. This site has some neat information about Sousa and sound clips of some of his more famous tunes. It also has lots of links, including ones to the bands of the U.S. military. Did you know that the United States Marine Corps band is called "The President's Own" and that it closes its weekly Washington, D.C., concert with a Sousa march? A few years ago, President Ronald Reagan named Sousa's "The Stars and Stripes Forever" as the national march. We guarantee you'll be humming his tunes and tapping your toes before you leave this page.

http://www.dws.org/sousa/

NET FILES

Everyone knows the Liberty Bell is cracked.

How did that happen?

Answer: It cracked the first time it was test rung, while it still at the English foundry where it was cast in 1752. It was given to a Philadelphia foundry to be recast in 1753. It was then hung in the tower of Philadelphia's Independence Hall. The most important time it rang was on July 8, 1776, when it was called people to hear the first public reading of the Declaration of Independence. Over the years, the crack in the bell became worse and worse, until by 1846 it was too damaged to be rung. There are several known recordings of the bell. Its sound was broadcast to all parts of the country on June 6, 1944, when Allied forces landed in France. Every year, it is symbolically "tapped" on the Fourth of July. Read more at http://www.libertynet.org/iha/libertybell

Links to Marching Bands

Do you love a parade? If you're a fan of *The Music Man* or if you're in a band yourself, this is the site for you. Bands by the score, of every description, abound. You can see pictures, statistics, contest standings, and lots of homecoming celebrations from all over the U.S. You can download sound clips, too. "Professional" bands, like the Right Reverend Al's Screamin' Hypin' Revival Band ("dedicated to the production of camaraderie and volume") vie with the 60 or so college bands. You'll find great variety here, from the straight-laced traditional bands like Michigan State to the newer "scramble" bands of the Ivy League schools. Take a look at "The World's Worst Marching Band" or the international bands (especially if you read Norwegian). Even if you don't play the glockenspiel, these links are good fun. Links to instrument jokes for every instrument and musical style are fun (although a few may be mildly racy).

http://seclab.cs.ucdavis.edu/~wetmore/camb/
other_bands.html

MUSIC GAMES
Hop Pop Town

Precious musical games let preschoolers record a song or experiment with notes and instruments. Here's a writing activity that makes a cute, illustrated story. It's easy to use, with a little help from an adult or older brother or sister; the little ones learn about music and the mouse, and the "helpers" learn how to think more creatively!

http://www.kids-space.org/HPT/

Mozart's Musikalisches Würfelspiel

Do you know anything about a minuet? Here's a hint: it has something to do with music, and it deals with timing. Play a game devised by the great composer Mozart. That's right, a *game*. He wrote the measures and instructions for a musical composition dice game. Tell your orchestra teacher about this. She will think you are crazy. Then show her the site, and she'll think you're a genius and promote you to first chair. Just follow the instructions and "compose" your own minuet.

http://204.96.11.210/jchuang/Music/Mozart/
mozart.cgi

Welcome to Philomel Records!

You know what an optical illusion is: a picture that can look like several different things all at once. (If you don't know, check the OPTICAL ILLUSIONS section in this book.) Are you ready for an audio illusion? Diana Deutsch's CD is called *Musical Illusions and Paradoxes,* and you can hear several samples at this Web site. Did you know that people hear sounds differently? Sometimes your brain can be tricked into hearing melodies that aren't really there. Sound impossible? Listen to the audio files here and see if you can identify the mystery tune.

http://www.philomel.com/

MUSICAL THEATER
Musicals.Net

You are a talented kid! If you can't decide between singing, dancing, or acting, you can do all three in musical theater. Hey kids, let's put on a show! Let's find one we like, first. At this site you can explore the stories, songs, and productions of favorite musicals old and new—from *Annie* to *The Wiz.* There's lots of news and up-to-date info on all the current shows, too, including *The Lion King.*

http://www.musicals.net/

NET FILES

Why is ROY G. BIV important?

Answer: *ROY G. BIV is the name scientists made up to help them remember the colors of the rainbow, in order from top to bottom: red, orange, yellow, green, blue, indigo, and violet. Read more about light at* http://nyelabs.kcts.org/nyeverse/
episode/e16html

**OPTICAL ILLUSIONS: now you
see them, now you don't!**

A
B
C
D
E
F
G
H
I
J
K
L
M
N
O
P
Q
R
S
T
U
V
W
X
Y
Z

On Broadway WWW Information Page

A live performance in a theater—there is nothing like it. Lights, stage props, music, and acting are all parts of what makes the theater great. If you've ever seen or participated in a play, you know it can be fantastic! Some of the best theatrical performances take place on Broadway in New York City. Want to know what's playing there right now, plus get reviews of the performances and maybe hear some sound clips? The Antoinette Perry (Tony) Award is presented annually for distinguished achievement in the professional theater. These are the best of the best, and if you like theater, take a look to see which plays have won.

http://artsnet.heinz.cmu.edu/OnBroadway/

The Phantom of the Opera Home Page

This page celebrates the popular musical about love between a singer and a ghost in the Paris Opera House. Or was he a ghost? Come experience the "Magic of the Night," but watch out for that chandelier! Lots of kids love the special effects in this production as much as they love the music. This page offers chat sessions about the musical as well as the story, sound clips, and a FAQ section.

http://phantom.skywalk.com/

ROCK GROUPS

Elvis Presley's Graceland

Ever heard of Elvisology? Neither had Net-mom until she dropped into this Web site to pay her respects to The King. It includes an official biography, a list of all the recordings and movies, and answers to frequently asked questions about Elvis. There is also lots of trivia, such as this statistic on Graceland in Memphis, TN: "Graceland, Elvis Presley's home and refuge for twenty years, is, today, one of the most visited homes in America, now attracting over 700,000 visitors annually. It is also the most famous home in America after the White House." If only the White House had a jungle room perhaps it would have ranked higher!

http://www.elvis-presley.com/

The Internet Beatles Album

A splendid time is guaranteed for all! Look here for Beatles history, interviews (sometimes as audio files), lots of photos, and some gossip. The information is classified using Beatles song titles. For instance, the section called I Want to Tell You debunks (or verifies) certain Beatles rumors. Is "Lucy in the Sky with Diamonds" about drugs? No. Four-year-old Julian Lennon's drawing of the same name gave John the inspiration, and you can look at the picture here. Eight Days a Week tells you what happened today in Beatles history. Nowhere Man explains and updates the "Paul is dead" rumors.

http://www.primenet.com/~dhaber/beatles.html

Marybeth's Memorable Melodies

The '50s and '60s were famous for a lot of memorable music. Some of it is enshrined in the Rock and Roll Hall of Fame. A lot of the rest of it is at this site. Listen to Real Audio of songs your parents loved: folk music, protest songs, girl groups, surfing music, even really classic stuff like "Itsy Bitsy Teenie Weenie Yellow Polka Dot Bikini." And your parents think the music *you* listen to is weird!

http://www.rockinwoman.com/

The Official Hanson Web Page

Out in "The Middle of Nowhere" in cyberspace is the Official Hanson Page, where you can "Mmm bop" 'till you drop. Find out the very latest updates from the brothers Hanson as they continue to take on the pop world by storm. There's also an official Hanson store where you can buy T-shirts, hats, posters, and even a current calendar. Check out the Hanson chat room but notice the warning that the brothers do not make unannounced chat appearances there, so if you think you're talking to Zak, you're probably not.

http://www.hansonline.com/

Crack open CODES AND CIPHERS.

Rock & Roll Hall of Fame + Museum

Are these really the 500 songs that shaped rock and roll? Well, it's a start, and if you have other ideas, you can always vote in the Ballot Box for your personal choice. The Rock and Roll Hall of Fame and Museum is in Cleveland, Ohio, and it is a little bit like the Baseball Hall of Fame in Cooperstown, New York. Read profiles of the rock legends who have been inducted into the Hall of Fame and listen to their audio files. You can also read about and listen to the 500 songs. If you take the virtual tour to the museum's exhibits, say "Hi" to Eddie the Elevator Man. What rock star was born on your birthday? A file in "Play Around" will tell you. And there are searchable archives and articles (from the *Cleveland Plain Dealer*) about "Cities That Formed Rock & Roll," such as Detroit, Los Angeles, and Liverpool, England.

http://www.rockhall.com/

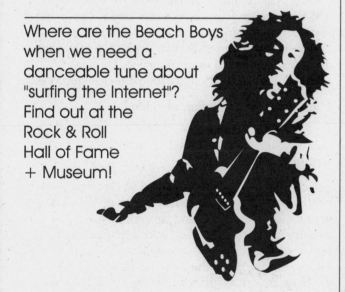

Where are the Beach Boys when we need a danceable tune about "surfing the Internet"? Find out at the Rock & Roll Hall of Fame + Museum!

SACRED MUSIC

Although some denominations like to share their religious songs on the Net, others feel the music is too sacred to be exposed in this way. We continue to seek out great sites containing sacred music from many faiths. If you find one or develop one, we would be very pleased to know about it.

The Cyber Hymnal

This site has more than 1,200 Christian hymns and sacred songs from many denominations. They are available in MIDI format for your listening pleasure. Don't remember the words? The lyrics are here too, and you can sing right along. You can also view hymns by topic, for example, Children's Hymns.

http://tch.simplenet.com/Default.htm

SACRED MUSIC—CHRISTIAN

Chant

In New Mexico is a Benedictine monastery called Christ in the Desert. The Brothers chant the Divine Office daily. It is a series of seven prayer sessions throughout the day and one at night. They have recorded some of their sacred chants so you can learn about them. This is a beautifully designed site.

http://www.christdesert.org/noframes/chant/
chant.html

Christian Music Online Welcome Page

For rock and other popular music with a message, look here. You'll find album covers, long biographies, and lyrics to songs by artists such as Amy Grant and Guardian. You can browse the artists alphabetically. There's also a link to two Christian magazines: *Christian Calendar* magazine has sample interviews with William Bennett and others; *Release* is specifically about Christian entertainment.

http://www.cmo.com/

A
B
C
D
E
F
G
H
I
J
K
L
M
N
O
P
Q
R
S
T
U
V
W
X
Y
Z

SACRED MUSIC—JEWISH

The Jewish Music Home Page

At this site you'll find CDs, videos, sheet music, and music books of interest to those of the Jewish faith. Many popular Jewish artists are featured (Mandy Patinkin, Barbra Streisand), but you'll also be able to explore children's recordings ("Because We Love Shabbat," "Aleph Bet Boogie," and more) as well as Passover and Chanukah songs. Audio files for many of the titles are available. Check out the links for more information.

http://www.jewishmusic.com/

WORLD MUSIC

Ceolas celtic music archive

Celtic music can be defined rather loosely as music from Ireland, Scotland, Wales, Brittany (France), and Galacia (Spain), with U.S. and Canada also contributing. This site is truly a Celtic cornucopia. The Ceolas Archive includes radio stations, magazines, events, and local information. "What is Irish Music?" "Hearing Irish Music," "Learning Irish Music," and "Studying Irish Music" are some good pamphlets from the Irish Traditional Music Archive. Ceolas: Tunes has links to GIF and "abc notation" formatted music. There are more links to tunes, listservs, newsgroups and mailing lists, festivals, and concerts. And all those interesting Irish instruments, like Uilleann pipes, bodhráns, and tin whistles, have explanatory essays.

http://celtic.stanford.edu/ceolas.html

JAMMIN REGGAE ARCHIVES Home Page

Immerse yourself in this deep reggae site. You'll find: a huge archive of articles, including a sketch of Rastafarian history; .au and .wav audio; and books, graphics, interviews, and biographies of artists. Find reggae radio stations near you. Check out tour schedules. Look at all the Bob Marley Web pages, plus many other artists' home pages. And there are associated Web sites on ska and Jamaica. Not all links have been checked.

http://niceup.com/

MAUI MUSIC PAGES

Listen to beautiful classical and contemporary music from Hawaii at this site. Definitely check out traditional slack key guitar music from Keola Beamer as well as the best-selling hits from Keali'i Reichel, who *swept* the Hawaiian Music Awards in 1995.

http://www.maui.com/~sbdc/music/

Music for a New Age

Just what is New Age music, you might ask? "What else can you call electronic synthesizers combined with the droning of the ancient Aboriginal didgeridoo?" says this site. All this, and more, can be found here. "Record Company Web Pages" starts with Windham Hill and has links to many more. In "Artists," you can find out about Kitaro, a Japanese "national living treasure." He once gave a free concert specifically for 2,000 pregnant women. Yanni, Ancient Future ("world fusion music"), Enya, Andreas Vollenweider, and many other artists have home pages. Other music sources include links to jazz sites, CD sources, a database of ambient musicians (including John Cage), and reviews of more than 100 artists. Parental advisory: Not all outbound links have been viewed.

http://www.his.com/~fjp/music.html

Tejano Home Page

Tejano (you pronounce this word "tay-yawno") is a cool music style that is a combination of Mexican sounds, American rock and roll, and a little bit of country music. If you are a fan of Tejano, or if you'd like to see what all the excitement is about, take a look at this page. All the best groups and solo artists are here, as well as birthdays of the stars, some great pictures, and the latest news on the Tejano scene. Parents, not all links have been checked.

http://www.OndaNet.com:1995/tejano/tejano.html

Whooooooo will you find in BIRDS?

NATIVE AMERICANS AND INDIGENOUS PEOPLES

Aboriginal Youth Network

Wow! This site is a perfect example of how the Internet can bring people with similar interests or backgrounds together no matter where they live. It can also provide information for those of us interested in a particular native topic. The Aboriginal Youth Network was established in 1995 to unify Aboriginal youth in Canada but since then it has gone into all corners of the world. Check out all kinds of information available as well as e-mail, chat lines, listings of events and programs, and more. We think you'll find it a very interesting place to spend some time.

http://ayn-0.ayn.ca/

Homes of the Past - ROM

What if you were an archaeologist and were exploring an ancient Iroquois village site? What could you learn about the culture from the clues left behind hundreds of years ago? This resource lets you imagine you are that scientist, trying to make sense out of hearths, post mould, storage pits, and pottery fragments. Based on a real dig site in Ontario, Canada, this page encourages you to make educated guesses based on the archaeological evidence.

http://www.rom.on.ca/digs/longhouse/

NATIVE LANGUAGES PAGE

Would you like to learn a little Navajo or a smattering of Ojibwe? Maybe you'd like to try using a Cherokee font or learn something about Mayan hieroglyphs. This page offers links to all of this and more!

http://www.pitt.edu/~lmitten/natlang.html

NativeWeb - an Internet Community

Did you know there are hundreds of federally recognized nations within the United States? Learn more about Native Americans at this site, which collects info on art, culture, government, languages, music, religious beliefs, and current tribal issues. You can read newsletters and see a calendar of upcoming events. Particularly interesting are the rules you should follow when attending a powwow, which is a ritual celebration including dance, singing, and drumming. To help find one near you, this site has event listings for the U.S., Canada, and Mexico. Lots of new links have been added to this site since the last edition. Parents: Not all links have been checked.

http://www.nativeweb.org/

NET FILES

What's the next number after a zillion?

Answer: *Actually, the number zillion doesn't exist—it is a slang word, meaning "a great many." But there are names for big numbers. According to Dr. Math, "Here's how the sequence starts (in the United States; British use different names):*

1,000,000 million
1,000,000,000 billion
1,000,000,000,000 trillion
1,000,000,000,000,000 quadrillion
1,000,000,000,000,000,000 quintillion
and so on. 'Vigintillion' is 1 with 63 zeroes after it. Some people use the word 'googol' to mean the number 1 with 100 zeroes after it. And a 'googol-plex' is a 1 with a googol zeroes after it—a VERY large number." Count on protak.8.29.96.html *for some math answers.*

A
B
C
D
E
F
G
H
I
J
K
L
M
N
O
P
Q
R
S
T
U
V
W
X
Y
Z

TOTEM POLES

If you've ever seen a totem pole, you might wonder why there are various figures and objects carved into it. According to this site, "Some of the things you might see are the eagle, raven, frog, killer whale, grizzly bear, and the mythical Thunderbird, among others. Less common figures include the owl, salmon, beaver, starfish, shark, halibut, bullhead, split person, mountain goat, moon, stars, and the rainbow." They all have meanings, and you can learn more at this most interesting site. There are also pictures of some totem polls and of people working on them. Among the totem polls listed is the tallest one in the world, located on the outskirts of the Nimpkish Reserve of Alert Bay, British Columbia. It is 173 feet tall. The 13 figures of this pole represent various groups of the Kwakawaka'wakw. If you explore elsewhere at this site, you will learn about the potlatch gift-giving ceremony and other traditions.

http://schoolnet2.carleton.ca/english/ext/
aboriginal/fnccec/umista/totem.html

NATIVE ABORIGINES

Aboriginal Art of Australia

Australian Aborigines—the original inhabitants of the continent—have been identified as the world's most primitive culture and the living representatives of the ancestors of mankind. Aboriginal culture, as anthropological work over the last hundred years has revealed, is a complex, subtle, and rich way of life. The Australian Aborigines see themselves as the custodians of their country. Aborigines belong to various clans, each having a spiritual ancestor from long ago in the Dreamtime. An individual experiences a personal connection with the ancestor by something called a *dreaming*, which bridges the present to the past. Their "dreaming" is not just of the land but of the song, dance, and mythology of the land. That dreaming has been transformed to canvas, and that artwork is well explained here, including many illustrations. Also, if you need a didgeridoo, you can buy one here.

http://www.ozemail.com.au/~hallpa/indexb.html

Indigenous People

This site, created in support of Australian schools, is a collection of links about Aborigines, the native peoples of the Australian continent. This culture is one of the oldest on Earth, with an oral tradition going back about 40,000 years! At these sites you can read more about the spiritual and cultural life of Australian Aborigines, the first ecologists. Don't miss the link to the Yothu Yindi band's Web site. This band combines traditional instruments and music with Western pop music sounds. The audio files of *yidaki* (didgeridoo or hollow log) music are haunting.

http://www.ozkidz.gil.com.au/Indigenous/

NATIVE AMERICANS

The First Americans

Originally designed for third-grade social studies classes, this site provides a brief introduction to the various native cultures in the U.S. You can study the Woodland culture, the Plains culture, the Northwest culture, the California-Intermountain culture, and the Southwest culture. You'll learn about houses, clothing, foods, and more. The site is nicely illustrated, and the addition of Indian legends adds another dimension to these cultures.

http://www.germantown.k12.il.us/html/intro.html

The Great Sioux Nation of the 19th Century

Twenty thousand people in seven tribes comprised the Great Sioux Nation of the nineteenth century. You might remember hearing about Sitting Bull and "Custer's Last Stand," the battle of Little Bighorn (near Billings, Montana). You can read all about that famous battle here, and you'll also learn much more about the Sioux—but, by the way, that word means "enemy." They were also known as the Lakota among their own people. That word means "people." This is part of the History Channel Web site and has lots of neat links to other Native American sites, as well as the rest of the History Channel.

http://www.historychannel.com/community/sioux/

A Guide to the Great Sioux Nation

The people of the Sioux Nation prefer to be called Dakota, Lakota, or Nakota, depending on their language group. On this South Dakota home page, you can learn about the languages, legends, and rich cultural traditions of these proud peoples. You'll see beautiful costumes, and maybe you can attend one of the powwows. You'll find a calendar of annual events here, so go get yourself some fry bread and enjoy the music and dance!

http://www.state.sd.us/state/executive/
  tourism/sioux/sioux.htm

National Museum of the American Indian

The Smithsonian Institution's National Museum of the American Indian is in New York City, not in Washington, D.C. (like their other museums). Most of the one million objects in its collection represent cultures in the United States and Canada, although there are also items from Mexico and Central and South America. You can see many artifacts of ancient and contemporary culture through the online exhibits of clothing, baskets, beadwork, and other objects. This museum displays sacred materials only with the permission of the various tribes and returns these materials on request. Chances are you've never seen things like this before! Imagine wearing a beautiful eagle-feather costume as you dance. "When a Ponca singer sings, the singing and the music make you dance. Some singers don't move you, but a Ponca singer will move you in your heart and mind; they make it easy to dance longer. These eagle feathers are stripped so they can hang down and flutter in the wind, like the ribbons on our shirts." (Abe Conklin, Ponca-Osage)

http://www.si.edu/nmai/

Native American Indian PlentyStuff

Want to learn about astronomy and traditional foods or read some stories written by kids at Native American schools? You'll find loads of annotated links to Maya, aboriginal, and other resources. There's also an HTML tutorial for eight-year-olds! This page is a must for anyone interested in Native American issues and current events. Not all links have been viewed.

http://indy4.fdl.cc.mn.us/~isk/mainmenu.html

Arvol Looking Horse is the 19th-generation Keeper of the Sacred White Buffalo Calf Pipe for the Lakota, Dakota, and Nakota nations. Two thousand years ago, the pipe (or sacred bundle) was given to the people by White Buffalo Calf Woman. She taught seven sacred ceremonies, including the sweat lodge and sun dance ceremonies, before she left the nations. She made a prophesy that she would come back for the pipe someday and that a sign of her coming would be the birth of a white buffalo calf. In 1994, a white buffalo calf was born in Wisconsin. You can read about the cultural and spiritual significance of this event at Native American Indian PlentyStuff.

Native Americans Home Pages

You have a report due on a Native American nation you've never heard of before. So you walk down to the public library to look for it. Trouble is, all the books on Native Americans have been checked out, and the reference books have just one paragraph on your topic! Now you can go straight to the source. Many nations have their own home pages, complete with historical and cultural information. They are listed here, at a site put together by a librarian who says she is "mixed-blood Mohawk urban Indian." You'll also find links to tribal organizations, colleges, businesses, powwows, singers, and more. This site is carefully tended and updated. We have not checked outside links.

http://www.pitt.edu/~lmitten/indians.html

Pony up to HORSES AND EQUESTRIAN SPORTS.

A
B
C
D
E
F
G
H
I
J
K
L
M
N
O
P
Q
R
S
T
U
V
W
X
Y
Z

A
B
C
D
E
F
G
H
I
J
K
L
M
N
O
P
Q
R
S
T
U
V
W
X
Y
Z

NativeTech: Native American Technology and Art

This site is really neat! It talks about a lot of Native American art and technologies like beadwork, clay and pottery, leather and clothes, toys and games, and more. We started at beadwork because it seems so interesting. There is information about the kinds of beads and their meanings. Wampum beads were made from shells and often decorated clothing. Long, woven wampum belts were often exchanged at treaty signings or other formal occasions. You can find out how the beads were made—it was a very difficult process! Let's mosey on over to porcupine quillwork, perhaps the oldest form of Native American embroidery. Native American artists sometimes decorate their clothing and birchbark containers with quills. At this site, not only do you learn the history of these fascinating art forms, but you can also learn these crafts. Maybe you should start with the cornhusk doll instructions, though, since corn's easier to find than porcupine quills.

http://www.lib.uconn.edu/NativeTech/

NET FILES

Where would you find a tiger's pug mark?

Answer: *On the ground—it's another word for a footprint or track. Its actual size is 5.5 inches (10.8 cm) by 4.5 inches (8.75 cm)! You can see a tiger's pug mark at* http://www.5tigers.org/pug.htm

New Perspectives on THE WEST

This is a companion site to the eight-part PBS television series *The West*. It is a history of the expansion of the American West, and we are including it because of the rich biographical information about famous Native Americans. Just click on "People in the West." You'll find short biographies about Sitting Bull, Chief Joseph, Chief Seattle, Crazy Horse, Sacagawea, and more.

http://www.pbs.org/weta/thewest/

Oneida Indian Nation

The Oneida were the first Native American nation to put up a Web page and claim territory in cyberspace. Net-mom was honored to have been a part of this history. The Oneida are located in central New York State, and they remain an unconquered nation. In fact, they were the only Native American tribe to fight on the side of the American colonists during the American Revolution. This fact, often left out of history books, is detailed on this site. In 1777–78, Washington's soldiers were enduring a hard winter at Valley Forge, Pennsylvania. Oneida people walked hundreds of miles south, carrying food and supplies, to come to their aid. Polly Cooper was an Oneida woman who helped the soldiers, and she taught them how to cook the corn and other foods the Oneida had brought with them. Although offered payment, she refused, saying it was her duty to help friends in need. She was thanked for her assistance by Martha Washington herself, who presented Polly with a fancy shawl and bonnet. The shawl has been a treasured Oneida relic since then, and you can see a photo of it here. You can also hear some Oneida words, take a tour of the cultural museum, read original treaties, learn why the cornhusk dolls have no face, and see some real wampum!

http://www.one-web.org/oneida/

Looking for the State Bird or the State Motto? It's in the UNITED STATES—STATES section.

Pocahontas Start Page

For a Native American perspective on the popular Disney movie, check this Web page. The true history of Pocahontas and Captain John Smith might make less of a story than the Disney version, since she was only about 11 or 12 years old when she begged for his life. See what some Native American kids and adults think about the cartoon and its look at their culture and history.

http://indy4.fdl.cc.mn.us/~isk/poca/pocahont.html

Pueblo Cultural Center

In the American Southwest desert in New Mexico, 19 Pueblo communities welcome visitors, both real and virtual. You can read descriptions of all of them here, as well as pick up maps to the pueblos, calendars of events, and even rules for attending dances (don't applaud—dance is a prayer, not a performance). Gaze at the stunning wall murals, with titles such as these: The One-Horned Buffalo Dance; The Sounds of Life and Earth as It Breathes; and Indian Maiden Feeding Deer. You can read biographies of the artists, too.

http://hanksville.phast.umass.edu/defs/
  independent/PCC/PCC.html

Sipapu — Chetro Ketl Great Kiva

Over a thousand years ago, there was a great civilization in what is now northwestern New Mexico, in the desert southwest of the United States. What remains now are cliff dwellings and other scattered hints about how these people lived and worked. One central part of their existence was the *kiva,* an underground enclosure used for sacred and other purposes. Young men would enter the kiva to learn secret languages and hidden lore of the tribe. The kiva was the central spiritual focus of the community. Large communities needed a Great Kiva, and this site reconstructs one for you to climb down in and visit virtually. It is based on the recently excavated Chetro Ketl Great Kiva, which is located in isolated Chaco Canyon, in northwestern New Mexico. You can choose the multimedia tour, with QuickTime VR, or you can try the less bandwidth-intensive version. The descendants of these ancient peoples now live in the various pueblos of the area. They also use kivas for ceremonies, and they are off-limits if you are a visitor to the pueblo.

http://sipapu.ucsb.edu/html/kiva.html

Southern Native American Pow Wows

This site was created by kids for the ThinkQuest competition. In it, you'll learn where to sit (and where not to sit) to watch the dancing, and you'll know what to do if you are a dancer. Don't forget to honor the Head Man and the Head Lady and give respect to the Drum, which has probably traveled a long way to give you beautiful music. Listen to the audio files of various songs, and check out the various styles of dances for both men and women. There is even advice for the new dancer and someone wishing to get involved with this tradition.

http://tqd.advanced.org/3081/

NATIVE ARCTIC PEOPLES

Arctic Circle: History & Culture

You'll find information here about many people who are native to the Arctic Circle region of the world. You'll learn not only about the Cree of northern Quebec and the Inupiat of Arctic Alaska, but also about the Nenets and Khanty of Yamal Peninsula, northwest Siberia, and the Sámi of far-northern Europe. Find out why the concept of "wilderness" is unknown to these people, who live in harmony with their natural surroundings.

http://www.lib.uconn.edu/ArcticCircle/HistoryCulture/

NATIVE HAWAIIANS

HAWAI'I - INDEPENDENT & SOVEREIGN NATION-STATE

In November 1993, President Bill Clinton signed into law U.S. Public Law 103-50, which is "To acknowledge the 100th anniversary of the January 17, 1893 overthrow of the Kingdom of Hawaii, and to offer an apology to Native Hawaiians on behalf of the United States for the overthrow of the Kingdom of Hawaii." Some native Hawaiians are trying to restore Hawaii to sovereign nation status. That means it would have its own leaders and could determine its own future. Read news about the Nation of Hawai'i, and find out about native island culture here.

http://hawaii-nation.org/nation/

A B C D E F G H I J K L M N O P Q R S T U V W X Y Z

NEWS, NEWSPAPERS, AND MAGAZINES

See also INTERNET—SEARCH ENGINES AND DIRECTORIES; TELEVISION—NETWORKS AND CHANNELS

Many sites, such as those found in INTERNET—SEARCH ENGINES AND DIRECTORIES offer customizable newspapers you can easily customize yourself. One example is <*http://edit.my.yahoo.com/config/login*>, but almost all the search engines and directories have something similar.

AJR NewsLink

Wow—stop the presses! Check this site: over 8,000 links to newspapers, broadcast stations, magazines, plus other special links from all over the world. You ought to be able to get all the news here! Have you started wondering about which college is right for you? Maybe you've got a sister, brother, or friend who's already gone away to one. One of the best ways to find out about a college is to check out its newspaper. You can keep up with campus news by reading the online versions of college newspapers from the *Arizona Daily Wildcat* to *The Yale Daily News* at this site. Or say you want the news directly from India about nuclear testing there. No problem, just click on Asia, then India to get daily papers from the region.

http://www.newslink.org/menu.html

CRAYON

Wouldn't it be great if you could design a newspaper with just the news *you* want to read? How about an all-sports newspaper or an all-music newspaper? How about adding the current weather map or the current stock price on a share of Toys 'R' Us? This interactive site lets you do just that and "publish" an updated paper anytime you want, to your very own Web browser.

http://crayon.net/

Go climb a rock in OUTDOOR RECREATION.

Media Awareness Network

This site provides support for media education in the home, school, and community. It's also a place where educators, parents, students, and community workers can share resources and explore ways to make media a more positive force in children's lives. If you have a fast connection, be sure to download "Privacy Playground: The First Adventure of the Three Little CyberPigs," a neat game that will help you understand what's good and bad about being on the Net.

http://www.screen.com/mnet/eng/

MediaINFO Links - Search Page

Editor & Publisher has been around for a long time, providing information for the news industry. Now they've got this great online media directory for you to use! You will find associations, city guides, magazines, newspapers, news services and syndicates, and radio and television Web sites listed both geographically and by media type. Check it out and find the newspaper in your community, the community where you used to live, or the community where you're moving to. If you've got a homework assignment about current events in, say, Bermuda, you can read the daily news from local newspapers there.

http://www.mediainfo.com/emedia/

Newseum, the Interactive Museum of News

Next time you take a family vacation to Washington, D.C., convince the folks to head across the Potomac river to Arlington, Virginia. That's where The Freedom Forum has built a museum dedicated to the news, known as the Newseum. But for those who don't plan to visit D.C. in the near future, you can visit the Newseum right on the Net. There's lots of cool information about the news that is happening right now as well as stuff from long ago. Read all about current challenges to the Bill of Rights and other attempts to trample constitutional rights. Parental advisory: This is a news site that you should explore with your children.

http://www.newseum.org/

PointCast Network - The leading broadcast news and information service on the Internet

A new wave is out there on the Web, and it's called "push" technology. That means the information is being pushed at you rather than having you click on it to request it, or "pull" it. Sort of like television broadcasting, except you tell them what shows you want to watch. One of the cool uses of this is customized news, including weather and sports scores. You select the types of stories you want to read and the news resources you want to have checked. You can choose to have new information pushed to you every few minutes, every hour, or every day. You can even have floating news stories or weather maps as your screen saver! You can download software to try one version of it here, but ask your parents before installing it to make sure you have the right hardware.

http://www.pointcast.com/

Timecast - Your RealAudio & RealVideo Guide

Now hear this! The news, that is. Yep, this site's for people who'd rather listen to the news than read it. You're going to want to grab your own version of the RealAudio player (it's free, courtesy of Progressive Networks) once you check out all the cool stuff you can hear. The RealAudio player software enables users to access RealAudio programming and play it back in an on-demand audio stream, which means you don't have to download those gigantic files first, which gets a little boring. Not to be missed is the news from French, Italian, and Japanese public broadcast networks (not to mention National Public Radio), political speeches from C-SPAN, the evening news from *ABC World News Tonight*, and broadcasts from Greenpeace ships around the world.

http://www.timecast.com/

Vanderbilt Television News Archive

Word for word, the abstracts of television network news broadcasts from August 5, 1968, to the present date are available at this site. The abstracts can be browsed by date or searched for keywords. The search returns specific items and the complete show. This site would be particularly helpful in developing a research paper about a specific event.

http://tvnews.vanderbilt.edu/

What's News? Current Events Challenge Plan

Step right up and try your hand at What's News, an ongoing competition where you and your classmates create the questions for a fast-paced game of current events investigation. The site also links you to a wide array of news sources where you will be able to research the questions and answers for this competition.

http://www1.minn.net/~schubert/WNplan.html

Yahoo! Get Local

All this national and international news is sometimes overwhelming! If you just want to focus on your local community news, this is the place. You need to set up a profile the first time you use it. You have to type in the name of your city, and sometimes your ZIP code, but that's about it. Then, every time you go to this page, it will bring up your local news! This may include links to your local TV and newspaper's Web sites, local team scores, movie listings, special event calendars, weather, and lots more. If you ever want to change to another city, a button at the top of the page will let you do that. You can "get local" in the U.S. or in many other countries.

http://local.yahoo.com/

NET FILES

How many quills does the average porcupine have?

Answer: *How would you like to be the one who has to count? It's been estimated that most have about 30,000 quills, and new ones grow back in when others have been lost in an enemy attack. Read more at http://www.ec.gc.ca/cws-scf/hww-fap/porcupin/porcupin.html*

A B C D E F G H I J K L M N O P Q R S T U V W X Y Z

A B C D E F G H I J K L M N O P Q R S T U V W X Y Z

MAGAZINES
Cyberkids Home

CyberKids magazine is chock-full of games, word searches, and crossword puzzles, but—watch out!—you could learn something before you know it. All the stories and artwork have been created by kids, of course. They've told about the first African American woman in space, how one family came from Vietnam to the United States, and about Egyptian gods. Also pretty great are the reviews of computer stuff, like software and printers. You can contribute your own stories, enter contests, and comment on other kids' ideas.

http://www.cyberkids.com/index.shtml

MidLink Magazine

Design an alien or visit a virtual haunted house at *MidLink*, where kids ranging in age from 10 to 15 years gather to share news of their schools and cities. And speaking of cities, why not take a virtual tour of kids' homes around the world while you're there? Or join a virtual voyage with a weather research vessel. And don't miss the Cool-School Home Pages. There is always something fun happening at this site, which gets better and better every time we see it!

http://longwood.cs.ucf.edu/~MidLink/

NET FILES

WHAT DO
Bob Hope, Henry Aaron, the Apollo 12 astronauts, John Wayne, Frank Sinatra, Gerald Ford, Pele, Walt Disney, Shannon Miller, and Carl Lewis
HAVE IN COMMON?

Answer: *They have all served as Grand Marshals of the Tournament of Roses Parade! Read more about it at* http://www.citycent.com/tournamentroses/rosegm.htm

NWF's Ranger Rick

The National Wildlife Federation has a magazine for kids that's about nature, wildlife, and wilderness, and some of it is online. You can sample articles from past issues, such as "Ladybug Lore," "Elephant Jokes," or "Far-out Numbers." Check out Ranger Rick!

http://www.igc.apc.org/nwf/rrick/

OWLkids Online

These Canadian kids' magazines have online versions full of stories, jokes, puzzles, crafts, and of course, links! Kids ages eight and up will love *Wired OWL*, while younger kids should try *Chickadee Net*. The Cybersurfer section in *Wired OWL* has a nice overview of the culture of the Net. There's also a new parenting section of this entertaining and educational resource.

http://www.owl.on.ca/

Reuters News

Click on a headline, and instantly you'll be taken to the complete story, whether it's the latest from Washington, D.C., or the batting average of your favorite player. General news is in Top News, while you'll have to click on CNNSI Sports to get the scores. The sports news here is awesome: you can get stats, schedules, box scores, game recaps and previews, and the very latest transactions. Since Time Warner, Inc.—the people who publish *Time, People, Sports Illustrated, Money, Fortune,* and lots of other famous magazines—runs this site, you can get the complete background on any subject right here.

http://pathfinder.com/news/latest/

Sports Illustrated for Kids

When was the last time you climbed a treacherous rock wall, shredded some ramps with the only pro female skateboarder in the country, or picked up some racing tips from the world's best BMX bicycle racer—all without leaving your computer? This online magazine is all about athletic challenges. If you've been wanting to try your hand at a new sport, this is where you can find out all about the moves, the lingo, and the equipment. Don't miss the interviews with sports heroes, hilarious comics, games, and a whole lot more.

http://www.sikids.com/

Stone Soup magazine

Stone Soup is a well-known magazine of stories, poems, and artwork by kids, for kids. Here at their home page, you can peek at a sample issue, plus read some online stories and poems. Maybe you'll be able to send them some of your own work. There is nothing like seeing your name in print, next to something you wrote, whether it's printed in a magazine, a book, or on the Net!

http://www.stonesoup.com/

Time For Kids

Time is a very popular news magazine for adults, but now there is an online version for kids, and it is HOT! You'll find current news stories on the front page, but dig deeper for cartoons, multimedia, and an archive of past issues. Recent stories included info on Chelsea Clinton's first car, photos of a rare albino koala bear, and a multimedia Build a Robot game.

http://pathfinder.com/TFK/

U.S. News Online

Do we even need to mention that a magazine called *U.S. News* is going to bring you news, news, and more news every week? Want more than just the week's news? Click on "News You Can Use," a weekly feature, full of some really helpful tips, like how to order healthy food at a restaurant, how to buy a new computer, and which colleges are the very best in the country.

http://www.usnews.com/usnews/

Welcome to TIME.com

Okay, okay, we know this is a news magazine for adults, but we've got a helpful homework hint for you. Say it's 8:00 P.M. and you've got a report due tomorrow on how Russians and Americans are cooperating in space, or on hurricanes, or on computer hackers. Are you in big trouble or what? Well, here's what you can do. Go to this home page, where you can search through magazines for articles. And there's a whole lot more than just *Time* magazine. Don't forget, *Time* has a bunch of sister magazines, including *Fortune*, *Money*, and *People*, and they're all right here. Just type in a word or a phrase, and let this Web site do the walking for the stories you need.

http://pathfinder.com/time/

WORLD Magazine @ nationalgeographic.com

National Geographic has been a family favorite for decades. They also have a magazine just for kids, called *WORLD*, and this is its online version. The contents of the issues vary, but we've enjoyed articles on the space station, pirates, and movies of an avalanche in action! There are links to challenging games, plus a way for you to get an international pen pal, too (click on "Kids" at the top of the screen).

http://www.nationalgeographic.com/media/world/

Yak's Corner

Imagine a magazine for kids run by a yak. There would be hard-hitting investigative journalism ("Is Lake Champlain Really a Great Lake?"), survey reports ("How High is Your Allowance?") and even behind-the-scenes sports stories ("How to Talk Hockey"). You'd also find some Yaktivities such as the Neverending Yak Story, where you can add to the adventures kids have already written, some yak jokes, and lots of fun and games. You don't have to imagine it—you can visit it!

http://www.yakscorner.com/

YES Mag Home Page

Canada's science magazine for kids has an electronic version! It includes book and software reviews, in-depth articles, and science news and projects. We particularly liked the "How Does That Work?" section, where we learned lots about telescopes, cameras, submarines, and other inventions.

http://www.yesmag.bc.ca/

NEWSPAPERS

NandoNext

NandoNext is a Web site created just for the interests and attitudes of the "next" generation, featuring stories and art from Raleigh, Durham, and Chapel Hill, North Carolina high school students. Don't miss their music, movie, and concert reviews. If you need to take a break, click on Features and check the "Cool Site of the Day!"

http://www2.nando.net/links/nandonext/next.html

A B C D E F G H I J K L M N O P Q R S T U V W X Y Z

A
B
C
D
E
F
G
H
I
J
K
L
M
N
O
P
Q
R
S
T
U
V
W
X
Y
Z

News Index

News Index claims to be the most comprehensive news search engine on the planet. It's time for a current events paper on the situation in the Middle East, says your teacher. This is the place to start. You will find breaking news stories from more than 300 newspapers and news sources from around the world. When we typed in the words "Middle East," there were 1,646 articles from which to choose!

http://www.newsindex.com/

The Paperboy - Online Newspapers

Quick quiz: Can you list the top 15 online newspapers in Slovakia? Quick answer: Just check thepaperboy.com. This site features an extensive listing of the top online newspapers, by country. You're just a click away from the *New York Times*, the *Washington Post*, the *Sydney Morning Herald*, and hundreds of other papers across the world—like the *Demokraticke Slovo* in Slovakia. If you only spoke the language! This is a great resource to quickly find news from all over the world.

http://www.thepaperboy.com/

The Positive Press: Good News Every Day

Sometimes it seems like the news is all bad. But that's not true—it's just that the news that's *reported* is all bad. There are plenty of positive, good things happening all the time in this beautiful world of ours. This Web site reports only on stories that say: Great! Wow! Terrific! and That's Wonderful! There's also a free mailing list so you can get an inspirational quote every day.

http://www.positivepress.com/

What did grandma do when she was a kid? There is a list of questions to ask in GENEALOGY AND FAMILY HISTORY.

Tomorrow's Morning!

When your family talks about what's going on in Washington or in the world, do you just sit there with a puzzled look on your face? After you've checked out *Tomorrow's Morning*, the first national weekly newspaper for kids from 8 to 14, you'll dazzle everyone with your knowledge of the news. What's really great is that the editors who put this paper together think being informed should be fun! Of course they've got the serious stuff, such as national and international news. But they throw in tons of fun stuff, too, like comic book news, Brainiac quizzes, science fiction updates, and news about kids from other parts of the country. Future business executives should be sure to take a look at Kid$tock$, to see how Coca-Cola, Nike, Toys 'R' Us, and lots of other stocks are doing.

http://www.morning.com/

USA Today

"Your news when you want it" is *USA Today*'s motto, and you're going to get exactly that at this site. You can go right to the sections you want by clicking on the buttons for News, Sports, Money, Life, or Weather. And speaking of weather, there's a ton of forecasts, fun facts, and lots of other goodies here, from information on tornadoes and hurricanes to tips on weather forecasting. Everything's just as readable and colorful as the actual newspaper. It's a whole lot more than a newspaper, though, because the news is updated every day and sports scores are updated every two minutes. Impress your family by downloading the interactive crossword puzzle and a special puzzle viewer so you can work it out offline.

http://www.usatoday.com/usafront.htm

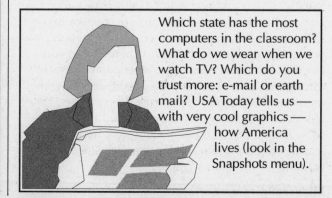

Which state has the most computers in the classroom? What do we wear when we watch TV? Which do you trust more: e-mail or earth mail? USA Today tells us — with very cool graphics — how America lives (look in the Snapshots menu).

OPTICAL ILLUSIONS

IllusionWorks Home Page

This is the coolest optical illusion site on the Net. Discover not only sight illusions but sound illusions! Try to figure out the distorted puzzles or the camouflaged hidden pictures. Some of these require Shockwave or Java-enhanced browsers. A caution to parents: Not all links leading off this site have been checked.

http://www.illusionworks.com/

Learning Studio On-Line Exhibits

Don't look now. At this site there are illusions that will make you think your computer is spinning, your palm is squirming, and Mona Lisa is frowning. If that's not enough to convince you to go to this site, there's a short story called "Ladle Rat Rotten Hut" that will completely confuse you, then amuse you. Remember, the moral of this very familiar story is: "Yonder nor sorghum stenches shut ladle gulls stopper torque wet strainers."

http://www.exploratorium.edu/
   learning_studio/lsxhibit.html

Mark Newbold's Animated Necker Cube

Do not try this illusion at home. Remember, we warned you. OK, well maybe you can try it at home, but make sure you have your seat belts fastened first and your tray and seat backs are fully upright. Prepare for your brain cells to get messed up as your perception of this seemingly innocent cube switches around. According to this site, "The Necker Cube is named after the Swiss crystallographer Louis Albert Necker, who in the mid-1800s saw cubic shapes spontaneously reverse in perspective." But don't try the Counter-Rotating Spirals Illusion—unless you want to have fun!

http://www.sover.net/~manx/necker.html

Optical Illusions

Now you see them, now you don't. Optical illusions are given wide representation here. Open up the doors of perception and come into this exhibit at the Cyberspace Middle School. Maybe you'll even be able to find your way back out!

http://www.scri.fsu.edu/~dennisl/CMS/activity/
   optical.html

The Stereogram Page

Can you see hidden 3-D images inside a stereogram? People who can see them describe tigers jumping through hoops, wild outer space landscapes, and more. Those who can't see them think everyone else is just making it up! This site includes a tutorial on how to make your own images like this.

http://stereogram.i-us.com/

Welcome to Philomel Records!

You know what an optical illusion is: a picture that can look like several different things all at once. Are you ready for an audio illusion? Diana Deutsch's CD is called *Musical Illusions and Paradoxes,* and you can hear several samples at this Web site. Did you know that people hear sounds differently? Sometimes your brain can be tricked into hearing melodies that aren't really there. Sound impossible? Listen to the audio files here and see if you can identify the mystery tune.

http://www.philomel.com/

Welcome to SandlotScience.com

They're all here: those illusional figures that leave you wondering. You'll see impossible illusions, like the animated triangle and the endless staircase. You'll also find camouflage illusions and hidden pictures, and finally, our favorite: moiré patterns. They're caused when two transparent patterns overlap. You will enjoy visiting this site, but don't be in a hurry—these illusions are irresistible!

http://www.sandlotscience.com/

A
B
C
D
E
F
G
H
I
J
K
L
M
N
O
P
Q
R
S
T
U
V
W
X
Y
Z

A
B
C
D
E
F
G
H
I
J
K
L
M
N
O
P
Q
R
S
T
U
V
W
X
Y
Z

World of Escher

Waterfalls that flow up? Stairs that seem to keep going down, yet, suddenly, they're back on top of a building? These inexplicable drawings by M. C. Escher must be seen to be believed!

http://lonestar.texas.net/~escher/

You Can Illusions

What you think you see is not always what's really there. Look at some famous optical illusions with Beakman and Jax, who explain things like whether that's a young lady wearing a hat or an old woman wearing a scarf.

http://www.beakman.com/illusion/illusions.html

ORGANIZATIONS

Cards for Kids

If you like to make greeting cards with crayons or rubber stamps, there's an organization that would love to hear from you. They ask you to send handmade cards to them for redistribution to very sick children. If you know a child who fits into this category and who would like to receive some fun, cheerful mail, you can suggest his or her name. Carefully read the card guidelines before creating a card, though. There are also suggested places for you to send old greeting cards, as well as contact addresses for similar projects.

http://www.cardsforkids.com/

Children's Defense Fund

Being a kid in the 1990s can be tough. Poverty, abuse, and negligence are a few of the problems kids confront. The Children's Defense Fund (CDF) is an organization designed to help kids with some of the difficult problems they face. To learn more about how kids can get a Head Start, a Healthy Start, a Fair Start, a Safe Start, and a Moral Start—find out what the CDF is doing.

http://www.childrensdefense.org/

The Giraffe Project

Giraffes are really special. They are so tall, they can see just a little bit farther ahead than everyone else. Some people are sort of like giraffes, too. Some of them see problems in the world. What do they do? They "stick their necks out" and try to find solutions. They become heroes and the world becomes a better place. Read stories about some of these "giraffes" who have made a difference in helping other people, the environment, and animals. Maybe you'll be inspired to become a giraffe yourself! These folks can help.

http://www.giraffe.org/giraffe/

Habitat for Humanity International

Wouldn't it be great if everyone in the world had a nice house to live in? Habitat for Humanity (HFH) thinks so too. HFH is a Christian organization that invites people of all faiths to help them build affordable housing for people in need. Can you drive a nail? Can you paint? Can you serve lunch to the other volunteers? Youth and campus affiliates are welcomed, from ages 5 to 25. Use the search engine at this site to find a group near you. Your church, scout troop, school, or family can get involved in this visionary program. Former U.S. President Jimmy Carter and his wife, Rosalynn, help build HFH houses every year; in 1998, 6,000 volunteers showed up to help them build 100 houses in Houston, Texas.

http://www.habitat.org/default.html

Kids Can Make A Difference

Around the world, every day, there are very poor families who never get enough to eat. At this Web page you can learn how to assist kids who need a helping hand. There are lots of ideas: for example, you can write letters to politicians, newspaper editors, and others to alert them to the problems of hunger. You can hold car washes or bake sales to raise money for relief organizations. One class "adopted" a family at a local homeless shelter, while others held a "hunger banquet" and collected canned food to stock a local food pantry. Take a look now—it'll make you feel good to learn how you can do something positive for your community and your world!

http://www.kids.maine.org/

Make-A-Wish® Foundation of America

Founded in the belief that lives are measured by memories and not by years, the Make-A-Wish Foundation has granted more than 50,000 wishes to American children between the ages of 2 1/2 and 18 who have terminal illnesses or life-threatening medical conditions. Since the first wish (granted in 1980 for a seven-year-old boy with terminal leukemia who wanted to be a policeman), 81 chapters have sprung up around the U.S. With the family's participation, the Foundation is committed to providing a memorable and carefree experience for these children, whose wishes are limited only by their own imaginations. If you know someone who would like to make a special wish, check the Chapter Listing to find the Make-A-Wish chapter nearest you. One of the most frequently requested wishes is to travel to Disneyland or Disney World, but many unusual wishes have been granted, and you can read about them here. Also, be sure to check out the story of Craig Shergold. Long ago, he had a life-threatening brain tumor and asked that people send him greeting cards so that he could get into the *Guinness Book of World Records.* They did. Then he had surgery and (hooray!) fully recovered. Trouble is, those original requests are still floating around the Internet! You may receive a request from a friend; tell your friend the truth. The Shergold family is swimming in cards, and they want it to stop. Make-A-Wish was never involved with the original request, but you'll find the whole story explained here about this Net chain letter.

http://www.wish.org/

National 4-H Council

What does it mean to be involved in 4-H? It can mean learning how to give a great speech, helping save the environment, raising animals, or working on a project with friends. From country lanes to city streets, kids are involved in 4-H activities, and 4-H kids are having fun and learning much. To get the inside scoop on 4-H, take a peek at this home page.

http://www.fourhcouncil.edu/

Welcome to SERVEnet!

Do kids care? You bet they do! Lots of kids find ways to volunteer their time with charitable organizations such as the Ronald McDonald House, the American Red Cross, and many homeless shelters. Do you want to show you care? Type in your ZIP code and search for volunteer opportunities in your city or region. This site won the 1998 NII Awards Promise category. Parental advisory: This site contains links to many different types of organizations and their Web sites; please preview.

http://www.servenet.org/

YMCAs on the WEB

Why would you go to the "Y," the YMCA? You could go for all kinds of reasons. You could go for a game of B-Ball, swimming or judo lessons, or even classes in basketry. The "Y" is a fun place for everybody in the family, and there are many YMCAs all over the Internet. Take a look at YMCAs on the Web to see if a "Y" near you has a presence in cyberspace.

http://www2.interaccess.com/ymcaweb/

NET FILES

Who invented Silly Putty®?

Answer: James Wright, back in 1943, was the guy who mixed silicon oil with boric acid, looking for a substitute for rubber. He worked for General Electric, which couldn't seem to find a use for this "nutty putty." Then in 1949, a man named Peter Hodgson attended a party where this item was the main entertainment. He immediately saw its potential as a children's toy, and he bought the production rights from G.E. for $147. At the time of his death in 1976, his estate was worth $140 million. Read more at *http://web.mit.edu/invent/www/inventorsA-H/sillyputty.html*

A
B
C
D
E
F
G
H
I
J
K
L
M
N
O
P
Q
R
S
T
U
V
W
X
Y
Z

SCOUTING

Camp Fire Boys & Girls

Camp Fire was originally founded as an organization for American girls. That was in 1910. In 1975, they decided to let boys join too. Headquartered in Kansas City, Missouri, approximately 670,000 kids are now Camp Fire members. The organization stresses self-reliance, making friends, and helping one's community. You can visit this page to find out about Camp Fire programs in your area.

http://www.campfire.org/

General Reference - Compass @Scouter

Your patrol is supposed to come up with a campfire skit or funny songs for Scout camp. No problem—just check some of the entertainment links here! You'll also find resources on international scouting, times and places for the next Jamboree or other scouting event, fund-raising ideas, discussion groups, and links to other pages for both Boy Scouts and Girl Scouts.

http://compass.scouter.com/General_Reference/

The InterNETional Scouting Pages

Scouting is *everywhere*. Girl Scouts, Boy Scouts, Explorers, the college fraternity Alpha Phi Omega—all are scouting organizations, and you can find them in just about every country in the world. Naturally, scouting groups are all over the Internet as well. To learn about scouting from A to Z, take a look at this page. You'll learn that scouting is more than tying knots and selling cookies! Download some of Baden-Powell's original scouting handbooks, or learn to use a compass or build backpacking equipment. Looking for camp songs and skits? They are collected here too, and many of them are wonderfully gross.

http://inter.scout.net/

> Volcanoes are an explosive subject. Find one in Earth Science.

OUTDOOR RECREATION

See also SPORTS

Go Climb a Rock!

Check the Climber's dictionary. They actually have an entry under "AAAAAAHHHHHHHH!!!" The definition is "a fall in progress!" Seriously, this is a site you need to traverse. Check climbing shoe ratings, technique tips, and a slew of links to climbing magazines and gear companies. There is also a listing of the top competitive climbers in the world. They are doing a great job of expanding the page and have links to other climbing pages, too.

http://www.traks.com/goclimb/climb.htm

GORP - Great Outdoor Recreation Pages

GORP stands for the hiker's staple food: good old raisins and peanuts! Do you love to play in the great outdoors? Is there anything more fun than hiking, camping, climbing, or seeing wildlife? GORP has it all. Check out the sections on places to go, things to do, good food to take, and staying healthy while traveling. If you are trying to get in the mood to go camping, enjoy the outdoor art, photography, cartoons, and, best of all, traveler's tales. Parental advisory: links off this page have not been checked.

http://www.gorp.com/

Lumberjack Entertainment and Timber Sports Guide (Lumberjack Guide Page One, records, contest and timbersports equipment)

Ever heard of timbersports? They include logrolling, crosscut sawing, and standing block chop. There are world records for lumberjack (or lumberjill) sporting events. If you haven't heard of this sport, you will. It's growing like crazy. On this page, you can see who holds the world record in a variety of timber competitions as well as see other information about this unusual sport, such as where to see a competition and where to buy the unusual equipment required. You can also find out when to watch this sport on ESPN!

http://www.starinfo.com/ljguide/lumberjack.html

Welcome to L.L. Bean

L.L. Bean has been in the outdoor recreation outfitting business for many years, and they have quite a wealth of knowledge on such things as fly-fishing, camping, cycling, winter camping, backpacking, and cross-country skiing. Also, don't forget snowshoeing, which is a really cool (no pun intended) activity! It's a bit easier for most people than cross-country skiing, and it allows you to do a little more exploring. This page is where you can find out what you need and how to get started. After reading the helpful hints, maybe you still have a few more questions. Chances are the answers are only a mouse click away. For example, did you know you can make an emergency snowshoe repair with duct tape? (Is there anything you *can't* fix with duct tape?)

http://www.llbean.com/aos/

It's like wearing tennis racquets on your feet! How do you get down a hill in snowshoes, anyway? Whatever you do, don't jump down—that can damage the shoe and the webbing. There are specific techniques for snowshoeing, and things like going up and down hills or walking backwards can get a little tricky. Stop in at the Welcome to L.L. Bean page for the tips you need.

YMCA SCUBA: Home Page

Scuba diving can be a wonderful, lifelong hobby, but you need to take lessons from an expert first. Where can you find an expert? Many times you can visit your local YMCA. They offer courses in everything from safe snorkeling to dive master. Discover more by getting your feet wet here.

http://www.ymcascuba.org/

FISHING

See also AQUARIUMS; FISH

Fishing Knots

Are you all thumbs when it comes to trilene? Do your hooks and sinkers fall off the line? You just need to know the moves when you're tying fishing knots. There are easy directions and pictures for a number of popular and useful knots at this site. If you go one level "back" to <http://www.anglersinfo.com/tips/> you'll find more good information, like the proper way to care for rods and reels.

http://www.anglersinfo.com/tips/fishing_knots.html

The Fishing Network

Something smells *fishy* here! That's because this page is full of fish-type information. Are you interested in learning about fly-fishing or do you just want to talk with others interested in this art? Speaking of art, how about some color clip art of fish? You can find that at this site, too. There are also lots of links to other fishing pages on the Web, for people who like to fish for everything from panfish to deep-sea monsters! This is the place to go. Hurry, before this one gets away!

http://sbinnie.rogerswave.ca/tfn/

NET FILES

When was the first camera made available to consumers?

Answer: The first consumer camera was marketed all the way back in 1888! The Kodak camera was priced at $25 and included film for 100 exposures. It was a little inconvenient to get your pictures developed, though: the whole camera had to be returned to Kodak in Rochester, New York for film processing! Click over to *http://www.eastman.org/timeline/timeline.html* for more on the history of photography.

GORP- Fishing - fly fishing, freshwater angling, saltwater fishing

Looking for the right *angle* on fishing? GORP is where they're biting! This is no *line*—you'll find everything from general fishing to fishing gear to information on fishing trips. There are lots of links to fishing hot spots in Scotland, Africa, and other places to cast your line. Stop by and catch your limit today.

http://www.gorp.com/gorp/activity/fishing.htm

Teach Your Kid to Fish

What is the biggest mistake parents make when they teach their kids to fish? It's thinking that they will get to fish, too. That's not how it works. According to this page, when kids are just starting to learn, they should do all the fishing. The parents do all the baiting of the hook, all the taking off of fish, and all of the falling in the water. OK, we made up that last part. The point is, the kids should associate fishing with fun and action. Kids would rather fish from the shore for 20 little ones than hang around in a boat all day waiting for a chance to catch a big one. Check out the other tips here, and be sure to let your mom and dad read them, too!

http://www.anglersinfo.com/feature_articles/
teachkids_jkumiski.html

GOLF AND MINIATURE GOLFING
Golfweb-Library-Fun and Games

There's no doubt about it: golf is fun! But sometimes just keeping score isn't enough. At this site, you can find the simple rules to dozens of different golf games. There are games for two, three, or four players, and there are team games for groups. And the best part is that they're all fun!

http://www.golfweb.com/glbb/index.htm

kidzgolf.com

Check this site to compare your golf scores with those of other kids. You can talk golf on the message boards, take some golf quizzes and play games, and catch up on the latest golf news.

http://www.golf.com/kidz/

Mika's Down Under Miniature Golf Course

Why not build your very own miniature golf course? These folks did! They built an 18-hole challenge consisting of nine hazards played in two directions. The "Down Under" course was constructed in their basement, using old toys, spare wood, and what looks like indoor-outdoor carpeting. After a few months their creation was destroyed "by random cat activity," but each hole is pictured and lovingly described as it appeared in its full glory. Now all you need is a scorecard and one of those little teeny pencils!

http://www.contrib.andrew.cmu.edu/~wall/course/

PGA Cool Kids

Would you like to improve your golf game? What? You don't even have a golf game? This site, from the Professional Golfers' Association, will give you beginner tips and help you get started. You can also find out about junior events as well as initiatives like The First Tee, which aims to develop small kid-friendly golf facilities. Former President George Bush is the honorary chairperson of this campaign.

http://www.pga.com/Cool_Kids/

NET FILES

Why do the temperate zones of the world have four seasons?

(Here at Pollywood Farm, we have only two seasons: four months of winter and eight months of bad skiing!)

Answer: Because of Earth's tilt in its orbit around the Sun, sometimes parts of Earth lean close to the Sun, and sometimes these parts lean farther away. Without the tilt of Earth's axis, we wouldn't have seasons at all! We would have about the same temperature year-round, according to the Missouri Botanical Garden. Find more info and a drawing of how this all works at http://www.mobot.org/MBGnet/vb/temp/4seasons.htm

NET FILES

You've always wondered if your brother was an alien from outer space. Now you get your photos back, and sure enough, he's got glowing red eyes!

What should you do?

Answer: Don't call NASA yet. According to Kodak, this effect sometimes occurs when you use a flash. It's actually the reflection of light from the flash off of the blood vessels inside the subject's eyes. To reduce red-eye, you need to reduce the size of your subject's pupils so there won't be so much reflective surface available. There are several ways to do this: increase the light level in the room by turning on all of the lights, or have your subject look at a bright light just before you take the flash picture. Also, some cameras have a red-eye reduction feature. To eliminate red-eye from pictures you have already taken, you need to manipulate the image electronically. If you have the equipment available to you, you can do it yourself, or you can take the prints to a Kodak digital enhancement station at a retail store. There's more information on that at http://www.kodak.com/global/en/consumer/pictureTaking/remedies/flash1.shtml where you'll also discover answers to more frequently asked questions about film and photography!

Putt-Putt Golf & Games - Fayetteville, NC

Net-mom loves to play miniature golf. Well, actually, Son of Net-mom really loves to play, because he usually *beats* Net-mom's score! (However, there was that one time, on Jekyll Island, Georgia...but then again, there were all those other times.) There are Putt-Putt mini golf courses in 34 states and seven other countries. The first course was built in North Carolina, in 1954, and the cost of a round of play was twenty-five cents! At this site, you can learn a little history and find a course nearby or near where you'll be on vacation.

http://www.putt-putt.com/

HIKING, ORIENTEERING, AND BACKPACKING

Appalachian Trail Home Page

The Appalachian Trail stretches from Springer Mountain, Georgia, to Mount Katahdin, Maine, a distance of 2,160 miles. If you walked it straight through, it would take you between four and six months before you emerged at the other end. At this outstanding site, you will see a map of the trail and read hikers' journals about their travels. Don't miss the story about Bill Irwin, a blind man who completed the trail accompanied by his trusty guide dog, Orient. There are also links to Web sites about major trail systems, such as the Pacific Crest Trail, the Natchez Trace, and several others.

http://www.fred.net/kathy/at.html

GORP - Hiking - for walkers, hikers and trekkers

This site covers trails all over the world. You can find tips on hiking equipment as well as a multimedia collection of links, books, and videos. You can read other hikers' stories of the trails they have traveled or check the jawboning in the discussion areas. There is also a very interesting section on historic routes, such as the Oregon Trail, the Santa Fe Trail, and others.

http://www.gorp.com/gorp/activity/hiking.htm

How to Use a Compass

On a hike, a compass will help you find your way, but first you have to learn to use one properly. You can learn in your own backyard, or in a park, or in a school playground. This site gives you a guided tour to a compass and its use. There are also tips on how to find your way in very difficult conditions, like fog or snow whiteouts.

http://www.uio.no/~kjetikj/compass/

HAY! Gallop over to HORSES AND EQUESTRIAN SPORTS.

A B C D E F G H I J K L M N O P Q R S T U V W X Y Z

A
B
C
D
E
F
G
H
I
J
K
L
M
N
O
P
Q
R
S
T
U
V
W
X
Y
Z

Orienteering

Does this sound like fun? You and your friends use a very detailed map and a compass to visit various checkpoint flags hidden in the forest. When you reach a checkpoint, you use a special hole punch (usually hanging by the flag) to verify that you found the flag. The punches make differently shaped holes in your control card. This fast-growing sport can be enjoyed as a simple family walk in the woods or as a competitive team race. Learn about getting started in orienteering here, and don't miss the explanation of orienteering clue symbols. Remember: a big asterisk means look for an ANTHILL!

http://www.williams.edu:803/Biology/
    orienteering/o_index.html

ROLLER AND INLINE SKATING

Rollerblade: Site Menu

This is a commercial site, developed by the Rollerblade company. It has lots of info on how to get started in rollerblading and catch up with your friends (or your parents, as the case may be). You'll learn about the scenes, the moves, the equipment, even the lingo. There's lots on safety, too, because "asphalt bites"!

http://www.rollerblade.com/site_menu.html

Skating the Infobahn

Are you looking for information on basic fitness rollerblading? Or maybe you're an aggressive skater looking for the latest moves. It's here! But remember, if you're going to skate, wear the gear—because "no one looks good wearing their brains on the outside." Check the tutorials (how to use that foot brake!), the directory of great places to skate, and more. Besides inline skating, you'll find great links for speed skating, roller hockey, and traditional roller skating. Parents: Not all links have been viewed.

http://www.skatecity.com/index/

DINOSAURS are prehistoric, but they are under "D."

SKYDIVING

Canadian Sport Parachuting Association

Do you think that people who jump out of airplanes are just plain nuts? Or are you one of those who live to skydive off into the wild blue yonder? Skydiving may be the sport for you, and this page could be your jumping-off point. This bilingual (French and English) page includes information on how to get involved in skydiving, links to other skydiving Web sites, and an area for people to talk about their skydiving experiences. You'll find some pretty funny stories here!

http://www.cspa.ca/

United States Parachute Association

This is the home page of the U.S. Parachute Association, and the first thing you need to know is that you can't skydive until you're 18 years old. Some drop zones will allow skydiving at 16 with parental consent, but keep in mind that this is an expensive sport. Expect to pay $150 to $300 for your first instruction. It does get cheaper after you've convinced an instructor that you know what you're doing. You should find an accredited teacher, too; there's a list here so you can find one near you.

http://www.USPA.org/

NET FILES

In the Pasadena Tournament of Roses Parade, each float must be completely covered with flowers or other organic material. What's the average number of flowers on each float?

Answer: An average float requires up to 100,000 blossoms. More than half a million roses are used in each parade, according to the City of Pasadena home page at http://ci.pasadena.ca.us/miscellany.html

PARADES

The Great Circus Parade - Wisconsin's National Treasure

Hey, look at this poster! It says: "Come to the Great Circus Parade! A two-hour processional over a three-mile route, authentically re-creating turn-of-the-century circus street parades. Features 60 historic wagons, 700 horses, cavorting clowns, wild animals in cage wagons, and the fabulous 40-Horse Hitch." Sounds like fun! Look over there—isn't that Buffalo Bill Cody in that beaded buckskin jacket? You can learn something about circus history, including circus trains, at this colorful, animated site. If you have Java, you'll also hear vintage calliope music!

http://www.circusparade.com/

Tournament of Roses

Alas, you won't be able to take time to smell the roses at this Web site, because there aren't any! But all the info is here about this traditional New Year's Day parade, held in Pasadena, California. All the floats must be completely covered with flowers or other natural, organic material.

http://www.rosebowl.com/

Trooping the Colour

One of the largest military parades in the world, the Trooping of the Colour is held every June to celebrate the official birthday of Elizabeth II of England. It's not on her real birthday but on her "official" birthday. It's a grand show of heraldry, music, prancing horses, and dashing soldiers. The presentation of the flag ("the colour") to Her Majesty is the highlight of the event. The flag is weighty and cumbersome, but no one would turn down the honor of carrying it, and the soldier who carries the flag during the ceremony must train for months. The ceremony requires strict adherence to military regulations. Anyone falling from a horse could get three months in jail! Learn about one of the most stirring parades in the world at this Web site. By the way, the official royal Web site at <http://www.royal.gov.uk/today/trooping.htm> also mentions a bit about this event.

http://www.buckinghamgate.com/events/features/
    trooping/trooping.html

MARDI GRAS

NEW ORLEANS.NET: CARNIVAL ON PARADE

Have you heard about Mardi Gras in New Orleans, Louisiana? The carnival season begins at the end of January and is celebrated right up until Fat Tuesday, the day before the Christian season of Lent begins. It's a series of parties, parades, and nonstop fun and foolishness! Over 70 parades are given by special clubs, called krewes. Everyone dresses up in outlandish costumes and yells, "Throw me somethin', Mister!" Then they line the streets to catch "throws" tossed from the krewes on the floats. Popular throws include doubloons, beads, cups, and sometimes coconuts (get out of the way if you see a coconut hurled your way!). You can see some of the fun and learn about the history of this gala event at this site, created by the *Times-Picayune* newspaper.

http://www.neworleans.net/carnpages/parades.html

NET FILES

When is the best time of year to get your piano tuned?

Answer: According to the Piano Home Page, the best times are in the fall, after your furnace has been on for about a month, and again in summer, after the air conditioning has been on for about a month, so that the instrument has stabilized with the humidity changes the seasons bring. You should also never try to fix or tune a piano yourself. Get a real piano technician to do it. And remember, just because someone can tune a piano doesn't mean he or she can tuna fish. Check out http://www.unm.edu/~jortiz/pnobtuying.html

A
B
C
D
E
F
G
H
I
J
K
L
M
N
O
P
Q
R
S
T
U
V
W
X
Y
Z

Official Site of Mardi Gras 1998

Take a trip through this site and learn all the lingo, the details on the parades, and how those elaborate floats are made. There are some games you can play, some recipes to try, and scenes from the last Mardi Gras. If you can't head to New Orleans and want to enjoy the ambiance from home, there are even places where you can order some of the special foodstuffs and other souvenirs, including the beads and doubloons that are thrown from floats.

http://www.mardigrasday.com/

NET FILES

Why is the capital of the United States located in Washington, D.C.?

Answer: There weren't a lot of choices back in the late 1700s. Some people thought New York would be a good place; others favored Philadelphia. Finally they decided on a site on the Potomac River, about halfway between the original northern and southern states. The area was wilderness. It was marshy and full of mosquitoes. The area was drained, and construction began. According to the White House for Kids home page, the French city planner, Pierre L'Enfant, "decided to place the Capitol Building on one hill and the 'President's House' on another hill." In between were parks and grand boulevards. You can read more White House history at http://www.whitehouse.gov/WH/kids/html/his_2.html

PEACE

Cranes for Peace

Sadako and the story of the thousand cranes has touched hearts worldwide. An old Japanese legend says that anyone who folds 1,000 origami cranes can have a wish. Sadako was a survivor of the atomic bomb attack on Hiroshima, Japan, in 1945. The radiation made her very ill, and she died before completing all her cranes. Her friends completed them for her. Sadako's story is not forgotten. Her inspiring statue stands today in the Hiroshima Peace Park. The year 1995 marked 50 years of peace between the U.S. and Japan, and many people around the world decided to fold cranes and send them to the Peace Park to honor Sadako and her gentle message of peace. Read the story of how many children's hands made these cranes, which flutter today over the park of peace.

http://www.he.net/~sparker/cranes.html

"We are pleased to present nearly 20,000 paper cranes made by children in 42 states and one Canadian province. The children were linked to each other and to Japan through the Internet, and they were linked by love and a desire for peace," said teacher Sharon O'Connell. She had carried brilliantly colored origami cranes to Hiroshima, Japan, for the 50th anniversary celebration of peace between the U.S. and Japan. Read about Sadako and the 1,000 paper cranes at Cranes for Peace.

Expect a miracle in RELIGION!

DEPARTMENT OF JUSTICE - KID'S PAGE

Your parents want you to say grace and thank the Lord before you eat lunch at school, but when you do, the other kids make fun of you and call you names. What should you do? You could stop saying grace, you could sit somewhere else, or you could talk to an adult about it. Each one of these choices has other consequences; compare them and see which is the right decision for you. The Attorney General of the United States presents this page about racial, religious, and other types of prejudice. Learn to recognize, and then do something, about hateful acts like these, whether it happens to you or to someone else.

http://www.usdoj.gov/kidspage/bias-k-5/

Development Journal 1996.1 — Seeds of Peace

This page is a couple of years old, but it still carries a strong message. The organization, Seeds of Peace, brings young people from the Middle East (Egypt, Israel, Jordan, Palestine, and Morocco) to the U.S. for a month of activities. Part of this month is spent at a summer camp, where the kids participate in coexistence workshops. They learn about each other's cultures and discuss issues that concern them all. This is an insider's view of what happens at one of these workshops.

http://www.waw.be/sid/dev1996/seeds-of-peace.html

Get Your ANGRIES Out!

Are you always yelling at your sister? Is there a bully bothering you at school? Are you mad and cranky a lot? This site gives you some useful ways to get your anger out in constructive ways. For example: "Check your tummy, jaws and your fists. See if the mads are coming. Breathe! Blow your mad out. Get your control. Feel good about getting your control. Stop and think; make a good choice. People are not to be hurt with your hands, feet or voice. Remember to use your firm words, not your fists." There are many more good ideas here, and don't forget to check the links about peace while you're dealing with your angries!

http://members.aol.com/AngriesOut/

I*EARN

The best way to understand people of a different nationality or race or religion is to get to know them. Basically, that's what the developers of this nonprofit site are doing, and it is a concept that has won them praise from all kinds of sources. Simply put, classrooms of children from kindergarten through secondary school work together in developing projects on a variety of subjects, using telecommunications to pave the way. School classes are invited to participate in a project already in progress or to begin something new. Like the idea? Read more about it and talk to your teacher. Soon your "classmates" could be kids from halfway around the world!

http://www.iearn.org/

International Day of Peace at the United Nations

As part of the United Nations International Day of Peace (September 16), kids from all over the world have collaborated on a "Peace Poem." Over 400 schools in 38 countries participated in the project. Each grade in each school could submit only one poem. Parts of the poem are in French and Spanish as well as English. If you could write just two lines describing your feelings about peace, what would they be? Here are some samples:

Peace on earth is like groovy tie-dyed shirts
Or tranquil baby birds on a bright spring morning.
(Cleveland Middle School, Cleveland, Oklahoma, U.S.A.)

As she soars through the hate, all wrong leaves her wing
It's amazing how much peace a small dove can bring.
(International School of Kuala Lumpur, Kuala Lumpur, Malaysia)

Peace doesn't need any words
just good hearts.
(Basic school, Masarykova, Kosice, Slovakia)

Intrigued? Read about the International Day of Peace, check out a discussion area, and find out more at this site.

http://www.un.org/Pubs/CyberSchoolBus/peaceday/

A B C D E F G H I J K L M N O P Q R S T U V W X Y Z

A
B
C
D
E
F
G
H
I
J
K
L
M
N
O
P
Q
R
S
T
U
V
W
X
Y
Z

Kids 4 Peace

What if for 1 DAY no gun were fired...
What if for 1 DAY we tried to get along...
Imagine what it could mean for us all...
Imagine how 1 DAY could change all the world...
1 DAY Of Peace, on January 1, in the Year 2000
Spread the word, the World has declared:
1 DAY Of PEACE, for all the world to share...

Kids for Peace wants to get everyone on the planet on board for this world day of peace. Learn how you can help!

http://members.aol.com/kidz4peace/

Kids' International Peace Museum

Welcome to the Kids' International Peace Museum, created for kids, by kids. Students in schools all over the world have contributed drawings, poems, essays, and other works to express their feelings on peace. Here's what Liana, a third grader from Dom Bosco School in Campo Grande, Brazil, wrote: "*Paz é um sentimento que nos traz amor e fé e nos faz viver em perfeita harmonia com as outras pessoas e com tudo que nos cerca. Paz entre os povos de todas as raças.*" (Translation: "Peace is a feeling that brings us love and faith and lets us live in perfect harmony with one another and everything that is around us. Peace through all people from all races.") After you have read what other kids wrote, check the first page and see how you and your classmates can participate.

http://www.ih.k12.oh.us/ps/peace/

Line Around the World

Here's something unusual, called a Web ring. Its creator wants to draw a line around the world, linking Web page to Web page, to show how we're all connected to each other on this little blue planet of ours. Register your home page, and within a few days, you'll receive the "line" to place on your page. You link back to the last person in the line, and the next person after you will link to your home page. Thus, you're standing in line between two strangers, but, oddly enough, it feels pretty good. By linking your home page, or your school's, into this big virtual "hug," you've agreed to perform a good deed. How far has the line gone so far? Check this page to find out!

http://www.stairway.bc.ca/latw/

The Peace Pilgrim Home Page

How far would you walk for peace? Maybe around the block? A mile? Five miles? How about 25,000 miles? That's what Peace Pilgrim did. "From 1953 to 1981 a silver haired woman calling herself only 'Peace Pilgrim' walked more than 25,000 miles on a personal pilgrimage for peace. She vowed to 'remain a wanderer until mankind has learned the way of peace, walking until given shelter and fasting until given food.' In the course of 28 years of walking she touched the hearts, minds, and lives of thousands of individuals all across North America. Her message was both simple and profound: 'This is the way of peace: overcome evil with good, and falsehood with truth, and hatred with love.'" You can read about her life, her journey, and her message at this site. Since her death in 1981, others have taken up similar quests, and you can read their stories here.

http://www.peacepilgrim.com/

Philips "Let's Connect"

According to a recent survey sponsored by Philips Consumer Communications, most parents and their preteen children spend less than one hour a day talking to each other; many spend less than 30 minutes! More than half the kids (57 percent) say their parents don't always give them a chance to explain themselves, but almost the same number of parents (51 percent) say their children don't let *them* explain themselves. Want to get your parents to really listen to what you're saying? Check the tips here.

http://www.philipsconsumer.com/letsconnect/

St. Julie Billiart School

"The key to peace starts with each of us. Many times peace is defined as not fighting. However broken feelings can be as painful as throwing a punch." This is one of the Peace Declarations published by several classes at St. Julie Billiart School in Hamilton, Ohio. This page opens with a large graphic; keep scrolling down to get to the declarations.

http://www.iac.net/~esimonds/stjulie.html

PEN PALS

eMail Classroom Exchange - K-12 Education Resource

Would your whole class or homeschool like to write to another class of kids on the other side of the world? You can, just by adding your information to the database here! Search for kids by city, state, country, grade/age, or language. There are also some real-time browser conferencing facilities here.

http://www.iglou.com/xchange/ece/

G.I.R.L.

G.I.R.L. (Girls Internationally wRiting Letters) is a cool club for girls ages 8 to 14. It began a few years ago with only four members; since then, lots more have joined, and the club has officers, a newsletter, and other interesting areas for you to explore. There are members from all over the world, and you can become one by registering here. Check the section on links for girls, too!

http://worldkids.net/girl/

NET FILES

What are the Cissoid of Diocles, the Pearls of Sluze, and the Witch of Agnesi?

Answer: *They are all famous mathematical curves, drawn from notable historic equations. They do look something like their namesakes; for example, the Witch of Agnesi does look like a witch's hat. According to this site, Maria Agnesi studied this equation in 1748 and wrote about it in her mathematics book. Be sure to find more famous curves at http://www-groups.dcs.st-and.ac.uk/~history/Curves/Curves.html.*

IECC, Intercultural E-Mail Classroom Connections

One of the great aspects of the Internet is that it provides children with the opportunity to reach well beyond their community to kids just about anywhere. Intercultural E-Mail Classroom Connections, or IECC, provides listserv discussions for teachers to find other teachers and classes interested in a pen pal exchange. If you are a teacher, definitely take a look. If you are a student, parent, or caregiver, mention IECC to a teacher. A whole new way of communicating may well open up, since at last count more than 7,300 teachers in 73 countries were participating. IECC provides connections for students of all ages, from grade school through college.

http://www.iecc.org/

KIDZMAIL

How would you like to contact kids from around the world and share messages? You could ask them about life in their countries. Make a new key pal (that's like a pen pal, but one you send e-mail to, using a keyboard rather than pen and paper for regular mail). KIDZMAIL is a good place to connect with kids the world over.

List Address: kidzmail@asuvm.inre.asu.edu
Subscription Address:
LISTSERV@ASUVM.INRE.ASU.EDU

Mighty Media Keypals Club

A part of the safe, fun Keypals Club, this is a good place to learn about others and the world around you as you practice the art of writing. If you're a student aged 14 or younger or a teacher looking for a classroom project, fill out a form with information about yourself, click a button, and ZAP! you've just joined the group! This site acts as a remailer and does not divulge your e-mail address.

http://www.mightymedia.com/keypals/

A B C D E F G H I J K L M N O P Q R S T U V W X Y Z

A
B
C
D
E
F
G
H
I
J
K
L
M
N
O
P
Q
R
S
T
U
V
W
X
Y
Z

Pen Pal Request Form

The Schoolnet folks have set up a service to help kids in Canada and elsewhere find pen pals. Interested in making contact with kids from all over the world? Take a look at this site. All you need is an e-mail address and a willingness to make new friends.

gopher://gopher.schoolnet.ca:419/11/
   K6.dir/penpals.dir

Penpal Box

Part of Net-mom's favorite site, Kids' Space, the Penpal Box offers kids aged from 6 to 16 the opportunity to have an e-mail friend. Actually, there is more than one box: look through the box for six and under, the box for ages seven and eight, the one for nine and ten, and so on. Remember to read the FAQ for safety tips, and remember not to give your home address to anyone.

http://www.ks-connection.com/penpal/penpal.html

Welcome to AGW's Pen Pal Spectacular!

Here's the good news: this site lets you safely exchange e-mail with girls aged 7 to 17 from around the world. Here's the bad news, guys: the site is for girls only! This is a system that takes your e-mail and remails it, giving you a member number instead. Your pen friend writes back to your "box number," the A Girl's World computer matches up your box number with your real e-mail address, and—poof!— your e-mail arrives at your regular mailbox. It sounds a lot more complicated than it is. Read some of these girls' descriptions: they sound really interesting and fun to get to know.

http://www.agirlsworld.com/geri/penpal/

WKN Fun Clubs

If you want a quick way to find other kids who are interested in space, animals, computers, books, writing, volunteering, entertainers, and more, try this site. For example, if you're a fan of *Star Trek*, transport into the USS *Jaguar* and take the turbolift to any deck to learn about the various officers and their duties on the ship. Then become an officer yourself and write to other officers all over the world! At this site, kids rule.

http://www.worldkids.net/clubs/clubs.htm

PEOPLE AND BIOGRAPHIES

See also AFRICAN AMERICANS; ASIAN AMERICANS; INVENTIONS AND INVENTORS; LATINO; NATIVE AMERICANS AND OTHER INDIGENOUS PEOPLES; QUEENS, KINGS, AND ROYALTY; REFERENCE WORKS; UNITED STATES—PRESIDENTS AND FIRST LADIES

America's West - Development and History

Return with us now to the days of yesteryear—of gold rush and ghost town, the heyday of cowboy and gunslinger. At this site, you'll discover links to information on America's westward expansion, famous Western trails, pioneers, trappers, and biographies of Kit Carson, Davy Crockett, Daniel Boone, Billy the Kid, Sitting Bull, Roy Rogers, and lots of other famous folks. There are links to movies about the West as well as to Western theme parks and dude ranches. A caution to parents: Not all the outbound links have been reviewed.

http://www.AmericanWest.com/

Biographical Dictionary

Sometimes you'll get an assignment in school to write about a famous person. Or maybe you're curious and you'd like to know some quick facts about a famous person. This site is the place to go for this type of info. Here you'll find 25,000 people listed, from both historical and current times. You can search by birth and death years, professions, literary and artistic works, and other achievements.

http://www.s9.com/biography/

"Use the source, Luke!"
and look it up in
REFERENCE WORKS.

Biography.com

Got a name? Get the facts! Here's a searchable online database from A&E TV and the *Cambridge Biographical Encyclopedia*. Discover the who, what, and why of 15,000 of the greatest names, past and present. Find out about current, best-selling biographies and then take the biography quiz.

http://www.biography.com/

Brittanica's Lives

Ever wonder who shares your birthday? Sure, it might be your mom or your dad or even your twin brother. But was anyone famous born on your birthday? (Besides you, of course!) Find out at this useful site. You can also discover which famous people in history share the same generation. For example, John McEnroe and Magic Johnson both turned 21 in 1980. Want to know more about each famous person? This site gives you short biographies.

http://www.eb.com/lives/lives.htcl

gauche! Left-Handers in Society

Bill Clinton is one. So is Queen Elizabeth II. Paul McCartney. Phil Collins. Larry Bird. For somewhere between 2 and 30 percent of the world's population, life is challenging because it seems like everything is being done backwards! This site will help all lefties to better understand "handedness." Also, solutions are provided for dealing with common everyday activities.

http://www.indiana.edu/~primate/lspeak.html

GreatKids on the Web

According to a 12-year-old named Cassie, a GreatKid is someone who has a great personality and a good sense of humor. Ten-year-old Carolyn says GreatKids get good grades, have opinions, and are nice to other siblings and people. And Konner, five years old, says GreatKids can be nice and sweet to their parents and teachers. Anyone can be a GreatKid and can have his or her story told here. Also, some GreatKids volunteer their time to help others, and if you want to be one of them, this site can help you find organizations that are looking for young volunteers. You'll also find some neat Web links.

http://www.greatkids.com/

The Invention Dimension!

Would you like to win half a million dollars? All you have to do is invent something so cool, so unique, and so compelling that everyone says, "Wow!" That's the idea behind the Lemelson-MIT Prize, which is presented every year to an American inventor-innovator for outstanding creativity. You can find out about the prize and its past winners here, and you'll also find a collection of material about other great inventors and inventions. Don't miss the Links area for more inventions and resources.

http://web.mit.edu/afs/athena.mit.edu/org/i/invent/www/invention_dimension.html

Man of the Year Home Page

Need biographies of famous people? Cruise over to this page for information about the man, woman, or idea considered by *Time* magazine to be the biggest influence on events each year since 1927. In 1982, the computer was "Man of the Year." You may want to select the text-only version of this page, since the graphics take a long time to load.

http://pathfinder.com/time/special/moy/moy.html

Your buddies (who like math as much as you do) invite you to the Pi Day celebration at the Exploratorium—but they've forgotten to tell you when it is and what time to show up!

What's your best guess?

Answer: Pi *Day is celebrated every year on March 14, at 1:59 in the afternoon. Third month? Fourteenth day? The value of pi to a few decimal places is 3.14159! This irrational celebration happens to coincide with Albert Einstein's birthday. Read about it at http://www.exploratorium.edu/pi/pi97/pi_one.html*

A
B
C
D
E
F
G
H
I
J
K
L
M
N
O
P
Q
R
S
T
U
V
W
X
Y
Z

MSU Vincent Voice Library

Wouldn't it be great to be able to hear the voices of some famous people? At this site, you can! Listen to sound files of many U.S. presidents as well as brief conversations with people such as George Washington Carver, Babe Ruth, and Amelia Earhart. Test: Teddy Roosevelt has left the building...he has left the building!

http://web.msu.edu/vincent/

World History : HyperHistory

Hey, your mom says you can have some friends over for lunch! She says to invite three people you admire from history—which heroes would you choose? You might get some ideas here. This site will teach you about important people from 1000 B.C. to the present. You'll find scientists, artists, musicians, authors, politicians, explorers, and many others. But that is not all. You can also trace events through history as well as look at important maps of time periods and the spread of civilizations.

**http://www.hyperhistory.com/online_n2/
    History_n2/a.html**

GIRLS

GIRL GAMES, INC. | PLANET GIRL

The president of Girl Games once told Net-mom that everyone in the Planet Girl office wears a tiara. Net-mom liked that, because at Net-mom International Headquarters, Net-mom herself often wears a tiara. So if you like tiaras, too, you'll like this site. Warning: you'd better like pink. Our favorite girl at this site is named "Phat." She writes a column and has exciting adventures. You might think the topics are sort of gross, but then they turn out to be really interesting. That Phat Girl will discuss anything: your period, your pimples, and fads, like *mehndi* (temporary henna body art). Parents: Preview the site for your kids.

http://www.girlgamesinc.com/plntgrl.html

A Girl's World

Looking for the space that's totally girl-powered? Explore a "girls-only" clubhouse, find a pen pal (your e-mail address is kept private), see stories about famous women, and have all sorts of fun. You'll also find crafts, links, and even ideas about starting your own business!

http://www.agirlsworld.com/

Welcome to Club Girl Tech

Did you ever hear of that great criminal Carmen Sandiego? Did you ever play with a Yak-back recording toy? If so, you're already acquainted with the inventor of this Web site. The site celebrates creative girls who like to think, whether it's about science or celebrities. There's also a fascinating section on women inventors. Check out book and movie reviews, take virtual field trips to places like NASA, and read stories about girls in the news. You go (there), girl!

http://www.girltech.com/Index_home.html

Who are **Nahuelito, Champ,** and **Ogopogo**?

Hint: If you can find them at all, they will be in water.

Answer: *Like Nessie of Loch Ness, they are all legendary lake monsters. Nahuelito supposedly inhabits Nahuel Huapi Lake (Argentina), while Champ is from Lake Champlain (between New York and Vermont). Ogopogo has been spotted in the waters of Lake Okanagan in British Columbia, Canada. Read more about them at* http://www.strangemag.com/nessie.home.html

INDIVIDUALS

Albert Einstein Online

Lots of people think Albert Einstein was the greatest physicist ever. His famous theory of relativity includes the equation $E=mc^2$. He even had an element named after him! Einsteinium, element 99, was discovered in 1952. Einstein won the Nobel Prize for Physics in 1921. Although he urged President Roosevelt to consider making an atomic bomb (the letter is at this site), he believed in peace. This site is a jumpstation to numerous links about Einstein; not all have been checked.

http://www.westegg.com/einstein/

Anne Frank Home Page

In 1942, 13-year-old Anne Frank and her family went into hiding in a house in Amsterdam. They were Jews, fleeing from Nazi terrorism. During her 24-month stay in "the Secret Annex," she kept a diary of her thoughts and ambitions. Ultimately, the secret hideout was discovered and Anne was captured; she later died at the age of 16. Her legacy remains. Her diary was published by her father, who survived the concentration camp experience. The diary has been translated into many languages and has sold over 25 million copies around the world. This site has photos of the Anne Frank House as well as pictures of the original diary. Parental warning: There are several grim photos of concentration camps in that section of this resource. See another Anne Frank site in the HISTORY—WORLD WAR II section of this book.

http://www.annefrank.nl/

Genghis Khan @ nationalgeographic.com

This legendary warrior lived in twelfth and thirteenth century Asia. He's pictured on today's Mongolian currency. Why is he so important? He managed to unite the rival tribes and create a nation that became the largest land empire the world has ever seen. At this site you can read biographical information and see the man through the eyes of a writer and a photographer on assignment for *National Geographic*.

http://www.nationalgeographic.com/features/97/
  genghis/

Seattle Times: Martin Luther King Jr.

In a thoughtful and moving Web site, *The Seattle Times* commemorates the life and legacy of Dr. Martin Luther King, Jr. You'll find a timeline of his life, along with many photos and audio files. You'll be able to hear part of his famous "I Have a Dream" speech as well as others. Check the sections on the history of the civil rights movement, and read about how the Martin Luther King, Jr. Day national holiday was created in memory of this great leader, called "America's Gandhi."

http://www.seattletimes.com/mlk/

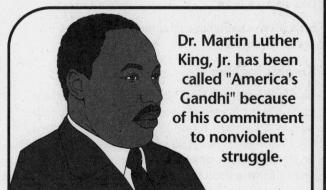

Dr. Martin Luther King, Jr. has been called "America's Gandhi" because of his commitment to nonviolent struggle.

Written on a plaque in the hotel room in which he was killed are these words:
"Behold here comes the dreamer.
Let us slay him, and we shall see
what becomes of his dream."
His dream lives on, despite the violent act that ended his life. Read about it at the Seattle Times: Martin Luther King, Jr. page.

The World of Benjamin Franklin

Hey! Who's that guy on the one hundred dollar bill, the hippie with the long hair? It's Ben Franklin: famous American scientist, statesman, and inventor. You remember him: he's the guy who supposedly flew the kite in the thunderstorm to learn about electricity. (Net-mom says don't try that—it's extremely dangerous.) Here are some classroom activities to help you learn more about some of the things that interested Franklin. He was interested in lots of things, too. For example, he was one of the original signers of the Declaration of Independence. And you know where it was signed, right? At the bottom!

http://sln.fi.edu/franklin/rotten.html

A B C D E F G H I J K L M N O P Q R S T U V W X Y Z

A
B
C
D
E
F
G
H
I
J
K
L
M
N
O
P
Q
R
S
T
U
V
W
X
Y
Z

KNIGHTS

Castles @ nationalgeographic.com

Wouldn't it be neat to live in a castle? Here's your chance to explore one built in Britain in the 1300s! We took the tour and met a lot of really neat people who are there to protect us, the castle owners. James, the archer, was one. He claims to be able to shoot a steel-tipped arrow more than 100 yards! With a few carefully placed clicks of your mouse on the mouse wandering around on the screen, you will be transported through this marvelous place. Watch for the ghosts, though. Now we're heading back to see what Peter the Jester has up his sleeve.

http://www.nationalgeographic.com/features/97/
     castles/enter.html

Knights for Hire

This is the story of Karl M. Kindt III, who became a knight. It is his way of showing tribute to his father, who was killed in World War II. After he reached adulthood, Karl had a set of armor made for him, and he studied all about knights. Now he travels around and talks to schoolchildren about knighthood and its history. He also has written a children's book entitled *Sir Kwain, the Armadillo and the Name Dragon.*

http://www.icon-stl.net/~kkindt/

PIRATES

Pirates at the City Art Centre

"Shiver me timbers!" If you don't know a pirate from a buccaneer, better sail over to this page. You'll learn lots about famous pirates, legends, and perhaps locations of buried treasure!

http://www.efr.hw.ac.uk/EDC/CAC/pirates/
     pirates.htm

Pirates! @ nationalgeographic.com

Can you solve these National Geographic adventures? You'll have to read clues and figure out which pirate, which ship, and which treasure star in each of the mysteries. Beware: if you get it wrong, you may have to walk the virtual plank and start all over again! There are also links to additional materials, books, and links about pirates.

http://www.nationalgeographic.com/features/97/
     pirates/maina.html

WOMEN

4000 Years of Women in Science

They've got to be kidding! Four thousand years of women in science? According to this site, the first "scientific literature" appeared some 4,000 years ago. Stone and bone records stretch back further than those first writings, but they don't give us the names of their authors. The very first technical writer's name was male: Imhotep, the architect of the first pyramid. The second technical name was female: En Hedu'Anna (c. 2354 B.C.). Learn more about other women in science right here.

http://www.astr.ua.edu/4000WS/4000WS.html

Distinguished Women of Past and Present

The biographies of women writers, educators, scientists, heads of state, politicians, civil rights crusaders, artists, entertainers, and more are listed at this site. Some were alive hundreds of years ago and some are living today. Some are famous and some are not as well known. No matter—their stories are interesting and would be a real plus for a school writing project. They're listed by fields of activity, so it is easy to find women in journalism, or architecture, or sports, or any other topic in which you're interested.

http://www.netsrq.com/~dbois/

NET FILES

It's been called Shovegroat, Slide-groat, and Shovel-penny in its long history. What is it?

http://www.duke.edu/~ishy/shuffle/about.html

Answer: Shuffleboard! This game, fun for all ages, gained popularity as a shipboard pastime during long ocean voyages. It was introduced as a land sport in 1913, in Daytona Beach, Florida. Find more fun shuffleboard facts at

The National Women's Hall of Fame

"Come Stand Among Great Women." That's the motto of the new official home page of the National Women's Hall of Fame, which is located in Seneca Falls, New York. That town was the site of the first Women's Rights Convention, back in 1848. The Convention led to the passage of the 19th amendment to the Constitution, which granted U.S. women the right to vote. Visit this site to learn about 136 women who have been inducted into the Hall of Fame. They include Sandra Day O'Connor, Ella Fitzgerald, Georgia O'Keeffe, Rosa Parks, and many others. Know of a woman who should be in the Hall of Fame? Check out the "How to Nominate" section—or perhaps the "The Wall of Fame"—where, for $100, you can make a personal tribute to an extraordinary woman of your choice.

http://www.greatwomen.org/

The National Women's History Project

Let's celebrate! That's what the National Women's History Project is all about. It celebrates women's diverse lives and historic contributions to society. The background of Women's History Month (in March) is here, along with links to each of the states showcasing their activities. Here's one quick question from the "Test Your Knowledge" section. Name the First Lady who traveled the country and the world to gather information about the problems and concerns of workers, children, minorities, and the poor. She wrote a daily newspaper column and made frequent radio broadcasts. Time's up. Did you guess Eleanor Roosevelt? If you did, head to the quiz for more interesting questions. If you didn't, go there anyway. You've got a lot to learn!

http://www.nwhp.org/

Women in American History

This collection of material on women in history is gathered in four time periods: Early America, the Nineteenth Century, At the Crossroads, and Modern America. It is presented in a time line beginning in 1587, with the birth of Virginia Dare, the first child in America born of English parents. It ends with the opening of a contemporary museum dedicated to the works of Georgia O'Keeffe in Santa Fe, New Mexico. Many of the items in the time line have links to more information about the woman or the event.

http://women.eb.com/

Women in Canadian History

Many women played important parts in Canada's history. Dr. Emily Jennings Stowe was the first woman to practice medicine in Canada. Lucy Maud Montgomery became known worldwide as the author of *Anne of Green Gables* and other books. Madeleine Jarrett Tarieu single-handedly defended an entire fort against invaders. And there are others. The stories here are very interesting! You'll also find quotes, trivia questions, and more.

http://www.niagara.com/~merrwill/

Women Mathematicians

These pages are an ongoing project by students at Agnes Scott College in Decatur, Georgia. You'll find brief comments on over 140 women in mathematics and expanded biographies, photos, and more information on at least ten of them. There are also extensive links to pages about women scientists, computer scientists, and others.

http://www.scottlan.edu/lriddle/women/women.htm

Ada Byron Lovelace is credited with the invention of programming for her work in explaining the details of how the analytical engine operated. The programming language Ada is named after her, as a tribute to her work. Read more about Ada and other women's achievements at Women Mathematicians.

A B C D E F G H I J K L M N O P Q R S T U V W X Y Z

A B C D E F G H I J K L M N O P Q R S T U V W X Y Z

PETS AND PET CARE

See also AMPHIBIANS; AQUARIUMS; BIRDS; CATS; DOGS AND DOG SPORTS; FARMING AND AGRICULTURE; HORSES AND EQUESTRIAN SPORTS; INSECTS AND SPIDERS; MAMMALS; REPTILES

Acme Pet-Your Guide to Pets on the Internet!

Pet enthusiasts, welcome! Here you'll find a current and complete source of pet information, discussion lists, and resources all over the Internet. Send in your facts, views, or opinions about pet-related topics on this home page. Whether you want to keep a pet gerbil or a pet prairie dog—check into it here first!

http://www.acmepet.com/

HealthyPet.com

The American Animal Hospital Association's pages include frequently asked questions on many types of pets, from birds to dogs, from felines to ferrets. There are also coloring book pages as well as a pet care library. If you own a pet or are thinking of getting one, the advice here is a must-see.

http://www.healthypet.com/

NET FILES

How many mosquitoes can one little brown bat catch in one hour?

Answer: It can catch 600 mosquitoes! Read more fascinating bat trivia at *http://www.batcon.org/trivia.html*

Heat stress can be a big summertime problem for your furry friends. Your dog will enjoy a splash in a hard plastic wading pool instead of a walk on hot, burning pavement. Or, freeze water in a closed gallon jug and leave it for your pet to "snuggle up to." Keep your pets cool in the shade, give them plenty of water, and don't EVER leave them in parked cars, even "for a minute." Summertime temperatures can soar in an enclosed space like your car. Know the signs and first aid tips for heat stress, located at HealthyPet.com. Heatstroke is a medical emergency; be sure to call your own veterinarian.

Hedgehog Hollow

Hedgehogs: the trendy pet of the '90s! Have you been considering getting a hedgehog as a pet, or are you just wondering what all the interest in those hedgehog things is about? Either way, this page is the place to go. Contrary to popular belief, hedgehogs are not related to porcupines. They make great pets, but some kinds make better pets than others; find out here. Some hedgehogs can even be trained to use a litter box! They eat a variety of foods, such as cat food, hard-boiled eggs, cottage cheese, oatmeal, fruit, mealworms, crickets, grasshoppers, earthworms...well, you get the picture.

http://www.pci.on.ca/~macnamar/hedgehogs/

The Pet Name Pages

Here you'll find names for all kinds of pets. Search for names by pet type, color, origin, personality, and more. Want to name your pet after a famous celebrity animal? Those names are here, too!

http://www.primenet.com/~meggie/petname.htm

Racine County dot Com - Pets

For a brief, funny guide to a lot of different kinds of dogs, cats, fish, and birds, you might explore this resource. What really sets it apart, though, is the pet's guide to selecting and caring for a human. For example, if a fish picks a human wearing a "power" tie, it is a safe bet that it'll get better-quality fish flakes in its tank; but if the fish chooses one that works too much, the person might forget to feed the fish at all, and that would be bad! Did you know that dogs and cats are really space aliens from the planet Kibble? Their mission is to enslave humans so that the planet can be colonized by animals. Does your cat control you? Ever notice how much your cat sits in the sun? That's because cats are really solar-powered. And when they get that really blank look in their eyes, cats are actually communicating with their home planet about plans for the upcoming invasion!

http://rcc.webpoint.com/pets/

Rainbow Bridge Tribute Pages

It's so sad to lose a pet. This gentle site gives one beautiful idea of what happens when a beloved pet crosses the "Rainbow Bridge" and waits with the other pets for their human friends to join them someday. You'll find pictures, poems, and thoughts about pets on this touching page, which always makes Net-mom cry. There are also numerous links to dealing with grief over the loss of a companion animal. You can also submit a memorial for your own pet by leaving a message in the guest book.

http://rainbowbridge.tierranet.com/bridge.htm

Welcome to NetVet Veterinary Resources and the Electronic Zoo

The doctor is in! You'll find information on animal care and behavior from breeders, vets, and researchers. This site features anything that walks, flies, hops, slithers, or swings through the trees. The NetVet resource contains some of the most respected and popular resources about pets on the Net.

http://netvet.wustl.edu/

VIRTUAL PETS

Adopt a Cyber Mascot

Lots of people seem to like to "adopt" a Web page mascot or guardian. This site will tell you the etiquette involved in adopting a cute animated graphic for your own pages. If you visit the "My Own Cyberpets" link at the bottom, you can find other sites from which you can adopt angels, fairies, unicorns, cows, and more.

http://www.geocities.com/Heartland/Meadows/
    6263/ring.html

Dogz and Catz, Your Virtual Petz are Here!

This site wants to sell you software, but you can download demos for free. Adopt a virtual dog, cat, or oddball creature. Train it, take care of it, play with it. Net-mom thought this was fun for at least 15 minutes. What do you think?

http://www.dogz.com/

Happy House - Your Virtual Rodent

Net-mom gives a lot of talks about the Internet. While waiting for the audience to assemble, she likes to put something attractive and fun up on the screen. Often, it's Happy House Hamster. Download it (Win or Mac), click on the basket, and meet your virtual hamster. Read the directions so you'll know what else to do.

http://www.maniform.com/stuff/hamster.htm

Sheri's Adopt A Petrock For Your Webpage

In the olden days before virtual electronic pets, people had pet rocks. Basically, people lined up to pay money for a rock in a box (OK, the box also had instructions to care for the new "pet"). At this site, you can adopt a pet rock to live on your computer desktop or Web page. You can also download a dancing Net baby and accessories for various holidays. It's wacky and silly, and you'll love it.

http://www.geocities.com/TimesSquare/Arcade/
    3412/petrock.html

A B C D E F G H I J K L M N O P Q R S T U V W X Y Z

A
B
C
D
E
F
G
H
I
J
K
L
M
N
O
P
Q
R
S
T
U
V
W
X
Y
Z

Virtual Dog

This is a neat adventure game you'll have to play for days. You adopt a virtual dog at the pound (you have to give your e-mail address). Take him "home" (oops, don't forget to buy dog food) and get some advice from the vet (go back and buy that chew toy). As days pass, will you become a super owner or will your pup run away? If you can't visit "home" for a few days, put your pooch in the kennel until you can play again.

http://www.virtualdog.com/

Virtual Pet Home Page

If you can't have a real pet, maybe you can own a virtual pet! There will be more than twenty GigaPets introduced in 1998, including Looney Tunes characters, Cabbage Patch pets, Rug Rats, circus, aquarium, and farm animals, and a lot more! Check this site for a collection of all known virtual pets. If this catches on, you may want to think about becoming a virtual veterinarian! Parents: We have not checked outbound links— preview please!

http://www.virtualpet.com/vp/

Welcome to SwineOnline!

Now don't get too attached to your little virtual piglet. You only have about a week to raise him to a hog, and at the end of the week, well, he'll either win a ribbon or wind up as pork chops. Think of this more as a game of luck, strategy, and fun. Can you beat out the other farmers and get high score of the week? Be sure to take really good care of your pig (he'll e-mail you if he's not happy). New games start every Friday.

http://www.swineonline.com/

WELCOME TO THE MOUSEPAD

At this site you can adopt a virtual orphan mouse, elephant, kitten, or other creature for your home page. You can also download accessories for your mouse and build a *hole* mouse house, called a mousepad. Lots of people are adopting these critters, and Net-mom admits they are pretty cute. Visit some of the elaborate mouse cities others have created! Note: If you adopt a "special needs" mouse you must also agree to link to a health-related site on your home page.

http://www.vikimouse.com/

PHOTOGRAPHY

Bob Miller's Light Walk

This site will really *illuminate* your knowledge of light and shadow. In fact, it's a *bright* idea to check it out if you have a science fair project due, since there are project directions for building your own pinhole camera, making your own "light walk," and performing more tricks of light. You'll find a whole spectrum of links here and a fascinating look into shadows. Don't be scared, just *lighten* up!

http://www.exploratorium.edu/light_walk/ lw_main.html

Center for Creative Photography Homepage

The University of Arizona maintains one of the largest and most accessible collections of fine photography in the world, with over 15,000 images. Renowned nature photographer Ansel Adams helped to found this institution, and his work, along with a who's who of other photographers, is well represented at this site. Along with rotating selections from its archives, the Center's home page also features information on its educational programs, library, research facilities, publications, and museum shop. Parental advisory: Not all photos have been previewed.

http://www.library.arizona.edu/branches/ ccp/ccphome.html

A complete guide to digital cameras and digital photography

There's a revolution happening right now in the photographic world. Film is being replaced by digital cameras, which save their pictures to memory rather than emulsion. Digital cameras have many advantages over older technologies, and since we know you'll want to learn about them, we've chosen this series of pages. There is an excellent—though long—tutorial in digital photography, a resource center and buying guide, and even a chat room so you can discuss digital cameras with others.

http://www.shortcourses.com/

Exposure - A Beginners Guide to Photography

Photography—is it technology or magic? Even if you have a nonadjustable camera, you can try some of these tips and tricks to jazz up your photos. If you do have a camera with a lot of controls on it, you can really change how the picture looks. You can learn how to set the camera so that the background blurs out of focus. This puts more emphasis on your main subjects in the foreground of the picture. On the other hand, you might want to make sure that as much of the scene as possible stays in focus. There is a special way to set the camera for that, too. You can try it all using Sim-Cam, a way-cool JavaScript applet that will teach you the mysteries of f-stops and aperture by letting you set a virtual camera, take a picture, and see immediate results!

http://www.88.com/exposure/lowrez_i.htm

George Eastman House

Explore the history of photography and view some very interesting early cameras and photographic experiments. George Eastman was the founder of the Eastman Kodak company. This is a tour of his house and gardens in Rochester, New York, which has been preserved as a photographic museum.

http://www.eastman.org/

NET FILES

"I do not like broccoli. And I haven't liked it since I was a little kid and my mother made me eat it. And I'm President of the United States and I'm not going to eat any more broccoli." Who said it?

Answer: George Bush, the 41st U.S. president, said it in 1990! Explore more famous quotes at the Quotations Home Page at
http://www.geocities.com/~spanoud/quote.html

Hoffer School Home Page

For over five years, the California Museum of Photography has collaborated with the students and teachers of Hoffer Elementary School in Banning, California. Students learn how to use photography and other multimedia tools to express themselves. The results are displayed in this engrossing Web page, which features pictures, voices, and written words of the student artists. They include a collection of their fun photos, montages, magazine collages, videos of motion toys, a collaborative e-mail "books project," and a history of the town of Banning in words and pictures. As more schools add their presence to the Internet, they would do well to follow this example. And as more high-powered graphic designers and ad agencies develop Web sites, it will be heartening to see that one of the best pages around was designed by third-graders! A caution to parents: The UCR/California Museum of Photography has other exhibits that contain adult subjects and may not be suitable for children; proceed to links off this page with caution.

http://www.cmp.ucr.edu/exhibitions/
    hoffer/hoffer.homepage.html

Konica Home Page English Menu

Have you always wondered how film is made? Here's a clue: it's made in the dark! At this site, you can take a virtual factory tour and see the steps of its manufacture. There's a nice little introduction to color photography and lots of tips and tutorials from Konica.

http://www.konica.co.jp/english/e_menu.html

Oatmeal Box Pinhole Photography by Stewart Lewis Woodruff

Shhh...don't tell the manufacturers of expensive photographic equipment: you can make pictures using an old oatmeal box! This page provides step-by-step detailed instructions on how to make a pinhole camera, load it with paper film, develop the film, and make prints. Just remember to eat the oatmeal first.

http://www.nh.ultranet.com/~stewoody/

Preserving Family Albums

If you want your great-great-great-grandchildren to see just what you looked like and how you lived, better start storing those photos properly. There's a special section at the George Eastman House home page that will tell you everything you need to know about preserving old and new photos.

http://www.eastman.org/education/album/album.html

Stereoscopic Photographs

Maybe your grandmother or great-grandpa had one of these neat gadgets that shows pictures in three dimensions. It is called a stereoscope. The person who developed this Web site must have had one, too, because a lot of the old slides are reproduced here. There is also a lot of information about the stereoscope and a picture of it. You can look at the slides. Follow the instructions for relaxing your eyes, and you'll see it in 3-D right on your computer screen. Want more? Try <http://www.vision3d.com/index.shtml> and also look at The Stereogram Page entry in the OPTICAL ILLUSIONS section.

http://www.stut-hs.odedodea.edu/Projects/
    stereograms/Stereoscopic_Photographs/
    Stereoscopic_Photographs.html

Welcome to Eastman Kodak Company

You would expect Kodak to have an active home page, and they do indeed. You can find all sorts of valuable information on photography here, whether your interests lie in producing professional-quality photographs or simple snapshots. A What's New section will keep you coming back regularly. One example is a section featuring the Top Ten Techniques for photographers to take and make good pictures.

http://www.kodak.com/

**Nothing to do?
Check CRAFTS AND HOBBIES
for some ideas.**

Want to take great pictures at the next ball game? Move in as close as you can!

If you have a telephoto lens, use that; otherwise, move yourself closer. Then, to freeze the sports action, use the fastest shutter speed your camera will allow. This will depend on the speed of the film you're using, so ask for some professional advice at the photo shop beforehand. It's also important to anticipate the peak of action, like when the bat cracks against the ball, when the runner jumps the hurdle, or when the basketball swishes through the hoop. Photos taken at the peak tend to be the most exciting! You can also freeze action by using a flash, but remember that your subject must be within about 15 feet of you for a flash to work. Get more great photo tips at the Welcome to Eastman Kodak Company page!

PHYSICS

Bill Nye the Science Guy's Nye Labs Online

It's Bill Nye the Science Guy, and is he loaded with science goodies to show you! If the graphics are too much, stop the page after part of it loads and click the TEXT Menu option. There are photos, sounds, and movies (caution: these are big files) in the Goodies area. Check out Today's Demo or visit the U-Nye-Verse to see what's happening in Bill's world of science. Lots of experiments and lessons on things scientific can be found here, plenty of fodder for your next science fair project. TV listings are also available if you want to find out when he's on the tube. There is even a chat area where you can post comments and see if anyone replies.

http://nyelabs.kcts.org/

How Things Work

Have you ever questioned some aspect of the science of physics? A professor of physics at the University of Virginia has listed answers to many questions, some of which are part of the basic physics courses he teaches at the university. A guide lists previous questions as well as a place where you can ask a new question. The search button will help you find whether one of the previously asked 5,500 questions is one you might also pose.

http://Landau1.phys.Virginia.EDU/Education/
    Teaching/HowThingsWork/

Physics - Welcome from the Mining Co.

Some people think physics is (a) too boring or (b) too difficult. Well, now you might want to add (c) very interesting. Do you know that a baseball pitcher throwing a curve ball is using the science of physics? Check it out right here! Were you aware that thermodynamics has a lot to do with the physics of air-conditioning? No? Well then, you've come to the right place!

http://physics.miningco.com/

ELECTRICITY

Bill Nye Episode Guide: ELECTRICITY

The Science Guy explains what electricity is and then comes up with a really neat experiment you can try at home—providing your mom or dad is helping you. By the way, did you know that electric eels use special organs in their bodies to make electricity? It would be cool never to need to buy batteries!

http://nyelabs.kcts.org/nyeverse/episode/e18.html

THE ELECTRIC CLUB

You'll want to visit this site to check out a great list of neat experiments to try, like creating lemon power. We know that the news may be *shocking*, but it's true: you can make a lightbulb light using lemons as the source of energy. There is another experiment called "charge it," which uses a comb, some bits of paper, and a head of hair (not a credit card)!

http://www.schoolnet.ca/math_sci/phys/electric-club/

INTERNET GUIDE TO BASIC ELECTRONICS

Do you know the difference between a parallel electrical circuit and one that is in series? You will within moments of opening this Web page! It's a real beginner's guide to the topic and includes many illustrations and clear explanations. There are also some cool calculators for Ohm's law and other topics, plus a guide to multimeter use and a handy chart of schematic symbols.

http://webhome.idirect.com/~jadams/electronics/

Theater of Electricity

Did you ever get zapped by touching a metal doorknob at home? Where'd the electricity come from? Static electricity built up on your shoes as you walked across a carpet. Scientists who need a lot of static electricity for an experiment use a Van de Graaff generator, which makes electricity from a revolving belt inside one of its towers. Read about its history and construction and all about lightning and electricity. You can see the huge original generator, built by Dr. Robert J. Van de Graaff, in the Theater of Electricity at the Museum of Science in Cambridge, Massachusetts, and on this World Wide Web site. You probably won't have a generator like this at home, but at this site you'll find some experiments you can do with balloons, paper bunnies, and static electricity!

http://www.mos.org/sln/toe/toe.html

EXPERIMENTS
Little Shop of Physics Online

Welcome to the Little Shop of Physics; nothing here will harm you (well, you might want to stay away from that disreputable-looking plant over in the corner!). They have concocted some interesting demonstrations using everyday objects that might amuse you and teach you something about physics. There are optical and auditory illusions plus lots of special effects you can try right on your computer screen. Come closer!

http://BrianJones.ctss.colostate.edu/

Beanie Babies rule in TOYS.

A
B
C
D
E
F
G
H
I
J
K
L
M
N
O
P
Q
R
S
T
U
V
W
X
Y
Z

Physics Experiments You Can Do At Home

How quickly do you react when someone throws you a ball or when a book drops from a table? Reaction time is one of several home experiments you can try, developed by a University of Wisconsin professor as part of a program he calls Wonders of Physics. Learn about the Doppler effect, take a "random walk," or try a vortex experiment. You'll soon be discovering lots of interesting new things.

http://scifun.chem.wisc.edu/WOP/HomeExpPhys.html

Science: Physical Sciences

Many fascinating science experiments are explained here in great detail. For example, a raw egg soaked in vinegar for several days will actually bounce (just don't try this on the new living room carpet)!

http://ericir.syr.edu/Virtual/Lessons/Science/Physical/

FORCES
Amusement Park Physics

As your roller coaster car rattles up to the tippy-top of the track, you think, "I hope the designer of this ride got an A in physics." As you practice your driving skills on the bumper cars, do you ever take time to thank Newton's third law of motion? Learn the physics behind many popular rides, and you'll never look at an amusement park the same way again.

http://www.learner.org/exhibits/parkphysics/

Bridge and Resonance (Multimedia Physics)

Can you imagine that a bridge could collapse because of a thing called resonance? Those of you who are string instrument players know that if you pluck a note on one string, another string matching that note often vibrates slightly too. The first string "talks" to the second string, which "answers." In 1940, the force of the wind got the Tacoma Narrows Bridge (Washington) swinging and swaying, and pretty soon the waves of the wind's frequency matched the natural resonance of the structure, and...well, you've got to see it to believe it.

http://www.ferris.edu/htmls/academics/
course.offerings/physbo/MultiM/bridge/bridge.htm

The Bubblesphere

You don't need a lot of skills to learn to blow soap bubbles, right? So what is with this guy who calls himself "Professor"? Turns out he really is an expert. At his home page, he reveals the ultimate soap solution for making the most colorful, sturdy bubbles. He explains how to make your own bubble-blowing tools from soup cans and coat hangers (ask your parents for help). But you don't even need anything special—he teaches you how to blow bubbles using only your HANDS! But wait, there's more. Check the bubble FAQ, bubble games, and the other wonders of the Bubblesphere.

http://bubbles.org/

Rocket Principles

This isn't exactly rocket science, but then again, this is where it all starts. Read all about Newton's first, second, and third laws of motion and forces and how they relate to rocketry. These basic laws rule all motion, not just rocketry. They explain why a basketball bounces, why a baseball goes so far when you hit it with a bat, and why you go over the handlebars if you run into a tree with your bike (you don't have to try the last one—just take our word for it!). Scroll to the bottom of the page and click on rockets, where you'll find some cool experiments to help you understand the laws of motion. Our personal favorite is the balloon-powered pinwheel!

http://www.lerc.nasa.gov/Other_Groups/K-12/TRC/
Rockets/rocket_principles.html

Roller Coaster Physics Book by Tony Wayne

As you swoosh around a roller coaster, you're probably not thinking very much about physics. But it's lucky for you that the designer of the roller coaster thought about physics a LOT when planning the engineering for the ride! A good coaster strikes a balance between thrills, speed, and safety—find out how the laws of physics can make sure you have fun at the amusement park. Explore one level out, at "The Physics Pavilion," for other interesting physics demos, downloadable calculator software, and some neat science tricks.

http://pen.k12.va.us/Anthology/Pav/Science/
Physics/book/

The Science Behind a Home Run

Time to grab a bag of peanuts, crank up the radio or TV, and listen to the sweet sound of the baseball bat against the ball as another one flies out of the park. Did you ever wonder how a person holding a narrow wooden bat could hit a baseball so hard that it could fly several hundred feet? It happens every day all across the country during the baseball season, and now you can read how physics and forces make it all happen. Remember the magic words *viscosity* and *density*, take a gulp of fresh air, and read on.

http://www.exploratorium.edu/learning_studio/news/
  september97.html

Soap Bubbles

Have you ever noticed that bubbles are always round, no matter what shape the wand you blow through is? Is that because your breath is shaped like a circle as it comes out of your lips? No. A bubble is round because of physical forces you can learn about here. You'll also learn that when a bubble looks gray or black, it is about to pop. Why does it lose its pretty colors? Find out here, and don't miss the Internet Resources section for more good, clean fun.

http://www.exploratorium.edu/ronh/bubbles/
  bubbles.html

NET FILES

St. Edward's Crown is the coronation crown of England, first used in 1661. It was used when Queen Elizabeth II was crowned in 1953. How much does the crown weigh?
(Hint: It is made from solid gold.)

Answer: The crown weighs nearly five pounds (2.2 kilograms) and is set with 444 semiprecious stones. You can read more about the British Crown Jewels and see a picture at *http://www.royal.gov.uk/faq/crowns.htm*

Toys in Space

In 1993, the space shuttle *Endeavor* took off with an interesting payload: a high-tech communications satellite and a chest full of toys! The idea was to see how the familiar toys performed in orbit, without the force of gravity. This site compares normal earth operation of the toys with the orbit results. You'll be very surprised!

http://observe.ivv.nasa.gov/nasa/exhibits/toys_space/
  toyframe.html

WaterWorks

Oh, the magic of water fountains! Some are tall, some are wide, others squirt in many directions at once. Discover what makes a fountain work and the forces it takes to make water do its tricks. Pictures of different types of fountains are shown, along with some that were made by students. There are even movies and sounds of the different fountains available (caution: the files are big!).

http://www.omsi.edu/sln/ww/

FORCES—CORIOLIS EFFECT
Bad Coriolis

Does draining water *really* turn one way in the Northern Hemisphere and the opposite way in the Southern Hemisphere? You'll learn a lot about Coriolis effect science—good and bad—at this site. Also, check how you can fake out your class into believing the equator runs right through your classroom.

http://www.ems.psu.edu/~fraser/Bad/BadCoriolis.html

Mr. Science: The Coriolis Effect Page

Because the Earth rotates, it has a special effect on the behavior of fluids on its surface. We see this when large low-pressure storms turn one way in the Northern Hemisphere and the other way in the Southern Hemisphere. This is known as the Coriolis effect. It has led to speculation that the same thing happens to water draining from a sink, bathtub, or toilet bowl. Go run some water in the sink and see which way the water drains: clockwise or counter-clockwise. Now go to this site and log your location and your results. Then see how the experiment is progressing by viewing the *current* standings.

http://chemlab.pc.maricopa.edu/mrscience.html

A B C D E F G H I J K L M N O P Q R S T U V W X Y Z

FORCES—MAGNETISM

Bill Nye Episode: MAGNETISM

Here's an experiment that explores the world of magnetism. Bill Nye the Science Guy guides you through a simple project that shows you how to make your own compass out of a needle and bowl of water. Did you know some animals use magnetism to find their way when they migrate? Is it magic? No, it's magnetism!

http://nyelabs.kcts.org/nyeverse/episode/e21.html

How to Use a Compass

One use of magnetism is finding your way with a compass. On a wilderness hike, a compass is necessary, but first you have to learn to use one properly. You can learn in your own backyard, or in a park, or in a school playground. This site gives you a guided tour to a compass and its use. There are also tips on how to find your way in very difficult conditions, like fog or snow whiteouts.

http://www.uio.no/~kjetikj/compass/

NET FILES

If you had 10 billion $1 notes and spent one every second of every day, how many years would it take for you to go broke?

Answer: According to the U.S. Bureau of Engraving and Printing, it would require 317 years!

http://www.bep.treas.gov/nptemp1.cfm

Magnetism

What's the *attraction*? Magnetism helps us find our way with a compass. It's what makes electric motors run. Did you know it's also responsible for the northern lights—the aurora borealis? Read about the history of magnetism and how it works. Drawings show how magnetic fields are made up of invisible field lines. There are also facts about the contributions of Michael Faraday and James Maxwell to the *field* of magnetism. May the *force* be with you!

http://www-spof.gsfc.nasa.gov/Education/
    Imagnet.html

LASERS

The Internet Webseum of Holography

Lasers can do some pretty amazing things. Did you know they are used to make interesting 3-D pictures that allow you to "look inside" and see around objects? That's called holography. Although lasers are needed to make a hologram, you don't need a laser to view one. You can view laser shows and holograms right here if you have the right plug-in. If you don't, there are links to get you the free software, so don't worry. Think it's all too complicated? Not at the Holo-kids area, which you can reach by clicking on Kids Page!

http://www.holoworld.com/

Laserium Home Page

The word "laser" is really an acronym, which stands for "light amplification by the stimulated emission of radiation." Lasers are used in many scientific and medical applications, but everyone agrees the most fun you can have with lasers is at a "laserium" show! Often held in planetarium buildings and performed to music, the laserist is a true artist, as he or she "plays" the laser controls to draw fabulous light effects on the domed ceiling. This page tells about the history of laser shows and explains the science behind the vibrant colors overhead.

http://www.laserium.com/

Overview of the Lasers Site

How many lasers do you think you encounter in a day? Go to the checkout line at the grocery store: lasers read the prices coded on those zebra-striped labels. Climb into the car and crank up some tunes on the CD player—lasers again. Every CD player has a tiny laser in it to read the digital code on the CD. Visit this site for more close encounters of the laser kind.

http://www.thetech.org/hyper/lasers/overview.html

LIGHT

Bob Miller's Light Walk

This site will really *illuminate* your knowledge of light and shadow. In fact, it's a *bright* idea to check it out if you have a science fair project due, since there are project directions for building your own pinhole camera, making your own "light walk," and performing more tricks of light. You'll find a whole spectrum of stuff here and a fascinating look into shadows. Don't be scared, just *lighten* up!

http://www.exploratorium.edu/light_walk/
lw_main.html

Soon there will be one currency for Europe, the euro. Everyone's familiar with the dollar sign, the symbol for the British pound, and the glyph for the Japanese yen. What will the symbol for the euro look like?

Answer: According to the official euro site, "It features an epsilon harking back to the cradle of European civilization and the first letter of Europe, crossed by two parallel lines to indicate the stability of the euro." You can see a picture of it at *http://europa.eu.int/euro/html/ rubrique-default5.html?Lang=&rubique=100*

Bubbles

Bet you didn't know that soap bubbles can teach you a lot about light and optics, right? Check the Light and Optics Activities to explore light, refraction, lenses, and lasers. Practice tricks with bubbles, including how to make a bubble within a bubble! You'll also find the secret to making long-lasting "tough" bubble mix here.

http://www.scri.fsu.edu/~dennisl/CMS/activity/
bubbles.html

Make a Splash with Color

Why do we see red apples, green grass, and blue sky? Is it the color of the object? Something to do with our eyes? Or have we just been the victims of a long-standing government conspiracy that makes us believe apples are red? (You're right, we made up that last one.) This site explores hue, shade, and other ways we talk about color. Then find out about what light is made of, and finally, experiment on your own with lots of online games, er, educational activities.

http://www.thetech.org/exhibits_events/online/
color/teaser/

MACHINES

Simple Machines

Did you ever think of a wedge as a simple "machine"? Or a screw? What about a pulley? A simple machine is a tool to make the "work" of a job easier. You can even try some demonstrations that will prove how machines help make life easier.

http://www.fi.edu/qa97/spotlight3/spotlight3.html

You Can & Levers

The basic principles of levers are explained nicely here by Beakman and Jax. All three classes of levers are shown in easy-to-understand diagrams. Did you know that many household devices are levers? Nail clippers, pliers, nutcrackers, and fly swatters are just a few. After reading this page, see if you can tell to which class of levers each device belongs.

http://www.beakman.com/lever/lever.html

A B C D E F G H I J K L M N O P Q R S T U V W X Y Z

SOUND

Bill Nye Episode: SOUND

Bill Nye the Science Guy has a sound project for you. It's not just educationally sound, it's *about* sound! With the help of a few household objects, learn how to make a sound-detecting device. You'll love the links to auditory experiments and demos elsewhere on the Web, too. Put on your lab coats and get out the fire extinguisher (just kidding), then prepare to *sound* off.

http://nyelabs.kcts.org/nyeverse/episode/e12.html

Characteristics of Sound

We'll bet you didn't know that the standard A musical note has a length of 16.4 inches. Its wavelength, that is! The calculation to prove it is right here on this page. There are comparison diagrams of a simple sine wave and of Bart Simpson saying, "Wow, cool, man." There are also comparisons of different sound levels, a diagram of how the ear works, and a chart showing the range of human hearing. *Sounds* great, huh?

http://jcbmac.chem.brown.edu/scissorsHtml/sound/
charOfSound.html

Interactive Experiments

Part of a larger site called Little Shop of Physics (see earlier entry under PHYSICS—EXPERIMENTS), this lets you experience two weird Shockwave demonstrations. The first is an illusion in sound—pure sound, that is. Do you hear the notes as going up or going down? Check the science behind this very strange auditory foolery! The second explains how they make that Emergency Broadcast signal sound so annoying. Check it out.

http://brianjones.ctss.colostate.edu/online.html

Kids, Percussion, and Stomp

Is pure rhythm really music, or is it just a cacophony of noise? If you go to a performance of STOMP, you will see and hear the cast members "play" Zippo lighters, push brooms, trash cans, newspapers, and other common objects. Visit this Web site to see and hear audio from the show, try some fun activities, and learn more about the science of sound.

http://www.usinteractive.com/stomp/studyguide/
contents.htm

PLANTS, TREES, AND GARDENS

See also FARMING AND AGRICULTURE

Great Plant Escape

Bud and Sprout are on hand to help Detective Le Plant solve some of the great mysteries of plant life. Case by case, you will check the clues, try experiments, and solve problems as Bud and Sprout journey into the world of plants. The detective promises lots of fun, but the outcome will remain a mystery until your investigative duties are completed. You can also find your way to some other great "green links." Get the *dirt* on soil—it's much more than you think. Do you know the difference between a daffodil bulb and a potato? Bud and Sprout will help you find out about a lot of plants, fruits, and vegetables, and they will even show you how to grow your own mango!

http://www.urbanext.uiuc.edu/gpe/

Plants and Our Environment

If you don't know a sepal from a cotyledon, this is the place for you! Learn all about plants at this site, which was one of the finalists in the 1998 ThinkQuest Junior competition. The handy A to Z glossary reveals that the cotyledon is the hard outer case of the seed, which holds the embryo (baby part of the plant) and gives it a food supply, whereas the sepals are the outer green parts of the base of the flower. Sepals protect the flower bud before it opens. The entire process of growth is explained, and the site includes lots of great graphics.

http://tqjunior.advanced.org/3715/

If you can read this, good! Now check BOOKS AND LITERATURE.

BOTANIC GARDENS

Access Arboretums: Boyce Thompson Southwestern Arboretum

If you're one of those people who think a cactus is just a prickly, ugly weed and the desert is a dry wasteland of sand, may we suggest taking a cyberwalk through Arizona's Boyce Thompson Southwestern Arboretum? There's not very much water to go around in the desert, but most deserts are not deserted! Many scientists think that the variety of life in the desert is second only to that found in the tropics. You won't want to miss the cactus garden, with its 800 different cacti, including tall saguaros, ground-covering prickly pears, and squat, spiky hedgehogs. So that the cactus can conserve what little water it has, some of its flowers last only one day—and that day happens to be captured here in lots of beautiful pictures.

http://ag.arizona.edu/BTA/btsa.html

The Butchart Gardens

A garden in an old rock quarry? Come to Vancouver Island, off the west coast of Canada, and see for yourself. Over a million bedding plants are used each year to ensure continuous bloom. And they plant 100,000 bulbs every fall to make a spectacular springtime display!

http://www.vvv.com/butchart/

Introduction to the Australian National Botanic Gardens

Ever hear a kookaburra laugh? The call of this bird is one of the most famous sounds of the Australian bush. You can listen to the calls of the kookaburra, the currawong, the peewee, and a bunch of other very strange birds at the Australian National Botanic Gardens. Birds love the gardens because it's a safe place, filled with lots of native plants and habitats that give them food and shelter. You can also find out how Aborigines—who have lived in Australia for at least 40,000 years—gathered everything they needed to live a healthy life from the land. At least half of what they ate came from plants, and one of the ways they encouraged new plants to grow was to burn all the old plants to the ground! And speaking of plants, don't miss the kangaroo paws and the wattles, just two of the many different kinds of plants grown halfway around the world.

http://osprey.erin.gov.au/anbg/anbg-introduction.html

Missouri Botanical Garden's What's It Like Where You Live?

This site is awesome. For example, explore the virtual biomes. A biome is a collection of plants and animals that live together in a specific region. Visit the desert, the tundra, the temperate forest, the grasslands, the rain forest, and the taiga. What's the taiga? It's the largest biome of all, stretching across parts of Canada, Europe, Russia, and Asia. The summers are warm and the winters are cold (with an average temperature of below zero six months of the year!). It doesn't have as many different kinds of animals and plants as the other biomes; still, you can learn all about moose, red fox, and other species that do thrive in this land. Wouldn't it be great to talk to some kids who lived in the taiga biome? You can! There are partner schools for each biome, so check them out.

http://www.mobot.org/MBGnet/

The New York Botanical Garden

Back before there was a New York City, a forest covered the whole island of Manhattan. Of course, there isn't much of a forest left these days, but 40 acres of the natural, uncut, 200-year-old forest has been saved at the New York Botanical Garden just as it was. The garden, one of the oldest and biggest in the world, also has 27 specialty gardens featuring everything from rocks to roses, all of which you can visit online. Make sure you read all about the garden's scientists, who travel the world looking for medicinal plants that may help to fight cancer and other diseases.

http://pathfinder.com/vg/Gardens/NYBG/

Attention everyone.
The Internet is closing.
Please go play outside.

A B C D E F G H I J K L M N O **P** Q R S T U V W X Y Z

A
B
C
D
E
F
G
H
I
J
K
L
M
N
O
P
Q
R
S
T
U
V
W
X
Y
Z

GARDENING (INDOOR AND OUTDOOR)

The Bonsai Primer

This excellent primer explains what bonsai is, and isn't. It is a small tree and pot, grown in visual harmony to give the impression that you're looking at an ancient tree, not a shrub. It is not a dwarf tree. The tree's branches have been trimmed carefully, sometimes wired and trained, in order to give the impression that you're looking at a very old tree, or in the case of *saikei*, an entire tiny landscape. You can learn the basics of this gardening hobby at this site, including which trees and shrubs lend themselves best to the art of bonsai.

http://www.wmin.ac.uk/~allen/main.html

Bonsai Web's Beginner's Guidelines

This page shows you step-by-step how to take a throwaway nursery plant and start it on the path to becoming a beautiful bonsai. There is a list of special tools you'll need if you want to take up this intriguing hobby.

http://www.bonsaiweb.com/forum/articles/begin/
   begin.html

bulb.com

After a long winter, there's nothing so cheerful to see as tiny crocuses blooming in the sun. Did you know that most spring-flowering bulbs are planted in the fall? At this site you can find out everything you'd ever want to know about bulbs, including how to "force" bulbs to bloom out of season, how to keep squirrels from eating all your bulbs, and what's the latest in the quest to develop a black tulip.

http://www.bulb.com/

The Butterfly Guide

You love butterflies, especially when they visit your yard. You wish they'd stay around longer, though. This site tells you what kinds of plants you need in your garden to attract caterpillars and butterflies, especially the really pretty and unusual ones. For example, if you want the beautiful, light blue spring azure butterfly to hang around, you need to plant aster, butterfly weed, and dogwood trees.

http://www.butterflies.com/guide.html

CANOE PLANTS OF ANCIENT HAWAII - Intro and Contents

When early Polynesian explorers set out for Hawaii, a journey of thousands of miles, they traveled in wooden canoes. They took with them, among other things, 24 species of plants thought to be essential to life. These "canoe plants" of ancient Hawaii included *awapuhi kuahiwi* (shampoo ginger), *ko* (sugar cane), and *niu* (coconut). They were all the new settlers needed for their food, rope, medicine, containers, and fabrics. Here's a guide to these life-sustaining plants. There are also fascinating links to early Polynesian wayfinding over these vast ocean reaches.

http://www.hawaii-nation.org/canoe/canoe.html

Carnivorous Plant Database

Imagine this if you can: a little fly takes a break from buzzing around by coming to rest on the leaf of a beautiful pink plant. What the fly doesn't know is that the leaf is very sticky. Slowly, the leaf edges curl up around the fly. Gulp. It's been eaten—by a plant! Trapping insects for food is what "carnivorous" plants do. They live in poor soil, so they have to get their nutrition from somewhere (or something). Here, you can see what they look like. A fun thing to do at this site is to click on "Database Entry Formats" to find the right abbreviation for where you live. Then enter the abbreviation into the search box to see if carnivorous plants are anywhere near you. If so, keep your pet flies tied up inside! There are also links to other sites on the Net with even more information and pictures of carnivorous plants.

http://www.hpl.hp.com/bot/cp_home

I wonder what the QUEENS, KINGS, AND ROYALTY are doing tonight?

The Farm @ InterUrban | Hydroponics 101

OK, you've got no dirt, no sunshine, and no space. No way can you start a garden, right? Wrong. Hydroponics to the rescue. Hydro-what? "Hydro," as in water, and "ponics," as in the Greek word *ponos*, which means labor. But you don't have to work very hard to grow plants hydroponically, which just means growing them in water mixed with fertilizer—no dirt is required. Plants use a lot of energy tunneling their roots into the dirt to get food. With the hydroponic method, vegetables, fruits, flowers, and herbs get big and fat by lying back and letting their roots hang down in some very nutritious water. Imagine making strawberry shortcake in the middle of January, with organic strawberries grown from your own "water farm" in your bedroom closet! Take a look at this site to find out how.

http://www.interurban.com/hydroponics/

Fern Care

Ferns don't have any flowers and they don't produce seeds, but they do have a way (or ways) to reproduce. Look on the underside of the frond. You may see tiny dots or a brown powder. That material is called spores, and it's one of the ways you could grow a new fern plant. Growing ferns from spores takes a long time. The experts are at this page to let you in on the secrets of fern propagation and culture. One recipe is at *<http://www.visuallink.net/fern/growcomm.htm>*.

http://www.inetworld.net/sdfern/ferncare.htm

Fine Gardening Online

Have you ever watched a butterfly head for a certain spot in the garden? Or seen a hummingbird swoop down on a particular flower? There's a reason, and this magazine has the answers. For kids who like to work with mom and dad in the garden or the yard, a lot of good ideas and answers can be found here. Create a mini water garden or make a handy twine dispenser. There are lots of other fascinating articles and features—dig in!

http://www.taunton.com/fg/

The Garden Gate

This great jumping-off point is blooming with links to help you figure out how to make your garden grow. You'll find resources on pest control, plant identification, wildflowers, water gardens, deer-resistant plants, composting, perennials, and much more. Be sure to visit this site when you've got time to smell the roses, because there's enough here to keep you busy all day!

http://www.prairienet.org/garden-gate/

GardeningGuides — Come Garden With Us!

Asparagus, beans, beets, broccoli, Brussels sprouts, cabbage, carrots, cauliflower, Chinese cabbage, corn, cucumbers, eggplant, garlic, greens, leeks, lettuce, onions, parsnips, peas, peppers, potatoes, tomatoes, and zucchini. You can grow 'em all and you can find out how right here! Remember what Santa Claus says to his gardener elves: "Hoe, hoe, hoe!"

http://www.gardenguides.com/

Kid's Valley Webgarden

Growing flowers and vegetables takes more than a few seeds and some dirt. It all begins with developing a plan and choosing the right place to plant. The people at Kid's Valley Webgarden will tell you when to plant (depending on the weather in your part of the world), what to plant, and how to do it. Then you've got to maintain the garden, but don't worry— they're ready to help. Water, fertilize, mulch, weed; water, fertilize, mulch, weed. Just when you get the *bugs* all worked out, the fruits of your labor will be ready to enjoy! You will love to visit this gardening bonanza.

http://www.arnprior.com/kidsgarden/index.htm

kinderGARDEN

This is a treasure trove of gardening links and projects just for kids and families, brought to you by Texas A & M. Whether growing a salad on your windowsill or sprouts in an eggshell, you'll find easy-to-understand projects here. There's even more: games, puzzles, and advice on the best gardening books for kids.

http://aggie-horticulture.tamu.edu/kinder/

A B C D E F G H I J K L M N O P Q R S T U V W X Y Z

A
B
C
D
E
F
G
H
I
J
K
L
M
N
O
P
Q
R
S
T
U
V
W
X
Y
Z

My First Garden

My first garden. Sounds pretty neat, doesn't it? Imagine what fun it will be. A lot of hard work is involved in planting a garden, but the end results make it all worthwhile. At this site, you will learn how to choose the seeds, clear the land, and tend the soil. You will learn about watering and weeding, and finally about harvesting the vegetables and clipping the flowers for a pretty dining room bouquet.

http://family.disney.com/Categories/Activities/
    Features/family_1997_06/famf/famf67garden/

National Gardening Association

Every year, the National Gardening Association awards Youth Garden Grants to 300 schools, neighborhood groups, community centers, camps, clubs, treatment facilities, and intergenerational groups throughout the United States. Each grant consists of tools, seeds, and garden products valued at an average of $750. To be eligible, an organization must plan to garden the following spring with at least 15 children between the ages of 3 and 18 years. Selection of winners is based on leadership, educational, social, and/or environmental programming, innovation, sustainability, need, and community support. All applicants will receive seeds and other materials to support their programs, thus ensuring that everyone is a winner. Check the details here and prepare to plant! Also inspect the seed swap, Q&A, and lots of other gardening info at this site.

http://www.wowpages.com/nga/

Rittners School Floral Education Center

You've spent the summer hoeing, pulling weeds, and watering, and now you have lots of beautiful flowers. Congratulations! Now pick some for the house and come inside. You are about to learn how to make arrangements that will make the neighborhood florists jealous of your talents! Well, maybe you're not ready to put them out of business yet, but several of the arrangements described at this Web site are simple to do. Ask your mom or dad to give you a hand and prepare to create an arrangement of beauty.

http://www.tiac.net/users/stevrt/RittnersGallery.html

Seeds of Change Garden

What's a Seeds of Change garden? It's a combination of green thumb and cultural exchange. Before Columbus arrived in the New World in 1492, there were "Old World" plants native to Europe and "New World" plants native to the Americas. People's food choices were limited to what grew nearby; if oranges didn't grow in their village, for example, they would never get to taste one. Exploration and trade with other nations changed all that. Read about how schools are growing Old World and New World gardens and a third garden based on seeds from traditional fruits and vegetables saved from their home kitchens. This terrific site will tell you all about the history of food crop plants and how you can create your own Seeds of Change garden! You'll find recipes here, too.

http://horizon.nmsu.edu/garden/welcome.html

The Succulent Plant Page

How do you repot a cactus? Very carefully, of course! Or, you could wrap the spiny beast in a roll of newspaper or paper towel, keeping it in place with twist-ties or a rubber band. That will prevent the spines from breaking off as well as keep your fingers safe. This page *bristles* with *pointed* information regarding the culture of our prickly pals in the cactus and succulent family.

http://www.graylab.ac.uk/usr/hodgkiss/succule.html

The Telegarden

Now here's a garden for the '90s, where Web cruisers gather to plant seeds and water plants by the remote control of an industrial robotic arm. This started as a real garden at the University of Southern California, although last year it moved to a server in Austria. The idea is to bring together a community of people to help tend a "shared garden." Click on "Guest Entrance" at the bottom of the page. You can explore the garden by clicking on a drawing of the robotic arm. This moves the arm—and a camera—to give you an up-to-the-minute picture of what's going on. Every so often, they clear the garden and start over. If you register as a member and visit the site regularly, you'll get to plant a seed.

http://www.usc.edu/dept/garden/

The Time Life Gardening Library

OK, you live in Colorado and have a shady front yard. You really like red flowers, but your soil is very poor. Is there anything you can plant? Search the Electronic Encyclopedia's database of thousands of plants to find out which ones will work, what they look like, and how to take care of them. Maybe you already know the name of the plant you want to grow and are just looking for some watering or pruning tips. Everything you need to know is here! When nothing can grow outside, search for a house plant in the House Plant Pavilion. If your parents find out about this site, watch out: you may get to do some weeding. But remember, a weed is just a plant for which a use has not yet been discovered.

http://pathfinder.com/vg/TimeLife/

Timeless Roses

Your grandma remembers she once had a beautiful rose garden, full of floribundas, grandifloras, and hybrid teas. Huh? Take your grandma down the garden path to visit this Web site, and see if she can spot some of her old favorites. The photos are beautiful. There are special sections on old-style roses, historical roses, and even the latest All-American Rose Society winners. If you need some cultivation hints, try the message boards.

http://www.timelessroses.com/

The Virtual Garden Homepage

Remember the flowers you planted early in the spring? The ones along the front wall of the house? The ones that are growing great? The ones that are white with a tinge of purple in the middle? If only you could remember what they are. Net-mom has a friend who can't tell a geranium from a gerbil! OK, that's a little extreme, but honestly, she has trouble recalling what that flowering red thing is. She—and you—should plan to spend some time checking this really neat site! The plant encyclopedia not only describes the flower, plant, or tree, but also shows a picture. (Note to Net-mom's friend: that plant in your front yard—it's known as the Martha Washington geranium; the animal in the pet cage—that's the gerbil.)

http://pathfinder.com/vg/

WebGarden Factsheet Database

Yikes! Your carrots have weevils all over them, and the bottoms of your tomatoes are covered with black spots. Who ya gonna call? Ohio State University's WebGarden Factsheet Database, that's who. It's a mega-collection of thousands of links to gardening fact sheets from the United States, Canada, and all over, complete with a handy little search form. In the case of your weird tomatoes, for example, all you have to do is type "tomatoes" and "black spot" into the title part of the form and choose "vegetables" as the category for expert advice and instant relief (bet you're watering too much or too little). Try the WebGarden main pages for a gardening dictionary and more on watching your garden grow.

http://hortwww-2.ag.ohio-state.edu/factsheet.html

Welcome to the Rose Resource

And the winners are: Betty Boop, Kaleidoscope, Candelabra, and Fourth of July. Bet we've got you guessing on this one! How could Betty Boop and a Candelabra be winners in the same contest? Wonder no more. They are 1999 prize-winning roses! Stop at this site to read about these magnificent flowers, including detailed descriptions and photos of the winners. You can also learn about designing your garden with roses.

http://www.rose.org/

TREES AND FORESTS

See also EARTH SCIENCE—LAND FEATURES—RAIN FORESTS

Ancient Bristlecone Pine

Imagine a tree that is nearly 5,000 years old! Back in the 1950s (that seems like a long time ago, but not when compared to the age of the tree), a man named Edmund Schulman was studying bristlecone pine trees in the White Mountains of California. He and fellow researchers discovered "Methuselah," which was found to be 4,723 years old. That was in 1957. Today, it remains the world's oldest known living tree. Read more here.

http://www.sonic.net/bristlecone/intro.html

A B C D E F G H I J K L M N O P Q R S T U V W X Y Z

A
B
C
D
E
F
G
H
I
J
K
L
M
N
O
P
Q
R
S
T
U
V
W
X
Y
Z

ArborKids: An Arbor Day Website for Young Folks

Trees provide us with shade, lumber, food, and fuel. Trees are great! *Wood* you ever think there's some way for you to get free trees? There is. What a re*leaf*. The Arbor Day Foundation folks will send kids five free seedlings—just send them a few dollars for shipping and handling.

http://www.arborday.net/kids/

E-Quarium: Habitats Path: Kelp Forest

Have you ever heard of a kelp forest? At the Monterey Bay Aquarium site, you can see photos and learn about this interesting forest, home to hundreds. They come in all shapes and sizes, from the gray whales who sometimes pass through to tiny hermit crabs on the sea floor below. You can even see some of these species through the "kelp cam."

http://www.mbayaq.org/hp/hp_kf.htm

Explore the Fantastic Forest @ nationalgeographic.com

You may want to tell people to *leaf* you alone while you trek through this fantastic forest, picking up clues along with maple leaves. We encountered a deer, a woodchuck, and some running buffalo clover. You can learn a lot about the forest and its inhabitants by spending an afternoon here.

http://www.nationalgeographic.com/features/96/ forest/html/forest.html

Massachusetts Maple Producers Association

Did you know that depending on the sweetness of the sap, it can take anywhere from 25 to 75 gallons of maple sap to make one gallon of maple syrup? The average, though, is 40 gallons raw to one gallon finished. It doesn't hurt the tree to be tapped, as long as you do it the right way. This page explains how you can make your own maple syrup. If you'd rather visit a commercial "sugar bush" and see how it's done, there's a directory of maple producers as well as lots of *sticky* links.

http://www.massmaple.org/

National Christmas Tree Association

Too bad they don't have "smell attribute" plug-ins (yet)! If they did, this site would smell terrific! The National Christmas Tree Growers page provides a dictionary of 16 evergreen types, from the Arizona cypress to the white spruce. You'll also find a directory of tree farms close to you (if you want to cut your own), selection tips, and interesting facts and figures.

http://www.christree.org/

Nature/Fitness Trail

Wonder what can be done in that wooded area near your school? Hey, how about building a nature trail? Read about how students and faculty of one elementary school turned land next to their building into an area that integrates fitness and academic subjects. The nature trail extends a quarter mile into a wooded area with all kinds of plants and trees. There is an outdoor classroom area, a bird study area, a pond study area, a vegetable garden, and a fitness trail. See how you can turn a plot of land into a great learning experience!

http://www.lex1.k12.state.sc.us/rbe/trail.htm

NET FILES

When was U.S. President Bill Clinton born?

Answer: He was born on August 19, 1946. You can find out more vital statistics and biographical information at http://www.giftcards.com/p000030.htm

Seuss Lorax Introduction

"I am the Lorax, I speak for the trees!" Even very little children will have fun trying to catch seeds in this Shockwave game inspired by Dr. Seuss. Use your mouse to position your basket just right. If you catch ten seeds you'll be able to replant the Truffula Forest, and the Truffula Forest is what everyone needs.

http://www.randomhouse.com/seussville/games/lorax/

The Wonderful World of Trees

This resource has several sections. Let's explore A Year in the Life of a Tree. Did you know that trees have flowers? Some are so small we don't even notice them, but they are necessary for the tree to reproduce. At this site, follow a Canadian tree through its four seasons. Click on the buds, the branches, the roots, and the leaves and see what's going on at each time. In the Formidable Forms section, you can learn how to classify trees by the properties they have in common. Other areas of this site discuss protecting trees, paper recycling, and an update on the devastating ice storms of the winter of 1997–1998. Hint: Click on the camera icon to open an encyclopedia of trees, with photos and information on each. If you click on the tic-tac-toe icon you'll discover several tree-related games and word-find puzzles.

http://www.domtar.com/arbre/english/start.htm

NET FILES

Maryland has an unusual official state sport. What is it?

Answer: It's the equestrian sport known as jousting! Read why at this informative Web page about Maryland's official symbols, which was created by fifth graders: http://www.inform.umd.edu/UMS+State/UMD-Projects/MCTP/Technology/School_WWW_Pages/pogs/Jason.html

POLLUTION

Campaign for Dark Skies

"The light from the rest of the Universe takes hundreds, thousands, or millions of years to reach our eyes. What a pity to lose it on the last moment of its journey!" Yet that's what happens when light from Earth "pollutes" the night sky. Instead of stars, we see a glowing sky, as light from cities, street lamps, and other terrestrial sources streaks upwards instead of down on the ground where we need it. This useless light is scattered by moisture and dust particles in the atmosphere, which produces the glowing effect. This is important to astronomers, who need as much darkness as possible, but it's also important to everyone else. A dark night sky, spangled with stars, is our heritage as humans. Read all about the various campaigns that say "Let there be dark!" A particularly good introduction may be found at <http://www.u-net.com/ph/cfds/info/inf003.htm>.

http://www.u-net.com/ph/cfds/

Noise Center Home Page

A jet aircraft taking off. A loud "boom car" driving by. Lawn mowers. Leaf blowers. All of these can produce noise pollution. So what? So it can damage your hearing! Studies also show that test scores go down when there is lots of noise in the environment. What can you do to reduce noise pollution? Choose quieter toys, turn down the volume on your CD player, and follow this site's advice for dealing with noise problems in the neighborhood.

http://www.lhh.org/noise/

U.S. EPA Explorers Club

Do you know what the EPA is? It's a governmental entity (how's that for a big word!) called the Environmental Protection Agency, and it makes sure everyone works to keep the air, land, and water safe and pure. We headed to the recycling section and found a lot of neat things about how we can reuse and recycle materials. There are a lot of other sites on this page that can help you understand the environment and our impact on it. This place is guaranteed to make you more aware of your surroundings so you and others can grow up in an environment that is safe for everyone.

http://www.epa.gov/kids/

A B C D E F G H I J K L M N O P Q R S T U V W X Y Z

A B C D E F G H I J K L M N O **P** Q R S T U V W X Y Z

AIR

Air Table of Contents

According to this site, "Americans make the equivalent of 3 million trips to the moon and back each year in cars, using up natural resources and polluting the air." Find out about the major kinds of air pollution and what you can do to help. There are lots of classroom activities, too—how about putting on a play about pollution? Maybe you can get the part of reporter Connie Lung!

http://www.igc.apc.org/nwf/atracks/air/

Burning Issues/Clean Air Revival

If you live in a snowbound part of the world, you may know that there's nothing like a nice, warm fire in the fireplace. It feels so cozy and is so relaxing to watch. Have you ever thought of how your wood smoke might be polluting the air? Particles from the smoke can drift far away before settling out of the air. Along the way, that smoke may be inhaled by anyone in the area. You have probably noticed the often pleasant-smelling smoke from a neighbor's fireplace yourself. Have you ever thought that your lungs may not think it's so pleasant? Read more about this issue here.

http://www.webcom.com/~bi/

US EPA Acid Rain Home Page

Acid rain is a scientific puzzle that was not easy to solve. It takes years for acid rain to cause problems, so its existence remained unknown for a long time. It can cause acid levels in lakes to increase so that fish and plant life cannot survive. Acid rain can also slowly eat away at buildings and structures, causing long-term damage. Where does it come from? What can be done about it? Two major chemicals combine to cause acid rain: sulfur dioxide and nitrous oxide. Although there are many sources of these two chemicals, coal-burning plants, cars, and trucks are the major contributors. This page, from the Acid Rain Program of the Environmental Protection Agency, describes some of the things that are being done to stop acid rain and the destruction it causes. For handy student resources, click on "students and teachers."

http://www.epa.gov/docs/acidrain/ardhome.html

You Can & Acid Rain

Beakman and Jax answer the question "How can rain be acid?" They talk about acid rain and show you how to make an acid tester. Use the acid tester to check the rain in your town to see if your area's being affected. Oops, there's one small detail you should know: you need to boil some cabbage to make the tester. So what, you say? Well, we'll let you discover that one on your own. :-)

http://www.beakman.com/acid/acid.html

TOXIC WASTE

Ocean Planet:perils-toxic materials

Out of about 65,000 chemicals used by industry, do you know how many of them are toxic? No? No one else does, either! Only a few hundred of them have been thoroughly tested to discover if they have a toxic effect on our environment. That leaves a whole lot of waste materials that could have an unknown effect on us and our future health. Read about how dredging harbors to make them deeper can stir up toxic problems that have long been "sleeping." There's also a success story about how oyster beds have recovered their vitality since a certain paint was banned from use on boats.

http://seawifs.gsfc.nasa.gov/OCEAN_PLANET/HTML/
    peril_toxins.html

WATER

NWF: Table of Contents

These fun K–8 activities teach the sources of pollution, the reach of a watershed, and the problems of discarded plastics in the sea. Can you solve the mystery of who is polluting the neighborhood's water? There's also a quick tutorial on water pollution. Sure sounds like a fun way of learning!

http://www.igc.apc.org/nwf/atracks/water/

The water we have on Earth now is all we will ever have, so we'd better take care of it. Did you know that one quart of motor oil can contaminate up to two million gallons of drinking water? Find out about the types of water pollution at NWF: Table of Contents, which is a National Wildlife Federation site.

Ocean Planet: Oceans in Peril

Did you know U.S. sewage treatment plants discharge more oil into the ocean than spills from oil tankers do? Medical waste, plastics, and other debris threaten not only water quality but also sea creatures' lives. You can learn more facts about pollution of the ocean and waterways by taking a look at this exhibit, presented by the Smithsonian Institution as part of a larger Internet exhibition on the ocean. You'll never think the same about water draining from your kitchen sink!

http://seawifs.gsfc.nasa.gov/OCEAN_PLANET/HTML/
ocean_planet_oceans_in_peril.html

Water Quality

This is a collection of reports to Congress that define the quality of U.S. lake, river, and stream water. The reports reveal findings about the different types of pollutants, such as metals and pesticides. There are sections on the sources of water pollution, ocean waters, wetlands, and ground water. The information is presented in graphics and text and is good material for a school project on water pollution. You can also find out about water quality in your state, although you need the free PDF Reader to view it (you'll find a link here to obtain the free PDF software).

http://www.epa.gov/305b/

PUPPETS AND MUPPETS

Henson.com - The Jim Henson Company

The main Henson page is a hoot. There's an online look at the Creature Shop, video clips of Jim Henson at work, and a trip to the company store. But be sure to take the Muppets link to visit <http://www.muppets.com/>. Before this site opened, while it was under construction, this was the message displayed on the screen: "Hi Ho, Kermit the Frog here. We are busy building Muppets.com, the first Virtual Reality, 5D, secured-socket, fully encrypted, dynamically interactive, bearly browserable, community based, Java-enabled, highly compliant, platform independent, frog-functional, scalable, backwardly compatible, indefinitely online, gif-animated, e-deliverable, sequentially tagged, third generation, CGI reciprocal, porcine promoted, plug-and-play, state of the art Web site. Unfortunately, last night Animal ate our hard drive. We're working hard to get that fixed. But for now, you can read all about us." Check out what they came up with after Animal coughed up the hard drive.

http://www.henson.com/

NET FILES

YOU'VE MADE IT INTO THE FORBIDDEN CITY, HOME OF CHINESE EMPERORS OF LONG AGO. NOW, CAN YOU FIND YOUR WAY OUT? HOW MANY ROOMS ARE THERE?

Answer: Beijing is the capital city of China. At its center is the Forbidden City, which was the home and audience hall of the Ming and Qing emperors. The Forbidden City contains over 9,000 rooms! It was originally built in the early 1400s. Read more about Beijing's 3,000-year-old history at http://www.ihep.ac.cn/tour/bj.html

A
B
C
D
E
F
G
H
I
J
K
L
M
N
O
P
Q
R
S
T
U
V
W
X
Y
Z

Muppets Home Page

All images, sounds, and scripts are at this site with permission from Jim Henson Productions. You'll relive lots of good memories with episode guides for *The Muppet Show, Fraggle Rock, Dinosaurs,* and even *Sesame Street*! Look for press releases from Jim Henson Productions to be posted here and lots of lists and reviews.

http://www.ncsa.uiuc.edu/VR/BS/Muppets/
muppets.html

When Jim Henson started producing short television programs and commercials for a local Washington, D.C., station back in the 1950s, he could not have dreamed what an international phenomenon his creations, the Muppets, would become. Visit the Muppets Home Page tribute to Kermit, Miss Piggy, Fozzie, and friends.

The Puppetry Home Page

Looking for a place to buy fake fur, foam rubber, and neoprene to build your own original puppets? Check the resources listed here. If your puppet-making aspirations are more along the old sock variety, you'll find links and patterns to help with that, too. Explore puppetry traditions around the world, from the Punch and Judy shows of France to the shadow puppetry of Asia. There are also links to ventriloquism resources on the Web, so you can learn to throw your voice in cyberspace, where no one can see your mouth move!

http://www.sagecraft.com/puppetry/

VIDEO AND SPY CAMS let you look in on interesting parts of the world.

Stage Hand Puppets * Activity Page *

Puppet theater requires a stage, puppets, and a play. Read puppet plays other kids have written, or try writing your own and submitting it here. There are also lots of ideas and patterns for making puppets from scrap and other materials around your house. You'll find performance tips, hand-shadow directions, and even information on ventriloquism!

http://fox.nstn.ca/~puppets/activity.html

Strings, Springs, and Finger Things

Here's the scoop on puppets—some string, some spring, some finger things! That's not all. You will learn about the various methods of puppetry and see examples of each. There are puppets from many countries. For example, *bunraqu* is a traditional form of Japanese puppetry, native to Osaka. Very large and elaborately jointed and costumed figures are operated in full view of the audience. It takes a whole team of people to manipulate these puppets! Then there are water puppets, which originated in Imperial China. A water puppet consists of two parts: the body, which stands out of the water, and the support, which acts as a floater. The entire production takes place in the water, and the puppeteer stands up to his waist! Want to learn more? Let your fingers take you to this site!

http://www.civilization.ca/membrs/arts/
ssf/ssf00eng.html

Walt Disney Home Video

The Muppets go on a treasure hunt. Join Jim Hawkins, Gonzo, Rizzo, Long John Silver, and, of course, Kermit as they travel the seas in their quest. Take the Statler and Waldorf tour that will (mis)guide you through movie clips and interviews. Read all about the puppeteers, production staff, crews, and filmmakers that make the story come alive. If you want to go on your own adventure, you can play the Muppet Treasure Island game and seek your own fortune. Click on the treasure map and dig in.

http://www.disney.com/DisneyVideos/
MuppetTreasure/

QUEENS, KINGS, AND ROYALTY

See also PEOPLE AND BIOGRAPHIES—KNIGHTS

The 700 Years of Grimaldi

Monaco's Grimaldi dynasty has ruled this small principality for the past seven hundred years! Your grandparents may remember how exciting it was in 1956, when the dashing Prince Rainier III married the American film star Grace Kelly. You can read about the stirring history of the Grimaldis, including biographies of Rainier and Prince Albert, his son. On a surprising historical note, Monaco did not join the United Nations until 1993.

http://www.monaco.mc/monaco/700ans/

Castles on the Web

King Arthur, eat your heart out! If you want to know anything (and we mean *anything*) about castles, this is the page for you. You'll find Castle Tours, Castle of the Week, Castle Questions and Answers, Castle Image Archive, and Castles for Sale. Maybe you can look up your family's ancestral castle. There's also a Glossary of Castle Terms so that even the novice castle lover can feel at home. Hey! Watch out for the (splash) moat.

http://fox.nstn.ca/~tmonk/castle/castle.html

A Glossary of European Noble, Princely, Royal and Imperial Titles

Can you tell a baronet from a marquis? How about a duchess from a countess? This interesting site tries to make sense of it all across various European nobility systems. If you're confused about how to address a sovereign, check <*http://www.heraldica.org/topics/preced.htm*>. That way, you'll know if you should use Highness, Royal Highness, or Most Serene Highness.

http://www.heraldica.org/topics/odegard/titlefaq.htm

Hawai'i: Queen Liliuokalani

Did you know that Hawaii was once a sovereign nation with its own monarch? The last queen of Hawaii was Lydia Liliuokalani, who was illegally deposed in 1893 by the American "Committee of Safety." Though briefly restored, the monarchy was over by 1894, when the Queen was arrested and imprisoned inside Honolulu's beautiful Iolani Palace. You can read about her life and history here. Although President Clinton has officially apologized to the Hawaiians, there is a movement to restore sovereignty to the Islands.

http://ha-waii-shopping.com/~sammonet/liliuokalani.html

THE IMPERIAL FAMILY OF JAPAN

Meet His Imperial Majesty the Emperor of Japan, Her Imperial Majesty the Empress, and their immediate family. This is not an official site, but the information appears to be accurate. There is also a very useful selection of links to Internet sites about other royalty.

http://www.geocities.com/Tokyo/Temple/3953/

King Ludwig II of Bavaria; His Life and Art

Ludwig II was known as "the Mad King" as well as "the Dream King." You have probably seen his fairy tale castle, Neuschwanstein, on many a travel poster. They say it even inspired one of the Disney castles. Net-mom and family visited this castle while on vacation in Germany. It is pretty and it has many unusual features in it. For example (as Net-mom recalls), in the ceiling over the King's bed were many pinprick holes. The floor above was lit with many lanterns, so the King could look up at his ceiling and pretend it was illuminated by stars. There is also a room decorated to look like a cave and a ballroom with a silent, smiling audience painted on the walls. This site offers details on the life of Ludwig II, who reigned in Bavaria from 1864 until he was deposed in 1886. An account of his mysterious death is also included.

http://www.geocities.com/Paris/LeftBank/4080/

A B C D E F G H I J K L M N O P Q R S T U V W X Y Z

A B C D E F G H I J K L M N O P Q R S T U V W X Y Z

THE MONARCHY IN BELGIUM

To see the background of one king, take a look at the *curriculum vitae* (that's Latin for "life's work") of King Albert II of Belgium. You'll see it's not easy to become a king, but then again, the perks of the job are probably really great! The Belgian monarch's position is well respected in Belgium, as he is responsible for keeping the country independent and free.

http://belgium.fgov.be/Engels/417/41709/41709.htm

Thailand: His Majesty King Bhumibol Adulyadej's Golden Jubilee Home Page

His Majesty King Bhumibol Adulyadej of Thailand was born in Cambridge, Massachusetts. He became King in 1946, and in 1996 he celebrated his Golden Jubilee—50 years as monarch. According to the information presented here, he is very popular among his subjects. He is involved in making technology and other scientific advances available to his people. Read about his agricultural and other reforms, and get a glimpse of the beautiful Jubilee celebration and its royal regalia. There are also Internet tutorials on this page, which shows how serious the King is about encouraging his people to learn about technology.

http://kanchanapisek.or.th/index.en.html

NET FILES

What is the oldest city in North America?

Answer: Founded by Champlain in 1608, Quebec City claims to be the oldest—and the only walled—city in North America. Find out lots more interesting facts about the land and people of Canada at http://www-nais.ccm.NRCan.gc.ca/schoolnet/quiz2/english/html/quiz_a_human.html

Welcome to the Royal Court of Sweden

This is the official Web site of the Swedish monarchy. Carl XVI Gustaf, who ascended the throne in 1973, is the 74th King of Sweden. The monarchy goes back over a thousand years. You will learn about the King, Queen Silvia, and the rest of the royal family here. Check the information on the palace and why it has a different architectural style on each of its four sides.

http://www.royalcourt.se/eng/

JORDAN

JordanView: The Royal family

This is the official site of Jordan's Royal Family. From it we learn that His Majesty King Hussein bin Talal is the 42nd generation direct descendant of the Prophet Muhammad (peace be upon him) through the male line of the Prophet's grandson Al-Hassan. He ascended the throne on May 3, 1953. King Hussein married Her Majesty Queen Noor Al-Hussein on June 15, 1978, and they have four children. Committed to peace in the Middle East, King Hussein is a tireless advocate and mediator. Also an accomplished sportsman, he enjoys water sports, karate, flying, and race-car driving among many other activities.

http://www.JordanView.net/royalfamily.html

Welcome to H.M. Queen Noor of Jordan's Web site

Her Majesty Queen Noor is one busy lady! She's involved in many national and international projects and yet she still finds time to help develop her own Web page and read the mail she gets from the Feedback form! At her site you can learn about her leadership in improving the education and health of Jordan's children, as well as her work with The Jubilee School, a magnet school for promising young Jordanian kids. Their new campus is wired and chock-full of computers. She has also won awards for her environmental activism. On top of all that, she's a mom of seven, including four of her own children, two step-children, and an adopted daughter.

http://www.noor.gov.jo/

RUSSIA

The Alexander Palace Time Machine

Once, a second-grade boy visited the library and found a book about the great tsars of Russia. He became fascinated with their stories and their palace lifestyle. As time went on, he read everything he could about the great palace, hoping someday to visit Russia to see it for himself. Incredibly, this boy grew up to do that very thing, and now he's written a comprehensive Web page all about it. This outstanding multimedia tour will give you a look into the past as you explore the life and times of Tsar Nicholas II and his family and friends.

http://www.alexanderpalace.org/palace/

Czars Lobby

Royalty's rule of Russia started with the Romanov Dynasty in 1613 and ended tragically with the Bolshevik Revolution of 1917. At this site you can meet some of Russia's fascinating leaders, such as Peter Alexeevich. The 14th child out of a family of 21 children, he grew to a height of seven feet at a time when the average person's height was even shorter than it is today. He was a skilled diplomat and a talented leader. It was under his rule that Russia became an empire, and he was given the title Emperor of All Russia, Great Father of the Fatherland. You may know him as Peter "the Great."

http://www2.sptimes.com/Treasures/

UNITED KINGDOM

The British Monarchy

This is the official Web site of the British monarchy. Here you will learn about the monarchy as it exists today as well as how it was in the past. You'll visit the palaces, the Crown Jewels, even find out why Elizabeth II keeps corgis as pets! There is a section on a typical day in the life of Her Royal Highness, and you can find out about the many ceremonial duties she must perform. There is also a special section on the life of Diana, Princess of Wales.

http://www.royal.gov.uk/

The Coronation of Queen Elizabeth II

Learn exactly what was said, sung, and done on June 2, 1953, when Elizabeth became the Queen of England. Word for word, the ceremony is re-created at this site.

http://www.oremus.org/liturgy/coronation/

Monarchs of Britain

They are all here: all the monarchs of England, from the Anglo-Saxon kings to Her Majesty Elizabeth II. This site is lavishly illustrated with portraits and photos. For example, learn about William the Conqueror, who started on his claim to fame when he became Duke of Normandy at age seven. Even after spending grueling days out in the field conquering his enemies, he still had to keep his guard up when relaxing back at the castle. The desire to be king among the ruling family members often led to assassination attempts and fatal "accidents." Learn more about William and his "unruly" family at this illustrated site. A long list of links is also provided so you can find out what the rest of the royals were up to during their time of rule.

http://www.britannia.com/history/h6f.html

Trooping the Colour

One of the largest military parades in the world, the Trooping of the Colour is held every June to celebrate the official birthday of Elizabeth II of England. It's not on her real birthday but on her "official" birthday. It's a grand show of heraldry, music, prancing horses, and dashing soldiers. The presentation of the flag ("the colour") to Her Majesty is the highlight of the event. The flag is weighty and cumbersome, but no one would turn down the honor of carrying it, and the soldier who carries the flag during the ceremony must train for months. The ceremony requires strict adherence to military regulations. Anyone falling from a horse could get three months in jail! Learn about one of the most stirring parades in the world at this Web site. By the way, the official royal Web site at <http://www.royal.gov.uk/today/trooping.htm> also mentions a bit about this event.

http://www.buckinghamgate.com/events/features/
    trooping/trooping.html

A B C D E F G H I J K L M N O P Q R S T U V W X Y Z

QUOTATIONS

Bartlett, John. 1901 Familiar Quotations

Project Bartleby, from Columbia University in New York, is an easy way to look for "phrases, proverbs, and passages" from works of literature. Keep in mind that you won't find anything contemporary here, just things prior to 1901. You can search for specific words or for entries from various authors. Want to know some famous Ben Franklin sayings? Just click on his name. Hmmm—"Early to bed and early to rise, makes a man healthy, wealthy and wise." And you thought your dad made that up! According to the notes, Franklin didn't make it up, either, but he helped popularize it.

http://www.columbia.edu/acis/bartleby/bartlett/

"The web of our life is of a mingled yarn, good and ill together."

Was Shakespeare a psychic? Did he predict the growth of the Internet, almost 400 years ago? Check more of his quotes at the Bartlett, John. 1901 Familiar Quotations home page and decide for yourself!

What is the water capacity of the Super Soaker CPS 3000?

Answer: Run away, run away! It packs two gallons of liquid! To soak up more information, go to *http://www.supersoaker.com/faq.htm*

Murphy's Laws

There are a lot of little rules in life. For example: "When all else fails, read the instructions." How about "A clean tie attracts the soup of the day"? Or "Experience is something you don't get until just after you need it." And the ever-popular "If you have watched a TV series only once, and you watch it again, it will be a rerun of the same episode." These quotes and sayings are fun to read and are sometimes more fun to try to figure out. For example, you've heard of Cole's Law, right? It's finely chopped cabbage. (Did you get it?) Parents might wish to preview this site for language suitability.

http://dmawww.epfl.ch/roso.mosaic/dm/murphy.html

Quotations Home Page

"A child of five could understand this. Fetch me a child of five." The comedian Groucho Marx said that. To find all kinds of quotes, from long ago and just yesterday, be sure to try this page. You'll find quotes from Miss Piggy to David Letterman here. There's a collection of the world's most annoying proverbs ("Haste makes waste") as well as Miscellaneous Malapropisms and student bloopers ("The Egyptians built the Pyramids in the shape of a huge triangular cube"). Don't miss "The Best of Anonymous" either ("Remember, a day without sunshine is like night"). This site is highly recommended!

http://www.geocities.com/~spanoudi/quote.html

RADIO

100 YEARS OF RADIO - HOME PAGE -

Today, we think nothing of turning on the TV and seeing events happen, live, on the other side of the world. This was not always the case. Before the development of fast communication technologies, news often took months to work its way across the globe. One of these great technological breakthroughs was radio— wireless communications. The year 1995 marked the 100th anniversary of its invention by Guglielmo Marconi. His first test radio experiments took place in Italy, in 1895. At first, radio communication was limited to a distance of about 100 miles from point to point. To make the invention a commercial success, long-distance communication had to take place. The first stations that Marconi built to meet this goal were in Poldhu, Cornwall, England, and on Cape Cod, Massachusetts. According to this page: "Unfortunately, gales in the autumn of 1901 blew down the antennas of both stations, so Marconi had to improvise for his first transatlantic experiment with a temporary antenna at Poldhu and portable receiving equipment at St. John's, Newfoundland. In December, 1901, the first radio signals were transmitted across the Atlantic Ocean from Poldhu, and were received by Marconi at St. John's. This proved to Marconi (but not to everyone else!) that transatlantic radio communications were possible." The signal sent was the letter *S* in Morse code: "click-click-click." Marconi set out to build his permanent stations, and he settled on Nova Scotia as his western Atlantic radio terminus. On December 15, 1902, Marconi sent the first wireless transatlantic message to Cornwall, England, thus making Glace Bay, on Cape Breton Island, Nova Scotia, the birthplace of transoceanic wireless communication. Read more and see historic photos of the stations and the original equipment at this most interesting site.

http://www.alpcom.it/hamradio/

Wolves are a howl in MAMMALS.

Broadcasting History

Can you imagine riding in a car without hearing tunes on the radio? Car radios weren't introduced until 1930. Radios were expensive back then, and not every home had one. In 1929, home radios were $120 each, which was a fortune! Before 1935, most radios broadcast only live music. After that, stations got record players and began spinning 33 1/3 or 78 rpm records. You say you don't remember records? Ask your parents about them! Radio plays were big, too: one of the biggest early successes was a western called *The Lone Ranger*, and one of its sponsors was Cheerios. Follow the amazing history of broadcast radio from the 1920s through the 1950s at this site.

http://www.people.memphis.edu/~mbensman/
    history1.html

Oatbox Crystal Set Project

It's easy and fun to build your own "crystal" radio set using only some simple components. You will need a soldering iron, some stuff from Radio Shack or your favorite electronics parts store, a Quaker oatmeal box (or other round, tall box), and some time. All the directions are explained at the URL lised below. If you want a more elaborate project, you can find an old cigar box and build a radio with a simple tuner. Cigar stores may have empty boxes; just ask. The directions for that project are at *<http://www.midnightscience.com/cigar.html>*.

http://www.midnightscience.com/project.html

The Original Old Time Radio (OTR) WWW Pages

Many years ago, before cable TV, even before any TV, there was radio. Not just talk and music on the radio, like today, but radio "shows." Radio shows were like today's TV shows, without the pictures. People enjoyed listening to comedies, dramas, mystery thrillers, and variety shows. It was a whole different kind of radio, at a whole different time, and now it is known as "old time radio." This page is entertainment and history all rolled into one, and it is packed with information, pictures, and sounds. Hear clips from such radio greats as *The Great Gildersleeve*. In the History section, you can take a fascinating virtual tour of the old NBC radio studios in Chicago's Merchandise Mart. Don't turn that dial!

http://www.old-time.com/

A B C D E F G H I J K L M N O P Q R S T U V W X Y Z

A
B
C
D
E
F
G
H
I
J
K
L
M
N
O
P
Q
R
S
T
U
V
W
X
Y
Z

AMATEUR RADIO

AA9PW's Amateur Radio Exam Practice Page

You knew "ham radio" was another name for amateur radio, didn't you? You didn't imagine knobs and buttons and an antenna sticking out of a ham, we hope. Ham radio is fun and exciting, and people of all ages have found it to be a useful hobby as well. You need to be licensed to operate a ham rig, and to get a license you have to take a test. At this site, you can take sample amateur radio licensing exams. How well can you do? This site will check your exam and suggest areas where you need more study.

http://www.biochem.mcw.edu/Postdocs/Simon/
   radio/exam.html

ARRLWeb: Welcome to Amateur Radio (Ham Radio)!

The American Radio Relay League, or ARRL, has been helping amateur radio enthusiasts since 1914. They now have over 170,000 members. At the ARRL site you can tune in to lots of information on getting started in the hobby. It's best to find a local radio club to help guide you, and there's a convenient directory at this site. You'll also learn about licensing rules, upcoming testing in your area, and lots more.

http://www.arrl.org/hamradio.html

Ham Radio.FAQ

Amateur radio has long been an exciting hobby for people of all ages all over the world. Would you like to set up your own equipment and broadcast from your home? Do you need to organize a team to provide mobile communications at special events and festivals? The "ham" is always ready to be "on the air." Absolutely anyone can do it in most countries, so find out how. If you're already a ham, find out more from this u-to-date FAQ. The collection of links at this site is first rate and includes all sorts of info, including scanner frequencies and satellite data.

http://www.mv.com/ipusers/wd1v/hamradio.faq.html

Ham Radio Online

Licensed ham radio operators use high-tech radios for communications with others (it's sort of like using a cellular phone, but without the cost of airtime charges). Hams meet new friends and "visit" with hams in countries all over the globe. They have even talked with astronauts orbiting Earth! Many U.S. and Russian astronauts are also licensed hams, ad they make contacts from space for educational uses and sometimes just for fun. If you're not already an amateur radio operator, get into the Education section. If you are a ham, here's where you'll keep up on all the newest amateur radio news and latest technological developments. Since hams often provide emergency communications in the event of a disaster (some systems evn have 911 emergency access), this site also has real-time links to earthquake and other disaster monitoring sites all over the globe. Other unusual features are real-time forecasts for auroral, solar, ad meteor shower activity. Don't forget to bring an umbrella if you're going out in a meteor shower!

http://www.hamradio-online.com/

RADIO STATIONS

Live Radio on the Internet

Want to listen to the latest tunes from India? Maybe catch a hot new band from New Zealand? Or maybe you're just homesick for that old radio station where you used to live. Many stations now send their broadcast feeds live over the Internet. You can take a world tour of live sounds and news here.

http://www.frodo.u-net.com/radio.htm

The MIT List of Radio Stations on the Internet

Is your favorite radio station's home page on the Internet? How about that great station you listen to when you visit your cousin in Boston? This is the place to find out. This site lists radio stations all over the world that have home pages on the Web. So whether it's that country music station in Nashville or that hot rocker on the dial in the Netherlands, you can get there from here!

http://wmbr.mit.edu/stations/

NetRadio Network - Listen to over 150 Free Music Channels

NetRadio was the first "radio station" just for the Internet. They don't broadcast anywhere but cyberspace. You can go to NetRadio and listen to music on your computer even while you surf somewhere else. There's lots of good music plus news to listen to. You can get the latest concert information, enter contests, win prizes, and vote in a monthly poll. It's all the fun stuff about radio right at your fingertips! Kids will like to listen to special children's selections and news on the KidzRadio channel. Parental advisory: Links from this site have not all been reviewed.

http://www.netradio.net/

NPR Online - National Public Radio

Many people think that National Public Radio (NPR) gives us the best news, feature stories, and music on the radio. This site gives you a lot of all these and lets you know where you can find NPR on your local radio dial. Like PBS on television, NPR is federally and privately funded programming. It's also commercial-free. This Web site has the same "Breaking News" and "Story of the Day" as the NPR radio broadcasts. Yes, you can actually listen to the most recent NPR news report right on your computer. You can also listen to past broadcasts of favorite NPR shows. Tune in and see what public radio has to offer.

http://www.npr.org/

Welcome to Vatican Radio

Staff from 50 countries prepare 400 hours of broadcast material every week in 37 different languages. Radio Vatican broadcasts on short wave, medium wave, FM, satellite, and the Internet. You can download Real Audio files or FTP features in several languages. As they say: "Listen, for heaven's sake!"

http://www.wrn.org/vatican-radio/

SHORTWAVE

Numbers Stations on Shortwave Radio

"So this is a shortwave radio. What do you guys listen to on these things? Wait, turn the knob the other way, slowly. Right there—stop! What in the world is THAT? It sounds like counting in a foreign language. What is that?" Could it be a math lesson in Russian? A language class in the U.K.? A spy sending secret code from some remote island? Or maybe someone in the U.S. is giving someone in Germany a company e-mail address? Hmmm, the spy answer is definitely the most fun—and it just might be the right one! The so-called "numbers stations" heard on shortwave radio make a fascinating topic. For many years, listeners came across them now and again, never really sure of their purpose. Even today, their origin and meaning are mysterious. Can you find the signals? What might they really be? This page helps you track them down and uncover the truth. Listen in! If you're really interested, you can subscribe to a mailing list via this site <*http://www.access.digex.net/~cps/numbers.html*>.

http://itre.ncsu.edu/radio/numbers.html

Shortwave/Radio Catalog (Page 1)

Shortwave radio enthusiasts can find lots of new information in each new issue of this page. There are links to basic information and resources that the radio hobbyist will use again and again. Hardware, software, and radio services are covered in depth. You'll find plenty of quality links to all kinds of radio information from all corners of the globe. This really is a one-stop radio information catalog for the Internet! Don't miss the "The WWW Shortwave Listening Guide" link to find out what programs are on right now, today: <*http://www.anarc.org/naswa/swlguide/*>.

http://itre.ncsu.edu/radio/

Shortwave/Radio Catalog (Radio Services)

What is shortwave radio? Technically, that's the name for radio frequencies between 2.3 and 30 MHz. Shortwave broadcasts can be received over long distances, making it possible to communicate internationally—yes, without the Internet! You can tune in radio broadcasts from around the world. Questions, anyone? The answers are here. Be sure to pay special attention to the links marked "Newbies take notice!"

http://itre.ncsu.edu/radio/RadioCatalogRS.html

A B C D E F G H I J K L M N O P Q R S T U V W X Y Z

RAILROADS AND TRAINS

See also MODELS AND MINIATURES—RAILROADS

Corey's Choo-Choo CAD

Thinking of building your own model railroad? If you have Java on your browser, you can start here by building your own railroad track and running your own little cybertrain. This program won't let you derail your train when you remove a piece of track, but you can make it turn angles that real trains can't. It is simple but entertaining fun, and it doesn't take up any space in the family room or basement.

http://kidshealth.org/kid/games/choo_choo/

Cyberspace World Railroad Home Page

This site has all the bells and whistles that train lovers adore. Hang out in the lounge car and check out the travel stories. Download train typefaces for your computer. Brush up on the General Code of Operating Rules. Listen to an actual recording of a train crew member's transmission as he is trapped on a runaway train. And if all the monthly articles about trains and transportation issues are still not enough, you can always switch tracks to one of the over 900 railroad links that will have you riding the rails all over the globe.

http://www.mcs.com/~dsdawdy/cyberoad.html

High Speed Trains around the World - by Oliver Keating

This site says that building a fast train is easy. What's hard is building a fast track and smart signaling system to work in conjunction with the fast train to make a supremely fast railroad. From this site you can visit high-speed trains such as Japan's bullet trains, France's TGV network, and the mag-levs (magnetically levitated trains), which set a new speed record in early 1998: 344 mph!

http://www.keating.ml.org/trains/

Interactive Model Railroad

Wow, that's a cool model train—too bad it's in Germany. Bet you'd love to play with it. Guess what? You can! Through the magic of forms and server-push technology, you can select one of two trains to control. Then select which platform the train should travel to. Then press GO and watch your train speed along past the miniature Bavarian town. Watch out for that alp!

http://rr-vs.informatik.uni-ulm.de/rr/

Jeremiah L. Toth Railroads Page

This site features information about Maryland railroad stations, Washington, D.C.'s colossal and historic Union Station, railroading in Delaware, Pennsylvania, New York, and Connecticut, and trolley, interurban, and heavy rail resources. This is a good, fact-driven resource center for railroad buffs looking for on-track information.

http://www.clark.net/pub/jltoth/trains.html

New York City Subway Resources

Net-mom likes subways. She's traveled on the El in Chicago, the Metro in Washington, D.C. and Montreal, the T in Boston, BART in San Francisco, and whatever they call the subway in Prague. This Web page is done by people who really *love* subways. Learn about the history of the New York subway system and take a virtual tour of some of the abandoned stations and tracks. There are also interesting links to information on subways, trolleys, and interurban rail systems all over the world.

http://www.nycsubway.org/

North American Steam Locomotives

While a rarity today, steam trains have not entirely vanished from the American landscape. This page provides information about steamers of the past and today's survivors, including schedules of currently running steam excursions, specifications of steam trains, and sections on trains that are "Lost Forever (but not forgotten)." There is also information on rail fairs, rail museums, and a special piece on the annual reenactment of the Golden Spike ceremony in Utah, featuring some terrific photographs; look for it in the Virtual Tours area.

http://www.arc.umn.edu/~wes/steam.html

A
B
C
D
E
F
G
H
I
J
K
L
M
N
O
P
Q
R
S
T
U
V
W
X
Y
Z

The Golden Spike was "driven" at Promontory, Utah, in 1869, completing the railroad track which joined the East and West coasts of the North American continent for the first time. There were really several ceremonial spikes, some silver and some gold. Now there is an annual reenactment of this event. For a full-color report on it and other steam locomotive events, run on over to the North American Steam Locomotives page.

Operation Lifesaver, Inc.

Trains are fascinating but dangerous. Did you know that a big, 150-car freight train traveling at 50 mph can take up to 1.5 miles to come to a complete stop? In the U.S., about 6,000 deaths and injuries per year involve trains and cars or pedestrians walking on the tracks. Most train accidents occur when the train is traveling 30 mph or slower. Even at 30 mph, the approximate stopping distance is 3,500 feet, or two-thirds of a mile! Operation Lifesaver educates adults and kids on trains and train safety. Make tracks to visit here soon.

http://www.oli.org/oli/

RailCams at RailServe - The Internet Railroad Directory

Interested in spotting a few real trains yourself? Visit this collection of train cams! For example, you might check trains on the Tehachapi Hill, "the busiest single tracked mainline in the world." It's Oone of the main north-south routes for rail traffic in California, and the RailCam is situated on a stretch featuring a 2.2 percent grade. That's nothing for a car, but it's a big deal for a train. The cam shows pictures of the last few trains spotted by the camera. Be sure to click on the Huh? button to find out more about what you can see in the photos.

http://www.railserve.com/switchyard/RailCams_Page/

TGV

A TGV (*train à grande vitesse*) is a high-speed system launched in the 1960s comprising train, track, and signaling technologies that when combined make high speeds possible. Its record so far is 320.3 mph. The TGV system is owned and operated by the French national railways, and it is an integral part of French rail travel. There are directions for "railfanning," or watching these trains as they whoosh by, but don't blink, or you'll miss it. A typical running speed is 186 mph.

http://mercurio.iet.unipi.it/tgv/tgvindex.html

Trains Magazine Online

Have you ever ridden on a train? They're really cool. You can get up and walk to the snack bar for a soda or lean your seat back and look out the window at the passing countryside. Since your parents don't have to drive, they can take time to play a game or read a book with you. This site has lots of neat stories about trains in places all over the world. You can link to the pages of lots of railway companies, check out railroad museums, get background information about railroads, and look at some great photos of trains. In fact, if you go on a ride and take a really good picture, you can send it to them. It might even appear on the Web page!

http://www.kalmbach.com/trains/trains.html

READING AND LITERACY

See also BOOKS AND LITERATURE

CLWG: Children's Literature Web Guide

"If my cunning plan works, you will find yourself tempted away from the Internet and back to the books themselves!" says David K. Brown, children's librarian. He's collected links to many outstanding reading experiences. You can find information on fictional people and places in children's books. Play Virtual Poohsticks at the 100 Acre Wood. Look at the links to Arthurian legend. Book series, such as Nancy Drew, Hardy Boys, and Goosebumps, also have their own pages. If you have a favorite author, like C. S. Lewis, or Dr. Seuss, look here for links to their pages. There are online children's stories and lists of award-winning books. And you'll find a whole section called Children's Writings and Drawings. If you want to put your work on the Net for the world to see, start here.

http://www.acs.ucalgary.ca/~dkbrown/

A
B
C
D
E
F
G
H
I
J
K
L
M
N
O
P
Q
R
S
T
U
V
W
X
Y
Z

Cyberkids Home

"Monster in the Park," "Mixed-Up Zoo," "Beyond the Barrier of Time," "Scary Stories That Make Your Mom Faint"—these are only some of the great stories written by kids that your family can read together in this online magazine. Like any magazine, there are writing and art contests, software and product reviews written by kids for kids, and cookie recipes, too. In addition to the fictional stories, the feature articles have crossword or word search puzzles along with them, to make learning about something new even more fun. The CyberKids Launchpad will link you to lots of other neat sites listed by subject area. If you have thoughts or ideas you want to share with other readers, be sure to send them in.

http://www.cyberkids.com/index.shtml

IPL Youth Division

Some kids really like to go to the library and spend time there: reading and rereading favorites, listening to CDs in the audiovisual (AV) department, maybe even doing a little homework. Here's another library to explore, with guides to help you. Like any good public library, the Internet Public Library, or IPL, has a vibrant children's room. There are lots of things to read, a story time (with illustrated folktales), homework help, and an Authors' Corner. If you go to the Story Hour, some stories have audio or animations; most of them are illustrated. If you like science, Dr. Internet will direct you to interesting sites on the Internet, where you can explore dinosaurs, earthquakes, geology, volcanoes, and weather. In the Authors' Corner, Matt Christopher, Jane Yolen, Avi, and Lois Lowry, among others, share their life stories and talk about their books. You can ask them questions, too. If you like contests, you'll find links to many Internet contests. And the hours are great—this library is always open.

http://www.ipl.org/youth/

KidPub WWW Publishing

Here's a great place to share your stories, poems, and news about where you live. Kids from all over the world have their writing published on this Web page. You'll find stories mostly from the U.S., but some are also from places such as Tasmania, Malaysia, Germany, and Singapore. Most of the young authors include their e-mail addresses, so you can write back to them. Writers also write a little bit about themselves. Contributors range in age from 4 to 15. Write on!

http://www.kidpub.org/kidpub/

NET FILES

Time magazine's annual "Man of the Year" has also been a woman and even an idea from time to time. Guess who the first woman was. (Hint: A king loved her so much that he gave up his throne to marry her.)

Answer: Wallis Warfield Simpson was *Time's* first "Woman of the Year," for the year 1936. Find out more at *http://pathfinder.com/time/special/moy/1939.html*

Parents and Children Together Online

Part of the fun of reading and writing can be the sharing of it. This site is fun to explore with your mom or dad or with a younger sister or brother. There are illustrated stories and articles for sixth grade and under. Some of the stories and articles have links to resources on the Internet. You can follow the links to find information on koalas, cats, or Scottish terrier dogs. The Scottie article even has a link to a site about U.S. President Franklin Delano Roosevelt, who had one! If you like to write stories, hunker down around The Global Campfire, where you can contribute your part to an ongoing story. And if you want a key pal, look here.

http://www.indiana.edu/~eric_rec/fl/pcto/menu.html

RECYCLING

The Consumer Recycling Guide: Commonly Recycled Materials

You recycle, right? Do you have questions about those cryptic markings on the bottoms of plastic containers— what do they mean? You'll find a description of them here. Also, you can learn what to do with items such as used motor oil or spent NiCad batteries. This is the one-stop answer place for recycling questions.

http://www.obviously.com/recycle/guides/
common.html

Your mom says this new juice is good for you, but you're not so sure you want to drink it. After all, the bottle has some other kid's name on it. There's this triangle with a "1" in it, and below that it says "PETE." Not to worry. That's a recycling symbol. It means the container is made out of polyethylene terephthalate (PET). Lots of soda and water containers and some other waterproof packaging have the same symbol. These markings help us know which plastics are recyclable and which are, well, trash. Find out more at The Consumer Recycling Guide: Common Recycled Materials.

Dumptown Game

Welcome to Dumptown! Look around—there's litter and pollution, lots of garbage cans and dumpsters, but no way to recycle. You can save Dumptown! You can make things better, but you've got to do so in a cost-effective way. It won't be easy, but you can discover how proper management of resources can make a difference in saving this community. There will be lots of help, because this site is run by the Environmental Protection Agency.

http://www.epa.gov/recyclecity/gameintro.htm

Garbage

The average American contributed 1,570 pounds of solid trash and 3,613 pounds of sewage to the world's waste this past year. Americans are generating waste products faster than nature can break them down! We're also using up resources faster than they can be replaced. At this site you can learn about the various types of waste and how we can begin to turn the tide. Don't miss the links on this site (which by the way is made from 100 percent recycled electrons).

http://www.learner.org/exhibits/garbage/

Rot Web Home Composting Information Site

This is the lowdown on dirt (for those of you who have a sense of *humus*). It gives basic information about home composting. You can find out how to build compost heaps of every description, some even including worms. If you want to see a heap in action, there's a nationwide list of Composting Demo Sites. It's a *rotten* Web site, and that's why we've included it!

http://net.indra.com/~topsoil/Compost_Menu.html

You Can Make Paper

This site will give you directions on making your own paper out of recycled materials. Making paper is fun, but it is pretty messy, so make sure an adult helps you!

http://www.beakman.com/paper/paper.html

REFERENCE WORKS

Electric Library Personal Edition

As this book goes to press: "The Electric Library currently contains 7,933,923 newspaper articles, 774,856 magazine articles, over 419,040 book chapters, 1,103 maps, 86,302 television and radio transcripts, and 57,303 photos and images!" There's also an encyclopedia, Monarch Notes, and a fair number of reference books. You can search topics for free, but if you want to read the full text of the articles, you must become a member. There's a 30-day free trial offer.

http://www.elibrary.com/

Fugitive Facts File

What do Henry ("Hap") H. Arnold, Omar N. Bradley, Dwight D. Eisenhower, Douglas MacArthur, and George C. Marshall have in common? They are the only men who have been five-star generals in the U.S. Army. You can find that here, along with a ton of information that could help you with a paper at school or let you impress family and friends. In fact, you'll get lots of neat information, from A (Actors' and actresses' real names—did you know that Tom Cruise was born Thomas Mapother?) to Z (it'll link you to a Web site about Zorro).

http://www.hennepin.lib.mn.us/catalog/fff.html

A B C D E F G H I J K L M N O P Q R S T U V W X Y Z

A
B
C
D
E
F
G
H
I
J
K
L
M
N
O
P
Q
R
S
T
U
V
W
X
Y
Z

ICONnect: KidsConnect

You've got a question and no one seems to have an answer—not your mother or your grandpa or your great-aunt, Gert. Just head to this site and ask your question to one of the school library media specialists throughout the world. They provide direct assistance to any student looking for resources. They'll help you learn how to use the Internet effectively for your class work, and you can tell Mom, Grandpa, and aAunt Gert that you've got the answer!

http://www.ala.org/ICONN/kidsconn.html

IPL Reference Center

With a reference desk and bookshelves arranged by subject, the only thing missing here is the smiling librarian! This site links to sites all over the Net, so be prepared to take some time to check all the different sources at the Internet Public Library.

http://www.ipl.org/ref/

Learn2.com - The ability utility

Do you know how to use chopsticks, or clean a freshly caught fish? Could you use a lesson in putting a golf ball or breaking in a new baseball mitt? How about tips on folding a shirt or cleaning up a stain? This truly great site will teach you all of the above and more!

http://www.learn2.com/

LibrarySpot

Just in time for term paper season, a new one-stop reference desk has opened on the Web. You may not need it today, but believe Net-mom, you'll need it in the future. Acronym dictionaries, biographical dictionaries, inventions, useful calculators (how much grass seed to buy, how to convert cooking measurements)—all are here for your use. There are also links to hundreds of library card catalogs all over the world. Explore numerous magazines and newspapers, phone books, mapping programs, and more. If you like Library Spot, you'll love its sister site, Book Spot <http://www.bookspot.com/> with links to the best-seller lists, authors, publishers, and what's new and old in award-winning books for kids and adults.

http://www.libraryspot.com/

Martindale's 'The Reference Desk'

Hotlist this one now. First off, find out what time it is, not only where you live but all over the world. You'll learn what the weather is, where the earthquakes are, and where the surf's up. Then move on to the calculators. There are over 6,400 of them. In fact, there is so much compelling information here we bet you can't take just one link! Unfortunately, each time you go back for a new one, the entire page has to reload, and it's very frustrating. Perhaps by the time you read this, Martindale will have divided up the Web site a little more for your navigating pleasure.

http://www-sci.lib.uci.edu/HSG/Ref.html

Research-It! - Your one-stop reference desk

This site's cool! Spell a word, conjugate a verb, find a quote, or locate facts about a famous person. Almost 30 quick reference tools are rolled into one easy-to-use site.

http://www.itools.com/research-it/

The Scholes Library Electronic Reference Desk

Groan...your paperback dictionary has disappeared. Hmmm, well, here's the *As* in the middle of the kitchen, and there are *B* through *F* down the basement stairs. Maybe it was the dog? Don't despair. You can use dictionaries online! This site also has encyclopedias, a thesaurus, maps, current news, historical documents, time zones, area codes, and more!

http://scholes.alfred.edu/Ref.html

Study WEB

Whatever your homework assignment is, this site is sure to have something you can use, with "more than 69,000" research-quality links, listed by subject category. The Reference Shelf is a good place to start, but the brief reviews of each site will also help you select just the right place to look. Tell your parents and teachers about this site too, because there is some neat stuff for them here as well.

http://www.studyweb.com/

Bring an umbrella, we're going to explore WEATHER AND METEOROLOGY resources!

ALMANACS AND GAZETTEERS

1997 World Factbook

Did you know that Kenya (569,250 square kilometers) is twice the size of Nevada? Did you know that in Denmark four languages are spoken (Danish, Faroese, Greenlandic, and German)? If you ever wanted to know facts like these about countries around the world, this is the place to look. You'll also find a section on oceans of the world. By the way, did you know that as of 1993 there were 215 million TV sets in the United States?

http://www.odci.gov/cia/publications/factbook/

Events for ...

Ho hum, today is just another day, right? It seems there are so few special days—like Christmas, your birthday, or the Fourth of July. Actually, every single day has been important in history, or there is some momentous event taking place somewhere, or someone great was born. To see why today is important, take a look here. Maybe you can use the information here as a good excuse for a party!

http://erebus.phys.cwru.edu/~copi/events.html

How far is it?

In the not-too-distant past, finding the distance from one part of the globe to another took a fair amount of work. It involved using complicated tables and converting map scales. Now, we have an alternative! On this page, all you need to know is the name of two locations, and the distance between the two is calculated for you. This service provides distance for almost all places in the United States and a good number of major cities elsewhere. If a city doesn't appear to be in the database, just put in the name of the country and see what cities are available.

http://www.indo.com/distance/

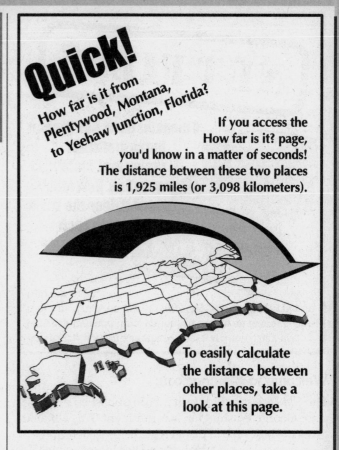

Quick! How far is it from Plentywood, Montana, to Yeehaw Junction, Florida?

If you access the How far is it? page, you'd know in a matter of seconds! The distance between these two places is 1,925 miles (or 3,098 kilometers).

To easily calculate the distance between other places, take a look at this page.

Information Please Home Page

This is great! We typed in "longest river" and up came a list starting with the Nile, about 4,180 miles in length. Then we tried typing "Michael Jordan birthday." No hits. So then we just tried "Jordan" and sure enough, under Sports Personalities there was an article on him. He was born February. 17, 1963. Then we tried "Dogs" just to see what we'd get—wow, a whole history of the dog, from the wolf to the American Kennel Club. Don't miss this site!

http://www.infoplease.com/

U.S. Gazetteer

A quick way to find the county, state, area code, ZIP code, and latitude and longitude of a place in the United States is to check this resource. It is linked to the XEROX PARC Map Viewer, so once you find out that Prague, Arkansas, is in Grant County, ZIP code 05053, latitude 34 17 12 N, longitude 92 16 50 W, you can click on those coordinates to view the map.

http://www.census.gov/cgi-bin/gazetteer/

NET FILES

A monster truck like Bigfoot burns methanol racing fuel instead of gasoline. How much of it does the truck burn in each 250-foot run?

Answer: Fuel efficient these trucks are not. They use between two and three gallons of fuel in an average 250-foot run. Truck on over to *http://www.bigfoot4x4.com/* to find out more.

Welcome to Almanac.com

The *Old Farmer's Almanac* has been published ever since George Washington was president. This almanac gives the best time to plant crops, helps to determine the weather long in advance, and has lots of cool old sayings (these are called aphorisms). People have used and enjoyed the *Old Farmer's Almanac* throughout history. Now, parts of this publication are available on the Internet. You can see weather predictions, read some old-timey quotes, and find a great history of the almanac. Whether you live on a farm or in a city high-rise apartment, you'll like this site!

http://www.almanac.com/

AWARDS

ALSC: The Randolph Caldecott Medal; The John Newbery Medal

There's no doubt that librarians know tons about books. Every year, children's librarians in the American Library Association give two awards to authors and illustrators of the best books for kids. The Caldecott Medal goes to the best illustrator of a children's book, and the Newbery Medal is given to the author of the finest kids' book. See the Caldecott winners at this Web site, then scroll to the bottom and click on the Newbery page for those winners; you'll find some librarian-tested and approved books!

http://www.ala.org/alsc/caldecott.html

Children's Book Awards

Every year, thousands of books are written for kids. Most of the books are good, but trying to decide which books to borrow from the library can be difficult. Fortunately, several organizations pick the finest books for children each year. These books are judged by a variety of criteria, including best for young children, best for elementary school kids, and so on. Some of the awards for the best children's books are listed on the Internet, and you can find convenient links to many of those lists here. Besides the Caldecott and the Newbery Awards, you'll find the Coretta Scott King Award and the Laura Ingalls Wilder Medal winners. This year, there are also many international awards, plus awards given to books selected by kids! If you're looking for a good book to read, take a glance here.

http://www.acs.ucalgary.ca/~dkbrown/awards.html

You are bored.

There's nothing good on TV. You've played all the video games a million times, and none of your friends are around. What to do? You can find a really great book to read! On the Children's Book Awards page, you'll find links to lists of some of the best books for kids of all time!

Emmy® Awards—Academy of Television Arts & Sciences

Have you ever heard the song by Bruce Springsteen, "Fifty-Seven Channels and Nothin' On"? Sometimes nothing good seems to be on TV, but many good shows are available. The Academy of Television Arts and Sciences selects some of the best programs and gives the winning shows and actors an award called an Emmy. To see who the most current winners are, check out this Web page. You'll learn television history, see who is being nominated, and get a behind-the-scenes look at the annual Emmy awards show.

http://www.emmys.org-/tindex.html

Famous parents and their kids who have both won Emmy®awards are: Danny and Marlo Thomas; James and Tyne Daly; and Carl and Rob Reiner. Find out more about the awards at the Emmy® Awards—Academy of Television Arts & Sciences page!

GRAMMY® Awards

Music is a universal language. Everybody likes music, whether it's pop sounds, rock and roll, rap, or R&B. Most music we listen to is recorded, either on tapes, CDs, the radio, or TV. The National Academy of Recording Arts and Sciences is an organization of recording specialists who vote on the best recordings each year. The winning recording artists receive an award called a Grammy. To see (and hear) who has won in the past and who is nominated for the upcoming awards, take a look at this page. It's the place to look if you like music, and who doesn't!

http://www.grammy.com/

The Nobel Foundation

Alfred Nobel was a Swedish-born inventor and international industrialist, most famous for the invention of dynamite. He died in 1896. His will founded the Nobel Prizes in the fields of physics, chemistry, literature, physiology/medicine and peace. Since 1901, they have been presented to the winners (called Nobel laureates) at ceremonies on December 10, the anniversary of Alfred Nobel's death. Most of the prizes are awarded in Stockholm, Sweden, while the Nobel Peace Prize is awarded in Oslo, Norway. Since 1969, the Sveriges Riksbank (Bank of Sweden) Prize in Economic Sciences in memory of Alfred Nobel has been awarded in Stockholm at the same time. You can get a list of all the winners, pictures of the medals awarded, plus a biography of Nobel and a history of his prizes at this site.

http://www.nobel.se/

On Broadway WWW Information Page

A live performance in a theater—there is nothing like it. Lights, stage props, music, and acting are all parts of what makes the theater great. If you've ever seen or participated in a play, you know it can be fantastic! Some of the best theatrical performances take place on Broadway in New York City. Want to know what's playing there right now, plus get reviews of the performances and maybe hear some sound clips? The Antoinette Perry (Tony) Award is presented annually for distinguished achievement in the professional theater. These are the best of the best, and if you like theater, take a look to see which plays have won.

http://artsnet.heinz.cmu.edu/OnBroadway/

Oscar® Awards—Academy of Motion Picture Arts and Sciences

If you're a movie fanatic, don't miss the Official Interactive Guide to the Academy Awards, designed to help you explore Oscar nominees and winners, past and present. There are pictures and lots of information on all of them. You may be surprised to find out that the Academy of Motion Picture Arts and Sciences does a lot more than just give out awards. They have an amazing movie history library, too. They also sponsor Student Academy Awards, designed to recognize excellence among college students enrolled in film courses throughout the United States.

http://www.ampas.org/ampas/

The Pulitzer Prizes

Joseph Pulitzer was an American newspaper publisher known for his innovative ideas and bold reporting style. When he died, his will established the Pulitzer Prizes. The first ones were awarded in 1917. Each year, achievements in American journalism, letters, drama, and music are recognized. Fourteen prizes are given in journalism. The prizes in "letters" are for fiction, history, poetry, general nonfiction, and biography or autobiography. There are also prizes for drama and music. At this site, you can read about the 1995, 1996, 1997, and 1998 winners; perhaps in the future the site will expand to include past years.

http://www.pulitzer.org/navigation/

A B C D E F G H I J K L M N O P Q R S T U V W X Y Z

Sidebar alphabet: A B C D E F G H I J K L M N O P Q R S T U V W X Y Z

BUYING GUIDES

Bottom Dollar

Find the best price for a book, CD, toy, movie, hardware, software, or other merchandise. For example, just type in the name of the book you want, and the search engine queries several online bookstores to discover the lowest price.

http://www.bottomdollar.com/

Welcome to Consumer Reports® Online

Consumer Reports is a non-profit organization that tests appliances, audio and TV equipment, cameras, cars, and all sorts of other things. They issue their opinions on which items are the best, based on the results of the tests they run on competing products. They accept no advertising in their magazine, so you can really trust what they have to say. Next time you want to buy something, see if it has been reviewed lately. You'll be glad you did. By the way, be sure to tell your parents this is online.

http://www.consumerreports.org/

CURRENCY CONVERTER

164 Currency Converter by OANDA

When is a dollar not a dollar? Wait a minute! Where did you get that dollar? Is that a U.S. dollar, or an Australian dollar, or a Namibian dollar? If it's a Namibian dollar, then it is likely worth less than half the U.S. dollar. The Australian dollar is worth more than the Namibian dollar but is still not worth as much as the U.S. dollar. Confused yet? What about the German mark, the Japanese yen, or the Slovenian tolar? Whoa! This stuff can get confusing. Luckily, at this site, with just a couple of clicks you can compare 164 currencies all over the world. Try it!

http://www.oanda.com/cgi-bin/ncc

DICTIONARIES

Acronym and abbreviation list

Do you know what an acronym is? It's a word that is formed by the letters or syllables of other words. For example, let's say we created an organization called American Cats Resting On New Yarn Mattresses—its acronym could be ACRONYM! If you want to look up and see what some real acronyms stand for (try UNESCO or PTA for fun), take a glimpse at this site.

http://www.ucc.ie/info/net/acronyms/acro.html

Casey's Snow Day Reverse Dictionary (and Guru)

Casey's a young girl who lives in Los Alamos, New Mexico. One day, there was a lot of snow and her school closed, so she went to work with her dad. While she was there, she got this great idea. Sometimes, people know what a word means, but they just can't think of the word—so how about a reverse dictionary? The programmers thought Casey's idea was great, so they came up with a way to do it. All you do is type in the definition, then you see a list of choices that match it. The programmers were so happy with it that they named it after Casey. If words have a habit of escaping you, a reverse dictionary might be just what you need!

http://www.c3.lanl.gov:8064/

Dictionary of Phrase and Fable

Are you forever forgetting the Riddle of the Sphinx? Want to know who Apollo was? Can't wait to find out what the seven wonders of the ancient and medieval worlds were? The current edition of this classic book is one of Net-mom's favorites, but you have to get it at the store. The 1894 edition is online and searchable.

http://www.bibliomania.com/Reference/
PhraseAndFable/

How is Kwanzaa celebrated? Find out in HOLIDAYS!

Hypertext Webster Gateway at UCSD

Have you ever tried to actually read a dictionary? There's not much of a story! However, dictionaries are very useful when you want to know the meaning of a word. You can use this page to enter a word and have a computer look it up for you in several dictionaries.

http://work.ucsd.edu:5141/cgi-bin/http_webster

The Internet Dictionary Project

This site lets you convert English words to Assyrian, French, German, Italian, Latin, Persian, Portuguese, or Spanish and back again. The catch is, the dictionary isn't very big, so often the word you want won't be found. If you know one of these languages, you can help the dictionary to grow!

http://www.june29.com/IDP/

LITTLE EXPLORERS by Enchanted Learning Software

Try this on very little kids. They can click on any letter in the alphabet, and link to lots of Web sites and activities that begin with that letter. This is an interactive picture dictionary, with hours of fun just waiting behind the letters. This page also has English-French, English-German, English-Portuguese, and English-Spanish versions. Much of the site is also available in Japanese.

http://www.EnchantedLearning.com/Dictionary.html

OneLook Dictionaries (Dictionary), The Faster Finder

Did you know that a lot of specialized online dictionaries are scattered all over the Net? There are dictionaries for medicine, sports, religion, art, music, and more. This site has cobbled together 287 of them to create a huge dictionary you can search with just one look (can you guess what it is called?). Be sure to check out the survey, too. It will ask you how you pronounce certain Net-related words. Past surveys have sampled world opinion on the correct way to say "GIF," "URL," and "FAQ." Vote for your favorite audio file and let your voice be counted!

http://www.onelook.com/

A Web of On-line Dictionaries

This exceptional resource collects links to over 500 online dictionaries and word lists in over 140 different languages. You'll also find other reference sources, such as thesauri, rhyming dictionaries, grammars, and more. Parental advisory: rRemember, some dictionaries may contain profanity and obscenity.

http://www.bucknell.edu/~rbeard/diction.html

WWWebster Dictionary - Search screen

Sure, you can look up words online and get the definitions from this famous dictionary publisher. But you can also read some of the fascinating features about interesting words, and scratch your head over some perplexing word puzzles. See what words Shakespeare coined, or trace the history of the word "phat." Find out how words get into the dictionary, too. This page explains how Merriam-Webster does it, and they should know the best way, because they have been doing it since the 1880s. There are almost 15 million citations for word uses in their database today.

http://www.m-w.com/netdict.htm

ENCYCLOPEDIAS
Knowledge Adventure Encyclopedia

The library's closed. You left your textbook in school. Your family doesn't own a set of encyclopedias. Try here: loads of links for those in need of homework help!

http://www.adventure.com/encyclopedia/

Smithsonian FAQs: Encyclopedia Smithsonian

For 150 years, the Smithsonian Institution collections have been a treasure trove. They house many wonders of history, science, and the natural world. Thousands of people visit the museums of the Smithsonian Institution in Washington, D.C., where the staff hears the same questions over and over. The Smithsonian folks took the answers to many of those questions and put them in an encyclopedia format on the Internet. You can get information on the history of the U.S. flag, great lists of books on animals, the inside scoop on the *Titanic*, and loads of other info!

http://www.si.edu/resource/faq/start.htm

A B C D E F G H I J K L M N O P Q R S T U V W X Y Z

A
B
C
D
E
F
G
H
I
J
K
L
M
N
O
P
Q
R
S
T
U
V
W
X
Y
Z

Welcome to Britannica Online

The *Encyclopedia Britannica* is available on the Internet. All those great articles on science, history, and geography are obtainable by point and click—the whole enchilada is here! However (and this is a big however), it costs money to subscribe to this service. You can, though, sample the Britannica Online to see if you want to purchase access. Use the Sample Search area to get partial information in answer to any question; sometimes that's enough. Also, all the details for cost and other subscription information are available. If you think you might be interested, take a look.

http://www.eb.com/

POPULATION

POPClock Projection—U.S. Population

The current estimated U.S. population is found at this site. The U.S. Census Bureau starts with the 1990 census and adds the births and subtracts the deaths. Then they factor in their best guesses about trends and come up with this estimated result. In case you wondered, only residents in the U.S. and the District of Columbia are counted and not families of military serving overseas or others living abroad.

http://www.census.gov/cgi-bin/popclock/

Population Reference Bureau — Informing people about population since 1929

The Population Reference Bureau has been providing the public with solid information on trends in world and U.S. population and demographics since 1929. This nonprofit organization has put together a useful and lively home page, which enables visitors to query the extensive World Population Data Sheet and read current and back issues of the magazine *Population Today*. There are also links to many other online population resources.

http://www.prb.org/prb/

U.S. Census Bureau Home Page

Do you know what Obi-wan Kenobi said to Luke Skywalker in *Star Wars*, when he had a question about the population of the United States? "Use the Source, Luke!" For such questions, go right to the source: the U.S. Census Bureau. How do they count the number of people in the U.S.? Find out here, plus learn lots of statistical info on jobs, housing, health, crime, income, education, marriage and family, race and ethnicity, aging, transportation and travel, and recreation. You might think that statistics are boring, but try this: of the U.S. population, 26 percent are under the age of 18! And if you don't have cable TV, tell your dad to get with the program, because 61 percent of American households have it.

http://www.census.gov/

W3C/ANU - Demography & Population Studies WWW VL

The world is a mighty big place, and this is a mighty big Web page. From here, the intrepid Internaut gathering data on population and demographics can click on over 150 links around the world, covering every aspect of the field. From tiny little sites dealing with local matters all the way up to massive data banks at major colleges and government institutions, this site has it all.

http://coombs.anu.edu.au/ResFacilities/
    DemographyPage.html

World POPClock Projection

Quick! If you wanted to send a letter to everyone in the world, how many stamps would you need? See an estimate of the world's current population at this site. You'll also find out how many births and deaths occur each minute.

http://www.census.gov/cgi-bin/ipc/popclockw/

World Population

Every 30 seconds, the world population clock at this site clicks to the latest figures. If you have Netscape 1.*x* or greater, you can have the clock animated as well. From here, you can check out the U.S. Census Bureau's national and world POPClocks with just a click and link to other related sites.

http://sunsite.unc.edu/lunarbin/worldpop/

World Population Trends

Check this site for United Nations world population statistics and trends. Included are population figures for countries and a brief list of historical milestones in world population. For example, the estimated world's population was one billion people in 1804. It took 123 years for it to double to two billion, in 1927. By 1974, 47 years later, it had doubled again to four billion. Estimates are that the world's population will double again, to eight billion, by 2021. Right now, it's just under six billion people. A note to parents: There's also a link here to world abortion policies as it applies to population trends.

gopher://gopher.undp.org:70/11/ungophers/
    popin/wdtrends

NET FILES

What is the Rosetta stone?

Answer: *Ancient Egyptian hieroglyphics had been seen for years, but no one could decipher their meanings. In 1799, one year after Napoleon captured the Nile delta area of Egypt, a French soldier found a black basalt slab while working on a fort near the Rosetta branch of the Nile. It held a message in hieroglyphs but also held translations of the message into other known languages—and this cracked the "code." The message turned out to be an edict from a 13-year-old pharaoh, dated March 27, 196 B.C.! Nowadays, people often describe the key to any mystery as "the Rosetta stone." The original is in the British Museum. Check out http://www.clemusart.com/archive/pharaoh/exhibit/glyphs.html*

SUN AND MOON RISE CALCULATION

Sunrise/Sunset computation: Online Data

Sometimes you have to get up awfully early to watch the sun rise. Exactly when the sun or moon rises or sets depends on where you live and the time of year. You can take the mystery out of when old Sol (that's another name for the sun) takes off in the morning by using this page from the U.S. Naval Observatory. All you have to do is plug in a date and a place, and through the magic of computers, the time of sun (and moon) rise and set is provided. For fun, enter your birthday and birthplace or pick an interesting date, like December 31, 1999.

http://aa.usno.navy.mil/AA/data/

THESAURI

ARTFL Project: ROGET Thesaurus Search Form

Sometimes words can be so frustrating. Have you ever had a homework assignment and found you were using the same word over and over again? You just couldn't think of another word that meant the same thing. To solve this problem, a guy named Peter Roget came up with a list that grouped similar words together. This list of similar words is called a thesaurus, and Roget's is considered one of the best. All you have to do is type in a word. Now you'll be able to impress your teachers with your growing—expanding, increasing, enlarging—vocabulary. Keep in mind that this is the edition from 1911, so newer words will not appear.

http://humanities.uchicago.edu/forms_unrest/
    ROGET.html

Plumb Design Visual Thesaurus

This resource offers a Java-based way to see relationships in English words. Imagine the starting word at the center of the screen, floating in space. Around it are the various synonyms of that word, arranged like spokes on a wheel. If you click on one of those words, you will see that word drift to the center, while new spokes for it appear., The link to the original word is still there for you to see, too. It's a visual dictionary. No, it's a flight simulator. No, it's just fun!

http://www.plumbdesign.com/thesaurus/

A B C D E F G H I J K L M N O P Q R S T U V W X Y Z

The Wordsmyth English Dictionary-Thesaurus

Why no one on the Web ever thought of this before, we don't know. This resource combines a dictionary with a thesaurus, so you can find synonyms and antonyms, as well as definitions. There are also regular contests, interesting word lists, and other diversions from folks who are obviously in love with language.

http://www.lightlink.com/bobp/wedt/

WEIGHTS AND MEASURES

The Beaufort Scale

Your kite instructions say that you need a 10-knot wind before you can launch. How do you know how fast that is? The Beaufort scale is a way to estimate wind speed without the use of instruments. For example, the description of Beaufort force 3 is this: "Leaves and small twigs in constant motion; wind extends light flag." That translates to a wind speed of 7 to 10 knots (8 to 12 mph, or 12 to 19 kph, or 3.4 to 5.4 mps). Find out the other indicators here.

http://www.anbg.gov.au/jrc/kayak/beaufort.html

Conversion of Units

This is another HUGE measurement converter. Written in English and German, at this site you'll be able to get the formulas to convert just about anything. Included are electronic measures, such as amperage and watts. Remember, this one doesn't convert—it just gives the formula.

http://www.chemie.fu-berlin.de/chemistry/
general/units_en.html

Martindale's 'The Reference Desk: Calculators On-Line'

Sure, you get the usual converted units: feet to meters, Celsius to Fahrenheit, and more. But then you go from the commonplace to the exotic: automotive, loan and budget, math and engineering, medical, and even fabulous miscellaneous calculators (calculate the size of the fish tank you need). There are guitar tuners, card games, even translation services to get your name in Hawaiian or Japanese. You can definitely *count* on this Web site!

http://www.sci.lib.uci.edu/HSG/RefCalculators.html

Scales of Measurement Version 1.7

Have you ever compared small things to bigger things, or hot things to colder things? This site lists various types of comparisons in orders of magnitude. For example, people are listed at about 1.8 meters tall, or long. On the smaller side of people, we find an "unraveled human DNA strand" with a length of 0.068 meters. On the other side, we have a blue whale, with a length of 30 meters. Your backyard's grass grows at a faster rate than the seafloor spreads, but that's still not as fast as the typical rate a glacier advances. Maybe they are checking the wrong grass; we seem to mow ours a lot around here!

http://physics.hallym.ac.kr/reference/scales/
scales1p.html

WORLD RECORDS

See name of sport or subject under SPORTS

ZIP AND POSTAL CODES

Postal Code Formats of the World

Ever wonder what all the letters and numbers mean in a Canadian postal code? Turns out that the first letter identifies the province or region of a province. The rest of the letters and numbers have specific meanings, too. If you're interested in what postal codes might look like for Singapore, Estonia, and Vatican City (under Italy), as well as many other countries, stop in here!

http://www.philatelic.com/faq/ch20.html

Postal Code Lookup—Canada

If you need to send a message to Canada (or if you're in Canada and you need postal code info), take a look here. A neat graphic shows you exactly where everything goes when you address an envelope. Toll-free 800 numbers are provided for assistance, and all sorts of info on the Canadian postal code system is available at this site.

http://www.canadapost.ca/CPC2/addrm/
pclookup/pclookup.html

USPS ZIP+4 Code Lookup

This is a very useful U.S. ZIP code lookup service. This site will provide, in most instances, a ZIP code for a street and town address you provide. This service is provided by the U.S. Postal Service. If you don't know your nine-digit ZIP code, this site will tell you, based on your address.

http://www.usps.gov/ncsc/lookups/lookup_zip+4.html

Zip Codes & Country Codes of the World

Besides U.S. and Canadian ZIP and postal codes, you'll find handy links to those of Denmark, Germany, Italy, South Africa, the United Kingdom, and several others.

http://www.escapeartist.com/global10/zip.htm

RELIGION AND SPIRITUALITY

See also HOLIDAYS; MUSIC AND MUSICIANS—SACRED MUSIC

APS Guide to Resources in Theology

This jumpstation contains briefly annotated links to resources on religious subjects, from Gregorian chant to the Anglican Church (including a link to Archbishop Desmond Tutu's texts in South Africa) to Buddhist, Islamic, and other texts and links. It is heavy on Christian resources but also lists resources on other religions that we have not mentioned elsewhere in this book.

http://www.utoronto.ca/stmikes/theobook.htm

Religious and Sacred Texts

If you go to church or temple services, you probably know a lot about your own religion. But have you ever wondered about other people's beliefs? This site contains electronic versions of texts sacred to followers of many of the world's major religions, including Judaism, Islam, and Hinduism. Also explore links to early Christian texts, Zen gardens, and a thematic guide to world scripture.

http://webpages.marshall.edu/~wiley6/

The Religious Freedom Home Page

Beginning with the U.S. Bill of Rights and continuing onward through the United Nations Universal Declaration of Human Rights, religious freedom has been a cornerstone of progressive government worldwide. This well-designed, nondenominational Web site, sponsored by the Christian Science Committee on Publication, explores what religious freedom really means and looks at the phenomenon both nationally and globally. It includes conflicting thoughts on controversial issues but always takes the viewpoint that individuals should be informed and educated about their right to worship freely.

http://www.religious-freedom.org/

APPARITIONS AND MIRACLES

All About Angels

Have you ever had a close call? Did you wonder if you had a guardian angel who saved you from a mishap? This angel page explains who's who when it comes to angels. Parental advisory: This site also contains information on fallen angels.

http://www.knight.org/advent/cathen/01476d.htm

CATHOLIC APPARITIONS OF JESUS AND MARY

An apparition is a supernatural sight. People have made various claims about apparitions all over the world. Did you ever wonder about which ones might have really occurred? Here's a list of reported apparitions, some of which are still ongoing! Some sites have been disproved by the Catholic Church, but others have been verified. This resource provides a code so that you can tell which is which. Decide for yourself whether you are a skeptic or a believer in these happenings. There is also information about some saints, and you can download a current calendar with the saint's important dates.

http://web.frontier.net/Apparitions/

A B C D E F G H I J K L M N O P Q R S T U V W X Y Z

Catholic Online Angels Page

Many people believe that angels, while invisible to the human eye, may be felt by the human heart. This is a good introduction to angels. Did you know that there are nine different kinds of angels? Most are described on this page, but not all. For the rest, visit this page as well: The Holy Angels at <*http://www.ocf.org/OrthodoxPage/reading/angels.html*>.

http://www.catholic.org/saints/angels.html

The Miracles Page

Crosses of light, weeping statues, healing waters, the Hindu milk miracle, the white buffalo—are these events hoaxes or real? One thing is sure: it's next to impossible to find information about them in a book (except *this* book!), since so many of them are new and facts are sketchy. Check the info at this site and see if you can make up your own mind from the information as it is presented. You might want to ask a parent or other trusted adult what he or she thinks about it all.

http://www.mcn.org/1/miracles/

The Shroud of Turin Website HOME PAGE

In a cathedral in Turin, Italy, sits a silver chest. Inside the chest is the mysterious Turin Shroud, which many believe to be the burial cloth that covered Jesus Christ. You'll view amazing photographs and research about the famous shroud. Examining the evidence, what do you see?

http://www.shroud.com/

BAHÁ'Í

A Bahá'í Faith Page

One of the world's fastest-growing religions, Bahá'í was founded in the mid-nineteenth century by Bahá'u'lláh, a Persian nobleman from Teheran. He gave up a comfortable and secure lifestyle for a life of persecution and deprivation. Learn more about his life and teachings here, in many different languages.

http://www.bcca.org/~glittle/

Soc.Religion.Bahai

Could many of the world religions be rolled into one? The Bahá'í believe that there have been many messengers from God, each one arriving during a different age. This online archive will show you other teachings, texts, sacred sites, and where to find more on the Bahá'í faith.

http://www.bcca.org/srb/

BIBLE STUDY

Bible Browser Basic Home Page

Can't seem to recall that Bible verse about the "lilies of the field"? Just visit this site. Type the target word, phrase, or verse into the search box and hit "Retrieve." Here it is, Mat 6:28.11 "And why are you anxious about clothing? Consider the lilies of the field, how they grow; they neither toil nor spin;" That's not much, so click on the button that lets you see more of the context of the quote. If you want to see a different translation rather than the King James Version, you have your choice of the Revised Standard Version or the Latin Vulgate. Be sure to read the FAQ to find out the particular scope of this collection and other important information. There is also an audio tutorial should you prefer to hear it rather than read it.

http://goon.stg.brown.edu/bible_browser/pbeasy.shtml

Blue Letter Bible

This resource combines both a King James Version Bible, a Bible concordance, and commentaries on the various passages. It's very extensive, and if you're into Bible study this site is very powerful. The Blue Letter Bible "now has over 1,100,000 links from the Word of God to over 85,000 pages of concordances, lexicons, dictionaries, and commentaries!"

http://www.khouse.org/blueletter/

BUDDHISM

Buddhist Studies WWW VL

You'll find an extensive collection of links here. See the art, read the literature, and find out about the four Noble Truths of Buddhism.

http://www.ciolek.com/WWWVL-Buddhism.html

A B C D E F G H I J K L M N O P Q R S T U V W X Y Z

CMCC - Sacred Art by the Tibetan Lamas of Drepung Loseling Monastery

This site follows the creation of a Tibetan sacred sand painting from the beginning to its end. Considered a healing ceremony, the area for the sand painting is claimed and blessed. Local spirits are asked for permission before construction begins. The monks draw an intricate geometric mandala on the floor. Colored grains of sand are painstakingly placed with precise movements. The process takes several days. The mandala's patterns have significance on many different levels; learn about them at this site. After the painting is complete, there is a dismantling ceremony. All the sand is swept up and deposited in a nearby body of water. Find out why.

http://www.civilization.ca/membrs/traditio/
    mandala/mandalae.html

Dharma The Cat

This site is a little hard to explain. There's this cat named Dharma. There's a young Buddhist monk named Bodhi. Then there's a mouse called Siam. They have brief cartoon adventures that explain various Buddhist concepts. If you don't "get it," there is a commentary you can read. In case you're of another faith, there are commentaries written by various ministers and a rabbi, too. The links collection is extensive, but we haven't visited all the destinations, so explore with a parent.

http://www2.one.net.au/~lourie/

Prayer Flags and Dharma Prints from Radiant Heart

For centuries, Tibetan Buddhists have planted prayer flags outside their homes and places of spiritual practice. The flags bear pictures of traditional Buddhist symbols, protectors, and enlightened beings. The idea is that the wind will carry their beneficent vibrations across the countryside. Prayer flags are said to bring happiness, long life, and prosperity to the flag planter and those in the vicinity.

http://www.asis.com/radiantheart/

Zen@SunSITE

Zen Buddhism is based on a philosophy of life taught by Gautama Buddha, who lived and taught in northern India in the sixth century B.C. The Buddha was not a god—*Buddha* means "enlightened one" or "one who is awake." The teachings of Buddhism are aimed solely to relieve beings from suffering. This meta-resource includes art, philosophy, meditation, and many fascinating links. Parental advisory: Not all links have been checked.

http://sunsite.unc.edu/zen/

CHRISTIANITY
Distinctive Church Collection!

Many churches have their own parishes in cyberspace these days. This site is trying to collect them all and selects "distinctive" ones to highlight each month. Churches from almost 50 countries are represented so far. It's interesting to drop in on many congregations and see what's happening. There are also (what else?) lots of links.

http://www.rwf2000.com/church.html

The Gallery

A great collection of Christian clip art and the "Six Days of Creation" screen saver are available at this site. There are several 3-D electronic paintings as well as images from the film *The Crossing*.

http://www.gospelcom.net/gf/gallery/

Virtual Church (SM)

This virtual church has a youth room just for kids. You'll find Bible stories with colorful graphics to go along with them. If you want to read an exciting one, try "The Men in the Fiery Furnace." If you're a younger kid, you can ask a parent to download coloring pages, and then send them back after you've colored them on your computer. Explore the other rooms in this church, too. The library, for instance, contains crossword puzzles, trivia quizzes, and word jumbles. Don't miss a peek at the skeletons in the closet! There is also an award-winning area all about Biblical angels.

http://www.virtualchurch.org/

A B C D E F G H I J K L M N O P Q R S T U V W X Y Z

CHRISTIANITY—AMISH, MENNONITE

The Amish And "The Plain People"

If you've ever been curious about the Amish, Mennonites, the Brethren, or the other "Plain People" of the Pennsylvania Dutch country, visit this page. You'll learn a little about their beliefs, their mode of dress, and their customs. Did you know that an Amish bride wears a blue wedding dress, or that kids attend school only through the eighth grade? You can also "Ask the Amish" and submit your own questions.

http://www.800padutch.com/amish.html

CHRISTIANITY—CATHOLIC

Blessed Virgin Mary: Catholic Cincinnati Info Web

Mary, the mother of Jesus: what is the history of this woman who has been revered by so many? How did the prophets know that a virgin would bear a son, long before it happened? Find out about the miraculous events and what some people think they mean. Here, too, you'll find the Little Internet Library of the Blessed Virgin Mary and several links.

http://www.aquinas-multimedia.com/
  arch/marian.html

Christus Rex

This is the definitive unofficial Vatican site. You'll also find an annotation for it in the ART—MUSEUMS section of this book (the Splendors of Christendom entry). It contains not only pictures of the Vatican museums but many more documents, and these items are in many languages. This site offers The Lord's Prayer in 210 languages, a worldwide tour of churches, cathedrals, and monasteries, and much more.

http://christusrex.org/www1/icons/

> # The Web in Pig Latin? Make it so in LANGUAGES.

The Holy See

The Vatican has established an official and attractive Web site under its own top-level country domain, ".va." Since this site was opened they have added a tremendous amount of material about the Pope, the structure of the Roman Catholic Church, history of the church and previous pontiffs, and information about the Vatican museums. This site is well worth checking—and you can do it in several different languages! Access is sometimes slow, but it's definitely worth the wait.

http://www.vatican.va/

HOLY YEAR 2000 - The Great Jubilee

Holy Year has been celebrated every 25 years from 1450 until the present time. The next one will be in the year 2000. People flock to Rome to ask forgiveness for their sins. They visit the great basilicas of Saint Peter, St. Paul, St. John Lateran, and St. Mary Major. Catholics believe that participating in these special ceremonies will grant them indulgences, which remove the penalties for their past sinful behavior. Each basilica has a holy door, which is sealed except during the term of the holy year. Pilgrims pass through the holy doors, and at the end of the year, the doors are walled up to await the next Jubilee. Learn the history of this holy event at this site.

http://members.truepath.com/fraoli/index.htm

The Marian Hour

Many Catholics around the world pray using a special set of beads called a rosary. They use the beads to count the various prayers they have said. You can learn about the Mysteries of the Rosary at this well-designed site as well as hear the various prayers for yourself. The organization will send a free rosary to anyone who wants one. This site has audio files in French as well as English and text files in many languages.

http://marianhr.bc.ca/

The Mary Page

Mary, the Mother of Jesus, is also known as Mary, The Blessed Virgin, Our Lady, Madonna, Notre Dame, Domina, and more. Learning more about Mary, some may acquire a fuller knowledge of Christ. The Mary Page holds the world's largest collection of printed information on Mary.

http://www.udayton.edu/mary/

St. Joseph Messenger's CATHOLIC KIOSK

The archdiocese of Cincinnati, Ohio, has an extensive collection. You can read the entire catechism of the Catholic Church as well as tour the Vatican and other Catholic art and architecture resources. You can also see a list of all the members of the College of Cardinals around the world, with links to their home pages, if they have them. Many religious orders have opened up abbeys and cloisters on the Web, and you can visit them here. There are links to saints' lives, Marian resources, and sources of Catholic news. Don't miss the link to the 1917 edition of *The Catholic Encyclopedia*. Parent alert: Many "right-to-life" links are included.

http://www.aquinas-multimedia.com/arch/

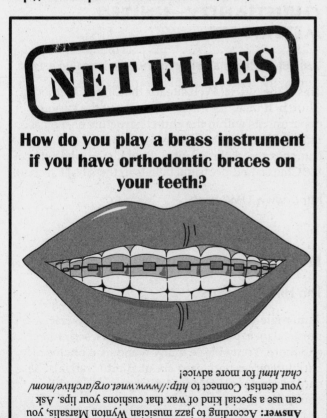

NET FILES

How do you play a brass instrument if you have orthodontic braces on your teeth?

Answer: According to jazz musician Wynton Marsalis, you can use a special kind of wax that cushions your lips. Ask your dentist. Connect to http://www.wnet.org/archive/mom/chat.html for more advice!

Welcome to Vatican Radio

Staff from 50 countries prepare 400 hours of broadcast material every week in 37 different languages. Radio Vatican broadcasts on short wave, medium wave, FM, satellite, and the Internet. You can download Real Audio files or ftp features in several languages. As they say: "Listen, for heaven's sake!"

http://www.wrn.org/vatican-radio/

CHRISTIANITY—CHRISTIAN SCIENCE

The official home page of the Church of Christ, Scientist

Here is a quote from this page: "Mary Baker Eddy (1821–1910) is the Discoverer and Founder of Christian Science, and author of Science and Health with Key to the Scriptures, a perennial best-selling book on healing. She was raised in New Hampshire by parents who were devout Congregationalists. The Bible was central to her religious and educational upbringing. Her early adult life included more than its share of serious personal tragedies and poor health. Over the next twenty years chronic illness led her to explore many curative methods. None resulted in permanent healing until her discovery of Christian Science." Although Christian Scientists believe the healing of disease can be accomplished by spiritual means alone, "its higher purpose is universal salvation from every phase of evil—including sin and death (see Matthew 10:8)."

http://www.tfccs.com/

CHRISTIANITY—THE CHURCH OF JESUS CHRIST OF LATTER-DAY SAINTS

LDSWorld

This is the place to go to find numerous sites of interest to the Latter-Day Saints. Here you can study the Gospel, meet other members, share ideas, and even shop for LDS products.

http://www.ldsworld.com/

A B C D E F G H I J K L M N O P Q R S T U V W X Y Z

A
B
C
D
E
F
G
H
I
J
K
L
M
N
O
P
Q
R
S
T
U
V
W
X
Y
Z

The official site of The Church of Jesus Christ of Latter-day Saints

The Church of Jesus Christ of Latter-day Saints was officially organized on April 6, 1830, with six members. Today, congregations of the Church are found in more than 160 nations and territories. With more than 10 million members, it is one of the fastest growing religions in the world and one of the largest Christian churches in the United States. Neither Protestant nor Catholic, the Church of Jesus Christ of Latter-day Saints is "a restoration of the ancient Church as established by Jesus Christ." This site outlines the beliefs of the church as well as the worldwide programs it offers. A detailed history of the church is also offered.

http://www.lds.org/

World Wide Web 1st Ward

At this site, you'll find a lively discussion of many topics of interest to Mormons. Be inspired by the Daily Devotional and the scripture class for Sunday school teachers and others. There is a ton of genealogy resources, Church news, and sacred texts and resources. Don't miss the Salt Lake City, Utah, Temple Square tour. Somewhat inexplicably, the "What Mormons Believe" resources are filed at the end of the tour, where you can also send e-mail to have a free Book of Mormon delivered to your house.

http://www.uvol.com/www1st/

Utah's state bird is the seagull, even though Utah is miles from any coastline! Seagull Monument stands in Temple Square, in Salt Lake City, as a reminder of a miracle that occurred there during the time of the Mormon pioneers. In the spring of 1848, their newly planted fields were being devoured by crickets. Without those crops, the settlers were sure to starve. However, seagulls appeared, gobbled up all the crickets, and saved the settlement. Read more about early Mormon history at World Wide Web 1st Ward.

CHRISTIANITY—SAINTS

Catholic Online Patron Saints Page

You can find the patron saint for just about any occupation or country or organization at this site. Did you know that there's a patron saint for broadcasters? And comedians? Check it out here!

http://www.catholic.org/saints/patron.html

The Saints: Catholic Cincinnati Info Web

At this site, you can read various saints' lives and check the calendar to see whose feast day it is. Check Nicholas of Myra, the patron saint of children—whom you may know better as Santa Claus! Here's your chance to look up Saint Nick, Saint Valentine, Saint Patrick, and other Catholic saints.

http://www.aquinas-multimedia.com/arch/saints.html

CHRISTIANITY—UNITED METHODIST

United Methodist Information

This is the official Web site for the United Methodist Church. It includes information about the various departments within the church structure as well as links to hundreds of resources for individual churches across the country. Find historical origins of the Church and doctrinal beliefs in the About section.

http://www.UMC.org/

HINDUISM

The Hindu Universe

At this site you can explore the Hindu universe: art, music, dance, philosophy, sages, gurus, scriptures, and more. You will see many wonderful photos of Hindu temples and learn about Hindu festivals. Be sure to send some Hindu digital postcards while you're visiting.

http://www.hindunet.org/home.shtml

Hinduism's Electronic Ashram

This site offers an introduction to Hindu belief and practice, including a link to *Hinduism Today*, "The Monthly Magazine Affirming Sanatana Dharma and Recording the Modern History of a Billion-Strong Global Religion in Renaissance." The current issue includes articles about saris, the lovely draped garment many Indian women wear.

http://www.hinduismtoday.kauai.hi.us/

Nine Questions about Hinduism

On July 4, 1990, the youth meeting of the Hindu Temple of Greater Chicago had a special visitor: Gurudeva, Sivaya Subramuniyaswami. He was asked to give "official" answers to nine questions, ranging from "Are Hindus idol worshippers?" to "What's this reincarnation thing?" to "Why do Hindu women wear the dot on the forehead?" It's a revealing look at what kids want to know about Hinduism. Hindu gods are described and illustrated in one link from this page (scroll to the bottom), and the top level at this site includes numerous outside links. Parental advisory: Links from this page have not been checked.

http://www.spiritweb.org/Spirit/Veda/
   nine-questions.html

Spirituality/Yoga/Hinduism Home Page

One of the first things you will learn in yoga class, besides where to take off your shoes, is the word *namasté*. Your instructor will say it to you, and you're expected to say it back. *Namasté* is derived from the Sanskrit word, *Namaskaar*, meaning "I bow to the divine in you." Yoga is from the Sanskrit word *Yug*, meaning "union with the Divine." This site is a great overview of major yogic disciplines, although it's kind of wordy. You'll also get an introduction to Hinduism and tips on learning Sanskrit.

http://www.geocities.com/RodeoDrive/1415/

Swami Chinmayananda

This is the home page of a great Indian spiritual Master, Swami Chinmayananda (1916–1993), who was chosen to act as a "President of Hinduism" at a meeting of the Parliament of World Religions in Chicago in 1993. Read his teachings and interpretations of the Bhagavad Gita, and learn why "Happiness depends on what you can give, Not on what you can get."

http://www.chinmaya-chicago.com/chinmaya.htm

INTERFAITH
Gobind Sadan

There is a place in India where the holidays of all faiths are celebrated with reverence. It is a farm-based spiritual place of pilgrimage for all people, under the guidance of Baba Virsa Singh Ji. He asks for no charity, he recruits no followers, yet people from all over the world, and all walks of life, come to this place to see him, hear his teachings, and perform short periods of voluntary service. The place, in South Delhi, is called Gobind Sadan, "House of God." There is a similar site in the U.S. near Central Square, New York. Babaji says, "All the Prophets have come from one Source. They did not come to build religious institutions as walled forts, they came to change our consciousness. They came to teach us how to live. Sectarian divisions have been created by religious 'authorities,' out of self interest. Ignore them—we are all sisters and brothers, with one parent." Babaji emphasizes that religion is not a matter of outer rituals. It is a loving inner surrender to God's eternal teachings. His farm communities, built on former waste lands, are now fertile and thrive with abundance. They are self-supporting and do not seek monetary donations. See the light at this site.

http://www.GobindSadan.org/

What is the sound of one router flapping?

A
B
C
D
E
F
G
H
I
J
K
L
M
N
O
P
Q
R
S
T
U
V
W
X
Y
Z

ISLAM

Dome of the Rock

Built in A.D. 692, the Dome of the Rock is one of the great Muslim monuments. The building looks like an enameled, multicolored jewel, capped by a shining golden dome. The Dome protects and houses the Sacred Rock of Jerusalem sandstone at the summit of Mount Moriah. Muslims believe that the prophet Muhammad (peace be upon him), guided by the archangel Gabriel, traveled to Jerusalem and rose to the presence of God from this Rock. The site is also sacred to other faiths, as it was formerly the location of the Temple of Solomon. This site also details costumes, foods, and other important sites in early Muslim history.

http://jeru.huji.ac.il/ee21.htm

FAQ on Islam

This is a very easy-to-understand look at Islam and "Who's a Muslim?" Find out what Muslims believe, and read about their sacred text, the Quran. You'll also find answers to questions like "What do Muslims think about Jesus?" and "What about Muslim women?"

http://darkwing.uoregon.edu/~kbatarfi/islam_1.html

Islamic Texts and Resources MetaPage (MSA @ University at Buffalo)

This is an excellent jumpstation to introductory material, scriptures, Islamic art and culture, and many other resources on the Net. According to this site, "Islam is derived from the Arabic root *salaama* [meaning] peace, purity, submission, and obedience. In the religious sense, Islam means submission to the will of God and obedience to His law." Muslims believe there have been 25 messengers and prophets. These include Noah, Abraham, Ishmael, Isaac, Moses, Jesus, and Muhammad (peace be upon him). Their messages were all the same: Submit to God's will and obey His law. Explore more at this fascinating site.

http://wings.buffalo.edu/student-life/sa/muslim/isl/isl.html

Masjid of the Ether: A Place of Prayer and Fellowship in Community

Devout Muslims pray several times a day at specific times. You can use the Prayer Calculator and a ZIP code or city to find out the correct times and the correct direction to face. See if your answers can be found in the FAQ area, and make a small visit to the Digital Tekke, a Sufi lodge in Web space. Parental advisory: Links off this site have not been checked.

http://www.ou.edu/cybermuslim/cy_masjid.html

USC Muslim Students Association Islamic Server

Explore the sacred pillars of this religion, its texts, and its practice. One interesting article states that the "Nation of Islam," among others, should not be calling itself that, based on Islamic writings.

http://www.usc.edu/dept/MSA/

JUDAISM

Josh's Bar Mitzvah Web Site

The bar/bat mitzvah ceremony (bar mitzvah for boys, bat mitzvah for girls) is celebrated when a Jewish boy turns 13 or a Jewish girl turns 12. The child embraces the Jewish tradition and assumes adult responsibility for fulfilling Jewish law. This site was created by Josh from Lawrenceville, New Jersey, as part of his bar mitzvah project. He relates his bar mitzvah requirements and offers suggestions on planning the reception, which is often as elaborate as a grown-up wedding.

http://www.geocities.com/TelevisionCity/1333/

Nurit Reshef: Shabbat

The Jewish sabbath, or *Shabbat*, begins just before sunset on Friday night. It can't begin until one lights the sabbath candles, and the lighting is usually done by a woman. She lights the candles, covers her eyes, and says a special blessing in Hebrew. Only then does she open her eyes to look at the sabbath light. Learn the traditions of the shabbat at this site, and see how good you are at a matching game and a word search. Other pages by the same author: From Pesach to Shavuot <*http://www.bus.ualberta.ca/yreshef/pesach/index.html*> and Funland Hebrew <*http://www.bus.ualberta.ca/yreshef/funland/funland.html*>.

http://bus-nt2.bus.ualberta.ca/yreshef/shabbat/
  index.html

Project Genesis: Torah on the Information Superhighway

Project Genesis works to establish a strong Jewish identity, expand Jewish knowledge, and encourage its participants to become more involved with Judaism and the Jewish community. A variety of classes are offered on-line, and additional information regarding Judaism is available. There are also links to other sites of Jewish interest.

http://www.torah.org/

SACRED SITES

"Biblelands," Virtual multimedia tour of the Holy Land

If you have the IPIX viewer, you can experience 360-degree views of various places in the Holy Land. You can download the viewer for free if you don't already have it. Zoom in to see the area of Jesus' Sermon on the Mount. Sit on the steps of Jerusalem's Damascus Gate. There are many places to visit; try them all!

http://www.mustardseed.net/html/places.html

Città del Vaticano

Take a virtual tour of St. Peter's Basilica in Rome, Italy, designed by Michelangelo. See photos of the domes and vaults, piazzas, and gardens at this multilingual site.

http://www.christusrex.org/www1/citta/0-Citta.html

Places of Peace and Power

Anthropologist and photographer Martin Gray has visited over 900 places of religious and spiritual pilgrimage. This resource offers many of his photos and writings about the sites, as well as a calendar listing of Gray's upcoming slide shows and appearances. See and read about Stonehenge, Mount Olympus, the Golden Temple, places in Jerusalem, and many more. Be sure to read what you'll have to go through if you want to kiss the Blarney Stone in Ireland!

http://www.sacredsites.com/

Washington National Cathedral

On the highest point in Washington, D.C., is a beautiful interfaith cathedral. It is decorated with 107 carved stone gargoyles and untold numbers of grotesques. A grotesque is like a gargoyle, except it has no pipe inside and the water runs over the outside of the carving. The cathedral also has wonderful stained glass windows inside. The western rose window contains over 10,500 pieces of glass! Along the inside aisle is another window commemorating the flight of *Apollo 11.* It holds a real piece of moon rock! In addition to many U.S. presidents, Dr. Martin Luther King, Jr. and Indira Gandhi have spoken from the pulpit. Helen Keller is among the famous Americans buried beneath the cathedral.

http://www.cathedral.org/cathedral/

A B C D E F G H I J K L M N O P Q R S T U V W X Y Z

A
B
C
D
E
F
G
H
I
J
K
L
M
N
O
P
Q
R
S
T
U
V
W
X
Y
Z

Westminster Abbey

This London landmark has been the site of every British coronation since 1066. Many kings and queens are entombed at the Abbey, notably Elizabeth I. You'll also find Chaucer's grave in the Poets' Corner, along with those of other famous English authors, including Lewis Carroll. The Abbey has been the scene of numerous royal ceremonies, including royal weddings and other occasions. The funeral of Diana, Princess of Wales, was held at Westminster Abbey on September 6, 1997. Admire the inspiring Gothic architecture as you wander around with the other tourists at this site.

http://www.westminster-abbey.org/

SIKHISM

The Sikhism Home Page

The Sikh religion, founded over 500 years ago, today has a following of over 20 million people worldwide. Sikhism "preaches a message of devotion and remembrance of God at all times, truthful living, [and] equality of mankind.... [It] denounces superstitions and blind rituals." The Sikh scripture is called the Sri Guru Granth Sahib, and it is considered a Living Guru, or spiritual teacher. It contains devotional hymns and poetry from many faiths.

http://www.sikhs.org/

TAO

Taoism Information Page

Taoism began about 2,500 years ago, in China. The Tao, or Way, is illuminated by several texts, one of which is the Tao-te-Ching. It is among the shortest of all sacred scriptures, containing only 5,000 words. Here are a few of them:

> *It is not the clay the potter throws,*
> *which gives the pot its usefulness,*
> *but the space within the shape,*
> *from which the pot is made.*

This site offers a good introduction to Taoism.

http://www.clas.ufl.edu/users/gthursby/taoism/

REPTILES

See also PETS AND PET CARE

Mike's Herpetocultural Home Page

Here's a herp, there's a herp, everywhere's a herp, herp. It's not Old MacDonald and it's not a farm, but this page is the place to go for information about reptiles. You'll learn about herpetoculture, the keeping and breeding of amphibians and reptiles. You'll find links to other herp home pages, research organizations, herp FAQs, journals and magazines, and much more.

http://gto.ncsa.uiuc.edu/pingleto/herp.html

Trendy's House of Herpetology

Everything you need to know about snakes, amphibians, lizards, turtles, and iguanas is here, including lots of great photos. Learn how to treat your turtle and how to coddle your chameleon. Whether you want to soothe your snakes or animate your amphibians, this page will surely be of use. Parental advisory: There are two versions of this page; the URL listed here is the K–12 version, but not all links off it have been checked.

http://fovea.retina.net/~gecko/herps/

CROCODILES AND ALLIGATORS

The Gator Hole

Much maligned and misunderstood, alligators have existed since the time of the dinosaurs. Hunted almost to extinction, they have made an astounding comeback. You will find an amazing collection of gator myth and fact lying around this virtual gator hole. Find out here if the stories you hear about alligators are true.

http://magicnet.net/~mgodwin/

St. Augustine's Alligator Farm

Chomp, chomp! Be careful, don't get too close. Visit the St. Augustine Alligator Farm, and remember: you should never feed wild animals. Don't forget to pick up your discount admission ticket at this Web site, too, should you ever visit the real zoological park in Florida. Lots of alligator info at this site.

http://www.alligatorfarm.com/

LIZARDS

Chameleons

That little statue-like lizard never moves, but you could swear those eyes follow you wherever you go. They do. Chameleons have globular independent eyes that can do almost a complete 360-degree turn without ever moving their heads. The fascinating behavior, unusual body shapes, and changing color of these creatures have kept collectors intrigued for decades. However, they often face one major challenge: delicate by nature, these critters tend to die easily. But the availability of quality information on raising chameleons and new restrictions on importing them has led to captive-bred lizards that are healthier and better adapted, increasing their chances of survival. Did you know you should buy food-quality crickets for your lizard and not bait cricks, which are often fed growth hormones? You'll find lots of great info here for general lizard care, too!

http://www.skypoint.com/members/mikefry/
    chams2.html

Heatherk's Gecko Page

Are you a "herper"? Perhaps you should stop by this site, just to be sure. Ask yourself the following questions, and be careful how you answer them. Do you carry a moisture-mister and spray yourself three times a day? Do you lick your lips and curl out your tongue when a bug lands near you? Is your house a field trip destination for the school's science classes? This page also has links to other herp interest sites, herp home pages, and care sheets for other lizards, not just geckos.

http://www.geckoworld.com/~gecko/

Iguana iguana

You really want to raise a reptile, but you can't stomach the thought of having to feed it icky insects. Then maybe you wanna iguana. These lovely lizards are very vegetarian, but they will swiftly snarf your pepperoni pizza if left alone all night. Find out what makes these captivating creatures the most popular pet from the reptile race.

http://fovea.retina.net/~gecko/herps/iguanas/

Tricia's Water Dragon Page

Looking for a new pet? How about a dragon? Water dragons, also known as *Physignathus cocincinus*, are easier to take care of than iguanas. Tricia's Web page shows that she certainly knows her dragons. She presents information on everything you could possibly need to know about selecting and caring for these two- to three-foot lizards, including tips on how to travel with your dragon if you can't bear to leave it home when the family goes on vacation.

http://www.icomm.ca/dragon/

SNAKES

An Interactive Guide to Massachusetts Snakes

You've found a snake you don't recognize sunning itself on your deck, and you want to know if it's safe to move it. Answer a series of questions at this interactive site, and you can quickly identify that suspect snake. If you already know the snake's name and want to know more about its lifestyle and habits, you can also find that here. But once you make an identification, remember: usually it's best to let a sleeping snake lie.

http://klaatu.oit.umass.edu/umext/snake/

Jason's Snakes and Reptiles

Do you have questions on housing your snakes, feeding them, or what diseases they can get? This page has the answers. Check out the care sheet for snakes, or get information on other snake sites, snake newsgroups, and Gopher (the Net protocol, not the rodent) sites.

http://www.shadeslanding.com/jas/

A
B
C
D
E
F
G
H
I
J
K
L
M
N
O
P
Q
R
S
T
U
V
W
X
Y
Z

A
B
C
D
E
F
G
H
I
J
K
L
M
N
O
P
Q
R
S
T
U
V
W
X
Y
Z

Fetch some fascinating info in DOGS AND DOG SPORTS.

King Cobra @ nationalgeographic.com

The king cobra is one snake you don't want to go messing with, but if you check him out here it will be relatively safe. Consider these facts about Mister KC: it has a head as big as a man's hand and can stand tall enough to look you straight in the eye. Its venom can stun your nervous system and stop your breathing. Ready for more? Its fangs are a half-inch long, and a little bite will deliver venom from glands attached to the fangs. Within minutes, neurotoxins stun the prey's nervous system, especially the impulses for breathing. Other toxins start digesting the paralyzed victim. We've had enough, but if you'd like more information, there's plenty available!

http://www.nationalgeographic.com/features/97/
    kingcobra/index-n.html

TURTLES

CALIFORNIA TURTLE & TORTOISE CLUB

When Net-mom was little, she read her King James Version of the Bible and saw in Song of Solomon 2:12 the following verse about spring: "The flowers appear on the earth; the time of the singing is come, and the voice of the turtle is heard in our land." Well Net-mom could not understand it, because her pet turtles never seemed to make any noise. (Years later, Net-mom figured out it was supposed to be an abbreviation for the turtledove, and the Revised Standard Version bears this out. Duhhh.) However, should you want to hear the real voices of real turtles, just visit this page and turn up your speakers. There is also an exhaustive selection of links and care sheets.

http://www.tortoise.org/

Reslider's Swamp

This site has extensive information on caring for pet red-eared sliders, a common type of turtle for sale in pet stores. You'll learn that they need cuttlefish bones to sharpen their "beaks," that raw meat is bad but live crickets and guppies are OK, and that it's important to filter the water in which your turtle is kept. There's a lot more to visit here in Reslider's Swamp: links to info about other species of turtles, a turtle cam, and a link to a turtle rescue site for those who (like Groundskeeper Willie on *The Simpsons*) want to "save the wee turtles." Slide on in, the water's fine!

http://www.altern.com/reslider/res.html

NET FILES

What is a
dream catcher?

Answer: It's a weblike object hung above a bed or cradle. According to Ojibwe legend, "mothers, sisters, & Nokomis (grandmothers) took up the practice of weaving magical webs for the new babies using willow hoops and sinew or cordage made from plants. It is in the shape of a circle to represent how giizis (the Sun) travels each day across the sky. The dream catcher will filter out all the bad bawadjigewin (dreams) and allow only good thoughts to enter into our minds.... You will see a small hole in the center of each dream catcher where those good bawadjige may come through. With the first rays of sunlight, the bad dreams would perish." Find out how to make one at http://www.lib.uconn.edu/
NativeTech/dreamcat/dreamcat.html

Turtle Trax - A Sea Turtle Page

Did you know that *all* species of marine turtles are either threatened or endangered? That's right, and a major reason for this is danger to their nests. These dangers include increased numbers of people on the beaches where the turtles dig their nests. Also, some people dig up the nests and sell or eat turtle eggs. Another problem is artificial lighting around beaches, which has a disorienting effect on little turtles—they can't find the safety of the sea. In addition to the nesting threats, don't forget about the environmental threats to turtles, which include water pollution and getting stuck in floating trash. These are just some of the most serious threats. For more information about marine turtles, their environment, and ways you can help, visit this page. Don't miss the series of pictures from the Amazing Way Cool Bogus Cam (hint: keep loading them—you'll get a surprise!).

http://www.turtles.org/

RIGHTS AND FREEDOMS

The Human Rights Web Home Page

Certain human rights are guaranteed to everyone by United Nations declarations and other international agreements. But people in some countries have had to struggle to make those rights a reality. The very existence of the Internet has made it easier for those folks to communicate with the rest of the world. This page clearly and thoroughly spells out what human rights are, how they are abused, and what you can do. The resources section features links to groups like Amnesty International, PEN International Writer's Union, and Physicians for Human Rights, among dozens of others. Middle school and high school kids will find this page an endless source of thought-provoking information.

http://www.hrweb.org/

Explore underwater archaeology in SHIPS AND SHIPWRECKS.

National Civil Rights Museum

The National Civil Rights Museum is located at the Lorraine Motel (Memphis, Tennessee), where Dr. Martin Luther King, Jr. was assassinated on April 4, 1968. Here you will find continuing exhibits, events, and links of interest. The virtual tour is arranged in chronological order. You'll learn about the Montgomery bus boycott, the freedom rides, Dr. Martin Luther King, Jr., the student sit-ins, the march on Washington, and the Chicago freedom movement. You can take a chronological tour or choose the exhibit you want to see. Each exhibit has a short paragraph about the subject and why it is important in civil rights history.

http://www.mecca.org/~crights/

Reebok and Human Rights

This well-designed page shines as an example of how corporations can become involved with more than just a ledger sheet. Since 1988, Reebok has been actively involved in the worldwide human rights movement. This isn't just a publicity stunt, either. They give their Human Rights Awards to people under the age of 30, and include a major cash donation to each recipient's organization of choice. They also have been promoting their Witness Program, which provides mass communications tools such as computers, video cameras, and fax machines to human rights groups, and their Project America has been responsible for getting thousands of people involved in community service organizations. Although sports shoe and other apparel manufacturing has come under scrutiny for poor labor practices in Asia and elsewhere, Reebok seems to be doing something positive about a situation that has existed in the industry for a long time.

http://www.reebok.com/humanrights/

The Religious Freedom Home Page

Beginning with the U.S. Bill of Rights and continuing onward through the United Nations Universal Declaration of Human Rights, religious freedom has been a cornerstone of progressive government worldwide. This well-designed, nondenominational Web site, sponsored by the Christian Science Committee on Publication, explores what religious freedom really means and looks at the phenomenon both nationally and globally. It includes conflicting thoughts on controversial issues but always takes the viewpoint that individuals should be informed and educated about their right to worship freely.

http://www.religious-freedom.org/

A B C D E F G H I J K L M N O P Q R S T U V W X Y Z

A School for Iqbal - A Bullet Can't Kill a Dream

If you think kids don't have much power, visit this page. Here are the main points you should know about the tragic story of a Pakistani child named Iqbal, as quoted from this site:

> Iqbal was sold into Child bonded labor at four years of age for the equivalent of $12. He escaped at age ten and began to speak out against child slavery and for freedom and schools for all Pakistani children. Iqbal won the Reebok Human Rights Youth in Action Award 1994. Easter Sunday, 1995, he was murdered. In response, students at Broadmeadow Middle School (Quincy, Massachusetts) formed a campaign in order to help fight for Iqbal's Dream."

There's good news. Recently, Net-mom heard from the kids at the school. They said, "With a lot of help from thousands of students and others in all 50 U.S. states and 28 countries, we did it! We built that School for Iqbal in Pakistan. It is open and giving education, love, and hope to 252 poor, working children who never went to school before. The 'School for Iqbal' is open, but more needs to be done for the millions still trapped in forced, child labor." Now these same kids are helping along the Rugmark Campaign. What's that? In some parts of the world, children are forced to make oriental rugs. Many rugs are made solely by adults, so how can you tell the difference? Until recently, there has been no good way to select a child-labor-free rug. Now, just look for the Rugmark symbol! You can find out more about the campaign, the school, and child labor at this site.

http://www.digitalrag.com/iqbal/

U.S. House of Representatives - Internet Law Library - Civil Liberties and Civil Rights

Human rights may be inalienable, but it takes a lot of documentation to put them into law. This page includes literally hundreds of important documents pertaining to human rights from nations in every corner of the globe and throughout history. If you're looking for the complete text of Thomas Paine's "Rights of Man" or the International Covenant on Civil and Political Rights, you'll find them only a click away here.

http://law.house.gov/93.htm

Various Historical Documents

Jon Shemitz, who also runs a homeschooling Web site at <http://www.midnightbeach.com/hs/>, has put the U.S. Declaration of Independence, the Constitution of the United States, and the United Nations Convention on the Rights of the Child, into HTML (Hypertext Markup Language) so that the documents can be read more easily with a Web browser. This presentation also makes the documents easy to search!

http://www.midnightbeach.com/jon/histdocs.htm

Y-Rights

Kids have rights, too! The question is, what rights do they have? Y-Rights is an electronic mailing list where discussion of the rights of kids and teenagers is front and center. Parents, teachers, kids, and others talk about the give-and-take of minors and their legal status. Younger children may have a hard time keeping up with the conversation, but teens may find this very interesting. For parents, keeping tabs and providing input on the rights of kids is essential.

List Address: y-rights@sjuvm.stjohns.edu
Subscription Address: listserv@sjuvm.stjohns.edu

ROBOTS

Bradford -Robotic -Telescope

OK, here's the deal. You register (free) with this site, then you get to use their telescope. Unfortunately, the 46-centimeter 'scope is high on the moors in West Yorkshire, England. Fortunately, the Bradford Robotic Telescope is robotic, and an astronomer does not need to be present. Anyone can direct the telescope to look at anything in the northern night sky. The observations are completed as time allows, so be prepared to wait awhile for your results. If you don't want to wait that long, you can browse through some of the completed jobs. Oh wow! Look at that! Wait, who's that waving from the Moon?

http://www.eia.brad.ac.uk/rti/

Cog, the Robot

Back in 1921, playwright Karel Capek coined the word "robot," and since then, books, movies, and television programs have all speculated about the form these mechanical creatures will take. Now a group of researchers at the Massachusetts Institute of Technology's Artificial Intelligence Lab are actually attempting this feat. Artificial intelligence is the process in which a computer takes in information and uses it to create new knowledge—a simulation of human thinking. Cog the Robot is a collection of sensors and motors that attempt to duplicate the sensory and manipulative functions of the human body. Coupled with artificial intelligence programming, Cog may eventually succeed in bringing science fiction's fantasies to reality. Move over Data, here comes Cog!

http://www.ai.mit.edu/projects/cog/Text/
    cog-robot.html

NET FILES

What are "storm chasers"?

Answer: Storm chasers are people who chase tornadoes! Not that they want to catch them, you understand. They just want to record information about them and study them. Meteorologists, college professors, students, and curious citizens can all be storm chasers. Training is strongly encouraged, and you can find out how to get it at http://www.gilbertzone.com/beginner/beginner.html

---

The truth is out there in UFOS AND EXTRATERRESTRIALS. Maybe.

Info on Hobby Robots (from comp.robotics.)

Why wait for George Jetson and Spacely Space Sprockets to build you a robot, when plenty of folks are building their own right now? This page gives you the lowdown on where to pick up inexpensive hobby kits for assembling your own robot! It also includes links to places where you can download hints and plans, information on building sensors, and the entire "6.270 Robot Builder's Guide," which is also available in hard copy from the Massachusetts Institute of Technology.

http://www.cs.uwa.edu.au/~mafm/robot/

The Planetary Society: Young Explorers: Red Rover

How would you like to explore Mars? These classrooms did—well, actually they explored a simulated version right here on Earth. The first step is to build a small Martian landscape. Put volcanoes, canyons, impact craters, rocks, and maybe a giant face on it for fun. Then you get to build your robot, called a Red Rover. You make it from a special LEGO Dacta kit, which allows you to operate the robot via computer software. This project simulates what scientists go through to control robots on other worlds. Other Red Rover teams around the world can control your Rrover by issuing commands over the Internet. The good news is that you can control their rovers, too. See some schools' elaborate landscapes in the Mars Sites Around the World section. You and your friends can join the fun, but you need to have your school buy some special equipment, and we warn you, it is expensive. Have a bake sale and a car wash! Tell a local business that if they sponsor the project, your rover will be named after their company. Get several local businesses to donate money and put their logos on your rover.

http://planetary.org/explorers-red-rover.html

A B C D E F G H I J K L M N O P Q R S T U V W X Y Z

A
B
C
D
E
F
G
H
I
J
K
L
M
N
O
P
Q
R
S
T
U
V
W
X
Y
Z

NET FILES

All dinosaurs are extinct . . . right?

(Hint: This involves the greatest fish story ever told!)

Answer: *Maybe not. In 1938, fishermen off the coast of South Africa found the first living coelacanth in recent history; another was reported in 1952, off the Comoros Islands (to the northeast, in the Mozambique Channel). The coelacanth (pronounced "see-la-kanth") is a 400-million-year-old "living fossil" fish, once thought to have become extinct long ago. The account at http://www.dinofish.com/discoa.htm reads like a mystery story. Check the "dinofish" home page at http://www.dinofish.com/ for pictures and more amazing details.*

Robots Exhibit — The Computer Museum

If you were going to build your own robot to explore Mars, or maybe creep into a live volcano, or perhaps entertain humans at a party—what would you need to consider in your design? You'd need to figure out how it gets power, how it moves around, and of course how it looks. This Shockwave simulation allows you to try out various choices in a robot lab and get feedback on your choices.

http://www.tcm.org/html/galleries/robots/

Catch a ride on a Carousel in AMUSEMENT PARKS.

The Telegarden

Now here's a garden for the '90s, where Web cruisers gather to plant seeds and water plants by the remote control of an industrial robotic arm. This started as a real garden at the University of Southern California, although last year it moved to a server in Austria. The idea is to bring together a community of people to help tend a "shared garden." Click on "Guest Entrance" at the bottom of the page. You can explore the garden by clicking on a drawing of the robotic arm. This moves the arm—and a camera—to give you an up-to-the-minute picture of what's going on. Every so often, they clear the garden and start over. If you register as a member and visit the site regularly, you'll get to plant a seed.

http://www.usc.edu/dept/garden/

WebINK: Auto Tour: So You Want To Make A Car...

Have you ever wondered how cars are made? This site takes you through all the steps, saving you from walking the 16 miles of conveyors that transfer car bodies from start to finish. That's more than 230 football fields in length! At this auto factory, over 260 programmable robots install, weld, and paint in order for those shiny new vehicles to roll off the line. Look over their shoulders (or whatever robots have) and see how cars are built. There are also some great links on car history, solar cars, and race cars.

http://www.ipl.org/autou/

Xavier

Where in the world is Xavier the Robot? Exploring the classrooms and halls of Carnegie Mellon University, of course! Check in at this Web site and find out where he is, plus see what he's "seeing" as he wanders around. You can even control his movements if you visit during certain times (check the schedule). See if you can think up some new jokes for him to tell when he encounters people; the ones on the list right now are real groaners: "I'm a screen Xavier."

http://www.cs.cmu.edu/People/Xavier/

SCHOOLS AND EDUCATION

See also separate PARENTING AND FAMILIES— EDUCATION *section at the end of the book, especially for resources aimed primarily at teachers*

ARTSEDGE: The National Arts and Education Information Network

If you dig deep enough at this site, you'll find a very nice selection of links about the arts. The "arts" doesn't just mean drawing and painting; it also includes performing arts, such as music, dance, and theater. You'll find discussion areas for students and teachers, news flashes, and even showcases of art by kids; teachers will enjoy the curriculum guides. There's a section for online exhibits, museums, and galleries.

http://artsedge.kennedy-center.org/

Ask An Expert Page

Got a question no one seems to know how to answer? Maybe you need to call in an expert. Experts are people who know a lot about a certain topic—so much, in fact, that they often write the textbooks themselves! Many scientists and others have offered to answer questions about science, math, medicine, history, and other topics. You won't usually get an answer overnight, though, so think ahead.

http://njnie.dl.stevens-tech.edu/curriculum/aska.html

B.J. Pinchbeck's Homework Helper

"Beege" is 11 years old and has collected over 440 resources that he uses with his school homework. Maybe they will work for you, too! You'll find everything from biographical dictionaries to flags of the world.

http://tristate.pgh.net/~pinch13/

Blue Web'n Learning Library

This site collects the cream of the crop of learning-oriented Web sites. All sites are rated and categorized by area, audience, and type. Each subject category has links to related tutorials, activities, projects, lesson plans, and more. You can also use their keyword search to explore their collection. Want more? Join the free mailing list for weekly updates. We found the sites listed here to be excellent resources for eager learners as well as educators looking for teaching materials.

http://www.kn.pacbell.com/wired/bluewebn/

Cisco Educational Archive and Resources Catalog

OK, you've got this great new computer sitting in front of you, with a super-fast modem. Now, how do you actually use it for your day-to-day homework? Are you looking for information about the dilophosaurus? Or perhaps you want to find out more about civil rights. Don't waste any time—go right to the door of the Virtual Schoolhouse! Investigate your questions here and "CEARCH" using a very fast search engine. Cisco's done an excellent job of collecting great resources for kids, teachers, and parents. You'll also find a list of online schools and links to their home pages. You may never have heard of Cisco, but your Internet service provider has, and chances are good that much of your Internet traffic travels through Cisco equipment. A note to teachers: Cisco often announces special grants and other opportunities for schools here, so check often.

http://sunsite.unc.edu/cisco/edu-arch.html

Homework Central. Study Hard

Net-mom first heard about this site from a really smart teacher she knows. It is a useful place to find information needed for a special project or paper, if you don't mind all the ads and animations. This site is definitely worth your time, and it might get you some extra points if you tell your teacher about it, too!

http://www.homeworkheaven.com/

A
B
C
D
E
F
G
H
I
J
K
L
M
N
O
P
Q
R
S
T
U
V
W
X
Y
Z

HomeWorkHelper! Welcome!

Kids, got a question? Your answer may be just a click away! Here you can submit your question, select any or all of the six source types, and GO. For older students, there is also a link to the Electric Library and Researchpaper.com, the Internet's largest collection of topics, ideas, and assistance for school-related research projects.

http://www.homeworkhelper.com/

ICONnect: KidsConnect

You've got a question and no one seems to have an answer—not your mother or your grandpa or your great-aunt, Gert. Just head to this site and ask your question to one of the school library media specialists throughout the world. They provide direct assistance to any student looking for resources. They'll help you learn how to use the Internet effectively for your class work, and you can tell Mom, Grandpa, and Aunt Gert that you've got the answer!

http://www.ala.org/ICONN/kidsconn.html

Kathy Schrock's Guide for Educators - Home Page

This site says it's for educators, but it's also for kids! The links in this guide are organized according to subject area. In World History, for instance, you'll get a breakdown of Web pages, from "Ancient World Web" to "World War II: The World Remembers." Each month, a list of new resources will point you to the latest and greatest.

http://www.capecod.net/schrockguide/

Multnomah County Library - Homework Center

This well-organized collection of links will pay off for you when the library's closed, when your CD-ROM encyclopedia won't load, and when your dad's taking a nap and can't help. The brief annotations help you find that diagram of the human eye you need, for example, or information on what kinds of foods were eaten by the ancient Egyptians. Remember to check here—this site was built by librarians!

http://www.multnomah.lib.or.us/lib/homework/

Surfing the Net with Kids

Barbara Feldman's syndicated column, "Surfing the Net With Kids," runs in almost 30 newspapers. Each week, she picks five great Web sites on a favorite topic, such as Beanie Babies, paper money, robots, and more. You can read her excellent column at her Web site and even subscribe to the e-mail edition for free.

http://www.surfnetkids.com/

LEARNING AND STUDY

CalRen Home Page

Something's clanking in the dryer. The dog is barking at a bike rider going by outside. You can smell dinner cooking, and you feel hungry. All of a sudden, a football whizzes by your bedroom window. So many distractions make it hard to study! Here are some tips to help you study better, listen, take notes, and take tests.

http://www-slc.uga.berkeley.edu/CalRENHP.html

How to be a Successful Student

Being a successful student isn't just about doing your homework. You have to discover your own learning style and find out how to avoid putting things off. You'll find a few tips here that will get you started.

http://marin.cc.ca.us/~don/Study/Hcontents.html

IPL Citing Electronic Resources

Using the Net to find information for research projects is great, but how do you cite all those electronic resources? This useful list from the Internet Public Library will show you the way. If the style sheet you need is not mentioned, try Karla's Guide to Citation Style Guides at *<http://bailiwick.lib.uiowa.edu/ journalism/cite.html>*.

http://www.ipl.org/ref/QUE/FARQ/netciteFARQ.html

IQ Test

Did you ever hear of your intelligence quota? It's a way to measure how smart you are, or at least some people think that! In just a few minutes you can answer some questions and determine just how intelligent you really are. Now, Net-mom wants you to remember that the first sign of intelligence is shown by kids who do NOT write in their name or provide any other information about themselves. You can take this test without divulging any specific information. OK, it's time to begin! Good luck!

http://www.iqtest.com/

Techniques to Manage Procrastination

Procrastination! What does it mean? It means we put off doing that term paper, report, or science project until it's too late to complete it! Why do we do that? There are lots of theories, but one thing's for sure: we all want to get over it! For techniques on how to conquer procrastination, check this site without waiting another minute. Here is one tip: "Break the task down into little pieces. Not: There's so much to do, and it's so complicated. I'm overwhelmed by my English term paper. Instead: I don't have to do the whole project at once. There are separate small steps I can take one at a time to begin researching and drafting my paper."

http://gbc-178-3.UGA.berkeley.edu/SLCHP.html

Welcome to TheBig6.com

Would you like to be able to answer any question? Try this methodical approach! There are six steps: 1. Define the problem; 2. Brainstorm how you might find answers; 3. Figure out where the resources might be, and get them; 4. Read the information and take notes; 5. Organize your information and present it; and 6. Evaluate your product and how effective it is in communicating the answers to the problem. Sounds so simple, doesn't it? It's amazing how many people can't even get started on a project. This method lets you break down your research into manageable steps. At the official site, you'll find lots more detail, examples, and sample lesson plans. Forget study tricks: go Big Six!

http://big6.syr.edu/

You Don't Have to Play Football to Score a Touchdown

Although this study skills page was designed for high school and college students, anyone can learn from these short tips. Did you know the best time to study is right after class? Did you know that when taking a test you should skip the hard questions, do the easy ones, and then return to spend time figuring out the more difficult problems? This page will help you take notes, manage your time, and learn to do your best to make and meet your goals. Be sure to take the link to "Study Skills Help Page" for more.

http://www.mtsu.edu/~studskl/hsindex.html

PROJECTS
Global SchoolNet Foundation Home Page

"Where in the World Is Roger?" "Roots and Shoots with Jane Goodall," "International CyberFair," "Global Schoolhouse Videoconferencing"—does any of that sound interesting? The folks in charge of GSN just keep collecting and coming up with more terrific ideas all the time. Always fresh and exciting, this is where K–12 innovation lives on the Net! Kids can find new contest announcements at this site, including ThinkQuest and other opportunities.

http://www.gsn.org/

NET FILES

What is a Zampoña? (Hint: it's not that big machine the guy at the ice rink rides around on.)

Answer: It's a South American pan pipe (a wooden flute of sorts). Blow on over to http://lykeko.rcp.net.pe/snd/snd_ingles.html and hear what it sounds like! To see a picture of one, try Lark in the Morning's catalog at http://www.mhs.mendocino.k12.ca.us/MenComNet/Business/Retail/Larknet/Andes

A
B
C
D
E
F
G
H
I
J
K
L
M
N
O
P
Q
R
S
T
U
V
W
X
Y
Z

A
B
C
D
E
F
G
H
I
J
K
L
M
N
O
P
Q
R
S
T
U
V
W
X
Y
Z

I*EARN

The best way to understand people of a different nationality or race or religion is to get to know them. Basically, that's what the developers of this nonprofit site are doing, and it is a concept that has won them praise from all kinds of sources. Simply put, classrooms of children from kindergarten through secondary school work together in developing projects on a variety of subjects, using telecommunications to pave the way. School classes are invited to participate in a project already in progress or to begin something new. Like the idea? Read more about it and talk to your teacher. Soon your "classmates" could be kids from halfway around the world!

http://www.iearn.org/

IECC, Intercultural E-Mail Classroom Connections

One of the great aspects of the Internet is that it provides children with the opportunity to reach well beyond their community to kids just about anywhere. Intercultural E-Mail Classroom Connections, or IECC, provides listserv discussions for teachers to find other teachers and classes interested in a pen pal exchange. If you are a teacher, definitely take a look. If you are a student, parent, or caregiver, mention IECC to a teacher. A whole new way of communicating may well open up, since at last count more than 7,300 teachers in 73 countries were participating. IECC provides connections for students of all ages, from grade school through college.

http://www.iecc.org/

KIDLINK: Global Networking for Youth through the age of 15

Wow! Kids from more than 118 countries have answered these four questions: Who am I? What do I want to be when I grow up? How do I want the world to be better when I grow up? What can I do now to make this happen? Once you've answered those questions to introduce yourself, you can take part in any of the KIDLINK projects. You can even have a dialogue in the KIDCAFE in languages such as Spanish, Japanese, and Portuguese. Make the world a better place through KIDLINK! This site is available in 13 different languages.

http://www.kidlink.org/

Visit the stars in ASTRONOMY.

ThinkQuest

Would you like to win thousands of dollars in scholarship money? Do you have a great idea for a new Web resource? You might be a fabulous C++ programmer, but you can't write interesting English prose very well. Or maybe you're terrific at graphics but can't code. Maybe you're not a computer nut at all but you really know how to research a topic. There is a place for all of you at ThinkQuest. First, you have to create a team to work on your project. Advertise your skills and your ideas at the Team Maker part of the site. Typically, teams are formed with four or five kids from all over the world; they have usually never met, and they usually come from schools or homeschools with widely varying levels of technology. You also need a coach or two, usually a teacher or a parent, but it could be someone else. You decide how to tackle the project and then spend many months building your Web resource on the server space provided by ThinkQuest. You and your team members use chat rooms to discuss the project as well as e-mail and other forms of communication. Eventually the contest deadline rolls around and your project is frozen in time so that the judges can take a look. If your site if chosen as a finalist, you and your team (and your coaches) are flown (all expenses paid) to Washington, D.C. Your site is inspected by the finals judges. You and your team are interviewed, and at long last, winners are chosen and placements are made. The winning team members each get $25,000 scholarships, and many of the finalist teams who place lower get scholarships as well. ThinkQuest has given away over one million dollars in scholarship money. There are two contests: one for elementary grades, called ThinkQuest Junior, and the original one for older kids. At this site you can explore past winners' sites and get information about the latest ThinkQuest competition schedule.

http://www.thinkquest.org/

Welcome to International Schools CyberFair 98!

The International Schools CyberFair invites schools to participate in a collaborative project to create world-class Web sites. Projects should "exploit the unique abilities of the World Wide Web to build relationships and alliances with different people and groups within their local community." One of the goals is to promote an "Internet style of learning" that encourages participants to reach out and use the Web for information gathering. There are prizes and incentives to encourage participation. Check out the list of prizes, rules, and past winners' sites. Be the hero who gets your school started in the CyberFair competition.

http://www.gsn.org/cf/

Where is the geographic center of the North American continent?

http://www.giness.com/tourism/html/Facts.html

more North Dakota facts at

miles south, 7 miles west of the city of Rugby. Learn

Answer: It's in the state of North Dakota, exactly 16

SCIENCE

See also under name of specific subject throughout the book

Frank Potter's Science Gems

This treasure chest of science gems includes links to resources on physical sciences, earth science, life science, engineering, and math. There are over 3,000 links here, which makes one wonder what Frank's life is like! The Web pages are arranged by subject and ordered by grade level. In some sections, a handy list shows which sites are popular and are most often "clicked."

http://www.-sci.lib.uci.edu/SEP/SEP.html

The JASON Project

Ever heard of The JASON Project? It was founded in Massachusetts in 1989, and here's how it got started. Dr. Robert D. Ballard had just discovered the wreck of the RMS *Titanic*. When he got back, he was overwhelmed by the letters he received from interested kids. He decided to develop a way for kids to interact with real science and take part in global field trips. In 1998, they're preparing for the next expedition to the Amazon Center for Environmental Education and Research, located in the Peruvian Amazon rain forest, but you can read all about other travels to Iceland, the Florida keys, Yellowstone, and similar exciting places. Past JASON projects have let kids control deep-sea submarines and make other real observations. You never know what JASON's going to do next! Do try the Dive for Sunken Treasure game, though.

http://www.jasonproject.org/front.html

Kinetic City

The Super Crew solves scientific problems and mysteries by gathering clues, performing experiments, and drawing conclusions. Can they help save the whales in Nova Scotia? Maybe. But then will they find out who sabotaged the robot contest? Help the eight young sleuths in the Cyber Club (you have to register, but it's free), or just look at the archives for their companion radio show. Have a science mystery or question of your own? Ask the crew; they may answer you on the air and on the Web!

http://www.kineticcity.com/

A
B
C
D
E
F
G
H
I
J
K
L
M
N
O
P
Q
R
S
T
U
V
W
X
Y
Z

A
B
C
D
E
F
G
H
I
J
K
L
M
N
O
P
Q
R
S
T
U
V
W
X
Y
Z

MadSci Net: Ask-A-Scientist (and more) on the WWW

Do you have a question about science that is stumping everyone you ask? Or maybe you have a really simple question you're too embarrassed to bring up in class. Look no further. You have just stumbled onto the solution. This site is a collaboration of scientists around the world gathered to answer your questions. You can search the archives and see if your question, or one like it, has already been answered.

http://www.madsci.org/

Newton's Apple Index

This is the *Newton's Apple* home page. This site is full of science-related lessons and experiments from the TV show. The lesson on "Arctic Nutrition" explains why Arctic explorers need a carbohydrate-rich diet to maintain their strength. Another lesson explains why you don't get a strong smell from garlic until it is cut or crushed. You'll find lots more here: experiment and learn, and you'll be sure to have fun!

http://ericir.syr.edu/Projects/Newton/

Quest: NASA K-12 Internet Initiative

Check the links to online interactive projects—new ones every year! Past projects have included "Live from Antarctica," "Online Jupiter 1997," and "Earth to Mars Activities." Ask the scientists questions, order interesting materials, and help NASA decide what they will do next.

http://quest.arc.nasa.gov/

Real-Time Data Access Page

Do you know what "real time" is? It's right now, as you're reading this. Want to see some live, real-time scientific observations? Check the current moon phase, see a map of where *Mir* space station is, gaze at radar weather maps, view volcano cams to see what's smokin', and more. Every *time* we visit here, there's more to see.

http://www.math.montana.edu/~tslater/real-time/

Science Friday Kids Connection

Every Friday, science guru Ira Flatow hosts a radio show on National Public Radio, called (what else?) "Science Friday." The companion Web site for kids is a real treasure for all listeners! Interested in the show topic? Find study questions, links, and resources to find out more about it. Recent topics have included comets, identifying smashed bugs on your car windshield, and HAL, the robot from the movie *2001: A Space Odyssey*.

http://www.npr.org/programs/sfkids/

Science From Kids' Perspective

"Most books now say our Sun is a star. But it still knows how to change back into a Sun in the daytime." This is a little collection of things kids have said on class exams, and you may think they are pretty funny. Don't use any of these on your next test, though!

http://w3.mit.edu/afs/athena/user/h/e/hershey/www/humor/random/random43.html

A Science Odyssey

We don't care what you're doing right now. Just get on the Net and visit this site. You will not be disappointed. Check out the Shockwave simulations in the You Try It section. In the Technology at Home area, you can scroll through the twentieth century and see what changes happen in the virtual home. Appliances appear and disappear, telephone equipment changes—what else will you notice? You can mouse over each item and see some facts about it: what it is, who invented it, and when it came into vogue or went out of style. Now try the other explorations: human evolution, radio transmission, probe the brain, atomic structure, and several more. When you get done with those, read the On the Edge comic books about various scientists and their discoveries. Did radio astronomer Jocelyn Bell really think she'd gotten a message from little green men in outer space? Find out here! Don't miss the hit game show That's My Theory! Question the three contestants to see which one is the real Einstein, the real Freud, and the real ENIAC.

http://www.pbs.org/wgbh/aso/

Science, Technology - Dr. Bob's Home Page

Dr. Bob is a scientist who also directs a Sylvan Learning Center and this Web page! He hopes to get kids ten years old and up really hooked on science. Mysterious lights at the thermal vents on the bottom of the ocean, or the case of the sliding boulders in the desert—do these topics sound interesting to you? How about the guy who lived for 13 years with a metal pipe stuck through his head (a photo of his skull is here, and it's very gross anatomy). If that is just too weird, skip it and read about the space shuttle or insects, or try some of the neat science links.

http://www.frontiernet.net/~docbob/science.htm

Welcome to Thinking Fountain!

From A to Z, you're going to find a lot of wonderful ideas and information at the Thinking Fountain. Allow us to demonstrate! A—Read about Anansi the Spider and then find out how to make your own sliding spider toy. G—Golf-O-Rama, a book about miniature golf, complete with everything you need but the ball and the putter, and a story about some kids who made their own mini-mini golf course. N—Noodle-ing around: learn to build a structure out of spaghetti. (Don't believe it? The secret is in the mini marshmallows!). Z—Zoo Machines: invent a machine to take care of all those animals. Keep going, you're sure to find lots more activities and ideas, galleries to show your work, books you can use, and surprises inspired by the Thinking Fountain!

http://www.sci.mus.mn.us/sln/tf/

Whelmers Science Activities

Before we go further, answer this: Is there iron in your cereal? Can a penny dance on the top of a soda bottle? Want to find out? Try these "whelmers"—activities that catch the mind and the eye of every student. At this really cool site, you can open up 20 different whelmers and have a lot of fun while actually learning some useful information! It will require gathering some simple materials and then reading instructions on how to complete the task. Remember, you can never be too whelmed by science, although you can be overwhelmed with homework.

http://www.mcrel.org/whelmers/

The Why Files

Your coach has really gone crazy this time. He's climbed to the top of the backboard, and he's dropping a round basketball and a flat basketball (with no air in it) at the same time. Which one will hit the floor first? Everybody guesses one or the other, but the answer is that they will strike the floor at the same time. Why? The answer is at this site, which is funded by the National Science Foundation. You'll also find current science news for kids, as well as archives of past whys (and wise) answers!

http://whyfiles.news.wisc.edu/

YES Mag Home Page

YES Mag is the place to go for the latest science news, info on how things work, some great science projects, and more. The projects are cool, too: make a toothpick bridge, a "telegraph," and investigate how red blood cells move through capillaries. Our favorite, though, is the "Geodesic Club House," a geodesic dome made out of rolled newspapers and staples.

http://www.yesmag.bc.ca/

You Can with Beakman and Jax

Why do feet smell? What's Jell-O really made of? What direction is down? Where are the latest Hubble Space Telescope photos? If it has something to do with science, you may find it collected here. Look for more Beakman information at the *Beakman's World* TV show home page by clicking on "TV Home Page."

http://www.beakman.com/

SCIENCE FAIRS

CMS - Science Fair 97

Are you stumped trying to think of an interesting project for the science fair at school? The Cyberspace Middle School's resource page will give you a great start! Lots of science fair ideas, projects, and tips are collected here. If your school doesn't have a science fair and you'd like to start one, several suggested books contain everything you'll need to know.

http://www.scri.fsu.edu/~dennisl/CMS/sf/sf.html

A B C D E F G H I J K L M N O P Q R S T U V W X Y Z

A
B
C
D
E
F
G
H
I
J
K
L
M
N
O
P
Q
R
S
T
U
V
W
X
Y
Z

Helping Your Child Learn Science

OK, it's really a brochure for parents, but you should check out the experiments here, because some of them would make neat science fair projects. You'll find lots of kitchen chemistry tricks and fun with static electricity, and don't miss "celery stalks at midnight"!

http://www.ed.gov/pubs/parents/Science/

IPL Science Fair Project Resource Guide

This is your first science fair project, and you're not really sure where to begin! The folks at the Internet Public Library can help: they have collected a lot of good information to get you going. You can even search by grade level, then by topic.

http://www.ipl.org/youth/projectguide/

Reeko's Mad Scientist Lab

It sure is dusty here in Reeko's basement science lab. Better put on this lab coat to keep your clothes clean, and this pair of goggles might not be a bad idea, either! Fun educational experiments in astronomy, chemistry, physics, and earth science may be found here if you look around a bit. In the archives, you can examine the experiments by level of difficulty or by category. Reeko's got a fun sense of humor, too; consider the description for Rocket Powered Pennies: "Ok, so maybe the term rocket powered is taking it a little too far. But we still get to propel an object. All we need for this simple experiment is an empty soda bottle and a penny (unless you are getting your Mad Scientist supplies from Dad, in which case—ask for a quarter)."

http://www.flash.net/~spartech/ReekoScience/
    ReekoIndex.htm

Science and Math Carnival

How about organizing a math and science carnival for your school? This site gives you a complete how-to manual. There is a list of all the equipment and materials you'll need, although the first thing you need to assemble is a long list of volunteers to help! Your ten hands-on exhibits will be fun for kids of all ages, but you need adults to help, because some of the exhibits involve electricity, liquid nitrogen, and other similar materials.

http://www.ca.sandia.gov/outreach/html/carnival.html

SCIENCE HOBBYIST

Are you into amateur science? If so, you've just found a great place to bookmark! This site has lots of science links. Sites are grouped in categories, such as amateur science, science projects, kids asking scientists, science suppliers/stores, and others. If you're looking for a place to browse for science stuff, be sure to experiment with this one, but get an adult to help you.

http://www.eskimo.com/~billb/

Virtual Science Fair

If you're looking for a way to dazzle the rest of the class with your science fair know-how, put your safety goggles on and take a look here! You'll learn how to make objects float, how to grow crystals, and how to tell if something is an acid or a base. Most of these kitchen chemistry experiments were designed by kids.

http://www.parkmaitland.org/sciencefair/

SCIENCE MUSEUMS
Exploratorium: ExploraNet

Do you know what makes a fruit fly grow legs out of its head? How would you like to take a "light walk" and explore the world of shadows? The Exploratorium, in San Francisco, California, is a huge hands-on science laboratory for kids of all ages. Discover the many interesting wonders that they have ported to the Web!

http://www.exploratorium.edu/

The Lost Museum of Sciences

No, they didn't lose the museum—the idea here is for you to get lost. No, we don't mean GET LOST, just lose yourself amidst all the stuff you'll find here. Now you're starting to get the picture. By the time you do find your way back, if you find your way back, you're sure to have learned something. No, we don't mean you'll learn how to find your way back, we mean you'll learn something scientific. Oops! If you like to be challenged, you can always play "Find The Exhibit." The first one to find it gets his or her name displayed here for all to see!

http://www.geocities.com/Athens/Delphi/9810/
    lostmuseum.html

Questacon

Australia's National Science and Technology Centre has a fabulous online museum! You can explore lots of interactive exhibits, puzzles, games, and more. Dinosaurs, meteors, optical illusions, and clever science activities abound here. This is one of the best sites on the Net for kids interested in science.

http://sunsite.anu.edu.au/Questacon/

SHARKS

See also FISH

Beyond Jaws

Sharks have terrible eyesight, right? Wrong. OK, but aren't sharks just brainless eating machines? Wrong again. Discover what is fact and what is fiction about these great ocean dwellers and learn shark no-no's when swimming in potentially shark-infested waters.

http://hockey.plaidworks.com/sharks/great-white.html

Fiona's Shark Mania

Shark! Good thing you're just surfing the Net and not the ocean. Actually, sharks do live in the ocean, but they can also be found in rivers, lakes, and other freshwater bodies. Sharks are saltwater fish, but they can live in fresh water for several days. This page celebrates "all things sharky." At this site, you'll find sharks in literature, shark info, shark photos, even shark clip art and graphics.

http://www.oceanstar.com/shark/

The Great White Shark

Carcharodon carcharias is the scientific name of the great white shark. It comes from the Greek *carcharos*, meaning "ragged," and *odon*, meaning "tooth." *Jaws* was a pretty scary movie, but it was just a story, after all. Discover the truth about great white sharks!

http://www.cybervault.com/users/D/dgrgich/
   shark.html

NOVA Online | Shark Attack!

According to this *Nova* site, "Some sharks can smell as few as 10 drops of liquid tuna in the volume of water it takes to fill an average swimming pool!" But smell is only one of the shark's six senses. Find out what in the world the others are, and learn all about shark tagging, anatomy, life cycle, and more.

http://www.pbs.org/wgbh/nova/sharks/

Zoom Sharks - Enchanted Learning Software

Did you know that sharks have no bones? Their skeletons are made of thick, fibrous cartilage. There are all sizes of sharks, too, from a shark that would fit on your hand to a shark as big as a bus—the whale shark can be over 50 feet long! At this site you can learn about types of sharks found around the world, how they are classified, what they eat, what their teeth look like, and more. You can also print out shark coloring pages to make a souvenir shark booklet.

http://www.EnchantedLearning.com/subjects/sharks/

SHIPS AND SHIPWRECKS

See also TREASURE AND TREASURE-HUNTING

Chesapeake Bay Maritime Museum

Although the museum is located in Maryland, the Chesapeake Bay's estuary runs 190 miles and touches several states, from the mighty Susquehanna River in Pennsylvania to Virginia's capes. At its widest point, the bay is 30 miles across, and its greatest depth is 174 feet. An interesting array of boats has developed around the bay's main occupations: crabbing, oystering, and waterfowling. Take the online museum tour to get a look at some of these sleek maritime beauties, and learn a lot about the Chesapeake Bay as you explore.

http://www.cbmm.org/

A B C D E F G H I J K L M N O P Q R **S** T U V W X Y Z

A
B
C
D
E
F
G
H
I
J
K
L
M
N
O
P
Q
R
S
T
U
V
W
X
Y
Z

Edmund Fitzgerald Bell Restoration Project

You may have heard the Gordon Lightfoot song commemorating the wreck of the *Edmund Fitzgerald*. On November 10, 1975, the 729-foot freighter was hauling a heavy cargo of iron ore pellets across Lake Superior and was caught in a severe storm that sent the ship suddenly to the bottom, killing its 29 crew members. This page describes the search for the wreck, the salvage effort, and the restoration of the ship's bell. Surviving family members asked that the bell be recovered as a memorial to the sailors who gave their lives in the maritime accident. A duplicate bell, inscribed with the names of the sailors, was left in the pilot house of the ship. The original bell was brought to the surface and dedicated on July 7, 1995. At the ceremony, the bell was rung 30 times: once for each of the 29 *Fitzgerald* crew members, and once for all mariners who have lost their lives at sea.

http://web.msu.edu/bell/

The legend lives on from the Chippewa on down
Of the big lake they called 'Gitche Gumee'
The lake, it is said, never gives up her dead
When the skies of November turn gloomy
With a load of iron ore twenty-six thousand tons more
Than the Edmund Fitzgerald weighed empty.
That good ship and true was a bone to be chewed
When the gales of November came early.

Read about the history of this famous shipwreck at the Edmund Fitzgerald Bell Restoration Project page.

Exploring Amistad: Race and the Boundaries of Freedom in Antebellum Maritime America

What has come to be known as the Amistad Revolt began in 1839 as a shipboard slave uprising off the coast of Cuba. It intensified into a debate on slavery, race, Africa, and the foundations of American democracy itself. Popularized by a recent movie, you can read the original accounts of the story at this informative site. The schooner the slaves took over was named *Amistad*, which means "friendship."

http://amistad.mysticseaport.org/main/welcome.html

La Salle Shipwreck Project of the THC

The Texas Historical Commission has quite a find on their hands! They are excavating a shipwreck believed to be that of the *Belle*, one of the ships brought by the French explorer René Robert Cavelier, sieur de La Salle. La Salle was the explorer who claimed the Mississippi River and all its tributaries for France. His ship was lost in 1686. It lies in about 12 feet of water in a bay about halfway between Galveston and Corpus Christi. Archaeologists built a special double-walled coffer dam around the wreck, then pumped out the water in the middle of this "doughnut." They were then free to explore and carefully record their findings. You can read about La Salle and the recovery of his ship and its artifacts at this very special site! In February 1998, they discovered a second shipwreck in the bay. Whose is it? Check this site and see.

http://www.thc.state.tx.us/belle/

MERCHANT MARINE AND MARITIME PAGES

Have you ever wondered what it takes to pass the Coast Guard exam for a marine engineer license? Here's your chance to take a quiz! Examine many kinds of ship engines and ship designs. Maritime poems are interspersed with drawings and photos of all kinds of freighters in many world ports. In the Photo Gallery, don't miss the Russian vessel in Kobe, Japan, "exporting" souvenir cars for each crew member. The cars sprout all over the deck, sticking out at all angles like porcupine quills! You'll find links to lots of other maritime sites around the Web, including virtual port authorities and research fleets. This Web site, written by a real merchant marine engineer, is a real winner.

http://www.pacifier.com/~rboggs/

> ## People are the true treasures of the Net.

Midway @ nationalgeographic.com

Long before you were born, battles took place during World War II. One of them involved some ships in the Pacific Ocean near Midway Island. Two United States ships, the USS *Yorktown* and the *Hammann,* were sunk. Join this expedition to the bottom of the ocean floor and see and read about the search for sunken vessels.

http://www.nationalgeographic.com/features/98/
  midway/

Polynesian Voyaging Society

The Polynesian Voyaging Society has built two replicas of ancient canoes—*Hokule'a* and *Hawai'iloa*—and conducted many voyages in the South Pacific to retrace ancient migration routes and recover traditional canoe-building and wayfinding (noninstrument navigation) arts. Discover this voyaging tradition at their official Web page.

http://leahi.kcc.hawaii.edu/org/pvs/

Wayfinding In the Middle of the Pacific

Journey back through time to the days of the early Hawaiians and see how they voyaged across the sea without instruments or a compass to guide them. They had only the stars and other natural "signposts" to show them the way. Some young people from several elementary schools in Hawaii thought that was really unusual and cool. So they did a lot of research about the early settlers of Hawaii and entered their Web page in the ThinkQuest Junior competition. You'll enjoy reading about how the original Hawaiians traveled and how they used stars to navigate. You can even play a game that will prove just how much you have learned!

http://tqjunior.advanced.org/3542/

Welcome to the Mary Rose

July 19, 1545: On the flagship, the Tudor king, Henry VIII, was having a lavish dinner. The *Mary Rose,* a four-masted warship built between 1510 and 1511, sailed nearby. French ships appeared and fired on the fleet. A little while later, the *Mary Rose* was lying at the bottom of the Solent, a body of water between Portsmouth, England, and the Isle of Wight. Most of the 500-person crew drowned. The ship was rediscovered in 1971 and was raised to the surface in 1982. This site takes you on a tour of the museum artifacts found on board as well as a dry dock containing what is left of the ship itself. You'll be fascinated at the technology used to raise the ship and the stories of shipboard life during those times. This site has a wonderful children's area, where you can take a tour led by Tudor Rat!

http://www.maryrose.org/

RMS TITANIC

Mediadome - Explore Titanic

This Java-based virtual reality experience lets you explore the wreck of the *Titanic* as you search for the missing safe. We didn't see Leonardo around anywhere, and we didn't find the safe either, but we did feel sort of wet after sloshing around in the sunken staterooms and corroded corridors for a while! How well can you do?

http://www.mediadome.com/Webisodes/Titanic/
  Explore/

Ocean Planet:How Deep Can they Go? - The RMS Titanic

For a truly impressive set of links on this famous shipwreck, don't miss Ocean Planet's RMS *Titanic* site. If you've got Java capabilities on your browser, you'll be able to see the ship traveling across your screen and hear the haunting toll of a ship's bell as you explore.

http://seawifs.gsfc.nasa.gov/OCEAN_PLANET/
  HTML/titanic.html

A
B
C
D
E
F
G
H
I
J
K
L
M
N
O
P
Q
R
S
T
U
V
W
X
Y
Z

A B C D E F G H I J K L M N O P Q R S T U V W X Y Z

NET FILES

What fruit, also called a "Chinese gooseberry," is sometimes used to patch bicycle tires? (Hint: You probably know it by a more common name.)

Answer: It's New Zealand's most famous fruit, the kiwi. Eat it, fix a puncture, make it into a pillowcase. But whatever you do, point your browser to *http://www.lonelyplanet.com.au/dest/aust/nz2.htm* and read all about it!

Titanic

You'll find lots of artifacts, annotated Web links, and facts, lore, and legend at this *Titanic* offering from *Encyclopedia Britannica*. Even if you think you've read everything about the *Titanic*, give this site a try too. One good thing that came out of this disaster was the establishment of an International Ice Patrol. About 1,000 icebergs are tracked each year during the iceberg season, from March to August. The U.S. Coast Guard broadcasts their locations twice daily via satellite and high-frequency radio facsimile.

http://titanic.eb.com/

Titanic Pages

The great movie, *Titanic*, has brought the disaster to life. Want to see how a Central New York newspaper reported the story at the time? The *Syracuse Post-Standard* has put a series of its original stories on their home page. You can read about all the people who were saved, as well as those who drowned. Put yourself in the place of those who were waiting at home for word of family members' fates. There are also links to many other pages about this famous shipping tragedy.

http://www.syracuse.com/news/special/titanic/

Titanic: the Movie

Nothing on Earth should come between you and this official Web site for the hit movie. You can send a "Marconigram" to a friend, learn a lot about the cast and special effects, download screen savers and wallpaper, and lots more.

http://www.titanicmovie.com/

VNP Exhibit of the Titanic

For many years, the sinking of the *Titanic* was thought to be a disaster in "modern" times. Now, the year 1912 seems long ago in the past. It has even become a distant memory for the dwindling number of people alive both then and now. Web sites such as this become excellent repositories for a great deal of information that could easily become lost. This page not only gives the hard facts of the sinking of the *Titanic* but also explores (through contemporary newspaper headlines, articles, and cartoons) how the average person of that time found out what was happening in the world—there was no cable TV satellite news back then!

http://www.lib.virginia.edu/cataloging/vnp/
titanic/titanic1.html

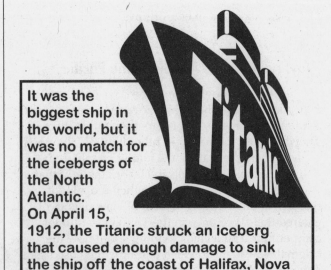

It was the biggest ship in the world, but it was no match for the icebergs of the North Atlantic. On April 15, 1912, the Titanic struck an iceberg that caused enough damage to sink the ship off the coast of Halifax, Nova Scotia. Read about it at the VNP Exhibit of the Titanic.

SPORTS

AudioNet - Sports Channel

You missed the big game? Check here to see if an audio broadcast is available. Some are live; others are here whenever you tune in. You'll also catch online shows with coaches and players, as well as special reports. Just about every sports team you can think of is listed here.

http://www.broadcast.com/sports/

Ballparks by Munsey & Suppes

Interested in baseball, football, hockey, or basketball? You should be interested in where the games are played, too, and this site will tell you about those fields, rinks, and courts. This site offers stadium facts, statistics, aerial views, and more! For example, explore baseball's American and National League parks of the past, present, and future. Ah, Ebbet's Field, home of Father of Net-mom's beloved Brooklyn Dodgers. Read all sorts of interesting trivia about it. For example, after World War II there was a big sign advertising Schaefer Beer on top of the right center scoreboard. When the officials said it was a hit, the *H* in the sign would light up; if there was an error, the *E* would be illuminated. Alas, Ebbet's Field was demolished in 1960.

http://www.ballparks.com/

CBS SportsLine

Scanning for up-to-the-minute scores, team news, and the latest on athletes and other figures in sports? This resource covers the NBA, NFL, baseball, NHL, golf, tennis, soccer, volleyball, skiing, boxing, and even horse racing events such as the Kentucky Derby.

http://www.sportsline.com/

College Nicknames

Teams usually pick a nickname to describe themselves, like the Wolverines or the Wildcats. Which names go with which U.S. colleges? Find out here! Did you know there's even a team nicknamed the White Mules? They're at Colby College, in Waterville, Maine.

http://www.afn.org/~recycler/sports.html

You've picked a really cool name for your new team: the Banana Slugs.

You figure that no one will have thought of that name before. But you'd be wrong. It's the nickname for teams from the University of California at Santa Cruz! Try College Nicknames to find out more about team nicknames.

ESPN SportsZone

Get the latest in up-to-the-minute sports reporting, including scores, from this site. There are columns and feature stories, too. Want to track Michael Jordan's progress since he came back to the NBA? Just do it. Or maybe you want to play Fantasy Football or get some industry insider information. If so, then this site is for you, from the folks who bring you ESPN, the all-sports cable TV network. To get all the features of this site, you must be a paid subscriber, but much is available for free.

http://espnet.sportszone.com/

IN FITNESS AND IN HEALTH

Ever wonder how exercise helps you maintain a healthy body? You can develop a fitness program and then track your progress when you hook up with the people at this site. Learn how to burn calories, determine your ideal weight and body fat, and check your favorite sport to see what benefits you gain from participating. You'll also learn how to prepare for being an athlete—warm-up exercises, proper clothing, and equipment are all explained for each sport.

http://www.phys.com/

A
B
C
D
E
F
G
H
I
J
K
L
M
N
O
P
Q
R
S
T
U
V
W
X
Y
Z

A
B
C
D
E
F
G
H
I
J
K
L
M
N
O
P
Q
R
S
T
U
V
W
X
Y
Z

The Locker Room....Sports For Kids!

Do you need basic information on how to hold a bat, kick a football, serve a volleyball, or shoot a hockey puck? Get it here. Besides "skills and drills," you'll find the rules of these sports and many others, their histories, fun facts about them, and a glossary of terms. There is also advice on how to do warm-up exercises and how to deal with team problems. If you don't have a big brother or sister to teach you this stuff, this page is the next best thing.

http://members.aol.com/msdaizy/sports/locker.html

Sports Illustrated for Kids

When was the last time you climbed a treacherous rock wall, shredded some ramps with the only pro female skateboarder in the country, or picked up some racing tips from the world's best BMX bicycle racer—all without leaving your computer? This online magazine is all about athletic challenges. If you've been wanting to try your hand at a new sport, this is where you can find out all about the moves, the lingo, and the equipment. Don't miss the interviews with sports heroes, hilarious comics, games, and a whole lot more.

http://www.sikids.com/

Winter Sports Foundation

This site will give you basic information on the following sports: Alpine skiing, cross-country skiing, biathlon, bobsled, figure skating, freestyle skiing, hockey, luge, ski jumping, snowboarding, speed skating, and telemark skiing. You'll learn how to get started in each sport: who to contact, what equipment is needed, and where to learn.

http://www.wintersports.org/

Beanie Babies rule in TOYS.

ARCHERY

Angus Duggan: Archery

Archery is hard! Making an arrow go where it's supposed to may seem easy, but it isn't. At the World Target Archery Records, you'll see who is the best in bending bows and slinging arrows. You'll also learn something about the history of archery and its equipment.

http://www.dcs.ed.ac.uk/home/ajcd/archery/

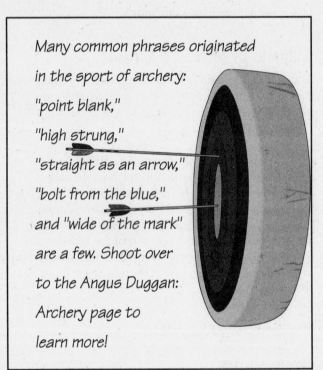

Many common phrases originated in the sport of archery: "point blank," "high strung," "straight as an arrow," "bolt from the blue," and "wide of the mark" are a few. Shoot over to the Angus Duggan: Archery page to learn more!

National Archery Association

Ever since Justin Huish won two Olympic gold medals (individual and team) in Atlanta for his archery skills, there has been renewed interest in this family sport. The National Archery Association governs the U.S. Olympic archery team, and you can read about the team members at this site. A handy spectator's guide will tell you what it means when the arrow hits various places on the target. You'll also learn about the different kinds of bows and other equipment. There is an online publication for youth archery, called The Edge, and its archives are available.

http://www.USArchery.org/

BADMINTON

Anita's Badminton Homepage

What's the world's fastest and oldest racket sport? Badminton! The "bird," or shuttlecock, has been clocked traveling up to 200 mph. And although the sport goes back to the fifth century B.C., badminton only recently became an Olympic sport—first appearing at the 1992 Olympics in Barcelona. Current world rankings, results from major badminton tournaments, photos, and links to other major badminton sites are collected here. Rules and regulations are here, too. If you want to organize your own tournament, why not use the Swiss Ladder System—the details are in the Programs area, where a computer program is available to do the calculations for you. There is a mirror site in the U.S. at *<http://www.web4free.com/badminton/>*.

http://huizen.dds.nl/~anita/badmint.html

BASEBALL

Baseball Links: Main Menu

This is a neat, annotated collection of Web sites, newsgroups, and graphics from all over the Net. You'll find links to baseball history, stats, Little League, coaching, and lots more here. How about softball, whiffleball, and the Irish and Swedish baseball teams? Yes, they are here, too, as well as a link to the U.S. Olympic baseball team's home page. Bring some peanuts and hot dogs—you'll be here all day!

http://www.baseball-links.com/main.shtml

The Baseball Online Library - CBS SportsLine

Some of the information here can be accessed only if you join, but the Today In Baseball History section is free, as are the featured player of the week and the Chronology of Baseball.

http://cbs.sportsline.com/u/baseball/bol/

The Baseball Server

This site is a hit, if you're just looking for the scores. From the majors to the minors, from Japanese to Korean teams, you'll find stats, standings, streaks, and records at this site. Also of interest are historical reports on past World Series, baseball heroes, and more.

http://www.nando.net/SportServer/baseball/

Baseball: The Game and Beyond

Baseball, apple pie, and motherhood: three American traditions. Everyone understands what motherhood is, and everyone knows how to eat an apple pie, but a lot of people don't really understand how baseball is played. Or why a pitcher throws a curveball one time and a fastball the next, or how physics is involved in this age-old sport. Well, wonder no longer. This ThinkQuest Junior finalist team has come up with a lot of the answers. If they could only tell us when the Red Sox will win the Series!

http://library.advanced.org/11902/

Black Baseball's Negro Baseball Leagues

Among the many great African American baseball players were Satchel Paige and Josh Gibson. Did you know there was a time in American history when major league teams didn't allow African American players on the same team with white players? It seems impossible to believe now. These fantastic players competed in what was called the Negro Baseball Leagues. You can find out all about their history and greatest athletes at this excellent site.

http://www.blackbaseball.com/

Fastball - The baseball site for Major League Baseball fans

Do you love major league baseball and hate when the season is over? Then this is the site for you. It is devoted to covering baseball during the off-season and has discussion areas and the latest news for each team. If you are hooked on baseball, this is one site that will make it easier for you to wait for spring training!

http://www.fastball.com/

A B C D E F G H I J K L M N O P Q R S T U V W X Y Z

Louisville Slugger

This maker of legendary baseball bats has a factory in Louisville, Kentucky, but they have a virtual museum in cyberspace, and you can visit it online. In business for over 112 years, they have supplied bats to Babe Ruth, Ty Cobb, and a host of other well-known baseball greats. Players can be very particular about their bats. Some like wood with a narrow grain, while some like a wider grain. They like different weights, different wood stains, and different dimensions. Ted Williams once said his newly received bats didn't feel right. They weren't. When measured, they were 5/1000ths of an inch off his specifications!

http://www.slugger.com/home.htm

ML Players' Uniform Numbers

On April 18, 1929, the New York Yankees introduced numbers on the backs of their players' uniforms. At that time, the number corresponded with the player's position in the batting order. Now one baseball fan has gathered the names to go with those numbers, listing both active and retired numbers and players. But those numbers go far past nine (the number of players in a batting order), and the listing contains more than 1,100 names!

http://www.wp.com/elondon/numbers.htm

Mudball

Austin "Mudball" Taylor's dream is to play baseball in the major leagues. At his Web site, you can follow his personal stats and his training progress through Little League. Check his secret training weapon—but make sure you have your parents' and coach's approval before you try it, and always remember to stretch and warm up first!

http://mudball.com/

The National Baseball Hall of Fame

Visit the Baseball Hall of Fame in Cooperstown, New York! Get information on exhibits and tours, and read *Around the Horn*, the Hall of Fame newsletter. You'll read about Babe Ruth's bat, Mickey Mantle's locker, and the special displays on Women in Baseball. You can also read about the baseball greats who have been inducted into the Hall of Fame as well as see pictures of this year's class of inductees.

http://www.baseballhalloffame.org/

Official Site of Little League Baseball International Headquarters

Do you play Little League baseball? Did you know that the Little League baseball organization has a Web site? This site gives you answers to frequently asked questions about Little League and its history. You'll also find summer camp information, Little League World Series news, and access to the Little League Gift Shop. No Little League near you? Talk Mom and Dad into starting one for you and your friends—contact names for starting the procedure are here!

http://www.littleleague.org/

Professional Baseball in Japan

Let's go, Yakult Swallows! Look out for the Hiroshima Toyo Carp! Baseball is huge in Japan, and this page is the place for information and stats on Japanese baseball. Some of the team's home pages are in Japanese, though.

http://www2.inter.co.jp/Baseball/

The Official Site of Major League Baseball

All the information you'd ever need to settle any World Series argument is here: all the stats, all the teams, everything but the hot dogs. You'll need to hotlist this site right away, because you'll need it all season. Here, you'll find official information on all the major league teams, expanded box scores for all the games, and a great photo gallery! A baseball team shop is here, too, as well as contests for kids and others.

http://www.majorleaguebaseball.com/

Who's On First

"Who's On First?" is one of the all-time great routines by Bud Abbott and Lou Costello, a pair of comedians known for their radio show in the 1940s and 1950s. You can hear their rendition if you visit the Baseball Hall of Fame in Cooperstown, New York. If you can't get there, you can check it out at this Web site.

http://www.ece.uc.edu/~pbaraona/stories/
   abbott_costello.txt

Yankees.com

During the summer, in cities all across the U.S., baseball teams head to the fields, umpires shout to let the games begin, and fans munch on salted peanuts and drink soda while waiting for their favorite team to win the big one. OK, our favorite team is listed here, but if you have another, just type the name in and chances are it will come up. For our team—Go Yanks!—there are listings of all the players, a schedule of the season's games, ticket information complete with a diagram of the park, and lots more. There are pictures of the Yankee greats, including Babe Ruth and Mickey Mantle. You can hear a sound bite of the day Babe hit one out of the park and the famous *New York, New York* played on the organ at the end of each game. It makes us want to head for the Big Apple and a trip to the stadium!

http://www.yankees.com/

BASKETBALL

The Basketball Page for Thinking Fans

All the stats, all the info, all the news about your team, your favorite players, and the game of basketball in general is right here! The most comprehensive schedule for all the NBA teams and when and where they are televised is available. There's also a great file of feature stories that have appeared at this site. Anyone who is a basketball fan will be spending some time checking this place out, we guarantee it!

http://www.alleyoop.com/

Harlem Globetrotters Online

One sports team has played before more people and has won more consecutive games over the last 70 years than any other: the Harlem Globetrotters, of course! Check out these funny athletes at their Web site, and play some fun basketball trivia games while you're here.

http://www.harlemglobetrotters.com/

History of College Basketball

One of the fun things about getting interested in sports is learning all the background info on a team or sport. If basketball is your favorite, this is the place to stop. All the info you want on basketball from 1938 to 1997 is right here, listed by year, by league, by player, and by team. Do you know how many players are ranked between Lew Alcindor (Kareem Abdul Jabbar) and James Worthy? There are 98, between number 1 Alcindor and number 100 Worthy. You'll learn a lot here, so when basketball comes up in a game of trivia, you'll be the champ.

http://www.businesscents.com/cci/

Hoops Nation

There are some people who love to play basketball. Then there are people who eat, sleep, dream, and LIVE basketball. Here are some guys who decided to travel all over the country and find the best places to play a pickup game of b-ball. They even wrote a book about the best courts, and their online diary talks about lots of cities they visited on their 30,000-mile trip. Did they come to your city? Did they beat you and your friends? Send in reports of your favorite place to play hoops; maybe they will come to play! Watch out for these guys—they are good.

http://www.hoopsnation.com/

NBA.com: The Official Site of the National Basketball Association

The official NBA Web site really lets you interact with the players and teams. You can't go one-on-one (yet), but they do have live chat sessions with all your favorite players, which are saved, so if you miss one you can go back and read the transcript! This site also gives you the latest news, schedules, results, and links to the home pages of the NBA teams. You can also read reports in Spanish and French, as well as follow international hoop tournaments.

http://www.nba.com/

A B C D E F G H I J K L M N O P Q R S T U V W X Y Z

A
B
C
D
E
F
G
H
I
J
K
L
M
N
O
P
Q
R
S
T
U
V
W
X
Y
Z

NBL Today - The National Basketball League of Australia website

It's not enough just to follow the NBA and the NCAA if you're a real basketball nut. You have to follow the sport wherever it's played! Head for this site and get the latest information on all the Australian teams, including schedules, standings, statistics, rumors, results, and box scores from the most recent NBL playoff series.

http://www.webtech.com.au/nbltoday/main.asp

Playerfile: Michael Jordan

Normally we wouldn't concentrate on just one sports figure. But for Michael Jordan...well, we just had to make an exception. See Michael dunking the ball. See Michael shooting a free throw. See Michael soaring through the air. See Michael driving around an opponent. See Michael smiling. You've got to love this guy! Then you can click on "Bulls Home" to check out the rest of his team.

http://www.nba.com/playerfile/michael_jordan.html

Women's National Basketball Association

Step aside, Michael. Move over, Shaquille. The women have made their mark in basketball history, and you can read all about it right here. The two-division, ten-team league features top names from college and Olympic play. This site has you sitting courtside, with highlights of the players and their teams. Ask a question, read the stats, and learn the history of the league and of women in basketball. You can even find out how to order a shirt or hat from your favorite team—but check with your parents before you do that!

http://www.wnba.com/

BICYCLES AND BICYCLING
ABA BMX Racing

In the early 1970s, kids in California took their 20-inch Stingray bikes to an abandoned lot and made a movie that started a new sport! They called it Bicycle Motocross, a name that was quickly shortened to BMX. How do you get started in BMX racing and learn the moves and tricks? It's all here, courtesy of the American Bicycle Association.

http://www.ababmx.com/

Bicycle Helmet Safety Institute Home Page

Bicycle helmets make good sense. Fifteen states and more than 55 localities in the U.S. plus all of Australia and parts of Canada require helmets. Other places are studying such laws and may require helmets as well. This all-volunteer organization tells you what types of helmets meet safety standards, where you can get inexpensive ones, and what's new and trendy at the bike equipment trade shows. If your dad is bald or has a very large head, there is advice for him here, too. According to this site, a round, smooth helmet is better than one with points that can snag on pavement. Visit this site for much, much more about bike and helmet safety.

http://www.helmets.org/

Mountain Bike Directory — MtBike.com

This site has been growing in popularity right along with the sport of mountain biking. There are thousands of links to everything from general information about mountain biking to clubs, trips, and classified ads. Looking for a bike? The various brand names are listed along with the URLs for their Web pages. Want to join a club or get one started in your area? Again, there are a number of sites to browse. There are even several magazines and newsletters to check out, some of which are online.

http://www.mtbike.com/

Mountain Biking

Let's say you live in Kansas but go on family vacations to California, and you love to go mountain biking there. Then you see on the news that there are wildfires in Point Reyes, and you wonder what might have happened to your favorite seaside trails. Your local newspapers and bike shops don't have any info on trails that far away, so what do you do? You connect to this Web site and read updates about the trail damage, of course! Here you'll find news, race information, and advice on riding and taking care of your mountain bike. You can also get information about cool mountain bike trails in the United States, Canada, Europe, Latin America, Asia, and Africa.

http://xenon.stanford.edu/~rsf/mtn-bike.html

BOBSLED AND LUGE

The International Bobsled & Skeleton Federation

Talk about fast-moving sports! According to this site, "From a standing start, the crew pushes the bobsled in unison for up to 50 meters. This distance is typically covered in less than six seconds and speeds of over 40 km/h are reached before the crew loads into the sled." This is the official home page of the organization that regulates world bobsled competition. You can find out the history of the sport, the equipment used, and the results of races past and present at this site.

http://www.bobsleigh.com/

Jamaica Bobsleigh... THE HOTTEST THING ON ICE!!

Get ready for some cool runnings at the official Jamaican bobsled team's home page! Since their 1988 Winter Olympic Games debut in Calgary, Alberta, the team has gained in popularity every year. At the Nagano Olympics, they finished 21st. Find out how their true story compares with the tale told in the Disney movie. It's always bobsleigh time at this site!

http://www2.cariboutpost.com/outpost/bobsleigh/

The Luge Home Page

Become a virtual slider as you hurtle down several famous luge courses! On the Lake Placid run, you have to remember to steer the turn that comes after the finish line, too. Find out about the sleds, the techniques, the history, and the standings in this slick, fast sport.

http://www.luge.com/

BOOMERANGS

Aboriginal Steve's Boomerang Page

This should be called Boomerangs for Dummies, because the instructions are very simple and easy to follow. Even Net-mom holds out hope that she might finally get a 'rang to return to her, by close adherence to these rules of thumb, er, wrist, er....

http://www.vcnet.com/abosteves/booms.html

United States Boomerang Association

"Aussie Round," "Fast Catch," and "Maximum Time Aloft" are some of the events you might see at a boomerang competition. Find out which types of boomerangs are best for each event, where you can get them, how you should throw them, and more at this site, to which you'll have many happy returns.

http://www.usba.org/

BOWLING

Professional Bowler Association

You're going to love this Web site. Are you having a hard time finding the latest news stories and results from the PBA tour? At this site, you can get the latest results, tour schedules, and the history of the PBA. The PBA is popular all over the world: tournaments have been held in Canada, Puerto Rico, Japan, South America, France, and England. Chat with other bowling enthusiasts in the real-time chat emporium. Maybe you'll even get to talk to a pro!

http://www.pba.org/

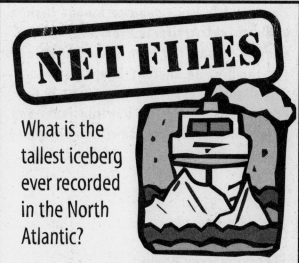

NET FILES

What is the tallest iceberg ever recorded in the North Atlantic?

Answer: According to the U.S. Coast Guard, "The tallest known iceberg in the North Atlantic was 550 feet high, extending out of the water to almost the height of the Washington Monument. This iceberg was sighted in Melville Bay, Greenland from the ice breaker USCGC Eastwind by CDR Dinsmore in March 1957." See a picture of it at http://webtac3.rdc.uscg.mil/iippages/faq/faq11.html

A
B
C
D
E
F
G
H
I
J
K
L
M
N
O
P
Q
R
S
T
U
V
W
X
Y
Z

Sports:Bowling: Complete Bowling Index

At this site, you can get bowling news from around the world, tournament dates and results, plus links to other bowling sites. But there's so much more: equipment, the lists of bowling organizations (including those for the disabled), and the history of bowling. You'll also find a link to information about the National Bowling Hall of Fame and Museum in St. Louis, Missouri. What is the probability of bowling a perfect game? Find out in the Reference section.

http://www.bowlingindex.com/

Bowling has been popular longer than you'd think! Artifacts from a game similar to bowling have been found in the tomb of an ancient Egyptian teen who died in approximately 5200 B.C. Find more interesting bowling facts and milestones at Sports:Bowling: Complete Bowling Index.

BOXING

ESPN SportsZone: Boxing

If you want up-to-the-minute information on boxing, try this page full of boxing news. You can see how your favorite boxer did in a recent fight and see the schedules for future fights. You'll find information on fights and about boxing, including items like a list of the top ten heavyweight boxers.

http://espn.sportszone.com/box/

CANOEING AND KAYAKING

See also BOATING AND SAILING

Bruce's Paddling Page

Paddling is a fun and exciting adventure for the "real outdoors type." This site is from Delaware, and there's some information of local interest, including some neat information on Chesapeake Bay; you can even get the local sea buoy meteorological readings. However, this site also has extensive material for paddlers everywhere. Answers to frequently asked questions, a list of resources, and a checklist of gear you really ought to have are all included. There's even a recipe page full of good "outdoor" eating. Paddle on over!

http://ssnet.com/~bef/BrucesPaddlingPage.html

The River Wild: Running the Selway @ nationalgeographic.com

Some people love to ride down a wild river, working their way through the rapids, braving the dangers of unknown waters. Others just like to read about such a trip. We'll take yet another route—riding the waters on the Internet. "Holy Smokes," "Galloping Gertie"—we're in some mighty fast waters here! They give these rapids some pretty interesting names. Watch it, here we come to "Ping Pong Alley"! That one was "No Slouch"! Don't know about you, but we think it is time for a rest. You forge on ahead if you wish; we'll be there later!

http://www.nationalgeographic.com/
   features/96/selway/

CHEERLEADING
The Cheer Starts Here

Gimme a B and an R and an I-A-N-N-E for Brianne, a student at Concordia College in Seward, Nebraska, who has a great cheerleading page! You can learn cheers and jumps and chants, tryout tips, how to organize a pep rally, and just about everything else you'll need to know about cheerleading. After that it's practice, practice, practice! Parents: There are a lot of links on this page, and we haven't checked them all.

http://www.geocities.com/Colosseum/8339/

Worldwide Cheerleading Homepage

"Hold that line, push 'em back, waaay back!" Sometimes it really helps to have someone cheering a team on. Family and friends are always good at that, but it's also great to have a whole cheerleading squad yelling and screaming for the team. If you are a cheerleader, you'll find some great cheerleading tips here.

http://www.telepath.com/jennifer/cheer/

COACHING

Coaching Youth Sports

You ask your mother to coach your basketball team this year. She says "Yes". As the season gets closer, she starts wondering about what she should do. How can you help? Check out this site, which offers some basic tips about coaching kids in sports.

http://www.chre.vt.edu/~/cys/

CRICKET

CricInfo - The Home of Cricket on the Internet

This site is a gold mine for all things related to the sport of cricket, which has thousands of players and fans around the world. Here you'll find statistics, player profiles, news, match results, and even humor and history. And now you can listen to cricket matches online!

http://www.-usa.cricket.org/

An Explanation of Cricket

What do rabbits, golden ducks, ferrets, and night watchmen have in common? No, we're not talking about Grimm's fairy tales or the night shift at the local zoo. They are all terms used in the sport of cricket. This site provides a good starting point for learning about cricket, the distant cousin of baseball.

http://www.ozsports.com.au/cricket/cricket_exp.html

NET FILES

What is Barbie's last name?

Answer: According to the official Mattel site, "The full name of Barbie® doll is 'Barbie Millicent Roberts.' She is from Willows, Wisconsin and went to Willows High School." Learn more about Barbie at http://www.barbie.com/collectors/guides/fun.html

Lord's, the home of cricket

This site features cricket news with splendid coverage of England's teams and news from everywhere. Lord's is devoted to providing the best coverage of this interesting sport. There's even a game called Kwik Cricket, which has become the rage with children throughout the United Kingdom. Read about it. Who knows, maybe your school could start a Kwik Cricket team!

http://lords.msn.com/

CURLING

Curling at Brown University

What sport uses a 42-pound granite rock and a broom? No, it's not a Flintstones version of stickball—it's curling. How is it played? You bowl a highly polished stone down an ice runway, you see, and try to knock your opponent's stone out of the "house," and your teammates run in front of the hurtling stone and sweep ice crystals out of its way, and…well, maybe you'd be better off going to this site for an explanation. You'll find a history of curling stones and info about the sport, including video clips of curling technique. It also gives links to other curling sites around the Net.

http://www.brown.edu/Students/
Brown_Curling_Club/

A B C D E F G H I J K L M N O P Q R S T U V W X Y Z

International Curling Information Network Group (ICING)

Curling is a game played on ice only in northern countries, right? Wrong! Curling is played all over the world, including South America and the whole region of Australasia. This site offers information about curling history, rules, and equipment, as well as links to organizations and clubs around the world. This is the best site yet for information on the sport of curling.

http://icing.org/

EXTREME SPORTS

Triathlon and triathlete

Some people think the triathlon is the most difficult sporting event of all. Actually, it's three events—running, biking, and rowing—thus the name *tri*athlon. Anyone interested in learning more about the distances involved in triathlon competition should be able to find the answers here. This site also provides links to triathlons around the world.

http://www.triathletes.com/index2.html

Ultramarathon World

What is an ultramarathon? Imagine people running races of 50 miles, 100 miles, even more! Consider the Sri Chimnoy ultramarathon: 1,300 laps around a one-mile loop. Or how about the Trans America Footrace, from Los Angeles to New York? Find out all this and more at this site.

http://fox.nstn.ca/~dblaikie/

The Comrades Marathon, in South Africa, may be the greatest ultramarathon in the world. It was first run in 1921 and now more than 10,000 runners annually participate. The route varies, but the distance is 55.89 miles (90 kilometers), and there is an elevation change of 2,500 feet (762 meters) along the course. Read more about it at Ultramarathon World.

Welcome to Eco-Challenge

It's a 24-hour-a-day, 300-mile race for teams over extremely demanding territory. It may involve running, hiking, scaling cliffs, canoeing, swimming, bicycling, or riding horseback. One of the unusual parts of this competition is that the entire team must finish together. If one team member can't go on because of injury or fatigue, the entire team is disqualified. This grueling race attracts worldwide media attention for environmental concerns, which are highlighted for each region where the race is held. In September 1998, Morocco hosts the Eco-Challenge. Be there, or be here to find out more.

http://www.ecochallenge.com/

FENCING

Fencing home

Everyone likes a great swordfight in the movies: Peter Pan, Zorro, a party of pirates, or a platoon of shiny knights, all jumping here and there, swiping at the opponent, all the while avoiding the other person's sharp sword. Sometimes it's scary, but it's always exciting. The sport of fencing is exciting, too. Fencing is an Olympic sport that is practiced almost everywhere. There may even be a fencing club near you. Find out.

http://www.architecture.ubc.ca:8080/vds96/
    gymnasium/fencing.htm

FIELD HOCKEY

Hockey's Home Page

In 1997, the United States Field Hockey Association (USFHA) celebrated its 75th year of constitutional history. The USFHA has over 11,000 members nationwide and promotes programs such as junior hockey, Olympic development, festivals, and educational programs. Read about some of the key players in field hockey here, and learn about the rules of the game.

http://www.fieldhockey.com/

FIGURE AND SPEED SKATING

Amateur Speedskating Union of the United States - ASU Home Page

When you take up the sport of speed skating, you are guaranteed to be hanging out with some "cool" people! Is it fast? You'd have to be crazy to go this fast. How crazy? Well, let's see: ice, blades, power, speed—sounds just crazy enough to be fun. And it is fun, for everyone from kids to seniors. If you're just thinking about starting, this page fills you in; if you're already a die-hard skater, you'll get advanced details on clubs and special events. It's great exercise, and it makes those long winters (and you) go really fast!

http://speedskating.org/

Figure Skater's Website

The life of a figure skater isn't as simple as it may seem. Many young people decide they're willing to devote the time and energy this sport demands, though. This Web site is especially for them. It lists the rules and regulations of competition, the judges' perspective, a calendar of upcoming events, and a lot more. There is a ton of "how to" articles, exercises for skaters, and links to other skating pages.

http://www.webcom.com/dnkorte/sk8_0000.html

Hockey Skating Tips

This site provides tips for ice skaters, rollerbladers, hockey players, roller hockey players, and others who strap blades or rollers on their feet. Try some of the speed and scoring drills described here, and explore the links off-site. Use your inside edge on your outside skate and shoot in here!

http://www.cs.toronto.edu/~andria/skating_tips.html

Recreational Figure Skating FAQ

What's the difference between a crossover and a progressive? Do you need to know how to execute a closed mohawk? How do you know when your skates need sharpening? At this site, you'll find the answers to these questions. In fact, chances are you'll find answers to most of your skating questions here.

http://www.cyberus.ca/~karen/recskate/

SkateWeb: The Figure Skating Page

Loads of links (some annotated) about the sport of figure skating. All the other figure skating pages link back to this site as "the ultimate." Net-mom appreciates the reference material on this particular page (frequently asked questions, rules, skating organizations, music, and much more), but parents should definitely monitor use of the rest of this site's offerings.

http://frog.simplenet.com/skateweb/reference.shtml

FOOTBALL

The Football Archive

Close your eyes. Breathe deeply and savor the smell of fall. It's football season, and it's time to read up on some of the history of the game, some of its greatest players, and a few of the plays used by your favorite team. You can also read about the top 50 players in the history of football. You can ask the questions you have and search the site for a particular team or moment in football history. It's all here, football fans, and this site was built by kids for the ThinkQuest contest. Enjoy!

http://library.advanced.org/12590/

Netguide: Superbowl special

Even before the season begins, football fans are ready to choose the teams that will make it to the Super Bowl. Whatever you like about football, there's probably plenty of information about it for you at this site. They also have a ton of links to other football pages, including the home page of each team in the league, fan pages for teams and players, and lots more!

http://www.netguide.com/
    special/superbowl/home.html

NFL.COM

The official NFL site provides the latest headlines and league statistics and even offers an opportunity to chat with the players. In the Fan area, you'll also find a complete digest of NFL rules (in English, Thai, Chinese, and Malay), the Pro Football Hall of Fame, and a library of historical facts and timelines.

http://www.nfl.com/

A B C D E F G H I J K L M N O P Q R S T U V W X Y Z

A
B
C
D
E
F
G
H
I
J
K
L
M
N
O
P
Q
R
S
T
U
V
W
X
Y
Z

NET FILES

Has a bird ever won a military medal?

Answer: At least one has. Cher Ami, a carrier pigeon, served in World War I and was awarded the French Croix de Guerre with Palm for his heroic service between the forts of Verdun. He died in 1919 as a result of his battle wounds. He was one of 600 birds owned and flown by the U.S. Army Signal Corps in France during World War I. His body was mounted and preserved and is now part of the Smithsonian Institution collections in Washington, D.C. At *http://www.si.edu/resource/faq/nmah/cherami.htm* you can read more about the exploits of this brave bird and the final message he carried.

Welcome to The Junior Seau Foundation

Junior (real name: Tiaina) Seau is a linebacker with the San Diego Chargers football team. He's also a really good guy who has his own foundation, and he helps a lot of people. Some of his projects include child abuse prevention efforts, drug and alcohol awareness, and programs to stop juvenile delinquency. On his Web site you can play some interactive games combining his native Samoan with football!

http://www.juniorseau.org/kids.html

FOOTBALL—AUSTRALIAN RULES
AFL Official Web Site - Home Page

This game resembles rugby. There are 18 people on a side, they use an oval ball, and they score by kicking the ball. This official Web site is a virtual photo scrapbook of your favorite Australian rules football players in action!

http://www.afl.com.au/home/

Australian Rules Football Frequently Asked Questions

What is the oldest form of "football"? Australian rules football dates back to the 1850s and predates American football, rugby, soccer, and Gaelic football. This site provides an overview of Australian rules football and lets you take a look at Australian football trading cards. It also answers a burning question: what is the Australian equivalent of the hot dogs that are eaten at American football games? The answer is Aussie meat pies!

http://www.ozsports.com.au/Football/FAQ4.html

FOOTBALL—CANADIAN RULES
OFFICIAL CFL WEB SITE HOME PAGE

Visit the official Web site for the Canadian Football League! Read the rules, the latest CFL news, and a history of the CFL. You can also look at a list of CFL records and awards and see the CFL Hall of Fame. There are also links to other sites on the CFL.

http://www.cfl.ca/

GYMNASTICS
Welcome to Gymn, an electronic forum for gymnastics!

Know the results of the gymnastics world championships and other current events by tumbling over to this site! Do you like to read articles about gymnasts? Would you like a list of gymnastics magazines with order forms? Find them here. You can take gymnastics trivia tests, too. Did you ever wonder about the "chalk" you see gymnasts rub on their hands? It's magnesium carbonate, and they use it to absorb sweat so that they won't lose their grip on the equipment.

http://gymn.digiweb.com/gymn/

Welcome to USA Gymnastics Online!

When the U.S. women's gymnastics team appeared at the 1996 Summer Olympics, it was truly a magical event! Their skill and courage inspired many kids. Where are they now? Keep up with the U.S. teams and other events in gymnastics at this site.

http://www.usa-gymnastics.org/

ICE HOCKEY

See also the Hockey Skating Tips *entry under* SPORTS—FIGURE AND SPEED SKATING

The Exploratorium's Science of Hockey: Home

There you are—center ice at the San Jose Arena. Join the San Jose Sharks as they explore the science of one of the most exciting sports. You will soon learn a lot about the game, starting with the surface it's played on. For example, did you know there is a difference between fast ice and slow ice? Fast ice is harder and colder with a smoother surface, while slow ice is warm and soft and may have a rough surface. Follow the Sharks as you learn about the ice, the skills, the equipment, and more. And when your mom tells you to be careful with your teeth, listen—she knows what she's talking about!

http://www.exploratorium.edu/hockey/

Why are rainbows so frequently seen during summer and not so frequently during winter?

Answer: To see a rainbow, you've got to have both rain and sunshine. In the winter, water droplets freeze into ice particles that do not produce a rainbow but scatter light in other very interesting patterns. Learn more about rainbows at *http://www.unidata.ucar.edu/staff/blynds/rnbw.html*.

NHLPA Home Page

You and a friend are talking hockey, but you disagree on the number of goals your favorite player has scored this season. Where do you go for the answer? The NHLPA site provides player stats for each NHL player, and these stats are updated each day! You can find pictures, personal information, stats for this season, and stats from past seasons—just like online hockey trading cards. And there's more. Check this site for the weekly hockey trivia challenge. Answer the questions correctly, and you may win an autographed NHLPA replica jersey.

http://www.nhlpa.com/

Welcome to Zamboni!

OK, hands in the air: how many of you really have the secret fantasy of driving the Zamboni around the ice rink? You know, that big machine that magically lays down a new layer of smooth ice for you and your friends to skate on. Net-mom usually plays "Slamboni" instead, at <*http://www.sikids.com/ games/slamboni/index_v1.html*>, but now she has discovered the official Zamboni site. You can learn the history of the company (they celebrate their 50th birthday in 1999), buy some cool Zamboni merchandise (including the fabulous "Zamboni Crossing" sign), and check out the trivia. For example, did you know that the top speed of a Zamboni ice resurfacing machine is 9 mph?

http://www.zamboni.com/

The Women's Hockey Web

This site provides player profiles, tournament results, and loads of links. You can also hook up with a hockey camp and score with a collectible hockey-related phone card or sports trading card, if that's your goal.

http://www.whockey.com/

WWW Hockey Guide

This site pulls together information about hockey from all over the Web, linking to over 1,100 other hockey sites. Would you like a list of all Stanley Cup finalists since the Stanley Cup started in 1893? How about a visit to the Hockey Hall of Fame? You'll find that here, as well as all official and unofficial home pages for your favorite National Hockey League teams. You can see the latest hockey news from ESPN or *USA Today*, too. If you can't get enough information about hockey, start with this site!

http://www.hockeyguide.com/

A
B
C
D
E
F
G
H
I
J
K
L
M
N
O
P
Q
R
S
T
U
V
W
X
Y
Z

A B C D E F G H I J K L M N O P Q R S T U V W X Y Z

JUMP ROPE

U.S.A. Jump Rope Federation

As easy as skipping rope? This competitive sport takes skill, and the U.S.A. Jump Rope Federation has all the info. Jump right in—there are photos and descriptions of some of the skills you'll need, plus links to famous jumpers and teams around the world. There are also jump rope camps and clinics all over. Maybe one is coming to your area soon; check here.

http://www.usajrf.org/

MARTIAL ARTS

Black Belt For Kids

Brought to you by the publishers of *Black Belt* magazine, *Karate Kung-fu Illustrated* magazine, and *Martial Arts Training* magazine, this site has interesting articles, schedules of events, lists of martial arts schools, and links to other sites. This link will take you to their Black Belt for Kids page. Remember, though, that the empty-handed master defeats another warrior with the most powerful weapon: the mind. Warning: This page is very graphics-heavy, so you may want to turn off automatic image loading.

http://www.blackbeltmag.com/bbkids/

Judo Information Site — Judo

Are you interested in judo? If you'd like to learn more about its history or see the results of tournaments like the World Judo Championships, then this site is for you! You'll find links to dojos and judo schools and e-mail addresses of other people who are interested in judo. There are also interesting links to Zen koans and other sources of martial arts inspiration.

http://www.rain.org/~ssa/judo.htm

THE MARTIAL ARTS MENU PAGE

Parental advisory: This site has hundreds of links to other martial arts sites on the Web, and you should explore this with your child. This is a very comprehensive starting point to information about martial arts around the world. You'll find sites for judo, karate, aikido, jujutsu, ninpo, wing chun, tai chi, and much more!

http://www.mindspring.com/~mamcgee/
   martial.arts.html

TKD Reporter Home Page

Would you like to read articles about tae kwon do, karate, hapkido, and other martial arts? The Tae Kwon Do Reporter is an online magazine that has martial arts news from around the world, a list of martial arts schools, and articles on training and techniques.

http://www.taekwondoreporter.com/

Welcome to International Judo Federation

Just opening this site is fun! There are some cool animations right from the start, as well as some really great pictures in the photo section. Judo's been around for more than 100 years, and it is one of the more popular Olympic sports for spectators. Now there are judo tournaments for men, women, and children. Read about the world championships, Olympics, and the World Cup.

http://www.ijf.org/

NETBALL

NETBALL AT THE AUSTRALIAN INSTITUTE OF SPORT

According to this site, the most popular women's sport in Australia is netball. The sport started in England way back in 1898. Before 1970, it was known in Australia as "women's basketball." It's like basketball, except it's played with something more like a soccer ball. It can be played on wood floors, grass, cement, or artificial surfaces, which may be either indoors or outdoors. Today, there are more than two million netball players in the world. Australia has won six world championships, more than any other country. Find out the history and rules of netball here!

http://www.ausport.gov.au/aisnet.html

If you forgot the words to "gopher guts" try lyrics in MUSIC AND MUSICIANS.

OLYMPICS

The Ancient Olympics

When you think of the Olympics, chances are you picture Atlanta or Nagano, lots of brightly colored uniforms, and men and women competing in a lot of different events. Well, the ancient Olympics were much different. There were fewer events, and only free men who spoke Greek could compete, instead of athletes from any country. Also, the games were always held at Olympia instead of moving around to different sites every time. This site tells you a lot about all of the Olympics and has a lot of very interesting information. A similar resource is at Dartmouth at <*http:// devlab.dartmouth.edu/olympic/*>.

http://olympics.tufts.edu/

Official Olympic Winter Games Site Nagano '98

The 1998 Winter Games were in Nagano, Japan. We just loved the official mascots for the games— Snowlets! These four birds represented the owls found in the forests of Nagano. Owls are found throughout much of the world, and they are a Greek symbol of wisdom, so they seemed like a good symbol to Net-mom. If you click in the "Fun" section, you can play some games with the Snowlets! This site has lots of information and photos about the Nagano games and the various medal winners.

http://www.nagano.olympic.org/

the olympic movement . le mouvement olympique

Here is the official site for the Olympics, where you can explore the past, present, and future of the Games. When new Olympic cities are announced, you can read news and updates here first. For example, the 2004 Summer Games will be held in Athens, Greece. You can keep track of progress through the Olympic.org page or go directly to the official link they provide at <*http://www. athens2004.gr/*>.

http://www.olympic.org/

Salt Lake Organizing Committee for the Olympic Winter Games of 2002

Did you go to the 1996 Olympics in Atlanta or the 1998 games in Nagano? Did you enjoy the experience? Are you wondering when the Olympics will come again to North America? The XIX Olympic Winter Games will be held in Salt Lake City, Utah, February 8–22, 2002! This site gives information on where the events will be held and where the Olympic Village will be located. If you live in the Salt Lake City area, there is information on how to join the volunteer program for the 2002 Olympics.

http://www.slc2002.org/

The Sydney 2000 Olympic Games

Where are the next Summer Olympics? In the year 2000, athletes will gather in Sydney, Australia! The official Sydney Olympics 2000 site is the place to go for early information. Approximately 5.5 million tickets will go on sale in 1999, and this site will be the first to provide information about ordering tickets. You'll find a lot of info here now, including an explanation of what the logo means.

http://www.sydney.olympic.org/

RACQUETBALL

The United States Professional Racquetball Association

You've wanted a racquetball racket for a long time, and finally you spot one at a garage sale. It needs new strings, but you're not sure if it can be restrung or if it's junk. What do you do? The USPRA Web site provides handy tips on restringing racquets and offers links to information about Olympic racquetball, official rules, and the schedules for televised racquetball on ESPN. You'll also find tips on improving your backhand stroke, and you can ask a certified referee all your tricky rule questions.

http://www.uspra.com/

A B C D E F G H I J K L M N O P Q R S T U V W X Y Z

ROWING AND SCULLING

See also BOATING AND SAILING

Rowing Frequently Asked Questions

"Stroke! Stroke! Stroke!" That's the call of the coxswain as the rowers propel the shell (that's what those sleek racing vessels are called) ahead in a race for the finish line. Rowing is a sport particularly enjoyed by colleges and university teams around the world, with many amateur clubs as well. There are several variations on the sport, and the boats, equipment, and rowers are different in many cases. Did you know that rowers are grouped in heavyweight and lightweight classes? Learn all about the sport of rowing here.

http://riceinfo.rice.edu/~hofer/Rowingfaq.html

RUGBY

Rugby Today

If you don't know anything about rugby, then this site is a good place to start. It gives you basic information about rugby, a short history of the sport, and a little bit about rugby in the U.S., as well as a link to the official World Cup site. Rugby is a fast-moving team sport played with a ball that looks like a football, only slightly larger. You also can't pass forward. And don't forget, it's not a scrimmage, it's a scrummage!

http://www.rugbynews.com/rnt.htm

SHUFFLEBOARD

National Shuffle Boarder's Association

Shuffleboard has been called Shovegroat, Slide-groat, and Shovel-penny in its long history. Though popularized in retirement communities, it's a fun game for all ages, combining skill and strategy. It's also good exercise! You can find the rules, top player rankings, tournament schedules, and more at this Web site. Work on your "schnog," and "slide and glide" on over!

http://www.duke.edu/~ishy/shuffle/

SKIING

Approved Surface Conditions Terms...

You're reading the ski reports for your favorite slopes, and the descriptions just don't make any sense! What is frozen granular? What is corn snow? Is it even worth getting out your equipment? If you check that report against the definitions provided at this site, you'll learn that corn snow, typical in spring conditions, is made up of large ice granules, which are loose when the temperature is above freezing but which freeze together if the temperature gets any colder.

http://www.travelbase.com/skiing/peek-n-peak/
   surface-term.html

GoSki — The Worldwide Snow Sports Guide

It's Friday, it's snowing, and your dad is calling you on the phone. "Pack the gear," he says. "We're going skiing this weekend." Not only is that a cool idea (especially if you've just purchased a snowboard with your summertime lawn mowing money), but your dad says you can pick the spot. Surf on over to the Web and type in this URL. You'll quickly discover why it's the place to be when you're looking for a place to be. It has listings of every ski area in every state, plus a ton of them in foreign countries. Hmmm...do you suppose Dad and Mom would care to head to Mount Parnassós in Greece? Parents: This site prints personal reports from skiers, so please proceed with caution.

http://www.goski.com/

A Resort Sports Network

You want to hit the slopes—but there's no snow. You can at least dream about it and see how much snow is on the ground at ski resorts across the U.S. and Europe. This site offers pictures taken daily at ski resorts, as well as weather forecasts. Come in out of the cold and ski the Net!

http://www.rsn.com/

Chase some waterfalls in EARTH SCIENCE.

The SkiCentral - Skiing and Snowboarding Index

They stay up all night, working in the freezing cold. They mix proteins into water and make "whales." Nothing pleases them more than the sight of fresh powder. Who are they? They are the folks who run the snow-making equipment at ski resorts! Did you know that dirty water makes better snow than clean water? This site is packed with information and articles about skiing, snowboarding, racing, clothing, and equipment, plus links to hundreds of other skiing and snowboarding sites. Parents: There are hundreds of links here, so explore with caution.

http://www.skicentral.com/

SkiNet

Get the latest in skiing techniques, reports on snow conditions, and skiing news from the editors of *Ski* magazine and *Skiing* magazine. You can even read articles from the pages of these magazines and join the SkiNet mailing list. The Technique area (click on the box at the bottom of the page and scroll to "technique") has a list of the top 100 ski instructors in the U.S. There are also online beginner tutorials for kids, teens, and tots.

http://www.skinet.com/

U. S. Ski Team Online

If you are a fan of the U.S. ski team, you can follow the standings, write to your favorites, and pick up the latest news about the slopes and competitions worldwide at this site. You'll also learn about the different styles of ski competition (Alpine, Nordic, disabled, freestyle, snowboard) and find out how you can get your own multicolored leopard hat like the Olympic champions wore at Nagano!

http://www.usskiteam.com/

SKIING—FREESTYLE
Fall-Line Mogul Skiing

Interested in learning about mogul skiing? Do you want to approach your first mogul run and not fall down? You'll find a great tutorial called Fall-line Mogul Skiing here, especially the "How to Cope with Moguls" section.

http://easyweb.easynet.co.uk/~michaell/skier/ch15/

Freestyle Skiing Venue

Imagine ballet on a tilted stage that's almost three football fields long, where the dancers turn cartwheels and do handsprings wearing skis and ski poles! Welcome to the strange world of freestyle, or acro/ballet, skiing. This site gives a good description of this winter sport, which now includes water pools at the bottom of the run—hard to believe, but true.

http://www.wintersports.org/freestyle/

SKIING—NORDIC SKIING
Cross Country Ski World

Are you interested in cross-country skiing but don't know how to start? This site is packed with information on the world's oldest skiing sport, including a special section just for junior skiers. You'll find out how to choose equipment, how to wax for various conditions, and competition results from around the world.

http://www.xcskiworld.com/

If you don't know your klister from your kick wax, better glide on over to Cross Country Ski World! There are lots of tips for skiing families about waxing and ski technique.

A B C D E F G H I J K L M N O P Q R S T U V W X Y Z

Sidebar: A B C D E F G H I J K L M N O P Q R **S** T U V W X Y Z

SKIING—SKI JUMPING

JUMP - Ski Jumping Archive

Welcome to this site, created by a ski jumper. Get up-to-date information on the World Cup and other ski jumping competitions, and check out the links to other ski jumping sites. There are four phases to the ski jump (no, they are not approaching the jump, looking at the jump, screaming, and running away): you have the inrun, the takeoff, the flight, and the telemark landing (one foot in front of the other). If you doubt that humans can fly, look at the photos at this site!

http://www.cdnsport.ca/jump/

SNOWBOARDING

Jump into Snowboarding

Just when you think they've done just about everything crazy on snow, up comes a new sport. This one is called snowboarding, and we thought we'd slide on over to this ThinkQuest Junior site (built by kids) and see what it's all about. The sport began in the early 1960s when an eighth grader in shop class decided to try a new way of heading down a snowy hill. The first snowboard was made of plywood; now they're fiberglass. This site tells you all about the special language used by snowboarders—try an "Indy Grab on a Halfpipe, Dude"—as well as the six snowboarding events in the 1998 Olympic competition.

http://tqjunior.advanced.org/3885/

Snwbrdr's Snowboarding Page

Snowboarding just keeps getting more popular and more respected by athletes. It's fun but not easy, and advanced boarders can do some amazing tricks. Find out who's ruling, where, and how at this great site in Finland. And check out those sweet action photos!

http://www.snwbrdr.com/

SOCCER

Federation Internationale de Football Association

Federation Internationale de Football Association (FIFA) is the organization behind all the World Cup and other official international soccer competitions. You'll find authoritative team standings, a history of FIFA, and lots of soccer news at this site. You'll also be able to read the official rule book, called the Laws of the Game (there are only 17 rules). Soccer, football, whatever you call it—what a kick!

http://www.fifa.com/

MLSNET: The Official Site of Major League Soccer

In North America, it's called soccer, but elsewhere in the world it's called football. Confused? Don't be—it will all become clear to you if you visit the Major League Soccer Web page. From there you can link to team pages, check standings, news, and more. You'll be able to see video highlights of great plays, hear interviews, and enjoy other multimedia treats if you have the right browser plug-ins.

http://www.mlsnet.com/

Soccer - AYSO Home Page (Main)

Still wondering why the sport is called "soccer" in some countries and "football" in others? OK, we'll tell you. The sport started as football in England. By the time it became popular in other parts of the world, some countries already had sports known as football: the U.S. had American football, and Australia had Australian rules football. In countries where football was already played, the sport became known as soccer, short for "association football," the original name for the sport in England. You can also visit the American Youth Soccer Organization from this site.

http://www.soccer.org/

The Soccer Patch

Does your soccer team have a patch? Or maybe you've gotten a different patch for each tournament in which you've participated. Is your team patch displayed on this page? If not, send it in! They have over 760 patches now, from all over the world! There are also lots of links to kids soccer pages, team pages, and news and information about the sport.

http://www.soccerpatch.com/

SPECIAL OLYMPICS

Special Olympics International

"Let me win, but if I cannot win, let me be brave in the attempt." This is the oath of the Special Olympics. What great inspiration this is for all athletes, not just "special" kids with physical, mental, or other challenges! The first International Special Olympic Games was held in 1968, at Soldier Field in Chicago, Illinois. It was organized by Eunice Kennedy Shriver. Since then, the Special Olympics have become the world's largest year-round program of physical fitness, sports training, and athletic competition. In the U.S., games at the local and chapter levels are held every year, with special summer and winter events held every four years.

http://www.specialolympics.org/

SQUASH

THE INTERNET SQUASH FEDERATION

Do you love squash? Yum: Hubbard, summer, acorn—even zucchini! But we're not talking veggies here; we're talking about the fast-paced game of squash ball, sort of like racquetball, except the court, equipment, and rules are different. All the rules are here, including those governing clothing, equipment, and more. Player profiles, tournament schedules, even satellite broadcast schedules are here. Also, you can keep up with the latest news on the campaign to make this an Olympic sport.

http://www.squash.org/

World Squash Federation

Squash has been played for over 130 years. You'll find a neat history of the game here, which explains that the name derives from the way the ball "squashes" against the wall as it hits! You'll also find the rules of the game as well as rankings.

http://www.squash.org/WSF/

SURFING

Surf - Global Oceanic Surf Links - Mountain Man Graphics, OZ.

This is the real thing, not this waterless digital surfing we've all gotten used to. Big surf, land surfing, swells—it's all here. See a live picture of Sunset Beach on Oahu, or check wave conditions in Australia. See some gnarly GIFs or check some equipment reviews. Keep scrolling—there are surf cams and beach reports from surfing cultures all over the world! A caution to parents: Not all links have been checked.

http://magna.com.au/~prfbrown/tubelink.html

NET FILES

What are "Moki Steps" and where can you climb them?

Answer: In the 1200s was a flourishing culture of cliff dwellers called the Anasazi in southwestern Colorado, in a beautiful place called Mesa Verde, now a national park. To climb from their cliffside homes to the top of the mesa to get water and harvest crops, they used the Moki Steps, which are handholds and footholds built right into the vertical cliff faces—hundreds of feet above the canyon floor. The Anasazi carved these in the rock in such a way that anyone who started climbing down with the wrong foot would be stuck halfway down! Travel back in history to http://artseek.com/anasazi/MesaVerde.html and read more about the Anasazi cliff dwellings and other mysterious places.

Surfrider Foundation USA

This organization is working to protect our coastlines. In addition to information on the group and its mission, you'll get numerous resources for surfers and some nice pictures and music clips. You can even take a look at today's waves on the Southern California coast. The resource list of links can send you coast to coast (USA), off to Hawaii, and all over the world. It's awesome, dude, hang ten!

http://www.surfrider.org/

SWIMMING AND DIVING

Open Water Swimming Tips

OK, you like to go swimming. The school pool is good, when that kid in the other class isn't there to do cannonball dives on your head. The backyard pool is nice, when the filter works. And you love the open water at the lake. But better yet, there's the ocean: the sand, the sun, and the surf. All of these are great, but open water swimming is not the same as swimming in a pool. For one thing, sometimes you can't even see the bottom under you! And there are other things to deal with, like the choppy water, the current, and those green, slimy things floating by. Here's the page that tells you all about swimming in the open sea. You'll find tips on everything from getting ready to swim to racing, plus good commonsense information on how to deal with hazards. The number one rule is never swim alone (but you can visit this site alone).

http://www.mindspring.com/~beyondwords/ owstips.htm

SWIMNEWS ONLINE

Do you swim? We're not talking about an occasional wade through the baby pool. We're talking about competitive swimming. You know: pruny looking fingers, webbed toes, red eyes, and gills. If that's you, then you need to see this online magazine! Virtually every major swim meet in the world is here, and the results are updated regularly. You'll find features on the world's best swimmers, and all the world records are here, too. Links? You bet. This is the diving platform for your lane.

http://www.swimnews.com/

Giorgio Lamberti of Italy swam the 200-meter freestyle in the world record time of 1:46.69 seconds on August 15, 1989. Will the record be broken soon? Who's favored in the next world championships?

The only real news is up-to-date information. Get the latest at SWIMNEWS ONLINE.

The Yellow Pages of Swimming

Are you a swimmer? Would you like to go to other swimmers' sites? Then this is the place for you: over 220 links to Web sites related to swimming and diving! You'll find governing bodies for swim competitions, college and high school swim team pages, swim club news, and more. Look for water polo, synchronized swimming, coaching, rankings, and triathlete links here, too.

http://www.netutah.com/swimlinx/

TABLE TENNIS

INTERNATIONAL TABLE TENNIS FEDERATION

At this official site, you will find official rules, championship and rankings information, and lots of table tennis links. This game has been around a long time. Around 1900, it was also called gossimar and whiff-whaff. By the way—did you know there's a way to fix dented ping pong balls? Put the balls in a pan, cover with a towel, pour hot water over them, and let them sit for about an hour. There, good as new!

http://www.ittf.com/

TENNIS

The Tennis Server

Would you like free tips from a tennis pro? Would you like to know how to avoid tennis elbow? Would you like information on tournaments, players, rankings, and equipment? How about links to other tennis sites? You get all this and more when you go to the Net for the WWW Tennis Server.

http://www.tennisserver.com/

How did a space-borne spider's web influence the design of earthly tennis racquets? Find out at the WWW Tennis Server, under equipment tips!

TENNIS WORLDWIDE

This Net magazine offers a world of information on tennis. Television schedules for tournaments, sources of supplies, and rankings are all here, plus feature articles, like how hard a junior player should practice! You'll also find info on wheelchair tennis, tennis camps, racquet repair, jokes about tennis, and more.

http://www.tennisw.com/

TRACK AND FIELD

Athletics Home Page

Who is the world's fastest Norwegian? Who is the best overall Italian athlete? What's the Moroccan record in the high jump? If you are a track and field statistics nut, then this is the site for you. It lists world's records, indoor and outdoor, for men and for women, as well as track and field records for many nations.

http://www.hkkk.fi/~niininen/athl.html

The Official Boston Marathon Web Site

What is the world's most well-known race? A lot of folks would argue it's the Boston Marathon. Learn its history and facts about the next race at this official site. You'll view video clips, see a map of the 26.2 mile course, and more! The first race was in 1897, and since then runners have only been able to improve on the winning time by 48 minutes, despite all the high-tech shoes and training methods they have now.

http://www.bostonmarathon.org/

Road Runners Club of America

Runners can find a mile and a half of track at this site! Online articles and magazines about running are appearing all over the Internet. This site links you to them and also gives you a list of other resources, including their own publications. The club is involved in a wide range of activities. There is general information on the club, their services, and an interactive map to let you find the local clubs and events in your own area. If you enjoy running and you want to stay current on running and amateur sports news, then jog on over!

http://www.rrca.org/

A
B
C
D
E
F
G
H
I
J
K
L
M
N
O
P
Q
R
S
T
U
V
W
X
Y
Z

A B C D E F G H I J K L M N O P Q R S T U V W X Y Z

The Running Page

Running can be a sport, a hobby, or an exercise. This is a nicely organized page for all kinds of runners, from casual to serious. There are many links to a wide variety of running sources, and even one to a chat site for runners. Serious runners can find race results, columns geared toward their level of interest, and lists of publications, frequently asked questions, and clubs. You'll also find articles and links on ultramarathons as well as running injuries. Basically, you can run in here to see what's new "out there." It's another way of getting from where you are to where you want to be!

http://sunsite.unc.edu/drears/running/running.html

Welcome to USA Track & Field

USA Track and Field is the governing body for track and field competition in the United States. This site gives you news on the latest happenings in track and field, with links to other sites. You'll really enjoy seeing the U.S. Track and Field Hall of Fame and reading about record performances and the athletes who made them (records are in the "Numerology" section). This is a great source for short sports biographies, too.

http://www.usatf.org/

TRACK AND FIELD—POLE VAULT

VaultWorld Pole Vault Page

What is the single most important thing in pole vaulting, besides getting over the top of the bar? Pole vaulters and coaches answer this and other questions at this site. You can even give your own answers to these questions. By the way, not all vaulters agree on the most important thing, but most of them agree that it is speed. You'll also find the top 100 vaulters, some great animations, and a place to trade used poles!

http://www.vaultworld.com/

VOLLEYBALL

NCAA Volleyball

The *USA Today* women's volleyball page provides the latest information on the sport. Want to know the latest National Collegiate Athletic Association (NCAA) volleyball rankings? How about information on volleyball win streaks? Check the sports stats and tournament schedules—it's all here!

http://www.usatoday.com/sports/volleyba/svcw/svcwd1.htm

Volleyball World Wide

Is beach volleyball an Olympic sport? Yes, it was, for the first time, in the 1996 Atlanta Olympics. What is wallyball? Where can you find information on international volleyball? What teams will play in the volleyball World Cup? If you love volleyball, start with this site, which has general volleyball info, including TV schedules, and links to organizations like USA Volleyball, Federation Internationale de Volleyball, and professional and college volleyball.

http://www.volleyball.org/

WATER POLO

United States Water Polo

Water polo is your favorite game and you love to watch a local college game every week. But your mom says you're moving, and you're worried there won't be a water polo club where you're going. What do you do? Check this site and find one. This official page offers rules and regulations, links to college and club teams, and other resources. Don't get in over your head with all the water polo info here!

http://www.uswp.org/

WATER SKIING

Canadian Water Ski WWW Page

Remember when water skiing was just a boat, two skis, and a lake? Oh yeah, and a skier, too. You might be surprised to see all there is to water skiing these days. Luckily, this page covers many different aspects of water skiing and answers many questions. Sure, you'll find plenty of material on traditional skiing, including slalom and jumping, and also links to barefoot and kneeboard sites. Did you think they would forget wakeboarding? It's here, too. You'll also find pictures here, and they are pretty exciting. You can even submit your own picture. (Hint: Don't take a picture of yourself while you're holding that tow rope. Get someone else to do it!) Parental advisory: There are lots of links here, and we didn't visit them all.

http://www.utoronto.ca/ski/water/

NET FILES

Where can you buy the rare *black tulip?*

Answer: You can't—it doesn't exist. According to this site, "The search for the fabled black tulip has been an epic quest for centuries. In 1850 Alexander Dumas, famed French author of 'The Three Musketeers' and 'The Man in the Iron Mask,' captured the popular fancy with 'The Black Tulip,' a romantic tale in which a fictional black tulip figures in a love story laced with murder...Dutch hybridizers have achieved some very, very deep purples. But achieving a true black tulip, say the experts, is not possible (yet still worth the try!)." For more tulip trivia, visit http://www.bulb.com/basics/mainfaq.html

WIND SURFING

windsurfer.com

If you're interested in boardsailing, you need to see this site, which has the expected tips on sailing, race schedules, world rankings, and links to other Web pages on this topic. But you'll also find a list of user reviews of various boards and user recommendations on the hottest travel destinations. Maps and other regional information will help you decide on where to beg your parents to take the next family vacation. You'll also find a handy calculator, which will convert knots to miles per hour, pounds to kilograms, feet to meters, and several other measurements. And if you're new to this sport, check the beginner's guide, called "Learn to Windsurf." Parental advisory: This site has many unchecked links.

http://www.windsurfer.com/

WRESTLING

Amateur Wrestling by InterMat: The Ultimate Amateur Wrestling Resource

You know, you don't have to look like Hulk Hogan to wrestle as an amateur. Lots of people participate in this sport, in all different weight classes. For the latest in international, collegiate, and high school wrestling, including rankings, try this site! Parental advisory: This site contains many unchecked links.

http://www.intermatwrestle.com/

Sumo Wrestling

Sumo wrestling has been practiced for over 1,500 years. Its origins stem from religious rites, which were matches performed to please the gods. Many ritual elements remain, including the symbolism of the *dohyo*, or wrestling ring. Above the ring there is always a roof resembling a Shinto shrine. Four giant tassels hanging from each corner signify the seasons of the year. At this site you can learn about sumo wrestling history, culture, and champions.

http://www.sumo.or.jp/index_e.html

The Web's Best of Amateur Wrestling by Tom Fortunato, Rochester, NY

This site will get a *hold* on you if you're into wrestling. Find info on the international, collegiate, high school, and youth wrestling scenes, and also unusual stuff like Mongolian wrestling, Celtic wrestling, and more. Check the Wrestling stamps from around the world and links to photo archives.

http://www.geocities.com/Colosseum/Sideline/9563/

Let balloonists take you to new heights in AVIATION AND AIRPLANES.

A B C D E F G H I J K L M N O P Q R **S** T U V W X Y Z

STAR TREK, STAR WARS, AND SPACE EPICS

The 2001 Internet Resource Archive

"Good afternoon, gentlemen. I am a HAL 9000 computer. I became operational at the H.A.L. lab in Urbana, Illinois, on the 12th of January, 1992." Long before we had Picard and Kirk and before we had Luke Skywalker and Princess Leia, we had HAL, the killer computer on the spaceship in *2001: A Space Odyssey*. This movie was released in 1968, and it explored the differences between humanity and technology. The story is told in a free-form kaleidoscope of images and sounds, and years later, people are still arguing about what it all means. This site gives you a lot of famous audio clips from the movie, as well as pictures and links to other resources about the film, including a HAL birthday Web site featuring the book's author, Arthur C. Clarke.

http://www.palantir.net/2001/

The Klingon Language Institute

How many languages do you speak? Have you checked the batteries in your universal translator? If you saw a snarling Klingon warrior, what would you say? Are you worried that your opportunities on the Klingon homeworld are limited because of the language barrier? If so, then this site is the place for you!

http://www.kli.org/KLIhome.html

PEOPLE Online - 30 Years of STAR TREK

In September 1996, the original *Star Trek* crew got back together for a 30th year anniversary party. *People* magazine was there to cover the event, and you can read some of the interviews and see how everyone looks now that they have retired from Starfleet service. Try the trivia quiz to see how good you are, and remember, Vulcans have green blood!

http://pathfinder.com/people/sp/trek/

STAR TREK: CONTINUUM

Resistance is futile. First this official site was free and open to all. There was much rejoicing. Then the Microsoft Network swallowed up most of the great *Star Trek* info that Paramount used to offer for free. You could still get to it if you were a subscriber to the Microsoft Network and had a password there. This year (1998) Net-mom is excited because it looks like the site is open to all again. All the great old stuff looks like it is there. It has plenty of new stuff too. Check it out.

http://www.startrek.com/startrek.asp

Star Wars: Welcome to the Official Web Site

Who is your favorite character in the *Star Wars* saga? Is it Jedi Knight Luke Skywalker, or do you prefer that scoundrel Han Solo? Maybe you'd like to be like courageous Princess Leia and have a couple of happy-go-lucky droids like C-3P0 or R2-D2 to give you a hand. Whether you like the old or the new digital version of these sci-fi classics, you're really going to like this Web site! There is also news about Episode I, the upcoming new movie. Visit the National Air and Space Museum's Star Wars: The Magic of Myth site at *<http://www.nasm.edu/StarWars/>*.

http://www.starwars.com/

Starbase 907 — Starfleet Ship Registry Database

Can't tell a Galaxy-class ship from a Miranda-class ship? Have you always wondered where the USS *Bozeman* went for 80 years? This site lists over 18 classes of Starfleet ships. Within the classes, you'll find descriptions, Starfleet ship registration numbers in that class, and some ship histories. Also check out photos of the new *Enterprise-E* from the movie *Star Trek: First Contact*.

http://www.webzone.net/rowan/sb907/ssrd/

U.S.S. Jaguar

Have you always wanted to be a crew member on a Starfleet mission? At this free online club for kids, you can—but first you have to pass a *Star Trek* trivia test. Son of Net-mom (Junior Lieutenant Oten'nan) really enjoys the mailing list, which includes discussions on real-life transporters, the uselessness of Borg assimilation techniques, and general rants about the Ferengi.

http://worldkids.net/jaguar/

NET FILES

How many yards of fabric have been used to make Barbie clothes since her debut in 1959?

Answer: According to the official Mattel site, "More than 105 million yards of fabric have gone into making Barbie® fashions. That makes Mattel one of the largest apparel manufacturers in the world!" Get more fun Barbie info at http://www.barbie.com/collectors/guides/fun.html.

SUMMER CAMPS

Camps & Conference Homepage

Any search of the Web will bring up well over a thousand summer camp home pages in the U.S. and elsewhere. What's nice about this site is that they feature a highly organized listing of many top-notch camps, organized by region or type or even alphabetically. You might be looking for a performing arts camp in Northern California, a ranch camp for girls in Texas, a space camp in Florida, or a listing of dozens of Boy Scout camps in Virginia. Whatever kind of summer camp experience interests you, you'll find detailed listings for each of the camps, including phone numbers, addresses, and sometimes even photographs. A "Camp-O'-The-Week" is featured here every seven days, plus links to environmental and outdoor educational centers, retreats, associations, online magazines, and a detailed calendar.

http://www.camping.org/

Peterson's: Summer Programs

Get your older brother or sister to apply for a job at camp! Peterson's (the educational directory publisher) posts lists of summer jobs here, mostly at summer camps, for both older teenagers and young adults. Phone numbers and e-mail contact addresses are included, making this a good place to look for that first-time job. There are also links to the American Camping Association's Directory of Accredited Camps and lots of information for international students. Your parents may want to explore the rest of the items at this comprehensive educational directory. They will find everything from K–12 schools to colleges, from studying abroad to career information.

http://www.petersons.com/summerop/

U.S. Space Camp

It's light years away from any other camp experience! You can visit Space Camp here on the Web and see pictures of some of the things kids (and adults) get to do there. How would you like to ride a space shuttle simulator or build your own satellite? Beam yourself up to this site; you'll definitely find intelligent life here!

http://www.spacecamp.com/

NET FILES

When the twenty-first century arrives, Fiji will be one of the first places to welcome it. Do you know why?

Answer: Fiji lies just west of the international date line. Thus, as the world turns to the first day of the new century, Fiji will enter that new day before most of the rest of the world. An 1879 ordinance moved all of Fiji west of the date line, with one foot in one day and the other in tomorrow. Kind of eerie, huh? Read about it at http://www.en.com/users/laura8/tav.html.

TELEPHONE

Inside AT&T Labs

Ever wonder how your telephone works? This site gives you an overview of what takes place when you make that call to your great-grandparents in Cleveland. You did remember to thank them for sending those cool handkerchiefs for your birthday, right? You'll also learn about fiber optics, Alexander Graham Bell, and what the phone company's going to do when they run out of phone numbers. There are also some fun interactive games to try.

http://www.att.com/attlabs/brainspin/

Telephony History

The name of this page is pronounced "teh-LEFF-oh-knee." If you're like most people, all you know about how a telephone works is that you talk in one part and listen through another. The rest of it is magic. When you're through checking out everything on this page, you'll know more than you ever dreamed there was to know about the telephone! This page contains links to the Alexander Graham Bell Home Page, the history of the telephone page, and an antique phone page. You'll find sites on telephone and communication technology from Sweden and France plus the Smithsonian Information Age exhibit page. Home pages for virtually all of the long-distance carriers and the big "baby bells" are collected here at the Media History Project.

http://www.mediahistory.com/phone.html

TELEPHONE BOOKS

AT&T Internet Toll Free Directory

You have a suggestion for a new toy, so you want to call the new products division at Mattel. How do you get the number? No problem. Fire up this Web site and search for the name Mattel, or look in the Toys and Games category. While not quite as thorough as AT&T's voice directory assistance, this handy Web tool features an easy-to-use interface. Search for toll-free numbers by category or name with a simple click.

http://www.tollfree.att.net/

BigYellow - The Biggest Online Yellow Pages Directory!

Do you need to look up a business somewhere? Why drag out that hefty telephone book, when this Web page is available? Let your mouse do the walking as you scour through millions of business listings in the U.S., organized by company names, categories, and even (yes!) phone numbers.

http://www1.bigyellow.com/

Four11 Directory Services

The name of this site is pronounced "Four-One-One." From the main menu, click on the Telephone area. If you're looking for a phone number, this resource has over 100 million! There are also directories of celebrities and famous folks in sports, entertainment, business, and government. You'll find lots of other cool services, too, such as free Web-based e-mail accounts.

http://www.Four11.com/

WhoWhere? Phone Numbers & Addresses

Finding addresses and phone numbers should always have been this easy. You can also find people's e-mail addresses and home pages with the search tools here. Another cool thing is to find other people interested in the same things you are—or people who went to the same school, or summer camp. That's called the "Communities" feature, so check it out! You can also find business home pages, toll-free phone numbers, and more (we find something new every time we visit). There are also English, French, and Spanish versions of this page. And if you didn't find who you were looking for, WhoWhere will keep looking and e-mail you if your friend ever turns up in the database.

http://www.whowhere.com/wwphone/phone.html

Did the groundhog see his shadow? Find out if it will be an early spring in HOLIDAYS.

TELEVISION

Emmy® Awards—Academy of Television Arts & Sciences

Have you ever heard the song by Bruce Springsteen, "Fifty-Seven Channels and Nothin' On"? Sometimes nothing good seems to be on TV, but many good shows are available. An organization called the Academy of Television Arts and Sciences selects some of the best programs and gives the winning shows and actors an award called an Emmy. To see who the most current winners are, check out this Web page. You'll learn television history, see who is being nominated, and get a behind-the-scenes look at the annual Emmy awards show.

http://www.emmys.org/tindex.html

MZTV Museum of Television / MZTV Musée de la Télévision

At the 1939 World's Fair in New York City, it was a big deal to have a TV camera pointed at you and to watch your image turn up on a nearby monitor. In fact, they gave everyone a little souvenir card to mark the event; it read: "This is to certify that (your name here) was televised at the RCA exhibit building New York World's Fair...." Why was this so unusual? In 1939, most people had never seen television before. NBC's first broadcast was on April 30, 1939. TV sets were expensive ($2,000 to $6,000 in the equivalent of today's dollars) and bulky. Find out all about the early history of TV at this online museum.

http://www.mztv.com/

Television History

Whether you're looking for the inventions that led to the development of television or the technologies that make direct satellite TV broadcast possible, you'll get a series of excellent links here. There are resources on general broadcasting technology as well as thoughtful essays on what we all have gained, and lost, through the spread of TV culture.

http://www.mediahistory.com/teevee.html

NETWORKS AND CHANNELS

C-SPAN

If you want to see the U.S. government at work, you'll see it here. Hearings, meetings, legislative sessions: this site will tell you what C-SPAN will be showing, and when. There are also classroom activities and lesson plans for the teachers among you. And aren't we all teachers, really? All you kids are teachers, and every truly great adult teacher knows that.

http://www.c-span.org/

CNN Interactive

CNN, the 24-hour news channel, has made it easy and fast to get the news of the moment over the Internet. And it's in a multimedia format that brings you lots more than words. You'll find that QuickTime movies and sound turn up in the most amazing places! Look for them in stories about belly-flop contests as well as space shuttle dockings. And if you want to know more about the news CNN is covering, you can link to thousands of newspapers, magazines, and broadcasts from all over the world. Don't forget that CNN covers entertainment, sports, style, and other fun stuff. Check out Billboard's weekly Top Ten list, featuring sound clips of each popular song.

http://www.cnn.com/

For breaking news, we can't steer you anywhere else but to CNN Interactive. Check here for updates on news as it happens. You can also look over a video archive of cool QuickTime movies. Search for your topic—there is probably video on it at this site!

A
B
C
D
E
F
G
H
I
J
K
L
M
N
O
P
Q
R
S
T
U
V
W
X
Y
Z

A
B
C
D
E
F
G
H
I
J
K
L
M
N
O
P
Q
R
S
T
U
V
W
X
Y
Z

Discovery Online

You'd expect to find background articles on many of the Discovery Channel's programs here, and you'd be right. There are stories and pictures from shows on history, nature, science, and people. Here are some examples: You can visit a baseball factory in Costa Rica or take a close-up look at elephants. There is even a Keiko-cam to let you keep an eye on the *Free Willy* whale. And there's more: links to The Learning Channel and Animal Planet programming and a way to search the archives of past fascinating stories!

http://www.discovery.com/

ESPN SportsZone

Hey, sports fans! If you're really into sports, then you probably already know about ESPN, the all-sports cable TV network. They do the same great job on their home page as they do on their network. This site offers the latest, up-to-the-minute sports news, scores, and game summaries. Let's say your favorite team is in Seattle and you live all the way across the country on the other coast. Chances are, it's a pain in the neck to get the latest news, stats, and player profiles on your favorite team. Hey, relax. Tune in to the "zone" and get it all right here: college, amateur, pro. They cover it all, and they let you talk back. After all, you have to make your opinion known, right?

http://espn.sportszone.com/

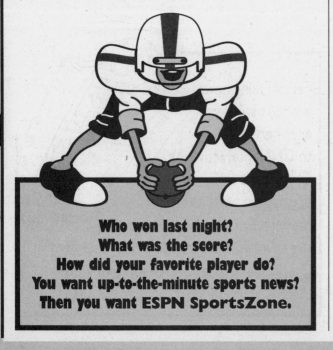

Who won last night?
What was the score?
How did your favorite player do?
You want up-to-the-minute sports news?
Then you want ESPN SportsZone.

FOX KIDS

This network is a favorite for Saturday morning and after-school entertainment. You may like *Power Rangers, Goosebumps,* and *Toonsylvania* among others. You can find some fun sound files and get news on the shows and contests here. This *sounds* like just the place for you!

http://www.foxkids.com/

NASA Television on CU-SeeMe

Did you know there is a NASA channel, where you can watch broadcasts from the space shuttle mission or whatever else NASA is broadcasting today? If you have the right kind of Internet connection, you can watch this stuff right on your computer screen! All you need to know is right here on this home page, where you'll also get a programming schedule.

http://btree.lerc.nasa.gov/NASA_TV/NASA_TV.html

Nick at Nite & TV Land

Everyone loves this stuff: *The Munsters, The Mary Tyler Moore Show, Bewitched, I Dream of Jeannie*...good ol' classic TV. Download the clever and funny ads used on the network. It's fun TV you can watch at night, and now you can visit those wacky characters on the Web. Lucy, I'm home!

http://www.nick-at-nite.com/

Nickelodeon Online-The Web Site for Kids

Ooze into this Web site, but please avoid the mess Ren and Stimpy made! Find your way into the TV Shows area to read up on the latest with all your favorites: *Kablam, Alex Mack, AAAHH!! Real Monsters, Doug,* and those wacky guys *Keenan and Kel.* Download some cool games for Macintosh or Windows, and make sure the rest of your family notices the links to Nick Jr. and Nick at Nite! Probably the most important part of this site, though, is The Big Help. Find out how you can get involved in cleaning up the environment, helping in your community, and making our world a better place to be.

http://www.nick.com/

PBS Online

If it's on PBS, it's educational, entertaining, excellent, or all three. Viewers support their local public stations, and these stations provide quality local programs as well as programs from PBS (Public Broadcasting Service). From Muppets to money, PBS brings us important issues and delightful special events. The Web site invites you to investigate what's on the schedule, what's going on inside the network, and what to try on in the network store. The online news reports keep you up to date, and links to your local station keep you in touch. Look for all the PBS kids shows in the Kids' area of this site. Did you know that you're the public? So it's your network!

http://www.pbs.org/

Sci-Fi Channel: The Dominion

If it's not of this world, then it must be from the sci-fi zone: UFOs, monsters, and vampires, *Star Wars*, Buck Rogers, *The Twilight Zone*, and all that cool stuff. It's far out—it's waaaaayyyy far out—and it's all out there on the Web. Can you get there? Can you get program schedules, highlights, and series information? Affirmative! Are there pictures, landscapes, sounds, and science fiction video clips? The sky isn't even the limit. There's a Schedulebot that knows what's on the Sci-Fi Channel right now; just look under the animated broadcasting tower and click on your area of the country. You'll also find a live chat area, where you can talk to actors, such as James Doohan, from the original *Star Trek* TV series. Explore the site beyond all others. Set your coordinates. Warp factor nine. Engage!

http://www.scifi.com/

UltimateTV — United States of America Television

A collection of all U.S. broadcast networks is here. If the network has a home page, you'll find a link to that. If the network has e-mail, you'll find that as well as fax and voice phone numbers and addresses. The cable broadcast and satellite channels are also listed, but you should peruse this list with your parents.

http://www.UltimateTV.com/tv/us/

The Weather Channel - Home Page

How's the weather where you are, or anywhere else, for that matter? Actually, anyone can find out just by visiting this page. Sure, you'll find up-to-date weather information from around the world, but that's only the beginning. This site has more weather stuff than anyone could imagine. It includes shareware to download, colorful maps, video clips, tips on getting started as a meteorologist, and special forecasts for sports fans. This site is really cool (in the north) and hot (down south)!

http://www.weather.com/homepage.html

Welcome to Warner Bros. Animation!

It seems like Warner Brothers has been making cartoons forever! Here's where you'll find their latest shows, the schedules, and even a historical look at some of the most famous cartoons of all time. But that's only part of this site. You'll find games to play and download, and you'll get a fascinating look at how cartoons are made. Stop in whenever you want to see, hear, or watch your favorite cartoon characters online, because the pictures, sounds, and video clips are right here. Shows included are: *Animaniacs, Freakazoid!, Pinky & The Brain, The Sylvester & Tweety Mysteries, and Earthworm Jim,* among others. Don't miss the karaoke songs!

http://wbanimation.warnerbros.com/

PROGRAMS

Barney

It's here: a site that celebrates Barney and all his pals! You'll find photos, merchandise, fan page links, audio, games, coloring pages, and more.

http://www.barneyonline.com/

Beakmaniac's World

Beakman is a kid's personal scientist. He answers questions that kids can't get the answers to in school, like stuff about embarrassing body functions or why cats purr. The show was canceled by CBS, but it lives on at this site. For answers to questions about the show, visit here. For some of your science questions, try the companion home page, You Can with Beakman and Jax, at <*http://www.beakman.com/*>.

http://www.geocities.com/TelevisionCity/Set/4567/

A B C D E F G H I J K L M N O P Q R S T U V W X Y Z

A
B
C
D
E
F
G
H
I
J
K
L
M
N
O
P
Q
R
S
T
U
V
W
X
Y
Z

Bill Nye the Science Guy's Nye Labs Online

It's Bill Nye the Science Guy, and is he loaded with science goodies to show you! If the graphics are too much, stop the page after part of it loads and click the TEXT Menu option. There are photos, sounds, and movies (caution: these are big files) in the Goodies area. Check out Today's Demo or visit the U-Nye- Verse to see what's happening in Bill's world of science. Lots of experiments and lessons on things scientific can be found here, plenty of fodder for your next science fair project. TV listings are also available if you want to find out when he's on the tube. There is even a chat area where you can post comments and see if anyone replies.

http://nyelabs.kcts.org/

Charlie Horse Music Pizza

Whether it's the waltz, the tango, or the fugue, it's served at Shari Lewis' Music Pizza Parlor. On the show, you can learn about musical instruments, while at this site you'll find coloring pages, games, and project activities. These change from time to time. Recently they had very silly jokes here such as the following:
Shari: Did you know it takes three sheep to make a sweater?
Lamb Chop: I didn't know sheep could knit!

http://www.pbs.org/charliehorse/

NET FILES

What country is considered to have the most skilled labor force in the world?

Answer: According to the Belgian Embassy, "Belgium has the most skilled labor force in the world and the most productive in Western Europe, having held this record for the last 15 years." Read much more about Belgium and its list of accomplishments at http://www.diplobel.org/usa/geninfos/didyknow.html

Clarissa Explains it All

We love to listen to Clarissa explain her rather strange life. It sounds more and more like ours all the time! They made only 65 episodes of this show at Nickelodeon, but we never tire of watching them. We've even been to the set complex at Universal Studios in Florida—OK, so we're fans, but we think perhaps you are, too. The Nick page on Clarissa is no longer available; we think this fan's resource is good.

http://www.ee.surrey.ac.uk/Contrib/Entertainment/
    Clarissa/

Encyclopedia Brady

The Brady Bunch is one of those TV shows that just seems to go on forever. Just about everybody has seen at least a few of the original episodes, featuring Marcia ("Marcia, Marcia, Marcia!"), Greg, and all the rest as they struggle through life in suburbia. If you're a Brady Bunch fan, this site is just for you. Included here are details about the Brady Bunch that would inform even the most dedicated Brady follower! For example, although the series was filmed on a sound stage, the exterior shots are of a real house. The address (near Los Angeles) is here, along with real Brady trivia, like the mysterious connection between the show and *Gilligan's Island*, another popular show.

http://www.primenet.com/~dbrady/

Ghostwriter - Welcome Page

What is Ghostwriter, anyway? The kids don't really know, but Ghostwriter "talks" to them by rearranging whatever printed words happen to be around or by using the computer keyboard. At this site you can meet the rest of the original Ghostwriter team and learn how they solve mysteries! Descriptions of the shows are included (teachers will like the classroom activity suggestions that correspond to the shows). You'll also find a complete list of all the Ghostwriter books and videos. The only surprise is that Ghostwriter doesn't have an e-mail account. You have to send snail mail, and the address is here. There's a NEW Ghostwriter series broadcast on CBS, and you can read about the cast and play some word puzzles at its home page at *<http://www.ctw.org/ghostwriter/>*.

http://www.pbs.org/ghostwriter/welcomepage.html

Mister Rogers' Neighborhood

This beloved TV show has entertained three generations of neighborhood visitors and has won every broadcast award there is. Kids have fears, dreams, hopes, and feelings—just like everyone else. Fred Rogers has always understood that, and his Web site shows that care and detail. He has everything from play activities (just right for your preschooler brother) to his favorite song lyrics to an annotated book list. Read Rogers' biography and hear a message from him. Don't miss the history of the show, and learn what happened when viewers were invited to the studio to celebrate Daniel Striped Tiger's birthday.

http://www.pbs.org/rogers/

The Morphing Grid — Power Rangers WWW Homepage

Who do you think is the best Power Ranger? According to the survey here, it's Tommy the White Ranger. The leader of the Power Rangers, Tommy stands for all things good and true. Did you know he started as a Green Ranger, lost all his power, and was reincarnated? Of course you knew that, because you love the show and really loved the movie! Who do you think is the best monster? Kids here have voted for Rito Revolto, younger brother of Rita Repulsa, who is married to Lord Zedd, of course. And the best villain is Lord Zedd himself, followed by Ivan Ooze. Learn all about the shows, discover powerful links, and discuss morph technology and other cool stuff with fans of the series.

http://ic.www.media.mit.edu/Personal/manny/power/

Newton's Apple Index

This insanely great science program covers everything from earthquakes to garlic, from the Hubble Space Telescope to the redwoods. We wish they listed the programs by topic so that all the Astronomy topics, for example, were together. Maybe they will, if they read this. You'll love the Science Try-it section, where you can learn to make your own barometer, and have fun with a Möbius strip.

http://ericir.syr.edu/Projects/Newton/

The Official Thomas The Tank Engine & Friends Web Site

Do you know *Thomas the Tank Engine & Friends*? If you're a fan of *Shining Time Station,* then you'll love the coloring book pictures and information on Thomas and the whole gang. The popular series used to be on PBS but moves to Fox in the fall of 1998. New shows are being produced, and new Really Useful Engines are being introduced on this site.

http://www.thomasthetankengine.com/

The Rosie O'Donnell Show!

Net-mom's visited the Rosie O'Donnell Show! Unfortunately, Rosie wasn't there. In fact, nobody was there except for the guide and 20 other people on the NBC tour in New York City. Still, Net-mom was able to gawk at the set, including the desk, the chairs, and the Coney Island roller coaster replica. If Rosie's your favorite talk show host, you should definitely see her Web page. You can find out who's going to be on the show, reminisce about who has been on (and see pictures!), and play a couple Shockwave games. Ask Rosie's Magic Ball anything you want, and see what it says. Let's see…Will Net-mom be invited to be on the show this year? The Magic Ball says: "YES—if you're good!"

http://rosieo.warnerbros.com/

Sesame Street Central

Home to the *Sesame Street* Web site, here you'll also find a link to the CTW (Children's Television Workshop) preschool series *Big Bag*. Numerous activities are here: an interactive storybook, online games, and coloring pages. Be sure to click on the topics button to go to a list of advice and tips from experts. This site has laughs for parents, too!

http://www.sesamestreet.com/sesame/

Want a snack? Learn to make one in COOKING, FOOD, AND DRINK.

A B C D E F G H I J K L M N O P Q R S T U V W X Y Z

A
B
C
D
E
F
G
H
I
J
K
L
M
N
O
P
Q
R
S
T
U
V
W
X
Y
Z

The Simpsons

Bart is just a good kid with a "few bad ideas...that are still being reviewed by the Springfield district attorney." Better get over to the official Fox Network Simpsons Web page before you have a cow! You'll find some fun Simpsons games, news about the show, and contests here in virtual Springfield.

http://www.foxnetwork.com/simpsons/simpson2.htm

Skinnamarink TV

You can watch Sharon, Lois, and Bram's *Skinnamarink TV* show on The Learning Channel and some PBS affiliates. You may know them from *The Elephant Show* or their lively recordings. Now they "run" a whole TV channel called Skinnamarink TV. Their broadcast "day" includes exercise shows, cooking shows, crafts, and of course music! Sometimes they push The Big Red Button on the control panel and then there's no telling what will happen. Hey, there's a Big Red Button on this Web page. What will happen if you push it?

http://www.skinnamarink.com/

Teletubbies

According to this site, "Tinky Winky, Dipsy, Laa-Laa and Po are four technological babies...[who live in] Teletubbyland, which hums with the play technology that supplies their every need: Tubby Toast, Tubby Custard, and a conscientious comic vacuum cleaner, Noo-Noo." Net-mom has never seen the show, but she has it on good authority that it's a real hit with the preschool set. The games offered on the Web site include simple matching and sequencing fun. Want more activities? "Telly-Tubbies" are on in the United Kingdom, too. Try the official British Broadcasting Corporation (BBC) site at *<http://www.bbc.co.uk/ education/teletubbies/logo.htm>*.

http://www.pbs.org/teletubbies/

The Theodore Tugboat Online Activity Centre

Here's a tugboat with a smile and appealing eyes, straight from the TV series. Toddlers will love the interactive story, in which they get to choose what happens next. Downloadable coloring book pages sail via the Net to your printer or graphics program. Little ones can even get their own postcard in the mail from Theodore Tugboat himself!

http://www.cochran.com/theodore/

TV Party tonight!

Back in the good old days, there were television shows the likes of which you have never seen. Well, until you visit this Web site, that is! You can actually view clips of some of those old shows and read about a lot more. Many of them were aired live, and no tapes exist. The names Tom Terrific, Soupy Sales, Wonderama, Scrub Club, Winky-Dink and You, Mighty Hercules, Jot, and Pinky Lee may mean nothing to you, but your parents and grandparents will have heard of them. Begin the journey into the yesteryear of television and discover these fascinating folks for yourself.

http://www.tvparty.com/

The UltimateTV Show List from UltimateTV

Are you a big fan of *Bewitched* or *Lost in Space*? Maybe you just love TV! If only you could find a Web site listing all the TV shows from the old days, and all the TV shows from today, and all the Web pages that are dedicated to them, and—STOP! That would have to be the grandest TV list of all. That would have to be the ultimate TV list, which this is! This list has over 10,461 links for 1,339 shows! Wondering if there's a Web page, FAQ, or newsgroup devoted to your favorite show? If there is, you can get there from here. Parental advisory: Just as you guide what your kids watch on TV, guide them in using this site; not all shows are appropriate, and not all links have been checked.

http://www.ultimatetv.com/UTVL/

The Web Site of Pete & Pete

What could be crazier than two brothers, both named Pete? Their surreal adventures, of course! This unofficial fan page has everything you've always wanted to know about the Wrigley family, including speculation on where they live. Don't miss the quotes from superhero Artie, the Strongest Man in the World, fond of such words of wisdom as "Physics makes me strong!"

http://www.cs.indiana.edu/entertainment/ pete-and-pete/

Welcome to Goosebumps!

Are you a fan of R. L. Stine? His *Goosebumps* series is the subject of this home page. Follow creepy links that lead you to Stine's biography, his photo, and the transcript of an online Halloween chat with Stine. Also read a ghoulish chapter from recent books in his series. Did you know you can get *Goosebumps* from TV? A link includes synopses of the TV episodes, identifying the book featured. Did you hear a noise? We're sure we heard something....

http://place.scholastic.com/goosebumps/

Where in Time is Carmen Sandiego?

It was late, and I was on my way to my office on an evening with snow coming down like caramel corn. Shaking the stuff off of my mukluks, I headed over to warm my hands by the hot computer. Yes, Acme Timenet was still booted up from this morning. It seemed so long ago. Like so many times before, I wanted to check the latest on Carmen and her gang. Later, gumshoes....

http://www.pbs.org/wgbh/pages/carmen/

Wishbone

How can a little dog know so much about literature? This PBS series features a Jack Russell terrier with a big imagination. You'll find descriptions of all the shows, the classic literature on which they are based, and suggested activities.

http://www.pbs.org/wishbone/

The X-Files

Are UFOs and extraterrestrials for real? *The X-Files* is a make-believe TV show about two FBI agents trying to answer that question. Join Special Agents Fox Mulder and Dana Scully as they investigate UFOs, extraterrestrial sightings, and many other bizarre cases. This Web site has in-depth character sketches, episode descriptions, and information about the show. A caution to parents: Some of the show descriptions are graphic.

http://www.TheX-Files.com/

Zoom

Zoom is a wonderful show for kids of all ages. That's not surprising, because kids help produce the show! Learn all sorts of "kid lore" like clapping games, crafts, embarrassing moments stories, and more. Then there are the jokes. Ah, the jokes. Example: What goes in one hole and out three holes? A person putting on a T-shirt. Get it?

http://www.pbs.org/wgbh/zoom/

SOUNDS AND THEMES
TV Jukebox

If it's been on TV in the last 30 years or more, then the theme song is probably at one of the sites listed here. If you want to see your mom and dad act nostalgic, just play some tunes, such as the theme song from *Captain Kangaroo* or *The Mickey Mouse Club.* Are you looking for a great TV sound bite for your computer's start-up sound? Then get here and start browsing! Another "hit" can be found at <*http://www.filecity.com/midi/television/*>. And you won't need to argue over the words to *Gilligan's Island* when you can check them for yourself at <*http://www.geocities.com/Hollywood/Academy/4760/*>.

http://stl.interspeed.net/TvJukebox/

NET FILES

Idaho has an official state horse. What breed is it?

Answer: It's the spotted Appaloosa! Possibly originating with the Nez Perce Indians, "Appys" can be seen today in parades, on ranches, and in horse shows. The coloring of the Appaloosa's coat is distinct in every individual horse and ranges from white spotted hips to a full leopard look all over. Find more fascinating facts at http://www.state.id.us/gov/symbols.htm

A
B
C
D
E
F
G
H
I
J
K
L
M
N
O
P
Q
R
S
T
U
V
W
X
Y
Z

A
B
C
D
E
F
G
H
I
J
K
L
M
N
O
P
Q
R
S
T
U
V
W
X
Y
Z

STATIONS

UltimateTV — US Television Online

Is your favorite local television station on the Internet? Maybe you can e-mail them with your complaints and your compliments. Maybe they have a Web page full of information on their news team. Maybe you can find out what's on tonight. Never mind maybe—this is the place to find out if they are on the Net! This site lists U.S. television stations that have Internet addresses. In many cases, mail addresses, fax and voice phone numbers, and Web pages are included. TV stations are there to entertain and serve you, so keep in touch!

http://www.ultimatetv.com/tv/us/stations1.html

UltimateTV — World Television

Where in the world can you find a television station that has an Internet address? Right here! A growing number of television stations and resources around the world are joining the Internet and "logging in." Some have e-mail capabilities and even Web pages. Find your favorite station, or just look around for someplace interesting. What's on TV in Iceland? You could find out here.

http://www.ultimatetv.com/tv/

You just found out your family's going to visit Great-Auntie Gwen in Great Britain! You're pretty excited, but then you realize you're going to miss two weeks of your favorite shows on Nickelodeon! What do you do? Before you get too depressed, check the UltimateTV—World Television page. It will tell you what TV stations and networks are available, all over the world! Nickelodeon is broadcast on cable channels in the United Kingdom, so hope that your great-aunt has cable. (But, you know, you should get out more.)

TIME

CALENDARS

@ February 29 LEAP DAY - LEAP YEAR 1996

Were you born on the leap year day, February 29? Your birthday only comes around every four years! When it isn't a leap year, do you celebrate your birthday on February 28 or March 1? Find other people facing the same dilemma. There are also fascinating resources from the Royal Greenwich Observatory about leap years and calendars in general.

http://www.clark.net/pub/stroh/leap.html

A Base for Calendar Exploration thru Time

"Thirty days hath September, April, June, and November. All the rest have thirty-one, except...." Except what? And when? It's about *time* someone came up with a site devoted to calendars! You will learn some fascinating information here, including the origins of the seven-day week, calendar structures and changes, and much more. By the way, what began above ends like this: "...excepting February alone: which hath but twenty-eight, in fine, till leap year gives it twenty-nine." Click on "An introduction to calendars" and learn all about the "Thirty days" rhyme.

http://ghs1.greenheart.com/billh/

Calendar

If you've ever needed a quick calendar, for, say, the year 1753, or maybe the year 3000, or anything in between, you'll love this site in Norway. Key in the year you want (try the year you were born), and like magic, a calendar is generated. Be sure to read the technical information on how the calendar program works.

http://www.stud.unit.no/USERBIN/steffent/kalender.pl

CalendarLand

Are you looking for a new calendar, or maybe an old one? This page has calendars that will calculate moon phases, holidays, and many other types of date-watching delights. You'll also find Islamic, Hebrew, Chinese, and other cultural or religious calendars. There is downloadable software, links to pages of interest (lots on the year 2000), including one on Calendar Reform (click on "reform"). Did you know that some people think we should have 13 months in the year? Others propose 12 equal months, with "blank days" that don't belong to any month at all and are celebrated as world holidays. One result of this idea is that you wouldn't need a new calendar every year, because the dates would always fall on the same days of the week. Calendar manufacturers are probably not happy with the idea.

http://www.calendarzone.com/

This Day in History - From the Archives of The History Channel

The date is May 4. The year is 1979. Do you know what was happening in world history? Margaret Thatcher was being elected prime minister of England. "This Day in History" will let you time-travel anywhere you want. In 1626 on this day, Governor Peter Minuit made a great deal on his purchase of a 20,000-acre island—what is now Manhattan, New York City. The price was $24 worth of cloth and brass buttons. Just punch in any date and year and see what bit of history you can learn.

http://www.historychannel.com/thisday/

Today Date and Time

"Today is Sunday, August 9, 1998. EDT is 4:53 PM. This is the 221st day of the year. Year of the Earth Tiger. Month of the Earth Ram. Day of the Earth Rat. Hour of the Metal Monkey. 18th day of the 6th month. Year 223 of American independence. 47th year of H.M. Elizabeth II, Queen of Canada....2nd year of the 694th Olympiad...Buddhist Year 2541...." There is more. Did anything interesting happen today in history, movies, or literary history? What's the current population of the world? What's the total national debt? Know about the moon phase? How about tidal charts? How much time until the next space shuttle launch? It's all collected for you here.

http://www.panix.com/~wlinden/calendar.shtml

CLOCKS

Earth and Moon Viewer

This isn't really a clock, but it will show you where it's day and where it's night—right now—all over the planet. Besides, this is one of our favorite places on the Internet. We hope you think so, too!

http://www.fourmilab.ch/earthview/vplanet.html

Foam Bath Fish Time

Kevin Savetz plays with bathtub foam fish toys. You will, too, at this site, which will tell you the time in several time zones—using FISH. Just get in here and see one of Net-mom's all-time favorite Internet toys.

http://www.savetz.com/fishtime/

Make a Two-Potato Clock

We just can't resist putting this page in the book. It gives you complete directions to make a clock powered by two potatoes. Be sure to have an adult help you with this, though. Will it work with other vegetables or fruits?

gopher://gopher.schoolnet.ca:419/00/K6.dir/
   trycool.dir/clock

Sundial Generator

Before we had digital clocks, even before we had analog clocks with hands, we had sundials. They didn't work very well when it was raining, and they also didn't work very well unless they were precisely "tuned" to your latitude. Since commercial sundial companies pretty much standardized on latitude 45, that left the rest of the world scratching their heads and asking each other, "Hey, anybody got the time?" This Web page changes all that. If you know your latitude, or even if you only know where you live, you can generate a perfect sundial for your area. Cut it out and follow the instructions for its use. Remember, sundials "count only sunny hours."

http://weber.u.washington.edu/~jlks/dial/

A
B
C
D
E.
F
G
H
I
J
K
L
M
N
O
P
Q
R
S
T
U
V
W
X
Y
Z

Time Service Dept.

The U.S. Naval Observatory in Washington, D.C., is the official timekeeper for the United States. This site is tied into the official clock—clocks, actually. U. S. Naval Observatory timekeeping is based on several unusual clocks: cesium beam and hydrogen maser atomic clocks. You can find out more about these at this site. They also use a network of radio telescopes to make sure they are always right on time. Why is that so important? Well, if a rocket engine burns a second too long, the rocket may end up miles from where it should be. Or if one computer sends a message but the other computer isn't "on" to receive it yet, that's a problem. These clocks are correct to the nanosecond level, which is a billionth of a second! At this site, you can also calculate the sunrise, sunset, twilight, moon rise, moon set, and moon phase percentages and times for a U.S. location.

http://tycho.usno.navy.mil/time.html

A Walk Through Time

Until about 5,000 or 6,000 years ago, there was no need to know the exact time. When the sun rose, people woke up and worked at getting food, fuel, and shelter. When it got dark, people went to bed. Nobody needed to ask "Is it time for *Seinfeld* yet?" or "Am I late for school?" At this site you can follow the evolution of timekeeping and clocks, from the Sumerians right up until today.

http://physics.nist.gov/GenInt/Time/time.html

The World Clock

Hey, what time is it, anyway? Are you curious about the clocks in Copenhagen? Or maybe you want to make inquiries in Istanbul. This page gives you the current time in over 100 locations on the globe! If you keep watching it, the page will automatically update every minute.

http://www.stud.unit.no/USERBIN/steffent/
 verdensur.pl

If you wonder whether tomorrow will ever come, just check The World Clock. You can find out where it's already tomorrow, in time zones all around the world!

GEOLOGIC TIME

Geology Entrance

Just when was the Paleozoic era? Find out here as you learn about how geologic time is measured and how the science of geology began. Remember, the oldest rocks are on the bottom!

http://www.ucmp.berkeley.edu/exhibit/geology.html

MILLENNIUM

The 21st Century and the Third Millennium

Many people think that we'll be celebrating a new millennium on January 1, 2000. Don't be fooled by false millennia! This site explains why that is not true and why there is still time for you to get New Year/Millennium party hats for December 31, 2000!

http://riemann.usno.navy.mil/AA/faq/docs/faq2.html

Countdown to year 2000

Everybody's excited about the year 2000. The guy who wrote this Web page just can't wait: he's counting down the days, hours, and seconds until we can all say "Happy New Year, 2000!" Wonder if he knows the third millennium doesn't start until the year after that.

http://www.stud.unit.no/USERBIN/steffent/aar2000.pl

Countdown!

How much time do you have before the big party on January 1, 2000, and the millennium party in 2001? Find out here! If you're wondering the number of seconds, hours, and minutes you've been alive, this site will figure that out for you too (why you'd want to know that, we're not sure!).

http://www.spiders.com/cgi-bin/countdown

Millennium Institute: Millennium Resources on the Internet

For a clearinghouse of millennium plans and events, the Millennium Institute is the place to go. Parents are strongly cautioned: we have not checked all links.

http://www.igc.org/millennium/links/millen.html

The Year 2000 Information Center/Millennium Bug

Many computers will have problems when the last two digits of the year roll around to "00," and you can find out the latest news on that here, along with some other useful links on timekeeping.

http://www.year2000.com/cgi-bin/y2k/year2000.cgi

TIME MACHINES

EDUNet's Timemachine - Home Page

About 1,200 years ago, someone wanted to name a new country. They came up with Aotearoa (which means "Land of the Long White Cloud"). Now we call that country New Zealand! You can find out about it by taking a ride on EduNET's Time Machine. Did Italy ever invade Ethiopia? Yes, indeed! It happened on October 7, 1935, and it was one of the first major wars that saw the use of combined arms tactics. You can learn so much at this site that all your friends and family members will think you are a genius! You probably are if you take our advice and give this site a try.

http://www.baxter.net/edunet/cat/timemachine/

PM TIME MACHINE MAIN PAGE

Popular Mechanics is *the* magazine for anyone interested in machines. They have built an Internet time machine to help you see how machines have improved over the last 90 or so years. See high-flying French balloons from the early 1900s and crazy car designs from 1960. It's a walk through history, and you won't even have to leave the chair in front of your computer! Your time machine comes with a lot of shiny buttons, and there's even an owner's manual. Let's see, what happens if we press this button right here?

http://popularmechanics.com/popmech/sci/time/
   1HOMETIME.html

The Time Machine by H. G. Wells

Probably the best story about time machines is one of the first—it was written by H. G. Wells, in 1898. This story, titled *The Time Machine,* has inspired a countless number of books, movies, and articles on time travel. Read a no-frills copy of the story right here on the Internet, and maybe you'll decide to write your own time travel tale!

http://www3.hmc.edu/~jwolkin/hum1/
   TimeMachine.html

TOYS

See also GAMES AND FUN; KITES; PETS AND PET CARE—VIRTUAL PETS

Balloon HQ

This is a colorful site where you can pop in to learn how to make animals and other items from balloons. Want to make a balloon bat? A Santa wearing a hat? A Power Ranger? Look in the Highlights and Features section. Before you begin, let us remind you that your mom or dad or another adult should be around when you try this, because it can be dangerous.

http://www.fooledya.com/balloon/

A
B
C
D
E
F
G
H
I
J
K
L
M
N
O
P
Q
R
S
T
U
V
W
X
Y
Z

A
B
C
D
E
F
G
H
I
J
K
L
M
N
O
P
Q
R
S
T
U
V
W
X
Y
Z

KidsHealth Toy & Game Reviews '97

Are Toobers and Zots a good gift for a four-year-old? How much fun are Zolos? What about that Brew Your Own Root Beer kit? Let Kyle, the KidsHealth train conductor, help you out. He rates games, toys, activities, even back-to-school stuff. First he finds out how much fun it is, using the Fun O Meter, and judges it from "fair" to "awesome." Then he rates it on whether a kid would need lots, some, a little, or no skill to like the toy. If a toy has exceptional special qualities that make it stand out from all the others and gets a high rating, it is awarded the KidsHealth Best Toy Award. By the way, Toobers and Zots *are* good for four-year-olds, and Zolos are awesome. Check it out!

http://kidshealth.org/kid/games/review/

Marble Collectors Society of America

Net-mom used to love playing with marbles when she was a kid. Still does, to tell the truth. But let us squelch the rumor that she was one of the first to enjoy collecting aggies and shooters. History shows that marbles were collected more than 3,000 years ago! Why, in England they've had a Good Friday tournament for more than 300 years. And the United States National Marbles Tournament is still held the third weekend of June in Wildwood, New Jersey. You'll find all kinds of information about collecting marbles here—including how to spot the antiques from the reproductions—as well as links to a lot of other great marble sites. For the rules of play, try Shooting Marbles, Mountaineer Style at <*http://www.iolinc.net/~marbles/*>.

http://www.blocksite.com/mcc/mcsa.htm

Matchbox Action Central | Garage

What should we do for fun today? How about playing with Matchbox cars online? All systems are go here at Matchbox Action Central! Check out the huge contest, a timeline of Matchbox history, and tons of cool info, including the hottest models of the year. Don't forget to design and equip your own custom pickup truck, select snazzy colors and decals, and print it for your collection.

http://www.matchboxtoys.com/garage/

The Official Ninja Turtle Web Site!

Cowabunga, dudes! It's the official Teenage Mutant Ninja Turtle page, and it's totally awesome! Michelangelo, Leonardo, Raphael, and Donatello want you dudes and dudettes to send them some fabuloso mail with your thoughts and opinions, so they can have the coolest place on the Net. Check in frequently to see what happens with the next mutation.

http://www.ninjaturtles.com/

Solving the Rubik's Cube

Take it out of the drawer, dust it off, and solve it once and for all. The instructions are at this site. Got one of those pyramid puzzles? There's a solution here for that, too.

http://www.unc.edu/~monroem/rubik.html

The Toy Zone

Do you go to McDonald's and buy their Happy Meals just to get the toy? Come on, admit it! You probably need to check out this site. It lists many of the Happy Meal promotions that McDonald's has done in the past and is doing now—and not just in the United States but also in countries like Germany and Australia. If you are interested in selling your Dalmatians or just trading them for Tamagotchis, you can post it in the Happy Stuff section. A McFAQ will answer questions about Happy Meal toys and provide more official McDonald's information and history. Enjoy this site, and happy meals to you.

http://www.TheToyZone.com/

Zometool

Net-mom's always looking for the perfect construction kit for icosahedral quasicrystalline models, and now she's finally found it. It's called Zometool, and you can learn all about it at this site. Unlike other modular construction kits, which force users to think in squares and angles, Zometool allows builders to think in terms of curves, spirals, fractals, and more. This is because Zometool has 62 different places (instead of four or six) to put the next adjoining piece. The struts between the connectors are flexible, as well. Move over Tinkertoys, here comes Zometool.

http://www.zometool.com/

BEANIE BABIES

Beanie Babies here at Billy Bear's Playground

Once again it's Billy Bear to the rescue when it comes to fun Web sites! This time he's set out some games involving your friends and Net-mom's—the Beanie Babies! Help Billy Bear "shop" for Princess in a crowded mall. Win at Beanie Tic-Tac-Toe or Concentration. Play dress up with Bongo or Princess. Then download some Beanie screen savers and wallpaper, clip art, and more. There are great Beanie links collected at this site too, for your further Beanie pleasure.

http://www.billybear4kids.com/beanie/babies.htm

Beanie Philes

Lots of Beanies are offered for sale or trade on the monitored postings area of this site. We also liked the up-to-date news, the Beanie biographies and name tag poems, and the Miracle Sightings area. While listening to the theme music from *Mission Impossible*, you can read reports from other collectors about where rare Beanies have turned up recently. Erin? Princess? Peace? Where are you? Come home to Net-mom!

http://www.geocities.com/~beaniephiles/main.html

Beaniemonium's Beanie Baby Rumors, Stories, News, & Graphics

This site has an up-to-date history of Beanies, several contests, a very nice dictionary presentation of every Beanie on Earth, and a place where you can get a kid pen pal just as nuts about Beanies as you are. If you're an adult, get a "Granniac" pen pal instead!

http://www.geocities.com/~beaniemonium/

The Official Homepage of the Beanie Babies

Are you bonkers for Beanie Babies? We're listing it, but the 1998 Ty site is a disappointment. Where they used to have a home page for each individual toy, complete with its poem, there is only a photo. They used to have games and news; now they don't. All is not lost, though. Every month there is a spotlight on an individual Beanie Baby's personal Internet diary, though it seems sort of contrived and fake. The guest book is very active—use it to get in touch with other Beanie Baby collectors.

http://www.ty.com/

DOLLS AND DOLLHOUSES

About Cornhusk Dolls

Have you ever wanted to make a cornhusk doll but didn't know how to get started? It only takes a few simple materials, which are listed here along with the easy-to-follow directions. Then, get creative in decorating your dolls—you'll be surprised at how quickly and easily you can grow your own personal cornhusk doll collection. You can dress your doll as a man or a woman, but remember that cornhusk dolls have no faces. Read the native legend about why this is so.

http://www.lib.uconn.edu/NativeTech/cornhusk/corndoll.html

NET FILES

You break a leg somewhere in the outback of Australia, but luckily you remembered to bring a two-way radio.

Who do you call?

Answer: Why, The Royal Flying Doctor Service of Australia, of course. For over 66 years, they have provided medical and health services to the remote locations of Australia's outback. The service uses a fleet of 38 aircraft and 27 doctors to cover 5,000 locations throughout four fifths of the Australian continent. They can be anywhere in Australia within 90 minutes! Read more about the service and its history at
http://www.csu.edu.au/australia/detail/flydoc.html

A
B
C
D
E
F
G
H
I
J
K
L
M
N
O
P
Q
R
S
T
U
V
W
X
Y
Z

Colleen Moore's Fairy Castle

The ultimate dollhouse is in the Chicago Museum of Science and Industry. It was created by Colleen Moore, a star of 1920s silent films, who decorated the interior with antiques, real gold, jewels, and other precious items. The dollhouse is located in a magic garden, with a weeping willow tree that really weeps! Who is to say fairies don't really live there? You'll see the Rock-a-Bye Baby cradle, Santa Claus' sleigh, and lots of other objects familiar from nursery rhyme lore and legend. The table is set in King Arthur's dining hall, and the Bluebird of Happiness sings in the princess' bedroom. Don't miss the attic— Rumplestiltskin's spinning wheel hangs from the rafters.

http://www.msichicago.org/exhibit/fairy_castle/
fchome.html

Dolls of Every Description

Do you or someone you know look like your Barbie doll? Of course not—Barbie doesn't look like a normal human! If you'd like to get a doll that does, check this site. Browse through the catalog and click on a boy or girl doll that looks friendly. You can pick skin color, hair color, age, and so many other things. For example, you can customize your doll to wear glasses, a hearing aid, or to use a wheelchair. You'll also find dolls with special medical conditions here.

http://www.teleport.com/~people/

Pleasant Company for American Girls

The American Girls Collection is about lovable dolls, each from a different period of American history. Each doll is beautifully dressed in the historical clothes and accessories of her time. Accompanying books invite you into their exciting times and show you that although their lives were very different, many of the traditions of girlhood (such as family, friends, and feelings) are still alive today. You can get the American Girl catalog here and also sign up for clubs and fun activities that focus on the interests and activities of American girls today.

http://www.americangirl.com/

Welcome to Barbie.com

Barbie's come a long way from that perky teenage fashion model in the striped bathing suit. Now she's a dentist, a veterinarian, or a teacher, and she even rides a Harley-Davidson motorcycle! At this site you can learn all about the many faces of Barbie. There are also many tips, trivia, and information for collectors.

http://www.barbie.com/

KALEIDOSCOPES
The Kaleidoscope Collector

Your view of everything created inside these tricky tubes is done with simple mirrors. It is the number of mirrors and how they are positioned that creates all the different patterns that you see. Scope out the different types of kaleidoscopes and their mirror configurations at this splendid site. Seeing double? You've probably got a Twin Two Mirror in your kaleidoscope.

http://www.kaleidoscopesusa.com/

Kaleidoscope Heaven

Did you ever sit in your bedroom on a cloudy afternoon, wishing you could think of something to do that could brighten up the day? Well, grab a kaleidoscope and start twirling. Don't have one? Look in the Info section to find out how to make one from a tubular potato chip can (which you may have in your house) and some Plexiglas and mirrors (which you may have to go buy). You'll also find something on the history of these clever toys, as well as links to online virtual kaleidoscopes and more fun.

http://kaleidoscopeheaven.org/

"A ship in the harbor is safe, but that is not what ships are built for."
—John A. Shedd

LEGOS

LEGO Worlds

Your dog chewed all the little pieces, and now you need some new ideas for other Lego projects to make with what's left! On the LEGO Information page, you can see pictures of other people's creations and discover how to make and play Lego games. You'll also find fun online games, screen savers, and other things to download for Lego-maniacs everywhere.

http://www.lego.com/

The Minifig Generator

This neat interactive site uses Lego body parts and JavaScript so you can have fun picking heads, torsos, and legs to create your own mini figure. How about a pirate's head on a doctor's lab coat, with skeleton legs? You can make your own choices or let the computer randomly pick its own. You can then name your creation and build it so that you can print out a copy. Cool, huh?

http://www.baseplate.com/toys/minifig/

TEDDY BEARS

Bear Story

Germany and the United States each have laid claim to the fame of originating the teddy bear, back in the early 1900s. Check out both stories and decide for yourself which one was *bear* first.

http://www.qvc.com/bearstry.html

Good Bears of the World

Have you offered a bear hug today? There are lots of lonely kids and others who could use a bear hug, and this organization tries to give it to them. You can join a "bear den" near you and help raise money to buy teddy bears to be distributed to local hospitals, police departments, and senior citizen homes. This nonprofit organization has affiliates worldwide; there is a directory at this site.

http://www.goodbearsoftheworld.org/

The Teddy Bear Project

The folks at I*EARN have a fabulous idea. They team pairs of schools around the world and have them exchange special teddy bear "ambassadors." The bears keep detailed diaries of their travels and often e-mail back home. Want to join in on the fun? This site will tell you how! Some schools have similar projects involving bears with accompanying backpacks full of postcards, coins, and other souvenirs for the other classroom. What a great way to learn about life in another part of the world.

http://www.ne.com.au/~gwps/teddybear.html

WATER GUNS

Super Soaker

Net-mom has run away from more Super Soaker water play than she cares to remember. Seems like every year Son of Net-mom just HAS to have the latest, greatest, and newest model. Luckily he hasn't discovered this Web site yet. And don't YOU tell him! He'd be entering the contest to win free water guns and drooling over the CPS 3000. No, Net-mom's going to keep this site a secret.

http://www.supersoaker.com/

Water Weapons of Mass Destruction

Want to know which water guns are the best? Check out the fan reviews at this site. You'll also be treated to water fight strategy, "war" stories, and maintenance tips. The most important thing is to empty those tanks and depressurize after each water fight. Otherwise, mildew will grow and clog the pipes, and your gun will turn into a colorful but useless plastic object.

http://members.xoom.com/waterweapons/

YO-YOS

American YoYo Association

What should you say to your friends if they tell you that last night they walked the dog, rocked the baby, hopped the fence, went around the corner, saw a flying saucer and a tidal wave, and entered into a time warp? Congratulate them for performing great yo-yo tricks, then check out this site. Maybe you'll find yourself reaching for the moon and perfecting a warp drive.

http://ayya.pd.net/

A B C D E F G H I J K L M N O P Q R S T U V W X Y Z

A
B
C
D
E
F
G
H
I
J
K
L
M
N
O
P
Q
R
S
T
U
V
W
X
Y
Z

Tomer's Page of Exotic Yo-Yo

Is your favorite yo-yo a looper or a sleeper? You should also know if it's a butterfly or an imperial. If you have trouble doing some yo-yo tricks, you may be using the wrong type of yo-yo for that particular trick! Should you ever wax your string? How do you untie those pesky knots? And what do you do when you feel like your finger is about to fall off? Find out here.

http://pages.nyu.edu/~tqm3413/yoyo/

TRAVEL

See also UNITED STATES—STATES; COUNTRIES OF THE WORLD *and* PARENTING AND FAMILIES *special sections*

DOS/CA: TRAVEL WARNINGS & CONSULAR INFO SHEETS

Have you ever fantasized you were an international spy? This site has links to all sorts of cool stuff! There are travel advisories and maps of all of the different countries. Check out the Central Intelligence Agency (CIA) publications and handbooks. Look at what's going on in different countries, what is necessary to get across the border, and what to take with you to be safe (besides your passport and your parents, that is).

http://travel.state.gov/travel_warnings.html

Excite Travel

If your family wants to travel and is looking for a fun place, then visit this site, which is a well-organized list of great places to go. Use the random destination link if you don't know where you want to go or if you want to find out about someplace new.

http://www.city.net/

GORP - Great Outdoor Recreation Pages

Is there anything more fun than hiking, camping, climbing, or seeing wildlife? GORP has it all. Check out the sections on places to go, things to do, good food to take, and staying healthy while traveling. If you are trying to get in the mood to go camping, enjoy the outdoor art, photography, cartoons, and, best of all, traveler's tales. Parental advisory: Links off this page have not been checked.

http://www.gorp.com/

History Channel - Traveler

How about a tour that re-creates the Civil War? Or one that helps you understand the Klondike gold rush in Alaska? This site will help you plan a vacation you'll remember forever. Once you have the plans made, better tell Mom and Dad you will need them to drive you there!

http://www.historytravel.com/

International Road Signs

OK, you and your folks have a great trip planned in Europe. That's great, but the adults on your trip insist on a road trip, and they want to do their own driving. Problem is, the rules of the road in European countries are different than in North America: signs are different, traffic lights vary, and so on. That's where this site comes to the rescue! Show your folks this page so they'll know how to turn, when to stop, and, most important, get you safely to all the fun places you want to see.

http://www.travlang.com/signs/

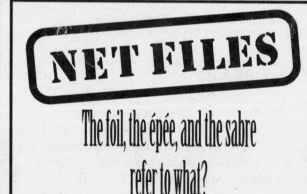

NET FILES

The foil, the épée, and the sabre refer to what?

a) Essential items for your next barbecue
b) Those little bones in your ear
c) The three weapons of fencing

Answer: C. Fencing is that sport where the players engage in, well, swordplay. You've seen them, with those cagelike masks on their faces. Fencing is a sport and, to many, an art. Concentration, quickness, and agility are all very important to the fencer. Go to *http://www.architecture.ubc.ca:8080/vds96/gymnasium/whatis.htm* to find out how fencing started and how it is done, scored, and won. It's not just for swashbucklers!

Klutz Press: Kid's Travel

You are on a 1,000-mile cross-country trip to visit Aunt Mabel. Your kid brother is singing "Do Your Ears Hang Low" for the umpteenth time, and your dad keeps going on and on about how he walked through the snow barefoot to school. In other words, you're bored out of your skull. Fight road boredom with some great travel games from this site. See license plates from around North America so you can quickly recognize which state cars are from (before anyone else). Learn a simple game called NIM that'll kill many road miles, and print off some matching games that'll keep your brother quiet and give you both fun times. You may even look forward to going to Aunt Mabel's now!

http://www.klutz.com/treefort/travel.html

Rec.Travel Library

Where in the world can you go to have fun? If you are asking yourself this question, check out this site, which is a collection of posted articles from the Usenet News section called rec.travel. You'll find recommendations for places to go, how to get there, what to do there, and much more! A caution to parents: Not all links off this page have been checked.

http://www.travel-library.com/

Tourism Offices Worldwide Directory

Where do you want to go on vacation? You have a lot of possible choices; where can you go to get information on each? You want official material, too, not just brochures from hotels and resorts. The same thing applies if you're doing a report on a state or a country: you want information from some authoritative source. Here it is! Just select the country or state you want, and the contact information (and sometimes, the Web page location) will appear on your screen. It will also tell you the last time the address was verified.

http://www.towd.com/

TREASURE AND TREASURE-HUNTING

See also SHIPS AND SHIPWRECKS

The Armchair Treasure Hunt Club: Home Page

Some years ago, publication of Kit Williams' beautifully illustrated book, *Masquerade,* caused an international sensation. Williams had buried a valuable Golden Hare and provided a series of cryptic visual clues and riddles in the book that revealed where the treasure was hidden. Intrepid treasure hunters did not have to go skulking about backyards and parks with shovels (although some did). Instead, they simply had to follow the clues and send in their guess to the publisher in order to win the gold. This could be done without leaving home—hence the advent of the phrase "armchair treasure hunting." Since then, similar puzzling treasure hunts have popped up with enough regularity that a home page has become essential to sort them all out. You'll find lists and links to an assortment of new and ongoing hunts, the solutions to old ones, and an invitation to join an Internet mailing list where armchair treasure hunters around the globe compare notes with each other.

http://treasure.mertec.co.uk/tathc/indextxt.html

International Treasure Hunters Exchange

Do you think the days of digging up buried treasure are over? Does the idea of stumbling onto a chest of pirate gold or digging up Genghis Khan's fabled lost tomb seem like something from storybooks? It doesn't happen daily, but many people are looking for fabulous treasures, and they are finding them more often than you'd think! This site covers the worldwide treasure hunting scene with a thoroughness that makes dropping in on their site a true joy for anyone who has ever fantasized about carrying armloads of pieces of eight. If you want to go out and hunt up some treasure, then this page is a must for you. Some solid information can be found here on metal detecting, shipwrecks, and online research sources.

http://www.treasure.com/

A B C D E F G H I J K L M N O P Q R S T U V W X Y Z

A
B
C
D
E
F
G
H
I
J
K
L
M
N
O
P
Q
R
S
T
U
V
W
X
Y
Z

No Quarter Given

"Whether ye be interested in the buccaneers and privateers of the Caribbean Sea, the Elizabethan Sea Dogs, or Jean Laffite's pirates of Barataria, we'll be havin' something of interest to ya." That's what the creators of this site are promising, and we're not about to disagree. The history, lore, romance, and sheer adventure of being a pirate or privateer is right here at "the source fer all things piratical." We'll add no more for fear of angering them—we wouldn't want to be walking any plank!

http://www.discover.net/~nqgiven/index.htm

Oak Island

Did you ever dig a hole? What if you dug a hole and found beams of wood? What if you then found a buried shaft? You'd probably be excited! That's exactly what happened to a young man years ago on Oak Island, just off the coast of Nova Scotia, in Maritime Canada. What's really intriguing is that many people have dug deeper into the shaft since then and found inscribed stones, coconut fiber, an iron plate, and oak wood, just as might be found in treasure chests. Problem is, the shaft is booby-trapped to flood with water, and no one has made it to the bottom. Is there treasure? No one knows. See more about this mystery at this Web page, or at *<http://unmuseum.mus.pa.us/oakisl.htm>*.

http://www.activemind.com/Mysterious/Topics/
    OakIsland/

The On-Line Treasure Hunter

This site has exciting stories of real treasure finds. Sometimes the best place to look for treasure is where others have already looked. With today's modern computerized, electronic equipment, treasure hunters can often revisit sites that were "cleaned out" many years ago and walk off with riches! This site offers plenty of detailed information for folks who would like to find wealth in the ground or the ocean, as well as solid equipment data, classified ads, question and answers, and links to other related pages. Some of the articles are written by kids.

http://www.onlinether.com/

Pirates at the City Art Centre

"Shiver me timbers!" If you don't know a pirate from a buccaneer, better sail over to this page. You'll learn lots about famous pirates, legends, and perhaps locations of buried treasure!

http://www.efr.hw.ac.uk/EDC/CAC/pirates/
    pirates.htm

Silver Bank @ nationalgeographic.com

"Spanish galleon *Nuestra Señora de la Pura y Limpia Concepción* set sail from Havana, Cuba, in September 1641. Eight days later a hurricane thrashed the ship. Leaking, she began a month-long limp toward Puerto Rico for repairs. Just short of salvation, the *Concepción* struck a shallow reef and began sinking slowly. Three hundred hapless passengers and crew perished, and a fortune in silver tumbled into the Atlantic, inspiring the reef's shiny new name: Silver Bank." That's the background. This site allows you to explore the last days of the ship, the wreck itself, and salvage efforts over the years. Treasure hunter Tracy Bowden is the most recent explorer of the Silver Bank, and you can see many artifacts at this site. There are links to other marine archaeology and treasure Web sites, too.

http://www.nationalgeo.com/
    features/98/silverbank/index.html

The Story of the Beale Ciphers

The Beale ciphers hold the key to one of the greatest unsolved puzzles of all time. The story goes that around 1820, a fellow named Beale hid two wagonloads of silver, gold, and jewels someplace near Roanoke, Virginia. He left three coded letters, supposedly detailing the location of the treasure, with a trusted friend. Then he left for the West and was never seen again. One of the letters, describing the treasure, has been deciphered. It is in a code based on the Declaration of Independence. It is believed the other letters are similarly coded to the same document or other public documents. You can read about the status of the Beale ciphers, and you might want to try solving them yourself (if you find this treasure, please let us know!).

http://www.treasure.com/j195.htm

Treasure Island - Home

It's a tale of adventure, pirates, tropical islands, and murder! "If this don't fetch the kids, why, they have gone rotten since my day," said Robert Louis Stevenson, when he wrote this book in 1881. The book is available online at this site. Besides a biography of the author, you'll find links to sites about pirates, islands, and buried treasure. This finely designed site also has some rainy-day suggestions for things to do—besides reading, of course.

http://www.ukoln.ac.uk/services/treasure/

Treasure Net

With so much treasure hunting activity on the Web these days, it must seem like a gold rush is going on. As a matter of fact, there is! This site has all the usual resources for equipment and advice, plus a nice assortment of maps and historical photos. There are also links to sources of old state and county maps, which could be a bonanza for treasure hunters. It's especially useful, though, for the message forums, where you can discuss treasure sites and technical tips with others interested in this hobby.

http://www.treasurenet.com/

What flag, with vertical bands of blue, yellow, and red, was flown with a hole cut out of its center?

cont-gi.html#steag
http://students.missouri.edu/~romsa/romania/html/
Romania's revolution. Read about it at
protest, making the flag with the hole a symbol of
In 1989, Romanians fighting for democracy cut it out in
Communist rule, a coat of arms was added to the flag.
Answer: The Romanian flag. During the years of

Worldwide Treasure Links, the worlds largest list of treasure sites

Treasure—everybody wants to find coins, jewelry, or other valuables hidden or lost. Finding treasure, though, takes skill, the right equipment, good clues, and maybe a bit of luck. If you want to be a treasure hunter, then this Web page is a good place to start. You'll find links to dozens of treasure-related resources on the Internet. Learn about the latest equipment, find tips from treasure hunters, and read about treasure sites around the world. Start mining for valuables now—right on the Net!

http://www.iwl.net/customers/norman/linkog1.htm

TRUCKS AND HEAVY EQUIPMENT

The Great Picture Book of Construction Equipment

Looking for a field guide to construction equipment? Dig into this one and learn how to distinguish (for example) a mud bulldozer from one that works better in a woodlot. There are QuickTime movies so you can watch them move, too! The picture book includes dump trucks, hydraulic excavators, bulldozers, cranes, front loaders, and lots of other things that dig, move, shovel, and tow.

http://www.komatsu.co.jp/kikki/zukan/e_index.htm

HCEA - Historical Construction Equipment Association

HCEA knows all about how roads were built, how fields were plowed, and how old construction equipment worked. This site has many photos of big, heavy machines and numerous links to companies that manufacture paving equipment, cranes, payloaders, bulldozers, trucks, and all sorts of neat vehicles.

http://www.bigtoy.com/index2.html

A B C D E F G H I J K L M N O P Q R S T U V W X Y Z

Jim's Farming Page

If you don't live close to a farm, you probably have no idea what a harrower is or how corn and beans are grown and harvested. Farmer Jim takes you on a tour of his fields through the growing season. See the big equipment Jim uses. If you explore this resource a little further, you can "Ask a Farmer" a question and see some neat agricultural links.

http://toybox.asap.net/farmsite/

Make a Strange Truck

Click on the cab, middle, or back section of the fire truck to make an all-new vehicle with a strange name. How about an ambu-garbage-van or a moving-dump-engine? How many real trucks can you match? This is perfect for preschoolers!

http://www.EnchantedLearning.com/Slidetrucks/
   Slidetruck.html

Terry the Tractor

Terry the Tractor starts out as a frame in a factory. Gradually he gets sprockets, an engine, and more parts until he emerges from the factory as a shiny new bulldozer. His new owner treats him roughly, and it looks like the scrap heap is going to be Terry's next home. But someone realizes there's still a lot of work left in Terry, if only the damage can be repaired. See what happens to this little dozer with the big heart.

http://www.butler-machinery.com/kids.html

TRUCKWORLD ONLINE

Interested in monster trucks, 4×4s, sport utility vehicles, and all kinds of street and off-road equipment? You'll love this site. Check the QuickTime video of the world record monster truck jump—see a 10,000-pound truck fly as Team Bigfoot clears a distance of 141 feet, 10 inches. Do visit the Team Bigfoot Web site, too, at <http://www.bigfoot4x4.com/>.

http://www.truckworld.com/

Welcome to Zamboni!

OK, hands in the air: how many of you really have the secret fantasy of driving the Zamboni around the ice rink? You know, that big machine that magically lays down a new layer of smooth ice for you and your friends to skate on. Net-mom usually plays "Slamboni" instead, at <http://www.sikids.com/games/slamboni/index_v1.html>, but now she has discovered the official Zamboni site. You can learn the history of the company (they celebrate their 50th birthday in 1999), buy some cool Zamboni merchandise (including the fabulous "Zamboni Crossing" sign), and check out the trivia. For example, did you know that the top speed of a Zamboni ice resurfacing machine is 9 mph?

http://www.zamboni.com/

FIRE TRUCKS

The Firehouse Museum's Home Page

Did you ever wonder how fires were fought in your grandparents' day? They didn't have the sleek, powerful fire trucks we have now! See some historic photos and memorabilia from this museum in San Diego, California, dedicated to firefighters all over the world. Check the steam fire engines and old fire extinguishers, and don't miss old La Jolla #1, a hand-drawn chemical fire truck.

http://www.globalinfo.com/noncomm/firehouse/
   Firehouse.HTML

The Florida State Fire College Kids Site

Follow Li'l Boots into the firehouse as he explains the features and uses of various kinds of firefighting vehicles, including pumpers, ladder and aerial trucks, and special-use equipment. How has fighting fires changed over the years? Find out at this site!

http://www.fsfckids.ufl.edu/fsfckids/

Try actual reality.

UFOS AND EXTRATERRESTRIALS

The Bermuda Triangle

There are two sides to every story, and this page takes the skeptic's side of the mysteries of the Bermuda Triangle. This page explains, in factual terms, why many of the mysterious events attributed to the Bermuda Triangle may be no more than products of "over-active imaginations."

http://icarus.cc.uic.edu/~jdrege1/toby/triangle/
tri.html

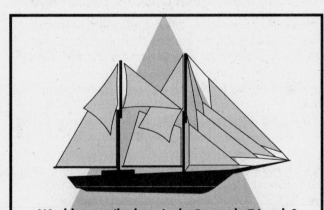

Would you sail a boat in the Bermuda Triangle? Wouldn't you be scared, because of all the mysterious boat and plane disappearances in that area of the Caribbean? The Salty Dog says there's no truth to all the rumors. Learn the facts he presents at The Bermuda Triangle page!

MUFON WWW Page

You'll find loads of unidentified flying object (UFO)–related links here. Parents are cautioned that we haven't checked them all. The Mutual UFO Network was founded in 1969, and it now has more than 5,000 members worldwide. Among other things, this resource will tell you what you need to do if you ever see something you think is a UFO. The first rule is: Observe carefully!

http://www.rutgers.edu/~mcgrew/mufon/

The Museum of Unnatural Mystery Homepage

Look up ahead. That's a strange little building. What's this—burning torches at the front door? Can you make out the lettering on the sign? Hmm, "Museum of Unnatural Mystery." Pushing open the door (it creaks, of course), we see a number of odd exhibits: Pirates; Lost Worlds; Odd Archaeology; and UFO Mysteries. Enter, if you dare.

http://unmuseum.mus.pa.us/unmuseum.htm

The Schwa Corporation

The best evidence that aliens have already landed and have a Web page of their own appears here. Good luck—you'll need it.

http://www.theschwacorporation.com/

Unusual Phenomena: Files From the FBI

Here are some of the Federal Bureau of Investigation's *real* X-Files! Released under the Freedom of Information Act, you can pore over 1,600 pages of UFO reports dating back to 1947 as well as one solitary page on the Roswell incident. You'll need the free PDF reader to look at the documents. Parents: All reports may not be suitable for your kids.

http://www.fbi.gov/foipa/ufo.htm

Who's Out There? A SETI Adventure

What if you were hired to search for life out there in the universe? How would you go about planning your investigation? What types of signals would you try to find? Where would you look? Try this adventure game to find some answers, but beware, it may open still more questions in your mind.

http://www.seti-inst.edu/game/

A
B
C
D
E
F
G
H
I
J
K
L
M
N
O
P
Q
R
S
T
U
V
W
X
Y
Z

A B C D E F G H I J K L M N O P Q R S T U V W X Y Z

UNITED STATES

CNN/Time AllPolitics

No matter where you live, your life is affected by politicians. They are everywhere! Politicians make laws about a lot of different things every day. CNN, one of the world's most trusted news sources, offers these pages dedicated to political news. From the federal budget to the presidential elections, look here for great leads on today's top stories.

http://allpolitics.com/1998/

Project Vote Smart

Have you ever wondered how the U.S. government works? Politicians are everywhere, and they are constantly making important decisions. Vote Smart keeps track of what politicians are doing. If you are writing a paper about a candidate, a political issue, or even a project that requires a cartoon or an audio clip, try this site. It has links to campaigns, educational material, and a political humor section. If you don't know who your elected officials are, just type in your ZIP code, and Vote Smart will tell you! You'll also learn about their voting records and how to contact them to tell them they are doing a good job or to complain if you don't agree with their stand on the issues so far.

http://www.vote-smart.org/

CITIES, COMMUNITIES, REGIONS

City.Net United States

City.Net combines the features of an atlas, gazetteer, and almanac, plus the best material from local guidebooks and newspapers. This page starts with a list of all the states and territories. Within each state, you'll find links sorted by city, county, or subject. Subjects include arts and entertainment, education, events, government, and more. Use the search function to find out if anything is available for a specific city or town. This is great for probing through local community newspaper and TV station Web pages to help you with that history or geography homework. Check it out!

http://www.city.net/countries/united_states/

USA CityLink Home Page

Homework can be fun with a resource like this to help! This is a nicely organized site; just click on Visit a City and then find the list sorted by state. Within each state are links to general state pages, city, and regional pages. So, if you needed to find information on places of interest in Syracuse, New York, for example, you could click on New York and select one of the Syracuse links for more info. There are also some interesting features on various holidays, Mardi Gras, and more.

http://banzai.neosoft.com/citylink/

FEDERAL GOVERNMENT
FedWorld Information Network Home Page

This is your one-stop location for finding information that's available online from the U.S. government. It's a master list of all the Net servers and resources, bulletin boards, and electronic documents the government has to offer. For example, check the new design and the new "security features" of the redesigned currency. You'll find GIFs and a press release at the U.S. Treasury server. You can find lots of cool stuff here, if you take time to look. If you want to look something up by keyword, try a search from the National Technical Information Service (NTIS) area of FedWorld. You can also browse by subject area, such as Health Care or Space Technology. Download (or order) a number of free catalogs, ranging from *Environmental Highlights* to *Occupational Safety & Health Multimedia Training Programs*. Government documents are a gold mine of information; "pick" some today!

http://www.fedworld.gov/

You know something the Net doesn't—create your own home page! Look in the INTERNET—WEBWEAVING AND HTML section to find out how!

Library of Congress Home Page

Did you know that the first American "postcards" were souvenir mailing cards sold at the Columbian Exposition in Chicago, all the way back in 1893? They didn't become popular, partly because you couldn't write on the back. What did people mail to their friends back home when they went on vacation? Luckily, on May 19, 1898, Congress passed a law that allowed private printers to publish and sell cards. The postage rate was one cent back then. This began the postcard era in the United States. This information was found in the American Memory Collection of the Library of Congress World Wide Web. This site has access to newspapers around the world and thousands of historical postcards, photographs, motion pictures, manuscripts, and sound recordings. Many Library of Congress exhibits are also available for viewing online.

http://lcweb.loc.gov/

NET FILES

Here comes a 150-car freight train traveling at 50 mph! If the engineer suddenly slams on the brakes, how far does the train travel before it comes to a complete stop?

Answer: It can take up to 1.5 miles to stop! Even at 30 mph, the approximate stopping distance is 3,500 feet, or two-thirds of a mile! Operation Lifesaver educates adults and kids on trains and train safety. Make tracks to visit http://www.oli.org/oli/hrfactsterns.html soon.

FEDERAL GOVERNMENT—EXECUTIVE

Air Force Kids Online

Make up a nickname for yourself, key in the password "aim high" and enter the Air Force for Kids Web site. Captain Zoom asks for your help in collecting supplies to be sent to the space station, but he's not very good in math, so Net-mom hopes *you* are, or the two of you will never get off the ground! After you survive that mission, you can play other games relating to planes, as well as have fun with the coloring book pages and word searches. Learn about the history of the Air Force and check out its most famous comic strip hero, Steve Canyon. You can also send friends electronic postcards featuring planes and images of the space shuttle.

http://www.af.mil/aflinkjr/

Bureau of Engraving and Printing

Did you know that Martha Washington is the only woman whose portrait has been on a U.S. currency note? It appeared on the face of the $1 silver certificate of 1886 and 1891 and on the back of the $1 silver certificate of 1896. There are lots more interesting facts to learn when you visit the Bureau of Engraving and Printing (BEP). If you are in Washington, D.C., you can visit in person, or you can do it right here if you are surfing the Internet. The BEP also has a really neat area especially for kids. Did you know that if you had 10 billion $1 notes and spent one every second of every day, it would require 317 years for you to go broke? Bill Gates had better start spending!

http://www.bep.treas.gov/

CIA Kids Page

Do you know what the Central Intelligence Agency does? They collect and analyze all kinds of information from all over the world, and they do it in the name of national defense. Besides men and women, the agents include spy dogs and even spy pigeons! Don't miss the Try on a Disguise Shockwave game in the Who We Are and What We Do section. We particularly like the way you can disguise the dog to look like a cat! You'll know a lot more about the CIA when you've finished spying on this site. Did we say spy? Shhhh!

http://www.odci.gov/cia/ciakids/

A
B
C
D
E
F
G
H
I
J
K
L
M
N
O
P
Q
R
S
T
U
V
W
X
Y
Z

The Department of Health and Human Services for Kids Page

The Department of Health and Human Services includes the Center for Disease Control, the Food and Drug Administration (FDA), and the National Institutes of Health, among other agencies. Their kids' page has a food safety coloring book as well as an introduction to vaccines that help you stay well. You'll find pages with information about smoking and drug abuse, as well as how to deal with bullies and dangerous situations. There are some bizarre things collected on this page of links, though. We're not sure what holiday and brain teaser links have to do with the subject.

http://www.hhs.gov/kids/

The Department of the Interior Kid's Page

The Department of the Interior is in charge of the U.S. Fish and Wildlife Service, the National Park Service, U.S. Geological Survey, and the Bureau of Indian Affairs, among other things. At the kids' version of their home page, you can visit the Hoover Dam, learn how coal is mined, and download some great American landmarks to color.

http://www.doi.gov/kids/

Department of Justice Kids and Youth Page

The Department of Justice (DoJ) oversees everything from the FBI to the DEA (that's the Federal Bureau of Investigation and the Drug Enforcement Administration, for those who aren't familiar with the acronyms). Take the DEA link to get the straight facts on drugs, or visit the FBI to see which criminals are on the Ten Most Wanted list. You can also see what happens inside a courtroom as you trace a case from its initial investigation through its appeals process. Older kids will learn a lot from the civil rights primer. When faced with racial, religious, or cultural prejudice, what would you do? Find out by exploring the scenarios in Hateful Acts Hurt Kids.

http://www.usdoj.gov/kidspage/

Department of State Digital Diplomacy for Students

The Department of State is responsible for carrying out our diplomatic policies and relationships with other nations of the world. They oversee U.S. Embassies abroad—there is an official list of links and addresses at this site—and our ambassadors to those countries. They also need to know the addresses of foreign embassies in the U.S., and there is a list of them here as well. The Department of State is also the custodian of the Great Seal of the United States, which is used on treaties and very important official documents. At this site you can also learn what the Secretary of State does, as you "tag along" on a recent trip. This site provides information on several different grade levels, but if you decide you have picked too young or too old, you can easily change to another level at any point.

http://geography.state.gov/htmls/plugin.html

The Department of the Treasury Kid's Page

The U.S. Customs Service, the Bureau of Alcohol, Firearms, and Tobacco, and the Bureau of Engraving and Printing are just a few of the many organizations working under the Department of the Treasury. Take the tour led by Trez the cat (does Socks know about this?). Someone call the Secret Service! No problem, they work for the Treasury Department, too. Don't miss the Dog of the Month—those customs service drug-sniffing dogs have their own trading cards on the Net! Our favorite part, though, is the "Start Your Own Business" game, where you can pretend to run a lemonade stand, operate a lawn-mowing business, or manage a rock band. What's involved in starting a business? Find out here.

http://www.ustreas.gov/kids/

VIDEO AND SPY CAMS lets you look in on interesting parts of the world.

U.S. EPA Explorers Club

Do you know what the EPA is? It's a governmental entity (how's that for a big word!) called the Environmental Protection Agency, and it makes sure everyone works to keep the air, land, and water safe and pure. We headed to the recycling section and found a lot of neat things about how we can reuse and recycle materials. There are a lot of other sites on this page that can help you understand the environment and our impact on it. This place is guaranteed to make you more aware of your surroundings so you and others can grow up in an environment that is safe for everyone.

http://www.epa.gov/kids/

Welcome to the White House

Besides a tour of the White House, you can learn a lot about President Bill Clinton and the First Family. This is also a gateway to information about the executive branch of the U.S. government, its cabinet offices, and independent agencies. Don't miss the White House for Kids tour, led by (who else?) Socks, the First Cat.

http://www.whitehouse.gov/WH/Welcome.html

FEDERAL GOVERNMENT—JUDICIAL

The Federal Judiciary Homepage: News and information about the Federal Courts

Order in the court! Hmmm, but which court? Supreme Court, Court of Appeals, bankruptcy court—more courts than a tennis tournament! This site is a clearinghouse of information on the U.S. federal judiciary system, and the hypertext links will give you a brief overview plus contact information for more in-depth help.

http://www.uscourts.gov/

Legal Information Institute - Supreme Court Decisions

Prepared by the Cornell University Law School in New York, these hypertext Supreme Court decisions date from 1991. Also included are a few famous cases that took place before this time.

http://supct.law.cornell.edu/supct/

FEDERAL GOVERNMENT—LEGISLATIVE

Congress.Org

Did you know that you have representatives in Washington? They are supposed to be working for you, but they are so far away, how can you check up on them? One way is across the Internet. Type in your ZIP code and find out how your representatives voted on recent legislation. You'll also find address books here so you can write to your congresspeople and express your opinions! If you're a little hazy about how all this government stuff works, this site will get you up to speed.

http://www.congress.org/

THOMAS — U.S. Congress on the Internet

It's Congress at your fingertips—you'll find lots of information at this site. Read a detailed account about how laws are made, find out what happened at the last Congress, or get the scoop on the hot bills now under consideration at this Congress. The full text of the Constitution of the United States is also available here, as well as other important documents.

http://thomas.loc.gov/

United States House of Representatives

The main function of Congress isn't to make headlines; it's to make laws. The whole process is outlined at this site (look in the Educational Resources area). Put your newfound knowledge into action immediately by checking out what the House of Representatives considered today and what they will talk about tomorrow. Find out who voted, how they voted, and best yet, how your own representative voted. Do you agree with what your representative did? Why not write a letter or e-mail—the addresses are available here too. There's also a twist on amendments to the Constitution at this site. Besides the ones that did pass and have become law, there is a section on the six amendments to the Constitution that have been proposed but never ratified (approved by 75 percent of the states).

http://www.house.gov/

A B C D E F G H I J K L M N O P Q R S T U V W X Y Z

United States Senate

Why are there two legislative houses, rather than just one? According to this site, "The two houses of Congress resulted from the 'Great Compromise' between large and small states reached at the Constitutional Convention in 1787. Membership of the House of Representatives is apportioned according to a state's population, while in the Senate each state has equal representation. The Constitution assigns the Senate and House equal responsibility...." At the Web site you can track Senate activity, write to your senators, and take a virtual reality tour of the Senate chambers. Learn about the special desks used in the Senate chambers. Traditionally, each senator carves his or her name in a desk drawer!

http://www.senate.gov/

NATIONAL PARKS

PARKNET:The National Park Service Place on the Web

This site, hosted by the U.S. National Park Service, is loaded with facts! It includes visitor information, statistics, conservation practices, and park history. You can find information on a specific park or historic site in a variety of ways. Try the alphabetical list, or use a clickable map to select from a list of sites for that state. A selection sorted by theme or keyword is also available. They even include a list of keywords to make the selection easier.

http://www.nps.gov/

USDA Forest Service Recreation Home Page

America's national forests belong to you, but when was the last time you visited one? To find out where they are and how to visit them, check the U.S. Department of Agriculture Forest Service guide, which lists every national forest, grassland, and park in the country. Click on any one of them to learn all about the area, including what kind of wildlife you can see and what there is to do, whether it's fishing, skiing, biking, kayaking, or camping. Once you've decided where you'd like to go, reserve your spot by downloading a reservation application.

http://www.fs.fed.us/recreation/

PRESIDENTS AND FIRST LADIES

Abraham Lincoln Online

Most of us know a few things about Abraham Lincoln, 13th president of the United States. But the facts found at this site go far beyond what we might learn in the average history book. Many of his speeches and letters are available, as are FAQs, historic sites, and links to other Web sites on Lincoln. The Abraham Lincoln Quiz provides a lot of great questions, like "Which two things would Lincoln not want you to know?" The answers are here too.

http://www.netins.net/showcase/creative/lincoln.html

The American Experience/The Presidents

This site has a timeline of U.S. presidents running across the top of the page. You can see who served when and for how many years. Click on any name to get more information. Look at the "Snapshot" for a picture and a brief overview. Then use the menu of choices on the left to find out more about the historical era and events of the times. You'll get a sense of what the president's domestic and foreign relations policies were as well. Some presidents rate expanded feature stories where you can learn a lot more. The material is presented in an appealing and interesting way; see what you think.

http://www.pbs.org/wgbh/pages/amex/presidents/
indexjs.html

A Day In The Life Of A President

Did you ever think about growing up to be president of the United States? If you think you have a busy schedule now—with school and sports and errands and homework—you should check this out! Taken directly from former President Gerald Ford's daily diary, read what a typical day in the life of the president is really like. The day is Monday, April 28, 1975. The day begins with breakfast at 6:50 A.M. and goes nonstop from there with staff meetings, press conferences, and various other meetings with important people from all over the world. At 9:15 P.M., the President and First Lady have dinner (hey, whatever happened to lunch?). Then, phone calls and more phone calls, and some pretty serious decision making in the Situation Room. At 12:05 A.M., the President finally returns to his second-floor bedroom so he can catch a few hours of sleep and then do it all over again.

http://sunsite.unc.edu/sullivan/ford/DayInTheLife.html

Dear Mr. Lincoln...

How would you like to take a trip back in history? More precisely, how about traveling back through the years to visit with Abraham Lincoln himself? That's right, Honest Abe, president number 16, is available for your questions. Through the magic of the Internet and a very knowledgeable actor who portrays Lincoln, you can send messages to a man many consider one of the greatest presidents of the U.S.

http://www.gettysbg.com/dearmr.html

The First Ladies

In recognition of the significant contribution to American history made by many of the presidents' wives, the First Ladies Web site has been added to the official White House Home Page. From Martha Dandridge Custis Washington to Hillary Rodham Clinton, read about their upbringing, their education, their courtships, their marriages, their children, and many interesting facets of their lives.

http://www.whitehouse.gov/WH/glimpse/firstladies/
    html/firstladies.html

Hillary Rodham Clinton, First Lady of the United States

Bet you didn't know that Hillary Clinton is a serious baseball fan! Her father used to take her to all the Cubs games at Wrigley Field in Chicago when she was young. She was even invited to throw out the first ball of the Cubs' 1994 season. Check out this official site for more interesting facts about the First Lady of the United States. Her speeches are also included here.

http://www.whitehouse.gov/WH/EOP/First_Lady/
    html/HILLARY_Home.html

Hillary Rodham Clinton - WIC Biography

From her close-knit family in Park Ridge, Illinois, to Yale Law School to First Lady of Arkansas to the White House, Hillary Rodham Clinton has expressed her special concerns for protecting children and their families. Read about her many activities and the programs she has pioneered.

http://www.wic.org/bio/hclinton.htm

Inaugural Addresses of the Presidents of the United States

George Washington's second-term inaugural speech remains the shortest on record, requiring only 135 words. William Henry Harrison delivered one of the longest, speaking for an hour and 45 minutes in a blinding snowstorm. He then stood in the cold and greeted well-wishers all day; he died a month later, of pneumonia. Read the speech here, but make sure you keep your hat on! Project Bartleby, at Columbia University in New York, houses a home page containing the inaugural addresses of the presidents. Also included is an article about presidents sworn in but not inaugurated and the Oath of Office itself. This is a good site for finding inaugural factoids, such as the revelation that Geronimo, the great Apache, attended the inauguration of Teddy Roosevelt and that attendees at Grover Cleveland's second inaugural ball were all agog at the new invention: electric lights!

http://www.columbia.edu/acis/bartleby/inaugural/

Inside the White House @ nationalgeographic.com

Imagine you've just been elected president of the United States! What would your first decision be? What can people expect of your presidency? You can let your imagination soar and get an idea of what it's like to sit in the president's Oval Office right here at this Web page. Best yet, you'll learn loads about presidents and U.S. history while having fun. Be careful of those pesky newspaper reporters and radio talk show hosts!

http://www.nationalgeographic.com/features/96/
    whitehouse/whhome.html

The Presidents of the United States

For some kids growing up in the United States, becoming president is the highest ambition. So far, only a few people have achieved that goal, and the job of president is a tough one. At this White House site, you can read quick facts about each president, find links to other informative Web pages, and get a sense of the times and struggles of each leader of the U.S. Who knows, maybe some day you'll grow up to be president, and your picture will be on these Web pages!

http://www1.whitehouse.gov/WH/glimpse/
    presidents/html/presidents.html

A B C D E F G H I J K L M N O P Q R S T U V W X Y Z

A
B
C
D
E
F
G
H
I
J
K
L
M
N
O
P
Q
R
S
T
U
V
W
X
Y
Z

Presidents of the United States IPL POTUS

This site is loaded with information about all of the U.S. presidents. You'll find a picture or photo, information about their elections, inaugurations, terms of office, and cabinet members. There are also links to other resources around the Net; for example, learning about "Thomas Jefferson," we can take a virtual visit to his home, called Monticello. There are also links to biographies, historical documents, and trivia. Did you know that Jefferson wrote his own obituary and did not mention that he had served as president of the United States?

http://www.ipl.org/ref/POTUS/

US Presidents Lists

What a great way to learn American history and master presidential trivia all at once! Which U.S. president said, "The only thing we have to fear is fear itself"? (Franklin Roosevelt) Which president was responsible for starting the National Park Service in 1916? (Woodrow Wilson) Who initiated the United Nations? (Harry Truman) How about the Peace Corps? (John F. Kennedy) You can find answers to these questions and much more as you zip through more than 200 years of American history. Read the brief biographies of each U.S. president. The entry for each president includes a description of his administration, its chief concerns, highlights of his years in office, and links to his inaugural speeches.

http://www.fujisan.demon.co.uk/USPresidents/
   preslist.htm

STATES

Do you need information about a U.S. state? We've found it for you! The "official" home page of each state's government, a direct link to each state's symbols, and the best tourism site we could find are all included. General information about each state can usually be found at either the "official" or the "tourism" site, and often at both. Expect to find information here on each state's history, culture, statistics, travel, and more.

50 States and Capitals

Pick a state, any state. Or pick a territory; they are here too. You'll get a page with lots of information about each area. For example, look at Nebraska, the Cornhusker State; its capital is Lincoln. See the state flag, the bird, the flower, the song, even links to other information about the state. Hey, did you know Nebraska was the birthplace of President Gerald R. Ford? You do now!

http://www.50states.com/

Color Landform Atlas of the United States

What state are you interested in? They are all here, but how about New York? At this site you can see a color physical map of the state, or a black-and-white map, or an 1895 map, or a counties map. There is also a satellite photo of the state, with its outlines marked. Here's the fun part. There are links to other specific types of information about New York. See New York watershed maps, find out where the toxic waste dumps are, explore national parks and historic sites in New York, and find out about roadside attractions such as the Cardiff Giant hoax. Parents: Be sure to explore the Roadside America part of the site with your kids.

http://fermi.jhuapl.edu/states/states.html

The Life of a Bill in Mississippi

Governments have lots of laws and rules for people and businesses to follow. When a new law is needed, it goes through a maze of committees and meetings. The proposed new law is called a *bill*. This page contains a nice chart that shows all the steps necessary for a bill to become a law in Mississippi.

http://www.peer.state.ms.us/LifeOfBill.html

State and Local Government on the Net

Hear ye, hear ye! Citizens that be among you wishing to partake of information from the category of state, federal, and tribal governments, assemble freely here. Delve ye deep within diverse agencies and departments. What ye find may astound you. Here be thy taxes at work.

http://www.piperinfo.com/state/states.html

Stately Knowledge

Stately Knowledge is one of Net-mom's favorites because it is part of the Internet Public Library Web site, and Net-mom's on the board of trustees there. Besides information on every state (and Washington, D.C.), you can play a state capitals game or a state flags game and find a great list of online resources for your assignment.

http://www.ipl.org/youth/stateknow/

Know your ALPHABET? Now try someone else's in LANGUAGES AND ALPHABETS.

ALABAMA

Located in the Deep South, Alabama is the 22nd state. Alabama is an Indian name for "tribal town." The state bird is the yellowhammer, and the flower is the camellia.

Official State Home Page:
AlaWeb Home Page
http://alaweb.asc.edu/

State Symbols:
Alabama Archives: Emblems and Symbols
http://www.asc.edu/archives/emblems.html

State Tourism:
AlaWeb - Tourism Page
http://alaweb.asc.edu/ala_tours/tours.html

ALASKA

Alaska is the largest state, in area, and is home to the tallest mountain in the United States, Mount McKinley (20,320 feet). It's both the westernmost and easternmost state at the same time! This curiosity is possible because, technically, part of the Aleutian Island chain of Alaska is located in the Eastern Hemisphere, while the rest of Alaska is in the Western Hemisphere. Alaska gets its name from an Inuit word for "great lands." It is the 49th state, and some of it lies above the Arctic Circle.

Official State Home Page:
State of Alaska Home Page
http://www.state.ak.us/

State Symbols:
Official Student Information Guide to Alaska
http://www.commerce.state.ak.us/tourism/student.htm

State Tourism:
Alaska Division of Tourism
http://www.commerce.state.ak.us/tourism/

ARIZONA

The 48th state, Arizona, is home to the largest gorge in the U.S.: the Grand Canyon. It is 277 miles long and one mile deep. The name is from the Aztec word *arizuma,* meaning "silver bearing." The official state bird is the cactus wren and the flower is the saguaro cactus. This western desert state has lots of cactus!

Official State Home Page:
Arizona State Web Site
http://www.state.az.us/

State Symbols:
Stately Knowledge: Arizona: Just the Facts
http://www.ipl.org/youth/stateknow/az1.html

State Tourism:
Arizona Guide
http://www.arizonaguide.com/

ARKANSAS

Rice grows in much of the lowlands of the 25th state. Midlands Arkansas is home to Hot Springs National Park, where people come from miles around to relax and soothe their tired muscles in the hot mineral baths. The name is from the Quapaw language and means "downstream people." The official state bird is the mockingbird.

Official State Home Page:
Welcome to the State of Arkansas!
http://www.state.ar.us/

State Symbols:
Welcome to the State of Arkansas
http://www.arkansasusa.com/Arkansas.html

State Tourism:
Arkansas - Vacation in The Natural State
http://www.1800natural.com/

A
B
C
D
E
F
G
H
I
J
K
L
M
N
O
P
Q
R
S
T
U
V
W
X
Y
Z

CALIFORNIA

California, the 31st state, was once part of Mexico. It is known for its national park, Yosemite. Also, the lowest point of land in the United States is Death Valley, at 282 feet below sea level. Located on the west coast, California is known as the Golden State. The state tree is the California redwood, and its flower is the golden poppy.

Official State Home Page:
Welcome to the California Home Page
http://www.state.ca.us/s/

State Symbols:
History and Culture - State Insignia
http://library.ca.gov/california/cahinsig.html

State Tourism:
CA Home Page: Traveling & Vacations
http://www.ca.gov/s/travel/

COLORADO

One of the Rocky Mountain states, Colorado has the highest average elevation of all the states, and over 50 of the highest mountain peaks in the U.S. are found there. Yes, skiing is popular in Colorado! The 38th state has had over 20,000 years of human habitation. Its state flower is the graceful Rocky Mountain columbine.

Official State Home Page:
State of Colorado Home Page
http://www.state.co.us/

State Symbols:
Colorado Emblems, Symbols, Flag and State Seal
http://www.state.co.us/gov_dir/gss/archives/
  arcembl.html

State Tourism:
Tourism and Recreation in Colorado
http://www.state.co.us/visit_dir/visitormenu.html

I wonder what the QUEENS, KINGS, AND ROYALTY are doing tonight?

Did the groundhog see his shadow? Find out if it will be an early spring in HOLIDAYS.

CONNECTICUT

Settled by the Dutch in the early 1600s, Connecticut was one of the original 13 colonies. It is the fifth state. The name of this East Coast state comes from a Mohican word meaning "long river place." The official state song is "Yankee Doodle."

Official State Home Page:
ConneCT - State of Connecticut Website
http://www.state.ct.us/

State Symbols:
State of Connecticut - Sites, Seals and Symbols
http://www.state.ct.us/emblems.htm

State Tourism:
Connecticut Tourism Home Page
http://www.state.ct.us/tourism/

DELAWARE

Delaware was the first state, becoming one in 1787. It's the second smallest state in area, ahead only of Rhode Island. Delaware was named after Lord De La Warr, a governor of Virginia. The motto of this eastern seaboard state is "Liberty and independence."

Official State Home Page:
State of Delaware
http://www.state.de.us/

State Symbols:
Delaware Facts
http://www.state.de.us/facts/history/delfact.htm

State Tourism:
Delaware Tourism
http://www.state.de.us/tourism/intro.htm

DISTRICT OF COLUMBIA

Although it's not a state at all, the District of Columbia is well known for its city of Washington, D.C. It's the special place where the United States government buildings and leaders are. The president of the U.S. lives there, and you can visit the White House and other historic buildings either in person or over the Net. The District of Columbia has its own "state" motto, "Justice for all," as well as an official flower (American beauty rose), tree (scarlet oak), and bird (wood thrush).

Official Home Page:
D.C. Home Page
http://www.ci.washington.dc.us/

Symbols:
Stately Knowledge: Washington D.C.: Just the Facts
http://www.ipl.org/youth/stateknow/dc1.html

Tourism:
Official Tourism Website of Washington, DC
http://www.washington.org/

FLORIDA

Florida has the distinction of being the flattest state. It is also home to the southernmost spot in the continental United States. Its peninsula divides the Atlantic Ocean from the Gulf of Mexico. Florida was named by Ponce de León in 1513; it means "flowery Easter." Lots of oranges and grapefruit grow here due to the mild, sunny climate. The 27th state's official flower is the orange blossom!

Official State Home Page:
Florida Government Services DIRECT
http://www.state.fl.us/

State Symbols:
Florida Symbols
http://www.dos.state.fl.us/symbols/

State Tourism:
Communities of Interests
http://fcn.state.fl.us/oraweb/owa/
www_index.show?p_searchkey=168&pframe=1

GEORGIA

Georgia is named after King George II of England. The Cumberland Island National Seashore is a coastal wilderness area located in Georgia, also famous for its sea islands. The 1996 Summer Olympics were held in Atlanta. The fourth state's official tree is the live oak.

Official State Home Page:
State of Georgia
http://www.state.ga.us/

State Symbols:
Georgia's Official State Symbols
http://www.sos.state.ga.us/museum/html/
state_symbols.html

State Tourism:
Georgia Department of Industry, Trade, and Tourism
http://www.georgia.org/

HAWAII

Hawaii's Mount Waialeale, on the island of Kauai, is the rainiest place in the world, with an average rainfall of over 460 inches a year. Also within this tropical state is the southernmost spot in the U.S., at Ka Lae on the Big Island of Hawaii. Hawaii is comprised of over 130 Pacific islands, but there are eight main islands. Its name is believed to have come from the native word *Hawaiki*, meaning "homeland." It is the 50th state, and its state tree is the candlenut. Some people in Hawaii are trying to return the state to sovereign nationhood. Please see the entry for the Nation of Hawai'i in the NATIVE AMERICANS AND OTHER INDIGENOUS PEOPLES—NATIVE HAWAIIANS section.

Official State Home Page:
Hawaii State Government Home Page
http://www.state.hi.us/

State Symbols:
Hawaii Information for School Reports
http://www.gohawaii.com/hokeo/school/report.html

State Tourism:
Hawaii Visitors & Convention Bureau
http://www.visit.hawaii.org/

A
B
C
D
E
F
G
H
I
J
K
L
M
N
O
P
Q
R
S
T
U
V
W
X
Y
Z

IDAHO

Idaho is known for its farming and its most famous crop, the Idaho potato. The deepest gorge in North America is in Hells Canyon, along the Idaho-Oregon border, measuring 7,900 feet deep. This Rocky Mountain state's official bird is the mountain bluebird. It is the 43rd state.

Official State Home Page:
State of Idaho Home Page
http://www2.state.id.us/

State Symbols:
Idaho Symbols
http://www2.state.id.us/gov/symbols.htm

State Tourism:
Idaho Travel and Tourism Guide
http://www.visitid.org/

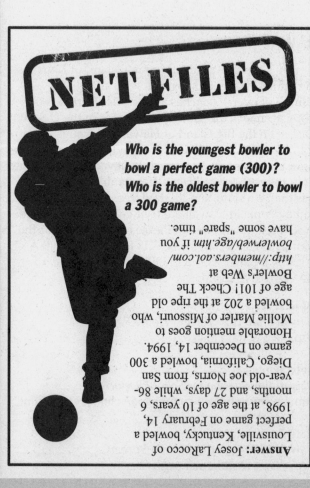

Who is the youngest bowler to bowl a perfect game (300)? Who is the oldest bowler to bowl a 300 game?

Answer: Josey LaRocco of Louisville, Kentucky, bowled a perfect game on February 14, 1998, at the age of 10 years, 6 months, and 27 days, while 86-year-old Joe Norris, from San Diego, California, bowled a 300 game on December 14, 1994. Honorable mention goes to Mollie Marler of Missouri, who bowled a 202 at the ripe old age of 101! Check The Bowler's Web at http://members.aol.com/bowlerweb/age.htm if you have some "spare" time.

ILLINOIS

Illinois is the Algonquin word for "warriors." The 21st state is also known as the Land of Lincoln, in homage to the 16th president, who lived and is buried in the Springfield area. The tallest building in the United States is the Sears Tower in Chicago, Illinois. The official bird of this Midwest state is the red cardinal.

Official State Home Page:
State of Illinois
http://www.state.il.us/

State Symbols:
State Symbols of Illinois
http://www.museum.state.il.us/exhibits/symbols/

State Tourism:
State of Illinois – Tourism
http://www.state.il.us/tourism/

INDIANA

The 19th state, Indiana means "land of the Indians." Indianapolis, its capital and largest city, is where the Indianapolis 500 auto race is held every year. This Midwest state's official tree is the tulip tree.

Official State Home Page:
Access Indiana Information Network
http://www.state.in.us/

State Symbols:
Some Emblems of the State of Indiana
http://www.ai.org/sic/emblems/

State Tourism:
Indiana Tourism
http://www.ai.org/tourism/

IOWA

A major producer of corn and soybeans, Midwest state Iowa is a Native American name for "beautiful land." It is the 29th state. Its state bird is the colorful and jaunty eastern goldfinch.

Official State Home Page:
State of Iowa Home Page
http://www.state.ia.us/

State Symbols:
Table of Contents for Iowa State Symbols
http://www2.legis.state.ia.us/Pubinfo/StateSymbols/

State Tourism:
Iowa Travel/Tourism
http://www.state.ia.us/tourism/

KANSAS

The geographical center of the lower 48 states is located near Lebanon, Kansas. Kansas is a Sioux word meaning "south wind people." Famous for farming and wheat fields, the 34th state is also known as the mythical home of Dorothy and Toto of *The Wizard of Oz*.

Official State Home Page:
State of Kansas (INK)
http://www.state.ks.us/

State Symbols:
Kansas State Symbols
http://skyways.lib.ks.us/kansas/KSL/Ref/
  GovDocs/Kan/symbols.html

State Tourism:
KANSAS SIGHTS
http://www.ukans.edu/heritage/kssights/

KENTUCKY

Kentucky, the "land of tomorrow," has what is possibly the largest cave system in the world, Mammoth Caves. The 15th state is also known for its many thoroughbred horse farms. Its state flower is the goldenrod.

Official State Home Page:
Commonwealth of Kentucky Homepage
http://www.state.ky.us/

State Symbols:
*Commonwealth of Kentucky - Web Server -
  Kentucky Facts*
http://www.state.ky.us/kyfacts/history.htm

State Tourism:
Official Kentucky Vacation Guide
http://www.state.ky.us/tour/tour.htm

> Bring your shovel and meet us in the TREASURE AND TREASURE-HUNTING section.

> Brother reading your diary again? Learn to encrypt in CODES AND CIPHERS.

LOUISIANA

This southern state is where the mighty Mississippi River enters the Gulf of Mexico. Its largest city, New Orleans, is famous for its Mardi Gras celebration, held every year on the last day before Lent. The 18th state's bird is the brown pelican, which also appears on the state flag.

Official State Home Page:
Welcome to INFO Louisiana
http://www.state.la.us/

State Symbols:
Louisiana Symbols
http://www.crt.state.la.us/crt/symbols.htm

State Tourism:
Louisiana Department of Tourism
http://www.crt.state.la.us/crt/tourism.htm

MAINE

This is the state where the lobster rules. It's also the easternmost point of the U.S. mainland. The 23rd state is also famous for Acadia National Park and its rugged coastline. The state bird is the playful black-capped chickadee, and the official tree is the eastern white pine.

Official State Home Page:
Maine State Government Web Site
http://www.state.me.us/

State Symbols:
Visitmaine.com - State Facts & Information
http://www.visitmaine.com/facts.html

State Tourism:
*Visitmaine.com and The Main Office of Tourism
  Welcome You*
http://www.visitmaine.com/

A
B
C
D
E
F
G
H
I
J
K
L
M
N
O
P
Q
R
S
T
U
V
W
X
Y
Z

A
B
C
D
E
F
G
H
I
J
K
L
M
N
O
P
Q
R
S
T
U
V
W
X
Y
Z

MARYLAND

The east coast of Maryland is near where the District of Columbia, the capital of the United States, is located. The national anthem, "The Star Spangled Banner," by Sir Francis Scott Key, was inspired by a battle in 1814 at historic Fort McHenry. Surrounding the Chesapeake Bay, much of eastern Maryland is known for its fishing industries, particularly for soft-shelled crabs. You may have read the horse story, *Misty of Chincoteague*, by Marguerite Henry. These stories were set at the Assateague National Seashore, which Maryland shares with neighboring Virginia. The seventh state, Maryland's state bird is the northern oriole.

Official State Home Page:
Maryland government - The Maryland Electronic Capital
http://www.mec.state.md.us/

State Symbols:
Maryland POGs
http://www.inform.umd.edu/UMS+State/ UMD-Projects/MCTP/Technology/ School_WWW_Pages/pogs/

State Tourism:
Maryland Tourism
http://www.mdisfun.org/

MASSACHUSETTS

The Pilgrims landed at Plymouth Rock, near Boston, on December 21, 1620. They later started one of the most traditional American feasts, Thanksgiving. Native Americans helped them to survive. Famous folks from Massachusetts include John F. Kennedy and Louisa May Alcott. The sixth state's official flower is the mayflower.

Official State Home Page:
Commonwealth of Massachusetts
http://www.state.ma.us/

State Symbols:
Massachusetts Facts
http://www.state.ma.us/sec/cis/cismaf/mafidx.htm

State Tourism:
Massachusetts Office of Travel and Tourism
http://www.mass-vacation.com/

MICHIGAN

Henry Ford's Detroit auto factory began an industry that has made Michigan the center of U.S. car manufacturing. Michigan gets its name from *mici gama*, the Chippewa words meaning "great water." Michigan is in two parts, the Upper and Lower Peninsulas. It has shoreline on four of the Great Lakes: Lake Michigan, Lake Huron, Lake Erie, and Lake Superior. The 26th state's official bird is the robin.

Official State Home Page:
Michigan State Government
http://www.migov.state.mi.us/

State Symbols:
Michigan's State Symbols
http://www.sos.state.mi.us/history/michinfo/ symbols/symbols.html

State Tourism:
Travel Michigan
http://www.michigan.org/

MINNESOTA

The Mississippi River starts here! Minnesota is from the Sioux word meaning "cloudy water," but it referred to the Minnesota River. This northern border state has over 15,000 lakes, left there by glaciers. The 32nd state's official bird is the common loon, and its flower is the pink and white lady's slipper.

Official State Home Page:
Minnesota Government Information and Services
http://www.state.mn.us/

State Symbols:
All About Minnesota Page 5
http://www.state.mn.us/aam/aamp5-6.html

State Tourism:
Welcome to Minnesota
http://www.exploreminnesota.com/

MISSISSIPPI

Southern state Mississippi's history dates back to the 1500s, when Spanish explorers visited the area. The French were first to settle it, however, in 1699. The 20th state was a center of attention in the 1960s with the activities of the civil rights movement. The state flower is the sweetly scented magnolia.

Official State Home Page:
State Of Mississippi
http://www.state.ms.us/

State Symbols:
U.S. Senator Thad Cochran — Mississippi Facts
http://www.senate.gov/member/ms/cochran/
general/facts.html

State Tourism:
Welcome to Mississippi, The South's Warmest Welcome
http://www.decd.state.ms.us/tourism.htm

MISSOURI

Two major rivers, the Missouri and the Mississippi, meet in the 24th state. Samuel Clemens, also known as Mark Twain, lived in Hannibal, Missouri, on the Mississippi River. The Ozark Mountains in this state contain more than 400 caves. A dam on the Osage River holds back the Lake of the Ozarks, one of the largest man-made lakes in the world. The official state tree is the hawthorn.

Official State Home Page:
Missouri State Government Home Page
http://www.state.mo.us/

State Symbols:
Missouri Facts & Figures
http://www.ecodev.state.mo.us/tourism/facts/

State Tourism:
The Official State of Missouri Division of Tourism Homepage
http://www.ecodev.state.mo.us/tourism/

MONTANA

Montana is "Big Sky Country," a nickname that came from the wide-open spaces that dominate the eastern grasslands. However, the Rocky Mountains in the west are responsible for its name, the Spanish word for "mountains." The 41st state's official tree is the ponderosa pine.

Official State Home Page:
Montana Online: Homepage For The STATE OF MONTANA
http://www.state.mt.us/

State Symbols:
MT KIDS: Montana Facts - State Symbols
http://kids.state.mt.us/db_engine/
subcat.asp?Subcat=State+Symbols

State Tourism:
Montana Travel Guide
http://travel.mt.gov/

NEBRASKA

Nebraska's name is from the Omaha word meaning "broad water," referring to the Platte River. The Agate Fossil Beds National Monument contains bones from animals over 22 million years old. This Great Plains state is known for farming and grazing land. The official tree of the 37th state is the cottonwood.

Official State Home Page:
State of Nebraska, Official Website
http://www.state.ne.us/

State Symbols:
Nebraska's State Symbols
http://visitnebraska.org/reports/symbols.txt

State Tourism:
GENUINE.NEBRASKA @ VisitNebraska.Org
http://visitnebraska.org/

A
B
C
D
E
F
G
H
I
J
K
L
M
N
O
P
Q
R
S
T
U
V
W
X
Y
Z

NEVADA

Nevada's Hoover Dam on the Colorado River is one of the tallest dams in the world. Tourists from around the world visit Las Vegas for its gambling and entertainment. The official flower of the 36th state is the pungent sagebrush.

Official State Home Page:
State of Nevada Home Page
http://www.state.nv.us/

State Symbols:
Nevada Information
http://www.travelnevada.com/visitorinfo/
　　nevada_info.html

State Tourism:
Welcome to Nevada
http://www.travelnevada.com/

NEW HAMPSHIRE

This state's motto is "Live free or die." Although New Hampshire was the ninth state to be admitted into the United States, it was the first colony to declare its independence from Britain. Its state flower is the sweetly scented purple lilac.

Official State Home Page:
*WEBSTER: The New Hampshire State Government
　　Online Information Center*
http://www.state.nh.us/

State Symbols:
The New Hampshire Almanac
http://www.state.nh.us/nhinfo/nhinfo.html

State Tourism:
*State of New Hampshire Information @
　　NH.com - Tourism & Travel*
http://www.nh.com/tourism/

NEW JERSEY

The third state admitted to the Union was New Jersey. Northeastern New Jersey is densely populated, with close ties to New York City. It is also known for Atlantic City, a popular seaside resort. The state flower is the purple violet.

Official State Home Page:
New Jersey Home Page
http://www.state.nj.us/

State Symbols:
Official Symbols of the State of New Jersey
http://www.state.nj.us/njfacts/njsymbol.htm

State Tourism:
NJ Travel and Tourism Home Page
http://www.state.nj.us/travel/

NEW MEXICO

The 47th state has many natural wonders. Carlsbad Caverns National Park has caves that are over 11,000 feet deep and 20 miles long. This western desert state claims the yucca as its official flower and the roadrunner as its bird.

Official State Home Page:
State of New Mexico Government Information
http://www.state.nm.us/

State Symbols:
More New Mexico Facts
http://stoper.nmt.edu/facts.htm

State Tourism:
*New Mexico Department of Tourism -
　　Enchantment USA*
http://www.newmexico.org/

You can always count on the info in MATH AND ARITHMETIC.

NEW YORK

From New York City to the Adirondack Mountains to Niagara Falls, New York has a diverse array of sights. Its history dates back to the 1620s, when the Dutch colonized Manhattan Island. The Baseball Hall of Fame is located in Cooperstown. The 11th state's official tree is the sugar maple. This state also has an official muffin!

Official State Home Page:
Welcome to New York State
http://www.state.ny.us/

State Symbols:
I LOVE NY - THE EMPIRE STATE
http://iloveny.state.ny.us/emblems.html

State Tourism:
I LOVE NY - TOURISM IN NEW YORK STATE
http://www.iloveny.state.ny.us/

NORTH CAROLINA

Orville Wright made his historic first flight at coastal Kitty Hawk, North Carolina. The first English settlement in the Americas was made on Roanoke Island in 1587, but three years later, the village was found abandoned and in ruins. What happened to these people remains a mystery to this day. The 12th state's official tree is the long-leafed pine.

Official State Home Page:
North Carolina Information Server
http://www.state.nc.us/

State Symbols:
Official State Symbols of North Carolina
http://statelibrary.dcr.state.nc.us/nc/symbols/
   symbols.htm

State Tourism:
The Official North Carolina Travel Guide
http://www.visitnc.com/cat/visitnc/index.html

You are your own network.

DINOSAURS are prehistoric, but they are under "D."

NORTH DAKOTA

This state is famous for its uneven territory known as the Badlands. The Badlands were justly named by early travelers, because they are almost impossible to cross. Dakota is a Sioux word, meaning "friend." A 2,063-foot TV tower in Blanchard, North Dakota, is the tallest man-made structure in the country. North Dakota's official flower is the wild prairie rose. It is the 39th state.

Official State Home Page:
The State of North Dakota
http://www.state.nd.us/

State Symbols:
Facts & Info
http://www.glness.com/tourism/html/Facts.html

State Tourism:
North Dakota Travel & Tourism
http://www.glness.com/tourism/

OHIO

Ohio is an Iroquois word, meaning "good river." Ohio was one of the ancient homes of the Mound Builders, who built thousands of earthen burial and ceremonial mounds, many of which can be seen today. The Pro Football Hall of Fame is located in Canton. The 17th state's official tree is the buckeye.

Official State Home Page:
Official Ohio Home Page
http://www.state.oh.us/

State Symbols:
Ohio Citizen's Digest
http://www.oplin.lib.oh.us/OHIO/OCJ/

State Tourism:
Ohio Division of Travel and Tourism
http://www.ohiotourism.com/

A B C D E F G H I J K L M N O P Q R S T **U** V W X Y Z

A
B
C
D
E
F
G
H
I
J
K
L
M
N
O
P
Q
R
S
T
U
V
W
X
Y
Z

RAILROADS are on track.

OKLAHOMA

The deepest well in the U.S. is located in Washita County. This gas well is 31,441 feet deep! Oklahoma gets its name from a Choctaw word, meaning "red man." The 46th state's official tree is the redbud. Yahoo! The National Cowboy Hall of Fame is in Oklahoma City.

Official State Home Page:
O K L A H O M A
http://www.state.ok.us/

State Symbols:
State Emblems
http://www.otrd.state.ok.us/StudentGuide/
   emblems.html

State Tourism:
Oklahoma Tourism and Recreation Department
http://www.otrd.state.ok.us/

OREGON

The deepest lake in the United States is Crater Lake, in Crater Lake National Park, with depths to 1,932 feet. This lake is located inside an ancient volcano and has no water flowing in or out. Oregon's west coast is known for its dense woods and beautiful, mountainous scenery. Its state tree is the Douglas fir. It is the 33rd state.

Official State Home Page:
Welcome to Oregon On-Line!
http://www.state.or.us/

State Symbols:
Oregon State Trivia
http://www.state.or.us/trivia.htm

State Tourism:
*Official Oregon Tourism Web Site: Planning An
   Oregon Vacation*
http://www.traveloregon.com/

PENNSYLVANIA

Pennsylvania was settled by Quakers from Great Britain in the 1680s. In 1863, during the Civil War, a famous battle was fought in Gettysburg. You'll also find the Liberty Bell in Philadelphia. Pennsylvania, which is the second state, has a small border on one of the Great Lakes, Lake Erie. Its official bird is the ruffed grouse.

Official State Home Page:
Pennsylvania Main Homepage
http://www.state.pa.us/

State Symbols:
Pennsylvania Fact Sheet
http://www.state.pa.us/visit/html/
   pennsylvania_fact_sheet.html

State Tourism:
Pennsylvania Visitors Guide
http://www.state.pa.us/visit/index2.html

RHODE ISLAND

Rhode Island is the smallest state in the U.S. It is also the 13th of the original 13 colonies and the 13th state. The first factory in the U.S. was built there in the 1790s. This east coast state's official bird is the Rhode Island red chicken.

Official State Home Page:
Rhode Island State Government
http://www.info.state.ri.us/

State Symbols:
Rhode Island State Emblems
http://www.state.ri.us/rihist/riemb.htm

State Tourism:
Visit Rhode Island
http://www.visitrhodeisland.com/index2.html

The wonderful world of worms may be admired in the section called INVERTEBRATES.

Find your roots in GENEALOGY.

SOUTH CAROLINA

The Civil War started in South Carolina, at Fort Sumter, in Charleston harbor. This historic east coast city is very well-preserved. Hilton Head and Myrtle Beach are well-known and popular seaside vacation sites. The eighth state's official bird is the Carolina wren.

Official State Home Page:
State of South Carolina-Public Information Home Page
http://www.state.sc.us/

State Symbols:
Symbols & Emblems - S.C. General Assembly – LPITR
http://www.lpitr.state.sc.us/symbols.htm

State Tourism:
Welcome to South Carolina
http://www.sccsi.com/sc/

SOUTH DAKOTA

Famous Mount Rushmore is located in the Black Hills of South Dakota. Four 60-foot heads of U.S. presidents have been sculpted on the side of a mountain. The Black Hills look "black" from a distance because they are covered with dense pine forests. The 40th state's official bird is the ring-necked pheasant.

Official State Home Page:
South Dakota Home Page
http://www.state.sd.us/

State Symbols:
Signs and Symbols of South Dakota
http://www.state.sd.us/state/sdsym.htm

State Tourism:
Department of Tourism
http://www.state.sd.us/state/executive/tourism/

TENNESSEE

Tennessee, the 16th state, is known for the Great Smoky Mountains National Park. Nashville is famous as a world center for country music. The official state flower is the iris.

Official State Home Page:
Tennessee Sounds Good to Me
http://www.state.tn.us/

State Symbols:
Tennessee Symbols and Honors
http://www.state.tn.us/sos/symbols.htm

State Tourism:
Department of Tourist Development Vacation Guide
http://www.state.tn.us/tourdev/vacguide.html

TEXAS

Cattle and oil dominate the economy of Texas. It's the second-largest state in area, after Alaska. A famous battle in 1836, between thousands of Mexicans and a few hundred Texans, took place at an old Spanish mission called the Alamo, located in San Antonio. "Remember the Alamo" is a famous battle cry. Texas is the 28th state, and its flower is the bluebonnet.

Official State Home Page:
State of Texas Government World Wide Web
http://www.state.tx.us/

State Symbols:
Texas, the Lone Star State
http://www.main.org/boyscout/texas.htm

State Tourism:
TravelTex: Texas it's Like a Whole Other Country
http://www.traveltex.com/

> "A ship in the harbor is safe, but that is not what ships are built for."
> —John A. Shedd

UTAH

Utah comes from a Navajo word, meaning "upper." Salt Lake City is the spiritual center of the Church of Jesus Christ of Latter-Day Saints (Mormon) religion. The Great Salt Lake in Utah is eight times saltier than the ocean. Utah is the 45th state, and its official bird is the seagull.

Official State Home Page:
State of Utah Navigational Network
http://www.state.ut.us/

State Symbols:
Symbols of Utah
http://www.state.lib.ut.us/symbols/symbols.htm

State Tourism:
Utah Travel and Adventure
http://www.utah.com/

VERMONT

Vert and *mont* are French for "green" and "mountain," respectively. The Green Mountains are located in Vermont. One interesting fact about Vermont is that it has no major cities. This makes it the most rural state in the country. Its official flower is the red clover, and it is the 14th state.

Official State Home Page:
State of Vermont Home Page
http://www.cit.state.vt.us/

State Symbols:
Vermont State Emblems
http://dol.state.vt.us/www_root/000000/html/
   emblems.html

State Tourism:
*A Vermont Travelers' Guide - The official Vermont
   Internet travel and tourism guide.*
http://www.travel-vermont.com/

NET FILES

When you're giving an opinion, sometimes you say that's your "two cents' worth." Where did that phrase originate?

Answer: According to Evan Morris, "Two cents or two-center has been a slang synonym for 'very cheap' since the middle of the nineteenth century, when the cheapest cigar available was literally a two-center. The U.S. Treasury Department actually issued a two-cent coin in 1864, which was, incidentally, the first U.S. coin to bear the motto 'In God We Trust.' The government, evidently feeling frisky in a monetary sort of way, also issued coins in three-cent and twenty-cent denominations during the same period." Read more at *http://www.word-detective.com/back-k.html#cents*

VIRGINIA

Virginia has been home to both George Washington and Thomas Jefferson, and you can tour their historic homes today. Jamestown became the first permanent English settlement in 1607. It is the tenth state, and the dogwood is both its official tree and flower.

Official State Home Page:
Virginia! Welcome to the Commonwealth
http://www.state.va.us/

State Symbols:
Virginia Legislature - Symbols of the Commonwealth
http://legis.state.va.us./vaonline/vc3.htm

State Tourism:
Virginia Visitor's Guide
http://www.state.va.us/home/visitor.html

A B C D E F G H I J K L M N O P Q R S T **U** V W X Y Z

WASHINGTON

Coastal Washington state is known for its many natural features. The Cascade Range is where Mount St. Helens erupted in 1980. Olympic National Park contains vast sections of ancient rain forest. It is the 42nd state, and the rhododendron is the official flower.

Official State Home Page:
Home Page Washington
http://www.state.wa.us/

State Symbols:
The Symbols of Washington State
http://www.leg.wa.gov/www/admin/legis/symbols.htm

State Tourism:
Washington State Tourism Home Page
http://www.tourism.wa.gov/

WEST VIRGINIA

West Virginia's natural features are dominated by the Appalachian Mountains. Mining in these mountains is a major industry, and coal is the main product. The 35th state's official bird is the brilliantly colored cardinal.

Official State Home Page:
WV State Main Page
http://www.state.wv.us/

State Symbols:
West Virginia Fun Facts for Kids
http://www.state.wv.us/tourism/emblems.htm

State Tourism:
West Virginia Travel/Recreation and Tourism
http://wvweb.com/www/travel_recreation/
   Tourism_Home_Page2.html

WISCONSIN

Wisconsin is a state with over 8,000 lakes, carved out by glaciers long ago. This state has more dairy cows than any other state, so it's no wonder that milk and cheese are its major products. Bordered by two Great Lakes, Lake Superior and Lake Michigan, Wisconsin is the 30th state. Its official flower is the wood violet.

Official State Home Page:
State of Wisconsin
http://www.state.wi.us/

State Symbols:
More Wisconsin Facts
http://www.state.wi.us/agencies/tourism/guide/
   morefaq.htm

State Tourism:
Wisconsin Department of Tourism
http://tourism.state.wi.us/

WYOMING

Wyoming means "large prairie place" in Algonquin. Yellowstone National Park is famous for its geysers and hot springs (fictional "Jellystone Park" is where Yogi Bear and Boo-Boo live). This rugged Rocky Mountain state was the 44th to be admitted to the Union. Its official flower is the Indian paintbrush.

Official State Home Page:
Welcome to the State of Wyoming
http://www.state.wy.us/

State Symbols:
General Wyoming Information
http://www.state.wy.us/state/wyoming_news/
   general/general.html

State Tourism:
Wyoming Tourism Information
http://www.state.wy.us/state/tourism/tourism.html

A B C D E F G H I J K L M N O P Q R S T U V W X Y Z

A
B
C
D
E
F
G
H
I
J
K
L
M
N
O
P
Q
R
S
T
U
V
W
X
Y
Z

TERRITORIES

AMERICAN SAMOA

American Samoa

This 76-square-mile island group sits in the middle of the South Pacific Ocean, 2,600 miles from Hawaii. Its citizens are considered U.S. nationals and can freely enter the United States. American Samoa has a large tuna fishery; other exports include coconuts, taro, yams, bananas, and breadfruit. You can't make a sandwich out of breadfruit, by the way. Well, maybe you can in the Sandwich Islands, but not in American Samoa! If you go to this site, you'll hear a greeting in Samoan. Check the links for more interesting information on this island group.

http://prel-oahu-1.prel.hawaii.edu/pacific_region/
am_samoa/

American Samoa Office of Tourism - Department of Commerce

The official site of the American Samoa Tourism Office offers a history of the islands, information on language and culture, maps, and even a link to today's weather forecast. Should you need to experience sunny, 80-degree beaches, this site offers everything you need to plan your family's vacation, too.

http://www.samoanet.com/americansamoa/

Talofa from American Samoa

Congressman Eni Faleomavaega is American Samoa's delegate to the House of Representatives. *Talofa* is the traditional greeting. At his home page you can read his statements before the House, see legislation he has sponsored and cosponsored, and catch up on current American Samoa news.

http://www.house.gov/faleomavaega/

BAKER ISLAND

The World Factbook page on Baker Island

This is a teeny, low-lying atoll in the North Pacific Ocean, about one-half of the way from Hawaii to Australia. It was mined for its guano deposits until 1891. The birds are still there, the guano is still there, but you'll need a permit to visit. Only offshore anchorage is possible, and be advised that there are no malls or fast-food restaurants. This island is also a National Wildlife Refuge.

http://www.odci.gov/cia/publications/factbook/
fq.html

GUAM

Guam

Guam, located near the international date line, is "where America's Day Begins." This island is in the West Pacific, 3,700 miles from Hawaii. Guamanians are U.S. citizens.

http://www.odci.gov/cia/publications/
factbook/gq.html

Guam (U.S. Territory)

Hafa Adai! On this page you can hear a greeting in Chamaro, look at a map of Guam, and take some interesting links to other pages on Guam. If you'd like to try snorkeling, Guam is the place to visit. More than 300 varieties of coral make Guam a diver's delight. There's lots more to learn about Guam, and this site is the place to start.

http://prel-oahu-1.prel.hawaii.edu/
pacific_region/guam/

Guam's Official Congressional Web Site

Robert A. Underwood is Guam's delegate to the House of Representatives, and he's got a terrific Web site. Find out about Guam's history, view some maps, check out the current time in Guam, and read current news. There is up-to-date information on Guam's quest to become a commonwealth with the right of self-determination.

http://www.house.gov/underwood/welcome.html

Welcome to Guam

Sirena loved to swim in the sea! One day, she forgot her chores and spent the day swimming. When she did not come home, her angry mother said she should just become a fish if she loved the sea so much! Sirena's godmother quickly said, "But let the part of her that belongs to me remain." Sirena, still swimming, suddenly felt strange. She looked down and realized the lower part of her body had become a fish! The legend of Sirena is from Guam. Read more about the story and see a statue of Sirena at this home page, in the LEGENDS area.

http://ns.gov.gu/legends.html

HOWLAND ISLAND

The World Factbook page on Howland Island

This tiny, sandy island is in the North Pacific Ocean, about one-half of the way from Hawaii to Australia. It's a National Wildlife Refuge, and you need permission from the U.S. Department of the Interior to visit it. The island is famous because of someone who never made it there. In 1937, an airstrip was constructed there as a refueling stop on the round-the-world flight attempt of Amelia Earhart and Fred Noonan. They had left Lae, Papua New Guinea, for Howland Island, but something happened, and they were never seen again. Their disappearance is truly one of the world's great unsolved mysteries; read about it at The Earhart Project at <http://www.tighar.org/Projects/AEdescr.html>. Earhart Light, on the island's west coast, is a day beacon built in memory of the lost aviatrix. The airfield is no longer serviceable.

http://www.odci.gov/cia/publications/
factbook/hq.html

You won't believe how the PLANTS, TREES, AND GARDENS section grew!

JARVIS ISLAND

The World Factbook page on Jarvis Island

This tiny coral island is in the South Pacific Ocean, about one-half of the way from Hawaii to the Cook Islands. It is a favorite nesting and roosting area for seabirds, and until the late 1880s, guano was mined there. Bird droppings are a rich source of fertilizer, but it seems like a long way to go to get some. You can't visit Jarvis Island without permission of the U.S. Department of the Interior, since it is considered a National Wildlife Refuge.

http://www.odci.gov/cia/
publications/factbook/dq.html

JOHNSTON ATOLL

The World Factbook page on Johnston Atoll

This strategically located atoll group is in the North Pacific Ocean, about one-third of the way from Hawaii to the Marshall Islands. It's closed to the public and has been used for testing nuclear weapons. About 300 people work there on military and other projects. All food and other equipment has to be imported, but they do have excellent communications through an underwater cable link. Maybe they will get a home page on their own server soon!

http://www.odci.gov/cia/
publications/factbook/jq.html

KINGMAN REEF

The World Factbook page on Kingman Reef

We're talking very tiny: only one square kilometer of land area. This reef is in the North Pacific Ocean, about one-half of the way from Hawaii to American Samoa. It's only about one meter in elevation, so it's often awash with waves! If you go, bring your boots, but you'll need permission from the U.S. Navy. This reef was used as a way station by Pan American flying boats in 1937 and 1938. Now, it's basically known as a maritime hazard.

http://www.odci.gov/cia/publications/
factbook/kq.html

A
B
C
D
E
F
G
H
I
J
K
L
M
N
O
P
Q
R
S
T
U
V
W
X
Y
Z

MIDWAY ISLANDS

Midway Atoll

If you read the most interesting history of this remote island, you'll know why it has been in the possession of the U.S. Navy for many years. However, on April 3, 1997, Secretary of the Navy John Dalton presented the "key to Midway" (in the shape of a Laysan albatross) to Department of the Interior Assistant Secretary Bonnie Cohen. Now Midway Atoll National Wildlife Refuge is managed by the U.S. Fish and Wildlife Service and visitors are welcomed. This site explains how to get there, what to expect, and what to do once you arrive (besides relax).

http://www.midway-atoll.com/

The World Factbook page on Midway Islands

This is an atoll group in the North Pacific Ocean, about one-third of the way from Hawaii to Tokyo, Japan. Over 400 U.S. military personnel are stationed there, and the area is recently opened to the public. This is a famous World War II battle site, with many sunken wrecks in the area.

http://www.odci.gov/cia/publications/
    factbook/mq.html

NAVASSA

Navassa Island

The webmaster must be a fan of Navassa Island, because he's created a page with maps, photos, and information that rivals many. Gaze at the lighthouse, rising more than 160 feet off the hillside. View the lighthouse keeper's house, now abandoned and in ruins. Access to Navassa is hazardous (check the photos: rope ladders going up the rocky cliffs) and is allowed only by permission from the U.S. Department of the Interior.

http://members.aol.com/davidpb4/navassa.html

The World Factbook page on Navassa Island

This Caribbean island is strategically located, about one-fourth of the way from Haiti to Jamaica, south of Cuba. Haiti disputes the U.S. claim to the territory. Haitians fishing there often camp on the island, which has steep cliffs and is populated by goats and cactus.

http://www.odci.gov/cia/
    publications/factbook/bq.html

NORTHERN MARIANA ISLANDS

Commonwealth of the Northern Mariana Islands

Between Guam and the Tropic of Cancer lie the 17 volcanic islands that make up this commonwealth. Its inhabitants are U.S. citizens, and tourism is becoming a major industry.

http://prel-oahu-1.prel.hawaii.edu/
    pacific_region/cnmi/

Marianas Visitors Bureau-Commonwealth of the Northern Marianas

Saipan is the largest island in this group, and it's famous for its crystal clear, warm waters, perfect for viewing the coral reefs. Tinian is still partially used by a U.S. military presence, but on the rest of the island they expect large casinos to be built soon. Rota, a third island, offers exciting diving opportunities as well as golf.

http://www.saipan.com/tourism/

PALMYRA ATOLL

The World Factbook page on Palmyra Atoll

Administered by the U.S. Department of the Interior, this atoll group lies in the North Pacific Ocean, about one-half of the way from Hawaii to American Samoa. It has only 12 square kilometers in land area, and its many tiny islets are densely covered with vegetation and coconut palms.

http://www.odci.gov/cia/publications/
    factbook/lq.html

A B C D E F G H I J K L M N O P Q R S T U V W X Y Z

PUERTO RICO

Congressman Carlos Romero-Barceló

Carlos Romero Barceló is the resident commissioner, elected to that post by the people of Puerto Rico. He serves as a delegate to the House of Representatives but cannot vote. He can participate in debates and offer amendments, however. At his Web site you can learn about Puerto Rico and follow the path of current legislation to make it into the union as the 51st state of the U.S.

http://www.house.gov/romero-barcelo/

Welcome to Puerto Rico!

The island of Puerto Rico is the smallest and the most eastern island of the Greater Antilles, in the Caribbean. Puerto Rico is Spanish for "rich port." Puerto Ricans are U.S. citizens. You may have heard of these famous Puerto Ricans: musician Pablo Casals, sports figure Roberto Clemente, and actress Rita Moreno.

http://welcome.topuertorico.org/

NET FILES

On a merry-go-round, the horses usually follow one special leader, known as the "king horse." How do you tell which horse is the leader?

Answer: Look carefully. There's usually one horse that's just a little bit bigger and just a little more elaborate in its decorations and trappings. Often it's a warhorse wearing armor, and sometimes it has the logo of the company prominently displayed. For other clues, see
http://www.learner.org/exhibits/parkphysics/carousel2.html

U.S. VIRGIN ISLANDS

Congresswoman Donna Christian-Green - Home Page

As the elected delegate to the House of Representatives, Congresswoman Christian-Green sits on several House committees. She holds a medical degree and works for many children's and environmental issues. At her site you can track her statements in Congress as well as learn more about the U.S. Virgin islands. There is also a background history of the area illustrated with many beautiful photos.

http://www.house.gov/christian-green/

The Government of the United States Virgin Islands

At this official site you can learn about the governmental structure of the U.S. Virgin Islands, as well as see the emblems and the flag. You can also take the link to America's Caribbean Paradise: United States Virgin Islands Tourist, Vacation, and Business Guide at <http://www.usvi.net/> for tourist and other information.

http://www.gov.vi/

United States Virgin Islands

The Caribbean islands of St. Thomas, St. John, and St. Croix are known as the U.S. Virgin Islands, and residents are U.S. citizens. Columbus stopped there in 1493. Tourism has become a huge industry; there is a national park on St. John, an island famous for its coral reefs.

http://www.odci.gov/cia/
   publications/factbook/vq.html

WAKE ISLAND

The World Factbook page on Wake Island

This almost flat volcanic island group is in the North Pacific Ocean, about two-thirds of the way from Hawaii to the Northern Mariana Islands. About 300 people live there, and a U.S. military base is located there. It is also used as an emergency stopover for transpacific commercial aviation.

http://www.odci.gov/cia/publications/
   factbook/wq.html

A B C D E F G H I J K L M N O P Q R S T U V W X Y Z

A
B
C
D
E
F
G
H
I
J
K
L
M
N
O
P
Q
R
S
T
U
V
W
X
Y
Z

VIDEO AND SPY CAMS

31 Online Guide to Better Home Video

This site was created by a professional photojournalist for a TV station in Huntsville, Alabama, and he has some great tips to improve your home video movies. According to this site, the biggest mistake amateurs make is panning and zooming the camera too much. He suggests we learn to think visually: our eyes can't zoom! Take a wide shot to establish the story, move in closer for a medium shot to focus interest, then use close-ups for detail. You should think of this as three separate shots that together tell a story. You'll find some great tips here!

http://spider.waaytv.com/waay/31_video.html

The Amazing Fish-Cam!

Yes, from wherever you are on the Web, you can watch fish swim around a tank in someone's office. These fish can be viewed by two different cameras (you get to pick), or you can choose the Continuously Refreshing Fish-Cam if you have a browser that is capable of automatic updates. Ah, a nice, salty glass of refreshing fish-cam—there's nothing quite like it!

http://www1.netscape.com/fishcam/

Big Brother In Demand by Bob Kerstein

From this one site, you can watch an observatory being built in Hawaii, check out the traffic in Hong Kong, or watch the planes at airports in San Diego and Denver. Are indoor cams more your style? OK, how about spying on the employees at Berkeley Systems? Watch them eat lunch or go down the slide. That's right, they have a slide in the employee lunchroom—sounds like a fun place to work! (This one is listed under California.) If you want to watch someone else's pets, try the piranha fish tank (especially entertaining when they clean it—any volunteers?). You can also monitor satellite weather and other forecasting models. Be sure to check real-time traffic reports for many cities, too! This is a very useful site, with thoughtful and current reviews.

http://www.bbod.com/

EarthCam for Kids

Parents, we have not looked at all the webcams listed at this site, but they do seem to be mostly animals, landscapes, and other family-friendly subjects—however, proceed with caution. We saw a litter of newborn kittens, a stadium under construction, and a working llama farm.

http://www.earthcam.com/cgi-bin/
    search_cam.cgi?subject:KID;key:k;file:KID

Finnra, border traffic at Vaalimaa

There's something satisfying about watching traffic waiting to cross the Finnish border into Russia. Check the map to see where this particular crossing is located. What's in that truck? Hey, that lady in the car—she looks just like Carmen Sandiego! What stories can you make up about the people and vehicles you see? This picture is only updated twice an hour, so don't hang around—someone might ask to see your passport!

http://www.tieh.fi/evideo.htm

Giraffe Cam

You've got to see the giraffes at the Cheyenne Mountain Zoo in Colorado Springs, Colorado. Sometimes they are in, sometimes they are out, but keep tuning in and you're bound to see a giraffe or two eventually. We did! They are normally visible from 10 A.M. to 4 P.M. (mountain time). This zoo is famous for successfully breeding giraffes in captivity.

http://c.unclone.com/zoocam.html

Interactive Model Railroad

This one is pretty cool. You get to give commands to an actual model train at the University of Ulm in Germany! You pick the train you want to control, tell it which station to go to, and if you're quick (and lucky) enough, you're in charge. A box on the page gives the domain name of whoever happens to be controlling the train at the time.

http://rr-vs.informatik.uni-ulm.de/rr/

Live Iguana Cam

Check out Dupree the green iguana as he lazes the day away. The best time to visit is between about 9 A.M. and 6 P.M. (Pacific time), Monday through Friday. Otherwise, he's out partying, and you'll just see a typical image, not a live one.

http://iguana.images.com/dupecam.html

Mawson Station, Antarctica

It's extremely "cool" to get a live image of Antarctica. This picture is usually updated automatically each hour. The date/time on the picture shows local Mawson time, which is six hours ahead of Universal Coordinated Time, or UTC (previously known as Greenwich Mean Time, or GMT). Gee, it's 1 A.M. there and the sky's pretty bright! Also, it's extremely depressing to find out that it's warmer at Mawson Station than it is outside our window. :-) To find out how your local temperatures compare, use the Celsius/Fahrenheit conversion entries listed in this book in the REFERENCE WORKS—WEIGHTS AND MEASURES section.

http://www.antdiv.gov.au/aad/exop/sfo/
   mawson/video.html

Oregon Coast Aquarium - Official Keiko Home Page

Did you ever see the *Free Willy* movies about the whale that was rescued from a small display aquarium? Did you know that "Willy" is really named Keiko? For the last few years he's been living in a two-million-gallon aquarium in Oregon. People have been watching him in person and over the Web every day. In September 1998, Keiko will be moved to a sea tank in Iceland, where he was originally captured. You may be able to see him in a webcam there.

http://www.aquarium.org/keikohome.htm

Pikes Peak Cam

Lieutenant Zebulon Montgomery Pike discovered the mountain in 1806, but he never climbed it—seems the snow was too deep. This page shows a live image of Pikes Peak, elevation 14,110 feet, near Colorado Springs, Colorado. The tourist info here says the best viewing time is from sunrise to noon. They say the sunsets are magnificent, too, and if you want to see the most spectacular lightning storms in the world, view the mountain between 3 P.M. and 5 P.M. (mountain time) in July and August.

http://www.softronics.com/peak_cam.html

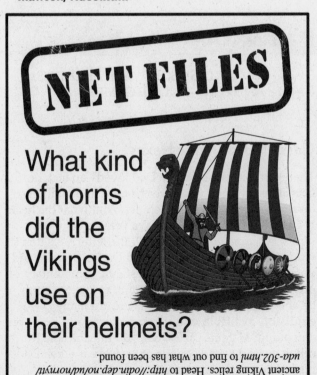

NET FILES

What kind of horns did the Vikings use on their helmets?

Answer: Helmets with horns have never been found among ancient Viking relics. Head to *http://odin.dep.no/ud/normynt/uda-302.html* to find out what has been found.

Visit Pikes Peak, Colorado!

In 1893, Katherine Lee Bates did. An author and teacher from Massachusetts, she was so inspired by the view that she composed the lyrics to "America the Beautiful," one of the most beloved patriotic songs.

You remember it: spacious skies, amber waves of grain, purple mountains' majesties, and so on. You can see a live view of the mountain behind the song at Pikes Peak Cam.

A
B
C
D
E
F
G
H
I
J
K
L
M
N
O
P
Q
R
S
T
U
V
W
X
Y
Z

A
B
C
D
E
F
G
H
I
J
K
L
M
N
O
P
Q
R
S
T
U
V
W
X
Y
Z

Room 100, Buckman Elementary School

What are the kids doing in Room 100 of the Buckman Elementary School in Portland, Oregon? What are they looking at under their video-equipped microscope? This spy cam will show you a recent view of the classroom, and maybe you'll get a picture of "the bee that just stung Ted" or something equally interesting.

http://buckman.pps.k12.or.us/room100/room100.html

San Francisco CityCam

Ah, the City by the Bay, where every nightclub crooner always manages to leave his or her heart. Now you can visit San Francisco over the Net and see a new view every five minutes. Station KPIX has a camera high atop the Fairmont Hotel on Nob Hill. Since the camera pans from the Golden Gate Bridge to the Bay Bridge, you may be able to catch video of both bridges, plus views of downtown, the famous Coit Tower, Fisherman's Wharf, the Marina district, and other attractions. Better hold onto your heart, though! If you miss the sunset, don't worry: you can view a series of time-lapse photos and relive the whole thing. And they have other new features: the Monterey cam, the Coliseum cam, the Wharf cam, and the Northstar at Tahoe ski resort cam.

http://www.kpix.com/live/

Steve's Ant Farm at A T O M I C W E B . C O M

Every time we visit this site showing an ant farm, the view reminds us of Auntie Em's farm in *The Wizard of Oz*. The cyclone's just struck, carrying Dorothy off, and everyone else is hiding in the root cellar. Yet, below the ground, the ants go on, industriously making molehills out of mountains. Check their activity, or lack of it, but keep an eye on the weather!

http://www.atomicweb.com/AntFarm2.html

WebCam Central

This is yet another collection of live webcams from around the world, including views of railroads, scientific instruments, landscapes, pets, the weather, and much more. Parents: There are lots of sites here, and we haven't checked them all.

http://www.camcentral.com/

WebCam Theater

Hey! Would you like to see a live picture from Antarctica? Oops, must be nighttime there. Well, how about Hawaii? Hmm, seems to be the middle of the night there, too. What about that office where they have the employee slide? (See the Big Brother In Demand entry earlier in this section.) Gosh, they seem to have closed for the weekend. Sometimes you want to show someone a live video picture from somewhere exciting, but all your favorite spy cams are dark! This site takes care of that little problem. It has them all in a database, which knows where it's daylight (in the case of outdoor views) or where activity is likely to be taking place (in the case of non-daylight-dependent cams). You can look up cams by subject. For example, try landscapes, animals, or cities and see which ones are likely to have a live picture right at the moment. This is also a good way to visit a lot of webcams at once, using the video jukebox feature.

http://wct.images.com/

VIDEO GAMES

See also COMPUTERS—SOFTWARE ARCHIVES; GAMES AND FUN—ONLINE GAMES

Classic Video Games Nexus

There's an old arcade game Dad loved—in fact, he gets all misty-eyed whenever he talks about all those quarters he put into the machines. And what the heck is a Pac-Man? (Download a Java version at *<http://www.csd.uu.se/~alexb/>*. If the letter keys don't work, try your arrow keys.) Lead Dad to this site and you're bound to hear a lot of nostalgic commentary on how great all those games were. In fact, you may be able to play some of them. There are many emulators available, and if you can get your hands on any old ROM game cartridges, you may be able to relive the sights and sounds of yesteryear when Dad played as many video games as you do now.

http://home.hiwaay.net/~lkseitz/cvg/nexus/

Computer Gaming World

How much do you know about video games? Do you know it all, or do you want to know more? *Computer Gaming World* has a very well-written collection of information about home computer video games. They have in-depth reviews, cheat codes, hints, tips, and previews of beta-release versions of games. You can never have enough great sources of gaming information. There are also links to almost every game manufacturer's home page. This site also features a text-only mode. Parents: Some games may not be suitable for your kids.

http://cgw.gamespot.com/

Electric Playground

Do you want the scoop on your favorite game? Click on the late-breaking news area to find out all that is hot in the world of gaming and all that is not! You can click on buttons for your computer or console platform and read reviews of new games. We prefer the other sites reviewed in this section, but try this one if the others are busy.

http://www.elecplay.com/

GameFun

This site was developed by a preteen devoted to what's new and fun in the world of computer and video gaming. Besides articles on the latest Nintendo, PlayStation, and online games, you'll find cheat codes, playing hints, sounds, and more. Don't miss reading the ongoing argument between Will and his dad regarding whether or not Nintendos are better than PCs. The argument has gone back and forth over the last few years, and some minds have been changed. Which do you think is better?

http://www.gamefun.com/

Games Domain Review

Are you stumped deciding which computer or video game you want next? Do you wish you could find out about the games available for your system? This online magazine covers reviews, news, previews, and an opinion section for games on PC and Macintosh computers, as well as dedicated console game systems. Add to the review database! Don't miss the links to Kids Domain and special software that's rated kid-friendly.

http://www.gamesdomain.com/gdreview/

Kid's Domain

Families who drop in on this site will find it a severe test of the storage capacity of their hard drives. :-) A wealth of kids' software is available on the Internet, and this is the place to look. This extensive, fully annotated collection gives each program its own page, including age recommendations, program sizes, and shareware fees, if any. The page is divided between Mac and PC archives, and a third section is devoted to downloadable commercial demo programs. This last section includes links to many pages of kids' software review sites.

http://www.kidsdomain.com/

Nintendo Power Source

Everybody loves Mario (although they may get tired of his theme song). That crazy plumber has appeared on computer screens everywhere for years. Visit this site for the latest games, news, and inside information on dozens of Nintendo games. This popular site is very busy and is often slow, though, so keep trying.

http://www.nintendo.com/

Sega Online

It's SEGA, home to the world's only blue hedgehog: Sonic. You'll find Sonic's fascinating biography here, in case you need to write a school report on a famous personality! You might also download hedgehog wallpaper for your computer screen. Check the latest news on all of SEGA's games, and get game hints! Do you need to know how to get extra air in Ecco the Dolphin? We'll "clam" up about it for now, but you can find out here.

http://www.sega.com/

Welcome to the World of PlayStation

Bandicoots are the coolest thing to come out of Australia since kangaroos! Take a "crash" visit to the Bandicoot's island to get the idea. You can also play other online games and find out about the latest titles for the Sony PlayStation.

http://www.playstation.com/global.html

A
B
C
D
E
F
G
H
I
J
K
L
M
N
O
P
Q
R
S
T
U
V
W
X
Y
Z

WEATHER AND METEOROLOGY

Bay Kids' Weather Page

It's summer, and the sky decides it's time for us to cook up some fun. Here are some interesting recipes; how about whipping up a nice afternoon thunderstorm? Let's see, check the ingredients: water vapor, dust particles, rising air, electricity potential. Yes, we seem to have all of those, now all we need to do is follow the instructions (and remember, really good lightning is shaken, not stirred). This ThinkQuest Junior entry, built by kids, will teach you all about weather events, jokes, myths, and much more.

http://tqjunior.advanced.org/3805/

DAN'S WILD WILD WEATHER PAGE

Do you want to know how clouds are formed or what to do if you are caught in a lightning storm? Just see Dan! He has info on almost any weather occurrence. From hurricanes to air pressure, Dan has it covered with colorful diagrams and graphics. Teachers and parents might learn a thing or two, as well.

http://www.whnt19.com/kidwx/

Meteorology Guide: the online guides

This resource includes lots of interesting weather material, including classifying clouds and predicting precipitation. But we want to focus your attention on the Light and Optics section, which starts at <http://ww2010.atmos.uiuc.edu/(Gh)/guides/mtr/opt/home.rxml>. Find out how particles of dust, water, and ice crystals combine to make spectacular sunsets, resplendent rainbows, and silver linings. Photos and drawings will help you understand each effect.

http://ww2010.atmos.uiuc.edu/(Gh)/guides/mtr/
   home.rxml

National Climatic Data Center (NCDC)

Was this the rainiest April ever in your city? What was the weather like the day you were born? You're just a few clicks away from finding out, when you cruise over to the National Climatic Data Center (NCDC), the world's biggest collection of weather information. In seconds, you can create graphs showing what the weather's been like just about anytime or anywhere in the world. Some of the weather statistics go all the way back to the late 1600s. Choose Inventory to see what choices you have in displaying the information.

http://www.ncdc.noaa.gov/onlineprod/drought/
   xmgr.html

Natural Disasters

This site is brought to you by a high school class on Canada's Prince Edward Island—the first ever to use the Internet there! They point you to some great natural disaster links, full of activities, pictures, and trivia on earthquakes, tornadoes, floods, and hurricanes. You could click around here for days, whether taking a virtual reality tour of Mount St. Helens at Volcano World or watching movies of hurricanes, clouds, or a space shuttle launch at NASA's Flood Management Page.

http://www.gov.pe.ca/educ/schools/themes/disasters/
   disaster.html

Severe Weather Safety

Would you know what to do if you heard a tornado was approaching? (Hint: Go to the basement or an interior room away from glass. Get out of cars and mobile homes. Lie flat in a ditch if necessary.) What if there were flash flood warnings, or a winter blizzard, hurricane, or other severe weather forecast? This site from the Federal Emergency Management Agency offers lots of information on how to prepare for, and survive, these disasters and more, including nuclear power plant emergencies.

http://www.fema.gov/pte/prep.htm

The University of Michigan Weather Underground

The Weather Underground has been on the Net for a long time, and they have lots of experience helping kids make their own weather observations. To participate in a K–12 collaborative project with kids from all over, visit One Sky, Many Voices. Do you think you could predict the weather better than the guys on TV? Your class could have a forecasting contest, using the rules and scoring methods outlined at *<http://groundhog.sprl.umich.edu/curriculum/ forecast_contest.html>*. All the resources you'll need are linked from this one page. For your observations, we recommend you use the University of Michigan's outstanding weather visualization program, called Blue Skies. There's a download area for Macintosh or Windows versions, or use the Java implementation online.

http://groundhog.sprl.umich.edu/

USA Today WEATHER

This site is the best-kept secret on the Net for weather information! You'll find a ton of special articles, fun facts, and lots of other goodies at this site, from information on tornadoes and hurricanes to tips on weather forecasting. Check the index. If you have a weather-related report due or if you're just interested in things meteorological, do not miss this excellent site.

http://www.usatoday.com/weather/wfront.htm

Weather and Climate from GEOGRAPHY WORLD

Net-mom is a real fan of teacher Mr. Bowerman and his extensive pages on all sorts of topics. But right now let's look at his collection of sites on climate and weather. You will discover fascinating links on how the seasons work, the water cycle, monsoons, aurora borealis, El Niño, and many other topics.

http://members.aol.com/bowermanb/weather.html

Weather Calculator

We admit it. The reason we picked this weather calculator page over the others is that this one offers something unique. Did you know you can make a pretty good guess at the outdoor air temperature by counting cricket chirps? On a hot night, just go out and count the number of times a cricket chirps in 15 seconds. Then plug that number in here and the calculation will be performed for you. For example: 45 cricket chirps in 15 seconds equals: 85.0 degrees Fahrenheit, or 29.4 degrees Celsius, or 302.6 Kelvin! Besides converting the weather observations of insects, this site offers many other weather calculators involving temperature, moisture, and pressure. If you have forgotten what "wet bulb" or "dewpoint" mean, there's also a convenient glossary.

http://nwselp.epcc.edu/elp/wxcalc.html

The Weather Channel - Home Page

Serious weather watchers and meteorologist wannabes should head over to the Weather Channel home page. Grab your own heat index or windchill charts from the Weather Whys and Teacher Resource areas. Find out how to become a meteorologist, a storm chaser for the National Weather Service, or even just a backyard observer. If you've still got questions about the weather, you can ask the Weather Channel meteorologists. They pick the best questions to answer online.

http://www.weather.com/twc/homepage.twc

Weather Dude

"Weather Dude" Nick Walker, a weathercaster for KSTW-TV in Seattle, Washington, specializes in making weather fun. Our favorite part of this site is Weather Resources for Kids, where you can download audio clips and sing along with songs from Nick's "Weather Dude: A Musical Guide to the Atmosphere." Don't miss his tips on how to get free stuff, like the Winter Survival Coloring Book and hurricane tracking charts.

http://www.nwlink.com/~wxdude/

A B C D E F G H I J K L M N O P Q R S T U V W X Y Z

A
B
C
D
E
F
G
H
I
J
K
L
M
N
O
P
Q
R
S
T
U
V
W
X
Y
Z

WeatherNet

Are you tired of surfing the Internet? OK, then maybe it's a good day for surfing in Maui! What's the latest view from above that hurricane swirling around in the Gulf of Mexico? And how does the weather look—right now—on the slopes of your favorite ski resort or on the streets of Hollywood? The answers can be found right here, along with links to over 300 great meteorology sites and 800 weather cams.

http://cirrus.sprl.umich.edu/wxnet/

CLOUDS
UIUC Cloud Catalog

If you can say "cumulonimbus" or "cirrostratus" and point out these kinds of clouds in the sky, you can call yourself a cloud expert! If you'd like to be one, check out the University of Illinois Cloud Catalog. There are some really great pictures to go along with all these huge words. You may be surprised to find out how much difference there is between clouds close to the ground and clouds much higher in the sky.

http://covis.atmos.uiuc.edu/guide/clouds/

EL NIÑO AND LA NIÑA
El Niño: online meteorology guide

From the Department of Atmospheric Sciences at the University of Illinois at Urbana-Champaign, this site provides an overview of what El Niño is, where it comes from, and what it does. You might also like the introduction at NASA's Goddard Space Flight Center at <*http://nsipp.gsfc.nasa.gov/ primer/ englishwelcome.html*>.

http://ww2010.atmos.uiuc.edu/(Gh)/guides/mtr/eln/ home.rxml

El Nino Theme Page-NOAA/PMEL/TAO

What kind of winter will you have this year, and how does the unusual combination of winds and currents known as El Niño affect the weather in your area? No one knows, but chances are that the National Oceanic and Atmospheric Administration's clearinghouse provides the best information. This site explains where the name comes from: "El Niño was originally recognized by fisherman off the coast of South America as the appearance of unusually warm water in the Pacific ocean, occurring near the beginning of the year. El Niño means 'The Little One' in Spanish. This name was used for the tendency of the phenomenon to arrive around Christmas (the birthday of the Christ Child)." Have you heard there is also La Niña ("girl child"), which refers to an unusually cold condition found in the same region? Could be she'll be putting in an appearance next! At this site are impressive climate visualization data graphics as well as real-time marine buoy readings.

http://www.pmel.noaa.gov/toga-tao/el-nino/home.html

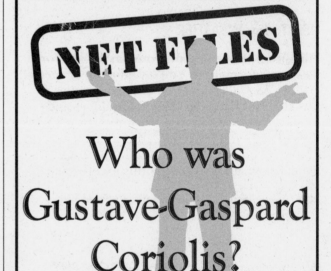

NET FILES

Who was Gustave-Gaspard Coriolis?

Answer: *In 1835, he provided a mathematical explanation for the behavior of fluids on the Earth's surface. We see this when large low-pressure storms turn one way in the Northern Hemisphere and the other way in the Southern Hemisphere. This is known as the Coriolis effect. It has led to speculation that the same thing happens to water draining from a sink; even though physicists say it has no effect, people still believe it! Find out more at http://www.usatoday.com/weather/ wcorioli.htm*

Have you written to your PEN PALS lately?

HURRICANES

Hurricane Season: 1998 Atlantic Basin

Print out this site's handy tracking chart map and keep an eye on this year's 'canes in the Atlantic, Caribbean, Gulf of Mexico, and the eastern Pacific. See up-to-the-minute satellite pictures of tropical storms or even full-blown hurricanes. Maps of hurricane tracks are available for the past 100 years. What was happening the year you were born? This site is available in English and Spanish.

http://www.met.fsu.edu/explores/canepage.cgi

Miami Museum of Science - Hurricane Main Menu

During Florida's Hurricane Andrew in 1992, the Benitez family huddled together in a closet while their whole farm was destroyed in 150-mph winds. "The part I thought was the worst was when we heard the windows break," says 11-year-old Patrick, whose family had nothing to eat for two days! Read this family's story and find out how they survived. Or maybe you'd like to try flying into the eye of a hurricane with a special, storm hunting plane. Check out Hurricane Andrew with 3-D glasses you can make, or learn how to create a model of a hurricane spiral.

http://www.miamisci.org/hurricane/

RAINBOWS

About Rainbows

The spectacular light shows known as rainbows are really just spread-out sunlight. People have been wondering about rainbows for a long time, but the first scientist to study them was René Descartes, over 350 years ago. He found out about rainbows by looking at just one drop of water and observing what happened when light fell on it. Learn all about the optics behind the magic of rainbows at this page, along with some fascinating facts. Did you know that no two people see the same rainbow? In fact, each of your two eyes sees its own rainbow!

http://www.unidata.ucar.edu/staff/blynds/rnbw.html

The Rainbow Maker Web Site Welcome to the Rainbow Maker

Meet rainbow maker Fred Stern, an artist who paints the sky! Using fire trucks or fire boats to pump water into the air, Fred only has to add sunlight to make rainbows of up to 2,000 feet across. He says if our planet had a flag it should be the rainbow, since it stands for peace and unity. To show how he feels, he recently created a rainbow over the United Nations Building that flew higher than the flags of all the nations. Want to stage a rainbow-making event in your town? Check out Fred's Web site to learn how.

http://www.zianet.com/rainbow/

SNOW AND ICE

Current Snow Cover

So you think you're sick of shoveling the snow out of your parents' driveway? See where kids have it worse than you do! Check out how deep the snow is today, all over the U.S., with this snow cover map. Hint: This map is very boring to look at in the summer.

http://wxp.atms.purdue.edu/maps/surface/ snow_cover.gif

Kids Snow Page

If you lived in the frozen North, you might have as many different words for snow as the Inuit do. There are words that mean falling snow, ground snow, smoky snow, and wind-beaten snow. Do you live in a snowy climate? Go on a scavenger hunt activity! Use the list of all the different kinds of snow and see how many you can find where you live. If you'd like to keep your snowflake finds, learn how you can do it with a piece of glass and some hair spray. Make an edible glacier, cut and fold paper snowflakes, and learn that soap bubbles won't pop if you blow them outside when it's –40 degrees Fahrenheit, as it is pretty often where the Teel family kids live—in Alaska.

http://www.teelfamily.com/activities/snow/

A B C D E F G H I J K L M N O P Q R S T U V W X Y Z

National Ice Center

Where does the sea ice end? Where are icebergs in the North Atlantic? Someone's tracking it all these days, largely as a result of that famous maritime disaster: the 1912 sinking of the *Titanic.* North Atlantic icebergs are tracked only during the "season" (it's variable, but it's usually 100 to 200 days in spring to midsummer), so you may not see a current map when you visit the Icebergs area of this site.

http://www.natice.noaa.gov/

National Snow and Ice Data Center

These scientists really know snow. Come explore the digital drifts of their site, especially the Cold Links section at *<http://www-nsidc.colorado.edu/NSIDC/coldlinks.html>*. You'll discover where the polar ice caps are today, where it's snowing now, and how people deal with snow removal when there's a blizzard. Learn about historical storms, weather records, and lots more. Don't miss the gallery of snowflake images.

http://www-nsidc.colorado.edu/NSIDC/EDUCATION/

U.S. Coast Guard International Ice Patrol/ North Atlantic Iceberg Detection and Forecasting

According to this site, "10,000 to 15,000 icebergs are calved each year, primarily from 20 major glaciers between the Jacobshaven and Humboldt Glaciers" in west Greenland. These drift south, melting as they go. Sometimes they reach the shipping lanes, and in the old days this was a cause for great concern. Historical reports indicate that the iceberg that sunk the *Titanic* was 50 to 100 feet high and 200 to 400 feet long. These days, icebergs are located by radar and carefully tracked, and one of the organizations responsible for that is the U.S. Coast Guard. Find out about their activities at this site. Don't miss the "Other Links" to their icebreaker vessels, the *Polar Sea* and the *Polar Star.* A new vessel, the *Healy,* may be launched by the time you read this. You can sometimes correspond with the crews via e-mail.

http://webtac3.rdc.uscg.mil/iippages/iip.html

THUNDERSTORMS AND LIGHTNING

Exploring: Weather

San Francisco's Exploratorium brings you the story of lightning, chock-full of trivia that will amaze you. Did you know that a lightning bolt has enough energy to lift a 2,000-pound car 62 miles high into the air? Or that a lightning flash jumps from the ground up to a cloud at 61,000 miles per second? You won't want to miss the story of Roy "Dooms" Sullivan, a former park ranger who holds the world's record for being zapped by lightning more than any other person: seven times. Now that's an electrifying personality!

http://www.exploratorium.edu/ronh/weather/weather.html

Lightning @ nationalgeographic.com

National Geographic brings you the whole shocking story of how lightning is striking the Earth about 100 times a second. Read the electrifying tale of what it's like to be hit by lightning, told by people who have survived the encounter. And, when you've found out everything you've always wanted to know about lightning, don't *bolt*—take a quiz and win the hottest prize in cyberspace.

http://www.nationalgeographic.com/features/96/lightning/

NASA/MSFC/ESSD - Shuttle Lightning Observations

Everybody's seen lightning from down here on Earth, but not many people get to see it from outer space. Lightning bounces around in some very weird ways out there. For a long time, pilots had been saying that they saw lightning that started at the tops of clouds and shot out into space, but nobody believed them. In 1989, space shuttle astronauts helped solve this mystery when they took pictures of this "vertical lightning." Check out their pictures and movies of some wild storms as seen from space.

http://wwwghcc.msfc.nasa.gov/skeets.html

Sparks and Lightning

It's impossible to see a lightning bolt; it happens too fast. If you could only speed yourself up, while everything else went on at normal speed! This page helps you find out what that would be like, as you examine an imaginary slow-motion lightning bolt strike on a nearby rooftop. Read this page and find out why lightning starts out as purple "St. Elmo's Fire." This page is not for the timid: at the end, it has you imagine what it would be like to be zapped and knocked unconscious, but you do learn a lot about electricity.

http://www.eskimo.com/~billb/tesla/spark.html

Nine out of ten Internet users find this page shocking! See what you think of the Sparks and Lightning page!

Storm Chaser Warren Faidley's Homepage

Thunderstorms, monsoons, and waterspouts are all just part of the incredible day's work of photographer Warren Faidley, the world's only full-time, professional storm chaser. His storm pictures have appeared in *National Geographic* and *USA Today*, in commercials and music videos, and even in a Michael Jordan sports video. His severe weather slide show will amaze you!

http://www.indirect.com/www/storm5/

You Can & Thunder

Wow! That was a LOUD storm! You can come out now. Let Beakman and Jax answer your questions about thunder. What's it made of, anyway? Is it hot? Is it cold? If we could see this event, what would it look like? Try these simple experiments to help you learn more about thunder.

http://www.beakman.com/thunder/thunder.html

TIDES

Tide Prediction - USA Coast

You're going to St. Petersburg, Florida, and you want to know when low tide is because you really want to find some shells and go beachcombing. When you get to St. Petersburg, tide tables will be easy to locate; in fact, they are often printed in the local newspapers. However, your family lives in New York. What morning should you beachcomb and what morning should you go to a theme park? You need to be able to plan your trip! This site predicts high/low tides months in advance for places as diverse as the Florida coast, Alaska, Honolulu, and all up and down the east and west coasts of the U.S. If that's not enough, the site at <http://www.nws.fsu.edu/buoy/> does the same thing in a slightly different way.

http://www.opsd.nos.noaa.gov/tideframe.html

TORNADOES

NWSFO Norman WWW Home Page - Spotter Guide

See what happens to a car during a tornado and why it's a bad idea to stay in one when these violent storms—some of them have winds of up to 300 mph—come around. (Hint: The car left the ground and never came back!) The Storm Spotter's Guide explains how these long-lasting storms, called "supercell" thunderstorms, cause most of our really bad weather, including tornadoes and big hail. Learn how you can stay safe during all the different kinds of bad storms. Be sure to read the *USA Today* weather information on tornadoes, at <http://www.usatoday.com/weather/wfront.htm>.

http://www.nssl.noaa.gov/~nws/spotterguide.html

A B C D E F G H I J K L M N O P Q R S T U V W X Y Z

A
B
C
D
E
F
G
H
I
J
K
L
M
N
O
P
Q
R
S
T
U
V
W
X
Y
Z

TSUNAMIS

Tsunamis

Tsunamis—walls of water, sometimes more than 100 feet high—are usually caused by earthquakes or big storms at sea. When you check out this collection of tsunami pictures, you'll see huge boats that have been thrown onto the shore like toys and amazing before-and-after pictures. See what happened to a five-story lighthouse that sat 40 feet above the sea until a tsunami came crashing ashore. Read a definition of a tsunami by clicking on "Main Menu."

http://www.ngdc.noaa.gov/cgi-bin/seg/m2h?seg/
slide2.men+Tsunamis

Welcome to Tsunami!

Tsunamis cause severe damage to coastal areas. Learn about the Tsunami Warning System and what you can do to protect yourself if one is issued for your area. But if you are ever near the ocean and feel a deep rumble in the earth, don't wait for an official warning—get moving. It could be the first sign of a tsunami, and once the wave gets to shore, you will not be able to outrun it. Another early sign of trouble is that sometimes, just before a tsunami, the water is sucked out to sea, exposing the ocean floor. This is a warning that you should move inland quickly or to a higher area, such as the top floors of a high-rise building. You'll also find detailed information about recent tsunami events as well as links to other tsunami sites.

http://www.geophys.washington.edu/tsunami/
welcome.html

WHY

Earth and Sky Homepage

Earth and Sky is a daily radio feature about science, heard on 950 stations around the world. The topics range from deep-ocean vents to the star nurseries in deep space. They also answer listener questions, some of which have been collected on this Web site. Why is the sky blue? Are soap bubbles round in weightless conditions? Why do leaves change color in the fall? *Earth and Sky* knows!

http://www.earthsky.com/

Frequently-asked Questions in Science and Physics

Why do stars twinkle? What's the purpose of all those dimples on a golf ball? Why does hot water freeze faster than cold? How do those "Dippy Bird" toys work? Seek here and ye shall find the answers.

ftp://rtfm.mit.edu/pub/usenet-by-group/
news.answers/physics-faq/part3

How Things Work

Have you ever questioned some aspect of the science of physics? A professor of physics at the University of Virginia has listed answers to many questions, some of which are part of the basic physics courses he teaches at the university. A guide lists previous questions as well as a place where you can ask a new question. The search button will help you find whether one of the previously asked 5,500 questions is one you might also be posing.

http://Landau1.phys.Virginia.EDU/Education/
Teaching/HowThingsWork/

NET FILES

If UFOs are real, how come no astronauts have ever reported seeing one?

Answer: Ah, but they have! Go to *http://www.ufomind.com/ufo/sighting/astronaut/* to see reports from various astronauts. The truth is out there, and some of it may be at this page!

New Scientist Planet Science: The Last Word Science Questions and Answers

Are you puzzled why penguins don't get frozen feet? Do you wonder how many times you can recycle paper? How about frozen carrots and a microwave—why do they produce sparks during the cooking process? Wait, there's more: Are we ever going to run out of words? Why do some people sweat when they eat cheddar cheese? Why do onions make us cry? How were battery sizes named? The answers to these and hundreds of other questions can be found at this site.

http://www.last-word.com/

OMSI Science Whatzit!

You name the topic, the Oregon Museum of Science has the info. Is there wood so dense it won't float? Why is the Earth round? How many stars are out there? How do fireflies light up? If you have a question, see if it's been answered at this site. If not, go ahead and ask it here.

http://www.omsi.edu/online/whatzit/home.html

ScienceNet - Database - Search

The ScienceNet database has answers to more questions than you could ask in any given day. Actually, maybe that should be any given week, or year! With topics ranging from archeology to earth science, biology to the social sciences, you're sure to find something of interest. Can dogs get addicted to something? How does the human eye work? What are dreams? Why is yawning "catching"? Are women "built" to talk more than men? Hint: First pick a large subject area, like sociology. Then click on "Browse Resources." Then choose a Database Topic, and you'll be able to browse the questions themselves.

http://www.campus.bt.com/CampusWorld/pub/
    ScienceNet/qpages/search.html

The Skinny On...

This site offers "the skinny on" a lot of unusual subjects. Why does bright light make you sneeze? How do sonic booms work? Why do you twitch sometimes when you're falling asleep? Why does eating beans give you gas? What color is snow (the answer will surprise you!).

http://www.discovery.com/area/skinnyon/
    skinnyon.html

Smart Stuff with Twig Walkingstick

Did you ever wonder if fish have ears? Why rabbits like carrots? Where the water goes during low tide? What causes heartburn? This Twig guy has the answers to these and a lot more questions in a wide variety of topics. Check it out, and you'll learn why the sea is blue in some places and green in others, among other things.

http://www.ag.ohio-state.edu/~twig/

Welcome to ScienceNet

Where is your funny bone? What's the Earth made of? Do identical twins have identical fingerprints? Search or browse the extensive database of scientific questions and see what answers scientists have given.

http://www.campus.bt.com/CampusWorld/pub/
    ScienceNet/first.html

Why do cat's eyes glow in the dark?

At night, if you shine a beam of light into a cat's eyes, they seem to glow back at you. You can also get this effect if you take a flash photo of a cat's face. What gives the eyes this spooky appearance? Find out at this site!

http://dialspace.dial.pipex.com/agarman/faq3.htm

A B C D E F G H I J K L M N O P Q R S T U V W X Y Z

A
B
C
D
E
F
G
H
I
J
K
L
M
N
O
P
Q
R
S
T
U
V
W
X
Y
Z

The Why Files

Your coach has really gone crazy this time. He's climbed to the top of the backboard, and he's dropping a round basketball and a flat basketball (with no air in it) at the same time. Which one will hit the floor first? Everybody guesses one or the other, but the answer is that they will strike the floor at the same time. Why? The answer is at this site, which is funded by the National Science Foundation. You'll also find current science news for kids, as well as archives of past whys (and wise) answers!

http://whyfiles.news.wisc.edu/

Why is the Ocean Salty

You could describe seawater as being a very diluted soup of pretty much everything on Earth: minerals, organic matter, even synthetic chemicals. Here's the strange thing: the ocean has the same degree of saltiness everywhere. There isn't one place that is saltier than another. Where did the salt come from? If freshwater rivers and streams keep flowing into the sea, why doesn't the sea become less salty? Find out here!

http://www.ci.pacifica.ca.us/NATURAL/SALTY/
salty.html

NET FILES

WERE THERE ANY WOMEN PIRATES?

Answer: Aye, there were at least two, but they fought in men's clothing. One was Mary Read, and the other was Anne Bonny. They plied the waters of the Caribbean in the early 1700s and were known as tough, salty ladies. Sail on over to http://www.efr.hw.ac.uk/ EDC/CAC/pirates/pirate.htm to find out more.

Why is the sunset red?

Did you ever wonder how a blue sky can have a red sunset? This site has a really neat experiment that will help you understand the phenomenon. All you need is a flashlight, a container of water (a fish tank is ideal), and a glass of milk. Hint: The colors of the sky and the sunset have to do with particles of dust in the air. The rest of the answer is here!

http://scifun.chem.wisc.edu/HOMEEXPTS/BlueSky.html

SEASONS

How the Seasons Work

At this Web site, you can learn how the weather is related to the tilt of the Earth and how it moves around the Sun. Did you know Earth is actually closer to the Sun in January (winter in the Northern Hemisphere) than it is in July? Find out all about it; the explanation at this site is both in English and in French.

http://www.pwc.bc.doe.ca/es/education/
education.a.html

Why are there seasons?

Can you put together the pieces of this puzzle? Separate fact from myth in this fun little Shockwave tutorial.

http://observe.ivv.nasa.gov/nasa/earth/seasons/
seasons1.html

Why Leaves Change Color in the Fall

Start at this site to see how a librarian searched the Web for the answer. You'll find sites for both elementary and older kids where this topic is discussed. At Simple Science, the first listed URL for elementary ages, we learn that chlorophyll gives leaves their green color. In some leaves, the chlorophyll goes away in the fall. Then we see red, orange, and yellow colors. These other colors were there all summer, but the green covered them up! Visit the sites to find out just why this happens.

http://www.ala.org/ICONN/KCFAQ/leaves.html

WORDS

See also REFERENCE WORKS—DICTIONARIES

A.Word.A.Day Home Page

Do you love words? Then you'll want to get on the A Word a Day (AWAD) mailing list. It's free! Each day you'll get a new word, definition, and brief quote showing how the word is used. Net-mom's on the AWAD list, along with 112,000 other people! The home page has sample words from today and yesterday, or you can look through the archives to see what the list is like.

http://www.wordsmith.org/awad/

Common Errors in English

Plenty of people use common words and phrases the wrong way, and this page aims to set them all straight. Learn when to use "its" and when to rely on "it's." Discover why being "very unique" is impossible. Is it "loose" or "lose"? "Immigrate" or "emigrate"? Could you "care less"? Find out here. By the way, at press time the derivation of Net-mom's "Surfing the Internet" listed here was incorrect, but we wrote to the author to ask him to read the real story behind the metaphor. You can find it at *<http://www.netmom.com/about/surfing_main.htm>*.

http://www.wsu.edu/~brians/errors/

Fake Out!

OK, give this multiple-choice quiz a try. The word "bleb" means: a) a Takis word for "blabbermouth"; b) a yellow fish with five fins and a long, blue tail; or c) the first movie that was ever on the big screen. If you said none of these, you'd be right, and you'll be a winner at this definition guessing game. The object of the game is to come up with word definitions so believable you fool other players into picking the wrong one.

http://www.eduplace.com/dictionary/

GRY Words

Have you heard this puzzle? Quick—name three words that end in "-gry." Having a hard time? Here are a list of -gry words, but the solution to the puzzle may be that the question is just phrased the wrong way! Another site weighing in on the problem is The Word Detective at *<http://www.word-detective.com/gry.html>*.

http://www.cruzio.com/~sclibs/internet/gry.html

I, Rearrangement Servant

Do you know what an *anagram* is? Take all the letters in a word or phrase, scramble them, and come up with a new word or phrase! For example, "Inert Net Grave Near Mars" is an anagram for "Internet Anagram Server." Type in ten or less letters and see what mysterious phrase you'll get. For anagrams of more than ten letters, use the "anagram by email" service.

http://www.wordsmith.org/anagram/

John's Word Search Puzzles

John certainly is a creative guy. He's developed word search puzzles about many different themes, including holidays, states, sports, the Bible, and other topics. Hidden words may be frontwards, backwards, on a diagonal, vertical, or horizontal.

http://www.thepotters.com/puzzles.html

Puzzlemaker

This is a neat site to make some fun party games or puzzles to add some interest to a school assignment or class newsletter. You can very easily create word search puzzles, hidden message puzzles, crossword puzzles, mazes, math squares, and more. Print them out and send them to your friends and family—everyone will wonder how you did it!

http://www.puzzlemaker.com/

A B C D E F G H I J K L M N O P Q R S T U V W X Y Z

A
B
C
D
E
F
G
H
I
J
K
L
M
N
O
P
Q
R
S
T
U
V
W
X
Y
Z

Secret Language

Psssst! Want to send a secret message to a friend, one that nobody else can possibly decipher? Head on over to this page at San Francisco's Exploratorium, where you can print out a copy of some substitution cipher wheels. Put one inside the other, twirl them around a little bit, and you're in the spy biz!

http://www.exploratorium.edu/ronh/secret/
secret.html

The Word Detective

This syndicated newspaper column has been running since 1953. William Morris started it, and now his son Evan does the honors. A short while after the columns run in newspapers, he posts them on this page. Morris answers readers' questions about the English language and its odd words and phrases, such as "busting chops," "lame duck," or "eyes peeled," and he does this cleverly, with wit and humor. He also has a sampling of *The Word Detective*, a newsletter that "aims for the large grey area between the *Oxford English Dictionary* and Monty Python."

http://www.word-detective.com/

Word.Net's Ambigram.Matic

It's a flipped out, backwards world at this site, the world's only ambigram generator. *Ambigrams* are words or phrases that can be read in at least two different ways, such as right side up and upside down. To find out how, cruise over to this silly site and try typing in your name.

http://ambigram.matic.com/ambigram.htm

WWWebster Dictionary - Search screen

Sure, you can look up words online and get the definitions from this famous dictionary publisher. But you can also read some of the fascinating features about interesting words and scratch your head over some perplexing word puzzles. See what words Shakespeare coined, or trace the history of the word "phat." Find out how words get into the dictionary, too. This page explains how Merriam-Webster does it, and they should know the best way, because they have been doing it since the 1880s. There are almost 15 million citations for word uses in their database today. Try the quick word games at this site, too.

http://www.m-w.com/netdict.htm

NET FILES

Massachusetts has an official folk hero. Who is he? (Hint: His first name is John.)

Answer: He is John Chapman, better known as Johnny Appleseed, who lived from 1775(?)–1845. This site describes him this way: "An American pioneer and hero of folklore, his planting of apple trees from New England to the Ohio River valley earned him his more popular name." Read the facts at *http://www.state.ma.us/sec/cis/cismaf/mf1a.htm*

MNEMONICS
The Mnemonic Number Alphabet

Mnemonics are handy little devices for jogging our memories. For example, the first letters of "My Very Educated Mother Just Served Us Nine Pickles" gives the initials, in order, of the nine planets. "Lucy Can't Drink Milk" provides the Roman numerals in order for 50, 100, 500, and 1,000. Some of these mnemonics have been helping students breeze through tests for years; now it's your turn to use them! Do you have trouble remembering dates in history class? Try the mnemonic alphabet system, which replaces numbers with consonants. Maybe you can make up some of your own, too.

http://www.curbet.com/speedlearn/chap10.html

TONGUE TWISTERS
Tongue Twisters

You'll find a couple dozen or so of these here, from the banal "How much wood could..." to the short and clever "Unique New York" and "Truly Plural." Go ahead—say them a few times.

http://www.geocities.com/Athens/8136/
tonguetwisters.html

WRITING

See also SCHOOLS AND EDUCATION—LEARNING AND STUDY

Cyberkids Home

"Monster in the Park," "Mixed-Up Zoo," "Beyond the Barrier of Time," "Scary Stories That Make Your Mom Faint"—these are only some of the great stories written by kids that your family can read together in this online magazine. Like any magazine, there are writing and art contests, software and product reviews written by kids for kids, and cookie recipes, too. In addition to the fictional stories, the feature articles have crossword or word search puzzles along with them, to make learning about something new even more fun. The CyberKids Launchpad will link you to lots of other neat sites listed by subject area. If you have thoughts or ideas you want to share with other readers, be sure to send them in.

http://www.cyberkids.com/

For Young Writers

If you dream about writing, or if you write and you want your writing to be better or published or just appreciated by others, it's all here! Get advice from professional writers and editors. Participate in chat sessions and discussions with other young writers. Find links to other useful writing sites. Submit your work to the Young Writer's Collection for Web publication. You may even get your first paid writing job by visiting the Market Info page, although most of the leads there are for nonpaying publications. Writing contests are listed too.

http://www.inkspot.com/young/

Glossary of Poetic Terms from BOB'S BYWAY

Your teacher has assigned a poetry project that's just gone from bad to "verse." There are so many unfamiliar words and lots of confusing jargon! Do you know the difference between a sestina and a sonnet? Can you write a poem in iambic pentameter? Visit this site to learn all these terms and more. Many are also illustrated with examples.

http://shoga.wwa.com/~rgs/glossary.html

Grammar and Style Notes

Are you a little shaky on the parts of speech? Can you tell a preposition from a present participle? The names may be strange, but you use these elements in everyday conversation. A *preposition* usually describes the object of the sentence and its location in time, space, or relationship to the rest of the sentence. For example, in the next sentence, the prepositions are capitalized: BEFORE the alarm rang, the cat was ON the table. A *present participle* just adds "-ing" to the rest of the verb: singing, sitting, walking. This resource teaches the parts of speech in a fun and easy way. You'll also learn about punctuation, building sentences and paragraphs, and yes—even spelling! Knowing the correct names for these grammatical terms becomes very important when you begin to learn another language. You'll want to know what the teacher means when talking about French subjunctives and superlatives!

http://www.english.upenn.edu/~jlynch/grammar.html

Kids' Space

This is every kid's home page! Do you want other kids to see your paintings? Do you want them to be able to hear you play your trombone? How about letting kids all over the world read your story or poem? Send your multimedia to this site for publication. Also, you can look for a pen pal to write to on the Internet; if you don't have a mailbox, use the bulletin board feature to let other kids know what you're thinking about, looking for, or dreaming about. Menus are in both Japanese and English.

http://www.kids-space.org/

Mind's Eye Monster Project: A Free Curriculum Based Language Arts Writing Project

This is a site that everyone is going to love—students, parents, teachers—you name it, stop here! It's simple. Your class draws a monster, but then you have to describe it well enough so that another class can re-create the monster just from the written description. Teachers, take a tour of the site and see how your classes can discover new excitement in creative writing.

http://www.win4edu.com/minds-eye/monster/

A
B
C
D
E
F
G
H
I
J
K
L
M
N
O
P
Q
R
S
T
U
V
W
X
Y
Z

A
B
C
D
E
F
G
H
I
J
K
L
M
N
O
P
Q
R
S
T
U
V
W
X
Y
Z

The Neverending Tale

Help kids and "young at heart" adults add to the stories here. Maybe you'd like to choose your own path through the 5,000 pages of The Haunted Castle. Or maybe the Space Station Delta story (900 pages) is more to your liking. Just start reading a story, and when you get to the bottom of the page you'll find a number of choices about what to do next. You can follow a path someone else has written, or you can easily add your own series of choices. The site is monitored for appropriate family content. One thing is for sure—there are two words you'll never find in any of these stories: The End.

http://www.coder.com/creations/tale/

Poetry Pals Internet Poetry Publishing Project for K-12 Students

Do you like to write poetry? If the answer is "Yes", by all means visit this site and share your poems with other kids from all over the world. If you've never written a poem in your life and you'd like to give it a try, click on Magnetic and take a peek at an online version of "magnetic poetry." Click on the words you like and drag them around to make a poem on your computer screen. There are several of these types of games on the Net, but this one is created especially for kids.

http://www.geocities.com/EnchantedForest/5165/

Purdue Online Writing Lab

Are those commas confusing? How about nouns, verbs, and adjectives—do they puzzle you? Are apostrophes getting you mixed up every time? And what's a preposition, anyway? Come to this writing lab to figure out how you should use all these things. Your reports, letters, and tests will look impressive!

http://owl.english.purdue.edu/

Strunk, William. 1918. The Elements of Style.

This little book of grammar was written a long time ago, but writers use it to this day, often referring to it as their "bible." You might be interested in checking the list of words and phrases commonly misused and misspelled.

http://www.columbia.edu/acis/bartleby/strunk/

Study WEB

To colon or semicolon, that is the question. For the answer, *dash* over here and *capitalize* on the grammar tips and tricks that *punctuate* this site. A variety of sources will help you organize your paragraphs, straighten your sentences, check your spelling, and keep those too-common commas and rogue apostrophes from running amok across the pages of your next assignment.

http://www.studyweb.com/

The UVic Writer's Guide Table of Contents

Your teacher assigns you a choice: you can write either an expository essay or a persuasive one. Huh? She explained it, but you still don't understand. This Web site explains various types of essays, then gives advice on how to get started writing an essay, how to proofread it, and how to solve common writing problems. If you're not up to writing a whole essay yet, there's a section on how to write paragraphs. Can't write a whole paragraph? Stick to the part about how to write a good topic sentence. There is something here for everyone! You'll also find a huge glossary of literary terms as well as grammar basics.

http://webserver.maclab.comp.uvic.ca/writersguide/
    Pages/MasterToc.html

GREETING CARDS

Blue Mountain Arts' Electronic Greeting Cards

Picture this: You're at school and suddenly realize today is your mom's birthday. No problemo. Just remember this site! Pick out a nice card for your mom—many have music and animations. Follow the instructions to send information about the card to your mom's e-mail account—it will be there the next time she reads her mail. This site offers birthday cards, holiday cards, and cards for all sorts of occasions. A new addition is a selection of cards for kids. You can also find awards to send, if you're not into cards. Send your mom a "Best Mom" award, or create a "Braveheart" award for a friend who stood up to a bully. Be sure to write in your own words to personalize whatever cards you send.

http://www.bluemountain.com/

X-FILES

See also UFOS AND EXTRATERRESTRIALS

The X-Files

Are UFOs and extraterrestrials for real? *The X-Files* is a make-believe TV show about two FBI agents trying to answer that question. Join Special Agents Fox Mulder and Dana Scully as they investigate UFOs, extraterrestrial sightings, and many other bizarre cases. This Web site has in-depth character sketches, episode descriptions, and information about the show. A caution to parents: Some of the show descriptions are graphic.

http://www.TheX-Files.com/

X-MEN

The X-Page Hotlist

X-Men? Look no further. All you could possibly want to know about "X-Men" comics (and other comics, too) is here. Somewhere. At least we think so, although we have not checked all the links.

http://x-page.com/hotlist/

NET FILES

What famous event occurred in 1989, marking the end of the Cold War?

(Hint: It attracted a huge flock of "wall woodpeckers.")

Answer: The demolition of the Berlin Wall, which had divided East and West Germany. Many people chiseled off pieces as souvenirs. With all their tapping, they were called "wall woodpeckers"! See the before and after photos at http://www.appropriatesoftware.com/BerlinWall/welcome.html

X-RAYS

NASA's Advanced X-ray Astrophysics Facility (AXAF)

In 1895, Wilhelm Roentgen, a German physicist, discovered something really strange. It was so strange he called it X-radiation. It was sort of like light, except it went right through things. These days, we have found many uses for X-radiation. X-rays are useful to see if bones are broken or if your teeth have cavities. Did you know x-ray astronomy is really hot? Scientists know X-rays are emitted from things like black holes, neutron stars, and other interesting stellar objects. The only problem is, the Earth's atmosphere absorbs X-rays coming in from space. Astrophysicists have to use special telescopes located in space in order to study these exotic locales. According to this page, "NASA's Advanced X-ray Astrophysics Facility (AXAF) is scheduled for launch in 1998. This telescope will contain four sets of nested mirrors and will be the premier X-ray observatory to date. It will detect sources more than twice as far away and will produce images with five times greater detail. The mirrors, already completed, have been polished to a smoothness of a few atoms. If the surface of the Earth were as smooth as the AXAF mirrors, the largest mountain would be less than 2 meters (7 feet) tall!"

http://xrtpub.harvard.edu/pub.html

XYLOPHONE

Musical Compositions by Kilvington Students

Why isn't this site listed in the MUSIC AND MUSICIANS section, you ask? It's because we like to have a few entries for each letter of the alphabet. And we thought these xylophone compositions, played by kids in Australia, were fun to listen to. We hope you like them. :-)

http://www.kilvington.schnet.edu.au/music/music.htm

A B C D E F G H I J K L M N O P Q R S T U V W X Y Z

A
B
C
D
E
F
G
H
I
J
K
L
M
N
O
P
Q
R
S
T
U
V
W
X
Y
Z

YOGA

Yoga Central

One of the first things you will learn in yoga class, besides where to take off your shoes, is the word *namasté*. Your instructor will say it to you, and you're expected to say it back. Namasté is derived from the Sanskrit word *Namaskaar*, meaning "I bow to the divine in you." Yoga is from the Sanskrit word *Yug*, meaning "union with the divine." This site offers Real Audio of many elements of a yoga class, from stretching to breathing to chanting and working out. It will let you see what a real class is like. There is probably a class or two in your area that you could join; check the phone book. A caution to parents: Links off this site have not been checked.

http://www.yogaclass.com/central.html

Yoga Studio

If you have Shockwave, you can create your own animated yoga class from the list of postures at this site. Whatever you pick will be demonstrated for you by the student on the screen. The virtual class takes place on a beach, accompanied by the sounds of waves, relaxing music, and crying seagulls. There are also many links to yoga magazines, associations, and Web sites.

http://www.timages.com/yoga.htm

ZOOLOGY

Australian A to Z Animal Archive

Do you know how the kangaroo got its name? When European explorers first saw a strange animal jumping around, they asked the Aborigines what it was. The Aborigines replied, "Kangaroo," which means "I don't understand," but the Europeans thought that was the strange animal's name. Check out this site and learn about other Australian animals.

http://www.aaa.com.au/A_Z/

The Electronic Zoo

Let a veterinarian loose on the Internet, and what do you get? A Web site filled with information on all kinds of animals, plus resources on veterinary medicine, agriculture, biology, environment, and ecology—and the list goes on and on. Do you think this guy loves his job and knows his stuff? You bet!

http://netvet.wustl.edu/e-zoo.htm

National Wildlife Federation's Homepage

What's for lunch at the National Wildlife Federation home page? Flamingos eat algae, and that's how they get their beautiful pink coloring. Even though algae is green, it has a special chemical that turns the birds' feathers pink! Koala bears are very picky eaters. They eat only one kind of food: eucalyptus leaves. Tree squirrels eat nuts, pine cones, and other foods that they bury for winter storage. When winter arrives, they search for the food they have buried. Squirrels have an excellent sense of smell and can sniff out food that has been buried in a foot of snow! Did you know that up to 100 species become extinct every day? You can help. Visit this site and find out how you can get involved in a project or organization working to help endangered species. You may even be able to "adopt" an endangered animal.

http://www.nwf.org/

CLASSIFICATION

Search Marine Species Index

You may know a sponge as something you use to wash your family's car, but do you know about the sponge sea animal? That's right, though it may look like a plant, the sea sponge is really an animal. Check out this site to learn all about sponges and other sea animals, such as flatworms and comb jellies. You'll also make your way to sea life with backbones, including various types of fish.

http://database.mbl.edu/SPECIMENS/
phylum.taf?function=form&page=2

Zoology Resource Guide - Animal Index

Did you know that you're a *Homo sapiens*? That's the scientific classification name for humans. All life can be organized and classified this way, using a system of scientific naming or nomenclature. Visit the Zoological Record Home Page, where you'll find information on the ordering of organisms into groups based on their relationships. You'll find the order, class, and kingdom for everything here, from people to dinosaurs. In addition, you'll find reports containing the symbol, scientific name, common name, and family for each member of the animal kingdom.

http://www.york.biosis.org/zrdocs/zoolinfo/
gp_index.htm

MIGRATION
Journey North 1998

Migration occurs every year with all kinds of animals, birds, and insects (even some grandparents like to go south for the winter). Journey North is a project where the Internet really shines. Each year, monarch butterflies migrate from Canada and the U.S. to their wintering grounds in Mexico and California. In the spring, they start their journey north again. Where are they now? Go outside—see any monarch butterflies? OK, now go back inside, and go to this site to report your findings. Your results will be combined with other reports from all over the U.S., and a map will be created to show where the migratory monarchs have landed. Butterflies aren't the only things monitored here. Besides tracking various animals and birds, this site tracks when the ice goes out of various lakes and rivers, where the tulips are blooming, and where the spring frogs are peeping.

http://www.learner.org/jnorth/

Be dazzled by the laser shows in PHYSICS.

ZOOS

The Birmingham Zoo

Look at the kudu antelope with that pair of oxpecker birds on its back. They're eating ticks and other "bugs" off of the antelope, bringing relief from an irritating source of discomfort. What's that black spot in the corner of that dik-dik's eye? It's a gland with black, sticky stuff that dik-dik antelopes rub on tree branches to mark their territory. Have you ever been on an African safari? These are some of the things you will see while taking a virtual safari through the Birmingham Zoo home page in Alabama. Have fun, and watch out for the leopards hiding in the rocks and trees!

http://www.birminghamzoo.com/

Giraffe Cam

You've got to see the giraffes at the Cheyenne Mountain Zoo in Colorado Springs, Colorado. Sometimes they are in, sometimes they are out, but keep tuning in and you're bound to see a giraffe or two eventually. We did! They are normally visible from 10 A.M. to 4 P.M. (mountain time). This zoo is famous for successfully breeding giraffes in captivity.

http://c.unclone.com/zoocam.html

National Zoo Home Page - Animals, Plants, People, Movies and More.

Admission is free. The only rule is: Don't feed the animals—and don't smudge the computer screen with your nose! Have you ever wondered what goes on behind the scenes at the National Zoo in Washington, D.C.? People, animals, and plants all play a part. How do cheetahs get their exercise at the zoo? Cheetah calisthenics! Yes, the cats actually warm up by playing ball, and then they run through a ropes course. Visit your favorite animal at the National Zoo home page.

http://www.si.edu/natzoo/

A B C D E F G H I J K L M N O P Q R S T U V W X Y Z

A
B
C
D
E
F
G
H
I
J
K
L
M
N
O
P
Q
R
S
T
U
V
W
X
Y
Z

Rhinos and Tigers and Bears — Oh My!

What's that hippo doing with a watermelon? And why is that tiger rolling a barrel? Those are special toys and enrichment activities for the zoo animals. Find out more about animal toys and learn lots of other interesting information about the diet and conservation of the animals at the Knoxville, Tennessee Zoo.

http://www.utenn.edu/uwa/vpps/ur/ut2kids/zoo/
    zoo.html

San Diego Zoo, San Diego Wild Animal Park

The San Diego Zoo is one of Net-mom's favorite travel destinations. The zoo started in 1916 with only 50 animals. Now the 100-acre park contains 3,800 creatures! Besides wandering around in Tiger River, Polar Bear Plunge, and Hippo Beach, Net-mom loves the beautiful landscaping and exotic plants around the park. You can see some of the attractions at this site, as well as play a few games and send some electronic postcards.

http://www.sandiegozoo.org/

ZooNet - All about Zoos!

ZooNet doesn't collect animals; they collect zoos! Their goal is to link to every zoo in the world, and so far they're doing a great job. They can link you to official home pages for private and specialized zoos or to zoo-related organizations. Don't forget to download some animal screen savers while you're here. The animal galleries offer herds of animal photos and images for your pleasure. Also, check the endangered species info and the links to many animal pages across the Net.

http://www.mindspring.com/~zoonet/

Be dazzled by the laser shows in PHYSICS.

Your report on giraffes is just about finished. It still needs some finishing touches, though. For example, it would be nice to have a picture! Hike over to the animal galleries at ZooNet - All about Zoos! and download or print your choice!

Zoos and Aquariums of AZA

The American Zoo and Aquarium Association has a members' directory with hot links to home pages, if the zoo or aquarium has one. Take a virtual visit to zoos all over the U.S. One fascinating section of this site is called the Species Survival Plan, found in the Programs area. Look up the natural history and endangered status of your favorite animals. For example, reading about the Asian elephant, we find there are 120 cows and 50 bulls in the captive breeding program. One of the problems is the lack of facilities that can manage an adult bull elephant. You'll learn that there are between 30,000 and 50,000 Asian elephants left in the wild. Their major threat is loss of habitat. Are you interested in pursuing a career as a zookeeper? Learn what sort of education and training you'll need to fulfill your dreams.

http://www.aza.org/

COUNTRIES OF THE WORLD

See also TRAVEL

Welcome to the Countries of the World! We've found some educational, entertaining, interesting, and fun Web pages about countries of the world. Some countries have many great Web resources, while others have only brief mentions in networked reference sources. In all cases, we thought of you at home, doing your homework and needing to find out what the flag of Latvia looks like, or the words to the national anthem of South Africa, or the major exports of Australia. So we tried to find resources to provide that information to you. Along the way, we also found some fascinating facts and bits of trivia. Check out some of the entries for any country, and you'll see what we mean. We didn't look for resources on uninhabited places, such as small islands. If you're looking for the Arctic or the Antarctic, also check the EARTH SCIENCE—LAND FEATURES—POLAR REGIONS section in the main part of this book. If you still can't find the place you need, check some of the general resources we have listed just below, before the individual countries. The ones to check first are Yahoo! Regional:Countries and the World Factbook home page.

NET FILES

Do fish sleep?

Answer: *According to the Florida Aquarium, "Fishes don't sleep like we do, but reef fishes have active and inactive times. Some prefer days; others are active at night. The reef is like a motel with day guests who leave at dusk when night guests arrive." For more answers about fish and ocean life, check http://www2.sptimes.com/ Aquarium/FA.3.1.html*

3D Atlas Online Home

What on earth are you looking for? It doesn't matter—you'll find it here. Check out research links for every country, current news, and a geographic glossary. For example, in Zimbabwe, you can see a photo of a mud hut home with a thatched roof, learn about the country's plateau and savanna, view its colorful flag, and link to other sites about this country. Also find an index to maps for each country and resources for students and teachers.

http://www.3DAtlas.com/

Africa Online: Kids Only

You've just discovered the best Africa site ever for kids. Learn all about Africa as you answer questions that test your knowledge on all things African. Visit African school home pages, play a word search game, and take a quiz to see what you've learned. This site welcomes your comments, so if you feel like doing so, be sure to tell them what you think.

http://www.africaonline.com/AfricaOnline/
    coverkids.html

ArabNet

If you need information on a country in the Middle East or North Africa, check this clearinghouse site. There are 22 countries represented and over 1,900 sites. You'll find maps and political and cultural information, plus links. They call this site a "magic carpet" for a good reason!

http://www.arab.net/

Asia Society:Links

This site lives up to the variety and vastness of its continent. Expect to find many Web sites related to Asia and its many cultures, businesses, politics, news, and discussions. It's an excellent place to start—and finish—if you want to expand your focus on Asia-specific resources.

http://www.asiasociety.org/

COUNTRIES OF THE WORLD

Asian Studies WWW VL

The Asian branch of the World Wide Web Virtual Library at the Australian National University has many selected and rated resources to search through. Links to and about all the Asian countries, from Turkey to Japan, are waiting here to be discovered. If you don't have a project that needs any of this information, browse around anyway and discover some of the exciting marvels to be found.

http://coombs.anu.edu.au/WWWVL-AsianStudies.html

AskAsia Homepage

Here's a site on Asia designed specially for K–12. There's an Information/News section, with news events about Asia, and a What's New area for recent additions to the site. For Educators contains Instructional Resources, a Communication Center, and School to School Connections. The Adult-Free-Zone has an Activity Corner, E-Pals, and a kids' feedback section called Kids Ask AskAsia. A final section, called Gateway to Asia, has links and Live From Asia, where live lectures and discussions featuring Asian and Asian American writers, artists, and educators are available.

http://www.askasia.org/

Database Europe

This is a geographical database that includes statistical information, economy, history, politics, culture, climate, and weather of all the European countries. It has been compiled by the students and teachers at the Albert Schweitzer Gymnasium in Erlangen, Bavaria. We hope they each got an A+ because they did a great job of gathering all sorts of information. There are wonderful maps of all the countries and of Europe. In addition, they link to many other sites filled with helpful information for a student working on a term paper or a family planning a vacation.

http://www.asg.physik.uni-erlangen.de/europa/
  indexe.htm

Electronic Field Trip to the United Nations

Learn all about the United Nations by taking this electronic field trip, and link to many other UN sites. Check the Classroom Activities area for discussion and debate topics related to the UN. If you need information about the United Nations, its history, and the work it does, this is a great place to begin.

http://www.pbs.org/tal/un/

The EmbassyWeb

Countries that are friendly towards each other often set up embassies in each other's countries, to help continue their good relationships. The embassies provide a place for businesses and individuals to get accurate and authoritative information about the other country. Embassies also provide a place for their own citizens to get help when they are away from home and for travelers to get visas (entry permits, not the credit cards) to the other country. Since embassies are in the information business, they can also be a valuable resource for researching facts about their countries.

http://www.embpage.org/

The European Directory: TED

This collection of Web sites focuses on sites that are located specifically within Europe. You can browse through categories including art, science, health, and sports. Sites are also categorized by country and region. There are many different languages in Europe, and these listings include non-English sites that are only available in the native language. If you're looking for sites in French, German, or other European languages, this is a good place to find them. However, many sites are in English or include an English version.

http://www3.ukshops.co.uk/

Lost your sheep? Find them in FARMING AND AGRICULTURE.

The European Union

According to this site, "The ultimate goal of the European Union is 'an ever closer union among the peoples of Europe, in which decisions are taken as closely as possible to the citizen: the objective is to promote economic and social progress which is balanced and sustainable, assert the European identity on the international scene and introduce a European citizenship for the nationals of the Member States." The European Union currently has 15 member states. It has its own flag, anthem, and "day" (May 9). One of the big initiatives is the launch of the euro currency. Find out about it at <http://europa.eu.int/euro/html/entry.html>.

http://europa.eu.int/abc-en.htm

Excite Travel: Countries & Territories

World geography homework never had it so good! Enjoy touring the world, looking for interesting places for that class project. Inside each country page are links sorted by categories, such as country information, culture and language, maps, and travel. At the bottom of each country page is an additional choice that lists links to all the countries in the same region or continent. Happy trails.

http://www.city.net/countries/

Geographica Homepage

The Interknowledge Corporation presents this professional-looking site that contains country-specific pages on many countries around the world. Each country site is both a pleasure to look at and a wealth of comprehensive information. This is a don't-miss site for worldly info-seekers.

http://www.geographia.com/

Governments on the WWW

And now for the political side of the Web: here is a collection of government sites for all the countries of the world. Links are included on parliaments, ministries, agencies, law courts, embassies, consulates, political parties, and parliamentary groups and youth organizations of political parties. All the government sites are grouped by continent, but you can also browse other categories such as multinational organizations and institutional sites on broadcasting, elections, statistics, tourism, and more.

http://www.gksoft.com/govt/en/

Index on Africa

This comprehensive index is maintained by the Norwegian Council for Africa (NCA). All Web sites within this collection (over 2,000) are focused on Africa and are sorted by news, country, and subject. Subjects include Children's Pages, Cooking, Health, History, Human Rights, and more. Another section includes Africa Update, which has daily news briefings from various African news sources. A search index is also included where you can search on the NCA collection only or the NCA collection plus over 150 sites at OneWorld, a site that focuses on human rights. Two additional Africa-specific search engines are included on the search page.

http://www.africaindex.africainfo.no/

K-12 Africa Guide

If you're trying to gather information for a homework assignment or a project about an African country, take a good look at this site. Find information about Africa's languages, customs, governments, environment, and people. You'll discover and learn about the heritage of the different African countries and their rich history. The Multimedia Archives offer maps, images of animals, flags, satellite images, and pictures of African face masks.

http://www.sas.upenn.edu/African_Studies/
    Home_Page/AFR_GIDE.html

Latin American Network Information Center (LANIC)

The Institute of Latin American Studies at the University of Texas at Austin has compiled this site of information on and from Latin America. Resources are indexed by 29 different countries, each with their own subcategories, such as Art, Government, and News. An additional section groups resources by 44 general categories, including Anthropology, K–12, Maps, Science, Music, and Food. Resources within these 44 categories are again grouped by countries and various appropriate categories. A search function spans all the collected resources. If it's Latin, it's in LANIC.

http://www.lanic.utexas.edu/

Library of Congress - Country Studies

Country Studies is part of a continuing series of books prepared by the Federal Research Division of the Library of Congress under the Country Studies/Area Handbook Program. This series presently contains studies of 85 countries. You will find accurate and detailed historical information. Learn about the people who make up each country's society, their origins, dominant beliefs and values, and their common interests as well as the issues on which they are divided.

http://lcweb2.loc.gov/frd/cs/cshome.html

Lonely Planet on-line

Although this is a tourist-oriented service, Lonely Planet can be an excellent source of information about a country. They publish some of the most popular travel books in the world. You'll find facts on the environment, history, culture, and more about each of the world's countries here. Of course, since it's for tourists, there's even info on getting there, attractions, events, and travelers' reports. All this adds up to some of the best stuff for reports and homework assignments, not to mention interesting reading for that virtual trip. Parental advisory: Sections of this site may be inappropriate for younger children.

http://www.lonelyplanet.com/

Micronations on the Web

"Micronations are attempts by groups or individuals to found their own nations, either to address what they see as deficiencies in current nations, as mental exercises, for self-aggrandizement, for earnest ideological motives, or for almost any reason at all. They are pursued with varying levels of seriousness, and have life-spans that range from weeks to decades." If you've ever dreamed about starting your own country, this is the place to visit. Of course, once you get started, you'll need to write a constitution, create some holidays, design a flag, schedule summit conferences, print some money, and, well, you get the idea. Actually, there are many justified reasons for some of these micronations to be in pursuit of sovereignty. Read through the pages on this site and see if you agree. Be sure to check out the Micropatrology Web Sites section for other Web sites on this subject.

http://www.geocities.com/CapitolHill/Senate/5385/

Multicultural Home Page

This site offers just what it says: a sampling of different cultures from all around the world. Hear Chinese folk music, or learn more about the history of the Canadian fur trade or details about historic Canadian women. How about a recipe for *brigadeiro* (a delicious Brazilian dessert) or a visit to the Taj Mahal in India? Not every country is listed here, but you'll find a good selection of diverse cultures from around the world, each listed with a color picture of the country's flag. If you haven't found the information you are looking for somewhere else, check out this site compiled by Purdue University.

http://pasture.ecn.purdue.edu/~agenhtml/agenmc/

Pacific Islands Internet Resources

Set sail for the Pacific and plot a course through the islands with help from the clickable map on this home page. Each map area takes you to a page with a list of sites on that country or island group. A pop-up menu takes you to other areas of the site. Pacific Islands Introduction includes the four major Pacific groups of Anglonesia, Melanesia, Micronesia, and Polynesia. The General Information Page includes Books, Document Collections, Media Resources, Travel & Tourist Info, and Newsgroups and Chat Rooms. The Geophysical Page has Maps & Images and Environmental Features. Are we there yet?

http://www2.hawaii.edu/~ogden/piir/

Summary of the Peri-Antarctic Islands

Here's an interesting collection of materials on the islands that surround Antarctica. These 19 islands and archipelagos include the somewhat familiar South Georgia and the South Sandwich islands and some not so familiar, like Iles Crozet and Iles Kerguelen. The peri-Antarctic islands include the sub-Antarctic ones and several others with associated features. This site provides brief information about each of the islands.

http://www.spri.cam.ac.uk/bob/periant.htm

The United Nations CyberSchoolBus

It won't take you 80 days to go around the world at this site, but you'd find plenty here to keep you busy if you wanted to take that long! Besides learning all about the United Nations and how and why it began, you could check Resource Source and learn about special celebration activities for days that are relevant to the entire world, such as World Environment Day. The City Profile section includes descriptions of cities around the world and an urban fact game. The Country At A Glance section contains information about all member countries of the United Nations. Quiz Quad offers several games. Test your knowledge of flags with the Flag Tag game or take quizzes from Doctor Data. The Professor's global quizzes on UNESCO's World Heritage site are lots of fun, too. Periodically, the Professor goes on a seven-week tour of historically and culturally significant sites around the world. Based on the hints from the postcards, you have to figure out where the professor has been. If you uncover all seven destinations, you'll win a prize and get your name listed on the Photo Quiz site. You'll also find lots of info on Model UN activities here.

http://www.un.org/Pubs/CyberSchoolBus/

NET FILES

What makes a rose smell like a rose?

Answer: According to the Timeless Roses site, "Fragrance is determined by the concentration of chemicals in the petals of the flower, and how these chemicals interact with each other and the atmosphere. Oils, resins, alcohols, fatty acids, and phenols all contribute to the character of scent. As a general rule, darker colored roses are more fragrant than white or yellow roses. Environmental factors which determine how a rose smells on a specific day include climactic conditions such as temperature, humidity, and time of day. Warm, sunny days with low humidity will bring out the best rose fragrance in the garden." Find out more at http://www.timelessroses.com/fragrant.htm

Virtual Tourist World Map

Virtual Tourist is a way to find Web pages around the world. You're first presented with a clickable world map. Pick a continent or region and zoom in to a more detailed map showing the countries. Click once more on a country, and you'll see a list of Web servers located in that country. The server may have information about that country along with other subject matter.

http://www.vtourist.com/webmap/

WashingtonPost.com: International

Try the Search the World database to find news, reference materials, and Internet resources for more than 220 countries and territories. This is a great place to look if you need the very latest information on a country! You can type in the name of a specific country or territory or just browse the countries alphabetically. Regional sections are updated weekly, with news and features from six different regions of the world.

http://www.washingtonpost.com/wp-srv/inatl/front.htm

Welcome to the Environmental Atlas

Are you interested in the environment and concerned about conservation and resource depletion? So is the Green Plan Center of the Resource Renewal Institute. They have treated this environmental atlas as an Internet-based tool for researching environmental policy worldwide. The map-based atlas lets you view information about a country's environmental policies—just click on the appropriate continent. Or, you can search a text-based atlas by continent or alphabetically by country. Stop at this site for a profile of your country's major environmental problems, a brief chronology of its environmental history, and any recent policy developments. Learn if global conditions are affecting your country's environment and how it is cooperating on environmental issues with neighboring countries and the world community. Preserving our world's natural resources is a global issue.

http://www.rri.org/envatlas/

Welcome to World Heritage

What do the Grand Canyon, the Galápagos Islands, Moenjodaro, Völklingen Ironworks, the Island of Gorée, and the Citadel of Haiti all have in common? Though each of these sites is located in a different part of the world, they share a common heritage as unique treasures. If environmental or political situations cause them to disappear, it would be a loss for each and every one of us. UNESCO (United Nations Educational, Scientific, and Cultural Organization) believes that preservation of this common heritage concerns us all. They have established a list of these sites, recognized as exhibiting "outstanding universal value." At press time, the World Heritage List included 552 cultural and natural sites. Find out if your country has any special sites on this list. Maybe your school can become part of the World Heritage Youth Project. Check the Just for Kids section, where you'll find out What Makes a Site and what a World Heritage site manager does, and take some Virtual Tours in the Let's Visit section.

http://www.unesco.org/whc/nwhc/pages/home/pages/
   homepage.htm

The World Clock

As you eat your breakfast cereal, you wonder what your pen pal is doing right now. What time is it where your pen pal lives, hundreds or thousands of miles away? Is it morning or is it the middle of the night? Here is a site that will answer this question for you. For more, try the Time Service Department, U.S. Naval Observatory, listed under the links as "Directorate of Time, USA." You'll find general information about time zones and telling time, and the FAQ area even has information on how to make a sundial (talk about retro!). This is one site you'll definitely want to refer to periodically.

http://www.stud.unit.no/USERBIN/steffent/
   verdensur.pl

World Factbook

It's the job of the Central Intelligence Agency (CIA) to know what's going on in the world. This involves gathering information about each country's government, its people, economy, and transportation facilities, including maps of each country. They have recently redesigned their home page, and it's a winner! There is also a text-only option.

http://www.odci.gov/cia/publications/factbook/

Yahoo! Regional:Countries

Brazil has its rain forests, Morocco has its desert, Chile has its mountains, and Yahoo has them all. Browse the world's countries here to your heart's content. Each country's links are sorted by up to 36 categories, such as government, health, libraries, culture, and more. Indices are also listed separately.

http://www.yahoo.com/Regional/Countries/

AFGHANISTAN

Afghanistan Online

Civilization in Afghanistan dates back as far as 4000 B.C., and many empires have controlled this region throughout the centuries. Afghanistan became a republic in 1973, after being ruled by monarchs for over 2,000 years. At this site you can check the latest news, learn about Afghan music, find information on cultural ceremonies, read historical facts, dream about some savory foods, and more!

http://www.afghan-web.com/

ALBANIA

Albanian Home Page

Albania's rugged mountains have earned it a reputation as a remote and mysterious country. The Albanian language is one of the oldest original languages in Europe. Albania was home to the late Mother Teresa, the nun who became famous throughout the world for her humanitarian efforts towards the poor and was awarded the Nobel Peace Prize. At this site, you can learn all sorts of facts about Albania, the country, and Albanians, the people.

http://www.albanian.com/main/

ALGERIA

Miftah Shamali- Algeria

France controlled this country from 1830 until independence in 1962. The government and economy have been struggling to stabilize ever since. Today, Algeria is a country of curfews and unrest, and foreigners are advised against travel there. Still, at this site you can learn a lot about this North African country.

http://i-cias.com/m.s/algeria/

NET FILES

Dad says I can eat dessert first "once in a blue moon." What's a blue moon, and when is the next one?

Answer: Calendar months are either 30 or 31 days long; the lunar month is 29 1/2 days. So every now and again, there are two full moons in the same month. The second full moon in the same month is called a *blue moon*. Go to http://www.ast.cam.ac.uk/~adh/astro/bluemoon.html to calculate blue moons in a given year (there will be two blue moons in 1999, and none before then). But remember to correct for time zones–this site is is in the United Kingdom. According to them, there was a blue moon in 1996 (full moons on July 1 and 30); but in the U.S., the two full moons were on June 1 and 30! See the time zone explanation at http://www.earthsky.com/Tools/comments. pl?show_date=1996-06-30

ANDORRA

ANDORRA TOURISM

The principality of Andorra is a small country situated between France and Spain, in the Pyrenees Mountains. Its size is about half that of New York City. Skiing is by far the most popular industry there, and the abundant wildlife and natural beauty make it an outdoor enthusiast's paradise. At this page you will also find links to the official government Web pages and others, but many did not have English versions when we checked. This page is available in English, Castellano, Català, and French.

http://www.turisme.ad/angles/angles.htm

ANGOLA

Angola:Welcome to the Official Web Site of the Republic of Angola

A colony of Portugal for 400 years, Angola gained its independence in 1975. Situated in equatorial Africa, Angola is rich in oil, gold, and other resources. Portuguese is the official business and international language, but Angola also has six national languages: Kikongo, Kimbundo, Umbundu, Chokwe, Mbunda, and Oxikuanyama. Political unrest has prevented development; according to the information here, the humanitarian crisis is still acute in Angola, and the United Nations and Red Cross relief efforts continue to help. In February 1997, Princess Diana of Great Britain visited Angola as a Red Cross volunteer. She focused world attention on the deadly legacy of years of military activity in the region: buried and forgotten land mines. Children and adults step on these hidden explosive mines and are sometimes killed or horribly maimed. A movement to demine the landscape is in progress, but the process is slow and the number of hidden mines is unknown.

http://www.angola.org/

Volcanoes are an explosive subject. Find one in EARTH SCIENCE.

ANGUILLA

See UNITED KINGDOM—DEPENDENCIES—ANGUILLA

ANTARCTICA

See EARTH SCIENCE— LAND FEATURES—POLAR REGIONS

ANTIGUA AND BARBUDA

Antigua & Barbuda - Official Travel Guide

These two West Indies islands are located about 250 miles southeast of Puerto Rico. Barbuda is known for its fantastic scuba diving, among other things. Most Antiguans are of African heritage, descendants of slaves brought to the island centuries ago to work the sugarcane fields owned by a British developer. According to the information on this page, "Antigua's history of habitation extends as far back as two and a half millenia before Christ. The first settlements... were those of the Siboney (an Arawak word meaning 'stone-people')...whose beautifully crafted shell and stone tools have been found at dozens of sites around the island."

http://www.interknowledge.com/antigua-barbuda/

ARGENTINA

Argentina!

At this site, you'll get facts on Argentina, nicely presented, and links to other regions, cities, and Internet resources. One of the interesting tidbits concerns the origin of the name Argentina. It comes from the Latin *argentum*, which means "silver." According to this page, "The origin of the name goes back to the voyages made by the first Spanish *conquistadores* (conquerors) to the Río de la Plata (Silver River). The shipwrecked survivors of the expedition mounted by Juan Díaz de Solís discovered Indians in the region who presented them with silver objects. The news about the legendary Sierra del Plata, a mountain rich in silver, reached Spain around 1524."

http://www.middlebury.edu/~leparc/htm/argent2.htm

Lonely Planet - Destination Argentina

This South American country is home to *los Gauchos*—Argentinian cowboys. Argentinians eat a lot of beef per person compared to the rest of the world, so they have many ranches to raise lots of cattle. Argentina is also known for the famous Latin dance, the tango! At this site, you can learn about the history, culture, music, and people of Argentina.

http://www.lonelyplanet.com/dest/sam/argie.htm

República Argentina - Secretaría de Turismo

Argentina has a diverse geography, including grasslands, glaciers, rain forests, and the sea. This site contains a wonderful virtual tour of the country and many pictures showing the beauty of the area. Some pages may be slow to load, but we think it's worth the wait.

http://turismo.gov.ar/g/menu.htm

NET FILES

True or false:
Most cartoons we
see on TV these
days are created
completely on
computers.

Answer: False. Computer animation is still rare in the world of television cartoons. In fact, while you might assume that the pictures are the first things to "go digital," it's sound that is usually stored and played back on computers and special keyboards. Cool, huh? There's lots of info on how cartoons are made at http://www.wbanimation.com/ani_04if.htm

ARMENIA

The Armenian Cause Home

Armenia is indeed an old, yet troubled, country. The country was born in 189 B.C. when it declared its independence from the Greeks. In A.D. 301, Armenia became the first country to adopt Christianity as its state religion. Read more at this site about Armenia's history from its beginning to the present, and learn about the country's developments and its wars.

http://armen-info.com/lacause/publcs/

Armenian Embassy Website

At this official site you can get lots of facts on all subjects Armenian. For example, the Armenian alphabet has 39 characters. It was created in A.D. 405 by a monk who thought only 36 letters were needed. Later on, people added three additional letters. According to this site, "The first work of literature with the new alphabet was the translation of the Bible from Greek." Find out much more about Armenia's heritage at this site, including facts about its people, religion, and architecture.

http://www.armeniaemb.org/

ARUBA

See NETHERLANDS—DEPENDENCIES—ARUBA

AUSTRALIA

Australian Commonwealth Government Entry Point

This official site offers lots of government information, including details about the national symbols. Australia's coat of arms features a shield containing the badges of the six Australian states. Supporting the shield on either side are a red kangaroo and an emu (a large bird). In the foreground are the yellow flowers of Australia's native wattle, also called acacia. Australia has never adopted an "official" bird, flower, or other emblems, according to this site. The national flag is currently a hot topic. If Australia becomes a republic, perhaps it should have a new flag. Read about the controversy here and at <http://www.ausflag.com.au/debate/debate.html>.

http://www.fed.gov.au/

Guide to Australia

This is your jumpstation to facts on Australia and all its regions. Find out about education, tourism, government, and natural history. Australia is the smallest continent but the sixth largest country. Many unusual animals inhabit Australia, including the koala and platypus.

http://www.csu.edu.au/australia/

Lonely Planet — Destination Australia

Lonely Planet, which publishes a travel book series, is based in Australia. So you might guess that they would create a terrific page about their home country—and they have! Here you will find photos and general information on Aussie government, culture, environment, and tourist destinations.

http://www.lonelyplanet.com/dest/aust/aus.htm

TERRITORIES—COCOS (KEELING) ISLANDS

Fact Sheet 103 - The Cocos (Keeling) Islands

This Australian tropical paradise is in the Indian Ocean. Residents voted to become part of Australia's Northern Territory in 1984. Cocos Islands (sometimes called the Keeling Islands) are two atoll groups containing 27 islands. This page has some brief facts about the islands.

http://www.aa.gov.au/AA_WWW/FactSheets/
   FS103.html

Ships On Stamps (Ayesha)

Here is a short bit of history illustrated by a souvenir sheet of stamps issued by the Cocos Islands (part of Australia's Northern Territory) in 1989. The *Ayesha* was a three-masted schooner commandeered by German soldiers from Port Refuge after their ship, *Emden,* was attacked and captured by the Australian cruiser *Sydney* during World War I. It's a great story; read about it here. If you are a stamp collector or you have a passion for ships and boats of all kinds, click on the arrow at the bottom of the page to see how "the history of water transport mirrors that of mankind itself." This site's really cool!

http://www.sron.ruu.nl/~erikp/ayesha/ayesha.html

TERRITORIES—NORFOLK ISLAND

Norfolk Island

The important facts about this tiny island in the Pacific, along with a map of the country, are here at this site.

http://www.odci.gov/cia/publications/factbook/
   nf.html

Norfolk Island - The Web Site

Before the first white man stepped ashore on Norfolk Island from the good ship *Resolution*, the island had long been a stopover for sea-roving Polynesians. Today, migratory birds make this lush, green island in the South Pacific Ocean their temporary resting place. Here, among the famed Norfolk pine trees that can reach 150 feet in height, no "fatal creature" dwells. Pretty peaceful, right? Yes, but it wasn't always like this. At one time, according to this site, it was home to "the most cruel British penal colony, ever." Set sail for the stunning images of Norfolk Island. Australia says Norfolk Island is an external territory of Australia. However, this page says there is no constitutional basis for that claim and that Norfolk Island is a British Crown colony.

http://www.ozemail.com.au/~jbp/pds/

AUSTRIA

Austrian National Tourist Office

This site is the Austrian National Tourist Board's North American edition. If you want to see another edition, just follow the handy link they have provided. Austria is rich with tradition. It was the home of Mozart, who created his first symphony when he was a boy. Austria is well known as the setting for the movie *The Sound of Music,* and the Austrian Alps are a famous place for skiing and outdoors adventure. This site has tourist-type info, as you might imagine.

http://www.anto.com/

Republik Österreich

The Federal Chancellery of Austria provides current news and information about this country's people, culture, history, and more at this site. Other areas include government facts and information about Europe in general.

http://www.austria.gv.at/e/

AZERBAIJAN

Virtual Azerbaijan Presents - Azerbaijan's History

Once part of the Roman Empire and later conquered by the Turks, Azerbaijan became part of the Soviet Union in 1922. It became an independent country in 1991 when the Soviet Union dissolved, but the country is still torn by political unrest. This page has facts on this country's history, culture, people, and more.

http://www-scf.usc.edu/~baguirov/azeri/
    azerbaijan4.htm

THE BAHAMAS

Welcome to the Bahamas, Nassau, Freeport and the Family Islands

The Bahamas refers to a group of 700 islands located off the peninsula of Florida. Of these, only 40 are inhabited! The Bahamas boasts the world's third largest barrier reef, built up from thousands of years of coral deposits. And there's more: you'll even find pine forests and limestone caves on some islands. The Morton Salt Company operates a salt factory on Inagua, producing over a million pounds of salt a year. Check out Abaco, where Disney is building a "fantasy island" for its new cruise ships to visit. If you want to learn how to take a vacation without impacting Mother Earth very much, look at the Eco-Bahamas area of this site for ecotourism ideas.

http://www.bahamasnet.com/index.shtml

BAHRAIN

Bahrain A Country Study

Bahrain is a group of 33 islands on the west side of the Persian Gulf. Of these islands, most are uninhabited except for the largest, also called Bahrain. Bahrain, once known as Dilmun, was a popular regional trading center as far back as 2000 B.C. Today, it's a well-developed country with a low crime rate and stable economy.

http://lcweb2.loc.gov/frd/cs/bhtoc.html

BANGLADESH

Virtual Bangladesh

Bangladesh is a tropical country of hot, humid summers. It's known as the "Land of Bengal Tiger." A major feature of this country is a large delta into which the Brahmaputra, Ganges, and Meghna Rivers empty into the sea. The delta forms a large, fertile area used as farmland. The heavy rains that fall during the monsoon season make this country one of the rainiest locations on Earth. In 1971, there was a war for independence between the Bengalis and the Pakistanis; over 10,000 Bengalis were killed (this site has disturbing photos in the Holocaust Museum). On the lighter side, at this site you can try some online Bangla language lessons and get recipes for Bangladeshi egg *haloa* (a dessert) and *sandesh* (it means "good news"), which is prepared by many Bengali families to celebrate good news or festivals.

http://www.virtualbangladesh.com/

NET FILES

The state of Ohio has an official rock song. What is it?

Answer: According to this site, 'Hang on Sloopy', a favorite of the Ohio State University marching band, became the state rock song in November 1985. Composed by Celina-born guitarist Rick Derringer, it was first recorded by The McCoys, a rock band from Dayton, in 1965." You have to go to *http://www.oplin.lib.oh.us/OHIO/OCJ/rocksong.html* and read the hilarious state resolution that goes along with the designation!

BARBADOS

Barbados Tourism Encyclopedia

The Portuguese and Spanish traveled to this island as early as the 1500s in search of gold. However, no permanent settlements were there until the English arrived in 1625. Sugar production became the island's main industry. The work was done by slaves, starting in the 1630s, and the first slaves were white indentured servants who had somehow displeased the Crown and were "Barbadoed" from Britain. Barbados gained its independence from England in 1966.

http://www.barbados.org/

BELARUS

The Virtual Guide to Belarus

Belarus is an ancient country situated between Poland and Russia. Its western border is about 300 miles east of Moscow. The region was occupied by Slavic tribes back as far as the first century. According to this site's history area, "The name Belarus means 'white Rus,' and there's still no exact version of its origin. Some historians believe that 'white' in old Slavic languages meant 'free,' pointing to the fact that Belarus was never invaded by the Tatars or under their control, unlike the other principalities later in the thirteenth to fifteenth centuries. Others think that this name is older and served as a difference between Kievan Rus—Black Rus—a small territory in the western part of modern Belarus, and the territory known as White Rus." You'll also find information here on the Chernobyl nuclear disaster. Although Chernobyl is in the Ukraine, when the plant exploded on April 26, 1986, the winds took 70 percent of the radioactive dust over Belarus, causing problems that still exist today. Note that this is not an official page, and many strong opinions are expressed by the scientists who maintain it.

http://www.belarusguide.com/

NET FILES

The most recent Winter Olympics were held February 7–22, 1998, in Nagano, Japan. Merchandise of all kinds bore the special Olympic logo mascots. What were they?

Answer: The four mascots were called Snowlets, representing baby owls from the forests of Japan. Each had a different quality: passion (fire), curiosity (wind), calmness and wisdom (earth), and romance (water). Find out more at http://www.nagano.olympic.org/fun/stories/stories/_e.shtml

BELGIUM

Belgium: Overview

This impressive site has many categorized links all about Belgium. Here, you'll find information for tourists, including sites focused on specific cities and towns. There are also Belgium-specific sites listed for food, arts, language, genealogy, news, and much more.

http://pespmc1.vub.ac.be/Belgcul.html

THE MONARCHY IN BELGIUM

Take a look at the curriculum vitae (that's Latin for "life's work") of King Albert II of Belgium. You'll see it's not easy to become a king, but, then again, the perks of the job are probably really great! The Belgian monarch's position is well respected in Belgium, as he is responsible for keeping the country independent and free.

http://belgium.fgov.be/Engels/417/41709/41709.htm

Welcome to the Embassy of Belgium in the United States

Check this official site, especially the Student's Corner, for fast facts. Did you know that Belgium has the world's finest lace? The world's 14th largest port, Antwerp, is also called the diamond capital of the world. Belgium is the largest producer of azalea plants, cobalt, radium, and cotton thread and has one of the largest glass industries in the world. Its capital, Brussels, is also the headquarters of the European Commission and therefore is the administrative capital of Europe.

http://www.diplobel.org/usa/default_en.asp

BELIZE

Lonely Planet - Destination Belize

Belize was once part of the 4,000-year-old Maya empire. It was taken over by the Spanish in the sixteenth century and then by Britain in the nineteenth century. Belize gained its independence from Britain in 1981. Along Belize's coast are numerous cays, islands, atolls, beaches, and the longest barrier reef in the Western Hemisphere. What this really means is that there are more water-related activities available than you can imagine.

http://www.lonelyplanet.com/dest/cam/belize.htm

BENIN

Benin Page

Benin is a small country on the west coast of Africa and is about the size of the state of Pennsylvania. It has undergone many changes in government since the French colonized it in the early 1700s. Previously known as Dahomey, it was also once part of French West Africa. Dahomey gained its independence from France in August 1960, and it has since changed its name to the People's Republic of Benin. Although the official language is French, over half the 4.5 million people speak Fon. Learn to say "good morning" in Fon: *AH-FON Ghan-Jee-Ah.* You'll find more handy phrases at this site!

http://www.sas.upenn.edu/African_Studies/
  Country_Specific/Benin.html

BERMUDA

See UNITED KINGDOM—DEPENDENCIES—BERMUDA

BHUTAN

The Bhutan web site [Tashi Delek]

Bhutan means "Land of the Thunder Dragon." It gets its name from the severe storms that come down from the Himalayas at the northern part of the country. Bhutan is a monarchy that gained its independence from India in 1949. It is an isolated country that tends to resist influences from the outside world; in fact, it limits the number of tourists to only 4,000 per year to help keep itself separated from the rest of the world. Some areas of this site are not yet translated into English and are available only in Japanese.

http://www.tashidelek.com/maine.html

BOLIVIA

Bolivian Home Page in South Africa

The Andes Mountains dominate the western part of Bolivia. They contain three of the highest mountain peaks in South America. Lake Titicaca, on the western border, is the highest commercially navigable lake in the world, at 12,506 feet above sea level. The 12,000-foot central plateau puts a large portion of this country higher than many of the rest of the world's mountains! This Web page has some info of its own and links to other pages about Bolivia, including a quick guide to Quechua, language of the Incas. For example, *K-MartMAN riyku* means "We have gone to K-Mart"! That link is at <*http://www-robotics.usc.edu/~barry/quechua/*>.

http://ufrmsa1.olivetti.za/~ivan/bolivia_0.html

Lonely Planet - Destination Bolivia

Visit Bolivia, the "Tibet of the Americas"! It's also a great place to see wildlife. Some of the animals you might see there include the spectacled bear, jaguar, vicuña, llama, alpaca, anteater, tapir, capybara, turtle, alligator, rhea, and condor. Bolivia's La Paz is the highest capital city in the world (11,929 feet). Did you ever wonder about the bowler hats the Bolivian women wear? According to this source, the hats are worn to the side if the wearer is single and on top if she's married.

http://www.lonelyplanet.com/dest/sam/bolivia.htm

BOSNIA AND HERZEGOVINA

About Bosnia

Once ruled by Croatian kings, Hungary, the Turks, Austria-Hungary, and Yugoslavia, Bosnia has undergone a long history of change. In recent years, Muslims, Croats, and Serbs have sought to gain control of the country. This continues today with clashes between the Serbs and Muslim-Croat confederation. This site puts the country's history and culture at your fingertips.

http://www.bosnet.org/bosnia/index.html-ssi

The Bosnian Virtual Fieldtrip

Take this multimedia tour and learn a lot more about the country and why it is split along ethnic lines. This is more of a tutorial than a field trip, since it keeps asking you to write paragraphs and answer questions, but it is a good way to learn about the history of the conflicts and the hope for their peaceful resolution.

http://geog.gmu.edu/projects/bosnia/default.html

Looking for the State Bird or the State Motto? It's in the UNITED STATES—STATES section.

BOTSWANA

African Alternatives - Botswana Travel Background

Imagine this: In the north the magnificent Okavango waterway, with its green and fertile plains, flows straight into a sea of sand, the Kalahari Desert, and vanishes. There is a lot of interesting information about the parks and natural history of Botswana at this site. You'll learn about animals and safaris and the national park system in that country.

http://www.ecoafrica.com/africa/south/btsw/btsw.htm

Botswana Page

This southern African country is about the size of Texas. Botswana's early inhabitants were Bushmen and Bantus. It became the British protectorate of Bechuanaland in 1886, but the name Botswana was adopted when it gained its independence in 1966.

http://www.africaindex.africainfo.no/africaindex1/
countries/botswana.html

Okavango @ nationalgeographic.com

This virtual safari into the jungles of Botswana will give you a close-up view of some of Africa's most unusual animals. Follow the tracks, then use your binoculars to see cheetah, wild dogs, antelope, and more. Remember, you don't need bug spray in cyberspace.

http://www.nationalgeographic.com/features/96/
okavango/

BRAZIL

Brazil Information

Here are some facts from this official site. Brazil is the fifth largest country in the world. Within its borders lies the Amazon jungle, the largest tropical rain forest in the world. The Amazon's trees are the world's largest source of oxygen. São Paulo and Rio de Janeiro are two of the ten most populated cities in the world. Rio was a candidate to host the Summer Olympics in 2004 but did not make it to the list of finalists this time. Look for them to try again, though.

http://www.embratur.gov.br/embingl/infhist.html

Brazilian Embassy/ Embaixada do Brasil, Washington, D.C.

The Brazilian embassy, in Washington, D.C., presents this comprehensive collection on the government as well as a large selection of links. Try its jumpstation to info on Brazilian culture, tourism, and education. Maybe you will find a link about Capoeira, a ritualized martial art combined with dance and music, or samba schools and the eagerly awaited thematic parades at Carnival.

http://www.brasil.emb.nw.dc.us/

Maria Brazil

This site is a wonderful collection of information tidbits about Brazil. Read all about Brazil's culture, cuisine, crafts, holidays, and folklore. It's complete with audio clips from Brazilian music and singers, plus many Brazilian recipes—especially desserts.

http://www.maria-brazil.org/

Meu Brasil by Sergio Koreisha

This is a lovingly crafted page about a country that is so large it touches almost all the other countries in South America. This site has tons of unchecked links! If you just want Brazil in a nutshell, go to "Information in a *Brazil* - Nutshell"; you'll love the collection of facts there.

http://darkwing.uoregon.edu/~sergiok/brasil.html

BRITISH VIRGIN ISLANDS

See UNITED KINGDOM—DEPENDENCIES—BRITISH VIRGIN ISLANDS

BRUNEI

Lonely Planet — Destination: Brunei

Brunei was once a larger country, with Borneo and part of the Philippines under its control. The British were largely responsible for shrinking Brunei's territory since their arrival in the seventeenth century. Oil was discovered there in 1929. A revolt in 1962 eventually led to its independence in 1984. Today, this Muslim country (properly called Negara Brunei Darussalam), although rich from its oil exports, is isolated and underdeveloped.

http://www.lonelyplanet.com/dest/sea/brunei.htm

BULGARIA

Embassy of The Republic of Bulgaria - Washington D.C.

At this site from the Bulgarian embassy in Washington, D.C., you will learn many facts about the government, the environment, geography, and more. There is also fascinating cultural information. Did you know that a Bulgarian folk song, "*Izlel e Delyu Haidutin*," was selected to be sent into space on the *Voyager* spacecraft? It was part of the disc mixed to represent Earth's culture, including a message of greeting from earthlings to other civilizations.

http://www.bulgaria.com/embassy/wdc/

COUNTRIES OF THE WORLD

Frequently Asked Questions about Bulgaria

Bulgaria is located south of Romania on the Black Sea. Its early ancestry started with the Slavs in the sixth century. In the seventh century, the Turkic Bulgars began their influence in the region and founded empires through the twelfth century. The Ottomans ruled for 500 years beginning in the late 1300s. Bulgaria became independent in 1908, but the Communists took power in the 1940s and abolished the monarchy. Since 1990, the Communist party has lost its power. This site offers everything from history to music, from how to make delicious baklava to Bulgarian holidays.

http://www.cs.columbia.edu/~radev/cgi-bin/bgfaq.cgi

BURKINA FASO

Burkina Faso Page

The Mossi tribe was the earliest to settle in this West African country as early as the eleventh century. After changing control with the Mali and Songhai empires over the centuries, France took control of the area in 1896. The region became known as Upper Volta in 1947 and gained its independence in 1960. It was renamed Burkina Faso in 1984. Most workers today are farmers, and many of them migrate to neighboring Ghana and Côte d'Ivoire every year to find additional work because of the poor farming conditions in their own country, due to drought.

http://www.sas.upenn.edu/African_Studies/
Country_Specific/Burkina.html

BURMA

See MYANMAR (BURMA)

What time is it, anyway? Check with the atomic clock in TIME.

BURUNDI

Burundi Information

Burundi is a small country in central Africa on the northeast shore of Lake Tanganyika, the second deepest lake in the world. Coffee is Burundi's major export, so its economy is largely dependent on good weather and the international coffee market.

http://www.sas.upenn.edu/African_Studies/
Country_Specific/Burundi.html

CAMBODIA

.asiatour / Welcome To Cambodia

This site offers fun and interesting information about the country of Cambodia and its climate, geography, and people. The photo gallery is a great way to learn the history of the country. You'll see Cambodian houses on stilts at Lake Tonle Sap—similar to those built by ancient civilizations dating back to 4000 B.C. Learn about ancient temples, royal palaces, and examples of how the French colonists influenced Cambodian architecture and culture. Parents: Not all links have been checked.

http://www.asiatour.com/cambodia/content1.htm

Lonely Planet — Destinations: Cambodia

Imagine being a teenager with the responsibility of ruling a whole country. That is what happened in 1941, when the French installed 19-year-old Prince Sihanouk on the Cambodian throne. King Sihanouk ruled this war-torn country up through 1995 and is now referred to as the Father of Cambodia. This is a great place to look for quick facts-at-a-glance about the history, culture, economy, and environment of Cambodia, along with a photo slide show. The map of the country clearly shows the major mountain ranges surrounding Cambodia on three sides, its only major port of Kampot in the south, and the dominant influence of the waters of the Mekong and Tonle Sap Rivers.

http://www.lonelyplanet.com/dest/sea/camb.htm

CAMEROON

The Home Page of the Republic of Cameroon

Cameroon is sometimes referred to as the hinge point of West and East Africa, since historically it has been a meeting place for diverse people and civilizations. Go to this page for information from Cameroonians about the Republic of Cameroon, its geography, its people and their warmth and friendliness, its government, its economy, its cultures and traditions, and its diversity of folklore. Listen to a MIDI version of the Cameroon national anthem. Be sure to check the Stepping Disks for some interesting links to other related sites, including a great large-scale map of Cameroon and sound clips of Cameroon music. You'll also find pictures of Cameroon's active volcano and its six national parks, where tourists can take pictures of Derby elan, rhinos, giraffes, and elephants in their natural habitat.

http://www.compufix.demon.co.uk/camweb/

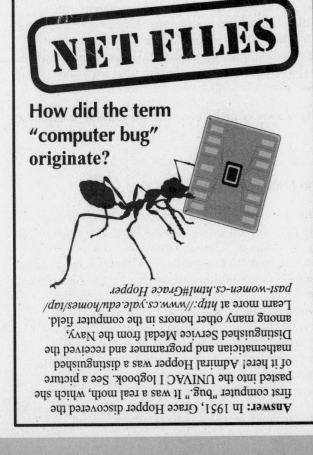

NET FILES

How did the term "computer bug" originate?

Answer: In 1951, Grace Hopper discovered the first computer "bug." It was a real moth, which she pasted into the UNIVAC I logbook. See a picture of it here! Admiral Hopper was a distinguished mathematician and programmer and received the Distinguished Service Medal from the Navy, among many other honors in the computer field. Learn more at http://www.cs.yale.edu/homes/tap/past-women-cs.html#Grace Hopper.

CANADA

Canada's SchoolNet-Rescol canadien

Explore this site and its many resources for K–12 students and educators. Everything has a Canadian focus, and everyone will be interested in the wonderful digital collections at <http://www.schoolnet.ca/collections/english/index.htm>. Here are some of the subjects: Celtic music, Cree hand signals, Canadian literature for young adults, sports heroes from Saskatchewan. And there's more!

http://www.schoolnet.ca/

The Canadian Flag

The beaver is the largest rodent in Canada. Beavers have played a significant role in the country's history and economic development. Hudson's Bay Company honored the furry little animal by putting it on the shield of its coat of arms in 1678. The beaver did attain official status as an emblem of Canada on March 24, 1975, but it didn't make it as the preferred symbol for Canada's distinct national flag (the maple leaf won out). This site presents a complete history of the first Canadian flags representing the alternating French and British colonization of Canada, right up through the lengthy debate and final selection of the single maple leaf design of the present national flag. Be sure to look at the National Archives at <http://www.archives.ca/www/com/english/flag/new.htm> to see sample drawings and flag suggestions that didn't get selected. In About Canada, you'll also find flag etiquette rules and information about the origin of the name Canada and other national symbols.

http://canada.gc.ca/canadiana/flag_e.html

Canadiana — The Canadian Resource Page

Looking for the words to the Canadian national anthem? Seeking Canadian schools and teachers to contact for projects? Want to link up to CBC radio news? This is a huge jumpstation to all things Canadian.

http://www.cs.cmu.edu/Unofficial/Canadiana/

From another galaxy? Learn about EARTH in the ASTRONOMY—SOLAR SYSTEM area!

The Coin Collection/Pièces de collection

In 1996, the Royal Canadian Mint introduced a two-dollar coin. The reasoning was simple: they last longer than paper money. A metal coin can survive circulation for about 20 years! The two-dollar bill was very popular, but the government had to replace them every year as they wore out! It costs more to make a coin, but over the coin's lifetime, Canadians will save millions. It's a very cool-looking coin, too. There is a smaller circle in the center, made of gold-colored aluminum bronze, while the outer ring is silver-colored nickel. There's a polar bear on the back. Kids call these coins "Twonies." Why? Just for fun, and to differentiate them from the one-dollar coins. The one dollar coin has a loon on it, and those coins are called "Loonies." Learn a lot about the Royal Canadian Mint and the history of currency here!

http://www.canniff.com/mint/

First Nations in Canada

Imagine yourself living thousands of years ago. You're traveling across a land bridge from Asia to North America and coming into the vast wilderness we now know as Canada. Maybe you would have hunted buffalo, moving your tipi and following the herds as they crossed the plains. Maybe you would have established a permanent village along the Pacific coast and fished for salmon and whales. Read all about the six distinct Canadian Indian cultures and the main tribes in each. Find out how they lived and hunted, what their dwellings looked like, and what they wore. This site takes you through the centuries of change the native populations have experienced, including progress in the last 30 years. This site is available in English and French.

http://www.inac.gc.ca/pubs/fnic/

Gander Academy's Canada Theme-Related Resources on the World Wide Web

If you can visit only one comprehensive reference site on Canada, make sure it's this one. All the emblems are listed in one place and you can find out about famous Canadians, Canada in space, national parks, Canadian place-names, and more.

http://www.stemnet.nf.ca/CITE/canada.htm

Hinterland Who's Who index

Lemmings—those are cute little computer game characters who run up and down hills and in and out of caves, right? Better check out this site! Real lemmings are mouselike rodents that live in the treeless areas of northern Canada. They are a very important species in Arctic ecosystems. The curious thing is that lemming populations fluctuate drastically, peaking about every four years and then crashing almost to extinction. One of the Inuit names for the collared lemming is *kilangmiutak*, which means "one who comes from the sky." Read about this Indian legend and the various theories on the rise and fall of the lemming population as well as interesting information about more than 80 other animals native to Canada's hinterlands. Put on your snowshoes and follow the animal tracks across northern Canada.

http://www.ec.gc.ca/cws-scf/hww-fap/eng_ind.html

The National Anthem of Canada

This resource is a music and history lover's delight. Not only do you get the official lyrics and sheet music for "O, Canada," Canada's national anthem, but you can also listen to the music, too. Then you can read the full history of this anthem, from its beginnings as a patriotic poem written by Sir Adolphe-Basile Routhier to when it was put to music by Calixa Lavallée in 1880. "O, Canada" was rewritten in 1908 by Robert Stanley Weir, in honor of the 300th anniversary of the founding of Quebec City. Despite the many English versions that have appeared over the years, the French lyrics have remained unaltered.

http://canada.gc.ca/canadiana/anthm_e.html

National Atlas on Schoolnet

You'll find maps of all kinds at this interactive learning site about the geography of Canada—in both English and French. You can Make-a-Map by defining map layer attributes from a preselected database, such as birds at risk or wetlands, or follow the link to Our Home: Atlas of Canadian Communities. Also in English and French, Notre Foyer lets you select a Canadian community and read what the kids who live there have written about it. Try your hand at the Interactive Geography Quiz, but don't think you have mastered it all just yet. Make sure you don't overlook the Canadian Geographical Names section—the ultimate Canadian trivia test—to find weird and wonderful answers to questions you never knew you wanted to know!

http://www-nais.ccm.emr.ca/schoolnet/

National Gallery of Canada - Virtual Tour

This multimedia site lets you wander through virtual galleries of Canadian painters with a knowledgeable guide by your side. If you have Real Audio, you will be able to hear the guide's narration. But even if you want to take a silent tour, the vibrant pictures will astound you.

http://national.gallery.ca/virtual_tour/

O Canada .... Information about this Great Country

This site takes awhile to load, but when you're done you'll find an excellent selection of links concerning all matters Canadian. Each site has a brief annotation, so you'll know what to expect. Try a trip to the Canadian Space Agency. Visit Parks Canada. Or pick a province, any province, and find useful resources. The main level of this site, at <http://www3.ns.sympatico.ca/manbenn/teach.htm>, is a must!

http://www3.sympatico.ca/s.bell/kids/ocanada.htm

PROVINCIAL HERALDRY

Do you need a really big, really detailed color picture of the Coats of Arms of all the Canadian provinces? Check in here. Short descriptions are included too.

http://www.ualberta.ca/~dgeorge/heraldry/
    provincial_heraldry.htm

The Royal Canadian Mounted Police Musical Ride

The Musical Ride of the Royal Canadian Mounted Police developed from a desire of early members to display their riding ability and entertain the local community. The series of figures that form the basis of the Musical Ride was developed from traditional cavalry drill movements. The Ride is performed by 32 regular member volunteers (male and female) who have had at least two years of police experience. The Ride contingent consists of 36 horses. It travels throughout Canada and sometimes into the U.S.

http://www.rcmp-grc.gc.ca/html/ride.htm

Welcome to Statistics Canada

Which animals are threatened or endangered in Canada? What is the cause of most forest fires: humans or lightning? Which one of the Great Lakes is the deepest? If you're looking for any kind of official statistic from Canada, begin at this site.

http://www.statcan.ca/

Welcome to the Canadian Museum of Civilization (CMC)

If you think museums are b-o-r-i-n-g, this one will change your mind! Be sure to register as a visitor, then hop the elevator to Level 2 to see the displays of folk art and fine crafts. Visit the Treasures Gallery to see why Canada is truly a cultural mosaic. Canada Hall is on Level 3. An interactive map lets you explore 1,900 years of Canadian history. Or take the voyage through all the regions of Canada and see a prairie curling rink, an Alberta oil rig, and lots more. Take a snack break if you need to, but don't leave the museum before venturing up to Level 5 to see the History in a Box Exhibit and find out what the colors and symbols on a mailbox can tell about the history of a country. Cool! Learning history was never so much fun.

http://www.cmcc.muse.digi-
    tal.ca/cmc/cmceng/welcmeng.html

NET FILES

What do comedians, animals, lost articles, and snake bite victims all have in common?

Answer: They all have a patron saint! St. Vitus takes care of comedians, St. Francis of Assisi looks after animals, St. Anthony of Padua may be a help with lost articles, and St. Hilary comforts snake bite victims. Here's the page where you can find these saints and more: *http://www.catholic.org/ saints/patron.html*

ALBERTA

Alberta's Endangered Species

Logging, oil and gas exploration, and other human activities have endangered many animal and plant species in Canada. The province of Alberta is passing legislation that will set aside portions of its six diverse natural regions (mountain, foothill, boreal, shield, parkland, and grassland) in order to protect endangered species. Each of these six habitats is mapped out and explained at this site, with a fact file and photo of the 12 Alberta species that are most in danger of becoming extinct. There are links to articles that define the difference between the terms extinct, extirpated, endangered, threatened, and vulnerable. Be sure to follow the link to the World Wildlife Fund of Canada, where you can search by province for fact sheets with lots more information on other Canadian and international endangered species.

http://www.afternet.com/~teal/species.html

Discover Alberta! The on-line travel planner for vacationing in Alberta

If you love outdoor recreation and the thrill of caving, hang gliding, white-water rafting, or downhill skiing in the Rockies, then here is a place you won't want to miss. Banff National Park, Canada's oldest national park, was established in 1855. Jasper National Park is home of the Columbia Icefields, the largest chunk of ice in the Rocky Mountains. Find out even more about Alberta's national parks from the clickable map and the link to the official Banff National Park Home Page. It is no wonder that the motto of this Canadian province is *"Fortis et Liber"* ("Strong and Free"). No time to explore a glacier? You can also stop here for quick facts, a little history, and a tour of Edmonton, the capital city.

http://www.discoveralberta.com/

BRITISH COLUMBIA

Government of British Columbia

Did you know that British Columbia, or B.C., is bigger in land area than France and Germany combined? This official site explains all about B.C. government, including the official emblems: Dogwood (provincial flower), Steller's jay (provincial bird), jade (provincial gemstone), western red cedar (provincial tree).

http://www.gov.bc.ca/

The Great Outdoors - BC Adventure Network

Here you can venture into the beautiful and fascinating wilderness areas of British Columbia and learn about the creatures that inhabit its forests and coasts. From badgers to wolverines, bald eagles to wood ducks, from Alpine fir to yellow cedar, practically everything you might want to know about the animals, birds, fish, forests, and wildflowers of this Canadian province is all right here. You can learn how to tell the difference between a bobcat and its larger cousin, the lynx. Peer into the eyes of the great horned owl. Wade right in and take a look at some weird-looking fish that you may never have seen before. If you're more of a land rover, learn to identify the wildflowers and plants that paint this Canadian province with such spectacular color.

http://bcadventure.com/adventure/wilderness/

MANITOBA
Explore Manitoba - A Visitor's Guide

This official site offers information on Manitoba's fishing and other outdoor activities, but you'll also find material on urban attractions and historical sites. You can also learn about the official emblems. The great grey owl is the official bird, the crocus is the flower, and the white spruce is the official tree. The province has an official tartan cloth; according to this site: "Each colour has its own significance: Dark Red Squares-natural resources of the province; Azure Blue Lines-Lord Selkirk, founder of Red River Settlement (Winnipeg); Dark Green Lines-the men and women of many races who have enriched the life of the province; and Golden Lines-grain and other agricultural products."

http://www.gov.mb.ca/itt/travel/

Government of Manitoba, gouvernement du Manitoba

This official site is your home base to find information about Manitoba's government. There is a great picture of the coat of arms, too. It has a very detailed description, explaining the symbology behind the beaver, the buffalo, the crocus, the unicorn, and the lion, among other things.

http://www.gov.mb.ca/cgi-bin/choose_home.pl

NET FILES

Assuming you're not a pig, why would you want to become

a ham?

Answer: "Ham" is a word commonly used to refer to an amateur radio operator. That's right, you can broadcast your own radio signals, even from your home. Do you copy? To find out the answers to all your questions about amateur radio, tune in to

http://www.mv.com/ipusers/wd1v/hamradio_faq.html/

NEW BRUNSWICK
Province of New Brunswick Home Page / Page d'accueil - Province du Nouveau-Brunswick

New Brunswick has some of the highest tides in the world, as it is bordered by the Bay of Fundy. The Bay of Fundy has its own Web page, and you can find it if you click on Tourism from the main page of this official government site. Looking for the official emblems? They are in the General Information section of the Tourism link. The purple violet is the official flower, and the black-capped chickadee is the provincial bird. The official tartan cloth is described this way: "These are represented in the design by the forest green of lumbering, the meadow green of agriculture, the blue of coastal and inland waters, all interwoven with gold, a symbol of the province's potential wealth. The red blocks represent the loyalty and devotion of the early Loyalist settlers, the Royal New Brunswick Regiment and all of our people. The red block also contains the grey and gold of the province's coat of arms and the regimental crest. Because the first weaving of the design was commissioned for Lord Beaverbrook, the province's eminent benefactor, the red blocks are highlighted by 'beaver' brown."

http://www.gov.nb.ca/

NEWFOUNDLAND
Government of Newfoundland and Labrador Home Page

Visit this official site and find out lots of interesting facts. For example, ever heard of "Iceberg Alley"? That's where the icebergs drift south from Greenland, sometimes all the way into the north Atlantic shipping channels. That's what happened to the *Titanic* in 1912. See some pictures, and find out where you can spot icebergs along the coasts.

http://www.gov.nf.ca/

> ## Wolves are a howl in MAMMALS.

NORTHWEST TERRITORIES

The Government of the Northwest Territories

This site takes you to Canada's Northwest Territories, which encompasses one-third of the land mass of Canada, about 1.3 million square miles. It is a land firmly rooted in the cultural past and old traditions of the Inuit, Inuvialuit, Dene, and Metis; it is a land of adventure and exploration, where some of the wildlife and scenery are like nowhere else on earth.

http://www.gov.nt.ca/

Leo Ussak Elementary School

These kids go to a cool school—we really mean it's cool there. This school is way up north. They live in the Northwest Territories, above the 60th parallel. At this site, you can learn about Inuktitut, the language of the Inuit people, and you can get a lot of information about what life is like in an Arctic village. Although the school is very Net-savvy (read about how they videoconference with a school in Hawaii) and modern, they honor the elders and their traditional ways; you'll find a good deal of cultural information here. For example, what kinds of foods do kids eat there? "Here in Rankin Inlet you can eat caribou (a lean, nutritious, delicious meat), delectable arctic char, lake trout, or grayling. In the fall you can pick ripe, juicy berries growing all over the tundra. You can sample seal, mukta (yes it's true, Inuit do consider it a delicacy to eat whale blubber!) and goose. You can also have a Pizza Hut pizza or Kentucky Fried Chicken if you want!" And how do people sleep when the sun stays above the horizon all "night"? "On June 21st, it is light almost all of the time. People sometimes put cardboard, plastic garbage bags or aluminum foil on their windows to help make it dark enough to sleep. It is darkest on December 21st when the sun rises at 9:45 in the morning and goes down at 2:45 in the afternoon. Sleeping is no problem then!"

http://www.arctic.ca/LUS/

NOVA SCOTIA

Government of Nova Scotia Canada

This official site is really a jumpstation to other useful sites about Nova Scotia. Each site has a brief annotation. As you look around you'll learn that the Coat of Arms includes a rearing unicorn, thistles, and a First Nations warrior. These are the oldest arms (granted in 1625) in the commonwealth, outside of Great Britain.

http://www.gov.ns.ca/

Titanic ~ The Unsinkable Ship and Halifax, Nova Scotia

After the maritime disaster that befell the *Titanic* on April 15, 1912, ships from Halifax, Nova Scotia, were sent to recover many of the bodies. They are buried in Halifax's city cemeteries, and you can find here a list of those who were identified. There is a J. Dawson, but it's not Jack—it's James. He was a 23-year-old "trimmer." At this site you can learn about artifacts and recovery efforts as well as see interesting photos and find a series of links to related sites.

http://titanic.gov.ns.ca/

NUNAVUT

Nunavut Planning Commission Home Page

At press time, Canada had ten provinces and two territories—the Yukon Territory and the Northwest Territories. These two territories together make up more than one-third of the entire country's land area. On April 1, 1999, the northern and eastern portion of the Northwest Territories will become Nunavut, Canada's third territory. Read all the background details of the establishment of Nunavut. Find out all kinds of facts about the Northwest Territories as a whole, its three regions, and its communities. Link to *Nunatsiaq News*, the weekly Nunavut newspaper, at <http://www.nunatsiaq.com/>.

http://npc.nunavut.ca/

NET FILES

What is an AFUCHE drum?
What does it look like?

Answer: It's a small, squat cylinder with a handle and a corrugated metal surface. A long string of beads wound loosely around it makes a scrabbly, swishy note when you shake it. There's a great picture of it at *http://www.cse.ogi.edu/ Drum/encyclopedia/a.html* where you can also find out what a *shekere* is, among other things.

ONTARIO

About Canada's Capital

Being a tourist in Ottawa is fun and educational. You can take a walking tour of the "Mile of History" in downtown Ottawa, the national capital region of Canada in the province of Ontario. Stroll through the famous Byward Market and learn about the Bytown Locks. Make sure to bring your sweater for ice skating on the Rideau Canal. And when you get too cold, you can take a virtual tour of some of Ottawa's historic museums: the Canadian Museum of Civilization, the Canadian War Museum, the National Library, and the National Aviation Museum, just to name a few. While you're there, view the city's culture, parks, and festivities.

http://www.capcan.ca/english/about/intro/

The Government of Ontario

This very well-organized page lists lots of facts and information about Ontario, including the official emblems. The bird is the loon, the flower is the white trillium, and the tree is the eastern white pine. There's an official gem, too: the amethyst.

http://www.gov.on.ca/

Ontario: History

Do you need to know about the Indian tribes that make up Ontario's First Nations? What about the specific kinds of trees in the forests that cover three-quarters of this province? Early settlements? Upper and lower Canada? This government site lets you time-travel through 400 years of Ontario history at a glance.

http://www.gov.on.ca/MBS/english/its_ontario/ ont-hist/

PRINCE EDWARD ISLAND

Prince Edward Island Information Centre: Main Home Page

What do Avonlea, Kindred Spirits, and Lover's Lane all have in common? You can find them all on Prince Edward Island, the birthplace of Lucy Maud Montgomery, who wrote the universally beloved book, *Anne of Green Gables*, first published in 1908. Her story was inspired by the land, the sea, and the people around her. *Anne of Green Gables* is so popular with young (and old) readers that it has been translated into 15 different languages and put on film. You'll enjoy all the stops on the "Anne" tour at this site, especially the Green Gables Farmhouse in Cavendish, which is preserved as a national museum. Check out the L. M. Montgomery literature links, and before you leave, don't forget to look through the IslandCam, Prince Edward Island's mobile digital camera located in Charlottetown.

http://www.gov.pe.ca/index.asp

QUÉBEC

CAMP 100% Pure Maple Syrup

Lots of maple syrup is produced in the Canadian province of Québec; in fact, it provides 70 percent of the world's production. This site will tell you about the history and techniques of maple syrup production in Québec. As a good source of three essential elements (calcium, iron, and thiamin), maple syrup is really good for you, too, so be sure to try some of the great recipes listed here. Happy eating!

http://neptune.ivic.qc.ca/abriweb/erable/camp.html

Site officiel du gouvernement du Québec

This is the official site of the province of Québec. It is also a jumpstation to other departments; for example, try the Department of Tourism, where you can take a Virtual Tour of the 19 different tourist regions of the province. Find a city or tour that interests you? It's easy to have a brochure sent to you via postal mail.

http://www.gouv.qc.ca/

SASKATCHEWAN

The Official Site For Tourism in Saskatchewan!

Sure, you'll find lots of information about tourism in this province, but if you're looking for emblems, they are at <http://www.sasktourism.com/info/emblems.html>. The sharp-tailed grouse is the official bird, and the western red lily is the flower. How did this province get its name? According to this site: "Plains Indians are credited with originating the name Saskatchewan. Their word was 'kisiskatchewan'—meaning the river that flows swiftly—in reference to the most important waterway running through their territory."

http://www.sasktourism.com/

Virtual Saskatchewan

If you think that Saskatchewan is, according to this site, "one big wheat field," then it's time for you to learn more. For example, Selwyn Lake uplands include tundra as well as boreal forest. There are ten more regions; read about them here.

http://www.virtualsk.com/

YUKON TERRITORY

GHOSTS OF THE KLONDIKE GOLD RUSH

It's 1898, and we're going to join the 100,000 others stampeding toward Canada's mysterious Yukon hoping to fulfill their dreams. We've survived avalanches and beat starvation, and we've made it as far as Dawson City. Now we're ready to pan for gold and strike it rich! You may not find "real" gold here, but you'll pick up nuggets of fact and fiction about this memorable time in history. Find out what motivated some of these prospectors by hearing what the grandchildren of a Klondike stampeder have to say.

http://www.gold-rush.org/

Government of Yukon Home Page

From this official government site you can take a link to the travel and tourism area. Sure, you'll find all kinds of info about visiting this section of the country, but you'll also find some fun. There's a Just for Kids section with a couple of quizzes and puzzles as well as a Shockwave game involving a snowmobile and its bear driver. Seems they have met with a little accident and there are pieces of snowmobile everywhere. If you get all the pieces back in the right places (it's hard!) a special key will appear and you'll see the snowmobile go. Hint: Press the Help button to get a clue where the pieces are supposed to go.

http://www.gov.yk.ca/

CAPE VERDE

Cape Verde Home Page (UNOFFICIAL)

Cape Verde, officially known as the Republic of Cape Verde (in Portuguese, it's *Republica de Cabo Verde*), is a chain of islands, or *archipelago*, in the Atlantic Ocean, off the northwest coast of Africa. Most of the information on this small and interesting country is located in the Main Information Index. You'll find information about Cape Verde's history and culture, from its discovery and colonization in the mid-1400s by the Portuguese to the wonderful blending of Christian and African traditions, art, and cuisine. This section also has lots of maps as well as individual pages for some of the islands, each with pictures and a bit about the island.

http://www.umassd.edu/SpecialPrograms/caboverde/

Fogo, Cape Verde

The ten islands of Cape Verde originated from volcanoes. The volcano on the island of Fogo burned almost continuously from 1500 to 1760 and served as something of a natural "lighthouse" to early sailors. Over hundreds of years, Fogo has developed as one massive volcanic cone, with an eight-kilometer-wide caldera that opens out to the east and offers some of the best farmland on the island. Naturally, the people who lived on the floor of this volcano were surprised by the most recent eruption of Fogo in April 1995.

http://volcano.und.nodak.edu/vwdocs/current_volcs/fogo/fogo.html

CAYMAN ISLANDS

See UNITED KINGDOM—DEPENDENCIES—
CAYMAN ISLANDS

CENTRAL AFRICAN REPUBLIC

Central African Republic

The Central African Republic was a part of French Equatorial Africa known as Ubangi-Shari-Chad. It became an autonomous republic within the French community in 1958 and fully independent in 1960. This site will give you some basic facts and figures about the geography, people, government, and economy of the Central African Republic.

http://www.africaindex.africainfo.no/africaindex1/
countries/car.html

CHAD

Chad

With 495,755 square miles of land area, Chad is the fifth largest country in Africa and Africa's largest landlocked state. By comparison, Chad is slightly more than three times the size of the state of California, but with only one-fifth the population.

http://www.africaindex.africainfo.no/africaindex1/
countries/chad.html

CHILE

Chile's Tourism

This official site discloses lots of information tourists need, plus unusual tidbits like the following on Chilean cuisine: "Chileans enjoy an enviable variety of fish, particularly the conger eel, trout, sole, *corvina* and salmon cultivated in the south. Cooks prepare shellfish, including *locos* (abalone), the world's only edible barnacle, and the unique *machas* (similar to razor clams), mussels and 'shoe-sized' mussels, with a variety of recipes, soups hot and cold being among the most common."

http://www.segegob.cl/sernatur/inicio2.html

Chile's Volcanoes

Of the 2,085 volcanoes in Chile, 55 are active. This site gives all the information you may ever want to know about them, including great aerial photos. Two of these volcanoes, located in the Lake Country region of Chile, are continuously smoking today. Based on the eruptive history detailed here, Volcan Villarrica has had an "event" about once every ten years. As its last major eruption was in 1984, Villarrica may be due for another big one anytime soon. During the summer season, it is estimated that as many as 150 tourists a day climb this volcano, despite the potential danger at the active crater (maybe they forgot to read this Web site!).

http://www.geo.mtu.edu/~boris/Chilehome.html

NET FILES

WHERE IS THE WORLD'S LARGEST COLONY OF BATS?

Answer: The largest known colony is at Bracken Cave, Texas. The 20 million Mexican free-tails eat 250 tons of insects nightly. The largest known colony in a city is in Austin, Texas, under the Congress Avenue bridge. The Austin bats eat 10,000 to 30,000 pounds of insects per night, including mosquitoes and numerous agricultural pests. According to Bat Conservation International, "This is the largest urban bat colony in North America. With up to 1.5 million bats spiraling into the summer sunset, Austin now has one of the most unusual and fascinating tourist attractions anywhere." See the bats at http://www.batcon.org/congress.html

Easter Island Home Page

The inhabitants of the island call their land Rapa Nui, but Dutch Admiral Roggeveen called this lonely, South Pacific island Easter Island, in honor of the day he encountered it in 1722. How people first found this small, volcanic island is only one of its mysteries. Rapa Nui is 2,485 miles (4,000 kilometers) from South America and 1,243 miles from the nearest neighboring island. Even more curious are the peculiar stone statues, or *moais*. These 10- to 20-feet-tall giants all face inward toward the island. They have short bodies with long heads and ears and are made of a yellow-gray volcanic rock, topped with red rock hats. Despite the island's annexation by Chile in 1888, the people of Rapa Nui continue to preserve their Polynesian culture and identity. Come visit this unique island, learn its history, and meet its friendly people!

http://www.netaxs.com/~trance/rapanui.html

Lonely Planet - Destination Chile & Easter Island

Described by some as an extravaganza of "crazy geography," Chile is characterized by a little bit of everything, from fertile river basins to snowcapped volcanoes to some of the driest desert on Earth. Zoom in and out of the interactive map. Read facts about Chile's climate, history, and culture. Or just flip through the photo album to view some of the most spectacular mountain peaks you'll ever see. If you're planning on more than a virtual visit to Chile, be sure to bring warm- and cold-weather gear! Are you still looking for more adventure? Take a detour to Rapa Nui (Easter Island), the world's most remote inhabited island.

http://www.lonelyplanet.com/dest/sam/chile.htm

Spotlight on Chile

In an ancient tradition that lives on today, the Mapuche people of this region still honor the Machi. The Machi are spiritual leaders that have unique talents—some are healers, some are seers of the future. People come from miles around to speak with the Machi to discuss their ailments and receive advice. Read about the Mapuche, Chilean society, its poets, and much more at this site.

http://www.localaccess.com/chappell/chile/

Pony up to HORSES AND EQUESTRIAN SPORTS.

Virtual World Jamboree '99

"Building Peace Together"—what could be a better theme? In 1999, thousands of young people from more than a hundred countries will meet at a hacienda just outside Chile's capital city of Santiago. These youngsters will be wearing colorful uniforms, and many of them will have kerchiefs around their necks. Welcome to the Virtual World Scouting Jamboree! This site is designed to provide information, multimedia presentations, and lots of images from the Jamboree site before, during, and after the actual event. Images and files will also be available at the Global ScoutNet Network for download. In addition to the Jamboree information, you'll find facts about the geography, history, people, and economy of Chile. Plus, there is an interesting map showing flying times and the different land regions of Chile from north to south. Did you know it takes more than five hours to fly from the northernmost city of Arica to Chile's southernmost city of Punta Arenas?

http://scoutnet.ch/events/jam99/

CHINA

Asiapac - 100 Celebrated Chinese Women

One hundred legendary women are listed, and there is detailed information about 60 of them, Yes, Mulan is listed under "Hua Mulan," but you can also read about what happened to Cannü, the Silkworm Girl, and others. The stories have beautiful illustrations. Parental advisory: Preview these to make sure they are suitable for your family.

http://www.span.com.au/100women/

China: Beyond the Great Wall

See some of China's most spectacular landmarks, including the Great Wall of China, Gugong: The Forbidden City, magnificent Mount Huang-shan, and breathtaking Jiuzhaigou Falls. Follow the link to Focus on China for even more fascinating details about this country's history, land, people, and culture. China has a recorded history of nearly 4,000 years! The Qinghai-Tibet Plateau is home to Mount Qomolangma on the Sino-Nepalese border. You may know it by another name: Mount Everest. It soars 29,028 feet (8,848 meters) above sea level and is the highest mountain peak in the world. China also boasts the highest population in the world, with more than 1.2 billion people. You'll even find a brief history of Chinese cooking, but unfortunately there is no taste test!

http://www.uncletai.com/china/china.html

China Maps

It's a lot harder to study the country of China if you don't know how to pronounce the names of all its provinces! Here is a great place to start. This is a clear and simple political map, and all the way at the bottom is a chart that shows the Chinese characters, Chinese name, and a pronunciation guide for each of China's provinces, autonomous (self-governing) regions, and special municipalities. Select "China: Administration 1991 (278K)" from the list on this page.

http://www.lib.utexas.edu/Libs/PCL/
    Map_collection/china.html

Space Exploration is a blast. Check out ASTRONOMY, SPACE, AND SPACE EXPLORATION.

China the Beautiful - Chinese Art and Literature

Calligraphy is as much beautiful abstract art as it is a way of writing. It dates back to the earliest days of Chinese history and is still widely practiced. Even after 2,000 years, the five major styles of calligraphy (seal script, clerical script, standard script, semicursive script, and cursive script) are still in use today. This site is also filled with Chinese history. The outline of Chinese chronology and timeline included here is especially useful because it includes a listing of events happening outside China at the same time. And if you need more maps of historic and present-day China, this is a good place to look. This site even includes audio files and flash cards for learning Chinese words (the latter is in A is for Love) and links to museums around the world that have Chinese art collections on their Web pages. There is also a Mulan FAQ for fans of the movie.

http://www.chinapage.com/china.html

China Today

China is *really* big—640 cities, 32 of them with a population of over one million people! These folks have loved music and art for a long time: as early as the first century B.C., more than 80 different kinds of musical instruments were already in use. Want more facts? Some Asians believe jade will bring them good luck and good health and can help them to get rid of bad luck. Did you know that the Chinese people love football (what Americans call soccer)? This is a huge, comprehensive site with lots of information. Parents: Too many links here for us to check them all.

http://www.chinatoday.com/

Chinese Embassy in Washington DC

The national emblem of China and the Chinese flag are only two items you'll find at this site. You can also hear the national anthem. Learn about the geography and flora and fauna. Did you know that some species are found only in China? These are the giant panda, golden monkey, white-lipped deer, takin, Chinese river dolphin, and Chinese alligator. There are also links to information on the regions and provinces of China.

http://www.china-embassy.org/

Condensed China: Chinese History for Beginners

If you're dazzled by dynasties, confused by Qing, muddled by Ming, or even hazy on the facts about the People's Republic of China, come to this site. The author says it is more like "Chinese History: the Cliff Notes version" or "Chinese History's Greatest Hits" than a full-fledged history. For the highlights, visit here!

http://www.asterius.com/china/

The Imperial Tombs of China in Orlando Florida

Long ago, when a Chinese emperor died, he was buried with fabulous treasures. One was buried with thousands of life-size terra-cotta soldiers and horses. One was buried in a special garment made of thousands of jade pieces held together by gold thread. Two hundred fifty objects from tombs spanning 2,500 years of Chinese history have been touring the world's museums.

http://www.omart.org/itoc/

SILK ROAD

Imagine it is the year 1271. The Venetian traveler, Marco Polo, is packing a caravan for his first long expedition to a country called Cathay. He travels across the deserts and mountains of Asia and finally comes to a place filled with beautiful riches he has never seen before: silk, ivory, spices, and rare jewels. He brings these treasures back to Europe, as well as knowledge of new cultures, customs, and inventions such as the compass. The historical trade route Polo followed was given its name, The Silk Road, by a French historian in 1887. Silk, however, was only one of the many items in the exchange between inland China, its western border, India, and the Middle East. Travel along this ancient passageway—through the province of Xinjiang in the west and across into Gansu and Xi'an in the east—and see some of China's historical sites along the way.

http://www.xanet.edu.cn/xjtu/silk1/eng/silk.html

Tour in China

China is the world's third largest country in area, after Russia and Canada. At this site, you will really get a sense of China's diverse climates and land regions as well as the culture and history of its people. For example, Xinjiang, the largest region in China, covers one-sixth of its total land area. This large province is the source of both the Huang He (Yellow River) and the Yangtze River. You'll also learn about Qinghai Lake, China's biggest saltwater lake. And check out Snake Island, near the port of Dalian in Liaoning province, which is home to more than 13,000 pit vipers!

http://solar.rtd.utk.edu/~china/tour/china_tour.html

Virtual China '98

Here's something different. Seventh graders at the Hong Kong International School are offered a choice of two trips: a one-week biking trip in rural southern China or a week-long trip to Xi'an, home of the famous terra-cotta soldiers. You can follow along in their diaries and read their impressions. When these trips first started in 1995, Hong Kong was still a British colony. In 1997, Hong Kong returned to the control of China. Based on these kids' observations, how do you think life there has changed? Some of the "perspectives" are hilarious—for example, read a description of a hotel lobby from the point of view of the couch (see the Virtual China '96 link at the bottom of the page). Links to the 1995 and 1997 trips are also here.

http://www.kidlink.org/KIDPROJ/VChina98/

AUTONOMOUS AREAS— HONG KONG

GoAsia - Asia Travel Guide

Cute little cartoon guys will guide you around this Web site on Hong Kong. There are islands to explore, with lots of photos. You can even teach yourself Chinese! Hear a few of the common phrases, and then say them out loud. Then you'll be able to find your way to all of the attractions for kids. Hong Kong has lots of them: beaches, parks, and amusement centers. Don't forget to visit the Great Buddha. It's the tallest bronze sculpture in the world.

http://www.goasia.com/

The Hong Kong Children's Choir

OK, on the count of three, everybody sing! This children's choir travels all around the world. At their site, you can even hear sound samples of their singing (these are quite large, so they will take time to come through your modem). Some are in English and some are in Chinese (the two official languages of Hong Kong). The boys and girls also learn to play instruments, dance, and paint.

http://www.hkcchoir.org.hk/

Hong Kong Home Screen

Kids who have been to Hong Kong will often tell you that their favorite part is the boat rides! Some people even live on their boats, in large groups that form a type of community. Adults will probably mention the shopping or the food in Hong Kong. This is a crowded, bustling place full of excitement! A British Crown colony for years, it returned to China as a special administrative region in July 1997. What has changed?

http://expedia.msn.com/wg/places/HongKong/
HSFS.htm

Hong Kong Tourist Association: WONDER NET

Festivals are the best in Hong Kong! Start with the Chinese New Year in Events and Festivals. Keep going—there's always a reason to celebrate! This site has videos of the people, city, and even the food. Be sure to click on "The Wonder of the Day" for something new.

http://www.hkta.org/

Lonely Planet — Destination Hong Kong

Hong Kong harbor has lots of junks. No, not the trashy kind of junk. A *junk* is a type of boat with a sail that is also a home for thousands of people in Hong Kong. Hong Kong at night is like fireworks in the sky; it's very spectacular. Read about some of the local customs—for example, you should never leave any rice uneaten at a meal (be a member of the "clean plate club" here!) and be sure not to place your chopsticks vertically in your bowl; we'll leave it up to you to find out why.

http://www.lonelyplanet.com/dest/nea/hong.htm

AUTONOMOUS AREAS—TAIWAN

The Government Information Office

Some countries recognize Taiwan as a free nation, although China declares it an autonomous region. This Taiwanese government site explains the dispute and provides a jumpstation to other resources.

http://www.gio.gov.tw/

The Office of the President of the Republic of China

Click on "English" if you don't speak Taiwanese. This official site offers a brief tour to the President's office in Taipei. While you are looking around, you notice there is information on the flag and the national symbols. You'll learn about the great seals of the Republic of China, used in marking official documents. One is made of emerald jade while the other is made of "sheep suet" white jade. Both materials are extremely rare and precious, but you can see them close-up at this Web site.

http://www.oop.gov.tw/

AUTONOMOUS AREAS—TIBET

Tibetan Government in Exile's Official Web Site

China calls Tibet an autonomous region, but others say China is taking away Tibetan culture and spiritual practices and abuses the human rights of the Tibetan people. The spiritual leader of Tibet, Tenzin Gyatso, His Holiness the Dalai Lama, leads a "government in exile" in India. This Web site gives a lot of information about the Dalai Lama, who received the Nobel Peace Prize in 1989. The citation reads, in part: "The Dalai Lama has developed his philosophy of peace from a great reverence for all things living and upon the concept of universal responsibility embracing all mankind as well as nature." This Web site outlines Tibetan Buddhist beliefs, culture, medicine, astrology, and more. It also details the charges against China, and many of them are disturbing and contain adult subject material.

http://www.tibet.com/

Have a whale of a time in MAMMALS.

COCOS (KEELING) ISLANDS

See AUSTRALIA—TERRITORIES—COCOS (KEELING) ISLANDS

COLOMBIA

Lonely Planet — Destinations: Colombia

Like the other Lonely Planet sites, you will find a map of Colombia and just the basics here. But you'll learn about the country's geography, history, population, and culture. Be sure to check the photo journal for some great shots of the Andes Mountains, a pre-Colombian stone statue, beautiful Spanish architecture, and more. Need some trivia tidbits to pique your interest? The jungle of Colombia's Pacific coast holds the record for the highest rainfall. There are more than 1,550 recorded species of birds (more than in the whole of Europe and North America combined), ranging from the huge Andean condor to the tiny hummingbird. Colombian author Gabriel García Márquez won the Nobel Prize for Literature in 1982 for his book, *One Hundred Years of Solitude*. And if you think you're an adventurous eater, you might want to try *Hormiga Culona*, a "sophisticated Colombian dish." You'll have to visit this site to find out the main ingredient, but here is a hint: it has six legs.

http://www.lonelyplanet.com/dest/sam/col.htm

Republica de Colombia

The official home page of the president of Colombia offers brief information on the government, the history, and the culture of this South American country.

http://www.presidencia.gov.co/

COMOROS

Action Comores Home Page

Have you ever seen a Livingstone's flying fox? Probably not, unless you have been to the Comoro Islands. Livingstone's flying fox is one of the rarest fruit bats in the world and is native there. Rapid population growth on these islands in the western Indian Ocean has caused the destruction of much of the upland forest habitat of these fruit bats. There may only be around 400 of this species left in the wild. At this site, find out why the slogan for the Action Comores conservation organization is "People Need Forests Need Fruit Bats!"

http://ibis.nott.ac.uk/Action-Comores/

NET FILES

It's a sunny winter day, about 10 degrees Fahrenheit outside. It's breezy, too, with the wind blowing about 5mph. Your mom says it's way too cold to go out and play. She keeps talking about something called "windchill"—what the heck is that?

Answer: Wind removes heat from your body.

☆ The windchill equivalent index measures the heat loss from any skin that's exposed to the air (where *did* you leave your mittens, anyway?).

☆ Heat loss is caused by a potentially dangerous combination of wind and low air temperature. Risk of frostbite from low windchill "temperatures" makes windchill a winter weather hazard.

Show Mom this windchill chart on the Net. It shows that at today's air temperature (10 degrees) and wind speed (5 mph), the apparent temperature will "feel like" 6 degrees Fahrenheit. It will be unpleasant, but not dangerous. Remember, the definition of a sweater is "what goes on a child when his mom feels cold." Check

http://www.weather.com/glossary/wx_glossary_w.html

The Comoro Islands' Home Page

The Comoro Islands resulted from volcanic activity along a crack in the seabed that runs between mainland Africa and the country of Madagascar in the Mozambique Channel. Today, three of the islands—Ngazidja (Grande Comore), Mwali, and Nzwani—make up the Federal Islamic Republic of the Comoro Islands. The fourth major island of the archipelago, Mayotte (Maore), continues to be administered by France even though it is claimed by the Republic of the Comoros. Get a sense of the geography, economy, and people of these islands and then visit each of the four main islands separately to learn its own special story. Hear a sample of music, which is a blend of cultural and musical influences from East Africa, the Middle East, Madagascar, and southern India. The Comoro Islands provide a unique habitat for several endangered species. Follow some of the extra links here to read more about the mysterious coelacanth fish living in the caves along the west coast of Grand Comore island. Be sure to follow the link to the "African Studies Program" for a great map showing the four main islands and information from the *World Factbook*.

http://www.ksu.edu/sasw/comoros/comoros.html

CONGO, DEMOCRATIC REPUBLIC OF THE

Africa Online: News & Information

The Democratic Republic of the Congo was once known as the Belgian Congo until it gained its independence in 1960, when its name changed to Zaire. After another rebellion, which began in 1996, it assumed its present name. While the country has a vast array of natural resources, such as gold, silver, oil, diamonds, copper, manganese, coal, and uranium, it is among the poorest nations on earth. Look to this site for strong, detailed facts and figures on the county's government, people, environment, and other useful information.

http://www.africaindex.africainfo.no/africaindex1/countries/congo-z.html

Democratic Republic of Congo

This official site is mostly in French, but the English version is promised soon. For now you can look at the pictures and listen to the music, if you don't read French.

http://drcongo.org/

CONGO, REPUBLIC OF THE

Congo Page

In addition to the *World Factbook* entry, which gives you basic facts about the economy, geography, government, and people of the Republic of the Congo, you'll find a small color picture of the flag and a nice map at this site.

http://www.sas.upenn.edu/African_Studies/Country_Specific/Congo.html

NET FILES

When was the planet Uranus discovered?

Answer: Uranus was discovered on March 13, 1781 by William Herschel. Check out the Chronology of Solar System Discovery at *http://seds.lpl.arizona.edu/billa/tnp/history.html* for an astronomical list of facts.

It never rains in cyberspace.

CongoWeb

This site says that it is not an official government site or a site from the opposition, but it does have good information on the Republic of the Congo. Learn about the government, the land, and the history of this country. There are also links to other related sites, as well as Congo in the News items.

http://www.congoweb.org/

COOK ISLANDS

See NEW ZEALAND—DEPENDENCIES—COOK ISLANDS

COSTA RICA

COCORI Complete Costa Rica Homepage

Costa Rica is located on the isthmus between North and South America. A lot of history and culture are packed into this small Central American country. Find out why it is sometimes referred to as the "Switzerland of the Americas." Be sure to stop into the Library (in the Articles section) to read more about Costa Rica's traditions and holiday celebrations. Christmas in Costa Rica means eating tamales for breakfast, lunch, dinner, and even coffee breaks. This delicious dish is prepared almost exclusively in December to eat during the year-end parties and celebrations, and it has been a country tradition for thousands of years. Visit Iguana Park, take a ride through a mangrove forest, or learn more about Costa Rica's tropical rain forests, sometimes referred to as "nature's crumbling cathedral."

http://www.cocori.com/

Costa Rica: A Natural Haven for the World

The Central American country of Costa Rica is one of the oldest democracies in America, as well as being a free and independent republic. In fact, this country is often described as an oasis of peace. The Costa Rican people are friendly to visitors and are anxious to show off their country's rich natural heritage. Costa Rica is a real paradise for nature lovers, volcano enthusiasts, and water sports fans, too. This small tropical country, situated between two oceans, offers the Canales of Tortuguero, a network of more than 62 miles of navigable canals and lagoons on the Caribbean side. If surfing is your thing, Playa Pavones on the Pacific Ocean side is internationally famous for having the longest waves in the world.

http://www.ticonet.co.cr/costa_rica/

Costa Rica Tourism Board

If you stare at this opening page long enough, the butterfly's wings flutter, the lizard's eyes blink, and a fish swims through the trees. Make your way through the rain forest and learn about some thrilling tourist destinations from this official tourism page. There are nine active volcanoes in this country, so steer clear of them. In the In Few Words section you can find out about the national symbols. Did you know the official flower is the cattleya orchid?

http://www.tourism-costarica.com/

Embassy of Costa Rica - U.S.A.

With 130 species of freshwater fish, 160 species of amphibians, 208 species of mammals, 220 species of reptiles, 850 species of birds (one-tenth of the world's total), 1,000 species of butterflies, 1,200 varieties of orchids, 9,000 species of plants, and 34,000 species of insects, Costa Rica is considered to have the greatest biodiversity of any country in the world. Check out this site for official facts and figures about this small country, called the "Coast of Plenty." Follow the link to Costa Rica! to a commercial resource with additional information.

http://www.costarica.com/embassy/

An Introduction to Costa Rica

In 1502, Christopher Columbus became the first European explorer to visit Costa Rica. Later, a Spaniard named Gil Gonzalez Davila gave the country its name, meaning "rich coast" because of the gold jewelry worn by the Costa Rican inhabitants. Learn about the civilization that existed there thousands of years before Columbus, and then get to know the Costa Ricans of today. They are a people who really care about their environment. They have set aside one-quarter of their land as protected areas and national parks. Besides the basic geography and history facts you'll find here, you'll get the chance to explore some of these national parks. In Braulio Carrillio National Park, one of the best features is the *Teleferico del Bosque Lluvioso*, or "rain forest tram." It is the only vehicle of its kind in the world, and unless you want to climb the trees, it is the only way to view the canopy, or life in the treetops. Drive up to the edge of an active volcanic crater in Poas National Park. Corcovado National Park on the Osa Peninsula is home to jaguars, crocodiles, and hammerhead sharks. Tortuguero National Park boasts the largest breeding population of green sea turtles in the world. This site will also link you to similar pages of other Latin American countries, as well as Africa, Asia, Europe, and the Caribbean.

http://www.interknowledge.com/costa-rica/

NET FILES

How does plain old air turn into a cloud, anyway?

Answer: Those magical, fluffy castles in the sky are caused by a process of air rising, expanding, and cooling to its saturation point, which then becomes visible as a cloud. Find out more and see some great cloud photos at *http://covis.atmos.uiuc.edu/guide/clouds/cloud.listing/html/listing.home.html*.

Watch your steps in DANCE.

CÔTE D'IVOIRE

City.Net Map of Cote d'Ivoire

If you need a clear map of Côte d'Ivoire, here's where to look. The map shows the capital city of Abidjian in the south, along the coast of the Gulf of Guinea, plus the other major cities, lakes, and rivers.

http://city.net/maps/view/?mapurl=/countries/ cote_divoire

Cote d'Ivoire Page

Côte d'Ivoire, formerly called the Ivory Coast, is a West African nation located on the Gulf of Guinea. The country gained independence from France in 1960, but because of the more than 60 ethnic groups and great number of local dialects, French was selected as the official language. Côte d'Ivoire is the world's largest producer of cocoa and the third largest producer of coffee, after Brazil and Colombia. This page is produced by the U.S. embassy in Côte d'Ivoire.

http://www.usia.gov/abtusia/posts/IV1/ wwwhdata.html

United in Majesty

Here is a picture of The Basilica of Our Lady of Peace, one of the largest churches in the world. It was the vision of one man, Félix Houphouët-Boigny, President of the Ivory Coast. The marble was imported from Italy and the stained glass was from France.

http://www.allenorgan.com.au/majesty.htm

CROATIA

The City of Split

Because of its central position on the eastern coast of the Adriatic Sea, the country of Croatia, and specifically the district of Split and Dalmatia, have always had an important cultural and historical role. The Roman emperor Diocletian built his spectacular limestone palace in the year 295, near Salona (present day Solin), which was then the capital of the Roman province of Dalmatia. During the Middle Ages, Diocletian's palace became the center of the medieval town of Split. The palace has been recognized and preserved as a famous architectural and cultural monument, and today it is on UNESCO's World Cutural Heritage list. Jump back in time and brush up on your Roman history with this brief entry about the life of Emperor Diocletian. Enter the huge courtyard, or *peristyle,* of the palace. You will think you have been transplanted back in time as you look at the carved door frames or parts of Diocletian's mausoleum, which in later centuries became the site of a Christian cathedral.

http://www.st.carnet.hr/split/

Republic of Croatia

Imagine you are in an airplane. You are flying low over the coast of Croatia. When you look down, you see the magnificent blue of the Adriatic Sea set off by steep cliffs, dark green trees, and white stone buildings of cities like Dubrovnik and Zadar. Then you visit the eastern border town of Slavonski Brod and the Serbian-occupied city of Vukovar. This sensitive map lets you click on many of the Croatian cities to see aerial photos, get historical chronologies, and learn about famous personalities. What stories do the ancient Roman ruins and archaeological items reveal about Croatia's historical heritage? The Croatian people are also dedicated to the preservation of their musical folklore. You may want to take a quick detour to learn about the stringed *tamburitza,* the most popular and most common Croatian folk instrument. A caution to parents: Some of the off-site war links and associated reportage include disturbing adult subject matter.

http://www.hr/hrvatska/HR.html

The Thousand Islands of the Croatian Adriatic

Croatia is a country with a thousand-year-old history. This horseshoe-shaped country has over 1,100 miles of mainland Adriatic shoreline and no fewer than 1,185 islands, islets, and reefs. These islands are known for their natural beauty and also for the hundreds of years of history and legend they represent. The famous feast of Our Lady of Snows is still celebrated every August on the island of Kukljica. Every summer, the people of Korcula Island re-create the old knight's dance of Moreska, which dates back to the fifteenth century, and they re-create the battles with the Moors. The ancient island of Zadar is dominated by its Roman monuments. Brac Island is known all over the world for its white stone, which was used in ancient times to build the Palace of Diocletian in the Croatian coastal city of Split and in the late 1700s to build parts of the White House in Washington, D.C.

http://islands.zems.fer.hr/

CUBA

CubaWeb

Bienvenidos al CubaWeb! Here's a different way to learn a country's history—from a culinary perspective! Did you know that pineapples are a symbol of hospitality? That custom was originally practiced by the indigenous Tainos living in Cuba. There is also a brief history of the Cuban flag. This site has interesting information, divided into a Business Library and a Culture Library. You'll find history, news, and maps in the Business Library. Check out art, literature, music, food, and sports in the Culture Library. A caution to parents: There is a link to a Cuban cigar manufacturer's home page.

http://www.cubaweb.com/eng/

Surf today, smart tomorrow.

Visit the CHEMISTRY section periodically.

Lonely Planet - Destination Cuba

Usually we think of Cuba as one large Caribbean island, but according to this site it also includes "4200-odd coral cays and islets, most of which are low lying and uninhabited." This site offers tourist information and an extensive history, as well as basic facts.

http://www.lonelyplanet.com/dest/car/cub.htm

CYPRUS

THE **CYPRUS** HOME PAGE

The small island of Cyprus, located in the northeast corner of the Mediterranean Sea, is a place rich in Greek heritage, legend, and fabulous weather. It is estimated that the people of Cyprus enjoy 300 sunny days each year! But the ongoing political tension between the Greek-Cypriots (well over three-quarters of the island's population) and the Turkish-Cypriots is a conflict that continues to plague the island. Since the Turkish invasion of July 1974, the northern 37 percent of the Cypriot Republic's territory has been under Turkish military occupation. Learn about present-day Cyprus from the maps, country profiles, and chronology of events, then step back into the history of this country at the crossroads of Europe and the Middle East. See the ancient Greek temples where Aphrodite, the Greek goddess of love and beauty, was worshipped. You'll find songs, folk art, lots of color pictures of Cyprus, and interesting facts and folklore about the birds of Cyprus, too. You might also want to click on "Kypros-Net" for more information and links.

http://www.kypros.org/Cyprus/

Kopiaste - Welcome to Cyprus

If you like sweet potatoes, you'll love *kolokasi*. This root vegetable (*Colocasia esculanta*) is a specialty of Cyprus. How about *eliopitta, lountza, kefalotiri, kaskavali, sfyrida,* or *loukoumades*? You'll have to visit this Web page, or any outdoor market on Cyprus, to find out about these other delicious foods! If you're eating *vasilopitta*, it must be New Year's Day. The Cyprus food calendar is lots of fun, as you find out which special foods are associated with different celebrations throughout the year. After sampling some of the taste treats of Cyprus, be sure to tour the collection of over 200 photos included here. You can really see why people love to visit this unique island.

http://www.cosmosnet.net/azias/cyprus/c-main.html

CZECH REPUBLIC

Czech Open Information Project

This site introduces Czech culture, music, art, history, and more. Travel through the countryside of the Czech Republic, visiting centuries-old châteaus and castles. Are you more into science than history? In Culture Information Service, read all about the founder of genetics, Johann Gregor Mendel, then turn to Czech's environmental concerns, and discover lots of other country information, too.

http://www.open.cz/project/here.htm

CZECH REPUBLIC

The Czech Republic contains beautiful cities, rugged mountains, rolling hills, and dense forests. Historically, the Czech Republic can be divided into three Czech lands: Bohemia in the west, and Moravia and Slovakia in the east. Lakes in the Czech Republic are usually artificial ponds for growing fish, mostly in south Bohemia, one of the least industrialized parts of the Czech lands. If you need business, news, and government information, visit this official site from the Ministry of Foreign Affairs.

http://www.czech.cz/

Prague Castle - Prazsky hrad

Open up the castle gates and visit the President of the Czech Republic at the Prague Castle. Net-mom and family have been at this castle, and it is really a treasure. We saw many fascinating things, including the crown jewels at St. Vitus' Cathedral, in the tomb of St. Wenceslas. If you can't visit in person, do visit this gem of a Web site.

http://www.hrad.cz/index_uk.html

DENMARK

Copenhagen Home Screen

Copenhagen is the largest city in Scandinavia. The beloved statue of The Little Mermaid is in the harbor of this capital city, but it's not Disney's Ariel, it's the original, from the fairy tale of the same name. The red brick homes are very close to the water, too. Some people can step right out of their homes and into a boat! Even more fun might be Tivoli Gardens, an amusement park. The story goes that Walt Disney was so impressed by the place that he hurried back to the U.S. to begin plans for a similar facility: Disneyland. How about a visit to the palace of the royal family? Amalienborg Palace is actually four different buildings, and if the Queen is in residence, you can watch the Changing of the Guard every day at noon. It is a city custom for spectators to follow the bearskin-capped guards from their barracks all the way to the palace.

http://expedia.msn.com/wg/places/Denmark/
    Copenhagen/HSFS.htm

Explore Denmark

Wow. Denmark—the land of the Vikings, the home of castles and queens, famed for fishing, furniture, and...Lego. Denmark's history is filled with names like Gorm the Old and Harald Bluetooth. The seafaring people of Denmark's past and present are a strong bunch. Visit this site and look at all that they've accomplished.

http://www.geocities.com/TheTropics/4597/

H.C. Andersen

Hans Christian Andersen (1805–1875) was a "Great Dane." No, he wasn't a dog! He often didn't attend school, and he left home at the young age of 14. He tried a lot of careers, but nothing clicked for him until he recognized that his imagination was his best quality. Later, he wrote some of the most delightful children's stories of all time (and you thought that Disney wrote *The Little Mermaid*). Check out this page; how many of his more than 160 fairy tales do you know?

http://www.geocities.com/WallStreet/2575/
    hcand.html

Royal Danish Embassy, Washington D.C.

Amazing fact: no one in Denmark is more than 52 kilometers from the sea. That's only 32 miles! But you might want to hop on a bike instead of a boat. You can bounce along the cobblestone streets. Amazing fact #2: the Danish line of 52 kings and queens is unbroken since its start. That's a world record. Queen Margrethe II's picture is on the site. She is a very well educated woman who loves to ballet dance and create artworks. In fact, she was a great fan of J. R. R. Tolkien, author of *The Hobbit* and *The Lord of the Rings*. In 1977, *The Lord of the Rings* was published with illustrations by Ingahild Grathmer, a "pen name" that the Queen used for her first works. She now uses her own name. You'll find her fascinating biography in History and Culture.

http://www.denmarkemb.org/

DEPENDENCIES—FAROE ISLANDS
Faroe Islands Travel Guide

The Faroe Islanders have home rule, but they are part of the kingdom of Denmark. In the summer, the sun never sets for three months! It gets low on the horizon, but it doesn't set. Photos of the villages are one of the best parts of this site, and they're picturesque. Many of the buildings have colorful roofs and siding. The green hills will entice you to hike around. Some footpaths are from olden times, before roads were built, but be sure to take a raincoat. It's foggy and drizzly there much of the time. The map is in the Around the Islands section.

http://www.puffin.fo/travel/

DEPENDENCIES—GREENLAND
Greenland Guide Index

Lemmings, those furry, cute little creatures, are on the stamps of Greenland. Other animals, famous people, plants, and scenes are on the stamps, too. Be sure to send away for a free brochure and booklet about the wonderful world of Greenland. In the northern part of this cold country, the ground stays frozen all year! Here are just a few of the unusual sights in Greenland, home to the Inuit people: icebergs, whales, reindeer, dog sleds, the northern lights, the midnight sun, kayaks, musk oxen, and the fjords. If you don't know what some of these are, just visit the site to find out. You can also read about the ice cap and people who travel down into it. Greenland is part of the kingdom of Denmark, but it has home rule and its own parliament, which you can find out about here. You can also look at Santa Claus' page, too! We thought he lived at the North Pole, but it turns out he has a place in Greenland, too.

http://www.greenland-guide.dk/

NET FILES

HERE IS THE SAME SOUND DESCRIBED IN SEVERAL LANGUAGES. WHAT SOUND IS IT?

Arabic (Algeria): *couak couak*

Chinese (Mandarin): *gua gua*

Finnish: *kvaak kvaak*

Japanese: *gaagaa*

Russian: *krya-krya*

Turkish: *vak, vak*

Answer: It's the sound of a duck quacking! Hear the duck for yourself and see what language you think says it best at *http://www.georgetown.edu/cball/animals/duck.html*

DJIBOUTI

Djibouti

Djibouti is a country in East Africa that was formerly known as the French Territory of the Afars and Issas and also as French Somaliland. It gained its independence in 1977. It's a mostly Muslim country, and the land is largely desert. The *World Factbook* entry is at <*http://www.odci.gov/cia/publications/factbook/dj.html*>.

http://www.africaindex.africainfo.no/africaindex1/countries/djibouti.html

DOMINICA

Dominica: Essential Information on the Caribbean's prime eco-tourism island

Are you wondering how on earth to pronounce Dominica? (We were pronouncing it wrong!) You can find out this and a whole lot more. Here's a fact for you: there are 365 rivers on this island—one for each day of the year. But there is only one stoplight. Parrot watching is popular, as are hiking, snorkeling, and other outdoor activities. See some photos and maps at this lovely site.

http://www.delphis.dm/basics.htm

Dominica Home Screen

Dominica is a Caribbean island; don't get it confused with the Dominican Republic, which is elsewhere. You'll find lots of natural attractions in Dominica, but you don't want to step in the Boiling Lake! The reason it's bubbling is because it's HOT. Since this is a volcanic island, you'll find other hot spots, too. Here's some trivia: most of the beaches have a certain color of sand. Knowing it's a volcanic area, can you guess what color? You'll also find beautiful waterfalls in the mountainous rain forest. The "mountain chicken" on the menu is really "*crapaud,* the legs of huge frogs that burrow in the woods."

http://expedia.msn.com/wg/Places/Dominica/HSFS.htm

DOMINICAN REPUBLIC

Consulate of the Dominican Republic

What is "the most beautiful land human eyes have ever seen"? According to this official page, it's the Dominican Republic, on the island of Hispaniola. Read about many different vacation destinations, most of which involve lots of sun and sea! The northern coast of this Caribbean land contains the world's largest deposit of amber. This site also offers a very detailed history of this country, which is illustrated with historic photos.

http://www.consudom-ny.do/

Dominican Republic Home Screen

Check the entry in this book for Haiti, which shares the island of Hispaniola with the country of the Dominican Republic. Christopher Columbus wasn't the only member of his family who landed here. According to this site, "Christopher Columbus dropped anchor here on his first voyage in 1492; four years later, his brother Bartolomeo founded the colony of Santo Domingo; 13 years after that, Christopher's son became the colony's governor!"

http://expedia.msn.com/wg/Places/
    DominicanRepublic/HSFS.htm

ECUADOR

Dorn's Ecuador Page

Ecuador sits right on the equator, in South America. Would you like to be a student in Ecuador for seven months? This guy did just that: he lived with a host family and had many adventures. He even visited a tribe in the rain forest! Sail your mouse on over to his site to look at the great pictures he took and the terrific links he has collected on Ecuador, the Galápagos Islands, the Maya, and Incas.

http://earth-art.com/ecuador/

Ecuador

This official page comes from the Embassy of Ecuador in Washington, D.C. You'll find lots of tourism and cultural information, as well as details on the national insignia. For example, the coat of arms includes many symbols. According to this site, "The condor perched at the top offers the country shelter and protection under its outstretched wings and stands ready to strike out against any enemy."

http://www.ecuador.org/

Virtual Galápagos

The Galápagos are islands off the coast of Ecuador. Some unusual plants and animals here aren't found anywhere else on Earth. Movies show a giant tortoise eating (what an appetite!) or lizards doing push-ups (lizard aerobics?). As you journey through the islands in virtual reality movies, you can even walk among the tortoises!

http://www.terraquest.com/galapagos/

EGYPT

See also ANCIENT CIVILIZATIONS AND ARCHAEOLOGY—ANCIENT EGYPT

Cleveland Museum of Art Pharaohs Exhibition

See kings and queens, pharaohs, and their treasures. See statues and carvings from long ago. Learn some fun facts about the pharaohs. Did you know that some of them were women? Construct a paper model of one of their death masks (the pattern is printable). Hut, hut, go King Tut!

http://www.clemusart.com/archive/pharaoh/

Egypt - Guardian's Egypt - Main Gate

Venture through the ruins of a real pyramid. Can you figure out its mysteries? The Sphinx has clues about its past, too. But what on earth happened to its nose? Hint: It didn't fall off as a result of erosion or weather! This site is a complete guide to links on both ancient and modern Egypt and includes info about music and art, language lessons in Arabic, a special kids' section, and more.

http://guardians.net/egypt/

EGYPT has it all !!

From the Red Sea coast to the oases in the interior, Egypt really does have it all. This official site has it all! You might want to visit a city like Luxor first. It has statues, carvings, and paintings. Perhaps you'd like to hop over to the Sinai. Its mountains tower above the sea, where you can snorkel. Check out the two-mile-long High Dam at Aswan, which supplies electricity for all of Egypt. Or maybe you'd rather sit back and see an automatic slide show of the whole tour.

http://its-idsc.gov.eg/tourism/

Egypt Information Highway

One of the best sites on this country is the official Egyptian Information Highway site. You will discover a lot of background information on Egypt plus carefully sorted and arranged links to other pages.

http://www.idsc.gov.eg/

Horus Web Site

Little Horus is ready to take you on a trip through Egypt! So sit back and click on any of the buttons. Horus says you should expect to find fun, knowledge, and joy. And the best news is that each month, Horus finds a new place in Egypt for you to visit, so plan to return often! For example, head for the Abdeen Palace. Horus says it is one of the most elegant places in the world!

http://www.horus.ics.org.eg/

Odyssey in Egypt

Join archaeologists in a real dig at this award-winning resource. You can tour the dig site and move around it in virtual reality. But Egypt is much more than old stuff. Get to know kids who live and work there. One weaves carpets in a store. Another helps on the farm with his family. How would you study and preserve a wall painting? Where would you dig for archaeological ruins next? Your ideas are valuable! You can help by solving problems in the SOS section of each week's material.

http://www.website1.com/odyssey/

EL SALVADOR

Lonely Planet - Destination El Salvador

Did you think that the only pyramids were in Egypt? Guess again! There are ruins of ancient pyramids in El Salvador, too. Take a look at these Central American designs and compare them to those in Egypt. Volcanoes, lakes, and beaches are a part of the landscape of El Salvador. You'll find lots of background info on the country here.

http://www.lonelyplanet.com/dest/cam/els.htm

ENGLAND

See UNITED KINGDOM—ENGLAND

What did grandma do when she was a kid? There is a list of questions to ask in GENEALOGY AND FAMILY HISTORY.

EQUATORIAL GUINEA

Equitorial.Guinea Page

One clue about where this country is located is in its name. Here's another: it's on a large continent shared with the countries of Egypt, Uganda, and Zaire, among others. An island off its coast has two volcanoes. If you know Spanish, you'll feel right at home in Equatorial Guinea. Spanish is the official language, since the country was formerly owned by Spain. Careful—this country has a lot of political unrest.

http://www.sas.upenn.edu/African_Studies/
    Country_Specific/Eq_Guinea.html

ERITREA

Eritrea Network Information Center

This country has been torn by war for many years. But if you look around, you'll see the potential for many good things there. Many farmers share their land, because it is owned by all of them. Gold mines abound. Located on the Red Sea and formerly a colony of Ethiopia, Eritrea got its name from the Greek word for just that—Red Sea. You can also get more info and links on Dehai Eritrea Online at <http://www.primenet.com/~ephrem/>.

http://www.eritrea.org/

ESTONIA

Estonia Country Guide

When the glaciers left this area, they also left behind—Estonia! It still is very cold in the winter, with a permanent snow cover for months. Estonia used to be part of the Soviet Union. In 1991, it broke off and became independent. You'll find lots of political and cultural links here to sites on music, museums, and stamps.

http://www.ciesin.ee/ESTCG/

ETHIOPIA

Embassy of Ethiopia

At this site, see the flag of Ethiopia and read the biographies of its leaders. Then read about the history, culture, foods, and people of this country. There are also tourism notes on the major cities as well as information on the climate, environment, and geography of this country located "in the heart of the Horn of Africa."

http://www.nicom.com/~ethiopia/

A Journey through Ethiopia

See Ethiopia in pictures. From a waterfall on the Blue Nile to people in native dress, from modern buildings to ancient obelisks, you will be amazed at the contrasts. Also read about Ethiopia's vast history, from 500 B.C. to the present, and how its struggle for unity continues on today.

http://home.wxs.nl/~spaansen/

OneWorld Magazine - ETHIOPIA, LAND OF ZION

This beautiful site contains a wealth of information about Ethiopia through magazine-quality stories created by journalists who traveled to this land. The articles range from a story about the original Ark of the Covenant to the prestige and power of Ethiopia's women.

http://www.envirolink.org/oneworld/focus/etiopia/
    toc.htm

FALKLAND ISLANDS

See UNITED KINGDOM—DEPENDENCIES—
FALKLAND ISLANDS

FAROE ISLANDS

See DENMARK—DEPENDENCIES—
FAROE ISLANDS

FIJI

Fiji Islands Travel Information Service

Besides travel information from the Fiji Visitors'
Bureau, you'll discover much historical and cultural
information at this site, including practice in saying a
few words and phrases in Fijian. There are also
wonderful folktales, including the Shark God, sacred
turtles, and firewalkers.

http://www.fijifvb.gov.fj/

Rob Jay's Fiji Islands Travel Guide

Fiji consists of over 300 islands of various sizes. If you
visit, you'll find all sorts of fun things to do:
kayaking, hiking to a volcano, sliding down a watery
slope, bird watching, scuba diving, and surfing. The
main attraction, though, according to this Web site's
author, is the people of Fiji. He says, "Fijian customs
reflect an utmost dignity and courtesy toward the
visitor. There are ceremonies for every occasion,
which may include the presentation of *tabua* (whale's
teeth), food or other gifts, or more commonly the
drinking of *yaqona* (kava), the national beverage."

http://www.fijiguide.com/

Scrapbook of Fiji

This journalist's site is subtitled "A scrapbook of six
months in paradise." Take a virtual vacation with the
author, and you'll see that the customs in Fiji are
unique. You'll get a sense of their ceremonies,
clothing, homes, and special events by looking at the
pictures and text. It's fun to attend a village wedding,
a 21st birthday party, and the installation of a new
tribal chief. You'll find a good collection of links
here, too.

http://www.en.com/users/laura8/

FINLAND

A blast through SW Finland by Greg Rubidge

This fellow took a trip through Finland, and now he
shares it on the Web. It's sort of a "What I Did on My
Vacation" report, and it gets kind of wordy, but the
stories are fabulous. He says it all boils down to the
people, the places, and the food. One of the
experiences he had was taking a "smoke sauna." They
have 4.5 saunas for every one person in Finland! As
for the food, he'll have you drooling with his
description of the sweets.

http://www.hype.com/finnart/

FINFO - INDEX - Facts about Finland

This is an official site, with the lowdown on
everything about Finland. A multimedia show awaits
you in the Picture Book area, including The Four
Seasons of Finland. It has beautiful pictures taken
during the year, along with the sounds of nature and
poetic text. Is that a woodpecker you hear in the
distance? Finland has six national nature symbols. See
if you can figure out what they might be. The Finnish
Way of Life section will tell you about the people's
festivities, origins, sayings, food, and more. Arts and
Entertainment has pictures of men and women in the
national costume.

http://virtual.finland.fi/finfo/findeng.html

The Finnish Sauna

OK, here are directions for taking a sauna bath. Hop
in the sauna room. It's about 175 to 210 degrees
Fahrenheit. When you're good and hot, get out of
there and run to the river, lake, or snowbank. Jump
in. When you're good and freezing, run back to the
sauna. Actually, there are better instructions at this
site. Learn how to take a sauna the way the Finns
really do. Along the way, you'll find out the history
behind this thousand-year-old tradition and learn
the vocabulary.

http://www.hut.fi/~icankar/sauna/

NET FILES

How many miles of book shelving does the Library of Congress maintain?

Answer: About 532 miles, spread out among three buildings. Read more about it at *http://lcweb.loc.gov/faq/25faq.html*

Welcome to Travel in Finland

From the reindeer in northern Lapland to the city of Helsinki in the south, there's lots to see in Finland. Would you like to take a canoe out on a lake or have an adventure with a snowmobile? How about swimming in ten pools under one roof? If you strap on your skis, and your courage, you can even learn to ski jump!

http://www.travel.fi/int/

FRANCE

See also ARCHITECTURE—GOVERNMENT AND PUBLIC BUILDINGS

The Chauvet Cave

You're about to explore a cave in France. Crawl down. As you clear a narrow passageway, you head further into a previously untouched cavern. Wait, what's that on the ground? Cave bear skeletons! Shine your headlamp over there on the wall. You can just make out some things. They are paintings of animals, all over the walls. Discover more about these ancient cave drawings at this site.

http://www.culture.fr/culture/arcnat/chauvet/
    en/gvpda-d.htm

The French Embassy

Friendship between France and the United States goes back a long, long way! At the French Embassy page you'll learn the history of that relationship. You can also spend time touring the countryside and even learn a verse or two of the French national anthem. This site has a special section just for kids and might be the place to head for help with a school project. *Vivé la France*!

http://www.info-france-usa.org/

Louvre W3

This museum was originally designed as a palace. In medieval times, it was a fortress. Now you can walk in what used to be the moats, but now your feet will stay dry! The collections include not just French art but also paintings, sculpture, and works of art from many countries and times. To jump right to the paintings on this site, go to The Collections and click on Paintings. Whose eyes are those peering out at you? Click on them to find out.

http://mistral.culture.fr/louvre/louvrea.htm

Official Website of the French President: The Elysée Palace

Walk right up the virtual red carpet and take a tour of the President of France's official residence. At this site you can also learn about the national symbols of France, including "Marianne," a sculpted figure representing liberty and wisdom. She is pictured on stamps, coins, and this Web page. The origin of the name is unclear. Another famous symbol is the Gallic rooster. It is a play on words: *gallus* means "rooster" in Latin as well as Gaul, the ancient name of the region of which current-day France was once a part. The rooster appears on the seal of state.

http://www.elysee.fr/ang/

An Overview of French Culture

Politics, customs, history, and of course, famous French art and architecture all get top billing at this site. Read about Charlemagne, Joan of Arc, the Notre Dame cathedral, and the influence of World War II on France. Discover a variety of facts on France—this is a great place to learn about the country or to use as a starting place for a school project on France.

http://www.france.com/culture/

Les Pages de Paris / The Paris Pages

Here's a more serious look at Paris. It's bilingual, with both French and English versions. The city, its culture, its tourist sites, train stations, museums, monuments—it's all here. In the Culture section are special expositions featuring historic postcards, including a photo history of the August 1944 liberation of Paris during World War II.

http://www.paris.org/

Welcome to the French Prime Minister's Website

Learn about the various duties of the president and the prime minister of France, how they are chosen, and how their jobs are similar, yet different. In the Quick Facts section, you know what you'll find! In the National Symbols area, you can find out about the history of the tricolor flag, read about Bastille Day, and hear the national anthem.

http://www.premier-ministre.gouv.fr/GB/

DEPENDENCIES— FRENCH GUIANA

Lonely Planet — Destination: French Guiana

This South American country is about the size of the state of Indiana. It is an overseas department of France. This page includes basic tourist information, but there isn't much!

http://www.lonelyplanet.com/dest/sam/fgu.htm

DEPENDENCIES—FRENCH POLYNESIA

Chris Davis' French Polynesia

Tahiti, Bora Bora, scuba diving, sunken treasure, black pearls. Interested? You can check it all out here and also learn the history, holidays, customs, and lots of other interesting information about these tropical islands. There are also links to other pages about French Polynesia.

http://www.cd-enterprises.com/french_polynesia/

TAHITI EXPLORER - The Ultimate Travel Guide for Tahiti

Maybe you've heard of Tahiti. It's the largest of the 115 islands that make up French Polynesia, an overseas territory of France. If you were going to imagine a perfect South Pacific island, this would be it: volcanoes in the background, lush plants and huts in the foreground. Ocean life all around includes sharks, dolphins, and coral reefs. This page has info about many of the French Polynesian islands, including the Marquesas, Moorea, Bora Bora, and more.

http://www.tahiti-explorer.com/

DEPENDENCIES—GUADELOUPE

Guadeloupe Home Screen

Chris Columbus landed here too, like so many other places. He gave it its name. Today, it's nicknamed "the butterfly," because it's shaped like one. It's also known as the "Island of Beautiful Waters" because of its waterfalls. The people who live there love music. Can you hear that Caribbean beat? There are still wooden huts right alongside the big hotels. Where would you rather stay? If you like to bike, you'll be able to get around Guadeloupe just fine. It's the craze there, besides diving. Guadeloupe is an overseas department of France. You'll find a lot of information here and also be able to link to other pages about this country.

http://expedia.msn.com/wg/Places/Guadeloupe/
   HSFS.htm

DEPENDENCIES—MARTINIQUE

The Ever Radiant Welcome Of Martinique

Martinique is a popular vacation destination in the Caribbean Sea. In fact, many Web sites about Martinique are produced by commercial travel agencies. This colorful site includes a picture- and music-filled guided tour in which flowers, rain forests, and sandy white beaches are featured. You can sit back and tour while listening to Caribbean music! There are also brief overviews of history, geography, climate, and population. Travelers may be interested to learn about shopping and food on the island. Some commercial promotions are found at this site, but they are nicely mixed with some Web-based Caribbean fun. This site is available in English and French, since the island is an overseas department of France.

http://www.martinique.org/

DEPENDENCIES—MAYOTTE

Discovering Mayotte

This site is based on information from the *World Factbook* entry, but with buttons for easy access to subjects and links to other atlas information. Mayotte is a small tropical island off of southern Africa, in the Mozambique Channel. It is a territory of France, and the almost 100,000 Mahoran people (the name for people from Mayotte) are Muslim. Mayotte flies the flag of France, exports something called *ylang-ylang* (a sweetly scented flower used in making perfume), and has no television stations! But there is much more to know about this island, and this fact-based site is a good place to get started.

http://www.i-helpdesk.com/pages/VE/carteide.html

DEPENDENCIES—NEW CALEDONIA

K-tour New Caledonia

It's a good news/bad news thing for New Caledonia. This group of islands east of Australia in the South Pacific boasts more than 20 percent of the world's nickel resources. That's good. It's too bad that in recent years the world demand for nickel has been slowing down. Crank up your Web browser and head to the site with all the facts on this French territory, which contrasts high mountains and dense forests with sparking lagoons and coral reefs.

http://www.ktour.nc/english.htm

DEPENDENCIES—REUNION

Reunion Island, touristic guide

Reunion Island is a volcanic island off the coast of Africa. As Reunion Island is a department of France, you can polish up your *français* here (although most of the page is also in English). You'll see beautiful color photos of people, animals, plant life, and beaches. As well, you'll get good background information on history, climate, and economic and social aspects of life there. A rainbow of people inhabit this island, which was first populated by 12 mutineers in 1646.

http://la-reunion.web-france.com/Aaccueil.htm

DEPENDENCIES—SAINT-PIERRE AND MIQUELON

Encyclopédie de Saint-Pierre et Miquelon

Saint-Pierre and Miquelon are the last remaining North American possessions of France, located just off Newfoundland. This site has a detailed history of the islands, including a list of those who died in World War II. There are links to Basque and Breton sites, language and politics, and locally produced Web pages. Much of this material is in French, but about 20 percent has been translated into English. Portions of the site are also available in Portuguese, Euskara, Galego, and Spanish. Have you heard of all of those languages before? If not, learn more here!

http://209.205.50.254/encyspmweb/english.html

DEPENDENCIES—WALLIS AND FUTUNA

Wallis and Futuna

This small South Pacific island group is an overseas territory of France. At this page, you'll find out that one of the big problems there is that the forests are being cut down for fuel. With no trees, the rocky ground is subject to erosion. The good soil washes into the sea, which affects how many crops they can grow. The islanders have to import a lot of food from other countries. How do they pay for it? They get money from selling off fishing rights to Japan and other countries. They also sell handicrafts.

http://www.odci.gov/cia/publications/factbook/wf.html

> "We're flooding people with information. We need to feed it through a processor. A human must turn information into intelligence or knowledge. We've tended to forget that no computer will ever ask a new question."
> —Admiral Grace Hopper

FRENCH GUIANA

See FRANCE—DEPENDENCIES—FRENCH GUIANA

FRENCH POLYNESIA

See FRANCE—DEPENDENCIES—FRENCH POLYNESIA

GABON

Welcome to the Official Site of Gabon

The famous humanitarian Albert Schweitzer did his work in Gabon. Now there's a museum and hospital in the city where he lived. Gabon is also the land of the African pygmy tribes and you can reach some areas of the jungle only by canoe. If you have any mahogany furniture in your home, it may have come from Gabon. Most of the trees there are red mahogany, a beautiful hardwood. If you thought that Florida was the only place where manatees lived, guess again. They live off the coast of this country, too. The lowland gorilla is another inhabitant, and there has been much research into their lives. Are we studying them, or is it the other way around?

http://www.presidence-gabon.com/index-a.html

GAMBIA, THE

The Republic of The Gambia's Web Page

This snake-shaped West African country follows the river Gambia. If you take a boat upriver, you'll see all kinds of wildlife, including hippos. With your jungle hat and some tropical clothing, you'll be set to explore. Since the climate is pleasant compared to much of West Africa, it should be an enjoyable trip! What do you suppose it was like, though, back in the days of the slave ships? Learn about the history of this land here at the official government page.

http://www.gambia.com/

GEORGIA

Welcome to the Parliament of Georgia

At this official page you will find photos, national symbols, and lots of information about the environment, history, and culture of Georgia. You can listen to a Georgian folk song. See lots of art. Read about the history (it used to be part of the Soviet Union). Uncover old relics, like temples and feudal fortresses. See the Caucasus mountains—one of them is called the "Pyramid of Ice." For more, try some of the links at <http://www.personal.psu.edu/users/d/x/dxc185/georgian.html>.

http://www.parliament.ge/

GERMANY

See also QUEENS, KINGS, AND ROYALTY

Chris De Witt's Berlin Wall Website

If Net-mom had written this book in 1989, it would have had two entries for Germany: one for East Germany and one for West Germany. In fact, the city of Berlin was divided by a huge wall, separating the western, Democratic side from the eastern, Communist side. Travel was very restricted between East and West. Border guards were always on the lookout for people trying to escape to the West. Some people were killed. But all that is over now, and the two sides are reunited into one Germany. Read about the history of the wall here.

http://www.appropriatesoftware.com/BerlinWall/welcome.html

Convention & Visitors Bureau Heidelberg

Heidelberg is an historic German city with a famous university, which was founded in 1386! Don't miss the Sightseeing section of this page and check the Student's Prison, which was sort of like detention in the 1700s. If a student played a trick on a teacher or participated in a duel with another student or was too loud or disorderly, then that student was sent off to "prison" for a few days. Supposedly, the prisoners were let out to go to class, but the rest of the time they had to stay there. You can still see the "artwork" on the walls! Don't miss the outstanding views of castles and other old buildings.

http://www.heidelberg.de/verkehrsverein/english/

Die Deutschekulturseite
(The German Culture page)

This site features a clickable map that lets you visit all 16 of Germany's states and find out info about them. The page also plays the German national anthem while you browse. There's also a section on Famous Germans, which lists many people, from Albert Einstein to Albert Schweitzer, along with brief biographies.

http://www.geocities.com/Athens/Olympus/5011/

German Embassy and German Information Center

At this official site you'll find up-to-date fast facts as well as cultural information, recipes, tourism info, and even tips on tracing your German ancestors. You can also order some free pamphlets online. Do you know Germany? You will if you visit this page!

http://www.germany-info.org/

Germany Home Screen

Germany was one of the founding countries in the European Union. Here are facts and super photos of some of the more famous German sights. Hint: If you want to see a larger picture, click on any photo. Maps and travel tips for three German cities will help if you want to visit them in person.

http://expedia.msn.com/wg/places/Germany/
HSFS.htm

Lonely Planet — Destination: Germany

From the industrial north to the alpine forests of the Bavarian south, Germany will charm you! Did the designers of the Disney World castle use Neuschwanstein Castle as their model? What do you think? See it at <http://www.majesty.org/europe/germany1.html>. One thing is for sure: There is no such thing as too much apple strudel! And why look at just any old map when you can click your way around this interactive map of Germany? A slide show and facts about the country will bring Germany to your desktop.

http://www.lonelyplanet.com/dest/eur/ger.htm

GHANA

Ghana

Traveling to this African coastal country would be an adventure. Here's a woman who actually went all that distance to take a drumming class, although she had never played the drums before. She really gives you a glimpse into what daily life is like. Learning to dance the native way, playing the drums, and eating *fou fou* (check it out) were all new things to try in this country. Learn how to make and tie a *lapa*, a long garment worn by women. There is also lots of information about kente cloth, batik, and other types of African textiles. And she suggests women splurge and get their hair braided! She kept her hair extensions in for seven weeks when she got home—they still looked great, but she got tired of them after that.

http://www.bpe.com/travel/africa/ghana/

The Republic of Ghana Home Page

At this site, you'll get loads of facts, tourist info, maps, and more. For example, you can see pictures of Ghanaian money. Can you spot the precious gems pictured on the one thousand Cedi note? They are diamonds, which are important exports.

http://www.ghana.com/republic/

GIBRALTAR

See UNITED KINGDOM—DEPENDENCIES—GIBRALTAR

GREECE

See also ANCIENT CIVILIZATIONS AND ARCHAEOLOGY—ANCIENT GREECE

EMBASSY OF GREECE: Home Page

Did you know that the history of Greece goes back 4,000 years? You can learn about its history at this official site, as well as explore cultural and other information. Visit many ancient monuments and archaeological sites, including the Acropolis in Athens and the numerous Greek islands.

http://www.greekembassy.org/

GoGreece.com: Your Internet Guide to Greece

At GoGreece, you can choose links on cooking, music, culture, religion, science, and current events. Visit Anna's Cyberhome for a look at Greek costume, poetry, and dance. Try the recipe section for tasty treats. How about making some sweet baklava, or savory moussaka? Parents: Please check outside links.

http://www.gogreece.com/

Greece Home Screen

Every country has its customs and manners. In Greece, it is impolite to leave any food on your plate. Of course, with all that wonderful Greek food, you won't want to quit eating! So get out your drachmas (Greek money) for some great meals. If you visit Athens, you'll be walking the same streets as Socrates and many other famous Greeks. The marathon (a 26-mile, 385-yard race) also started in Greece, when a runner was sent to tell others of a victory in battle. Aren't you glad we have telephones, radio, and the Net now?

http://expedia.msn.com/wg/places/Greece/HSFS.htm

Hellas On Line - Greek Pages

Hellas is another name for Greece. The interactive map here will show you a photo of each city as you click on it. There sure are a lot of islands! Now let's go back in time. The Mythology & History section is great to help you keep track of all those Greek gods, Fates, Muses, and semigods. A family tree and other info will help you get them straight.

http://www.hol.gr/greece/

If you forgot the words to "gopher guts" try lyrics in MUSIC AND MUSICIANS.

THE HISTORY OF GREEK COSTUME

Do you think only of togas when you think of ancient Greek costume? Actually, their clothing changed through the centuries. They used a lot of cloth in their flowing dresses, and it must have cost a lot to weave threads of silver and gold into the costumes. You'll see many designs here, but parents, early ones are very revealing. How do you suppose we know what they wore if they didn't have photos back then? Find out here.

http://www.firstnethou.com/annam/costhist.html/

The Olympic Games in the Ancient Hellenic World

Click on a room of this virtual museum to find out about the ancient Greek Olympics. Read about the history of the games. (Did you know that they were held every four years, even back then?) Wander around Zeus' temple in virtual reality. A slide show of the ruins and modern-day cities gives you a look at Greece then and now. They didn't have as many different sports back then as we have now. How many are the same now as then? Visit this site and see!

http://devlab.dartmouth.edu/olympic/

GREENLAND

See DENMARK—DEPENDENCIES—GREENLAND

GRENADA

Grenada Home Screen

Grenada is also known as the Caribbean "spice island." Lots of spices are grown here, including nutmeg, allspice, and cinnamon. A nutmeg pod even appears on its flag! Perhaps you'd like a hike through the rain forest? Bring your machete along, because you'll need it to hack away the plants. Or, if you'd rather snorkel, the reefs are beautiful. Watch out for the jellyfish and other critters, though. This site offers basic information and a wealth of outside links.

http://expedia.msn.com/wg/places/Grenada/HSFS.htm

Grenada - Official Travel Guide

Escaping to a tropical island can sound pretty good sometimes. Grenada is in the Caribbean. It's lush as can be, and no building may be taller than a coconut palm. Plus, it has an extinct volcano! The waterfalls will make you want to splash around underneath them. When Christopher Columbus sailed by this island, he named it something else. To find out this little tidbit and other history about Grenada, you'll need to go to the site.

http://www.interknowledge.com/grenada/

GUADELOUPE

See FRANCE—DEPENDENCIES—GUADELOUPE

GUATEMALA

About Guatemala

In this land of volcanoes, caves, and the ancestors of the Maya people, you'll see amazing sights. Check out the toucans or the green and red quetzal (the national bird), which appears on the flag. You'll also see photos of the ancient Maya ruins at this site.

http://www.ualr.edu/~degonzalez/Guatemala.html

Guatemala

Guatemala is in Central America, bordering the Caribbean Sea, between Honduras and Belize and bordering the North Pacific Ocean, between El Salvador and Mexico. It is hot and has frequent tropical storms and hurricanes.

http://www.odci.gov/cia/publications/factbook/gt.html

GUERNSEY

See UNITED KINGDOM—DEPENDENCIES—GUERNSEY

GUINEA

Guinea Republic General

Waterfalls, rain forests, and wildlife are special sights. Street musicians will share their talents with you in the city. If you like spicy food, then the dishes of Guinea will suit you just fine (pass the water, please—quickly!). The *World Factbook* page on Guinea is at <http://www.odci.gov/cia/publications/factbook/gv.html>.

http://www.wtgonline.com/country/gn/gen.html

GUINEA-BISSAU

Guinea-Bissau General

Guinea-Bissau is a West African country that sits right near Guinea. It used to belong to Portugal, and the official language is still Portuguese. If you like to eat nuts, you'll go nuts in Guinea-Bissau! They are one of the main exports. The businessmen don't wear suits and ties. Instead, they wear safari suits to work (and we thought business casual was invented in the U.S.). The *World Factbook* page is at <http://www.odci.gov/cia/publications/factbook/pu.html>.

http://www.wtgonline.com/data/gnb/gnb.asp

GUYANA

The Guyana World Wide Web Handbook

Did you think that the Netherlands was the only low-lying country protected by a seawall? Nope. Guyana's capital city also sits below sea level. Hey, there's a jaguar in the forest! Jaguars are on the national coat of arms, too, along with sugarcane and rice. Many races live in this South American country. If you explore the history, you'll understand why.

http://www.guyana.org/Handbook/handbook.htm

HAITI

The Embassy of the Republic of Haiti, Washington D.C.

At this site you'll learn about Haitian government and tourism, but you can also explore an extensive collection of links on everything from voodoo to the *Kreyòl* language. You can also view Haitian handicrafts and even purchase them from their makers.

http://www.haiti.org/embassy/

Haiti MC Page

Click! Each spot on the map will take you to the history of that area of Haiti. This country shares the Caribbean island of Hispaniola with another country. Can you find out which one? The style of paintings from Haiti really make you feel like you're right there in the tropics. You'll see lots of colors, green being the main one. And the music! It will have you moving with the beat. Would you like to try a taste of pumpkin soup or fried plantain (banana)? Along with the happier part of this island country, though, is the darkness of poverty and unrest. You'll also find voodoo links at this site since many Haitians practice it.

http://pasture.ecn.purdue.edu/~agenhtml/agenmc/haiti/haiti.html

HOLLAND

See NETHERLANDS

HOLY SEE

Città del Vaticano

The art treasures of the Vatican are truly astounding. This site includes hundreds of masterpieces in exquisite detail, including Michelangelo's remarkable Sistine Chapel ceiling. It is not to be missed by anyone who appreciates beautiful art and architecture.

http://www.christusrex.org/www1/citta/0-Citta.html

The Holy See

While Vatican City is just a tiny group of buildings entirely within the city of Rome, Italy, it is also considered an independent nation. As the global spiritual center of the entire Roman Catholic Church, its importance on the international scale is equal to that of many other countries. This is the official Web site of the Vatican, and it is the place to go for news from the Church, pronouncements and messages from the Pope, looks at some of the Church's vast collections of magnificent art, and the latest information on the upcoming celebration of the year 2000. You can find photographs, biographies, and other fascinating information on the last four Popes.

http://www.vatican.va/

Welcome to Vatican Radio

Staff from 50 countries prepare 400 hours of broadcast material every week in 37 different languages. Radio Vatican broadcasts on short wave, medium wave, FM, satellite, and the Internet. You can download Real Audio files and features in several languages. As they say: "Listen, for heaven's sake!"

http://www.wrn.org/vatican-radio/

HONDURAS

Lonely Planet - Destination Honduras

Do you know Spanish and have a love of adventure? Then you might want to visit this country in Central America. There are still primitive tribes living in some areas of the rain forest but you may need to paddle a wooden dugout canoe in order to visit them! Or maybe a visit to the Maya's ancient city of Copán would suit you. There are more questions about the Maya than there are answers. Maybe you could help solve the puzzle.

http://www.lonelyplanet.com/dest/cam/hon.htm

HONG KONG

See CHINA—AUTONOMOUS AREAS—HONG KONG

HUNGARY

HUNGARIAN IMAGES AND HISTORICAL BACKGROUND

The Hungarian national anthem and other music are here for your enjoyment. Our favorite is Beethoven's "King Stephen Overture." This first King of Hungary later became a saint. You'll get to look at his royal crown and jewels here. The national costumes are beautiful, with fancy hats, aprons, and embroidery. And there is an interesting section on Transylvania, which was part of the kingdom of Hungary until 1921 and is now part of Romania.

http://www.msstate.edu/Archives/History/
   hungary/hungary.html

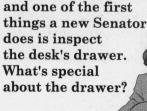

When a new U.S. Senator is elected, he or she gets a desk in the Senate debate chamber. Each desk has a long history, and one of the first things a new Senator does is inspect the desk's drawer. What's special about the drawer?

Answer: The names of the desk's previous owners are carved inside. "Today, the history of each desk may be traced by reading the names carved inside the desk drawers. These inscriptions are a twentieth-century tradition, and not all the names were personally inscribed by the senators. However, in recent decades, senators have adhered more closely to a tradition of personally inscribing their desks." Learn more at http://www.senate.gov/curator/sdesk.htm

HUNGARY Home Page

Right smack in the middle of Europe—that's where you'll find Hungary. In this decade, we've seen the Communists give up their power. Now, Hungary is a democracy. The best part of this site is the tour of Budapest, the capital. It used to be three towns. One was named "Pest," and one was named "Obuda." Can you guess what the other town was?

http://www.fsz.bme.hu/hungary/homepage.html

Lonely Planet — Destination: Hungary

Hungary is a mixture: old and new, Islam and Christianity, mosques and cathedrals, water and land, city and country. The slide show at this site will show you the contrasts.

http://www.lonelyplanet.com/dest/eur/hun.htm

ICELAND

The Embassy of Iceland - Washington, DC

So how cold is Iceland, anyway? According to this official site, due to the moderating effect of the Gulf Stream current, winter temperatures are in the low 30s while July brings a heat wave all the way up to the low 50s. At this site you can take a virtual tour of Iceland and learn about culture, history, and the national symbols. The coat of arms "is a silvery cross in a sky-blue field with a fiery red cross in the silvery one. The shield-bearers are the four guardian spirits of the land: A bull to the right of the shield, a giant to the left, a vulture to the right above the bull, and a dragon to the left above the giant. The shield rests on a slab of basalt."

http://www.iceland.org/

IGI Home

The real gems of this site are the pictures: winter photos of kids playing in the snow; trees covered with crystals of ice; summer pictures of the countryside and the fjords; even the midnight sun! Santa Claus lives in Iceland (according to this site), and his helpers, the Yule Swains, have some mighty crazy names. Gully-guy? Keyhole-sniffer? What will Santa think of next? Find out in the IGI Where, what, how, who section.

http://www.zocalo.net/iceland/

Reykjavik

The Icelandic word for the capital, Reykjavik, means "smoky bay." But the explorers who discovered it weren't really seeing smoke. They were seeing steam from the hot springs! Residents even heat their homes with the hot water from these springs. You can swim in outdoor heated pools right next to the snow and ice. This site is almost as attractive as the city. You'll love the icy-looking colors.

http://www.rvk.is/

Virtually Virtual Iceland

You could spend days at this site, written by an Icelandic man. The section on Norse mythology is illustrated. Other goodies jump out at you; for example, take the link to learn how to make your own pair of Viking shoes from the patterns and instructions at <*http://www.spoon.demon.co.uk/vikes/vikshoe.htm*>. Or, learn some Icelandic words from original sounds. Or you can figure out what your name would be if you went by traditional Icelandic naming customs. Interactive maps link you to photos and stamps of the country. This site is hot, and it's not just from Iceland's geothermal springs!

http://www.itn.is/~gunnsi/gardar1.htm

INDIA

Discover India

This official, comprehensive site will teach you about Indian politics, sports, clothing, art, dance, music, festivals, foods, films, history, and more. For example, did you know that 15 national languages are recognized by the Indian constitution? These languages together have over 1,600 variations or dialects! This site also provides information on the anthem, flag, and national symbols of India. The national bird is the peacock. Once hunted, they are now a protected species. The national fruit is the mango, and the national tree is the banyan. India's saffron, green, and white flag features a central Dharma Chakra, known as the wheel of law.

http://www.indiagov.org/

Hello, India! Home Page

Head right to the Parent's Corner section, because it's the best part. You'll read illustrated stories from Indian folklore. One is about a bedbug (yes, a bedbug) that lives in the king's mattress. What do you think happened when the king let his feet poke out from under the covers? The story about a lion might remind you of another fable.

http://www.helloindia.com/

An Introduction to India

Hop on board a camel and take a trek through the valleys of the Himalayas. Or visit the Taj Mahal; people say it is the world's most beautiful building. Did you know that some of the most advanced civilizations lived in ancient India? Moving into more modern times, you can learn about Mahatma Gandhi at this site. He was a peaceful leader. This Web page is very, very wordy, but the information is good and the pictures are lovely.

http://www.interknowledge.com/india/

Khazana: India Arts Online

Sitar, sarode, tabla, santur—what are those? They are just a few of the musical instruments of India. Some are stringed instruments, and others are drums. Hear the unusual sounds coming right out of your computer. You'll also get to see folk paintings in two different styles, as well as bronze castings and clothing designs. Explanations tell you about the traditions behind the art.

http://www.khazana.com/

Lonely Planet — Destination: India

The Lonely Planet guide offers traveler's tips as well as facts on India. Photos, maps, and slide shows will give you a taste of this busy, crowded country. But hey, don't fall off that mountaintop! Some of the tallest peaks in the world are in India, and it's a long way down. There is a lot more to see. View the colorful temples, and see if you can find out why so many small flags are flying in the wind.

http://www.lonelyplanet.com/dest/ind/ind.htm

Welcome to Indiahorizons

In 1997, India celebrated its 50th year of independence. Show your support! Send a free cybercard to a friend. Choose from all sorts of Indian designs for your greeting card. An art gallery features Indian artists. Try out an Indian recipe. At this site, you can even enjoy the top 25 Hindi movie songs or try the Shockwave games in the Kids' section.

http://www.att.com./indiahorizons/

Welcome to the Non-violence Home Page

Mohandas K. Gandhi was a great leader of India who believed in nonviolence. His family has formed the Gandhi Institute to carry on his beliefs. At this site, you'll find quotes from Gandhi, such as "Your character must be above suspicion, and you must be truthful and self-controlled" and "Truth is what the voice within tells you." He also gave us his Seven Blunders of the World, and his grandson has added an eighth. What would the world be like if everyone lived as Gandhi did?

http://www.cbu.edu/Gandhi/

INDONESIA

BEAUTIFUL INDONESIA ONLINE - Home Page

The Indonesian archipelago (that means island group) consists of 17,500 islands and spans more than 3,000 miles from east to west, 1,200 miles from north to south. About 3,000 of these islands have people living on them. Indonesia has a total population of more than 190 million, making it the fourth most populous nation in the world! This site has lots to see. Wander around the largest Buddhist temple in the world. It's kind of like a pyramid, built of stone and fitted just right. This site also has a lot of photos and info on the art, culture, nature, and history of Indonesia. You've never heard of an ox-like creature called the *anoa*? That's because it's only found on the island of Sulawesi. Have you ever heard of Sulawesi? Click on Forests and then on Fauna to read more.

http://www.travel-indonesia.com/

Lonely Planet — Destination: Indonesia

Active volcanoes, hot springs, tribal masks, and an island way of life. That's Indonesia, a country of many islands. They are home to unusual exotic plant and animal species. Not only that, but over 300 languages are spoken there!

http://www.lonelyplanet.com/dest/sea/indo.htm

> **It's hard to remember, but mnemonic memory tricks are in WORDS.**

Tourism Indonesia Homepage

This official government tourism page is where you can learn about the traditional gamelan orchestra, batik textiles, and native Orang Utan primates! Indonesia is a country of over 30,000 flowering plant species, 90 species of bats, and over 17 percent of the world's species of birds. And don't forget the monkeys, the world's smallest bear, and the flying possums. That's a lot of wildlife!

http://www.tourismindonesia.com/

www.indonesiatoday.com

At this site, get the facts about Indonesia, its people, and places to see. Tour the great dive sites of underwater Indonesia, then get out of the water and make some Indonesian recipes (rice is a staple food). After that, you can relax in the tropical forests section and learn all about the birds, beats, and plants native to the area.

http://www.indonesiatoday.com/

IRAN

IRAN: An Introduction

So many things are done differently in Iran! For example, the Persian alphabet has 32 letters, compared to 26 in English. A pronunciation guide will help you here. Persian is written left to right, and it's very beautiful. This site also looks at the history, cities, pilgrimage centers, behavior rules, and literature of the culture.

http://knight3.cit.ics.saitama-u.ac.jp/hobbies/iran/farsi.html

Salam Iran Homepage

Visit this official site to learn many details about Iranian life. In the Women's section, view the varieties of traditional women's dress. In the Kids' section, you can hear the national anthem. There is also tourism information, including descriptions of foods and drinks. Did you know that you can drink diluted yogurt? Yogurt is called *mast* in Iran. According to this site, "It is served as a soft drink in summer....They dilute it with water, add a pinch of salt, spearmint, and call it *abdugh*. Iranians, particularly in rural areas, keep abdugh on hand and serve it to their family and guests on hot summer days."

http://www.salamiran.org/

IRAQ

ArabNet — Iraq

Iraq is sometimes called the "Cradle of Civilization." The earliest cultures lived between its two great rivers, the Tigris and the Euphrates. Many of the Bible's ancient cities (Nineveh, Ur, and Babylon) were in the area we now know as Iraq. This site gives a virtual tour and information on culture, history, and the government of Iraq. There is also information on the Gulf War and the invasion of Kuwait by Iraq's Saddam Hussein.

http://www.arab.net/iraq/iraq_contents.html

IRELAND

Eolas ar Sátt na hÉirwann - Information on the Irish State

The official site for the government of Ireland is filled with facts and information about Ireland and its government. You can read speeches by the current president and biographies of all the past presidents. Take a tour of the public reception areas, state dining rooms, and meeting rooms of *Áras an Uachtaráin*, the official residence of the president. Look at those Waterford crystal chandeliers—beautiful!

http://www.irlgov.ie/

An Interactive Travel Guide to the best of Ireland

Visit them all—Dublin, Cork, Belfast, Limerick, Galway, Waterford, and everywhere in between! This site also includes a virtual tour to Blarney Castle at <http://www.iol.ie/~discover/blarney.htm>. According to legend, if you kiss a special stone there, you will gain powerful and persuasive speaking skills. Kissing the real Blarney stone requires an athletic feat, but you can kiss it virtually at <http://www.irelandseye.com/blarney/1.html>. Don't get too many marks on your computer monitor, though.

http://www.iol.ie/~discover/welcome.htm

Ireland the in/complete Guide

Anyone interested in Ireland, studying Ireland, or planning a trip to Ireland should make a first stop here. Cook up some Irish recipes, trace your Irish roots, and learn about the birds, animals, and trees of the Emerald Isle.

http://www.irelandseye.com/contents.html

Irish Tourist Board

This official site will get you in the mood for a trip to Ireland! Learn about Irish scenery (it's not always green!), places to visit, food and drink, and more.

http://www.ireland.travel.ie/

Lonely Planet — Destination Ireland

This is a brief overview of travel in Ireland, as well as short facts on its history and culture. Did you know that Ireland is called "The Emerald Isle"? That's because its landscape is said to have 50 shades of green!

http://www.lonelyplanet.com/dest/eur/ire.htm

A Wee Bit O' Fun

Leprechaun followers finally have a Web site on Saint Patrick's Day and everything that goes along with it. Here, you can learn how Saint Patrick was kidnapped by pirates at the age of 16. Read how he eventually became the patron saint of Ireland. Check out the section of lucky things to do on Saint Patrick's Day!

http://www.nando.net/toys/stpaddy/stpaddy.html

ISLE OF MAN

See UNITED KINGDOM—DEPENDENCIES—ISLE OF MAN

ISRAEL

Infotour

Here's a great site for people who want to travel to Israel—either by air or by modem! Visit all the cities of this fascinating country. You'll read about museums and cultural events, learn where you can make a religious pilgrimage, visit the sites, find a place to eat—just about everything about Israel is here!

http://www.infotour.co.il/main.html

Israel Ministry of Tourism

What part of Israel would you like to visit first? Perhaps the historic Galilee area to the north? Or maybe Jerusalem, with sites sacred to three different religions: Christianity, Judaism, and Islam. This official government tourism site will give you lots of ideas, pictures, and even a brief QuickTime movie!

http://www.travelnet.co.il/tnet/mtoursm/

Maven - More than 6,000 Jewish/Israel Links!

There are two words to describe this site: neat and complete. As the title says, there are thousands of links to sites with Jewish or Israeli stuff in them. Topic sections include Youth & Students, Sports & Hobbies, Entertainment, Holocaust & Anti-Semitism, Law, Communities & Synagogues, and many more.

http://www.maven.co.il/

Nurit Reshef: 100 Years of Zionism

An excellent site that celebrates Israel's 50th anniversary. Find out about the Israeli flag, symbols, and national anthem. There's a time line, biographies of leaders and other personalities, and some fun games involving Hebrew and other subjects!

http://www.bus.ualberta.ca/yreshef/zionism/
index.html

Virtual Jerusalem

OK, here is a joke: How do you flavor your virtual latkes? With CyberSpice! Besides acting as a gateway to the Web, Virtual Jerusalem's home page is a destination for Internet users seeking Israeli and Jewish headline news, daily features, study classes, an Israel vacation guide, an extensive online Jerusalem photo gallery, and advertisements. Virtual Jerusalem also provides a chat feature where kids can discuss issues with other kids from around the world. And you can even take a virtual tour!

http://virtual.co.il/

Welcome to the State of Israel Web Site

Want to know about the Knesset, the Israeli Parliament? That information is in the National Institutes area, but in other areas you'll find links to other government departments and more. The Ministry of Tourism offers a wealth of tourist information and a jumpstation to other sites.

http://www.knesset.gov.il/israel.htm

ITALY

See also HOLY SEE

There's a real gem of a site in EARTH SCIENCE—GEOLOGY!

GF's Leaning Tower of Pisa Web Page

On August 9, 1173, they started building a bell tower in Pisa, Italy. Little did they know that, years later, people would travel from all over the world to wonder at this tower and its famous gravity-defying lean. This Web site is a *towering* achievement. It offers a real *foundation* of education and scholarship that you'll enjoy, especially the section on Leaning Tower of Pisa humor. What's new in plans to save the tower? Study the recent news stories, then contact them if you have any *tips* of your own.

http://www.endex.com/gf/buildings/ltpisa/ltpisa.html

Lonely Planet — Destination Italy

In Italy, an archaeological treasure, historical building, or church is never far from sight. At this site, learn about the history and culture of Italy, including a look at its regions and what makes them special. You can also click on further information about the major cities, including Rome and Florence, among others. And don't forget to have a look at the links!

http://www.lonelyplanet.com/dest/eur/ita.htm

Mama's Learn to Speak Italian

Ragu, maker of Italian sauces and foods, presents Mama to teach you a little useful Italian. Some are actually phrases your parents might use, such as *Hai già fatto il tuo compito per casa?* (Have you done your homework yet?) It's funny and entertaining, plus there are Real Audio files so you can hear the phrases.

http://www.eat.com/learn-italian/

Welcome to Italy - Embassy of Italy - Washington, D.C.

Listen to the national anthem of Italy as you visit this official site. You can also download the sheet music and lyrics if you want to sing along. Find info on the government, history, and tourist regions in the links provided under General Information.

http://www.italyemb.org/

IVORY COAST

See CÔTE D'IVOIRE

JAMAICA

Jamaica Bobsleigh... THE HOTTEST THING ON ICE!!

Get ready for some Cool Runnings at the official Jamaican bobsled team's home page! Since their 1988 Winter Olympic Games debut in Calgary, Alberta, the team has gained in popularity every year. At the Nagano Olympics, they finished 21st. Find out how their true story compares with the tale told in the Disney movie. It's always bobsleigh time at this site!

http://www2.cariboutpost.com/outpost/bobsleigh/

Jamaica everything you need to know and more...De web site on Jamaica.

Sell mi tree poun a swimps (Sell me three pounds of shrimps). Can you speak patois? It's called either an island dialect of English or Real English, depending on who you are talking to! You can learn some phrases in Jamaican patois here, as well as get a look at island culture, music, and history. A caution to parents: Preview this site to see if it is appropriate for your family; some parts are mildly racy.

http://www.jamaicans.com/jam.htm

The Land of Jamaica

According to this site, Jamaica's name is derived from an Aarawak word *Xaymaca*, meaning "land of wood and water." After 300 years as a British colony, Jamaica became independent in 1962, although it remains part of the British commonwealth. Learn more about its history here.

http://www.webcom.com/~travel/jam1.html

Welcome to Jamaica

Do you like beaches? How about sun and sand and fabulously fresh foods? "Come to Jamaica and feel all right," says this snappy Web site. After you look at the material for tourists, do spend some time at the wonderful collection of links. There are historical and cultural sites you won't want to miss. Hint: Click on the subject categories to bring up additional pages of links. Pay your respects to Jamaica's national heroes at *<http://jamaicaway.com/Heroes/>*.

http://www.jamaicatravel.com/

JAPAN

ASIJ Elementary School Home Page

How would you feel about attending a Japanese tea ceremony for the first time? Would you know what to do? If someone gave you a chance to try playing a large stringed instrument—a *koto*—what would it be like? The kids at The American School in Japan have done all that and more! They've written about their experiences, and you'll learn all sorts of things from their Web page. For example, the tea used in a tea ceremony is bitter, so make sure you get a piece of candy in your mouth first! Be sure to read about Japanese holidays, too, especially the New Year's celebrations.

http://www.asij.ac.jp/elementary/Welcome.html

THE IMPERIAL FAMILY OF JAPAN

Meet His Imperial Majesty the Emperor of Japan, Her Imperial Majesty the Empress, and their immediate family. This is not an official site, but the information appears to be accurate. There is also a very useful selection of links about other royalty on the Internet.

http://www.geocities.com/Tokyo/Temple/3953/

Japan: Images of A People

These examples of Japanese painting will help you better understand and appreciate the culture of Japan. This site includes lessons that have been adapted from materials developed by the education department of the Smithsonian Institution's Freer Gallery of Art and Arthur M. Sackler Gallery—the two national museums of Asian art.

http://educate.si.edu/lessons/art-to-zoo/japan/
   cover.html

Japan Information

This is the best general-interest site we could find. You can hear "Kimigayo," Japan's national anthem, plus try some links to Japanese sites on travel, culture, history, and more. You might try the Japanese art of origami or bonsai, the art of growing small trees in miniature potted landscapes. This site even has a map of the subway system! You'll find it under Japan Maps.

http://SunSITE.sut.ac.jp/asia/japan/

Japan Travel Updates

This official site is for those who need travel information and suggested places to visit in Japan. You will learn a lot about various Japanese cities at this site, but you can also find out about theme parks! Try Nikko Edo Mura if you want to experience historic Japan with ninjas and shogun generals. Or maybe you'd prefer the Fuji-Q amusement park. Besides the thrilling rides, a tamer Thomas the Tank Engine attraction opened in 1998.

http://www.jnto.go.jp/

The Japanese Tutor

This extensive guide to Japanese culture and language will let you hear everyday Japanese words and phrases. You'll also learn the polite way to count on your fingers and how to use chopsticks!

http://www.missouri.edu/~c563382/

Crack open CODES AND CIPHERS.

Kid's Window

This is a great site for children. Here, kids can visit a virtual library with stories and a picture dictionary, a restaurant filled with delicious Japanese dishes (and how to pronounce them), a school with language and crafts areas, and a gallery of art created by kids aged 3 to 18. This site was a semifinalist in the 1996 National Information Infrastructure (NII) Awards.

http://www.jwindow.net/KIDS/kids_home.html

KIDS WEB JAPAN

This site provides a look into the life and culture of Japanese children. Many Japanese kids eat miso soup, pickled vegetables, and rice for breakfast. A school lunch might consist of fish, meat, sea vegetables, and fruit. But what do they like to eat in a fast-food restaurant? Hamburgers, fried chicken, and other delights! You can find out the answers to many questions about Japanese daily life at this entertaining and informative site.

http://www.jinjapan.org/kidsweb/

Living in Tokyo is....

This excellent winner from a recent Cyberfair was created by over 40 kids from a school in Japan. They will tell you from experience that living in Tokyo is fun, delicious, interesting, challenging, and inspiring! You'll discover the fascinating material they present on Japanese customs, theater and music, sumo wrestling, foods, and more.

http://cyberfair.gsn.org/smis/contents.html

JERSEY

See UNITED KINGDOM—DEPENDENCIES—JERSEY

JORDAN

ArabNet — Jordan, Contents

Jordan's entry in ArabNet is one of the most fact-filled sites you can find concerning the country. It has an overview section that covers all the info you could find at the *World Factbook* site, plus it has a section devoted to history, geography, business, culture, government, transportation, a tour guide, and links, too. One of the crafts available in Jordan is blown glass. Originally made from sand—Jordan's deserts supplied a lot of that—now these beautiful fragile artworks are made of recycled bottles. Hungry? Jordan's national dish is called *mansaf*, which is a whole stewed lamb cooked in a yogurt sauce and served on a bed of rice.

http://www.arab.net/jordan/jordan_contents.html

JordanView: The Royal family

This is the official site of Jordan's Royal Family. From it we learn that His Majesty King Hussein bin Talal is the 42nd-generation, direct descendant of the Prophet Muhammad (peace be upon him) through the male line of the Prophet's grandson, Al-Hassan. He ascended the throne on May 3, 1953. King Hussein married Her Majesty Queen Noor Al-Hussein on June 15, 1978, and they have four children. Committed to peace in the Middle East, King Hussein is a tireless advocate and mediator. Also an accomplished sportsman, he enjoys water sports, karate, flying, and race-car driving, among many other activities.

http://www.JordanView.net/royalfamily.html

National Information System

King Hussein bin Talal, the King of Jordan, ascended the throne when he was only 17 years old! He immediately instituted some reforms, notably freedom of speech and freedom of the press. So it's no wonder that his government has a very beautiful and informative Web site. You'll find information on the royal family, a history of Jordan, a map, and what attracts tourists to this land.

http://www.nic.gov.jo/

Welcome to H.M. Queen Noor of Jordan's Web site

Her Majesty Queen Noor is one busy lady! She's involved in many national and international projects and yet she still finds time to help develop her own Web page and read the mail she gets from the Feedback form! At her site you can learn about her leadership in improving the education and health of Jordan's children, as well as her work with The Jubilee School, a magnet school for promising young Jordanian kids. Their new campus is wired and chock-full of computers. She has also won awards for her environmental activism. On top of all that, she's a mom of seven, including four of her own children, two step-children, and an adopted daughter.

http://www.noor.gov.jo/

KAZAKSTAN

Kazakstan WWW VL

Part of the collaborative WWW Virtual Library project, the Interactive Central Asia Resource Project (ICARP) hosts a very informative site for those looking for information on Kazakstan. With maps, flags, culture, links, and more, you can't go wrong.

http://www.rockbridge.net/personal/bichel/kazakh.htp

Lonely Planet - Destination Kazakstan

Half the size of the United States, Kazakstan is largely a desolate country in central Asia potentially rich in minerals but with only a few cities. Its land is scarred from Russian rocket and nuclear testing that has taken place since the 1940s. The country has not fared well since its separation from Russia.

http://www.lonelyplanet.com/dest/cas/kaz.htm

"Use the source, Luke!" and look it up in REFERENCE WORKS.

KENYA

Kenya

The author of this page has cobbled together lots of useful resources and links on Kenyan history and culture. The symbols on the Kenyan flag include a shield and two spears. You can hear the national anthem here and follow along with it in English or Swahili. Don't miss the traditional recipes.

http://www.rcbowen.com/kenya/

Welcome to Kenyaweb - Kenya's Definitive Internet Resource

KenyaWeb is the one-stop site for Kenya information and resources. You can find general information, such as history, culture, and geography, as well as government information, commercial information, tourist information, and education information. There are over 40 ethnic groups in Kenya, and you can find information on many of them here. Also famous for its national parks, Kenya's wildlife is world famous. Did you know that in Swahili, *safari* means "a journey"?

http://www.kenyaweb.com/

NET FILES

You are very hip to the latest fashions: Your front teeth have inlaid pyrite, obsidian, jade gemstones, and you wear a lot of quetzal feathers and a big hat. You can't wear jaguar sandals, though, since they are reserved for the chief only. You're a member of an ancient civilization. Who are you?

Answer: You're a Maya. Discover more classic Maya beauty tips at *http://www.halfmoon.org/beauty.html*

KIRIBATI

Welcome to Kiribati

A country of many small coral atolls, Kiribati was a former colony of Great Britain. Its flag shows a yellow frigate bird flying in front of a sunrise over the blue sea. There are complex rules of behavior you need to know in case you ever visit: for example, never touch anyone on the head or walk across their outstretched legs! At this site, read more about proper etiquette in this Pacific island nation.

http://www.travisa.com/Kiribati/Kiribati.htm

KOREA, NORTH

DPRK - Democratic People's Republic of Korea

This site is a jumpstation to many resources about "The People's Korea," including general information, travel info, and political and current events. This is an interesting perspective; contrast it with views on North Korean topics from other news sources around the world.

http://www.kimsoft.com/dprk.htm

KOREAN CENTRAL NEWS AGENCY

If you want to know what the news is in North Korea, this site will provide today's stories as well as an archive of old articles. What's interesting is that there is no news at all about anything bad, such as the famine that has swept the country in the last few years.

http://www.kcna.co.jp/

North Korea - A Country Study

Also known today as the Democratic People's Republic of Korea, North Korea contains excavations revealing that humans inhabited the peninsula half a million years ago. Its history has been influenced by China as long ago as the fourth century B.C. and more recently by Russia and Japan. This site has extensive information about North Korea, but it was compiled in 1993, so recent information is not included.

http://lcweb2.loc.gov/frd/cs/kptoc.html

KOREA, SOUTH

CHONG WA DAE

Would you like to visit the President of South Korea? Maybe even send him a postcard? Here's an opportunity to do just that without leaving the comfort of your own home. You will learn about President Kim Dae-jung and about his home, Chong Wa Dae, also known as the Blue House. There's also a terrific area for kids at this site, where you can learn about the national symbols, tigers, and the Korean language.

http://www.bluehouse.go.kr/english/

Korea Government Homepage

The *Taegukki* is Korea's national flag. It contains symbols of peace, unification, creation, light, and eternity. Purity, harmony, and balance are also represented in the flag by the colors it contains. Read a brief outline of the country's history, its people, and culture as you navigate through this site.

http://www.gcc.go.kr/ehtm/ushome.html

Korea Kidsight

This highly polished site has an excellent array of resources about Korea aimed at kids. Don't be fooled, though: the information here is not trivial. You'll find Korean art, complete with descriptions, Korean recipes, and annotated pictures of traditional Korean clothing. There's also an accounting of Korean history dating back to the legend of Tan'gun and how he established Choson, Land of the Morning Calm, over 4,000 years ago.

http://korea.insights.co.kr/forkid/

Korea Window

Explore South Korea in detail. The Culture and the Arts section is particularly interesting, featuring traditional handicrafts and music. There is much more to discover at this site about Korean society, economy, history, and art, so plan to stay awhile.

http://www.kocis.go.kr/

> There's some funny business going on in the CIRCUSES AND CLOWNS section!

Seoul Focus

This is the official home page of the capital of South Korea, the city of Seoul. You can learn all about the city and its mayor, cultural festivals, tourist sights, and more. The city has a new emblem and a new mascot; read about them here.

http://www.metro.seoul.kr/

KUWAIT

The State of Kuwait - Ministry of Information Office, Washington, DC, USA

Do you have a question about Kuwait? Here's an official source of information. Although known for its oil production, Kuwait also has a long maritime tradition. In fact, the national emblem of Kuwait is a "falcon with outspread wings embracing a *dhow* (a boat) sailing on blue and white waves."

http://www.kuwait.info.nw.dc.us/

KYRGYZSTAN

Kyrgyzstan WWW VL

The WWW Virtual Library page on Kyrgyzstan includes loads of links to material on this nation in central Asia, carved out of the former Soviet Union. The history of the people is very interesting—the record goes back as far as 2 B.C.! The Kyrghyz people began as an alliance of nomadic tribes; in fact, one interpretation of the word *Kyrghyz* is "forty tribes."

http://www.rockbridge.net/personal/bichel/kyrgyz.htp

LAOS

Discovering Laos

Laos, or Lao People's Democratic Republic, used to be called Lane Xang, "The Land of a Million Elephants." Its culture is primarily based on Buddhist philosophy, reflected by its many Buddhist temples, statues, and art. Much of this site is separated into pages about Laos' various provinces, with a description of each.

http://www.laoembassy.com/discover/

My Travel in Laos

This site is a collection of beautiful pictures of Laos taken during a 16-day trip started on December 29, 1995. There are images of the countryside, temples, animals, and children. Share this journey with the photographer and return with some lasting ideas about life in Laos.

http://www2.gol.com/users/akihito/html/laos.html

LATVIA

Embassy of Latvia - Washington, D.C.

Latvia is one of the Baltic nations (the others are Lithuania and Estonia) located on the Baltic Sea. It achieved independence in 1991 due to the breakup of the Soviet Union. Latvians have a long history of cultural and artistic tradition—and they love to sing! According to this page, "More than 1.4 million folk songs, or 'dainas,' almost always four-line couplets reflecting the ethics, morals and lifestyles of ancient Latvians, have been identified, thanks largely to the pioneering work of Krisjanis Barons (1835 -1923)." There is also an interesting history of the Latvian National Emblem at <http://home.earthlink.net/ ~ibezdechi/gerb.htm>. Lions, griffins, sun, and stars— what do they all mean?

http://www.virtualglobe.com/latvia/

Learning Latvian Online

This resource teaches just a little Latvian with audio files and crossword puzzles! You can also see and hear the letters of the alphabet and learn some of the history of the language.

http://www.codefusion.com/latvianasp/latonline.asp

LEBANON

Embassy of Lebanon

The Embassy of Lebanon in Washington, D.C., has a very nicely designed page that gives a lot of background information on the country. You can take a virtual tour to many cities, including Bsharri, birthplace and gravesite of Kahlil Gibran, Lebanon's famous poet, artist, and mystic.

http://www.embofleb.org/

lebanon-online

Lebanon has a narrow coastline on the Mediterranean Sea, backed by mountain ranges. It has an average of 300 sunny days a year, so bring your hat and sunglasses. This site is a jumpstation to many Web pages about Lebanon.

http://www.lebanon-online.com/

Ministry of Tourism Official Web Site

This site contains many interesting facts about Lebanon. For instance, did you know that this country dates back as far as the fourteenth century B.C.? That's a *very* long time ago. However, it wasn't until the Phoenicians established a small trading station, about the ninth century B.C., that the area really became settled. Then along came the Romans, and then the Crusades, and, well, we don't want to spoil the ending—stop by this site and read the story for yourself.

http://www.lebanon-tourism.gov.lb/main.htm

LESOTHO

Lesotho

Lesotho is one of only two independent states in the world that is completely surrounded by another country. Lesotho is located inside the country of South Africa (the other independent state is the Holy See, Vatican City, surrounded by Italy). *O a utlwa?* In other words, are you listening? You should be! This page has a lot to say. You'll find a description and picture of the national flag of Lesotho, links (including one to learn some of the language), maps, and more.

http://www.sas.upenn.edu/African_Studies/
    Country_Specific/Lesotho.html

LIBERIA

Ijoma Flemister's Fokpah Liberia WebSpace

Ijoma Robert Flemister has been called to the special station of *fokpah*—someone who will put personal interests aside and try to heal the country and its people. His site is very interesting. Here is an example: "We, Elders of the Land of Liberia, assembled at Zouzon by the Grace of the Almighty and under the commanding authority of the Ancestors, present these sentiments. Let them that have ears hear, know and act. We, Elders of the Land of Liberia, hear the roar of Liberia's silence. We fear the rumble of the storm of poverty and see the fury of ignorance. We hear the cry of our people... 'How long,...how long?' Our children have failed us and we have failed our children. We are on bended knee for the blood that has flowed across our land during these shameless dark days. Yet, we lift our eyes unto the hills from whence cometh our help. The incredible atrocities of war that we inflict on ourselves shall end; the blatant denial of hope shall pass; the rape and waste of our natural resources shall cease; the overwhelmimg fear of brother for brother shall fade away; peace, unity and common sense shall prevail; we shall sing and dance once again - soon, very soon...."

http://www.infinet.com/~ijoma/

The Liberian Connection News Magazine

At this site, you will find answers to questions about Liberian statistics, community events, pictures, history, and government. Also read current Liberian news, check the community events, and visit the Liberian embassy page. Parents: Outside links have not been checked.

http://www.gis.net/~toadoll/

LIBYA

ArabNet — Libya

Libya has a long history of name changes. In 1951, it was *Al-Mamlaka Al-Libiya Al-Motahidda* (The United Kingdom of Libya). On September 1, 1969, the day of the Libyan revolution, it was *Al-Jamhooriya Al-Arabiya Al-Libiyah* (The Libyan Arab Republic). On March 8, 1977, it was *Al-Jamahiriya Al-Arabiya Al-Libiyah Ash-Shabiya Al-Ishtrakia* (The Socialist People's Libyan Arab Jamahiriya). The flag of the country has changed each time. Presently, it is a plain, dark green rectangle with no symbols or any other ornament on it. At this site, read about how Libya's history reaches back as far as the twelfth century B.C., when it was inhabited by the Phoenicians.

http://www.arab.net/libya/libya_contents.html

Libyana

This site is perfect for anyone needing information for a report on Libya. Read about the Sahara Desert, "the great sand sea," and the oases scattered through it, which provide water and refuge. Find a link to some outstanding maps in the History section and read through sections on art, crafts, poetry, music, food, and more.

http://www.libyana.org/

LIECHTENSTEIN

Liechtenstein

Tiny Liechtenstein has an area of only 61 square miles, and it has a population of 300,000 people. This guide, from the Liechtenstein National Tourist Office, takes you on a virtual vacation to this beautiful country. Admire the pictures and learn the history of Liechtenstein. The actual date on which the Principality of Liechtenstein was founded was January 23, 1719, although settlements had been there since 800 B.C.

http://www.searchlink.li/tourist/

Liechtenstein News

This official newspaper site is more than just current events. It is also a history and information site. For example, you can find out about the history of the royal family (H.S.H. Prince Hans-Adam II and family) in one area, then you can shoot over to Art Market and check out some of the latest Liechtenstein art. Or if you are into stamp collecting, try that section. The first Liechtenstein postage stamps went on sale in early 1912. They are beautiful and cover many subjects. Sales of stamps account for about 3 percent of the country's revenues; you can order them online.

http://www.news.li/

LITHUANIA

Lithuania Academic and Research Network Litnet

We know what you want. You want a great site that has Lithuanian information. Guess what? Here it is. You can find tourist tips, country statistics, geography, Lithuanian Internet information, and much more. The section on Traditions (in Cultural Heritage) lists the following holiday, which sounds strangely familiar: "Zemaitija, the Lithuanian Lowlands in the western part of the country, is famous for its Uzgavenes masquerades when groups of both children and grown-ups, disguised as animals, birds, and fantastic beasts can be seen roaming the streets of villages and towns. Zemaitija is also famous for its woodcarvers specializing in masks for the Uzgavenes carnivals." Hmmm. We wonder how to say "Trick or Treat!" in Lithuanian.

http://www.ktl.mii.lt/

Lithuanian Folk Culture Centre

The highlight of this site is the collection of great recipes for tasty Lithuanian food. After you stop drooling, you can check out a couple of online Lithuanian books or see what's coming up on the events schedule. If that doesn't satisfy you, click on the link to other cultural sites, where you can look at detailed color drawings of the national costume through history.

http://neris.mii.lt/heritage/lfcc/lfcc.html

IN MODERN TIMES, WHAT FAMOUS PEOPLE WERE BORN ON DECEMBER 25?

Answer:
* Rod Serling, creator of *The Twilight Zone*
* Conrad Hilton, founder of the Hilton Hotel chain
* Louis Chevrolet, auto racer and designer, whose name is on General Motors cars
* Clara Barton, founder of the American Red Cross
And many others. Find out who shares your birthday at *http://www.eb.com/lives/lives.htcl*

LKL - Lithuanian Basketball League

One of the fastest-growing crazes in Lithuania is basketball. Team Lithuania took a bronze medal at the Olympics, and now, more and more Lithuanians are getting excited about the sport. There are even Lithuanians on NBA teams! You can learn about the Lithuanian Basketball League right here.

http://www.lkl.lt/

LUXEMBOURG

A visit to Luxembourg

The Grand Duchy of Luxembourg is a constitutional monarchy, located between Belgium, France, and Germany. It is only 51 miles long and 36 miles wide. Its major export is steel, although it is known as a world financial center, too. This site has a nice tour, loads of links, and beautiful photos.

http://www.geocities.com/TheTropics/6434/

MACAU

See PORTUGAL—DEPENDENCIES—MACAU

MACEDONIA, THE FORMER YUGOSLAV REPUBLIC OF

Macedonia

The Republic of Macedonia is located on the Balkan Peninsula, an area situated at the crossroads of the three continents of Europe, Asia, and Africa. It borders on Greece, the Republic of Serbia, Bulgaria, and Albania. Archaeologists have found remnants of ancient cities in Macedonia, and so Macedonia is really a country of old and new. It has many cultural art treasures, religious icons, and natural beauty, including high mountains and thermal hot springs.

http://www.soros.org.mk/mk/en/

MADAGASCAR

Madagasikara - The Rainbow Island

Madagascar is an unusual country surrounded by the Indian Ocean. This Web site provides a wonderful look at this fascinating island. History, climate, and culture are described here, along with unusual subjects like fauna (it's a sanctuary for lemur species), music (listen to sound samples), and tourism (they say there are only two seasons in Madagascar: the rainy season and the season when it rains). If you want to learn about Madagascar, you've come to the right place.

http://www.dstc.edu.au/AU/staff/andry/Mada.html

MALAWI

MALAWI

What would you like to know about the Republic of Malawi? Where is it? How is the weather? What is the capital? You can find the answers to those questions at this site and probably at many other sites, too. But do you have other questions? What about e-mail—is it available in Malawi? What is the latest news about Malawi? What does Malawi look like? There are answers to those and a lot more questions here as well. There are some great pictures, too! Find a little more information at the University of Pennsylvania's African Studies Malawi Page by clicking on links. You'll also find a lot of other pages about Malawi.

http://spicerack.sr.unh.edu/~llk/

You know something the Net doesn't—create your own home page! Look in the INTERNET—WEBWEAVING AND HTML section to find out how!

MALAYSIA

Education In Malaysia

Here's your opportunity to visit real schools in Malaysia. Many high schools in Malaysia have home pages, and most have text in English. By starting on this page of links for Malaysian universities, schools, and libraries, you can find high school and lower schools under the Schools section. Many of the school home pages include picture tours of the school and interesting histories. If you like to browse, and you would like to visit some schools in Malaysia, start right here! Maybe you can get your school to "link up" to a school in Malaysia.

http://www.jaring.my/msia/newhp/educ/educ.html

MALAYSIA HOMEPAGE

About 80 percent of the land of Malaysia is covered with tropical rain forests. This beautiful country is in Southeast Asia. To find out its history, go to this Web page! This home page is so full of wonderful information about Malaysia and its people that you could do a whole report just on Malaysia's national flower, the hibiscus. But there is a great deal more, complete with maps and pictures. You'll find the latest news, links to government and tourism sites, and a background section that is very educational, too.

http://www.jaring.my/

RTM.Net

If you've ever wondered what's on the radio or television in a foreign country, then you should visit this site. Here you can listen to six different radio stations in Malaysia. You will hear the actual, live broadcasts over the Internet, and you may hear Bahasa Malaysia, English, Mandarin, or Tamil. Check out the television schedule in Malaysia. How many TV programs do you recognize? You will also find information on the history of television and radio in Malaysia. Explore the many sounds of Malaysian radio broadcasts, from music to educational fare. Tune in!

http://www.asiaconnect.com.my/rtm-net/

Visit Malaysia

At this official site you can send e-postcards of colorful Malaysian scenes, get recipes for three sample menus, and discover 12 different tourist destinations. There are also numerous audio files, including popular and traditional Malay music.

http://www.tourism.gov.my/

Welcome To The Star Online Malaysia

Do you want to know what's happening in Malaysia? Extra, extra, you can read all about it! A weekly edition of *The Star* Online can be delivered right to your computer. Not all of this weekly online newspaper is light reading, but there is quality coverage of current Malaysian news in areas such as politics, sports, technology, education, business, and weather. If you really want to know what's happening in Malaysia, you have to check it out.

http://www.jaring.my/~star/

MALDIVES

Maldives - The Last Paradise

The Maldives is a nation of over 1,000 small coral islands in the Indian Ocean. A quarter of a million tourists visit the Maldives each year. At this commercial Web site, a tour of the Maldives, full of beautiful pictures and useful information, begins in the capital city of Malé (pronounced "maa lay"). Why not see the sights of the Maldives and learn about this unusual country, too?

http://www.asiaville.com/corporate/maldives/

Visit Maldives

Only about 200 of the 1,190 small islands of the Maldives are inhabited. This country, located off the southern tip of India, is a favorite of tourists, but natives rarely mingle with the visitors. Many islands are covered with beautiful tropical vegetation and palm trees. Others are only sand and coral. Set sail for this official site to find facts about the Maldives as well as tourist information.

http://www.visitmaldives.com/

MALI

An Introduction to Mali

True to its name, this site is a good introduction to this African nation. Most famous for the city of Timbuktu and the long Niger River, Mali is the largest country in western Africa. Learn about the legendary cities of Timbuktu and Djenne, the great river Niger, and the Sahara Desert. Now climb down off that camel and look around!

http://www.interknowledge.com/mali/

MALTA

FOCUS on MALTA

This exceptionally thorough Web site includes lots of valuable information about Malta. Malta is known as the "Cradle of the Mediterranean." Its heritage is rich in culture and history, dating back over six thousand years. Today, it's a seaside paradise with a pleasant climate and lots of warm Mediterranean hospitality.

http://focusmm.com.au/malta/ma_anamn.htm

It's Malta

Among the most popular recreational activities on Malta are scuba diving and golf. But other sports, such as windsurfing, boating, soccer, and tennis, are popular too. It's easy to see why the Maltese people are usually considered friendly and relaxed. It's also easy to see why so many people visit Malta. Visiting Malta is even fun on the World Wide Web. See for yourself!

http://www.visitmalta.com/

MAGNET HOME PAGES

You'll find information about every aspect of this country at this "Official Website of the Maltese Government." Information about the geography, history, and people of the country is yours in a click, as are a large assortment of photos taken in various parts of Malta.

http://www.magnet.mt/

Everyone's flocking to BIRDS!

MARSHALL ISLANDS

Marshall Islands

This group of atolls and reefs is in the North Pacific Ocean, about one-half of the way from Hawaii to Papua New Guinea. The group has a population of over 60,000 people. It has had a free association agreement with the U.S. since 1990 and became an independent nation in 1991. One of the atolls is Bikini, famous for the first military atomic bomb tests. You can read an account of these tests and see a photo at <http://magic.geol.ucsb.edu/~fisher/bikini.htm>. The bikini swimsuit, a very explosive new fashion, was invented about the same time as the weapon, and it was named for this atoll. Nearby islands with indigenous people were evacuated in 1948; some of them, and their descendants, are asking to be repatriated to their homelands.

http://www.escapeartist.com/marshall/marshall.htm

Marshall Islands Internet Guide (RMI Online)

This is the official site of the Republic of the Marshall Islands' U.S. embassy. You can see the flag, the official seal, the national anthem, and many maps of many atolls. Check out the audio phrasebook of Marshallese and information on traditional tattooing and foods. There's also a very interesting section on ordering stamps from the Marshall Islands. Subjects include Diana, Princess of Wales, Elvis, and folklore from the Islands.

http://www.rmiembassyus.org/

MARTINIQUE

See FRANCE—DEPENDENCIES—MARTINIQUE

MAURITANIA

Africa Online: News & Information

This site is comprised mainly of factual information commonly found in the *World Factbook*, except that this site includes a larger, more detailed map, in color. Mauritania is a hot and dry country in northwestern Africa that has suffered through many droughts. Start your journey to Mauritania here, gathering facts, and then cross the Sahara and search the Web for more!

http://www.africaonline.com/AfricaOnline/
    countries/mauritania.html

The Embassy of Mauritania

Welcome to the embassy of Mauritania. Mauritania is situated on the northern coast of Africa, bordered on the north by Algeria and the Sahara, in the east by Mali, and on the south by Senegal. Approximately three-fourths of Mauritania's territory is covered by the Sahara Desert. Minerals currently mined include iron ore, gypsum, copper, and phosphate. Mauritanians receive free schooling and health care from the government.

http://www.embassy.org/mauritania/

MAURITIUS

LSE SU Mauritian Society: Mauritius

Mauritius is a small island country in the Indian Ocean, located several hundred miles east of Madagascar. The island was formed by volcanoes, but they are no longer active. The now-extinct dodo bird originated here. Mauritius is a popular travel destination and features the attraction of the séga dance and music, which was connected with the early slave trade.

http://www.lse.ac.uk/clubs/mtiansoc/mauritius.htm

Mauritius Welcomes You

Children of Indian, Chinese, French, Creole, and English descent are the welcoming faces on this official page of the Tourist Promotion Authority. They are smiling from ear to ear, and no wonder: The sun is shining brightly and the waves are gently lapping onto the white sand beach. Mark Twain once visited this paradise and said, "God created Mauritius and then the heaven."

http://www.mauritius.net/

MAYOTTE

See FRANCE—DEPENDENCIES—MAYOTTE

MEXICO

The Art of Mexican Native Children

Kids everywhere like to paint and draw. True to form, kids in Mexico like to do artwork, and it's fantastic. See samples of drawings from Mayo, Tzeltal, and Maya children at this Web page. The colors will grab you, and the world they paint is filled with animals, musicians, and festivals. Brighten your day and take a look now!

http://www.embamexcan.com/KidsPage/k-artof.html

The Azteca Web Page

Did you know that many kids in the United States are of Mexican descent? They are proudly called *Chicanos y Chicanas*. Understanding what it means to be Chicano is about many things: music, history, culture, and language. To learn about this fascinating culture, this page is a good pace to start.

http://www.azteca.net/aztec/

Cinco de Mayo

Do you like a really good party? Well, every May 5, many Latino Americans and citizens of Mexico celebrate a grand event, and they have a party in the process. In 1862, on Cinco de Mayo (that's Spanish for the fifth of May), a handful of Mexican troops defeated a much larger and better-armed force of soldiers from France. This victory showed that a small group, strengthened by unity, can overcome overwhelming odds. Ever since, Cinco de Mayo is celebrated with music, tasty food, parades, and a party.

http://latino.sscnet.ucla.edu/cinco.html

Day of the Dead

On November 2, Mexicans celebrate the annual Day of the Dead. It's not a sad occasion. They make special foods and prepare a feast to honor their ancestors. They have picnics on their relatives' graves so the dead can join in the festivities, too. One of the special foods is called "Bread of the Dead" (*pan de muerto*). The baker hides a plastic skeleton in each rounded loaf, and it's good luck to bite into the piece with the skeleton! People also give each other candy skeletons, skulls, and other treats with a death design. The holiday has complex social, religious, and cultural meanings. Learn more about this celebration here.

http://www.public.iastate.edu/~rjsalvad/
    scmfaq/muertos.html

DAY OF THE DEAD - DIA DE LOS MUERTOS

Learn many of the traditions and rituals surrounding this Mexican holiday, when the dead pay a visit to their old homes and are welcomed with special foods and festivities. This site has a rich section with links to explore, but parents should note that we didn't get to look at all of them.

http://www.mexconnect.com/mex_/feature/
    daydeadindex.html

There's a very important desk in the U.S. Senate chambers. It's one particular desk in the back row, and there's something in it that the Senators sometimes need to help them make laws. What is it?

Answer: It's candy! The "candy desk" was a tradition started by Senator George Murphy (R-CA). He "originated the practice of keeping a supply of candy in his desk for the enjoyment of fellow senators. This desk was subsequently passed on to other members for use, but the tradition of keeping candy in the desk that occupies that particular place in the back row of the chamber continues." Read more about it at
http://www.senate.gov/curator/sdesk.htm

Embassy of Mexica in Canada

This official home page was under construction when we visited, but we especially liked the Kid's Pages. Learn about the toys and games kids play in Mexico. Ever heard of a piñata? It's a papier-mâché figure filled with candies and fruits. The piñata is hung over a tree branch, suspended by a rope. Someone holds onto and controls the opposite end of the rope. Blindfolded children take turns swinging at the piñata with a stick, but it is pulled out of the way at the last minute. Eventually, someone takes a lucky swing, the piñata breaks, and everyone scrambles for the treats. Surprisingly, the piñata is thought to have been invented in China, not Mexico. You can learn to make one at this site.

http://www.embamexcan.com/

Lotería: Mexican Bingo Games

Latinos like to play a fun game called *Lotería*. It's like Bingo, but it has colorful pictures with Spanish names instead of numbers and letters. Would you like to play the game? Go to the Lotería page on the World Wide Web. It's fun!

http://www.mercado.com/juventud/loteria/loteria.htm

MayaQuest '98

Who were the Maya, and what happened to their civilization? This site tells you all about the history and cultures of this lost nation. The ancient Maya had an apparently healthy culture from around A.D. 250. They were masters of mathematics, building huge pyramids in the jungles of what is now Mexico and Central America. They had complex astronomical calendars and engineering for improving agriculture. During the ninth century, their civilization collapsed. No one knows exactly where they went or what happened to them. From this site, you can follow an expedition team called MayaQuest, searching the jungle for archaeological answers in 1995, 1996, and 1997.

http://mayaquest.classroom.com/

Mexico: an Endless Journey

This is the official home page of the Ministry of Tourism. It describes the various states and regions of Mexico, which vary from temperate to torrid as the geography moves from the seaside to the jungle. Mexico has a long prehistory. Its original settlers may have come from Asia, over the Alaskan land bridge. According to this site, Olmec, Toltec, Maya, and Aztec cultures all left their marks on the land: "The architectural remnants of these civilizations can be found in virtually every corner of the country; more than 11,000 archaeological sites are registered." You can also read all about Mexican food and festivals here. And remember, the Mole Festival is *not* about small rodents. It celebrates *mole* (pronounced "MOH-lay"), which is "a rich, thick sauce made from various chilies, ground peanuts, spices, sesame seed, and chocolate."

http://www.mexico-travel.com/

Have an order of pi in MATH AND ARITHMETIC.

MICRONESIA, FEDERATED STATES OF

Welcome to the FSM Government Home Page

This island group, called the Federated States of Micronesia, is in the North Pacific Ocean, about three-quarters of the way from Hawaii to Indonesia. Its landscape varies from low coral atolls to high forested mountains. About 123,000 people live on these islands, which achieved independent nation status in 1991. Chuuk is a famous destination for scuba divers who want to explore a sunken Japanese fleet. Rural Kosrae has the smallest land mass. Pohnpei is famous for gourmet pepper. Yap consists of one volcanic complex of four islands plus 11 inhabited outer islands and atolls. Here you can learn something about each of these states.

http://www.fsmgov.org/

MOLDOVA

Virtual MOLDOVA - The Home Page

Moldova is a country in Eastern Europe, northeast of Romania. For a long time, Moldova was a part of the Soviet Union (U.S.S.R.), but it became independent in 1991. Moldova and Romania have many similarities; in fact, it would be very hard to tell if a person were speaking Moldovan or Romanian. The languages are almost the same! Find out more about this young independent nation by visiting this page.

http://www.info.polymtl.ca/zuse/tavi/www/Moldova.html

MONACO

The 700 Years of Grimaldi

Monaco's Grimaldi dynasty has ruled this small principality for the past seven hundred years! Your grandparents may remember how exciting it was in 1956, when the dashing Prince Rainier III married the American film star Grace Kelly. You can read about the stirring history of the Grimaldis, including biographies of Rainier and Prince Albert, his son. Surprisingly, Monaco did not join the United Nations until 1993.

http://www.monaco.mc/monaco/700ans/

Monaco

The Principality of Monaco is a tiny country on the southern border of France. Monaco's beautiful coastline is on the Mediterranean Sea. How small is Monaco? The land area is about one square mile! If it's facts about Monaco's geography, people, government, and climate you're after, then you've come to the right little Web page.

http://www.intergo.com/Library/ref/atlas/
   europe/mn.htm

The Monaco Guide

Monaco is one of the most fascinating places in the world. It has a long and captivating history of kings, lords, and princes. Today's Monaco is a favorite for tourists around the world. The climate is neither too hot nor too cold. Swim with the fishes, or travel a short distance to ski. Visit the glamorous city of Monte Carlo, with its exciting Casino Square flashing at night. There is a tremendous cultural side to Monaco, too, with much theater, music, and art. This page is very thorough, containing information on everything from history to entertainment. The sights are beautiful. See for yourself!

http://www.monaco.mc/monaco/guide_en.html

MONGOLIA

Mongolia Resource Page

Mongolia is a beautiful country where lush forests meet stark deserts. Nomads still travel the lands as they did hundreds of years ago. But one major change in recent years is that Mongolia has now become a democracy, and it's recently gotten on the Net. Visit this informative Web page from the Soros Foundation and learn about Mongolia, including information on traditional tentlike homes, called *ger* (called yurts by non-Mongolians).

http://www.soros.org/mongolia.html

Virtual Mongol

Not everyone can travel to Mongolia. But you can virtually visit Mongolia on your screen! This WWW site contains dozens of quality pictures of beautiful and historic Mongolia. The picture index identifies the subject of each image. The shots are divided into categories: nature, people, religion, and history. There are links to other sites about this fascinating country, too. Don't miss the throat singing pages, and see if you can learn to make those haunting multitoned sounds.

http://www.kiku.com/electric_samurai/
   virtual_mongol/virtual_mongol.html

MONTENEGRO

See SERBIA AND MONTENEGRO

MONTSERRAT

See UNITED KINGDOM—DEPENDENCIES—
MONTSERRAT

MOROCCO

Morocco Guided Tour

When you take the online guided tour of Morocco, you hear the music, see the sights, and even get a taste of Moroccan cooking. Well, maybe not an actual taste, but several recipes are here. You'll find a description of dining customs in Morocco, too. So even if your computer can't give you an actual taste of Moroccan food, with a little imagination, reading this page can be just like being there. Hey, do you smell *meshwee*?

http://www.dsg.ki.se/morocco/

Welcome to Morocco

Click on the Foundation section to get to the facts on this country. You can also read a short biography of His Majesty, King Hassan II, and see photos of him and the rest of the royal family. There is a gallery of plant and animal life, too, and you can admire some of the minerals found in Morocco: agate, malachite, and desert rose, which does indeed look like a frozen flower. If you want to see beautiful floral patterns and other designs, try the link to the Carpets of Rabat.

http://www.mincom.gov.ma/english/e_page.html

MOZAMBIQUE

Mozambique Page

Mozambique is an African country fortunate enough to be rich in natural resources. Unfortunately, it struggled with a civil war for years. The war finally ended in 1992, and today the country is still rebuilding from its effects. The coastline of Mozambique is long, and fishing is important to the economy. Prawns and shrimp are major exports. Get the facts on Mozambique here.

http://www.sas.upenn.edu/African_Studies/
Country_Specific/Mozambique.html

MYANMAR (BURMA)

Destination: Myanmar (Burma)

Although Myanmar (Burma) is trying to promote tourism, many people are refusing to travel there, because reports of an oppressive government, slave labor, and other disturbing stories have surfaced. You should be aware of the issues. This page collects not only general information on the country but also links to sites where you can learn more about the Free Burma movement. A caution to parents: The Myanmar (Burma) story is violent.

http://www.lonelyplanet.com/dest/sea/myan.htm

Myanmar Home Page (The Goldenland)

Myanmar is the new name of the country formerly known as Burma. It has a long history, with archaeological evidence of settlement as early as 5,000 years ago! This home page will give you a good introduction to its symbols and culture. For example, you can learn about the wet and wild holiday called the Thingyan Water Festival. Celebrated in April and lasting three days, it symbolizes the change (*Thingyan*) from the old year to the new. Since water is a symbol of cleanliness and rebirth, everybody is splashed with large amounts of water—even tourists, so bring your rain gear!

http://www.myanmar.com/gov/tourist/wel.htm

NAMIBIA

REPUBLIC OF NAMIBIA

Namibia is a large country in southwest Africa. Despite the country's size, its population is quite small. The reason is because Namibia is one of the driest countries on Earth. Almost half of Namibia is desert, and droughts are common. Incredibly, some areas are rich in wildlife. Namibia has been an independent country since 1990. Learn about the struggles, and triumphs, of this interesting African country by visiting this official Web site.

http://www.republicofnamibia.com/

NET FILES

What do you get if you walk the dog correctly on your first try?

Answer: Five points when competing in the American Yo-Yo Association Competition. Find out more at http://ayya.pd.net/list.html

NAURU

Nauru Index Page

Coconut trees sway gently in the tropical breeze. You stretch out on the sandy beach and watch the sunset. You're uneasy. But why? Why wouldn't you be content on the pleasant South Pacific island of Nauru? There is no unemployment, and Nauruans have high incomes. Maybe it's the sinking feeling of knowing that the island's sustaining industry must end soon. The phosphate mining will be exhausted by 2000. Or it could be that you sense the danger of near-complete dependence on other nations for food and water, other than what rainwater can be collected in rooftop storage tanks (most fresh water is imported from Australia). Check out this site for clues to what makes life so uncertain for an island republic that is only a tenth the size of Washington, D.C. The *World Factbook* page on Nauru is at <http://www.odci.gov/cia/publications/factbook/nr.html>.

http://www.tcol.co.uk/nauru/nauru.htm

NEPAL

Department of Tourism (Nepal)

This official site has wonderful photos of Nepal, as well as facts, figures, and more. Find out about the elephant polo matches, the living goddess, and the only country with a nonrectangular flag. See a picture of the flag at <http://fotw.digibel.be/flags/np.html>.

http://www.south-asia.com/dotn/

A Visit to Nepal

"Please do not disturb the monkeys. This temple belongs to them." That's one unusual sign Scott Yost found during a six-week visit to Nepal. Learn about this enchanting country and what it took to get there and back, through the eyes of a man who had admittedly "never done anything like this before." Now, he has made a way for us to discover Nepal through his detailed personal journal entries, which are linked to trek maps, a searchable index, and rich photography. Make your own cybervisit to Nepal through Yost's beautifully executed site. You might also like the Nepal Home Page (look in "Nepal on the Web" under "General Nepal Pages") for basic information and lots more.

http://www.vic.com/nepal/

NETHERLANDS

The Flying Dutchman's Page - main

The name Netherlands is derived from the Dutch word *neder*, meaning "low," referring to the fact that much of this country is below sea level. A system of dikes and canals has allowed the Netherlands to reclaim land and use it for farming and other purposes. According to this page, "Approximately a third of the entire country lies below sea level at high tide. Another 25% is so low-lying that it would be subject to [flooding] if it were not for the surrounding dunes and dikes and the regular pumping of excess water. The lowest point is 6.7 m (22 ft.) below mean sea level, immediately to the northeast of Rotterdam." This page has lots of general interest info on the Netherlands and its people and culture.

http://www.proqc.com.tw/~jeroen/main.html

Gouda

Yes, it's like the cheese. But Gouda is also the name of a medieval Dutch city. A stop at this site on the virtual Netherlands tour is rich with different things to do and see. Learn about the unique role that water has played in the life of Holland and the city of Gouda in particular. Read the illustrated stories of some of the more bizarre goings-on over the years. Take a look at the products of the region: cheese (of course), clay pipes, candles, and more. The beautiful, original photography will give you a feel for the Dutch way of life as you stroll Gouda's virtual streets.

http://www.xs4all.nl/~eleede/

The Holland Site

Windmills? Wooden shoes? Tulips? Distinctive women's headgear? Yes, you've got all those in Holland (also known as the Netherlands), but did you know about Van Gogh's connection to the "low country"? Did you know about the castles (over 300 of them) or extensive cycling opportunities? See it all, with lots of great color photos, as you easily navigate this attractive and informative site from the official Board of Tourism. From how to get there to how to get around once you're there, this is the place to go to glimpse the historic past and the future of this beautiful land. And with the 20 questions and answers for the "Holland uninitiated," you might just get by without the locals seeing "tourist" written all over your face.

http://www.nbt.nl/holland/

Teylers Museum

Teylers Museum is the oldest museum in Holland. It has the traditional stuff you'd expect from a great gallery. In addition to its excellent permanent exhibits, it also has rotating exhibits that feature the coolest new stuff. This site has lots of graphics, whose clever design is to carry you from one great find to the next. If you can't make it to the Netherlands this year, do the next best thing and take a leisurely tour of the anything-but-boring Teylers Museum.

http://www.nedpunt.nl/teylersmuseum/engels/
    hal.html

DEPENDENCIES—ARUBA

Aruba - Original Official Travel Guide

Aruba is a small, desertlike island just off the coast of Venezuela. Aruba is part of the Dutch realm. Formerly part of the Netherlands Antilles, Aruba was on its way to independence. However, in 1990, Aruba requested and received cancellation of the Netherlands' agreement to give independence to the island in 1996. Aruba's official language is Dutch. Its 85-degree weather and white sand beaches make it a favorite vacation spot. If you like sailing, scuba diving, or windsurfing, you'll love Aruba.

http://www.interknowledge.com/aruba/anscripts/
    default.asp?

DEPENDENCIES—NETHERLANDS ANTILLES

Bonaire / Official Travel Guide

The Antilles island group is a Dutch protectorate. It is made up of two island groups; the largest islands are Curaçao and Bonaire. Papiamentu, the native tongue of many of these islands, is a mix of Spanish, Dutch, Portuguese, French, English, Caribbean Indian, and some African. At this page, you can learn a lot about this language, plus find out what you can do for fun if you're ever in the islands.

http://www.interknowledge.com/bonaire/

The Islands of the Netherlands Antilles

As you listen to some snappy tunes, you can learn about history, industry, people, government, country facts, fun, and sun. Check out the food: soursop ice cream sounds strange, but it's a fruity and cool delight. So if you can't talk your parents into a family vacation on these islands, make a virtual visit to the Netherlands Antilles to learn and enjoy.

http://www.travelnetguide.com/CARIBB/ANTILLES/

NETHERLANDS ANTILLES

See NETHERLANDS—DEPENDENCIES—
NETHERLANDS ANTILLES

NEW CALEDONIA

See FRANCE—DEPENDENCIES—NEW CALEDONIA

NEW ZEALAND

Lonely Planet - Destination New Zealand

So this Polynesian guy named Kupe finds it in A.D. 950, names it *Aotearoa* ("Land of the Long White Cloud"), then poof, a thousand years later we've got New Zealand! Where else can you take in the Golden Shears Sheep-Shearing Contest, watch the earth bubble, hiss, and spew, learn about a fascinating native people, and snow ski from June through August (that's their winter, you know)? This cybersampler gets you in the mood to visit (virtually or otherwise) with great slide shows, interactive maps, and other cool links (including the Mountain Biking in New Zealand page). The only thing missing on this techno tour is the country's friendly people. Just browse it!

http://www.lonelyplanet.com/dest/aust/nz.htm

Mount Ruapehu

It was clear the day Mount Ruapehu blew. We know, because this site's stunning photograph from the NOAA-14 satellite shows it. On that day in June of 1996, the photo from space showed the beautiful, green North Island of New Zealand under the long, red ash cloud that spewed from this active volcano. Make a stop here for facts on the violent history of the mountain. Read about living near a volcano and what must be done when it threatens to erupt. And link to other great volcano sites. Whether you're interested in the five levels of a volcanic alert or the stunning pictures of Ruapehu's stormy past, these are must-see New Zealand pages.

http://inform.dia.govt.nz:8080/mocd/nz_volcs/
ruapehu/ruapehu.html

NET FILES

NORTH POLE

What is Santa Claus' postal code?

Answer: In Canada, it's H0H 0H0. This is a special promotion used around the Christmas holidays. Try *http://www.philatelic.com/faq/ch20.html* for more information on postal codes of the world!

National Library of New Zealand Home Page

What will the library of the future look like? Sign onto the National Library of New Zealand's site to see. Check out how online versions of journals and books will become available in the "Library without Walls." But it's not all about the future. This online library has beautiful and interesting summaries of current and past local exhibits. And there are links to other New Zealand library resources, too. Here is a center of learning that reaches out to all of New Zealand's people and does it with cutting-edge flair. Of particular interest is the collection of Maori materials. The Maori are the people indigenous to the area.

http://www.natlib.govt.nz/

New Zealand Government Online

At this site you can learn all about New Zealand's parliament, the cabinet, and governmental agencies. See a picture of the flag and learn about its symbols. You can even hear the national anthem and get the words in both English and Maori. The Treaty of Waitangi, considered New Zealand's founding document, was signed in 1840 by representatives of the British Crown and Maori chiefs; you can read English and Maori versions of it here.

http://www.govt.nz/

DEPENDENCIES—COOK ISLANDS

The best kept secret in the Pacific - The Cook Islands

Put on your *rito*, a hat made from the uncurled fiber of the coconut palm. We are going to meet with Cook Islands women to make a *tivaevae*. *Tivaevae*, the making of patchwork quilts by hand, is a major art form peculiar to the Cook Islands. It was originally brought to these Polynesian islands by the Europeans, but the patterns and techniques used for these quilts have evolved over time into styles distinct to the Cooks. The *tivaevae* represent the native surroundings of the islands with designs of flowers, leaves, birds, fish, insects, and animals. Imagine the rhythmic drumming on the *pate* as you read about the art of dance in the Cooks. The name Cook Islands was actually given to the group by the Russians in the early 1800s, in honor of the great English navigator Captain James Cook. But this nation of 15 islands, which spreads over 850,000 square miles in the middle of the South Pacific, has a rich and interesting history that dates back hundreds of years before then. Read about each island as you visit "the heart of Polynesia." This site is available in English and French.

http://www.ck/

DEPENDENCIES—NIUE

Visit Niue

What do passion fruit products, pawpaw, footballs, and stamps have in common? They are all exports of Niue. This is a tiny, self-governing territory in free association with New Zealand. Niue, one of the world's largest coral islands, is situated in the South Pacific Ocean, east of Tonga.

http://www.visit.nu/

DEPENDENCIES—TOKELAU

Escape Artist Tonga & Tokelau

Tokelau is a territory of New Zealand. It's an island group that's approximately six square miles in total area. It has no airports, no railroads, and no port. However, here is a page containing a few links to information about the island.

http://www.escapeartist.com/tonga/tonga.htm

NICARAGUA

Lonely Planet — Destination: Nicaragua

Ten thousand years ago, humans and animals ran toward the lake of *Lago de Managua* to escape nature's onslaught (we know because their footprints have been found buried under layers of volcanic ash). Another nearby lake, *Lago de Nicaragua,* is the largest lake in Central America. In it lives the world's only freshwater shark species. From its warthogs and boas to jaguars and howler monkeys, from its rain forest jungles to its plains, Nicaragua is a land waiting to be explored. Why did the Sandinistas come to power? Why did the Contra rebels fight them? What was Irangate? Come to this site and learn of the history and culture of this beautiful tropical country.

http://www.lonelyplanet.com/dest/cam/nic.htm

NIGER

Focus on Niger

The market for Niger's largest export, uranium, was booming during the 1970s and 1980s. Now, for many reasons, there is less demand, and the country has seen uranium revenues drop almost 50 percent. How will they replace this income? You might find some ideas at this page, which also has some wonderful photos from former Peace Corps volunteers and others. Parents: Outside links have not been checked.

http://www.txdirect.net/users/jmayer/fon.html

Did the groundhog see his shadow? Find out if it will be an early spring in HOLIDAYS.

NIGERIA

Nigeria by Index on Africa

In 1926, he traveled to Nigeria from England, where he served as an administrative officer until 1946. Armed with a Roloflex camera, G. I. Jones began taking photographs of the art and culture that he had come to profoundly respect. Now you can see 1930s southeastern Nigeria through the lens of a master. This site showcases the art and people of that time and place with simple brilliance. And after you've browsed a sample of his work, the world of African art is just a mouse click away, with great links to places like the National Museum of African Art at the Smithsonian Institution. But don't leave before reading about the man himself (he was also called "Sherlock Jones"). Parents: Outside links have not been checked.

http://www.africaindex.africainfo.no/africaindex1/
    countries/nigeria.html

NIUE

See NEW ZEALAND—DEPENDENCIES—NIUE

NORFOLK ISLAND

See AUSTRALIA—TERRITORIES—NORFOLK ISLAND

NORTH KOREA

See KOREA, NORTH

NORTHERN IRELAND

See UNITED KINGDOM—NORTHERN IRELAND

NORWAY

Introducing Norway: Homepage

Brown goat's cheese is found in virtually every Norwegian home. It's "a rather sweet cheese made of goat's milk and cow's milk." Yum! This is just one of the things you'll learn at this very cool site designed just for kids. Norway does a lot of things just for kids. In fact, the government has a special official, called an *ombudsman*, whose job it is to take care of issues kids think are important. Kids can just call up the ombudsman if they have any problems. We wonder if they can get help with homework, too! Learn about Norway's history, culture, and much more at this page that combines great content with great fun. By the way, the paper clip is a Norwegian invention. Really, it is—go to Bytes and Pieces (page two) and see! This site was created by the Royal Norwegian Ministry of Foreign Affairs.

http://odin.dep.no/ud/publ/96/norway/

The Ministry of Foreign Affairs' article service

Do you want to know about Norse trolls and other folklore? How about snacking on some nice *lutefisk*? Or maybe you'd prefer learning about famous Norwegians, such as Roald Amundsen, who was the first person to reach the South Pole. This site has lots of information about Norwegian royalty, culture, and tourism.

http://odin.dep.no/ud/nornytt/

The Viking Network Web

From A.D. 800 to A.D. 1050, they raided, they traded, and they sailed their longships and merchant ships. Sure we're talking about Vikings here, but do you really know them? This truly awesome site, with just the right balance of text and graphics, lets you breeze as easily through Viking history, culture, religion, and commerce as they sliced through the Atlantic. Use the site's maps and search features to sing Viking shipbuilder raps, visit the places that they visited, take Viking quizzes, and do Viking math (seriously, check it out). And while you're at it, participate in a collaborative Viking project. Write a story, draw a picture, get involved! A Viking would.

http://www.viking.no/

A WWW Railway Page for Norway

Norway has trains. Norwegians are serious about trains. And serious strategic planning about railroads is happening there. Immerse yourself in the towns and country of Norway with a visit to this train lover's paradise site. Read about railroad history in Norway, and see their trains of days gone by and of the not-too-distant future. If you're planning a trip, Norway's rail network information and timetables are here, too. All aboard!

http://www.ifi.uio.no/~terjek/rail/

DEPENDENCIES—SVALBARD

NN: Geography, history, religion, people - Svalbard

Svalbard is called the "land of cold coasts," and they're not kidding. One thing that keeps it so cold is the fact that the land never completely thaws out in the summer. Only the top few feet warm up, which means you won't find any deep-rooted vegetation. Still, some 164 species of plants are found on the island. Svalbard is part of the kingdom of Norway. Since the opening of an airport in 1979, tourism has increased. A vacation at Svalbard includes experiencing beautiful coastlines and desert—Arctic desert, that is. Don't pack a swimsuit, unless, of course, it's fur-lined!

http://odin.dep.no/ud/nornytt/uda-297.html

Svalbard - A Polar Experience

The term "polar expedition" takes on a whole new meaning at this site, because your travel guide is a polar bear! Just follow the bear for some of the most exquisite photos you've ever seen, from hiking on snow-covered mountains in the summer to incredible shots of the aurora borealis (northern lights) in the winter.

http://home.sol.no/~okleven/

OMAN

THE NOT-SO-LOST CITY OF UBAR

Long ago, frankincense was worth its weight in gold; in fact, it was one of the treasures laid at the feet of the baby named Jesus. Ubar, the ancient Arab center of the frankincense trade, is referred to in *The Thousand and One Nights* (The Arabian Nights) and the Koran. So was this city only mythical or was it real? Thanks to space-age technology, we find that it was very real indeed. In 1982, a remote spacecraft "peered" under the dry sand of modern-day Oman and found it! Come and read this amazing tale and share the excitement of discovery. This beautiful site is rich with stunning information and photos, and it links you to other awesome sites on this archaeological find.

http://kidsat.jpl.nasa.gov/kidsat/exploration/
    explorations/ubarpage/

OMAN.ON.LINE

Oman, on the southern end of the Arabian peninsula, has been on the trade routes of civilization since 3000 B.C. Frankincense, vital to the religious rites of almost every civilization in the ancient world, was a rare item found only in Oman and a few other places in the world. This commodity became the lifeblood of the country and was its primary source of income for over 4,000 years. This site offers information on current tourism, business development, and culture of this land and its peoples.

http://oman-online.com/

PAKISTAN

Lonely Planet - Destination Pakistan

The Islamic Republic of Pakistan is a land of contrasts: the landscape is dotted with Buddhist monuments, Hindu temples, and Islamic landmarks. Make this page on Pakistan your destination for history, geography, current events, links, and more.

http://www.lonelyplanet.com/dest/ind/pak.htm

Pakistan - A Tourist's Paradise

The world's earliest human settlements—the prehistoric Indus Valley Civilization—are known to have started in Pakistan. Most of this site is partitioned according to province. In each section, you'll find information about the province's history, culture, religion, government, and architecture, complete with pictures.

http://www.tourism.gov.pk/

PALAU

Palau (PAM) World Travel Guide

Palau, and its 17,000 people, is 600 miles east of the Philippines. It consists of several hundred volcanic islands and a few coral atolls, but only eight islands are inhabited. It has mineral resources, including gold, but its main industry is tourism. It is a world-famous area for scuba diving. Look at some stunning photos and get a little more information at the Under Watercolour Palau Pages at <http://www.underwatercolours.com/palaupg.html>.

http://www.wtgonline.com/data/plw/plw.asp

PALESTINE

Palestine Information Center

Where is Palestine? According to this site, "Palestine nowadays refers to the holy and historic region that extends from the Jordan River in the east to the Mediterranean Sea; and from the Golan Heights and Lebanon in the north to the Sinai and the Red Sea in the south." While not an official country, this region has deep-rooted historical and religious significance. So much about this region is controversial and interpretive that it's difficult to find objective information. However, you'll find a well-organized collection of facts and stories about Palestine here that should help you understand this region's situation.

http://www.alquds.org/palestine/

PALESTINE.ON.LINE

This site is a collection of articles and links on Palestine, organized into various categories. Many countries have conflicting views on its heritage, and Palestine has more than its share of controversy. If you have an interest in this region, then this site is an excellent jumpstation for gathering facts and stories about this land rich in history and Biblical importance.

http://www.palestine-online.com/

PANAMA

Panama

Two and a half million people live in the Republic of Panama. Learn the pertinent facts about Panama and view a map as well at this site.

http://www.odci.gov/cia/publications/factbook/pm.html

The Panama Puzzle

Spin back in time to 1900 and take a trip with Major Walter Reed, U.S. Army Medical Corps. Your destination is Panama, where the now-famous Panama Canal is being dug. But there's a problem. Hundreds of men are dying of a disease they call "yellow jack." The major describes what was known of the disease and the popular theories regarding its outbreak, and he leads you down a series of paths that might explain it. Your answers will bring you closer to the cause that he and his colleagues discovered nearly a century ago. This site is rich in history and science and is a fun challenge to your reasoning skills. So put on your lab coat and get ready to sweat!

http://www-micro.msb.le.ac.uk/Tutorials/Panama/Panama.html

Welcome to The Panama Canal's Web Site

The Republic of Panama is located in Central America. Running through it is the Panama Canal, which connects the Caribbean Sea to the Pacific Ocean. Thousands of trips through the canal are made each year by commercial vessels, cruise ships, and private pleasure yachts. Most people think the Panama Canal runs east-west, but it really goes northwest-southeast. It's a 50-mile (80 kilometer) ocean-to-ocean trip, and ships must be raised 85 feet to the man-made Lake Gatun and Gaillard Cut and then lowered again to sea level. At this site you can view a live video feed from the Miraflores Locks. The site will be returned to Panamanian control at noon, December 31, 1999. Learn more about the treaty at *<http://www.pananet.com/pancanal/public/organiza/treaty /treaty.htm>*.

http://www.pancanal.com/

NET FILES

Here is the answer:
The 'Possum Trot Line, The Flash Between East and West, and the Route of the Great Big Baked Potato.
What is the question?

Answer: The question is "What were the slogans of the following railroads: Reader Railroad, Quanah, Acme and Pacific, and Northern Pacific?" Remember more mottoes from the past at *http://www.spikesys.com/Trains/rr_signs.html*

The northwest patrol

It's 1926. An expeditionary force set out through the mountains to do what had not been done by the governments of Papua or the Mandated Territory of New Guinea. The force was to cross New Guinea at its widest point, not knowing what kind of reception they would get from the local tribe. How did they fare? Thankfully, only one life was lost to disease and not one shot was fired in anger. Fast-forward 70 years to a group of Australians and Papua New Guineans who sought to retrace the steps of the earlier Northwest Patrol, only this time with helicopter resupply and remote satellite data updates to this Web site. Read and see the bold story of both parties.

http://rses.anu.edu.au/NWP/

PAPUA NEW GUINEA

This country, located north of Australia, occupies half of the island of New Guinea. Stone tools and other agricultural techniques have been found on the island dating back well over 10,000 years. However, due to its rugged terrain, which discouraged large, developed communities, the country is divided into more than 700 languages and tribes, many of which are untouched by outside influence even today!

http://203.22.79.34/png/

PARAGUAY

Lonely Planet - Destination Paraguay

These pages define *tranquilo* as a "state of mind that lulls you into a cheery, relaxed peace." Maybe *tranquilo* is found in the Chaco. The Chaco is one of South America's great wilderness areas and makes up 60 percent of Paraguay's landscape. In it live Indian peoples who trace their ancestry back to the 1500s. Animal life abounds: jaguar, puma, ocelot, and other wildlife. It hasn't always been cheery in Paraguay, though. Years of dictatorship and isolation are only recently giving way to brighter days.

http://www.lonelyplanet.com/dest/sam/par.htm

PERU

NOVA Online/Ice Mummies of the Inca

Sometime in the 1500s, she was taken to the top of Sara Sara in the Cordillera Mountains of Peru and offered as a human sacrifice. The frozen and mummified remains of this child, now known as "Sarita," were recently uncovered there. Now, through NOVA Online, you can share in the discovery. Read the story of the expedition that reclaimed her from the ice, and see beautiful photographs of the Peruvian landscape, the local children, and the expedition and its discoveries. Listen to a native melody, a bilingual "Happy Birthday," and the sounds of the picks and shovels of the dig. This finely crafted site is a joy to experience. Don't miss it!

http://www.pbs.org/wgbh/nova/peru/

PERU EXPLORER

In Peru are 84 of the world's known ecological zones and 28 different climates. The result is that kernels of corn grow as big as Buicks there (okay, a bit of an exaggeration). This site doesn't just give you the facts about Peru (loads of great "report stuff" like language, religion, currency, culture, climate, and history); it refuses to let you browse on by until you've had fun doing it. Walk the Inca Trail or visit the Sacred Valley, but by all means, have some of that corn! Maybe that's what the scarlet macaws at the top of the page are pecking. Okay, it's touristy, but it's, well, good.

http://www.peru-explorer.com/

Some Peruvian Music...

The soft sound of the zampona (the South American pan pipe) is a musical signature of the Andes mountains. On this page, you will hear its haunting melodies along with other native instruments of Peru. A dozen or so sound samples give you a good feel for the music of the land. Sure, you'll have to wait a few minutes to hear them, but good things truly are worth the wait.

http://ekeko.rcp.net.pe/snd/snd_ingles.html

Tales From the Peruvian Amazon

Have you ever dreamed about exploring the Amazon jungle? Ron Belliveau, Project Amazonas staff biologist, did more than dream—he packed his bags and did it! Ease your canoe into the water and join him as he tells his tale in words and pictures. Climb onto the river bank and into the dense rain forest that envelops you. You almost hear the songs and screeches of exotic Amazon birds. You almost feel one unlucky adventurer's shock of running his metal collection net into an electric eel! Whether you're looking at a photo of butterflies quietly sipping in a pool or the grin of a saber-toothed characin (enough to make a piranha envious), you'll hardly believe your eyes.

http://www.amazon-ecotours.com/tales/

PHILIPPINES

The Department of Tourism of The Philippines

Some of the data at this official site is not current, but the timeless cultural information is very interesting. You'll learn about various types of handicrafts, such as basketry and woodcarving. Furniture descriptions are unusual: "The *gallinera*, a type of bench used to sit visitors, is also a Filipino innovation. It is so-called because its slatted bottom half is a pen for keeping the guests' roosters."

http://www.sequel.net/RPinUS/Tourism/

Land of the Morning

Come to a virtual exhibit of the art and artifacts of Filipino culture from A.D. 500 to A.D. 1900. The stone carvings, ceramics, metalwork, wood carvings, textiles, and jewelry appear before you through the rich photography and text descriptions of each piece. Click on a map of the Philippines to read about the history and culture of the islands. Then view the objects in their context by hyperlinking to them as you read. This is a beautiful site; no Web study of the Philippines would be complete without a visit here. The gallery is always open!

http://www.laurasian.org/LOM_home.html

Lonely Planet - Destination The Philippines.

The Philippines consists of over 7,100 islands, some of them with active volcanoes. Mount Pinatubo erupted in 1991 and left a moonlike landscape that tourists now visit by jeep. The Philippines are also notable for being the only Christian country in Asia. Ferdinand Magellan arrived in 1521 and erected the first cross, claiming the land for Spain. At the time, the natives did not think much of this idea. You'll find lots of general info at this site.

http://www.lonelyplanet.com/dest/sea/phil.htm

A Philippine Leaf

More than a thousand years ago, documents were written on leaves. In India and Southeast Asia, such communication was often made on palm leaves. Now, as we near a new millennium, a one-time aerospace computer systems engineer digs deeply into the ancient writing of the Philippines. He shares his results on the "leaf" of today's communication: the Web page. This site is rich in the history of the Philippines and Filipino writing systems, languages, and scripts that predate the Spaniards. Take a journey back to the ancient Philippines, "the way she was before the West found her."

http://www.bibingka.com/dahon/

Philippine Prehistory

Who were the Austronesians? How did they get where they were going? What three domestic animals were always with them? (Hint: Lassie, Porky, and Henny Penny.) The answers all tie in with today's Filipino people. In this "glimpse of the prehistory and pre-contact culture of the Philippines," we learn of their weapons, including the feared swivel gun. We discover their incredible ocean navigation and fishing skills and the religious beliefs of these very early people of the Philippines. And for those mystery lovers among you, see and read about the "tiger bells" and muse over their meaning.

http://www.he.net/~skyeagle/prehist.htm

Underwater Photos - Philippines

Who would have ever thought that a moray eel's eyes look like those on a cartoon fish? Normally, the first thing anyone would notice is the menacing jaws, but in Chuck Gardner's photographs the sea creature keeps its mouth shut long enough for us to notice its eyes. These brilliant pictures of what lies under the waves of the Philippines (and a few topside shots of the beaches, the palms, the dusty streets, and the landscape) are a feast for the eyes. And if you grow tired of stunning beauty, go to Chuck's home page and read about his role in the early development of the Internet and the World Wide Web in the Philippines. Don't miss this site!

http://super.nova.org/uw/Index.html

PITCAIRN ISLANDS

See UNITED KINGDOM—DEPENDENCIES—PITCAIRN ISLANDS

POLAND

Explore Poland

This is a jumpstation to many sites on Polish history, culture, and more. You might want to try the link to the State Ethnographical Museum in Warsaw, established in 1888 (click Travel, then Sightseeing, then Museums). It features folk culture in Poland, Europe, and other continents. The museum owns 50,000 works from Central Europe and Poland and 20,000 works from other countries. The works include folk costumes, sculpture and painting, handicrafts, and ritual objects. Small pictures of some of these items are shown on the home page. One exhibition of paintings is also featured. Parental advisory: There are links to sites on the death camps of WWII.

http://www.explore-poland.pl/

GoPoland! Web Travel Guide to Poland

This travel guide contains a history about the country in addition to individual histories on 11 (when we last checked) different Polish cities and towns. Find brief descriptions on local sights, museums, galleries, and more here for each location.

http://www.gopoland.com/

Poland Country Guide

A tribe known as Polians, or "dwellers of the field," claimed Poland as their own in the early ninth century. At this site, you can learn about Polish history, people, and culture. If you explore the site, you'll find interesting details. For instance, defensive castles became an integral part of the Polish landscape in the fourteenth century in the reign of Casimir the Great, who "found Poland built of wood and left her built of stone." The Education section includes links to the major universities in Poland.

http://ciesin.ci.uw.edu.pl/poland/poland-home.html

Poland Home Page

This official site is your passport to many interesting links to government ministries and departments, as well as other useful sites dealing with the environment, culture, tourism, health, and more. Many of the resources are in Polish, and English versions are under development.

http://poland.pl/

POLAND - Polish National Tourist Office

Have you ever visited a salt mine? You can, if you visit some of the unique sites highlighted by this official Web page. The Wieliczka salt mines are world famous. The underground tour route winds about two miles through old salt works, plus some surprises: ornate chapels, carved entirely from salt. Even the chandeliers are made from glittering salt. See a picture of it at this site.

http://www.polandtour.org/

POLISH NATIONAL PARKS

Explore 22 different national parks in Poland, complete with pictures and geological histories and descriptions of the areas. The geology ranges from the seashores in Wolinski to the snow-covered mountains in Tatrzanski, from the caves in Ojcowski to the gorges in Pieninski. Take a virtual vacation through Poland's parks here, and learn some geology on the way.

http://hum.amu.edu.pl/~zbzw/ph/pnp/pnp.htm

PORTUGAL

Algarve Info Page

This is a warm welcome from a mild climate. This part of Portugal receives many tourists, and this page explains everything a visitor might want to know about the area. There's information on weather, news, exchange rates, current Internet access, and links to various things Portuguese.

http://www.nexus-pt.com/alg/info.htm

A collection of home pages about Portugal

Why did Portugal send so many explorers out to the New World? Maybe it's because Portugal is the westernmost point in Europe. It ranks as one of the world's longest-established countries. Portugal's boundaries have remained unchanged since the thirteenth century. Start your virtual journey at this huge collection of sites. Assembled are many of the available English language sources and some in Portuguese. You'll even find a "how to use the Net" guide here—in Portuguese!

http://www.well.com/user/ideamen/portugal.html

Portuguese Embassy in Tokyo - Cultural Services

Learn basic facts about Portugal, including details on the anthem and the national symbols, at this official site. Did you know the Portuguese language is spoken all over the world? According to this site, "Portuguese is spoken in seven countries: Angola, Brazil, Cape Verde, Guinea-Bissau, Mozambique, Portugal and São Tomé...and territories of Macao and East-Timor, as well as in the African, Portuguese and Brazilian communities living throughout the World."

http://www.pnsnet.co.jp/users/cltembpt/

DEPENDENCIES—MACAU

Macau Official Homepage

This is an official site, created and maintained by the government. Macau is currently a Chinese territory under Portuguese administration, but it will return to China's sovereignty on December 20, 1999. After that, it will be governed as a Special Administrative Region of Macau (SARM). It is an island off the southeast Chinese coast, connected to the mainland by two bridges.

http://www.macau.gov.mo/indexe.shtml

Welcome to Macau Tourism HomePage

This Web page features a look at some of the sights, such as the oldest temple in Macau, the Temple of the Goddess A-Ma: "According to the legend, A-Ma, a poor girl looking for passage to Canton, was refused by the wealthy boat owners, but a lowly fisherman took her on board. A storm blew up and wrecked all but the boat carrying the girl. On arrival in Macau she vanished, to reappear as a Goddess on the spot where the fishermen built her temple."

http://turismo.macau.gov.mo/

Find your roots in GENEALOGY.

QATAR

Ministry of Foreign Affairs, Qatar - Entrance

This, the official site of the Ministry of Foreign Affairs of Qatar, has absolutely splendid graphics. If you like the game of *Myst*, you'll appreciate this site. "Hot News" is offered in both English and Arabic. You'll find the emir's latest speeches and recent photos. Although the site is under construction, you'll get a feel for how Qatar sees itself.

http://www.mofa.gov.qa/

QATAR.ON.LINE

The discovery of oil in 1939 has enabled Qatar to establish and maintain a high standard of living for its people. The sale of oil accounts for about 75 percent of the country's export earnings. This site is both an information resource about Qatar as well as a gateway to many useful Web resources on this country. Everything is categorized to help you easily find the information you need.

http://www.qatar-online.com/index-e.htm

REUNION

See FRANCE—DEPENDENCIES—REUNION

ROMANIA

Discover Romania

At this site you'll find a clickable map, general information, history, people, politics, economy, and sports. In "Celebrities," famous Romanians past and present, including Dracula and Ceausescu, are presented, with good descriptions of their lives. You may have to expand your browser window to see these choices.

http://students.missouri.edu/~romsa/romania/

Embassy of Romania, Washington D.C.

Is the Black Sea in Romania really black? No, the Turks gave it the name Karadeniz ("black") because they feared the sea's storms. The embassy's FAQ section answers this and other questions you might have about Romania. You'll also find good links to other Romanian sites in Romania on the Net and Other Official Romanian Sites on the Internet. And there are up-to-date links to newspapers and magazines, in Romanian and English.

http://embassy.org/romania/

ROMANIA

This Romanian source surveys everything from generalities, geography, and history to tourism and culture. A country in transition, Romania is still reeling from the fall of the Communist government in 1989. For decades, the Romania Communist party was the only party. After its demise, however, more than 200 parties sprang up. Cultural and political restructuring have been more difficult than anticipated. Transylvania is in Romania, and five centuries ago it was home to a man so infamous he is remembered to this day. This man was Vlad Tepes, also known as Vlad Dracula. "Tourism" contains a brief history of the man in history and in legend, as well as a portrait and pictures of two of his castles.

http://indis.ici.ro/romania/romania.html

Virtual ROMANIA

This up-to-date site has a little more depth than official sites. Explore news from Romania, facts about Romania, statistics, and culture (including fragments of Romanian folk music you can listen to). Also, in Culture, enjoy Romanian/English quotations, such as Întrebarea trece marea, Cine întreabă nu greseste ("He that nothing questions, nothing learns"). A section called Etc. includes information on Romanian adoption, recipes (Romanians apparently love sour foods), Romanian soccer, Jewish roots in Romania, computers in Romania, and much, much more.

http://www.info.polymtl.ca/zuse/tavi/www/
    rom_eng.html

RUSSIA

Czars Lobby

Royalty's rule of Russia started with the Romanov Dynasty in 1613 and ended tragically with the Bolshevik Revolution of 1917. At this site you can meet some of Russia's fascinating leaders, such as Peter Alexeevich. The 14th child out of a family of 21 children, he grew to a height of seven feet at a time when the average person's height was even shorter than it is today. He was a skilled diplomat and a talented leader. It was under his rule that Russia became an empire, and he was given the title Emperor of All Russia, Great Father of the Fatherland. You may know him as Peter "the Great."

http://www2.sptimes.com/Treasures/

Friends of Tuva

We knew someone would eventually look up Tuva in this book, so we included this entry just for you! Tuva is an autonomous republic of Russia. You can find pictures of its flag and national symbols here. Richard Feynman made Tuva famous. Feynman was an American physicist, bongo drum player, and engineer. He helped develop the atomic bomb in 1945, and he also helped solve the mystery behind the Challenger space shuttle disaster. Feynman was fascinated with Tuva, the land of triangular postage stamps and throat singing. Many of Feynman's fans started an organization to advance the world's knowledge of Tuva, and Friends of Tuva was born.

http://www.feynman.com/tuva/

Museums of Russia

Tour major museums in Russia, from history (natural and otherwise) to literature to music to space flight. As you sift through this site, you'll find the menu for Nicholas and Alexandra's coronation dinner, hear "Flight of the Valkyrie," and see Russian portraits, architecture, and cultural artifacts. Most of the sites have English versions, but even the ones that don't are worth viewing.

http://www.museum.ru/defengl.htm

The Official Guide to Russia

This is the official site of the Russian National Tourist Office, and it offers good Web value. A clickable timeline presents basic Russian history, from ancient Russia through the Soviet era. You'll see pictures of cities and natural wonders. Read an enlightening essay on Russian art and architecture. The history and culture of Moscow and St. Petersburg are also presented. You can learn about the Trans-Siberian Railway and find out a little bit about the magnificent 13-foot Siberian tiger.

http://www.interknowledge.com/russia/

Research Exchange with PIN

A *dino*-mite exhibition is currently being shown at the University of California Museum of Paleontology site. It's a virtual visit to the Paleontological Institute in Moscow, the world's largest paleontological institute. The exhibit displays photographs of dinosaurs from Siberia and Mongolia, plus early mammals. The architectural features of the Moscow museum are also noted, including door hinges shaped like elk and three-story mosaics.

http://www.ucmp.berkeley.edu/pin/pin.html

Russia Alive!

This site is good for current news, weather, and culture of Russia. Newspapers such as the *St. Petersburg Times* and others publish up-to-the-minute reports. There are links to Russian magazines and an interview with Ovod, a 121-year-old former spy. And when you go to the section about Ovod, just ignore the part about "illegal entry—arrest warrant issued"—it's a joke! If you need to know about a specific city, it's probably got a Web page on this site. Russia Alive! also includes a page just for children, where you'll find postings from kids in Kamchatka and Novgorod. For an interesting look at current Russian home pages, try the All-Russian Hedgehog Award links.

http://www.alincom.com/russ/

Russian History

Russian history is like none other. The mix of cultures, invasions, religions, and politics creates a fascinating and complex entity. You can spend hours at this site. Learn about the very first settlements in Russia. The Greek historian Herodotus noted that Russian wheat sustained the builders of Athens' Parthenon in the fifth century B.C. The Vikings, the Byzantine Empire, and Genghis Khan all played their parts in early Russian history. Find out why the Russians use the Cyrillic alphabet. And just how terrible was Ivan the Terrible? There is also information on the rise and fall of the Soviet Union and other recent happenings, as well as a very useful set of general links.

http://www.bucknell.edu/departments/russian/
history.html

Russian Life

Russian Life is "the Monthly Magazine of Russian History, Culture, Business and Travel." Originally *USSR,* then *Soviet Life,* the newly named *Russian Life* was reborn in 1993. It is now a 32-page monthly magazine, a little bit like *Life* magazine in the U.S. *Russian Life* archives its front-page stories. You can find out about Catherine the Great, schools in Siberia, democracy in Russia, and marriage in Russia. Read about the birth of the samovar and why the samovar is so important to Russians. There are also departments such as Survival Russian (which mixes Cyrillic text with English), Russian Cuisine, and Travel Journal. Also, you can read letters to the editor and follow links to other Russian pages. A caution to parents: Not all links have been viewed.

http://www.friends-partners.org/rispubs/RL-TOP.HTM

RWANDA

Rwanda- Embassy of the Republic of Rwanda

This page gives an official history of this troubled country, including the recent genocide and the search for peace. You will also find information about the business and economic development of this country.

http://www.rwandemb.org/

Rwanda Page

This page, assembled by the African studies department of the University of Pennsylvania, brings together many sources about Rwanda. You'll find Rwanda's constitution, the *World Factbook* article, maps, and background information about the civil war and genocide of 1994. There is also a link to the Ethnologue, a catalog of the world's languages, which describes the languages of Rwanda. A caution to parents: Violent events are described.

http://www.sas.upenn.edu/African_Studies/
Country_Specific/Rwanda.html

SAINT HELENA

See UNITED KINGDOM—DEPENDENCIES—SAINT HELENA

SAINT KITTS AND NEVIS

Accenting St. Kitts and Nevis - Official Travel Guide

These two islands look like a baseball and bat. Considering the colonial British history of this Caribbean nation, however, the residents would probably liken it more to a cricket ball and bat. This twin island nation became independent on September 19, 1983. At this site, you'll find more than just tourist information. There's a long article on Horatio Nelson, the famous British admiral, who married Francis Nisbet on Nevis in 1787. The Nelson Museum on Nevis has the largest collection of Nelson memorabilia in the Western Hemisphere. Information on the history and culture of Saint Kitts and Nevis is also available. Nature is held in high regard there—by law, no building can be higher than the palm trees around it.

http://www.interknowledge.com/stkitts-nevis/

NET FILES

Who invented the microscope?

Answer: The first true microscope was invented by Zacharias Jansen in 1595. Read all about the history of the compound microscope at http://www.utmem.edu/personal/thjones/hist/hist_mic.htm

SAINT LUCIA

Official Guide to Saint Lucia

Part of the Lesser Antilles, Saint Lucia has the Atlantic Ocean lapping at its eastern shores, while its western beaches touch the Caribbean Sea. The terrain includes rain forests and volcanoes. There's much to celebrate in Saint Lucia—they have Independence Day in February, Emancipation Day in August, and National Day in December. This island is truly multicultural: a visitor can drive on the British (left) side of the road to a French town for an Indian meal. And, although French was outlawed by the British in the nineteenth century, Creole patois is commonly spoken. According to this page, Saint Lucia is the site of the world's only drive-in volcanic crater (Diamond Head on Oahu may make a similar claim).

http://www.interknowledge.com/st-lucia/

SAINT-PIERRE AND MIQUELON

See FRANCE—DEPENDENCIES—SAINT-PIERRE AND MIQUELON

SAINT VINCENT AND THE GRENADINES

St. Vincent & the Grenadines

This island group lies about 1,600 miles southeast of Miami, Florida. At this Web page, you'll find out about location and climate, as well as other background information on this country. Sites and Side Trips offers interesting anecdotes about the history and culture of the islands. For instance, St. George's Anglican Cathedral, which was built in the early 1800s, has a red-robed angel in a stained glass window. "The stained glass was originally commissioned by Queen Victoria to honour her first grandson, who later became King Edward VIII. Although it was destined to hang in St. Paul's Cathedral in London, the venerable queen took exception to the scarlet angel, believing the Bible specified that all angels wore white. As a result, the window found its way to Kingstown as a gift to the bishop and the diocese in St. Vincent."

http://www.cpscaribnet.com/destin/stvincent/ stvgeni.html

SAMOA

The Government of Western Samoa

"Polynesia at its purest." That's what this, the official Web site for the Government of Western Samoa, has to say about its country. They just might be right! You'll see lots of beautiful sites as you stroll through these pages, and you will learn a lot about this country.

http://www.interwebinc.com/samoa/

HAY! Gallop over to HORSES AND EQUESTRIAN SPORTS.

SAMOA

It may be hard to believe, but the tropical resort islands of Samoa are the home of World Rugby Cup Champions the Manu Samoa. The famous writer Robert Louis Stevenson ended his days there, and the island's natural beauty is much as it has been for the last 5,000 years. This site, designed to promote environmentally friendly tourism, is a great place to take a virtual visit.

http://www.pi.se/~orbit/samoa/welcome.html

SAN MARINO

Information About San Marino

San Marino is a small but old nation. It is found within Italy, but it is a separate democratic republic that has been electing officials since 1243. The boundaries of San Marino have remained unchanged since 1463. In 1797, Napoleon Bonaparte offered to help the country expand its boundaries and increase revenue; the consuls politely declined. San Marino has a centuries-long tradition of asylum and hospitality. During the Second World War, it took in over 100,000 refugees, which is remarkable—especially when compared to their present population of only 24,000.

http://inthenet.sm/det_smgb.htm

SAO TOME AND PRINCIPE

Sao Tome and Principe Page

These islands are off West Africa, straddling the equator. This site includes a flag, a map, and general information on population, geography, and economy of the area. You can also hear the national anthem. Their major export is cocoa! Additional information and a few photos can be found at <http://www.sao-tome.com/english.html>.

http://www.emulateme.com/saotome.htm

SAUDI ARABIA

ArabNet — Saudi

Here you'll find fascinating tidbits among the population, government, and history facts. For instance, Saudi Arabia is home to the Arabian oryx, thought by some to be the inspiration for the legendary unicorn. This fabulous beast is perfectly suited to its desert habitat and according to this site, it can go for years, if necessary, without drinking. The oryx gets water from the plants it eats and from licking dew from desert plants. The site also explains the Islamic calendar, which is based on a lunar year instead of the solar one used in the West. Islamic months rotate, rather than coming in the same seasons each year. You'll learn a little bit about the *gahwa* ritual (coffee making). Also, the once-a-year hajj pilgrimage to Makkah (Mecca) is described in some detail. It differs from the pilgrimage to Mecca at any other time of year. There are even short articles on natural toothbrushes and Bedouin tents.

http://www.arab.net/saudi/saudi_contents.html

Royal Embassy of Saudi Arabia

This page is maintained by the Royal Embassy of Saudi Arabia in Washington, D.C. You'll find lots of information on the history, culture, economy, and government of the country. Religion is an important part of Saudi Arabian life. Be sure to take a look at the section on the history and practice of Islam. There is also a search engine that looks for terms appearing anywhere in the site. And look to the Multimedia Presentation for lots of pictures in categories such as health, Islam, sports and recreation, and energy.

http://www.saudi.net/

Saudi Arabia

This entry in the Encyclopedia of the Orient has brief articles on the political situation, the economy, health and education, religions and people, and history of Saudi Arabia. Look here for a more Western view of the country. Challenges facing Saudi Arabia are mentioned.

http://i-cias.com/e.o/saudi.htm

NET FILES

What would you be looking at if you were holding a copy of the "Dunlap Broadside"?

Answer: You'd be looking at one of only 24 known surviving copies of the first printing of the Declaration of Independence, printed by a Philadelphia printer John Dunlap on July 4, 1776. Read more interesting facts surrounding the creation of this famous document at http://lcweb.loc.gov/exhibits/declara/declara4.html

Welcome to Saudi Arabia

This site is less official than some, with links to recipes, Arabian horses, newsgroup postings, Operation Desert Storm, and Saudi Arabian resources. While not all links work at all times, you will find information collected here that is hard to find elsewhere.

http://www.uoregon.edu/~kbatarfi/saudi.html

SCOTLAND

See UNITED KINGDOM—SCOTLAND

SENEGAL

The Official Home Page of the Republic of Sénégal

Senegal is the westernmost African country and a cultural crossroads. An overview of Senegal's current life and culture is provided on this home page. You can dip into information on art, recipes, and popular sporting events. "National Parks" gives you an idea of the kinds of animals native to the country (including hippos and warthogs). The *World Factbook* entry is included, so you can get the facts on population statistics and terrain.

http://www.earth2000.com/senegal/

SERBIA AND MONTENEGRO

MONTENEGRO - Presented by MonteNet

Montenegro's history is both complex and challenging. Its history can be traced back to before the sixth century A.D. when the area was inhabited by the Illyrians. About that time, the Slavs colonized the Balkan peninsula and are considered the ancestors of the Montenegrins. You can read much more about the complex series of events that eventually lead up to Montenegro's assimilation into the country of Yugoslavia, and its present situation. This country's religious and cultural histories are also complex, and along with sections on politics, art, geography, and more, this site has much to offer. As opinions on some of the politics and other topics vary, you should also explore other sites about Montenegro and Serbia to get the whole story. Look in the Links section for more.

http://www.montenet.org/

DINOSAURS are prehistoric, but they are under "D."

Serbia Info

This site, created by the Ministry of Information, states that: "The Republic of Serbia, together with the Republic of Montenegro, is a constituent part of the Federal Republic of Yugoslavia." This new republic, however, is not officially recognized by the U.S. State Department as of March 1, 1998. Explore this site's presentation on Serbia's national monuments, national parks, caves, and mountains. Take a virtual Guided Tour through archaeological sites, mountain peaks, and the wildlife in a place where more than 40 different nations live.

http://www.serbia-info.com/

Yugoslavia

Look at different sites for different views of Serbia and Montenegro. Although Serbia and Montenegro have asserted the formation of a joint independent state, it is unrecognized as yet by the United States. This site has information on culture, news, and economy of the area, plus a library of links. "Culture" is worth a look for the museums and descriptions of the people. You'll find lots of recipes here, too. And "Food" is a good place to look for Christmas and other holiday foods.

http://www.yugoslavia.com/

SEYCHELLES

Seychelles Online

A group of islands in the Indian Ocean, northwest of Madagascar, Seychelles is a beautiful tropical nation. Seychelles is home to giant tortoises and unique fruit bats, as well as 72,300 people. Tourism is an important part of Seychelles' economy. It has been developed in an environmentally sound manner—only 200,000 tourists are allowed per year. As the country didn't have an airport until 1971, it has developed its own unique culture. At this site you will be able to visit links to the official Republic of Seychelles page as well as keep up with current news.

http://www.seychelles-online.com.sc/

SIERRA LEONE

Sierra Leone Web

Current news of Sierra Leone will be found at this site. You'll learn about some language tidbits, too: proverbs and lorry (truck) slogans. Here's a sample in Krio: *Nius noh geht fut, boht i de waka* ("News has no feet, but it travels"). There are also links to various Sierra Leone pages including some on local recipes, literature, some local schools, and pages maintained by Peace Corps volunteers.

http://www.Sierra-Leone.org/

SINGAPORE

National Heritage Board: Homepage

"Preserving the heritage of the people of Singapore," this home page offers one-stop access to four of Singapore's museums. The National Archives of Singapore features building plans, old photographs, and audio clips (in Chinese). For instance, there's an interesting photograph collection of rickshaw drivers at the turn of the century. The Asian Civilisations Museum focuses on ancestral cultures of Singaporeans. Look for pictures and descriptions of art objects from all over Asia. The Singapore History Museum includes dioramas and famous monuments. Look for contemporary art at the Singapore Art Museum, with exhibitions and highlights.

http://www.museum.org.sg/nhb.html

Singapore Government

This is the official clearinghouse site for the various ministries of the Singaporean government. You'll see many, many links, including one to Istanga Singapore at <http://www.gov.sg/istana/>, the official residence and home page of the President of Singapore.

http://www.gov.sg/

Singapore infomap

This site introduces and indexes Singapore resources on the Internet. You may find everything you need in "One-Minute Singapore." It has links to basic information on the country's climate, people, education, and government, and more. The "country profile" section has in-depth information on many of the same topics. If you have more time, delve into the many links related to sports and recreation, history, culture, business, and tourism. There are links to current newspaper articles as well. Parents: Off-site links have not been checked.

http://www.sg/

Singapore unofficial food ... Cook it yourself!

This is Singapore's unofficial food site. Foods from China, Thailand, Vietnam, and Malaysia all contribute to the delicious cuisine of Singapore. You can read about Asian restaurants in Singapore and all over the world. Also, there's a sizable collection of authentic recipes, with ingredients such as *pandan* leaves and *galangal*. Don't worry, another page of the site describes Asian ingredients, with pictures included. If you're traveling and want to find a good Asian restaurant, this site will clue you in to the best and the worst. Don't miss the link to "hawker food," which is what you'd find in the equivalent of a mall food court.

http://www.sintercom.org/makan/recipes.html

SLOVAKIA

SLOVAK REPUBLIC - FAQ

This site contains bits of information about Slovakia—mostly useful tourist tidbits, such as local customs, currency regulations, phone numbers and addresses for long distance connections, embassies, and travel. Short descriptions of each region—High Tatras, Central Region, and Eastern Region—are here, each with tourist help, hotel and restaurant locations, and sites to visit. Links to additional Slovakia-related sites are listed at the bottom of the page. An in-depth history of Slovakia from 500 B.C. through 1992 is located at <http://www.adc.sk/english/slovakia/slovakia.htm>.

http://photo.net/bp/slovak-FAQ.html

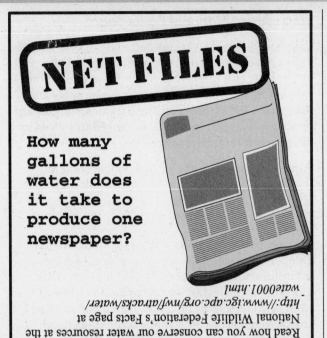

NET FILES

How many gallons of water does it take to produce one newspaper?

Answer: The whole process takes 280 gallons of water to produce one Sunday newspaper! It takes 7 to 25 gallons of water to produce one gallon of gasoline! Read how you can conserve our water resources at the National Wildlife Federation's Facts page at http://www.igc.apc.org/nwf/atracks/water/wate0001.html

SLOVAKIA DOCUMENT STORE

Since before the Roman Empire, this region has undergone many political and cultural changes. In this century, Slovakia was under Communist rule from 1948 until 1989 as part of Czechoslovakia. It struggled economically and politically for three years to establish its independence, and it did so on January 1, 1993. This site has a collection of links and local information arranged in categories that include geography, cities, culture, history, news, and pictures.

http://www.eunet.sk/slovakia/slovakia.html

SLOVENIA

Connection to Slovenia Page

Hope you like accordion music—you get a nice peppy polka to listen to while you explore this site. Most of the information is in the Slovenian Links section, which is a collection of resources on Slovenia-related news, facts, recipes, maps, music, and more. Parents: Outside links have not been checked.

http://plaza.v-wave.com/accordion/slovenia.htm

The President of the Republic of Slovenia

Milan Kucan became the first president of the independent Republic of Slovenia in 1992. He was reelected to a five-year term in 1997. At this site you can read some of his major addresses as well as follow recent events and appearances.

http://www.sigov.si/upr/ang/

SOLOMON ISLANDS

Solomon Islands

A flag of blue and green with white stars and a yellow stripe waves over the Solomon Islands, located in the South Pacific Ocean. At this site, you will learn a lot about the country—for example, it used to be called the British Solomon Islands but achieved independence in 1978.

http://www.odci.gov/cia/publications/factbook/bp.html

Solomon Islands Home Page

The answer is 998! The question is exactly how many islands, atolls, and reefs make up the Solomon Islands? Furnished with a tropical climate, forests, mountain ranges, unspoiled beaches, butterflies as big as birds, underwater volcanoes, tons of history, and a location just a stone's throw from Australia, the Solomon Islands are truly the "happy isles." This site is a trove of information on the people, climate, geography, history, commerce, and government. Just one visit to this site will explain why the Solomon Islands are also referred to as the "pearl of the Pacific." You may find more current information at the *World Factbook* site.

http://www.spacelab.net/~solomons/

SOMALIA

ArabNet — Somalia

Did you ever wonder what frankincense is and where it comes from? It's a gum resin from the *Boswellia* tree, and it is an ingredient of incense and perfumes. Along with uranium, copper, gypsum, iron, marble, manganese, tin, and oil, it is one of the natural resources found in Somalia. Somalia is located in the easternmost part of the African continent. It has a hot and arid climate, rugged plateaus, and sandy coastal plains. Wildlife is plentiful in this African nation, but because of the harsh climate, plant life is limited. Much of the historical information at this site deals with Somalia's turbulent past, although its present is just as stormy.

http://www.arab.net/somalia/somalia_contents.html

SOUTH AFRICA

Nkosi Sikelel' iAfrika - South Africa's National Anthem

In many ways, the story of South Africa's national anthem mirrors the development of the country. The "Nkosi Sikelel' iAfrika" was composed in 1897 by Enoch Sontonga, from the Mpinga clan of the Xhosa nation. He taught at a Methodist Mission School. He wrote the tune and the first verse (in Xhosa), and the song of peace and healing always moved its audiences. In 1927, a further seven verses were published, added by a South African poet. It became an anthem of the oppressed, spreading beyond the borders of South Africa to Tanzania and Zambia. The problem was that white South Africa already had an official national anthem. When sweeping governmental reforms changed the policies that divided the races, South Africa also changed its national anthem. In 1994, parts of both anthems were combined. You can find the words to all three anthems here. Sontonga's burial site has been declared a national monument. Don't miss the story of the difficulty of locating his grave so that he could be honored.

http://www.anc.org.za/misc/nkosi.html

South Africa National Parks Board

Visit South Africa's various national parks at this site. The parks are located in the coastal regions, the mountains, and in the desert. These parks are home to hundreds of species of birds and mammals that have made Africa famous. The park descriptions are brief, but some of the words are linked to a glossary offering further explanations.

http://www.ecoafrica.com/ntpks/npbhome.htm

The South Africa Page

This site lists many links related to South Africa. Categories range from agriculture, arts, and the environment to news, politics, and tourism. This collection is not as large or up to date as some of the other link collections on South Africa, but most of the links we checked were valid and the collection had quality sites.

http://www.mwc.edu/~geogrph/sa/aboutsa/

Welcome to South Africa

For too many years, the mere thought of South Africa brought visions of a nation in which the black majority lived under a bigoted and constricting system known as apartheid. But that was then, and this is now. Apartheid has been abolished, Nelson Mandela has been released from prison and elected president, and South Africa is emerging into a world in which all of its people are citizens and all are represented. This official site, from the South African embassy in Washington, D.C., is a wonderful source for historical, cultural, and social information.

http://www.southafrica.net/

SOUTH GEORGIA AND THE SOUTH SANDWICH ISLANDS

See UNITED KINGDOM—DEPENDENCIES—SOUTH GEORGIA AND THE SOUTH SANDWICH ISLANDS

SOUTH KOREA

See KOREA, SOUTH

SPAIN

ALL ABOUT SPAIN - Travel and Tourism in Spain

This colorful, well-designed site is an excellent resource for information "all about Spain." Check the Regions section for a list and map of all the provinces, each of which includes a description and further links to some of the cities of that province. There's a searchable database of hotels, camping, country houses, and restaurants. Don't miss the Photo Tour of selected locations, which links to a page full of small pictures of the sites at that location. You can then enlarge each picture or link to a description of the site. The Culture and Popular Customs section has its own subsections, including a General section, where you will discover history, architecture, and tourist info. Other subsections in General include Flamenco, Fiestas and Folklore, and Gastronomy (food). Finally, a search feature lets you search the entire site.

http://www.red2000.com/spain/

Discover Spain with the Tourist Office of Spain

Of course this site is tourist-oriented, but don't let that keep you from giving it a visit. It has all the usual country facts, such as geography, history, and government. It also has really neat sections on people, social customs, transportation, communications, and things to do in the country. Be sure to check out the World Heritage in Spain section and the descriptions of the 15 World Heritage Site locations. For those really tough questions, there are even addresses for local tourist offices worldwide.

http://www.spaintour.com/indexe.html

Si, Spain

This official site is from the Directorate General for Cultural Affairs at the Spanish Foreign Ministry. It not only covers the history and culture of Spain but also gives practical information for tourists, including online Spanish lessons. If you are looking for specific info on Spain and can't seem to find it, then try the internal search engines here. There's even a search engine just for fiestas!

http://www.DocuWeb.ca/SiSpain/

SRI LANKA

Embassy of Sri Lanka

This official site offers a wealth of beautiful pictures and history of this island republic. A great map is even included. By the way, did you know that Sri Lanka used to be called Ceylon? Its main exports are tea, rubber, coconuts, garments, gems, desiccated coconut, and cinnamon, among others. One of the fascinating things to see in Sri Lanka is the Sacred Bo Tree, which is in the city of Anuradhapura. According to this site, it is the world's oldest tree: "a branch of the very Bo Tree beneath which the Buddha himself found Enlightenment. It was brought to Sri Lanka in the third century B.C."

http://piano.symgrp.com/srilanka/

Lonely Planet — Destination: Sri Lanka

Where would you go to wash your elephant? The bathtub? No, it would leave footprints in the soap, and besides, your parents would never understand. The automatic car wash is probably out of the question, too—think of all the elephant wax you'd need. The only solution is to take your elephant to Sri Lanka, where they have elephant baths. You can see a picture of one at this site ("Jumbo bath") and find out lots of other interesting facts about the country of Sri Lanka, including information about the ethnic unrest there.

http://www.lonelyplanet.com/dest/ind/sri.htm

SUDAN

Sudan page

Sudan is the largest country on the continent of Africa. It also has some of the largest problems: civil war, border disputes, a declining economy, overpopulation, drought, and military coups, just to name a few. Each year, thousands of Sudanese citizens flee to the neighboring countries to escape the harsh conditions in their own country. Find basic information and suggested links at this site.

http://www.sas.upenn.edu/African_Studies/
    Country_Specific/Sudan.html

The Sudan Page

Almost as old as man himself (and possibly just as old, according to this site), Sudan has been inhabited for nine million years. With an area of nearly a million square miles of mostly desert, Sudan contains most of the upper Nile river and is the largest country in Africa. In addition to its large size, Sudan also contains 132 living languages spread among 90 Arabized tribes. Its people are mostly farmers and animal breeders, while others are nomadic herders, businesspeople, and merchants.

http://www.sudan.net/

SURINAME

Lonely Planet — Destination: Suriname

The original inhabitants of this South American country were Carib Indians. The English founded a settlement there in A.D. 1650 and established sugar and tobacco plantations. Twenty years later, the Dutch traded New Amsterdam for Suriname in order to take over and develop the plantations. What was New Amsterdam is now called New York City.

http://www.lonelyplanet.com/dest/sam/sur.htm

Parbo

Paramaribo is Suriname's capital and home to two-thirds of the population. Visit this site and discover what Suriname is all about. Since the 1970s, 250,000 Surinamese have emigrated to Holland (most of the population is of Dutch descent). Read more about the people, culture, religion, and the government of Suriname.

http://www.parbo.com/

Tropical Rainforest In Suriname

Save the rain forests! They are up for sale and are being destroyed at an alarming rate. This excellent site gives a close-up look at the rain forest, its plants, animals, people, and sounds. Don't miss it!

http://www.euronet.nl/users/mbleeker/
    suriname/suri-eng.html

SVALBARD

See NORWAY—DEPENDENCIES—SVALBARD

SWAZILAND

Swaziland

Swaziland is known as the "emerald of Africa." High mountains, grassy hills, tribal villages, luxury hotels, a temperate climate, wildlife, and...well, you get the idea. There is plenty of wildlife. Much of it is protected in one of Swaziland's several huge wildlife preserves. This small, landlocked South African kingdom also has the last remaining ruling monarchy on the continent.

http://www.africaindex.africainfo.no/africaindex1/
    countries/swaziland.html

SWEDEN

Passagen Smorgasbord

If you happen to be doing a report on Sweden, this is the most comprehensive site you will find. Whatever facet of Swedish life you're interested in, you'll find it described here—everything from their history (starting with the Vikings), government, society, and industry to their food and recreation. For example, have you heard of Everyman's Right? According to this site, "The Right of Public Access" (*Allemansrätten*) is unique and the most important base for recreation in Sweden, providing the possibility for each and everyone to visit somebody else's land, to take a bath in and to travel by boat on somebody else's waters, and to pick the wild flowers, mushrooms, berries." You can't destroy property, and if you want to pitch your tent for more than a day, you have to have permission of the landowner. You might also enjoy reading about the Swedish educational system and comparing it to the one you know.

http://smorgasbord.navigo.se/

The Saami - people of the sun and wind

The Saami are northern Scandinavia's indigenous people. Their traditional homeland crosses five national borders, and about 20,000 Saami currently live in the Swedish part. Although originally hunters and gatherers, they are now better known for their large herds of reindeer. There are eight distinct seasons in reindeer herding; find out about them here. The Saami now have their own parliament under Swedish law, and its task is to provide the Saami with a way to determine their own political future.

http://www.sametinget.se/english/

> "A ship in the harbor
> is safe, but that is not
> what ships are built for."
> —John A. Shedd

Virtual Sweden Introduction

Sweden is about the size and shape of California, and you'll find a good map here. You'll also find other information about its geography, people (including King Carl XVI Gustaf), and the country in general. There's even a recipe section so you can try Swedish food, although some of the ingredients might be a little hard to find: stinging nettles and reindeer heart! But you might try the recipe for delicious waffles, traditionally eaten on March 25, Annunciation Day. According to this site, "They are also very popular in Swedish mountain resorts, where they generally are served together with whipped cream and cloudberry jam." Now if we could just find some cloudberry jam, we'd be all set!

http://www.sr.se/rs/virtual/

Welcome to the Royal Court of Sweden

This is the official Web site of the Swedish monarchy. Carl XVI Gustaf, who ascended the throne in 1973, is the 74th King of Sweden. The monarchy goes back over a thousand years. You will learn about the King, Queen Silvia, and the rest of the royal family here. Check the information on the palace and why it has a different architectural style on each of its four sides.

http://www.royalcourt.se/eng/

SWITZERLAND

Information About Switzerland

That's just exactly what this site provides: basic information about Switzerland, and more. You find the usual area, population, and government statistics and a map. An interesting section further down lists famous people from Switzerland, such as William Tell (remembered for the famous apple incident), St. Nicholas (Santa Claus), and psychoanalyst Carl Jung, just to name a few. A good portion of this site is in German and English.

http://www.ethz.ch/swiss/Switzerland_Info.html

(NMBE) Saint Bernard Dog

It is winter, in the year 1800. At the summit of Switzerland's Great St. Bernard Pass, 8,100 feet above sea level, Napoleon Bonaparte's soldiers struggle against the "White Death" of snow and ice fog. They flounder in the deep snow, trying to find the way back to the right path. Just as they despair of ever finding it again, they hear a friendly bark! A huge fluffy dog bounds up to them. It's "Barry," one of the distinctive dogs owned by the nearby monastery. Since the eleventh century, the monks have offered travelers shelter from the fierce mountain storms, and their big working dogs have been adept at finding lost people and saving lives. The dog leads the soldiers back to the warm monastery buildings, called a hospice. As this site says, "The existence of such dogs has been documented in paintings and drawings dating back to 1695 and in written official documents of the Hospice since 1707." Read more about the early history of the Saint Bernard dog, and see wonderful pictures of this remarkable breed.

http://www-nmbe.unibe.ch/abtwt/saint_bernard.html

Swiss Embassy in Washington DC

This official site presents a history of the country, tourist information, and a link to the 2006 Winter Olympics campaign to bring the games to Switzerland. You'll also find out the connection between the Swiss flag and the Red Cross organization.

http://www.swissemb.org/

Switzerland Home Screen

Did you know that Geneva is the birthplace of the World Wide Web? Tim Berners-Lee started it, way back in 1989. Visit <http://www.w3.org/People/Berners-Lee-Bio.html/> to learn about Berners-Lee, and then go to the site listed here for info on Switzerland. Check out the history, the culture, the geography, and the art of Switzerland at this site. Also find additional in-depth information on Geneva and Zurich.

http://expedia.msn.com/wg/places/
   Switzerland/HSFS.htm

SYRIA

ArabNet — Syria

The modern state of Syria was not established until 1946, after the Second World War, but it is a land that has been inhabited since ancient times. An overview of the history, geography, people, business, culture, government, and more is found at this site. It also links to other Arab countries.

http://www.arab.net/syria/syria_contents.html

Lonely Planet — Destination Syria

If you're looking for information on just about every subject having to do with Syria, then here it is. Syria boasts the oldest capital, Damascus. The first written alphabet came from Syria, and bronze was invented there. It was the scene of many battles during the Crusades. Three continents meet in Syria: Asia, Africa, and Europe. It was also a trade crossroads between the Caspian Sea, the Indian Ocean, the Black Sea, and the Nile River. The Silk Road, a famous trade route to China, also went through Syria. This site offers both tourist and general background information on the country.

http://www.lonelyplanet.com/dest/mea/syr.htm

NET FILES

What's the longest-lived mammal on Earth? What's the second longest-lived mammal?

Answer: Man has the longest life of all mammals, but the spiny anteater comes in second with a life expectancy of 50 years. Read more about this unusual egg-laying mammal at *http://edx1.educ.monash.edu.au/~juanda/vcm/gary.htm.*

TAIWAN

See CHINA—AUTONOMOUS AREAS—TAIWAN

TAJIKISTAN

Tajikistan Resource Page

Formerly part of the Soviet Union, Tajikistan is bordered by China to the east, Uzbekistan to the west, Kyrgyzstan to the north, and Afghanistan and Pakistan to the south. It is a country of political unrest, and life there is uncertain. Do yetis (Abominable Snowmen) really live in the inaccessible mountain wilderness there? Some people think so!

http://www.soros.org/tajkstan.html

TANZANIA

The Sukuma Home Page

The Sukuma culture is the largest in Tanzania. They live near the equator close to Lake Victoria, the second largest lake in the world. Visit the Sukuma Museum and learn about Sukuma culture, religious practices, and dances. You'll read about the traditional Sukuma healers and learn "that their power for healing is dependent on the goodwill of their ancestors." There is much more to read and learn about these people and their lives, and the text has many pictures that can be enlarged by clicking on them.

http://photo.net/sukuma/

Tanzania Website

This official Tanzanian embassy site features facts on the country, its symbols and flag, and some nice maps. You can also view some photos of Mount Kilimanjaro and find out about the Uhuru Torch. First lit in 1961, it sends symbolic light and hope beyond the borders to wherever there is despair in the world.

http://www.tanzania-online.gov.uk/

THAILAND

Lonely Planet — Destination: Thailand

At this site you'll find tons of all the usual info you'll ever need for reports, papers, or whatever. There's even a recommended reading section with books, articles, and travel guides on Thailand. Just watch out for the land mines on the Cambodian border—read the warning here.

http://www.lonelyplanet.com/dest/sea/thai.htm

Thailand: His Majesty King Bhumibol Adulyadej's Golden Jubilee Home Page

His Majesty King Bhumibol Adulyadej of Thailand was born in Cambridge, Massachusetts. He became King in 1946, and in 1996 he celebrated his Golden Jubilee—50 years as monarch. According to the information presented here, he is very popular among his subjects. He is involved in making technology and other scientific advances available to his people. Read about his agricultural and other reforms, and get a glimpse of the beautiful Jubilee celebration and its royal regalia. There are also Internet tutorials on this page, which shows how serious the King is about encouraging his people to learn about technology.

http://kanchanapisek.or.th/index.en.html

Tourism Authority of Thailand

The Emerald Buddha. The Golden Royal Barges. Thai horoscopes. This well-written and beautiful site gives you a fascinating look at Thailand, from its prehistory to its current monarchy. You'll also learn about sights, foods, and a provincewide guide to local information and attractions.

http://www.tat.or.th/

Not everything on the Net is true.

TIBET

See CHINA—AUTONOMOUS AREAS—TIBET

TOGO

Togo's OFFICIAL Web Page

This small African nation is about the size of West Virginia, with a population of about 4.5 million people. Its southernmost border is comprised of less than 30 miles of coastline on the North Atlantic. This site has a map and lots of statistics about Togo that would be useful for a geography class report.

http://www.afrika.com/togo/

TOKELAU

See NEW ZEALAND—DEPENDENCIES—TOKELAU

TONGA

Welcome to the Kingdom of Tonga

If we ask you to meet us just west of where the international date line crosses the Tropic of Cancer, where would we be? In the Kingdom of Tonga! Made up of three island groups, Tonga has about 171 islands, the newest of which is Metis Shoal, created by volcanic activity in June 1995. With its coral reefs, rain forests, and volcanic islands, Tonga was the first South Pacific nation to establish national parks and reserves to protect its unique ecology. While you're visiting this site, you can hear a welcome message from Tonga's Crown Prince Tupouto'a and even see a film of one of their native dances.

http://www.vacations.tvb.gov.to/

NET FILES

What's the most visited national park in the U.S.?

(Hint: We mean national park, not national recreation area, parkway, or national monument.)

Answer: Nope, it's not the Grand Canyon in Arizona (5.4 million visitors a year). It's not Yosemite in California (5.2 million tourists). And Yellowstone in Montana, Idaho, and Wyoming is about the same (5.2 million). The winner is: the Great Smoky Mountains National Park in Tennessee. Almost six million people a year come to see its beautiful forests and mountain vistas! Find out more parks trivia at
http://www.ngd.nps.gov/stats/fiscal93397.htm

TRINIDAD AND TOBAGO

Discover Trinidad and Tobago

You're enjoying a holiday at a lush Caribbean resort, strolling through throngs of brightly dressed families playing music and singing and dancing. Suddenly you're doused with sprays of multicolored paint! Welcome to the Phagwa Festival, celebrated annually by the many Hindu residents of the islands of Trinidad and Tobago. This site explains many of the holidays celebrated in the region. Also, check the Reference section for basic facts, maps, and photos.

http://www.carib-link.net/discover/main.html

> ## You won't believe how the PLANTS, TREES, AND GARDENS section grew!

True True Trini:The Trinidad-Online! Homepage

The locals call it "T&T," and everyone knows this dual island nation as the birthplace of calypso and steelpan steel band music. The islands are among the largest producers of oil and natural gas in the Caribbean. But with the festive and bustling cities of Trinidad and the quiet, unspoiled beaches of Tobago, they are a haven for tourists the world over. Parts of this site were apparently under construction when we received this site, but the information here was well presented and unique, so we couldn't pass it up. Check the Wildlife and Nature, Trini Photo Album, Trini People, and Trinidadian Culture sections for some good reading.

http://www.smith.edu/~nbland/trinidad2.html

TUNISIA

ArabNet — Tunisia

Thousands of years ago, Carthage was home to the Phoenicians, and it rivaled the Roman Empire. It was from there that Hannibal led an army—mounted on elephants—across the Alps to invade Rome itself. Years later, the Romans retaliated and destroyed Carthage, leveling it to the ground. The city that rose atop the ruins became the capital of Tunisia, and it is a living remnant of those ancient times. This Web site allows you to explore the wonders and history of Tunisia. It features magnificent color photographs of the people and landmarks.

http://www.arab.net/tunisia/tunisia_contents.html

Welcome to the travel and tourism guide to Tunisia

As you glance at these beautiful color photographs of Tunisian towns such as Tunis and Carthage, you may think that some of the views look familiar. Did you see the movie *Star Wars*? The area known as Matmata, where people live underground to escape the heat of the Sahara Desert, was used as Luke Skywalker's home. Sixteen other cities are listed in the Places section, with pictures and descriptions. Also visit the museums and festivals in Culture for a complete experience.

http://www.tourismtunisia.com/

TURKEY

A Travel at Warp Speeds in Turkey

Hop aboard the Turkish time machine! Travel at warp speeds through ten thousand years and a multitude of civilizations. Mehmet Kurtkaya designed this clever cyberguide to Anatolia, now known as Turkey, as it developed from the Neolithic ages on through the twentieth century. It is truly amazing what is known about the people who lived in this area a hundred centuries ago. The time travel is complemented by a section called The Jewels of Anatolian History, featuring a dozen mind-boggling features and events of the region. According to legend, King Midas magically turned everything he touched to gold. While the legend is just a story, Midas was a real king of Gordion, located in central Turkey. And Gordion, too, is a place with its own legend: the Gordion Knot. Many wise and powerful people tried to untie the knot for years, believing that the one who could successfully untie it would be given magical powers. Alexander the Great conquered Gordion with his armies and came up with his own solution. He cut the knot open with his sword!

http://www.twarp.com/turkwarp.htm

TURKISH LANDSCAPE

Nestled comfortably between Europe and Asia, Turkey is the home of ancient cities built along historical silk and spice trade routes. Once you've seen Turkey, you simply can't confuse it with anywhere else. This site explores the look of Turkish architecture and styles of its people—see natural, historical, and cultural landscapes. Turkey is described here as the "crossroads of history," where East meets West. The Ottoman army blazed a trail across Europe in the sixteenth century, operating out of Turkey. They made it as far as the gates of Vienna in Austria, where they were driven back. The retreating armies left behind sacks of Turkish coffee, introducing the beverage to Europe. Even today, Vienna's coffee cafes are world famous.

http://www.turknet.com/turkey/landscape/

TURKISH STYLE

"The Turkish home is a living tradition whose refinements has continued uninterrupted for over 10,000 years, from the earliest recorded dwellings of Central Anatolia to the modern Istanbul townhouse." This site is a companion to the book by the same title. It is filled with pictures of Ottoman, traditional, and contemporary houses and architecture found in Turkey. The History and Traditions chapter describes the history and evolution of Turkish culture as it relates to Turkish architecture. This site provides a wonderful insight into the country, and the pictures are beautifully done.

http://www.arzu.com/turknet/turkishstyle/

TURKMENISTAN

Turkmenistan Resource Page

This former Soviet Republic, now an independent nation, is wedged between Iran, Afghanistan, Uzbekistan, Kazakhstan, and the Caspian Sea. You can't get there by train, so most visitors go by airplane. Turkmenis have been famous for their wool carpets for over two thousand years, and many of the ones made today use designs similar to those of long ago. You can also learn about the Akhal-Teke horses, an ancient breed once known as a cavalry mount, now popular as a show horse. They have an unusual diet, which includes eggs and butter. This Web site organizes lots of useful information concerning Turkmenistan. Here you'll find the latest news, arts, culture, business, government, human rights information, and just about anything else you might want to know about this nation.

http://www.soros.org/turkstan.html

TURKS AND CAICOS ISLANDS

See UNITED KINGDOM—DEPENDENCIES—TURKS AND CAICOS ISLANDS

NET FILES

Master chefs often wear very tall hats with 100 pleats in them. Why?

Answer: Chefs have worn special hats ever since ancient times. According to http://www.civilization.ca/membrs/canhist/hats/sp20eng.html "the pleats in a chef's hat—of which there should be 100—denote the number of ways in which a master chef could prepare eggs, since eggs were regarded by the ancient Persians, Greeks, and Romans as symbolic of the universe and hence as a special food. Its towering height, whiteness and stiffness give the chef's hat an air of authority, even in the paper version often seen today."

TUVALU

Tuvalu World Travel Guide

Tuvalu, a stamp-sized nation of just 8,000 people living on nine tiny atolls, coincidentally lists postage stamps as its main source of international trade. Formerly known as the Ellice Islands, it is located in the western Pacific Ocean, north of Fiji.

http://www.wtgonline.com/data/tuv/tuv.asp

UGANDA

Buganda Home Page

Buganda is a large region in the southern part of Uganda, comprising most of Uganda's shoreline on Lake Victoria. The people of Buganda are known as Baganda, and they are the largest of Uganda's 40 different ethnic groups. Within the Baganda are 46 different clans officially recognized by the government. According to this site, "A clan represents a group of people who can trace their lineage to a common ancestor in some distant past." Read more about the different clans, Bugandan history, and languages at this site. Various words on the pages are linked to additional information on other sites, but they don't all work. However, even without the links, you'll find a wealth of reading here.

http://ozric.eng.wayne.edu/~ssemakul/buganda.htm

THIS IS UGANDA

Winston Churchill called Uganda the "pearl of Africa." Once you've toured this site and seen what Uganda has to offer with its scenery and wildlife, you may agree. With information about Ugandan history, government, education, geography, business, health, human rights, and other important facts, this site offers rich insights into this developing nation.

http://www.africa-insites.com/uganda/

Uganda

Surprisingly, even though this page was developed by a travel agency trying to get people to vacation in Uganda, it is still quite frank about the brutal history of the country and its two terrible dictators. For good hard, historical facts about Uganda, this may be the site to see.

http://www.kilimanjaro.com/uganda/uganda.htm

UKRAINE

Kiyiv-Pechesrsk Lavra

This site explores the cultural side of the Ukraine. Most notable here is the truly in-depth exploration of the 900-year-old Lavra monastery and its network of caves and catacombs in Kiev, Ukraine's capital city. In fact, the Ukrainian word *pechery,* which means "caves," is where the monastery gets its name. Also to be found here is a look at a recently unearthed collection of carved stone artwork done by Cossack warriors of the eighteenth and nineteenth centuries. Plus, you'll discover an exhibition of breathtaking woodcuts by Ukrainian artist Jackues Hnizdovsky, a history of the last five years of Ukrainian independence, and much more. Parts of this site are in the Ukraine language, but the sections mentioned above are all in English.

http://www.lavra.kiev.ua/

Welcome to Kyiv

Kyiv (or Kiev) is the capitol and sports center of the Ukraine. It's known for having produced world-class champions in track, weight lifting, boxing, and wrestling. Tour The Lost Churches of Kyiv in the Culture section, where you'll find pictures and brief histories of 20 churches that were demolished in the 1930s when Stalin's Soviet Union occupied the city. On April 26, 1986, an episode at the nearby Chernobyl nuclear power plant marked the world's worst peacetime nuclear disaster. Read about these events and more at this site. You'll find much about Kyiv here, although all sections were not yet functioning when we visited.

http://www.kyiv.com.ua/index_e.htm

Welcome to Ukraine

Moroccan boots, beautifully decorated eggs, and *holubtsi* (stuffed cabbage) are a few of the traditional icons of the Ukraine that you can read about at this site. For example, traditionally, eggs painted with magical symbols were believed to protect one from evil. After Christianity was introduced, the meaning of the eggs changed, and they were said to have been formed from Christ's tears. However, many of the original meanings have survived, such as: "Buds and leaves represent birth, growth and the continuity of life." As you explore this site, you will discover much more about the people and their lifestyles and the culture of the Ukraine. The government section was not available in English when we visited the site.

http://www.ukraine.online.com.ua/

UNITED ARAB EMIRATES

United Arab Emirates

Here's a good look at the United Arab Emirates, a very young and extremely wealthy country. Although mostly arid, in the past conditions were different. Paleontologists have found fossils that date back nearly 300 million years, and some of these fossils are of river-dwelling creatures. Apparently the region was once well watered, lush, and green. At this site you'll find extensive information about the history of the U.A.E., its geology and wildlife, its culture, and its government.

http://www.uaeinteract.com/

United Arab Emirates

This site presents a brief overview of the country, including descriptions of the six emirates that joined together on December 2, 1971, to form the United Arab Emirates (U.A.E.). Another joined in 1972. Read about traditional children's games and fishing techniques, complete with pictures. Enjoy the sights with a photo tour of the country. There is also a biography of Sheikh Zayed Bin Sultan Al Nahayan, the President of the U.A.E.

http://www.emirates.org/

UNITED KINGDOM

The British Monarchy

This is the official Web site of the British royals. Here you will learn about the monarchy as it exists today as well as how it was in the past. You'll visit the palaces, the crown jewels, even find out why Elizabeth II keeps corgis as pets! There is a section on a typical day in the life of Her Royal Highness, and you can find out about the many ceremonial duties she must perform. If you're interested in exactly what was said, sung, and done back on June 2, 1953, when Elizabeth became an anointed sovereign, the Queen of England, you can follow the complex procedure at *<http://www.oremus.org/liturgy/coronation/>*.

http://www.royal.gov.uk/

BritSpeak

In America, a man would have no trouble complimenting a woman on the pants she wears, but in Britain, "pants" refers to one's underwear! Other strange bits of Britspeak: "public school" means private school, "homely" means pleasant, "presently" means soon, and "pavement" is a sidewalk. A speed bump on the road is called a "sleeping policeman." "Bob's your uncle" is what Brits say instead of "That's all there is to it," and a really brainless person is as "thick as two short planks." You'll find British to American and American to British dictionaries here as well as links to other similar pages. A caution to parents: Some common American words translate into rude British language and vice versa.

http://pages.prodigy.com/NY/NYC/britspk/main.html

Dr. Dave's UK Pages

The United Kingdom includes England, Wales, Scotland, and Northern Ireland. Dr. Dave's pages give you a look at the assorted cultures that make up the kingdom. You will find detailed looks at the cities, towns, and villages and a wonderful collection of photographic images organized by subject matter, such as castles, pub signs, and British cartoons and caricatures.

http://www.neosoft.com/~dlgates/uk/ukpages.html

Monarchs of Britain

They are all here: all the monarchs of England, from the Anglo-Saxon kings to Her Majesty Elizabeth II. This site is lavishly illustrated with portraits and photos. For example, learn about William the Conqueror, who started on his claim to fame when he became Duke of Normandy at age seven. Even after spending grueling days out in the field conquering his enemies, he still had to keep his guard up when relaxing back at the castle. Among the other family members the desire to be king often led to assassination attempts and fatal "accidents." Learn more about William and his "unruly" family at this illustrated site. A long list of links is also provided so you can find out what the rest of the royals were up to during their time of rule.

http://www.britannia.com/history/h6f.html

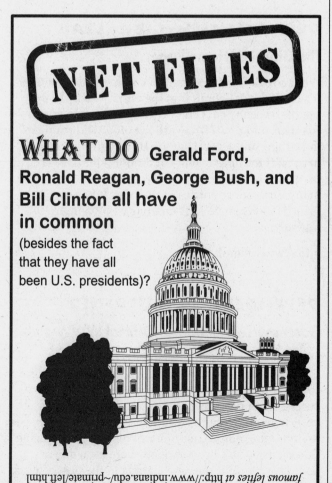

NET FILES

WHAT DO Gerald Ford, Ronald Reagan, George Bush, and Bill Clinton all have in common

(besides the fact that they have all been U.S. presidents)?

Answer: *They are all left-handed! Find out more about famous lefties at* http://www.indiana.edu/~primate/left.html

DEPENDENCIES—ANGUILLA

Anguilla's Home Page

This small British dependency is located at the northern end of the Leeward Islands in the Caribbean Sea. It was discovered by Christopher Columbus in 1493 and was formerly the British colony administered as Saint Kitts-Nevis-Anguilla. In 1982, Anguilla became a separate British dependent territory. Anguilla has beautiful island scenery with lots of beaches and coral reefs that are great for snorkeling. Stay away from the manchineel trees (the ones with the green apples). The sap can burn and irritate the skin.

http://anguillahomepage.ai/

DEPENDENCIES—BERMUDA

Welcome to Bermuda and Bermuda Online!

Bermuda is a group of islands almost 600 miles east of North Carolina and 700 miles south of Nova Scotia. It was discovered by accident in 1503 by Juan de Bermudez, a Spanish navigator. However, Bermuda wasn't colonized until the British Admiral Sir George Somers wrecked his ship there in 1609. This became the first permanent settlement. One of the "castaways" from the wreck was John Rolfe, who later became the husband of Pocahontas, the Native American girl who twice saved the life of Captain John Smith. Today, the islands officially have the dual name of Somers Isles and Bermuda. From this site, you can link to many other sites on Bermuda, as well as all government departments and officials.

http://www.bermuda-online.com/

DEPENDENCIES—BRITISH VIRGIN ISLANDS

BVIWelcome On-line Caribbean Destination Interactive Magazine

This group of about 50 islands is located about 60 miles east of Puerto Rico. Its subtropical climate and island environment make the British Virgin Islands a popular tourist resort. All the islands are volcanic except Anegada, which is a coral and limestone atoll. Visit this site and read about the history, the shipwrecks, the snorkeling, and all the fun you can have if you go!

http://www.bviwelcome.com/

DEPENDENCIES—CAYMAN ISLANDS

Cayman Web World

The Cayman Islands motto is "He hath founded it upon the seas." The sea has definitely played a major role in the history of these three small islands in the Caribbean. Cayman's historical beginning (officially at least) was on May 10, 1503, when Christopher Columbus encountered the then-uninhabited islands of Little Cayman and Cayman Brac. You may have also heard of the notorious Edward Teach (or Thatch), better known as Blackbeard the pirate, who lived in the Caymans and offered refuge to other buccaneers and their stolen treasures. Today, tourists come from all over the world to enjoy Cayman's beautiful beaches and the natural wonders of the islands' waters.

http://cayman.com.ky/

Class 5M - Red Bay Primary School

The kids here want you to know all about how they live and work in their beautiful Cayman Island communities. Take a look at how they celebrate Pirate's Week and Christmas in this tropical land. White beach sand is usually brought inside homes to be "pretend snow." Although these kids have never seen real snow, they know what it's like, and you can read their poems about it! You can also learn about the special programs to protect and support marine turtles.

http://www.monmouth.com/~bmeekings/5m.html

Online Guide to the Cayman Islands: Welcome

Pirates, iguana, sea turtles, coral—you'll find them all on the Cayman Islands. Well, all but the pirates, unless you come to visit the last week of October and join in the annual Pirate's Week Festival. Any week of the year, you can see the other popular sights in Cayman, such as the endangered blue iguana in Queen Elizabeth II Botanic Park or green sea turtles at the Cayman Turtle Farm. Maybe you'd like to explore the mysteries of the ocean—take a dive and experience the spectacular Cayman Wall and the fascinating undersea world of sponges and coral. You can't beat the year-round temperatures in the Caymans; just remember to bring your sun lotion!

http://cs.fit.edu/~jgoddar/

DEPENDENCIES—FALKLAND ISLANDS

Showcase - Falkland Islands

The Falklands, or Islas Malvinas, are claimed as part of the United Kingdom, which went to war to prove it when Argentina thought otherwise. At this site, you can learn a little about the history of the islands and the people, animals, and birds that inhabit them. Check the penguins. You'll see pictures and read about the different species. Isn't that rockhopper cute, with its tuft of feathers on top? You can get a good idea of how close the Falklands are to both Argentina and Antarctica at <http://www.tbc.gov.bc.ca/cwgames/country/Falklands/falkland.html>.

http://www.vni.net/~kwelch/penguins/showcase/showcase_Falklands.shtml

DEPENDENCIES—GIBRALTAR

The Gibraltar Home Page

What a rock! You've seen it in commercials and logos. It's the Rock of Gibraltar at the entranceway to the Mediterranean Sea. Did you know that wild apes roam around on it? They are the only wild primates in Europe, and legend says that something will happen if the apes leave—find out at this site! The history of Gibraltar shows how it has been ruled by many different countries in the past. It has been a British colony since 1704 and has its own internal self-rule.

http://www.gibraltar.gi/

DEPENDENCIES—GUERNSEY

Guernsey Tourist Board. Official WWW Site

Tucked right between England and France, this Channel Island is famous for its cows. Yes, Guernsey cows. You're just as likely to see one of them on the beach as in a pasture. Did pirates sail past Guernsey or did they land there with their loot? See these pages to find out. Another reminder of history is the Castle Cornet. They still fire a cannon there each day at noon. And look at the new stamps in the post office: cats, flowers, and movie detectives!

http://www.guernsey.net/~tourism/

DEPENDENCIES—ISLE OF MAN

Welcome to the Isle of Man

Legend has it that two fierce warriors battled between England and Ireland. In the course of the battle, a large chunk of Ireland was hurled, but it missed its target and fell into the North Irish Sea. And that is how the Isle of Man was created! Well, believe what you like, but know for certain that this Web site contains a good overview of this historical island country, a British Crown dependency. Its history (wow, Vikings), its geography and climate (not too hot or cold), and its people (Irish and English settlers) are all explored briefly here. And there are great pictures, too! Check out the Basking Shark project and the Home for Old Horses. What is the story behind the national symbol: three running legs connected in the center? Find out here.

http://www.isle-of-man.com/

DEPENDENCIES—JERSEY

JerseyWeb - Home Page

Jersey Web has information on just about anything you need to know about this Channel Island. With links to other helpful sites, tourism info, and more, this is a great site if you are planning a trip or you just want some information about the island, which is only 14 miles from France. Heard of Jersey cows? (Or is that "herd" of Jersey cows?) They come from there.

http://www.jersey.co.uk/

NET FILES

What carnivorous "bear" isn't really a bear after all and doesn't even eat meat?

Anwer: The giant black and white pandas in China. Pandas actually belong to a family of their own, closely related to raccoons. The panda has the digestive system of a carnivore but long ago adapted to a vegetarian diet and now feeds almost entirely on the stems and leaves of bamboo in the forests of southwestern China. Find out more at http://www.wwfcanada.org/facts/panda.html

States of Jersey Home Page

This page is the official site of Jersey's government. As the largest of the Channel Islands, it is a British Crown dependency. Heritage, sports, government, business, and tourism are covered at this site.

http://www.jersey.gov.uk/

DEPENDENCIES—MONTSERRAT

Official Montserrat Tourist Board Web Site

Currently, this Caribbean island is in crisis. Montserrat's volcano explosively erupted on September 17, 1996, depositing 600,000 tons of ash on the southern part of the island. Volcanic activity continues today. You can read about the volcanic history of the island, scientific studies of the volcano, and daily reports on volcanic activity at this site.

http://www.geo.mtu.edu/volcanoes/west.indies/
soufriere/govt/

DEPENDENCIES—PITCAIRN ISLANDS

Pitcairn Island Web Site

Isolation: see Pitcairn Island. This is a place where it takes months for mail and news to arrive. You could always call one of the 50 islanders on the phone. Not "their" individual phone, *the* phone. There is only one phone on the island. How could a place that is this far out of the mainstream possibly interest anyone? This site answers that question with a wealth of current local happenings, a list of who's who on the island, history (including the settlement by HMS *Bounty* mutineers), and more. View the local crafts and place your order. Look at the scenes and faces of the island. Read the musical scores, poems, and stories about Pitcairn. Just don't sail by! This is a great spot on the Web.

http://www.wavefront.com/~pjlareau/pitc1.html

DEPENDENCIES—SAINT HELENA

Saint Helena, South Atlantic Ocean

It's a good thing you can visit Saint Helena on the Web. It's very difficult to get there in person. Tiny Saint Helena is remote (1,200 miles from Africa, 1,800 miles from Brazil), and it's almost inaccessible. The only way you can get there is by mail boat, which sails six or seven times a year. The island's volcanic terrain has prevented any airports and runways from being built. But Saint Helena has a fascinating history and unique plant and animal life. Napoleon Bonaparte spent the last six years of his life there, in exile. At this page, you can see a picture of the wirebird, learn about island life today, and even find out how to get to the island. Take the spectacular photo tour, too, especially if you don't think you'll get there very soon. The island is a British dependent territory, and the people there are called "Saints." Larger islands dependent on Saint Helena are Ascension and Tristan da Cunha, even though they are miles and miles away!

http://geowww.gcn.ou.edu/Ascension/sh.htm

DEPENDENCIES—SOUTH GEORGIA AND THE SOUTH SANDWICH ISLANDS

South Georgia and The South Sandwich Islands

Name a city in South Georgia. Waycross, you say? Yes, that's right, but the world has more than one South Georgia. The one we're talking about is officially called South Georgia and the South Sandwich Islands. These islands are overseas British territories. But they are also claimed by the South American nation of Argentina. Fairly close to Antarctica, some of these islands have permanent ice and snow cover, and one has a herd of reindeer (the reindeer are not native; the species was brought there). A bit more about these islands can be found at <http://www.tcol.co.uk/part_v/sth-georgia.html>.

http://www.odci.gov/cia/publications/ factbook/sx.html

DEPENDENCIES—TURKS AND CAICOS ISLANDS

Welcome to Turks & Caicos!

Recent evidence points to the Grand Turk Island as being the first place Columbus landed in the New World. Not too long afterward, the people who greeted Columbus vanished, and the islands were uninhabited for two hundred years. Pirates made the Turks and Caicos Islands their hideout for a long time. This site will provide you with a good overview of these Caribbean islands and why they are so popular with tourists and divers.

http://www.interknowledge.com/turks-caicos/

ENGLAND

Guy Fawkes Day

On November 5 every year, people in England shoot off fireworks, light bonfires, and make a lot of noise. Why? They are celebrating a foiled plot to blow up the Parliament Buildings way back in 1605. It seems one Guy Fawkes and his group wanted to kill the King and all the members of Parliament. Thirty-six barrels of gunpowder were discovered just in time, and the traitors were executed. "Burning the Guy" is another tradition, where an *effigy*, or pretend figure, representing Guy Fawkes is thrown onto the bonfire. Children ask for "pennies for the Old Guy"—and they buy firecrackers with the money! It is the English version of trick or treating, and you can read about this holiday here. For an explanation with a little more detail, written by an English schoolgirl, try <http://www.kidlink.org/KIDPROJ/MCC/mcc0422.html>.

http://web.idirect.com/~redsonja/guy/

The Tower of London

The Traitor's Gate. The Bloody Tower. The Ceremony of the Keys. The Crown Jewels. What an incredible history this building has. The Tower of London has been a treasury, a prison, and a government building for a thousand years. It is said that if the ravens that inhabit the Tower green ever leave, the Commonwealth of Great Britain will fall. You can take a tour of the Tower and its grounds right here. But don't scare the ravens!

http://www.camelot-group.com/tower/

Westminster Abbey - Place of Worship, and House of Kings

This London landmark has been the site of every British coronation since 1066. Many kings and queens are entombed at the Abbey, notably Elizabeth I. You'll also find Chaucer's grave in the Poets' Corner, along with those of other famous English authors, including Charles Dickens. The Abbey has been the scene of numerous royal ceremonies, including royal weddings and other occasions. The funeral of Diana, Princess of Wales, was held at Westminster Abbey on September 6, 1997. Admire the inspiring Gothic architecture as you wander around with the other tourists at this site.

http://www.westminster-abbey.org/

NORTHERN IRELAND

Official Guide to Northern Ireland

This Tourist Board site offers a look at the historical and cultural context of Northern Ireland. But the site looks at the sweetness and light, and not the dark side of "the troubles," as the civil unrest there is called.

http://www.interknowledge.com/northern-ireland/

SCOTLAND

The Internet Guide to Scotland: the Highlands and Islands

It's really *Eigg*-citing news! The Isle of Eigg is now owned by a coalition of its residents and a nonprofit organization willing to help preserve the unique natural and cultural heritage of this small Hebridean Island, located ten miles offshore, south of the Isle of Skye. What's it like there? According to this site, "Its 7,400 acres of heather moorland, wooded glens, fertile fields and spectacular beaches are dominated by the massive basalt ridge of An Sgurr." Eigg, by the way, comes from a Gaelic word meaning "notch." This site has lots of info on all regions of Scotland, including all the small isles.

http://ourworld.compuserve.com/homepages/
  RJWinters/scotland.htm

Scottish Tourist Board

This site is a rich treasure trove of kilts, Loch Ness monsters, castles, historic battlefields, and, yes, bagpipes. According to this site, the Scottish didn't invent bagpipes, although they have elevated the playing of them to a real art form. Bagpipes consist of a sheepskin bag and five wooden projections. One is the mouthpiece, three are drone pipes, and one is called the chanter, which is the one your fingers actually play. Bagpipes only have one volume: loud! You can't vary the volume level at all. Luckily, Scotland has all those lonely heaths and moors, with all kinds of room to play, where no one will be disturbed. To read more about bagpipes and how you can get one, visit this excellent site.

http://www.holiday.scotland.net/practical_info.htm

NET FILES

Worldwide, what can you buy for the equivalent of about $4 of U.S. money?

Answer: *In Singapore, you can buy five cans of Coca Cola or one Big Mac, or for something different, a bowl of laksa (a curry noodle dish), one glass of soybean milk, and a bowl of ice kachang (a multicolored, multi-ingredient ice dessert). In Nigeria, that much money could pay your monthly rent, or it could buy 50 pounds or more of rice, 50 pounds of flour, or 10 pounds of meat. Send in your own answers at* http://www.winmera.net.au/CurrComp/CurrComp.html

WALES

The Castles of Wales

At this site you'll find pictures and descriptions of over 150 castles, most of them in Wales. The others are in England, on the often-disputed "marcher" lands between the English and Welsh borders. You can learn a lot of historical facts, including some hints about castle construction (should you ever get enough Legos to do such a thing). If you don't know a *portcullis* from a *trebuchet*, not to worry—there is a very cool dictionary of castle terms here. Don't forget the moat!

http://www.castlewales.com/home.html

Official Wales Tourist Board Web Site

Ireland has Saint Patrick, and Wales has March 1—Saint David's Day, which is celebrated by Welsh people all over the world. You wouldn't wear a shamrock, though, because the national emblems of Wales are the leek and the daffodil (in Welsh, the word for leek and the word for daffodil are almost the same: *cenhinen* means "leek," and *cenhinen pedr* means "daffodil"). As the legend goes at this site, "St. David advised the Britons, on the eve of a battle with the Saxons, to wear leeks in their caps so as to easily distinguish friend from foe. This helped to secure a great victory. It is also thought that the same thing occurred when Welsh archers fought with Henry V at the battle of Agincourt. Hence, the wearing of leeks on St. David's Day. It is still a surviving tradition that soldiers in the Welsh regiments eat a raw leek on St. David's Day." This excellent site explains many Welsh cultural themes and highlights lots of interesting regions and places to visit. Be sure to stop in at *Llanfair-pwllgwyngyllgogerychwyrndrobwllllantysiliogogogoch*, which has the longest name of any village in Wales. The name means "Saint Mary's (church) in the hollow of the white hazel near a rapid whirlpool and Saint Tysilio's (church) by the red cave." Its home page is at <*http://www.nwi.co.uk/llanfair/*>, and you can practice saying the name along with the audio recording.

http://www.tourism.wales.gov.uk/

UNITED STATES

See UNITED STATES *in the main section of this book*

URUGUAY

URUGUAY - Country of Encounter

Uruguay, once known as Banda Oriental, is one of the oldest democracies in South America. Its two political parties go back to the 1830s. On these pages, you will find a well-written history of the nation, a monthly calendar of events, tourism information, maps, weather reports, geological data, and lots more. You'll have to scroll to the bottom of General Info to find most of the links for that area.

http://www.turismo.gub.uy/index-e.html

UZBEKISTAN

Cyber Uzbekistan

Uzbekistan, a former Soviet Republic, is a study in contrasts. The nation, standing at the crossroads of Asia, is mostly wide expanses of sandy nothingness. The capital city of Tashkent, however, despite being over 2,000 years old, is almost entirely modern. Most of the old city was destroyed in an earthquake in 1966, and the new city was built up over the ruins. There are factories, theaters, even a subway system. This Web site explores all of Uzbekistan, including photographs of Tamerlane's Tomb, the Market Place of Bukhara, and the infamous Tower of Death. Get news reports and a short list of English-Uzbek phrases here as well.

http://www.advancenet.net/~k_a/uzbekistan/

Uzbekistan Resource Page

In early times, Uzbekistan was a thoroughfare for travelers on the Great Silk Road, a land passage from Europe to Asia, so it played an important role on the world scene. At the end of the fifteenth century, new sea routes from Europe to India were discovered, and Uzbekistan lost its strategic economic importance. It was colonized by Tsarist Russia in 1860 and became independent in 1991. Uzbekistan is now enjoying world exposure again.

http://www.soros.org/uzbkstan.html

VANUATU

Vanuatu - A Canadian's Perspective

Ever wonder what life would be like on a tropical island? There is a big difference between having a vacation and actually living there. The author of this site spent five years living and working in Vanuatu, where 170-mile-per-hour cyclones are a fact of life and lolling under a coconut tree can be deadly if a coconut happens to fall off. The author describes and contrasts life in Vanuatu's city and country areas and includes a number of photographs and links, not all of which may be appropriate for all members of your family.

http://www.silk.net/personal/scombs/vanuatu.html

VANUATU: AN INTRODUCTION

For people who have seen the movie and musical *South Pacific*, this very tiny island nation is more well known as "Bali Hai." Actually, *South Pacific* wasn't really filmed there but in Hawaii instead (they just pretended to be in Vanuatu). The Robin Williams movie *Club Paradise*, which was not set in Vanuatu, actually *was* filmed there. Formerly known as the New Hebrides, the islands were jointly run by the French and the English, but since 1980, it has been an independent country. This site is full of breathtaking photographs and written impressions of the place people think of when they envision tropical islands. There is much to explore, see, and even hear on these pages. The webmaster recommends you take your time, just as you would if you were strolling around Vanuatu itself.

http://www.clark.net/pub/kiaman/vanuatu.html

Welcome to Vanuatu Online

Vanuatu means "Land Eternal," according to this page, which claims to be the largest and most up-to-date Web site on this nation. There is a link to Vanuatu Weekly's online edition and information on the use of Vanuatu as a confidential tax haven for financial and estate planning matters. There is also a description of several of the islands, including Tanna, home of a smoldering volcano, wild horses, and traditional villages.

http://www.vanuatu.net.vu/

VATICAN CITY

See HOLY SEE

VENEZUELA

La Cocina Venezolana

Venezuelans must love terrific food, judging by the variety of wonderful recipes at this site, translated as "The Venezuelan Cuisine." Many of the recipes are written in Spanish, but a large number of them are available in English as well. Some are also translated into Japanese. You can discover how to make delicious main dishes, such as *tequeños* (fried cheese pastries) and *cachapas* (corn pancakes), or sweet desserts, such as *churros* and flan. There are links to other Latin American recipe pages as well.

http://members.tripod.com/~cocinavzla/

Lonely Planet — Destination: Venezuela

Venezuela is home to a strange variety of animals, such as the jaguar, ocelot, tapir, armadillo, anteater, and the longest snake in the world, the anaconda. Angel Falls, the world's highest waterfall (16 times the height of Niagara Falls) is there, and the Amazonian jungles are full of beauty and mystery. Designed for travelers looking for exciting places to visit, the Lonely Planet Venezuelan page is chock-full of fascinating information about the country.

http://www.lonelyplanet.com/dest/sam/ven.htm

Venezuela Is Beautiful

Tour Venezuela's beautiful scenery at this site with a multitude of photos complete with descriptions and historical information. You won't regret the load time after you've seen a few of these pages. Another site with a scenic tour of this beautiful land is Venezuela in Postcards at <*http://www.coroweb.com/venez.htm*>.

http://venezuela.mit.edu/tourism/brochure/

VIETNAM

Lonely Planet - Destination Vietnam

Since Vietnam was opened up to American travelers a couple of years ago, it has become a popular tourist destination. Vietnam's French and Asian traditions blend to make it the home of unique contrasts. Ho Chi Minh City (once known as Saigon) is full of hustling, bustling street vendors and exotic shops and peaceful, scenic pagodas and cathedrals. The Lonely Planet travel pages offer a surprisingly thorough and balanced guide to Vietnam's environment, culture, history, and well-known and off-the-beaten-track attractions. The fast-loading, mostly text page also offers links to beautiful photographs.

http://www.lonelyplanet.com/dest/sea/vietnam.htm

Vietconnection.com Home

Your parents probably have very strong emotional feelings concerning Vietnam. However, it has been over 20 years since the long war with that nation ended, and the people at Viet Connection have determined to use this Web site to take down cultural barriers between the Vietnamese people and the rest of the world. Here you can get news reports, shop for Vietnamese books, hear broadcasts from Radio Vietnam, and even get online language lessons! The news reports on the Web site have not been updated as frequently as promised, but we hope that this unique voice continues.

http://vietconnection.com/

Welcome to VietGATE

This site claims to be the "Yahoo of the Vietnamese online community." With a searchable collection of over 90,000 Vietnam-related pages, there's a good chance you'll find most of the Net's Vietnamese resources right here. Look in the VN Art, Culture & History link under Useful Stuff to find an extensive illustrated section on Vietnam's culture and past. And if you've ever wanted to try some Vietnamese cooking, there are many recipe links in VN Cooking Recipes to spice up your life. There's much more to explore here, so bookmark this site, because you'll want to come back for more.

http://www.vietgate.net/

NET FILES

How many people are on Earth?

Answer: Quite a few! For the latest estimate, check the world population clocks at http://sunsite.unc.edu/lunarbin/worldpop/

WALES

See UNITED KINGDOM—WALES

WALLIS AND FUTUNA

See FRANCE—DEPENDENCIES—WALLIS AND FUTUNA

WESTERN SAHARA

Western Sahara Home Page

Western Sahara is a nation that has been struggling for decades to keep its existence. Bordering Morocco has claimed the country as its own, and many of the Western Saharan people live in huge refugee camps. This desert country is the home of tent-dwelling nomads and has very little in the way of industry, cities, or farming. The site features a number of photographs that spell out the harsh conditions there better than words, and it offers links to an assortment of other Web pages offering background information. One that gives a view of life in the refugee camps is in the Land and People section.

http://www.oneworld.org/guides/sahara/

YEMEN

ArabNet — Yemen

Yemen, a small, mostly desert country on the Arabian peninsula, has pretty much avoided contact with the outside world for over a thousand years. This site is a good place to get an overview of Yemen's 3,000-year history. Around 2,700 years ago, a great dam was built there, making the area a rich agricultural center for growing spices that were traded around the world. In the year A.D. 570, the dam burst, and Yemen quickly became arid desert. In the 1970s, Yemen split into two countries, one of which was the first-ever Marxist Arabian state. In 1990, the two states joined together to become a republic.

http://www.arab.net/yemen/yemen_contents.html

Auracea Yemen

While most of the world considers Yemen to be a desert nation, it actually has a huge, mostly unexplored coastline teeming with underwater life. For the last 15 years, Daniel Jouvance and the International Marine Science Committee have been studying the wealth of the underwater world. Some of the things they discovered may lead to new antibiotics or other medicines. The Auracea Expedition explored ocean life off the coasts of Tunisia, Yemen, and Mozambique. See some of their incredible photographs here!

http://djouvance.com/history/h03c.html

YUGOSLAVIA

See SERBIA AND MONTENEGRO

ZAIRE

See CONGO, DEMOCRATIC REPUBLIC OF THE

ZAMBIA

THIS IS ZAMBIA

Zambia's geologic resources include a wealth of minerals. Eighty percent of its export earnings are from the sale of copper. Its gems are also known worldwide. Emeralds, amethysts, garnets, tourmalines, and agates are some of the minerals that are mined there and sold on the world market. Most anything you might want to know about Zambia can be found at this extensive site.

http://www.africa-insites.com/zambia/

Zambia Page

Prolific wildlife, spectacular sunsets, and unforgettable Victoria Falls (354 feet high)—all these are images of Zambia you may already know. For what you don't know, check this page or perhaps the World Factbook page on Zambia, which is linked at this site.

http://www.sas.upenn.edu/African_Studies/
    Country_Specific/Zambia.html

ZIMBABWE

Lonely Planet - Destination: Zimbabwe

Among the sites in Zimbabwe are Victoria Falls, one of the largest and most unspoiled major waterfalls in the world. The falls and the Zambezi River form a border with Zambia to the north, and Zambia claims the falls, too. Another popular tourist site is the Chipangali Wildlife Orphanage, where exotic animals once raised as pets are set loose in a protective environment.

http://www.lonelyplanet.com/dest/afr/zim.htm

INTRODUCTION

ASK NET-MOM: WHAT PARENTS ASK ME ABOUT KIDS AND THE INTERNET

In my travels as Net-mom, I do many radio and press interviews. I also do book signings, talks, and other appearances. Everywhere I go, people have the same questions: "How can I keep my kids safe on the Net?" is number one, followed by "Is there anything on the Net about <insert favorite subject here>?" The answers to some of these questions follow. Internet addresses referenced in the text are provided at the end of this introduction.

First, though, I know you're busy. You may want to save the long version for when you have more time. For the quicker version, here's a handout I wrote, with six short tips, which many people find useful.

Net-mom's "Don't Let the Information Superhighway Drive You Nuts"

1. Rules of the road: Buckle up!

Learn a few basic safety rules and find out about Internet culture and etiquette.

- Child Safety on the Information Superhighway: National Center for Missing and Exploited Kids, <http://www.missingkids.org/html/ncmec_default_child_safety.html>
- The Net: User Guidelines and Netiquette, <http://www.fau.edu/~rinaldi/net/>

2. Get a map.

How do you keep your kids from taking a "wrong turn" and ending up in a cyber-neighborhood that's not so nice? Best: be a parent and teach your values. Use my book, *The Internet Kids & Family Yellow Pages*, 3rd Edition, as a guidebook, too! Samples, free newsletter, and more info: <http://www.netmom.com/>

Interested in filters and other technology toolkit solutions?

- Larry Magid's Safe Kids and Safe Teens sites, <http://www.safekids.com/>
- Technology Inventory, <http://www.research.att.com/projects/tech4kids/>

3. Start your engines. Become an Internet-savvy parent!

If you feel left in the silicon dust by your far more skillful progeny, do something about it!!

- "Yahoo Internet Life Surf School," <http://www3.zdnet.com/yil/filters/surfjump.html>
- InterNIC's 15-Minute Series, <http://rs.internic.net/nic-support/15min/>
- Internet Coach CD ROMs Search for the Black Rhino, Mission to Planet X, Liftoff to Lizard Island, APTE, <http://www.apte.com/>

4. Get up to speed. Know how to use Internet search tools!

Too much information is sometimes worse than none at all!

- Net-mom's Seven Secrets of Internet Searching, <http://www.netmom.com/rescue/secrets.htm>
- Trico Academy Internet Training for Educators CD-ROM, <http://www.trico-associates.com/>

5. Are we there yet? Are we having fun yet?

Seven places to have too much fun on the Net.

- Socks' special tour to the White House, <http://www.whitehouse.gov/WH/kids/html/kidshome.html>
- San Francisco's Exploratorium, <http://www.exploratorium.edu/>
- Cyber Jacques' Cyber Seas Treasure Hunt, <http://www.cyberjacques.com/>
- ThinkQuest Competitions, <http://www.thinkquest.org/>
- Safe Chat areas: Freezone<http://www.freezone.com>, Headbone <http://www.headbone.com>
- The Teel Family Home Page, <http://www.teelfamily.com/>

6. Don't forget to pull over and park.

The Internet isn't everything; you need to remember to experience actual reality. Attention everyone, the Internet is closing! Please go play outside!

All About Net-mom

Q: How did you become Net-mom?

A: I first got on the Internet in 1991, and I had been involved in electronic bulletin board systems (BBS) and online conferencing at the WELL[1] long before that. In fact, from 1985–87, I ran a BBS[2] at the public library where I worked. Modems and home computer telecommunications were still new back then, and I did help many people take their first "baby steps" on the Net. Since I was a public librarian, I was used to answering a lot of "new user" questions. I think Dan Umstead at the Oneida Indian Nation[3] of New York was one of the first to call me "Mother Internet"—

which was later shortened to Net-mom. I got the Internet domain Net-mom.com in 1995 and registered the trademark in 1996. We subsequently got the domain Netmom.com too.

Q: Did you really coin the phrase "Surfing the Internet"?

A: Yes. NEXIS credits me with its first published use (1992). Read the original article and hear the tale at Birth of a Metaphor at my home page.[4]

This has become a cause célèbre in surfing circles, where some equate the phrase with mindless "channel surfing." Certainly no harm was intended: in fact it was meant to compare respectfully to a sport that takes great skill and ability. And that is what you needed back in 1991–92 if you wanted to use the Internet for anything besides e-mail.

You have to remember that in 1991–92, the Internet was not as we know it today. It was *much* harder to use, there were no indices as we have now, and you had to know a lot of arcane commands. It was an art, not a science. Today, we navigate ships using GPS satellites; in those days, navigating the Net was more like ancient Polynesian wayfinding: memorizing star pairs at each horizon, reading patterns of phosphorescence in the waves, and knowing the habits of pelagic birds.

In the article referenced above, I explain it like this: "In casting about for a title for the article, I weighed many possible metaphors. I wanted something that expressed the fun I had using the Internet, as well as hit on the skill, and yes, endurance necessary to use it well. I also needed something that would evoke a sense of randomness, chaos, and even danger. I wanted something fishy, net-like, nautical.

"At that time I was using a mouse pad from the Apple Library in Cupertino, CA, famous for inventing and appropriating pithy sayings and printing them on sportswear and mouse pads (e.g. 'A month in the Lab can save you an hour in the Library'). The one I had pictured a surfer on a big wave. 'Information Surfer' it said. 'Eureka,' I said, and had my metaphor."

Scroll down on the Birth of a Metaphor page mentioned above to see the original mousepad that inspired the phrase. I should mention that the closest I have come to surfing is that I wandered into a surf shop once, I have seen it on TV, and I paid homage to the Duke Paoa Kahanamoku statue on Waikiki Beach the last time I was in Honolulu (he is considered the father of modern surfing.[5]

Q: How can I contact you?

A: You can write to me by following the instructions at the following Web page: <*http://www.netmom.com/feedback.htm*>. Or, you can contact the publisher of this book.

Connecting to the Internet

Q: Why would I want to connect to the Internet?

A: Everyone has a different reason. Some parents first get a Net e-mail address because they discover they can write to their kids in college and get a quick answer back! Others go to the Net to find current information that is hard to find elsewhere: medical information, government information, or news from across the country or across the seas. Some people want to research their family trees, find old school roommates, or shop online. Kids want to play online games, get help with homework, and chat with their friends.

Sometimes people say, "Oh, I'm not interested in computers." Then I talk to them and find out that they are interested in dogs, or Asian cooking, or telescopes. So I tell them the types of things they can find on the Net that deal with those subjects. Usually they can't wait to find the nearest network connection after that!

Q: Why don't some people want to connect to the Internet?

A: The same thing happens with other types of technology. Some people don't choose to have a telephone. Some decide not to have a television. Some don't subscribe to magazines or newspapers. We all know people who don't own cars or don't cook in microwave ovens or will not use a credit card.

Why don't they use these things? In some cases it's because they don't want outside influences, cultural or otherwise, to intrude into their lives. Or they might see TV, newspapers, or the Net as an addictive "time sink," ready to eat up precious minutes better spent communicating directly with their kids. They might want to eat food that's not "nuked," or they might want to live as simply as possible. It follows that some people will also not want an e-mail address, a Web page, or a 56K modem. This is OK. The Net's not a necessity of life.

What's not OK is to avoid the Net because you think everyone else on it is a pedophile and every other Web page is full of porn. It's just not the case.

Q: But isn't it expensive to get on the Net?

A: These days, there are lots of ways to get on the Internet. Most U.S. Internet service providers (ISPs) will charge you about $10–$20 per month as a flat rate. This includes e-mail, Web access, and sometimes your own Web page. Internet service will become even more inexpensive. You can find a list of over 4,800 local, national, and international Internet service providers at The List.[6]

Remember that when you want to connect to the Internet it's not just the monthly service charge you have to consider; there are a number of associated costs. Expenses include the price of a computer, use of a phone line, and the monthly Internet service charge. Or in the case of WebTV,[7] it is the cost of the TV, the cost of the WebTV terminal, the use of the phone line, and monthly service subscription. For those using a cable modem, such as Road Runner,[8] it is the cost of your computer and the cost of the cable modem service (note that this type of access does not use a phone line).

Also, your time is valuable. Like anything else, you have to expect to spend some time on the Net in order to learn how to use it and to see if, and how, it fits into your family's life. Some types of Net connections are still hard to set up, and some of the more esoteric applications are difficult to use, especially the ones that use multimedia. The good news is that for the most common uses, it is now easier to use the Net than it is to program your VCR.

Q: What if we can't afford it?
A: Many U.S. public libraries offer some type of free Internet access. Some also provide Internet classes and other technical help. Check with your local librarians.

Another source to investigate: there may be a nearby community network or Free-net. There is an international list of these,[9] which is maintained by Peter Scott. Some offer low-cost or no-cost access, training, e-mail, and more.

For sources of free e-mail accounts,[10] free Web space,[11] and more, please see the INTERNET section in this book.

How to Protect Yourself and Your Family on the Net

Q: Isn't there a lot of pornography on the Net?
A: Some of the Web pages we've seen in the course of our research for this book include: legal and illegal pornography, racism, hate speech, gambling, drugs, alcohol, weapons, Satanism, propaganda, and other political and cultural influences to which you may not want your family exposed. These things are available on the Net, just as they are in real life.

No one company or organization regulates the Internet; it is a network of networks, each with its own policies and accountability. You can't control what happens on the Internet, but you can control your view of what's happening.

It's important to remember that the Internet is not the enemy. The Net is only the transport method; in that regard, it's like the telephone system. What you may want to filter out are the places you can call, some of which may not be appropriate for your family. You also want to control who "calls" you. The good news is that there are many tools to help you choose what you want to see.

Q: How do parental controls and filtering software tools work?
A: Parental control software can guide your kids to great places on the Net and it can keep them from getting into places you don't want them to visit. Some programs have many other features;[12] please check the PARENTING AND FAMILIES—INTERNET—INTERNET TOOLKIT section of this book.

Filtering the Internet generally works with either "forbidden" site lists or "allowed" lists. If users try to go to a site that is not allowed, the filter notices and prevents it from appearing on the computer screen; this is also called *blocking* a site. A "safe harbor" list works the other way: it includes only allowed or rated sites, and users can go *only* to sites included on that list, not anywhere else.

Many parents and public facilities will elect to use filtering software. You should be aware of how the filtering is done: who chooses what is on the forbidden or the allowed lists? How flexible is it to modify? Can parents make the filter more restrictive in general, or less restrictive, or can they choose to allow or restrict on a site-by-site basis? You should also find out how easy or difficult the software is to uninstall if you want to try something else!

Q: What kinds of questions should I ask filtering software companies?
A: Here are just a few:

- What are your criteria for rating sites?

- How can I find out what sites you have blocked?

- Please give me examples of forbidden sites in each category.

- How often are your lists/your product updated?

- Do I have to download a new list of blocked sites every day/week/month? Is it automatic?

- If I think a site should be/shouldn't be blocked, what should I do?

- Does your software support self-ratings schemes such as RSACi or SafeSurf or other PICS implementations? (See below for discussion of these terms.)

- Can I easily allow or disallow sites for my family?

- Can these changes be enabled "on the fly"?

- Is there a limit to the number of local changes I can save for my family's use? Is there a limit to the size of this file?

- Can I set up your software so that it will be more restrictive for my 6-year-old and less restrictive for my 14-year-old? And can I use the computer without controls for myself?

- How easy is it to install your software? Will it work with my current computer system?

- How easy is it to uninstall your software if I change my mind?

- What other features do you offer that would differentiate your product from the others?

- Can you tell me where and when your product has been reviewed so I can look up those articles?

Q: I have heard that filters don't work very well. What's the story?

A. I don't think any filter manufacturer will claim 100 percent accuracy. Sometimes blocks are made on sites that should be allowed, while other sites that should have been marked as blocked are allowed to pass. I think you should look at a number of opposing viewpoints[13] and data and make up your own mind about it. This information is in the PARENTING AND FAMILIES—INTERNET—INTERNET TOOLKIT section of the book.

The danger remains that in an effort to keep the view of the Net as noncontroversial as possible (whatever that means, given a global arena), blocking will be done with too broad a brush, or worse, with a hidden, undisclosed agenda. It is not hard to imagine, for example, a revisionist secretly blocking sites about the Holocaust.

Who would you trust to rate a Web site for you (besides Net-mom, that is!)? How about asking the webmaster of the site itself? Read on for more about RSACi and PICS.

Q: What is PICS and what is RSACi, and do I really need to know anything about them?

A: You should be aware of both PICS[14] and RSACi.[15] PICS stands for Platform for Internet Content Selection. It was developed by the World Wide Web Consortium (W3C) and is still in active development by member organizations. The W3C is located at the MIT Laboratory for Computer Science (LCS) in Cambridge, Massachusetts, and at the Institut National de Recherche en Informatique et en Automatique (INRIA) in Rocquencourt, France.

PICS is not software; it is a specification. It proposes a standard method of placing "metadata" tags within the source code of Web pages. These tags are readable by browsers, such as Microsoft's Internet Explorer, and some filtering software. You can get a complete list of PICS-compliant browsers and software at the PICS Web site.

RSAC is the Recreational Software Advisory Council. It began life as a voluntary industry rating organization for disclosing levels of violence in video games. You can read about its history at the Web site noted, but what interests us now is the RSACi, or RSAC Internet, ratings hierarchy. It implements the PICS specifications, but it is by no means the only organization with a PICS-compliant ratings system. However, the parental controls for Microsoft's Internet Explorer software use the RSACi ratings system by default. (Parents can choose to install and use other ratings systems.)

At publication date, about 80,000 Web sites have rated themselves using the RSACi system. Yes, that's right: the RSACi ratings are not done by organizations but by webmasters themselves. Do you want to rate your own home page? Do you know a little basic HTML (HyperText Markup Language)? Just go to the RSACi site and answer a few simple questions about the level of nudity, violence, and other adult subjects at your site. Based on your answers, you will be given a metadata HTML tag to insert in the header of your pages. You're also supposed to insert the "We Rated with RSACi!" graphic on each of your pages and have it link back to the RSAC page. As you can tell, it involves some effort and extra steps for webmasters. All rating is done "on the honor system," that is, no one from RSACi checks to see if the webmasters have rated their sites accurately. They do have to agree to be bound by RSACi terms—find out more about this at the RSACi Web site. Will RSACi become the standard PICS implementation, or will one of the many others surface as the industry leader? Time and market share will tell.

Q: Is there any way to tell if a page has been rated?

A: Yes, if it is an implementation of the PICS standard. Did you know that (depending on the browser you're using) you may be able to view the source code behind any Web page? For example, in Netscape, use the View pull-down menu and choose View Document Source. Depending on how you have Netscape configured, the source code (with all those HTML tags) either will show up in a new browser window or will be saved to disk as a simple text file that can be opened with a word processor.

The metadata tags will be at the top of the file. You may find that a particular site has no rating. Or, it may be a collector of ratings: one from SafeSurf, a Safe for Kids rating, and a RSACi rating. You may even find others.

My RSACi ratings tag for *<http://www.well.com/user/polly/>* is:

```
<META http-equiv="PICS-Label" content='(PICS-1.0
"http://www.rsac.org/ratingsv01.html" l gen true
comment "RSACi North
America Server" by "polly@well.com" for
"http://www.well.com/user/polly" on
"1997.03.10T13:03-0500" exp
"1997.07.01T08:15-0500" r (n 0 s 0 v 0 l 0))'>
```

Looks confusing, doesn't it? This translates into:

Nudity	0
Sex	0
Violence	0
Language	0

Q: You say there is parental control software in my browser? Where?

A: First, check your browser. Recent versions of Microsoft's Internet Explorer offer something called Content Advisor. Enable it by first clicking on the View menu, then on Options. From there, click on the Security tab and choose Enable Ratings. Just follow the instructions to set your limits in the RSACi categories: Sex, Nudity, Violence, and Language. There is a zero-to-four tolerance level; each is explained. You don't have to use the RSACi ratings files, either. At the Internet Explorer home page[16] is a FAQ (Frequently Asked Questions) file about the Content Advisor and instructions for changing from the RSACi ratings system to another one.

Not to be outdone, Netscape has announced NetWatch, which had not yet been released in the stand-alone version of Navigator as of press time. However, it has been released in Netscape's Communicator 4.5 beta (which includes Navigator, among other applications). According to a press announcement,[17] "NetWatch...will allow control over Web page viewing so users access only the Internet content they want to see. NetWatch provides a mechanism for screening Internet content based on two PICS-compliant rating systems—RSACi and SafeSurf—for adult language, violence, and nudity, both of which will be supported in future versions of the Netscape Navigator browser. Through NetWatch, parents can ensure that children only see those sites they are allowed to view. For instance, when a user tries to access a Web site by either typing a Web address or clicking on a hyperlink or bookmark, Navigator compares ratings embedded in that particular Web page to the preselected NetWatch rating settings established by the user. If the rating of a given Web site passes the screening process, the user then sees the Web page. But if the ratings do not comply with predetermined user preferences, that Web page is blocked and the user sees an 'alert' page that informs the user that the page was blocked due to the content's rating. In addition, NetWatch gives parents the option to block unlabeled or unrated sites."

Q: I'm using American Online (AOL). Any tips?

A: Yes! Under the Members menu item, you'll find Parental Controls. Did you know that you can create up to five free individual screen names under your Master Account screen name? Give each of your kids his or her own screen name. Then you can set the parental controls differently for each child. Complete directions will walk you through this process. It is very easy. AOL suggests that kids under 12 be limited to the Kids Only area. Any screen name account designated as Kids Only cannot send or receive Instant Messages. Also, they are very limited in browsing the Web. Kids can't enter member-created chat rooms, and they can't send or receive e-mail with attachments or embedded pictures.

AOL offers other parental choices: Young Teen is for ages 13–15 and Mature Teen is for ages 16–17. Each level gives more access to various AOL services and the Internet.

You can fine-tune your settings with Custom Controls. These allow you to decide if your child can use AOL chat rooms, send or receive instant messages, enter Usenet newsgroups, download materials, or access the Web. You can even put restrictions on the kinds of e-mail your kids can receive and from whom they can receive it.

Q: Filters, PICS—I still can't decide. Net-mom, what should I do?

A: Spend time on the Net with your kids. See what's out there. Better yet, teach kids how to deal with information and evaluate it for themselves, whether it's finding the "gotchas" in advertising or knowing when a resource of any kind is "too adult" for them. One of the great gifts parents can give their children is the ability to evaluate information on their own—whether it comes in print, on TV or radio, or on the Internet.

Here at Net-mom's Pollywood Farm, we don't use filtering software. But we support the right of parents to evaluate it and see if it meets their needs.

Q: What's the Great Debate about use of filters and rating systems in public libraries?

A: A 1997 National Commission on Libraries and Information Science study[18] reports that nearly 61 percent of U.S. public libraries are connected to the Internet and provide some type of public access.

Libraries offer the Internet to their customers in many ways. Some, by necessity or choice, offer "text only" access to the Web, thereby avoiding display of explicit graphic material. Others allow full access, using Netscape, Internet Explorer, or other graphical user interface (GUI) browsers.

Historically, libraries have been constrained in their materials selection by limited funds and limited shelving. Moreover, libraries have purchased materials in line with a carefully worded selection policy. The Internet is outside these selection policies.

In fact, the Internet effectively gives access to materials not commonly found in public libraries, both expensive reference works and cheap pornography.

Many libraries report no problems, while others detail incidents where clients have retrieved, viewed, and printed material, which left other library patrons and some library employees experiencing a gamut of emotions from discomfort to outrage.

Although installation of filtering software might seem to be a simple solution, there is the possibility that filters would also block constitutionally protected speech. The Council of the American Library Association, a body elected by ALA members, says "that the use of filtering software by libraries to block access to constitutionally protected speech violates the Library Bill of Rights."[19] The Library Bill of Rights[20] is a document that most, if not all, American public libraries choose to adopt and support.

The American Library Association's Office for Intellectual Freedom (OIF) has issued a Statement on the Library Use of Filtering Software, which advises that libraries may not and should not use filtering software. ALA's OIF instead recommends that libraries "facilitate user access to Web sites that satisfy user interest and needs, create and promote library Web pages designed both for general use and for use by children, consider using privacy screens or arranging terminals away from public view to protect a user's confidentiality, provide information and training for parents and minors that remind users of time, place and manner restrictions on Internet use, and establish and implement user behavior policies."

There is bitter debate in the public library community over the ALA stance on use of filters. Those willing to consider filtering or "deselecting" some Internet content are labeled "censors" by free speech absolutists.

For librarians and others interested in at least investigating filter options, there are two sites on your must-see list.

One site that collects comprehensive information (pro and con) on the library filtering issue is called Filtering Facts.[21] Filtering Facts says most libraries want to block only hard-core pornographic sites. Filtering Facts recommends filtering software products meeting its criteria for home and institutional use.

Also notable is another volunteer effort, The Internet Filter Assessment Project (TIFAP),[22] which puts many filtering packages through a barrage of tests to see where the dust falls and the filters fail. TIFAP is the subject of a book which was released in late 1997, though its author admits TIFAP is a nonscientific study and Filtering Facts (above) refutes some of its claims.

Public libraries have long been defenders of free speech and pride themselves on offering quality materials on many facets of many subjects, even issues unpopular in the library's community. But it's disingenuous to say that library resources haven't already gone through a number of "filters" before they are offered on the shelf. Materials enter the library because they fit the library's selection policy. They are chosen because they have been reviewed well in library professional media, like *Library Journal*, which chooses what it will evaluate and review.

Publishers choose what to publish, based on salability, author's reputation, and so on. Acquisition editors choose what to acquire from authors. So, before material ever arrives in the library, it has gone through many qualifiers or filters.

The public perception of the public library is that the materials there are well reviewed and are for general audiences, including both adults and kids. No one walks into an American public library and expects to find photos and manuals about how to have sex with infants. No one expects to find child pornography, which is illegal.

That's the perception. However, the library has not done a good job of communicating what it *is* willing to do. ALA will tell you that they would assist anyone, including a minor, to try to borrow material like the above on interlibrary loan. They say they might not like to do it, but it's their duty as part of upholding intellectual freedom. Of course there is little chance of actually getting such material, since no public library collects it.

However, that type of thing is readily available on the Internet. The concept of intellectual freedom and free speech, which we hold so dear, collides with illegality at a public library terminal. Pornography involving children is illegal. The Department of Justice has told me it's even illegal to have it temporarily in your browser's cache, if you know it's there, let alone stored on your hard drive. Shouldn't libraries block unquestionably court-designated illegal materials? For example: an offshore site (outside the reach of U.S. laws) announces that it has child porn. Its address never changes. Will the library block that one site, yes or no?

It boils down to this: if there is a difference between ALA's perception of what public libraries are and what communities think they are, there will be trouble ahead. It is noble to wrap yourself in the mantle of the first amendment, but some taxpayers may not want their public libraries to provide a safety net for "home computer have-nots" who can't get to illegal material in their own living rooms and want public funds to provide it for them.

Q: Do you believe public libraries should filter the Internet?
A: As a former public librarian and as a member of the American Library Association, I can say I believe it is very much a local issue, and I'll defer to local library boards to sort it all out with their communities. State and national library associations should stay out of it and not try to tell local communities what to do.

However, since you asked what I think, I'll tell you. I believe libraries should stay within the law. That doesn't mean they should just stop at the free speech guarantees of the first amendment and read no further. All laws of the land must be upheld, and because of this, libraries should filter material that the courts have determined is illegal. Child porn, for example, is illegal in the U.S., and sites distributing it should be filtered from use at public libraries.

Also, I think that library patrons should be able to filter their own view of the Internet while using library machines, if they choose to. They should also have the right to use an unfiltered Internet, as long as the illegal material is blocked, as above. Libraries can easily have it both ways by installing a reasonably priced flexible filtering system, like GuardiaNet.[23]

Additionally, libraries uphold the right of minors to access any library materials, regardless of what the parent's wishes may be. This is a "sacred cow" in the library profession, and in my opinion it is wrong if parents are still going to be legally responsible for the child's overdue library materials fines. If parents are responsible for fines, they should also be able to say what materials may be borrowed and used. Perhaps the parent may wish to block the child from borrowing R-rated videos, or they may limit him or her to no computer time at all or a filtered view of the Net. As I see it, "Whoever pays the piper gets to call the tune."

And finally, libraries may decide to filter such things as extremely hard-core porn and suspected child porn if their legal counsel suggests the library may be found to be in opposition to local laws on endangering children, gambling, etc.

Some libraries that refuse to filter the Net instead rely on signage that says something like "Don't go to bad sites on this machine." Or they have library users sign "acceptable use policies." Both of these so-called solutions put the librarian in the unenviable role of police officer: "Excuse me, but can you move a little so I can look over your shoulder and see what you're doing? Is that a bad site?" How bad is bad? There will be a different level of tolerance for all librarians in the building! I would much rather that the library filter out a quality-controlled definition of what's unacceptable on the way to the computer screen. I don't want anyone hanging over me, snooping on what I'm doing.

What should be done in your library? That's up to your community. Check into it.

Q: What about e-mail? Won't my child get a lot of junk mail, some of it advertising adult services?
A: It's true that anyone with an electronic mailbox will get junk e-mail, and it is also true that some of it will be of the "make money fast!" variety and some will be advertising adult fare. You may hear this called SPAM, but since that term is a registered trademark owned by the Hormel company, you will also see it referred to as UCE (unwanted commercial e-mail).

There is current legislation to prohibit abuses of e-mail, and the best place to track the progress of that is at the CAUCE (Coalition Against Unsolicited Commercial Email) home page.[24] CAUCE is a nonprofit, volunteer organization.

For those using America Online and other services, there are parental controls (see above) that let you designate the addresses from which your child (or you!) can receive mail. There are also ways members can choose to not receive mail if it comes from anyone on AOL's Spammer's list. If you get mail that slips around these controls, you can also choose to ignore future mail from that person. Check with AOL to find out how to set your preferences to use these mail controls.

Others may want to try some of the e-mail filtering software available at many shareware and freeware download archives.[25] These work in different ways, but most look for patterns. For example, many spammers use a particular bulk e-mail system with known errors, which show up in the e-mail "headers" (address areas) of the mail. Your incoming e-mail is filtered against this error-checker. If there is a match, the offending mail is dumped into your e-mail trash can. Often, incoming mail is filtered against a list of known spammer addresses in order to weed out UCE.

The problem is that many spammers/UCE mailers use false e-mail addresses! In fact, they often try to hide their true origins by relaying their mail through several unrelated host names. The fact that this can be done is a security hole that can be fixed, if the host's system administrator is aware of the problem. Sometimes sites don't even know that they have been used in this manner, unless unusual mail server activity is noticed. When complaining about junk

mail, I notify everyone up the chain, just to make sure they are aware that their servers are being used as waystations by the spammers.

You need to find out the real origin of the offending mail. Find the name of the Internet host machine that sent the original mail and send an e-mail complaint to abuse@hostname and postmaster@hostname. Replace "hostname" with the actual host name of the offending site. These are standard, generic addresses—most legitimate host systems have them just for this purpose. How do you find out the real host name? Instructions, along with many other suggestions for avoiding or fighting spam, are provided at several sites.[26]

If you get no response to your complaints of abuse to the postmaster at the offending machine host name, go to the next level: the Internet service provider (ISP) that gave the transport for all that unwanted mail from the spammer. Send the unwanted mail and a complaint to the ISP. In many cases, they are not aware that the abuse is going on, and they often shut off service to spammers. To trace the company that provides Internet service to the suspect host name, contact the sites noted in the preceding paragraph.

Q. OK, but what do YOU do about junk e-mail, Net-mom?
A: I use Eudora[27] to read my e-mail. It allows me to set up filters. Then, when telltale signs of UCE are detected, the mail goes directly to my trash folder; I don't see it.

Still, UCE often gets by my filters. I have gotten pretty good at spotting it from looking at the subject line, so I don't even open the mail—I just delete it. What tips me off? First, I look and see if I recognize the name of whoever sent me the mail. If I do, fine; I'll read it. If not, I look at the subject of the mail. Subjects like "Come Visit Me;" "About Your Web Site;" and "Make Money Fast" are usually UCE. "$250 Cookie Recipe" and "Bill Gates wants to give you $1000" are hoaxes (read about hoaxes in the question below on the Good Times Virus).

If I open a piece of mail and see that it's UCE, either I ignore it or I complain about it as described above. One thing I do not do is respond to it. The reason is that it will flag your address as active, and you may just get more junk mail! Sometimes junk mailers will say, "Go to our Web site to remove your name from our mailing list." Don't do it. For one thing, you may have to look at a porn site. For another, if you enter your e-mail address at a site that looks legitimate, it also proves that your address is current. You may be removed from that spammer's list, but you may be sold to another's marketing database.

Not all online marketing is bad. In fact, I have actually signed up to be on many such lists. But I hate to have my e-mail box so clogged with junk that I can't find the mail from my friends and business associates.

Q: What about computer viruses? Can't you get them from the Internet?

A: A *virus* is a little program that piggybacks onto another program. This virus may slide unnoticed into your computer, only to resurface later to do something cute or malevolent to your system or your files. You should have some type of virus protection on your computer. See some of the entries listed in the COMPUTERS—SOFTWARE ARCHIVES section of this book for sources of virus protection software. Much of it is free.

As I write today, a computer can get a virus only from a program that is run or executed. You can't get a virus from e-mail you open and read. However, your computer could get a virus from an infected program attached to an e-mail message, if you ran that program.

Q: Hey, but what about the Good Times Virus? It comes in e-mail!

A: That particular one is a hoax! There is a link below from an even more authoritative source than Net-mom. Check CIAC Internet Hoaxes[28] to help sort out the truth from the hype. The U.S. Department of Energy's Computer Incident Advisory Capability says it spends more time debunking bogus virus reports than it does reporting real ones.

For technical virus and security information on the Net, try the equally authoritative resource page at the Computer Emergency Response Team (CERT) site.[29]

Q: Yeah, but...

A: It's smart to be suspicious, and it's smarter to keep up to date. Check the home page for your browser and e-mail application of choice; some security information may be there. For example, Netscape offers a security page of its own.[30] Net-mom's favorite resource for debunking viruses, hoaxes, and more is the Computer Virus Myths Home Page.[31] For an adult's guide to chain letters of the world (by the way, they are sometimes illegal),[32] you should visit The Curse of a Thousand Chain Letters.[33]

Q: OK, but what about those "magic cookies" I keep hearing about?

A: Sounds like something from *Alice's Adventures in Wonderland*, doesn't it? A *cookie* is a little file of settings a host computer tries to send you, which will stay resident on your computer. You can set your browser to ask you before you accept a cookie. You *can* turn down a cookie! Net-mom refuses cookies all day (well, except chocolate chip!).

Cookies can be good: they let you set your preferences. For example, at an airline reservation site, cookies remember that you like aisle seats and Asian vegetarian meals. Cookies can be annoying, but harmless. For example, cookies can track which advertising has been shown to you—which things interested you, and which did not.

Cookies can also be bad if they report on your personal Web activities to others and this fact isn't disclosed to you. For example, this information can include which ads you have clicked on, which pages you have seen, and what information you have requested.

You can control your cookies—and lose them if you have to! Browser software allows you to set a few security features, and one of them involves cookies. If you choose to have your browser ask you for permission to accept a cookie each time one is presented, you will be shocked at how many cookies are offered to you at each Web page! This is all explained at the Cookie Central site.[34]

Other Miscellaneous Questions

Q: Isn't the Net mostly people's opinions, old information, and misinformation?

A: Misinformation is out there, just as misinformation is in any other kind of media. How do you recognize authoritative information in the things you read in newspapers and magazines? How do you recognize authenticity on radio and television?

You need the same skills to evaluate the information you discover on the Net. Just as you read the *New York Times* instead of the *National Enquirer*, you may want to stick to authoritative hosts, such as NASA or the Library of Congress or CNN. That's what we did when we picked the sites in this book!

Q: I hear the Net is slowing down and breaking all the time. Why does it take so long for pages to load into my browser?

A: "Death of the Net predicted; film at 11" is a common theme on the Net these days.

If you're dealing with pages that never seem to load, hosts that can't be reached, time outs, "not found" messages, and so many other annoyances, it may seem that the prediction is true.

What causes the "World Wide Wait"? It takes a little bit of explanation. First, you have the two end points: your desktop computer, which is trying to get the Web page, and the host computer, which is trying to send you the Web page. Then you have everything else in between.

Maybe your own computer is too pokey. Your processor can be slow to translate Web pages and display them to your screen—especially graphics. Many browsers allow you to turn graphics off. You might find this mode useful when trying to quickly move through a familiar location and don't want to wait for all the graphics to load. With graphics turned off, you can still decide to manually load images; they just won't come in automatically.

Perhaps the host computer system at the other end is busy with other users. If there is a general slowness of response, you may get a "Connection Refused" message. Or perhaps there has been a power failure and the host is truly unreachable—this happens more often than you might think!

Between these two end points, a lot can happen to your "send me this Web page" request. The first stop is the domain name system (DNS) server, which is probably operated by your Internet service provider (ISP). (Your company or school may choose to run its own DNS instead or in addition to the server operated by the ISP.)

Say you want to go to http://www.yahoo.com. You type that into your browser. Domain names are easy for humans to use, but computers understand only numerical Internet addresses. So, your yahoo.com request has to go through a DNS to be translated into its correct numerical address, in this case 204.71.177.71, before the actual request can go through.

What happens if the DNS server your ISP runs is down? Usually that is not a problem, because they operate more than one, and your Internet software should be set up to try several DNS servers. But if both are down, or unreachable, your browser returns a message that "the server does not have a DNS entry." Obviously, you know Yahoo has a DNS entry! In most cases, you should just try again in a few minutes; the routes will probably come back to life in the interim. If this happens a lot, you should

complain to your service provider. But if all is well and your Web page request to see www.yahoo.com is translated, then you're now on your way.

Simply put, the physical network connection itself can "break," or become so congested that you don't get the Web page you want, at three possible places:

- The line between you and your Internet service provider
- The line between the site you're trying to reach and its service provider
- Anywhere along the route between the two service providers—this route may be very indirect (once I traced the route of a message going from New York to California: it went via the United Kingdom).

If congestion appears anywhere along these connection paths, slowness and other problems can occur. The physical lines are connected by special computers called *routers*. These routers can "blink" or "flap" on and off. They can suffer power outages. That is not supposed to matter, since there are many ways to get from one place to another in cyberspace, but it can cause delays in your experience of using the Net.

In all the confusion, "dropped packets" can and do occur. I'll explain packets and why we don't want to see one dropped. Information is shuttled along the Internet not as a whole but broken up into "packets." Here's an example. Think of sending a physical photo print of your beagle to a friend. You put the photo in an envelope, address it, put a stamp on it, and go down to the post office. The mail moves by trucks, planes, and postal carriers, and in a few days your buddy can open the envelope, take out the photo, and admire it.

When you send a digitized photo over the Net, things are a little different. The digitized file is too big—contains too much data—to cram into one "envelope." So Internet protocols kick in, take the picture apart and divide it into neat jigsaw puzzle pieces. Each piece is deposited in its own envelope, or packet—with reassembly instructions—and is sent on its merry way. At the other end, the packets are opened and reassembled, and your buddy gets to see your cute little dog.

Sometimes things go wrong. Some of the packets can get delayed along the way, which will make your friend wait longer to see the picture put back together. Worse, if the Internet connections between you and your friend have "blinked" during this transaction, packets can be dropped into la-la land, never to return. So packet #1 and packet #3 will sit around, waiting to join up with packet #2, which has not arrived. Eventually your browser says, "Hmm, I'd better ask the Web server to send packet #2 again." Your computer sends the request back to the other end ("Hey! I got one and three, send two again!"). Sometimes the missing part is sent, the picture loads, and all is well. Other times, there's so much delay in response from the other computer that your browser gives up and says something to you like "Connection timed out."

What can you do? The best strategy is to click the stop button on your Web browser, wait a couple of seconds, and try the site again. For fun, try looking at the Internet Weather Report,[35] which looks not at real-time weather fronts but Internet traffic jams. You might also be able to use some of the new network monitoring tools for civilians, such as Net.Medic,[36] and you can find out lots more information about connectivity problems at Keynote Systems.[37]

Q: Can't you just wake me when this Internet thing is over?

A: Uh, no. Millions of users, hundreds of thousands of computers serving Web pages, a WWW address on every TV commercial and print ad—it's everywhere. It's impossible to sleep through it anymore.

That said, welcome to the Net. You belong here; welcome home.

Notes

[1] The WELL: <http://www.well.com/>

[2] "Everything I Need to Know I Learned in the Public Library": <http://www.netmom.com/about/everything.htm>

[3] Oneida Indian Nation: <http://www.one-web.org/oneida/>

[4] Birth of a Metaphor: <http://www.netmom.com/about/surfing_main.htm>

[5] Father of modern surfing: <http://planet-hawaii.com/duke/>

[6] The List: <http://thelist.iworld.com/>

[7] WebTV subscription: <http://www.webtv.net/>

[8] Road Runner cable modems: <http://www.rdrun.com/>

[9] Free-Nets & Community Networks list: <http://www.lights.com/freenet/>

[10] Free E-mail accounts: <http://www.emailaddresses.com/>

[11] Free Web space: <http://www.yahoo.com/Business_and_Economy/Companies/Internet_Services/Web_Services/Free_Web_Pages/>

[12] Parental controls Technology Inventory: <http://www.research.att.com/projects/tech4kids/>

[13] Opposing viewpoints on filtering are discussed in depth in the PARENTING AND FAMILIES—INTERNET—INTERNET TOOLKIT section of this book. In addition, we list two sites here. On the pro side, you should read Filtering Facts at <http://www.filteringfacts.org/>. For the opposite side, see Peacefire at <http://www.peacefire.org>, which takes the view that filters violate kids' rights.

[14] PICS: <http://www.w3.org/PICS/>

[15] RSACi: <http://www.rsac.org/>. (Disclosure: I am on the board of this organization.)

[16] Microsoft Internet Explorer Content Advisor FAQ: <http://www.microsoft.com/ie/ie3/ratefaq.htm>

[17] Netscape's NetWatch feature press release: <http://sitesearch.netscape.com/newsref/pr/newsrelease623.html>

[18] John Carlo Bertot, Charles R. McClure, and Douglas L. Zweizig (1997). The 1997 National Survey of U.S. Public Libraries and the Internet: <http://www.ala.org/oitp/research/plcon97sum/>

[19] American Library Association's Office for Intellectual Freedom: <http://www.ala.org/oif.html>

[20] The Library Bill of Rights: <http://www.ala.org/work/freedom/lbr.html>

[21] Filtering Facts: <http://www.filteringfacts.org>

[22] The Internet Filter Assessment Project: <http://www.bluehighways.com/tifap/>

[23] GuardiaNet: <http://www.GuardiaNet.net>. (Disclosure: I do have a business relationship with the manufacturers of GuardiaNet. However, I would not endorse this software unless I had used it myself and was confident that it lived up to its claims and was a good product, useful to parents, libraries, businesses, and schools.)

[24] CAUCE—Join the Fight Against Spam: <http://www.cauce.org/>

[25] Software archives like Tucows <http://www.tucows.com/> offer spam filters in their e-mail tools sections.

[26]SPAM (UCE): An easy guide on what to do about unwanted e-mail: <http://www.oitc.com/Disney/WhatToDo.html>.

For even more spam/UCE info:

Fight Spam on the Internet!: <http://spam.abuse.net/>
Tracing an E-mail message: <http://digital.net/~gandalf/spamfaq.html>
Blacklist of Internet Advertisers: <http://math-www.uni-paderborn.de/~axel/BL/>. (Warning: This one has some coarse language.)
The Net Abuse FAQ: <http://www.cybernothing.org/faqs/net-abuse-faq.html>

[27]Eudora is a popular e-mail client for both Mac and Windows. Download free "Lite" versions: <http://www.eudora.com/>

[28]CIAC Internet Hoaxes: <http://ciac.llnl.gov/ciac/CIACHoaxes.html>

[29]CERT: <http://www.cert.org/>

[30]Netscape's security page: <http://home.netscape.com/products/security/index.html>

[31]Computer Virus Myths Home Page: <http://www.kumite.com/myths/>

[32]U.S. Postal Inspection Service on Chain Letters: <http://www.usps.gov/websites/depart/inspect/chainlet.htm>

[33]The Curse of a Thousand Chain Letters <http://www.personal.psu.edu/users/d/r/drl146/curses/index.htm>

[34]Cookie Central: <http://www.cookiecentral.com/>

[35]Internet Weather Report: <http://www.internetweather.com/>

[36]Net.Medic: <http://www.vitalsigns.com/>

[37]Keynote's tips for Internet users: <http://www.keynote.com/user/us_content.html>

Do you know the way to San Jose? If not, check a map in GEOGRAPHY.

Internet Safety for Kids: A Word from Net-mom

I hear from many parents who are frightened by the Internet. They are so scared that they are not sure they want their kids to get online at all. As noted elsewhere in this book, my feeling is that this would be a shame. There are many ways to protect your kids online. These range from simple "house rules of use" to the installation of filtering software or use of a "clean" Internet service provider, with all sorts of ideas in-between. Parents need to know that there are plenty of ways for kids to have safe Internet experiences.

I have touched on this gamut of safety solutions in two places in this book. In the main section you will find safety tips to share with your children under INTERNET—SAFETY. In this section of the book, you'll find PARENTING AND FAMILIES—INTERNET—INTERNET TOOLKIT. From there you will be able to read about many types of filters as well as information from sites both for and against their use.

I first met Donna Rice Hughes last year, during planning sessions for the Kids Online White House summit meetings. I was immediately impressed with her tireless advocacy for families. She's techno-savvy and her anti-illegal porn message is certainly one Net-mom cares to support.

When Donna told me she was writing a book, I knew right away it would be something special. She asked me to read chapters of her book while it was in progress, and I was delighted to provide some suggestions and advice.

Her publisher, Baker Book House, graciously agreed to allow me to excerpt Chapter Five of Donna's book and share it with my readers. Each of Donna's chapters opens with a brief scenario involving one family and their experiences online. Against that narrative backdrop, you'll learn how to match problems with practical solutions. You can get more information about the book at the Baker Book House Web site <http://www.bakerbooks.com/>. Donna's book is highly recommended by Net-mom.

(Net-mom's note: Due to space considerations, Donna Rice Hughes' end notes have not been included in this brief excerpt. Attribution has been incorporated into the text.)

AN EXCERPT FROM "KIDS ONLINE: PROTECTING YOUR CHILDREN IN CYBERSPACE"

by Donna Rice Hughes with Pamela T. Campbell

Chapter Five: The First Line of Defense

- How can I build a trust relationship with my child?
- When are children ready to use a computer or go online?
- What should I tell my child about the risks and dangers of cyberspace?
- What kinds of rules and limitations regarding online activity do I need to set for my child?

Susan sat on Lily's bed and thought about the pornographic e-mail her daughter had received. *Thank goodness, I was here when it happened! And thank goodness, Lily talked to me about it! But what if I hadn't been home? What if she had replied to the message or seen something even worse on the screen?*

The encounter had confirmed Susan's greatest fears about having a computer with Internet access—a dangerous stranger from cyberspace had approached her daughter there in her own family room…and in Susan's presence!

Susan didn't want to restrict Lily's online time. That would be punishing Lily for the stranger's intrusion. At the same time, she was more determined than ever to make sure that Lily's online experience would be safe.

"Mom, I'm sorry about reading the e-mail and seeing that picture," Lily said softly, hanging her head as she sat down next to Susan.

"It's not your fault, Lily," Susan responded as she put her arm around Lily's waist and pulled her closer. "In fact it's really your dad's and my responsibility to take some safety precautions. And we should have sat down as a family and set some safety rules for all of us when we go online."

"What if the person who sent that stuff to me comes to our house?"

"I don't think there's any way for that person to know where we live, Lily," Susan said calmly. "But even if the person discovers where we live, your dad and I can protect you, along with the police and Murphy."

"Murphy's just a little dog!"

"Ahhh, he may be a little dog but he has a very big bark that lets Daddy and me know if anyone is in our yard or near the house. We can count on him!"

Most parents wouldn't dream of sending a nine-year-old into a new situation—the first day at a new school, the first time at a new playground, the first time without supervision at a large mall—without explaining what to expect and defining acceptable behavior for that new situation. But like Susan, many parents do not realize the same principle applies to the Internet. Parents need to establish the rules for the Information Superhighway, spelling out what kids can do, what they should avoid, and how to respond to messages and material that make them uncomfortable.

The TV set served as a baby-sitter for many years until the arrival of the personal home computer. Many of us couch potatoes sat for hours watching *The Andy Griffith Show, The Brady Bunch,* and our favorite cartoons. Whereas TV may have sequestered us into a world of our own, computer use—particularly, Internet use—puts us in contact with a large number of people throughout the world. For this reason, when children use the Internet, specific guidelines need to be in place. The ideal is that an adult is present and involved. When a latchkey child, who arrives home several hours before a parent, or a lonely child with low esteem has unrestricted access to the Internet, he or she is vulnerable and at risk.

Just as parental involvement is necessary to help children avoid other pitfalls in life, such as alcohol or drug abuse, our active participation in online experiences is critical. We bear the primary responsibility for teaching our children to be wise and safe on the Internet. To do that, we need to be aware of practical and helpful resources, safety tips, and technological solutions that guard against online risks. In an era of two-career families and single-parent families, however, many of us cannot do the job alone. It may not be possible (or even desirable) for parents to supervise their children all of the time, and the home is not the only point of access to the Internet. The problem is further complicated by the fact that some parents are not yet computer literate.

Ultimately we must educate our children about online safety, including the possibility of encountering pornographic material and pedophiles. Depending on their age, this may mean exploring cyberspace alongside our children, implementing software solutions, and talking to them about the real dangers of the Internet. We must ensure our children's protection online and be mentors for wise decision making.

Establishing an Atmosphere of Trust

Regardless of your level of technical know-how now, it is important for you to become comfortable using your computer and the Internet. Then you will be able to discuss intelligently with your child online experiences that either of you have. Maintaining a continuing dialogue with your child is one of the keys to building an atmosphere of trust around your computer. If you want to encourage such an atmosphere, then you must make it clear to your child that he or she can safely bring online incidents to your attention without being blamed or having the Internet banned from your home. If you neglect to build a trust relationship with your child, you will probably never hear what happens online, whether in your home, at school, or in the library.

In a recent *20/20* interview a group of teenagers were asked if they had ever encountered pornography or sexual predators online. The answer was a unanimous "yes." When asked if they shared this disturbing information with their parents, the answer was an overwhelming "no way!"

Trust building must be an intentional process. It doesn't happen automatically. It requires commitment and time, and your children may test you on both of these. There is no substitute for spending quality time with a child over an extended period. By regularly committing to going online together (for example, 10 to 20 minutes a day), you can experience educational and recreational adventures that bring you and your child closer together.

You can build a trust relationship with your child by giving him or her a problem-solving task that requires your child to work side by side with you or another family member. For example, you might ask your computer-literate child to help you locate some information online about how to build a birdhouse. As the two of you search the Internet, discover and discuss solutions, and help each other accomplish the goal, bonds will be built. Cooperation is your main goal. As you accept and welcome your child's input, he or she will begin to recognize the value of his or her opinion and computer literacy.

When children perceive that we are genuinely interested in them, they will be more willing to trust us with their insecurities, frustrations, and fears. Sadly the opposite is also true. If they perceive that we don't care to listen, trust will not be built. Take opportunities to talk with and listen to your child around the dinner table or on the way to school. Parents need to stimulate discussion, dialogue, and a sharing of ideas. Every time you get together, ask questions of each other, exchange views, weigh decisions together, air feelings. This disclosure will draw you closer together. Try to get beyond the small talk and share deeply with your child. This does not mean you must bare your soul, but rather that you are honest and open with him or her. The more empathic you are, the more secure your child will feel when sharing with you a distressing or uncomfortable experience on the Internet.

In a healthy family each person feels included and appreciated. If a child is shy or less outgoing than other children, make sure he or she is affirmed and accepted. Affirming your child's value and unique abilities is crucial to the growing process of trust. This affirmation can come in relationship to the computer. Compliment your child for his or her grasp of the technology or for a discovery he or she has made online. Your affirmation encourages your child to share deeper experiences and feelings. Many reclusive children become more active and self-confident as they become more aware of their family's admiration and respect for them and their technological giftedness. Try telling your child why you appreciate him or her and what strengths you admire, particularly in the area of computer skills and savvy. Kids need positive feedback to reassure them that others think they are okay. Then they feel free to be open about their feelings and experiences.

When children are able to express their anger, struggles, and frustrations with what they may perceive as our overprotectiveness regarding Web surfing, we need to respond with empathy, support, and encouragement. Then we will be able to talk through possible solutions to the potential dangers that concern us regarding the Internet and set guidelines for appropriate behavior and safe conduct online. Our calm, grounded approach will give us a foundation from which to hold our children accountable while giving them some freedom to fail.

===

It is *very* important that you place your computer in a central family location. This will enable you to supervise the computer without always actively participating with your child.

===

Rules for the Road

Children hear about the wonders and exciting places to visit on the Internet from their friends, their teachers, and the media. Unfortunately they don't hear often enough about the risks of Internet use—except from their parents. We must accept the preventive (and often criticized) role of setting limits that keep our kids safe from harmful material and predators. There are ten concerns that I believe every parent should discuss with his or her child as soon as the child begins to use the Internet, regardless of his or her age.

Top 10 Things to Tell Your Child

1. *Never* fill out questionnaires or any forms online or give out personal information (such as name, age, address, phone number, school, town, password, schedule) about yourself or anyone else to anyone without Mom and/or Dad's permission.

2. *Never* agree to meet in person with anyone you have spoken to online without Mom and/or Dad's presence.

3. *Never* enter a chat room without Mom and/or Dad's presence or supervision. Some "kids" you meet in chat rooms may not really be kids; they may be adults with bad intentions. Remember, people may not be who they say they are.

4. *Never* tell anyone online where you will be or what you will be doing without Mom and/or Dad's permission.

5. *Never* respond to or send e-mail to new people you meet online.

6. *Never* go into a new online area that is going to cost additional money without first getting Mom and/or Dad's permission.

7. *Never* send, without Mom and/or Dad's permission, a picture over the Internet or via regular mail to anyone you've met on the Internet.

8. *Never* buy or order products online or give out any credit card information online without Mom and/or Dad's permission.

9. *Never* respond to any belligerent or suggestive contact or anything that makes you feel uncomfortable. End such an experience by logging off and telling Mom and/or Dad as soon as possible.

10. *Always* tell Mom and/or Dad about something you saw, intentionally or unintentionally, that is upsetting. (It is better for your child's mental health to be able to discuss exposure to pornography than for it to become a dark and confusing secret.)

[Adapted from Stephen J. Kavanagh, *Protecting Children in Cyberspace* (Springfield, Va.: Behavioral Psychotherapy Center, 1997)]

When Is My Child Ready to Go Online?

While going online together is a wonderful opportunity to instill cautious and responsible use of the Internet into your child, I realize that this may not be a realistic option for many parents. So let me just suggest that whenever possible, join your child as he or she explores the valuable resources online. If your child knows more about getting around the Internet than you do, ask him or her to be your guide! This is a great way for you to empower and build self-confidence in your child. Sharing the experience of surfing the Net is an effective, proactive parenting technique. Leaving kids alone for hours at a time on the Internet is not. Check the computer screen periodically and let your children know that you are interested in what they are learning online. Just as watching a TV program with your child is more effective than letting him or her watch alone, surfing the Net together gives you the opportunity to answer questions and talk about anything that comes up.

Very little formal research has been done to identify how information technology affects children of different ages and when is the best time to start various activities, such as computer usage. But common sense tells us that younger children need more supervision than older ones. Younger children, of course, would need more restrictive software tools to safeguard their online experiences. As kids get older, less supervision and less restrictive software measures may be required. In addition, children differ in their maturity, emotional development, and skills. The Children's Partnership, a national nonprofit organization with a mission to raise public awareness about the needs of America's children, has developed some age-appropriate guidelines, based on the advice of child development experts. The following tips, adapted from their Parents' Guide to the Information Superhighway, are given for the earliest age group applicable. They may, however, apply at later stages as well.

Ages Two to Three

Computers need not play much of a role in a two- to three-year-old's life, but you may choose to introduce your toddler to computers. A child's motor skills become more highly developed between eighteen and twenty-four months. At that age you may want to let your child sit in your lap and tap the keyboard and touch the mouse. Put your hand over your child's on the mouse to show how it works. While a little one's tiny hands won't work well initially on adult-size accessories, you may be surprised at how adept your child will become if he or she has regular contact with a computer. There are games and interactive activities on CD-ROMs or other software (rather than online activities) that are geared to the level of a two to three year old.

==

The Children's Partnership <*http://www. childrenspartnership.org/*> is a national, nonprofit organization with a mission to increase public awareness of children's needs and engage leaders and the public in finding ways to help children. It offers online, for free, the full text of its useful guide, *The Parents' Guide to the Information Superhighway: Rules and Tools for Families Online* (1998), prepared by The Children's Partnership with the National PTA and the National Urban League. A printed version of the guide is also available.

==

Ages Four to Seven

Children at this age begin to make greater use of computer games and educational products. Older children in this age range, with their parents, may also begin exploring online children's areas. Children learn intuitively and quickly, but at this age they still depend on parents for reading and interpreting directions.

Between the ages of four and seven, children begin to form their first friendships, grasp the basics of gender differences, and acquire morally relevant rules and behaviors. This is a good time to begin talking about rules for using the computer and going online.

Spend as much time as you can with your child while he or she uses the computer. Print work your child has done on the computer or resources he or she has found on the Internet. You and your child should have the same address, so you can oversee his or her mail and discuss correspondence. Check with your child's teachers and librarians for suggestions for good online activities.

Ages Eight to Eleven

At eight to eleven years of age most children begin to directly encounter and appreciate more fully the potential of online experiences. For example, they can begin to use online encyclopedias to do research and download graphics and photos for school reports. They may correspond via e-mail with pen pals around the world. They may also be exchanging information with faraway relatives and online friends. Be aware of your child's e-mail habits and do not allow correspondence with strangers. Get to know your children's online friends just as you would get to know their friends at school or in the neighborhood. Remember, even in cyberspace, the most vulnerable children are those with low self-esteem. Encourage your children to find friends and interests outside of the Internet.

Just as many conscientious parents limit the amount of time that their children spend watching movies and TV or playing video games, they need to apply the same principle to online time. Set clear guidelines as to how much time is spent online. Even if a child's online experience is educational, recreational, and enriching, relating to a machine will never offer the benefits of relating to other people face-to-face. If you observe your child withdrawing from family or friends to sit at the computer, you may want to reduce the amount of time your child is spending both on the computer and on the Internet. Help your child to learn not to rely on a computer for companionship.

Children between the ages of nine and eleven are the most likely victims of child sexual abuse. Make sure that your child is aware that not all "friends" whom he or she meets on the Internet will be well-meaning. Teach your child to end any experience online when he or she feels uncomfortable or scared by logging off and telling you or a trusted adult as soon as possible. Discuss the unique aspect of anonymous behavior in cyberspace and what it means for your child and others. Explain to your child that many of the people that he or she will meet on the Internet do not use their real identities. For example, a man may identify himself as a woman, or, in some cases, adults may attempt to pass themselves off as children. Explain that while these actions may seem funny and harmless, many children are often seduced and lured into dangerous situations by such predators.

As your child moves toward independence, you need to stay "hands-on" and help guide him or her to appropriate online content. Children of this age are also prime targets for programmers and advertisers. Help your child evaluate content and understand what's behind advertising. Marketers have devised a variety of techniques to compile personal information and profiles on children. Tracking technologies make it possible to monitor every interaction between a child and an advertisement. Discuss the difference between advertising and educational or entertainment content. Show your child examples of each. Begin to show your child the difference between sources of information that are credible and those that are not.

Ages Twelve to Fourteen

Adolescents are capable of using the sophisticated research resources of the Internet, accessing everything from the Library of Congress's collection of magazines and newspapers to letters and archives from around the world.

Just as most teenagers are interested in chatting on the phone, many will want to be involved in chatting online. Some online commercial services have chat rooms that are appropriate for preteens and teenagers. However, as I have mentioned previously, these areas are often the playgrounds of pedophiles, criminals, and unscrupulous marketers who may target your child.

According to Ernie Allen, president of the National Center for Missing and Exploited Children, thirteen- to fifteen-year-old teenagers are at the greatest risk of sexual exploitation by Internet predators. NCMEC has produced a brochure, "Teen Safety on the Information Highway," which is an excellent resource for you and your teenager. It is available at <http://www.missingkids.org/> or author Larry Magid's own site <http://www.safeteens.com/>.

While you (and your teen!) may feel that he or she doesn't need the same restrictions that are placed on younger children, I want to encourage you to consider the risks of allowing your teenager unlimited Internet freedom. This age group is more likely to explore out-of-the-way nooks and crannies in cyberspace. They're also more likely to reach out to people outside their peer groups. And because they're more likely to explore on their own, they are more easily preyed upon by pedophiles and other sexual predators.

Parents must set up clear rules for teenagers. This means agreements about Internet access at and away from home, time limits, and periodic check-ins. Help your child understand the laws governing online behavior (including pornography, predators, and stalking) and the consequences to them or anyone else for breaking them. Remind your son or daughter that possession, distribution, and production of some pornographic material is illegal. Ask your teenager very specific questions like:

Have you seen any pornographic pictures?
Has anyone online talked dirty to you?
Have you met anyone online whom you don't know?
Has anyone asked you for personal information?
Has anyone asked to meet you in person?

If you decide to allow your teen to spend some time in chat rooms, clarify the rules and decide which groups are acceptable. Because chat rooms can be so dangerous, I recommend that you supervise your child whenever he or she enters that area. The exception would be monitored chat rooms offered by some online services. Discuss with your young teen what actions he or she can take if people harass or do anything inappropriate online.

If your teen has computer magazines, review them and discuss any objectionable material. Don't forget to look at ads, new games, and software packages. If you find questionable products in your child's possession, take the time to have a discussion about them. Pay attention to games that your teen has downloaded or copied. Many are great fun, but others are extremely violent. A good way to dissolve the atmosphere of trust that you have attempted to create with your child is by destroying one of his or her games or CD-ROMs. Remember: Trust works both ways. Discuss why a game or program is objectionable and allow your teen to decide that it's not worth having in his or her library.

Ages Fifteen to Nineteen

Teenagers often want to have a computer in their bedroom. In spite of a teenager's need for privacy and independence, I do not recommend that a computer with Internet access be placed in his or her bedroom. It's very difficult for a parent to monitor a teen's online activities when the computer is behind a closed door. Some parents have reported seeing a blue glow coming from under their teen's door in the middle of the night. Later when they received their phone bill, they put the puzzle together and discovered unauthorized computer use. When it comes to Internet access, keeping the computer in a common area of the home is the safest option.

Older teens can use the Internet to search for information about job opportunities, internships, and colleges or universities. With their increased skills, curiosity, and freedom come more ways to run into undesirable and even dangerous experiences. Parents must find creative ways to stay in touch with their teenage children about online activities.

===

For Parents Only

- Become more computer literate and develop Internet savvy so that you can keep up-to-date on products, news, and opinions surrounding the issues of children's safety on the Internet.

- Place your computer in an area of your home where you can easily monitor your child's Internet activity.

- Talk with your kids about their online friends and activities.

- Implement parental controls available on your online service, install protective software on your home computer, or use a clean Internet Service Provider (ISP).

- Block adult chat rooms and instant/personal messages from people you and your child don't know.

- Some OSPs (Online Service Providers), such as America Online, offer subscribers the ability to create online profiles of personal information. Do not permit your child to have an online profile. With this restriction, he or she will not be listed in directories and is less likely to be approached in chat rooms where pedophiles often search for prey.

- Many Internet sites allow children to set up free home pages. Discuss with your child what information he or she can have on the page. For example, interests and hobbies are probably okay, but a home phone number is not!

- Check with your child's school to see if kids' projects, artwork, or photos (where material is identified by name) are being put on school home pages. Schools often want to post school newsletters or sports scores, but every time a full name is displayed, there is vulnerability. Schools need to be reminded of that risk.

- Monitor the amount of time your child spends on the Internet, and at what times of day. Excessive time online, especially at night, may indicate a problem.

- Establish online rules and an agreement with your child about Internet use away from home (i.e., at a friend's house, at school, at the library, etc.).

- Watch for changes in your child's behavior (mention of adults you don't know, secretiveness, inappropriate sexual knowledge, sleeping problems, etc.).

===

House Rules

Every family should draft their own Internet use policy. In appendix E [of Donna's book], you will find several sample family contracts or Internet use policies from which to draw ideas for your own house rules.

When you sit down with your family to write the rules for your house, keep in mind the top ten list of concerns given earlier in this chapter. Your rules should govern every family member's behavior online.

The possible scenarios in the following family pledge were adopted from The Direct Marketing Association's brochure Get CyberSavvy! and may help you make choices regarding your own house rules. <http://www.the-dma.org/pan7/parents-cybrsvvy7b1.shtml>

Being Cybersavvy: Your Family Pledge

I (we), member(s) of the _____ family, believe it is my (our) duty to use the Internet responsibly and safely and to follow the pledge we have created for our family. By signing this agreement, I (we) promise to explore the Internet safely and to uphold the responsibilities we have written below.

If I want to explore parts of the Internet or an online service, I will

_____

If a person I meet online asks for my address, phone number, school name, password, or other personal information, I will

_____

If I receive a scary or threatening e-mail message, I will

_____

If I want to visit a Web site or play a game and have to fill out a registration form, I will

_____

If I want to buy something from a store I have visited online, I will

_____

If I come across pornography, I will

_____

If someone says something to me online that makes me feel uncomfortable, I will

_____

If someone I meet online asks to see me in person, I will

_____

Special Family Amendments

If_____

I will

_____

Signed,

_____

On the_____day of_____in the year _____

Breaking the Rules

In the event that you discover your child has violated your house rules, try to meet the transgression with an appropriate discipline. For example, replying to unsolicited e-mail that contains obscenities is a far worse (and more dangerous) offense than spending too much time online.

If your child has received, downloaded, printed, viewed, or uploaded a pornographic message or photo, consider suspending his or her Internet privileges. Take the opportunity to discuss the dangers of viewing pornography and how viewing more and more pornography is harmful and may lead to sexual addiction. Share one of the stories from chapter 3 [in Donna's book] on how pornography can easily become a destructive habit.

I'm often asked how I make my own family's experience online a safe one. At first, my husband, Jack, and I had Internet access at our offices and so we elected not to have an online service at home. Knowing what is available on the Internet with a few clicks of a mouse, we didn't feel we would be able to properly monitor our computer-literate teenagers as much as we'd like to since we both work full-time.

Recently we purchased a home computer and after careful evaluation, we have chosen a major service as our Internet provider. Jack and I have instituted our own house rules for behavior, both online and off.

To teach Sean and Mindy how to conduct themselves as responsible teenagers and, later, adults, my husband, Jack, often uses the following word picture to make it easier for them to visualize the concept. It goes something like this:

Jack's Box: Picture your life as operating inside a box. As you consistently demonstrate increasing levels of personal responsibility, the box gets larger, and your world of opportunity increases. When you do not act responsibly, the box shrinks, and we start over again. As the parent responsible for training you in the right way to live, I control the box. At a point in the future, when you have reached adulthood, I expect to turn the control of your box over to you.

In regard to Internet use, as our children comply with general safety practices, our specific house rules, and their school's Internet policy, their freedoms may be expanded. With violations and demonstrations of broken trust, Internet and computer privileges are restricted.

In addition to house rules, we utilize the parental controls on our ISP. In the next chapter [of Donna's book], we'll look at the technological solutions available to parents, including parental controls and blocking and filtering software programs.

Your supervision and communication of expectations are the keys to your child having a safe and enjoyable experience on the Internet. While technological solutions will provide some protection and safety features, no software will substitute for your supervision. Use the suggestions and age-appropriate guidelines in this chapter to help your child earn that "license" to drive on the Information Superhighway.

Excerpted from Kids Online: Protecting Your Children in Cyberspace, by Donna Rice Hughes with Pamela T. Campbell.

Baker Book House
ISBN 0-8007-5672-X
$11.99 paper, August 1998.

PARENTING AND FAMILIES

The entries in this part of the book are primarily for adults. You will find sites on divorce, sites on death and grief, and sites on sensitive health matters. We have also listed sites on Internet filtering software and other controls here. Plus, you will find many sites on parenting. Please note that some subject headings are duplicated in the main part of this book. However, the sites in this parents area are different. Adults should check both the kids and the parents parts of this book for complete coverage of a topic.

Teachers will be especially interested in the EDUCATION section. Join the discussions with your peers about alternative assessment, charter schools, and more. We also have pointers to sites with lesson plans. Teachers should remember to look in SCHOOLS AND EDUCATION in the main part of the book in order to see all our suggestions.

Finally, parents need to have some terrific sites that only they know about—that can be "pulled out of the hat" on a rainy day. Look in both the FAMILY FUN and the PRESCHOOLERS sections for these surefire sites!

ADOPTION

Faces Of Adoption, America's Waiting Children

If your family is thinking about adopting but you still have lots of unanswered questions, then be sure to check out this site. First browse the photolistings of American children waiting for adoption. Then check the AdoptionQuest section for useful information on how to begin the adoption process, what kinds of questions to ask the agency, and articles on key issues, such as single parent and older parent adoptions, tax credits, and the latest court rulings. There are book reviews and lists of books for both adults and children, lists of state agency contacts, and links to the National Adoption Center (NAC) and Children Awaiting Parents (CAP) for additional information. This site was the children's category winner of the 1996 National Information Infrastructure Awards.

http://nac.adopt.org/

Welcome to Adoption.com

Whether you're a birth mother, an adoptee, a health care professional, or a member of a family trying to adopt a child, you will find something of interest at this site. Browse the international photolistings of children by country, age, or gender. You'll also find answers to frequently asked questions about international adoption, general articles about adoption issues and concerns, and a comprehensive listing of agencies to contact for more information.

http://www.adoption.com/

BABIES

The Baby Booklet

You've got a new baby, who is so adorable when sleeping. But what do you do when he/she wakes up and cries, and wets, and needs a bath, and is hungry, and gets diaper rash, or some other kind of rash, and so on? If you are feeling a little overwhelmed and need answers to even the most basic baby care questions, then this is a good place to look. Written by Dr. Lewis Wasserman, a pediatrician from Florida, this booklet provides a guided tour to babies, with useful information about baby skin care, normal growth patterns (including weight tables), colic, and other common concerns of new parents (or "old" parents who may have forgotten!). Also useful is the health care schedule, which includes a complete list of vaccinations and the ages at which they should be given.

http://members.aol.com/AllianceMD/booklet.html

The HALLWAY At Tommy's CyberNursery Preemie Web Site

If you are a parent or grandparent of a premature baby (a *preemie*) or if you have friends going through this experience, you won't want to miss this site. You'll find emotional support as well as valuable information and insight about what families go through when their baby is born too early. The information here is written by a father whose son was born at 25 weeks (more than three months early) about his family's experiences in the neonatal unit at the hospital. The Babies On The Web section provides links to other parents' personal stories about their special baby. Whether you want information on the special feeding needs of preemies or a knitting pattern for a preemie hat, it's all here.

http://www.flash.net/~cyberkid/

Interactive Pregnancy Calendar: Parents Place.com

Provide some basic information at this site, and you'll get a day-by-day personalized calendar detailing the development of your baby, from the day of conception through the day of birth. There are also discussion boards where you can talk to other parents "due" the same month you are. In addition, an "Ask an Expert" section provides important information on a wide variety of topics involving kids of all ages.

http://www.pregnancycalendar.com/

La Leche League International

Breast milk is the best milk for most babies. Moms can breast-feed an adopted baby, too, and that info is here! This site will give you all the facts and encouragement you need to start it, continue it, or help other moms with it. The La Leche League is a nonprofit, nonsectarian group that gives education and support. Their Web page explains how they got their name: "La Leche is Spanish for 'the milk,' and is pronounced 'la LAY-chay.' The idea came from a statue in St. Augustine, Florida (USA) honoring '*Nuestra Senora de la Leche y Buen Parto*,' which translated, means 'Our Lady of Happy Delivery and Plentiful Milk.' When La Leche League was founded in the mid 1950s, polite people didn't use words like 'breastfeeding' in public. The Spanish term became an informal code-word for our meetings and our function. La Leche League meetings could be listed in newspapers without offending anyone."

http://www.lalecheleague.org/

Natal Care - Development of the Baby

Your kid has heard the big news: Mom, an aunt, or someone else is pregnant! He or she may have questions about what the heck is happening! The answer is available at FamilyWeb's page, which teaches the stages in pregnancy and what it feels like for a woman to be pregnant. Lots of technical terms are here, but you can share the pictures of the baby's growth with your child.

http://www.familyweb.com/pregnancy/natal/
   natpt103.html

Pampers Parenting Institute

Wow! Are you experiencing information overload, with nurses and doctors and well-meaning relatives and friends all giving you information and advice about caring for your new baby? It's hard to sort it all out, and you don't want to call your pediatrician with every little question. But how *do* you take care of your newborn's belly button? You'll find Well Baby and Skin Care clinics, staffed by pediatricians, here. And everyone's favorite pediatrician, Dr. T. Berry Brazelton, is available here to answer your child development questions online.

http://www.pampers.com/

The Preemie Ring Homepage

Meet the miracle babies on the Internet! This site links you to other home pages of children born prematurely. Scroll down and connect with The Early Edition, a bimonthly newsletter of collected wisdom all about preemies.

http://members.aol.com/liznick1/preemiering.htm

Pregnancy & Childbirth Information - Childbirth.org

This is an excellent site, offering good, factual information about fertility, episiotomies, doulas, breast-feeding, and more. But it's not all serious stuff. Wondering if your baby will be a boy or a girl? A handy "calculator" here may give you the answer, based on a combination of old wives' tales and folk wisdom. For example, if you've been craving meats and cheese, the baby's a boy, but if you're carrying high, the baby's a girl!

http://www.childbirth.org/

Stork Site

Whether you're looking for baby names, choosing the menu for a baby shower, or looking up the definitions of all those confusing medical words, this site is a nice, friendly place to start. Become a "storkie"—it's free—and participate in the chats and other members-only areas. For example, you can set up a "Family Album" page and get a free e-mail address. Your other storkie friends can see when you're logged on to the site, and you can trade stories over the virtual picket fence.

http://www.storksite.com/

Welcome to "THE BABIES PLANET"

At this site, you'll find a thoughtful collection of briefly annotated links in subject areas such as Morning Sickness, Crack Babies, S.I.D.S., and more general topics, such as making your own baby food, the diaper dilemma, and more. It's definitely worth a look, even if this is not your first child or if you're a grandparent on baby-sitting duty!

http://www.thelastplanet.com/babyhp.htm

NAMES

10 Free Helpful Baby Name Hints

Need a new baby name? You should definitely check the hints here. One tip is to make sure the initials of the first, middle, and last names don't spell out something with negative connotations, such as PIG or DUM. If you're looking for new baby shower games and stunts, check out this link! A lot of these games sound hilarious.

http://www.dfcreations.com/nh.html

Baby Names from The Babies Planet

Your new family addition is on his or her way or maybe is already here—now all you need is a name! Try some of the links here; some let you search for names by gender or by meaning of the name. For example, did you know the name Elvis means "elf-wise friend"? (Perhaps Elvis isn't dead—he's just gone to live with those cookie-making elves!)

http://www.thelastplanet.com/bbnames.htm

Eponym

This is an outstanding collection of links to "name the baby" sites. What really sets this one apart is that you can click on a map of the world to get to links containing names from that region. For example, click on the British Isles to get a list of currently popular names there (no surprise, a lot of girls are named Diana) as well as some really unusual gems such as unisex names or a reversed name. An example of the latter is Cire—Eric spelled backwards. (What these have to do with the British Isles we don't know, but that is where this site files them.) Also, there is a short list of chat rooms where you can "try out" a proposed name on other parents from around the world.

http://student-www.uchicago.edu/users/smhawkin/
  names/

> ### Want to get your hobby off the ground? Try Rocketry in MODELS AND MINIATURES.

BABY-SITTING

The BabySitters International Club

It's one thing for your preteen to want to try baby-sitting, but it's another to know just what is involved. Your child can probably take a course through school or a scout troop or 4-H or other club, but this site is great for reminders about the basic safety tips and other rules regarding the care of someone else's children. Kids can earn good money baby-sitting, but first make sure they are completely qualified to take on this responsibility.

http://worldkids.net/babysit/

BABYSITTING SAFETY TIPS

Your child's got a job baby-sitting. It's a very big and important job, and there is so much to remember! Help him or her learn to be a safe baby-sitter by taking a look at this page from the Phoenix Arizona Police Department, which has loads of commonsense tips to make baby-sitting easier and more fun. For example, before accepting the job, baby-sitters should get specific instructions about bedtimes, allowed snacks for themselves and the kids, and other information about what is expected. This will make both the baby-sitter and the parents feel more confident.

http://www.ci.phoenix.az.us/POLICE/babysit.html

BIRTHDAY PARTIES

Billy Bear's Birthday Party

Happy Birthday to YOU! Happy Birthday to YOU! This site is a present from Net-mom to YOU! Your kids can play virtual pin the tail on the donkey, bake a virtual cake, pick out some virtual party favors, color some pictures, and more. This site also suggests that the kids make their own Web page with the party icons supplied here.

http://www.billybear4kids.com/holidays/birthday/
  party.htm

Disney Online - NY - Best-Ever Birthday Party Planner

When your child's birthday appears on the calendar's horizon, do you recoil in horror at the thought of yet another competitive party where parents try to outdo each other with entertainment, food, and party favors? It's time to relax and learn to plan a sane, safe, homespun party. Kids will have lots of fun, and you won't end up too frazzled to enjoy the celebration! This site offers tips, including Ten Pitfalls to avoid. There are links to themes, games, foods, entertainment, and more. For a frugal but fun party plan, try <http://www.stretcher.com/stories/960603a.htm>.

http://family.disney.com/Categories/Activities/
    Features/family_0000_01/dony/Parties/Parties.html

CONSUMER INFORMATION

Consumer Information Center Main Page

Are you on a limited budget? Learn how to stretch it a bit further with publications from the Consumer Information Center. Many of them are right on this page in text or HTML format. Or you can order the publications online and have them sent to you. You can also find pamphlets on how to help your kids learn to read, book lists of great reading for kids, info on colleges, mortgages, online scams, birdhouses, landscaping, and more.

http://www.pueblo.gsa.gov/

Consumer World: Everything Consumer

Teach your kids that they have consumer power and that manufacturers listen to consumers regardless of their age. While you're here, you can also find out how to avoid online scams, determine if products have been recalled, and check out a company via a link to the Better Business Bureau. You'll also find out how to contact many companies and other sources of consumer information. Check out the links to Smart Money Interactive and Best Fares for the latest and best airline fares, hotel deals, and more.

http://www.consumerworld.org/

Guide to Toys and Play

Play is essential to your child's development. But how do you know which toys are safe, which ones are best for which ages, and how to select the best toy for your child when faced with a megamall toy store? It's all so confusing. Fortunately, this site provides articles and links to make it all seem like child's play. The information provided is from the Consumer Products Safety Commission and the American Toy Institute.

http://www.kidsource.com/kidsource/content/
    toys_ply.html

The Oppenheim Toy Portfolio: the independent guide to kids' media!

Your kids seem to know about the latest in toys, games, books, software, and other stuff—but do you know what works, what doesn't, what's a waste of money, or what's a good value? The Oppenheim Toy Portfolio is a consumer organization dedicated to providing independent reviews of the best products for children.

http://www2.toyportfolio.com/toyportfolio/
    default.htm

DEATH AND GRIEF

Children And Grief

Grief is a painful experience for both kids and grown-ups, and sometimes parents will try to protect their children from this pain by not allowing them to participate in the funeral of a loved one. Read about one little girl's struggle with the loss of a close family friend. The author of this article delivers some very useful advice on helping kids through a "healthy" grief process. Kids need the support of friends and family, too, and attending funeral services is often an important part of saying good-bye.

http://www.funeral.net/info/chilgrf.html

> It's hard to remember, but mnemonic memory tricks are in WORDS.

Pets Loss Grief Support, Rainbow Bridge, Monday Candle Ceremony

The loss of a pet is a difficult time. Many people like to remember their pets with the Monday Candle Ceremony, which is described in several languages at this site. Rainbow Bridge is one idea of where beloved pets go when they die. There is also a list of online grief support groups that meet every week on many of the online services.

http://www.petloss.com/

Talking to Kids About Death

The topic of death and dying is a very difficult one to talk about, both for parents and for kids. This article gives you guidelines and hints on how to begin the discussion and help children to understand death and to grieve.

http://family.disney.com/Features/family_1998_05/
metp/metp58death/metp58death.html

DIVORCE

The Divorce Support Page: Child Custody, Alimony, Support, Family Law

Are you experiencing or contemplating divorce? At this site you can find out how to get a divorce and also how to avoid getting one. Questions about custody, alimony, and other topics are answered in "Ask a Divorced Guy" and "Ask a Divorced Woman." Visit the links to learn more about spousal rights, visitation, domestic violence, and much more. In particular, pay attention to the 12-step Divorce Recovery area, which will help you get back on track again.

http://www.divorcesupport.com/

DivorceNet

This site presents lots of legal and other factual information about divorce. The On-line Newsletter covers all aspects of divorce, including child custody issues, visitation, and child support. There is an interactive bulletin board where parents can post questions and read about the concerns of other families in similar situations. Separation and divorce are situations that affect all family members.

http://www.divorcenet.com/

EDUCATION

Access Excellence

This site is renowned for its design, content, and collaborative activities. Focusing on the biological sciences, the activities collection is truly excellent. Online "seminars" put you in touch with scientists and science teachers. Offerings include "Local Habitats," "Science of Amber," and "Emerging Diseases." Collaborative classroom projects like "Fossils Across America" help in sharing resources.

http://www.gene.com/ae/

AERO - The Alternative Education Resource Organization

As Mark Twain said, "I have never let my schooling interfere with my education." There are many alternatives to traditional schools, and information and links may be found at this site from the Alternative Education Resource Organization. It also functions as a companion site to a book called *The Almanac of Education Choices*. The book is a directory to charter schools, independent schools, Montessori schools, Waldorf schools (based on the teachings of Rudolf Steiner), Quaker (or Friends) schools, local and national homeschool organizations, and more.

http://www.edrev.org/

Blue Web'n Learning Library

This site collects the cream of the crop of learning-oriented Web sites. All sites are rated and categorized by area, audience, and type. Each subject category has links to related tutorials, activities, projects, lesson plans, and more. You can also use their keyword search to explore their collection. Want more? Join the free mailing list for weekly updates. We found the sites listed here to be excellent resources for eager learners as well as educators looking for teaching materials.

http://www.kn.pacbell.com/wired/bluewebn/

BookSpot feature - Children's Books from Alcott to Seuss

Just about anything you'd like to know about great books for children is at this site. It has information on all the award winners and the recommended-reading listees. Look for this surefire reading material on your next trip to the library. But this particular page is just a feature on kids' books. For everything else, take the link to the BookSpot main page for general book reviews, best-seller lists, movies made from books, book club discussion groups (some are online!), and more.

http://www.bookspot.com/childrensbooks.htm

Classroom Connect

Classroom Connect is one of our favorite magazines. Their Web site doesn't disappoint, either. Check it out for info on upcoming conferences, a jumpstation to great Web links, newsgroups, FTP sites, a Web toolkit, and more. This is a commercial publisher, but they know their market, so stop in and browse!

http://www.classroom.net/

ERIC - Educational Resources Information Center

Custom-build your own curriculum! The Educational Resources Information Center (ERIC) is a vast collection of data, ideas, research, lesson plans, literature, and more. This site will be of interest to parents who want to supplement their child's education at home or learn about parenting techniques. Teachers will find classroom ideas that go above and beyond textbook-type learning as well as professional information. They can also use the renowned AskERIC service. If you're an education professional (librarian, teacher, administrator, homeschooler, and so on) you can e-mail questions to AskERIC's Net-savvy information specialists; within 48 hours, you'll have suggestions and solutions drawn from customized ERIC database searches, ERIC digests, and Internet resources. If you've always wanted to talk to the reference librarian of the Internet, you can start with these folks. If you want to browse on your own, check AskERIC's Virtual Library, which contains over 700 lesson plans plus material drawn from the archives of *Newton's Apple*, *CNN Newsroom*, and the Discovery Channel.

http://ericir.sunsite.syr.edu/

The truth is out there in UFOS AND EXTRATERRESTRIALS. Maybe.

Gifted and Talented (TAG) Resources Home Page

Being gifted is being blessed—it means having special talents beyond the average. While being gifted is good, it can also lead to complications. Sometimes school can be boring and unchallenging for gifted kids, and finding other kids who share the same interests can be difficult. The Internet offers a way for gifted children to explore the world in a challenging environment and to find other kids with similar gifts; this is a good place to find information on how to accomplish this.

http://www.eskimo.com/~user/kids.html

Global SchoolNet Foundation Home Page

"Where in the World Is Roger?" "Roots and Shoots with Jane Goodall," "International CyberFair," "Global Schoolhouse Videoconferencing"—does any of that sound interesting? The folks in charge of GSN just keep collecting and coming up with more terrific ideas all the time. Always fresh and exciting, this is where K–12 innovation lives on the Net! Kids can find new contest announcements at this site, including ThinkQuest and other opportunities.

http://www.gsn.org/

Inclusion: School as a Caring Community

Kids with special needs are no longer in "special ed." classes—they are welcomed into the "ordinary ed." classroom. This is called inclusion. If you're a teacher, you wonder how this works, and if you're a parent, you're concerned for your child. This site puts many questions to rest as you hear success stories from teachers with inclusive classrooms in elementary through secondary schools. Read the Handbook to find out specifics. The message here is "You are not alone."

http://www.quasar.ualberta.ca/ddc/incl/intro.htm

Kathy Schrock's Guide for Educators - Home Page

The links in this guide are organized according to subject area. In World History, for instance, you'll get a breakdown of Web pages, from "Ancient World Web" to "World War II: The World Remembers." Each month, a list of new resources will point you to the latest and greatest. Kathy Shrock's list is a lifesaver for teachers!

http://www.capecod.net/schrockguide/

Literacy Resources Online

What can parents do to help their kids become readers? This Web site offers pointers to several pamphlets and articles on how to prevent reading difficulties in young children as well as how to encourage reading in older kids. For example, there is a link to the Department of Education's Web page, "Simple Things You Can Do to Help All Children Read Well And Independently By The End of Third Grade." It's divided into things parents, schools, grandparents, caregivers, and community groups can do to promote literacy. One of these tips is the following: "Ask your children to describe events in their lives. Talking about their experiences makes children think about them. Giving detailed descriptions and telling complete stories also helps children learn about how stories are written and what the stories they read mean."

http://www.mcrel.org/resources/literacy/litonline.html

Multiple Intelligences

"It's not how smart you are, it's how you are smart," says this site. Did you know that people learn and think differently? Howard Gardner of Harvard University came up with this theory of "multiple intelligences"—and so far he has identified nine different ways people learn. These include kids who learn visually, or through activity, music, or other mode. How do these multiple intelligences work? This site offers ten links per intelligence category so you can get a feeling for each one. In which categories does your child fit?

http://www.interserf.net/mcken/im.htm

The National Clearinghouse for Bilingual Education

"Can you read this? Thank a teacher." Have you seen that bumper sticker? Lots of kids can't read it because English isn't their first language. The buzzword is that they have Limited English Proficiency (LEP). Bilingual education means classroom instruction is done in two languages. This is important for LEP students because it allows them to keep up with their studies while they learn "academic" English as a second language. It has recently become a hot topic in education, and this site acts as a clearinghouse for starting points, methods, success stories, and more.

http://www.ncbe.gwu.edu/

The One-Room School Homepage

Mom of Net-mom went to school in a one-room schoolhouse in Terre Haute, Indiana. When she was little, Net-mom heard all kinds of tales about what it was like to have six kids in your grade, and all the grades in the same room. Now, you could write to Mom of Net-mom and ask her to tell you all those stories, too, or you could visit this Web page. Hear it all from a former one-room schoolhouse teacher! Remember the beloved nursery rhyme "Mary Had a Little Lamb"? See the picture of the one-room schoolhouse that may (or may not) have inspired the tail, er, tale. Follow this link: <http://www.wayside.org/research.html>.

http://www.msc.cornell.edu/~weeds/SchoolPages/welcome.html

Project Gutenberg

Numerous full-text, public domain books appear on the Internet. Many are collected as part of Project Gutenberg and are at this site; others may be found via The On-Line Books Page at Carnegie Mellon at <http://www.cs.cmu.edu/books.html> and The Modern English Collection at the Electronic Text Center, University of Virginia, at <http://etext.lib.virginia.edu/modeng.browse.html>. If your kids are browsing through these large archives, parental guidance is very strongly suggested. Most of the books you will find are retrieved as flat text files. If you prefer reading them as HTML hypertext, try the archives at <http://www.cs.cmu.edu/People/rgs/rgs-home.html>.

http://www.promo.net/pg/

Quest: NASA K-12 Internet Initiative

This site has links to directories of which schools are online. Is your school listed? No? Everybody at your school wants to get hooked up to the Net, but nobody knows exactly how to do it! NASA will help you get started with all the ins and outs of getting online (look in the Bring the Internet to Your Classroom area). Then they've got links to online interactive projects—new ones every year! Past projects have included "Live from Antarctica," "Online Jupiter 1997," and "Earth to Mars Activities." Ask the scientists questions, order interesting materials, and help NASA decide what they will do next.

http://quest.arc.nasa.gov/

Reggio Emilia

This is a very hot topic in preschool education these days. Reggio Emilia is a city in northern Italy. The educational philosophy there is that children have many "languages" besides words to express themselves. These may take the form of art, music, or other creative works. Reggio schools are more homelike than schoollike, and in fact a beautiful environment is thought of as "the third teacher." The first two teachers are the parents and the classroom teacher, who work in collaboration. For an introduction, try <http://www.nauticom.net/www/cokids/reggio.html>. The idea is that kids are empowered to do their own learning, with the teacher and parent as guides. At the same time, it is important to document this learning, although the documentation may take many forms. Reggio Emilia's methods offer a challenge to revisit entrenched educational views. Check some of the links here and see what you think.

http://ericps.crc.uiuc.edu/eece/reggio.html

SchoolHouse Rock

This is not an official site, but you'll probably find everything you're looking for here. We know you want the lyrics to songs from *Grammar Rock*, *Multiplication Rock*, *America Rock*, and more.

Not only will you find the lyrics of the songs at this site, but you'll also be able to hear the songs and view the video!

http://genxtvland.simplenet.com/SchoolHouseRock/

TEACHERS HELPING TEACHERS

Teachers, don't you just hate to read "advice" from someone who has never set foot in the classroom? Instead, here are your teaching peers, who know *exactly* what you are going through and how to help.

http://www.pacificnet.net/~mandel/

U.S. Department of Education (ED) Home Page

The Department of Education has an easy-to-use site with some useful and welcome features. This site is worth a look if you're concerned with any of the following topics: improving education on a local or national level, learning from other schools in other communities, application procedures for education grants, and student financial aid. The Picks O' the Month section highlights important resources you won't see elsewhere.

http://www.ed.gov/

NET FILES

It's said that sharks have six senses. What are they?

Answer: The usual five: sight, smell, hearing, taste, and touch—plus extreme sensitivity to detecting electromagnetic fields. This allows them to find prey and locate tasty crabs buried under the sand. Find out more at *http://www.pbs.org/wgbh/nova/sharks/tidbits.html*

Urban Education Web

UEweb is connected with the ERIC (Educational Resources Information Center) clearinghouses. They offer vast numbers of articles, manuals, and other publications about urban education. Just one example is their "Strong Families, Strong Schools" handbook (click on "Urban/Minority Families"). One of UEweb's best features is its searchable ERIC databases. These hold lesson plans, publications, and educational research.

http://eric-web.tc.columbia.edu/

US Charter Schools Web Site

This site provides a definition of a charter school, from *Education Week*: "The basic charter concept is simple: Allow a group of teachers or other would-be educators to apply for permission to open a school. Give them dollar for dollar what a public school gets for each student. Free them from the bureaucracy that cripples learning and stifles innovation at so many public schools....The school generally operate[s] under a 'charter' or contract with the local school board or the state. And while exempt from most state and local laws and regulations, to gain charter renewal, the schools must prove that their students have gained the educational skills specified in that initial contract." Would you like to learn more and perhaps start a charter school in your community? This site will help you through the process of starting a school, running it, and evaluating it. There are also discussion groups so you can talk to others sharing similar experiences.

http://www.uscharterschools.org/

Web Sites And Resources For Teachers

Many subject areas are covered here, but let's take math as an example. Teachers will get not only lesson plans but also online math applications, like a calorie calculator and even a magic square checker. Online board games such as Mancala (the great strategy game that teaches critical thinking) and dozens of puzzles will challenge kids to go beyond worksheet math.

http://www.csun.edu/~vceed009/

Welcome to the National PTA

One hundred years ago, the National PTA was founded by Alice McLellan Birney and Phoebe Apperson Hearst as the National Congress of Mothers. Birney said, "Let us have no more croaking as to what cannot be done; let us see what can be done." Today, this large organization is doing many things. Here, you can get more information about educational initiatives, health and welfare programs, and legislative issues.

http://www.pta.org/index.stm

Yahoo! - Education

Here's a searchable page chock-full of education resources. Everything from special education to online teaching to alternative education is accessible from Yahoo. As an aside, did you know that two graduate students started Yahoo as a hobby and developed it into the indispensable information service we know today?

http://www.yahoo.com/Education/

EDUCATIONAL TECHNOLOGY
From Now On—Educational Technology for Schools

Internet use policies. Assessment. Libraries of the future. Grants. Parenting. This site tackles all those topics and more. It is a vast collection of feature articles, Web sites, and other resources for the home, classroom, and community. Learn how to cut out the "mind kandy" and the "new plagiarism" of indiscriminate cut and paste. Jamie McKenzie tells it like it is. Don't waste any more time without visiting his site.

http://fromnowon.org/

Judy's Rat

Did your school get some money for technology and networking? Need a little help figuring out how to get networking cable through the school walls? This rat can help. She has been trained to pull wire via the shortest route from classroom to classroom, and she works for candy gummi bears! We are not making this up. This is a very cute site, and you'll be a fan of Judy's Rat right away! Be sure to check out the theme song.

http://www.judyrat.com/

Web66 Home Page

If your kid's school or the school you teach in has its own Web server, it should be linked here. It's the largest collection of all the schools with Web sites in the world! If the school doesn't have a Web site yet, a cookbook here will give your school the recipe to create one: where to get the software, how to write the HTML, and more. Teachers: Can't tell a LAN from a WAN? You just found out administration wants the fifth grade to run ethernet around the building? No fear, stop here. You'll find technical info anyone can understand, plus acceptable use policies as well as other technology planning musts. You want links on top of all that? No surprise, they've got 'em.

http://web66.coled.umn.edu/

The Well-connected Educator

This site features real teachers doing real things with technology in real classrooms. Read articles like these: "Computers: What Do You Do After You've Opened the Box?" and "So You're Finally Online. Now What?" Find out how to get a multimedia, multidisciplinary project going—with classrooms on the other side of the planet. Talk to your peers about what works, and what doesn't. Gwen Solomon and a slew of savvy teachers can help you—don't miss this site!

http://www.gsh.org/wce/

HOMESCHOOLING

The Christian Homeschool Forum Web Site

If you were to decide to homeschool, how would you get started? This information desk has tips to help you take the plunge. You'll also find answers to questions you might have, lists of books and magazines, links to support groups, and lots of tips. You'll find plenty of encouragement here, whether or not you homeschool from a Christian perspective.

http://www.gocin.com/homeschool/

Homeschool World: The #1 Homeschooling Site on the Web

Some kids don't "go" to school; they stay home. Every state in the U.S. and many foreign countries permit homeschooling in some form. If you're thinking of making the switch to more independent learning at home or if you already teach your kids at home, you'll find lots of ideas, news, links, and more at this site from the publishers of *Practical Homeschooling, Big Happy Family,* and *Homeschool PC.*

http://www.home-school.com/

Homeschooling Information and Homeschool Resource Pages

This is a fine ecumenical resource with information about everything you want to know about homeschooling and unschooling, sponsored by *Home Education* magazine and its online version. You can get a free copy of the "Homeschooling Information and Resource Guide" as well as explore many carefully organized links to homeschooling resources around the Net. The site offers numerous free information files, which may be ordered for delivery by an e-mail autoresponder.

http://www.home-ed-press.com/

What extremely well-known science fiction movie was partially filmed in a place where it is so hot that people live underground?

Answer: The movie was *Star Wars,* and Tunisia was the site of Luke Skywalker's uncle's moisture farm on Tatooine. Find out more at http://us.imdb.com/M/title-more?locations+Star Wars (1977)

Homeschooling Information - France & Associates

Visit this excellent selection of homeschooling resources for an overview of what's current and what's useful. You'll find thoughtful, briefly annotated links to homeschooling associations, magazines, newsgroups, and more. Some of the most interesting are a site started by a teenager about how to "do high school" at home and Real Audio files with interviews of interest to homeschooling families. For example, you can listen to Susannah Sheffer, author of *A Sense of Self: Listening to Homeschooled Adolescent Girls.* Don't miss the links to selected high-energy homeschooling families, and scroll to the bottom to find some great software to support homeschooling (and other) families.

http://www.dimensional.com/~janf/
homeschoolinfo.html

Jon's Homeschool Resource Page

If you could choose only one page on homeschooling, this would be it. Will your children fit into the "real world" if they don't go to school? Will they do as well academically in homeschool? Will they be able to get into college? Research shows that the answer to all of these questions is a loud Yes! This site also has a collection of home pages and photos from families; check out what they're doing and learning.

http://www.midnightbeach.com/hs/

The Teel Family Web Site

Brrrr! Snow is falling all around, and you're harnessing the dogs to the sled. Get ready for a trip to Alaska to visit the Teel family. There is no such thing as a typical homeschooling family, but you'll find out what interests the Teels on their homeschool Web page. See what curriculum they are working on this week, and explore some of their favorite links. Watch out for the polar bears, though!

http://www.teelfamily.com/

> Be dazzled by the laser shows in PHYSICS.

ENTERTAINMENT

Broadcast.com

If you have audio capabilities on your computer, you should visit a live broadcast site like this one. Here's how Broadcast.com describes itself: "On broadcast.com we offer more than 50,000 hours of programming every week! Our programming choices include live play-by-play broadcasts of more than 350 sports teams, more than 360 live radio and TV stations, and our AudioBook Channel and CD Jukebox where you can listen to more than 2,100 full length CDs and over 360 full-length audiobooks. In addition there are hundreds of political, business and special events every week! All you have to do is pick what you want and enjoy it." It's in the parents part of the book because some of the programs are about health topics and relationships, which you need to preview for your kids.

http://www.broadcast.com/

CelebSite

Parental warning: Preview this site before your kids get to it. If your child's a Leo fan, a Spice Girls or Hanson fan, a Rosie O'Donnell or Jerry Seinfeld fan, a Michael Jordan fan, or a fan of Brandy, Mariah, or Mick—he or she will love this site. There are brief biographies of all the celebrities we know, and some we don't know (yet): athletes, actors, musicians, models, even publishers! There are annotated links to the best sites on each celebrity and information on where to send fan mail. This is a quick way to find information on the albums and artists that rock your child's world.

http://www.celebsite.com/

Center For Media Education

Here's an interesting statistic. By age 70, most Americans will have spent ten years of their lives watching TV. Kids watch an average of three to four hours of TV every day. According to this site, "By the time children complete elementary school, the average child will witness more than 100,000 acts of violence on TV, including 8,000 murders. These numbers double to 200,000 acts of violence and 16,000 murders by the time they graduate from high school." What effect does watching this violence have on kids? Read about it at this site. Did you know the Federal Communications Commission requires TV stations to air three hours of educational and informational programming per week? This site tells you how to keep local TV stations accountable to the rules. There are also sections on how to teach kids to evaluate TV commercials and how to safeguard Internet privacy.

http://www.cme.org/

How to Analyze News

This site has a tremendous amount of very solid information, as well as suggestions on how to get kids thinking about news stories. Who gathered the information, who reports it, what's the slant, who sponsors the program—all these things and more should be evaluated when we hear a news story. Make sure your kids are media-aware! Visit the main level of this site for more.

http://www.screen.com/mnet/eng/med/class/
   teamedia/htan.htm

PBS Teacher Connex

There are so many TV programs! How do you select the best ones for your kids? Here are descriptions of the shows on public television, grouped by month or subject area. Teacher guides, info on taping rights, and links to related sites—they're all here in one place.

http://www.pbs.org/learn/tconnex/

MOVIES

Hollywood Online

Parental advisory: This site lists all movies, not just G-rated ones. This is the place for the latest on all the hottest movies. It's got all the video, sound bites, pictures, and production notes you could possibly want. Don't miss the Movietunes link for information and audio from recent soundtrack albums! Find out what the rating and the running time are before you drop the kids off at the theater. Try the interactive press kits and other media for favorite movies.

http://www.hollywood.com/

The Movie Mom's Guide to Family Movies and Videos

Nell Minow is an author and a critic, but most importantly she is a mom. She calls herself "Movie Mom" and gives lots of advice to kids and families on the best movies to see. According to Movie Mom, no one should grow up (or be a grown-up) without seeing *The Muppet Movie*, *Tom Thumb*, *The Absent-Minded Professor*, and *Captains Courageous*, among others. Take a look at this site to read her reviews and to find out other movies you must see. The authors of a new book called *The Practical Guide to Practically Everything* liked her opinions so much they included them in their book!

http://pages.prodigy.com/moviemom/moviemom.html

MovieLink | 777-FILM Online

Parental advisory: This site has links to other movies besides G-rated ones. Let's go to the movies—but which one? And where's it playing? If you live in a major American city, the best place to find out is here at MovieLink, which calls itself "America's online source for movie information." Type in your city or ZIP code and find out what's playing near you and what the show times are. From there, you can read movie reviews and even check out the Parents' Guide. If your kids loved the movie, you can download posters and movie trailers as electronic souvenirs.

http://web18.movielink.com/

MUSIC

The International Lyrics Server - Find your favourite song lyrics!

What are the lyrics to that song your teen's been playing over, and over, and over? You can't quite understand the words. If you know the name of the artist or the name of the song, you can often find the lyrics via this site. You can also look up the "oldies" you once enjoyed.

http://www.lyrics.ch/

Welcome to the Ultimate Band List

This is a good place to preview lyrics for CDs your kids want to buy. For other uses, please explore this site with your children. Prepare to spend the day sifting through this vast list. It's an interactive guide to band Web pages and digitized music and lyrics servers. There are also listings by genre, such as pop/rock/alternative, metal/hard rock/industrial, country/western, jazz/blues/R&B, even classical and New Age. You can browse alphabetically or by type of music or resource, which includes newsgroups, mailing lists, FAQ files, lyrics, guitar tablature, digitized songs, and many, many WWW pages.

http://www.ubl.com/

REVIEWS

Dove Family Approved Movies and Videos

Free Willy 2: The Adventure Home, *The Baby-Sitter's Club*, and *Babe* are just three of the movies that have won the Dove Foundation's seal of approval for being "family friendly." So far, this group, whose motto is "Families everywhere deserve a choice," has approved over 1,400 movies. If you still can't decide what to see, just fill out a simple online form and search by viewer age group or type of movie, including action, adventure, classic, and lots more.

http://www.dove.org/

Be swampwise in EARTH SCIENCE.

SCREEN IT! ENTERTAINMENT REVIEWS FOR PARENTS

These movie, video, and music reviews are astonishingly complete, scoring each title in a variety of sensitive areas that might be of concern to parents. How much violence? How much bad language? How many instances of disrespectful behavior or nudity? This site helps parents "know before you go" so there will be no surprises later.

http://www.screenit.com/

FAMILY FUN

See also GAMES AND FUN—ONLINE GAMES and PARENTING AND FAMILIES—PRESCHOOLERS

Berit's Best Sites For Children

Over 850 sites are reviewed by librarian Berit, who rates them on a five-point scale. Check out anything that got a five out of five and you'll find a real gem of a Web site. Arranged in general categories such as Holidays, Just for Fun, and Serious Stuff, you'll also discover sites to help your kids find a pen pal or a safe chat room. This site is part of the popular Theodore Tugboat home page, which has a separate review in the TELEVISION—PROGRAMS section of this book.

http://db.cochran.com/li_toc:theoPage.db

Bonnie's Favorite Games

Bonnie has looked all over the Internet for fun games for families, and she's found a lot of them! You can select from her "Easy" collection or "Play a Harder Game" selection. There are some of Net-mom's favorites here, too, so enjoy!

http://www2.arkansas.net/~mom/game.html

Bonus.com The SuperSite for Kids TM

This site has lots of family-safe places to visit. Head in any direction and encourage your kids to play a game, enter a contest, find homework help, or learn about dinosaurs or the United States or what's under the sea. For rainy-day fun, remember this site!

http://www.bonus.com/

Funbrain

Math games can add up to "sum" fun edutainment. How about playing math baseball with your kids? They can pick how difficult the math questions should be and decide if they want addition, subtraction, multiplication, division, or all of the above. Then the computer will ask an arithmetic question. Can they get it right? Swing—wow, it's a triple! After that, have them see how good they are at making change of a dollar. How many pennies, nickels, dimes, or quarters in change should they receive after a certain purchase is made? There are some other fun games, too, including a concentration matching game.

http://www.funbrain.com/

funschool.com - Free Interactive, educational software for Kids

This site has more fun, engaging, and educational Java games than any other site we've seen for this edition. There are separate sections for preschoolers, kindergartners, first graders, and second graders. If your kids fall into third through sixth grade, there is one catchall section for them. Let's focus on preschool activities. There are 18 of them: matching games, concentration, ordering, opposites, even animal homes. Sometimes Java games take quite a while to load; this site even gives you something to do during the download process! Play with an online kaleidoscope while you wait.

http://www.funschool.com/

GusTown: Fun, Games, Cartoons, and the CyberBuds!

Meet Gus, Rant, Rave, and the rest of the CyberBuds in this colorful town full of animations, articles, games, recipes, crafts, and links for kids and parents! Head over to the toy store for fun games like Ice Going. Picture a frozen lake with a lot of holes in the ice. Click on one hole—hey, a penguin pops up. Click on another hole—a whale is under that one. Too bad, they don't match. With a splash, both creatures dive back into the holes, and you can try again to make a match. Hint: Click on the Index link to look at a quick map to all the fun on this site.

http://www.gustown.com/home/gustownsummer.html

Kid's Domain - KIDS

What a great place to introduce your kids to the Internet. Lots of games and pictures to color, software downloads, clip art, and a list of links to similar sites. Click on Surf Safe and talk to your youngsters about what rules they should follow when using the computer. Or go to Kids Can Program and find software that will help them develop their computer skills. Finally, take a minute (or lots of minutes) to scroll through the What's New section to find new games, ideas, activities, and more. This is a must-see site for all families!

http://www.kidsdomain.com/kids.html

Kids' Space

What fun—this is everybody's home page! Here your family can submit music or drawings and hear and see what other children around the world have done, too. The Story Book is where kids write their own stories, using the pictures and themes provided. There is even a beanstalk that keeps growing each month in the Craft Room. Pick an artwork and create a story for it, or choose a story already written and draw a picture for it. All commands at this site include pictures with them, so even the youngest child (who may be still developing reading skills) can enjoy this interactive learning experience.

http://www.kids-space.org/

KRN Software's Java Edutainment - Free Online Educational Games for Kids

There are many fine games here, but let's go into the Edutainment area and try Cargo Bay. Triangles, squares, and circles are floating around in the spaceship's cargo bay—can you sort them into the right bins? Wait until this Java game loads completely and you see your grabbing tool. It looks sort of like starship *Voyager*. Then click on the floating shape you want, and the tool will move over to it and grab on. It makes a loud noise, so be sure the volume on your speakers isn't too high. Then click the bin where you want the cargo to be stored, and if you're right, it will go there.

http://www.worldnetoh.com/krnsoft/

Whooooooo will you find in BIRDS?

The Multnomah County Library KidsPage!

It's fun, it's fabulous, and now it's famous. This is one of the best library sites on the Web. Whether your kids are looking for homework help, info on a current craze, or a suggestion for a good book to read, check this out. Don't miss the Library Joke of the Week. Example: When a librarian goes fishing, what goes on her hook? A bookworm, of course!

http://www.multnomah.lib.or.us/lib/kids/

Pass the Pigs

Here's some family fun for all. It seems like such a simple game, but it can be challenging playing against the computer. You roll a couple of tiny virtual piggies. If one lands on its razorback, that's worth five points. If one lands on its snout, that is worth 10 points. What happens if they both land on their sides? That's "pig out," and you don't get any points. You can roll again as long as you don't get a pig out. If you do, you lose all your points gained on that round. Change the challenge level in the options area, where you can make the computer into a beginner instead of an expert.

http://www.ultranet.com/~gkramer/PassThePigs.shtml

Platypus Garden of Goodies

If you love to give your brain a workout, come on in! You'll discover mazes, word search puzzles, jigsaws, and more. Many of them were designed for kids, by kids! You'll also find family activities, music, pages that *talk* and *sing* (if you have the right plug-ins and hardware), and much more. We particularly enjoyed the "Shareware Carol." This site is available in English and Spanish, and there are some songs in Japanese.

http://www.platypus-share.com/

The Prince and I

The teenage prince lives in a beautiful castle, but there's a small problem. How can he be king someday if he can't read? He needs some friends to help him learn! Become a "Friend of the Prince" (it's free!), and you can submit stories to be posted at this site. Some of them are very imaginative and funny. There's even a mission you can go on to explore the village (if you can—we got lost), make your way through the forest (we got lost there, too), find the missing prince, and give him a message. Hint: Don't play the Shockwave version; play the regular version. Make a map. If you get lost, click on Help and watch for the hands on the screen. They will point you in the right direction. If you lose the Forward button and the hand says to go forward, just click where the button used to be. This royal site is produced by the National Film Board of Canada

http://www.nfb.ca/Kids/

VIRTUAL DESSERT MACHINE

This site is from Breyers Ice Cream, and it's delicious. Pick your dish or waffle cone. Now pick the ice cream flavor you like best. Sauce? You bet. Add toppings, tropical fruits, berries, candies, nuts, and as much gooey stuff as you want. Now preview your creation, and change it if you're not satisfied. Got it all set? Now e-mail it to a friend and challenge him or her to make an even messier dessert! Remember, this site is entirely fat-free.

http://www.icecreamusa.com/cgi-bin/icusa/ vrsundae/vrsundae

HEALTH AND SAFETY

See also HEALTH AND SAFETY *in the main part of this book*

Achoo Healthcare Online - Home Page

With thousands of resources on health, you're sure to find some information on your topic. Whether it's baby care, parenting, alternative medical care, or even a directory to medical products, give this site a try. Don't miss the Site of the Week and the past archives for it. This will give you a good overview of some of the best resources on health the Net offers. This is a site for adults, not kids.

http://www.achoo.com/

American Dental Association Online

This is the home page for the professional society of dentists, probably best known for bestowing the "American Dental Association Seal of Acceptance" on various dental gels, flosses, pastes, mouthwashes, and other products for both consumer and professional use. Surprisingly, the first report on toothpastes was published in 1866! You can get a list of all the approved products here, as well as lots of pamphlets on tooth sealants, kids' teeth, and more. Need a root canal? They have a great online pamphlet that explains everything, at <http://www.ada.org/consumer/endo.html>.

http://www.ada.org/

Ask the Dietitian(tm)

Staying healthy means practicing good nutrition, but it's hard to know what's good and bad for you and your kids. Some people say that some fat is good; others say it's all bad. Some say sugar is unhealthy; others say it's OK for you. What to do? You can ask a dietitian! Here you'll find information on many frequently asked questions about nutrition from an expert who knows what foods are good for you.

http://www.dietitian.com/

CenterWatch Clinical Trials Listing Service

Here's a useful site. Currently there are many experimental and other drug therapies in clinical trials all over the world. If you need to find out where research is going on for a specific disease or condition, check here, as over 5,000 are listed. You'll see a state-by-state listing of research studies, with links to a description and contact names and addresses. There are also lists of resources for further information on each disease. And there is a confidential e-mail notification service if new material is added on a therapeutic subject of interest to you.

http://www.centerwatch.com/MAIN.HTM

Eating Disorders Awareness and Prevention

Anorexia nervosa. Bulimia nervosa. We know the words, but do we know the warning signs? This site offers Ten Things Parents Can Do to prevent eating disorders and gives tips on how to help a friend with a suspected eating disorder. One thing everyone can do is educate others about the seriousness of eating disorders. It is not "just a girl's problem." Find out more here.

http://members.aol.com/edapinc/

> Can't tell a hawk from a handsaw? Look it up in BIRDS.

Facts For Families

The American Academy of Child and Adolescent Psychiatry provides many information fact sheets here. They provide concise and up-to-date material designed to educate parents and families about a wide variety of concerns affecting children and adolescents. Issues covered include bed-wetting, stepfamilies, learning disabilities, gay and lesbian teens, grief, adoption, AIDS, and much more. This material is revised and updated regularly and is offered in three languages: English, Spanish, and French.

http://www.aacap.org/web/aacap/factsFam/

Family Health Home Page

Staying healthy means learning all kinds of facts. One way to learn some facts about staying healthy is to listen to doctors giving good information on how to be healthy. Here you'll find Real Audio sound files, lasting approximately two minutes, on health topics from acne to weight loss. Give these a listen—it'll be good for your health!

http://www.fhradio.org/

healthfinder

This is an easy-to-use clearinghouse of links to health information from various government and other agencies. Read an online magazine, search a database, or find a self-help or support group for topics as diverse as adoption to substance abuse. The variety will surprise you. You can locate statistics on playground injuries, information on vaccine safety, guidance on suicide prevention, and more. These are selected publications, so you're assured it's just the "good stuff"!

http://www.healthfinder.gov/

KidsHealth - Children's Health & Parenting Information

Quite simply, this is currently the best children's health resource on the Net. It is divided into sections for kids and parents, with an area for health professionals as well. The kids' section has Shockwave games and animations, tips on nutrition, fun recipes, and a sensitive section on feelings, including a Kid's Guide to Divorce. The resources for adults detail childhood diseases, explain medical tests, and answer questions like "How can I tell if my child has attention deficit disorder?" and "What do I tell my child about surgery?" plus many more. This site is well designed and built with love, and it doesn't go overboard with multimedia like so many others. It is sponsored by The Nemours Foundation and is staffed by professionals from The duPont Hospital for Children and The Nemours Children's Clinic, among others.

http://kidshealth.org/

Martindale's Health Science Guide

It's huge! It's got "over 49,000 teaching files; over 124,000 Medical Cases, 864 Multimedia Courses/Textbooks; 1,350 Multimedia Tutorials; over 3,350 Databases, and over 10,300 Movies"—and a really long download time! Still, if you haven't found what you're looking for at any of the other sites we've reviewed, do take a few hours and look around in Martindale's virtual library. It's an excellent resource, and it will be good for your health.

http://www.sci.lib.uci.edu/HSG/HSGuide.html

Mayo Clinic Health Oasis: Daily News on Disease, Treatment, Drugs, Diet

The Mayo Clinic is a world-renowned source for authoritative health information. Their Web site does not disappoint. Read articles on all sorts of topics, from Alzheimer's to asthma. Browse through features on pregnancy and pediatrics. Search for information on drugs in the Mayo PharmaCenter. You can also Ask a Physician or Ask a Dietitian if you have more questions. There is a current news area, which is updated several times a week, where you can find out about new treatments and research. You can also subscribe to House Call, a free e-mail newsletter.

http://www.mayohealth.org/

Med Help International - The Virtual Medical Center for Patients

If you or your child has been diagnosed with a particular medical condition and you'd like to talk to other families dealing with the same thing, you might try registering here in the Patient Network Support area. Let's face it—we all get sick once in a while. Sometimes it can just be annoying, and other times it can be scary. At the Med Help Library Search area, you can learn about all kinds of sicknesses. Sometimes just knowing what's happening can help you feel better. The texts are written in a nontechnical style, and relevant links to the rest of the Internet are included for each entry. There are also several medical forum areas where you can get answers from medical staff at various hospitals and well-known clinics.

http://www.medhelp.org/

PEDINFO Home Page

This site holds an archive of information for pediatricians and others interested in children's health. You'll find current information (and links!) on disorders, diseases, and syndromes. Visit many pediatrics departments in teaching hospitals all over the world, and examine some interesting information you won't find elsewhere. There is also a very useful collection of info on parental control of Internet access.

http://www.uab.edu/pedinfo/

Virtual Children's Hospital Home Page

The Children's Hospital of Iowa has a wonderful Web site for parents, patients, kids, and kids who are patients. The kids area has a very nice selection of outside links to specific health sites for children on such topics as Crohn's disease, asthma, and various medical procedures. You'll even find a couple of virtual hospital tours. Parents will appreciate the peer-reviewed Web site links to resources on common medical problems. You can find it by digging in the Patient information section, or use this direct path: <http://www.vh.org/Beyond/PeerReviews/PeerReviewHomePage.html>.

http://vch.vh.org/

DIABETES

Children with Diabetes on-line Community

This site contains many features and resources to help your family deal with diabetes. There is an overview of diabetes as well as current research, plus reviews of medical monitors and other equipment. Browse through a list of summer camps catering to diabetic kids. Hang out in the chat room or post a message on the message board. Notice you can find e-mail addresses of other families in the Friends area; on the Internet, your diabetic child can find another kid who really understands because he or she is going through the same thing. There are also many links to other useful sites.

http://www.childrenwithdiabetes.com/

Kids Learn About Diabetes

This site was created as an Eagle Scout project. It was written to help kids learn to understand diabetes and manage it, especially during special times, like sporting events, parties, and summer camp. Users will learn about testing, complications, fears and feelings, and what's new in research. Best of all, this site isn't written in "doctor-ese" and it's understandable to all.

http://www.geocities.com/HotSprings/6935/

DRUGS, TOBACCO, AND ALCOHOL

Close to Home Online

When school lets out, five teens face some really big decisions about life, love, and alcohol and substance abuse. This innovative site lets you peek into their rooms to discover clues about their decisions so far in this 13-week soap opera. The comic-book style is gritty and true to life and may not be for all families. For others, though, it is a real discussion starter, and Net-mom believes we all need to talk to our kids more. A bulletin board allows readers to discuss the story, characters, and substance abuse issues.

http://www.wnet.org/closetohome/

> ## OPTICAL ILLUSIONS: now you see them, now you don't!

DEA - Publications - Get It Straight! - Cover

Written by kids, this straight talk describes "What's up with" all kinds of drugs, from anabolic steroids and over-the-counter medications to heroin and cocaine. Besides the solid information, there are suggested activities to extend the antidrug message into the community. For example, there are planning ideas for a drug-free dance or neighborhood fair.

http://www.usdoj.gov/dea/pubs/straight/cover.htm

Does your friend have an alcohol or other drug problem? A guide for teens

Did you ever wonder how to help a young person having problems with alcohol or drugs? This brochure was designed for teens wishing to help their friends. They talk about how to see the symptoms, how to help friends who won't admit that they have a problem, what to do to get that help, and where to write or call. There is a listing at the end of the brochure with names and phone numbers of agencies in every state in the country.

http://www.health.org/pubs/guidteen.htm

FIRST AID
Active First Aid Online v2.5

Ouch! Insect bites, scrapes, cuts, sprained ankles, nosebleeds, and other injuries are never fun. When these bumps and bruises happen, always check with your physician. If help isn't immediately available, check this site, written by an Australian paramedic. He teaches that remembering the acronym DRABC (danger, response, airway, breathing, and circulation) is the most important consideration when assessing any injury. This is all explained at this site. No online service is a substitute for your doctor, but for minor injuries, this is a good place to remember.

http://www.parasolemt.com.au/afa/

Excerpts: "All Stings Considered..."

This site lists the first aid and medical treatment for marine injuries in Hawaii—including what to do for a sea snake bite, a sea urchin puncture, a sting from a sponge, and lots more. Many of the descriptions have photos of the marine life. There is also general wound care information.

http://www.aloha.com/~lifeguards/alsting1.html

Poison Center Answer Book

This informative site contains fact sheets on everything from spider bites to food poisoning. You'll learn how to poison-proof your house, and you might consider getting some "Officer Ugg" stickers to put on household chemicals. They are free upon request from this site.

http://wellness.ucdavis.edu/safety_info/
     poison_prevention/poison_book/

KIDS WITH DISABILITIES

Autism Network International

Autism Network International (ANI) is an organization run "by and for autistic people." They promote peer support, information sharing, self-help, and help with educating the public about autism. There is also a wonderful collection of links to resources on other syndromes, such as ADD, Fragile X, hyperlexia, and Tourette's, among many others.

http://www.students.uiuc.edu/~bordner/ani.html

Autism Resources

This resource is a large collection of autism-related sites on the Net. It includes an autism FAQ, autism mailing lists, advice to parents, treatment methods, facilitated communication, research information, and organizations.

http://web.syr.edu/~jmwobus/autism/

Blindness Resource Center: a service of the New York Institute for Special Education

Explore this clearinghouse for information on everything concerning blindness, from the history of braille to accessible Web design. On the latter topic, you'll get a lot of advice. For example, webmasters should construct their pages so that they can be read out loud by a screenreader. Sites that automatically "push" music while browsing cause problems for those who are trying to listen carefully to a screenreader. At this site you will also find online resources on disabilities besides blindness, including low vision and other visual conditions.

http://www.nyise.org/blind.htm

Children and Adults with Attention Deficit Disorder

ADD, ADHD—it's all just a bunch of letters. All you do know is that your child really has trouble paying attention in school. You're not alone! In the U.S., 3.5 million kids have been diagnosed with attention deficit disorder (ADD). At this site you can click on the map of the United States and see if a CH.A.D.D. (Children and Adults with ADD) chapter is near you. CH.A.D.D. is a nonprofit, parent-based organization providing family support, advocacy, and education. Read articles and information on upcoming events and current laws relating to students with ADD.

http://www.chadd.org/

Cystic Fibrosis

It used to be that kids with cystic fibrosis, a lung disease, rarely lived long enough to become adults. That has changed. Many people with cystic fibrosis, or CF, can look forward to a long life. If you have CF or if you know someone who does, you have to take a look at this page. You'll find some easy-to-understand information about CF and also the latest news about this disease.

http://cf-web.mit.edu/

The Web in Pig Latin? Make it so in LANGUAGES.

Deaf World Web

This site includes lots of news and resources for persons with hearing disabilities. Look through the Deaf Encyclopedia and the American Sign Language Dictionary. There's also a Deaf CyberKids section where kids can find a pen pal, submit a story, picture, or poem, or join the discussion forum.

http://dww.deafworldweb.org/

Down Syndrome Title Page

The information here has been compiled by members of the Down listserv. It includes information about support organizations, conferences, educational issues, medical resources, and parenting (and brothering or sistering) your special child (or sibling).

http://www.nas.com/downsyn/

Facilitated Communication

This site points out that "Not being able to speak is not the same as having nothing to say." Facilitated Communication (F.C.) is a method of expression for those who have trouble speaking. This can be because of autism, Down syndrome, mental retardation, or other reasons. F.C. is controversial, and there is a lot of research currently in progress. The Facilitated Communication Institute is a center for research, training, and public education on the techniques employed.

http://soeweb.syr.edu/thefci/

Family Village

Although the main purpose of this site is to support families and friends of mentally disabled or other special needs kids, the site is a wealth of information for all parents. Check the Coffee Shop to find online groups, listservs, and other resources for parents, grandparents, and siblings. The Library has information on specific diagnoses. The Hospital has links to a current medical breakthroughs page, while the Mall has listings for special adaptive technologies, toys, clothing, and other items. Special Olympics links are also here, along with camps and other outdoor opportunities for special kids and special families. There is a lot to learn at this excellent site!

http://www.familyvillage.wisc.edu/

How Can I Help? (CP Booklet)

What's it like to raise a child with a disability? If you have not shared that unique experience, it may be hard for you to understand and imagine how it feels. "It's just a different place," says Emily Kingsley in her article, "Welcome To Holland." For friends or relatives of a child with cerebral palsy, this site offers valuable advice on how to provide empathy and support for the family, as well as information on what they may be experiencing and other ways you can help.

http://www.iinet.com.au/~scarffam/cpa.html

KIDS TOGETHER, INC.

This site helps you create a vision for your child with disabilities. One part of the vision is that individuals everywhere start using "People First" language. That means we should focus on the person first and the disability second. So, don't say "wheelchair-bound" or "victim of" or "is afflicted with." And as this site says, "Children are not born with birth defects. They are born with congenital disabilities; they are not defective—toasters might be, babies aren't." You'll find useful and important material on a variety of topics: educational inclusion, assistive technology, pertinent legislation, and lots more.

http://www.kidstogether.org/

LD OnLine: Learning Disabilities Resources

Did you know that Walt Disney, Winston Churchill, and Albert Einstein all had learning disabilities of some kind? According to this site, actor Tom Cruise is dyslexic and learns his lines by listening to them on tape. This site is a real encyclopedia of information on learning disabilities and disorders (LD). You'll find lots of info on Developmental Speech and Language Disorders, Academic Skills Disorders, and Other Learning Differences. One of the treasures this site offers is the First Person stories. Discover how kids and adults deal with and overcome their disabilities to celebrate their abilities. One of the great tales involves Paul Orfalea, founder of Kinko's copy and office stores. Check it out!

http://www.ldonline.org/

Our-Kids Website

For a little support and a lot of information, browse the Our Kids archives and then join the hundreds of others on this e-mail discussion list who are sharing stories about their children's accomplishments and challenges with other families facing similar situations. If you are a parent, relative, or friend of a child with any kind of developmental delay, this site is a must. There's also a good list of adaptive technologies and how to contact the manufacturers. Be sure to try some of the links to special education institutions, medical research organizations, and others for more valuable information.

http://rdz.stjohns.edu/lists/our-kids/

Parents Helping Parents

The Family Resource Center provides links to many other sites of interest to parents and their special needs children. If you haven't found what you are looking for at any of the other sites mentioned in this section, be sure to try this one. Ketogenic and Feingold diet information, seizure disorders, and Tourette's are only a few of the support group areas at this site. There are links to disability, health, and child care information, and lots, lots more.

http://www.php.com/

Special Olympics International

"Let me win, but if I cannot win, let me be brave in the attempt." This is the oath of the Special Olympics. What great inspiration this is for all athletes, not just "special" kids with physical, mental, or other challenges! The first International Special Olympic Games was held in 1968, at Soldier Field in Chicago, Illinois. It was organized by Eunice Kennedy Shriver. Since then, the Special Olympics have become the world's largest year-round program of physical fitness, sports training, and athletic competition. In the U.S., games at the local and chapter levels are held every year, with special summer and winter events held every four years.

http://www.specialolympics.org/

You are your own network.

You can always count on the info in MATH AND ARITHMETIC.

Virtual Assistive Technology Center

This site is so loaded with information about all kinds of assistive technologies (AT) that you won't want to miss it. Look for links to software for Mac, PC, and Windows that will supercharge your computer so it talks to you, among other things. There are also pointers to organizations and other Web sites with more resources, as well as a fully annotated and carefully selected list of suggested books. Be sure to read about the webmaster of this site: she types with her toes and says, "Feet, don't fail me now!"

http://www.at-center.com/

LICE

American Head Lice Information Center - Home Page

Cooties! Nits! Over 12 million Americans, mostly kids, are affected each year. This number has doubled from the rate of ten years ago. Why? The scourge of classrooms, once thought under control by gallons of chemical remedies, is back with a new "super louse." This ugly creature has developed a resistance to the active ingredients in many common antilouse shampoos and other treatments. As it turns out, olive oil smothers the insects. You use it as part of the following five-step battle plan outlined on the site and in an award-winning video: how to safely apply a louse medicine, how to correctly time and apply a series of olive oil treatments to disrupt the life cycle of the louse and kill the medicine-resistant lice, how to comb out the nits, how to clean the home environment, and how to perform an effective nit check. The video also provides tips for kids on how to avoid an infestation.

http://www.headliceinfo.com/

Headlice Information, Laboratory of Public Health Entomology, Harvard School of Public Health

"Why did they send my child home from school?" "Can the infestation be spread from the dog or the cat?" "Do I have to clean out my car?" They answers to these questions are at this site. Wondering if that's really a louse or just dandruff? Send your suspected head lice to Harvard, and receive identification back in a self-addressed, stamped envelope.

http://www.hsph.harvard.edu/headlice.html

SAFETY

Consumer Product Safety Commission's Kids Page

There are a variety of information sheets on the CPSC's Kid Page, and you may want to print out one or two to share with your children. Topics include baby-sitting tips, info on bicycle helmets, and facts on bicycles, in-line skating, playground, and other safety areas. Most are in PDF format (the site explains what this is and how to read them). Others have no pictures and may be accessed the usual way. Just click on the No pictures choice.

http://www.cpsc.gov/kids/kids.html

Lowe's Knows-Safety Archives

Does your family have a disaster plan? Do you know what supplies you should have on hand in the event of a hurricane? This site has all those answers and more. Everyone should take a look at the child safety tips at this resource, including how to make sure toys are safe and household dangers are kept to a minimum.

http://www.lowes.com/noframes/safety/encycl/

National Center for Missing and Exploited Children

Some families are looking for their missing children. Check their photos. Have you seen any of these kids? Maybe you can help! This site lets you search by state, physical description, and other characteristics. If you have a Web page of your own, check the How You Can Help area. It will tell you how to put a link at your page that will show photos of recently missing kids to your Web site visitors, like the pictures on milk cartons.

http://www.missingkids.org/

NATURAL DISASTER PROGRAM FOR FAMILIES

Tornado! Flood! Hurricane! Forest fire! Earthquake! Natural disasters are those times when Mother Nature seems to go a little crazy. You and everyone in your family can learn how to be prepared for natural disasters by looking at the Natural Disaster Preparedness pages from the North Carolina Cooperative Extension Service. Take the time and learn how to set up a Family Disaster Kit (remember to pack games for kids!), how to cook without electricity, how to save your saltwater-soaked plants, and much more helpful information.

http://www.ces.ncsu.edu/depts/fcs/disaster/

INTERNET

Deja News and Newsgroups

Usenet is like a huge e-mail party where people get together to exchange messages on all kinds of subjects. Part of Usenet is just for kids. However, it is IMPORTANT to remember the following: Even in areas set aside for kids, adults can send messages. You might even find adults pretending to be kids. Also, sometimes the kids in these discussion groups can say things your kids might not like. Usenet offers many parenting and K–12 discussion groups. To search for information contained in newsgroups or to find newsgroups of potential interest to you, we recommend DejaNews.

http://www.dejanews.com/

Web66 Home Page

If your kid's school or the school you teach in has its own Web server, it should be linked here. It's the largest collection of all the schools with Web sites in the world! If the school doesn't have a Web site yet, a cookbook here will give the recipe to create one: where to get the software, how to write the HTML, and more. Teachers: Can't tell a LAN from a WAN? You just found out they want the fifth grade to run ethernet around the building? No fear, stop here. You'll find technical info anyone can understand, plus acceptable use policies as well as other technology planning musts. You want links on top of all that? No surprise, they've got 'em.

http://web66.coled.umn.edu/

INTERNET TOOLKIT

See also INTERNET—SAFETY *in the main part of this book*

The Center for Democracy and Technology

The CDT works for government policy in the interest of protecting citizens' privacy and civil liberties. Besides their take on filtering, you can learn all about encryption, digital wiretaps, and more.

http://www.cdt.org/

Center For Media Education

This excellent site will tell you how to safeguard your family's Internet privacy. Find out how online marketeers are targeting children, and discover what you can do about it. While you're visiting this site, be sure to read the information about violence in TV programming, local TV station educational programming requirements, and how you can make your kids media-literate.

http://www.cme.org/

Children in Cyberspace

Be sure you visit this excellent resource about online marketing and the privacy rights of kids. All the facts on the issue are mentioned in a neutral way. There is also a calm and clear section on the filtering debate, and it should be required reading for every parent.

http://www.privacyrights.org/fs/children.htm

Cyberliberties

The American Civil Liberties Union has published several reports on filtering, notably "Fahrenheit 451.2 Is Cyberspace Burning?" You can read these reports online, plus follow current news on the filtering and cyberliberties scene.

http://www.aclu.org/issues/cyber/hmcl.html

CyberTipline

CyberTipline, sponsored by the National Center for Missing and Exploited Children (NCMEC), is a national clearinghouse for tips and leads regarding the sexual exploitation of children in cyberspace. Anyone may use the report form on this site to report incidents of suspicious or illegal Internet activity, including the distribution of child pornography online or situations involving the online enticement of children for sexual exploitation. You can also call your report into the Center's toll-free, 24-hour tipline at 800-843-5678. Net-mom salutes the supporters and sponsors that made this service possible.

http://www.missingkids.com/cybertip/

DMA Privacy Action Now/Parents Get CyberSavvy!

Get cyber-savvy! A Family Guide includes "What should I do if..." situations to help parents begin a dialog with their kids about specific Net hazards. Don't miss the main level of this very interesting site from The Direct Marketing Association at <http://www.the-dma.org/>.

http://www.the-dma.org/pan7/
    parents-cybrsvvy7b1.shtml

NET FILES

YOU'RE IN MOROCCO, AND YOU ARE GIVEN SOME MESHWEE, TAGINES, AND COUSCOUS. SHOULD YOU EAT, DRINK, OR WEAR THEM?

Answer: *You should eat them, but be careful so you won't wear them, too! Not only are they all delicious foods, but in Morocco, one is expected to eat some from each dish served. About silverware: leave it at home. In Morocco, the thumb and first three fingers are used when eating. Find out other interesting facts about this north African country when you take the guided tour at* http://www.dsg.ki.se/morocco/cuisine/about/

The Electronic Frontier Foundation

Founded in 1990, the Electronic Frontier Foundation is one of the oldest organizations solely dedicated to protecting civil liberties on the Net. Their site includes a vast array of useful documents. One of the latest additions is "Protecting Yourself Online: The Definitive Resource on Safety, Freedom & Privacy in Cyberspace." Read it to learn how to guard against e-mail spamming and viruses and how to protect yourself from identity theft and fraud.

http://www.eff.org/

Enough is Enough Home Page

Enough Is Enough says it's "Lighting the way to protect children and families from the dangers of illegal pornography and online predators." They have an informative Web site, which includes a white paper on Child Safety at <http://www.enough.org/summit/whitepaper.htm>. Many child advocacy groups and individuals worked on this white paper, including Net-mom. It illuminates some of the safety issues on the networked table, plus the need for the shared responsibility of parents, industry, community, and law enforcement to help solve them.

http://www.enough.org/

Filtering Facts

Filtering Facts supports use of filters in public libraries and schools. At this site you can read an extensive collection of articles, editorials, quotes, news stories, and other material on both sides of the argument. There is a section on recommended filters and a useful FAQ, which among other things debunks the story that filters mistakenly block sites about "breast cancer." Inform yourself here.

http://www.filteringfacts.org/

Internet Online Summit: Focus On Children

Net-mom was a participant in a December 1997 summit meeting about kids online. This page tells you what happened at the summit and gives information about America Links Up, a national education campaign.

http://www.kidsonline.org/

Parents Guide to the Internet

This brief introduction to the Internet, from the Department of Education, is aimed at parents who are not quite as techno-savvy as their kids. You'll learn Internet basics as well as Net safety tips. Explore suggested search engines and other links (Net-mom's site is listed!), including a section on Net resources for children with disabilities. There's a handy glossary, too.

http://www.ed.gov/pubs/parents/internet/

A Practical Guide to Internet Filters

This is a companion site to the book by the same name, written by librarian Karen Schneider. The book is based on admittedly nonscientific research done during the summer of 1997 by Schneider and a group of librarian volunteers as part of The Internet Filter Assessment Project (TIFAP). This site provides some product updates, news on filtering issues, and presentation slides on the "Should a library filter the Internet?" debate. There is also a link to the TIFAP material, methods, and results.

http://www.bluehighways.com/filters/

Technology Inventory

There's been a lot of talk in the news about the Internet having stuff on it that is inappropriate for kids. The overwhelming majority of information is OK, but those news stories can make you nervous. Some people are even talking about keeping kids off the Net entirely, which would be terrible! We think that access to information is a good thing. But we also recognize that parents may want to use filtering software and other tools in the digital toolbox. This page, from research by Dr. Lorrie Cranor at AT&T, will tell you what's available. Tools are arranged into categories and are explained in great detail in the report.

http://www.research.att.com/projects/tech4kids/

Tips & Tools for Parents: Keeping Kids Safe Online

The Children's Partnership, in cooperation with the National PTA and the National Urban League, presents a very nice overview of some of the dangers kids face on the Net and what parents can do about each one. One of the main things parents should know is that when kids meet the Internet, it always merits parental attention.

http://www.childrenspartnership.org/safety.html

Welcome to Safe Kids

The Internet is a wonderful communications medium: your family can learn a lot, make new friends, and have a whole new world opened to them. However, there may be parts of the Internet you don't want your kids to see. As with some television programs, or books, or magazines, or parts of town, you decide what they can and cannot view. There are a variety of software products you can install on your computer to help guide what they see. See what is available and get answers to questions about how to make your Internet experiences great! Larry Magid, syndicated columnist, is your friendly guide.

http://www.safekids.com/

MOVING

ALLIED VAN LINES, INC. - The official website of Allied Van Lines: Relocation and Moving Specialists

This is a don't-miss site! You'll find lots of informative facts here, and the main reason we like this site is the thoughtful treatment it gives to taking care of kids' special needs before, during, and after a move. A psychologist offers answers to commonly asked questions about families on the move, including emotional support, school-related issues, and family teamwork. Also, a Carton Capers area gives step-by-step instructions on how to use empty Allied packing cartons to build a navy, an express train, and other exciting stuff (we're not sure kids really need directions on what to do with the huge empty boxes, but if they run out of ideas, try here!).

http://www.alliedvan.net/

The Atlas Van Lines Interchange

How are you going to move that aquarium? Those plants? And your computer equipment? This site will tell you that, and more. Check the Sites area for links to places chock-full of stuff, like the Employee Relocation Council.

http://www.atlasvanlines.com/

Family.com: Chesapeake Family - Moving With Kids

This site offers tips on how to explain an upcoming move to your kids and what to expect in the way of reactions! There are plenty of things you can do to ease the transition. You can enlist the kids' help in gathering information about the new city, to help conquer fear of the unknown. Depending on the child's age, he or she can help you plan the logistics of the move, help pack, and scout out potential houses and schools. If you're in for a *moving* experience, visit this site for ideas.

http://family.disney.com/Features/
family_1997_05/cspk/cspk57moving/
cspk57moving.html

PARENTING

The Bilingual Families Web Page

If you live in a family where more than one language is spoken, your kids are so lucky! They are growing up with an advantage many kids don't have. Other kids may have to study for years in order to approach your kids' knowledge of another language. This resource is for families who want to network with other multilingual families and share what works best for them. Some of the best suggestions are collected at this site, including links to everything from children's folk songs to language summer camps.

http://www.nethelp.no/cindy/biling-fam.html

Children Now

How do you talk to your kids about tough issues like drugs, sexuality, and abuse? Sometimes it's hard for parents to begin these conversations. In fact, it's sometimes so difficult that parents don't do it at all! According to this site, "By age 13, the most common source of information about difficult issues such as AIDS changes from parents to friends and the entertainment media." This children's advocacy group wants to turn that statistic around. In the online publication "Talking With Kids About Tough Issues" you'll find 13 essential rules of thumb for talking with your child about anything. Don't miss the additional publications, such as "There are Hundreds of Ways to Help America's Children"—even if you can only spare an hour a week. Check their suggestions! There are also extensive links to other children's advocacy groups and information around the Net.

http://www.childrennow.org/

The Coroner's Report - Gangwar.com

How much do you know about gangs? Do you think you could spot warning signs that might indicate your child was involved with a gang? If you need a quick education on gangs, graffiti "tagging," and hand signals, visit this site and its associated links. Created by an outspoken retired coroner, this Web site may shock you. The page offers this quote: "The choice today is no longer between violence and nonviolence. It's either nonviolence or nonexistence."—Dr. Martin Luther King, Jr.

http://www.gangwar.com/

DEPARTMENT OF JUSTICE - KID'S PAGE

You want your child to say grace and thank the Lord before she eats lunch at school, but when she does, the other kids make fun of her and call her names. What should you do? Your child could stop saying grace, she could sit somewhere else, or she could decide to talk to an adult about it. Each one of these choices has other consequences; discuss them with your child and decide which is best for you. The Attorney General of the United States presents this page about racial, religious, and other types of prejudice. Learn to recognize, and then do something, about hateful acts like these, whether it happens to your family or to someone else.

http://www.usdoj.gov/kidspage/bias-k-5/

Dr. Gayle Peterson: Marriage and Family Therapist

This collection of columns by Dr. Gayle Peterson is part of ParentsPlace, a great Web site for parents and families. Dr. Gayle answers all kinds of questions, such as "How can I help my sensitive eight-year-old deal with moving?" and "My sons fight constantly; what should I do?" Net-mom appreciates Dr. Gayle's thoughtful and caring answers. She never belittles her readers or makes them feel guilty.

http://www.parentsplace.com/cgi-bin/objects/family/

Family.com Home Page

Presented by Disney Online, this site offers lots of intriguing feature articles on family activities, travel, recipes, education, and more. A recent peek revealed these articles: "Out of the Woods: Camp Crafts to Make at Home," "Preparing for Kindergarten: What Your Preschooler Needs to Know," and "A Primer for Grandparents: Generational Do's and Don'ts." Besides this, you can Go Local for links to parenting news in your city or state. We were able to find out about this week's family activities in our town. Coverage is currently limited to the U.S. and its territories, Canada, and Australia.

http://family.disney.com/

Fathers' Resource Center

Whether you are a new dad, a single dad, or a seasoned dad, this site has something for you. The quarterly online newsletter, Father Times, offers insightful articles and advice designed to "support, educate, and advocate" fathers. The list of links to other father-focused resources, personal stories, and online magazines is great.

http://www.visi.com/~frc/

Foster Parent Home Page

Whoever said "I never promised you a rose garden" must have been referring to foster care. So says one dedicated foster parent, who shares her personal story here. This is a wonderful site for foster parents to find lots of information and support on all issues relating to foster care and the child welfare system. There are feature articles on topics such as foster care and the news media, medical, addiction, and educational concerns, plus transracial/cross-cultural issues. Intended as an interactive forum specifically for foster parents, this site has enlightening information for all parents.

http://fostercare.org/FPHP/welcome.htm

May the force be with you in PHYSICS.

Get Your ANGRIES Out!

Are you always yelling at your kids? Is there a bully bothering them at school? Are you mad and cranky a lot? This site gives you some useful ways to get your anger out in constructive ways, with hints for adults, couples, and kids. Here is a sample for kids: "Check your tummy, jaws and your fists. See if the mads are coming. Breathe! Blow your mad out. Get your control. Feel good about getting your control. Stop and think; make a good choice. People are not to be hurt with your hands, feet or voice. Remember to use your firm words, not your fists." There are many more good ideas, and don't forget to check the links about peace here while you're dealing with your angries!

http://members.aol.com/AngriesOut/

KidsCampaigns

Sponsored by the Benton Foundation, this site is a clearinghouse of child advocacy activity. Learn what individuals and groups are doing to improve the lives of kids in the U.S. There's a state-by-state archive so you can find out what's happening in health care, education and literacy, and financial security. Join a discussion group or sign up for the free newsletter so you can keep up on the issues and solutions as they are identified. This is an excellent, thought-provoking site.

http://www.kidscampaigns.org/

KidSource OnLine Welcome Page

Wasn't that toy recalled? Find out here! Families, be sure to check out this outstanding parenting site. The reviews of kid-tested software are written from a family perspective, with both negative and positive comments. The Education section includes articles and book lists and, best of all, annotated links and more links! The Health section has everything from vaccination schedules to growth charts, and the ComputingEDGE is a way to match needy schools with computer equipment. We highly recommend this site for annotated pointers to sites about dealing with angry kids, raising only children, and figuring out such things as alternative assessment in education.

http://www.kidsource.com/

National Parent Information Network

You are not the only one out there struggling with issues such as how much TV your child should be watching or how to get your kids to clean up their rooms or develop better study habits. The National Parent Information Network (NPIN) is sponsored by the ERIC Clearinghouses on Urban Education and on Early Childhood Education. There are lots of choices: a parenting discussion list and a Q&A service through AskERIC are only two. You can search the ERIC database on all topics relating to child development, child rearing, and parenting children from birth to adolescence. *Parent News* monthly newsletter offers feature articles on a wide range of topics and periodically lists information about organizations of special interest to parents and how to subscribe to other publications, such as *Pp* (parents and preschoolers) *Newsletter* and *Single Mother Newsletter*.

http://www.npin.org/

The National Parenting Center

The content changes daily here, with articles for parents of babies through teens. There's also a focus on soon-to-be parents, too! You'll find articles on how to prepare for a parent-teacher conference, how to deal with bed-wetting, how to help your child change schools, and much, much more. There are also live chat opportunities as well as discussion groups. This site is programmed by ParentsPlace, which has a separate listing in this book.

http://www.tnpc.com/

The Natural Child Project

"All children behave as well as they are treated." That's the motto at The Natural Child Project. The site includes many areas: articles by noted parenting authors, parenting advice columns, even laws around the world pertaining to child advocacy. Look for the "parenting site of the month."

http://www.naturalchild.com/

ParenthoodWeb

Here new parents and parents of young children can "Ask the Pros," browse the library for child care and parenting articles, find out about children's product recalls, and participate in the open discussion board. Don't miss the links to software and movie reviews.

http://www.parenthoodweb.com/

Parenting Matters: Respectful, Democratic, and Non-Punitive

This site supports the parenting theory of "how reward and punishment as a disciplinary technique can be replaced by limited choices and 'natural and logical consequences.'" Everyone's trying to have a role in life, and if kids feel powerless, there can be problems. As this site puts it: "If they can't 'count' in a positive way, a negative way will do." Learn how to short-circuit misbehavior by trying some of the techniques described here for both parents and grandparents.

http://lifematters.com/parentn.html

Parenting on the Go

This site is subtitled "Expert suggestions for parenting with discipline." Learn how to set up a disciplined environment, how to increase communication, and how to respond to misbehavior. You'll also read suggestions on dealing with sibling wars and, when all else fails, how to "start all over." One thing you can do is rehearse new responses to whatever your "triggers" are. Instead of blowing up when your child does something wrong, try a more neutral comeback answer, such as "What's your best guess as to what I'm about to do now?" It's important to teach your child to rehearse too, to avoid potential sources of conflict; for example, you could say: "Kari is probably going to want to play with your new toy alone. What can you say to her?" This is an excellent site, with solid suggestions.

http://www.mentor-media.com/

Parenting Q & A

If you're looking for expert answers to questions on child development, discipline, motherhood, fatherhood, or special needs, you've come to the right place. Search by broad topic, age level, or keyword. For example, say your child is having a problem with a bully on the school bus. At this site you will find tips on dealing with bullies, suggested books, and additional links to other sources of information. The most important tip is that children's complaints about bullies should not be ignored. Find out why at this site. There is also a link to the Cybermom dot com Web site if you'd like to chat about issues with other parents.

http://www.parenting-qa.com/

Parents.com

From the publishers of *McCall's, Family Circle, Parents,* and *Child* comes the type of quality Web site you'd expect. It answers questions like "You're Pregnant! Now What?" and "How Can I Raise a Responsible Child?" If you join as a member (free), you can participate in the chat rooms and choose to receive specialized content targeted to your situation. The only drawback to this site is the heavy advertising, much of which pops up in an annoying second browser window.

http://www.parents.com/

Parents Without Partners Online Home Page

Whether you have never married, are separated, divorced, or widowed, there's one thing for sure: you love your kids and want to be the best single parent you can be! If you are already a member, you can join the chat and discussion areas to meet other single parents and share ideas and friendship. Not yet a member? Find a local chapter in your area and attend some of their events. Still not sure? There are several online resources here, plus lots of links to get you started.

http://www.parentswithoutpartners.org/

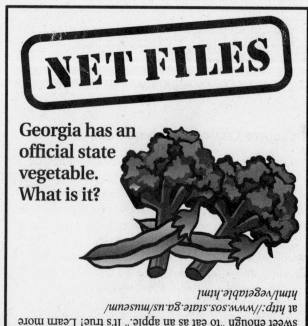

NET FILES

Georgia has an official state vegetable. What is it?

Answer: The Vidalia onion. Although the seeds grow into pungent onions everywhere else, when planted in the fields around Vidalia and Glennville they turn out sweet enough "to eat as an apple." It's true! Learn more at http://www.sos.state.ga.us/museum/html/vegetable.html

Philips "Let's Connect"

According to a recent survey sponsored by Philips Consumer Communications, most parents and their preteen children spend less than one hour a day talking to each other; many spend less than 30 minutes! More than half the kids (57 percent) say their parents don't always give them a chance to explain themselves, but almost the same number of parents (51 percent) say their children don't let *them* explain themselves. Want to get your kids to really listen to what you're saying? Check the tips here.

http://www.philipsconsumer.com/letsconnect/

POSITIVE PARENTING (ON-LINE!)

Parents know that dealing with kids can sometimes be a real battle of wills. This site provides support and advice on how to handle the most difficult situations with your kids. "Nine Things to do Instead of Spanking," "Bedtime Without Struggling," and "Saying I Love You" are only a few features. This site includes a great set of links on parenting and affinity groups and organizations.

http://www.positiveparenting.com/

SGT MOM'S The Internet Site for Military Families

It's hard to parent from a distance when you're in the military and your family is on the other side of the planet. Sergeant Mom knows how it is. Her site aims to help military families (and military "brats") cope with it all. Be sure to grab a ride on Sergeant Mom's "Tank Taxi" to get a tour of the entire base, er, Web site.

http://www.sgtmoms.com/

Talk_About_Violence

This page points out some alarming statistics. Homicide is the second leading cause of death for all youths aged 15 to 24. It is the leading cause of death for young African American males in this age group. What can parents do to help stop the violence? One of the most powerful concepts found at this site is the following: "Help your child to adopt healthy responses to conflict. Avoid situations in which 'losing face' becomes an issue by recognizing the kind of behavior which leads to a fight. Assess the conflict for what you want, not for what the other person wants." Some good suggestions are found here, plus pointers to organizations and other resources across the Net.

http://www.dnai.com/~children/toughissues/
  Talk_Violence.html

PARENTING COMMUNITIES

Canadian Parents Online

Here is a good place for parents to help each other in a comfortable, community atmosphere in which to connect and communicate about diverse issues, such as stepparenting, foster parenting, or raising special-needs children. Be sure to check out the Library for monthly feature articles or ask one of the resident experts questions about nutrition, family finances, or child rearing.

http://www.canadianparents.com/

Parent Soup

Remember the story of Stone Soup? Some soldiers boasted that they could make a nourishing soup out of stones. Then they said, does anyone have an onion? A carrot? A potato? Some salt? And soon, everyone in the village brought something to add to the simmering pot. In the end, everyone marveled that such a good soup could be made out of simple stones! This site is sort of like that. It's made up of a community of parents just like you, each bringing some new element to the pot. The content here is based on what other users can add to the mix of real-time chat and discussion groups. Want to ask for help with your shy preschooler? Want someone to talk to while your partner watches football? Want some health, crafts, or entertainment suggestions? Try the Parent Soup community!

http://www.parentsoup.com/

Parents Place.com: Pregnancy, Parenting, Parents, Baby, Pregnancy, Kids, Family

Parents, whether you are on your first child, your tenth, or somewhere in between, join the hundreds of other parents who come to ParentsPlace to chat, get support, and share information on the adventures and challenges of child rearing. Whether you are looking for directions to make invisible ink or the latest in toy safety labeling requirements, you'll find it here. Feature articles in the reading rooms include information on parenting twins, stepparenting, at-home dads, and single parents; but that's just the beginning. You can "Ask the Pediatrician" questions about children's health or check with other experts on various aspects of parenting. This Web site is sure to be one of your favorites.

http://www.parentsplace.com/

Working Moms' Internet Refuge

Kids, work, husband, house, outside interests—help! Sound familiar? If you are a working mom with a lot of plates, watermelons, and anvils to juggle, this site might be just the place to take a break! There are all kinds of articles and advice on topics ranging from getting organized and reducing stress to telecommuting, dealing with finances, potty training, day care, and what to cook for dinner. You'll find lots of sound advice here—and an occasional column or poem that reminds us all that life does require a good sense of humor!

http://www.moms-refuge.com/

PRESCHOOLERS

Children's Storybooks Online

Explore these stories with your little prereaders, who will be delighted by the busy animations, charmed by the animal noises, and enchanted by the tales themselves. There are stories for older kids too.

http://www.magickeys.com/books/

Children's Storybooks Online - Alphabet Letters

Is your child just learning his or her ABCs? This series of alphabet pages will surely help. Each letter is illustrated with a cute animation. The "B is for Bear" winks and stretches, the "H is for Helicopter" hovers around the computer screen, and the "N is for Nest" hatches out some baby birds. Can you guess what "Z" is for?

http://www.pacificnet.net/~cmoore/alphabet/

Idea Box - Early Childhood Education and Activity Resources

Crafts for little hands, finger plays, recipes, games, and online stories are just a few of the ideas we found here. Parents will love these on a rainy day!

http://www.theideabox.com/

Kindergarten Kafe

Each issue of this online newsletter offers a finger play, a story, suggested books, crafts, activities, and more. For example, the Back to School issue features the theme "Apples." There's a little apple poem, a couple of suggested Web sites, and a tasty snack made of apple slices, peanut butter, and a few mini-marshmallows. Scrolling down, we find an apple printing craft and picture books with an apple flavor. Look through back issues for holiday crafts and other activities.

http://members.aol.com/CharleneWP/kkafe.htm

KRN Software's Java Edutainment - Index of our Educational Games for Kids

There are many fine games here, but let's try Cargo Bay. Triangles, squares, and circles are floating around in the spaceship's cargo bay—can you sort them into the right bins? Wait until this Java game loads completely and you see your grabbing tool. It looks sort of like starship *Voyager*. Then click on the floating shape you want, and the tool will move over to it and grab on. It makes a loud noise, so be sure the volume on your speakers isn't too high. Then click the bin where you want the cargo to be stored, and if you're right, it will go there.

http://www.worldnetoh.com/krnsoft/Java-edu/
  Index-edu.html

Meddybumps

On the island of Meddybumps, jelly beans grow on vines, like grapes. You can learn all about the ritual and lore of gourmet bean tasting (yes, they sell them here, too). But that's not the best part. You can check out some wonderful and imaginative stories, such as "Frogwart and the Tooth Fairies." But that's not the best part either. Visit the Learning Activities section and the Young Writer's Workshop. Read a "story starter" to your child and ask him or her to finish the story; write it all down. Make a whole library of your child's own stories! But that's *still* not the best part. In the Learning area, click on Online Activities, then have some fun playing games with frogs, fire engines, clowns, and rutabagas. And *that's* the best part!

http://www.meddybemps.com/

Miss Mouse -STCPL

Where is Miss Mouse? She's gone into one of these colorful houses, but which one? Let's try the orange house. Oops, there's a fire truck in there. How about the green house? Nope, just an old shoe. Keep clicking until you find her. Every game is different.

http://www.st-charles.lib.il.us/low/missmouse.htm

Seussville Games

Just pick up the clover containing the entire Who civilization and place it back in Horton's trunk. Seems easy, right? Not when the screen is dark! Then scramble your brains with the Cat in the Hat's concentration game, or see if you can match the right kooky teacher with her classroom in Diffendoofer School. Try to sort out Sneetches with stars on their bellies from those without them, and then play Net-mom's favorite, the Lorax's Save the Trees game.

http://www.randomhouse.com/seussville/

Virtual Farmland

At Davis' Farmland in Massachusetts, you can discover what's old in farming: rare and endangered farm animal breeds. Click on the farm fun page to see a variety of common farm animals and hear the sounds they make; click on "more animal sounds" to hear elephants, lions, and other nonbarnyard creatures! You can also download coloring pages of farm life and activities, plus play a farm crossword puzzle.

http://www.davisfarmland.com/index2.htm

Webcrawler : Kids & Family : CTW Family Workshop

Children's Television Workshop's area offers new ideas, activities, and fun for your preschooler. Net-mom writes the Best of the Web column, and Foam Bath Fish Time's Kevin Savetz writes Family Tech Tips. Visit us soon!

http://webcrawler.com/ctw/

> **Never give your name or address to a stranger.**

TRAVEL

Family.com: Travel Category Page

Whether you're traveling by car or by plane, don't miss the great information here on how to keep your kids entertained. There are activities and games, travel snacks (what would any family trip be without food?), packing tips, and lots more in the Advice section.

http://family.disney.com/Categories/Travel/

HEALTHY FLYING With Diana Fairechild

Flying takes less time than going by car, but it can be less comfortable. The airplane air is drier. The pressure changes quickly as the plane takes off and lands. Flying to places in different time zones can leave passengers with *jet lag*, that tired feeling that surfaces when you are in one place but your body thinks it is still someplace else! The solutions to most of these problems are inexpensive and can be brought with you on the plane. Read Diana's secrets for comfortable flying and share them with your family. She should know: she's a retired flight attendant.

http://www.flyana.com/

Rand McNally Online: Parents' Corner

Rand McNally, famous for maps, offers this site with travel planning tips, activities to keep the backseat passengers happy, and lots more. Remember, it's hard for kids to anticipate how bored they can get after the initial excitement passes. Be sure they understand that sometimes they will be responsible for entertaining themselves, and help them plan accordingly before you pull out of the driveway.

http://www.randmcnally.com/parentsCorner/

The Travelite FAQ : How to travel with just one carry-on bag

This wonderful site was created by a librarian who knows how to travel well yet travel light. Her system involves using a special kind of travel pack, although she reviews many other types of luggage and discusses their pros and cons. There's a wealth of information here, including an extensive and well-organized section of links, which will assist you in any travel experience, whether you want to try one-bag travel or not.

http://members.tripod.com/~travelite/

Index

Alphabetical List of Sites

Internet Coach®

Buy two and get the third FREE!
see order form-

Liftoff to Lizard Island
Join Izzy the Lizard on his Internet flying machine. You'll travel the world and at every stop learn a new Web feature. Packed with games, learning activities and zany humor, this award winning CD charms and delights the youngest Web-ster.

Field Trap
An exciting introduction to U.S.A. cultural history. The greedy Museum Monster has stolen history facts from the Web. You'll need to put the true facts back. Packed with biographies, animated stories, games and other learning activities, **Field Trap** captivates the imagination of the youngest learner.

Ages 5-9

Not just thrilling cyber games, these CDs are essential learning tools for the Internet!

Ages 9-Adult

Search for the Black Rhino
Sharpen your Internet research skills as you trail the rare Black Rhino. You are the Web expert on a scientific team. They need you to unravel the mysteries of Enki Island and save the Rhino. You'll use a special search engine to find accurate geological and zoological information. This 3D adventure is the ultimate learning challenge for Internet explorers.

Mission to Planet X
You'll need all your Web moxie to escape the alien traps on Planet X. E-mail your secret agent on Mars. Download hidden videos from Pluto or search Venus' Web site for an encrypted map of Planet X. Only those with courage and Web smarts will ever return from Planet X.

Parents! Be as Web savvy as your kids!

Internet Coach® for Netscape Navigator and Communicator
Internet Coach® for Microsoft Internet Explorer
In minutes you'll be a Web Pro. Learn about browsing, searching, e-mail, newsgroups, downloading and much more. No wonder **Internet Coach®** is the world's most popular software for learning the Web.

Internet Coach® for Net Safety
The perfect ammo against Web villains! Learn how to keep your whole family safe from Web dangers. This CD includes an encyclopedia of safety information, kids safety games and much more.

Ages 12-Adult

All Ages

apte
APTE, Inc.

Order Form ➞

No Web connection necessary to use these CD's

Internet Coach®

Internet Kids & Family Yellow Pages Special!!
Buy two, get one FREE!!

Name _____

Address _____

_____

City _____ State / Zip _____ _____

Phone # (___)_____

E-mail address: _____

School discounts available! Please contact us.

☐ Check / Money Order enclosed, payable to APTE, Inc.

☐ Visa ☐ MC ☐ Am Ex

Card # _____-_____-_____-_____

Expiration Date _____/_____

Signature _____

Products	Quantity*	Cost	Total
(all hybrid CD-ROMs unless indicated)			
Internet Coach® for Adults			
Net Safety (all ages)	_____	$28.95	_____
Netscape Navigator	_____	$28.95	_____
Netscape Navigator and Communicator	_____	$28.95	_____
Microsoft Explorer(Win only) 3.0__ 4.0__	_____	$28.95	_____
Internet Coach® for Kids			
Mission to Planet X	_____	$38.95	_____
Liftoff to Lizard Island	_____	$38.95	_____
Search for the Black Rhino	_____	$38.95	_____
Field Trap(available fall 98!)	_____	$38.95	_____

If you buy two, indicate FREE on the third program!

Illinois residents add 8% tax Tax _____

Shipping/Handling Shipping _____

$5.00 or 6% of order, whichever is higher

All sales for end user use only. Not for resale.

TOTAL: $_____

offer expires September 30, 1999

Fax or mail this form to:
APTE, Inc.
Northwestern University/Evanston Research Park
1840 Oak Ave., Evanston, IL 60201
voice: 847/866-1872 fax: 847/866-1873 e-mail: mail@apte.com

An important new way

to keep your kids safe on the Internet.

★ ★ ★ ★ ★
Highest Rating
"We can honestly say that GuardiaNet is by far the most effective Parental Control program we have ever seen"
– 5 Star –

You probably know that the Internet is an extraordinary reference tool that can help your children excel in school. However, valuable as it is, the World Wide Web has its dangers. Besides information and entertainment, the World Wide Web can be a source of pornography - plus other material that contradicts your family's values.

You set the standards and GuardiaNet does the rest .... automatically.

Now you can have up-to-the-minute protection with GuardiaNet, the automatic Internet filtering service. Because your family is unique, GuardiaNet gives you the flexibility to create personalized access for each family member. Best of all, you can rest easy as your children safely browse the Internet, protected by the same patented technology used by banks to secure their sensitive data.

GuardiaNet does not rate or review sites - we let you choose from lists of websites created by first-class companies like SafeSurf and the Recreational Software Advisory Council.

Turn over for details › › › ›

GuardiaNet - www.safekid.com
3511 West Market Street • Suite 100 Greensboro, NC 27403
1-888-638-7007 Ext. 250

GuardiaNet

ABOUT THE CD-ROM

HOW TO USE THE ELECTRONIC BOOK

The accompanying CD contains a special electronic edition of the text of this book, created by Modern Age Books. Using the powerful Modern Age V-Book™ search engine, you can locate web sites, Usenet discussion groups, mailing lists, and other resources offline on your PC or Macintosh. You can then connect to the site of your choice using your browser.

SYSTEM REQUIREMENTS

This electronic book CD will run on any of the following computers: a Macintosh (68K or Power PC), Mac Performa, iMac or Powerbook with System 7 or higher (8MB RAM); or a PC with Microsoft Windows 3.1, 3.11, Windows 95 or Windows 98 (8MB RAM). For Macintosh users: You can install the entire book on your hard drive for best performance or run it from the CD to conserve hard drive space.

INSTALLATION

To use the CD, you must first install it on your system. To start the installation program, please choose the procedure below that is right for your system.

Windows 3.1x Users

1. Insert the CD-ROM into your CD drive.
2. From Program Manager, choose RUN from the File menu.
3. Type **d:\setup.exe** (or the appropriate drive letter) and press ENTER.
4. Click "Yes" and follow the instructions on the screen.

Windows 95/98 Users

Insert the CD-ROM into your CD drive. The install program should start up automatically within a few seconds. If for some reason it does not start automatically, do the following:

1. From the Start menu choose **Run**.
2. Type **d:\setup.exe** (or the appropriate drive letter) and press ENTER.*
3. Click "Yes" and follow the instructions on the screen.

Please note: If you are unsure of what letter your CD-ROM drive is assigned by your system, open Windows Explorer (In your Start Menu under Programs) and find the icon for your CD-ROM drive in the left pane. This is the letter you should enter in the **Run** dialog box.

Macintosh Users

1. Insert the CD-ROM into your CD drive. The "Modern Age Books" CD icon will appear on your desktop.
2. To install the electronic version of the book, drag and drop the "Modern Age Books" CD icon onto your hard drive icon.

DISNEY'S BLAST ONLINE

SYSTEM REQUIREMENTS

PC	Macintosh
Windows 95 operating system	MacOS 7.5.5 or higher
Pentium Processor	PowerMac or compatible PowerPC Macintosh
16MB or more of RAM	24MB or more of RAM. Preferred size of browser memory set to 12MB or more
14.4 kbps or faster modem (28.8 kbps is recommended)	14.4 kbps or faster modem (28.8 kbps is recommended)
3.x and above class Internet browsers. If your ISP is AOL, you must have AOL 3.0 for Windows 95.	4.0 and above Internet browsers. If your ISP is AOL, you must have AOL 3.0 for Macintosh.

PC USERS: LAUNCHING DISNEY'S BLAST ONLINE AFTER INSTALLATION

1. Double-click the Disney Blast (D-Ball) icon on your desktop.
2. When the Connect screen appears, enter your Internet Service Provider (ISP) information. If you are already connected, select the second option and click **Connect**.
3. At the Login screen, click **Login** if you are a signing up for the first time. If you are currently a Disney Blast member, scroll down to **Guest**, enter your Member Name and Password where prompted, and click **Login**.

For more help, you can call Disney Blast Member Service at 1-972-389-3970, 8am to 11pm ET or send e-mail from http://www.disneyblast.com/preview/email.html

APTE'S INTERNET COACH

Take a tip from the Coach®, "This is the coolest way to be an Internet Pro!" Taste a tidbit from each of these exciting learning adventures from Internet Coach®. Something fun for every member of the family! The Internet is simulated so you can practice and learn safely. No Web connection needed. Mac or Win!

To run a program, click on the Internet Coach icon at the startup screen. Wait a second and you should see the Internet Coach Product Sampler. Click on Product List at the right of the screen to bring up a list of the games below. Clicking on any of the games will run the demo.

FOR YOUNG WEB-STERS: AGES 5–9

Liftoff to Lizard Island: Internet Coach® Help Izzy tour the world and build a plane to get home!...and learn Internet basics with this award-winning, engaging cartoon.

Field Trap: Internet Coach® A field trip to a museum of U.S. history gone awry! Unravel the mystery with the simulated Internet to gather historical information, read maps, solve puzzles, and more, to find out where your teacher is!

FOR AGES 9–ADULT

Mission to Planet X: Internet Coach® If you cleverly avoid alien traps, solve perplexing problems and mind-boggling games, you can warp to Planet X to rescue StarSurfer. As you visit every planet, practice basic Internet skills.

Search for the Black Rhino: Internet Coach®   Join the team of scientists on mysterious Enki Island in the desperate effort to rescue a rare rhino from predators. Polish your Internet research skills, learn interesting scientific facts, but keep your wits about you to avoid tropical traps, carnivorous plants and more!

FOR AGES 12–ADULT

Internet Coach® for Net Safety   Knowledge is power! Filtering and blocking software is not enough. This educational program contains a clever safety game for kids and extensive information about inappropriate content, password and identity protection, scams, viruses, and much more.

Internet Coach® for Netscape Navigator, Internet Coach® for Microsoft Internet Explorer   Originally developed for the White House, Coach® is the most popular software for learning the Web. Coach takes the mystery out of the Internet for newcomers and provides a handy reference tool for experienced surfers.

SYSTEM REQUIREMENTS

No web connection is necessary.

PC	Macintosh
486-based PC	68040 Processor or Power PC
Windows 3.1, 95, or NT	System 7.1
16MB RAM	16MB RAM
No disk space required	No disk space required
4-speed CD-ROM drive	4-speed CD-ROM drive
256 color video adapter	256 color monitor

If you have questions about Internet Coach, please call APTE at **1-847-866-1872**.

TRICO ACADEMY: INTERNET TRAINING FOR EDUCATORS

WHAT IS TRICO ACADEMY?

Are you a parent and you want to learn what your kids already know about the Internet? Are you a teacher and you want to know how to use the Internet in the classroom? There is an answer: Trico Academy Internet Training for Educators.

Parents and teachers can learn to capture the power of the Internet with this self-paced CD-ROM. Featuring cool graphics, humorous lesson plans, and much more, this program guides you through everything from Internet basics to building your own Web pages!

This CD-ROM is packed with information and it's fun! You can take several "courses" on various net.topics or jump to the "Lounge" where you overhear a bunch of alpha-geek teachers discussing computers and the Net—just click on them to translate their words into understandable, jargon-free English. The "Study Hall" lets you go back to basics or hone your skills even more.

As Jean Armour Polly, author of *The Internet Kids & Family Yellow Pages* and famous Net-mom, says, "Trico Academy is a winner and every school should buy it for its computer lab. Parents can also learn a lot from the CD. This Net Tutorial CD shines."

SYSTEM REQUIREMENTS

To run the Trico Academy tutorial, your system must meet the following minimum requirements:

PC	Macintosh
133Mhz Pentium or better PC	Power Macintosh
Windows™ 95 or newer	System 7.5 or newer
QuickTime™ 2.1.2 for Windows	QuickTime™ for Macintosh
Sound card with a Windows Sound driver	
4-speed CD-ROM or faster	4-speed CD-ROM or faster
16-bit color display at 640 x 480 pixels	16-bit color display at 640 x 480 pixels
Arial™ font (TrueType)	Arial™ font (TrueType)
12MB available RAM	12MB available RAM
External speakers	External speakers

INSTALLATION TIPS

Macintosh:

- Make sure Arial Font has been installed
- Make sure that you have QuickTime™ software installed
- Double-click on the Academy_Mac icon

Windows 95:

- Make sure that you have QuickTime™ 2.1 (32-bit) software installed. QuickTime™ 2.1 (32-bit) has been included on the demo CD for your convenience. To find QuickTime™ 2.1 on the demo CD, click on the right mouse button while selecting "Internet for Kids Demo" and select "Open." Then you can double-click on the Trico folder and view the Readthis.txt file.

   NOTE: *QuickTime™ 2.1.2 (16-bit) and 3.0 are NOT compatible.*

- Double-click on the ForWIN95.exe icon

Both:

After you see a short set of screens with music, click on one of the icons—"Requirements," "Credits," or "Main Menu"—and you will begin your journey in the Academy.

   NOTE: *If you try loading the software and get a blank screen with music but do not see anything, it's probably because you don't have QuickTime™ 2.1 (32-bit) software installed. As noted above, QuickTime™ 2.1.2 (16-bit) and 3.0 are NOT compatible. Please install QuickTime™ 2.1 (32-bit) from the demo CD and try again.*

CONTACTING TRICO ASSOCIATES

At Trico Associates we believe technology shouldn't be so hard and can actually be fun! We provide training, consulting, and innovative products to help people use technology to achieve personal and organizational goals. We are very interested in your experiences with Trico Academy and would love to hear from you. Please send an electronic message to:
feedback@trico-associates.com
or call us toll free at **1-877-277-8311.**

ONEPLACE'S GUARDIANET

Based on the technology trusted by banks to secure their data, GuardiaNet keeps your children safe on the Internet! Continuous, automatic updating locks out forbidden sites. Flexible controls let parents create personalized access for each family member. For Windows only.

SYSTEM REQUIREMENTS

- Windows 95, IBM-Compatible, Intel 386 Enhanced
- Random Access Memory (RAM—8MB or higher)
- 4MB of hard disk space for Windows 95
- Connection to the Internet
- Netscape Navigator Versions 3.0 or Higher
- Microsoft Internet Explorer Version 3.0 or Higher

GUARDIANET INSTALLATION AND USER REGISTRATION PROCEDURES

The following instructions should be followed if you are installing from a CD with an Icon menu including GuardiaNet. These procedures outline the steps needed for installing and registering users for GuardiaNet. Before you start please have the following handy:

- Your GuardiaNet Family Group Code   The family group code is obtained by calling prior to Installation. The GuardiaNet Technical Support is **1-888-638-7007**.

- A pencil and paper to write down User ID and Access Codes as they are set up.

Typical Installation and User Registration Instructions

IMPORTANT: *Before installing GuardiaNet, using your existing Internet Service Provider, dial up and establish an open connection to the Internet. Wait until your service is connected before proceeding.*

1. Click on the GuardiaNet icon from the CD menu.
2. The GuardiaNet Welcome Window will appear; click Next.
3. The License Agreement will display; click on "Yes" if you accept the terms.
4. You will be presented with two installation options, Typical or Custom. The steps below follow a Typical Installation. Select the Typical Option. For instructions on the Custom installation, refer to "Custom Installation and User Registration Instructions" below.
5. The installation will detect all Internet browsers that are installed on your PC.
6. From the list of browsers found, select the browser that you wish to use in combination with GuardiaNet. *Other browsers will be disabled.*
7. The installation will install all necessary files to your hard drive. Please be patient—this process may take a few seconds.
8. Next, the Registration window will gather all user information.
9. On the Registration window, enter your family group code. The family group code is obtained by calling GuardiaNet Technical Support at **1-888-638-7007**.
10. On the Registration window, enter the First Name, Last Name, and Access Code (user supplied) for your family's Administrator.
11. On the Registration window, enter the First Name, Last Name, and Access Code (user supplied) for each member of your family. Except for the administrator, who assigns access codes, each member of the family should know only his or her own access code, allowing differing access levels.
12. When you are finished defining information for all members of your family, click on Next.
13. The Registration Confirmation window will display. Proof the information that you entered for the members of your family. If the information is correct, click on Next.
14. If the information is not correct, click Back to correct the information.

15. The registration procedure now sends the information that you entered about all family members to the server for registration. Please be patient while each member of the family is registered with the GuardiaNet Server.
16. When the registration process with the server is complete you will see a Member User Ids Window. You will need to write down the User ID for the family administrator; once you have done that, click Next. *The User ID information is automatically saved to a file called "users.log" and can be found in the directory where GuardiaNet is installed, which for the typical installation is c:\sgate.*
17. You have completed the installation and registration process for GuardiaNet; click on Finish.

Custom Installation and User Registration Instructions

A custom installation allows you to define installation parameters such as Installation Directory Setting, Internal Firewall Address, Custom Deny Message, and Security Key Storage.

The instructions below will guide you through a GuardiaNet custom installation.

NOTE: *If you are accessing the Internet through a LAN connection that is protected by a firewall, you need to select Custom Installation.*

IMPORTANT: *Using your existing Internet Service Provider, dial up and establish an open connection to the Internet. Wait until your service is connected before proceeding.*

1. Click the GuardiaNet icon.
2. The GuardiaNet Welcome Window will appear; click Next.
3. The License Agreement will display; click on "Yes" if you accept the terms.
4. You will be presented with two installation options, Typical or Custom. The steps below follow a Custom Installation. Select the Custom Option.
5. Appearing now is the "Choose Destination Location" window. The default directory that GuardiaNet is installed to is c:\sgate. Click "Next" to accept the defined destination, or browse and select an alternate location.
6. The next window that appears is the Firewall Address Window. If you are accessing the Internet via a LAN connection that is protected by an internal firewall, please enter the Firewall's IP Address in the field provided and click on Next. *Consult your LAN administration for the Firewall's IP Address.*
7. Now the Security Key Storage Window displays. This window presents you with three locations to store GuardiaNet Security Keys for each user. Please select one of the storage options on this screen and click on Next. *If you are a family using GuardiaNet on a home PC, choose Security Key on Hard Disk. If you plan on using multiple PCs, you can choose to store the security key on a floppy diskette; there are two floppy drive settings available.* Please refer to Advanced Topics in the User Documentation for use of a Floppy Diskette Security Key.
8. The installation will detect all Internet browsers that are installed on your PC.
9. From the list of browsers found, select the browser that you wish to use in combination with GuardiaNet. *Other browsers will be disabled.*
10. Next you will see the GuardiaNet Response window. This window allows you to customize the deny title and message that users will see when they request an Internet Site that is blocked from their access. Define a deny title and message in the fields provided and click on Next.
11. A window will confirm all custom settings that you have defined. To verify these settings and continue, click on Next.
12. The installation will install all necessary files to your hard drive. Please be patient—this process may take a few seconds.
13. The Registration window will gather all user information.
14. On the Registration window, enter your family group code. The family group code is obtained by calling GuardiaNet Technical Support at **1-888-638-7007**.
15. On the Registration window, enter the First Name, Last Name, and Access Code for your family's Administrator.
16. On the Registration window, enter the First Name, Last Name, and Access Code for each member of your family.
17. When you are finished defining information for all members of your family, click on Next.
18. The Registration Confirmation window will display. Proof the information that you entered for the members of your family. If the information is correct, click on Next. If the information is not correct, click Back to correct the information.
19. The registration procedure now sends the information that you entered about all family members to the server for registration. Please be patient while each member of the family is registered with the GuardiaNet Server.
20. When the registration process with the server is complete, you will see a Member User Ids window. You will need to write down the User ID for the family administrator; once you have done that, click on Next. *The User ID information is*

automatically saved to a file called "users.log" and can be found in the directory where GuardiaNet was installed, which for the typical installation is c:\sgate.

21. You have now completed the installation and registration process for GuardiaNet; click on Finish.

STARTING GUARDIANET

1. Using your existing Internet Service Provider, dial up and open a connection to the Internet.
2. Double-click the GuardiaNet icon on your desktop.
3. Select the User that is the administrator for your family to access the Internet.
4. You will be required to enter your access code for the selected user. After you enter it, the GuardiaNet Server will verify who you are and what Internet Access rights you have. Each user is assigned default Guardian Level "smart filter" when they are registered.
5. Next, the browser that you selected to use will automatically start. GuardiaNet automatically marks your browser's Home Page to www.guardianet.net. The next step you need to take as the family administrator is to set up all registered users with the correct Guardian Level. The Guardian Level will control the user's Internet Access Rights. In order to do this you must access the Members Only Entrance of the GuardiaNet site.
6. From the GuardiaNet Home Page, click on "Enter Member Services".
7. You will now need to enter your User ID, Family Group Code, and Admin Password.
   - *User ID* is the ID number that the user registration procedure returned for the administrator you registered. If you do not know your User ID you can find this information in the "users.log" file installed in the GuardiaNet directory. You can open this file with a word-processing package such as Windows' Notepad or WordPad.
   - *Family Group Code* is a unique key code needed to unlock your family's Internet settings. The family group code is obtained by calling GuardiaNet Technical Support at **1-888-638-7007**.
   - *Admin Password* is set to the default value of "guardian" until you as the administrator change it.
8. Click on "OK"

Upon successful Members Only entry, you will be on the Members Only Home Page. Inside of the Members Only site, you will be able to set up all Internet Access Controls for each member of your family. You will find additional documentation on GuardiaNet inside the Members Only Home Page by selecting the Documentation button along the top menu bar.

TECHNICAL SUPPORT

If you experience any problems with the GuardiaNet installation and need technical support, or would like assistance in setting up access levels or simply have a question, please contact us at this toll-free number: **1-888-638-7007**.

SURF MONKEY

Surf Monkey™ is a Web browser and online service designed exclusively for kids, Surf Monkey is the safe and easy way to learn and have fun on the Internet. Surf Monkey transports kids safely into the world of cyberspace exploration on a "Rocketship" browser, offering tips and tricks designed to entertain and amuse them during their journey. Surf Monkey, the animated talking agent, serves as an Internet tour guide for kids ages 7 and up. The Rocketship browser lets kids surf the Web, exchange multimedia e-mail, and enjoy comic chat rooms. Enabled with SurfWatch® filtering (the leading filtering technology), e-mail Buddy Lists, and an extensive network of safety features, Surf Monkey offers parents flexible controls to protect their kids in cyberspace. From exploding Web pages to providing links to encyclopedias and kid-friendly sites, Surf Monkey makes the Internet experience fun and educational.

Surf Monkey works with any Internet service provider, is easy to use, and is child's play to install. The character even appears onscreen during installation, talking users through the process and entertaining them along the way.

SYSTEM REQUIREMENTS

- Windows 95 or Windows 98
- 133Mhz Pentium or better
- 16MB RAM—with more you'll experience better performance
- 16-bit (high-color) video card (800 x 600 pixels)
- Hard drive space—30MB minimum

If you have any questions about the software, please contact **support@surfmonkey.com**

You can also check the Customer Services and Tech Support areas on Surf Monkey's web site at **www.surfmonkey.com** for answers to frequently asked questions.

WARNING: BEFORE OPENING THE DISC PACKAGE, CAREFULLY READ THE TERMS AND CONDITIONS OF THE FOLLOWING COPYRIGHT STATEMENT AND LIMITED CD-ROM WARRANTY.

Copyright Statement

This software is protected by both United States copyright law and international copyright treaty provision. Except as noted in the contents of the CD-ROM, you must treat this software just like a book. However, you may copy it into a computer to be used and you may make archival copies of the software for the sole purpose of backing up the software and protecting your investment from loss. By saying, "just like a book," The McGraw-Hill Companies, Inc. ("Osborne/McGraw-Hill") means, for example, that this software may be used by any number of people and may be freely moved from one computer location to another, so long as there is no possibility of its being used at one location or on one computer while it is being used at another. Just as a book cannot be read by two different people in two different places at the same time, neither can the software be used by two different people in two different places at the same time.

Limited Warranty

Osborne/McGraw-Hill warrants the physical compact disc enclosed herein to be free of defects in materials and workmanship for a period of sixty days from the purchase date. If the CD included in your book has defects in materials or workmanship, please call McGraw-Hill at 1-800-217-0059, 9am to 5pm, Monday through Friday, Eastern Standard Time, and McGraw-Hill will replace the defective disc.

The entire and exclusive liability and remedy for breach of this Limited Warranty shall be limited to replacement of the defective disc, and shall not include or extend to any claim for or right to cover any other damages, including but not limited to, loss of profit, data, or use of the software, or special incidental, or consequential damages or other similar claims, even if Osborne/McGraw-Hill has been specifically advised of the possibility of such damages. In no event will Osborne/McGraw-Hill's liability for any damages to you or any other person ever exceed the lower of the suggested list price or actual price paid for the license to use the software, regardless of any form of the claim.

OSBORNE/McGRAW-HILL SPECIFICALLY DISCLAIMS ALL OTHER WARRANTIES, EXPRESS OR IMPLIED, INCLUDING BUT NOT LIMITED TO, ANY IMPLIED WARRANTY OF MERCHANTABILITY OR FITNESS FOR A PARTICULAR PURPOSE. Specifically, Osborne/McGraw-Hill makes no representation or warranty that the software is fit for any particular purpose, and any implied warranty of merchantability is limited to the sixty-day duration of the Limited Warranty covering the physical disc only (and not the software), and is otherwise expressly and specifically disclaimed.

This limited warranty gives you specific legal rights; you may have others which may vary from state to state. Some states do not allow the exclusion of incidental or consequential damages, or the limitation on how long an implied warranty lasts, so some of the above may not apply to you.

This agreement constitutes the entire agreement between the parties relating to use of the Product. The terms of any purchase order shall have no effect on the terms of this Agreement. Failure of Osborne/McGraw-Hill to insist at any time on strict compliance with this Agreement shall not constitute a waiver of any rights under this Agreement. This Agreement shall be construed and governed in accordance with the laws of New York. If any provision of this Agreement is held to be contrary to law, that provision will be enforced to the maximum extent permissible, and the remaining provisions will remain in force and effect.

TECHNICAL SUPPORT: If you have any problem with the electronic book included on the CD-ROM, please visit the Modern Age Books website at http://www.modernagebooks.com. At the Modern Age Books home page, go to Support.

For other technical support information, please refer to the "About the CD-ROM" section that precedes this warranty.